thesaurus—Latin for "treasure house"

Webster's New World Thesaurus is a treasure house of *words* designed to provide you as quickly as possible with the perfect word for the proper occasion. Renowned writing expert Charlton Laird has organized this word finder with listings of synonyms and antonyms under the most commonly used versions of particular words. This remarkable improvement on the traditional thesaurus will enable you to discover with speed the word you need without reading long lists or flipping from page to page.

Comprehensive word choice and attention to wide areas of meaning make this reference work indispensable to anyone who needs the right word—right away.

Look for these outstanding
reference books
at your local bookstore:

*Webster's New World Dictionary of
The American Language*

*A Dictionary of Synonyms and
Antonyms*

A New Guide to Better Writing

*Webster's Red Seal Crossword
Dictionary*

Webster's New World Thesaurus

Published by
WARNER BOOKS

WEBSTER'S
NEW WORLD
THESAURUS

Charlton Laird

WARNER BOOKS

A Warner Communications Company

BY WAY OF INTRODUCTION

The book in your hands was intended to be the readiest word-suggester. It should be easy to use, for the book was planned and designed to make it easy, almost natural, to rely on. Still, some explanation may help. Many people have never learned to use a thesaurus at all, and those who have may find that this book differs from others they have tried. (Meanwhile, if you want capsule advice for using the book turn to page x).

Mainly, the book is an assortment of synonyms, but we mean something different by the word *synonym* than have some editors, and we have brought terms together differently. Partly we are recognizing that relationships among words are complex and subtle, and this subtlety becomes involved in word choice, as some foreign-born gentlemen learning English as a second language are said to have discovered. Having no professional teacher, they would read English books and meet together at one another's houses to talk English.

On this evening Mr. X was entertaining his friends. The conversation started like this:

"Good evening, Mr. X. I have the pleasure to ask after your health, and the health of your wife and children."

"Thank you, Mr. Y. I am well, and so is my wife, but it is my great sorrow that I have no children. My wife is unbearable."

"That is a great tragedy, Mr. X. You will forgive me what I say now, but you know we have the obligation to correct one another. I understand that the proper English word for Mrs. X's unfortunate condition is, she is impregnable."

At this point Mr. Z spoke up. "And you will forgive me, Mr. Y, but I must tell you that the proper English word for Mrs. X's most unfortunate condition is that she is inconceivable."

Of course these reflections on the infertility of the hostess were not intended as the insults they seem to be. A woman need not be un-bearable because she cannot bear children; she is not necessarily impregnable because she cannot be impregnated, and she is not inconceivable because she cannot conceive a child. Families of words are like families of people in this, that the family has grown a long time, that each term has gone its own way, and no one of them is exactly like any other. A word may be able to take over the job of a word similar in sound or meaning, but it may not. How is one to know? The knowing is not easy, but good books on words can help, particularly if the person using the books knows what each of them can be expected to do.

i

So now we come to what a book like this one can do. It should be able to suggest a word you want but have not been able to think of. That is its business; telling you very much about such a word is not its business. That kind of help should be given, if you need it, by other books, but trying to crowd descriptions of words into this book—along with what properly belongs here—would be to make the book clumsy and confusing.

To use this book most effectively, you will need other information, wherever you get it. The best source may be you. For example, assume you have thought of using the word *define,* but you are aware that it will not do just what you want in the sentence you are planning. So you look up the word *define* in a thesaurus. As soon as you see the synonym *discriminate* you know it is the word you want. You are already acquainted with it; you have seen it or heard it dozens of times in such contexts that you sense at once that it can do what you want done. You need waste no more time; you can use it and get on with the job.

Now let us change the example a bit. Suppose you look up *define* and find *discriminate,* but you are not entirely happy with it. You know that it puts the emphasis on the difference between two things, implying what this difference is and how it occurs. But that is not quite what you want. You are dealing with only one thing, and you need a word that will reveal how far it extends and no farther. Then you see the word *demarcate.* Can this be it? You recognize the prefix *de-* and know about what it can do. You know that *-ate* can be used to identify a verb. What about the *-marc-* syllable? It suggests the word *mark.* Can the word mean that if you demarcate something you lay it out very much as though you were putting marks around it?

Using Various Word Books

Now is the time to get some help from books other than a thesaurus and from resources other than your own memory. The readiest book usually is a dictionary. The publishers of this thesaurus also publish the excellent WEBSTER'S NEW WORLD DICTIONARY, *Popular Library Paperback Edition.* Or you may wish to use the more extensive WEBSTER'S NEW WORLD DICTIONARY, *Second College Edition,* of which the *Paperback Edition* is an abridgment. People much interested in writing and speaking may want a dictionary of usage, one of etymology, a slang dictionary, specialized dictionaries, as of medicine, law, or engineering, or a historical dictionary, such as the *Dictionary of Americanisms,* or the *Oxford English Dictionary.* Which word books a writer or speaker needs, and how many of them, each user will have to answer for himself.

For the moment we need notice only this: anybody who uses a thesaurus should have at least one other word book, probably several. He needs a thesaurus to suggest words or phrases he cannot remember, or to suggest terms new to him that he may want to use. He needs at least one other sort of book to tell him more about each of these words, once he has a likely candidate.

Seeking Synonyms

Now we might try more examples to see how you can make a thesaurus work with other word books to help you say what you want to. Let us assume you are doing some explaining, and you find yourself repeating the word *explain* in a way that becomes awkward. If you are a skillful writer, you will be able to eliminate some of these repetitions by tightening your sentence structure, but no matter how clever you are, if you must discuss the subject much you will need some synonyms.

At this point you are likely to turn to a dictionary. Actually, since your problem is thinking of a word, not defining it, you might do better to turn to a thesaurus at once. But if you are like most Americans you will not have the thesaurus habit, and you will have learned, with good reason, to trust dictionaries. If you look up the word in my favorite dictionary you will find the following:

explain, . . . 1. to make clear, plain, or understandable 2. to give the meaning or interpretation of; expound 3. to account for; state reasons for

Here you have a good start, enough for many purposes. You may decide that you do not quite mean *expound,* nor do you mean *account for.* But in the first use you have three good phrases: *make clear, make plain, make understandable.* All these are rather general, and you may be aware that if you write a paragraph in which you keep repeating *make,* the whole will sound as childish as if you were to keep repeating *explain.*

So now, if not earlier, you will do well to turn to a thesaurus. If you were using the present book you would find the following under *explain:*

interpret, explicate, account for, elucidate, illustrate, clarify, illuminate, make clear, describe, expound, teach, reveal, point up *or* out, demonstrate, tell, read, translate, paraphrase, put in other words, define, justify, untangle, unravel, make plain, come to the point, put across, throw light upon, comment *or* remark upon *or* on, make *or* prepare *or* offer an explanation *or* an exposition (of), resolve, clear up, get right, set right, put (someone) on the right track, spell out, go into detail, get to the bottom of, figure out, cast light upon, get across *or* through, bring out, work out, solve, put in plain English.

Now you have dozens of possibilities with various shades of meaning and differences in usage.

You may decide at once that some terms like *unravel, untangle,* and *comment upon* give you the emphasis upon complexity that you want. You may prefer words like *illustrate* or *demonstrate* to introduce detail. Or you may want to avoid all big or rare words, and welcome phrases made up of common words like *set right* and *get to the bottom of.* But you may also be puzzled by some of these words. What, after all, is the difference between *explicate* and *elucidate?* Here the dictionary can help you again. You can look these words up, and for some few words you will find that your dictionary has discriminated close synonyms, with examples. For these two synonyms my dictionary has the following:

> ... **explicate** implies a scholarly analysis or exposition that is developed in detail [the *explication* of a Biblical passage]; **elucidate** implies a shedding light upon by clear and specific explanation, illustration, etc. [to *elucidate* the country's foreign policy] ...

Dealing with Words for Things

Thus for rather general words like *explain, arrangement,* and *definition,* a thesaurus and a dictionary work very well together; the user can go back and forth from one to the other, and sooner or later he can be pretty sure to find what he wants. On the other hand, for concrete and specific words, like *boat, doctor,* and *language,* a dictionary by its nature cannot help much. Consider the first. For *boat* the dictionary I have been citing offers the following:

> ... 1. a small, open vessel or watercraft propelled by oars, sails, or engine. 2. a large vessel; ship: landsman's term 3. a boat-shaped dish [a gravy *boat*] ...

As dictionary definitions these leave little to be desired; they tell us, briefly and accurately, what the word *boat* can be used for. But inevitably they do not help us to many synonyms, except to suggest that *boat* can be a landsman's term for what is more properly called a ship. The fact is, of course, that there are no very good synonyms for *boat,* as *expound* is a good synonym for *explain* in one sense. There is no other common, single word for all "small, open watercraft."

Here we might remind ourselves of a principle not always observed by inexperienced writers, but well known to every teacher of composition. Much writing is weak because the writer uses terms that are more general than they need be. If he would use words that are as concrete and -specific as possible, he could strengthen his sentences. *Jaguar convertible* is more specific than *car,* and in many sentences would tell us more.

Thus a thesaurus can help by providing words that are not very close synonyms but do provide the writer with a better way of saying what he wants to, especially by using concrete words, names for real things. Consider the entry for *boat* in this book; it is too long to quote here, but it begins:

> Types of small boats include the following: ... rowboat, shell, scull, kayak, dugout, canoe, scow, raft, launch, motorboat. ...

The list continues, including *skiff, outrigger,* and even *catamaran.* That is, the book recognizes that often when a writer looks for a synonym he may not want a synonym at all. He may not be looking for another term as much as possible like the one he has rejected. What he is probably seeking is a more concrete, more exact, more picturesque, or more revealing term.

English has many such words for real things, of which the two others mentioned above, *doctor* and *language,* provide examples. The user who looks up *doctor* in this book will find a list of more specific terms for various sorts of doctors, *physician, surgeon, interne, chiropractor, general practitioner,* and the like, along with slang or colloquial terms like *doc* and *sawbones.* Then he will find a highly detailed list of specialists, such as *pediatrician, obstetrician, anesthetist,* and *gynecologist.* The entry for *language* gives terms that may be substituted for the word *language,* like *sound* and *utterance;* it provides words useful in the study of language, like *morphology* and *phonetics;* it includes words identifying the types of languages, like *synthetic* and *computer,* and it lists dozens of important languages all over the world. That is, a thesaurus, along with being a reference tool, can within limits become a textbook in composition, suggesting to the user ways in which he can make his writing clearer, sharper, more dramatic, more interesting.

A Thesaurus: A Treasure House

Earlier, the editor of this book said it differs from other books having similar titles. Some of these differences reveal why the book has been made as it was, and suggest how it should be used. Part of them go back to an engaging Englishman of Swiss ancestry, named Peter Mark Roget.

Roget, a young intellectual—he would probably have been a graduate student in our day—was much interested in philosophy. He was thrown into jail for political reasons. A gentle person, he had done nothing wrong, but he was kept there for more than a year. To while away the time, and to sharpen his perception of ideas, he tried to divide all thought into a thousand sorts, and to use these categories for what he called a "repertory" of words embodying ideas. Released from prison, he led a long and useful life as a professor, a doctor, and a city planner, but he continued to add words to his collection, and after he had retired, he turned once more to his repertory.

By now it had become to him a treasure house—*thesaurus* means treasure house in Latin—in which he stored the wonderful words he had assembled. He published it. It became immediately popular, not among the philosophers for whom Roget had originally intended his collection, but among writers who found that it helped them find synonyms. It became so famous for this purpose that Roget's term, *thesaurus,* is now the general name for a word-finder, and the word *Roget* itself has become the name for a collection of synonyms, as *Johnson* in England and *Webster* in the United States have become names for a dictionary.

Some of the limitations of such books stem from Roget's original idea. He set out to classify words under headings, very much as a botanist may classify plants—a plant exists, and hence it must resemble certain plants and differ from others. Similarly, Roget realized, words can appropriately be put together with other like-words and kept separate from unlike-words; in fact, the word *synonym* is made up of two Greek terms meaning *together with* and *name*. Synonyms are names for the same or similar objects or ideas. None of them can be exactly alike, of course, since no two words can do exactly the same things for all users of the language and in all uses.

Books that classify things can be helpful, whether the objects classified are nouns or varieties of tomatoes, but the modern user of a thesaurus is not mainly interested in classifying philosophic terms, as was Roget. He wants to write or speak better. He wants to find a different way of saying something, and if possible a better way. Roget's book helped them, as do more recent books that have been reedited from Roget, but not so much as they might if they were planned for the people who now use them.

Roget, in effect, asked himself: "How should I classify this word for philosophers?" A modern compiler of a thesaurus needs to ask himself: "How can I make this book most useful to writers and speakers?" And to solve this problem, he has to ask himself other questions: "How would a writer or speaker want to use this book? When would he use it? What would he want to get out of it?"

Once the questions are asked, most of the answers are obvious. A writer or speaker turns to a thesaurus when he has thought of one way to say something, but, for whatever reason, does not want to say it that way. The editor's job is to try to figure out what he would want to say, and suggest it to him.

Brains and the Thesaurus

Thus a thesaurus should be made to fit into the way brains work, when brains are used with language. Not all brains work alike, and an editor can only guess how a particular user will want to use his book. The editor will make blunders, of course, but that should be his theory, and it is the theory back of this volume. It has implications for every part of the book.

Take the entry list, the words printed in boldface at the left of the column, the words the user "looks up." On the whole, these are the words he has thought of, but does not, on this occasion, wish to use. They are likely to include words like *thing, really,* and *order*. They are not likely to include *thermonuclear, Weltschmerz,* and *cotangent,* although those are useful words and may belong among the synonymies. That is, the entry list of a thesaurus—although not of a dictionary—should be made of the commonest words in the language, those that come most readily to the mind of an average person. A likely word may include even slang and colloquialisms such as *keep the ball rolling* and *get going*. Those are just the sorts of terms a writer may think of, but not want to use.

Similarly, within the synonymies, some words and phrases may not be synonyms, or even come very close to being "like-names." For some words there may be nothing even approaching a synonym, but there is always another way to say something. Almost all of the so-called *wh*-words, that is, terms like *who, when, where,* and *what,* have no synonyms although they are very common words. For example, under *why* the present volume has the following:

> why . . . for what reason? how so? how? how is it that? on whose account? what is the cause that? to what end? for what purpose? on what foundation? how do you explain that? how come?

These are not synonyms in the sense that any of them can be substituted for *why* without change in construction, but they do suggest another way of saying what may be implied in *why.*

The natural way with words determines the order, also. Some kind of order we must have; something has to be first and something last. For the entry list, the alphabetical order is the most convenient; the alphabet helps you find a starting place. But within a list of synonyms, the alphabet is not useful. *Zero* is a handy synonym for *nothing* although it begins with *z,* whereas *annihilation,* although it begins with *a,* is seldom needed as a synonym. Instead, we have assumed that the user of the book would want to find his preferred synonym as soon as possible, and we have tried to put early those terms we thought he was most likely to want, and to put far on in the list those terms he was least likely to use. In making our judgments we guessed the user was most likely to want another common word; thus the first synonyms for *notify* in the sense of providing information are *declare, announce, inform, make known.* Terms like *promulgate* and *circularize* appear farther down. Or we thought the user might want a relatively exact like-word, even though it is rare, and hence *ascertained* and *descried* occur early among the synonyms of *discovered* because they are relatively exact, just what a discriminating writer might be looking for.

This is one of the ways in which we hope the book will be easy and quick to use. You need only look up the word you have thought of. It may well be a main entry, and you are likely to find the synonym you want without working through the whole list. First choose the use you want, since common words have several or even many uses. For *fair,* this book recognizes three, quite different: *just, moderately satisfactory,* and *not stormy.* For *to get* the editors recognized eleven groups of synonyms and dozens of phrases. Once you have chosen the use you have in mind, you are likely to find the synonym you want very quickly just by following the printed order.

Cross-references, A Necessary Nuisance

The need for convenience and low cost determined also the handling of cross-references. Cross-references are a nuisance; nobody likes them. They always require looking up at least one more entry. In fact, they are such a nuisance that the editor of one word-finder decided he would have no cross-references at all. The result was that his book is big and clumsy and quite expensive, and even so it lacks thousands of familiar items. He had to repeat so many synonymies that very common words and phrases are omitted, even those any user might want. Accordingly, we decided we had to have cross-references, but we would do what we could to keep them from being much bother.

We relied mainly on two devices. One of these sorts is usually identified by the phrase "see also." For example, assume you have intended writing, "We had to consider the language of our proposed bill." For *language,* in this specialized sense, most of the likeliest synonyms appear elsewhere in the book, not under the entry **language,** and consequently after the first use for *language* you will find a cross-reference: "see also **dialect, jargon 2, writing 1, 2.**" This means that if you do not find the synonym you want under the entry **language,** try **dialect,** the second use of **jargon,** or both the first and second uses of **writing.** Thus the user of this book will find cross-references at the end of many main entries, which will lead him to different but related lists if he wants them.

Then we included what we thought of as mainly cross-references, although to the casual user of the book they may seem to be small entries. The entry for *first-class* will provide an example. This is only one of dozens of terms that mean *good, fine, excellent.* If we had provided full treatment for each of them, and for other sets of terms having much in common, the book would be many times as big as it is and much more expensive. Accordingly, for practicaly reasons, we had to treat *first-class, first-rate,* and dozens more as cross-references to *excellent,* which for a number of reasons we had chosen as a good word to be a main entry. The readiest way, then, would be to have an entry like the following:

   first-rate, *a.* see **excellent.**

But you will find no such entry in this book. Instead, we guessed that if you look up *first-rate* you want one of a relatively few common but rather exact synonyms. If we could guess what this synonym is, we could in effect change the cross-reference to an entry, at least in use. Accordingly, the entry for this word is as follows:

   first-rate, *a.* prime, very good, choice; see **excellent.**

Here you have, in effect, four synonyms—since the cross-reference will usually supply a synonym in itself, even the most common one —and if we have been moderately shrewd in our guess, in a high percentage of such entries you will have the synonym you want without ever looking up the cross-reference.

A few other matters may warrant attention. First, there are the clusters that are sometimes called verb sets. These are verbs made up of at least two words, which taken together mean something other than the words used separately. Notice the following: *Having inherited money, he* started to live it up, *and got a reputation he* could not live down. That is, *live up* and *live down* do not mean living in two directions. Such verbs have been much neglected in thesauruses; we have tried to be more generous in our inclusion of such phrases than have most wordbooks.

Antonyms and What to Do About Them

Something should be said about antonyms. We considered leaving them out; many words have no antonyms. What is the antonym of *eye* or *who?* Besides, writers ʔ ɔ not often need antonyms. To save space we considered doing without them, but occasionally having an antonym is handy. So we compromised; where we found good antonyms we included a few at the end, usually three, but to be sure the user of the book could find as many antonyms as he might need, we always made one of these antonyms a main entry and printed it in boldface, like the other cross-references. That is, if you want an antonym for *heavy* in the sense of weighty, you will find that the antonyms provided are *light, bouyant, feather-light.* If you do not want any of these, you have only to look up **light** where you will find dozens more. If, however, you want an antonym for *heavy* in the sense of burdensome, you will find no antonyms at the entry for that term—because we are treating this use mainly as a cross-reference—but you will have references to **difficult 1, disturbing.** These will all have antonyms with cross-references to dozens more. Thus, in the interest of economy, you may find that antonyms take a little more time than synonyms; you may need to use two cross-references instead of one.

What a Thesaurus Is Not Meant For

Some things this book is not meant for. It will not replace a dictionary. As we noted above, it is intended to suggest terms, not to describe them. It is not a grammar; it does have grammatical categories (abbreviations like *a.* for adjective or adverb appear immediately after the entry), but these are intended as classification, not as grammatical statements. On the whole, if you have a cross-reference from a noun you should look at the noun use of the word provided in the reference. Words are not defined, but we have tried to assort them for convenience into groups. *Tranquil* is divided into *For persons* and *For weather,* since this seemed to be the readiest way to distinguish words like *sane* and *thoughtful* from words like *windless* and *still,* although *tranquil* certainly does not mean *for persons.* Incidentally, these groups of words will often not be the same as the uses recognized in a dictionary. We have had to devise our own classifications, since a thesaurus is not a special kind of dictionary but a different sort of book, with its own principles.

Other information usual in dictionaries is omitted or treated lightly here. There are no pronunciations or etymologies. We have shown only one spelling of a word, although several may be acceptable. *Gaol* is an acceptable British spelling for a place of incarceration, but we have shown only the American spelling, *jail.* We have done little with usage. That is a complex problem, partly because a term that is slang in one context may not be slang in another, and words change their currency and respectability. A few years ago, *teenager* was clearly slang, but now some of the most up-to-date dictionaries treat it as a standard Americanism. We have gone so far as to alert the user of the book to some questionable or local terms by placing an asterisk before them. These asterisks are meant to suggest that the word or phrase may have a slang or colloquial or dialectal flavor in the use we have in mind. The reader is cautioned to consider whether that term is appropriate to the context in which he wishes to use it.

How to Use this Book

For convenience, here is a summary of things you may want to have in mind while you use the book:

1. Look up any word you have thought of but do not want to use.

2. Unless you have thought of a rare word you should find: (a) a main entry, with many alternate terms, some antonyms, and possibly a "see also" cross-reference, or (b) a brief entry, with two to four synonyms and one or more cross-references.

3. If you have turned to a main entry, check to see whether more than one use is recognized, and if so, pick the one you want. The various uses will be numbered in boldface figures.

4. Work through the list, looking for a term that will suggest what you need, trying the cross-reference at the end if you need it.

5. If you find a word or phrase you may want, but do not know very well, look it up in at least one dictionary.

6. If you have looked up a brief entry, it is probably for the most part a cross-reference, but it will have a few common synonyms. If you do not want any of them, turn to the main entry or entries provided in the cross-reference. The entry to which you are referred may have more than one grammatical use—*fast* can be an adjective, adverb, noun, or verb. Prefer the grammatical category that corresponds to the use of the word from which you got the cross-reference.

In short, this book is intended to help you find the word or phrase you want. The editors wish you happy hunting!

Charlton Laird
University of Nevada, Reno
Reno, Nevada

Key: *a.* = adjective or adverb (i.e., modifier)
   n. = noun
   v. = verb
   * = nonformal (i.e., slang, colloquial, dialectal, etc.)

A

a, *a.* and *prep.* **1.** [The indefinite article; before vowels, written *an*] some, one, any, each, some kind of, some particular, any (one) of, a certain.—*Ant.* the, this, that. **2.** [An indication of frequency] per, every, at the rate of; see **each 2.**

abandon, *v.* **1.** [To give up] leave *or* go off, quit, withdraw (from), discontinue, give over *or* up, throw over, break off, let go, cease, cast off *or* away *or* aside, discard, vacate, give away, part with, evacuate, surrender, yield, desist, concede, renounce, abdicate, lose hope of, go back on, secede (from), waive, forgo, back down from, lay down *or* aside, dispose of, have done with, *throw in the towel, break the pattern *or* habit. **2.** [To leave someone *or* something in trouble] desert, forsake, ostracize, back out on, break (up) with, run away, defect, reject, disown, cast off, maroon, depart from, give over, throw overboard, jettison, leave behind, slip away from, *stand up, leave in the lurch, turn one's back upon, *run *or* skip out, *doublecross, let down, *drop.

abandoned, *a.* deserted, desolate, destitute, desperate, empty, given up, unused, vacated, left, neglected, relinquished, lonely, forsaken, solitary, hopeless, cast away *or* aside *or* off, forgotten, shunned, forlorn, avoided, outcast, rejected, helpless, unfortunate, alone, discarded, scorned, lost, doomed, friendless, *in the wastebasket, thrown overboard, *out on a limb, *waiting at the church, left in the lurch *or* in the cold *or* *holding the bag.—*Ant.* inhabited, used, in use.

abbreviate, *v.* shorten, cut, condense; see **decrease 2.**

abbreviation, *n.* contraction, abridgment, sketch, brief, abstract, synopsis, reduction, abstraction, condensation, digest, outline, summary, short form; see also **summary.**

abdicate, *v.* relinquish, give up, withdraw; see **abandon 1.**

abdomen, *n.* midsection, belly, bowels; see also **stomach.**

abduct, *v.* steal away, seize, carry off; see **kidnap.**

abide, *v.* **1.** [To lodge] stay (at), room, reside; see **dwell. 2.** [To submit to] put up with, bear (with), withstand; see **endure 2.**

abide by, *v.* follow, observe, comply with; see **follow 2.**

ability, *n.* aptitude, intelligence, innate qualities, powers, potency, worth, talent, gift, genius, capability, competence, proficiency, adeptness, qualification(s), knowledge, self-sufficiency, tact, finish, technique, craft, skill, artistry, cunning, skillfulness, dexterity, facility, finesse, mastery, cleverness, deftness, experience, ingenuity, strength, understanding, faculty, comprehension, makings, sense, *what it takes, brains, knack, hang, *know-how.—*Ant.* ignorance, ineptitude, awkwardness.

able, *a.* apt, agile, adept, intelligent, ingenious, worthy, talented, gifted, fitted, capable, effective, efficient, qualified, masterful, adequate, competent, expert, experienced, skilled, learned, clever, suitable, smart, crafty, cunning, bright, knowing, dexterous, endowed, deft, alert, adaptable, smooth, ready, versatile, equal to, suited (to), wellrounded, mighty, powerful, strong, robust, sturdy, brawny, vigorous, courageous, fit for, sharp, cut out for, *having an ear for.—*Ant.* stupid, bungling, unadaptable.

able-bodied, *a.* fit, powerful, sturdy; see **strong 1.**

abnormal, *a.* strange, irregular, unnatural; see **unusual 2.**

abnormality, *n.* peculiarity, singularity, malformation; see **irregularity.**

aboard, *a.* on board, on ship, shipped, loaded, on board ship, freight on board (F.O.B.), being shipped, en route, consigned, in transit, being transported, embarked, afloat, at sea, on deck, traveling.

abolish, *v.* suppress, eradicate, terminate, exterminate, obliterate, annul, remove, revoke, end, finish, nullify, set aside, annihilate, repeal, subvert, reverse, rescind, prohibit, extinguish, cancel, erase, root out, pull up, uproot, demolish, invalidate, overturn, overthrow, make or declare null and void, do away with, stamp or crush out, undo, throw out, put an end to, inhibit, dispense with, cut out, raze, squelch, *not leave one stone upon another; see also **destroy 1.**

abort, *v.* miscarry, fall short, miss; see **fail 1.**

about, *a.* and *prep.* **1.** [Approximately] roughly, closely, almost, around, very close, not quite, more or less, practically, just about, generally, comparatively, nearly, in general; see **approxi-**

mately. 2. [Concerning] regarding, respecting, touching, of, on, in relation to, relative or relating to, as regards, in or with regard to, on or in which, with or in respect to, in the matter of, in or with reference to, referring to, so far as (something) is concerned, in connection with, connected or concerned with, thereby, hereof, wherein, as to or for, concerning. 3. [Around] surrounding, round about, on all sides; see **around.**

***about to,** a. and prep. on the verge of, at the point of, just about; see **almost.**

above, a. and prep. 1. [High in position] over, high, higher, superior, beyond, on high, raised, above one's head, in a higher place, aloft, overhead, toward the sky; see **higher, over 1.** —Ant. low, below, beneath. 2. [Referring to something earlier] before, foregoing, earlier; see **preceding.**

above all, a. in the first place, chiefly, especially; see **principally.**

aboveboard, a. candidly, honestly, frankly; see **openly 1.**

abreast, a. level, equal, side by side; see **beside.**

abroad, a. away, at large, adrift, wandering, elsewhere, overseas, traveling, touring, outside, distant, far away, gone, out of the country, removed.

abrupt, a. 1. [Said of things, usually landscape] uneven, rough, rugged; see **steep.** 2. [Said of people or acts of people] terse, hasty, gruff; see **rude.**

absence, n. 1. [The state of being elsewhere] truancy, nonattendance, nonappearance, inexistence, loss, vacancy, *cut. 2. [The state of lacking something] deficiency, need, inadequacy; see **lack 1.**

absent, a. away, missing, elsewhere, vanished, gone (out), not at home, not present, out, wanting, lacking, abroad, lost, out of sight, nowhere to be found, on vacation, AWOL, playing hooky, *split.

absent-minded, a. preoccupied, abstracted, dreamy, listless, lost, absent, thoughtless, oblivious, inattentive, daydreaming, unconscious, unaware, withdrawn, removed, faraway, distracted, remote, forgetful. —Ant. attentive, observant, alert.

absolute, a. 1. [Without limitation] total, complete, entire, infinite, fixed, settled, supreme, full, unrestricted, unlimited, unconditional, independent, wholehearted, sheer, pure, unmitigated, utter, unabridged, thorough, clean, outright, downright, ideal, simple, perfect, full, blanket, all out, out-and-out.—Ant. restricted, limited, qualified. 2. [Without limit in authority] authoritarian, domineering, supreme, arbitrary, official, autocratic, tyrannical, fascist, fascistic,

overbearing, czarist, nazi, totalitarian, communistic, oppressive, browbeating, antidemocratic, imperative, dogmatic, commanding, controlling, compelling, despotic, intimidating, fanatic, dictatorial, arrogant, with an iron hand.— Ant. lenient, tolerant, temperate. 3. [Certain] positive, unquestionable, undeniable; see **certain 2.**

absolutely, a. 1. [Completely] utterly, unconditionally, thoroughly; see **completely.** 2. [Positively] unquestionably, certainly, definitely; see **surely.**

absolve, v. pardon, set free, clear; see **excuse.**

absorb, v. digest, suck or take or drink in or up, ingest, appropriate, embody, use up, assimilate, osmose, blot, imbibe, swallow, consume, incorporate, sop or soak or sponge up.—Ant. **flow,** expel, discharge.

absorbed, a. assimilated, taken in, swallowed up, consumed, drunk, imbibed, dissolved, united, incorporated (into), digested.—Ant. **removed,** unassimilated, unconsumed.

absorbent, a. porous, spongy, permeable, dry, soft, pervious, penetrable, receptive, retentive, thirsty.

absorbing, a. engaging, exciting, enthralling; see **interesting.**

absorption, n. assimilation, digestion, osmosis, saturation, penetration, fusion, intake, union, consumption, ingestion, swallowing up, taking in, reception, retention, incorporation, appropriation, drinking in, suction, sopping or soaking or drying or blotting or sponging up, inhalation.—Ant. **removal,** ejection, discharge.

abstain, v. refrain (from), renounce, desist, withhold, avoid, stop, deny oneself, refuse, decline, hold back, shun, evade, dispense with, do without, fast, starve, have nothing to do with, let (well enough) alone, do nothing, keep from, keep one's hands off, swear off, *lay off, turn over a new leaf, have no hand in, take the pledge. —Ant. indulge, **join,** gorge.

abstinence, n. abstaining, temperance, denial, self-denial, self-control, selfrestraint, continence, fasting, frugality, renunciation, avoidance, sobriety, austerity, refraining, nonindulgence, moderation, soberness, Puritanism.—Ant. indulgence, overindulgence, intemperance.

abstract, a. general, intellectual, ideal; see **obscure 1.**

absurd, a. preposterous, ridiculous, ludicrous; see **stupid 1.**

absurdity, n. improbability, foolishness, senselessness; see **nonsense 1, 2.**

abundance, n. bounty, more than enough, profusion; see **plenty.**

abundant, a. sufficient, ample, copious; see plentiful 2.

abundantly, a. plentifully, lavishly, richly, handsomely, in large measure, profusely, amply, sufficiently, generously, inexhaustibly, *many times over, to one's heart's content, on the fat of the land; see also adequately.

abuse, n. perversion, misapplication, debasement, degradation, desecration, injury, damage, harm, hurt, wrong, injustice, violation, malevolence, mishandling, mismanagement, pollution, defilement, prostitution.—Ant. respect, care, veneration.

abuse, v. insult, injure, hurt, harm, damage, impair, offend, overwork, ill-treat, ill-use, misuse, maltreat, mistreat, wrong, persecute, molest, victimize, oppress, ruin, mar, spoil, do wrong by or to, mishandle, pervert, profane, prostitute, desecrate, pollute, harass, manhandle, do an injustice to, violate, defile, impose upon, deprave, taint, debase, corrupt.—Ant. defend, protect, befriend.

abused, a. wronged, injured, harmed; see hurt.

academic, a. scholastic, erudite, scholarly; see learned.

academy, n. preparatory school, boarding school, finishing school, secondary school; see school 1.

accelerate, v. quicken, speed up, hurry; see hasten 2.

acceleration, n. speeding up, hastening, increase of speed, quickening, hurrying, stepping up, picking up speed; see also speed.

accent, n. beat, stroke, emphasis, pitch, accentuation, inflection, intonation, rhythm, meter, cadence.

accept, v. admit, be resigned, give into, surrender, suffer, endure, grant, allow, tolerate, take in one's stride, consent (to), acquiesce (in); see agree.

acceptable, a. satisfactory, agreeable, pleasing; see pleasant 2.

acceptance, n. recognition, assent, approval; see agreement 1.

accepted, a. taken, received, assumed, approved, adopted, recognized, endorsed, verified, acclaimed, welcomed, engaged, hired, claimed, delivered, used, employed, affirmed, upheld, authorized, preferred, acknowledged, accredited, allowed, settled, established, sanctioned, unopposed, authentic, confirmed, chosen, acceptable, popular, formally admitted, stereotyped, orthodox, standard, conventional, current, taken for granted, credited, OK'd; see also popular 1, 3. —Ant. refused, denied, nullified.

access, n. admittance, entree, introduction; see entrance 1, 2.

accessible, a. approachable, obtainable, attainable; see available.

accessories, n. pl. frills, ornaments, adornments, decorations, additions, attachments, *gimmicks, *doodads.

accessory, n. 1. [An accomplice] helper, aid, assistant; see associate. 2. [Something added] adjunct, attribute, accompaniment, attachment, consequence, attendant, complement, supplement.

accident, n. luck, adventure, fortune, contingency, occurrence, conjecture, circumstance, event, occasion; see also chance 1.

accidental, a. adventitious, chance, coincidental; see aimless.

accidentally, a. unintentionally, involuntarily, unwittingly, unexpectedly, inadvertently, casually, by chance, haphazardly, incidentally, randomly, not purposely. —Ant. deliberately, voluntarily, intentionally.

accommodate, v. 1. [To render a service] help, aid, comfort, make comfortable, oblige, suit, serve, gratify, please, arrange, settle, benefit, tender (to), supply, furnish, assist, support, sustain, do a favor (for), indulge, humor, pamper, accept, put oneself out for, do a service for. 2. [To suit one thing to another] fit, adapt, correspond; see also adjust 1. 3. [To provide lodging] house, rent, give lodging to; see entertain 2.

accommodations, n. pl. quarters, rooms, lodging, housing, apartment, hotel, room and board, roof over one's head; see also housing.

accompanied, a. attended, escorted, squired, tended, shown (around or about), not alone.

accompaniment, n. harmony, instrumental music, musical background; see music 1.

accompany, v. escort, attend, tend, be with, follow, keep company (with), guard, guide, show in or around, show the way, conduct, go along (with), chaperon, associate with, go hand in hand with, go side by side with.

accomplice, n. confederate, helper, aid; see associate.

accomplish, v. fulfill, perform, finish; see achieve, succeed 1.

accomplished, a. 1. [Done] completed, consummated, concluded; see finished 1. 2. [Skilled] proficient, expert, skillful; see able.

accomplishment, n. execution, fulfillment, attainment; see success 2.

accordingly, a. in consequence, consequently, equally, respectively, duly, in respect to, thus, hence, therefore, as a result, as a consequence, as the case may be, on the ground, under the circumstances, as things go, to that end, in that event.

according to, *prep.* in accordance with, as, to the degree that, conforming to, just as, in keeping with, in line with, in agreement with.

account, *n.* bulletin, annual, report; see **record 1.** —give a good account of oneself, boast, rationalize, justify one's actions; see **declare.** —on account, charged, in *or* on layaway, on call; see **unpaid 1.** —on account of, because of, by virtue of, since; see **because.** —on no account, for no reason, no way, under no circumstances; see **never.** —on someone's account, because of, for someone's sake, in someone's behalf *or* interest; see **because.** —take account of, judge, evaluate, investigate; see **examine 1.** —take into account, judge, allow for, weigh; see **consider.**

accountant, *n.* bookkeeper, cashier, teller; see **assistant.**

account for, *v.* clarify, resolve, elucidate; see **explain.**

accumulate, *v.* hoard, get together, gather (into a mass), collect, heap, store, concentrate, compile, provide, pile (up), scrape *or* stack up, stockpile, store up, acquire, gain, load up, rake up, unite, add to, profit, build up, gain control, drag *or* haul *or* rake *or* roll in, *bank; see also **get 1.**

accuracy, *n.* efficiency, exactness, precision, correctness, skillfulness, sharpness, incisiveness, mastery, dependability, strictness, certainty, sureness. —*Ant.* error, inaccuracy, mistake.

accurate, *a.* 1. [Free from error] exact, correct, perfect; see **right 1.** 2. [Characterized by precision] deft, reliable, trustworthy, true, correct, exact, specific, dependable, skillful, methodical, systematic, distinct, particular, realistic, authentic, genuine, careful, close, critical, detailed, factual, severe, rigorous, rigid, strict, meticulous, punctilious, faithful, punctual, scientific, objective, matter-of-fact, rational, unmistakable, reasonable, right, explicit, definite, defined, *(right) on the button, *on the spot, *on the nose.—*Ant.* incompetent, faulty, slipshod. —be accurate, *v.* be precise *or* exact *or* careful, hit the nail on the head, not miss, restrain oneself; see also **check 2, control 1, verify.**

accurately, *a.* correctly, precisely, exactly, certainly; see **carefully 1.**

accusation, *n.* indictment, denunciation, slur, complaint, citation, charge, insinuation, *beef, smear, *frame-up.

accuse, *v.* censure, charge, prosecute; see **blame.**

accused, *a.* arraigned, indicted, incriminated, charged with, under suspicion, alleged to be guilty, apprehended, held for questioning, liable, involved, under attack, under fire, up for.—*Ant.* discharged, acquitted, cleared.

accuser, *n.* prosecutor, plaintiff, adversary; see **opponent 1.**

accustomed, *a.* usual, customary, habitual; see **conventional 1.**

accustomed to, *a.* in the habit, used to, wont to; see **addicted to.**

ache, *n.* twinge, pang, spasm; see **pain 2.**

ache, *v.* pain, throb, be sore; see **hurt.**

achieve, *v.* complete, end, terminate, conclude, finish (up *or* off), do, perform, execute, fulfill, carry off *or* out *or* on *or* through, bring about *or* off, settle, effect, bring to an end *or* a conclusion, close, stop, produce, realize, actualize, discharge, wind up, work out, adjust, resolve, solve, accomplish, make an end of, enact, manage, contrive, negotiate, sign, seal, bring to pass, see (it) through, get done, close up, put the lid on, carry to completion, follow through, take measures, lose oneself in, deliver, *knock off, *fill the bill, round out, come through, *polish off, *clean *or* mop up, *put across, *pull over *or* off, make short work of, put through, *go all the way, *go the limit, *call it a day, *put the finishing touch on.—*Ant.* **abandon,** fail, give up.

achievement, *n.* fulfillment, feat, exploit, accomplishment, triumph, hit, success, realization, creation, completion, execution, masterpiece, performance, deed, act, enactment, victory, conquest, attainment, feather in one's cap.—*Ant.* **failure,** blunder, collapse.

acid, *a.* sharp, tart, biting; see **sour 1.**

acid, *n.* 1. [A sour substance] acidulous compound, corrosive, Lewis acid, hydrogen-ion concentration; see also **element 2.** 2. [A drug] D-lysergic acid diethylamide *or* LSD, di-methyl triptamine *or* DMT, mescaline; see **drug 2.** Common acids include the following—vinegar, verjuice, lemon juice; citric, ascorbic, nicotinic, boric, acetic, sulfuric, hydrochloric, hydrosulfurous, phosphoric, carbolic, nitric, benzoic, amino acid.

acidity, *n.* sourness, bitterness, tartness, sharpness, pungency, harshness, causticity.

acknowledge, *v.* 1. [To admit] concede, confess, declare; see **admit 2.** 2. [To recognize the authority of] endorse, certify, confirm, uphold, support, recognize, ratify, approve, defend, subscribe to, attest to, take an oath by, defer to.

acknowledged, *a.* admitted, confessed, recognized, unquestioned, accepted, authorized, confirmed, received, sanctioned, accredited, approved.

acknowledgment, *n.* greeting, reply, answer, response, nod, confession, statement, apology, guarantee, return, support, signature, receipt, letter, card, contract, applause, vote of thanks, I.O.U.

acquaintance, *n.* colleague, associate, neighbor; see **friend**.

acquainted (with), *a.* introduced, on speaking terms, having some connections; see **familiar with**.

acquaint with, *v.* introduce, make acquainted, present; see **introduce** 3.

acquire, *v.* take, earn, procure; see **get** 1.

acquired, *a.* reached, inherited, given, accrued, derived, granted, endowed, transmitted, handed down, bequeathed, allowed, awarded, passed on, willed to, attained, accomplished, learned, adopted, earned, collected, gathered, secured, procured, obtained, captured, realized, *got by the sweat of one's brow, *dug out, *raked in, *cornered, *netted, *salted away, grabbed; see also **won**.

acquisition, *n.* inheritance, gift, donation, grant, wealth, riches, fortune, profit, gain, earnings, wages, salary, income, winnings, return(s), proceeds, benefit, prize, reward, award, accomplishment, achievement, premium, bonus, fee, commission, pension, annuity, allowance, guaranty, security, gain, dividend.

acquit, *v.* clear, absolve, vindicate; see **excuse**.

acquittal, *n.* absolution, clearance, exoneration, dismissal, deliverance, amnesty, discharge, pardon, reprieve, exemption, liberation, release, freedom.—*Ant.* **punishment**, sentence, imprisonment.

acre, *n.* plot, acreage, bit of land, estate; see **property** 2.

acrobat, *n.* tumbler, clown, aerialist, equalibrist, trapeze artist, contortionist, performer, tightrope walker, somersaulter, bar swinger, rope dancer, flying trapezist, circus athlete, stunt man, figure skater, vaudeville performer, ballet dancer, aerial gymnast, gymnast, balancer.

across, *a.* and *prep.* crosswise, crossed, to the opposite side of, over (against), (directly) opposite, on the other side, from side to side of, from one side to another, in a crossing position, in front of, opposite (to), beyond.

across the board, *a.* impartially, fairly, equivalently; see **equally**.

act, *n.* 1. [An action] deed, performance, exploit; see **action** 2. 2. [An official or legal statement] law, proposal, judgment, commitment, verdict, amendment, order, announcement, edict, ordinance, decree, statute, writ, bull, warrant, summons, subpoena, document, bill, code, clause, *law of the land. 3. [A division of a play] scene, curtain, prologue, epilogue, introduction; first act, second act, third act, etc. 4. [A pose] falsification, feigning, affectation; see **pretense** 1.

act, *v.* 1. [To perform an action] do, execute, carry out *or* on, operate, transact, accomplish, achieve, consummate, carry into effect, perpetrate, persist, labor, work, officiate, function, preside, serve, go ahead *or* about, step into, take steps, play *or* take a part, begin, move in, enforce, maneuver, create, practice, develop, make progress, interfere, interpose, be active, intrude, commit, fight, combat, respond, keep going, answer, put forth energy, *hustle, *get going.—*Ant.* **wait**, await, rest. 2. [To conduct oneself] behave, seem, appear, carry *or* acquit *or* comport *or* bear oneself, give the appearance of, represent oneself (as), take on, play one's part, impress one as, *put on airs, *cut a figure; see also **behave**. 3. [To take part in a play] perform, impersonate, represent, act out, simulate, pretend, mimic, burlesque, parody, feign, portray, rehearse, take a part (in), dramatize, star, play *or* act the part of.

act for, *v.* do the work of, replace, fill in; see **substitute**.

acting, *a.* substituting, alternate, deputy; see **temporary**.

acting, *n.* pretending, feigning, simulating, gesturing, ranting, dramatizing, performing, behaving, playing, impersonation, depiction, portrayal, pantomime, rendition, dramatics, stagecraft, theatricals, performance, dramatic action.

action, *n.* 1. [Any state opposed to rest and quiet] activity, conflict, business, occupation, work, response, reaction, movement, industry, bustle, turmoil, stir, flurry, animation, vivacity, enterprise, energy, liveliness, alertness, agility, vigor, life, commotion, rush, motion, mobility, haste, speed, *go, life, doings. 2. [An individual deed] feat, exploit, performance, performing, execution, blow, stroke, maneuver, step, stunt, achievement, act, deed, thing, stratagem, something done, accomplishment, commission, effort, enterprise, manipulation, move, movement, doing, effect, transaction, exertion, operation, handiwork, dealings, procedure, manufacture. —**bring action**, accuse, start a lawsuit, take to court; see **sue**. —**see action**, do battle, engage in combat, conflict; see **fight**. —**take action**, become active, do, initiate activity; see **act** 1.

actions, *n. pl.* deportment, conduct, manner(s); see **behavior** 1.

activate, *v.* stimulate, initiate, arouse; see **begin** 1.

active, *a.* busy, lively, *dynamic, energetic, alive, mobile, rolling, hasty, going, motive, rapid, progressive, exertive, pushing, walking, traveling, movable, acting, bustling, humming, efficient, functioning, working, moving, restless, swarming, rustling, flowing, in process or effect or action or play, simmering, overflowing, stirring, effective, at work, operating, agitated, brisk, industrious, enthusiastic, agile, quick, nimble, rapid, dexterous, spry, fresh, sprightly, wiry, alert, ready, sharp, keen, wide-awake, animated, enlivened, ardent, purposeful, resolute, aggressive, forceful, intense, determined, diligent, hardworking, assiduous, enterprising, inventive, vigorous, strenuous, eager, zealous, bold, daring, high-spirited, *hopping, going full blast, *in high gear, *snappy, *on the ball.

activity, *n.* motion, movement, liveliness; see **action** 1.

act one's age, *v.* act properly, comport oneself, be orderly; see **behave.**

actor, *n.* player, performer, character, star, comedian, dramatis persona, leading man or woman, entertainer, artist, television star, villain, motion picture actor, stage actor or player, professional actor, mimic, mime, clown, ventriloquist, pantomimist, understudy, tragedian, protagonist, *bit player, *ham, movie idol; see also **cast** 2.

actress, *n.* comedienne, tragedienne, leading lady; see **actor, cast** 2.

actual, *a.* original, real, exact; see **genuine** 1.

actually, *a.* truly, in fact, as a matter of fact; see **really** 1.

act up, *v.* carry on, be naughty, create a disturbance; see **misbehave.**

act upon or **on,** *v.* 1. [To act in accordance with] adjust, regulate, behave; see **act** 1, 2. 2. [To influence] affect, sway, impress; see **influence.**

acute, *a.* 1. [Crucial] decisive, important, vital; see **critical.** 2. [Sharp] severe, keen, cutting; see **intense.** 3. [Shrewd] clever, sensitive, penetrating; see **intelligent.**

acutely, *a.* keenly, sharply, severely; see **very.**

*ad, *n.* announcement, display, notice; see **advertisement.**

adage, *n.* aphorism, saying, maxim; see **proverb.**

adapt, *v.* modify, revise, readjust; see **alter** 1.

adaptability, *n.* changeability, flexibility, versatility, adjustability, conformability, pliancy, docility, compliancy, pliability, plasticity.

adaptable, *a.* pliant, tractable, pliable; see **flexible.**

add, *v.* 1. [To bring together, usually by mathematics] total, sum (up), figure (up), compute, calculate, count or add up, do simple addition, append, annex, continue, run over, enumerate, tell off,

*hitch or clap on.—*Ant.* subtract, decrease, take away. 2. [To make a further remark] append, say further, continue, write further, annex, supplement, affix, add a postscript, reply.

addict, *n.* habitué, practitioner, *fiend, *hophead, *head, *dope fiend, *drug fiend, *mainliner, *junkie, *nut, *hard case, *freak.

addicted (to), *a.* given over, given or disposed to, inclined, habituated, prone, accustomed, attached, abandoned, wedded, devoted, predisposed, used to, imbued with, fanatic about, obsessed with.

addiction, *n.* fixation, inclination, bent; see **habit** 2, **obsession.**

addition, *n.* 1. [That which has been added] interest, raise, additive, adjunct, bonus, supplement, reinforcement, appendage, appendix, accessory, attachment, extension, increase, annex.—*Ant.* loss, reduction, shrinkage. 2. [A real estate development] annex, annexation, subdivision, shopping center, development, extension, expansion, branch, construction.

additional, *a.* supplementary, new, further; see **extra.**

address, *n.* 1. [A formal speech] oration, lecture, sermon; see **speech** 3. 2. [Place at which one may be reached] (legal) residence, home, (living) quarters, dwelling, headquarters, place of business or residence, box number; see **home** 1.

address, *v.* 1. [To provide directions for delivery] label, mark, prepare for mailing; see **write** 2. 2. [To speak formally to an assemblage] lecture (to), discuss, give or deliver a talk or speech or address, take the floor, orate, declaim, harangue, rant, sermonize, *spout (off), *spiel.

add to, *v.* augment, amplify, expand; see **increase** 1.

add up, *v.* be plausible or probable or reasonable or logical, stand to reason, hold water; see **make sense.**

add up to, *v.* indicate, signify, imply; see **mean** 1.

adept, *a.* skillful, proficient, capable; see **able.**

adequate, *a.* sufficient, equal to the need, satisfactory; see **enough** 1.

adequately, *a.* sufficiently, appropriately, suitably, fittingly, satisfactorily, abundantly, acceptably, tolerably, decently, presentably, modestly, fairly well, well enough, capably, good enough, to an acceptable degree, competently; see also **well** 1, 2.—*Ant.* inadequately, badly, insufficiently.

adhere (to), *v.* 1. [To serve] follow, be devoted to, practice; see **obey.** 2. [To stick to] attach, cling, hold fast; see **stick** 1.

adhesive, *a.* gummy, clinging, sticking fast; see **sticky.**

adjacent, *a.* beside, alongside, bordering; see **near 1.**

adjective, *n.* modifier, article, determiner, attribute, attributive, qualifier, descriptive word *or* term, limiting word, dependent, adjectival construction, identifier, qualifying word *or* term, adjunct, accessory, addition, dependent.

adjourn, *v.* leave, postpone, discontinue; see **suspend 2.**

adjournment, *n.* intermission, pause, break; see **recess 1.**

adjust, *v.* 1. [To bring to agreement] settle, arrange, conclude, complete, accord, reconcile, clarify, conform, sort, allocate, grade, tally, regulate, organize, methodize, systematize, coordinate, straighten, standardize, clean up. 2. [To place or regulate parts] fix, connect, square, balance, regulate, tighten, fit, repair, focus, readjust, rectify, correct, set, mend, improve, overhaul, grind, sharpen, renovate, polish, bring into line, align, put in working order, temper, service.

adjustable, *a.* adaptable, stretchable, tractable; see **flexible.**

adjustment, *n.* settlement, arrangement, pay, remuneration, reimbursement, compensation, compromise, reconciliation, agreement, making up, improvement, regulation, arrangement, correction, mutual understanding.

administer, *v.* 1. [To manage] conduct, direct, control; see **manage 1.** 2. [To furnish] extend, proffer, give; see **offer 1.**

administration, *n.* 1. [The direction of affairs] government, supervision, command; see **management 2.** 2. [Those who direct affairs] directors, administrators, officers, supervisors, superintendents, advisers, command, executives, strategists, officials, committee, board, board of directors, executive, executive branch, legislature, president, presidency, chief executive, cabinet, ministry, commander, chairman, general, admiral, commander in chief, central office, headquarters, the management, bureau, consulate, embassy, legation, department, Washington, party in power, *brass, *front office, the powers that be, *the man. 3. [The period in which an administration, sense 2, is operative] term of office, tenure, reign; see **sense 2.**

administrative, *a.* executive, controlling, deciding; see **governing.**

administrator, *n.* manager, head, chief; see **executive.**

admirable, *a.* worthy, attractive, good; see **excellent.**

admiration, *n.* praise, deference, approval, estimation, regard, fondness, esteem, respect, appreciation, favor, adoration, applause, glorification, idolatry, honor, recognition, prizing, valuing, liking, love, high regard, high opinion, reverence, veneration, homage.—*Ant.* objection, disregard, distrust.

admire, *v.* esteem, honor, applaud, praise, respect, approve, revere, venerate, laud, boost, glorify, reverence, hold dear, appreciate, credit, commend, value, treasure, prize, look up to, rate highly, pay homage to, idolize, adore, hail, put a high price on, have a high opinion of, think highly of, think well of, take great stock in, put on a pedestal.—*Ant.* censure, deride, blame.

admirer, *n.* supporter, believer, patron; see **follower.**

admissible, *a.* proper, suitable, right; see **permitted.**

admission, *n.* 1. [The act of granting entrance] acceptance, admittance, permission, reception, welcome, recognition, acknowledgment, confirmation, selection, initiation.—*Ant.* removal, rejection, expulsion. 2. [The entrance fee] (cover) charge, fee, check, dues, charges, demand, toll, tax, minimum, donation, *cover, gate. 3. [Something acknowledged] statement, disclosure, confession, acknowledgment, divulgence, declaration, confirmation, assertion, testimony, allegation, deposition, affidavit.—*Ant.* denial, disallowance, repudiation.

admit, *v.* 1. [To grant entrance] receive, give access to, allow entrance to; see **receive 4.** 2. [To confess] acknowledge, own, indicate, disclose, bare, unveil, uncover, expose, proclaim, declare, open up, bring to light, go over, go into details, confide to, tell, relate, narrate, enumerate, divulge, reveal, communicate, make known, tell the whole story, break down and confess, plead guilty, let slip, own up, talk, *sing, *cough up, *come clean, *spill the beans.—*Ant.* hide, cover up, obscure. 3. [To permit] let, allow, grant; see **allow 1.**

admonish, *v.* reprove, chide, rebuke; see **scold.**

adolescence, *n.* minority, puberty, teens; see **youth 1.**

adolescent, *a.* pubescent, juvenile, youthful; see **young 1.**

adolescent, *n.* youngster, minor, teenager; see **youth 3.**

adopt, *v.* 1. [To take as a son or daughter] pick, choose, select, transfer, father, mother, name, take in, raise, make one's heir, take as one's own (child), naturalize, foster. 2. [To take as one's own] embrace, appropriate, seize, take up *or* over, choose, assume, use, utilize, imitate, borrow, make one's own, mimic.—*Ant.* deny, repudiate, reject.

adoption, *n.* choosing, appropriation, choice; see **selection 1.**

*****adorable,** *a.* delightful, lovable, cute; see **charming.**

adoration, *n.* devotion, homage, veneration; see **worship 1.**

adore, *v.* 1. [To worship] venerate, revere, glorify; see **worship 2. 2.** [To love] cherish, treasure, prize; see **love 1.**

adorn, *v.* beautify, embellish, ornament; see **decorate.**

adorned, *a.* trimmed, decked, garnished; see **ornate 1.**

adult, *a.* of age, grown, developed; see **mature 1.**

adult, *n.* mature person, grown-up, fully developed member of a species; see **man 2, woman 1.**

adulterate, *v.* dilute, lessen, taint; see **pollute, weaken.**

adultery, *n.* unlicensed intercourse, infidelity, cuckoldry; see **fornication.**

advance, *n.* 1. [The act of moving forward] impetus, progression, motion; see **progress 1. 2.** [Promotion] enrichment, betterment, increase; see **improvement 1. 3.** [Loan] accommodation, allowance, credit; see **loan.**

advance, *v.* 1. [To move forward physically] progress, proceed, move on, forge ahead, press on, push ahead, go on, go forth, gain ground, make headway, step forward, come to the front, conquer territory, march *or* get on, move onward, continue ahead, push *or* press on.—*Ant.* halt, stop, stand still. 2. [To propose] set forth, introduce, suggest; see **propose 1. 3.** [To promote] further, encourage, urge; see **promote 1. 4.** [To lend] loan, provide with, furnish; see **lend 1. 5.** [To improve] develop, make progress, get better; see **improve 2.**

advanced, *a.* 1. [Superior] precocious, first, exceptional; see **excellent. 2.** [Aged] seasoned, venerable, time-honored; see **old 1, 3. 3.** [Progressive] radical, unconventional, ahead of the times; see **liberal.**

advancement, *n.* 1. [Promotion in rank] preferment, elevation, raise; see **promotion 1. 2.** [Progress] gain, headway, progression; see **progress 1.**

advantage, *n.* luck, favor, approval, help, aid, sanction, leeway, good, patronage, support, preference, choice, odds, protection, start, leg-up, helping hand, upper hand, leverage, hold, opportunity, dominance, superiority, supremacy, lead, influence, power, mastery, authority, prestige, recognition, position, eminence, sway, precedence, *****pull, *****edge, *****ace in the hole.—*Ant.* handicap, disadvantage, weakness. —**have the advantage of,** be superior, have the opportunity, be privileged; see **succeed 1.** —**take advantage of,** exploit, profit by, opportunize; see **use 1.**

adventure, *n.* happening, experience, story; see **event.**

adventurer, *n.* explorer, pirate, soldier of fortune, daredevil, hero, pioneer, mountain climber, wild game hunter, record breaker; see **pioneer 2, traveler.**

adventurous, *a.* bold, adventuresome, courageous; see **brave.**

adverse, *a.* unpropitious, inopportune, disadvantageous; see **unfavorable.**

adversely, *a.* negatively, resentfully, unsympathetically; see **unfavorably.**

adversity, *n.* misfortune, reverse, trouble; see **difficulty 1, 2.**

advertise, *v.* publicize, proclaim, herald, announce, declare, notify, warn, display, exhibit, show, reveal, expose, disclose, unmask, divulge, uncover, communicate, publish abroad, issue, broadcast, print, circulate, show off, parade, propagate, disseminate, inform, celebrate, propagandize, spread, call public attention to, give out, *****press agent, *****plug, *****play up; see also **declare.**

advertised, *a.* announced, posted, noted, publicized, billed, printed, made public, broadcast, emphasized, pointed out, displayed, exhibited, shown, offered, presented, put on sale, flaunted, *****plugged, boosted, built up, *****pushed.

advertisement, *n.* announcement, notice, publicity, exhibit, exhibition, display, circular, handbill, placard, poster, public notice, broadcast, bill, proclamation, classified advertisement, sample, endorsement, (want) ad, build-up, *****plug, ballyhoo, *****blurb, *****(color) spread, *****classified.

advice, *n.* guidance, instruction(s), consultation(s), suggestion(s), preaching, information, admonition, warning, caution, a word to the wise, injunction, lesson, directions, opinion, counsel, advisement, encouragement, persuasion, dissuasion, prescription, recommendation, proposition, proposal, view, help, aid, judgment.

advise, *v.* recommend, prescribe, guide, direct, admonish, warn, point out, instruct, counsel, advocate, suggest, urge, prompt, show, tell, inform, move, caution, charge, encourage, preach, teach, persuade, offer an opinion to, forewarn, prepare, *****wise up, straighten out, give the facts.—*Ant.* deceive, misdirect, lead astray.

adviser, *n.* counselor, instructor, consultant; see **friend, teacher.**

advisory, *a.* consulting, having power to advise, prudential; see **helping.**

advocate, *v.* bolster, push, further, advance; see **promote 1.**

aerial, *a.* in the air, atmospheric, airy; see high 2.

aeroplane, *n.* airplane, airship, flying machine; see plane 3.

aesthetic, *a.* creative, appreciative, inventive; see beautiful.

affair, *n.* 1. [Business; *often plural*] concern, responsibility, matter, duty, topic, subject, case, circumstance, thing, question, function, private concern, personal business, calling, employment, occupation, profession, pursuit, avocation, obligation, job, province, realm, interest, mission, assignment, task; see also job 1. 2. [An illicit love affair] liaison, rendezvous, intrigue, intimacy, romance, relationship.

affect, *v.* impress, sway, induce; see influence.

affected, *a.* 1. [Being subject to influence] moved, touched, melted, influenced, sympathetic, stimulated, stirred, grieved, overwhelmed, moved to tears, hurt, injured, excited, struck, impressed, overwrought, devoured by, concerned, reached, compassionate, tender, sorry, troubled, distressed.—*Ant.* indifferent, unmoved, untouched. 2. [Assumed artificially] insincere, pretentious, melodramatic, self-conscious, unnatural, stilted, superficial, awkward, mannered, theatrical, stiff, strained, overdone, ostentatious, hollow, shallow, showy, *arty, *put-on.—*Ant.* simple, natural, genuine.

affection, *n.* love, friendship, liking, attachment, good will, partiality, passion, ardor, zealous attachment, friendliness, concern, regard, desire, closeness, kindness, devotion, tenderness, fondness. — *Ant.* hatred, dislike, enmity.

affectionate, *a.* kind, tender, friendly; see loving.

affidavit, *n.* testimony, sworn statement, affirmation; see oath 1.

affinity, *n.* 1. [Attraction based on affection] fondness, liking, closeness; see affection. 2. [Similarity] likeness, resemblance, correspondence; see similarity.

affirmative, *a.* agreeing, consenting, concurring, approving, assenting, supporting.—*Ant.* negative, contradictory, noncommittal. —in the affirmative, favorable, in assent *or* agreement, with an affirmative answer; see yes.

afflict, *v.* try, torment, trouble; see hurt.

affliction, *n.* trouble, trial, hardship, plight; see difficulty 1, 2.

affluent, *a.* wealthy, opulent, well-to-do; see rich 1.

afford, *v.* have enough for, make both ends meet, allow, be able to, have the means for, be financially able, stand, be in the market for.

afire, *a.* flaming, on fire, blazing; see burning.

afloat, *a.* adrift, at sea, sailing; see floating.

afoot, *a.* on foot, hiking, marching; see walking.

afraid, *a.* hesitant, anxious, apprehensive, disturbed, frightened, fearful, nervous, uneasy, fidgety, alarmed, intimidated, discouraged, perplexed, worried, perturbed, upset, panic-stricken, scared, terrified, terrorized, shocked, frozen, aghast, alarmed, startled, aroused, horrified, petrified, stunned, rattled, struck dumb, trembling, distressed, *jittery, *jumpy, *leery, *shaky.—*Ant.* confident, self-assured, poised.

Africa, *n.* Terms for areas in Africa include the following—Senegal, Chad, Republic of the Congo *or* Zaire, Dahomey, Gabon, Ivory Coast, Madagascar, Rwanda, Togo, Upper Volta, Algeria, Libya, Mauritania, Mali, Guinea, Portuguese Guinea, Liberia, Nigeria, Niger, Sudan, Ethiopia, Zambia, Mozambique, Kenya, Democratic Republic of Congo, Tanzania, Angola, Rhodesia, Uganda, Central African Republic, Cameroon, Ghana, Morocco, Tunisia, Gambia, Somalia, Republic of South Africa, United Arab Republic, Spanish Sahara, Sierra Leone, Equatorial Guinea, Malawi, Mali, Botswana, Lesotho, Swaziland, French Somaliland, Burundi.

African, *a.* 1. [Concerning a part of Africa] North African, Moroccan, Egyptian, Libyan, Algerian, Saharan *or* Saharian, Sudanese *or* Sudanic, East African, Kenyan, Tanzanian, Ugandan, Ethiopian, Abyssinian, Eritrean, Ethiop, Somali, West African, Liberian, Ghanaian, Nigerian, Dahomian, Senegalese, Congolese, Angolan, Central African, Zambian, Rhodesian, South African. 2. [Concerning the inhabitants of Africa] Negro, negroid, black, Bantu, Zulu, Swazi, Matabele, Hottentot, Bushman, Pygmy, Afrikaaner, Boer, Colored, Cape Colored, Yoruba, Ibo, Hausa, Ashanti, Masai, Kikuyu, Somali, Ethiopian, Egyptian, Arab, Moor, Moorish.

aft, *a.* abaft, rearward, behind; see back.

after, *a.* and *prep.* 1. [Behind in space] back of, in the rear, behind; see back. 2. [Following] next, later, subsequent; see following.

after all, *a.* at last, when all is said and done, in the end; see finally 2.

afternoon, *n.* post meridian, P.M., early afternoon, late afternoon, mid-afternoon, teatime, cocktail hour, evening.

afterward, *a.* later, after, subsequently, in a while, a while later, afterwards, by and by, eventually, soon, on the next day, ultimately, another time, thereafter, then, thereupon, ensuingly, at a later time.

again, *a.* anew, afresh, newly, once more, once again, repeatedly, over (and over), from the beginning, on and on, another time, over again, a second time, recurrently, ditto, repeat.—*Ant.* once, once only, at first. —**as much again,** doubled, twice as much, multiplied; see **double.**

again and again, *a.* repeatedly, once again, continuously; see **again.**

against, *a.* and *prep.* 1. [Counter to] in the face of, into, toward, adverse to, versus, opposite to, facing. 2. [In contact with] on, upon, in collision with, in contact with; see also **next 2.** 3. [Contrary to] in opposition to, opposed to, counter to, adverse to, in violation of, versus, in contrariety to, over against. 4. [Opposite] facing, fronting, abreast, corresponding; see **opposite 3.**

age, *n.* 1. [The period of one's existence] span, lifetime, duration; see **life 4.** 2. [A particular point of time in one's life] infancy, childhood, girlhood, boyhood, adolescence, adulthood, youth, middle age, old age, dotage, senility. 3. [A period of time] epoch, era, period, time, century, decade, generation, interval, term, in the days *or* time of someone *or* something; see also **life 4.** —**of age,** adult, twenty-one, having attained (one's) majority; see **mature 1.**

age, *v.* grow feeble, decline, wane, advance in years, wrinkle, waste away, *have one foot in the grave, *go over the hill.

aged, *a.* gray, elderly, worn; see **old 1, 2.**

agency, *n.* 1. [Place where business is transacted] firm, bureau, company; see **office 3, business 4.** 2. [An instrumentality] power, auspices, action; see **means 1.**

agenda, *n.* list, plan, schedule; see **program 2.**

agent, *n.* broker, promoter, operator, representative, salesman, assistant, appointee, servant, executor, attorney, lawyer, go-between, surrogate, mediary, deputy, factor, minister, envoy, canvasser, middleman, commissioner, delegate, proxy, substitute, steward, functionary, solicitor, ambassador, proctor, negotiator, advocate, coagent, press agent, claim agent, employment agent, actor's agent.

aggravate, *v.* exasperate, annoy, provoke; see **bother 2.**

aggravation, *n.* 1. [A cause of aggravation] worry, affliction, distress; see **difficulty 1, 2, trouble 2.** 2. [*Annoyance] irritation, provocation, exasperation; see **annoyance.**

aggression, *n.* offensive, assault, invasion; see **attack 1.**

aggressive, *a.* warlike, attacking, combative, threatening, advancing, offensive, disruptive, disturbing, hostile, intrusive, destructive, intruding, invading, assailing, barbaric, up in arms, on the warpath.—*Ant.* peaceful, peace-loving, **serene.**

agile, *a.* nimble, quick, spry, deft, vigorous, frisky, spirited, lithe, sprightly, supple, dexterous, easy-moving, rapid, active, ready, alive, buoyant, energetic, stirring, brisk, lively, swift, alert, bustling.—*Ant.* awkward, slow, clumsy.

agility, *n.* nimbleness, dexterity, spryness, quickness, briskness, swiftness, friskiness, rapidity, readiness, liveliness, promptitude, promptness, alertness.

aging, *a.* declining, getting on *or* along, maturing, stale, developing, fermenting, wasting away, wearing out, growing old, fading, *one foot in the grave.

agitate, *v.* stir, move, arouse; see **excite.**

agitated, *a.* disturbed, moved, upset, aroused; see **excited.**

ago, *a.* gone, since, past; see **before.**

agony, *n.* suffering, torture, anguish; see **pain 1, 2.**

agree, *v.* coincide, get along (with), side with, concur, stand together, parallel, go well *or* along with, fit in, accord, attune, suit, say yes (to), conform, go hand in hand (with), equal, correspond (to), go together, synchronize, measure up (to), *square with, *click, hit it off (with), *see eye to eye.—*Ant.* **differ,** disagree, debate.

agreeable, *a.* pleasing, satisfactory, acceptable; see **pleasant 1, 2.**

agreeably, *a.* kindly, politely, pleasantly, genially, cheerfully, peacefully; see also favorably.—*Ant.* disagreeably, **opposite,** antagonistically.

agree about, *v.* come to terms, *see eye to eye, settle; see **agree on.**

agreement, *n.* 1. [The state of being in accord] conformity, friendship, accord, accordance, accommodation, correspondence, harmony, concord, unison, concert, common view, understanding, brotherhood, affiliation, alliance, intimacy, fellowship, companionship, goodwill, cooperation, assent, approval, compromise, treaty, pact, contract, bargain, settlement, satisfaction, affinity, closeness, balance, equality, kinship, peace, love, unity, union, tie.—*Ant.* **disagreement,** enmity, disunity. 2. [An expression of agreement, sense 1] approval, treaty, contract; see **deal 1.**

agree on, *v.* come to terms, close a deal, make a bargain, see **settle.**

agree to, *v.* admit, consent (to), approve; see **accept 2.**

agree with, v. coincide, accord, harmonize; see **agree.**

agriculture, n. tillage, cultivation, horticulture; see **farming.**

ahead, a. before, earlier (than), in advance (of), ahead of, advanced, preceding, foremost, leading, in the lead, at the head of, in the foreground, in lee of, to the fore, in the van, first, in front of, preliminary.—*Ant.* behind, back, toward the end. **get ahead**—advance, prosper, progress; see **succeed.**

ahead of, a. in advance of, before, above; see **ahead.** —**get ahead of,** outdo, excel, subordinate; see **exceed.**

aid, n. comfort, benefit, favor; see **help 1.**

ailing, a. ill, feeble, weak; see **sick.**

ailment, n. sickness, infirmity, disease; see **illness 1, 2.**

aim, n. intention, object, plan; see **purpose 1.** —**take aim,** sight, level (at), train (on); see **aim 2.**

aim, v. train, steer, level (at), direct, set up, set the sights, sight, take aim, zero in on, draw a bead on.

aimed, a. proposed, marked, intended for, directed, designed, calculated, leveled, trained, steered, set, planned, anticipated.

aimless, a. purposeless, pointless, erratic, thoughtless, careless, heedless, rambling, wandering, blind, random, unsettled, flightly, capricious, wayward, without aim *or* end, chance, haphazard, to no purpose, drifting, stray, accidental, undirected, casual, indecisive, irresolute, fitful, fanciful, fickle, eccentric, unplanned, helpless, unpredictable, shiftless.—*Ant.* purposeful, careful, planned.

air, n. 1. [The gaseous envelope of the earth] atmosphere, stratosphere, troposphere, wind, breeze, draft, the open air, sky, oxygen, the open, ventilation, *the out of doors. 2. [The apparent quality] look, mien, demeanor; see **looks.** —**off the air,** not being broadcast, closed, signed off; see **quiet 2.** —**on the air,** broadcasting, transmitting, reporting; see **on the air.** —**up in the air,** undecided, unsettled, unsure; see **uncertain 2.**

air, v. ventilate, open, freshen, air out, air-condition, circulate air, expose to air, draw in air, fan, refresh, cool, purify.

aired, a. 1. [Exposed to the air] ventilated, opened, freshened, purified, hung out, sunned, dried.—*Ant.* closed, stuffy, dark. 2. [Exposed to public attention] exposed, disclosed, discussed, revealed, told, unveiled; see also **exposed.** —*Ant.* secret, undisclosed, concealed.

air force, n. aviation service, air power, air cover; see **army 1.**

airline, n. air carrier, commercial airline, air freight carrier; see **business 4.**

airman, n. copilot, flight engineer, navigator; see **pilot.**

airplane, n. aircraft, aeroplane, airliner, glider; see **plane 3.**

airport, n. airfield, spaceport, flying field, landing field *or* airstrip, hangar, heliport, installations.

airs, n. pl. affectation, pretense, show; see **pretense 2.**

airtight, a. impermeable to air, closed, shut (tight); see **tight 2.**

airy, a. windy, breezy, draughty, exposed, ventilated, open, spacious, lofty, well-ventilated, atmospheric, aerial, out-of-doors, outdoors, in the open.

aisle, n. passageway, opening, way, walk, path, course, clearing, avenue, corridor, passage, gangway, alley, lane.

alarm, n. drum, siren, horn, signal, fog horn, fire siren, call, SOS, red light, hoot, blast, shout, warning sound, danger signal, cry, yell, scream, air raid siren.

alarmed, a. frightened, fearful, aroused; see **afraid.**

alarming, a. frightening, foreboding, distressing; see **disturbing.**

Alaska, n. the Klondike, the 49th state, the frozen North, the gold country, land of the sourdough.

album, n. collection, stamp book, register, index, snapshots, scrapbook, notebook, photograph album, portfolio.

alcohol, n. spirits, liquor, intoxicant; see **drink 2.**

alcoholic, a. spirituous, fermented, distilled; see **strong 8.**

alcoholic, n. addict, heavy drinker, sot; see **drunkard.**

alcoholism, n. intoxication, insobriety, dipsomania; see **drunkenness.**

alert, a. wary, on guard, wide-awake; see **observant.** —**on the alert,** watchful, aware, vigilant, on guard; see **observant.**

alert, v. inform, put on guard, signal; see **warn.**

alibi, n. proof of absence, plea, explanation, declaration, defense, statement, case, allegation, avowal, assurance, profession, excuse, assertion, answer, reply, retort, vindication.

alien, a. exotic, strange, unknown; see **foreign.**

alien, n. foreigner, stranger, refugee, displaced person, outsider, migrant, colonist, immigrant, guest, visitor, newcomer, barbarian, Ishmael, settler, stateless person, intruder, squatter, interloper, invader, noncitizen, man without a country.—*Ant.* inhabitant, native, citizen.

alienate, *v.* estrange, turn away, set against, withdraw the affections of, make unfriendly, come between, disunite, separate, divide, part, *turn off.—Ant.* unite, reconcile, acclimate.

align, *v.* arrange, straighten, regulate; see **adjust 1, 3.**

alike, *a.* like, same, equal, identical, matching, self-same, akin, similar, comparable, parallel, resembling, related, approximate, equivalent, allied, of a kind, twin, one, indistinguishable, facsimile, duplicate, matched, mated, chip off the old block, one and the same, all one, in the same boat.

alimony, *n.* upkeep, maintenance, provision; see **payment 1.**

alive, *a.* live, animate, living, breathing, existing, existent, vital, not dead, mortal, organic, extant, viable, growing, having life, conscious, *alive and kicking, *above ground, among the living.—*Ant.* dead, lifeless, inanimate.

all, *a.* **1.** [Completely] totally, wholly, entirely; see **completely. 2.** [Each] every, any, each and every, any and every, every member of, for everybody *or* anybody *or* anyone *or* anything *or* everything, *barring no one, bar none, *beginning and end, from A to Z.—*Ant.* no, not any, none. **3.** [Exclusively] alone, nothing but, solely; see **only 1.**

all, *n.* everything, everyone, every person, sum, collection, group, ensemble, total, totality, quantity, unit, entity, whole kit and caboodle; *lock, stock and barrel, *the works.—*Ant.* none, nobody, nothing. —**after all,** nevertheless, in spite of everything, despite; see **although.** —**at all,** to the slightest degree, in the least, none; see **never, not.** —**in all,** all told, collectively, on the whole; see **altogether.**

allegedly, *a.* assertedly, according to the statement, supposedly; see **apparently.**

allegiance, *n.* fidelity, homage, fealty; see **loyalty.**

allergic to, *a.* sensitive to, affected by, subject *or* susceptible to, repelled by, oversensitive *or* hypersensitive to.—*Ant.* immune, unaffected by, hardened to.

allergy, *n.* hypersensitive bodily reaction, hypersensitivity, antipathy to certain substances; see **illness 2.**

alley, *n.* back street, lane, rear way; see **road 1.** —*up or* down one's alley, suited to one's abilities *or* tastes *or* interest(s), enjoyable, useful; see **fit 1.**

alliance, *n.* **1.** [The state of being allied] connection, membership, affinity, participation, co-operation, support, union, agreement, common understanding, marriage, kinship, relation, collaboration, federation, friendship, partnership, coalition, association, affiliation, confederation, implication, bond, tie. **2.** [The

act of joining] fusion, combination, coupling; see **union 1. 3.** [A union] league, federation, company; see **organization 3.**

allied, *a.* unified, confederated, associated; see **united 2.**

allot, *v.* earmark, designate, dole; see **assign, distribute 1.**

allotment, *n.* portion, lot, part; see **share.**

all-out, *a.* total, entire, complete; see **absolute 1.**

allow, *v.* permit, let, sanction, grant, consent to, tolerate, favor, yield, bear, approve (of), give leave, endorse, certify, have no objection, release, pass, authorize, license, warrant, put up with, *give the green light *or* the go-ahead *or* the high sign.—*Ant.* deny, forbid, prohibit.

allowable, *a.* permissible, proper, legal; see **admissible.**

allowance, *n.* salary, wage, commission, fee, hire, remittance, stipend, gift, grant, pension, alimony, annuity, settled rate, endowment, scholarship, fellowship, prize, subsidy, pay, bequest, legacy, inheritance, contribution, aid, handout, pocket money. —**make allowances (for),** weigh, excuse, rationalize; see **consider.**

allow for, *v.* take into account *or* consideration, provide for, set apart; see **consider.**

alloy, *n.* compound, mixture, combination; see **metal.** Common metal alloys include the following—ferromanganese, ferrosilicon, pewter, chromesteel, nichrome, tungsten-steel, stainless steel, non-magnetic steel, chromium steel, chrome-nickel steel, high tensile steel, cobalt-steel, tungsten-chromium-cobalt, finishing steel, structural steel, carbon steel, brass, bronze, green gold, nickel-silver, magnalium, zinc-aluminum, aluminum-bronze, boron bronze, copper-aluminum, aluminum-manganese-copper, manganese-copper, tin-manganese, tin-copper, antimony.

all right, *a.* **1.** [Adequately] tolerably, acceptably, passably; see **adequately. 2.** [Yes] agreed, very well, of course; see **yes. 3.** [Certainly] without a doubt, definitely, positively; see **surely. 4.** [Uninjured] safe, well, unhurt; see **whole. 5.** [Correct] exact, precise, right; see **right 1.**

all-time, *a.* unsurpassed, record-breaking, to the greatest extent; see **best 1.**

all told, *a.* in all, in toto, on the whole; see **altogether.**

ally, *n.* confederate, partner, collaborator; see **associate.**

almanac, *n.* calendar, yearbook, annual, register, world almanac, chronicle, journal, record, register of the year.

almighty, *a.* **1.** [Omnipotent] invincible,

all-powerful, mighty; see **powerful 1. 2.** [Omnipresent] infinite, eternal, godlike, all-knowing, all-seeing, deathless, immortal, celestial, divine, godly, pervading.

almighty, *n.* all-ruling, omnipotent, all-powerful; see **god.**

almost, *a.* all but, (very) nearly, approximately, roughly, to all intents, as good as, near to, substantially, essentially, in effect, on the edge *or* verge of, relatively, for all practical purposes, to that effect, not quite, about to, with some exceptions, in the vicinity of, bordering on, within sight of, with little tolerance, close upon, in the neighborhood of, about, just about, not quite, most, around, within a hair of, *by a narrow squeak.

aloft, *a.* on high, overhead, up; see **above 1, over 1.**

alone, *a.* lone, lonely, solitary, deserted, abandoned, individual, forsaken, desolate, detached, friendless, unaccompanied, isolated, lonesome, apart, by oneself, single, widowed, unattached, unconnected.—*Ant.* accompanied, attended, escorted. —**let alone, 1.** [Besides] not to mention *or* speak of, also, in addition to; see **besides. 2.** [Neglect] ignore, isolate, refrain from disturbing; see **neglect 2.** —**let well enough alone,** forget, ignore, let alone; see **neglect 2.**

along, *a.* **1.** [Near] by, at, adjacent; see **near 1. 2.** [Ahead] on, onward, forward; see **ahead 2. 3.** [Together with] with, accompanying, in addition to, in company with, along with, side by side, along that (this) line, coupled with, at the same time, simultaneously. —**all along,** all the time, from the beginning, constantly; see **regularly.** —**get along, 1.** [Succeed] prosper, get by, make ends meet; see **succeed 1. 2.** [Advance] progress, move on, push ahead; see **advance 1. 3.** [Agree] accord, stand together, equal; see **agree.**

alongside, *a.* and *prep.* parallel to, close by, close at hand, by or at the side of, along the side, side by side, equal with, on the same plane with, almost touching, neck and neck.—*Ant.* beyond, ahead, behind.

aloof, *a.* remote, reserved, distant, secluded; see **indifferent.**

aloud, *a.* vociferously, audibly, lustily, noisily; see **loudly.**

alphabet, *n.* letters, runes, pictograph, ideograph, characters, symbols, signs, hieroglyphs, cryptograms, phonemes, morphemes, sounds; see also **letter 1.**

alphabetical, *a.* systematic, logical, consecutive, progressive, one after another, step by step, graded, planned, ordered, letter by letter, from A to Z, indexed.

alphabetize, *v.* arrange alphabetically, index, systematize; see **order 3.**

alpine, *a.* mountainous; high, lofty, snow-capped, rocky, soaring, rangy, snow-clad, elevated, towering; see **high 1, 2.**

already, *a.* previously, by now, now, even now, by this time, at present, just now, in the past, up to now, by that time, then.

also, *a.* too, likewise, besides, as well (as), in addition (to), additionally, along with, more than that, over and above, in conjunction with, thereto, together with, ditto, more, moreover, further, furthermore, including, plus, to boot.—*Ant.* excluding, without, otherwise.

alter, *v.* **1.** [To change for a purpose] vary, turn, diminish, replace, mutate, warp, alternate, remodel, renovate, evolve, translate, disguise, restyle, revolutionize, reduce, substitute, reorganize, increase, intensify, shape, shift, modify, transform, remake, convert, reform, tailor, adjust, adapt, invert, reverse, reconstruct. **2.** [To become different] convert, develop, decay; see **change 2.**

alteration, *n.* exchange, modification, revision; see **change 1.**

altered, *a.* modified, qualified, revised; see **changed 2.**

alternate, *a.* alternative, substitute, make-shift; see **temporary.**

alternate, *n.* replacement, equivalent, double; see **substitute.**

alternate, *v.* [To take or do by turns] substitute, follow in turn, happen by turns, follow one another, do by turns, do one then the other, relieve, fill in for, exchange. **2.** [To fluctuate] vary, rise and fall, shift; see **waver.**

alternative, *n.* option, discretion, opportunity; see **choice.**

although, *conj.* though, even though, despite, still, despite the fact that, in spite of, even if, while, however, for all that.

altitude, *n.* elevation, distance, loftiness, eminence; see **height.**

altogether, *a.* all told, collectively, on the whole, in the aggregate, in sum total, bodily, all in all, all things considered, by and large, all, taking all things together, as a whole, for the most part.

always, *a.* **1.** [Constantly] periodically, continually, ceaselessly; see **regularly. 2.** [Forever] ever, perpetually, eternally, evermore; see **forever.**

A.M., *abbr.* after midnight, morning, early hours, before noon, forenoon, dawn, sunup.

amass, *v.* gather, hoard, store up, garner; see **accumulate.**

amateur, *n.* beginner, novice, learner, nonprofessional, dabbler, recruit, dilettante, hopeful, neophyte, initiate, apprentice, freshman, tenderfoot, *rookie, greenhorn, cub.–*Ant.* **veteran,** professional, expert.

amaze, *v.* bewilder, astonish, perplex, astound; see **surprise.**

amazement, *n.* astonishment, awe, bewilderment; see **wonder 1.**

amazing, *a.* astonishing, astounding, marvelous; see **unusual 1.**

ambassador, *n.* representative, envoy, minister; see **diplomat.**

ambiguity, *n.* doubtfulness, incertitude, vagueness; see **uncertainty 2.**

ambiguous, *a.* equivocal, enigmatic, vague; see **obscure 1.**

ambition, *n.* hope, earnestness, aspiration, yearning, eagerness, longing, craving, passion, lust, itch, hunger, thirst, appetite, energy, ardor, zeal, enthusiasm, spirit, vigor, enterprise, *get up and go, *what it takes.–*Ant.* indifference, apathy, laziness.

ambitious, *a.* aspiring, longing, hopeful, zealous, hungry, thirsty, industrious, goal-oriented, enthusiastic, inspired, energetic, avid, sharp, climbing, ardent, designing, earnest, enterprising, aggressive, resourceful, pushing.

ambush, *n.* pitfall, snare, deception; see **trap 1.**

ambush, *v.* waylay, ensnare, lay for, set a trap, keep out of sight, decoy, entrap, hook in, lurk, lie in wait for, surround, hem in; see **attack.**

amend, *v.* correct, mend, revise; see **alter 1.**

amendment, *n.* bill, measure, act, clause, motion, revision, supplement, rider.

America, *n.* 1. [One or both of the continents of the western hemisphere] North America, Latin America, South America, Central America, the New World, the western hemisphere. 2. [The United States of America] U.S., the fifty states, Land of the Free, Land of Liberty, *the U.S. of A., *Uncle Sam, the States.

American, *a.* 1. [Related to the Western Hemisphere] continental, North American, Latin American, South American, Central American, Pan-American. In reference to specific countries of the Western Hemisphere, the following are used—Canadian, Mexican, Nicaraguan, Costa Rican, Guatemalan, Honduran, San Salvadorian, Panamanian, Cuban, Haitian, Puerto Rican, Colombian, Venezuelan, Guianan, Brazilian, Peruvian, Ecuadorian, Chilean, Argentinian, Uruguayan, Paraguayan, Bolivian, etc. 2. [Related to the United States of America] republican, constitutional, democratic, patriotic, freedom-loving, all-American.

American, *n.* citizen of the United States, United States national, Yankee, Northerner, Southerner, Indian, pioneer.

Americanism, *n.* patriotism, nationalism, isolationism, provincialism, flag waving, clean living, fair play, friendly rivalry, free enterprise, America first, the competitive system, *spirit of '76.

amiable, *a.* pleasant, genial, charming; see **friendly 1.**

ammunition, *n.* Types of ammunition include the following—projectile, charge, grenade, buckshot, gunpowder, cartridge, bullet, bomb, missile, hand grenade, fuse, shrapnel, torpedo, shell, ball, cannonball, shot, *ammo; see also **bomb, bullet, explosive, gas 3, shot 1.**

among, *prep.* between, in, in between, in the midst *or* middle of, surrounded by, in connection *or* association with, amid, amongst, amidst, in the company of.

amount, *n.* 1. [The total of several quantities] sum, product, sum total; see **whole.** 2. [Price] expense, output, outlay; see **price.** 3. [Quantity] bulk, mass, number; see **quantity.**

amount to, *v.* reach, extend *or* mount to, come to, effect, be equal to, approximate, check with, total *or* sum *or* foot up to, be in all, be in the whole, total, tally with, add up to.

ample, *a.* sufficient, plenty, adequate; see **enough 1.**

amplify, *v.* expand, augment, magnify, elaborate; see **increase.**

amply, *a.* enough, sufficiently, copiously; see **adequately.**

amputate, *v.* cut off, sever, cut away; see **remove.**

amuse, *v.* divert, cheer, enliven; see **entertain 1.**

amusement, *n.* recreation, pastime, play; see **entertainment.**

amusing, *a.* engaging, diverting, enchanting; see **entertaining.**

analysis, *n.* study, investigation, search; see **examination 1.**

analyze, *v.* dissect, examine, investigate, separate, break down *or* up, disintegrate, resolve into elements, determine the essential features of, decentralize.

anarchy, *n.* turmoil, chaos, mob rule; see **disorder.**

anatomy, *n.* physique, form, figure; see **body 1.**

ancestor, *n.* progenitor, forebear, founder of the family; see **forefather.**

ancestral, *a.* inborn, congenital, old, inherited; see **inherent.**

ancestry, *n.* lineage, heritage, parentage, pedigree; see **family.**

anchor, *n.* stay, tie, grapnel, mooring, grappling iron, support, mainstay, ballast, safeguard, security, protection, hold, fastener, grip, defense, protection, foothold.

anchor, v. make port, tie up, moor, berth, bring a ship in, lay anchor.

ancient, a. antique, antiquated, aged; see **old 1, 2, 3**.

and, conj. in addition to, also, including, plus, together with, as well as, furthermore, moreover.

anecdote, n. tale, incident, episode; see **story**.

anemic, a. pallid, weak, sickly; see **pale 1**.

anesthetic, n. hypnosis, gas, opiate; see **drug 2**.

angel, n. Angel of Death, good angel, dark angel, archangel, guardian angel, spirit, cherub, celestial spirit, winged being, saint.—Ant. **devil**, demon, satan.

angelic, a. saintly, good, humble, heavenly, spiritual, kind, radiant, beautiful, divine, holy, pure, lovely, devout, virtuous, above reproach, righteous, cherubic.—Ant. demonic, evil, **bad**.

anger, n. wrath, rage, fury, passion, temper, bad temper, animosity, indignation, hatred, resentment, ire, hot temper, impatience, vexation, annoyance, provocation, violence, turbulence, excitement, frenzy, tantrum, exasperation, huff, irritation, *dander.—Ant. **patience**, mildness, calm.

anger, v. infuriate, annoy, irritate; see **enrage**.

angle, n. 1. [Figure or plane formed at an intersection] notch, crotch, elbow, fork, cusp, incline, decline, Y, V, point where two lines meet.—Ant. **curve**, arc, oval. 2. [Point of view] standpoint, outlook, perspective; see **viewpoint**.

angle for, v. plot, scheme, maneuver; see **plan 1**.

angler, n. fisher, fisherwoman, sportsman; see **fisherman**.

angrily, a. heatedly, indignantly, irately, grouchily, crisply, sharply, savagely, hotly, fiercely, tartly, bitterly, furiously, wildly, violently.—Ant. **calmly**, softly, quietly.

angry, a. enraged, fierce, fiery, irate, raging, fuming, infuriated, furious, wrathful, stormy, indignant, cross, vexed, resentful, irritated, bitter, ferocious, offended, sullen, hateful, annoyed, provoked, displeased, riled, affronted, huffy, hostile, rabid, *flown off the handle, mad, *up in the air, *hot under the collar, boiling, *steamed up, *at the boiling point, with one's back up, all worked up (about), up in arms.—Ant. **calm**, quiet, restrained.

anguish, n. wretchedness, pain, agony; see **pain 1**.

angular, a. sharp-cornered, intersecting, crossing, oblique, divaricate, with corners, Y-shaped, V-shaped, crotched, forked, bent, crooked, pointed, triangu-

lar, rectangular, jagged, staggered, zigzag.—Ant. **round**, parallel, side-by-side.

animal, a. bestial, beastly, swinish, brutish, wild, beastlike, untamed, mammalian, bovine, canine, feline, reptilian.

animal, n. living thing, creature, human being, beast, being, fish, crustacean, amphibian, vertebrate, invertebrate, reptile, insect, bird, wild animal, domestic animal, mammal; see also **bird 1, fish, insect, man 1**.

animate, v. activate, vitalize, inform, make alive, arouse, give life to, energize, put life into, breathe new life into.

animated, a. spirited, gay, lively; see **happy 1**.

animosity, n. dislike, enmity, displeasure; see **hatred**.

ankle, n. anklebone, joint, tarsus; see **bone, foot 2**.

annex, n. expansion, additional quarters, new wing; see **addition 1, 2**.

annex, v. append, attach, affix; see **add**.

annihilate, v. demolish, exterminate, obliterate; see **destroy**.

anniversary, n. holiday, saint's day, birth date, birthday, yearly observance of an event, feastday, ceremony, annual meeting, biennial, triennial, quadrennial, quintennial, silver anniversary, golden anniversary, diamond jubilee, jubilee, festival, fiesta, centennial, red-letter day.

announce, v. proclaim, publish, state; see **declare 1**.

announced, a. reported, given out, told, broadcast(ed), issued, circulated, proclaimed, declared, published, disclosed, divulged, released, made known, disseminated, revealed, publicized, made public.—Ant. **hidden**, unannounced, unrevealed.

announcement, n. declaration, notification, prediction, proclamation, communication, publication, report, statement, advertisement, decision, news, tidings, returns, brief, bulletin, edict, white paper, message, notice, interim report, survey, advice, item, detail, communiqué, speech, release, handbill, poster, pamphlet, circular, billboard, brochure, form letter, telegram, wire cable, letter, leaflet; see also **advertisement**.—Ant. ban, secret, silence.

announcer, n. program announcer, broadcaster, television announcer, telecaster, commentator, sportscaster, newscaster, radio announcer, disc jockey.

annoy, v. pester, irritate, trouble; see **bother 2**.

annoyance, n. 1. [A feeling of annoyance] vexation, irritation, pique, uneasiness, disgust, displeasure, provocation, nervousness, exasperation, indignation, touchiness, perturbation, moodiness, mortification, vexation, worry, distress, unhappiness, discontent, heartache, misery, aches and pains, dissatisfaction, impatience, *peeve.—*Ant.* pleasure, joy, delight. 2. [A source of annoyance] worry, inconvenience, nuisance; see **difficulty 1, 2, trouble 2.**

annoying, *a.* irritating, bothersome, vexatious; see **disturbing.**

annual, *a.* yearly, each year, every year, once a year, lasting a year, anniversary, seasonal.

annually, *a.* each year, once a year, periodically; see **yearly.**

annul, *v.* invalidate, render void, repeal, revoke; see **cancel.**

annulment, *n.* invalidation, nullification, dissolution, see **cancellation.**

anonymous, *a.* unsigned, nameless, unknown, unacknowledged, unnamed, unclaimed, unidentified, secret, of unknown authorship, without a name, bearing no name, incognito, pseudo.—*Ant.* named, signed, acknowledged.

another, *a.* 1. [Additional] one more, a further, added; see **extra.** 2. [Different] a separate, a distinct, some other; see **unlike.**

another, *n.* someone else, a different person, one more, addition, something else.—*Ant.* same, **one, each.**

answer, *n.* 1. [A reply] response, return, statement, retort, echo, repartee, password, rebuttal, approval, acknowledgment, sign, rejoinder, comeback.—*Ant.* **question,** query, request. 2. [A solution] discovery, find, disclosure, revelation, explanation, interpretation, clue, resolution, key, the why and the wherefore.

answer, *v.* 1. [To reply] reply, respond, rejoin, retort, acknowledge, give answer, say, echo, return, refute, react, rebut, argue, plead, claim, remark, *give, talk, come back.—*Ant.* **question,** inquire, make inquiry. 2. [To provide a solution] solve, elucidate, clarify; see **explain.**

answerable, *a.* responsible, liable, amenable; see **responsible 1.**

answer for, *v.* be responsible (for), take (the) blame (for), accept the responsibility (for), take upon oneself, sponsor, do at one's own risk, *take the rap (for).

answer to, *v.* be responsible to, be ruled by, respect the authority of; see **respect 2.**

antagonism, *n.* enmity, hostility, opposition; see **hatred.**

antagonistic, *a.* opposing, hostile, inimical; see **unfriendly.**

antecedent, *a.* preliminary, previous, prior; see **preceding.**

antenna, *n.* aerial, TV antenna, receiving wire; see **wire.**

anthem, *n.* hymn, divine song, melody; see **song.**

antibiotic, *n.* antitoxin, wonder drug, miracle drug; see **medicine 2.**

antibody, *n.* virus, bacteria, microbe, bacillus; see **germ 3.**

antic, *n.* caper, frolic, trick; see **joke.**

anticipate, *v.* expect, forecast, prophesy, predict, hope for, look forward to, wait for, count *or* plan on, have a hunch, bargain for, hold in view, have in prospect, assume, suppose, divine, conjecture, promise oneself, lean upon, entertain the hope, await, reckon *or* count on, *have a funny feeling, look into the future, feel it in one's bones.—*Ant.* **fear,** be surprised, be caught unawares.

anticipated, *a.* foreseen, predictable, prepared for; see **expected, likely 1.**

anticipation, *n.* expectancy, outlook, trust, promise, prospect, impatience, preoccupation, hope, prevision, presentiment, intuition, foresight, inkling, premonition, apprehension, foreboding, awareness, forethought, *hunch, a feeling in one's bones.—*Ant.* **surprise,** shock, wonder.

antidote, *n.* antitoxin, counteractant, remedy; see **medicine 2.**

antique, *a.* ancient, archaic, prehistoric; see **old 3.**

antique, *n.* relic, artifact, heirloom, survival, rarity, monument, vestige, ruin.

antiseptic, *a.* clean, germ-free, sterilized; see **pure 2.**

antiseptic, *n.* detergent, prophylactic, preservative, preventive, preventative, counterirritant, sterilizer, immunizing agent, germicide, insecticide, disinfectant, deodorant; see **medicine 2.**

antitoxin, *n.* vaccine, antibody, serum; see **medicine 2.**

antlers, *n. pl.* horns, tusks, prongs; see **horn 2.**

anxiety, *n.* concern, trouble, misgiving; see **fear.**

anxious, *a.* 1. [Disturbed in mind] apprehensive, concerned, dreading; see **troubled.** 2. [Eager] desirous, eager, fervent; see **zealous.**

any, *a.* either, whatever, any sort, any kind, any one, in general, each, some, several, each and every, all, one and all; see also **each 1, some 1.—*Ant.* only, **one,** single.

anybody, *pron.* anyone, everyone, everybody, all, the whole world, the public, the rabble, the masses, each and every one, any person, any of.—*Ant.* **nobody,** no one, somebody.

anyhow, *a.* in any event, so, at any rate, nevertheless, at all, in spite of, however, in any case, regardless, anyway, in any way, in whatever way, however, under any circumstances, in one way or the other, in any respect, in either way, whatever happens, *irregardless, somehow or other.

anyone, *pron.* a person, one, anyone at all; see **anybody.**

***anyplace,** *a.* everywhere, wherever, in any place; see **anywhere.**

anything, *pron.* everything, all, anything at all, anyone, any one thing, whatever one wants, *you name it, anything around.—*Ant.* nothing, something, one thing.

any time, *a.* whenever, at your convenience, when you will, no matter when, any time when, at any moment, *anytime.

anyway, *a.* in any event, however, in any manner; see **anyhow.**

anywhere, *a.* wherever, in any place, all over, everywhere, in whatever place, wherever you go, *anyplace.—*Ant.* nowhere, in no place, somewhere. —get anywhere, prosper, thrive, advance; see succeed 1.

apart, *a.* 1. [Separated] disconnected, distant, disassociated; see **separated.** 2. [Distinct] separate, special, isolated; see **individual.** 3. [Separately] freely, exclusively, alone; see **independently.** 1. — **take apart,** dismember, dissect, reduce; see **analyze, divide.** —**tell apart,** characterize, discriminate, differentiate; see **distinguish 1.**

apartment, *n.* rooms, quarters, flat, suite, penthouse, residence, home, duplex, *pad, walk-up.

apartment house, *n.* tenement, hotel, apartment building, condominium, high-rise apartments.

apathetic, *a.* unemotional, cold, unconcerned; see **indifferent.**

apathy, *n.* dullness, insensitivity, unconcern; see **indifference.**

ape, *n.* gorilla, orangutan, chimpanzee, baboon; see **monkey.**

ape, *v.* copy, mimic, impersonate; see **imitate 1.**

apiece, *a.* respectively, separately, individually; see **each.**

apologetic, *a.* regretful, self-incriminating, explanatory, atoning, rueful, contrite, remorseful, sorry, penitent, *down on one's knees.—*Ant.* stubborn, obstinate, unregenerate.

apologize, *v.* beg or ask pardon, excuse oneself, atone, ask forgiveness, make amends, make apology for, purge, give satisfaction, clear oneself, make up with, confess, admit one's guilt, retract, withdraw, *eat crow, eat one's words.—*Ant.* insult, offend, hurt.

apology, *n.* excuse, plea, justification; see **explanation.**

apostle, *n.* messenger, witness, companion; see **follower.**

appall, *v.* amaze, horrify, dismay; see **shock 2.**

appalling, *a.* horrifying, shocking, dreadful; see **frightful.**

apparatus, *n.* appliances, machinery, outfit; see **equipment.**

apparel, *n.* clothes, attire, suit; see **dress 1.**

apparent, *a.* 1. [Open to view] visible, clear, manifest; see **obvious 1.** 2. [Seeming, but not actual] probable, possible, plausible; see **likely 1.**

apparently, *a.* obviously, at first sight or view, in plain sight, unmistakably, at a glance, indubitably, perceptibly, plainly, patently, evidently, clearly, openly, supposedly, overtly, conspicuously, palpably, tangibly, presumably, possibly, supposedly, manifestly, most likely, reasonably, seemingly, reputedly, as if, as though, to all appearances, in almost every way, allegedly, as it seems or were, on the face of it, to the eye.—*Ant.* surely, certainly, undoubtedly.

appeal, *n.* 1. [A plea] request, bid, claim, suit, petition, question, entreaty, prayer, invocation, supplication, address, demand, call, requisition, application, proposition, proposal.—*Ant.* denial, refusal, renunciation. 2. [Attractiveness] charm, glamour, interest, seductiveness, sex appeal, *class.

appeal, *v.* 1. [To ask another seriously] urge, request, petition; see **beg.** 2. [To attract] interest, engage, tempt; see also **fascinate.**

appear, *v.* 1. [To become visible] emerge, rise, come in view, come forth or out or forward, be in sight, become plain, loom, arrive, come to light, enter the picture, recur, materialize, become visible, loom up, break through, show (up), crop up, burst forth, turn up, stand out, *poke up, *see the light (of day), meet or catch the eye, break cover.—*Ant.* depart, disappear, vanish. 2. [To seem] look, have the appearance, resemble; see **seem.**

appearance, *n.* 1. [Looks] bearing, demeanor, features; see **looks.** 2. [That which only seems to be real] impression, idea, image, reflection, sound, mirage, vision, facade, dream, illusion, semblance, seeming.—*Ant.* being, **fact,** substance. —**keep up appearances,** be outwardly proper or decorous, hide one's faults or failures, *keep up with the Joneses; see **deceive.** —**make or put in an appearance,** appear publicly, be present, come; see **arrive.**

appease, *v.* do, be enough, serve; see **satisfy 1, 3.**

appeasement, *n.* settlement, amends, reparation; see **satisfaction 2.**

appendix, *n.* supplement, attachment, index; see also **addition 1.**

appetite, *n.* hunger, thirst, craving, longing, dryness, need for liquid, starvation, empty stomach, thirstiness, ravenousness, desire; see also **hunger, thirst.**—*Ant.* indifference, satiety, surfeit.

appetizing, *a.* savory, tasty, delectable; see also **delicious.**

applaud, *v.* cheer, clap, acclaim; see **praise 1.**

applause, *n.* ovation, cheers, hurrahs; see **praise 2.**

apple of (one's) eye, *n.* pet, idol, ideal; see **favorite.**

***apple polisher,** *n.* flatterer, toady, flunkey; see **flatterer.**

appliance, *n.* instrument, machine, apparatus; see **device 1.** Common electric household appliances include—broiler, deep-fryer, broom, can opener, carving knife, coffee maker, blender, mixer, frypan, portable oven, hair dryer, toaster, dishwasher, disposal, clothes dryer, clothes washer, stove, oven, refrigerator, freezer, water heater. toothbrush, waffle iron, iron, sewing machine, vacuum cleaner, tape recorder; see also **radio 2, record player, television.**

applicable, *a.* suitable, appropriate, usable; see **fit.**

applicant, *n.* petitioner, claimant, appellant; see **candidate.**

application, *n.* **1.** [Putting to use] employment, appliance, utilization; see **use 1. 2.** [The ability to apply oneself] devotion, zeal, diligence; see **attention 2. 3.** [A request] petition, entreaty, demand; see **appeal 1. 4.** [The instrument by which a request is made] petition, form, blank, paper, letter, credentials, certificate, statement, requisition, draft, check, bill.

applied, *a.* used, related, enforced, practiced, utilized, brought to bear, adapted, devoted, tested, adjusted, activated.

apply, *v.* **1.** [To make a request] petition, demand, appeal; see **beg. 2.** [To make use of] utilize, employ, practice, exploit; see **use 1. 3.** [To be relevant] be pertinent, pertain, bear on *or* upon, have bearing on, relate to, allude (to), concern, touch (on *or* upon), involve, affect, regard, have reference (to), connect, refer, suit, be in relationship, hold true, *come into play.

apply (oneself), *v.* attend to, dedicate oneself, address oneself, be occupied with, keep one's mind on, direct oneself to, concentrate on, persevere *or* persist in, be industrious, *buckle down (to).

appoint, *v.* select, designate, elect; see **delegate 1, 2.**

appointed, *a.* selected, chosen, delegated; see **named 2.**

appointment, *n.* **1.** [The act of appointing] designation, election, selection, nomination, approval, choice, promotion, assignment, authorization, installation, delegation, certification, empowering. **2.** [An engagement] interview, meeting, rendezvous, assignment, invitation, errand, something to do, date.

appraisal, *n.* examination, evaluation, assessment; see **estimate.**

appraise, *v.* **1.** [To set a price on] assess, price, assay; see **price.**

appreciable, *a.* considerable, sizable, tangible; see **large 1.**

appreciate, *v.* **1.** [To be grateful] welcome, enjoy, be *or* feel obliged, be indebted, acknowledge, never forget, give thanks, overflow with gratitude; see **thank.**—*Ant.* find fault with, minimize, **complain,** object. **2.** [To recognize worth] esteem, honor, praise; see **admire 1.**

appreciation, *n.* **1.** [Sense of gratitude] thankfulness, recognition, gratefulness; see **gratitude. 2.** [Favorable opinion] esteem, enjoyment, love, affection, sensitivity, attraction, commendation, high regard; see also **admiration.**

appreciative, *a.* grateful, obliged, satisfied; see **thankful.**

apprehend, *v.* **1.** [To understand] perceive, comprehend, grasp; see **understand 1. 2.** [To arrest] seize, place under arrest, take into custody; see **arrest.**

apprehension, *n.* **1.** [Foreboding] trepidation, dread, misgiving; see **fear. 2.** [Understanding] comprehension, grasp, perspicacity; see **judgment 1. 3.** [Arrest] capture, seizure, detention; see **arrest.**

apprehensive, *a.* fearful, worried, uncertain; see **troubled.**

apprentice, *n.* beginner, student, learner; see **amateur.**

approach, *n.* **1.** [A way] path, entrance, gate; see **way 2, 3. 2.** [Plan of action] method, program, procedure; see **plan 2.**

approach, *v.* **1.** [To approach personally] appeal *or* apply to, address, speak *or* talk to, propose, request, make advances *or* overtures to, take aside, talk to in private, *buttonhole, corner, descend on *or* upon.—*Ant.* avoid, shun, turn away. **2.** [To come near in space] drift *or* go *or* move toward, loom up, creep *or* drive up, near, go *or* draw near, close in, surround, come near *or* up (to), bear down (on *or* upon), edge *or* ease up to, *head into; see also **appear 1.** —*Ant.* leave, recede, depart. **3.** [To come near in time] be imminent *or* forthcoming, threaten, near, draw near, impend, *stare one in the face.—*Ant.* **increase,** extend, stretch out. 4. [To approximate] come near, take after, come close to; see **resemble.**

approaching, *a.* nearing, advancing, impending, oncoming, touching, approximating, coming, drawing near, (next) to come, threatening, rising, moving closer, gaining.

appropriate, *a.* proper, suitable, suited, fitting; see **fit.**

appropriate, *v.* 1. [To seize] secure, usurp, take (possession of); see **get** 1. 2. [To provide money] set aside *or* apart, allocate, assign (to a particular use), reserve, apportion, devote, appoint, allow (for), budget, allot.

appropriately, *a.* fittingly, suitably, justly, aptly, rightly, properly, agreeably, happily, fortunately.—*Ant.* **badly,** inappropriately, improperly.

appropriation, *n.* stipend, grant, fund, allotment, allowance, allocation, contribution, cash, budget, gift, remuneration, donation, support, pay, the wherewithal.

approval, *n.* 1. [Favorable opinion] regard, esteem, favor; see **admiration.** 2. [Sanction] endorsement, support, consent; see **permission.**

approve, *v.* ratify, affirm, encourage, support, endorse, seal, confirm, license, favor, consent *or* agree to, sanction, empower, charter, validate, legalize, recognize, accredit, recommend, authorize, second, subscribe to, allow, go along with, maintain, vote for, advocate, establish, pass, O.K., *give the green light, hold with.—*Ant.* **oppose,** reject, veto.

approved, *a.* certified, authorized, validated, passed, affirmed, legalized, ratified, sanctioned, permitted, endorsed, vouched for, praised, recognized, recommended, backed, supported, upheld, made official, agreed to, allowed, proven, ordered, established, *O.K.'d. — *Ant.* **refused,** censured, disapproved.

approximate, *a.* rough, inexact, uncertain, guessed, imprecise, imperfect, close, surmised, unscientific, by means of trial and error, almost, more or less, not quite, coming close, fair, nearly correct.

approximately, *a.* nearly, closely, roughly, close *or* near to, almost, around, about, very near, very close, in general, in round numbers, not quite, not far from, more or less, practically, just about, on the edge of, for all practical purposes, bordering on, generally, comparatively.

apron, *n.* cover, smock, bib; see **clothes** 1.

apt, *a.* 1. [Quick to learn] adept, clever, bright; see **intelligent** 1. 2. [Inclined] prone, tending, liable; see **likely** 4.

aptitude, *n.* capability, competence, capacity; see **ability.**

Arabia, *n.* Arabian peninsula, Near East, Mesopotamia; see **Asia.**

Arabian, *a.* Arabic, Semitic, from Arabia, Syrian, Jordanian, Lebanese, Iraqi, Egyptian, Tunisian, Libyan, Algerian, Morrocan, Saudi Arabian, Mesopotamian, Middle Eastern, Near Eastern, Moorish.

arbitrary, *a.* willful, tyrannical, unsatisfactory, temporary, unpremeditated, irrational, generalized, deceptive, superficial, unscientific, unreasonable, whimsical, fanciful, determined by no principle, optional, uncertain, inconsistent, discretionary, subject to individual will, halfway.

arbitrate, *v.* settle, adjust, reconcile; see **negotiate.**

arbitrator, *n.* arbiter, referee, mediator; see **judge.**

arc, *n.* bend, curve, segment of a circle; see **arch.**

arch, *n.* arc, curve, vault, dome, cupola, bend, arching, archway, curvature, cove.

arch, *v.* extend, hunch, round, stretch, curve, bend, shape, hunch, cover, hump, hook, arch over.—*Ant.* **straighten,** unbend, smooth.

archaic, *a.* antiquated, old, obsolete; see **old-fashioned.**

architect, *n.* planner, designer, draftsman, artist, engineer, builder, master builder, environmental engineer, designer of buildings.

architecture, *n.* construction, planning, designing, building, structure, housebuilding, shipbuilding, bridge-building, environmental engineering.

archives, *n. pl.* repository, vault, treasury; see **museum.**

arctic, *a.* polar, frozen, icy; see **cold** 1.

ardent, *a.* fervent, impassioned, warm; see **zealous.**

arduous, *a.* hard, severe, laborious; see **difficult** 1.

area, *n.* section, lot, neighborhood, plot, zone, sector, patch, square, quarter, block, precinct, ward, field, territory, district, ghetto, township, region, tract, enclosure, parcel, division, city, parish, diocese, principality, dominion, kingdom, empire, state; see also **measure** 1.

arena, *n.* field, pit, ground, park, coliseum, square, football field, gridiron, stadium, playing field, baseball field, amphitheater, hippodrome, circus, bowl, stage, platform, course, gymnasium *or* *gym.

argue, *v.* plead, appeal, explain, justify, show, reason (with), dispute, contend, wrangle, oppose, battle, demonstrate, establish, have it out, put up an argument, bicker (over), (have a) brush with. —*Ant.* **neglect,** ignore, scorn.

argument, *n.* 1. [An effort to convince] discussion, exchange, contention; see **discussion.** 2. [Verbal disagreement] debate, quarrel, row; see **dispute.**

argumentative, *a.* hostile, contentious, factious; see **quarrelsome.**

arid, *a.* parched, desert, dried; see **dry 1.**

arise, *v.* 1. [To get up] rise, stand (up), turn out, get out of bed, get out of a chair, get to one's feet, jump up, roll out, *hit the deck.—Ant.* **fall, sit, lie.** 2. [To ascend] mount, go up, climb; see **rise 1.**

aristocracy, *n.* nobility, privileged class, superior group, ruling class, noblemen, the elite, gentry, high society, upper class(es), persons of rank, patricians, class of hereditary nobility.

aristocrat, *n.* nobleman, peer, lord, noble, baron, earl, prince, patrician, ruler, gentleman, thoroughbred, duke, viscount, count, emperor, empress, queen, princess, duchess, countess, baroness, knight, lady, marquis; see also **king 1, lady 2.**

aristocratic, *a.* noble, refined, well-bred; see **noble 1, 2, 3.**

arithmetic, *n.* addition, subtraction, calculation; see **mathematics.**

arm, *n.* 1. [The upper human limb] member, appendage, forelimb, forearm, *fin, *flapper, *soupbone.* 2. [Anything resembling an arm, sense 1] bend, crook, projection, cylinder, sofa-end, branch, limb, rod, bough, off shoot, wing, prong, stump, hook, handle, bow. —**at arm's length,** aloof, distant, remote; see **unfriendly.** —**with open arms,** warmly, affectionately, joyously; see **friendly.**

arm, *v.* furnish weapons, load, give firearms, issue weapons, equip with arms, outfit, fit out.—*Ant.* **disarm,** demilitarize, deactivate.

armchair, *n.* easy chair, rocker, recliner; see **chair.**

armed, *a.* equipped, outfitted, in battle formation, loaded, provided with arms, fortified, protected, fitted out, in arms, well-armed, heavily armed.—*Ant.* **unarmed,** vulnerable, unprotected.

armistice, *n.* treaty of peace, cease-fire, temporary peace; see **peace.**

armor, *n.* tanks, tank force, Panzer divisions, armored personnel carriers (APC's), armored column, gun carriers, armor divisions.

armory, *n.* ordnance headquarters, training center, drilling place, depot, arsenal, gymnasium, drill center, shooting range, National Guard building, reserve corps headquarters.

arms, *n. pl.* armament, armor, ammunition, firearms, munitions, guns, small arms, instruments of war, deadly *or* lethal weapons, pistols, rifles, machine guns, submachine guns, equipment, supplies, ordnance, artillery, material, hardware, *ammo; see also **weapon, —bear arms,** carry weapons, be armed, be militant; see **arm.** —**take up arms,** go to war, rebel, do battle; see **fight 2.** —**up in arms,** hostile, indignant, willing to fight; see **angry.**

army, *n.* 1. [Military land forces] armed force, standing army, regulars, soldiery, troops, men, cavalry, infantry, artillery, air corps, reserves. 2. [A unit of an army, sense 1] division, regiment, armored division, airborne division, infantry division, battalion, company, corps, brigade, flight, wing, amphibious force, task force, detail, detachment, squad, troop, blocking force, patrol, unit, command, formation, point, column, legion, platoon, outfit.

aroma, *n.* fragrance, perfume, odor; see **smell 1, 2.**

around, *a.* and *prep.* 1. [Surrounding] about, in this area, on all sides, on every side, in circumference, neighboring, in the vicinity (of), all around, round (about), encompassing, nearby, approximately, in a circle, along a circuit, all about, close to *or* about, nearly in a circle, on various sides, round and round, right and left.—*Ant.* **distant,** remote, far-off. 2. [Approximately] almost, about, close to; see **approximately.** —**have been around,** worldly, sophisticated, knowledgeable; see **experienced.**

arouse, *v.* move, stir (up), stimulate; see **excite 1, 2.**

arrange, *v.* 1. [To put in order] order, regulate, systematize; see **order 3.** 2. [To make arrangements] determine, plan, devise, contrive, prepare for, get *or* make ready, draft, scheme, design, provide, make preparations, set the stage, prepare, put into shape, make plans for, line up, organize, adjust, manage, direct, establish, decide, resolve. —*Ant.* **bother,** disorganize, disturb.

arrangement, *n.* 1. [The result of arranging] method, system, form; see **order 3.** 2. [An agreement] settlement, adjustment, compromise; see **agreement 1.** 3. [A design] pattern, composition, combination; see **design.**

arrest, *n.* appropriation, imprisonment, apprehension, commitment, confinement, incarceration, capture, captivity, protective *or* preventive custody, taking by force, taking into custody, constraint, duress, seizure, detention, *bust.—Ant.* **freedom,** acquittal, release. —**under arrest,** arrested, in custody, apprehended; see **captured.**

arrest, *v.* apprehend, hold, place under arrest, take into custody, capture, imprison, jail, incarcerate, detain, secure, seize, get, catch, take (prisoner), nab, pick up, *bust.—*Ant.* free, liberate, parole.

arrival, *n.* **1.** [The act of arriving] entrance, advent, coming, entry, appearance, landing, homecoming, debarkation, approach, return, meeting.—*Ant.* departure, leaving, leave-taking. **2.** [That which has arrived] passenger, visitor, tourist, guest, newcomer, delegate, representative, traveler, cargo, freight, mail, shipment, package, parcel.

arrive, *v.* enter, land, disembark, alight, dismount, halt, roll up, reach, get to or in, visit, make shore, cast or drop anchor, reach home, appear, get to, *hit, *touch, *blow in or into, *breeze or check or pull in, *hit town.—*Ant.* leave, go, depart.

arrogance, *n.* insolence, smugness, vanity, audacity, haughtiness; see also **pride 2.**

arrogant, *a.* domineering, autocratic, sneering; see **proud 1.**

arrogantly, *a.* proudly, haughtily, insolently, loftily, *with one's nose in the air.

arrow, *n.* shaft, dart, missile; see **weapon.**

arson, *n.* pyromania, firing, deliberate burning of property; see **crime.**

art, *n.* representation, illustration, abstraction, imitation, modeling, description, portrayal, design, performance, personification, sketching, molding, shaping, painting, characterization, creating, sculpting, carving; see also **architecture, dance 1, literature 1, music 1, painting, sculpture.**

artery, *n.* **1.** [Main channel of communication or travel] highway, line, supply route, canal; see **road 1, way 2. 2.** [Blood vessel] tube, aorta, arterial passageway; see **vein 1.**

artful, *a.* clever, adroit, ingenious; see **able.**

article, *n.* **1.** [An individual thing] object, substance, commodity; see **thing 1. 2.** [Nonfiction appearing in a periodical] essay, editorial, commentary; see **writing 2.**

articulate, *v.* **1.** [To speak clearly] enunciate, pronounce, verbalize; see **speak 1. 2.** [To join] fit (together), combine, connect, link; see **join 1.**

artificial, *a.* unreal, synthetic, counterfeit; see **false 3.**

artillery, *n.* gunnery, arms, weapons; see **arms.**

artist, *n.* master, creator, painter, composer, virtuoso, musician, poet, novelist, dramatist, essayist, actress, actor, playwright, writer, performing artist, cartoonist, opera singer, dancer, ballet performer, ballerina, sculptor, etcher, engraver, designer, architect, photographer.

artistic, *a.* inventive, skillful, artful, crafty, imaginative, discriminating, creative, graceful, talented, accomplished, well-executed, well-wrought, pleasing, sublime, ideal, cultured, tasteful, exquisite, sensitive, fine, elegant, harmonious, grand, stimulating, elevated, noble, beautiful.

artistry, *n.* workmanship, skill, proficiency; see **ability.**

as, *a., conj.* and *prep.* **1.** [While] in the process of, in the act of, on the point of; see **while 1. 2.** [Because] since, inasmuch as, for the reason that; see **because. 3.** [To a degree] in the same way, in the same manner, equally, comparatively, similarly. **4.** [For a given purpose, end, use, etc.] just as, just for, serving as, functioning as, acting as, being, in and of itself, by its nature, essentially.

as a matter of course, *a.* ordinarily, commonly, customarily; see **regularly.**

as a matter of fact, *a.* truly, actually, indeed; see **really 1.**

as a rule, *a.* usually, commonly, ordinarily; see **regularly.**

as a whole, *a.* in all, all told, all in all; see **altogether.**

ascend, *v.* go or move upward, sprout, soar; see **rise 1.**

ascent, *n.* ascendance, climbing, ascension; see **rise 1.**

as far as, *a.* to the extent that, to the degree that, up to the time that, insofar as.

as good as, *a.* the same as, tantamount, practically; see **equal.**

ashamed, *a.* embarrassed, shamed, regretful, meek, repentant, penitent, apologetic, debased, abashed, conscience-stricken, mortified, uncomfortable, hesitant, perplexed, bewildered, shamefaced, bowed down, disconcerted, sputtering, stammering, stuttering, gasping, floundering, rattled, muddled, confused, blushing, flustered, distraught, submissive, feeling like a jackass, off balance, *in a hole, taken down a peg, *red in the face, looking silly or foolish, at a loss.

ashes, *n. pl.* dust, powder, cinders, slag, embers, charcoal, soot.

Asia, *n.* the Orient, the East, the mysterious East. Terms for parts of Asia include the following—*Far East:* China, Taiwan, Japan, North Korea, South Korea, Mongolia, Tibet, Siberia, North Vietnam, South Vietnam, Laos, Cambodia, Thailand, Burma, India, Bhutan, Sikkim, Nepal, Pakistan, Bengladesh, Ceylon or Sri Lanka, Malaysia, Indonesia; *Near and Middle East:* Turkey, Syria, Armenia, Kurdistan, Trocial

States, Iraq, Iran, Jordan, Israel, Lebanon, Saudi Arabia, Yemen, Aden, Muscat and Oman, Kuwait, Qatar, Afghanistan, Pakistan.

Asiatic, *a.* Oriental, Mongolian, almond-eyed, yellow-skinned, slant-eyed, Chinese, Hindu, Japanese, Asian, Mongoloid.

aside, *a.* to the side, to *or* on *or* by one side, at rest, out, by oneself, apart, by the side of, at one side, by itself, alone, alongside, out of the way, aloof, away, in safekeeping, beside, sidewise, sideways, abreast, at a short distance, by.

aside from, *prep.* beside, in addition to, excluding; see **besides.**

as if, *a.* and *conj.* just as (if), (just as) though, as it were, in such a way that, as if it were, supposing, quasi, so to speak, as would be if, as might be, (just) like.

*****as is,** *a.* as it stands, as usual, just the same, the same way.

as it were, *a.* so to speak, figuratively speaking, in a way, as it seems, as it would seem, in some sort, in a manner, so to say, *kind of, in a manner of speaking, *sort of.

ask, *v.* request, query, question, interrogate, examine, cross-examine, demand, pose *or* raise *or* put a question, inquire, frame a question, order, command, put questions to, requisition, bid, charge, petition, call upon, invite, urge (to), challenge, pry into, scour, investigate, hunt for, quiz, grill, *needle, *sound out, *pump, *put through the third degree.—*Ant.* answer, refute, rejoin.

asked, *a.* requested, questioned, urged; see **invited.**

asleep, *a.* sleeping, dreaming, quiet, resting, snoring, in a sound sleep, fast *or* sound asleep, slumbering, reposing, taking a siesta, hibernating, dozing, wakeless, napping, unconscious, *dead to the world, in the Land of Nod, *snoozing, *conked out, *out like a light.—*Ant.* awake, waking, alert.

as long as, *conj.* since, during, whilst; see **while 1.**

aspect, *n.* 1. [Looks] countenance, face, features; see **looks.** 2. [View] perspective, regard, slant; see **viewpoint.**

aspiration, *n.* yearning, eagerness, inclination; see **ambition.**

aspire, *v.* strive, struggle, yearn; see **try 1.**

aspiring, *a.* ambitious, hopeful, enthusiastic; see **zealous.**

as regards, *a.* and *prep.* concerning, regarding, respecting; see **about 2.**

ass, *n.* 1. [A stupid person] dolt, dunce, blockhead; see **fool.** 2. [A donkey] burro, jackass, jennet; see **animal 1.**

assailant, *n.* antagonist, foe, enemy; see **opponent.**

assassin, *n.* murderer, slayer, butcher; see **killer.**

assassinate, *v.* slay, slaughter, put to death; see **kill 1.**

assassination, *n.* killing, shooting, slaying; see **murder.**

assault, *n.* 1. [An attack] charge, advance, onslaught; see **attack.** 2. [A rape] attack, abduction, violation; see **rape.**

assault, *v.* 1. [To attack] assail, advance, strike; see **attack.** 2. [To rape] attack, violate, ravish; see **rape.**

assemble, *v.* 1. [To bring together] rally, call, convoke, muster, round up, group, convene, summon, mobilize, call together, accumulate, amass, invite guests, gather, collect, hold a meeting, unite, pack them in, *throw a party, *herd together, rally round, gather around, *gang around.—*Ant.* scatter, break up, send away. 2. [To put together] piece *or* fit together, set up, erect, construct, join, unite, solder, mold, weld, glue, model.—*Ant.* break, disassemble, break down.

assembly, *n.* 1. [A gathering of persons] assemblage, meeting, association; see **gathering.** 2. [The process of bringing parts together] construction, piecing together, fitting in, joining, modeling, assembling, attachment, adjustment, collection, welding, soldering, molding, fixing.—*Ant.* separation, dismantling, wrecking.

assent, *n.* approval, authorization, consent; see **permission.**

assert, *v.* state, say, affirm; see **declare 1.**

assertion, *n.* affirmation, statement, report; see **declaration 1.**

assess, *v.* 1. [To tax] charge, exact tribute, exact from; see **tax 1.** 2. [To estimate] judge, reckon, guess; see **estimate.**

assets, *n. pl.* holdings, possessions, capital; see **property.**

assign, *v.* commit, commission, authorize, hand over, earmark, allocate, detail, appoint, allot, prescribe, nominate, name, select, hold responsible, empower, entrust, allow, cast, deputize, attach, charge, accredit, hire, elect, ordain, enroll, relegate, draft.—*Ant.* maintain, reserve, keep back.

assignment, *n.* 1. [An appointment] designation, authorization, nomination; see **appointment 1.** 2. [Something assigned] job, responsibility, task; see **duty 2.**

assimilate, *v.* 1. [To absorb] take up, digest, osmose; see **absorb 2.** 2. [To understand] grasp, learn, sense; see **understand 1.**

assist, v. support, aid, serve; see **help.**

assistance, n. comfort, support, compensation; see **help** 1.

assistant, n. aid, deputy, henchman, friend, follower, adherent, auxiliary, lieutenant, associate, companion, colleague, partner, helper, apprentice, fellow-worker, secretary, helping hand, patron, backer, bodyguard, aide-de-camp, ally, accessory, clerk, collaborator, confederate, mate, helpmate, co-aid, co-operator, accomplice, copartner, co-worker, flunky, man Friday, *right arm, *yes-man, right-hand man, *friend in need.—*Ant.* enemy, rival, antagonist.

associate, n. comrade, brother-in-arms, peer, colleague, partner, copartner, friend, ally, buddy, accomplice, assistant, aid, attendant, henchman, confederate, auxiliary, co-operator, co-worker, co-helper, helper, collaborator, fellow-worker, helping hand, *right-hand man, man Friday, teammate; see also **assistant.**—*Ant.* enemy, foe, antagonist.

associate, v. 1. [To keep company with] work with, join with, get along with, be friendly with; see **go with, join** 2. 2. [To relate] correlate, link, connect, join; see **compare.**

association, n. 1. [The act of associating] frequenting, fraternization, friendship, acquaintanceship, co-operation, assistance, relationship, affiliation, agreement, participation, companionship, fellowship, familiarity, friendliness, camaraderie, membership, acquaintance, mingling, union, community.—*Ant.* **disagreement,** severance, rupture. 2. [The process of intellectual comparison] connection, relation, mental connection, train of thought, connection of ideas in thought, recollection, impression, remembrance, suggestibility, combination. 3. [An organization] union, federation, corporation; see **organization** 3.

assorted, a. varied, miscellaneous, mixed; see **various.**

assortment, n. variety, combination, group; see **collection.**

as such, a. in itself, by itself, alone, intrinsically.

assume, v. suppose, presume, posit, understand, gather, find, collect, theorize, presuppose, ascertain, draw the inference, judge at random, divine, get the idea, have an idea that, suspect, postulate, regard, consider, imply, hypothesize, guess, conjecture, suppose as fact, deem, imagine, surmise, opine, judge, estimate, speculate, fancy, take the liberty, be of the opinion, dare say, deduce, infer, conclude, put two and two together, be inclined to think, hold the opinion, think, calculate, hope, feel, be afraid, believe, have faith, take (it),

expect, allow, *reckon.—*Ant.* **doubt,** be surprised, be unaware that.

assumed, a. presumed, understood, presupposed, counted on, inferred, given, granted, taken as known, conjectured, accepted, supposed, hypothetical, hypothesized.

assumption, n. 1. [The act of taking for granted] supposition, presupposition, presumption, conjecture, assuming, accepting, suspicion, surmise, theorization, hypothesization.—*Ant.* **proof,** demonstrating, establishing. 2. [Something assumed] hypothesis, theory, postulate; see **opinion** 1.

assurance, n. 1. [A guaranty] insurance, support, pledge; see **promise** 1. 2. [Confidence] conviction, trust, certainty; see **faith** 1.

assure, v. 1. [To guarantee] vouch for, aver, attest; see **guarantee.** 2. [To convince] prove, persuade, induce; see **convince.**

assured, a. 1. [Certain] sure, undoubted, guaranteed; see **certain.** 2. [Confident] self-possessed, bold, unhesitating; see **confident.**

as though, a. and conj. 1. [As if] just as, just as if, just as though; see **as if.** 2. [Seemingly] evidently, supposedly, presumably; see **apparently.**

astonish, v. shock, amaze, astound; see **surprise.**

astonishing, a. surprising, startling, extraordinary; see **unusual** 1.

astonishment, n. surprise, amazement, bewilderment; see **wonder** 1.

astound, v. amaze, shock, startle; see **surprise.**

astray, a. straying, roaming, adrift; see **wandering** 1.

astronaut, n. space traveler, cosmonaut, spaceman, space pilot, rocket pilot, rocketeer, rocket man, space walker, explorer.

asunder, a. apart, in two or half, to shreds, in or into (little) (bits and) pieces, dismantled, dissected, in two parts, divided, into separate parts, separated, disjoined, rent, carved, dismembered, torn or broken apart, split; see also **broken** 1, **torn.** —*Ant.* whole, together, sound.

as well as, a. together or along with, in addition to, plus; see **including.**

as yet, a. still, not yet, till now; see **yet** 2.

at, prep. 1. [Position] on, by, near to, about, occupying the precise position of, in the vicinity (of), placed or situated at, found in, in front of, appearing in; see also **in** 1, **near** 1. 2. [Direction] toward, in the direction of, through; see **to** 1.

at all, a. anyhow, ever, in any way or wise, in any case or respect, under any condition or circumstances, anywise, in the least, in any manner or degree, to any extent, in the least degree, *anyways.

at all events, a. anyway, regardless, at least; see **anyhow.**

at a loss, a. in a quandary, perplexed, puzzled; see **doubtful 1.**

at arm's length, a. distant, afar, off, aloof; see **away 1.**

at ease, a. relaxed, untroubled, carefree; see **comfortable 1.**

at fault, a. in the wrong, in error, to blame; see **guilty.**

at first, a. in the beginning, in the first place, *first off; see **first.**

at hand, a. 1. [Near] nearby, accessible, convenient; see **available.** 2. [Imminent] approaching, near, impending; see **coming.**

atheism, n. irreligion, heresy, agnosticism, ungodliness, impiety, positivism, disregard or denial of God, iconoclasm, disbelief in God, irreverence, rationalism, dogmatic or skeptical atheism, infidelity, materialism, skepticism, freethinking, disbelief; see also **doubt.**

athlete, n. acrobat, gymnast, player, contestant, champion, sportsman, amateur, professional, semi-professional, contender, challenger, letterman, *muscle man, *jock. Athletes include the following—baseball player, football player, basketball player, soccer player, boxer, wrestler, swimmer, golfer, tennis player, badminton player, jockey, trackman, javelin thrower, high-jumper, discus thrower, shot putter, skier, ski jumper, slalom racer, runner, relay runner, broad-jumper, pole vaulter, hurdler, bowler, billiard player, polo player, hockey player, skater, bicyclist, fencer, swordsman, marksman, cricket player, *ball hawk, *netman, *spike digger, miler, *bamboo topper, *puck chaser, *dead-shot.

athletic, a. muscular, husky, heavy-set, wiry, springy, slim, fast, solid, strapping, hardy, robust, strong, vigorous, powerful, brawny, sinewy, sturdy, manly, well-built, well-proportioned, Herculean, Amazonian, *built like an ox.—Ant. **sick,** weak, fat.

athletics, n. pl. gymnastics, acrobatics, games; see **sport 3.**

atlas, n. book of maps, charts, tables; see **book.**

at last, a. ultimately, in conclusion, at the end; see **finally 2.**

at length, a. 1. [Finally] after a while, at last, in the end; see **finally 2.** 2. [Fully] unabridged, extensively, without omission; see **completely.**

atmosphere, n. 1. [The air] layer of air, gaseous envelope, air pressure; see **air 1.** 2. [A pervading quality] sense, impression, taste; see **character 1,** **characteristic.**

atmospheric, a. climatic, meteorological, aerial; see **airy.**

at odds, q. disagreeing, at variance, discordant; see **quarrelsome.**

atom, n. grain, mite, speck, particle, molecule, iota; see also **bit 1.** Parts and forms of atoms include the following—electron, proton, neutron, positron, neutrino, positive electron, neutral electron, cathode ray, alpha ray, beta ray, gamma ray; see also **element 2.**

atomic, a. microscopic, tiny, diminutive; see **minute 1.**

at once, a. 1. [Simultaneously] at the same time, concurrently, contemporaneously; see **together 2.** 2. [Immediately] directly, without delay, now; see **immediately.**

atone for, v. compensate (for), do penance, make amends; see **pay for.**

at one's disposal, a. ready, on call, accessible; see **available.**

at rest, a. relaxed, inactive, undisturbed; see **resting 1.**

atrocity, n. 1. [Brutality] inhumanity, wickedness, barbarity; see **cruelty.** 2. [A cruel deed] offense, outrage, horror; see **crime.**

at stake, a. in danger, risked, involved, implicated, in jeopardy or question, hazarded, concerned, endangered.

attach, v. 1. [To join] connect, append, add; see **join 1.** 2. [To attribute] associate, impute, ascribe; see **give 1.**

attachable, a. adjustable, connective, portable, movable, detachable, separable, in sections, prefabricated or *prefab.—Ant. **whole,** in one piece, inseparable.

attachment, n. 1. [Affection] fondness, liking, devotion; see **affection.** 2. [Something attached] accessory, adjunct, annex; see **addition 1.**

attack, n. 1. [Offensive tactical action] assault, raid, onslaught, advance, charge, thrust, offense, drive, aggression, onset, outbreak, skirmish, encounter, volley, shooting, barrage, siege, firing, trespass, blockade, cross fire, invasion, offensive, intrusion, intervention, onrush, inroad, encroachment, incursion.—Ant. **withdrawal,** retreat, retirement. 2. [Verbal attack] libel, slander, denunciation; see **blame.** 3. [Illness] seizure, breakdown, relapse; see **disease 1.** 4. [Rape] assault, violation, defilement; see **rape.**

attack, v. 1. [To fight offensively; used of an army] assault, beset, besiege, invade, storm, advance, infiltrate, raid, assail, march against, shell, board, take by surprise, make a push, bombard, bomb, go over the top, lift a hand against, lay siege to, open fire, lay into or at, launch an attack, ambush, strafe, waylay, engage, tilt against, torpedo, stone, push, combat, attempt violence to, trespass against, make aggression on, charge, strike the first blow, bayonet, saber, stab, tackle, rake, *light or sail into.—*Ant.* retreat, fall back, recoil. 2. [To assault; *used of an individual*] molest, beat, overwhelm; see **fight, rape.** 3. [To assail with words] revile, refute, reprove; see **blame.** 4. [To proceed vigorously] take up, deal with, start on; see **act 1.**

attacked, *a.* assaulted, bombed, bombarded, assailed, stoned, torpedoed, fired upon, stormed, under attack, strafed, invaded, besieged; see also **ruined 1.**

attacker, *n.* aggressor, fighter, assailant, antagonist, invader, foe, enemy, criminal, plunderer, intruder, trespasser, violator, ravager, spoiler, felon.—*Ant.* victim, prey, martyr.

attain, *v.* win, achieve, accomplish; see **succeed.**

attempt, *n.* trial, struggle, endeavor; see **effort.**

attempt, *v.* endeavor, strike, venture; see **try 1.**

attend, *v.* be present at, frequent, sit in on, visit, be a guest, revisit, haunt, be a member, be an habitué, make an appearance.—*Ant.* **leave,** be missing, absent oneself.

attendance, *n.* 1. [The act of attending] presence, participation, appearance, being present, putting in an appearance, being in evidence, turning or showing up.—*Ant.* **absence,** nonappearance, nonattendance. 2. [The persons attending] audience, spectators, assembly; see **gathering.**

attendant, *n.* aid, orderly, valet, nurse, usher, bell hop, servant, domestic, secretary, understudy, disciple, pupil, auditor, steward, stewardess, maid; see also **assistant.**

attend school, *a.* undergo schooling, learn, go to school, be educated, receive instruction, matriculate, study, take courses, be a student, enroll; see also **register 4, study.**

attention, *n.* observation, observance, regard, vigilance, mindfulness, inspection, heed, heedfulness, watching, listening, consideration, intentness, study, alertness, thought, application, diligence, caution, preoccupation, thoroughness, recognition, observance, regard, vigilance, mindfulness, inspection.

attitude, *n.* mood, opinion, idea about, belief, air, demeanor, condition of mind, state of feeling, position, reaction, bias, set, leaning, bent, inclination, propensity, cast, emotion, temper, temperament, sensibility, disposition, mental state, notion, philosophy, view, orientation to, nature, make-up, frame of mind, character; see also **viewpoint.**

attorney, *n.* attorney at law, barrister, counsel; see **lawyer.**

attract, *v.* 1. [To draw] pull, drag, bring; see **draw 1.** 2. [To allure] entice, lure, charm; see **fascinate.**

attraction, *n.* 1. [The act of drawing toward] magnetism, drawing power, allurement, fascination, temptation, pull, gravitation, affinity, inclination, tendency, enticement; see also **appeal 2.** 2. [An event] spectacle, display, demonstration; see **event.**

attractive, *a.* good-looking, winning, engaging; see **beautiful, handsome.**

attribute, *n.* peculiarity, quality, trait; see **characteristic.**

attribute, *v.* ascribe, impute, associate or connect with; see **give 1.**

auction, *n.* disposal, bargain, bankruptcy sale; see **sale.**

auction, *v.* put on sale, sell at auction, put under the hammer; see **sell.**

audible, *a.* perceptible, discernible, distinct, actually heard, loud enough to be heard, capable of being heard, within earshot, within hearing distance, hearable, sounding, resounding, loud, deafening, roaring, aloud, clear, plain, emphatic; see also **heard.**

audience, *n.* witnesses, spectators, patrons; see **gathering.**

audit, *n.* checking, scrutiny, inspection; see **examination 1.**

audit, *v.* examine, check, inspect; see **examine 1.**

auditorium, *n.* hall, lecture room, theater, playhouse, movie house, reception hall, amphitheater, assembly hall, opera house, music hall, concert hall, chapel, assembly room. Sections of an auditorium include the following—stage, proscenium, orchestra, parquet, stalls, boxes, pit, orchestra circle, dress circle, balcony, gallery, top gallery, tiers, box office.

auger, *n.* bit, twist drill, screw auger; see **drill 2.**

augment, *v.* enlarge, expand, magnify; see **increase.**

aunt, *n.* mother's sister, father's sister, uncle's wife, grandaunt, great-aunt, auntie; see also **relative.**

auspices, *n. pl.* protection, aegis, support; see **patronage 1.**

austere, *a.* harsh, hard, ascetic; see **severe 1, 2.**

austerity, *n.* sternness, severity, strictness, harshness, sharpness, hardness, grimness, stiffness, seriousness, rigidity, gravity, rigor, formality; see also **determination.**

Australia, *n.* Commonwealth of Australia, Australasia, the antipodes, southern or sixth continent, *down under.

Australian, *a.* Australasian, Austronesian, Anzac, antipodean, *Aussie, *from down under, *digger.

authentic, *a.* 1. [Reliable] trustworthy, authoritative, factual; see **reliable**. 2. [Genuine] real, true, actual; see **genuine 1**.

authenticate, *v.* verify, confirm, validate; see **prove**.

author, *n.* writer, journalist, columnist, dramatist, playwright, poet, poetess, novelist, short story writer, essayist, authoress, contributor, script writer, correspondent, reporter, copywriter, literary man, ghost writer, encyclopedist, lexicographer, scholar, publicist, advertisement writer, critic, annotator, hack writer, free lance, *ad-man, *ghost, *scripter; see also **editor, writer**.

authoritative, *a.* 1. [Official] well-supported, well-documented, authentic; see **reliable**. 2. [Authorized] lawful, legal, mandatory; see **approved, authorized**. 3. [Suggestive of authority] dogmatic, officious, domineering; see **absolute 2**.

authority, *n.* 1. [Power based on right] right, authorization, jurisdiction; see **power 2**. 2. [The appearance of having authority, sense 1] prestige, political influence, esteem; see **influence**. 3. [One who knows] expert, veteran, professional; see **specialist**.

authorization, *n.* sanction, signature, support; see **permission**.

authorize, *v.* 1. [To allow] permit, tolerate, suffer; see **allow**. 2. [To approve] sanction, ratify, affirm, endorse; see **approve**.

authorized, *a.* allowed, official, legal, administrative, lawful, mandatory, authoritative, ruling, sovereign, decisive, valid, standard, sanctioned, confirmed; see also **approved**.

auto, *n.* car, vehicle, passenger car; see **automobile**.

autobiography, *n.* memoirs, personal history, self-portrayal, confession, life, experiences, self-account, adventures, biography, life story, journal, letters, nonfiction book.

autocratic, *a.* bigoted, domineering, aggressive; see **absolute 2**.

autograph, *n.* handwriting, seal, *John Hancock; see **signature**.

automated, *a.* mechanical, mechanized, motorized, computerized, automatic, electronic, programmed, cybernetic, untouched by human hands; see also **automatic**.

automatic, *a.* self-starting, motorized, self-regulating, automated, mechanized, under its own power *or* steam, having the power of self-motion, cybernetic, self-moving, self-acting, self-propelling, computerized, programmed, push-button, involuntary, unthinking, mechanical, instinctive, spontaneous, reflex, intuitive, unintentional, unforced, unconscious, unwilling.

automobile, *n.* motor car, car, vehicle, passenger car, machine, auto. Types of automobiles include the following—passenger car, limousine, sedan, hardtop, compact, sports car, convertible, station wagon, taxicab, bus, truck, lorry, motor bus, bus, jeep, *crate, *job, *buggy, *wreck, *clunker, *jalopy, *boat, *heap. Principal parts of an automobile include the following—wheels, tires, fenders, chassis, motor, radiator, engine, fan, cylinder, carburetor, exhaust, muffler, throttle, gear, gear shift, clutch, steering wheel, transmission, universal joint, brake drum, generator, distributor, magneto, self-starter, oil gauge, speedometer, spark plug, ammeter, axles, emergency brake *or* hand brake, accelerator, chains, shock absorber, radius rod, piston, intake and exhaust valves, fuel pump, gas tank, control panel, steering column.

autonomous, *a.* self-governing, self-ruling, independent; see **free 1**.

autonomy, *n.* liberty, independence, sovereignty; see **freedom 1**.

autopsy, *n.* post-mortem examination, dissection, necropsy; see **examination 2**.

autumn, *n.* harvest time, Indian summer, fall, autumnal equinox, close of the year, one of the four seasons.

auxiliary, *a.* 1. [Subsidiary] secondary, accessory, subservient; see **subordinate**. 2. [Supplementary] reserve, supplemental, spare; see **extra**.

available, *a.* accessible, usable, ready, convenient, serviceable, prepared, handy, on call, ready for use, open to, derivable from, obtainable, attainable, practicable, achievable, feasible, possible, realizable, reachable, within reach, at one's disposal, at one's beck and call, at hand, at one's elbow, *on tap, *on deck.—*Ant.* occupied, unavailable, unobtainable.

avalanche, *n.* mudslide, snowslide, landslide, landslip, rockslide, large mass of falling snow, snowslip, icefall.

avenue, *n.* street, boulevard, parkway, promenade; see **road 1**.

average, *a.* ordinary, medium, mediocre; see **common 1**.

average, *n.* midpoint, standard, center, median, norm, middle, normal individual, standard performance, typical kind, rule, average man.—*Ant.* extreme, highest, lowest.

average, *v.* 1. [To compute an average] strike a balance, reduce to a mean, split the difference; see **balance 2**. 2. [To do, on an average] perform, make, receive, do at the rate of; see **do 1, earn 2, perform 1**. —**average out,** stabilize, balance, to arrive at an average; see **equalize**. —on the average, usually, commonly ordinarily; see **regularly**.

avert, v. turn aside, sidetrack, shove aside, shunt, turn away from, look away, break one's eyes away, look another way, cast one's eyes down.

aviation, n. flying, flight, aeronautics, theory of flight, aeronautical engineering or navigation, piloting, dynamics, airmanship.

aviator, n. flier, navigator, bombardier; see **pilot 1**.

avid, a. eager, keen, greedy, desirous; see **zealous**.

avoid, v. keep away or flee or escape from, evade, shun, fall back, elude, dodge, give one the slip, draw back, hold off, turn aside, recoil from, keep at arm's length, withdraw, stay off or back out of, shirk off or out of, let alone, keep out of the way, keep clear of, keep at a respectful distance, let well enough alone, avert the eyes, keep in the background, keep one's distance, keep away from, refrain from, steer clear of, *lay off, *pass up, shake off, *fight shy of.—*Ant.* face, meet, undertake.

avoidance, n. evasion, delay, elusion, escape, retreat, restraint, passive resistance (against), evasive action, temperance, flight, recoil, recession, escape mechanism, slip, *brush, dodge, *duck.—*Ant.* **meeting**, encounter, participation.

await, v. wait for, attend, anticipate, expect; see **anticipate**.

awake, a. attentive, vigilant, observant; see **conscious**.

awake, v. open one's eyes, become aware, gain consciousness, see the light, stir, get up, come out of sleep, rub one's eyes, rise up, stretch one's limbs, show signs of life, arise, turn or roll out, *hit the deck, *pile out, *rise and shine.—*Ant.* **sleep**, doze off, slumber.

awaken, v. awake, call, play reveille, arouse, rouse, *roll someone out, turn someone out.

awakening, n. rebirth, arousal, renewal; see **revival 1**.

award, n. citation, honor, scholarship; see **prize**.

award, v. grant, confer, bestow; see **give 1**.

aware, a. knowledgeable, cognizant, apprised; see **conscious**.

awareness, n. sensibility, mindfulness, discernment, cognizance, consciousness, alertness, keenness, attentiveness, recognition, comprehension, perception, information, apprehension, appreciation, experience.

away, a. absent, not present, distant, at a distance, not here, far afield, at arm's length, remote, from home, out of, far off or apart, beyond, off.—*Ant.* **here**, present, at hand. —do away with, eliminate, get rid of, reject; see **abandon 1**.

awe, n. fright, wonder, reverential fear; see **reverence**.

awesome, a. striking, moving, exalted; see **grand**.

awful, a. 1. [Frightful] horrible, terrible, dreadful; see **frightful**. 2. [Shocking] appalling, disgusting, repulsive; see **offensive 2. 3.** [Very great] gigantic, colossal, stupendous; see **big 1**.

awfully, a. 1. [*Badly] poorly, incompletely, clumsily; see **badly 1. 2.** [Very] very much, indeed, truly; see **very**.

awhile, a. for a or the moment, briefly, momentarily, for a short time, for some time, not for long, temporarily, for a little while, *for a spell.—*Ant.* **forever**, permanently, for a long time.

awkward, a. clumsy, bungling, ungraceful, gawky, floundering, stumbling, ungainly, unwieldy, slovenly, lacking dexterity, without skill, inexpert, unskilled, inept, unfit, inexperienced, shuffling, uncouth, gauche, incompetent, rusty, unused to, green, amateurish, butterfingered, messy, all thumbs, with two left feet.—*Ant.* **able**, dexterous, smooth.

awkwardly, a. clumsily, unskillfully, ineptly, ponderously, uncouthly, gracelessly, inelegantly, incompetently, artlessly, amateurishly, ungracefully, stiffly, woodenly, rigidly, with difficulty, with embarrassment.—*Ant.* **gracefully**, skillfully, adroitly.

awkwardness, n. ineptitude, inability, incompetence, botchery, artlessness, crudeness, ignorance, heavy-handedness, ungainliness, ungracefulness, oafishness, gracelessness, butterfingers, *handful of thumbs.—*Ant.* **ability**, grace, competence.

awl, n. bit, drill, pick; see **tool 1**.

awning, n. canvas covering, canopy, tent; see **cover 1**.

ax, n. hatchet, adz, mattock, tomahawk, battle-ax, poleax, pickax, cleaver, broadax, hand ax, double-bitted ax. —*get the ax, be fired or dismissed or discharged, be dropped from the payroll, get in(to) trouble; see **get it 2. —*have an ax to grind**, want something, have a purpose, hope to get something; see **want 1**.

axis, n. shaft, pivot, axle, pole, stem, support, dividing line, spindle, arbor, line of symmetry or rotation or revolution.

axle, n. shaft, spindle, pin; see **axis**.

B

babble, *n.* jabber, chatter, twaddle; see **nonsense 1.**

babble, *v.* talk incoherently *or* foolishly *or* nonsensically, rant, rave, drivel, gush, run on, gossip, murmur, chat, chatter, prattle, twaddle, gabble, tattle, jabber, blurt, patter, *run off at the mouth, *talk off the top of one's head, rattle (on), *gab, cackle, blab, sputter, gibber, *blabber, clatter; see also **talk 1.**

baby, *a.* youthful, babyish, juvenile; see **childish.**

baby, *n.* nursling, suckling, babe (in arms), child, toddler, tot, youngling, brat, young one, little one, papoose, pickaninny, chick, *kid, cherub, *little shaver, *little stranger *or* newcomer, *(little) accident, *bundle from heaven, *bundle of joy, *another mouth to feed, brat.—*Ant.* **man**, adolescent, grown-up.

baby, *v.* pamper, coddle, pet, spoil, fondle, caress, dandle, nurse, cherish, foster, cuddle, make much of, humor, indulge, mollycoddle; see also **pamper.**

babyhood, *n.* infancy, nursery days, *diaper days; see **childhood.**

baby-sit, *v.* watch, care for, sit; see **guard.**

bachelor, *n.* unmarried *or* single man, celibate, misogynist, virgin, womanhater, *bach, *lone wolf.—*Ant.* married man, **husband**, benedict.

back, *a.* rear, hinder, after, back of, in the wake of, backward, hindmost, behind, astern, hind, rearward, aft, to *or* in the rear, dorsal, caudal, following, at the heels of, posterior, terminal, in the wake, in the background, final.—*Ant.* **front**, forward, head.

back, *n.* 1. [The rear part *or* side] hinder part, posterior, stern, poop, aft, tailpiece, tail, *back end.—*Ant.* **front**, fore part, fore. 2. [The rear of the torso] posterior, dorsum, spinal portion; see **spine 2.** 3. [One who plays behind the line, especially in football] linebacker, fullback, halfback; see **football player.** **—behind one's back**, in secret, slyly, hidden; see **secretive.** **—(flat) on one's back**, ill, defeated, helpless; see **sick.** **—*get off one's back**, let alone, ignore, stop nagging; see **neglect 2.** **—get one's back up**, become angry, be stubborn, lose one's temper; see **rage 1.** **—go back on**, betray, reject, turn against; see **deceive.** **—in back of**, at the rear, behind, coming after; see **following.** **—turn one's back on**, reject, desert, fail;

see **abandon 1.** **—with one's back to the wall**, desperate, cornered, stopped; see **hopeless.**

back, *v.* 1. [To push backward] drive back, repel, reverse; see **turn 2.** 2. [To further] uphold, stand behind, encourage; see **support 2.** 3. [To equip with a back] stiffen, cane, line; see **line 1, strengthen.**

back and forth, *a.* zigzag, in and out, from side to side; see **to and fro.**

backbone, *n.* 1. [Line of bones in the back supporting the body] spinal column, vertebrae, chine; see **spine 2.** 2. [Determination] firmness, fortitude, resolution; see **determination.**

back down, *v.* withdraw, recoil, back out; see **retreat.**

backed, *a.* 1. [Propelled backward] driven back, shoved, repelled, repulsed, pushed, retracted.—*Ant.* **ahead**, moved forward, impelled. 2. [Supported] upheld, encouraged, approved, heartened, aided, assisted, advanced, promoted, sustained, fostered, favored, championed, advocated, supplied, maintained, asserted, established, helped, bolstered, propped, furthered, seconded, prompted, served, pushed, boosted, primed.—*Ant.* discouraged, **opposed**, obstructed. 3. [Supplied with a back, *or* backing] stiffened, built up, strengthened; see **reinforced.**

backer, *n.* benefactor, supporter, follower; see **patron.**

backfire, *v.* 1. [To explode] burst, erupt, detonate; see **explode.** 2. [To go awry] boomerang, ricochet, bounce (back); see **fail 1.**

background, *n.* 1. [Setting] backdrop, framework, environment; see **setting.** 2. [The total of one's experiences] education, qualifications, preparation, grounding, rearing, credentials, capacities, accomplishments, achievements, attainments, deeds, actions; see also **experience, knowledge 1.**

backhanded, *a.* obscure, sarcastic, unfavorable; see **indirect.**

backhouse, *n.* latrine, outdoor toilet, outhouse; see **toilet 2.**

backing, *n.* 1. [Assistance] subsidy, encouragement, aid; see **help 1.** 2. [Support] reinforcement, buttress, lining; see **support 2.**

backlash, *n.* response, repercussion, resentment; see **reaction.**

back off, *v.* fall back, withdraw, retire; see **retreat.**

back out of, v. withdraw, shrink from, escape; see **retreat.**

backslide, v. apostatize, break faith, fall from grace; see **relapse.**

backstop, n. screen, net, barrier; see **fence.**

back up, v. 1. [To move backward] fall back, withdraw, reverse; see **retreat** 2. [To support] aid, assist, help; see **support** 2.

backward, a. 1. [To the rear] rearward, astern, behind, retro-, retrograde, regressive, reflex.—*Ant.* **forward,** progressive, onward. 2. [Reversed] turned around, counterclockwise, inverted; see **reversed** 3. [Behind in development] underdeveloped, slow, slow to develop, retarded, delayed, arrested, checked, behindhand, late, undeveloped, underprivileged; see also **dull** 3. —**bend over backward,** try (hard) (to please), appease, be fair; see **try** 1.

back yard, n. patio, terrace, enclosure, play area, garden spot, lawn, grass, court; see also **garden, yard** 1.

bacon, n. flitch, gammon, side pork, beef bacon, Danish bacon, Canadian bacon; see **meat.** —***bring home the bacon,** earn a living, prosper, get paid; see **succeed** 1.

bacteria, n. pl. bacilli, microbes, organisms; see **germ.**

bad, a. 1. [Wicked] evil, sinful, immoral, wrong, corrupt, base, foul, gross, profane, naughty, degenerate, decadent, depraved, heartless, degraded, debauched, indecent, mean, scandalous, nasty, vicious, fiendish, devilish, criminal, murderous, sinister, monstrous, dangerous, *rotten, dirty, crooked.—*Ant.* **good,** honest, pure. 2. [Spoiled] rancid, decayed, putrid; see **rotten** 1, 2, 3. [Below standard] defective, inferior, imperfect; see **poor** 2. 4. [In poor health] ill, diseased, ailing; see **sick.** 5. [Injurious] hurtful, damaging, detrimental; see **harmful.** —***in bad,** in difficulty, unwanted, unwelcome; see in **trouble.** —***not bad,** all right, (pretty) good, passable; see **fair** 2.

badge, n. 1. [Outward evidence] marker, symbol, identification; see **emblem.** 2. [A device worn as evidence] pin, emblem, seal, medal, insignia, shield, ribbon, device, medallion, brassard, brand, token of office, motto, official star, marker, feather, rosette, cuff band, clasp, button, signet, crest, star, chevron, stripe.

badger, v. harass, annoy, pester; see **bother** 2.

badly, a. 1. [In an ineffectual or incompetent manner] wrongly, imperfectly, ineffectively, inefficiently, poorly, unsatisfactorily, crudely, boorishly, unskillfully, defectively, weakly, haphazardly, clumsily, carelessly, negligently, incompetently, stupidly, blunderingly, mistakenly, awkwardly, faultily, shiftlessly, abominably, *awfully, terribly.—*Ant.* **carefully,** competently, adequately. 2. [Not well] unwell, poorly, feeble; see **sick.** 3. [To a marked degree] severely, seriously, greatly; see **very.**

baffle, v. perplex, puzzle, bewilder; see **confuse.**

bag, n. purse, pocket, sac(k), pouch, grip, handbag, tote (bag), knapsack, backpack, carpetbag, kit, satchel, saddlebag, gunny sack, suitcase, brief case, attaché case, duffel bag, pack, container, feedbag, quiver, packet, pocketbook, poke, holster, vanity bag, valise, case, wallet, holdall, carryall. —**in the bag,** absolute, sure, definite; see **certain** 2. —**left holding the bag,** deceived, tricked, deserted; see **abandoned.**

bag, v. trap, seize, get; see **catch** 1.

baggage, n. luggage, gear, bags, trunks, valises, suitcases, overnight cases, parcels, paraphernalia, effects, equipment, things, movables.

baggy, a. slack, unshapely, bulging; see **loose** 1.

bail, n. bond, surety, recognizance, pledge, pawn, warrant, guaranty, collateral.

bail, v. 1. [To dip] scoop, spoon out, dredge; see **dip** 2. 2. [To empty] clear, drain, deplete; see **empty.**

bail out, v. release, give security for, post bail for, assure, underwrite, guarantee, warrant, insure, deliver, go bail for, spring.

bait, n. lure, inducement, bribe; see **attraction.**

bait, v. 1. [To torment] anger, nag, tease; see **bother** 2. 2. [To lure] entice, attract, draw; see **fascinate.**

bake, v. roast, toast, warm; see **cook.**

baked, a. parched, scorched, dried, toasted, warmed, heated, cooked, grilled, burned, charred, roasted, incinerated.

baker, n. pastry cook, chef, confectioner; see **cook.**

bakery, n. bake *or* pastry shop, pastry kitchen, confectionery, cook shop, bread *or* cake *or* biscuit factory, bread bakery, cake bakery.

balance, n. 1. [Whatever remains] excess, surplus, residue; see **remainder.** 2. [An equilibrium] poise, counterpoise, symmetry, offset, equivalence, counterbalance, tension, equalization, equality of weight, parity.—*Ant.* imbalance, inconsistency, topheaviness. 3. [An excess of credits over debits] surplus, dividend, cash on hand; see **profit** 2. —**in the balance,** undetermined, undecided, critical; see **uncertain** 2.

balance, v. 1. [To offset] equipoise, counterpoise, counterbalance; see sense 2. 2. [To place in balance] place in equilibrium, steady, stabilize, neutralize, set, level, equalize, support, poise, oppose, even, weigh, counteract, make equal or level or steady, compensate, tie, adjust, square, parallel, coordinate, readjust, equate, match, level or pair off, attune, harmonize, tune, accord, correspond.— *Ant.* topple, **upset,** turn over. 3. [To demonstrate that debits and credits are in balance] estimate, account (for), audit; see **check 2.**

balanced, *a.* 1. [Made even] equalized, poised, offset, in equilibrium, evened, counterweighted, equivalent, stabilized, symmetrical, counterpoised, counterbalanced, on an even keel.—*Ant.* unstable, unbalanced, unequal. 2. [Audited] validated, confirmed, certified; see approved.

balance of power, *n.* equilibrium, distribution, apportionment; see also **balance 2.**

balcony, *n.* gallery, veranda, terrace; see **upstairs.**

bald, *a.* hairless, shaven or shaved, bare, featherless, glabrous, shiny, smooth, *like a billiard ball; see also **smooth 3.** —*Ant.* hairy, covered, bearded.

balderdash, *n.* senseless talk, gibberish, bombast; see **nonsense 1.**

bale, *n.* bundle, bunch, parcel; see **package.**

balk, *v.* turn down, demur, desist; see **refuse.**

balky, *a.* contrary, obstinate, perverse; see **stubborn.**

ball, *n.* 1. [A spherical body] drop, knot, marble, globe, spheroid, sphere, balloon, orb, globule, globular or rounded or spherical object, pellet, pill. 2. [A game played with a ball] baseball, football, catch; see **sport 3.** 3. [A dance] grand ball, promenade, reception; see **party 1.** —*carry the **ball,** assume responsibility, take command or control, bear the burden; see **lead 1.** —*get or keep the **ball rolling,** initiate action, commence, start; see **begin 1.** —*have something on the **ball,** skilled, alert, efficient; see **able.**

ballad, *n.* carol, chant, primitive song; see **song.**

ballast, *n.* sandbags, counterbalance, counterweight; see **weight 2.**

ballet, *n.* toe dancing, choreography, tap dancing; see **dance 1.**

ballet dancer, *n.* (prima) ballerina, danseuse, danseur; see **dancer.**

balloon, *n.* dirigible, aircraft, airship, weather balloon, free balloon, captive balloon, kite balloon, lighter-than-air craft, toy balloon, zeppelin, observation balloon, weather balloon, radar balloon, *blimp, gasbag, *zep.

ballot, *n.* tally, ticket, poll; see **vote 1.**

*ball up, *v.* confound, jumble, tangle; see **confuse.**

balm, *n.* 1. [Anything healing and soothing] solace, consolation, comfort, relief, refreshment, remedy, cure. 2. [An ointment of resin] salve, lotion, dressing; see **medicine 2.**

bamboozle, *v.* swindle, trick, dupe; see **deceive.**

ban, *n.* taboo, prohibition, limitation; see **refusal.**

ban, *v.* outlaw, prevent, declare illegal; see **forbid, prevent.**

banal, *a.* dull, trite, hackneyed; see **common 1.**

band, *n.* 1. [A beltlike strip] circuit, meridian, latitude, circle, ring, orbit, zodiac, circumference, zone, ribbon, belt, line, strip, stripe, tape, sash, twine, scarf, bandage, girdle, thong, wristband, bond, tie, binding, stay, truss, belt, harness, brace, strap, binding, waistband, collar, hatband, cable, rope, link, chain, line, string, guy (wire). 2. [A company of people] group, collection, association; see **gathering.** 3. [A group of musicians] orchestra, company, troupe, group, *combo. Kinds of bands include the following—military, brass, street, concert, parade, jazz, stage, dance, Dixieland, jug, rock.

bandage, *n.* compress, cast, gauze; see **dressing 3.**

bandage, *v.* tie, swathe, truss; see **bind 1, fasten.**

bandit, *n.* highwayman, thief, brigand; see **robber.**

bang, *n.* 1. [A loud report] blast, roar, detonation; see **noise 1.** 2. [A blow] hit, cuff, whack; see **blow. 3.** [*A thrill] enjoyment, pleasant feeling, *kick; see **excitement.**

bang, *v.* 1. [To beat] strike, slam, whack; see **hit 1.** 2. [To make a noise] crash, clatter, rattle; see **sound 1.**

banish, *v.* exile, deport, cast out, expel, expatriate, ostracize, rusticate, excommunicate, proscribe, transport, outlaw, extradite, isolate, dismiss.—*Ant.* receive, welcome, accept.

banishment, *n.* expatriation, deportation, expulsion; see **exile 1.**

banister, *n.* railing, baluster, balustrade; see **rail 1.**

bank, *n.* 1. [Ground rising above adjacent water] ledge, embankment, edge; see **shore. 2.** [A financial establishment] national bank, state bank, commercial bank, savings bank, savings and loan association, Federal Reserve Bank, private bank, countinghouse, investment firm, banking house, credit union, (mutual) fund, trust company, treasury.

bank, *v.* 1. [To deposit money] save, put in the bank, enter an account; see deposit 2. 2. [To tilt on a curve] lean, pitch, bend, slope; see **lean 1**.

banker, *n.* treasurer, teller, officer of the bank, broker, financier, capitalist, investment banker, money-lender.

banking, *n.* investment, funding, money-lending; see **business 1**.

***bank on**, *v.* rely *or* depend on, believe in, be sure about; see **trust 1**.

bankrupt, *a.* failed, out of business, *broke; see **ruined 4**.

bankruptcy, *n.* insolvency, destitution, distress; see **failure 1**.

banner, *n.* colors, pennant, flag; see **emblem**.

banquet, *n.* repast, feast, festivity; see **dinner**.

baptism, *n.* dedication, christening, initiation; see **ceremony 2**.

baptize, *v.* immerse, purify, regenerate, sprinkle, dip, christen, name, administer baptism to, *give the water cure.

bar, *n.* 1. [A relatively long, narrow object] strip, stake, stick, crossbar, boom, rib, crosspiece, pole, spar, rail, lever, rod, crowbar, shaft, slab. 2. [A counter serving refreshments, especially drinks] bar room, tavern, cocktail lounge, saloon, public house, counter, hotel, inn, canteen, beer parlor, cabaret, restaurant, cafeteria, road house, brass rail, snack bar, beer garden, *dive, *pub (British), *grill. 3. [The legal profession] lawyers, counselors, barristers, solicitors, jurists, attorneys, bar association, advocates, judiciary. 4. [An obstruction] hindrance, obstacle, hurdle; see **barrier**. 5. [A relatively long, narrow area] strip, stripe, ribbon; see **band 1**.

bar, *v.* 1. [To raise a physical obstruction] barricade, dam, dike, fence, wall, erect a barrier, brick up, blockade, clog, exclude, shut *or* lock (out), keep out, bolt, cork, plug, seal, stop, impede, (set up a) roadblock.—*Ant.* open, free, clear. 2. [To obstruct by refusal] ban, forbid, deny, refuse, prevent, stop, boycott, ostracize, preclude, shut *or* keep out, exclude, exile, reject, outlaw, condemn, discourage, interfere with, restrain, frustrate, circumvent, override, segregate, interdict, *freeze out.—*Ant.* allow, admit, welcome. 3. [To close] shut, lock, seal; see **close 4**.

barbarian, *n.* savage, brute, Hun, cannibal, Goth, rascal, ruffian, monster, Yahoo, wild Indian, Philistine, troglodyte, clod; see also **beast 2**.

barbaric, *a.* inhuman, brutal, fierce; see **cruel**.

barbarity, *n.* savageness, fierceness, brutality; see **cruelty**.

barbecue, *n.* 1. [A grill] roaster, grill, broiler; see **appliance**. 2. [A picnic] cookout, wiener roast, picnic; see **meal 2**.

barbecue, *v.* grill, sear, broil; see **cook**.

barbed wire, *n.* fence wire, fencing, barb-wire; see **fence**.

bare, *a.* 1. [Without covering] uncovered, bald, stripped; see **naked 1, open 4**. 2. [Plain] unadorned, simple, unornamented; see **modest 2**. 3. [Without content] barren, void, unfurnished; see **empty**.

barefaced, *a.* 1. [Open] unconcealed, clear, apparent; see **obvious 1, 2**. 2. [Impudent] shameless, audacious, bold; see **rude 2**.

barefoot, *a.* shoeless, barefooted, unshod; see **naked 1**.

barely, *a.* almost, scarcely, just; see **hardly**.

bargain, *n.* 1. [An agreement] pact, compact, contract; see **deal 1, 2**. 2. [An advantageous purchase] good value *or* deal, discount, reduction, marked-down price, *buy, *steal, *giveaway, deal. — *into the bargain, in addition, too, additionally; see **also**.

bargain, *v.* 1. [To trade] barter, do business, merchandise; see **buy, sell**. 2. [To negotiate] make terms, arrange, confer; see **negotiate 1**.

bargain for, *v.* expect, plan on, foresee; see **anticipate**.

bargaining, *n.* trade, transaction, haggling; see **business 1**.

bark, *n.* 1. [An outer covering, especially of trees] rind, skin, peel, shell, case, crust, peeling, cork, husk, hide, pelt, coat. 2. [A short, explosive sound] yelp, yap, grunt; see **noise 1**.

bark, *v.* yelp, yap, bay, howl, cry, growl, snarl, yip, woof, *arf.

bark up the wrong tree, *v.* miscalculate, mistake, misconstrue; see **misjudge 2**.

barn, *n.* outbuilding, shed, outhouse, shelter, lean-to, coop, hutch, sty, pen, kennel, stable.

barnyard, *n.* feedyard, pen, corral, stableyard, lot, feed-lot, run.

barred, *a.* 1. [Equipped or marked with bars] striped, banded, stripped, streaked, pleated, pied, motley, calico, mottled, dappled, veined, ribbed, crosshatched, ridged, marked, piped, lined. 2. [Prohibited] banned, outlawed, unlawful; see **illegal**.

barrel, *n.* cask, keg, vat, tub, receptacle, pipe, container, vessel.

barren, *a.* 1. [Incapable of producing young] impotent, infertile, childless; see **sterile 1**. 2. [Incapable of producing vegetation] fallow, unproductive, fruitless; see **sterile 2**.

barricade, *n.* obstacle, bar, obstruction; see **barrier**.

barricade, v. obstruct, block, fortify; see **bar 1.**

barrier, n. bar, obstruction, difficulty, hindrance, obstacle, hurdle, stumbling block, fence, sound or sonic or transonic barrier, restriction, restraint, impediment, drawback, check, stop, stay, bulwark, barricade, rampart, wall, earthwork, embankment, blockade, barbed wire, bamboo curtain, iron curtain.—*Ant.* way, path, trail.

barroom, n. tavern, saloon, *pub; see **bar 2.**

barter, n. trade, exchange, traffic; see **business 1.**

barter, v. trade, bargain, *swap; see **buy, sell.**

base, n. 1. [A point from which action is initiated] camp, field, landing field, airport, airfield, airstrip, port, headquarters, terminal, base camp, home base, fire base, base of operations, center, depot, supply base, dock, harbor, station. 2. [The bottom, thought of as a support] root, foot, footing; see **foundation 2. 3.** [Foundation of a belief or statement] principle, authority, evidence; see **basis. 4.** [A goal, especially in baseball] mark, bound, station, plate, post, goal, first base, second base, third base, home plate. —*off base,* erring, mistaken, incorrect; see **wrong 2.**

baseball, n. ball, little league, *the national pastime; see **sport 3.**

baseball player, n. pitcher, catcher, infielder, batter, shortstop, left or right or center fielder, first or second or third baseman, hitter, *slugger.

based, a. confirmed, planted, founded; see **established 2.**

basement, n. cellar, excavation, storage room, wine cellar, furnace room, vault, crypt.

base on, v. institute, found, build; see **establish.**

bashful, a. retiring, reserved, timid; see **humble 1, modest 2.**

basic, a. essential, central, primary; see **fundamental, necessary 1.**

basically, a. fundamentally, primarily, radically; see **essentially.**

basin, n. pan, tub, bowl; see **container.**

basis, n. support, foundation, justification, reason, explanation, background, source, authority, principle, groundwork, assumption, premise, backing, sanction, proof, evidence, nucleus, center.

bask, v. relax, enjoy, *swim in; see **wallow.**

basket, n. bushel, crate, bin; see **container.**

basketball, n. court game, cage meet, *hoopfest; see **sport 3.**

bastard, a. illegitimate, natural, false, mongrel, baseborn, misbegotten.—*Ant.* legitimate, well-born, **true.**

bastard, n. 1. [An illegitimate child] natural child, whoreson, love child, *come-by-chance, *woods colt, *Sunday's child. 2. [A rascal] scoundrel, cheat, SOB; see **rascal.**

baste, v. 1. [To sew temporarily] stitch, catch, tack; see **sew. 2.** [To dress cooking meat with fat or sauce] moisten, grease, season; see **cook.**

bat, n. 1. [A club, especially one used in sports] club, racket, mallet; see **stick.** —**blind as a bat,** sightless, unseeing, blinded; see **blind 1.** —*go to bat for,* intervene for, support, back up; see **defend 2.** —*have bats in one's belfry,* mad, eccentric, peculiar; see **insane.** —*not bat an eye or eyelash,* not be surprised or shocked or amazed, ignore, remain unruffled; see **neglect 1.** —*(right) off the bat,* at once, without delay, instantly; see **immediately.**

bat, v. strike, whack, sock; see **hit 1.**

batch, n. stack, group, shipment; see **bunch.**

bath, n. 1. [The act of cleansing the body] washing, sponge bath, shower, tub, bath, steam bath, sauna (bath), *soak, dip, *soaking. 2. [An enclosure prepared for bathing] bathroom, toilet, shower, washroom, powder room, lavatory, steam room, sauna (bath), public baths, shower room.

bathe, v. soap, scour, scrub; see **wash 1.**

bathrobe, n. housecoat, duster, smock; see **clothes.**

bathroom, n. shower, toilet, lavatory; see **bath 2, toilet 2.**

battalion, n. unit, force, corps; see **army 2.**

batter, n. 1. [One who bats] hitter, pinch-hitter, switch-hitter; see **baseball player. 2.** [Baking mixture] dough, mix, paste, recipe, concoction, mush; see also **mixture 1.**

battery, n. 1. [Cells which generate or store electricity] dry or wet or storage cells, storage battery, energy unit, flashlight battery, solar battery, atomic battery, electric cell. 2. [The act of beating] assault, attack, thumping, beating, physical violence, mugging.

battle, n. strife, contention, struggle, combat, bombing, fighting, bloodshed, clash, onslaught, onset, barrage, conflict, warfare, fray, assault, crusade, military campaign, hostilities, havoc, carnage; see also **fight.** —*give or do battle,* fight back, struggle, engage in a battle or encounter; see **attack, fight.**

battlefield, n. field of battle or war, battleground, front, theater of war, disputed territory, no man's land.

battleship, n. man o' war, floating fortress, *battlewagon; see **ship.**

bawl, v. weep, shed tears, sob; see **cry 1.**

bawl out, v. chide, berate, admonish; see **scold.**

bay, n. inlet, gulf, bayou, loch, bight, sound, fiord, firth, estuary, strait, narrows, road, arm of the sea, mouth, lagoon, cove, harbor.

bayonet, n. spike, lance, pike; see **knife.**

B.C., a. before Christ, ante-Christian, pre-Christian; see **old 3.**

be, v. live, stay, be alive, exist, remain, continue, endure, go on, stand, subsist, breathe, last, prevail, abide, survive, move, act, do, hold, have place.—*Ant.* **die,** disappear, stop. 2. [To mean] signify, denote, imply; see **mean 1.**

beach, n. seaside, sand, the coast; see **shore.**

beached, a. stranded, marooned, aground; see **abandoned.**

beacon, n. flare, lantern, guide, signal fire or light or beam, lighthouse, lamp, beam, radar, sonar, airline beacon, radio beacon, air control beacon.

bead, n. drop, droplet, pellet, grain, particle, speck, dot, dab, pea, shot, pill, driblet.

beads, n. pl. necklace, pendant, string of jewels; see **necklace.**

beak, n. nose, prow, bill, mandible, projection, proboscis, snout, nozzle.

beam, n. 1. [A relatively long, stout bar] timber, brace, scantling, rafter, stringer, stud, two-by-four, strut, joist, bolster, axle, girder, sleeper, stay, crosspiece, prop, support, trestle, spar, pole, crossbar, T-beam, I-beam, steel beam, boom, post, column, pillar, sill, jamb, cantilever, shaft, scaffolding; see also **bar 1.** 2. [Radio waves intended as a guide] direction finder, unidirectional radio signal, radar; see **beacon.** —*off the beam,* faulty, incorrect, inaccurate; see **wrong 2.** —*on the beam,* alert, keen, efficient; see **able.**

beam, v. 1. [To emit] transmit, broadcast, give out; see **send 1.** 2. [To shine] radiate, glitter, glare; see **shine 1.** 3. [To smile] grin, laugh, smirk; see **smile.**

beaming, a. 1. [Giving forth beams] radiant, glowing, gleaming; see **bright 1.** 2. [In very genial humor] grinning, animated, sunny; see **happy.**

bean, n. Varieties include the following— kidney, navy, lima, soy, castor, black, pinto, string, black-eyed or black-eye, green, wax; see also **vegetable.** —*full of beans,* 1. lively, vital, energetic; see **active.** 2. mistaken, erring, incorrect; see **wrong 2.** —*spill the beans,* divulge information, tell secrets, talk; see **tell 1.**

bear, n. grizzly, polar bear, brown or black bear; see **animal.**

bear, v. 1. [To suffer] tolerate, support, undergo; see **endure 2.** 2. [To support weight] sustain, hold up, shoulder; see

support 1. 3. [To give birth to] be delivered of, bring to birth, bring forth; see **produce 1.**

bearable, a. endurable, tolerable, passable, admissible, supportable, sufferable.

beard, n. whiskers, brush, Van Dyke, chin whiskers, imperial, muttonchops, goatee, spade beard, forked beard, side whiskers.

bearded, a. bewhiskered, bushy, unshaven; see **hairy.**

bear down on or **upon,** v. 1. [To press] squeeze, compress, push; see **press 1.** 2. [To try] endeavor, strive, attempt; see **try 1.**

bearing, n. 1. [A point of support] frame, ball bearing, roller bearing; see **support 2.** 2. [Manner of carriage] mien, deportment, manner; see **behavior, posture 1.**

bear out, v. confirm, substantiate, support; see **prove.**

bear up, v. withstand, persevere, carry on; see **endure 2.**

bear upon, v. pertain, refer to, relate to, regard; see **concern 1.**

bear with, v. tolerate, ɔe patient, suffer, put up with; see **endure 2.**

bear witness, v. affirm, attest, give evidence; see **testify 1.**

beast, n. 1. [A large animal] brute, creature, lower animal; see **animal.** 2. [A person of brutish nature] monster, brute, degenerate, animal, fiend, swine, pervert, lout, savage, barbarian, pig, satyr, goat, hog, monstrosity, glutton, gargoyle, Bluebeard; see also **pervert.**

beastly, a. brutal, savage, coarse, repulsive, gluttonous, obscene, unclean, piggish, hoggish, irrational, boorish, brutish, depraved, abominable, loathsome, vile, low, degraded, sensual, foul, base, disgusting, inhuman, gross, vulgar.—*Ant.* refined, sweet, nice.

***beat,** a. weary, fatigued, worn out; see **tired.**

beat, n. 1. [A throb] thump, pound, quake, flutter, pulse, pulsation, cadence, flow, vibration, turn, ripple, pressure, impulse, quiver, shake, surge, swell, palpitation, undulation, rhythm. 2. [A unit of music] accent, vibration, division, stress, measure, rhythm.

beat, v. 1. [To thrash] hit, punish, whip, pistol-whip, flog, trounce, spank, scourge, switch, lash, slap, cuff, box, strap, birch, cane, horsewhip, buffet, pommel, tap, rap, strike, bump, pat, knock, pound, club, punch, bat, flail, batter, maul, whack, hammer, clout, smack, bang, *swat, *slug, *beat black and blue, *pound to a paste, *whale, *belt, *whack, *beat or knock the tar or daylights or hell or stuffing out of, *wallop, *lick, *paste, *bash, *work over, thwack. 2. [To pulsate] pound, thump, pulse; see **throb**. 3. [To worst] overcome, surpass, conquer; see **defeat 2, 3. 4.** [To win] be victorious, gain the prize, triumph; see **win 1. 5.** [To mix] stir, whip, knead; see **mix 1.**

beat around the bush, v. quibble, avoid the issue, hesitate; see **evade**.

beaten, a. 1. [Defeated] worsted, humbled, thwarted, bested, disappointed, frustrated, baffled, conquered, overthrown, subjugated, ruined, mastered, trounced, undone, mastered, overwhelmed, overpowered, *licked, *done in or for, *kayoed, mugged, *skinned, *trimmed, *had it, *washed up, *sunk.—Ant. victorious, **successful,** triumphant. 2. [Made firm and hard] hammered, tramped, stamped, rolled, milled, forged, trod, pounded, tramped down, tamped.—Ant. **soft,** spongy, loose. 3. [Made light by beating] whipped, frothy, foamy, mixed, churned, creamy, bubbly, meringued.

beater, n. whipper, mixer, egg-beater; see **appliance**.

beating, n. thrashing, whipping, drubbing; see **defeat**.

beatnik, n. Bohemian, hippie-type, nonconformist; see **radical**.

beautiful, a. lovely, attractive, appealing, comely, pleasing, pretty, fair, fine, nice, dainty, good-looking, delightful, charming, enticing, fascinating, admirable, rich, graceful, ideal, delicate, refined, elegant, symmetrical, well-formed, shapely, well-made, splendid, gorgeous, brilliant, radiant, exquisite, dazzling, resplendent, magnificent, superb, marvelous, wonderful, grand, awe-inspiring, imposing, majestic, excellent, impressive, handsome, divine, blooming, rosy, beauteous, statuesque, well-favored, bewitching, personable, taking, alluring, slender, svelte, lissome, lithe, bright-eyed, *classy, *easy on the eyes, *long on looks, built. —Ant. **ugly,** deformed, hideous.

beautifully, a. gracefully, exquisitely, charmingly, attractively, prettily, delightfully, appealingly, seductively, alluringly, elegantly, gorgeously, splendidly, magnificently, ideally, tastefully, sublimely, handsomely, superbly, divinely.

beauty, n. 1. [A pleasing physical quality] grace, comeliness, fairness, pulchritude, charm, delicacy, elegance, attraction, fascination, allurement, shapeliness, majesty, attractiveness, good looks, glamour, loveliness, bloom, *class, *spiff, *tone.—Ant. **ugliness,** homeliness, deformity. 2. [A beautiful woman] goddess, belle, attraction, siren, enchantress, seductress, Venus, femme fatale, *looker, *charmer.—Ant. **witch,** blemish, fright.

because, conj. on account of, in conse-

quence or view of, by cause or reason of, for the reason that, for the sake of, in behalf of, on the grounds that, in the interest of, as a result of, as things go, by virtue of, in that, since, by the agency of, *due to, *being as how, owing to.

be certain, v. be sure, make certain, have confidence; see **know 1.**

beckon, v. signal, motion, sign; see **summon**.

become, v. develop or change or turn or grow into, eventually be, emerge as, turn out (to be), come to be, shift, assume the form or shape or state of, be reformed or remodeled, be reduced or converted to, convert, mature, shift toward, incline to, melt into; see also **grow 2.**

becoming, a. attractive, beautiful, neat, agreeable, handsome, seemly, comely, tasteful, well-chosen, fair, trim, graceful, flattering, effective, excellent, acceptable, welcome, nice.

bed, n. 1. [A place of rest] mattress, cot, couch, bedstead, berth, bunk, *hay, *sack, *rack, *feathers, roost. Beds include the following—single or double bed, davenport, cot, four-poster, trundle bed, twin bed, fold-away bed, hammock, feather bed, double-deck bed, stretcher, folding bed, bunk bed, litter, cradle, crib, bassinet, king-size bed, queen-size bed, hospital bed, circular bed, day bed. 2. [A foundation] base, bottom, groundwork; see **foundation 2. 3.** [A seed plot] patch, row, planting; see **garden**.

bedding, n. bedclothes, (bed) linen, (thermal) blankets, covers, bedcovers, pillows, coverlets, sheets, quilts, spreads, comforters.

bed down, v. turn in, retire, *hit the hay; see **sleep**.

bedlam, n. confusion, pandemonium, clamor; see **confusion, noise 2.**

bedridden, a. incapacitated, confined to bed, laid up; see **disabled**.

bedroom, n. sleeping room, guest room, master bedroom; see **room 2.**

bedspread, n. spread, quilt, comforter; see **bedding**.

bedtime, n. slumbertime, time to hit the hay, *sack time; see **night**.

beef, n. 1. [Bovine flesh used as food] cow's flesh, steer beef, red meat; see **meat. 2.** [A grown animal of the genus Bos] bovine, bull, steer; see **cow. 3.** [A complaint] dispute, protestation, *gripe; see **objection**.

beef up, v. intensify, augment, increase; see **strengthen**.

beer, n. malt beverage, malt liquor, brew, *suds. Varieties include the following—lager, bock beer, ale, stout, porter, pale or light beer, heavy or dark beer, black beer.

beetle, *n.* bug, scarab, crawling thing; see **insect**.

before, *a.* previously, earlier, (in the) past, since, gone (by), in old days, heretofore, former(ly), back, sooner, up to now, ahead, in front *or* advance, facing.—*Ant.* in the future, **afterward**, to come.

before, *prep.* prior *or* previous to, in front *or* ahead of, under jurisdiction of, antecedent to.—*Ant.* **behind**, following, at the rear.

beforehand, *a.* previously, already, in anticipation; see **before**.

befriend, *v.* encourage, advise, stand by; see **help**.

beg, *v.* entreat, implore, beseech, supplicate, crave, solicit, pray for, urge, plead, sue, importune, petition, apply to, request, press, call *or* appeal to, requisition, conjure, abjure, apostrophize, canvass; see also **ask**.—*Ant.* **admit**, concede, accede.

beggar, *n.* pauper, poor man, hobo, tramp, indigent, poverty-stricken *or* destitute person, dependent, ghetto-dweller, bankrupt, *panhandler, *moocher, *bum.

begging, *a.* anxious, in need, imploring, supplicating; see **wanting 1**.

begin, *v.* 1. [To initiate] start, cause, inaugurate, make, occasion, impel, produce, effect, set in motion, launch, mount, start in *or* on *or* up *or* off, induce, do, create, bring about, get *or* set going *or* about, institute, lead up to, undertake, enter on *or* upon, open, animate, motivate, go into *or* ahead, lead the way, bring on, bring to pass, activate, initiate, make active, act on, generate, drive, actualize, introduce, originate, found, establish, set up, trigger, give birth to, take the lead, plunge into, lay the foundation for, break ground.—*Ant.* **end**, finish, terminate. 2. [To come into being, or to start functioning] commence, get under way, set *or* start (in *or* out), come out, enter *or* embark upon, arise, rise, proceed *or* result from, enter, dawn, sprout, originate, spring, spring *or* crop up, come to birth, come into the world, be born, emanate, come into existence, occur, burst *or* issue *or* come forth, bud, grow out of, flower, blossom, break out, set to work, kick off, *jump off, *go to it, *dig in, *take up *or* off, *see the light of day.—*Ant.* **stop**, cease, subside.

beginner, *n.* novice, freshman, apprentice; see **amateur**.

beginning, *n.* 1. [The origin in point of time or place] source, outset, root; see **origin 2**. 2. [The origin, thought of as the cause] germ, heart, antecedent; see **origin 3**.

begun, *a.* started, initiated, instituted, under way, in motion *or* progress, on foot, inaugurated, happening, proceeding, going, active, existing, operative, working, in force.

behalf, *n.* interest, benefit, sake; see **welfare**.

behave, *v.* act with decorum, observe the golden rule, do unto others as you would have others do unto you, be nice *or* good *or* civil, mind one's p's and q's, be orderly, play one's part, live up to, observe the law, reform, mind one's manners, comport *or* deport *or* manage *or* discipline *or* behave oneself, be on one's best behavior, act one's age, avoid offense, toe the mark, play fair.

behavior, *n.* bearing, deportment, comportment, demeanor, air, presence, carriage, conduct, manner(s), action(s), attitude(s), way of life, speech, talk, tone, morals, habit(s), tact, social graces, correctness, decorum, form, convention, propriety, taste, management, routine, practice, what's done, style, expression, performance, code, role, observance, course, guise, act, deed, ethics, way, front.

behind, *a.* and *prep.* 1. [To the rear in space] back of, following, after; see **back**. 2. [Late in time] tardy, dilatory, behind time; see **late 1, slow 2**. 3. [Slow in progress] sluggish, slow-moving, delayed, backward, underdeveloped, retarded, behind schedule, belated; see also **slow 2**.—*Ant.* **fast**, rapid, on time.

behind (one's) back, *a.* deceitfully, foully, faithlessly; see **falsely**.

behind the times, *a.* antiquated, out-of-date, obsolete; see **old-fashioned**.

being, *n.* 1. [Existence] presence, actuality, animation; see **life 1**. 2. [The essential part] nature, core, marrow; see **essence 1**. 3. [A living thing] creature, conscious agent, beast; see **animal**.—**for the time being**, temporarily, tentatively, for now *or* the present; see **briefly, now**.

belated, *a.* remiss, tardy, overdue; see **late 1, slow 3**.

belief, *n.* idea, opinion, faith, feeling, hope, intuition, view, expectation, acceptance, trust, notion, persuasion, position, understanding, conviction, confidence, suspicion, knowledge, conclusion, presumption, surmise, hypothesis, thinking, judgment, certainty, impression, assumption, conjecture, fancy, theory, guess, conception, inference.

believable, *a.* trustworthy, creditable, acceptable; see **convincing**.

believe, *v.* accept, hold, think, understand, consider, swear by, conceive, affirm, conclude, be of the opinion, have faith, have no doubt, take at one's word, take one's word for, be convinced, be certain of, give credence to, rest assured.—*Ant.* doubt, deny, suspect.

believe in, *v.* swear by, look to, put *or* have faith in; see **trust 1**.

believer, *n.* convert, devotee, adherent, apostle, disciple, prophet, confirmed believer; see also **follower**.

believing, *a.* maintaining, trusting, presuming, assuming, holding, accepting, impressed with, under the impression.

belittle, *v.* lower, disparage, criticize; see **abuse**.

bell, *n.* chime(s), siren, signal, gong, buzzer; see also **alarm**.

belligerent, *a.* warlike, pugnacious, hostile; see **aggressive**.

bellow, *n.* howl, cry, roar; see **cry 1**.

bellow, *v.* howl, call, shout; see **cry 2**, **yell**.

belly, *n.* paunch, abdomen, gut; see **stomach**.

***bellyache,** *v.* whine, grumble, protest; see **complain**.

belong, *v.* **1.** [To be properly placed] fit in, have a place, be one of; see **fit 1**. **2.** [To be acceptable in a group; *said of persons*] fit in, have (a) place, have (its) place, be born so, be a member, take one's place with, be one of, be classified *or* counted among, be included *or* contained in, owe allegiance *or* support to, be a part of, be one of the family.—*Ant.* **differ,** fight, not fit (in).

belongings, *n. pl.* possessions, goods, *things; see **property 1**.

belong to, *v.* pertain *or* relate to, be held *or* occupied *or* enjoyed *or* owned by, be in the hands *or* possession of, be at the disposal of, be the property *or* right of, concern, come *or* go with, fall under.—*Ant.* **escape,** be free, have no owner.

beloved, *a.* loved, adored, worshiped, cherished, dear, favorite, idolized, precious, prized, dearest, yearned for, revered, treasured, favored, doted on, nearest to one's own heart, dearly beloved, after one's own heart, darling, admired, popular, well-liked, cared for, respected, pleasing.—*Ant.* **hated,** abhorred, disliked.

beloved, *n.* fiancé, sweetheart, object of one's affection; see **lover 1**.

below, *a.* and *prep.* **1.** [Lower in position] beneath, underneath, down from; see **under 1**. **2.** [Lower in rank or importance] inferior, subject, under; see **subordinate**. **3.** [*In written work,* farther along] later, on a following page, in a statement to be made, hereafter, subsequently.—*Ant.* earlier, **above,** on a former page. **4.** [On earth] existing, in this world, here below, under the sun, on the face of the earth, in this our life, here. **5.** [In hell] in the underworld, damned, condemned; see **damned 1**.

below the belt, *a.* unjust, foul, unsporting; see **unfair**.

below par, *a.* inferior, below average, second-rate; see **poor 2**.

belt, *n.* girdle, ribbon, string; see **band 1**. **—tighten one's belt,** endure hunger *or* privation, suffer, bear misfortune; see **endure 2**. **—under one's belt,** past, finished, complete(d); see **done 1**.

bench, *n.* **1.** [A long seat] pew, seat, stall; see **chair 1**. **2.** [A long table] workbench, desk, counter; see **table 1**.

bend, *n.* crook, bow, arch; see **curve**.

bend, *v.* twist, contort, deform, round, crimp, flex, spiral, coil, crinkle, detour, curl, buckle, crook, bow, incline, deflect, double, loop, twine, curve, arch, wind, stoop, lean, waver, zigzag, reel, crumple, meander, circle, swerve, diverge, droop.—*Ant.* **straighten,** extend, stretch.

bending, *a.* twisting, veering, curving, buckling, twining, spiraling, looping, doubling, drooping, leaning, inclining, bowing, arching, curling, winding, stooping, crumpling, waving, wavering.

beneath, *a.* and *prep.* **1.** [Under] below, underneath, in a lower place; see **under 1**. **2.** [Lower in rank or importance] subject, inferior, under; see **subordinate**.

beneath contempt, *a.* offensive, contemptible, despicable; see **offensive 2**.

benefactor, *n.* helper, protector, *angel; see **patron**.

beneficiary, *n.* recipient, receiver, inheritor; see **heir**.

benefit, *n.* gain, profit, good; see **advantage**.

benefit, *v.* serve, profit, avail; see **help**.

bent, *a.* curved, warped, hooked, beaked, looped, twined, crooked, bowed, contorted, stooped, doubled over, wilted, drooping, humped, slumped, hunched, humpbacked, bowlegged, inclined; see also **twisted 1**. —*Ant.* rigid, **straight,** erect.

bent, *n.* leaning, tendency, propensity; see **inclination 1**.

bequeath, *v.* grant, hand down, pass on; see **give 1**.

berry, *n.* Common berries include the following—raspberry, blackberry, blueberry, loganberry, boysenberry, cranberry, huckleberry, gooseberry, currant, strawberry, mulberry.

berth, *n.* place, situation, employment; see **job 1**, **profession 1**. **—give a wide berth,** keep clear of, evade, stay away (from); see **avoid**.

beside, *a.* and *prep.* at the side *or* edge of, adjacent *or* next *or* parallel *or* close (to), adjoining, alongside, near, close at hand, by, with, abreast, side by side, bordering on *or* upon, neighboring, overlooking, next door to, to one side, nearby, connected with.

besides, a. in addition to, additionally, moreover, over and above, supplementary or added to, likewise, further, furthermore, beyond, exceeding, secondly, more than, apart from, extra, in excess of, plus, (and) also, in other respects, exclusive of, with the exception of, as well as, not counting, other than, too, to boot, on top of (all) that or this, aside from, else.

beside the point, a. extraneous, not pertaining to, not connected with; see **irrelevant.**

best, a. 1. [Generally excellent] first, greatest, finest, highest, transcendent, prime, premium, supreme, incomparable, crowning, paramount, matchless, unrivaled, unparalleled, second to none, unequaled, inimitable, beyond compare, superlative, foremost, peerless, *boss, *tough, *cool, first-rate; see also **excellent.** —Ant. **worst,** poorest, lowest. 2. [Applied especially to actions and persons] noblest, sincerest, most magnanimous or creditable or illustrious or glorious or honorable or praiseworthy; see **noble.**

best, n. first, favorite, choice, finest, top, pick, prime, flower, cream, *cream of the crop. —all for the best, favorable, fortunate, advantageous; see **helpful 1, hopeful 2.** —as best one can, skillfully, ably, capably; see **able.** —at best, good, highest, most favorable; see **best.** —at one's best, well, in one's prime, capable; see **able, strong 1.** —get or have the best of, outdo, surpass, defeat; see **exceed.** —make the best of, suffer, tolerate, get by; see **endure 2.** —with the best, excellently, well, ably; see **able.**

best, v. worst, get the better of, overcome; see **defeat 3.**

bestow, v. bequeath, present, offer; see **give 1.**

bet, n. gamble, wager, venture, pot, hazard, toss up, stake, speculation, betting, raffle, uncertainty, chance, lottery, game of chance, sweepstake(s), risk, ante, *long shot, *shot in the dark.

bet, v. wager, gamble, stake, bet on or against, venture, hazard, trust, play against, speculate, play (for), put or lay money down or on, risk, chance, make a bet, take a chance, *lay down, *buy in on, lay odds, *lay even money. —you bet, certainly, by all means, yes, indeed; see **surely, yes.**

betray, v. 1. [To deliver into the hands of an enemy] delude, trick, double-cross; see **deceive.** 2. [To reveal] divulge, disclose, make known; see **reveal.**

betrayal, n. treason, treachery, disloyalty; see **deception, dishonesty.**

betrayer, n. renegade, deceiver, conspirator; see **traitor.**

better, a. 1. [Superior] greater, finer, preferred, bigger, stronger, higher; see also **best.** 2. [Recovering health] convalescent, improved in health, improving, on the road to recovery,, on the mend.—Ant. **sick,** failing, wasting away. —for the better, favorable, fortunate, helpful; see **hopeful 2.** —get or have the better of, outdo, overcome, defeat; see **exceed.**

better, v. ameliorate, revamp, refine; see **improve 1.**

between, prep. separating, within, enclosed or bound(ed) by, amidst, amid, among, in, in between, mid, intervening, in the midst of, in the middle, centrally located, surrounded by, midway, halfway, in the thick of; see also **among.**

between you and me, a. confidentially, privately, personally; see **secretly.**

beverage, n. liquor, refreshment, draft; see **drink 3.**

bewilder, v. confound, upset, disconcert, puzzle; see **confuse.**

bewildered, a. confused, amazed, misguided, lost, astonished, thunderstruck, shocked, muddled, upset, dazed, giddy, dizzy, reeling, puzzled, misled, uncertain, surprised, baffled, disconcerted, appalled, aghast, adrift, at sea, off the track, awed, stupefied, astounded, struck speechless, breathless, befuddled, startled, struck dumb, dumbfounded, dazzled, stunned, electrified, confounded, staggered, petrified, awe-struck, flabbergasted, flustered, *all balled up, rattled, *up in the air, *stumped, *goofy.

beyond, a. and prep. on the other or far side, over there, in advance of, away, out of range, a long way off, yonder, past, free or clear of, farther back or off, ahead, behind, more remote.—Ant. on this side, here, nearer.

bias, n. bent, preference, leaning; see **inclination 1.**

bible, n. the Good Book, God's word, the Word, the Scriptures, the Canon, the Testaments, Sacred History, the Writings of the Apostles and Prophets, Holy Writ, the Holy Bible, the Word of God, Testament.

bibliography, n. catalogue, compilation, list of books; see **list.**

bicker, v. wrangle, squabble, dispute, argue; see **quarrel.**

bicycle, n. cycle, *bike, *two-wheeler; see **vehicle.**

bid, n. proposal, proposition, declaration; see **suggestion 1.**

bid, v. 1. [To propose a price for purchase] venture, bid for, submit a bid; see **offer 1.** 2. [To order] demand, charge, direct, instruct; see **command 1.**

big, a. 1. [Of great size] huge, great,

swolfen, fat, obese, bloated, overgrown, gross, mammoth, wide, grand, vast, immense, considerable, substantial, massive, extensive, spacious, colossal, gigantic, titanic, monstrous, towering, mighty, magnificent, enormous, giant, tremendous, *whopping.—*Ant.* tiny, small, little. 2. [Grown, or partially grown] grown-up, full-grown, adult; see **mature** 1. 3. [Important] prominent, significant, influential; see **important** 1, 2. 4. [Pompous] presumptuous, pretentious, imperious; see **egotistic**. 5. [Generous] magnanimous, liberal, unselfish; see **generous**.

bigot, *n.* dogmatist, fanatic, opinionated person, partisan, enthusiast, extremist, diehard, *crank, *red-neck; see also **radical**.

bigoted, *a.* biased, dogmatic, opinionated; see **prejudiced**.

bigotry, *n.* intolerance, narrow-mindedness, injustice; see **fanaticism**, **prejudice**.

***big shot,** *n.* *big wheel, *bigwig, *big man on campus *or* BMOC; see **executive**.

bill, *n.* 1. [A statement of account] itemized account, statement of indebtedness, request for payment; see **statement** 2. 2. [A piece of paper money] Federal Reserve note, currency, gold *or* silver certificate; see **money** 1. 3. [A statement prepared for enactment into law] measure, proposal, (piece of) legislation; see **law** 3. 4. [A beak] nib, mandible, projection; see **beak**. —**fill the bill,** meet requirements, be satisfactory, serve the purpose; see **satisfy** 3.

bill, *v.* dun, solicit, render *or* send account of indebtedness, draw upon.

billboard, *n.* bulletin board, display panel, poster board; see **advertisement**, **announcement**.

billfold, *n.* card case, pocket book, purse; see **wallet**.

bin, *n.* storeroom, granary, silo; see **container**.

***bind,** *n.* dilemma, tight situation, quandary; see **predicament**.

bind, *v.* 1. [To constrain with bonds] truss *or* tie up, shackle, fetter, cinch, clamp, chain, leash, constrict, manacle, enchain, lace, pin, restrict, hamper, handcuff, muzzle, hitch, secure, yoke, pin *or* peg down, fix, strap, tether, bind up, lash (down), *clamp down on, *hogtie. 2. [To hold together or in place] secure, attach, adhere; see **fasten**. 3. [To obligate] oblige, necessitate, compel; see **force**. 4. [To dress] treat, dress, bandage; see **heal** 1. 5. [To join] unite, put together, connect; see **join** 1.

binding, *a.* obligatory, requisite, required; see **necessary** 1.

binding, *n.* 1. [The act of joining] merging, coupling, junction; see **union** 1. 2. [Anything used to bind] tie, adhesive, binder; see **fastener**. 3. [A cover] wrapper, jacket, book cover; see **cover** 1.

biography, *n.* life story, saga, memoir, journal, experiences, autobiography, life, adventures, life history, confessions, personal anecdote, profile, sketch, biographical account *or* sketch; see also **record** 1, **story**.

biological, *a.* organic, life, living, zoological, botanical, concerning life.

biology, *n.* science of organisms, ecology, natural science *or* history, nature study, life science; see **science** 1.

bird, *n.* Common birds include the following—sparrow, starling, robin, blue jay, crow, hawk, meadow lark, owl, vulture, buzzard, turkey buzzard, woodpecker, cardinal, kingfisher, canary, chickadee, swallow, skylark, nightingale, nuthatch, whippoorwill, thrush, bluebird, cuckoo, bobolink, wren, gull, eagle, osprey, blackbird, dove, duck, goose, pheasant, chicken, parakeet, crane, heron, mockingbird, auk. —**eat like a bird,** fast, starve, restrain one's appetite; see **diet**. —**for the birds,** ridiculous, absurd, useless; see **stupid** 1, **worthless**.

birth, *n.* delivery, parturition, nativity, beginning, blessed event, visit from the stork, *act of God.—*Ant.* death, decease, demise. —**give birth to,** bring forth, have a child, reproduce; see **produce** 1.

birthday, *n.* natal day, name day, celebration; see **anniversary**.

biscuit, *n.* cracker, wafer, roll; see **bread**.

bishop, *n.* father, archbishop, primate; see **minister** 1, **priest**.

bit, *n.* 1. [A small quantity] piece, fragment, crumb, dot, particle, jot, trifle, mite, iota, whit, splinter, parcel, portion, droplet, trickle, driblet, morsel, pinch, snip, shred, atom, speck, molecule, shard, chip, fraction, sliver, segment, section, lump, slice, shaving, sample, specimen, scale, flake, excerpt, scrap, part, division, share, trace, item, chunk, paring, taste, mouthful, stub, butt, stump, *a drop in the bucket, *peanuts, *chicken feed, *gob, *hunk. 2. [A small degree] jot, minimum, inch, hairbreadth, trifle, iota, mite, fraction, tolerance, margin, *whisker, *hair, skin of one's teeth *or* nose. —**do one's bit,** participate, share, do one's share; see **join** 2. —**every bit,** wholly, altogether, entirely; see **completely**.

bite, *n.* 1. [What one takes in the mouth at one time] mouthful, chew, taste, spoonful, forkful, morsel, nibble. 2. [The result of being bitten] wound, sting, laceration; see **injury**. **3.** [A quick meal] snack, nibble, brunch; see **food**.

bite, *v.* **1.** [To seize or sever with the teeth] snap, gnaw, sink (one's) teeth in, nip, nibble, chew (up), mouth, gulp, worry, taste, masticate, clamp, champ, munch, bite into, crunch, mangle, chaw; see also **eat 1, taste 1. 2.** [To be given to biting] snap, be vicious, attack; see **hurt. 3.** [To cut or corrode] rot, decay, decompose; see **rust. —put the bite on,** pressure, ask for a loan, *touch; see **borrow.**

biting, *a.* **1.** [Acidulous] sharp, keen, tangy; see **sour 1. 2.** [Sarcastic] caustic, acrimonious, bitter; see **sarcastic.**

bitten, *a.* chewed, torn, lacerated, slashed, gulped, gnawed, nibbled, tasted, devoured, eaten, stung, pierced, mangled, punctured, cut, ripped.

bitter, *a.* **1.** [Acrid] astringent, acid, tart; see **sour 1. 2.** [Intense] sharp, harsh, severe; see **intense. 3.** [Sarcastic] acrimonious, caustic, biting; see **sarcastic.**

bitterness, *n.* tartness, piquancy, pungency, acidity, sourness, acridity, brackishness, brininess.

bizarre, *a.* odd, fantastic, grotesque; see **unusual 2.**

blab, *v.* disclose, tell, divulge; see **reveal.**

black, *a.* **1.** [Opposite to white] dark, blackish, raven, coal-black, dusky, dingy, murky, inklike, somber, swarthy, swart, jet, inky, ebony, pitch-black, black as coal *or* pitch, sooty, gun-metal, flat black, jet black, *black as the ace of spades, *black as night, *black as a crow.—*Ant.* white, colored, colorful. **2.** [Without light] gloomy, shadowy, clouded; see **dark 1. 3.** [Negroid] colored, African, black-skinned; see **black,** *n.* **2.**

black, *n.* **1.** [A chromatic color least resembling white] carbon, darkest gray, jet, sable, ebony, blackness.—*Ant.* white, blond, brightness. **2.** [A Negro] colored man *or* woman, Ethiopian, negro, African, Black Panther, Black Muslim, Afro-American, black man. **—in the black,** successful, lucratively, gainfully; see **profitably.**

blacken, *v.* darken, deepen, make black; see **shade 2.**

black magic, *n.* sorcery, witchcraft, necromancy; see **magic 1, 2.**

blackmail, *n.* hush money, tribute, *protection; see **bribe.**

blackmail, *v.* extort, exact, coerce; see **bribe, force.**

blackness, *n.* gloom, duskiness, murkiness; see **darkness 1.**

black out, *v.* **1.** [To delete] rub out, eradicate, blot out; see **cancel, erase. 2.**

[To faint] pass out, lose consciousness, swoon; see **faint. 3.** [To darken] put out the lights, make dark, batten; see **shade 2.**

blade, *n.* **1.** [A cutting instrument] edge, brand, sword; see **knife. 2.** [A relatively long leaf] frond, spear, flag, shoot; see also **leaf 1.**

blame, *n.* disapproval, condemnation, denunciation, disparagement, depreciation, opposition, depreciation, abuse, disfavor, objection, reproach, criticism, repudiation, reprimand, invective, slur, accusation, reproof, attack, chiding, rebuke, impeachment, complaint, diatribe, tirade, charge, indictment, recrimination, arraignment, implication, calumny, frowning upon.—*Ant.* praise, commendation, appreciation. **—be to blame,** guilty, at fault, culpable; see **wrong 2.**

blame, *v.* charge, condemn, criticize, arraign, challenge, involve, attack, brand, implicate, arrest, sue, prosecute, slander, impeach, bring to trial, connect with, indict, impute, *put the finger on, *smear, *point the finger at, bring home to.

blameless, *a.* faultless, not guilty, inculpable; see **innocent 1.**

bland, *a.* flat, dull, insipid; see **tasteless 1.**

blank, *a.* white, clear, virgin, fresh, plain, empty, untouched, pale, new, spotless, vacant, hollow, meaningless.

blank, *n.* **1.** [An empty space] void, hollow, hole, cavity, vacancy, womb, gulf, nothingness, hollowness, abyss, opening, vacuum, gap, interval; see also **emptiness. 2.** [A form] questionnaire, data sheet, information blank; see **form 5. —draw a blank,** fail *or* be unable to remember, lose one's memory, disremember; see **forget.**

blanket, *n.* quilt, robe, comforter, featherbed, throw, electric blanket, thermal blanket, rug, mat, cloak.

blanket, *v.* envelop, conceal, bury; see **cover 1.**

blank out, *v.* delete, black out, cross out; see **cancel, erase.**

blast, *n.* **1.** [An explosion] burst, eruption, detonation; see **explosion. 2.** [A loud sound] roar, din, bang; see **noise 1. 3.** [An explosive charge] gunpowder, TNT, dynamite; see **explosive. —(at) full blast,** at full speed *or* capacity, rapid, quick; see **fast 1.**

blast, *v.* blow up, dynamite, detonate; see **explode.**

blast off, *v.* rocket, climb, soar up; see **rise 1.**

blaze, *n.* conflagration, combustion, burning; see **fire.**

blaze, *v.* flame, flash, flare up; see **burn.**

bleach, v. blanch, wash out, whiten; see **fade**.

bleak, a. dreary, desolate, bare, cheerless, wild, exposed, barren, blank, disheartening, weary, melancholy, lonely, flat, somber, distressing, depressing, comfortless, joyless, uninviting, dull, sad, mournful, monotonous, waste, gloomy, dismal, unsheltered, unpopulated, desert, deserted, scorched, stony, burned (over), bulldozed, cleared, frozen.—*Ant.* verdant, **green,** fruitful.

bleed, v. lose blood, shed blood, be bleeding, (have a) hemorrhage, gush, spurt, be bled, open a vein, draw blood; see also **flow**.

blemish, n. flaw, defect, stain, spot, smudge, imperfection, disfigurement, defacement, blot, blur, chip, taint, tarnish, smirch, stigma, brand, deformity, dent, discoloration, mole, pock, blister, birthmark, wart, scar, impurity, speckle, bruise, freckle, pimple, patch, lump.—*Ant.* flawlessness, purity, **perfection**.

blench, v. flinch, quail, shrink back; see **wince**.

blend, n. combination, compound, amalgam; see **mixture 1**.

blend, v. combine, mingle, compound; see **mix 1**.

bless, v. baptize, canonize, glorify, honor, dedicate, make *or* pronounce holy, exalt, give benediction, absolve, anoint, ordain, hallow, consecrate, beatify, sanctify, enshrine, offer, render acceptable to, sacrifice, commend.

blessed, a. 1. [Marked by God's favor, especially in heaven] saved, redeemed, glorified, translated, exalted, rewarded, resurrected, sanctified, glorious, beatified, holy, spiritual, religious.—*Ant.* lost, doomed, accursed. 2. [Consecrated] sacred, dedicated, sanctified; see **divine**.

blessing, n. 1. [Benediction] commendation, sanctification, laying on of hands, absolution, baptism, unction, consecration, Eucharist.—*Ant.* damnation, **curse**, anathema. 2. [Anything which is very welcome] boon, benefit, good, advantage, help, asset, good fortune, stroke of luck, godsend, windfall, miracle, manna from heaven.—*Ant.* obstacle, disadvantage, **nuisance**.

blight, n. disease, withering, mildew; see **decay**.

blight, v. decay, spoil, ruin; see **spoil**.

blind, a. 1. [Without sight] sightless, unseeing, eyeless, blinded, visionless, in darkness, dim-sighted, groping (in the dark), deprived of sight, sun-blind, undiscerning, stone-blind, moon-blind, blind as a mole *or* bat.—*Ant.* **observant**, perceptive, discerning. 2. [Without looking] obtuse, unseeing, by guesswork *or* calculation, with instruments; see **blindly, unaware**. 3. [Without passage]

obstructed, blocked, without egress; see **tight 2, 3. 4.** [Random] chance, accidental, unplanned; see **aimless**.

blind, v. darken, shadow, dim; see **shade 2**.

blindly, v. at random, wildly, in all directions, frantically, heedlessly, carelessly, recklessly, passionately, thoughtlessly, impulsively, inconsiderately, willfully, unreasonably, without (rhyme or) reason, senselessly, instinctively, madly, pell-mell, purposelessly, aimlessly, indiscriminately.—*Ant.* directly, considerately, **carefully**.

blindness, n. sightlessness, stone blindness, purblindness, myopia, astigmatism, night *or* day *or* snow *or* moon *or* color blindness.—*Ant.* **sight,** vision, seeing.

blind spot, n. oversight, failing, unseen area; see **fault 1, weakness 1**.

blink, v. 1. [To wink rapidly] flicker, bat one's eyes, flick *or* flutter one's eyelids; see **wink**. 2. [To twinkle] glimmer, sparkle, shimmer; see **shine 1**.

bliss, n. joy, rapture, ecstasy; see **happiness**.

blister, n. vesicle, sac, weal, welt, blood blister, water blister, second-degree burn; see also **sore**.

blister, v. scald, irritate, mark; see **hurt**.

blizzard, n. snowstorm, tempest, blast, gale; see **storm 1**.

bloc, n. cabal, group, ring; see **faction**.

block, n. 1. [A mass, usually with flat surfaces] slab, chunk, piece, square, cake, cube, slice, segment, loaf, clod, bar, hunk. 2. [The area between streets] vicinity, square, lots; see **neighborhood**. 3. [The distance of the side of a block, sense 2] street, city block, intersection; see **distance 3. 4.** [An obstruction] hindrance, bar, obstacle; see **barrier**. —*knock someone's block off*, thrash, hit, beat up (on); see **beat 1**.

block, v. 1. [To impede] interfere with, prevent, close off; see **hinder**. 2. [In sports, to impede a play] throw a block, tackle, check; see **stop 1**.

blockade, n. barricade, encirclement, bar; see **barrier**.

block out, v. 1. [To obscure] conceal, screen, cover; see **hide 1**. 2. [To plan] outline, sketch, chart; see **plan 2**.

block up, v. obstruct, barricade, dam; see **bar 1**.

blond, a. fair, fair-skinned, pale, light, lily-white, white-skinned, creamy, whitish, milky, albino, pearly, platinum, gray-white, towheaded, snowy, light-haired, golden-haired, fair-haired, yellow-haired, sandy-haired, ashblond, bleached, strawberry-blond, *peroxide-blond.

blood, n. life's *or* heart's blood, vital fluid *or* juices, gore, sanguine fluid. — *bad blood,* malice rancor, feud; see **an-**

ger, hatred. —**in cold blood,** cruelly, intentionally, indifferently; see **deliberately.** —**make one's blood boil,** disturb, infuriate, agitate; see **enrage.** —**make one's blood run cold,** terrify, horrify, scare; see **frighten.**

bloodless, a. pallid, wan, anemic; see **pale 1.**

bloodshed, n. slaughter, butchery, gore; see **battle, murder.**

bloodshot, a. inflamed, streaked, red; see **bloody 1.**

bloody, a. 1. [Showing blood] bleeding, bloodstained, blood-spattered, gaping, unstaunched, grisly, crimson, open, wounded, dripping blood, raw, blood-soaked.—Ant. unhurt, whole, uninjured. 2. [Fiercely fought] savage, heavy, murderous; see **cruel.**

bloom, n. blossom, floweret, efflorescence; see **flower.**

bloom, v. flower, burst into bloom, open, bud, prosper, grow, wax, bear fruit, thrive, germinate, flourish, be in health, blossom, come out in flower, be in flower.

blooming, a. flowering, blossoming, in flower; see **budding, growing.**

blossom, n. bloom, floweret; bud; see **flower.**

blossom, v. flower, blow, burst into blossom; see **bloom.**

blossoming, n. blooming, flowering, budding; see **budding, growing.**

blot, n. spot, stain, smudge; see **blemish.**

blot, v. smudge, blotch, soil; see **dirty.**

blot out, v. 1. [To mark out] deface, cross or scratch out, delete; see **cancel.** 2. [To obscure] darken, blur, shroud; see **shade 2.**

blouse, n. pullover, overblouse, slipover; see also **clothes, shirt.**

blow, n. hit, strike, swing, bump, wallop, rap, bang, whack, thwack, cuff, box, uppercut, knock, clout, slam, bruise, swipe, kick, stroke, (rabbit) punch, jab, gouge, lunge, thrust, swat, poke, prod, slap, *the old one-two, *belt, *lick, *crack, *a knuckle sandwich, *kayo or K. O.

blow, v. 1. [To send forth air rapidly] puff, blast, pant, fan, whiff, whisk, whisper, puff away, exhale, waft, breathe, whistle. 2. [To carry on the wind] waft, flutter, bear, whisk, drive, fling, whirl, flap, flip, wave, buffet, sweep. 3. [To play a wind instrument] pipe, toot, mouth; see **play 3.** 4. [To sound when blown] trumpet, vibrate, blare; see **sound 1.** 5. [To give form by inflation] inflate, swell, puff or pump up; see **fill 1.** 6. [*To fail] miss, flounder, miscarry; see **fail 1.** 7. [*To spend] lay or pay out, waste, squander; see **spend 1.**

*blow a fuse, v. rant, have or throw a tantrum, become enraged or angry or irate; see **rage 1.**

blowing, a. blasting, puffing, fanning, panting, whisking, breathing, gasping, fluttering, flapping, waving, streaming, whipping, drifting, tumbling, gliding straining; see also **flying.**—Ant. standing still, **falling,** hovering.

blown, a. buffeted, fluttered, fanned; see **blowing.**

blowout, n. eruption, blast, detonation, tear, break, puncture, rupture, leak, gap, seam, flat tire, flat.

blow out, v. 1. [To extinguish] put out, dampen, snuff; see **extinguish.** 2. [To burst] shatter, erupt, rupture; see **explode.**

blow up, v. 1. [To fill] pump or puff up, swell, inflate; see **fill 1.** 2. [To explode] erupt, rupture, go or blow off; see **explode.** 3. [To destroy with explosives] bomb, dynamite, detonate; see **attack, destroy.** 4. [*To lose one's temper] become angry or enraged, rave, lose self-control; see **rage 1.**

blue, a. and n. 1. [One of the primary colors] Tints and shades of blue include the following—indigo, sapphire, turquoise, lapis lazuli, aquamarine, blue-black, azure, sky-blue, blue-green; royal, Prussian, navy, powder, baby, cobalt, Chinese, robin's egg, pale, light, dark, deep, livid, electric, etc., blue; see also **color.** 2. [Despondent] depressed, moody, melancholy; see **sad 1.** —**once in a blue moon,** rarely, infrequently, once in a while; see **seldom.** —**out of the blue,** unpredicted, unforeseen, surprising; see **unexpected.**

blues, n. pl. 1. [A state of despondency; often with the] depressed spirits, melancholy, dejection; see **gloom.** 2. [Rhythmic lamentation in a minor key] dirge, lament, torch song; see **music 1.**

bluff, n. 1. [A bank] cliff, precipice, steep; see **hill, mountain 1.** 2. [A trick] ruse, deception, delusion; see **trick 1.**

bluff, v. fool, mislead, trick; see **deceive.**

blunder, n. mistake, lapse, oversight; see **error.**

blunt, a. 1. [Dull] unsharpened, unpointed, round; see **dull 1.** 2. [Abrupt] brusque, curt, bluff; see **rude 2.**

blur, v. obscure, blur, blear; see **shade 2.**

blurt out, v. speak unthinkingly, jabber, utter; see **talk 1.**

blush, v. change color, flush, redden, turn red, glow, have rosy cheeks.

blushing, a. coloring, dyeing, staining, reddening, turning red or scarlet, flushing, glowing, changing color, burning, red as a rose, rosy-red, *with burning cheeks.

bluster, v. brag, swagger, strut; see **boast.**

board, n. 1. [A piece of thin lumber] plank, lath, strip; see **lumber.** 2. [Meals] food, fare, provisions; see **food, meal 2.** 3. [A body of men having specific responsibilities] jury, council, cabinet; see **committee.** —**across the board,** general, universal, common; see **universal 2.** —**go by the board,** be lost, go, vanish; see **fail 1.** —**on board,** present, in transit, en route; see **aboard.**

board, v. 1. [Cover] plank, tile, paper; see **cover 1.** 2. [Go aboard] embark, cast off, go on board ship; see **leave 1.** 3. [Take care of] lodge, room, accommodate; see **feed.**

boast, n. brag, vaunt, source of pride, pretension, self-satisfaction, bravado.

boast, v. gloat, triumph, swagger, bully, exult, show off, vaunt, swell, brag, strut, bluff, flaunt, bluster, flourish, *blow, *sound off, crow, *pat oneself on the back, *blow one's own trumpet, attract attention.—Ant. **apologize,** humble oneself, admit defeat.

boastful, a. bragging, pretentious, bombastic; see **egotistic.**

boat, n. Types of small boats include the following—sailboat, yacht, steamboat, craft, rowboat, shell, scull, kayak, dugout, canoe, scow, raft, launch, motorboat, dory, catboat, tartan, hydrofoil, speedboat, yawl, sloop, cutter, ketch, schooner, lifeboat, barge, punt, outrigger, dinghy, racer, hydroplane, catamaran, skiff, gondola, longboat, war canoe, flatboat, river boat, canal boat. —*in the same boat, in unison, in the same or a similar situation or condition, concurrently; see **together 2.** —*miss the boat, miss, fall short, neglect; see **fail 1.** —*rock the boat, upset, disturb, distort; see **confuse.**

bobsled, n. sleigh, coaster, toboggan; see **sled.**

bodily, a. carnal, fleshly, gross, somatic, solid, physical, unspiritual, tangible, material, substantial, human, natural, normal, organic; see also **biological, physical 1.**

body, n. 1. [The human organism] frame, physique, form, figure, shape, make, carcass, build, make-up. 2. [A corpse] cadaver, *corpus delecti* (Latin), dust, clay, carcass, dead body, relics, the dead, the deceased, mummy, skeleton, ashes, carrion, bones, remains, *cold meat, *stiff, *goner. 3. [The central portion of an object] chassis, basis, groundwork, frame, fuselage, assembly, trunk, hull, bed, box, skeleton, scaffold, anatomy, *bones, *guts. 4. [Individuals having an organization] society, group,

party; see **organization 2. 5.** [A unified or organized mass] reservoir, supply, variety; see **collection.** —**keep body and soul together,** stay alive, endure, earn a living; see **survive 1.**

boil, v. steep, seethe, stew, bubble, simmer, steam, parboil, boil over, evaporate; see also **cook.**

boil down, v. condense, summarize, sum up; see **decrease 2, summarize.**

boiling, a. stewing, steeping, percolating, steaming, bubbling, seething, simmering, evaporating, boiling over; see also *cooking.

boisterous, a. tumultuous, uproarious, noisy; see **loud 2, rude 2.**

bold, a. 1. [Courageous] intrepid, fearless, daring; see **brave.** 2. [Impertinent] brazen, audacious, presumptuous; see **rude 2. 3.** [Prominent] strong, clear, plain; see **definite 2.**

boldly, a. 1. [Said of animate beings] impetuously, headlong, intrepidly, fearlessly, recklessly, courageously, dauntlessly, daringly, valiantly, stoutly, resolutely, brazenly, firmly.—Ant. **cowardly,** fearfully, cravenly. 2. [Said of inanimate objects] prominently, conspicuously, saliently, sharply, clearly, plainly, openly, abruptly, steeply, eminently, vividly, strongly, palpably, commandingly, compellingly, showily.—Ant. **vaguely,** inconspicuously, unobtrusively.

boldness, n. audacity, hardihood, self-reliance; see **courage.**

bolster, v. prop, hold up, reinforce, sustain; see **support 1, 2.**

bolt, n. staple, brad, nut, skewer, peg, rivet, pin, spike, stud, coupling, key, pin, pipe; see also **nail, screw.**

bomb, n. weapon, high explosive, charge; see **explosive.** Types of bombs include the following—incendiary, (multiple) warhead, high explosive, demolition glider, jet propulsion, time, smoke, delayed action, antipersonnel bomb; atom(ic) bomb or A-bomb, cobalt bomb or C-bomb, hydrogen bomb or H-bomb, torpedo, depth charge, cherry bomb, hand grenade, *pineapple, *Molotov cocktail, stink bomb.

bomb, v. shell, bombard, torpedo, napalm, blow up, wipe out, blast, attack from the air, zero in on, raid, dive-bomb.

bombing, n. bombardment, shelling, an attack; see **attack.**

bond, n. 1. [A link] attachment, union, obligation, connection, relation, affinity, affiliation, bond of union, restraint; see also **friendship, marriage 1, relationship 2.** 2. [A secured debenture] security, warranty, debenture, certificate, registered bond, government bond, municipal bond, long or short term bond. 3. [Bail] surety, guaranty, warrant; see **bail.**

bondage, n. servitude, thralldom, subjugation; see **slavery 1.**

bone, n. Bones of the human body include the following—cranium or skull, frontal, temporal, parietal, occipital, zygomatic or cheekbone, mandible or jawbone, spinal column or vertebrae or backbone, costal or ribcage, clavicle or collarbone, scapula or shoulder blade, humerus, radius, ulna, carpal, metacarpal, phalanges, pelvis, illium or hipbone, femur or thighbone, patella or kneecap, tibia or shinbone, fibula, tarsal, metatarsal. —**feel in one's bones,** be convinced, expect be sure or positive; see **trust 1.** —**have a bone to pick,** have a complaint or quarrel, be angry, express an objection; see **complain.** —***make no bones,** confess, reveal, expose; see **admit 2.**

bonus, n. gratuity, reward, special or additional compensation; see **gift 1, tip 2.**

bony, a. emaciated, skinny, scrawny; see **thin 2.**

book, n. publication, work, volume, booklet, pamphlet, work, reprint, preprint, offprint, hardcover, text, edition, brochure, folio, copy, monograph, writing, scroll, periodical, magazine, paperback. Kinds of books include the following—manual, handbook, reference book, children's or juvenile book, atlas, cookbook, guidebook, story book, song book, trade book, textbook, workbook, hymnbook, bible or Bible, treatise, tract. —**by the book,** according to the rules, properly, correctly; see **well 3.** —**in one's book,** in one's opinion, for oneself, to one's mind; see **personally 2.** —**in the book,** practiced, done, established, prevalent; see **known 2.** —**know like a book,** understand, comprehend, be aware of; see **know 1.** —***one for the books,** source of amazement, shock, novelty; see **surprise 2.** —**on the books,** listed, noted, set down; see **recorded.** —***throw the book at,** accuse, charge with every possible offense, be overzealous with; see **blame.**

bookkeeper, n. controller or comptroller, accountant, auditor; see **clerk.**

boom, n. 1. [A loud noise] roar, blast, blare; see **noise 1.** 2. [Sudden increase, especially sudden prosperity] rush, growth, inflation; see **increase.**

boom, v. 1. [To make a loud sound] roar, reverberate, thunder; see **sound 1.** 2. [To increase rapidly] prosper, expand, swell; see **grow 1.** —***lower the boom (on),** take action or move (against), beat, overcome; see **attack.**

boon, n. benefit, good fortune, help; see **blessing 2.**

boor, n. peasant, yokel, rustic, lout, clown, (country) bumpkin, churl, oaf, lubber, boob, booby, bear, plowman, lumpkin, gaffer, *hick, *rube, *hayseed, clod, clodhopper.

boorish, a. awkward, clumsy, churlish; see **rude 1, 2.**

boost, n. 1. [Aid] assistance, aid, helping hand; see **help 1.** 2. [An increase] addition, advance, *hike; see **increase 1.**

boost, v. 1. [To raise] shove, hoist, advance; see **raise 1.** 2. [To promote] encourage, support, advertise; see **promote 1, 2.** 3. [To increase] raise, heighten, expand; see **increase.**

boot, n. hip-boot, bootie, wader, galoshes, laced boot, high shoe, hiking boot, ski boot, cowboy boot, climbing boot, riding boot. —**bet your boots,** be certain, rely on it, trust in it; see **depend on.**

booth, n. stall, counter, nook, corner, pew, berth, compartment, shed, manger, cubbyhole, coop, pen, hut, enclosure, stand, cubicle, box.

booty, n. plunder, spoil, winnings, stolen goods, (ill-gotten) gains, seizure, prize, haul, pickings, loot, *take.

*booze, n. liquor, alcohol, whiskey; see **drink 2.**

border, n. 1. [Edge] hem, end, trim; see **decoration 2, fringe 2.** 2. [Boundary] frontier, outpost, perimeter; see **boundary, edge 1.**

border, v. be adjacent to, adjoin, abut (on); see **join 3.**

bordering, a. rimming, bounding, neighboring, fringing, edging, lining, verging, connecting, on the edge (of); see also **near 1.**

border on, v. lie next to, abut, touch; see **join 3.**

bore, n. nuisance, pest, tiresome or tedious person; see **trouble.**

bore, v. 1. [To pierce by rotary motion] drill, ream, perforate; see **penetrate.** 2. [To weary] fatigue, tire, put to sleep; see **tire 2.**

bored, a. wearied, fatigued, jaded, dull, irked, annoyed, *bored to death, in a rut, sick and tired, *bored stiff or silly, *fed up; see also **tired.**—Ant. exhilarated, excited, thrilled.

boredom, n. lack of interest, tiresomeness, apathy, doldrums, listlessness, monotony, tedium, indifference.

boring, a. tedious, stupid, monotonous; see **dull 3, 4.**

born, a. intrinsic, innate, inherent; see **natural 1.**

borrow, v. accept the loan of, obtain the use of, take a loan, go into debt, get temporary use of, use, rent, hire, obtain, give a note for, *sponge (on or off of), *hit up or for, *bum, beg, *chisel, *mooch.—Ant. lend, loan, give back.

borrowed, a. appropriated, taken, acquired, assumed, adopted, hired, plagiarized, imported, cultivated, imitated.—Ant. owned, possessed, titular.

boss, *n.* supervisor, manager, administrator; see **executive.**

botanical, *a.* concerning plants, vegetable, floral, arboreal, herbaceous, morphological, cytological, agricultural; see also **biological.**

botany, *n.* phytology, natural history, study of flora *or* vegetation *or* plant life; see also **biology, science.**

botch, *v.* bungle, spoil, mar, ruin, wreck, mutilate, fumble, distort, blunder, mishandle, do clumsily, muddle, make a mess of, trip, flounder, err, fall down, be mistaken, misjudge, mismanage, miscalculate, misconstrue, misestimate, execute clumsily, do unskillfully, stumble, *put one's foot in it, *goof (up), butcher, *screw *or* mess *or* trip up, *put out of whack; see also **fail 1.** — *Ant.* **succeed,** fix, do well.

both, *a.* the two, (both) together, the one and the other, the pair *or* couple, one as well as the other.

bother, *n.* 1. [Worry] vexation, distress, anxiety; see **care 2.** 2. [A cause of worry] problem, concern, care; see **difficulty 1, 2, trouble.**

bother, *v.* 1. [To take trouble] put oneself out, fret, go out of one's way, make a fuss about, fuss (over), take pains, make an effort, exert *or* concern oneself, be concerned (about), worry (about). 2. [To give trouble] plague, vex, annoy, perplex, pester, molest, irritate, irk, provoke, insult, harass, heckle, aggravate, badger, discommode, discompose, mortify, goad, intrude upon, disquiet, pursue, hinder, impede, carp at, scare, exasperate, bore, afflict, taunt, torment, torture, bedevil, browbeat, tease, tantalize, ride, rub the wrong way, pick on, nag, *needle, *bug, *get under one's skin.—*Ant.* **help,** please, delight.

bothered, *a.* annoyed, agitated, disturbed; see **troubled.**

bothersome, *a.* vexatious, vexing, troublesome; see **disturbing.**

bottle, *n.* flask, flagon, decanter, cruet, jug, urn, canteen, cruse, jar, gourd, carafe, hip flask, vial *or* phial, caster, vacuum bottle, glass. —**hit the bottle,** get drunk, imbibe, become an alcoholic; see **drink 2.**

bottom, *n.* underside, base, nadir, foot, depths, bed, floor, lowest *or* deepest part, sole, ground.—*Ant.* **top,** peak, pinnacle. —**at bottom,** fundamentally, basically, actually; see **really 1.** —**be at the bottom of,** originate, be the reason for, activate; see **cause.** —*bet one's bottom dollar,** bet, risk, wager; see **gamble.**

bottomless, *a.* deep, unfathomable, boundless; see **infinite.**

bottoms, *n. pl.* low land, marsh, bottomland; see **swamp.**

bough, *n.* limb, arm, fork; see **branch 2.**

bought, *a.* purchased, procured, budgeted (for), requisitioned, paid for, on order, to be delivered, contracted for, included in the purchase; see also **ordered 1.** — *Ant.* **stolen,** sold, given away.

boulder, *n.* (field) stone, slab, crag; see **rock 2.**

boulevard, *n.* street, avenue, highway; see **road 1.**

bounce, *v.* ricochet, recoil, glance (off), spring (back), leap, hop, bolt, vault, skip, bob, buck, jump, bound, jerk up and down, fly *or* bounce *or* snap *or* kick back, boomerang, backlash.

bound, *a.* 1. [Literally confined in bonds] fettered, shackled, trussed up, manacled, enchained, handcuffed, hobbled, captive, pinioned, muzzled, in leash, tied (up), harnessed, bound hand and foot, lashed fast, pinned *or* pegged down, tethered, picketed, secured, roped, gagged. —*Ant.* **free,** unrestrained, loose. 2. [Figuratively constrained] impelled, compelled, obliged, obligated, restrained, under compulsion, constrained, forced, coerced, driven, pressed, urged, necessitated, under necessity, made, having no alternative, required.

bound, *v.* 1. [To move in leaps] leap, spring, vault; see **jump 1.** 2. [To rebound] bounce, ricochet, recoil; see **bounce.** 3. [To set limits] restrict, confine, circumscribe; see **define 1.** —**out of bounds,** off limits, not permitted, restricted; see **illegal.**

boundary, *n.* outline, border, verge, rim, beginning, end, confine, bounds, radius, terminus, landmark, march, extremity, fence, compass, side, hem, frame, skirt, termination, margin, line, barrier, frontier, outpost, perimeter, extent, circumference, horizon, periphery, fringe, mark, confines, limit, borderland.

bounded, *a.* limited, enclosed, bordered; see **surrounded.**

boundless, *a.* limitless, endless, unlimited; see **infinite.**

bound to, *a.* certain *or* sure *or* destined to; see **inevitable.**

bounty, *n.* prize, premium, bonus; see **pay 1, 2.**

bouquet, *n.* nosegay, bunch of flowers, garland, vase (of flowers), flower arrangement, wreath, spray; see also **wreath.**

bow, *n.* longbow, crossbow, single-piece bow; see **weapon.**

bow, *n.* 1. [Front of a boat] forepart, bowsprit, prow, head, stem, fore; see also **front 1.** 2. [A bend from the waist] nod, curtsey, bowing and scraping; see **acknowledgement.** —**take a bow,** accept praise, be congratulated, feel honored; see **bend**.

bow, v. 1. [To bend] curtsey, stoop, dip; see **bend**. 2. [To submit] surrender, acquiesce, capitulate; see **yield 1**.

bowels, n. pl. viscera, entrails, guts; see **insides**.

bowl, n. vessel, tureen, pot, saucer, crock, jar, urn, pitcher, basin, casserole, boat; see also **container, dish**.

bowling, n. ninepins, tenpins, bocce ball; see **sport 3**.

bow out, v. withdraw, resign, quit; see **abandon 1**.

box, n. receptacle, crate, carton; see **container**.

box, v. 1. [To enclose in a box] confine, package, crate; see **pack 2**. 2. [To fight for sport] spar, punch, slug; see **fight**.

boxer, n. pugilist, fighter, fisticuffer; see **fighter 1**.

boxing, n. pugilism, fisticuffs, the fights; see **sport 3**.

boy, n. lad, youth, stripling, fellow, schoolboy, youngster, whippersnapper, male child, junior, little gentleman; see also **child**.

boycott, v. withhold patronage, hold aloof from, ostracize; see **avoid, strike 2**.

boyhood, n. schoolboy days, formative period, adolescence; see **childhood, youth 1**.

boyish, a. puerile, boylike, adolescent; see **childish, young 1**.

boy scout, n. cub scout, explorer (scout), troop member; see **scout 2**.

brace, n. prop, bolster, stay, support, lever, beam, girder, block, rib, buttress, reinforcement, bearing, upholder, bracket, strengthener, band, bracer, stirrup, arm, splint, boom, bar, staff, rafter, jack, crutch.

brace, v. prop, bolster, hold up; see **support 1**.

bracelet, n. armband, ornament, bangle; see **jewelry**.

brag, v. swagger, exult, gloat; see **boast**.

braggart, n. boaster, blowhard, windbag, trumpeter, swaggerer, strutter, peacock, blusterer, bragger, *know-it-all.

brain, n. 1. [The organ of intelligence] cerebrum, gray matter, brain cells; see **head 1**. 2. [The intelligence] intellect, genius, mentality; see **mind 1**. 3. [*A very intelligent person] academician, scholar, *egghead; see **intellectual**. — **have on the brain,** be obsessed or involved (with), fuss, stew; see **bother 2**.

brainwash, v. indoctrinate, instill, catechize; see **convince, influence, teach**.

brake, n. check, hamper, curb, deterrent, obstacle, damper, hindrance, retarding device, governor.

bramble, n. brier, thorn, burr, (stinging) nettle, prickly shrub, goose grass, thistle, shrub, bramble bush, hedge, spray.

branch, n. 1. [A part, usually of secondary importance] member, office, bureau; see **division 3**. 2. [A secondary shoot] bough, limb, offshoot, sprig, twig, bud, arm, fork, growth.

branch off, v. diverge, separate, part; see **divide**.

branch out, v. expand, extend, add to; see **grow 1, increase 1**.

brand, n. stigma, scar, sear, welt, range brand, mark of the branding iron, earmark, owner's sign or mark.

brand, v. blaze, stamp, imprint; see **mark 1**.

brandish, v. flourish, gesture, warn; see **threaten**.

brass, n. 1. [An alloy of copper and zinc] copper alloy, pinchbeck, Muntz's metal, mosaic gold, yellow metal, prince's metal, brass leaf or Dutch gold, brass powder. 2. [*High-ranking officials] officers, *front office, brass hats; see **officer 3**. 3. [Impudence] effrontery, impertinence, audacity; see **rudeness**.

brat, n. impudent or unruly child, youngster, *kid; see **child**.

brave, a. fearless, daring, dauntless, valiant, intrepid, undaunted, undismayed, confident, unabashed, chivalrous, valorous, heroic, bold, imprudent, adventurous, reckless, foolhardy, dashing, venturesome, forward, audacious, gallant, resolute, militant, defiant, hardy, unafraid, stout, stout-hearted, lion-hearted, manly, firm, plucky, high-spirited, unshrinking, strong, stalwart, unflinching, unyielding, indomitable, unconquerable, *spunky, game, nervy, *gutsy. —Ant. cowardly, timid, craven.

bravely, a. courageously, fearlessly, valiantly, boldly, daringly, dauntlessly, intrepidly, heroically, gallantly, hardily, stoutly, manfully, staunchly, with courage or fortitude, resolutely, valorously, spiritedly, firmly, audaciously, chivalrously, indomitably, *with guts, *like a man.—Ant. cowardly, fearfully, timidly.

bravery, n. valor, intrepidity, fearlessness; see **courage, strength**.

brawl, n. fuss, squabble, riot; see **fight 1**.

breach, n. violation, infringment, transgression; see **crime, violation**.

bread, n. loaf, baked goods, the staff of life. Types of bread include the following—whole wheat, rye, leavened, unleavened, corn, sourdough, raisin, pumpernickel, French, white, black, dark brown, Boston brown, potato, hardtack. Breadlike foods include the following—spoon bread, cake, dumpling, turnover, bun, cookie, English muffin, corn bread, scone, shortbread, Indian bread. —**break bread,** partake, have a meal, indulge;

see eat 1. —**know which side one's bread is buttered on**, be prudent or cautious or shrewd, save, *look out for number one; see **understand** 1.

breadth, n. largeness, extent, vastness, compass, magnitude, greatness, comprehensiveness, amplitude; see also **size** 2.

break, n. 1. [The act of breaking] fracture, rift, split, schism, cleavage, breach, rupture, eruption, bursting, failure, collapse.—*Ant.* mending, **repair**, maintenance. 2. [A pause] intermission, interim, lapse; see **pause**. 3. [*Fortunate change or event; *often plural*] good luck, accident, favorable circumstances; see **luck** 1.

break, v. 1. [To start a rupture] burst, split, crack, rend, rive, sunder, sever, fracture, tear, cleave, break into or through, force open, puncture, split, snap, slash, gash, dissect, slice, disjoin, separate; see also **cut** 2. 2. [To shatter] smash (to atoms), shiver, crash, break up, crush, splinter, pull to pieces, break (all) to pieces or smithereens, fall apart or to pieces, collapse, break down, come apart or unstuck or unglued or off, get loose, fall off or down, cave in, go to wrack and ruin, get wrecked, *bust, split up, *go on the fritz or haywire; see also **disintegrate** and sense 1. 3. [To bring to ruin or to an end] demolish, annihilate, eradicate; see **destroy**. 4. [To happen] come to pass, occur, develop; see **happen** 2.

breakable, a. fragile, delicate, frail; see **weak** 2.

breakage, n. harm, wreckage, ruined goods; see **damage** 2.

breakdown, n. collapse, rupture, disruption; see **failure** 1.

break down, v. 1. [To analyze] examine, investigate, dissect; see **analyze** 2. 2. [To malfunction] fail, stop, falter, misfire, give out, cease, backfire, *conk or peter or fizzle out, collapse, *go kaput, *come unstuck or unglued, *run out of gas.

breakfast, n. morning meal, first meal of the day, early meal, breaking the fast; see also **meal** 2.

break in, v. 1. [Train] educate, instruct, prepare; see **teach**. 2. [Intrude] rob, burglarize, trespass; see **meddle** 2, **steal**.

breaking, a. bursting, splitting, cracking, rending, sundering, parting, severing, exploding, erupting, shattering, splintering, fracturing, tearing, cleaving, snapping, separating, smashing, shivering, crashing, splintering, disintegrating, collapsing, caving in, falling, *busting, *going to pot.—*Ant.* enduring, **strong**, stable.

break in or **upon**, v. cut in (on), intrude, intervene; see **interrupt**.

break off, v. end, cease, discontinue; see **stop** 2.

break out, v. 1. [To start] begin, commence, occur; see **begin** 2. 2. [To escape] burst out, flee, depart; see **leave** 1. 3. [To erupt] acquire blemishes, have acned skin, become diseased, get pimples.

breakthrough, n. discovery, finding, invention; see **discovery**.

break through, v. penetrate, force away, intrude; see **penetrate**.

break up, v. 1. [To scatter] disperse, disband, separate; see **disintegrate**, **divide**. 2. [To stop] put an end to, halt, terminate; see **stop** 2. 3. [*To distress] hurt, sadden, wound; see **hurt**. 4. [*To end relations] halt, break off, drop; see **end** 1.

breast, n. 1. [The forepart of the body above the abdomen] thorax, heart, bosom; see **chest** 2. 2. [A protuberant mammary gland] bosom, dug, teat, mammilla, tit, nipple, bust, udder, *boob. —**beat one's breast**, repent, humble oneself, be penitent or sorry or remorseful; see **apologize**, **regret** 1. —**make a clean breast of**, confess, reveal, expose; see **admit** 2.

breath, n. inspiration, expiration, inhalation, exhalation, breathing, gasp, sigh, pant, suspiration, wheeze. —**below** or **under one's breath**, quietly, subdued, murmuring; see **whispering**. —**catch one's breath**, rest, stop, slow down; see **pause**. —**in the same breath**, simultaneously, concurrently, at the same time; see **together** 2. —**out of breath**, gasping, choking, out of wind; see **breathless**. —**save one's breath**, be quiet, stop talking, never mind; see **shut up** 1. —**take one's breath away**, thrill, stimulate, invigorate; see **excite**.

breathe, v. respire, use one's lungs, inhale, exhale, draw in, breathe in or out, gasp, pant, wheeze, snort, sigh, take air into one's nostrils, scent, sniff.

breathless, a. out of breath, winded, spent, exhausted, used up, gasping, choking, windless, wheezing, short-winded, panting, puffing, short of breath, *out of wind.

breed, n. strain, variety, kind; see **race** 1.

breed, v. 1. [To produce] give birth to, deliver, bring forth; see **produce** 1. 2. [To cause] bring about, effect, occasion, produce; see **begin** 1.

breeze, n. zephyr, flurry, blast; see **wind** 1. —**in a breeze**, effortlessly, readily, jauntily; see **easily** 1. —**shoot** (or **bat**) **the breeze**, converse, chat, chatter; see **talk** 1.

brew, n. concoction, preparation, instillation, liquor, blend, beer, homebrew, ale, stout; see also **drink** 1, 2.

brew, *v.* concoct, ferment, mull; see **cook.**

bribe, *n.* fee, reward, hush money, lure, gift, graft, compensation, protection, bait, tip, blackmail, price, present, gratuity, *payola.

bribe, *v.* corrupt, get at *or* to, influence by a gift, reward, tip, give a bribe *or* price to, coax, hire, entice, tempt, influence, buy back *or* off, *fix.

brick, *n.* cube, Roman brick, pressed brick, block, slab, cement *or* concrete *or* cinder block, glass brick; see **stone.**

bridal, *a.* nuptial, marriage, wedding, matrimonial, marital, conjugal, connubial, wedded.

bride, *n.* spouse, mate, helpmate; see **wife.**

bridegroom, *n.* groom, benedict, spouse; see **husband.**

bridge, *n.* 1. [An elevated structure] viaduct, platform, pontoon, catwalk, gangplank, drawbridge, trestle, aqueduct, scaffold, transit, tram. Types of bridges include the following—arch, pier, gantry, suspension, cantilever, bowstring, tubular, bascule, pontoon, swing, turnpike, steel arch, vertical lift, hoist, truss. 2. [A game at cards] contract bridge, auction bridge, duplicate bridge; see **game** 1. 3. [A link] connection, bond, tie; see **joint** 1, **link.**

bridge, *v.* connect, span, link; see **join** 1.

brief, *a.* 1. [Abrupt] hasty, curt, bluff; see **rude** 2. 2. [Short in time] short-term, fleeting, concise; see **short** 2.

briefing, *n.* instruction, preamble, discussion; see **introduction** 4, **preparation** 1.

briefly, *a.* shortly, curtly, abruptly, quickly, hastily, hurriedly, momentarily, temporarily, in passing, casually, lightly, briskly, in brief *or* outline, in a few words, in a capsule, in a nutshell.

bright, *a.* 1. [Shining *or* vivid] gleaming, shiny, glittering, luminous, lustrous, burnished, polished, sparkling, mirrorlike, glowing, flashing, scintillating, shimmering, incandescent, twinkling, illumined, light, golden, silvery, illuminated, shining, irradiated, glistening, radiant, burning, glaring, beaming, glimmering, splendid, resplendent, brilliant, dazzling, aglow, lighted (up), full of light, ablaze, flamelike, moonlit, sunlit, on fire, phosphorescent, blazing, glossy, colored, colorful, tinted, intense, deep, sharp, rich, tinged, hued, touched with color, clear, ruddy, psychedelic.—*Ant.* dull, clouded, dark. 2. [Intelligent] clever, quick, alert; see **intelligent.** 3. [Not rainy] clear, sunny, mild; see **fair** 3. 4. [Cheerful] lively, vivacious, gay; see **happy.**

brighten, *v.* 1. [To become brighter] clear up, lighten, grow calm, improve, grow sunny, glow, kindle. 2. [To make brighter] polish, intensify, lighten; see **shine** 3.

brightly, *a.* lustrously, radiantly, splendidly, brilliantly, dazzlingly, shinily, gaily, freshly, vividly, colorfully, cleverly, sunnily.—*Ant.* dully, dingily, darkly.

brightness, *n.* shine, luster, illumination; see **light** 1.

brilliant, *a.* 1. [Shining] dazzling, gleaming, sparkling; see **bright** 1. 2. [Showing remarkable ability] ingenious, profound, penetrating; see **intelligent.**

brilliantly, *a.* 1. [Very brightly] shiningly, radiantly, blazingly; see **brightly.** 2. [With superior intelligence] cleverly, shrewdly, knowledgeably; see **intelligently.**

brim, *n.* margin, rim, border; see **edge** 1.

bring, *v.* 1. [To transport] convey, take along, bear; see **carry** 1, **pick up** 6. 2. [To be worth in sale] sell for, earn, bring in; see **pay** 2. 3. [To cause] produce, effect, make; see **begin** 1.

bring about, *v.* 1. [To achieve] do, accomplish, realize; see **achieve, succeed** 1. 2. [To cause] produce, effect, do; see **begin** 1, **manage** 1.

bring around, *v.* 1. [To convince] persuade, prove, induce; see **convince.** 2. [To revive] restore, refresh, resuscitate; see **revive** 1.

bring forth, *v.* deliver, bear, yield; see **produce** 1, 2.

*bring home the bacon, *v.* provide for, triumph, achieve; see **earn** 2, **provide** 1, **succeed** 1, **support** 5.

bring home to (one), *v.* make apparent, convince, make one realize; see **emphasize.**

bring in, *v.* 1. [To import] ship in, introduce, import; see **carry** 2. 2. [To produce] yield, bear, accrue; see **produce** 1.

bringing, *n.* fetching, carrying, transporting, accompanying, introducing, shipping, bearing, hauling, bringing in, getting, providing.

bring off, *v.* accomplish, realize, execute; see **achieve, succeed** 1.

bring on, *v.* cause, lead to, provoke; see **begin** 1.

bring out, *v.* 1. [To excite] elicit, arouse, evoke; see **excite.** 2. [To publish] print, issue, put out; see **publish** 1. 3. [To produce a play] present, put on the stage, exhibit; see **perform** 2. 4. [To intensify] heighten, sharpen, magnify; see **emphasize, increase.**

bring to bear, *v.* pressure, apply, concentrate; see **exercise** 2, **influence, use** 1.

bring to one's senses, v. restore, bring to reason, persuade; see **convince**.

bring up, v. 1. [To rear] educate, teach, train; see **raise 2, support 5**. 2. [To discuss] tender, submit, advance; see **discuss, propose 1**.

bring with, v. get, accompany, stop for; see **pick up 6**.

brink, n. limit, brim, rim; see **edge 1**.

brisk, a. sharp, keen, invigorating; see **stimulating**.

briskly, a. energetically, quickly, brusquely, rapidly, impulsively, nimbly, agilely, dexterously, decisively, firmly, actively, promptly, readily, vigorously, in a brisk or lively manner; see also **emphatically.—Ant.** listlessly, slowly, sluggishly.

bristle, n. hair, fiber, quill; see **point 2**.

Britain, n. Great Britain, United Kingdom, England, Scotland, Wales, and Northern Ireland; see **England**.

British, a. Anglo-Saxon, Celtic, Anglian; see **English**.

brittle, a. fragile, crisp, inelastic; see **weak 2**.

broad, a. 1. [Physically wide] extended, large, extensive, ample, spacious, deep, expansive, immense, wide, roomy, outstretched, thick, widespread, full.—Ant. narrow, thin, slender. 2. [Culturally wide] cultivated, experienced, cosmopolitan; see **cultured 3**. [Tolerant] progressive, open-minded, unbiased; see **liberal**.

broadcast, n. radio program, newscast, telecast; see **performance**.

broadcast, v. announce, relay, telephone, send out, telegraph, radio, transmit, televise, telecast, air, put on the air, go or be on the air; see also **send 2**.

broadcasting, n. radio transmission, announcing, television, airing, putting on a radio program, telecasting, newscasting, being broadcast, transmitting, reporting.

broaden, v. widen, expand, increase; see **grow 1, increase 1**.

broad-minded, a. tolerant, progressive, unprejudiced; see **liberal**.

brochure, n. handout, circular, pamphlet; see **advertisement**.

broil, v. sear, bake, roast; see **cook**.

broiler, n. oven, grill, barbecue; see **appliance**.

broke, a. bankrupt, out of money, indebted; see **ruined 4**. —*go for broke, gamble, wager, risk everything; see **risk**. —*go broke, become penniless or bankrupt, lose everything; be reduced to poverty; see **fail 1, lose 2**.

broken, a. 1. [Fractured] shattered, hurt, ruptured, burst, splintered, shivered, smashed, in pieces, collapsed, destroyed, pulverized, crumbled, mutilated, bruised, injured, damaged, rent, split, cracked, mangled, dismembered, fragmentary, disintegrated, crippled, shredded, crushed, slivered.—Ant. sound, **whole**, intact. 2. [Not functioning properly] defective, inoperable, in need of repair, in disrepair, out of (working) order, *busted, *gone to pot, *screwed up, *shot, (gone) haywire, *on the fritz or blink, gone to pieces, out of joint or gear or commission; see also **faulty**. 3. [Discontinuous] spasmodic, erratic, intermittent; see **irregular 1, 4**. 4. [Incoherent; said of speech] muttered, unintelligible, mumbled; see **incoherent**.

broken down, a. shattered, dilapidated, battered; see **old 2**.

brokenhearted, a. despondent, crushed, grieved; see **sad 1**.

brood, n. flock, offspring, young; see **family, herd**.

brood, v. 1. [To hatch] set, cover, incubate, warm, sit; see also **produce 1**. 2. [To nurse one's troubles] think, meditate, gloom, grieve, fret, sulk, mope, ponder, consider, muse, deliberate, dwell upon, speculate, daydream, reflect, dream, chafe inwardly, give oneself over to reflections, be in a brown study, eat one's heart out; see also **worry 2**.

brook, n. creek, stream, streamlet; see **river**.

broom, n. (carpet) sweeper, whisk (broom), mop, feather duster, swab, (floor) brush.

broth, n. brew, concoction, soup, potage, consommé, purée, bouillon, borsch, stock, chowder, gumbo, porridge, hodge-podge, potpourri; see also **food, soup**.

brotherhood, n. fellowship, equality, kinship, intimacy, (blood) relationship, affiliation, association, society, common humanity, family, race, comradeship, cameraderie, friendship, amity.

brotherly, a. kindly, humane, sympathetic; see **friendly, kind, loving**.

browbeat, v. bully, intimidate, frighten; see **threaten**.

brown, a. and n. Shades and tints of brown include the following—tan, bay, chestnut, nutbrown, copper-colored, mahogany, bronze, russet, chocolate, cinnamon, hazel, reddish-brown, sorrel, sepia, tawny, ochre, rust, rust-colored, brownish, puce, fawn, liver-colored, beige, dust, drab, coffee, khaki, maroon, cocoa, umber, brick, ginger, light brown, dark brown, auburn, buff; see also **color 1**.

brown, v. toast, scorch, sauté; see **cook, fry**.

browse, v. skim, peruse, scan, glance at, flip or look or run through, look or glance or check or run over, survey, inspect loosely, examine cursorily, go through carelessly, dip into, *wander here and there.

bruise, *n.* abrasion, wound, swelling; see blemish.

bruise, *v.* beat, injure, wound; see damage, hurt.

brunet, *a.* dark, dark-complexioned, tawny, dusky, brown, tanned, swarthy, dark-haired, dark-skinned.—*Ant.* fair, light, light-complexioned.

brush, *n.* 1. [A brushing instrument]—Varieties include the following—bristle, fiber, nail, clothes, camel's hair, rotary, paint, tooth, scrubbing, floor, hair, bath, dust. 2. [A touch] rub, tap, stroke; see touch 2. 3. [Underbrush] bush, thicket, undergrowth, second growth, chaparral, cover, brushwood, shrubbery, canebrake, grove, hedge, fern, underwood, scrub, brake.

brush, *v.* 1. [To cleanse by brushing] sweep, whisk, wipe; see clean. 2. [To touch lightly] stroke, smooth, graze; see touch 1.

***brush off,** *v.* reject, get rid of, send away; see dismiss.

brush up, *v.* reread, look over, review; see study.

brutal, *a.* pitiless, harsh, unmerciful; see cruel.

brutality, *n.* savageness, grossness, unfeelingness; see cruelty.

brutally, *a.* ruthlessly, cruelly, callously, relentlessly, mercilessly, heartlessly, grimly, viciously, meanly, inhumanly, inhumanely, brutishly, savagely, in a ruthless *or* cruel *or* heartless manner *or* way, pitilessly, barbarously, remorselessly, unkindly, wildly, fiercely, hardheartedly, murderously, ferociously, diabolically, barbarically, in cold blood.—*Ant.* gently, nicely, kindly.

bubble, *n.* sac, air bubble, balloon, foam, froth, spume, effervescence, lather.

bubble, *v.* froth, foam, gurgle, gush, well, trickle, effervesce, boil, percolate, simmer, seep, eddy, ferment, erupt, issue, fester.

bucket, *n.* pail, canister, can; see container, pot 1. —*kick the bucket, expire, lose one's life, pass away; see die 1.

buckle, *n.* clasp, clamp, harness, fastening; see fastener.

buckle down, *v.* apply oneself, attend to, keep one's mind on, be occupied with; see concentrate 2.

***buck up,** *v.* cheer, comfort, hearten; see encourage.

bud, *n.* shoot, incipient flower, germ; see flower. —nip in the bud, check, halt, stop; see prevent.

budding, *a.* maturing, developing, opening, blossoming, bursting (forth), putting forth shoots, vegetating, flowering, blooming, promising, young, sprouting, germinating, immature, latent, embryonic, in bud; see also growing.

buddy, *n.* peer, companion, *pal; see associate, friend.

budge, *v.* stir, change position, shift; see move 1.

budget, *n.* estimates, estimated expenses, allocations, accounts, financial statement *or* plan, cost of operation, funds; see estimate.

budget, *v.* allocate expenditures, balance income and outgo, forecast, plan outgo, allow for, figure in *or* on, estimate necessary expenditures; see also estimate.

bug, *n.* 1. [An insect] beetle, pest, gnat; see insect. 2. [*A microbe] bacillus, disease germ, virus; see germ. 3. [*A defect] flaw, fault, imperfection; see blemish, defect. 4. [*An enthusiast] devotee, zealot, fanatic; see follower.

***bug,** *v.* 1. [To annoy] irritate, plague, pester; see bother 2, disturb. 2. [To install hidden microphones] spy, overhear, listen in on, wiretap *or* tap; see eavesdrop.

build, *v.* create, form, erect, frame, raise, rear, make, manufacture, put *or* fit together, fabricate, contrive, carpenter, assemble, put *or* set up, mold, hammer together, pile stone on stone, sculpture, fashion, compose, evolve, compile, cast, produce, forge, bring about, devise, carve, weave.—*Ant.* destroy, demolish, wreck.

building, *n.* edifice, erection, construction, fabrication, house, framework, superstructure, frame, structure, apartment house, barn, castle, church, factory, home, hotel, motel, skyscraper, temple, pile; see also architecture.

build on, *v.* extend, enlarge, add (on) to, develop; see increase 1.

build up, *v.* 1. [To increase] strengthen, add to, expand; see increase 1. 2. [To construct] make, erect, establish, construct; see build.

built, *a.* constructed, fabricated, manufactured, made, put together, produced, assembled, contrived, reared, raised, remodeled, completed, joined, perfected, finished, realized, created, actualized, finalized; see also formed.

bulb, *n.* globe, globule, ball, knob, corn, tuber, protuberance, head, bunch, swelling, tumor, tube.

bulge, *n.* swelling, bunch, lump, protuberance, hump, bump, bulb, outgrowth, sagging, growth, prominence, excess, bagginess, appendage, projection, tumor, egg, sac, knob, horn, ridge, wart, promontory.

bulk, *n.* greater *or* better *or* main *or* major *or* best part, most, majority, plurality, biggest share, greater number, nearly *or* almost all, body, more than half, best, gross, lion's share.—*Ant.* bit, remnant, fraction.

bulky, *a.* massive, big, huge; see **high 1, large 1, long 1.**

bull, *n.* 1. [The male of the bovine species] steer, calf, ox; see **cow. 2.** [Nonsense] balderdash, rubbish, trash; see **nonsense 1.**

bullet, *n.* shell, cartridge, ball, projectile, missile, trajectile, (piece of) ammunition, slug, *ammo; see also **shot 1.**

bulletin, *n.* release, notice, communiqué; see **announcement.**

bully, *n.* ruffian, rowdy, tough; see **rascal.**

bully, *v.* tease, domineer, harass; see **threaten.**

bum, *n.* hobo, tramp, vagrant; see **beggar.**

bump, *n.* 1. [A jarring collision] knock, bang, bounce, jounce, jar, box, smash, pat, crack, jolt, crash, sideswipe, punch, hit, clap, push, shove, thrust, boost, shock, clash, impact, stroke, rap, tap, slap, clout, jab, jerk, crash, prod, jolt, slam, nudge, buffet, *swat, *bash, *wallop, *belt, *bat, *swipe, *thump, *whack, *poke, *clump, *plump, *clunk, *thwack, *sock, *whop, *lick, *smack, cuff, *slug. 2. [A swelling] projection, protuberance, knob; see **bulge, lump.**

bump, *v.* 1. [To collide with] collide, run against, strike; see **crash 4, hit 1, 3. 2.** [To make a bumping sound] thud, whack, sock; see **sound 1.**

bumper, *n.* cover, guard, protector; see **defense 2, fender.**

bun, *n.* muffin, scone, hot cross bun; see **bread, roll 1, 2, pastry.**

bunch, *n.* clump, group, batch, spray, sheaf, tuft, shock, stack, thicket, group, gathering, host, galaxy, bundle, knot, collection, *passel, *mess, *slug, *oodles.

bundle, *n.* packet, parcel, bunch; see **package.**

bungle, *v.* blunder, fumble, mishandle; see **botch, fail 1.**

bungler, *n.* fumbler, botcher, blunderer, flounderer, muddler, numskull, featherbrain, dolt, scatterbrain, dunce, clod, ignoramus, idiot, duffer, addlebrain, butterfingers, *bonehead, *blockhead, spoiler, *goof off, clumsy oaf, *bull in a china shop, harebrain, *klutz, *block.

bungling, *a.* clumsy, unskillful, inept; see **awkward, incompetent.**

bunk, *n.* 1. [A bed] berth, cot, pallet; see **bed 1. 2.** [*Anything untrue, silly, or unreliable] rubbish, rot, hogwash; see **nonsense 1.**

buoy, *n.* float, drift, floating marker; see **float.**

burden, *n.* 1. [Something carried] lading, freight, pack; see **load 1. 2.** [Anything hard to support or endure] encumbrance, punishment, weary load; see **difficulty 2, misfortune.**

burden, *v.* weigh down, force, hinder, encumber, overwhelm, hamper, strain, load (with), saddle with, handicap, obligate, tax, overtask, afflict, vex, try, trouble, pile, bog down, crush, depress, impede, overload, oppress, make heavy, press down.—*Ant.* **lighten,** relieve, unload.

burdensome, *a.* heavy, oppressive, troublesome; see **difficult 1, 2, disturbing.**

bureau, *n.* 1. [Committee] commission, authority, board; see **committee. 2.** [Chest of drawers] highboy, dresser, chiffonier; see **chest 1, furniture.**

bureaucracy, *n.* the Establishment, the authorities, the system; see **government 1, 2.**

burglar, *n.* thief, housebreaker, robber; see **criminal.**

burglary, *n.* housebreaking, stealing, robbery; see **crime, theft.**

burial, *n.* last rites, interment, obsequies; see **funeral.**

burn, *n.* scorch, wound, impairment; see **blister.**

burn, *v.* ignite, kindle, incinerate, burn up *or* down, blaze, flame, flare, burst into flame, rage, consume, enkindle, cremate, consume with flames, set a match to, set on fire, set ablaze *or* afire, sear, singe, scorch, brand, fire, light, roast, toast, heat, bake; see also **cook.**—*Ant.* **extinguish,** put out, quench.

burned, *a.* scorched, charred, seared, burnt, singed, branded, cauterized, marked, blistered, scalded.

*burned up,** *a.* angered, enraged, infuriated; see **angry.**

burning, *a.* fiery, blazing, glowing, ablaze, afire, on fire, smoking, in flames, aflame, inflamed, kindled, enkindled, ignited, redhot, scorching, turning to ashes, searing, in a blaze, blistering, red-hot, white-hot; see also **passionate 2.** —*Ant.* **cold,** frozen, out.

burnt, *a.* scorched, singed, charred; see **burned.**

burst, *n.* 1. [An explosion] blowout, blast, blowup; see **explosion. 2.** [A sudden spurt] rush, outburst, spate; see **fit 2.**

burst, *v.* 1. [To explode] blow up, erupt, rupture; see **break 2, disintegrate, explode. 2.** [To break] crack, split, fracture; see **break 1, destroy.**

burst into tears, *v.* weep, start crying, break into tears; see **cry 1.**

bury, *v.* 1. [To inter] lay in the grave, entomb, enshrine, deposit in the earth, embalm, hold funeral services for, hold (the) last rites for, lay out. 2. [To cover] conceal, secrete, stow away; see **hide 1. 3.** [To defeat] overcome, win over, beat, conquer; see **defeat 2, 3.**

bus, *n.* autobus, passenger bus, limousine, sightseeing bus, motor coach, common carrier, public conveyance, *Greyhound (trademark).

bus, *v.* transport, ship, redistrict; see **carry.**

bush, *n.* bramble, thicket, hedge, shrubbery, briar bush, rose bush; see also **plant.** —**beat around the bush,** speak indirectly *or* evasively, avoid the subject, be deceptive; see **evade.**

bushy, *a.* fuzzy, disordered, thick, shaggy, rough, full, tufted, fringed, woolly, nappy, fluffy, furry, crinkly, stiff, wiry, rumpled, prickly, feathery, leafy, bristly, heavy.—*Ant.* thin, sleek, smooth.

busily, *a.* diligently, actively, energetically, strenuously, eagerly, earnestly, seriously, intently, rapidly, dexterously, industriously, carefully, intently, studiously, hurriedly, briskly, purposefully, ardently, arduously, fervently, nimbly, zealously, vigorously, restlessly, enthusiastically, speedily, hastily, persistently, *like hell *or* the dickens *or* the devil.—*Ant.* listlessly, idly, **slowly.**

business, *n.* 1. [Industry and trade] commerce, exchange, trade, traffic, barter, commercial enterprise, gainful occupation, buying and selling, negotiation, production and distribution, dealings, affairs, sales, contracts, bargaining, trading, transaction, banking, marketing, undertaking, speculation, market, mercantilism, wholesale and retail, capital and labor, free enterprise, *game, *racket. 2. [Occupation] trade, profession, vocation; see **job** 1. 3. [One's proper concerns] affair, concern, activities; see **affair** 1. 4. [A commercial enterprise] firm, factory, mill, store, company, shop, corporation, concern, combine, conglomerate, cooperative, establishment, enterprise, partnership, institution, house, market, syndicate, cartel, trust, monopoly, holding company. —**do business with,** deal *or* trade with, patronize, employ; see **buy** 1, **sell** 1, **treat** 1. —*get the business,** be mistreated *or* abused, endure, tolerate; see **suffer** 1. —*give the business,** mistreat, bother, victimize; see **abuse.** —*mean business,** be serious, stress, impress; see **emphasize.**

businesslike, *a.* purposeful, methodical, systematic; see **practical** 1.

businessman, *n.* industrialist, capitalist, employer, tycoon, broker, retailer, stockbroker, manager, buyer, operator, backer, financier, systems expert, company man, comptroller, (certified public) accountant, investor, speculator, entrepreneur, purchasing agent, storekeeper, tradesman; see also **executive.**

busy, *a.* 1. [Engaged] occupied, diligent, employed, working, in conference, in a meeting, in the field, in the laboratory, on an assignment, with a customer *or* client *or* patient, etc., on duty, on the job, (hard) at work, busy with, on the move *or* run, on the road, hard-working, *busy as a bee, hustling, *up to one's ears, *(hard) at it, having other fish to fry.—*Ant.* idle, unemployed, unoccupied. 2. [In use] employed, occupied, (already) taken; see **rented.**

busybody, *n.* meddler, tattletale, troublemaker; see **gossip** 2.

but, *conj.* or *prep.* 1. [Indicating contrast] however, on the other hand, in contrast, nevertheless, still, yet, though, on the contrary, but then, but as you see; see also **although.** 2. [Indicating an exception] save, disregarding, without, not including, not taking into account, let alone, aside from, with the exception of, not to mention, passing over, barring, setting aside, forgetting; see also **except.** 3. [Indicating a limitation] only (just), merely, simply, barely, solely, purely, just, no more, exactly, no other than, without; see also **only** 1.

butcher, *v.* 1. [To slaughter for human consumption] stick, pack, dress, clean, cure, smoke, salt, cut, put up. 2. [To kill inhumanly] slaughter, slay, massacre; see **kill** 1. 3. [To ruin] mutilate, spoil, wreck; see **botch, destroy** 1.

butt, *n.* base, tail end, bottom, hilt, extremity, tail, tip, remnant, stump, stub, bottom, seat, posterior; see also **bottom.**

butt, *v.* hit, ram, push headfirst, bump, batter, knock, collide with, run into, smack, strike, gore, buck, toss, crash into.

butter, *n.* Varieties of butter include the following—creamery, sweet, dairy, cube, country, tub, vegetable, soy.

button, *n.* knob, catch, disk; see **fastener.** —*on the button,** correctly, precisely, accurately; see **right** 1.

button, *v.* close, clasp, make firm; see **fasten.**

*buy,** *n.* value, good deal, *steal; see **bargain** 2.

buy, *v.* purchase, get, bargain *or* barter for, procure, gain, contract *or* sign for, get in exchange, go marketing, buy and sell, order, invest in, make an investment, shop for, acquire ownership of, procure title to, pay (cash) for, redeem, pay a price for, buy into, *score.

buyer, *n.* purchasing agent, purchaser, customer, client, prospect, consumer, representative, patron, user, shopper.—*Ant.* **seller,** vendor, dealer.

buying, *n.* purchasing, getting, obtaining, acquiring, paying, investing, exchange, bartering, bargaining, procuring, trafficking. —*Ant.* **selling,** vending, auctioning.

buy off, *v.* corrupt, influence, *fix; see **bribe.**

buzz, *v.* drone, hum, whir; see **sound** 1.

buzzer, *n.* siren, signal, bell, see **alarm, warning, whistle** 1.

by, *prep.* 1. [Near] close *or* next to, by the side of, nigh; see **near** 1, **next** 2. 2. [By stated means] over, with, through, by means of, in the name of, at the hand of, along with, through the medium of, with the assistance *or* aid of, on, supported by.

by–pass, *v.* miss, evade, detour around; see **avoid.**

bystander, *n.* onlooker, watcher, spectator; see **observer.**

by the book, *a.* strictly, according to rule, rigidly; see **legally** 1, **officially** 1.

by the same token, *a.* similarly, likewise, furthermore; see **besides.**

by the way, *a.* casually, incidentally, offhand; see **accidentally.**

C

cab, n. taxi, taxicab, *hack; see automobile, vehicle.

cabin, n. log house, cottage, hut; see home 1, shelter.

cabinet, n. (advisory) council, authority, bureaucracy, committee, bureau, governing body, administrators, assembly, assistants, department heads, (body of) advisors, United States Cabinet, ministry, backstairs cabinet, brain trust; see also government 2.

cable, n. cord, preformed cable, wire twist; see chain, wire 1.

cackle, v. chuckle, snicker, giggle; see laugh.

cactus, n. Cactuses include the following—giant, saguaro, barrel, choya, hedgehog, cochineal, nipple, prickly pear, night-blooming cereus, century plant, mescal; see also plant.

cad, n. rogue, scoundrel, rake; see rascal.

cadence, n. rhythm, meter, flow; see beat 2, measure 3.

cafe, n. cafeteria, lunchroom, coffee shop; see restaurant.

cage, n. coop, jail, crate; see enclosure 1, pen 1.

cake, n. 1. [A flattish, compact mass] cube, bar, loaf; see block 1. 2. [Sweet baked goods] Kinds of cake include the following—wedding, birthday, angel food, devil's-food, corn, sponge, fruit, burnt-sugar, caramel, German chocolate, upside-down, pound, Martha Washington, maple, orange, white lemon, citron, walnut, almond, layer, white mountain, spice, marble, Lady Baltimore, coffeecake, jellyroll, gingerbread, shortbread; see also bread, pastry. —*take the cake, excel, outdo, win the prize; see exceed.

cake, v. crust, solidify, pack; see freeze 1, harden, thicken.

calamity, n. cataclysm, distress, trial; see catastrophe, disaster, misfortune, tragedy 1.

calculate, v. count, measure, reckon, enumerate, totaling, figure (up), account, compute, sum (up), divide, multiply, subtract, add, work out, cipher, tally, *lump off, *dope out; see also estimate.

calculation, n. 1. [The act of calculating] adding, totaling, count; see estimate, guess. 2. [A forecast] prediction, divination, prognostication; see forecast.

calendar, n. list, program, record, timetable, schedule, annals, journal, diary, daybook, chronology, log, logbook, table, register, almanac, agenda, docket; see also almanac.

calf, n. young cow or bull, yearling, maverick; see cow.

California, n. Golden Bear State, Gold Rush State, Golden Poppy State, Bear Flag State, Gold Coast, Sunny California, Cal.

calisthenics, n. exercises, workout, *slimnastics; see exercise 1, gymnastics.

call, n. 1. [A shout] yell, whoop, hail; see alarm, cry 1. 2. [Characteristic sound] twitter, tweet, shriek; see cry 2. 3. [A visit] visiting, a few words, afternoon call; see visit. 4. [Word of command] summons, battle cry, reveille; see alarm, command, cry 1. 5. [An invitation] bidding, solicitation, proposal; see invitation, request. —on call, usable, ready, prepared; see available. —within call, close by, approximate, not far away; see near 1.

call, v. 1. [To raise the voice] shout, call out, exclaim; see yell. 2. [To bring a body of people together] collect, convene, muster; see assemble 2. 3. [To address] denominate, designate, term; see name 1. 4. [To invite] summon, request, ask; see invite.

call a halt to, v. suspend, check, stop; see halt.

call (at, on or upon), v. attend, make a visit, stay with; see visit.

call attention to, v. point out, indicate, note; see remind, warn.

*call down, v. rebuke, chide, admonish; see scold.

called, a. christened, termed, labeled; see named 1.

call for, v. 1. [To ask] inquire or ask for, request, make inquiry about; see ask. 2. [To need] require, want, lack; see need. 3. [To come to get] come or stop (for), collect, fetch; see get 1, pick up 6.

call in, v. 1. [To collect] collect, remove, receive; see withdraw. 2. [To invite] ask for, request, solicit; see beg, summon.

calling, n. occupation, vocation, work; see job 1, profession 1, trade 2.

call names, v. defame, slander, attack; see curse 2, insult.

call off, v. cancel, postpone, cease; see halt, stop 2.

call on, v. stop in, have an appointment with, go to see; see visit 1.

callous, a. unfeeling, hardened, insensitive; see indifferent.

call up, v. 1. [To remember] recollect, recall, summon up; see remember 1,

summon. 2. [To summon] send for, bid, order; see **invite.** 3. [To telephone] phone, call, ring (up); see **telephone.**

calm, *a.* 1. [*Said especially of persons*] dignified, reserved, cool, composed, collected, unmoved, level-headed, cool-headed, impassive, detached, aloof, unconcerned, disinterested, unhurried, neutral, gentle, sedate, serene, unanxious, unexcited, contented, meek, satisfied, pleased, amiable, temperate, placid, civil, kind, moderate, confident, poised, tranquil, self-possessed, restful, relaxed, dispassionate, mild, still, self-controlled, patient, untroubled, cool as a cucumber, *unflappable; see also sense 2, **patient** 1. —*Ant.* violent, excited, furious. 2. [*Said often of things*] quiet, undisturbed, unruffled, comfortable, moderate, in order, soothing, at peace, placid, smooth still, restful, harmonious, peaceful, pacific, balmy, waveless, windless, serene, motionless, slow; see also sense 1, **quiet.**—*Ant.* rough, agitated, aroused.

calm, *n.* 1. [Peace] stillness, peacefulness, quiet; see **peace 2, rest 1, silence 1.** 2. [Composure] serenity, tranquillity, peace of mind; see **composure, patience 1, restraint 1.**

calm, *v.* tranquilize, soothe, pacify; see **quiet 1.**

calm down, *v.* compose *or* control *or* calm *or* restrain oneself, keep oneself under control, keep cool, take it easy, get organized, rest, get hold of oneself, *cool it, cool off *or* down, simmer down, *keep one's shirt on; see also **relax.**

calmly, *a.* quietly, unexcitedly, tranquilly, unconcernedly, serenely, confidently, sedately, collectedly, composedly, placidly, smoothly, restfully, motionlessly, peacefully, naturally, comfortably, unhurried, without anxiety *or* fuss, dully; see also **easily, evenly.**—*Ant.* excitedly, agitatedly, disturbedly.

calmness, *n.* quietness, tranquillity, calm; see **composure, patience 1, peace 2.**

camera, *n.* cinematograph, *kodak. Kinds of cameras include the following—cinecamera, X-ray machine, microcamera, photomicroscope, photostat, spectrograph, motion-picture, television *or* TV, press, movie, flash, still, electron-diffraction, box, stereo, zoom-lens, Polaroid (trademark), single-lens reflex, double-lens reflex, spectroscopic, three-dimensional *or* 3-D, telescopic.

camouflage, *n.* dissimulation, masquerade, simulation, cloak, shade, shroud, veil, blackout, masking, paint, netting, deceit; see also **disguise, screen 1.**

camouflage, *v.* cover, conceal, veil; see **deceive, disguise, hide 1.**

camp, *n.* 1. [A temporary living place] camping ground, campground, campsite, encampment, campfire(s), tents, tent city, wigwams, tepees, wickiups. 2. [Temporary living quarters] tent, lean-to, cottage, tilt, shack, hut, lodge, (log) cabin, chalet, shed, log house, summer home, cottage. —break camp, dismantle, depart, pack up; see **leave 1.**

camp, *v.* bivouac, stop over, make camp, encamp, dwell, nest, locate, pitch camp, pitch a tent, tent, quarter, lodge, sleep out, station, put up for the night, camp out, rough it, sleep under the stars.

campaign, *n.* operations, crusade, warfare; see **attack, fight.**

campaign, *v.* crusade, electioneer, run (for), agitate, contend for, contest, canvass (for), solicit (votes), lobby, barnstorm, mend fences, *go to the grass roots, stump, *beat the bushes, whistle stop; see also **compete.**

campus, *n.* seat of learning, (buildings and) grounds, (physical) plant, faculties, alma mater, quad (British); see also **college, university.**

can, *n.* 1. [A container] tin (can), canister, receptacle, package, jar, bottle, quart can, bucket, gallon can, vessel; see also **container.** 2. [*Jail*] prison, penitentiary, *stir; see **jail.** 3. [*A toilet*] lavatory, restroom, washroom; see **toilet.**

can, *v.* 1. [To preserve] bottle, put up, keep; see **preserve 3.** 2. [To be able] could, may, be capable of *or* equal to *or* up to, lie in one's power, be within one's area *or* control, manage, can do, take care of, make it *or* the grade, make out (to), *cut the mustard, *have it made.

canal, *n.* waterway, trench, ditch; see **channel, water 2.**

cancel, *v.* repudiate, nullify, ignore, invalidate, suppress, countermand, call off, set aside, rule out, refute, rescind, remove, repeal, counteract, recall, retract, abrogate, discharge, (make or render) void, put an end to, abort, offset, revoke, overthrow, scratch, drop; see also **abolish.**—*Ant.* sustain, approve, uphold.

cancellation, *n.* cancelling, annulment, nullification, abrogation, dissolution, invalidation, revocation, repudiation, repeal, abolition, retraction, reversal, voiding, recall, overruling, undoing, withdrawing, abandoning; see also **removal.**

cancer, *n.* growth, tumor, malignancy; see **growth 3, illness 2.**

cancerous, *a.* carcinogenic, virulent, mortal; see **harmful.**

candid, *a.* straightforward, sincere, open; see **frank, honest 1.**

candidate, *n.* aspirant, possible choice, nominee, applicant, political contestant, office-seeker, successor, competitor, bidder, solicitor, petitioner, *job-hunter; see also **contestant.**

candle, *n.* taper, rush, torch; see **light 3.** —**burn the candle at both ends,** dissipate, squander, use up; see **waste 1, 2.** —**not hold a candle to,** unequal to, subordinate, inferior; see **poor 2.**

candlestick, *n.* candelabrum, candelabra, taper holder, flat candlestick, menorah, candleholder.

candy, *n.* confection, confectionery, sweetmeat, bonbon. Varieties of candy include the following—chocolate, maple, coconut, fruit, etc., caramel; sugar, orange, molasses, etc., taffy; chocolate, vanilla, maple, etc., fudge; orange, lemon, walnut, etc., cream; lemon, peppermint, licorice, etc., drop; cotton candy, nougat, peanut brittle, praline, fruit roll, marshmallow, crystallized fruit, coconut bar, Turkish delight, lollipop, halvah, marchpane, gum drop, divinity *or* sea foam, toffee, after-dinner mint, *Life Saver* (trademark), stick, hard, spun-sugar, all-day sucker.

cane, *n.* walking stick, staff, pole; see **stick.**

canned, *a.* bottled, conserved, kept; see **preserved 2.**

cannon, *n.* Types of cannon include the following—self-propelled, muzzle-loading *or* muzzle-loader, breech-loading *or* breechloader, tank destroyer, turret, mountain, siege, coast defense, field, antiaircraft, railway, antitank gun, knee mortar, recoilless rifle, howitzer.

canoe, *n.* kayak, dugout, outrigger; see **boat.**

canon, *n.* decree, rule, order; see **command, declaration, law 3.**

canonize, *v.* saint, sanctify, beatify; see **bless, love 1, worship.**

canopy, *n.* awning, sunshade, umbrella; see **cover 1.**

canteen, *n.* jug, flask, water supply; see **bottle, container.**

canvas, *n.* **1.** [A coarse cloth] tenting, awning cloth, sailcloth, duck, coarse cloth; see also **cloth. 2.** [Anything made of canvas] sail, awning, tarpaulin *or* *tarp; see **cover 1, tent. 3.** [A painting on canvas] portrait, still life, oil; see **art, painting 1.**

canyon, *n.* gulch, gorge, gully; see **ravine, valley.**

cap, *n.* **1.** [Hat] beret, mortarboard, bonnet; see **hat. 2.** [*Capsule] dose, pill, tablet; see **medicine 2.**

capability, *n.* capacity, skill, aptitude; see **ability, inclination 1.**

capable, *a.* proficient, competent, fitted; see **able, intelligent 1.**

capacity, *n.* contents, limit, space, room, size, volume, holding power, extent, compass, magnitude, spread, expanse, scope, latitude, bulk, dimensions, measure, range, quantity, size, reach, holding ability, sweep, proportions, mass, sufficiency.

cape, *n.* **1.** [Land jutting into the water] headland, peninsula, foreland, point, promontory, jetty, head, tongue, point *or* neck of land, ness, mole, finger, arm. **2.** [An overgarment] cloak, wrapper, mantilla, mantle, shawl, wrap, overdress, poncho; see also **coat 1.**

caper, *n.* prank, trick, escapade; see **joke.**

caper, *v.* frolic, gambol, cavort; see **play 1, 2.**

capital, *n.* **1.** [A seat of government] metropolis, principal city, capitol; see **center 2, city. 2.** [Money and property] cash, assets, interests; see **estate, property 1, wealth. 3.** [A letter usually used initially] initial, upper case, majuscule; see **letter 1.**

capitalism, *n.* capitalistic system, free enterprise, private ownership *or* possessions; see **democracy, economics, government 2.**

capitalist, *n.* entrepreneur, investor, landowner; see **banker, businessman, financier.**

capitol, *n.* statehouse, state capitol, seat of government; see **center 2.**

capsize, *v.* overturn, invert, tip over; see **upset 1.**

caption, *n.* inscription, title, subtitle; see **heading.**

captive, *a.* restrained, incarcerated, jailed; see **bound 1, 2, restricted.**

captive, *n.* hostage, convict, *con; see **prisoner.**

captivity, *n.* imprisonment, jail, restraint, slavery, bondage, subjection, servitude, duress, detention, incarceration, enslavement, constraint, the guardhouse, custody; see also **confinement.**—*Ant.* liberty, freedom, independence.

capture, *n.* capturing, arrest, recovery, seizing, taking, seizure, acquisition, obtaining, securing, gaining, winning, occupation, appropriation, ensnaring, abduction, laying hold of, grasping, catching, trapping, commandeering, apprehending, confiscation, taking into custody *or* captivity, apprehension, fall.—*Ant.* liberation, freeing, setting free.

capture, *v.* seize, take, apprehend; see **arrest 1, seize 2.**

captured, *a.* taken, seized, arrested, apprehended, detained, grasped, overtaken, grabbed, snatched, kidnapped, abducted, netted, hooked, secured, *collared, *nabbed, bagged; see also **under arrest.**—*Ant.* released, unbound, loosed.

car, *n.* auto, motor (car), automotive vehicle; see **automobile, vehicle.** Types of cars include the following—passenger car, limousine, sedan, hardtop, compact, sportscar, convertible, town car, ranch wagon, station wagon, taxicab, squad car, prowl car, staff car, bus, truck, jeep, dune buggy.

carcase, *n.* corpse, cadaver, remains; see **body 2.**

card, *n.* cardboard, ticket, sheet, square, Bristol board, fiberboard. Varieties of cards include the following—poster, window card, show card, ticket, fortune-telling *or* tarot cards, label, badge, tally, check, billet, voucher, pass; calling, playing, address, visiting, credit, greeting, registration *or* filing, recipe, index, check-cashing, police, social security, identification *or* I.D. card; see also **paper 1.** —**in** *or* **on the cards,** probable, predicted, possible; see **likely 1.** —**put** *or* **lay one's cards on the table,** reveal, tell the truth, expose; see **admit 2.**

care, *n.* **1.** [Careful conduct] heed, concern, caution, consideration, regard, thoughtfulness, forethought, attention, precaution, wariness, vigilance, watchfulness, watching, diligence, nicety, pains, application, conscientiousness, thought, discrimination, exactness, exactitude, watch, concentration; see also **attention, prudence.**—*Ant.* carelessness, neglect, negligence. **2.** [Worry] concern, anxiety, distress; see **worry 2. 3.** [Custody] supervision, administration, keeping; see **custody. 4.** [A cause of worry] problem, care, concern; see **disaster, misfortune.** —**have a care** *or* **take care,** be careful *or* cautious, beware, heed; see **mind 3, watch out.** —**take care of,** protect, attend to, be responsible for; see **guard.**

care, *v.* **1.** [To be concerned] attend, take pains, regard; see **consider. 2.** [To be careful] look out for, be on guard, watch out; see **mind 3.**

care about, *v.* cherish, be fond of, hold dear; see **like 2, love 1.**

career, *n.* occupation, vocation, work; see **job 1, profession 1.**

care for, *v.* **1.** [To look after] provide for, attend to, nurse; see **raise 2, support 5. 2.** [To like] be fond of, hold dear, prize; see **like 2, love 1.**

carefree, *a.* lighthearted, cheerful, jovial; see **happy 1, calm 1.**

careful, *a.* thorough, concerned, deliberate, conservative, prudent, meticulous, particular, rigorous, fussy, finicky, prim, exacting, wary, sober, vigilant, watchful, suspicious, alert, wide-awake, scrupulous,

religious, hard to please, discriminating, sure-footed, precise, painstaking, exact, on one's guard, on the alert, conscientious, attentive, calculating, mindful, cautious, guarded, considerate, shy, circumspect, discreet, noncommittal, self-possessed, self-disciplined, solid, cool, calm, farsighted, frugal, thrifty, stealthy, observant, on guard, apprehensive, leery, choosy, *picky, feeling one's way *or* ground, seeing how the land lies, going to great lengths.—*Ant.* heedless, careless, haphazard.

carefully, *a.* **1.** [Scrupulously] conscientiously, exactly, rigidly, correctly, strictly, precisely, minutely, painstakingly, faithfully, honorably, attentively, rigorously, providently, deliberately, reliably, particularly, solicitously, concernedly, meticulously, laboriously, thoroughly, dependably, in detail.—*Ant.* neglectfully, **haphazardly,** indifferently. **2.** [Cautiously] prudently, discreetly, watchfully; see **cautiously.**

careless, *a.* loose, lax, remiss, unguarded, incautious, forgetful, unthinking, unobservant, reckless, unheeding, indiscreet, inadvertent, unconcerned, wasteful, regardless, imprudent, unconsidered, hasty, inconsiderate, heedless, mindless, untroubled, negligent, neglectful, thoughtless, indifferent, casual, not seeing the forest for the trees, oblivious, absent-minded, listless, abstracted, nonchalant, undiscerning, offhand, slack, blundering; see also **rash.**—*Ant.* attentive, **thoughtful,** careful.

carelessly, *a.* heedlessly, negligently, neglectfully, thoughtlessly, nonchalantly, offhandedly, rashly, unconcernedly; at random, happen what may, incautiously, improvidently, wastefully, without caution *or* care, without concern, with no attention, *like crazy.

carelessness, *n.* unconcern, nonchalance, heedlessness, rashness, omission, slackness, delinquency, indolence, procrastination, dereliction, neglect, negligence, disregard, imprudence, haphazardness; see also **indifference.**—*Ant.* care, consideration, caution.

caress, *n.* embrace, stroke, *feel; see **hug, kiss, touch 2.**

caress, *v.* embrace, cuddle, pat; see **love 2, touch 1.**

caretaker, *n.* porter, keeper, janitor; see **custodian, watchman.**

care to, *v.* prefer, desire, wish; see **like 1, want 1.**

cargo, *n.* shipload, baggage, lading; see **freight 1, load 1.**

carnal, *a.* fleshly, bodily, sensuous; see **lewd 2, sensual 2.**

carnival, *n.* side show, circus, fair; see **entertainment, show 1.**

carol, *n.* hymn, Christmas song, ballad; see **song.**

carpenter, *n.* mason, craftsman, builder; see **laborer, workman.**

carpet, *n.* wall-to-wall carpet, (indoor *or* outdoor) carpeting, linoleum, floor covering, matting; see also **rug.** —(called) **on the carpet,** reprimanded, censured, interrogated; see **in trouble 1.**

carriage, *n.* 1. [The manner of carrying the body] walk, pace, step, attitude, aspect, presence, look, cast, gait, bearing, posture, pose, demeanor, poise, air; see also **behavior.** 2. [A horse-drawn passenger vehicle] buggy, surrey, coach, coach-and-four, buckboard, cart, dogcart, two-wheeler, trap, gig, sulky, hansom, coupe, four-wheeler, stagecoach, chariot, hack, hackney coach; see also **wagon.**

carrier, *n.* aircraft carrier, escort carrier, *flattop; see **ship.**

carry, *v.* 1. [To transport] convey, move, transplant, transfer, cart, import, transmit, freight, remove, conduct, bear, take, bring, shift, haul, change, convoy, relocate, relay, lug, tote, fetch; see also **send 1.** 2. [To transmit] pass on, transfer, relay; see **send 1.** 3. [To support weight] bear, sustain, shoulder; see **support 1.** 4. [To give support] corroborate, back up, confirm; see **approve, support 2, strengthen.** —**be** *or* **get carried away,** zealous, aroused, exuberant; see **excited.**

carry on, *v.* 1. [To continue] keep going, proceed, persist; see **achieve, continue 1, 2, endure 1.** 2. [To manage] conduct, engage in, administer; see **manage 1.** 3. [To behave badly] blunder, be indecorous, *raise Cain; see **misbehave.**

carry (oneself), *v.* appear, seem, behave; see **act 2, walk 1.**

carry out, *v.* complete, accomplish, fulfill; see **achieve, complete, succeed 1.**

carry over, *n.* holdover, vestige, remains; see **remainder.**

carry over, *v.* continue, persist, survive; see **endure 1.**

carry (something) off, do, triumph, accomplish, handle, take care of, make it *or* good; see **achieve, succeed 1.**

cart, *n.* truck, wheelbarrow, (little) wagon, tip cart, handcart, gig, dray, two-wheeler, pushcart, gocart, two-wheeled cart; see also **carriage 2, wagon.** —**put the cart before the horse,** reverse, be illogical, err; see **mistake.**

cartoon, *n.* caricature, parody, joke; see **ridicule.**

carve, *v.* create, form, hew, chisel, engrave, etch, sculpture, incise, mold, fashion, cut, shape, model, tool, block out,

scrape, pattern, trim; see also **cut 1, engrave.**

carved, *a.* incised, graven, cut, chiseled, chased, furrowed, formed, hewn, hewed, etched, sculptured, scratched, slashed, done in relief, scrolled, grooved, sliced, scissored; see also **engraved.**—*Ant.* **plain,** cast, molded.

case, *n.* 1. [An example] instance, illustration, sample; see **example 1.** 2. [Actual conditions] incident, occurrence, fact; see **circumstance 1, event, fact 2, state 2.** 3. [A legal action] suit, litigation, lawsuit; see **trial 2.** 4. [An organized argument] argument, petition, evidence; see **claim, proof 1.** 5. [A container or its contents] carton, canister, crate, crating, box, baggage, trunk, casing, chest, drawer, holder, tray, receptacle, coffer, crib, chamber, bin, bag, grip, cabinet, sheath, scabbard, wallet, safe, basket, casket; see also **container.** —**in any case,** in any event, anyway, however; see **anyhow 1.** —**in case (of),** in the event that, provided that, supposing; see **if.**

cash, *n.* money in hand, ready money *or* assets, currency, legal tender, principal, available means, working assets, funds, payment, capital, finances, stock, resources, wherewithal, investments, savings, riches, reserve, treasure, moneys, security; see also **money 1, wealth.**

cash, *v.* cash in, change, draw; see also **pay 1.**

cashier, *n.* purser, treasurer, receiver; see **clerk.**

cash in, *v.* realize, change, exchange, turn into money, discharge, draw, pay.

cash on delivery, *a.* cash *or* money down, collect, C.O.D.; see **paid.**

cast, *n.* 1. [A plaster reproduction] facsimile, duplicate, replica; see **copy, sculpture.** 2. [Those in a play] persons in the play, list of characters, players, roles, parts, dramatis personae, company, troupe, producers, dramatic artists. 3. [Aspect] complexion, face, appearance; see **looks.** 4. [A surgical dressing] plaster-of-Paris dressing, plaster cast, arm cast, leg cast, knee cast, body cast, splint(s); see also **dressing 3.** 5. [A tinge] hue, shade, tint; see **color 1.**

cast, *v.* 1. [To throw] pitch, fling, hurl; see **throw 1.** 2. [To form in a mold] shape, roughcast, wetcast; see also **form 1.** 3. [To select actors for a play] appoint, designate, decide upon, determine, pick, give parts, detail, name; see also **assign, choose.**

cast away, *v.* dispose of, reject, throw out; see **abandon 1.**

castle, *n.* stronghold, manor, seat, villa, fortress, château, citadel, keep, fort, hold, safehold; see also **fortification.**

cast off, *v.* reject, jettison, throw away; see **abandon 1**.

cast out, *v.* evict, ostracize, expel; see **banish, eject**.

castrate, *v.* emasculate, sterilize, asexualize, mutilate, cut, spay, geld, unman, steer, caponize, effeminize, deprive of virility *or* manhood; see also **maim**.

casual, *a.* 1. [Accidental] chance, unexpected, unplanned; see **spontaneous 2**. 2. [Nonchalant] blasé, apathetic, unconcerned; see **careless, indifferent**.

casually, *a.* 1. [Accidentally] unintentionally, by chance, inadvertently; see **accidentally**. 2. [Nonchalantly] indifferently, coolly, unemotionally; see **carelessly, easily**.

casualty, *n.* fatalities, losses, death toll; see **loss 3**.

cat, *n.* 1. [A domestic animal] tom(cat), kitten, kit, tabby, puss, pussy, mouser, kitty. House cats include the following—Maltese, Persian, Siamese, Manx, Burmese, Angora, tortoise shell, alley, tiger, calico; see also **animal**. 2. [A member of the cat family] lion, tiger, leopard, puma, wildcat, cheetah, lynx, bobcat, mountain lion, ocelot, cougar, jaguar; see also **animal**. —**let the cat out of the bag**, expose, tell a secret, let slip; see **reveal**.

catalogue, *n.* register, file, directory, schedule, inventory, index, bulletin, syllabus, brief, slate, table, calendar, list, docket, classification, record, draft, roll, timetable, table of contents, prospectus, program, rent roll; see also **list**.

catastrophe, *n.* calamity, mishap, mischance, misadventure, misery, accident, trouble, casualty, infliction, affliction, stroke, havoc, ravage, wreck, fatality, grief, crash, devastation, desolation, hardship, blow, ruin, reverse, emergency, scourge, convulsion, tragedy, adversity, bad luck, upheaval, down; see also **disaster**.

*****catch,** *n.* 1. [A likely mate] boyfriend, sweetheart, fiancé; see also **lover 1**. 2. [Something stolen] capture, grab, *haul; see **booty**. 3. [A trick] puzzle, trick, trap; see **joke**. 4. [A hook] clasp, clamp, snap; see **fastener**.

catch, *v.* 1. [To seize hold of] snatch, take, take hold (of), snag, grab, pick, pounce on, fasten upon, snare, pluck, hook, claw, clench, clasp, grasp, clutch, grip, nab, net, *bag; see also **seize**. 2. [To bring into captivity] trap, apprehend, capture; see **arrest, seize 2**. 3. [To come to from behind] overtake, reach, come upon; see **pass 1**. 4. [To contract a disease] get, fall ill (with), become infected (with), incur, become subject *or* liable to, fall victim to, take, succumb to, break out (with), receive,

come down with.—*Ant.* ward off, escape, get over.

catching, *a.* contagious, communicable, infectious, epidemic, endemic, pestilential, noxious, dangerous, pandemic; see also **contagious**.

catch on, *v.* 1. [To understand] grasp, comprehend, perceive; see **understand 1**. 2. [To become popular] become fashionable *or* prevalent *or* common *or* widespread *or* acceptable, grow in popularity, find favor; see **succeed 1**.

catch (on) fire, *v.* inflame, ignite, burst into flame; see **burn**.

catch one's breath, *v.* rest, wait, stop; see **hesitate, pause**.

catch the eye, *v.* attract notice, engage attention, interest; see **fascinate**.

catch up, *v.* catch, join, equal; see **reach 1**.

catch up with *or* **to,** *v.* overtake, join, overcome; see **reach 1**.

category, *n.* level, section, classification; see **class 1, division 2, kind 2**.

cathedral, *n.* temple, house of God, house of prayer, Holy place, basilica; see also **church 1**. Parts of a cathedral include the following—altar, sanctuary, holy of holies, sacristy, sacrarium, holy table, baptistery, chancel, apse, choir, nave, aisle, transept, crypt, pew, seat, pulpit, confessional. Famous cathedrals include the following—St. Peter's, Rome; St. Paul's, London; Notre Dame, Paris; St. John the Divine, New York; St. Patrick's, New York. Famous cathedrals are also at; Rouen, Beauvais, Rheims, Milan, Pisa, Florence, Cologne, Canterbury, Lincoln, Wells, Nidaros, Madrid, Mexico City.

cattle, *n.* stock, cows, steers, calves, herd, beef cattle, dairy cattle; see also **cow**.

caught, *a.* taken, seized, arrested; see **captured, under arrest**.

cause, *n.* 1. [Purpose] motive, causation, object, purpose, explanation, inducement, incitement, prime mover, motive power, mainspring, ultimate cause, ground, matter, element, stimulation, instigation, foundation, (the why and) wherefore; see also **basis, reason 3**. —*Ant.* effect, result, outcome. 2. [Moving force] agent, case, condition; see **circumstances**. 3. [A belief] principles, conviction, creed; see **belief, faith 2**.

cause, *v.* originate, provoke, generate, occasion, let, kindle, give rise to, lie at the root of, be at the bottom of, bring to pass *or* to effect, sow the seeds of; see also **begin**.

caution, *n.* care, heed, discretion; see **attention, prudence**.

cautious, *a.* circumspect, watchful, wary; see **careful**.

cautiously, *a.* tentatively, prudently, discreetly, watchfully, wisely, sparingly, thoughtfully, heedfully, delicately, mindfully, anxiously, with care or caution, gingerly, with forethought, slowly.

cave, *n.* rock shelter, cavern, grotto; see **hole.**

cavern, *n.* cave, hollow, grotto; see **hole.**

cavity, *n.* 1. [Sunken area] pit, depression, basin; see **hole.** 2. [Hollow place in a tooth] dental caries, distal pit, gingival pit; see **decay.**

cease, *v.* desist, terminate, discontinue; see **halt, stop** 1, 2.

ceaseless, *a.* continual, endless, unending; see **constant, eternal.**

celebrate, *v.* 1. [To recognize an occasion] keep, observe, consecrate, hallow, dedicate, commemorate, honor, proclaim, ritualize.—*Ant.* forget, overlook, neglect. 2. [To indulge in celebration] feast, give a party, carouse, rejoice, kill the fatted calf, revel, go on a spree, *make whoopee, *blow or let off steam, have a party or a ball, *kick up one's heels, *let loose or go, *live or whoop it up, make merry, *kick up a row, *beat the drum.

celebrated, *a.* well-known, renowned, noted; see **famous, important** 2.

celebration, *n.* commemoration, holiday, anniversary, jubilee, inauguration, installation, coronation, presentation, carnival, revelry, spree, festivity, festival, feast, merrymaking, gaiety, frolic, hilarity, joviality, merriment, remembrance, ceremonial, keeping, observance, fete, Mardi Gras, birthday.

celebrity, *n.* famous man or woman, hero, heroine, leader, notable, magnate, dignitary, worthy, figure, personage, famous person, man of note, someone, somebody, *VIP, luminary, lion, lioness, star, *bigwig, *big gun, *big shot, ace.

cell, *n.* 1. [A unit of a living organism] corpuscle, cellule, micro-organism, vacuole, spore, plastid, organism, egg, ectoplasm, embryo, germ, follicle. 2. [A room] vault, hold, pen, cage, tower, hole, coop, keep, bastille, chamber, den, recess, retreat, alcove, manger, crypt, crib, nook, burrow, stall, closet, booth, cloister, compartment, lockup; see also **room** 2.

cellar, *n.* half basement, underground room, basement apartment; see **basement.**

cement, *n.* glue, putty, tar, gum, mortar, paste, adhesive, rubber cement, epoxy (resin), bond, *mud.

cement, *v.* mortar, plaster, connect; see **fasten, join** 1.

cemetery, *n.* burial ground, memorial park, funerary grounds, churchyard, necropolis, potter's field, catacomb, city of the dead, tomb, vault, crypt, charnel house, sepulcher, graveyard, mortuary, (last) resting place, Golgotha, *boneyard.

censor, *v.* control, restrict, strike out, forbid, suppress, ban, withhold, enforce censorship, control the flow of news, inspect, oversee, abridge, expurgate, review, criticize, exert pressure, conceal, prevent publication, blacklist, throttle the press, debase freedom of speech, blue pencil, cut, black out; see also **restrict.**

censorship, *n.* licensing, restriction, forbidding, controlling the press, infringing the right of freedom of speech or press, governmental control, security blackout, news blackout, thought control, iron curtain; see also **restraint.**

censure, *n.* criticism, reproof, admonition; see **blame, objection.**

censure, *v.* 1. [To blame] criticize, judge, disapprove; see **blame.** 2. [To scold] rebuke, reprove, attack; see **scold.**

census, *n.* statistics, enumeration, valuation, account, registration, listing, evaluation, demography, figures, statement, numbering, registering, roll (call), tabulation, tally, poll, count, counting, nose count; see also **count.**

cent, *n.* penny, Indian penny, 100th part of a dollar; see **money** 1.

center, *a.* mid, middle, inmost, inner, midway, medial, deepest, at the inmost, innermost, internal, interior, at the halfway point; see also **middle.**—*Ant.* outer, **outside,** exterior.

center, *n.* 1. [A central point] point, middle, focus, nucleus, core, place, heart, hub, navel, point of convergence or concentration, focal point, midst, middle point, centrality, marrow, centriole, kernel, bull's eye, pivot, axis, pith, dead center; see also **middle.** 2. [A point that attracts people] city, town, metropolis, plaza, capital, shopping or trading center, station, hub, mart, market, crossroads, mall, social center, meeting place, club, market place. 3. [Essence] core, gist, kernel; see **character** 1.

center, *v.* concentrate, centralize, focus, intensify, unify, unite, combine, converge upon, join, meet, gather, close on, consolidate, bring to a focus, center round or in, gather or flock together, collect, draw or bring together, focus attention, attract; see also **meet** 1. —*Ant.* decentralize, **spread,** branch off.

central, *a.* middle, midway, equidistant, medial, focal, nuclear, midmost, mean, inner, median, inmost, middlemost, intermediate, interior, in the center of; see also **middle.**—*Ant.* peripheral, **outer,** verging on.

centrally, *a.* in the middle, focal, middlemost, in the center, in the heart of; see also **central.**

century, n. 100 years, centenary, era; see **age 3, time 1.**

ceramics, n. earthenware, crockery, porcelain; see **pottery, sculpture.**

cereal, n. corn, breakfast food, seed; see **grain 1.**

ceremonial, a. ritual, formal, stately; see **conventional 3.**

ceremony, n. 1. [A public event] function, commemoration, services; see **celebration 1, 2.** 2. [A rite] observance, ritual, rite, service, solemnity, formality, custom, tradition, liturgy, ordinance, sacrament, liturgical practice, conformity, etiquette, politeness, decorum, propriety, preciseness, strictness, nicety, formalism, conventionality.

certain, a. 1. [Confident] calm, assured, sure, positive, satisfied, self-confident, undoubting, believing, secure, untroubled, unconcerned, undisturbed, unperturbed, (fully) convinced, assertive, cocksure; see also **confident.** 2. [Beyond doubt] indisputable, unquestionable, assured, positive, real, true, genuine, plain, clear, undoubted, guaranteed, unmistakable, sure, incontrovertible, undeniable, definite, supreme, unqualified, infallible, undisputed, unerring, sound, reliable, trustworthy, evident, conclusive, authoritative, irrefutable, unconditional, incontestable, unerring, unquestioned, absolute, unequivocal, inescapable, conclusive, *in the bag, *on ice, *done up, *salted away; see also **true 1, 3.** 3. [Fixed] settled, concluded, set; see **definite 1, determined 1.** 4. [Specific but not named] special, definite, individual, marked, specified, defined, one, some, a few, a couple, several, upwards of, regular, particular, singular, precise, specific, express; see also **some 1.** —**for certain,** without doubt, absolutely, certainly; see **surely.**

certainly, a. positively, absolutely, unquestionably; see **surely.**

certificate, n. declaration, warrant, voucher, testimonial, credential(s), license, testament, endorsement, affidavit, certification, coupon, document, pass, ticket, warranty, guarantee, testimony, receipt, affirmation, docket, record; see also **record 1.**

certify, v. swear, attest, state; see **declare, testify 2.**

chain, n. 1. [A series of links] series, train, set, string, connection, cable, link, (charm) bracelet, ring series, shackle, manacle; see also **series.** 2. [A sequence] succession, progression, continuity; see **series.**

chain, v. connect, attach, secure; see **fasten, hold 1.**

chair, n. 1. [A single seat] seat, place, room, space, cathedra; see also **furniture.** Chairs include the following—stool,

throne, footstool, rocker, wing chair, armchair, easy chair, wheel chair, highchair; occasional, dining-room, desk, kitchen, deck, lawn, swivel, folding chair. 2. [A position of authority] throne, professorship, fellowship; see **influence.**

chairman, n. president, administrator, director, toastmaster, speaker, moderator, monitor, leader, principal, captain, master of ceremonies *or* M.C. *or* emcee; see also **leader 2.**

chalk up, v. credit, enter, register; see **add 1, record 1, score 1.**

challenge, n. dare, provocation, threat; see **objection.**

challenge, v. 1. [To invite to a contest] defy, denounce, invite competition; see **dare 2, threaten.** 2. [To question] dispute, inquire, search out; see **ask, doubt, question.**

champion, n. vanquisher, conqueror, victor; see **hero 1, winner.**

chance, a. accidental, unplanned, unintentional; see **aimless, incidental 2.**

chance, n. 1. [The powers of uncertainty] fate, fortune, hazard, casualty, lot, accident, luck, good luck, bad luck, destiny, outcome, cast, lottery, gamble, adventure, contingency, happening, future, doom, destination, occurrence, *Lady Luck, turn of the cards, *heads or tails.—*Ant.* aim, **purpose,** design. 2. [A possibility] opening, occasion, prospect; see **opportunity 1, possibility 2.** 3. [Probability; *often plural*] likelihood, feasibility, indications; see **odds.** —**by chance,** by accident, as it happens, unexpectedly; see **accidentally.** —**on the off chance,** in case, in the event that, supposing; see **if.**

chance, v. venture, stake, hazard, wager, jeopardize, speculate, tempt fate *or* fortune, play with fire, take a shot *or* leap in the dark, buy a pig in a poke, *go out on a limb, chance it, have *or* take a fling at, put all one's eggs in one basket, skate on thin ice, run the risk; see also **risk.**

change, n. 1. [An alteration] modification, correction, remodeling, switch, reformation, reconstruction, shift, reform, conversion, transformation, revolution, rearrangement, adjustment, readjustment, reorganization, reshaping, renovation, realignment, redirection, reprogramming, variation, addition, refinement, advance, development, diversification, turn, turnover, enlargement, revision, qualification, distortion, compression, contraction, widening, narrowing, lengthening, flattening, shortening, fitting, setting, adjusting, rounding, gone every which way, ups and downs. 2. [Substitution] switch, replacement, exchange; see **shift 1.** 3. [Variety] diversity, novelty, variance; see **difference 1, variety 1. 4.** [Small coins] silver, coins, *chicken feed; see **money 1.**

change, v. **1.** [To make different] vary, turn, alternate; see **alter 1. 2.** [To become different] alter, vary, modify, evolve, be converted, turn into or from, resolve into, grow, ripen, mellow, mature, transform, reform, moderate, adapt, adjust; see also **become. 3.** [To put in place of another] displace, supplant, transpose; see **exchange 1, replace 1, substitute 2. 4.** [To change clothing] undress, disrobe, make one's toilet; see **dress 1.**

changeable, a. **1.** [Said of persons] fickle, flighty, unreliable; see **unstable 2. 2.** [Said of conditions] variable, unsteady, unsettled; see **uncertain 2.**

changed, a. **1.** [Exchanged] substituted, replaced, traded; see **returned. 2.** [Altered] qualified, reconditioned, modified, limited, reformed, shifted, moved, mutated, deteriorated, aged, run down, rewritten, conditioned, modernized, remodeled, reprogrammed, rescheduled, redone, done over, brought up or down to date, edited, moderated, innovated, deviated, diverted, fluctuated, chopped, warped, passed to, recreated, converted, transfigured, metamorphosed, transmuted.—Ant. **unchanged,** final, **permanent.**

changeless, a. permanent, unchanging, enduring; see **constant, regular 3.**

change one's mind, v. decide against, alter one's convictions, modify one's ideas; see also **alter 1, choose.**

changing, a. changeful, changeable, mobile, dynamic, alternative, unstable, inconstant, uncertain, mutable, fluid, mercurial, declining, deteriorating, unsteady, irresolute, degenerating, wavering; see also **uncertain 2.**—Ant. stable, fixed, unchanging.

channel, n. conduit, tube, canal, duct, course, gutter, furrow, trough, runway, tunnel, strait, sound, race, sewer, main, artery, vein, ditch, aqueduct, canyon; see also **way 2.**

chant, n. religious song, chorus, incantation; see **song.**

chant, v. intone, chorus, carol; see **sing.**

chaos, n. turmoil, anarchy, discord; see **confusion, disorder 2.**

chaotic, a. disorganized, disordered, uncontrolled; see **confused 2.**

chapel, n. place of worship, tabernacle, God's house; see **church 1.**

chapter, n. part, section, book; see **division 2.**

character, n. **1.** [The dominant quality] temper, temperament, attitude, nature, sense, complex, mood, streak, attribute, badge, tone, style, aspect, complexion,

spirit, genius, humor, frame, grain, vein; see also **characteristic. 2.** [The sum of a person's characteristics] personality, reputation, constitution, repute, individuality, estimation, record, caliber, standing, type, shape, quality, habit, appearance; see also **kind 3. 3.** [A symbol, especially in writing] sign, figure, emblem; see **letter 1, mark 1. 4.** [A queer or striking person] personality, figure, personage, original, eccentric, *crank, *nut, *oddball, *weirdo, *freak, *psycho. **–in character,** consistent, usual, predictable; see **conventional 1. –out of character,** inconsistent, unpredictable, unusual, see **unexpected.**

characteristic, a. innate, fixed, essential, distinctive, distinguishing, marked, discriminative, symbolic, individualizing, representative, specific, personal, original, peculiar, individualistic, individual, idiosyncratic, unique, special, particular, symptomatic, private, exclusive, inherent, inborn, inbred, ingrained, native, indicative, inseparable, in the blood; see also **natural 2, typical.**—Ant. erratic, **irregular,** aberrant.

characteristic, n. flavor, attribute, quality, faculty, peculiarity, individuality, style, aspect, tone, tinge, feature, distinction, manner, bearing, inclination, nature, personality, temperament, frame, originality, singularity, qualification, virtue, mark, essence, caliber, complexion, particularity, idiosyncrasy, trick, earmark, mannerism, trademark, badge, symptom, disposition, specialty, mood, character, bent, tendency, component, thing, *bag.

characterize, v. delineate, designate, portray; see **define 2, describe.**

charge, n. **1.** [A charged sale] entry, debit, credit; see **price. 2.** [An attack] assault, invasion, outbreak; see **attack. –in charge (of),** responsible (for), controlling, managing; see **responsible 1.**

charge, v. **1.** [To ask a price] require, sell for, fix the price at; see **price. 2.** [To enter on a charge account] debit, put to account, charge to, run up an account, take on account, put on one's account, incur a debt, put down, credit, encumber, sell or buy on credit, chalk up, put on the books, carry, put on the cuff; see also **buy, sell. 3.** [To attack] assail, assault, invade; see **attack 4.** **4.** [To accuse] indict, censure, impute; see **blame.**

charged, a. **1.** [Bought but not paid for] debited, placed on the account of, unpaid, on credit or account, on time, owing, owed, *on the cuff, *on the tab; see also **bought, due. 2.** [Accused] taxed, confronted with, arraigned; see **accused.**

charitable, *a.* open-handed, liberal, philanthropic; see **generous, kind.**

charity, *n.* 1. [Kindness] benevolence, magnanimity, compassion; see **kindness 1, tolerance 1.** 2. [An organization to aid the needy] charitable institution, eleemosynary corporation *or* foundation; see **foundation 3.**

charm, *n.* 1. [An object thought to possess power] amulet, talisman, fetish, mascot, good-luck piece, lucky piece, rabbit's foot. 2. [The quality of being charming] grace, attractiveness, attraction; see **beauty 1.**

charm, *v.* enchant, captivate, voodoo, possess, enrapture, enthrall, transport, delight, please, entrance, bewitch, mesmerize; see also **fascinate.**

charmed, *a.* enchanted, bewitched, enraptured, entranced, captivated, attracted, lured, tempted, enticed, bedazzled, hypnotized, mesmerized, under a spell, in a trance, spellbound, moonstruck, possessed, obsessed, *psyched, *out of it; see also **fascinated.**

charming, *a.* enchanting, bewitching, entrancing, captivating, cute, fascinating, delightful, lovable, sweet, winning, irresistible, attractive, amiable, appealing, alluring, charismatic, pleasing, nice, graceful, winsome, seducing, seductive, desirable, enticing, tempting, inviting, ravishing, enrapturing, glamorous, elegant, infatuating, dainty, delicate, absorbing, tantalizing, engrossing, titillating, engaging, enthralling, rapturous, electrifying, lovely, intriguing, thrilling, fair, exquisite, likable, diverting, fetching, provocative, delectable, *sexy, sharp, *smooth.—*Ant.* disgusting, offensive, unpleasant.

chart, *n.* graph, outline, diagram; see **map, plan 1.**

chart, *v.* map, outline, draft; see **plan 2.**

charter, *n.* contract, settlement, pact; see **agreement 3, treaty.**

chase, *v.* trail, track, seek; see **hunt 1, pursue 1.**

chaste, *a.* immaculate, unstained, clean, innocent, virginal, unblemished, unsullied, moral, modest, proper, decent, uncontaminated, virgin, celibate, platonic, controlled, unmarried, unwed, spotless, infallible, strong; see also **innocent 2.**—*Ant.* corruptible, **weak, frail.**

chastise, *v.* scold, discipline, spank; see **punish.**

chastity, *n.* innocence, purity, virtue, uprightness, honor, celibacy, integrity, decency, devotion, delicacy, cleanness, goodness, bachelorhood, unmarried state, demureness, abstinence, morality, chasteness, modesty, sinlessness, continence, coldness, restraint, virginity, spotlessness.—*Ant.* adultery, **lewdness,** licentiousness.

chat, *v.* converse, prattle, chatter; see **talk 1.**

chatter, *v.* gossip, chat, prattle; see **babble.**

cheap, *a.* 1. [Low in relative price] inexpensive, low-priced, moderate, family-size, economy-size, budget, utility (grade), depreciated, slashed, cut-rate, on sale, competitive, lowered, thrifty, bargain, irregular, reduced, cut-priced, low-cost, at a bargain, reasonable, marked down, half-priced, popular-priced, worth the money, *dime-a-dozen, *dirt-cheap, *peanuts, for a song, second, bargain-basement; see also **economical 2.**—*Ant.* expensive, dear, costly. 2. [Low in quality] inferior, ordinary, shoddy; see **common 1, poor 2.** 3. [Dishonest or base] dirty, tawdry, low; see **dishonest, mean 3,** vulgar.

cheapen, *v.* spoil, depreciate, demean; see **corrupt, damage.**

cheaply, *a.* economically, inexpensively, advantageously, at a bargain *or* a good *or* fair price, on sale, at cost, below cost, discounted, at a discount, reduced, at a reduced price, sacrificed, *dirt cheap, *given away, *stolen.

cheat, *n.* rogue, cheater, confidence man, quack, charlatan, conniver, fraud, swindler, chiseler, beguiler, fake, bluff, deceiver, inveigler, hypocrite, trickster, pretender, dodger, humbug, crook, wolf in sheep's clothing, *con man, *shark, *fourflusher, *shill; see also **criminal.**

cheat, *v.* defraud, swindle, beguile; see **deceive.**

cheated, *a.* defrauded, swindled, deprived of, tricked, imposed upon, victimized, beguiled, trapped, foiled, lured, *taken in, bamboozled, hoodwinked; see also **deceived.**

cheating, *n.* lying, defrauding, deceiving; see **deception, dishonesty.**

check, *n.* 1. [An order on a bank] money order, letter of credit, traveler's check, bank *or* teller's *or* cashier's check, counter check, note, remittance, deposition; see also **money 1.** 2. [A control] poll, roll call, rein; see **restraint 2.** 3. [An examination] investigation, analysis, inquiry; see **examination 1, 3. 4.** [The symbol √] cross, ex, sign, line, stroke, score, dot; see also **mark 1. 5.** [A pattern in squares] patchwork, checkered design, checkerboard; see **design. —in check,** controlled, under control, checked; see **held.**

check, *v.* 1. [To bring under control] bridle, repress, inhibit, control, checkmate, counteract, discourage, repulse, neutralize, squelch; see also **restrain.**—*Ant.* free, liberate, loose. 2. [To determine accuracy] review, monitor, balance accounts, balance the books, keep account of, correct, compare, find out, investigate, count, tell, call the roll, take (an) account of, take stock, go through, *go over with a fine-toothed comb, *keep tab(s) on or track of; see also **examine**. **3.** [To halt] hold, terminate, cut short; see **halt, stop 1.**

check in, v. appear, sign in, come; see **arrive, register 4.**

check off, v. mark off, notice, correct; see **mark 2.**

check out, v. depart, pay one's bill, settle up; see **leave 1, pay 1.**

check up on, v. watch, investigate, control; see **examine.**

cheek, n. jowl, gill, chop; see **face 1.**

cheer, n. **1.** [An agreeable mental state] delight, mirth, glee; see **joy. 2.** [An encouraging shout] roar, applause, hurrah, hurry, college yell, approval; see also **yell.**

cheer, v. **1.** [To hearten] console, inspirit, brighten; see **comfort 1, encourage, help. 2.** [To support with cheers] applaud, shout, salute; see **support 2, yell.**

cheerful, a. **1.** [Said especially of persons] gay, merry, joyful; see **happy. 2.** [Said especially of things] bright, sunny, sparkling; see **comfortable 2, pleasant 2.**

cheerfully, a. cheerily, gladly, willingly, happily, merrily, joyfully, lightheartedly, blithely, brightly, vivaciously, airily, genially, jovially, sportively, elatedly, winsomely, pleasantly, gleefully, gaily, mirthfully, playfully, hopefully, breezily, briskly, with good cheer.—Ant. unwillingly, reluctantly, **sadly.**

cheers, inter. here's to you, to your health, skoal (Scandinavian); see **toast 1.**

cheer up, v. enliven, inspirit, exhilarate, inspire, brighten, rally, restore, perk up, boost, *buck up, pat on the back; see **improve 1.**

cheese, n.—Varieties of cheese include the following—mild, American, (aged) cheddar, Monterey jack, Dutch, Philadelphia cream, creamed cottage, Edam (Cheddar), jack, Roquefort, Brie, mozzarella, provolone, Gorgonzola, Swiss, Camembert, Liederkranz, Neufchâtel, Gruyère, Parmesan, Stilton, Gouda, Limburger, muenster, Port du Salut, pot, ricotta, Romano; see also **food.**

chemical, a. synthetic(al), artificial, laboratory, ersatz; see **false 3.**

chemical, n. substance, synthetic, compound; see **drug, element 2, medicine 2.**

chemistry, n.—Branches of chemistry include the following—pure, quantitative, qualitative, organic, inorganic, theoretical, physical, physiological, pathological, metallurgical, mineralogical, geological, applied, agricultural, pharmaceutical, sanitary, industrial, technical, engineering chemistry, biochemistry, electrochemistry, zoochemistry; see also **medicine 3, science 1.**

cherish, v. treasure, value, adore; see **love 1, 2.**

cherry, a. ruddy, reddish, rosy; see **red.**

chest, n. **1.** [A box-like container] case, box, coffer, cabinet, strongbox, receptacle, crate, locker, bureau, coffin, casket, treasury; see also **container. 2.** [The ribbed portion of the body] breast, thorax, bosom, rib cage, heart, upper trunk, pulmonary cavity, peritoneum, ribs.

chew, v. bite, champ, munch, crunch, masticate, nibble (at), feast upon, gnaw, gulp, grind, rend, scrunch, ruminate; see also **eat 1.**

chicken, n. **1.** [A barnyard fowl] chick, hen, rooster; see **fowl. 2.** [Flesh of the chicken] giblets, dark meat, white meat; see **meat. 3.** [*A coward] recreant, dastard, craven; see **coward. —count one's chickens before they are hatched,** rely (on), depend on, put trust in; see **anticipate.**

chief, a. leading, first, foremost; see **main, principal.**

chief, n. principal, manager, overseer, governor, president, foreman, proprietor, supervisor, director, chairman, ringleader, general, master, dictator, superintendent, head, prince, master, emperor, duke, majesty, monarch, overlord, lord, potentate, sovereign, chieftain, ruler, captain, commander, *bigwig, *prima donna, boss, *it; see also **leader.**

chiefly, a. mainly, particularly, in the first place; see **principally.**

child, n. newborn, infant, youth, adolescent, youngster, daughter, son, grandchild, stepchild, offspring, innocent, minor, juvenile, tot, cherub, papoose, tot, *moppet, *kid, *kiddie, whelp, brat, imp, small fry; see also **boy, girl.**—Ant. **parent,** forefather, adult. **—with child,** bearing or carrying a child, going to have a baby, fertile; see **pregnant.**

childbirth, n. delivery, childbearing, parturition, childbed, labor, nativity, delivering, accouchement, lying in, confinement, procreation, reproduction, propagation, giving birth, *blessed event; see also **birth.**

childhood, n. infancy, youth, minority, school days, adolescence, nursery days, babyhood, boyhood, girlhood, teens, puberty, immaturity, tender age.—Ant. maturity, **age,** senility.

childish, a. childlike, foolish, stupid, baby, infantile, juvenile, youthful, babyish, boyish, girlish, adolescent, green, soft, immature; see also **naive, simple 1, young 2.**—Ant. adult, **mature,** grown.

chill, *n.* crispness, coolness, coldness; see **cold 1.**

chill, *v.* 1. [To reduce temperature] frost, refrigerate, make cold; see **cool, freeze 1.** 2. [To check] dispirit, dishearten, dampen; see **depress 2, discourage.**

chilly, *a.* brisk, fresh, crisp; see **cold 1, cool 1.**

chime, *v.* tinkle, clang, toll; see **ring 2, sound 1.**

chimney, *n.* smokestack, fireplace, furnace, hearth, flue, vent, pipe, funnel, smokeshaft, stack.

chin, *n.* mentum, mandible, jawbone; see **jaw.**

China, *n.* an Asiatic country, Chung Kwoh, Chinese Republic, Red China, the Celestial Kingdom, the Middle Kingdom, Chinese Empire, the East, the Orient, the Mysterious East; see also **Asia.**

china, *n.* earthenware, pottery, crockery; see **dish.**

chinese, *a.* Sinaic, Asian, Asiatic; see **Oriental.**

chip, *n.* fragment, slice, wedge; see **bit 1, flake, part 1.** —**having a chip on one's shoulder,** ready to fight, disturbed, agitated; see **angry.** —**when the chips are down,** in a crisis, having trouble, in a difficult position; see **in trouble 1.**

chip, *v.* slash, hew, hack, crumble, snip, fragment, incise, whittle, crack off, splinter, notch, sliver, cut (off), chop, split, slice, chisel, clip, break, crack, flake, cut away, nick, shiver, reduce, shear; see also **break.**

chip in, *v.* contribute, pay, *pitch in; see **share 1.**

chirp, *v.* twitter, warble, cheep; see **sound 1.**

chisel, *n.* gouge, blade, edge; see **knife, tool 1.**

chisel, *v.* 1. [To work with a chisel] carve, hew, incise; see **cut 1.** 2. [*To get by imposition] impose upon, defraud, gyp; see **deceive, steal.**

chivalrous, *a.* courteous, heroic, valiant; see **brave, noble 1, 2, polite.**

chivalry, *n.* valor, gallantry, fairness; see **courtesy 1.**

chock-full, *a.* packed, crammed, stuffed; see **full 1.**

choice, *a.* superior, fine, exceptional; see **best 1.**

choice, *n.* selection, preference, alternative, election, substitute, favorite, pick, *a good bet *or* guess; see **judgement 2.**

choke, *v.* asphyxiate, strangle, strangulate, stifle, throttle, garrote, drown, noose, smother, grab by the throat, wring the neck, stop the breath, gag, gasp, suffocate, choke off, be choked, die out, die by asphyxiation; see also **die.**

choke up, *v.* give way to one's feelings, weep, break down; see **cry 1.**

choose, *v.* decide (on), take, pick out, draw lots, cull, prefer, make a choice of, accept, weigh, judge, sort, appoint, embrace, will, call for, fancy, take up, separate, favor, determine, resolve, discriminate (between), make a decision, adopt, collect, mark out for, cut out, arrange, keep, take up, make one's choice *or* selection, pick and choose, settle on, use one's discretion, determine upon, fix on *or* upon, place one's trust in *or* on, glean, single out, espouse, exercise one's choice *or* option, make up one's mind, set aside *or* apart, commit oneself, separate the wheat from the chaff, incline toward, opt (for), burn one's bridges; see also **decide.**—*Ant.* discard, reject, refuse.

choosing, *n.* selecting, picking, judging; see **choice.**

chop, *v.* fell, cut with an ax, whack; see **cut 1.**

chord, *n.* harmonizing tones, triad, octave; second, third, fourth, fifth, etc., chord, diminished chord, augmented chord, inverted chord, broken chord; primary, secondary, tertiary chord; tetrachord, perfect fourth, arpeggio, common chord; see also **harmony 1, music 1.**

chore, *n.* task, routine, errand; see **job 2.**

chorus, *n.* 1. [A body of singers] choir, singing group, choristers, voices, glee club, singing society, church singers, male chorus, female chorus, mixed chorus, operatic group; see also **music 1.** 2. [A refrain] melody, strain, tune; see **song.**

chosen, *a.* picked, elected, preferred; see **named 2.**

Christ, *n.* the Saviour, Jesus, Jesus of Nazareth, the Redeemer, Messiah, Immanuel, the Word, the Son, the Son of Man, the Son of God, God the Son, the Son of David, the Son of Mary, the Risen, the King of Glory, the Prince of Peace, the Good Shepherd, the King of the Jews, the Lamb of God, the Only Begotten, King of Kings, Lord of Lords, Christ Our Lord, the Way, the Door, the Truth, the Life, the Light of the World, the Incarnate Word, the Word made Flesh, Rose of Sharon; see also **God.**

christen, *v.* immerse, sprinkle, dedicate (to God); see also **baptize, bless, name 1.**

Christian, *a.* pious, reverent, devoted; see **humble 1, religious 1, 2.**

Christian, *n.* Protestant, Catholic, gentile; see **church 3, saint 1.**

Christianity, *n.* 1. [A religion based upon the divinity of Christ] teachings of Christ, the Gospel, the Faith; see

faith 2, religion 2. 2. [The body of Christian people] Christendom, Christians, followers of Christ; see **church 3. 3.** [An attitude associated with Christianity, senses 1 and 2] Christian mercy *or* spirit, loving-kindness, forgiving disposition; see **kindness 1, tolerance 1.**

Christmas, *n.* Xmas, Noel, Yule; see **holiday, winter.**

chronic, *a.* inveterate, confirmed, settled, rooted, deep-seated, continuing, persistent, stubborn, incurable, lasting, lingering, deep-rooted, perennial, fixed, continual, incessant, long-standing, recurring, continuous, of long duration, long-lived, protracted, ceaseless, sustained, lifelong, prolonged, recurrent, obstinate, inborn, inbred, ingrained, ever-present; see also **constant, habitual, permanent 2.**—*Ant.* acute, **temporary,** casual.

chronicle, *n.* narrative, annals, account; see **history, record 1.**

chronological, *a.* temporal, historical, tabulated, classified, according to chronology, in the order of time, sequential, consecutive, properly dated, measured in time, in sequence, progressive in time, ordered, in order, in due time *or* course.

chubby, *a.* plump, round, pudgy; see **fat.**

chuckle, *n.* giggle, smile, grin; see **laugh.**

chuckle, *v.* giggle, smile, snigger; see **laugh.**

*chummy, *a.* affectionate, intimate, constant; see **friendly.**

chunk, *n.* piece, mass, lump; see **part 1.**

chunky, *a.* stocky, thickset, stout; see **fat.**

church, *n.* 1. [A building consecrated to worship] cathedral, house of God, Lord's house, temple, synagogue, mosque, place *or* house of worship, meeting house, chapel, basilica, tabernacle, abbey, sanctuary, house of prayer, mission, shrine, pagoda. 2. [A divine service] rite, prayer(s), (prayer) meeting, Sunday school, (divine) worship, Mass, Lord's Supper, sacrament, the holy sacrament, rosary, ritual, religious rite, morning service, evening service, congregational worship, fellowship, devotion(s), office, revival meeting, chapel service, sermon, communion; see also **ceremony. 3.** [An organized religious body] congregation, gathering, denomination, sect, chapter, body, order, communion, faith, religion, religious society *or* order, affiliation, persuasion, belief, faction, doctrine, creed, cult. Christian churches include the following—Methodist, Presbyterian, Unitarian, Episcopalian, Baptist, Christian Science, Latter-day Saint *or* Mormon, Congregational, Lutheran, (Roman) Catholic, (Greek) Orthodox, Russian, Pentecostal, Church of England,

Church of the Nazarene, Society of Friends *or* Quakers.

churn, *v.* stir, beat, agitate; see **mix 1.**

cigarette, *n.* *fag, smoke, *coffin nail; see **tobacco.**

cinema, *n.* film, photoplay, the movies; see **movie.**

circle, *n.* 1. [A round closed plane figure] ring, loop, wheel, sphere, globe, orb, orbit, zodiac, bowl, vortex, hoop, horizon, perimeter, periphery, circumference, full turn, circuit, disk, meridian, equator, ecliptic, cycle, bracelet, belt, wreath. 2. [An endless sequence of events] cycle, course, succession; see **progress 1, series, sequence 1. —come full circle,** go through a cycle *or* series, come around *or* back, revert; see **return 1.**

circle, *v.* round, encircle, loop, tour, circumnavigate, ring, belt, embrace, encompass, wind about, revolve around, circumscribe, curve around, circuit, enclose, spiral, coil, circulate, detour, wind, roll, wheel, swing past, go round about, evade; see also **surround 1.**—*Ant.* divide, bisect, cut across.

circuit, *n.* circumference, course, circle; see **orbit 1, revolution 1.**

circular, *a.* spherical, cyclical, globular; see **round 1, 3.**

circular, *n.* handbill, broadside, leaflet; see **advertisement, pamphlet.**

circulate, *v.* 1. [To go about] move *or* get around, get *or* fly *or* go about, wander; see also **travel, walk 1. 2.** [To send about] diffuse, report, broadcast; see **distribute.**

circulation, *n.* 1. [Motion in a circle] rotation, current, flowing; see **flow, revolution 1.** 2. [Number of copies distributed] transmission, apportionment, dissemination; see **distribution.**

circumference, *n.* perimeter, periphery, border; see **circle 1.**

circumscribe, *v.* encircle, encompass, girdle; see **surround 1.**

circumstance, *n.* 1. [An attendant condition] situation, condition, contingency, phase, factor, detail, item, fact, case, place, time, cause, status, element, feature, point, incident, article, stipulation, concern, matter, event, occurrence, crisis, coincidence, *happenstance. 2.** [An occurrence] episode, happening, incident; see **event 1.**

circumstances, *n. pl.* 1. [Condition in life] worldly goods, outlook, prospects, chances, means assets, prosperity, financial status *or* condition, resources, standing, property, net worth, financial standing, credit rating, terms, way of life, rank, class, degree, capital, position, financial responsibility, footing, income, sphere, substance, stock in trade, lot, prestige, what one is worth, place on the ladder; see also **state 2, wealth. 2.**

[Attendant conditions] situation, environment, surroundings, facts, particulars, factors, features, motives, controlling *or* governing factors, the times, occasion, basis, grounds, setting, background, needs, requirements, necessities, course of events, legal status, change, life, fluctuation, phase, case, condition, state of affairs, surrounding facts, *the score, *the scene, the story, *where it's at, how the land lies, the lay of the land, current regime, ups and downs. — **under no circumstances**, under no conditions, by no means, absolutely not; see **never**. —**under the circumstances**, conditions being what they are, for this reason, because of; see **because**.

circumstantial, *a.* presumptive, inferential, inconclusive; see **uncertain 2**.

circumvent, *v.* 1. [To go around] encircle, encompass, entrap; see **surround 1**. 2. [To avoid] dodge, elude, shun; see **avoid, evade**.

circus, *n.* hippodrome, spectacle, fair; see **entertainment**.

citation, *n.* bidding, charge, summons; see **command**.

citizen, *n.* inhabitant, denizen, national, subject, cosmopolite, commoner, civilian, urbanite, taxpayer, member of the community, householder, native, occupant, settler, voter, dweller, immigrant, naturalized person, townsman, the man on the street, villager, *John Q. Public; see also **resident**.

city, *a.* metropolitan, civil, civic; see **municipal**.

city, *n.* town, place, municipality, capital, megalopolis, metropolis, suburb, county seat, (trading) center, inner city, downtown, shopping center *or* district, business *or* financial district, incorporated town, village, metropolitan area, township, port; see also **center 2**.

civic, *a.* civil, urban, municipal; see **public 1, 2**.

civil, *a.* 1. [Civic] local, civic, public; see **municipal**. 2. [Polite] formal, courteous, refined; see **polite**.

civilian, *n.* (private) citizen, noncombatant, person not in the armed forces; see **citizen**.

civilization, *n.* cultivation, polish, enlightenment, refinement, civility, illumination, advancement of knowledge, elevation, edification, culture, advancement, social well-being, degree of cultivation, material well-being, education, breeding; see also **culture 1, progress 1**.—*Ant*. barbarism, savagery, degeneration.

civilize, *v.* enlighten, cultivate, enrich, reclaim, refine, acculturate, spiritualize, humanize, edify, uplift, tame, foster, instruct, promote, indoctrinate, idealize,

elevate, educate, advance, ennoble; see also **develop 1, teach**.

civilized, *a.* enlightened, refined, humanized; see **cultured, educated**.

civil rights, *n. pl.* civil liberties, equality, four freedoms; see **choice, freedom 2**.

claim, *n.* demand, declaration, profession, entreaty, petition, suit, ultimatum, call, request, requirement, application, case, assertion, plea, right, interest, title, part; see also **appeal 1**. —**lay claim to**, demand, challenge, stake out a claim (to); see **own 1**.

claim, *v.* 1. [To assert a claim to] demand, attach, lay claim to; see **own 1**. 2. [To assert] insist, pronounce, pretend; see **believe, declare 1**.

clam, *n.* bivalve, mollusk, shellfish; see **fish**.

clammy, *a.* moist, damp, soggy: see **cold 1, wet 1**.

clamor, *n.* din, outcry, discord; see **noise 2, uproar**.

clamp, *n.* snap, clasp, catch; see **fastener, lock 1**.

clan, *n.* group, clique, moiety; see **organization 2, race 2**.

clang, *n.* ring, clatter, jangle; see **noise 1**.

clank, *n.* chink, bang, clink; see **noise 1**.

clap, *v.* 1. [To applaud] cheer, acclaim, approve; see **praise 1**. 2. [To strike] bang, slap, slam; see **hit 1**.

clarification, *n.* exposition, elucidation, description; see **definition, explanation 2, interpretation**.

clarify, *v.* interpret, define, elucidate; see **explain**.

clarity, *n.* limpidity, clearness, purity, brightness, precision, explicitness, exactness, distinctness, plain speech, openness, directness, evidence, prominence, salience, transparency, conspicuousness, certainty, lucidity.—*Ant*. **darkness**, haze, obscurity.

clash, *n.* 1. [Collision] crash, encounter, impact; see **collision 1**. 2. [Disagreement] opposition, conflict, argument; see **disagreement 1, dispute**.

clash, *v.* be dissimilar, mismatch, not go with; see **contrast, differ 1**.

clasp, *n.* buckle, pin, clamp; see **fastener**.

clasp, *v.* clamp, pin, buckle; see **fasten**.

class, *n.* 1. [A classification] degree, order, rank, grade, standing, genus, division, distinction, breed, type, kingdom, subdivision, phylum, subphylum, superorder, family, sect, category, rate, collection, denomination, department, sort, species, variety, branch, group, genre, range, brand, set, kind, section, domain, nature, color, origin, character, frame, temperament, school, designation, sphere, spirit, vein, persuasion, province, make, grain, source, name, mood, habit, form, selection, stamp, status, range, property, aspect, disposition, tone; see also **classification**. 2. [A group organized for study] lecture, seminar, study session; see **school** 1. 3. [A division of society] set, caste, social level; see **family**. —**in a class by itself**, unusual, different, one of a kind; see **unique**.

class, v. identify, rank, grade; see **classify**, **mark** 2.

classic, n. opus, masterwork, exemplar; see **masterpiece**.

classical, a. 1. [Of recognized importance] standard, first-rate, established, ideal, flawless, distinguished, paramount, esthetic, superior, artistic, well-known; see also **excellent**.—*Ant*. modern, **popular**, transitory. 2. [Concerning ancient Greece or Rome] humanistic, academic, classic; see **old** 3.

classification, n. arrangement, assortment, grouping, ordering, allotment, organization, gradation, co-ordination, disposition, categorizing, apportionment, analysis, division, assignment, designation, assorting, distribution, allocation, categorization; see also **class** 1, **order** 3.

classified, a. assorted, grouped, classed, indexed, filed, orderly, recorded, listed, registered, detailed, arranged, regulated, compiled, co-ordinated, ranked, distributed, catalogued, separated, labeled, numbered, systematized, tabulated, alphabetized, typed, on file, rated.—*Ant*. confused, **mixed**, jumbled.

classify, v. arrange, order, pigeonhole, tabulate, organize, distribute, categorize, systematize, co-ordinate, correlate, incorporate, label, alphabetize, place in a category, range, form into classes, divide, allocate, number, rate, class, rank, catalogue, segregate, distinguish, allot, analyze, regiment, name, group, tag, type, put in order, break down, assort, sort, index, grade, match, size, reduce to order; see also **file** 1, **list** 1.—*Ant*. **disorganize**, disorder, disarrange.

clatter, v. rattle, clash, crash; see **sound** 1.

clause, n. 1. [A provision] condition, codicil, ultimatum; see **limitation** 2, **requirement** 1. 2. [A grammatical structure] limiters, sentence modifiers, transformations; see **grammar**.

claw, n. talon, hook, spur, paw, grappling iron or hook, forked end, clutching hand, grapnel, crook, barb, pincers, fingernail.

claw, v. tear, scratch, rip open; see **break** 1, **hurt**, **rip**.

clay, n. loam, earth, till, marl, potter's clay, clayware, green pottery, terra cotta, green brick, china clay, porcelain clay, adobe; see also **mud**.

clean, a. 1. [Not soiled] spotless, washed,

stainless, laundered, untarnished, unstained, neat, tidy, clear, blank, white, unblemished, unspotted, snowy, well-kept, dustless, cleansed, immaculate, unsoiled, unpolluted, *spic and span, *clean as a whistle.—*Ant*. soiled, **dirty**, stained. 2. [Not contaminated] unadulterated, wholesome, sanitary; see **pure** 2. 3. [Having sharp outlines] clear-cut, sharp, distinct; see **definite** 2. 4. [Thorough] complete, entire, total; see **absolute** 1, **whole** 1. 5. [Fair] reliable, decent, lawful; see **fair** 1, **honest** 1. — *come clean, confess, reveal, expose; see **admit** 2.

clean, v. cleanse, clean or clear up or out, purify, soak, shake out, wash down, scrub off, disinfect, tidy up, deodorize, swab, polish, sterilize, scrape, sweep out, scour, launder, vacuum, scald, dust, mop, cauterize, rinse, sponge, brush, dress, comb, whisk, scrub, sweep, wipe (up), clarify, rake, clean away, make clear, lave, bathe, soap, erase, neaten, shampoo, refine, flush, blot, *do up, spruce up, *slick up; see also **wash** 1, 2.—*Ant*. **dirty**, soil, smear.

cleaner, n. detergent, disinfectant, cleaning agent; see **cleanser**, **soap**.

cleaning, a. cleansing, purgative, detergent, washing, delousing, dusting, sweeping, scouring, soaking, sterilizing, laundering, vacuuming, scalding, purifying.

cleaning, n. cleansing, purge, scrubbing, scouring, purification, scrub, sweeping, brush, prophylaxis, sterilizing, washing, brushing, purifying, deodorizing, catharsis.

cleanliness, n. cleanness, neatness, pureness, tidiness, trimness, spruceness, immaculateness, spotlessness, dapperness, orderliness, whiteness, disinfection, sanitation.—*Ant*. **filth**, dirtiness, griminess.

cleanse, v. 1. [To remove dirt from the surface] launder, wash, scrub; see **clean**. 2. [To remove impurities from within] refine, disinfect, purge; see **clean**, **purify**.

cleanser, n. cleansing or cleaning agent, abrasive, lather, solvent, purgative, deodorant, fumigant, soap flakes, polish, disinfectant, antiseptic, purifier, cleaning or scouring powder, spray cleaner, cleaner, detergent, soap powder, cleaning fluid, dry cleaner, suds; see also **soap**. Cleansers include the following—water, soap and water, soap, washing powder, scouring powder, oven cleaner, naptha, furniture polish, borax, lye, household ammonia, solvent, bluing, carbon tetrachloride, toilet-bowl cleanser, baking soda, chlorine compound, silver-polish, kerosene, gasoline, vinegar, rug shampoo.

clear, a. 1. [Open to the sight or understanding] explicit, plain, manifest; see **obvious 1, 2. 2.** [Offering little impediment to vision] lucid, pure, transparent, apparent, limpid, translucent, crystal, crystalline, thin, crystal clear.—*Ant.* opaque, dark, muddy. **3.** [Unclouded] sunny, bright, rainless; see **fair 3. 4.** [Freed from legal charges] free, guiltless, cleared, exonerated, blameless, innocent, sinless, dismissed, discharged, absolved; see **innocent 1.**—*Ant.* accused, **guilty**, blamed. **5.** [Audible] loud enough to be heard, distinct, definite; see **audible.** — **in the clear**, guiltless, not suspicious *or* suspected, cleared; see **free 2, innocent 1.**

clear, *v.* **1.** [To free from uncertainty] clear up, relieve, clarify; see **explain. 2.** [To free from obstacles] disentangle, rid, unloose; see **free, remove 1. 3.** [To profit] realize, net, make; see **receive 1.**

clear-cut, *a.* precise, plain, evident; see **obvious 1, 2.**

cleared, *a.* **1.** [Emptied] cleaned, unloaded, cleared away; see **empty. 2.** [Freed of charges] vindicated, freed, set right; see also **discharged, free 2.**

clearing, *n.* **1.** [The act of clearing] clearance, freeing, removing; see **removal 1. 2.** [A cleared space] (open *or* empty) space, opening, clearance; see **area, court, expanse, yard 1.**

clearly, *a.* **1.** [Distinctly; *said of sight*] plainly, precisely, lucidly, purely, brightly, perceptibly, unmistakably, in full view, in focus, discernibly, decidedly, incontestably, undoubtedly, noticeably, admittedly, before one's eyes, beyond doubt, prominently, obviously, openly, overtly, observably, certainly, apparently, manifestly, recognizably, conspicuously, in plain sight, definitely, markedly, surely, visibly, positively, seemingly, evidently, *to the eye, at first blush *or* sight, to all appearances, on the face of.—*Ant.* dully, **hazy**, cloudily. **2.** [Distinctly; *said of sounds*] sharply, acutely, ringingly, penetratingly, audibly, bell-like.—*Ant.* indistinct, mutteringly, unclearly.

clearness, *n.* brightness, distinctness, lucidity; see **clarity.**

clear out, *v.* **1.** [To remove] clean out, dispose of, get rid of; see **eliminate 1, excrete. 2.** [To leave] depart, go, remove oneself; see **leave 1.**

clear up, *v.* **1.** [To become clear; *said especially of weather*] improve, blow over, stop raining *or* snowing *or* storming, run its course, die *or* pass (away), die down, show improvement, pick up, lift, become fair, have fair *or* fine weather. **2.** [To make clear] explicate, clarify, make plausible *or* explicable *or* reasonable, etc; see **explain.**

clench, *v.* grip, grasp, double up; see **hold 1.**

clergy, *n.* priesthood, prelacy, pastorate; see **ministry 2.**

clergyman, *n.* pastor, rabbi, preacher; see **minister 1, priest.**

clerical, *a.* **1.** [Concerning clerks] subordinate, stenographic, accounting, bookkeeping, secretarial, typing, written, assistant, on the sales force. **2.** [Concerning the clergy] ministerial, priestly, apostolic, monastic, monkish, churchly, cleric, papal, episcopal, canonical, pontifical, ecclesiastic, sacred, holy, ecclesiastical, in God's service, devoted to the Lord, in the Lord's work.

clerk, *n.* salesgirl, saleswoman, saleslady, shopgirl, shop assistant, salesclerk, salesman, salesperson, counterman, seller, auditor, bookkeeper, recorder, registrar, stenographer, office girl, office boy, timekeeper, cashier, teller, office worker, notary, controller, copyist, law clerk, switchboard operator, *steno; see also **secretary 2.**

clever, *a.* **1.** [Apt, particularly with one's hands] skillful, expert, adroit; see **able. 2.** [Mentally quick] smart, bright, shrewd; see **intelligent, sly.**

cleverly, *a.* neatly, skillfully, tactfully, dexterously, ingeniously, resourcefully, deftly, nimbly, agilely, adroitly, proficiently, expertly, smoothly, quickly, speedily, readily; see also **easily.**—*Ant.* **awkwardly,** clumsily, unskillfully.

cleverness, *n.* skill, adroitness, ingenuity; see **ability.**

cliché, *n.* commonplace, platitude, stereotype, proverb, saying, slogan, trite phrase *or* remark, stereotyped saying, vapid expression, triteness, banality, triviality, staleness, hackneyed phrase *or* idea *or* expression; see also **motto.**

click, *n.* tick, snap, bang; see **noise 1.**

click, *v.* **1.** [To make a clicking sound] tick, snap, bang; see **sound 1. 2.** [*To be successful] match, go off well, meet with approval; see **succeed 1.**

client, *n.* customer, patient, patron; see **buyer.**

cliff, *n.* bluff, crag, steep rock; see **hill, mountain 1, wall 1.**

climate, *n.* characteristic weather, atmospheric *or* meteorologic conditions, aridity, humidity, (weather) conditions; see also **cold 1, heat 1, weather.**

climax, *n.* peak, apex, highest point, culmination, acme, pinnacle, crest, zenith, summit, apogee, extremity, limit, pitch, utmost extent, highest degree, turning *or* crowning point; see also **maximum, top 1.**—*Ant.* anticlimax, **depression,** nadir.

climax, *v.* culminate, tower, end, top, conclude, reach a peak, come to a head, reach the zenith, break the record; see also **achieve**.

climb, *n.* 1. [The act of climbing] climbing, clamber, mounting; see **rise**. 2. [An ascending place] slope, incline, dune; see **grade 1, hill**.

climb, *v.* scale, work one's way up, ascend gradually, scramble *or* clamber *or* swarm up, start up, go up, ascend, labor *or* struggle up, get *or* climb on, progress upward, rise, lift, rise hand over hand, come up, creep up, escalate, surmount, *shinny up, shoot up.

climb down, *v.* step off, come down, dismount; see **descend**.

cling, *v.* adhere, clasp, hold fast; see **stick 1**.

clip, *v.* snip, crop, clip off; see **cut 1, decrease 2**.

clippers, *n.* shears, cutting instruments, barber's tools; see **scissors**.

clique, *n.* coterie, clan, club; see **faction, organization 2**.

clock, *n.* timekeeper, timepiece, timemarker, timer, *ticker. Kinds of clocks include the following—alarm, cuckoo, electric, grandfather, pendulum clock; hourglass, stop watch, sundial, wrist watch; see also **watch 1. —around the clock,** continuously, continually, twenty-four hours a day; see **regularly**.

clock, *v.* time, measure time, register speed *or* distance; see **measure 1**.

clog, *v.* stop up, seal, obstruct; see **close 2, hinder**.

close, *a.* 1. [Nearby] neighboring, across the street, around the corner; see **near 1. 2.** [Intimate] confidential, intimate, familiar; see **private. 3.** [Compact] dense, solid, compressed; see **thick 1. 4.** [Stingy] narrow, parsimonious, niggardly; see **stingy. 5.** [Stifling] sticky, stuffy, unventilated, moldy, heavy, motionless, uncomfortable, choky, stale-smelling, musty, stagnant, confined, suffocating, sweltering, tight, stale, oppressive, breathless; see also **uncomfortable 2.**—*Ant.* **fresh,** refreshing, brisk. **6.** [Similiar] resembling, having common qualities, much the same; see **alike, like**.

close, *n.* termination, adjournment, ending; see **end 2.**

close, *v.* 1. [To put a stop to] conclude, finish, terminate; see **end 1. 2.** [To put a stopper into] shut, stop down, choke off, stuff, clog, prevent passage, shut *or* turn off, lock, block, bar, dam, cork, seal, button; see also **close 2.**—*Ant.* **open,** uncork, unseal. **3.** [To come together] meet, unite, agree; see **join 1. 4.** [To shut] slam, close *or* shut down *or* up, seal, fasten, bolt, clench, bar, shutter, clap, lock, bring to.

closed, *a.* 1. [Terminated] ended, concluded, final; see **finished 1. 2.** [Not in

operation] shut (down), out of order, (temporarily) out of service, bankrupt, closed up, padlocked, *folded up; see also **broken 2. 3.** [Not open] shut, fastened, sealed; see **tight 2**.

closely, *a.* approximately, similarly, exactly, nearly, strictly, firmly, intimately, jointly, in conjunction with; see also **almost.**—*Ant.* separately, **individually,** one by one.

closet, *n.* cabinet, recess, cupboard, buffet, locker, wardrobe, receptacle, safe, bin, drawer, chest of drawers, vault, cold storage, clothes room.

clot, *n.* lump, bulk, clotting, curdling, coagulation, mass, clump, coagulum, thickness, coalescence, curd.

clot, *v.* coagulate, set, lump; see **thicken**.

cloth, *n.* fabric, material, stuff; see **goods**.

clothe, *v.* attire, dress up, costume; see **dress 1**.

clothed, *a.* clad, invested, costumed, robed, shod, dressed, attired, decked, disguised, covered, draped, veiled.—*Ant.* **naked,** exposed, stripped.

clothes, *n.* (wearing) apparel, raiment, clothing, garments, garb, vesture, vestments, attire, array, casual *or* informal wear, evening clothes, work clothes, suit of clothes, costume, wardrobe, trappings, gear, underclothes, outfit, get-up, rags, *toggery, *togs, *duds, things; see also **coat 1, dress 1, 2, hat, pants 1, shirt.** Men's clothes include the following—business suit, jacket and slacks, trousers, shorts, breeches, *knickers, tuxedo *or* *tux, dress suit, dinner jacket, uniform, shirt, body shirt, hiphugger pants, continental suit, socks; long underwear *or* *long johns. Women's clothes include the following—housecoat, negligee, morning dress, evening gown, kimono, shorts, frock, blouse, jumper, slip, shirtwaist, robe, underwear *or* *unmentionables, slacks, panties, brassiere *or* bra, girdle; nightgown *or* *nightie, pajamas *or* P.J.'s, dress, street dress, suit, cardigan, sweater, pullover, slipover sweater, house dress, dickey, nylon stockings *or* nylons, mini-skirt, maxi-skirt, shift, muumuu, hiphugger slacks, smock, skirt, coat, petticoat, hat, bonnet. Clothes worn by both men and women include the following—blue jeans, levis, turtleneck, sweat shirt, kimono, raincoat, tights, bell-bottom pants, *cut-offs. Children's clothes include the following—rompers, playsuit, coveralls, snow suit, leggings. Work clothes include the following—overalls, windbreaker, blue jeans, coveralls, jumper, *cords.

clothing, *n.* attire, raiment, garb; see **clothes, dress 1**.

cloud, *n.* haze, mist, fogginess, haziness, film, puff, billow, frost, smoke, veil, cloud cover, overcast. Types of clouds include the following—cirrus, cumulus, stratus, nimbus, cirro-cumulus, cirro-stratus. —in the clouds, fanciful, fantastic, romantic; see **impractical**. —under a cloud, suspect, dubious, uncertain; see **suspicious 2**.

cloudy, *a.* 1. [Hazy] overcast, foggy, sunless; see **dark 1.** 2. [Not clear] dense, nontransparent, nontranslucent; see **opaque 1**.

clown, *n.* buffoon, fool, a joker, harlequin, punch, funnyman, humorist, jester, comedian, *cut-up; see also **actor**.

club, *n.* 1. [A social organization] association, order, society; see **faction 1, organization 3.** 2. [A cudgel] bat, hammer, mallet; see **stick**.

club, *v.* batter, whack, pound; see **beat 1, hit 1**.

clue, *n.* evidence, trace, mark; see **proof 1, sign 1**.

clue, *v.* leave evidence, give information, leave tracks *or* traces; see **tell 2**.

clump, *n.* cluster, bundle, knot; see **bunch 1**.

clumsily, *a.* crudely, gawkily, stumblingly; see **awkwardly**.

clumsiness, *n.* crudity, ineptitude, boorishness; see **awkwardness 1**.

clumsy, *a.* ungainly, gawky, inexpert; see **awkward 1**.

cluster, *n.* group, batch, clump; see **bunch**.

clutch, *v.* grab, grasp, grip; see **hold 1, seize 1**.

clutches, *n.* control, grasp, keeping; see **power 2**.

clutter, *n.* disarray, jumble, disorder; see **confusion 2**.

coach, *n.* 1. [A carriage] fourwheeler, chaise, victoria; see **carriage 2, vehicle**. 2. [An instructor] mentor, drillmaster, physical education instructor; see **teacher, trainer**.

coach, *v.* train, drill, instruct; see **teach**.

coagulate, *v.* curdle, clot, congeal; see **thicken 1**.

coal, *n.* sea coal, stone coal, mineral coal; see **fuel**. —haul *or* rake *or* drag over the coals, reprimand, criticize, castigate; see **blame**.

coalition, *n.* compact, conspiracy, association; see **faction**.

coarse, *a.* 1. [Not fine] rough, rude, unrefined; see **crude**. 2. [Vulgar] low, common, base; see **rude 1, vulgar 1**.

coast, *n.* shoreline, beach, seaboard; see **shore**.

coast, *v.* glide, float, ride on the current; see **drift, ride 1**.

coat, *n.* 1. [An outer garment] topcoat, overcoat, cloak, suit coat, tuxedo, dinner jacket, sport coat, dress coat, mink coat, fur coat, ski jacket, mackintosh, raincoat, jacket, windbreaker, peacoat, three-quarter length coat, wrap, leather jacket, sou'wester, slicker; see also **clothes.** 2. [The covering of an animal] protective covering, husk, shell, crust, scale, fleece, epidermis, rind, ectoderm, pelt, membrane; see also **fur, hide, skin.** 3. [An applied covering] coating, layer, set, wash, primer, finish, glaze, crust, painting, overlay, whitewashing, varnish, lacquer, gloss, tinge, prime coat, plaster; see also **finish 2**.

coat, *v.* surface, glaze, enamel; see **paint 2, varnish**.

coating, *n.* crust, covering, layer; see **coat 3**.

coax, *v.* persuade, cajole, inveigle; see **influence, urge 2**.

cocktail, *n.*—Cocktails include the following—(dry) *Manhattan, (dry) Martini, old-fashioned, champagne, sidecar, Margarita, pink lady, whisky sour, black Russian, Daiquiri, Bacardi, Alexander; see also **drink 2**.

code, *n.* codex, method, digest; see **law 2, system 2**.

coerce, *v.* impel, compel, constrain; see **force**.

coercion, *n.* compulsion, persuasion, constraint; see **pressure 2, restraint 2**.

coexist, *v.* exist together, synchronize, be contemporary; see **accompany**.

coexistence, *n.* order, conformity, accord; see **peace 1, 2**.

coffee, *n.* beverage, decoction, *java; see **drink 2**. Prepared coffee includes the following—Turkish, Armenian, drip, percolated, vacuum, instant, French roast, coffee with cream, demitasse, camp coffee.

coffin, *n.* box, casket, sarcophagus, stone *or* lead *or* wood coffin, burial *or* funerary urn *or* vase, funerary box, mummy case; see also **container**.

cohabit, *v.* *shack up (with), *play house (with), be roommates (with); see **accompany**.

coherence, *n.* stickiness, viscosity, gumminess, cementation, soldering, adhesiveness, sticking together, coagulation, viscidity, adherence, set, fusion, sticking, union, adhesion, cohesiveness, consistency.

coherent, *a.* comprehensible, sound, intelligible; see **logical 1, understandable**.

coil, *n.* curl, turn, ring, wind, convolution, twine, twist, twirl, lap, loop, curlicue, corkscrew, roll, spiral, helix, scroll; see also **circle 1**.

coil, *v.* scroll, wind, loop, twist, fold, twine, intertwine, entwine, convolute, lap, twirl, spire, wreathe; see also **curl**. —*Ant.* unfold, unwind, ravel.

coin, *n.* legal tender, gold *or* silver piece, copper coin; see **money 1**.

coin, *v.* 1. [To mint money] mint, strike, stamp; see **manufacture 1.** 2. [To invent a word, etc.] mint, create a phrase, make up; see **invent 1**.

coincide, *v.* accord, harmonize, match; see **agree.** 2. [Happen] eventuate, come about, befall; see **happen 2**.

coincidence, *n.* incident, happening, event; see **accident, chance 1**.

coincidental, *a.* 1. [Occurring simultaneously] concurrent, concomitant, contemporaneous; see **simultaneous.** 2. [Apparently accidental] chance, casual, unplanned; see **random**.

cold, *a.* 1. [*Said of the weather*] crisp, cool, icy, freezing, frosty, frigid, wintry, bleak, nippy, brisk, keen, penetrating, snowy, frozen, blasting, cutting, snappy, piercing, chill, bitter, numbing, severe, stinging, glacial, intense, Siberian, chilly, sharp, raw, nipping, arctic, polar, below zero, biting.—*Ant.* warm, hot, heated. 2. [*Said of persons, animals, etc.*] cold-blooded, frozen, clammy, stiff, chilled, frostbitten, shivering, blue from cold. — *Ant.* hot, perspiring, thawed. 3. [*Said of temperament*] unconcerned, apathetic, reticent; see **indifferent, reserved 3**.

cold, *n.* 1. [Conditions having a low temperature] coldness, frozenness, chilliness, frostiness, draft, frostbite, absence of warmth, want of heat, chill, shivers, coolness, shivering, goose flesh, numbness, iciness, frigidity, freeze, glaciation, refrigeration; see also **weather.**—*Ant.* warmth, **heat**, hot wave. 2. [An aural or respiratory congestion] cough, hack, sore throat, cold in the head, sinus trouble, cold on one's chest, bronchial irritation, ague, common cold, laryngitis, hay fever, whooping cough, influenza *or* *flu, asthma, bronchitis, strep throat, strep, sniffles, frog in one's throat; see also **illness 2.** —**catch** *or* **take cold**, come down with a cold, have a chill, get a cold; see **sicken 1.** —**have** *or* **get cold feet**, go back on one's word, hold back, back down; see **fear, stop 2.** —**(out) in the cold**, forgotten, ignored, rejected; see **neglected.** —**throw cold water on**, dishearten, squelch, dampen; see **discourage**.

cold-blooded, *a.* relentless, callous, unfeeling; see **cruel**.

collaborate, *v.* work together, conspire, work with; see **co-operate**.

collapse, *n.* breakdown, downfall, destruction; see **failure 1., wreck**.

collapse, *v.* drop, deflate, give way; see **fail 1., fall 1, 2**.

collar, *n.* neckband, neckpiece, dicky; see **clothes**.

collateral, *n.* security, guarantee, pledge; see **insurance, money 1, wealth**.

colleague, *n.* partner, collaborator, coadjutor; see **associate**.

collect, *v.* 1. [To bring into one place] amass, consolidate, convoke; see **accumulate, assemble 2, concentrate 1.** 2. [To come together] congregate, assemble, flock; see **gather.** 3. [To obtain funds] solicit, raise, secure; see **get 1**.

collected, *a.* 1. [Composed] poised, self-possessed, cool; see **calm 1.** 2. [Assembled] accumulated, amassed, compiled; see **gathered**.

collection, *n.* specimens, samples, examples, extracts, gems, models, assortment, medley, accumulation, pile, stack, group, assemblage, compilation, mass, quantity, selection, treasury, anthology, miscellany, aggregation, combination, number, store, stock, digest, arrangement, concentration, discoveries, clone, finds, batch, mess, lot, heap, bunch.

collector, *n.* authority, historian, hobbyist, fancier, (serious *or* informed) amateur, gatherer, discoverer, curator, compiler, finder, assembler, hoarder, librarian; see also **scientist, specialist**.

college, *n.* institute, institution, professional school, organization, association, community college, liberal arts college, teachers college, junior college, state college, denominational college, seminary; see also **university**.

collide, *v.* 1. [To come into violent contact] hit, strike, smash; see **crash 4.** 2. [To come into conflict] clash, conflict, disagree; see **oppose 1**.

collision, *n.* impact, contact, shock, accident, encounter, crash, colliding, bump, jar, jolt, sideswipe, strike, hit, slam, blow, thud, thump, knock, smash, butt, rap, head-on crash, head-on, *fender-bender; see also **disaster**.

colonial, *a.* pioneer, isolated, dependent, planted, transplanted, settled, provincial, frontier, Pilgrim, emigrant, immigrant, territorial, outland, distant, remote, daughter, early American, overseas, protectoral, dominion, established, hard, raw, crude, harsh, wild, unsettled, limited, uncultured, new, unsophisticated.—*Ant.* old, cultured, decadent.

colonization, *n.* immigration, (pioneer) settlement, founding; see **foundation 2**.

colonize, *v.* found, migrate, pioneer; see **establish 2, settle 7**.

colony, *n.* settlement, dependency, subject state, colonial state, dominion, offshoot, (political) possession, province, group, new land, protectorate, hive, daughter country, satellite state *or* province, community, group migration; see also **nation 1**.

color, *n.* hue, tone, tint, shade, tinge, dye, taint, dash, touch, complexion, brilliance, undertone, value, iridescence, intensity, coloration, discoloration, pigmentation, coloring, cast, glow, blush, wash, tincture. Colors include the following—*colors in the solar spectrum*: red, orange, yellow, green, blue, violet; *physiological primary colors*: red, green, blue; *psychological primary colors*: red, yellow, green, blue, black, white; *primary colors in painting*: red, blue, yellow; see also **black 1, brown, green 1, orange 1, pink, red, yellow 1.** —**change color**, flush, redden, become red in the face; see **blush.** —**lose color**, become pale, blanch, faint; see **whiten 1.**

color, *v.* gloss, chalk, daub, gild, enamel, lacquer, suffuse, stipple, pigment, glaze, tinge, tint, stain, tone, shade, dye, wash, crayon, chrome, enliven, embellish, give color to, adorn, imbue, emblazon, illuminate, rouge; see also **decorate, paint 1, 2.**

colored, *a.* 1. [Treated with color] hued, tinted, tinged, shaded, flushed, reddened, glowing, stained, dyed, washed, rouged; see also **painted 2.** 2. [Belonging to a dark-skinned race] brown, black, red; see **negro.**

colorful, *a.* vivid, picturesque, realistic; see **bright 1.**

colorless, *a.* achromic, pale, neutral; see **dull 2, transparent 1.**

colors, *n. pl.* banner, standard, symbol; see **emblem.**

colossal, *a.* huge, enormous, immense; see **large 1.**

colt, *n.* foal, filly, yearling; see also **horse.**

column, *n.* 1. [A pillar] support, prop, shaft, monument, totem, pylon, obelisk, tower, minaret, cylinder, mast, monolith, upright, pedestal; see also **post 1.** 2. [Journalistic commentary] comment, article, editorial; see **news 1.**

columnist, *n.* newspaperman, journalist, correspondent; see **reporter, writer.**

coma, *n.* unconsciousness, trance, stupor; see **sleep.**

comb, *n.* hair comb, currycomb, graining instrument; see **brush 1.**

comb, *v.* untangle, disentangle, cleanse, scrape, arrange, straighten, lay smooth, smooth.

combat, *n.* struggle, warfare, conflict; see **battle, fight.**

combat, *v.* battle, oppose, resist; see **fight.**

combination, *n.* 1. [The act of combining] uniting, joining, unification; see **union 1.** 2. [An association] union, alliance, federation; see **organization 2.** 3. [Something formed by combining] compound, aggregate, blend; see **mixture 1.**

combine, *v.* 1. [To bring together] connect, couple, link; see **join 1.** 2. [To become one] fuse, merge, blend; see **mix 1, unite.**

combined, *a.* linked, mingled, connected; see **joined.**

combustion, *n.* flaming, kindling, oxidization; see **fire 1.**

come, *v.* 1. [To move toward] close in, advance, draw near; see **approach 2.** 2. [To arrive] appear at, reach, attain; see **arrive 1.** 3. [To be available] appear, be at one's disposal, be ready, be obtainable, be handy, be accessible, be able to be reached, show *or* turn up, be convenient; see also **appear 3.** 4. [*To have an orgasm] to reach sexual fulfillment, ejaculate, eject passionately; see **achieve, copulate.** —**as good as they come,** excellent, superior, fine; see **best.** —*how come?**, for what reason? how so? what is the cause of *or* the reason for that? see **why.**

come about, *v.* occur, take place, result; see **happen 2.**

come across, *v.* 1. [To find] uncover, stumble upon, notice; see **discover 1, find 1.** 2. [*To give] deliver, pay, part with, hand over; see **give 1.**

come again, *v.* 1. [To return] come back, go again, go back; see **return 1.** 2. [*To repeat] reiterate, retell, restate; see **repeat 3.**

come along, *v.* 1. [To accompany] accompany, go with, attend; see **arrive 1, advance 1.** 2. [To progress] show improvement, do well, prosper; see **improve 2.**

come around, *v.* 1. [To recover] improve, recuperate, rally; see **recover 3, revive 2.** 2. [*To visit] call on, stop by, drop in on; see **visit.**

come back, *v.* 1. [To return] come again, reappear, re-enter; see **return 1.** 2. [To reply] retort, rejoin, respond; see **answer 1.** 3. [*To recover] do better, triumph, gain; see **improve 2, win 1.**

*comeback,** *n.* 1. [Improvement] revival, progress, betterment; see **improvement 1, recovery 1, 2.** 2. [Witty answer] retort, reply, rejoinder; see **answer 1.**

come between, *v.* intervene, interpose, interrupt; see **happen 2, meddle 1.**

come by, *v.* 1. [To pass] go by, overtake, move past; see **pass 1.** 2. [To acquire] get, win, procure; see **get 1.**

*come clean,** *v.* confess, reveal, acknowledge; see **admit 2.**

comedian, *n.* comic, jester, entertainer; see **actor, clown.**

comedown, *n.* reversal, blow, defeat; see **failure 1.**

come down, *v.* worsen, decline, suffer; see **decrease 1, fail 1.**

come down on or **upon,** v. rebuke, reprimand, *land on; see **attack, scold.**

comedy, n. comic drama, satirical comedy, musical comedy, farce, tragicomedy, satire, burlesque, slapstick, light entertainment; see **drama.**

come for, v. call for, accompany, come or try to get or collect, etc.; see **pick up 6.**

come forward, v. offer oneself, appear, make a proposal; see **volunteer.**

come in, v. pass in, set foot (in), intrude; see **enter.**

*come in for, v. get, be eligible for, acquire; see **receive 1.**

*come in handy, v. be useful, have a use, aid; see **help 1.**

come into, v. 1. [To inherit] fall heir to, succeed (to), acquire; see **inherit, receive 1.** 2. [To join] enter into, associate with, align; see **join 2.**

come off, v. 1. [To become separated] be disconnected, be disengaged, be severed, be parted, be disjoined, be detached, be disunited; see also **divide.** 2. [To happen] occur, befall, come about; see **happen 2.**

come on, v. encounter, come across, come upon; see **meet 6.**

come out, v. 1. [To be made public] be published, be made known, be announced, be issued, be brought out, be reported, be revealed, be divulged, be disclosed, be exposed; see also **appear 1.** 2. [To result] end, conclude, terminate; see **succeed 1.**

come out for, v. announce, state, affirm; see **declare, support 1.**

come out with, v. report, declare, announce; see **advertise, declare, publish 1.**

come through, v. 1. [To be successful] accomplish, score, triumph; see **achieve, succeed 1.** 2. [To survive] live through, persist, withstand; see **endure 2.** 3. [To do] accomplish, achieve, carry out; see **perform 1.**

come to, v. 1. [To recover] rally, come around, recuperate; see **recover 3, revive 2.** 2. [To result in] end in, terminate (by), conclude; see **happen 2, result.**

come to life, v. recover, regain consciousness, live; see **revive 2.**

come to pass, v. result, befall, occur; see **happen 2.**

come to the point, v. cut the matter short, make a long story short, *get down to brass tacks; see **define 2.**

come up, v. appear, arise, move to a higher place; see **rise 1.**

come upon, v. locate, identify, recognize; see **discover 1, find 1.**

come up to, v. 1. [To equal] match,

resemble, rank with; see **equal.** 2. [To reach] extend (to), get or come to, near; see **approach 1, 2, arrive 1, reach 1.**

come up with, v. 1. [To propose] suggest, recommend, offer; see **propose 1.** 2. [To find] uncover, detect, stumble on; see **discover 1, find 1.**

comfort, n. rest, quiet, relaxation, repose, relief, poise, well-being, cheer, abundance, sufficiency, gratification, luxury, warmth, plenty, creature comforts, pleasure, happiness, contentment, restfulness, peacefulness, cheerfulness, exhilaration, complacency, *bed of roses; see also **ease 1, enjoyment, satisfaction 2.**—Ant. **weakness,** discomfort, uneasiness.

comfort, v. [To console] condole, solace, grieve with, cheer, gladden, uphold, hearten, pat on the back, put (someone) in a good humor, sustain, support, help, aid, confirm, reassure, refresh; see also **encourage, pity 1.**—Ant. be indifferent, **discourage,** depress. 2. [To make easy physically] alleviate, relieve, make comfortable, assuage, soothe, mitigate, gladden, quiet one's fears, help one in need, lighten one's burden, encourage, calm, revive, sustain, aid, assist, nourish, support, compose, delight, divert, bolster up, invigorate, refresh, put at ease, reassure, warm, lighten, soften, remedy, release, restore, free, make well, revitalize; see also **ease 1, help, strengthen.**—Ant. make uneasy, **weaken,** worsen.

comfortable, a. 1. [In physical ease] contented, cheerful, easy, at rest, relaxed, at ease, untroubled, healthy, rested, enjoying, pleased, complacent, soothed, relieved, strengthened, restored, in comfort, made well, at home (with), without care, *snug as a bug in a rug; see also **happy, satisfied.**—Ant. ill, uneasy, disturbed. 2. [Conducive to physical ease] satisfactory, snug, cozy, warm, sheltered, convenient, protected, cared for, appropriate, useful, roomy, spacious, luxurious, rich, satisfying, restful, in comfort, well-off, well-to-do; see also **pleasant 2.**—Ant. poverty-stricken, **shabby,** tumble-down.

comfortably, a. luxuriously, in comfort, restfully, snugly, cozily, pleasantly, warmly, conveniently, adequately, with ease, competently, amply; see also **easily.**—Ant. **inadequately,** insufficiently, poorly.

comforting, a. sympathetic, cheering, encouraging, invigorating, health-giving, warming, consoling, sustaining, reassuring, refreshing, upholding, relieving, soothing, lightening, mitigating, alleviating, softening, curing, restoring, releasing, freeing, revitalizing, tranquilizing.—Ant. **disturbing,** distressing, upsetting.

comic, *a.* ridiculous, humorous, ironic; see **funny 1.**

comical, *a.* witty, amusing, humorous; see **funny 1.**

coming, *a.* **1.** [Approaching] advancing, drawing near, progressing, nearing, in the offing, coming in *or* on, arriving, gaining upon, pursuing, getting near, near *or* close at hand, almost on *or* upon, immediate, future, in view, preparing, to come, eventual, fated, written, hereafter, at hand, in store, due, about to happen, looked *or* hoped for, deserving, close, imminent, prospective, anticipated, forthcoming, certain, ordained, impending, to be, expected, near, pending, foreseen, in *or* on the cards, in the wind; see also **expected, likely 1.**—*Ant.* going, **distant,** leaving. **2.** [Having a promising future] promising, advancing, probable; see **able, ambitious. 3.** [Future] lying ahead, pending, impending; see **expected 2, future.**

coming, *n.* approach, landing, reception; see **arrival 1.**

command, *n.* order, injunction, direction, dictation, demand, decree, prohibition, interdiction, canon, rule, call, summons, imposition, precept, mandate, charge, behest, edict, proclamation, instruction, proscription, ban, requirement, dictate, subpoena, commandment, dictum, word of command, writ, citation, notification, will, regulation, ordinance, act, fiat, bidding, word, requisition, ultimatum, exaction, enactment, order of the day, caveat, prescript, warrant; see also **law 3, power 2, request.**

command, *v.* **1.** [To issue an order] charge, tell, demand; see **order 1. 2.** [To have control] rule, dominate, master; see **control.**

commandeer, *v.* appropriate, sequester, confiscate; see **seize 2.**

commander, *n.* commandant, officer, head; see **administration 2, administrator, chief 1, leader 2.**

commanding, *a.* **1.** [Ruling] leading, directing, determining, ordering, charging, ruling, instructing, dictating, dominating, compelling, managing, checking, curbing, forcing, coercing, requiring, restraining, in command *or* authority, in charge, regulating. **2.** [Important] decisive, impressive, significant; see **important 1.**

commemorate, *v.* solemnize, honor, memorialize; see **admire, celebrate 1.**

commemoration, *n.* recognition, remembrance, observance; see **celebration, ceremony, custom.**

commemorative, *a.* dedicatory, in honor of, observing; see **memorable 1.**

commence, *v.* start, enter upon, originate; see **begin 2.**

commend, *v.* laud, support, acclaim; see **approve, praise 1.**

commendable, *a.* praiseworthy, laudable, deserving; see **excellent.**

commendation, *n.* tribute, approval, approbation; see **honor, praise 1.**

comment, *n.* report, commentary, editorial; see **discussion, explanation, remark.**

comment, *v.* observe, remark, criticize, notice, state, express, pronounce, assert, affirm, mention, interject, say, note, touch *or* remark upon, disclose, bring out, point out, conclude; see also **mention, talk 1.**

commentary, *n.* criticism, analysis, explication; see **explanation, interpretation.**

commerce, *n.* buying and selling, trading, marketing; see **business 1, economics.**

commercial, *a.* trading, business, financial, economic, materialistic, practical, profitable, mercantile, merchandising, bartering, exchange, fiscal, monetary, trade, market, retail, wholesale, marketable, in the market, for sale, across the counter; see also **industrial, profitable.**

commercial, *n.* message from the sponsor, commercial announcement, plug; see **advertisement.**

commercialize, *v.* lessen, degrade, cheapen; see **abuse.**

commission, *n.* **1.** [An authorization] order, license, command; see **permission. 2.** [A committee] commissioners, representatives, board; see **committee. 3.** [A payment] royalty, fee, *rake-off; see also **pay 2, payment 1. —out of commission,** damaged, not working *or* running, out of order; see **broken 2.**

commission, *v.* send, delegate, appoint, authorize, charge, depute, empower, constitute, ordain, commit, entrust, send out, dispatch, consign, deputize, assign, accredit, engage, employ, inaugurate, invest, name, nominate, hire, enable, license, command, elect, select; see also **delegate 1.**

commissioner, *n.* spokesman, magistrate, government official; see **executive.**

commit, *v.* **1.** [To perpetrate] do something bad *or* wrong, be guilty of, complete; see **perform 1. 2.** [To entrust] confide, delegate, relegate (to), leave to, give to do, promise, consign, turn over to, put in the hands of, charge, invest, rely upon, depend upon, confer a trust, bind over, make responsible for, put an obligation upon, empower, employ, dispatch, send, vest in, invest with power, authorize, deputize, grant authority to, engage, commission; see also **commis-**

sion 2.—*Ant.* relieve of, **dismiss**, discharge.

commitment, *n.* engagement, responsibility, assurance; see **duty 1, promise 1.**

commit suicide, *v.* kill oneself, take an overdose (of any dangerous drug), slash one's wrists, slit one's (own) throat, take one's own life, *end it all, *commit hara-kiri.

committee, *n.* consultants, board, bureau, council, cabinet, investigators, trustees, appointed group, board of inquiry, representatives, soviet panel, investigating committee, executive committee, standing committee, planning board, *ad hoc* (Latin) *or* special committee, grand jury, referees, court, subcommittee; see also **representative 2.**

commodity, *n.* goods, article(s), merchandise, wares, materials, possessions, property, assets, belongings, thing(s), stock in trade, consumers' goods, line, what one handles, what one is showing.

common, *a.* 1. [Ordinary] universal, familiar, natural, normal, everyday, accepted, commonplace, characteristic, customary, bourgeois, conventional, passable, general, conformable, habitual, prevalent, probable, typical, prosaic, simple, current, prevailing, trite, household, second-rate, banal, unvaried, homely, colloquial, trivial, stock, oft repeated, indiscriminate, tedious, worn-out, hackneyed, monotonous, stale, casual, undistinguished, uneducated, artless, workaday, provincial, unsophisticated, unrefined, untutored, plain, uncultured, vulgar, unadorned, ugly, obvious, average, orthodox, mediocre, humdrum, well-known, insipid, stereotyped, patent, moderate, middling, abiding, indifferent, tolerable, temperate, innocuous, undistinguished, *run-of-the-mill *or* of the mine, garden variety, warmed-over, *fair-to-middling, so-so, *nothing to write home about; see also **conventional 1, dull 4, popular 1, 3, traditional.**—*Ant.* unnatural, **unique,** extraordinary. 2. [Of frequent occurrence] customary, constant, usual; see **frequent 1, habitual, regular 3. 3.** [Generally known] general, prevalent, well-known; see **familiar, traditional.** 4. [Low] cheap, inferior, mean; see **poor 2, subordinate. 5.** [Held or enjoyed in common] shared, joint, mutual; see **co-operative, public 2. —in common,** shared, communal, mutually *or* commonly held; see **public 2.**

commonly, *a.* usually, ordinarily, generally; see **regularly.**

commonplace, *a.* usual, hackneyed, mundane; see **common 1, conventional 1, 3.**

common sense, *n.* good sense, practicality, *horse sense; see **sense 2, wisdom.**

commotion, *n.* violence, tumult, uproar; see **disturbance 2, fight.**

communal, *a.* shared, co-operative, mutual; see **public 2.**

commune, *n.* community, village, municipality; see **city, co-operative, neighborhood.**

communicate, *v.* 1. [To impart information] impart, inform, advise; see **teach, tell 1.** 2. [To be in communication] correspond, be in touch, have access to, reach, hear from, be within reach, be in correspondence with, be near, be close to, have the confidence of, associate with, establish contact (with), be in agreement with *or* about, confer, talk, converse, chat, discourse *or* speak together, deal with, write to, reply, answer, have a meeting of minds, find a common denominator; see also **agree.** —*Ant.* be out of reach, **differ,** be removed from.

communication, *n.* talk, utterance, announcing, extrasensory perception *or* ESP, publication, writing, picturing, drawing, painting, radioing, broadcasting, televising, correspondence, disclosure, speaking, description, mention, announcement, conference, presentation, interchange, expression, narration, relation, declaration, assertion, elucidation, transmission, reception, news, ideas, announcement, statement, speech, language, warning, communiqué, briefing, bulletin, summary, information, report, account, declaration, publicity, translation, printed work, advice, tidings, conversation, converse. Means of communication include the following—book, letter, newspaper, magazine, radio, proclamation, broadcast, dispatch, radio report, telecast, telephone call, telegram, cable, radiogram, broadside, circular, notes, memorandum, (picture) post card, poster, billboard; see also **mail, news 1, 2, radio 2, telephone, television.**

communications, *n.* mass media, airmail, telephone; see **communication.**

communism, *n.* state socialism, Marxism, dictatorship of the proletariat, collectivism, state ownership of production; see **government 2.**

communist, *n.* Marxist, *commie, *red; see **radical.**

community, *n.* 1. [A town] village, colony, hamlet; see **city, town 1. 2.** [Society] the public, the people, the nation; see **society 2.**

commute, *v.* 1. [To exchange for something less severe] reduce, alleviate, mitigate; see **decrease 2. 2.** [Travel] go back and forth, drive, take the subway *or* bus *or* train; see **travel.**

commuter, *n.* suburbanite, city worker, daily traveler; see **driver, traveler.**

companion, *n.* attendant, comrade, escort, chaperon, protector, guide, friend, bodyguard.

companionship, *n.* fraternity, rapport, association; see **brotherhood, fellowship 1, friendship.**

company, *n.* 1. [A group of people] assembly, throng, band; see **gathering.** 2. [People organized for business] partnership, firm, corporation; see **business 4.** 3. [A guest or guests] visitor(s), caller(s), overnight guest(s); see **guest 1.** —keep (a person) company, stay with, visit, amuse; see **entertain 1.** —part company, separate, part, stop associating with; see **leave 1.**

comparable, *a.* 1. [Worthy of comparison] as good as, equivalent, tantamount; see **equal.** 2. [Capable of comparison] similar, akin, relative; see **alike, like.**

comparatively, *a.* relatively, similarly, analogously; see **approximately.**

compare, *v.* 1. [To liken] relate, connect, make like, notice the similarities, associate, link, distinguish between, bring near, put alongside, reduce to a common denominator, declare similar, equate, match, express by metaphor, correlate, parallel, show to be similar or analogous, identify with, bring into meaningful relation with, collate, balance, parallel, bring into comparison, estimate relatively, set over against, compare notes, exchange observations, weigh one thing against another, set side by side, correlate, measure, place in juxtaposition, note the similarities and differences of, juxtapose, draw a parallel between, tie up, come up to, stack up with; see also **distinguish 1.** 2. [To examine on a comparative basis] contrast, set against, weigh; see **analyze, examine.** 3. [To stand in relationship to another] match, vie, rival; see **equal, match 3.** —beyond or past or without compare, incomparable, without equal, distinctive; see **unique 1.**

compare to or **with,** *v.* put beside or side by side, relate to, equate; see **compare 1.**

comparison, *n.* likening, metaphor, resemblance, analogy, illustration, correspondence, relation, correlation, parable, allegory, similarity, likening, identification, equation, measurement, example, contrast, association, parallel, connection, paralleling; see also **association 2.**

compartment, *n.* section, portion, subdivision; see **part 1.**

compassion, *n.* sympathy, consideration, clemency; see **kindness 1, pity 1.**

compatible, *a.* agreeable, congruous, cooperative; see **harmonious 2.**

compel, *v.* enforce, constrain, coerce; see **force.**

compensate, *v.* recompense, remunerate, requite; see **pay 1, repay 1.**

compensation, *n.* remuneration, recompense, indemnity, satisfaction, remittal, return for services, commission, gratuity, reimbursement, allowance, deserts, remittance, salary, stipend, wages, hire, earnings, settlement, honorarium, coverage, consideration, damages, repayment, fee, reckoning, bonus, premium, amends, reward, advantage, profit, benefit, gain, *kickback; see also **pay 2, payment 1.**—*Ant.* loss, deprivation, confiscation.

compete, *v.* enter competition, take part, race (with), strive, struggle, vie or cope with, be in the running, become a competitor, enter the rolls or lists, run for, participate (in), engage in a contest, oppose, wrestle, be rivals, battle, bid (for), spar, fence, collide, face, clash, encounter, match wits or strength (with), play, grapple, take on all comers, *go in for, lock horns (with), go out (for); see also **fight.**

competence, *n.* capability, skill, fitness; see **ability.**

competent, *a.* fit, qualified, skilled; see **able.**

competition, *n.* race, match, contest, meet, fight, bout, boxing match, game of skill, trial, sport, athletic event, wrestling; see also **game 1, sport 1, 3.**

competitive, *a.* competing, antagonistic, opposing; see **rival.**

competitor, *n.* foe, rival, antagonist; see **contestant, opponent 1.**

compile, *v.* collect, arrange, assemble; see **accumulate, edit.**

complacent, *a.* self-satisfied, contented, self-righteous; see **egotistic, happy, satisfied, smug.**

complain, *v.* disapprove, accuse, deplore, criticize, denounce, differ, disagree, dissent, charge, report adversely (upon), reproach, oppose, grumble, whine, whimper, remonstrate, fret, protest, fuss, moan, make a fuss (about), take exception to, object (to), deprecate, enter a demurrer, demur, defy, carp, impute, indict, attack, refute, *kick, *bitch, grouch, croak, *gripe, *grunt, *beef, *bellyache, *kick up a fuss.—*Ant.* sanction, approve, countenance.

complaining, *a.* objecting, lamenting, murmuring, mourning, regretting, bewailing, deploring, weeping, moaning, protesting, charging, accusing, disapproving, grumbling, fretting, whining, imputing, resenting, dissenting, registering a protest, filing a complaint, making an adverse report, kicking.—*Ant.* enjoying, appreciating, praising.

complaint, n. 1. [An objection] charge, criticism, reproach; see **accusation, objection.** 2. [An illness] ailment, disease, infirmity; see **illness 1.**

complementary, a. paired, mated, corresponding; see **alike, matched.**

complete, a. 1. [Not lacking in any part] total, replete, entire; see **full 1, whole 1.** 2. [Finished] concluded, terminated, ended; see **finished 1.** 3. [Perfect] flawless, unblemished, impeccable; see **perfect, whole 2.**

complete, v. execute, consummate, perfect, accomplish, realize, perform, achieve, fill out, fulfill, equip, actualize, furnish, make (up), elaborate, make good, make complete, develop, fill in, refine, effect, carry out or off, crown, get through, round out; see also **create.**—*Ant.* start, begin, commence.

completed, a. achieved, ended, concluded; see **built, done 2, finished 1.**

completely, a. entirely, fully, totally, utterly, wholly, perfectly, exclusively, simply, effectively, competently, solidly, bodily, absolutely, unanimously, thoroughly, en masse, exhaustively, minutely, painstakingly, extensively, conclusively, unconditionally, finally, to the or one's utmost, ultimately, altogether, comprehensively, to the end, from beginning to end, on all counts, in all, in full measure, to the limit or full, in full, to completion, to the nth degree, *to a frazzle, downright, through thick and thin, down to the ground, through and through, *hook, line, and sinker, rain or shine, in one lump, from A to Z, from head to foot.—*Ant.* somewhat, **partly,** partially.

completion, n. finish, conclusion, fulfillment; see **end 2.**

complex, a. 1. [Composed of several parts] composite, heterogeneous, conglomerate, multiple, mosaic, manifold, multiform, compound, complicated, aggregated, involved, combined, compact, compounded, miscellaneous, multiplex, multifarious, variegated; see also **mixed 1.** 2. [Difficult to understand] entangled, tangled, circuitous, convoluted, puzzling, mixed, mingled, muddled, jumbled, impenetrable, inscrutable, unfathomable, undecipherable, bewildering, intricate, perplexing, complicated, involved, enigmatic, hidden, knotted, meandering, winding, tortuous, snarled, rambling, twisted, disordered, devious, discursive, cryptic, inextricable, knotty, roundabout; see also **confused 2, difficult 2.**—*Ant.* understandable, plain, apparent.

complex, n. phobia, mania, repressed emotions or fears or desires or hates; see also **fear, insanity 1.**

complexion, n. tone, glow, color, coloration, general coloring, tinge, cast, flush, skin texture, tint, hue, pigmentation; see also **skin.** Descriptions of complexions include the following—blond, fair, pale, sallow, sickly, dark, brunet, olive, bronze, sandy, rosy, red, ruddy, brown, yellow, black, *peroxide or drugstore blond, *strawberry and cream.

complicate, v. combine, fold, multiply, twist, snarl (up), associate with, involve, obscure, confound, muddle, clog, jumble, interrelate, elaborate, embarrass, implicate, tangle, conceal, mix up, impede, perplex, hinder, hamper, handicap, tie up with, *ball up; see also **confuse, entangle.**—*Ant.* simplify, clear up, unfold.

complicated, a. intricate, various, mixed; see **complex 2, confused 2, difficult 2.**

complication, n. complexity, dilemma, development; see **confusion 2, difficulty 1, 2.**

compliment, n. felicitation, tribute, approval, commendation, endorsement, confirmation, sanction, applause, flattery, acclaim, adulation, notice, regards, honor, appreciation, respects, blessing, ovation, veneration, admiration, congratulation, homage, good word, sentiment; see also **praise 2.**—*Ant.* censure, **abuse,** disapproval.

compliment, v. wish joy to, remember, commemorate, pay one's respects, honor, cheer, salute, hail, toast, applaud, extol, celebrate, felicitate, pay tribute to, be in favor of, commend, endorse, sanction, confirm, acclaim, please, satisfy, pay a compliment to, sing the praises of, speak highly of, exalt, applaud, worship, eulogize, glorify, magnify, fawn upon, *butter up, puff (someone) up, *hand it to (someone); see also **praise 1.**—*Ant.* denounce, disapprove of, censure.

complimentary, a. flattering, laudatory, approving, celebrating, honoring, respectful, congratulatory, well-wishing, highly favorable, praising, singing the praises of, with highest recommendations, with high praise; see also **polite.**

compose, v. 1. [To be the parts or the ingredients] constitute, comprise, go into the making of, make up, enter or merge or go into or in, be a component or ingredient, be an element or portion of, belong to, consist of, be made of; see also **comprise, include 1.** 2. [To create] fabricate, produce, write (music), score, orchestrate, forge, discover, design, conceive, imagine, make up, turn out, draw up; see also **design, invent 1.**

composed, a. 1. [Made] created, made up, fashioned; see **formed.** 2. [Calm] poised, confident, *cool; see **calm 1, confident 2.**

composer, n. arranger, song-writer, musical author; see **author, musician, poet, writer.**

composition, *n.* creation, making, fashioning, formation, conception, presentation, invention, fiction, novel, tale, play, drama, verse, stanza, symphony, concerto, quartet, song, rhapsody, melody; see also **biography, literature 2, music 1, poetry, writing 2.**

composure, *n.* serenity, peace of mind, calm, calmness, self-possession, nonchalance, cool-headedness, control, self-control, balance, contentment, tranquility, stability, harmony, assurance, self-assurance, poise, serene *or* calm *or* composed state of mind, even temper, equanimity, coolness, level-headedness, fortitude, moderation, gravity, sobriety, a cool head, presence of mind, equilibrium, aplomb, self-restraint, ease, evenness, complacence, tolerance, content, quiet, command of one's faculties, forbearance, *cool; see also **patience 1, peace 3.—Ant.** exuberance, passion, zeal.

compound, *n.* composite, union, aggregate; see **mixture 1.**

comprehend, *v.* grasp, discern, perceive; see **know 1, understand 1.**

comprehension, *n.* understanding, perception, cognizance; see **awareness, knowledge 1.**

comprehensive, *a.* extensive, sweeping, complete; see **absolute 1, general 1, infinite, large 1.**

compress, *v.* condense, compact, press together, consolidate, squeeze (together), tighten, cramp, contract, crowd, constrict, abbreviate, shrivel, make brief, reduce, dehydrate, pack, shorten, shrink, narrow, abridge, bind tightly, wrap closely, wedge, boil down, cram; see also **press 1, tighten 1.—Ant.** spread, stretch, expand.

comprise, *v.* comprehend, contain, embrace, include, involve, enclose, embody, encircle, encompass, sum up, cover, consist of *or* in, be composed *or* made up of, constitute, incorporate, span, hold, engross, take into account *or* consideration, be contained in, add up to, amount to, take in; see also **compose 1, include 1.—Ant.** bar, lack, exclude.

compromise, *n.* covenant, bargain, give and take; see **agreement.**

compromise, *v.* agree, conciliate, find a middle ground; see **negotiate 1.**

compulsion, *n.* 1. [Force] drive, necessity, need; see **requirement 2.** 2. [An obsession] preoccupation, obsession, engrossment; see **requirement 2.**

compulsive, *a.* driving, impelling, besetting; see **passionate 2.**

compulsory, *a.* obligatory, required, requisite; see **necessary 1.**

compute, *v.* count, figure, measure; see **calculate.**

computer, *n.* electronic *or* electric brain, electro-computer, thinking machine, IBM (trademark), calculator, data processor, electronic circuit, cybernetic device, analog computer, digital computer, programmer; see also **machine.**

computer language, *n.* macroinstruction system, machine language, programming language, computer-processed instructions. Some computer languages include the following—FORTRAN (Formula translation), COBOL (Common Business Oriented Language), MAD (Michigan Algorithmic Decoder), Jovial (Jule's own version of the International Algebraic Language), SEPOL, LISP, ACE, ACOM, ADAPT, NL-1, PL-1, TABSOL, SLIP, ALGOL, SNOBOL, SIMSCRIPT; see also **language 1.**

comrade, *n.* confidant, confidante, intimate; see **associate, friend.**

con, *a.* conversely, opposed to, in opposition; see **against 1.**

*con, *n.* deception, swindle, fraud; see **trick 1.**

*con, *v.* cheat, dupe, mislead; see **deceive.**

concave, *a.* curved, sunken, cupped; see **round 3.**

conceal, *v.* screen, secrete, cover; see **hide 1.**

concealed, *a.* covered, obscured, unseen; see **hidden 2.**

concealment, *n.* hiding, covering, camouflage; see **disguise.**

concede, *v.* yield, grant, acknowledge; see **admit 2, 3, allow.**

conceit, *n.* arrogance, self-admiration, narcissism; see **vanity.**

conceited, *a.* vain, arrogant, *stuck up; see **egotistic 2.**

conceivable, *a.* understandable, credible, believable; see **convincing 2, imaginable, likely 1.**

conceive, *v.* 1. [To form a concept or image of] consider, formulate, speculate; see **imagine, think 1. 2.** [To become pregnant] come with child, get pregnant, be impregnated, *get in the family way.

concentrate, *v.* 1. [To bring or come together] amass, mass, assemble, combine, consolidate, compact, condense, reduce, hoard, garner, centralize, store, bring into a small compass, bring toward a central point, embody, localize, strengthen, direct toward one object, constrict, fix, cramp, focus, reduce, intensify, crowd or draw or flock together, contract, muster, bunch, heap up, swarm, conglomerate, stow away, congest, narrow, compress, converge, center, collect, cluster, congregate, huddle; see also **accumulate, gather 2, pack 2. 2.** [To employ all one's mental powers] think intensely, give attention to, meditate (upon), ponder, focus attention on, direct attention to one object, weigh, consider closely, scrutinize, regard carefully, contemplate, study deeply, examine closely, brood over, put one's mind to, be engrossed or absorbed in, attend, give exclusive attention to, occupy the mind or thoughts with, fix one's attention, apply the mind, give heed, focus (one's thought), give the mind to, direct the mind upon, center, think hard, rack one's brains, *get or be on the beam, *keep one's eye on the ball, *knuckle or buckle down; see also **analyze, examine, think 1.**–*Ant.* be inattentive, **drift,** ignore.

concentrated, *a.* 1. [Undiluted] rich, unadulterated, straight; see also **strong 8, thick 1. 2.** [Intense] intensive, deep, hard; see **intense.**

concentration, *n.* 1. [Anything brought together] company, audience, miscellany, band, party, flock, herd, mass, group, array; see also **collection 2.** 2. [Attention] close attention, concern, application; see **thought 1. 3.** [Density] solidity, consistency, frequency; see **congestion, density.**

concept, *n.* idea, theory, notion; see **thought 2.**

conception, *n.* 1. [The act of conceiving mentally] perception, apprehension, comprehension, imagining, speculating, meditation, dreaming, cogitating, deliberating, concentrating, meditating, realization, consideration, speculation, understanding, cognition, mental grasp, apperception, forming or formulation of an idea or principle or mental image; see also **thought 1. 2.** [The act of conceiving physically] inception, impregnation, insemination; see **fertilization 2.**

concern, *n.* 1. [Affair] business, matter, interest; see **affair 1. 2.** [Regard] care, interest, solicitude; see **attention.**

concern, *v.* 1. [To have reference to] refer or pertain or relate or be related or have relation to, have significance for, bear on or upon, regard, be concerned or connected with, be about, have to do with, be a matter of concern to, have a bearing on, have connections with, be applicable to, depend upon, be dependent upon, answer to, deal with, belong to, touch upon, figure in; see also **influence, treat 1. 2.** [Concern oneself] be concerned, become involved, take pains; see **bother 1, care, worry 2.**

concerning, *a.* respecting, touching, regarding; see **about 2.**

concert, *n.* (musical) selections, musicale, recital; see **performance.**

concise, *a.* succinct, brief, condensed; see **short 1.**

conclude, *v.* 1. [To finish] terminate, bring to an end, complete; see **achieve. 2.** [To deduce] presume, reason, gather; see **assume.**

conclusion, *n.* 1. [An end] finish, termination, completion; see **end 2. 2.** [A decision] determination, resolve, resolution; see **judgment 3.** –**in conclusion,** lastly, in closing, in the end; see **finally 1.**

conclusive, *a.* final, decisive, absolute; see also **certain 2.**

concord, *n.* harmony, consensus, accord; see **agreement, unity 1.**

concrete, *a.* 1. [Specific] particular, solid, precise; see **definite 1, detailed, real 2. 2.** [Made of concrete] cement, poured, prefabricated, precast, concrete and steel, compact, unyielding; see also **firm 2.**

concrete, *n.* concretion, ferroconcrete, reinforced concrete; see **cement, pavement.**

concur, *v.* accord, be consonant with, be in harmony (with); see **agree, approve, equal.**

concurrent, *a.* synchronal, parallel, coexisting; see **simultaneous.**

concussion, *n.* rupture, gash, crack; see **fracture, injury.**

condemn, *v.* doom, sentence, damn, pass sentence on, find guilty, seal the doom of, pronounce judgment, prescribe punishment; see also **convict, punish.**–*Ant.* acquit, **excuse,** exonerate.

condemnation, *n.* denunciation, disapprobation, reproach; see **accusation, blame, objection.**

condense, *v.* 1. [To compress] press together, constrict, consolidate; see **compress, contract 1, decrease 1, 2. 2.** [To abridge] abbreviate, summarize, digest; see **decrease 2.**

condensed, *a.* 1. [Shortened] concise, brief, succinct; see **short 2. 2.** [Concentrated] undiluted, rich, evaporated; see **thick 3.**

condescend, *v.* stoop, lower oneself, agree, humble or degrade or demean oneself, submit with good grace, assume a patronizing air, lower one's tone, descend, comply, oblige, favor, concede, grant, accord, accommodate to, *come down a peg or off one's high horse; see also **patronize 2.**

condescending, *a.* patronizing, complaisant, superior; see **egotistic.**

condition, *n.* 1. [A state] situation, position, status; see **state 2. 2.** [A requisite] stipulation, contingency, provision; see **requirement 1. 3.** [A limitation] restriction, qualification, prohibition; see **limi-**

tation 2, **restraint** 2. 4. [State of health] fitness, tone, shape; see also **health**. 5. [*Illness] ailment, infirmity, temper; see **illness 1, 2.**

condition, *v.* adapt, modify, work out; see **practice 1, train 1.**

conditional, *a.* provisional, subject, contingent, limited, restricted, relying on, subject to, restrictive, guarded, not absolute, granted on certain terms; see also **dependent 3.**

conditionally, *a.* provisory, provisionary, hypothetically, with the condition *or* stipulation (that), with reservations *or* limitations, tentatively, possibly; see also **temporarily.**

conditioned, *a.* altered, disciplined, modified; see **trained.**

conditions, *n.* environment, surrounding(s), setting; see **circumstances 2.**

condominium, *n.* 1. [Co-operative apartment dwelling] commonly owned apartment house, jointly owned dwelling, *co-op; see also **apartment, home 1.**

condone, *v.* pardon, excuse, overlook; see **approve.**

conduct, *n.* 1. [Behavior] deportment, demeanor, manner; see **behavior. 2.** [Management] supervision, plan, organization; see **management.**

conduct, *v.* 1. [To guide] escort, convoy, attend; see **accompany, lead 1. 2.** [To manage] administer, handle, carry on; see **manage 1.**

conduct (oneself), *v.* comport oneself, act properly, acquit oneself well; see **behave.**

conductor, *n.* 1. [That which conducts] conduit, conveyor, transmitter; see **channel, wire 1, wiring. 2.** [One who conducts] orchestra leader, pilot, head; see **administrator, guide, leader 2. 3.** [One in charge of a car or train] trainman, railroad man, ticket taker, brakeman, streetcar conductor, motorman, bus driver; see also **driver.**

Confederacy, *n.* Confederate States of America, Confederacy, the South; see also **south.**

confederate, *a.* allied, associated, in league; see **joined, united.**

confer, *v.* converse, deliberate, parley; see **discuss.**

conference, *n.* conversation, discussion, interchange; see **gathering.**

conferring, *a.* discussing, conversing, in conference; see **talking.**

confess, *v.* acknowledge, own, concede; see **admit 1.**

confession, *n.* 1. [The act of confessing] concession, allowance, owning to *or* up, revelation, disclosure, publication, affirmation, assertion, declaration, telling, exposure, narration, exposé, proclamation, making public; see also **acknowledgment.**—*Ant.* concealment, denial,

disclaimer. 2. [A sacrament] absolution, contrition, repentance; see **sacrament.**

confidant, *n.* adherent, intimate associate, companion; see **friend.**

confide, *v.* disclose, admit, divulge; see **reveal, tell 1.**

confidence, *n.* self-confidence, self-reliance, morale, fearlessness, boldness, resolution, firmness, sureness, faith in oneself, tenacity, fortitude, certainty, daring, spirit, reliance, grit, *cool, heart, backbone, nerve, *spunk; see also **courage, determination.**

confident, *a.* self-confident, assured, able, being certain, fearless, having faith in, sure of oneself, dauntless, bold, presumptuous, hopeful, depending *or* counting *or* relying on, self-sufficient; see also **certain 1.**

confidential, *a.* classified, intimate, privy; see **private, secret 1, 3.**

confidentially, *a.* privately, personally, in confidence; see **secretly.**

confidently, *a.* in an assured manner *or* way, with *or* having conviction, assuredly; see **boldly 1, positively 1.**

confine, *v.* 1. [To restrain] repress, hold back, keep within limits; see **hinder, restrain. 2.** [To imprison] cage, incarcerate, shut up; see **enslave, imprison.**

confined, *a.* 1. [Restricted] limited, hampered, compassed; see **bound 1, 2, restricted. 2.** [Bedridden] on one's back, ill, laid up; see **sick. 3.** [In prison] behind bars, locked up, in bonds *or* irons *or* chains, in jail, imprisoned, jailed, immured, incarcerated, detained, under lock and key, *on ice.—*Ant.* free, released, at liberty.

confinement, *n.* restriction, limitation, constraint, repression, control, coercion, keeping, safekeeping, custody, curb, bounds, check, bonds, detention, imprisonment, incarceration; see also **jail.**—*Ant.* freedom, release, independence.

confines, *n.* bounds, limits, periphery; see **boundary.**

confining, *a.* limiting, restricting, bounding, prescribing, restraining, hampering, repressing, checking, enclosing, imprisoning, incarcerating, detaining, keeping locked up, keeping behind bars.

confirm, *v.* 1. [To ratify] sanction, affirm, settle; see **approve, endorse 2. 2.** [To prove] verify, authenticate, validate; see **explain, prove.**

confirmation, *n.* 1. [The act of confirming] ratification, proving, authentication, corroboration, support, endorsement, sanction, authorization, verification, affirmation, acceptance, passage, validation, approval, attestation, assent, admission, recognition, witness, consent, testimony, agreement, evidence; see also **agreement, proof 1.**—*Ant.* annulment, **cancellation,** disapproval. 2. [A sacrament] rite, consecration, liturgy; see **ceremony, sacrament.**

confirmed, *a.* 1. [Firmly established] proved, valid, accepted; see **certain 2, established 2, guaranteed.** 2. [Inveterate] ingrained, seasoned, regular; see **chronic, habitual.**

confiscate, *v.* appropriate, impound, usurp; see **seize 2, steal.**

conflict, *n.* struggle, strife, engagement; see **battle, fight.**

conflict, *v.* clash, contrast, contend; see **differ 1, fight, oppose 1, 2.**

conform, *v.* comply, accord, submit, accommodate, live up to, fit, suit, acclimate, accustom, be regular, harmonize, adapt (oneself), be guided by, fit the pattern, be in fashion *or* the mode, reconcile, settle (down), obey (rules), grow used to, do as others do, get in line, fall in with, go by, adhere *or* adjust *or* keep *or* assimilate to, keep up, get one's bearings, keep up with the Joneses, chime in with, join the parade, play the game, go according to Hoyle, follow the beaten path, toe the line *or* mark, follow suit, run with the pack, follow the crowd, do in Rome as the Romans do; see also **agree, follow 2, obey.**—*Ant.* conflict, **differ,** disagree.

conforming, *a.* agreeing, in line with, in agreement *or* conformity; see **harmonious 2.**

conformist, *n.* conformer, conventionalist, advocate; see **follower.**

conformity, *n.* 1. [Similarity] congruity, correspondence, resemblance; see **similarity.** 2. [Obedience] willingness, submission, compliance; see **agreement.**

conform to, *v.* correspond, parallel, fit; see **agree, compare 1.**

confound, *v.* puzzle, perplex, bewilder; see **confuse.**

confounded, *a.* confused, bewildered, disconcerted; see **doubtful.**

confront, *v.* brave, defy, repel; see **dare 2, face 1.**

confrontation, *n.* meeting, battle, strife; see **dispute 1, fight 1.**

confuse, *v.* upset, befuddle, mislead, misinform, puzzle, perplex, confound, fluster, bewilder, embarrass, daze, astonish, disarrange, disorder, jumble, blend, mix, mingle, cloud, fog, stir up, disconcert, abash, agitate, amaze, worry, trouble, snarl, unsettle, muddle, clutter, complicate, involve, rattle, derange, baffle, frustrate, perturb, dismay, distract, entangle, encumber, befog, obscure, mystify, make a mess of (it), throw off (the scent), cross *or* foul *or* mix *or* ball up, lead astray, stump, rattle, make one's head swim; see also **disturb, tangle.**—*Ant.* clear up, clarify, untangle.

confused, *a.* 1. [Puzzled in mind] disconcerted, abashed, perplexed; see **doubt-**

ful. 2. [Not properly distinguished] mistaken, jumbled, snarled, deranged, bewildered, out of order, disarrayed, confounded, mixed (up), chaotic, disordered, muddled, fuddled, befuddled, slovenly, untidy, messy, involved, misunderstood, blurred, obscured, topsy-turvy, *balled *or* fouled *or* screwed up, in a mess, *haywire, *snafu; see also **obscure 1, tangled.**—*Ant.* discriminated, **distinguished,** ordered.

confusing, *a.* disconcerting, confounding, baffling, puzzling, disturbing, unsettling, upsetting, embarrassing, agitating, obscuring, blurring, befuddling, tangling, snarling, cluttering, muddling, disarranging; see also **difficult 2, obscure 1.**—*Ant.* reassuring, **orderly,** clear.

confusion, *n.* complication, intricacy, muss, untidiness, complexity, difficulty, mistake, bewilderment, turmoil, tumult, pandemonium, commotion, stir, ferment, disarray, jumble, convulsion, bustle, trouble, row, riot, uproar, fracas, distraction, agitation, emotional upset, daze, astonishment, surprise, fog, haze, consternation, racket, excitement, chaos, turbulence, dismay, uncertainty, irregularity, maze, interruption, stoppage, clutter, entanglement, backlash, clog, break, breakdown, knot, obstruction, trauma, congestion, interference, nervousness, disorganization, muddle, mass, lump, snarl, snag, *to-do, hubbub, tie-up, botch, rumpus, scramble, shuffle, mess, hodgepodge, stew, *going round and round, *jam, *fix, bull in a china shop; see also **disorder 2.**—*Ant.* quiet, calm, **order.**

confute, *v.* confound, dismay, invalidate; see **deny, oppose 1.**

congenial, *a.* kindred, compatible, suitable; see **friendly, harmonious 2.**

congestion, *n.* profusion, crowdedness, overpopulation, ghetto conditions, press, traffic (jam), overcrowding, overdevelopment, too many people *or* things, too much *or* many, concentration, surplus; see also **excess 1.**

congratulate, *v.* felicitate, wish joy to, toast; see **compliment, praise 1.**

congratulations, *interj.* best wishes, compliments, bless you; see **compliment.**

congregate, *v.* convene, meet, converge; see **gather 1.**

congregation, *n.* meeting, group, assemblage; see **gathering.**

congress, *n.* [*Often capital C*] parliament, deliberative assembly, legislative body; see **committee, government, legislature.**

conjunction, *n.* 1. [Act of joining together] combination, connection, association; see **union 1.** 2. [A syntactic connecting word]. Conjunctions include the following—and, but, if, for, or, nor, so, yet, only, else, than, before, since, then, though, when, where, why, both, either, while, as, neither, although, because, unless, until.

conjure up, *v.* call, invoke, materialize; see **summon, urge 2.**

connect, *v.* 1. [To join] combine, unite, attach; see **join 1.** 2. [To associate] relate, equate, correlate; see **compare 1.**

connected, *a.* 1. [Joined together] united, combined, coupled; see **joined.** 2. [Related] associated, applicable, pertinent; see **related 2, relevant.**

connecting, *a.* joining, linking (to), combining (with), uniting, associating, relating, tying *or* bringing *or* cementing *or* knitting *or* fusing *or* hooking together, clinching, fastening, mixing, mingling, welding, pairing, coupling; see also **joined.**

connection, *n.* 1. [Relationship] kinship, association, reciprocity; see **association 2, relationship.** 2. [A junction] combination, juncture, consolidation; see **union 1.** 3. [A link] attachment, fastening, bond; see **link.** —**in connection with,** in conjunction with, associated with, together with; see **with.**

connotation, *n.* implication, intention, essence; see **meaning.**

conquer, *v.* subdue, overcome, crush; see **defeat 2.**

conqueror, *n.* vanquisher, master, champion; see **hero 1, winner.**

conquest, *n.* triumph, success, conquering; see **victory.**

conscience, *n.* moral sense, inner voice, the still small voice; see **duty 1, morals, shame 2.** —**have on one's conscience,** be culpable, blamable *or* responsible for; see **guilty.** —**in (all) conscience,** rightly, fairly, properly; see **justly 1.**

conscience-stricken, *a.* remorseful, repentant, chastened; see **sorry 1.**

conscientious, *a.* fastidious, meticulous, complete; see **careful, reliable.**

conscientiousness, *n.* exactness, care, honor; see **care 1, duty 1, honesty, responsibility 1.**

conscious, *a.* cognizant, informed, sure, certain, assured, discerning, knowing, sensible, sensitive, acquainted, attentive, watchful, mindful, vigilant, understanding, keen, alert, awake *or* alert *or* alive *or* sensitive to, conscious *or* mindful *or* cognizant of, *hep to, *on to, *with it; see also **intelligent.**—*Ant.* unaware, insensitive, inattentive.

consciousness, *n.* alertness, cognizance, mindfulness; see **awareness, knowledge 1.**

consecrate, *v.* hallow, sanctify, anoint; see **bless.**

consecrated, *a.* blessed, sanctified, hallowed; see **divine.**

consecration, *n.* making holy, sanctification, exalting; see **celebration.**

consecutive, *a.* continuous, chronological, serial, in turn, progressive, connected, in order *or* sequence, sequential, going on, continuing, one after another *or* the other, serialized, numerical; see also **constant, regular 3.**

consecutively, *a.* following, successively, continuously; see **gradually.**

consensus, *n.* consent, unison, accord; see **agreement.**

consent, *n.* assent, approval, acquiescence; see **permission.**

consent, *v.* accede, assent, acquiesce; see **agree, allow, approve.**

consequence, *n.* 1. [Effect] outgrowth, end, outcome; see **result.** 2. [Importance] moment, value, weight; see **importance.** —**take the consequences,** accept the results of one's actions, suffer, bear the burden of; see **endure 2.**

conservation, *n.* maintenance, keeping, preservation, preserving, conserving, guarding, storage, protecting, saving, safekeeping, upkeep, economy, keeping in trust *or* in a safe state; see also **preservation.**—*Ant.* waste, destruction, misuse.

conservative, *a.* saving, holding to, keeping, unchanging, unchangeable, stable, constant, steady, traditional, reactionary, conventional, moderate, unprogressive, firm, obstinate, inflexible, opposed to change, cautious, sober, Tory, not speculative, taking no chances, timid, fearful, unimaginative, right-wing, *in a rut *or* groove; see careful, moderate 3.—*Ant.* radical, risky, changing.

conservative, *n.* reactionary, rightwinger, die-hard, Tory, Whig, Federalist, champion of the status quo, opponent of change, classicist, traditionalist, unprogressive, conventionalist, John Bircher, mossback, old fogy, *fossil.—*Ant.* radical, progressive, liberal.

consider, *v.* allow *or* provide for, grant, take up, concede, acknowledge, recognize, favor, value, take under advisement, deal with, regard, make allowance for, take into consideration, keep in mind, reckon with, play around with, toss *or* throw *or* bat around, see about; see also **reconsider, think 1.**—*Ant.* deny, refuse, reject.

considerable, *a.* 1. [Important] noteworthy, significant, essential; see **important 1.** 2. [Much] abundant, lavish, bountiful; see **much 2, plentiful 1.**

considerate, *a.* charitable, kind, solicitous; see **polite, thoughtful** 2.

consideration, *n.* 1. [The state of being considerate] kindliness, thoughtfulness, attentiveness; see **courtesy** 1, **kindness** 1, **tolerance** 1. 2. [Payment] remuneration, salary, wage; see **payment** 1. 3. [Something to be considered] situation, problem, judgment, notion, fancy, puzzle, proposal, difficulty, incident, evidence, new development, occurrence, state, pass, occasion, emergency, idea, thought, trouble, plan, particulars, items, scope, extent, magnitude; see also **idea** 1, **plan** 2. **—in consideration of,** because of, on account of, for; see **considering.** **—take into consideration,** take into account, weigh, keep in mind; see **consider.** **—under consideration,** thought over, discussed, evaluated; see **considered.**

considered, *a.* carefully thought about, treated, gone into, contemplated, weighed, meditated, investigated, examined; see also **determined** 1.

considering, *prep.* and *conj.* in light *or* view *or* consideration of, pending, taking into account, everything being equal, inasmuch *or* insomuch as, with (something) in view.

consign, *v.* convey, dispatch, transfer; see **give** 1, **send** 1.

consistency, *n.* 1. [Harmony] union, compatibility, accord; see **agreement, symmetry.** 2. [The degree of firmness or thickness] hardness, softness, firmness; see **density, texture** 1.

consistent, *a.* compatible, equable, expected; see **logical** 1, **rational** 1, **regular** 3.

consist of, *v.* embody, contain, involve; see **comprise, include** 1.

consolation, *n.* sympathy, compassion, fellow feeling; see **pity** 1.

console, *v.* cheer, sympathize with, gladden; see **comfort** 1, **encourage.**

consolidate, *v.* connect, mix, unify; see **compress, pack** 2.

consolidation, *n.* alliance, association, federation; see **union** 1.

consonant, *n.* Linguistic terms referring to consonant sounds include the following—voiceless, voiced; stop, fricative *or* spirant, resonant, sibilant; implosive, plosive, nasal, click, glide, continuant, trill. In spelling, English consonants are as follows—b,c,d,f,g,h,j,k,l,m,n,p,q,r,s,t,v, w,x,y,z; see also **letter, sound** 2, **vowel.**

conspicuous, *a.* outstanding, eminent, distinguished, celebrated, noted, notable, illustrious, striking, prominent, well-known, arresting, remarkable, renowned, famed, notorious, flagrant, glaring, important, influential, noticeable, standing out like a sore thumb; see also **promi-**

nent 1.—*Ant.* unknown, inconspicuous, unsung.

conspiracy, *n.* intrigue, collusion, connivance; see **trick** 1.

conspirator, *n.* betrayer, schemer, cabalist; see **traitor.**

conspire, *v.* plot, scheme, contrive; see **plan** 1.

constant, *a.* steady, uniform, perpetual, unchanging, continual, uninterrupted, unvarying, connected, even, incessant, unbroken, nonstop, monotonous, standardized, regularized; see also **regular** 3.

constantly, *a.* uniformly, steadily, invariably; see **regularly.**

constituency, *n.* (the) voters, electorate, body politic, electors, voting public, balloters, the nation, the people; see **voter.**

constituent, *n.* component, element, ingredient; see **part** 1.

constitute, *v.* 1. [To found] establish, develop, create; see **establish** 2. 2. [To make up] frame, compound, aggregate; see **compose** 1.

constitution, *n.* 1. [Health] vitality, physique, build; see **health.** 2. [A basic political document] custom, code, written law; see **law** 2.

constitutional, *a.* representative, republican, safeguarding liberty; see **democratic.**

constrain, *v.* necessitate, compel, stifle; see **force, urge** 2.

constraint, *n.* 1. [The use of force] coercion, force, compulsion; see **pressure** 2. 2. [Shyness] bashfulness, restraint, humility; see **reserve** 3. 3. [Confinement] captivity, detention, restriction; see **arrest, confinement.**

constrict, *v.* contract, cramp, choke up; see **tighten** 1.

construct, *v.* make, erect, fabricate; see **build, create.**

construction, *n.* 1. [The act of constructing] formation, manufacture, building; see **architecture, building, production** 1. 2. [A method of constructing] structure, arrangement, organization, system, plan, development, steel and concrete, contour, format, mold, cast, outline, type, shape, build, cut, fabric, formation, turn, framework, configuration, brick and mortar, prefab.

constructive, *a.* useful, valuable, effective; see **helpful** 1.

consult, *v.* take counsel, deliberate, confer, parley, conspire *or* counsel *or* be closeted with, compare notes about, put heads together, commune, treat, negotiate, debate, argue, talk over, call in, ask advice of, turn to, seek advice; see also **ask, discuss.**

consultation, *n.* interview, conference, deliberation; see **discussion.**

consume, *v.* 1. [To use] use, use up, wear out; see **spend** 1, **use** 1. 2. [To eat or drink] absorb, feed, devour; see **eat 1.**

consumer, *n.* user, customer, shopper; see **buyer.**

consumption, *n.* using, spending, expense; see **destruction 1, use 1, waste 1.**

contact, *n.* touch, junction, connection; see **meeting 1.**

contact, *v.* speak to, reach, make contact with; see **communicate 2, talk 1.**

contagion, *n.* poison, virus, illness; see **illness 1.**

contagious, *a.* communicable, infectious, transmittable, spreading, poisonous, epidemic, deadly, endemic, tending to spread; see also **catching.**

contain, *v.* 1. [Include] comprehend, embrace, be composed of; see **include 1.** 2. [Restrict] hold, keep back, stop; see **restrain 1.**

container, *n.* receptacle, basket, bin, bowl, dish, tub, cauldron, holder, vessel, capsule, package, packet, chest, purse, pod, pouch, cask, sack, pot, pottery, jug, bucket, canteen, pit, box, carton, canister, crate, pail, kettle; see also **bag, can 1, case 5, jar 1, vase.**

contaminate, *v.* pollute, infect, defile; see **corrupt, dirty.**

contamination, *n.* disease, contagion, taint; see **pollution 1.**

contemplate, *v.* ponder, muse, speculate on; see **study, think 1.**

contemporary, *a.* present, fashionable, current; see **modern 1, 3.**

contempt, *n.* scorn, derision, slight; see **hatred.**

contend, *v.* contest, battle, dispute; see **fight.**

content, *a.* appeased, gratified, comfortable; see **happy, satisfied.**

contented, *a.* happy, pleased, thankful; see **happy, satisfied.**

contention, *n.* 1. [A quarrel] struggle, belligerency, combat; see **competition, dispute, fight.** 2. [An assertion supported by argument] explanation, stand, charge; see also **attitude, declaration.**

contentment, *n.* peace, pleasure, happiness; see **comfort 1, ease 1, satisfaction 2.**

contents, *n.* gist, essence, meaning, significance, intent, implication, connotation, text, subject matter, sum, substance, sum and substance, details; see also **ingredients, matter 1.**

contest, *n.* trial, match, challenge; see **game 1, sport 1.**

contest, *v.* oppose, battle, quarrel; see also **dare, fight 2.**

contestant, *n.* competitor, opponent, participant, rival, challenger, contester, disputant, antagonist, adversary, combatant, player, team member; see also **player 1.**

context, *n.* connection, text, substance; see **meaning.**

continent, *n.* mainland, (continental) land mass, body of land; see also **Africa, America, Asia, Australia, Europe.**

continual, *a.* uninterrupted, unbroken, connected; see **consecutive, regular 3.**

continually, *a.* steadily, continuously, constantly; see **frequently, regularly.**

continuation, *n.* succession, line, extension, increase, endurance, sustaining, preservation, perseverance, correction, translation, revision, supplement, complement, new version; see also **addition 1, sequence 1.**—*Ant.* end, pause, delay.

continue, *interj.* keep on, carry on, keep going, keep talking, keep reading, etc.; keep it up.

continue, *v.* 1. [To persist] persevere, carry forward, maintain, carry or roll or keep or go or run or live on, never stop, sustain, promote, progress, uphold, forge ahead, remain, press onward, make headway, move ahead, keep the ball rolling, *leave no stone unturned, *chip away at; see also **advance 1, endure 1.**—*Ant.* cease, end, give up. 2. [To resume] begin again, renew, begin or carry over, return to, take up again, begin where one left off, be reinstated or reestablished or restored; see also **resume.**—*Ant.* discontinue, halt, postpone.

continuing, *a.* persevering, carrying on, progressing; see **constant 1, regular 3.**

continuity, *n.* continuousness, constancy, continuance, flow, succession, unity, sequence, chain, linking, train, progression, dovetailing, extension; see also **continuation.**—*Ant.* interruption, stop, break.

continuous, *a.* unfaltering, repeated, perpetual; see **consecutive 1, constant 1, regular 3.**

contort, *v.* deform, misshape, twist; see **distort 2.**

contortion, *n.* deformity, distortion, grimace, twist, ugliness, pout, wryness, crookedness.

contour, *n.* profile, silhouette, shape; see **form 1.**

contraband, *n.* plunder, smuggling, illegal goods or trade; see **booty.**

contraceptive, *n.* prophylactic, birth-control device, preventative. Contraceptives include the following—birth-control or hormone pill or *the Pill, condom or *safe, *rubber, diaphragm, IUD, loop, *coil, foam, (vaginal) douche.

contract, *n.* agreement, compact, stipulation, contractual statement or obligation, understanding, promise, pledge, covenant, obligation, guarantee, settlement, gentleman's agreement, commitment, bargain, pact, arrangement, the papers, deal; see also **agreement, treaty.**

contract, *v.* 1. [To diminish] draw in *or* back, shrivel, weaken, shrink, become smaller, decline, fall away, subside, grow less, ebb, wane, lessen, lose, dwindle, recede, fall off, wither, waste, condense, constrict, deflate, evaporate; see also **decrease** 1.—*Ant.* stretch, expand, strengthen. 2. [To cause to diminish] abbreviate, narrow, condense; see **compress, decrease** 2. 3. [To enter into an agreement by contract] pledge, undertake, come to terms, make terms, adjust, dicker, (make a) bargain, agree on, limit, bound, establish by agreement, engage, stipulate, consent, enter into a contractual obligation, sign the papers, negotiate a contract, accept an offer, obligate oneself, put something in writing, swear to, sign for, give one's word, shake hands on it, initial, close; see also **agree.** 4. [To catch; *said of diseases*] get, incur, become infected with; see **catch** 4.

contraction, *n.* shrinkage, shrinking, recession, reduction, withdrawal, consumption, condensation, omission, deflation, evaporation, constriction, decrease, shortening, compression, confinement, curtailment, omitting, abridgment, cutting down, consolidating, consolidation, lowering, editing; see also **abbreviation, reduction** 1, **shrinkage.**—*Ant.* expansion, **increase,** extension.

contractor, *n.* builder, jobber, constructor; see **architect.**

contradict, *v.* differ, call in question, confront; see **dare** 2, **oppose** 1.

contradiction, *n.* incongruity, inconsistency, opposition; see **difference** 1, **opposite.**

contrary, *a.* 1. [Opposed] antagonistic to, hostile, counter; see **against** 3, **opposed.** 2. [Unfavorable] untimely, bad, unpropitious; see **unfavorable** 2. 3. [Obstinate] willful, contradictory, headstrong; see **stubborn.**

contrast, *n.* divergence, incompatibility, variation, variance, dissimilarity, inequality, distinction, oppositeness, contradiction, diversity, disagreement, opposition; see also **difference** 1.—*Ant.* agreement, similarity, uniformity.

contrast, *v.* contradict, disagree, conflict, set off, be contrary to, diverge *or* depart *or* deviate *or* differ from, vary, show difference, stand out; see also **differ** 1, **oppose** 1.—*Ant.* agree, concur, be identical.

contribute, *v.* add, share, endow, supply, furnish, bestow, present, confer, bequest, commit, dispense, settle upon, grant, afford, donate, dispense, assign, give away, subscribe, devote, will, bequeath,

subsidize, hand out, *ante up, chip *or* kick in, have a hand in, get in the act, *go Dutch; see also **give** 1, **offer** 1, **provide** 1.—*Ant.* receive, accept, take.

contributing, *a.* aiding, helpful, supporting, secondary, subordinate, valuable, sharing, causative, forming a part of, not to be overlooked, to be considered, coming into the picture; see also **helpful.**

contribution, *n.* donation, present, bestowal; see **gift** 1, **grant.**

contributor, *n.* subscriber, giver, grantor; see **donor, patron.**

contrive, *v.* make, improvise, devise; see **create, invent** 1.

control, *n.* 1. [The power to direct] dominion, reign, direction; see **power** 2. 2. [The document executed to bind a contract, sense 1] deposition, paper, evidence; see **proof** 1, **record** 1.

control, *v.* 1. [To hold in check] constrain, master, repress; see **check** 1, **restrain.** 2. [To direct] lead, rule, dominate, direct, determine, master, conquer, conduct, administer, supervise, run, coach, head, dictate, manage, influence, prevail, domineer, constrain, charge, subdue, push, coerce, oblige, train, limit, officiate, drive, move, regulate, take over, *rule the roost, *crack the whip, *call the signals; see also **govern.**

controlling, *a.* ruling, supervising, regulating; see **governing.**

controversial, *a.* disputable, debatable, suspect; see **uncertain** 2.

controversy, *n.* contention, debate, quarrel; see **difference** 1, **discussion.**

convene, *v.* unite, congregate, collect; see **assemble** 2, **gather** 1.

convenience, *n.* 1. [The quality of being convenient] fitness, availability, accessibility, suitability, appropriateness, decency, acceptability, receptiveness, openness, accord, consonance, adaptability, usefulness. 2. [An aid to ease or comfort] ease, comfort, accommodation, help, aid, assistance, means, support, luxury, personal service, relief, cooperation, promotion, advancement, satisfaction, service, benefit, contribution, advantage, utility, labor *or* time saver, lift; see also **advantage, appliance.** —**at one's convenience,** suitable, conveniently, when convenient; see **appropriately.**

convenient, *a.* 1. [Serving one's convenience] ready, favorable, suitable, adapted, available, fitted, suited, adaptable, roomy, well-arranged, appropriate, well-planned, decent, agreeable, acceptable, useful, serviceable, assisting, aiding, beneficial, accommodating, advantageous, conducive, comfortable, opportune, timesaving, labor-saving; see also **helpful.**—*Ant.* disturbing, unserviceable, disadvantageous. 2. [Near] handy, close (by or in), easy to reach; see **near** 1.

convention, n. 1. [An occasion for which delegates assemble] assembly, convocation, meeting; see **gathering.** 2. [Custom] practice, habit, fashion; see **custom** 1, 2.

conventional, a. 1. [Established by convention] accustomed, prevailing, accepted, customary, regular, standard, orthodox, normal, typical, expected, usual, routine, general, everyday, commonplace, ordinary, plain, current, popular, prevalent, predominant, expected, wellknown, stereotyped, in established usage; see also sense 2; see also **common** 1, **familiar, habitual.**—Ant. atypical, **unusual,** unpopular. 2. [In accordance with convention] established, sanctioned, correct; see **popular** 3. 3. [Devoted to or bound by convention] formal, stereotyped, orthodox, narrow, narrow-minded, dogmatic, parochial, strict, rigid, puritanical, inflexible, hidebound, conservative, conforming, believing, not heretical, literal, bigoted, obstinate, straight-laced; see also **prejudiced.**—Ant. **liberal,** broad-minded, unconventional.

conversation, n. talk, discussion, communion, consultation, hearing, conference, gossip, chat, dialogue, discourse, expression of views, mutual exchange, questions and answers, traffic in ideas, getting to know one another, general conversation, questioning, talking it out, heart-to-heart talk, powwow, *bull session, chitchat; see also **communication, speech** 3.

converse, n. inverse, antithesis, reverse; see **opposite** 2.

conversion, n. turn, spiritual change, regeneration, rebirth, being baptized, seeing the light, new birth.

convert, n. proselyte, neophyte, disciple; see **follower.**

convert, v. 1 [To alter the form or use] turn, transform, alter; see **change** 2. 2. [To alter convictions] regenerate, save, baptize; see **reform** 1.

convertible, n. open car, sportscar, hardtop; see **automobile.**

convey, v. pass on, communicate, conduct; see **send** 1, 2.

convict, n. captive, malefactor, felon; see **criminal, prisoner.**

convict, v. find or p.onounce guilty, sentence, pass sentence on, doom, declare guilty of an offense, bring to justice, send up, *rap, *put the screws to; see also **condemn.**—Ant. acquit, **free,** find not guilty.

conviction, n. persuasion, confidence, reliance; see **belief, faith** 2.

convince, v. prove (to), persuade, establish, refute, satisfy, assure, demonstrate, argue into, change, effect, overcome, turn, win over, bring around, put across, bring to one's senses, bring to reason, gain the confidence of, cram or put into one's head, sell (a bill of goods); see also **prove, teach.**

convinced, a. converted, indoctrinated, talked into something; see also **changed** 2.

convince oneself, v. be convinced or converted, persuade oneself, make up one's (own) mind; see **believe, prove.**

convincing, a. trustworthy, credible, acceptable, reasonable, creditable, plausible, probable, likely, presumable, possible, dependable, hopeful, worthy of confidence, to be depended on; see also **reliable.**

convulsion, n. paroxysm, epilepsy, attack; see **fit** 1.

cook, n. short-order cook, chef, head cook; see **servant.**

cook, v. prepare, fix, warm (up or over), stew, simmer, sear, braise, scald, broil, parch, scorch, poach, dry, chafe, fricassee, percolate, steam, bake, griddle, brew, boil (down), seethe, barbecue, grill, roast, pan fry, pan broil, deep or French fry, brown; see also **fry, heat** 1.

cooking, a. simmering, heating, scalding, brewing, stewing, steeping, frying, broiling, griddling, grilling, browning, roasting, baking; see also **boiling.**

cooking, n. cookery, dish, dainty; see **food.**

*cook up, v. make up, concoct, falsify; see **arrange** 2, **plan** 1, 2.

cooky, n. small cake, sweet wafer, bun; see **bread, cake** 2, **pastry.** Common varieties of cookies include the following—cream, lemon, icebox, oatmeal, vanilla, chocolate, sugar, ginger, molasses, etc., cooky; gingersnap, fig bar, raisin bar, Scotch shortbread, doughnut, macaroon, tart, fruit bar, brownie, Marguerite, wafer.

cool, a. 1. [Having a low temperature] cooling, frigid, frosty, wintry, somewhat or a little or moderately or rather cold, chilly, shivery, chill, chilling, refrigerated, air-conditioned, snappy, nippy, biting; see also **cold** 1.—Ant. tepid, **warm,** heated. 2. [Calm] unruffled, imperturbable, composed; see **calm** 1. 3. [Somewhat angry or disapproving] disapproving, annoyed, offended; see **angry, indifferent.** 4. [*Excellent] neat, *keen, groovy; see **excellent.** —play it cool, hold back, underplay, exercise restraint; see **restrain.**

cool, v. lose heat, lessen, freeze, reduce, calm, chill, cool off, become cold, be chilled to the bone, become chilly, moderate, refrigerate, air-cool, air-condition, pre-cool, frost, freeze, quick-freeze; see also **freeze** 1.—Ant. **burn,** warm, defrost.

*cool it, v. quiet down, hold back, be sensible; see **calm down**.

co-operate, v. unite, combine, concur, conspire, pool, join forces, act in concert, stand *or* hold *or* stick together, comply with, join in, go along with, make common cause, unite efforts, share in, second, take part, work in unison, participate, work side by side (with), side with, take sides with, join hands with, play along (with), play fair, throw *or* fall in with, **be in cahoots, **chip in, stand shoulder to shoulder, pull together; see also **agree.**—*Ant.* act independently, **differ,** diverge.

co-operation, n. collaboration, participation, combination, concert, union, confederacy, confederation, conspiracy, alliance, society, company, partnership, coalition, federation, clanship, unanimity, concord, harmony; see also **agreement, unity 2.**—*Ant.* discord, disagreement, separation.

co-operative, a. co-operating, agreeing, joining, combining, collaborating, coactive, uniting, concurring, participating, in joint operation; see also **helpful, united.**

cooperative, n. marketing cooperative, consumer's cooperative, communal society *or* business *or* enterprise *or* establishment, kibbutz, commune, collective, **co-op; see also **unity 2.**

co-ordinate, v. harmonize, regulate, organize; see **adjust 1,** agree.

co-ordinator, n. superintendent, supervisor, organizer; see **executive.**

cope with, v. encounter, suffer, confront; see **endure 2, face 1.**

copied, a. 1. [Reproduced] dittoed, duplicated, transcribed; see **printed, reproduced. 2.** [Imitated] made in facsimile, mimicked, aped; see **imitated.**

copper, n. Cu (chemical symbol), biological trace element, major element of the alloys bronze and brass; see **element 2, metal.**

copulate, v. sleep with, make love, go to bed, unite, couple, cover, lie with, know, have relations, have sexual *or* marital *or* extramarital relations, be carnal, unite sexually, have (sexual) intercourse, breed, cohabit, fornicate, lay, fool around, screw, do *or* make it, get it on.—*Ant.* **abstain,** be continent, be celibate.

copulation, n. coitus, intercourse, sex, sex act, sexual union *or* congress, coupling, mating, coition, carnal knowledge, love, **screwing; see also **sex 1, 4.**

copy, n. imitation, facsimile, photostat, likeness, print, similarity, mimeograph sheet, simulation, mirror, impersonation, offprint, Xerox (trademark), semblance, imitation of an original, forgery, coun-

terfeit, reprint, rubbings, transcript, carbon, replica, typescript, cast, tracing, counterpart, likeness, portrait, model, reflection, representation, study, photograph, carbon *or* examined *or* certified *or* exemplified *or* office *or* typed *or* pencil *or* fair copy, ditto; see also **duplicate, reproduction 3.**

copy, v. 1. [To imitate] follow, mimic, ape; see **imitate 1. 2.** [To reproduce] represent, duplicate, counterfeit, forge, cartoon, depict, portray, picture, draw, sketch, paint, sculpture, mold, engrave; see also **reproduce 2.**

cord, n. string, cordage, fiber; see **rope.**

cordial, a. genial, hearty, warm-hearted; see **friendly.**

core, n. 1. [Essence] gist, kernel, heart; see **essence 1. 2.** [Center] hub, focus, pivot; see **center 1.**

cork, n. stopper, tap, spike; see **plug 1.**

corn, n. oats, millet, maize; see **food, grain 1.**

corn bread, n. hoe cake(s), corndodgers, corncakes, hot bread, johnnycake, hush puppies, corn pone, spoon bread; see also **bread, cake 2.**

corner, n. 1. [A projecting edge] ridge, end, projection; see **edge 1, rim. 2.** [A recess] niche, nook, indentation; see **hole 1. 3.** [A sharp turn] bend, veer, shift; see **curve, turn 2. 4.** [The angle made where ways intersect] V, Y, intersection; see **angle 1. 5.** [**Difficulty] impediment, distress, knot; see **difficulty 2.** —**around the corner,** immediate, imminent, next; see **near 1, soon 1.** —**cut corners,** cut down *or* back, shorten, reduce; see **decrease 2.**

corner, v. trap, trick, fool; see **catch 1,** deceive.

cornerwise, a. cornerways, diagonally, cater-corner, obliquely, askew, slanting, aslant, from corner to corner, on the bias, angling, diagonalwise, kitty-cornered, cater-cornered, **catawampus; see also **oblique.**

*corny, a. stale, trite, stereotyped; see **dull 4, stupid 1.**

corporation, n. partnership, enterprise, company; see **business 4.**

corps, n. troops, brigade, regiment; see **army 2, organization 2.**

corpse, n. carcass, remains, cadaver; see **body 2.**

correct, a. 1. [Accurate] exact, true, right; see **accurate 2. 2.** [Proper] suitable, becoming, fitting; see **fit.**

correct, v. better, help, remove the errors *or* faults of, remedy, alter, rectify, accommodate for, make right, mend, amend, fix (up), do over, reform, remodel, review, reconstruct, reorganize, edit, revise, make corrections, put to rights, put in order, **doctor, touch up, polish; see also **repair.**

corrected, *a.* rectified, amended, reformed; see **changed 2.**

correction, *n.* revisal, reexamination, rereading, remodeling, rectification, editing, righting, reparation, mending, fixing, amending, changing; see also **repair.**

corrective, *a.* restorative, curative, healing; see **medical.**

correctly, *a.* rightly, precisely, perfectly; see **right 1.**

correctness, *n.* 1. [Accuracy] precision, exactness, rightness; see **accuracy,** **truth.** 2. [Propriety] decency, decorum, fitness; see **propriety 1.**

correlate, *v.* connect, equate, associate; see **compare 1.**

correlation, *n.* interdependence, alternation, equivalence; see **relationship.**

correspond, *v.* 1. [To be alike] compare, match, be similar *or* identical; see **resemble.** 2. [To communicate, usually by letter] write to, reply, drop a line; see **answer 1, communicate 2.**

correspondence, *n.* 1. [The quality of being like] conformity, equivalence, accord; see **agreement, similarity.** 2. [Communication, usually by letter] messages, reports, exchange of letters; see **communication.**

corresponding, *a.* identical, similar, coterminous; see **like.**

correspond to, *v.* accord, concur, harmonize; see **agree.**

corrode, *v.* rot, degenerate, deteriorate; see **rust.**

corrupt, *a.* exploiting, underhanded, mercenary, fraudulent, crooked, nefarious, profiteering, unscrupulous, *shady, *fixed, *padded, *crooked as a dog's hind leg; see **dishonest.**

corrupt, *v.* pervert, degrade, demean, lower, pull down, reduce, adulterate, depreciate, deprave, debauch, defile, demoralize, pollute, taint, contaminate, infect, stain, spoil, blight, blemish, undermine, impair, mar, injure, harm, hurt, damage, deface, disfigure, deform, abuse, maltreat, ill-treat, outrage, mistreat, misuse, dishonor, disgrace, violate, waste, ravage, cause to degenerate *or* deteriorate; see also **rape, weaken 2.—** *Ant.* purify, **clean,** restore.

corruption, *n.* 1. [Vice] baseness, depravity, degradation; see **crime, evil 1.** 2. [Conduct involving graft] extortion, exploitation, fraudulency, misrepresentation, dishonesty, bribery, racket; see also **crime.**

cosmetic, *n.* beautifier, beauty *or* cosmetic preparation, get-up, *face; see also **make-up 1.** Cosmetics include the following—hair, body, sun tan, etc., oil; hair, eye, cold, cleansing, hormone, complexion, skin, hand, etc., cream; after-

shave, hand, sun tan, etc., lotion; talcum, face, bath, tooth, etc., powder; eyebrow pencil, mascara, eye shadow, eye liner, lipstick, nail polish, moisturizer, foundation, powder, perfume, toilet water, cologne, hair tonic, hair dye, hair bleach, mouthwash, tooth paste, shampoo, shaving soap *or* cream *or* foam, depilatory, deodorant, antiperspirant; see also **lotion, perfume, soap.**

cosmic, *a.* vast, empyrean, grandiose; see **universal 1.**

cosmopolitan, *a.* metropolitan, gregarious, catholic; see **international, public 2.**

cosmos, *n.* solar system, galaxy, star system; see **universe.**

cost, *n.* payment, value, charge; see **price, value 1.**

cost, *v.* require, take, be priced *or* marked *or* valued (at), be worth, amount to, be for sale (at), command a price of, mount up to, bring in, sell for, set one back.

costing, *a.* as much as, to the amount of, priced at, no less than, estimated (at), selling (for), on sale (at), reduced (to), a bargain *or* steal (at).

costly, *a.* high-priced, dear, precious; see **expensive.**

costs, *n.* price, outgo, living costs; see **expenses. —at all costs,** by any means, in spite of difficulties, without fail; see **regardless 2.**

costume, *n.* attire, apparel, garb; see **clothes, dress 1.**

cottage, *n.* cot, cabin, small house; see **home 1.**

cotton, *n.* Cotton cloth includes the following—chinz, organdy, dotted swiss, voile, cambric, calico, flannel, denim, ticking, net, muslin, crinoline, flannelette, gingham, jersey, lace, monk's cloth, poplin, velveteen, gabardine, crepe, twill, canvas, percale, terry cloth, sailcloth, cheesecloth, theatrical gauze.

couch, *n.* sofa, lounge, davenport; see **chair 1, furniture.**

cough, *n.* hem, hack, frog in one's throat; see **cold 2, illness 2.**

cough, *v.* hack, convulse, *bark; see **choke 2.**

council, *n.* advisory board, cabinet, directorate; see **committee.**

counsel, *n.* 1. [Advice] guidance, instruction, information; see **advice, suggestion 1.** 2. [A lawyer] attorney, legal adviser, barrister; see **lawyer. —keep one's own counsel,** be secretive, conceal oneself, keep quiet; see **hide 1.**

counsel, *v.* admonish, direct, inform; see **advise, teach.**

counselor, *n.* guide, instructor, mentor; see **teacher.**

count, *n.* number, enumeration, account, listing, statistics, returns, figures, tabulation, tally, poll, sum, outcome; see also **result, whole.**

count, *v.* compute, reckon, enumerate, number, add up, figure, count off *or* up, *foot (up), count noses; see **add, total.**

counter, *n.* board, shelf, ledge; see **bench 2, table 1. —under the counter,** black-market, underhanded, unofficial; see **illegal.**

counteract, *v.* frustrate, check, invalidate; see **halt, hinder, prevent.**

counterfeit, *a.* sham, spurious, fictitious; see **false 3.**

counterfeit, *v.* print *or* copy money *or* stamps, make (counterfeit) money, circulate bad money; see **forge.**

countless, *a.* innumerable, incalculable, numberless; see **infinite, many.**

count off, *v.* number, get numbers for, give numbers to; see **count, total.**

count on, *v.* rely *or* depend on *or* upon, count *or* lean *or* build *or* rest upon, expect from, take for granted, believe in, swear by; see **trust 1.**

count out, *v.* remove, mark off, get rid of; see **eliminate.**

country, *a.* 1. [Said of people] rural, homey, unpolished; see also **ignorant 2, rude 1.** 2. [Said of areas] rustic, agrarian, provincial; see **rural.**

country, *n.* 1. [Rural areas] farms, farmland, farming district, rural region *or* area, range, country district, back country, bush, forests, woodlands, backwoods, sparsely settled areas, *sticks, the *boondocks *or* *boonies; see also **farm, forest.—Ant.** city, borough, municipality. 2. [A nation] government, a people, sovereign state; see **nation 1. 3.** [Land and all that is associated with it] homeland, native land, fatherland; see **land 2.**

countryside, *n.* rural area *or* district, farmland, woods; see **country 1.**

count up, *v.* compute, get a total for, bring together; see **add, total.**

county, *n.* province, constituency, shire; see **area, region 1.**

couple, *n.* 1. [A pair] two, set, brace; see **pair.** 2. [*A few] two, several, a handful; see **few.**

couple, *v.* unite, come *or* bring together, link; see **copulate, join 1.**

coupon, *n.* token, box top, order blank, detachable portion, (premium) certificate, ticket; see also **card, ticket 1.**

courage, *n.* bravery, valor, boldness, fearlessness, spirit, audacity, audaciousness, temerity, manliness, pluck, mettle, enterprise, stoutheartedness, firmness, self-reliance, hardihood, heroism, gallantry, daring, prowess, power, resolution, dash, recklessness, defiance, the courage of one's convictions, *spunk, grit, backbone, *guts, *what it takes, nerve; see

also **strength.—Ant.** cowardice, fear, timidity.

courageous, *a.* daring, gallant, intrepid; see **brave 1.**

course, *n.* 1. [A route] passage, path, way; see **route 1.** 2. [A prepared way, especially for racing] lap, cinder path, cinder track; see **road 1.** 3. [A plan of study] subject, studies, curriculum; see **education 1.** 4. [A series of lessons] classes, lectures, seminar; see **education 1. —in due course,** in due time, properly, conveniently; see **appropriately. —in the course of,** during, in the process of, when; see **while 1. —of course,** certainly, by all means, indeed; see **surely. —off course,** misdirected, erratic, going the wrong way; see **wrong 2. —on course,** on target, correct, going in the right direction; see **accurate 2.**

court, *n.* 1. [An enclosed, roofless area] square, courtyard, patio; see **yard 1.** 2. [An instrument for administering justice] tribunal, bench, magistrate, bar, session. Types of courts include the following—the Supreme Court of the United States, appellate court of the United States, Federal court, State supreme court, district court, county court, justice's court, magistrate's court, mayor's court, police court. 3. [A ruler and his surroundings] lords and ladies, attendants, royal household; see **government 2, royalty, ruler 1.** 4. [An area for playing certain games] arena, rink, ring; see also **field 2.**

court, *v.* attract, allure, solicit, beseech, entice, pursue, accompany, follow, plead, make love, pay court, pay attentions to, pay court (to), make overtures, go courting, propose, ask in marriage, *set one's cap for, *pop the question, go steady, *go together *or* with, *make a play for; see also **date 2.**

courteous, *a.* courtly, affable, cultivated; see **polite.**

courteously, *a.* civilly, affably, obligingly; see **politely.**

courtesy, *n.* 1. [Courteous conduct] kindness, friendliness, affability, courteousness, gentleness, consideration, thoughtfulness, sympathy, geniality, cordiality, graciousness, tact, good behavior *or* manners, politeness, refinement, chivalry, gallantry, respect, deference, polished manners, good breeding; see also **generosity, kindness 1.** 2. [Courteous act] compassion, generosity, charity; see **kindness 2.**

cousin, *n.* kin, an aunt's child, an uncle's child; see **relative.**

cove, *n.* inlet, sound, lagoon; see **bay.**

cover, *n.* 1. [A covering object] covering, ceiling, canopy, hood, sheath, sheet, awning, tent, umbrella, dome, stopper, lid, canvas, tarpaulin, book cover, folder, wrapper, wrapping paper, jacket, case, spread, *tarp; see also **blanket**, **envelope**, **folder**, **roof**. 2. [A covering substance] paint, varnish, polish; see **coat 3**, **sheet 2**. 3. [Shelter] harbor, asylum, refuge; see **retreat 2**, **shelter**. —**take cover**, conceal oneself, take shelter, go indoors; see **hide 1**. —**under cover**, secretive, hiding, concealed; see **hidden**.

cover, v. 1. [To place as a covering] carpet, put on, overlay, surface, board (up), superimpose, black in or out; see also **spread 3**. 2. [To wrap] envelop, enshroud, encase; see **wrap**. 3. [To protect] shield, screen, house; see **defend 1, 2**, **shelter**. 4. [To hide] screen, camouflage, mask; see **disguise**, **hide 1**. 5. [To include] embrace, comprise, incorporate; see **include 1**. 6. [To travel] traverse, journey over, cross; see **travel 2**. 7. [To send down in plenty] drench, engulf, overcome; see **flood**. 8. [To report upon, especially for a newspaper] recount, narrate, relate; see **broadcast**, **record 3**.

covered, a. 1. [Provided with a cover] topped, lidded, roofed, wrapped, enveloped, bound, painted, varnished, coated, camouflaged, sheltered, shielded, separated, disguised, masked, secreted, protected, concealed; see also **hidden**.—Ant. revealed, obvious, exposed. 2. [Plentifully bestrewn] scattered with, sprinkled over, spattered, spangled, dotted, strewn with, starred, starry with, flowered, spotted with, sown, dusted over, powdered, spread with.—Ant. bare, **empty**, unfurnished. 3. [Attended to] noted, taken note of, reported, recorded, written, included, marked, explored, regarded, scrutinized, examined, surveyed, investigated, observed, looked to, cared for; see also **done 1**, **recognized**.—Ant. unheeded, unnoticed, passed over.

covering, n. concealment, top, spread; see **cover 1**.

cover up for, v. front or lie for, *take the rap for, *be the goat; see **defend 1, 2**, **shelter**.

covet, v. desire, envy, wish for; see **want 1**.

cow, n. heifer, milk cow, dairy cow, critter, bossy; see also **cattle**.

coward, n. sneak, milksop, shirker, deserter, weakling, alarmist, *slacker, *quitter, *chicken, *lily-liver, *scaredy-cat, *chicken-heart, *fraidy-cat, *yellow-belly.

cowardice, n. cowardliness, timidity, effeminacy, faint-heartedness, (abject) fear, weakness, quailing, lack or want of courage, apprehension, shyness, dread, fearfulness, *yellow streak, cold feet; see

also **fear**.—Ant. bravery, valor, fearlessness.

cowardly, a. timid, frightened, afraid, fearful, shy, backward, cowering, apprehensive, nervous, anxious, dismayed, faint-hearted, panicky, scared, scary, *jittery, craven, mean-spirited, weak, soft, *chicken-livered, *lily-livered, *yellow, skulking, sneaking, cringing, trembling, shaken, crouching, running, quaking, shaking like a leaf, *shaking in one's boots; see also **afraid**, **weak 3**.—Ant. **brave**, fearless, open.

cowboy, n. cowhand, hand, wrangler, rider, herder, vaquero, gaucho, illanero (all Spanish), cattle-herder, drover, *cowpuncher, *cowpoke, buckaroo; see also **rancher**.

cower, v. cringe, shrink, fear, run, quake, shiver, tremble, shake, snivel, flinch, quail; see also **grovel**.

coy, a. bashful, shy, demure; see **humble 1**.

cozy, a. secure, sheltered, snug; see **comfortable 2**, **safe 1**.

crab, n. crayfish, crustacean, seafood; see **shellfish**.

*crack, a. first-rate, first-class, skilled; see **able**, **excellent**.

crack, n. 1. [An incomplete break] chink, split, cut; see **hole 1**. 2. [A crevice] cleft, fissure, rift; see **hole 1**. 3. [A blow] hit, thwack, stroke; see **blow 4**. [*A witty or brazen comment] return, witticism, jest; see **joke 2**, **remark**.

crack, v. 1. [To become cracked] cleave, burst, split; see **break 2**. 2. [To cause to crack] cleave, splinter, sever; see **break 3**. [To damage] injure, hurt, impair; see **damage**. 4. [*To become mentally deranged] become insane, go crazy, *blow one's mind; see **crack up 2**. 5. [To solve] figure out, answer, decode; see **solve**. —**get cracking**, get going, go, start; see **begin 2**, **move 1**.

*crack a book, v. study, read, scan; see **examine**, **study**.

crack a joke, v. quip, jest, jape; see **joke**.

cracked, a. shattered, split, fractured; see **broken 1**.

cracker, n. wafer, cookie, soda cracker, oyster cracker, biscuit, saltine, hardtack, sea biscuit, wheat biscuit; see also **bread**.

crack up, v. 1. [*To crash a vehicle] collide, be in an accident, smash or break up; see **crash 4**. 2. [*To fail suddenly in health, mind, or strength] go (all) to pieces, fail, deteriorate, sicken, go or become insane or crazy or demented, *freak out, *blow one's mind, go out of one's mind, *go off one's rocker, *blow a fuse, *go off the deep end; see also **weaken 1**. 3. [*To laugh] roar, howl, roll in the aisles; see **laugh**.

cradle, *n.* trundle bed, crib, basinet; see also **bed 1, furniture.**

craft, *n.* 1. [Skill] proficiency, competence, aptitude; see **ability.** 2. [Trade] occupation, career, work; see **job 1, profession 1.** 3. [Ship] vessel, air *or* water vehicle, airplane; see **boat, ship.**

craftsman, *n.* artisan, skilled worker *or* tradesman *or* workman, journeyman, maker, technician, manufacturer, machinist, handcraftsman, mechanic; see also **artist, laborer, specialist.**

crafty, *a.* clever, sharp, astute; see **intelligent.**

cram, *v.* 1. [To stuff] crush, jam, press; see **compress, pack 2.** 2. [To study hurriedly] read, teach, review; see **study.**

cramp, *n.* spasm, crick, pang; see **pain 2.**

cramped, *a.* narrow, confined, restraining; see **restricted, uncomfortable 1.**

cranium, *n.* brain, cerebrum, cerebellum, brain encasing, brainpan, skull (of a vertebrate); see **head 1.**

crank, *n.* 1. [A device for revolving a shaft] bracket, turning device, bend; see **arm 2, handle 1.** 2. [A person with an obsession] eccentric, fanatic, monomaniac; see **character 4.** 3. [*An ill-natured person] eccentric, misanthrope, complainer; see **grouch.**

cranky, *a.* disagreeable, cross, perverse; see **irritable.**

crash, *n.* 1. [A crashing sound] clatter, clash, din; see **noise 1, sound 2.** 2. [A collision] wreck, accident, shock; see **collision.**

crash, *v.* 1. [To fall with a crash] overturn, upset, break down, plunge, be hurled, pitch, smash, dive, hurtle, lurch, sprawl, tumble, fall headlong, fall flat, drop, slip, collapse; see also **fall 1, 2.** [To break into pieces] shatter, shiver, splinter; see **break, smash.** 3. [To make a crashing sound] clatter, bang, smash; see **sound 1.** 4. [To have a collision] collide (with), run together, run *or* smash *or* bump *or* bang into, meet, jostle, bump, butt, knock, punch, jar, jolt, crack up; see also **hit 1.** 5. [*To collapse] fall asleep, pass out, become unconscious; see **faint, sleep.** 6. [*To go uninvited] disturb, invade, intrude; see **interrupt, meddle 1.**

crash program, *n.* crash project, immediate undertaking, intensive *or* telescoped program, around-the-clock endeavor, revised plan, speed-up; see also **emergency.**

crass, *a.* gross, doltish, stupid; see **ignorant 1, 2, vulgar 1.**

crate, *n.* carton, box, cage; see **container, package.**

crater, *n.* hollow, opening, abyss; see **hole 1.**

craving, *n.* need, longing, yearning; see **desire 1.**

crawl, *v.* creep, worm along, wriggle, squirm, slither, move on hands and knees, writhe, go on all fours, worm one's way, go on one's belly; see also **grovel, sneak.**

crayon, *n.* chalk, pastel, colored wax; see also **pencil.**

crazily, *a.* furiously, irrationally, hastily, madly, rashly, insanely, psychotically, maniacally; see also **violently, wildly.**

crazy, *a.* crazed, demented, mad; see **insane 1.**

cream, *n.* 1. [The fatty portion of milk] rich milk, creamy milk, coffee cream, whipping cream, ice cream, half-and-half, butterfat; see also **milk.** 2. [A creamy substance] emulsion, salve, jelly; see **cosmetic, lotion.**

creamy, *a.* smooth, buttery, creamed; see **rich 2, soft 2.**

crease, *n.* tuck, overlap, pleat; see **fold, wrinkle.**

crease, *v.* double, rumple, plait; see **fold 2, wrinkle.**

create, *v.* make, produce, form, perform, cause (to exist), bring *or* call into being *or* existence, build, fashion, constitute, originate, generate, construct, discover, shape, forge, design, plan, fabricate, cause to be, give birth to; see also **compose 2, invent 1, produce 2.**

creation, *n.* 1. [The process of creating] imagination, production, formulation; see **conception 1, making.** 2. [All that has been created] cosmos, nature, totality; see **earth 1, universe.** 3. [A work of art] labor of love, masterpiece, brain child; see **production 1.**

creative, *a.* formative, inventive, productive; see **artistic, original 2.**

Creator, *n.* First Cause, Deity, Maker; see **god.**

creature, *n.* creation, being, beast; see **animal.**

credential, *n.* declaration, warrant, voucher; see **certificate, record 1.**

credibility, *n.* likelihood, probability, chance; see **possibility 2.**

credible, *a.* trustworthy, dependable, sincere; see **reliable.**

credit, *n.* 1. [Belief] credence, reliance, confidence; see **faith 1.** 2. [Unencumbered funds] assets, stocks, bonds, paper credit, (bank) account, mortgages, liens, securities, debentures, cash; see also **wealth.** 3. [Permission to defer payment] extension, respite, continuance, trust (in future payment); see also **loan.** —**do credit to,** bring approval to, please, do honor to; see **satisfy 1.** —**give credit to,** believe in, rely on, have confidence in; see **trust 1.** —**give one credit for,** believe in, rely on, have confidence in; see **trust 1.** —**on credit,**

on loan, delayed, postponed; see **unpaid 1. —to one's credit**, good, honorable, beneficial; see **worthwhile**.

creditor, *n*. realtor, lender, mortgager; see also **banker**.

creed, *n*. belief, doctrine, dogma; see **faith 2**.

creek, *n*. stream, spring, brook; see **river. —*up the creek**, in difficulty, desperate, lost; see **in trouble 1**.

creep, *v*. slither, writhe, worm along; see **crawl**.

creeping, *a*. crawling, worming, squirming, writhing, wriggling, crouching, cowering, slinking, skulking, inching, dragging, lagging, limping, faltering, shuffling, hobbling, sneaking, moving slowly, barely moving, going at a snail's place, worming along.

crevice, *n*. chasm, cleft, slit; see **gap 3**.

crew, *n*. 1. [Company of seamen] seafarers, sailors, hands, (able) seamen, ship's company, mariners, sea dogs, *gobs. 2. [A group of men organized to do a particular job] company, troupe, squad; see **organization 2, team 1**.

crime, *n*. transgression, misdemeanor, vice, outrage, wickedness, immorality, infringement, depravity, evil behavior, wrongdoing, misconduct, corruption, delinquency, wrong, trespass, malefaction, dereliction, lawlessness, crime in the streets, atrocity, felony, capital crime, offense, scandal, infraction, violation, cold-blooded crime, mortal sin, homicide, voluntary manslaughter, involuntary manslaughter, simple assault, aggravated assault, battery, larceny, robbery, burglary, holdup, kidnapping, swindling, fraud, defrauding, embezzlement, smuggling, extortion, bribery, mugging, rape, statutory rape, attack, sexual molestation, breach of promise, malicious mischief, breach of the peace, libel, perjury, fornication, sodomy, conspiracy, counterfeiting, inciting to revolt, sedition; see also **corruption, evil 2, murder, rape, sin, theft, treason**.

criminal, *a*. unlawful, felonious, illegal; see **bad 1**.

criminal, *n*. lawbreaker, felon, crook. Criminals include the following—murderer, killer, desperado, thug, gangster, gang leader *or* *the brains, burglar, safecracker, swindler *or* *clip artist *or* *griffer, confidence man *or* *con man, thief, bandit, *second story man, cattle thief *or* rustler, horse thief, automobile thief, pickpocket, counterfeiter, forger, smuggler, extortionist, kidnapper, gunman *or* *trigger man, accomplice, informer *or* stool pigeon, *squealer, *convict *or* *con, dope peddler *or* *pusher.

crimson, *a*. blood-red, bright red, scarlet; see **color 1, red**.

cringe, *v*. flinch, quail, wince; see **cower, crawl**.

crinkle, *v*. coil, wind, crease; see **wrinkle**.

cripple, *v*. stifle, mangle, injure; see **hurt**.

crippled, *a*. maimed, mutilated, mangled; see **deformed, disabled**.

crisis, *n*. straits, urgency, necessity, dilemma, puzzle, pressure, embarrassment, pinch, juncture, pass, change, contingency, situation, condition, plight, impasse, deadlock, predicament, corner, trauma, quandary, extremity, trial, crux, moment of truth, turning point, critical situation, *pickle, stew, *fix, *big trouble, *hot water. —*Ant*. normality, **stability**, regularity.

crisp, *a*. 1. [Fresh and firm] green, plump, firm; see **fresh 1, ripe 1. 2**. [Brisk] fresh, invigorating, bracing; see **stimulating**.

criterion, *n*. basis, foundation, test, standard, rule, proof, scale, prototype, pattern, example, standard of judgment *or* criticism, archetype, norm, original, precedent, fact, law, principle; see also **measure 2, model 2**.

critic, *n*. 1. [One who makes adverse comments] faultfinder, censor, quibbler, detractor, slanderer, complainer, doubter, nagger, fretter, scolder, worrier, *mud-slinger.—*Ant*. praiser, **believer**, supporter. 2. [One who endeavors to interpret and judge] commentator, reviewer, analyst, connoisseur, writer of reviews, cartoonist, caricaturist, expert; see **examiner, writer**.

critical, *a*. 1. [Disapproving] faultfinding, trenchant, derogatory, disapproving, hypercritical, demanding, satirical, cynical, nagging, scolding, condemning, censuring, reproachful, disapproving, disparaging, exacting, sharp, cutting, biting; see also **sarcastic. 2**. [Capable of observing and judging] penetrating, perceptive, discerning; see **discreet, observant 1. 3**. [Crucial] decisive, significant, deciding; see **important 1**.

criticism, *n*. 1. [A serious estimate or interpretation] study, analysis, critique; see **judgment 2, review 1. 2**. [An adverse comment] caviling, carping, faultfinding; see **objection**.

criticize, *v*. 1. [To make a considered criticism] study, probe, scrutinize; see **analyze, examine. 2**. [To make adverse comments] chastise, reprove, reprimand; see **blame**.

***crook**, *n*. 1. [Criminal] swindler, thief, rogue; see **criminal. 2**. [A bend] fork, V, notch; see **angle 1**.

crooked, *a*. 1. [Having a crook] curved, curving, hooked, devious, winding, bowed, spiral, serpentine, not straight, zigzag, twisted, meandering, tortuous, sinuous; see also **angular, bent, oblique.**—*Ant.* unbent, **straight**, direct. 2. [Dishonest] iniquitous, corrupt, nefarious; see **dishonest.**

crop, *n.* harvest, yield, product, crops, reaping, hay, fodder, grain(s), vintage, fruits; see also **produce.**

cross, *a.* jumpy, easily annoyed, pettish; see **critical, irritable.**

cross, *n.* 1. [Religious symbol, especially of Christianity] crucifix, cruciform, Greek cross, swastika, papal cross, Maltese cross, Latin cross, Calvary cross. 2. [A tribulation] affliction, trial, misfortune; see **difficulty 2.** 3. [A mixed offspring] mongrel, crossbreed, half-breed; see **hybrid, mixture 1.**

cross, *v.* 1. [To pass over] traverse, move or go or pass across or over, pass, ford, cut across, span. 2. [To lie across] intersect, lean on, rest across; see **divide.** 3. [To mix breeds] mingle, interbreed, cross-pollinate; see **mix 1.**

cross-examine, *v.* investigate, check, interrogate; see **examine, question.**

crossing, *n.* 1. [A place to cross] intersection, overpass, crosswalk; see **bridge 1.** 2. [A mixing of breeds] hybridization, interbreeding, cross-pollination; see also **mixture 1.**

crossroad, *n.* service road, junction, driveway; see **road 1.**

crosswise, *a.* across, cross, perpendicular, transversely, vertically, horizontally, at right angles, awry, over, sideways, crisscross, askew, crossways; see also **angular.**

crotch, *n.* 1. [Angle] fork, corner, elbow; see **angle 1, curve 1.** 2. [Loins] pubic area, groin, pelvic girdle; see **body 1.**

crouch, *v.* 1. [To stoop] dip, duck, bow; see **bend.** 2. [To cower] cringe, flinch, quail; see **cower, crawl.**

crowd, *n.* host, horde, flock, mob, company, swarm, press, crush, surge, legion, rout, group, body, pack, army, drove, party, flood, throng, troupe, deluge, multitude, congregation, cluster, assembly, crew, herd, bunch, gang, batch; see also **gathering.**

crowd, *v.* stuff, jam, squeeze; see **pack 2, push 1.**

crowded, *a.* packed, huddled, crushed; see **full 1.**

crown, *n.* diadem, headdress, tiara, coronet, circlet.

crown, *v.* commission, authorize, invest, enable, sanction, inaugurate, fix, exalt, raise, heighten, set up, ennoble, establish; see also **delegate 1.**

crucial, *a.* 1. [Critical] decisive, climatic, deciding; see **important 1.** 2. [Severe] trying, taxing, hard; see **difficult 1.**

crude, *a.* rude, rough, unpolished, in a raw state, homemade, homespun, thick, coarse, harsh, rudimentary, roughhewn, unfashioned, unformed, undeveloped, in the rough, raw, immature, sketchy; see also **unfinished 1.**—*Ant.* **finished,** polished, refined.

crudely, *a.* clumsily, coarsely, impudently; see **rudely.**

cruel, *a.* malevolent, spiteful, depraved, wicked, vengeful, evil, sinful, degenerate, brutish, demoniac, rampant, outrageous, tyrannical, gross, demoralized, evil-minded, vicious, brutal, rough, wild, bestial, ferocious, monstrous, demoniacal, debased, destructive, harmful, mischievous, callous, unnatural, merciless, sadistic, unpitying, unmerciful, unyielding, remorseless, pitiless, unfeeling, inflexible, bloodthirsty, unrelenting, relentless, grim, inhuman, atrocious, harsh, heartless, stony, unconcerned, knowing no mercy, turning a deaf ear, hard as nails—*Ant.* **merciful,** kindly, compassionate.

cruelly, *a.* savagely, inhumanly, viciously; see **brutally.**

cruelty, *n.* brutality, barbarity, sadism, inhumanity, barbarism, mercilessness, wickedness, coarseness, ruthlessness, severity, malice, rancor, venom, coldness, unfeelingness, insensibility, indifference, fierceness, bestiality, ferocity, savagery, grimness, monstrousness, inflexibility, fiendishness, hardness of heart, bloodthirstiness, relentlessness, torture, persecution, harshness, heartlessness, atrocity; see also **evil 1, 2, tyranny.**—*Ant.* benevolence, **kindness,** humanity.

cruise, *n.* voyage, sail, jaunt; see **journey.**

cruise, *v.* voyage, navigate, coast; see **sail 2, travel.**

cruiser, *n.* cabin cruiser, boat, privateer; see **ship.**

crumb, *n.* particle, scrap, pinch; see **bit 1.**

crumble, *v.* fall apart, decay, break up; see **disintegrate.**

crumbly, *a.* breaking up or down, falling to pieces, decayed, degenerated, perishing, deteriorating, soft, corroded, rusted, rotted, worn away, friable, fragile, brittle, frail, rotten, breakable, apt to crumble, eroded, disintegrated, tumbling down; see also **decaying, gritty.**—*Ant.* sound, **firm,** undecayed.

crumple, *v.* rumple, crush, crease; see **wrinkle.**

crush, *v.* 1. [To break into small pieces] smash, pulverize, powder; see **grind.** 2. [To bruise severely] press, mash, bruise; see **beat 1, break 1.** 3. [To defeat utterly] overwhelm, beat or force down, annihilate; see **defeat 2.**

crust, *n.* 1. [A crisp covering] hull, rind,

piecrust; see **shell 1. 2.** [The edge] verge, border, band; see **edge 1.**

cry, *n.* **1.** [A loud utterance] outcry, exclamation, clamor, shout, call, battle cry, halloo, hurrah, hullabaloo, cheer, scream, shriek, yell, whoop, yawp, squall, groan, bellow, howl, bawl, holler, uproar, acclamation, roar; see also sense 2; see also **noise 2.**—*Ant.* whisper, murmur, silence. **2.** [A characteristic call] howl, hoot, wail, bawl, screech, bark, squawk, squeak, yelp, meow, whinney, nicker, moo, chatter, bay, cluck, crow, whine, pipe, trill, quack, clack, cackle, caw, bellow, coo, whistle, gobble, hiss, growl; see also **yell. 3.** [A fit of weeping] sobbing, wailing, shedding tears, sorrowing, mourning, whimpering; see also **tears. —a far cry (from),** unlike, dissimilar, opposed (to); see **different.**

cry, *v.* **1.** [To weep] weep, sob, wail, shed tears, snivel, squall, lament, bewail, bemoan, moan, howl, keen, whimper, whine, weep over, complain, deplore, sorrow, grieve, fret, groan, burst into tears, choke up, cry one's eyes out, break down *or* up, blubber, bawl.—*Ant.* rejoice, **laugh,** exult. **2.** [To call; *said of other than human creatures*] howl, bark, hoot, scream, screech, squawk, squeak, yelp, grunt, roar, shriek, meow, whinney, nicker, moo, bawl, snarl, chatter, bay, cluck, crow, whine, pipe, trill, coo, whistle, caw, bellow, quack, gabble, hiss, growl, croak, cackle, twitter, tweet; see also **yell.**

crying, *n.* shrieking, sorrow, sobbing; see **tears.** —*for crying out loud, for God's *or* heaven's sake; oh, no; *for the love of Mike *or* Pete; see **curse, no.**

crystallize, *v.* become settled *or* definite, take form *or* shape, be outlined; see **form 4.**

cub, *n.* young, offspring, whelp; see **animal.**

cube, *n.* six-sided solid, hexahedron, die; see **solid.**

cuddle, *v.* snuggle, huddle, curl up; see **nestle.**

cue, *n.* prompt, warning signal, opening bar(s); see **sign 1.**

cuff, *n.* **1.** [Edge of a sleeve or pants leg] French cuff, armband, wristband; see **band 1. 2.** [A blow] slap, punch, hit; see **blow.** —*off the cuff, extemporaneous, unofficial, offhand; see **informal.** —*on the cuff, on credit, charged, delayed; see **unpaid 1.**

culminate, *v.* finish, close, end up; see **end 1.**

culprit, *n.* offender, felon, fugitive; see **criminal.**

cult, *n.* clique, clan, band; see **faction, religion 2.**

cultivate, *v.* **1.** [Plant] till, garden, seed; see **harvest, plant. 2.** [Educate] nurture, refine, improve; see **teach.**

cultivation, *n.* horticulture, agriculture, gardening; see **farming.**

cultural, *a.* educational, socializing, refining, refined, constructive, influential, nurturing, disciplining, enlightening, civilizing, instructive, humanizing, beneficial, learned, educative, polishing, enriching, promoting, elevating, uplifting, ennobling, raising, broadening, expanding, widening, developmental.—*Ant.* barbaric, crude, **primitive.**

culture, *n.* **1.** [Civilizing tradition] folklore, folkways, instruction, education, study, law, society, family, convention, habit, inheritance, learning, arts, sciences, custom, mores, knowledge, letters, literature, poetry, painting, music, lore, architecture, history, religion, humanism, the arts and the sciences; see also **civilization.**—*Ant.* barbarism, **disorder,** chaos. **2.** [Refinement and education] breeding, gentility, enlightenment, learning, capacity, ability, skill, science, lore, education, training, art, perception, discrimination, finish, taste, grace, dignity, politeness, savoir-faire, manners, urbanity, dress, fashion, address, tact, nobility, kindness, polish; see also **courtesy 1, elegance, experience.**—*Ant.* **ignorance,** crudeness, vulgarity.

cultured, *a.* cultivated, educated, informed, advanced, accomplished, enlightened, polished, well-bred, genteel, elegant, courteous, intellectual, sophisticated, sensitive, intelligent, *au courant* (French), able, well-read, up-to-date, well-informed, traveled, experienced, tolerant, understanding, appreciative, civilized, literary, urbane, mannerly, gently bred, chivalrous, erudite, gallant, lettered, *high-brow, high-class; see also **liberal, polite, refined 2.**—*Ant.* narrow, **prejudiced,** backward.

cunning, *a.* clever, skillful, ingenious; see **intelligent.**

cup, *n.* vessel, bowl, goblet, mug, tumbler, beaker, stein, bumper, tea *or* coffee cup, measuring cup, chalice; see also **can 1, container.**

cupboard, *n.* closet, locker, storeroom; see also **furniture.**

curable, *a.* improvable, subject to cure, not hopeless, correctable, capable of improvement, healable, restorable, mendable, not too bad.

curb, *n.* **1.** [Restraint] hindrance, chain, check; see **barrier, restraint 2. 2.** [Edge] border, ledge, lip; see **edge 1, rim.**

curb, v. retard, impede, subdue; see **hinder, restrain, restrict.**

curdle, v. coagulate, condense, clot; see **thicken 1.**

cure, n. restorative, healing agent, antidote; see **medicine 2.**

cure, v. make healthy, restore, make whole; see **heal.**

curfew, n. late hour, (time) limit, check-in time; see **limitation 2.**

curiosity, n. 1. [Interest] concern, regard, inquiring mind, inquisitiveness, thirst for knowledge, a questing mind, questioning, interest, desire to know, interest in learning, scientific interest, healthy curiosity. 2. [An unusual object] exoticism, rarity, marvel; see **wonder 2.**

curious, a. 1. [Strange or odd] rare, queer, unique; see **unusual 2.** 2. [Interested] inquiring, inquisitive, questioning; see **interested 1.**

curl, n. coil, spiral, wave; see **hair 1.**

curl, v. curve, coil, bend, spiral, crinkle, wind, twine, loop, crimp, scallop, lap, fold, roll, contort, form into a spiral or curved shape, meander, ripple, buckle, loop, zigzag, wrinkle, twirl.—*Ant.* uncurl, straighten, unbend.

curly, a. curled, kinky, wavy, waving, coiled, crinkly, looped, winding, wound; see also **rolled 1.**

currency, n. coin, bank notes, cash; see **money 1.**

current, a. prevailing, contemporary, in fashion; see **fashionable, modern 1.**

current, n. drift, tidal motion, ebb and flow; see **flow, tide.**

curse, n. 1. [Profanity] oath, blasphemy, sacrilege, anathema, ban, cursing, profanity, denunciation, damning, cuss word, cussing, naughty words. Common exclamations and curses include the following—Lord, oh God, (the) Devil, bless my soul, bless me, mercy, gracious, goodness, oh my, oh me, in Heaven's name, great Caesar's ghost, *gee, *sakes (alive), *good night, *darn, hang it all, *dang, *blast, damn it, *damn, *double-damn, *by golly, *damn-it-to-hell, *for crying out loud, *Judas Priest, *Jesus H. Christ, *Lord-a-mercy, *hell's bells, *geez. 2. [*Menstruation] menses, period, *red letter days, see **flow.**

curse, v. blaspheme, profane, swear profanely, use foul language, be foulmouthed, be obscene, take the Lord's name in vain, damn, *turn the air blue, abuse, revile, swear at, insult, call down curses on the head of, blast, doom, fulminate, denounce, call names, *cuss (out).

cursed, a. blighted, doomed, confounded; see **damned 1.**

curt, a. brief, concise, terse; see **short 2.**

curtain, n. hanging, screen, shade, drape, drapery, window covering, blind. Kinds of curtains include the following—draw curtain, roller shade, shutter, portiere, arras, vertical blind(s), Venetian blind(s).

curve, n. sweep, bow, arch, circuit, curvature, crook. Types of curves include the following—bell or bell-shaped curve, hairpin curve, S-curve, sine curve, extrapolated curve, hyperbolic curve, parabolic curve, normal curve, logarithmic curve, French curve, circle, ellipse, arc.

curve, v. bow, crook, twist; see **bend.**

curved, a. bowed, arched, rounded; see **bent.**

cushion, n. mat, seat, rest; see also **pillow.**

custodian, n. superintendent, porter, cleaner, cleaning man or woman, attendant, caretaker, building superintendent, keeper, gatekeeper, night watchman; see also **watchman.**

custody, n. care, guardianship, supervision, keeping, safekeeping, watch, superintendence, auspices, safeguard; see also **management.** —take into custody, capture, apprehend, seize; see **arrest.**

custom, n. habit, practice, usage, wont, fashion, routine, precedent, use, form, addiction, rule, procedure, observance, characteristic, second nature, matter of course, *beaten path, rut, manner, way, mode, method, system, style, vogue, convention, habit, rule, practice, formality, form, mold, pattern, design, type, taste, character, ritual, rite, attitude, mores, dictate of society, unwritten law, etiquette, conventionality, matter of course.—*Ant.* deviation, **departure,** shift.

customarily, a. usually, commonly, generally; see **regularly.**

customary, a. usual, wonted, habitual; see **common 1, conventional 1, 2.**

customer, n. clientele, patron, consumer; see **buyer.**

cut, a. 1. [Formed] shaped, modeled, arranged; see **formed.** 2. [Reduced] lowered, debased, marked down; see **reduced 1, 2, 3.** 3. [Severed] split, divided, sliced through; see **carved.**

cut, n. 1. [The using of a sharp instrument] slash, thrust, dig, prick, gouge, penetrating, dividing, separation, severance, slitting, hack, slice, carve, chop, stroke, incision, cleavage, penetration, gash, cleft, mark, nick, notch, opening, passage, groove, furrow, slit, wound, fissure; see also **hole 1, injury 2.** 2. [A reduction] decrease, diminution, lessening; see **reduction 1.** 3. [The shape] fashion, figure, construction; see **form 1.** 4. [A section] segment, slice, portion; see **part 1, piece 1.** 5. [A piece of butchered meat] piece, slice, chunk; see **meat.** 6. [*An insult] indignity, offense, abuse; see **insult.** —a cut above, superior, higher, more capable *or* competent *or* efficient, etc.; see **better 2**.

cut, *v.* 1. [To sever] separate, slice (through), cleave, mow, prune, reap, shear, dice, chop (down), slit, split, cut apart, rip, saw through, chisel, cut away *or* through *or* off, snip, chip, quarter, clip, behead, scissor, bite, shave, dissect, bisect, amputate, gash, incise, slash, notch, nick, indent, score, mark, scratch, rake, wound, gouge; see also **carve**. 2. [To cross] intersect, pass, move across; see **cross 1**. 3. [To shorten] curtail, delete, lessen; see **decrease 2**. 4. [To divide] split, sever, separate; see **divide 1**. 5. [*To absent oneself] shirk, avoid, stay away; see **evade**. 6. [To record electronically] make a record, film, tape; see **record 3**.

cutback, *v.* reduce, curtail, shorten; see **decrease 2**.

cute, *a.* dainty, attractive, delightful; see **charming, pleasant 1, 2**.

cut off, *v.* 1. [To remove] lift up, tear out, pull off; see **remove 1**. 2. [To interrupt] intrude, break in, intervene; see **interrupt**.

cut out, *v.* pull out, extract, carve; see **remove 1**.

cut out for, *a.* suitable, adequate, good for; see **fit**.

cut short, *v.* finish, halt, quit; see **end 1, stop 1, 2**.

cut up, *v.* 1. [To chop] chop up, slice, dice; see **cut 1, 2**. 2. [To cavort] show off, play jokes, fool around; see **joke, play 2**.

cycle, *n.* succession, revolution of time, period; see **age 3, sequence 1, series**.

cylinder, *n.* 1. [An automobile part] compression chamber, expansion chamber, machine *or* engine part; see **automobile**. 2. [A geometrical form] circular solid, barrel, stand pipe; see **circle 1**.

cynic, *n.* misanthrope, mocker, satirist, scoffer, pessimist, sarcastic person, sneerer, unbeliever, egotist, egoist, manhater, skeptic, doubter, questioner, detractor, doubting Thomas; see also **critic 1**.—*Ant.* optimist, **believer**, idealist.

cynical, *a.* sardonic, unbelieving, sneering; see **sarcastic**.

cynicism, *n.* doubt, denial, disbelief; see **sarcasm**.

D

dabble, v. trifle (with), engage in superficially, amuse oneself with, dally, be an amateur, putter, idle away time, work superficially, putter (around), *fool with or around, *dip into.—*Ant.* study, work at, become an expert.

dad, n. *daddy, male parent, sire; see **father, parent.**

dagger, n. stiletto, point, blade; see **knife.** —**look daggers at,** glower, look at with anger *or* hatred, scowl (at); see **dislike.**

daily, a. diurnal, per diem, every day, occurring every day, issued every day, periodic, cyclic, day after day, once daily, by day, once a day, during the day, day by day, from day to day; see also **regular 3.**

dainty, a. delicate, fragile, petite, frail, thin, light, pretty, beautiful, lovely, graceful, fine, neat, elegant, exquisite, precious, rare, soft, tender, airy, lacy, nice, *darling, *cute, sweet; see also **charming, weak.**—*Ant.* coarse, **rough,** gross.

dairy, n. creamery, dairy farm, ice-cream plant, cheese factory, buttery, milk station, pasteurizing plant; see also **farm.**

dairy products, n. produce, cottage industry, farm products; see **butter, cheese, cream 1, milk, produce.**

dally, v. dawdle, trifle with, putter; see **dabble.**

dam, n. dike, ditch, wall, bank, embankment, gate, levee, irrigation dam, diversion dam; see also **barrier.**

dam, v. hold (back), check, obstruct, bar, slow, retard, restrict, stop (up), close, clog, choke, block (up), impede, confine; see also **hinder, restrain.**—*Ant.* advance, **release, free.**

damage, n. 1. [Injury] harm, hurt, wound, bruise, wrong, casualty, suffering, illness, affliction, accident, catastrophe, adversity, outrage, hardship, disturbance, mutilation, impairment, mishap, evil, blow, devastation, mischief, reverse, crack-up, crash landing, cave-in, knockout; see also **disaster, injury, misfortune.**—*Ant.* **blessing,** benefit, boon. 2. [Loss occasioned by injury] ruin, breakage, ruined goods, wreckage, waste, shrinkage, depreciation, pollution, corruption, blemish, contamination, defacement, degeneration, deterioration, erosion, disrepair, debasement, corrosion, *wear and tear, foul play; see also **destruction 2, loss 1.**—*Ant.* return, profit, recompense.

damage, v. ruin, wreck, fade, water-soak, tarnish, burn, scorch, dirty, rot, smash, batter, discolor, mutilate, scratch, smudge, crack, bang up, abuse, maltreat, mar, deface, disfigure, mangle, contaminate, crumple, dismantle, cheapen, blight, disintegrate, pollute, sap, stain, tear, undermine, gnaw, corrode, break, split, stab, cripple, rust, warp, maim, mutilate, wound, taint, despoil, incapacitate, pervert, bruise, spoil, wear away, abuse, defile, wrong, corrupt, infect; see also **break, destroy.**

damaged, a. 1. [Less valuable than formerly] injured, in need of repair, in poor condition; see **broken 1, 2. 2.** [Reduced in value because of damage] second hand, used, left over; see **cheap 1.**

damages, n. reparations, costs, reimbursement; see **expense, expenses.**

damn, v. curse, accurse, ban, doom, banish, excommunicate, sentence, convict, cast into hell, consign to the lower regions, torment, condemn to hell *or* eternal punishment, *call down curses on the head of, *send to a warm climate; see also **condemn.**—*Ant.* bless, **forgive,** elevate. —*not give (*or* care) a damn, not care, be indifferent, reject; see **neglect 1.** —*not worth a damn, useless, unproductive, valueless; see **worthless.**

damnation, n. damning, condemnation, doom; see **blame, curse.**

damned, a. 1. [Consigned to hell] cursed, condemned, accursed, lost, infernal, *hell-bound, *gone to blazes; see also **unfortunate.**—*Ant.* saved, **blessed,** on high. 2. [*Disapproved of] bad, unwelcome, *blamed, *blankety-blanked, *blasted, *bloody, *danged, *darned, *doggoned, *double-damned; see also **bad 1, undesirable.**—*Ant.* desirable, **welcomed,** favorite. —*do (*or* try) one's damnedest, endeavor, do one's best, give one's all; see **try 1.**

damp, a. moist, sodden, soggy; see **wet 1.**

dampen, v. sprinkle, water, rinse; see **moisten.**

dance, n. 1. [Rhythmic movement] hop, jig, shuffle, fling, *hoedown. Dances include the following—*social:* fox trot, polka, rhumba, tango, cha-cha, rock-and-roll, jitterbug, two-step, box-step, Charleston; *theatrical:* ballet, modern ballet, tap dance, soft-shoe; *traditional:* cotillion, polonaise, beguine, bolero, fandango, square dance, minuet, tarantella, schottische, (Virginia) reel; *folkloristic and primitive:* sun dance, ghost dance, sword dance, snake dance, fertility dance, Highland fling, flamenco, Irish jig, tarantella, hula. 2. [A dancing party] (grand) ball, dress ball, reception, *shindig, *prom; see also **party 1.**

dance, v. waltz, step, tread, jig, two-step, fox-trot, cha-cha, mambo, tango, polka, reel, hop, skip, jump, leap, bob, scamper, jiggle, bounce, sway, swirl, sweep, swing, *trip the light fantastic, *cut a rug, *rock; see also **move 1.**

dancer, n. (prima) ballerina, chorus girl, dancing student; ballet, tap, toe, figure, hula, belly, taxi, go-go, folk, square, modern, flamenco, geisha, etc., dancer; *hoofer, *stripper, *rock-and-roller.

*dandy, a. (very) good, fine, first-rate; see **excellent.**

danger, n. uncertainty, risk, peril, jeopardy, threat, hazard, insecurity, exposure, venture, menace, vulnerability; see also **chance 1.—Ant. safety,** security, certainty.

dangerous, a. perilous, critical, serious, pressing, vital, vulnerable, exposed, full of risk, threatening, alarming, hazardous, risky, menacing, threatening, serious, ugly, nasty, formidable, terrible, deadly, insecure, precarious, ticklish, delicate, unstable, touchy, treacherous, bad, thorny, breakneck, *shaky, *on a collision course, *hairy, *under fire, unhealthy, *hot; see also **endangered, uncertain 2, unsafe.—Ant. certain,** sure, secure.

dangerously, a. desperately, precariously, severely; see **seriously 1.**

dangle, v. droop, sway, suspend; see **hang 1, 2.**

dare, v. 1. [To be courageous] take a chance, venture, adventure, undertake, stake, attempt, endeavor, try (one's hand), hazard, *take heart, *take the bull by the horns, go ahead, take or run a chance; see also **chance, risk, try 1.—Ant. avoid,** dread, fear. 2. [To defy] meet, confront, oppose, disregard, brave, cope, scorn, insult, resist, threaten, spurn, denounce, bully, mock, laugh at, challenge, *call out, gather courage, *look big, *kick against, *put one's feet down, have the nerve, have the courage of one's convictions, *face the music, face up to, call one's bluff; see also **face 1.—Ant. avoid,** shun, evade.

daredevil, n. stunt man, madcap, gambler; see **adventurer 1.**

daring, a. bold, courageous, fearless; see **brave 1.**

dark, a. 1. [Lacking illumination] unlighted, unlit, dim, shadowy, somber, cloudy, foggy, sunless, lightless, indistinct, dull, faint, vague, dusky, murky, gloomy, misty, obscure, shady, shaded, clouded, darkened, overcast, opaque, without light, *pitchy; see also **black 1,**

hazy.—Ant. **bright,** lighted, illuminated. 2. [Dark in complexion] brunet, swarthy, dark-complexioned; see **black 1. 3.** [Evil] bad, immoral, corrupt; see **bad 1.**

dark, n. gloom, evening, dusk; see **darkness 1. —in the dark,** uninformed, unaware, naive; see **ignorant 1.**

darken, v. 1. [To grow darker] cloud up or over, deepen, become dark; see **shade 3. 2.** [To make darker] cloud, shadow, blacken; see **shade 2.**

darkness, n. 1. [Gloom] dark, dusk, murkiness, dimness, shade, blackness, lightlessness, pitch darkness, twilight, eclipse, nightfall, obscurity, cloudiness; see also **night 1. 2.** [Evil] wickedness, sin, corruption; see **evil 1. 3.** [Secrecy] concealment, isolation, seclusion; see **privacy, secrecy.**

darling, n. lover, sweetheart, dear one, beloved, (dear) heart, heart's desire, dearest, *pet, *angel, love, *sweetie-pie, *sugar, *honey, *precious, *sweetie, *hon, *light of my life, *baby, *one and only.

darn, v. mend, knit, embroider; see **repair, sew.**

dart, n. missile, barb, arrow; see **weapon.**

dart, v. shoot (up or out), speed, plunge, launch, thrust, hurtle, fling, heave, pitch, dash, go like an arrow, spurt, skim, fly, *fire off, *scoot; see also **move 1.—Ant. stop,** amble, loiter.

dash, n. 1. [A short, swift movement] spurt, sortie, rush; see **run 1. 2.** [Punctuation marking a break in thought] em, em dash, em quad, quad, quadrat, en, en quad, en dash; see also **mark 1, punctuation. 3.** [A little of something] little, a few drops, hint, sprinkle, scattering, seasoning, zest, touch, grain, trace, suspicion, suggestion, squirt; see also **bit 1, part 1.—Ant. too much,** quantity, excess.

dash, v. 1. [To discourage] dampen, dismay, dispirit; see **discourage. 2.** [To sprint] race, speed, hurry; see **run 1.**

data, n. evidence, reports, details, results, notes, documents, abstracts, testimony, matters of direct observation, facts, raw materials, memorandums, statistics, figures, measurements, conclusions, information, circumstances, experiments; see also **declaration, knowledge 1, proof 1.**

date, n. 1. [A specified period of time] epoch, period, era, generation, day, term, course, spell, duration, span, moment, year, while, reign, hour, century; see also **age 3, time 2, year. 2.** [An appointment] assignation, rendezvous, engagement, interview, call, visit; see also **appointment 2. 3.** [Person with whom one has a date, sense 2] partner, girl or boyfriend, *steady; see **friend, lover** 1. —out of date, passé, old, obsolete; see **old-fashioned**. —to date, until now, as yet, so far; see **now** 1. —up to date, modern, contemporary, current; see **fashionable**.

date, v. 1. [To indicate historical time] appoint, determine, assign a time to, measure, mark (with a date), fix the date of, fix the time of, chronicle, isolate, measure, put in its place; see also **define** 1, **measure** 1, **record** 1. 2. [To court or be courted] escort, associate with, take out, keep company (with), *go (out) with, *go together, *make a date, *go steady; see also **accompany**.

daughter, n. female child, girl, offspring, descendant, stepdaughter, infant, *her mother's daughter; see **child, girl**.

dawn, n. dawning, sunrise, daybreak; see **morning** 1.

day, n. 1. [The time of light or work] daylight, daytime, full day, working day, daylight hours, eight-hour day, good, bad, hot, cold, etc., day; *sizzler, *scorcher. 2. [A special day] feast day, celebration, festival; see **holiday** 3. [A period of time] term, days, years; see **age** 3. —*call it a day, finish, quit working, end; see **stop** 1. —from day to day, without thought or plan for the future, changing, irresponsibly; see **irregular**.

day after day, a. continually, day by day, steadily; see **regularly**.

day by day, a. gradually, monotonously, persistently; see **regularly**.

daydream, n. reverie, vision, fantasy; see **dream** 1.

day in and day out, a. consistently, steadily, every day; see **daily, regularly**.

daylight, n. daytime, daylight hours, broad day; see **day** 1. —*scare (or beat or knock) the daylights out of, frighten, scare, beat; see **threaten**.

daze, n. stupor, distraction, bewilderment; see **confusion**.

dazed, a. confused, bewildered, perplexed; see **doubtful**.

dead, a. 1. [Without life] not existing, deceased, perished, lifeless, inanimate, late, defunct, breathless, no longer living, devoid or deprived of life, departed, gone, *dead as a doornail, *no more, *done for, *gone the way of all flesh, *gone to one's reward, *gone to meet one's Maker, *out of one's misery, *snuffed out, *pushing up daisies, *rubbed out, *washed up, *gone by the board, *resting in peace.—Ant. alive, animate, enduring. 2. [Without the appearance of life] inert, still, stagnant; see **dull** 2. 3. [Numb] insensible, deadened, anesthetized; see **numb** 1, unconscious. 4. [*Exhausted] wearied, worn, spent; see **tired**.

deaden, v. blunt, impair, dull, repress, slow, paralyze, etherize, chloroform, gas, freeze, anesthetize, put to sleep, numb, knock out, incapacitate, depress, stifle, frustrate, injure, exhaust, tire, retard, consume, destroy, *KO, *dope; see also **hurt, weaken** 2.—Ant. animate, excite, invigorate.

deadlock, n. standstill, stalemate, cessation; see **pause**.

deadly, a. fatal, lethal, murderous, mortal, deathly, poisonous, bloody, destructive, venomous, malignant, injurious, suicidal, bloodthirsty, cannibalistic, harmful, violent; see also **dangerous**.

deaf, a. stone-deaf, unable to hear, without hearing, deaf and dumb, deafened, hard of hearing, *deaf as a post or a doorknob.

deafening, a. thunderous, overpowering, shrieking; see **loud** 1, 2.

deal, n. 1. [An agreement] pledge, compromise, pact; see **agreement, contract**. 2. [*A secret or dishonest agreement] swindle, robbery, graft; see **crime, theft**. 3. [A lot] much, abundance, superabundance; see **plenty**. —a good (or great) deal, a lot, quite a bit, a considerable amount; see **much**. —*make a big deal out of, expand, magnify, blow up; see **exaggerate**.

deal, v. trade, bargain, barter; see **buy, sell**.

dealer, n. bursar, vendor, changer; see **businessman, merchant**.

dealings, n. business, trade, sale; see **business** 1, 4.

deal with, v. handle, manage, have to do with; see **treat** 1.

dear, a. precious, endeared, cherished; see **beloved**.

dear, n. loved one, sweetheart, love; see **darling, lover** 1.

dearly, a. 1. [In an affectionate manner] fondly, affectionately, yearningly; see **lovingly**. 2. [To a great extent] greatly, extremely, profoundly; see **very**.

death, n. decease, dying, demise, passing, loss of life, departure, release, parting, quietus, end of life, grave, tomb, paradise, heaven, hell, extinction, mortality, *exit, end, *finish, *the way of all flesh, *the Grim Reaper, eternal rest; see also **destruction** 1.—Ant. birth, beginning, life. —at death's door, failing, wasting away, nearly dead; see **dying** 1, 2. —to death, very much, extremely, to the extreme; see **much** 1. —to the death, to the end, constantly, faithfully; see **loyally**.

debatable, a. disputable, unsettled, up for discussion; see **controversial, questionable** 1.

debate, n. contest, match, controversy; see discussion.

debate, v. confute, refute, oppose, question, contend, contest, reason, answer, ponder, weigh, differ, dispute, argue the pros and cons of, *jaw, *chew the fat; see also argue, discuss.—*Ant.* agree, concur, concede.

debit, n. deficit, obligation, liability; see debt.

debris, n. rubbish, ruins, wreckage; see trash 1.

debt, n. liability, obligation, (chattel) mortgage, debit, duty, arrears, deficit, note, bill, accounts outstanding or collectable, claim, indebtedness, account; see also obligation.—*Ant.* credit, asset, capital.

debtor, n. purchaser, borrower, mortgagor; see buyer.

decadence, n. deterioration, decline, degeneration; see decay, evil 1.

decadent, a. immoral, wicked, degenerate; see bad 1.

decay, n. decline, decrease, consumption, decomposition, collapse, downfall, decadence, depreciation, corruption, spoilage, wasting away, degeneration, dry rot, putrefaction, corruption, adulteration, rottenness, spoiling, carrion, mold, rust, atrophy, emaciation, blight, mildew, deterioration, ruination, extinction, disintegration, ruin, crumbling, waste, corrosion, wear and tear, *way of all flesh, *crack-up.

decay, v. blight, rot, wither; see spoil 1.

decayed, a. decomposed, putrid, spoiled; see rotten 1.

decaying, a. rotting, crumbling, spoiling, breaking down or up, wasting away, falling, deteriorating, wearing away, disintegrating, worsening, tumbling down; see also rotten 1.

deceased, a. late, former, defunct; see dead 1.

deceit, n. fraud, trickery, duplicity; see deception, dishonesty.

deceitful, a. tricky, cunning, insincere; see dishonest.

deceive, v. mislead, swindle, outwit, fool, delude, rob, defraud, not play fair, falsify accounts, victimize, hoax, betray, beguile, take advantage of, entrap, ensnare, hoodwink, dupe, fleece, *bamboozle, *take for, *cross up, *bilk, *gouge, *clip, fake, *gyp, *beat out of, *put on, *burn, *sell (out), *chisel, *double-cross, *shake down, *make a sucker out of, *take to the cleaners, *take for a ride, *snow, *slip or put (one) over on, *take in, *pull the wool over one's eyes, *flimflam, *give some the runaround, *do a snow job (on), *play upon, *make a monkey of, *stack the cards; see also trick.

deceived, a. duped, fooled, humbugged, hoaxed, snared, trapped, decoyed, baited, played, hoodwinked, betrayed, *bamboozled, *sucked in, *conned; see also cheated.—*Ant.* trusted, dealt with openly, informed.

deceiver, n. conniver, swindler, impostor; see cheat.

decency, n. propriety, seemliness, respectability; see honesty, virtue 1.

decent, a. 1. [In accordance with common standards] seemly, standard, approved; see conventional 3. 2. [In accordance with the moral code] nice, proper, seemly, chaste, modest, pure, ethical, reserved, free from obscenity, spotless, respectable, prudent, mannerly, virtuous, immaculate, delicate, stainless, clean, trustworthy, upright, worthy, untarnished, unblemished, *straight; see also good 1.

deception, n. trickery, double-dealing, untruth, insincerity, craftiness, juggling, treachery, treason, betrayal, pretense, falsehood, trickiness, lying,. deceitfulness, deceit, duplicity, cunning, *fast one, *snow job, *hokum; see also dishonesty.—*Ant.* honesty, frankness, naivete.

deceptive, a. unreliable, ambiguous, illusory; see false 2, 3.

decide, v. settle, determine, judge, conclude, compromise, choose, terminate, vote, poll, make a decision, come to a conclusion, form an opinion or judgment, make up one's mind, make a selection, select, pick, make one's choice, commit oneself, come to an agreement, *have the final word; see also agree, resolve.—*Ant.* delay, hesitate, hedge.

decided, a. 1. [Determined] settled, decided upon, arranged for; see determined 1. 2. [Certain] emphatic, determined, clear; see definite 1.

deciding, a. determining, crucial, conclusive; see important 1, necessary 1.

decipher, v. interpret, translate, explain; see solve.

decision, n. resolution, result, declaration; see judgment 3, opinion 1.

decisive, a. final, definitive, absolute; see definite 1, determined 1.

deck, n. 1. [The floor of a ship] level, flight, story, layer, tier, topside; see also floor 1, 2. 2. [Cards sufficient for a game] pack, set, pinochle-deck, playing cards, the cards; see also card. —*on deck, prepared, available, on hand; see ready 2.

declaration, n. statement, assertion, utterance, information, affirmation, profession, manifesto, announcement, document, bulletin, denunciation, proclamation, confirmation, ultimatum, notice, resolution, affidavit, testimony, charge, indictment, allegation, canon, bill of rights, constitution, creed, article of faith, presentation, exposition, communication, disclosure, explanation, revelation, publication, answer, advertisement, saying, report, oath, admission, acknowledgment; see also **acknowledgment, announcement.**

declare, v. assert (oneself), announce, pronounce, claim, tell, state, point out, affirm, maintain, attest or testify or certify to, confess, reveal, swear, disclose, impart, represent, indicate, state, notify, repeat, insist, contend, advance, allege, argue, demonstrate, propound, bring or put forward, set forth, stress, cite, advocate, pass, proclaim, acknowledge, profess, give out, certify, swear; see also **report** 1, **say.**—*Ant.* hide, equivocate, withhold.

decline, n. deterioration, dissolution, lessening; see **decay.**

decline, v. 1. [To refuse] desist, beg to be excused, send regrets; see **refuse.** 2. [To decrease] degenerate, deteriorate, backslide; see **decrease** 1.

decompose, v. rot, crumble, break up; see **disintegrate.**

decomposition, n. dissolution, breakdown, disintegration; see **decay.**

decorate, v. adorn, beautify, ornament, paint, color, renovate, enrich, brighten, enhance, festoon, embellish, illuminate, spangle, elaborate, enamel, bead, polish, varnish, grace, garnish, finish, tile, redecorate, add the finishing touches, perfect, dress up, fix up, *deck out, *pretty up.

decorated, a. adorned, ornamented, embellished; see **ornate** 1.

decoration, n. 1. [The act of decorating] adornment, ornamentation, embellishment; see **design, improvement** 1. 2. [Something used for decorating] tinsel, thread work, lace, ribbon, braid, gilt, color, curlicue, scroll, wreath, glass, flourish, tooling, inlay, figure work, spangle, finery, filigree, design, ornament, extravagance; see also **jewelry, paint** 1. 3. [An insignia of honor] citation, medal, ribbon; see **emblem.**

decorative, a. embellishing, beautifying, florid; see **ornate** 1.

decoy, n. imitation, bait, fake; see **camouflage, trick** 1.

decrease, n. shrinkage, lessening, contraction; see **discount, reduction** 1.

decrease, v. 1. [To grow less] lessen, diminish, decline, modify, wane, deteriorate, degenerate, dwindle, sink, settle, lighten, slacken, ebb, melt (away), lower, moderate, subside, shrink, shrivel (up), depreciate, soften, quiet, narrow (down), waste, fade (away), run low, weaken, crumble, let or dry up, slow or calm down, burn away or down, die away or down, decay, evaporate, slack

off, wear off or away or out or down, *slump; see also **contract** 1.—*Ant.* **grow,** increase, multiply. 2. [To make less] cut, reduce, check, curb, restrain, quell, tame, compose, hush, still, sober, pacify, blunt, curtail, lessen, lower, subtract, abridge, abbreviate, condense, shorten, minimize, diminish, slash, dilute, shave, pare, prune, modify, digest, limit, level, deflate, compress, strip, thin, make smaller, curtail, clip, lighten, trim, rake or level off, take from or off, roll back, hold or step or scale or boil down, let up, cut off or down or short or back, *chisel, *wind down, *knock off; see also **compress.**—*Ant.* increase, expand, augment.

decree, n. edict, pronouncement, proclamation; see **declaration, judgment** 3.

dedicate, v. devote, apply, give, appropriate, set aside, surrender, apportion, assign, give over to, donate; see also **give** 1.

dedication, n. sanctification, devotion, glorification; see **celebration.**

deduct, v. take away or from, diminish (by), subtract; see **decrease** 2.

deduction, n. 1. [The act of deducing] inferring, concluding, reasoning; see **thought** 1. 2. [A conclusion] result, answer, inference; see **judgment** 3, **opinion** 1. 3. [A reduction] subtraction, abatement, decrease; see **discount, reduction** 1.

deed, n. 1. [An action] act, commission, accomplishment; see **action** 2. 2 [Legal title to real property] document, release, agreement, charter, (title) deed, record, certificate, voucher, indenture, warranty, lease; see also **proof** 1, **record** 1, **security** 2. —**in deed,** in fact or reality or actuality, actually, really; see **surely.**

deep, a. 1. [Situated or extending far down] low, below, beneath, bottomless, submerged, subterranean, submarine, inmost, deep-seated, immersed, dark, dim, impenetrable, buried, inward, underground, down-reaching, of great depth, depthless, immeasurable, yawning; see also **under** 1.—*Ant.* shallow, near the surface, surface. 2. [Extending laterally or vertically] extensive, far, wide, yawning, penetrating, distant, thick, fat, spread out, *to the bone, *up to the hilt; see also **broad, long** 1.—*Ant.* **narrow,** thin, shallow. 3. [Showing evidence of thought and understanding] penetrating, acute, incisive; see **profound.** *—**go off the deep end,** 1. [To act rashly] go to extremes or too far, lose one's good sense, rant; see **exaggerate, rage** 1. 2. [To break down] collapse, lose control (of oneself), become irresponsible or insane; see **crack up** 2.

deepen, v. intensify, expand, extend; see develop 1, grow 1, increase.

deeply, a. surely, profoundly, genuinely; see sincerely, truly.

deer, n. doe, buck, fawn, roe, stag, venison, member of the deer family, cervine or cervid animal. Creatures popularly called deer include the following—spotted, white-tailed, mule, red, musk; antelope, American elk or wapiti, moose, caribou, reindeer, roebuck.

deface, v. disfigure, scratch, mutilate; see destroy.

default, n. failure, lack, error, offense, failure to act, wrongdoing, transgression, imperfection, oversight, neglect, shortcoming, inadequacy, insufficiency, failure to appear or pay, lapse, fault, weakness, vice, blunder; see also failure 1. —in default of, lacking, insufficient, failing; see wanting.

defeat, n. repulse, reverse, rebuff, conquest, tour, overthrow, subjugation, destruction, breakdown, collapse, extermination, annihilation, break, check, trap, ambush, breakthrough, withdrawal, setback, stalemate, ruin, blow, loss, butchery, massacre, Waterloo, beating, whipping, thrashing, fall, comedown, upset, *battering, *pasting, *walloping, *whaling, slaughter, massacre, *KO, *the old one-two; see also loss 1.—Ant. triumph, victory, conquest.

defeat, v. 1. [To get the better of another] master, subjugate, overwhelm; see overcome. 2. [To worst in war] overcome, vanquish, conquer, rout, entrap, subdue, overrun, best, overthrow, crush, smash, drive off, annihilate, overwhelm, scatter, repulse, halt, reduce, outflank, finish off, encircle, slaughter, butcher, outmaneuver, ambush, demolish, sack, torpedo, sink, shipwreck, drown, swamp, *wipe out, decimate, obliterate, roll back, *mop up, *chew up, *mow down, trample under foot; see also destroy, ravage.—Ant. yield, give up, relinquish. 3. [To worst in sport or in personal combat] beat, overpower, outplay, trounce, win (from), knock out, throw, floor, pommel, pound, flog, outhit, outrun, outjump, thrash, *edge, *shade, *lay low, *skin, *lick, *wallop, *clean up on, *beat up, take, *KO, *put down, *beat the pants off of, pulverize, *steamroll, *plow under, *smear; see also beat 1.—Ant. suffer, be defeated, fail.

defeated, a. crushed, overcome, conquered; see beaten 1.

defect, n. imperfection, flaw, drawback; see fault 1.

defect, v. fall away from, run away, forsake; see abandon 2, desert, leave 1.

defective, a. imperfect, incomplete, inadequate; see faulty, poor 2, unfinished 1.

defend, v. 1. [To keep off an enemy; often used figuratively] shield, shelter, screen; see protect. 2. [To support an accused person or thing] plead, justify, uphold, second, exonerate, back, vindicate, aid, espouse the cause of, befriend, say in defense, guarantee, endorse, warrant, maintain, recommend, rationalize, plead one's cause, say a good word for, argue or speak or stand up or put in a good word or apologize for, *go to bat for, *cover (up) for, *stick up for; see also support 2.—Ant. convict, accuse, charge.

defendant, n. the accused, defense, offender; see prisoner.

defended, a. protected, guarded, safeguarded; see safe 1.

defender, n. champion, patron, sponsor; see guardian 1, protector.

defense, n. 1. [The act of defending] resistance, protection, safeguard, preservation, security, custody, stand, front, backing, guardianship, the defensive, precaution, inoculation, excusing, apologizing, explaining, justifying, exoneration, explanation.—Ant. offense, retaliation, aggression. 2. [A means or system for defending] trench, bulwark, dike, stockade, machine-gun nest, bastille, bastion, fortification, fort, chemical and biological warfare, barricade, garrison, rampart, fence, wall, embankment, citadel, fortress, armor, antiaircraft, camouflage, (gas) mask, shield, screen, stronghold, parapet, buttress, strong point, guard; see also fortification, trench.—Ant. attack, siege, blitzkrieg. 3. [In law, the reply of the accused] denial, plea, answer; see declaration, proof 1, statement 1.

defensive, a. protecting, guarding, watchful; see protective.

defensively, a. suspicious, on the defensive, at bay; see also carefully 1.

defer, v. put off, postpone, shelve; see delay 1, suspend 2.

deference, n. veneration, acclaim, homage; see reverence.

deferred, a. delayed, prolonged, held up; see postponed.

defiance, n. insubordination, rebellion, insurgence; see disobedience.

defiant, a. resistant, obstinate, disobedient; see rebellious.

deficiency, n. want, need, loss; see lack 2.

deficient, a. insufficient, skimpy, meager; see inadequate.

deficit, n. shortage, paucity, deficiency; see lack 2.

defile, v. ravish, violate, molest; see hurt, rape.

define, v. 1. [To set limits] bound, confine, limit, outline, fix, settle, circumscribe, mark, set, distinguish, establish, encompass, mark the limits of, determine the boundaries of, fix the limits of, curb, edge, border, enclose, set bounds to, fence in, rim, encircle, hedge or wall in, envelop, flank, stake (out); see also limit.—*Ant*. confuse, distort, mix. 2. [To provide a name or description] determine, entitle, label, designate, characterize, elucidate, interpret, illustrate, represent, individuate, find out, popularize, spell out, translate, exemplify, specify, prescribe, nickname, dub; see also describe, explain, name 1, 2.—*Ant*. misunderstand, misconceive, mistitle.

definite, a. 1. [Determined with exactness] fixed, exact, precise, positive, accurate, correct, decisive, absolute, clearly defined, well-defined, limited, strict, explicit, specific, settled, decided, prescribed, restricted, assigned, unequivocal, special, conclusive, categorical, particular, unerring, to the point, beyond doubt; see also certain 2, determined.—*Ant*. obscure, indefinite, inexact. 2. [Clear in detail] sharp, visible, audible, tangible, distinct, vivid, unmistakable in meaning, straightforward, obvious, marked, plain, not vague, well-drawn, clearly defined, well-marked, well-defined, clear-cut, explicit, unmistakable, distinguishable, undistorted, crisp, bold, graphic, downright, undisguised, in plain sight, clear as day, *standing out like a sore thumb.—*Ant*. confused, vague, hazy. 3. [Positive] sure, beyond doubt, convinced; see certain 1.

definitely, a. clearly, unmistakably, unquestionably; see surely.

definition, n. meaning, terminology, signification, diagnosis, analogue, synonym, exposition, interpretation, explication, clue, key, translation, comment, rationale, commentary, explanation, representation, characterization, solution, answer; see also description, explanation.

definitive, a. final, ultimate, conclusive; see absolute 1.

deflate, v. exhaust, flatten, void; see empty 1, 2.

deflect, v. swerve, diverge, curve; see turn 3, 6.

deform, v. disfigure, deface, injure; see damage.

deformed, a. damaged, distorted, misshapen, disfigured, crippled, misproportioned, malformed, cramped, badly made, disjointed, unseemly, ill-favored, dwarfed, hunchbacked, warped, mangled, crushed, unshapely, clubfooted, curved, contorted, gnarled, crooked, grotesque, lame, irregular; see also twisted 1, ugly 1.—*Ant*. regular, shapely, well-formed.

deformity, n. malformation, ugliness, unsightliness; see contortion, damage 1.

defraud, v. hoax, dupe, cheat; see deceive.

defy, v. insult, resist, face; see dare 2, oppose 1, 2.

degenerate, a. depraved, immoral, corrupt; see bad.

degradation, n. depravity, corruption, degeneration; see evil 1.

degrade, v. demote, discredit, diminish; see humble.

degraded, a. disgraced, debased, depraved; see bad.

degree, n. 1. [One in a series used for measurement] measure, grade, step, mark, interval, space, measurement, gradation, size, dimension, shade, point, line, plane, step in a series, gauge, rung, term, tier, stair, ratio, tenor, period, level; see also division 2. 2. [An expression of relative excellence, attainment, or the like] extent, station, order, quality, development, height, expanse, length, potency, range, proportion, compass, quantity, standing, strength, reach, intensity, scope, caliber, pitch, stage, sort, status, rate; see also rank 3. 3. [Recognition of academic achievement] distinction, testimonial, honor, qualification, dignity, eminence, credit, credentials, baccalaureate, doctorate, *sheepskin; see also diploma, graduation. —**by degrees**, step by step, slowly (but surely), inch by inch; see gradually. —**to a degree**, somewhat, partially, to an extent; see partly.

dehydrate, v. dessicate, parch, drain; see dry 1.

dejected, a. depressed, dispirited, cast down; see sad 1.

delay, n. deferment, adjournment, putting off, procrastination, suspension, moratorium, reprieve, setback, stay, stop, discontinuation, *cooling-off period, *holdup; see also pause.

delay, v. postpone, defer, retard, hold up, deter, clog, choke, slacken, keep, hold, keep back, impede, discourage, interfere with, detain, stay, stop, withhold, arrest, check, prevent, repress, curb, obstruct, inhibit, restrict, prolong, encumber, procrastinate, adjourn, block, bar, suspend, table, slow, put aside, hold back or off, hold everything, bide's one's time, slow up, stall, put off, restrain, *put on ice, *shelve, *pigeonhole; see also hinder, interrupt.—*Ant*. speed, accelerate, encourage.

delayed, *a.* held up, slowed, put off; see **late 1, postponed.**

delegate, *n.* legate, emissary, proxy, deputy, substitute, consul, appointee, minister, alternate, nominee, ambassador, congressman, senator, *stand-in, *sub, *pinch hitter; see also **agent, representative 2.**

delegate, *v.* 1. [To give authority to another] authorize, commission, appoint, name, nominate, select, choose, assign, license, empower, deputize, swear in, ordain, invest, elect, *give one the green light, *give one the go-ahead; see also **approve.**—*Ant.* **dismiss,** repudiate, reject. 2. [To give duties to another] entrust, authorize, hold responsible for; see **assign.**

delegation, *n.* 1. [The act of assigning to another] assignment, giving over, nomination, trust, commissioning, ordination, authorization, charge, deputation, referring, transferring; see also **appointment 1.** 2. [A group with a specific mission] representatives, deputation, commission; see **committee, gathering, organization 2.**

deliberate, *a.* thought out, predetermined, conscious, advised, prearranged, fixed, with forethought, well considered, cautious, studied, intentional, planned in advance, done on purpose, willful, considered, thoughtful, purposed, planned, reasoned, calculated, intended, purposeful, premeditated, voluntary, designed, cold-blooded, resolved, cut-and-dried; see also **careful.**

deliberately, *a.* resolutely, determinedly, emphatically, knowingly, meaningfully, voluntarily, consciously, on purpose, willfully, premeditatedly, in cold blood, with malice aforethought, advisedly, after mature consideration, freely, independently, without any qualms, by design, intentionally, purposely, all things considered, pointedly, to that end, *with eyes wide open; see also **carefully 1.**

delicacy, *n.* 1. [Fineness of texture] airiness, daintiness, transparency, flimsiness, softness, smoothness, subtlety, tenderness; see also **lightness 2.** 2. [A rare commodity, especially for the table] tidbit, luxury, gourmet dish *or* food, dainty, dessert, sweet, delight, party dish, imported food, delicatessen, *chef's special; see also **food.**

delicate, *a.* 1. [Sickly] susceptible, in delicate health, feeble; see **sick, weak 1.** 2. [Dainty] fragile, frail, fine; see **dainty.**

delicately, *a.* deftly, skillfully, cautiously; see **carefully 1.**

delicatessen, *n.* 1. [Ready-to-serve foods] Varieties of delicatessen include the following—cold meats, luncheon meats, salad, dairy products, salami, pastrami, bologna, wurst, sausage, frankfurters, olives, sauerkraut, pickled peppers, pickled fish, dill pickles, sweet pickles, kosher pickles, gherkins, caviar, anchovies, liver paste; see also **bread, cheese, dessert, fish, fruit, meat, wine.** 2. [A place that sells delicatessen, sense 1] food store, butcher store, grocery; see **market 1.**

delicious, *a.* tasty, savory, good, appetizing, choice, well-seasoned, well-done, spicy, sweet, rich, delectable, exquisite, dainty, luscious, tempting, *fit for a king; see also **excellent, rich 4.**—*Ant.* **rotten,** flat, stale.

delight, *n.* enjoyment, joy, pleasure; see **happiness.**

delight, *v.* fascinate, amuse, please; see **entertain 1.**

delighted, *a.* 1. [Greatly pleased] entranced, excited, pleasantly surprised; see **happy.** 2. [An expression of acceptance of pleasure] thank you, by all means, to be sure, of course, certainly, splendid, excellent, overwhelmed, charmed, so glad.

delightful, *a.* charming, amusing, clever; see **pleasant 1.**

delinquent, *a.* 1. [Lax in duty] slack, behindhand, tardy, procrastinating, criminal, neglectful, faulty, blamable, negligent, derelict, remiss; see also **careless.**—*Ant.* **punctual,** punctilious, scrupulous. 2. [Not paid on time; *said especially of taxes*] owed, back, overdue; see **due, unpaid 1.**

delinquent, *n.* defaulter, tax evader, offender, dropout, reprobate, loafer, derelict, bad debtor, poor risk, felon, law breaker, wrongdoer, sinner, juvenile offender *or* delinquent *or* JD, outlaw, *black sheep, *fallen angel; see also **criminal.**

delirious, *a.* demented, crazy, irrational; see **insane.**

deliver, *v.* 1. [To free] set free, liberate, save; see **free.** 2. [To transfer] pass, remit, hand over *or* in; see **give 1.** 3. [To speak formally] present, read, give; see **address 2.** 4. [To bring to birth] bring forth, be delivered of, provide obstetrical attention; see **produce 2.** 5. [To distribute] allot, dispense, give out; see **distribute.**

delivered, *a.* brought, deposited, transported, checked in, forwarded, expressed, hand-delivered, mailed, dispatched, at the door, sent out by truck, trucked, laid down; see also **mailed.**

delivery, *n.* 1. [Bringing goods into another's possession] consignment, carting, shipment, transfer, portage, freighting, dispatch, conveyance, mailing, special delivery, parcel post, giving *or* handing over, cash on delivery (C.O.D.);

see also **transportation**. 2. [Delivery of a child] birth, parturition, confinement, childbirth, labor, bringing forth, midwifery, obstetrics, Caesarian operation or section; see also **birth**. 3. [The manner of a speaker] articulation, enunciation, accent, utterance, pronunciation, emphasis, elocution; see also **eloquence**.

delusion, n. phantasm, hallucination, fancy; see **illusion**.

demand, n. 1. [A peremptory communication] order, call, charge; see **command**. 2. [Willingness to purchase] trade, request, sale, bid, need, requirement, interest, call for, rush, search, inquiry, desire to buy; see also **desire** 1.—Ant. **indifference**, lack of interest, sales resistance. —**in demand**, sought, needed, requested; see **wanted**. —**on demand**, ready, prepared, usable; see **available**.

demand, v. charge, direct, command; see **ask**.

demanding, a. fussy, imperious, exacting; see **critical**.

demented, a. crazy, bemused, unbalanced; see **insane**.

demerit, n. bad or low mark, loss of points or credit or distinction, poor grade; see **fault** 1, **punishment**.

demobilize, v. disband, disperse, withdraw; see **disarm**.

democracy, n. justice, the greatest good for the greatest number, equality, popular suffrage, individual enterprise, capitalism, laissez faire, rugged individualism, freedom of religion, freedom of speech, freedom of the press, the right to work, private ownership, emancipation, political equality, democratic spirit, *the Four Freedoms, *the American Way; see also **equality**, **freedom** 2.—Ant. dictatorship, feudalism, tyranny.

democrat, n. republican, Social Democrat, state socialist, advocate of democracy, constitutionalist, individualist.—Ant. **dictator**, Nazi, autocrat.

Democrat, n. Southern Democrat, constitutional Democrat, Jeffersonian Democrat, *Dixiecrat, *Fair Dealer, *Great Society Democrat, *New Dealer; see also **Republican**.—Ant. **Republican**, Tory, Socialist.

democratic, a. popular, constitutional, representative, free, equal, common, bourgeois, individualistic, communal, laissez-faire.

demolish, v. wreck, devastate, obliterate; see **destroy**.

demolition, n. extermination, annihilation, wrecking; see **destruction** 1, **explosion**.

demon, n. imp, vampire, incubus; see **devil**.

demonstrate, v. 1. [To prove] show, make evident, confirm: see **prove**. 2.

[To present for effect] exhibit, manifest, parade; see **display**.

demonstration, n. 1. [An exhibition] showing, presentation, exhibit; see **display**, **show** 1. 2. [A mass rally] picket line, (peace) march, sit-in; see **protest**.

demoralize, v. weaken, unman, enfeeble; see **discourage**.

demoralized, a. unnerved, weakened, depressed; see **sad** 1.

demote, v. downgrade, lower, *bust; see **decrease** 2, **dismiss**.

den, n. 1. [The home of an animal] cavern, lair, cave; see **hole** 1. 2. [A private or secluded room] study, hideout, recreation or rec room; see **retreat** 2, **room** 2.

denial, n. repudiation, disclaimer, rejection, refutation, rejecting, retraction, dismissal, renunciation, refusing or refusal to recognize or acknowledge; *the cold shoulder, *the brush-off; see also **opposition** 2.—Ant. acknowledgement, avowal, confession.

denomination, n. 1. [A class] category, classification, group; see **class** 1. 2. [A religious group] belief, creed, sect; see **church** 3.

denounce, v. condemn, threaten, charge, blame, accuse, indict, arraign, implicate, incriminate, upbraid, impugn, prosecute, revile, stigmatize, ostracize, reproach, castigate, brand, boycott, rebuke, dress down, take to task, damn, impeach, scold, reprimand, reprove, condemn openly, charge with, blacklist. expose, *knock, *pitch or rip into, give away, blackball; see also **deny**.—Ant. praise, laud, commend.

dense, a. 1. [Close together] solid, compact, impenetrable; see **thick** 1. 2. [Slow-witted] stupid, half-witted, imbecilic; see **dull** 3, **ignorant** 2.

density, n. solidity, thickness, impenetrability, consistency, quantity, bulk, heaviness, body, compactness, denseness; see also **mass** 1, **weight** 1.—Ant. **lightness**, rarity, thinness.

dent, n. indentation, depression, impression, dimple, nick, notch, dip, cavity, cut, incision, sink, pit, trough, furrow, scratch; see also **hole** 1.

dent, v. hollow, depress, indent, gouge, sink, dig, imprint, mark, dimple, pit, notch, scratch, nick, make a dent in, perforate, ridge, furrow.—Ant. **straighten**, bulge, make protrude.

dentist, n. D.D.S., dental practitioner, specialist; see **doctor**.

deny, v. contradict, disagree (with), disprove, disallow, gainsay, disavow, disclaim, negate, repudiate, controvert, revoke, rebuff, reject, renounce, discard, not admit, take exception to, disbelieve, spurn, doubt, veto, discredit, nullify, say "no" to, *not buy, deny flatly; see also denounce, refuse.—*Ant*. admit, accept, affirm.

deodorant, *n*. disinfectant, deodorizer, fumigator; see cleanser, cosmetic.

depart, *v*. go, quit, withdraw; see leave 1.

departed, *a*. 1. [Dead] defunct, expired, deceased; see dead 1. 2. [Gone away] left, disappeared, moved; see gone 1.

department, *n*. 1. [The field of one's activity] jurisdiction, activity, interest, occupation, province, bureau, business, capacity, dominion, administration, station, function, office, walk of life, vocation, specialty, field, duty, assignment, bailiwick; see also job 1. 2. [An organized subdivision] section, office, bureau, precinct, tract, range, quarter, area, arena, corps, agency, board, administration, circuit, territory, ward, state office, district office, force, staff, beat; see also division 2.

department store, *n*. variety store, supermarket, shopping center, shopper's square, mall, drygoods store, ready-to-wear, mail-order house, bazaar, fair, bargain store; see also market 1.

departure, *n*. going, departing, separation, embarkation, taking leave, sailing, withdrawal, hegira, evacuation, passage, setting out *or* forth, parting, take-off, taking off, becoming airborne, starting, leaving, flight, exodus, exit, walkout, getaway; see also retreat 1.—*Ant*. arrival, landing, invasion.

depend (on *or* upon), *v*. 1. [To be undecided] be held up, be uncertain *or* doubtful, hang in suspense, hang in the balance, *hang by a thread. 2. [To be contingent] be determined by, rest with *or* on, be subordinate to, be dependent on, be based on, be subject to, hinge on, turn on *or* upon, be in the power of, be conditioned (by), revolve on, trust to, be at the mercy of. 3. [To rely upon] put faith in, confide in, believe in; see trust 1.

dependable, *a*. trustworthy, steady, sure; see reliable.

dependence, *n*. need of, servility, inability to act independently, subordination to the direction of another, subjection to control, subservience; see also necessity 3.

dependent, *a*. 1. [Subordinate] inferior, secondary, lesser; see subordinate. 2. [Needing outside support] helpless, poor, immature, clinging, not able to sustain itself, *on a string; see also weak 5. 3. [Contingent] liable to, subject (to), incidental to, conditioned, sustained by, unable to exist without, subordinate, accessory to, subservient, controlled *or* regulated *or* determined by; see also conditional.

depending (on), *a*. contingent upon,

regulated *or* controlled *or* determined by, in the event of, on the condition that, subject to, providing, provided, secondary (to), growing from; see also conditional.

depleted, *a*. emptied, exhausted, spent; see wasted.

depletion, *n*. exhaustion, consumption, deficiency; see emptiness.

deport, *v*. exile, ship out *or* away, expel (from a given place); see banish, dismiss.

deposit, *v*. 1. [To lay down] drop, place, put; see install. 2. [To present money for safekeeping] invest, amass, store, keep, stock up, bank, hoard, collect, treasure, lay away, put in the bank, entrust, transfer, put for safekeeping, *put aside for a rainy day, *salt away; see also accumulate, save 2.—*Ant*. spend, withdraw, pay out. —on deposit, hoarded, stored, saved; see kept 2.

depot, *n*. station, base, lot, freight *or* passenger *or* railway *or* railroad depot, terminal, railway station, railroad *or* loading *or* unloading yards, stockyards, sidetrack, loading track, ammunition dump, ticket office, waiting room, junction, central station, airport, harbor, station house, stopping-place, destination.

deprave, *v*. pervert, debase, degrade; see corrupt.

depraved, *a*. low, mean, base; see bad.

depreciate, *v*. deteriorate, lessen, worsen; see decrease 1.

depreciation, *n*. harm, reduction, shrinkage; see loss 3.

depress, *v*. 1. [To bring to a lower level] press down, squash, settle; see flatten, press 1. 2. [To bring to a lower state] reduce, dampen, dishearten, debase, degrade, abase, dismay, sadden, mock, darken, scorn, reduce to tears, deject, weigh *or* keep *or* cast *or* beat down, chill, dull, oppress, lower in spirits, *throw cold water on; see also discourage, disgrace, humble, humiliate.—*Ant*. urge, animate, stimulate.

depressed, *a*. discouraged, pessimistic, cast down; see sad 1.

depressing, *a*. discouraging, disheartening, saddening; see dismal, sad 1.

depression, *n*. 1. [Something lower than its surroundings] cavity, dip, sink; see hole 1. 2. [Low spirits] despair, despondency, sorrow, unhappiness, gloom, dejection, melancholy, misery, trouble, worry, discouragement, hopelessness, distress, desperation, desolation, dreariness, dullness, cheerlessness, darkness, bleakness, oppression, gloominess, dumps, blues, doldrums; see also grief, sadness.—*Ant*. joy, cheer, satisfaction. 3. [Period of commercial stress] decline, unemployment, slack *or* hard *or* bad times, inflation, crisis, over-production, economic decline *or* stagnation, recession, panic, *crash, slump; see also **failure** 1.

deprive, *v.* strip, despoil, divest; see **seize** 2.

depth, *n.* 1. [Vertical or lateral distance] lowness, pitch, extent down from a given point, downward *or* upward measure, perpendicular measurement from the surface *or* bottom; see also **expanse.**—*Ant.* **height,** shallowness, flatness. 2. [Deepness] profundity, intensity, abyss, pit, base, bottom of the sea; see **bottom.** 3. [Intellectual power] profundity, weightiness, acumen; see **wisdom. —in depth,** extensive, broad, thorough; see **detailed.**

deputy, *n.* lieutenant, appointee, aide; see **assistant, delegate.**

derail, *v.* run *or* go off the rails, be wrecked, fall off; see **crash** 1, **wreck.**

derange, *v.* madden, craze, unbalance; see **confuse, disturb.**

deranged, *a.* demented, crazy, mad; see **insane.**

deride, *v.* scorn, jeer, mock; see **ridicule.**

derision, *n.* scorn, mockery, disdain; see **ridicule.**

derivation, *n.* root, source, beginning; see **origin** 3.

derive, *v.* determine, work out, conclude; see **assume.**

derogatory, *a.* belittling, faultfinding, detracting; see **critical, sarcastic.**

descend, *v.* slide, settle, gravitate, slip, dismount, topple, plunge, sink, dip, pass downward, pitch, light, deplane, tumble, move downward, come down on *or* upon, slump, trip, stumble, flutter down, plummet, submerge, step *or* climb *or* get *or* tumble *or* go *or* swoop down *or* off; see also **dive, drop** 1, **fall** 1.—*Ant.* **climb,** ascend, mount.

descendants, *n.* offspring, kin, children; see **family** 1.

descent, *n.* 1. [A downward incline] declivity, fall, slide; see **hill, inclination** 2. 2. [The act of descending] slump, downfall, drop, lapse, subsiding, falling, coming down, sinking, reduction, landslide, tumble, decline; see also **fall** 1.—*Ant.* **rise,** mounting, growth. 3. [Lineal relationship] extraction, origin, lineage; see **family** 1, **relationship.**

describe, *v.* delineate, characterize, portray, depict, picture, illuminate, make clear *or* apparent *or* vivid, give the details of, specify, give meaning to, elucidate, report, draw, paint, illustrate, detail, make sense of, relate, express, narrate, label, name, call, term, write up, *give the dope on, *spell out; see also **define, explain.**

description, *n.* narration, story, portrayal, word picture, account, report, delineation, sketch, specification(s), characterization, declaration, rehearsal, information, definition, record, brief, summary, depiction, explanation, write-up; see also **record** 1.

descriptive, *a.* designating, identifying, definitive, photographic, describing, narrative, expository, interpretive, characterizing, expressive, clear, true to life, illustrative, lifelike, vivid, picturesque, circumstantial, eloquent, detailed, pictorial, indicative, revealing; see also **characteristic, explanatory, graphic** 1, 2.—*Ant.* **dull,** analytical, expository.

desert, *n.* waste, sand, wastelands, barren plains, arid region, deserted region, (sand) dunes, lava beds, infertile area *or* region, salt *or* alkali flats, abandoned country *or* land; see also **wilderness.**

desert, *v.* defect, be absent without leave, abandon one's post, sneak off, run away from duty *or* military service, violate one's oath, leave unlawfully, *go AWOL, *go over the hill; see also **abandon** 2.—*Ant.* obey, stay, do one's duty.

deserted, *a.* left, forsaken, relinquished; see **abandoned** 1, **empty** 1.

deserter, *n.* runaway, fugitive, refugee, truant, defector, derelict, delinquent, lawbreaker, betrayer, traitor, backslider, slacker; see also **criminal, traitor.**

desertion, *n.* abandonment, flight, escape, departure, leaving, defection, defecting, renunciation, withdrawal, avoidance, evasion, elusion, truancy, retirement, resignation, divorce, backsliding, *running out on, *going back on; see also **escape.**—*Ant.* **loyalty,** cooperation, union.

deserve, *v.* merit, be worthy of, earn, be deserving, lay claim to, have the right to, be given one's due, be entitled to, warrant, *rate, *have it coming.—*Ant.* fail, be unworthy, usurp.

deserved, *a.* merited, earned, justified, appropriate, suitable, equitable, right, rightful, proper, fitting, just, due, well-deserved; see also **fit.**

deserving, *a.* needy, rightful, fitting; see **worthy.**

design, *n.* pattern, layout, conception, diagram, drawing, (preliminary) sketch, draft, blueprint, picture, tracing, outline, depiction, chart, map, plan, perspective, treatment, idea, study; see also **composition, form** 1, **purpose** 1.—*Ant.* confusion, jumble, mess. —**by design,** on purpose, with intent, purposely; see **deliberately.**

design, *v.* block out, outline, sketch; see **plan** 2.

designate, *v.* indicate, point *or* mark out, name; see **choose.**

designation, *n.* classification, key word, appellation; see **class 1, name 1.**

designer, *n.* planner, draftsman, modeler; see **architect, artist, sculptor.**

desirable, *a.* 1. [Stimulating erotic desires] seductive, fascinating, alluring; see **charming.** 2. [Having many good qualities] good, welcome, acceptable; see **excellent.**

desire, *n.* 1. [The wish to enjoy] aspiration, wish, motive, will, urge, eagerness, propensity, fancy, frenzy, craze, mania, hunger, thirst, attraction, longing, yearning, fondness, liking, inclination, proclivity, craving, relish, *hankering, *itch, *yen; see also **ambition, greed.**—*Ant.* **indifference,** unconcern, apathy. 2. [Erotic wish to possess] lust, passion, hunger, appetite, fascination, infatuation, fervor, excitement, nymphomania, sexual love, libido, sensual appetite, carnal passion, eroticism, biological urge, *rut, *heat.—*Ant.* **abstinence,** coldness, frigidity.

desire, *v.* covet, crave, long *or* wish for; see **need, want 1.**

desk, *n.* 1. [A piece of furniture] secretary, bureau, box, lectern, frame, case, pulpit; see also **furniture, table 1.** 2. [A department of an editorial office] jurisdiction, occupation, bureau; see **department.**

desolate, *a.* 1. [Left unused] deserted, forsaken, uninhabited; see **abandoned 1, isolated.**

desolation, *n.* bareness, barrenness, devastation, havoc, ruin, dissolution, wreck, demolition, annihilation, extinction; see also **desert.**

despair, *n.* hopelessness, depression, discouragement; see **desperation, gloom 2.**

despairing, *a.* hopeless, despondent, miserable; see **sad 1.**

despair of, *v.* lose hope *or* faith *or* heart *or* courage, give up (hope), abandon (all) hope, have no hope, have a heavy heart, lose faith in, abandon oneself to fate; see also **abandon 1.**

desperado, *n.* outlaw, bandit, ruffian; see **criminal.**

desperate, *a.* 1. [Hopeless] despairing, despondent, downcast; see **hopeless, sad 1.** 2. [Reckless] incautious, frenzied, wild; see **careless, rash.**

desperately, *a.* severely, harmfully, perilously; see **carelessly, seriously 1.**

desperation, *n.* despondency, despair, depression, discomfort, dejection, distraction, distress, desolation, anxiety, anguish, agony, melancholy, grief, sorrow, worry, trouble, pain, hopelessness, torture, pang, heartache, concern, misery, unhappiness; see also **fear, futility, gloom.**—*Ant.* **hope,** hopefulness, confidence.

despicable, *a.* contemptible, abject, base; see **mean 3.**

despise, *v.* scorn, disdain, condemn; see **hate 1.**

despite, *a.* and *prep.* in spite of, in defiance of, even with; see **anyhow.**

despondent, *a.* dejected, discouraged, depressed; see **sad 1.**

dessert, *n.* sweet, tart, cobbler, jelly, custard, ice, sundae, compote, fruit salad, pudding, ice cream; see also **cake 2, candy, cheese, delicacy 2, fruit, pastry, pie.**

destination, *n.* objective, goal, aim; see **purpose 1.**

destined, *a.* fated, compulsory, foreordained, menacing, near, forthcoming, threatening, in prospect, predestined, predetermined, compelled, condemned, at hand, impending, inexorable, that is to be, in store, to come, directed, ordained, settled, sealed, closed, predesigned, in the wind, in the cards; see also **doomed, inevitable.**—*Ant.* **voluntary,** at will, by chance.

destiny, *n.* fate, future, fortune; see **doom.**

destitute, *a.* impoverished, poverty-stricken, penniless; see **poor 1.**

destroy, *v.* ruin, demolish, exterminate, raze, tear *or* throw down, plunder, ransack, eradicate, overthrow, root up *or* out, devastate, butcher, consume, liquidate, break up, dissolve, blot out, quash, quell, level, abort, stamp out, suppress, squelch, scuttle, undo, annihilate, lay waste, overturn, impair, damage, ravish, deface, shatter, split (up), crush, obliterate, knock *or* break to pieces, abolish, crash, extinguish, wreck, dismantle, upset, bomb, mutilate, smash, trample, overturn, maim, mar, end, nullify, blast, neutralize, gut, snuff out, erase, sabotage, repeal, pull down *or* to pieces, terminate, conclude, finish, bring to ruin, stop, put a stop to, wipe out, do in, do *or* make away with, finish off, make short work of, *total (out), *cream, destruct, self-destruct, put an end to; see also **defeat, ravage, stop 1.**—*Ant.* **build,** construct, establish.

destroyed, *a.* wrecked, annihilated, killed, lost, devastated, wasted, demolished, overturned, overwhelmed, upset, nullified, undone, put to an end, shattered, smashed, scuttled, ravished, engulfed, submerged, overrun, extinguished, eradicated, devoured, consumed, burned up *or* down, gone to pieces, razed, lying in ruins, sacked; see also **broken 1, dead 1, ruined 1.**—*Ant.* **saved,** protected, restored.

destroyer, *n.* 1. [A destructive agent] assassin, executioner, slayer; see **criminal, killer, weapon.** 2. [A swift armed surface vessel] light unit, battleship, fighting vessel; see **ship**.

destruction, n. 1. [The act of destroying] demolition, annihilation, eradication, slaughter, liquidation, overthrow, extermination, elimination, abolition, murder, assassination, killing, disruption, bombardment, disintegration, extinction, annihilating, wreckage, dissolution, butchery, sabotage, sacking, extinguishing, eliminating, crashing, falling, felling, tearing down; see also **damage 1, disaster.**—*Ant.* production, formation, erection. 2. [The condition after destruction] waste, ashes, wreck, annihilation, remnants, devastation, vestiges, desolation, ruins, overthrow, decay, loss, remains, havoc, prostration, injury, downfall, end, starvation, plague, shipwreck, dissolution, disorganization; see also **damage 2, wreck 2.**

destructive, a. 1. [Harmful] hurtful, injurious, troublesome; see **harmful.** 2. [Deadly] fatal, ruinous, devastating; see **deadly, vicious.**

detach, v. separate, withdraw, disengage; see **divide.**

detached, a. 1. [Cut off or removed] loosened, divided, disjoined; see **separated.** 2. [Disinterested] apathetic, uninvolved, unconcerned; see **indifferent.**

detail, n. item, portion, particular, trait, specialty, feature, aspect, article, peculiarity, minutia, fraction, specification, article, technicality; see also **circumstance, part 1.**—*Ant.* entirety, whole, synthesis. —**in detail**, item by item, thorough, comprehensive; see **detailed.**

detail, v. itemize, exhibit, show, report, relate, narrate, tell, designate, catalogue, recite, specialize, depict, enumerate, mention, uncover, reveal, recount, recapitulate, analyze, set forth, produce, go into the particulars, *get down to cases; see also **describe.**—*Ant.* dabble, summarize, epitomize.

detailed, a. enumerated, specified, explicit, specific, particularized, individual, individualized, developed, itemized, definite, minute, described, precise, full, narrow, complete, exact, fussy, particular, meticulous, point by point, circumstantial, accurate, unfolded, disclosed, elaborated, complicated, comprehensive, at length, gone into; see also **elaborate 2.**—*Ant.* general, brief, hazy.

details, n. analysis, trivia, minutiae, particulars, bill, (itemized) account, trivialities, fine points, items; see also **detail.**

detain, v. hold, keep, inhibit; see **delay, restrain 1.**

detect, v. distinguish, recognize, identify; see **discover.**

detection, n. apprehension, exposure, disclosure; see **discovery, exposure.**

detective, n. policeman, agent, plainclothesman, *private eye, narcotics agent, police sergeant or officer, FBI man, wiretapper, investigator, criminologist, prosecutor, patrolman, sleuth, *shadow, eavesdropper, spy, *flatfoot, *dick, *G-man, *copper, *cop, *fed, *nark; see also **policeman.**

detention, n. custody, impediment, quarantine; see **arrest, confinement, restraint 2.**

deter, v. caution, stop, dissuade; see **prevent, warn.**

detergent, n. cleansing agent, disinfectant, washing substance; see **cleanser, soap.**

deteriorate, v. depreciate, lessen, degenerate; see **decrease 1.**

deterioration, n. decadence, rotting, degeneration; see **decay.**

determinable, a. definable, discoverable, capable of being determined; see **definite 2.**

determination, n. resolution, certainty, persistence, stubbornness, obstinacy, resolve, certitude, decision, assurance, conviction, boldness, fixity of purpose, hardihood, tenacity, courage, independence, self-confidence, purposefulness, fortitude, self-assurance, firmness, self-reliance, nerve, heart, bravery, fearlessness, will, energy, vigor, stamina, perseverance, strength of will, a brave or bold front, a stout heart, enterprise, *guts, *spunk, *a stiff upper lip; see also **confidence, faith 1, purpose 1.**

determine, v. 1. [To define] limit, circumscribe, delimit; see **define 1, restrict.** 2. [To find out the facts] ascertain, find out, learn; see **discover.** 3. [To resolve] fix upon, settle, conclude; see **decide, resolve.**

determined, a. 1. [Already fixed or settled] decided, agreed, acted or agreed upon, concluded, contracted, set, ended, resolved, closed, terminated, achieved, finished, over, at an end, checked, measured, tested, budgeted, passed, given approval, *given the green light or the go-ahead, over and done with; see also **approved.**—*Ant.* unfinished, argued, suspended. 2. [Having a fixed attitude] resolute, firm, strong-minded; see **stubborn.**

deterrent, n. hindrance, impediment, obstacle; see **restraint 2.**

detest, v. abhor, loathe, despise; see **hate.**

detonate, v. touch off, discharge, blast; see **explode, shoot 1.**

detour, n. temporary or alternate route, byway, back road, service road, alternate highway, secondary highway, bypass, circuit, roundabout course.

detract, *v.* decrease, take away a part, subtract from, draw away, diminish, lessen, withdraw, derogate, depreciate, discredit; see also **slander.**

devastate, *v.* ravage, sack, pillage; see **destroy.**

devastation, *n.* destruction, defoliation, waste; see **desolation.**

develop, *v.* 1. [To improve] enlarge, expand, extend, promote, advance, magnify, build up, refine, enrich, cultivate, elaborate, polish, finish, perfect, deepen, lengthen, heighten, widen, intensify, fix up, *shape up; see also **grow 1, improve 1, 2, strengthen.**—*Ant.* damage, disfigure, spoil. 2. [To grow] mature, evolve, advance; see **grow 1.** 3. [To reveal slowly] unfold, disclose, exhibit, unravel, disentangle, uncover, make known, explain, unroll, explicate, produce, detail, tell, state, recount, account for, give account of; see also **reveal.**—*Ant.* hide, conceal, blurt out. 4. [To work out] enlarge upon, elaborate (upon), go into detail; see **explain, increase.**

developed, *a.* grown, refined, advanced; see **matured, perfected.**

development, *n.* growth, unfolding, elaboration, maturing, progress, ripening, maturation, enlargement, addition, spread, (gradual) evolution, evolving, advancement, improvement, growing, increasing, spreading, adding to, making progress, advancing; see also **improvement 1, increase, progress 1.**—*Ant.* reduction, decrease, lessening.

deviate, *v.* deflect, digress, swerve, vary, wander, stray, turn aside, keep *or* stay aside, go out of control, shy (away from), depart from, break the pattern, not conform, go out of the way, veer, fly *or* go off on a tangent, *go haywire, *swim against the stream; see also **differ 1.**—*Ant.* conform, keep on, keep in line.

deviation, *n.* change, deflection, alteration; see **difference 1, variation 2.**

device, *n.* 1. [An instrument] invention, contrivance, mechanism, gear, equipment, appliance, contraption, means, agent, tackle, rigging, harness, material, implement, utensil, construction, apparatus, outfit, article, accessory, gadget, *whatnot, *whatsit, *whatchamacallit; see also **machine, tool 1.** 2. [A shrewd method] artifice, scheme, design, trap, dodge, trick, pattern, loophole, wile, craft, ruse, expedient, subterfuge, plan, project, plot, racket, game, finesse, *catch; see also **discovery, method 2, trick 1.**

devil, *n.* Satan, fiend, adversary, error,

sin, imp, mischiefmaker, Beelzebub, fallen angel, hellhound, Mammon, Moloch, Hades, Lucifer, Mephistopheles, diabolical *or* satanic force, the Tempter, Prince of Darkness, Evil One; see also **evil 1.**—*Ant.* angel, Christ, God. —**give the devil his due,** give one credit, give credit where credit is due, recognize; see **acknowledge 2.** —**go to the devil,** 1. [To decay] degenerate, fall into bad habits, *go to pot; see **fail 1.** 2. [A curse] go to hell, damn you, be damned; see **curse.** —**raise the devil,** cause trouble, riot, be boisterous *or* unruly; see **disturb, fight 2.**

devious, *a.* foxy, insidious, shrewd; see **dishonest, sly.**

devote, *v.* apply, consecrate, give; see **bless, dedicate.**

devoted, *a.* dutiful, loyal, constant; see **faithful.**

devotion, *n.* allegiance, service, consecration, devotedness, adoration, piety, zeal, ardor, earnestness, faithfulness, fidelity, deference, sincerity, adherence, observance; see also **loyalty, worship 1.**—*Ant.* indifference, apathy, carelessness.

devotions, *n.* religious worship, church services, prayers; see **church 2, worship 1.**

devour, *v.* gulp, swallow, gorge; see **eat 1.**

devout, *a.* devoted, pious, reverent; see **faithful, holy, religious 2.**

diagnosis, *n.* analysis, determination, investigation; see **summary.**

diagonal, *a.* slanting, inclining, askew; see **oblique.**

diagonally, *a.* cornerways, slanting, askew; see **cornerwise.**

diagram, *n.* sketch, layout, picture; see **description, design, plan 1.**

dial, *n.* face, control, gauge, indicator, meter, register, measuring device, compass; see also **index.**

dialect, *n.* idiom, accent, local *or* regional speech, broken *or* pidgin English, brogue, lingo, trade language, *lingua franca,* usage level, pig Latin, jargon, cant, vernacular, patois; see also **language 1.**

dialogue, *n.* talk, exchange, remarks; see **conversation.**

diameter, *n.* breadth, measurement across, broadness; see **width.**

diametrical, *a.* contrary, adverse, facing; see **opposite 3.**

diamond, *n.* 1. [A crystalline jewel] (precious) stone, solitaire, engagement ring, brilliant, diamond chips *or* flakes, crystal, ring, *stone, *rock, *sparkler, *glass, *ice; see also **jewel.** 2. [Shape or figure] lozenge, solid, rhombus; see **form 1.** 3. [A baseball playing field, particularly the infield] lot, ball park, *sandlot; see **field 2, park 1.**

diary, *n.* chronicle, journal, log; see **record 1.**

dicker, *v.* trade, barter, bargain; see **argue, buy, sell.**

dictate, *v.* speak, deliver, give forth, interview, compose, formulate, verbalize, record, orate, give an account; see also **talk 1.**

dictator, *n.* autocrat, despot, tyrant, czar, fascist, absolute ruler, oppressor, terrorist, master, leader, caesar, ringleader, magnate, lord, commander, chief, adviser, overlord, taskmaster, disciplinarian, headman, *cock of the walk, *man at the wheel; see also **leader 2, ruler 1.**

dictatorial, *a.* despotic, authoritarian, arbitrary; see **absolute 2.**

dictatorship, *n.* despotism, unlimited rule, coercion; see **government 2, tyranny.**

diction, *n.* style, enunciation, expression, wording, usage, choice of words, command of language, locution, rhetoric, fluency, oratory, articulation, vocabulary, language, *line, *gift of gab; see also **eloquence, speech 2.**

dictionary, *n.* word book, word list, lexicon, thesaurus, reference work, glossary, encyclopedia, Webster, dictionary of synonyms.

die, *v.* **1.** [To cease living] expire, pass away *or* on, depart, perish, succumb, go, commit suicide, suffocate, lose one's life, cease to exist, drown, hang, fall, meet one's death, be no more, drop dead, *be done for, *fade away, *rest in peace, *go to one's last home, pass over to the great beyond, give up the ghost, *go the way of all flesh, *turn *or* return to dust, *cash in, *push up daisies, *kick the bucket, bite the dust, lay down one's life, breathe one's last, *croak, *conk out, *check out, *kick off, *go by the board.—*Ant.* live, thrive, exist. **2.** [To cease existing] disappear, vanish, become extinct; see **stop 2. 3.** [To decline as though death were inevitable] fade, ebb, wither; see **decay, weaken 2.**

die away, *v.* decline, go away, sink; see **stop 2.**

die down, *v.* decline, disappear, recede; see **die 2, 3, decrease 1.**

die-hard, *n.* zealot, reactionary, extremist; see **conservative.**

die off *or* **out**, *v.* go, cease (to exist), disappear; see **vanish.**

diet, *n.* **1.** [What one eats] menu, fare, *daily bread; see **food. 2.** [Restricted intake of food] weight-reduction plan, fast, abstinence from food, starvation diet, *bread and water.

diet, *v.* go without, starve oneself, lose weight, slim down, go on a diet, reduce, *tighten one's belt.

differ, *v.* **1.** [To be unlike] vary, modify, not conform, digress, take exception, turn, reverse, qualify, alter, change, diverge (from), contrast (with), bear no resemblance, not look like, jar with, clash *or* conflict with, be distinguished from, diversify, stand apart, depart from, go off on a tangent, sing a different tune; see also **contrast.**—*Ant.* **resemble**, parallel, take after. **2.** [To oppose] disagree, object, fight; see **oppose 1.**

difference, *n.* **1.** [The quality of being different] disagreement, divergence, non-conformity, contrariness, deviation, opposition, antithesis, dissimilarity, inequality, diversity, departure, variance, discrepancy, separation, differentiation, distinctness, separateness, asymmetry; see also **contrast, variety 1.**—*Ant.* **agreement**, similarity, resemblance. **2.** [That which is unlike in comparable things] deviation, departure, exception; see **variation 2. 3.** [Personal dissension] discord, estrangement, dissent; see **dispute.** —**make a difference**, change, have an effect, affect; see **matter 1.** —**split the difference**, compromise, go half way, come to an agreement; see **agree.** —**what's the difference?**, what does it matter? what difference does it make? *so what?; see **why.**

different, *a.* **1.** [Unlike in nature] distinct, separate, not the same; see **unlike. 2.** [Composed of unlike things] diverse, miscellaneous, assorted; see **various. 3.** [Unusual] unconventional, strange, startling; see **unusual 1.**

differentiate, *v.* contrast, set apart, separate; see **distinguish 1.**

differently, *a.* variously, divergently, individually, distinctively, creatively, uniquely, separately, each in his own way, severally, diversely, incongruously, abnormally, not normally, nonconformably, asymmetrically, in a different manner, with a difference, otherwise.—*Ant.* **evenly**, uniformly, invariably.

difficult, *a.* **1.** [Hard to achieve] laborious, hard, unyielding, strenuous, exacting, stiff, heavy, arduous, painful, labored, trying, bothersome, troublesome, demanding, burdensome, backbreaking, not easy, wearisome, onerous, rigid, crucial, uphill, challenging, exacting, formidable, ambitious, immense, tough, heavy, *no picnic, stiff; see also **severe 1.**—*Ant.* **easy**, wieldy, light. **2.** [Hard to understand] intricate, involved, perplexing, abstruse, abstract, delicate, hard, knotty, thorny, troublesome, ticklish, obstinate, puzzling, mysterious, mystifying, subtle, confusing, bewildering, confounding, esoteric, unclear, mystical, tangled, hard to explain *or* solve, profound, rambling, loose, meandering, inexplicable, awkward, complex, complicated, deep, stubborn, hidden, formidable, enigmatic, paradoxical, incomprehensible, unintelligible, inscrutable, inexplicable, unanswerable, not understandable, unsolvable, unfathomable, concealed, unaccountable, ambiguous, equivocal, metaphysical, inconceivable, unknown, deep, over one's head, too deep (for), not making sense, Greek to; see also **obscure 1, 3.**—*Ant.* clear, obvious, simple.

difficulty, *n.* 1. [Something in one's way] obstacle, obstruction, stumbling block, impediment, complication, hardship, adversity, misfortune, distress, deadlock, dilemma, hard job, maze, stone wall, barricade, impasse, knot, opposition, quandary, struggle, crisis, trouble, embarrassment, entanglement, thwart, mess, paradox, muddle, emergency, matter, standstill, hindrance, perplexity, bar, trial, check, predicament, *hot water, *pickle, *fix, stew, scrape, hard nut to crack, hitch, dead end, snag, *monkey wrench in the works, pinch, *deep water, *jam, the devil to pay, *hang-up; see also sense 2; **barrier.**—*Ant.* aid, assistance, **help.** 2. [Something mentally disturbing] trouble, annoyance, to-do, ado, worry, weight, complication, distress, oppression, depression, aggravation, anxiety, discouragement, touchy situation, embarrassment, burden, grievance, irritation, strife, puzzle, responsibility, frustration, harassment, misery, predicament, setback, pressure, stress, strain, charge, struggle, maze, *jam, *hangup, mess, *pickle, pinch, scrape; see also sense 1; **crisis, emergency.** — *Ant.* ease, comfort, happiness.

*dig, *n.* 1. [Insult] slur, innuendo, cut; see **insult.** 2. [Excavation] digging, archaeological expedition, exploration; see **expedition.**

dig, *v.* 1. [To stir the earth] delve, spade, mine, excavate, channel, deepen, till, drive (a shaft), clean, undermine, burrow, dig out, gouge, dredge, scoop *or* tunnel *or* hollow *or* clean out, muck, stope, grub, cat, bulldoze; see also **shovel.**—*Ant.* embed, fill, **bury.** 2. [To remove by digging] dig up, uncover, turn up; see **harvest.** 3. [*To like] enjoy, love, appreciate; see **like 1, 2.** 4. [*To understand] comprehend, recognize, follow; see **understand 1.**

digest, *n.* epitome, précis, condensation; see **summary.**

digest, *v.* transform food, consume, absorb; see **eat 1.**

digestible, *a.* eatable, absorbable, good to eat; see **edible.**

dig in, *v.* 1. [To begin] commence, rise, spring; see **begin 2.** 2. [To entrench] delve, burrow, undermine; see **dig 1.**

dig into, *v.* investigate, research, probe; see **examine.**

digit, *n.* symbol, arabic notation, numeral; see **number.**

dignified, *a.* stately, somber, solemn, courtly, reserved, ornate, elegant, classic, lordly, aristocratic, majestic, formal, noble, regal, superior, magnificent, grand, eminent, sublime, august, grave, distinguished, magisterial, imposing, portly, haughty, honorable, decorous, lofty, proud, *classy, *snazzy, *sober as a judge, slick; see also **cultured, refined 2.**—*Ant.* rude, undignified, boorish.

dignify, *v.* exalt, elevate, prefer; see **praise 1.**

dignity, *n.* nobility, self-respect, lofty bearing, grand air, quality, culture, distinction, stateliness, elevation, worth, character, importance, renown, splendor, majesty, *class, *something on the ball; see also **honor, pride 1.**—*Ant.* humility, lowness, meekness.

dig up, *v.* find, uncover, excavate; see **dig 2, discover.**

dilemma, *n.* quandary, perplexity, predicament; see **difficulty 1.**

diligence, *n.* alertness, earnestness, quickness, perseverance, industry, vigor, carefulness, intent, intensity; see **attention, care 1.**—*Ant.* carelessness, sloth, laziness.

dilute, *v.* mix, reduce, thin; see **weaken 2.**

dim, *a.* faint, dusky, shadowy; see **dark 1.**

dime, *n.* ten cents, thin dime, ten-cent piece; see **money 1.**

dimensions, *n.* size, measurements, extent; see **height, length 1, 2, width.**

diminish, *v.* lessen, depreciate, abbreviate; see **decrease.**

din, *n.* clamor, commotion, hubbub; see **confusion, noise 2.**

dine, *v.* lunch, feast, sup; see **eat 1.**

dingy, *a.* grimy, muddy, soiled; see **dirty 1.**

dining room, *n.* Varieties include the following—dining hall, breakfast nook, dinette, tea shop, lunch counter, lunch room, cafeteria, café, ice-cream parlor, drug store, grill, coffee shop, inn, hotel, soda fountain, steak house, sandwich shop, diner, mess hall, galley, cookshop, automat, *greasy spoon; see also **restaurant.**

dinner, *n.* feast, banquet, principal *or* main meal, supper, repast; see also **meal 2.**

dip, *n.* 1. [The action of dipping] plunge, immersion, soaking, ducking, drenching, sinking; see also **bath 1.** 2. [Material into which something is dipped] preparation, solution, suspension, dilution, concoction, saturation, mixture; see also **liquid.** 3. [A low place] depression, slope, inclination; see **hole 1. 4.** [A swim] plunge, bath, dive; see **swim.**

dip, *v.* **1.** [To put into a liquid] plunge, lower, wet, slosh, submerge, irrigate, steep, drench, douse, souse, moisten, splash, slop, water, duck, bathe, rinse, baptize, dunk; see also **immerse, soak 1, wash 1. 2.** [To transfer by means of a vessel] scoop, shovel, ladle, bale, spoon, dredge, lift, draw, dish, dip up *or* out, offer; see also **serve.**—*Ant.* empty, pour, let stand. **3.** [To fall] slope, decline, recede, tilt, swoop, slip, spiral, sink, plunge, bend, verge, veer, slant, settle, slump, slide, go down; see also **dive, drop 2, fall 1.**

diploma, *n.* degree, graduation certificate, credentials, honor, award, recognition, commission, warrant, voucher, confirmation, *sheepskin; see also **graduation.**

diplomacy, *n.* artfulness, skill, discretion; see **tact.**

diplomat, *n.* ambassador, consul, minister, legate, emissary, envoy, agent; see also **representative 2, statesman.**

diplomatic, *a.* tactful, suave, gracious, calculating, shrewd, opportunistic, smooth, capable, conciliatory, conniving, sly, artful, wily, subtle, crafty, sharp, cunning, contriving, scheming, discreet, deft, intriguing, politic, strategic, astute, clever; see also **polite.**

dipped, *a.* immersed, plunged, bathed, ducked, doused, drenched, soused, covered, dunked; see also **soaked, wet 1.**

dire, *a.* dreadful, terrible, horrible; see **frightful 1.**

direct, *a.* **1.** [Without divergence] in a straight line, straight ahead, undeviating, uninterrupted, unswerving, shortest, nonstop, as the crow flies, *straight as an arrow, point-blank; see also **straight 1.**—*Ant.* zigzag, roundabout, crooked. **2.** [Frank] straightforward, outspoken, candid; see **frank, honest. 3.** [Immediate] prompt, succeeding, resultant; see **immediate.**

direct, *v.* **1.** [To show the way] conduct, show, guide; see **lead 1. 2.** [To decide the course of affairs] regulate, govern, influence; see **manage 1. 3.** [To aim a weapon] sight, train, level; see **aim. 4.** [To command] command, bid, charge; see **order 1.**

directed, *a.* supervised, controlled, conducted, sponsored, under supervision, assisted, counseled, guided, serviced, managed, organized, orderly, modern, purposeful, functioning; see also **aimed, organized.**

direction, *n.* **1.** [A position] point of the compass, objective, bearing, region, area, place, spot; see also **way 2.** Points of the compass include the following—north (N), south (S), east (E), west (W), NE, NW, SE, SW, NNE, NNW, SSE, SSW,

ENE, ESE, WNW, WSW. **2.** [Supervision] management, superintendence, control; see **administration 2. 3.** [A tendency] bias, bent, proclivity; see **inclination 1.**

directions, *n.* (formal) instructions, advice, notification, specification, indication, order(s), assignment, recommendation(s), summons, directive, regulation, prescription, plans.

directly, *a.* instantly, at once, quickly; see **immediately.**

director, *n.* manager, supervisor, executive; see **leader 2.**

directory, *n.* list, syllabus, notice, register, record, almanac, roster, dictionary, gazetteer, telephone book, Yellow Pages, city directory, Social Register, Who's Who, blue book; see also **catalogue, index.**

dirt, *n.* **1.** [Earth] soil, loam, clay; see **earth 2. 2.** [Filth] rottenness, filthiness, smut; see **filth.**

dirty, *a.* **1.** [Containing dirt] soiled, unclean, unsanitary, unhygienic, filthy, polluted, nasty, slovenly, dusty, messy, squalid, sloppy, lousy, disheveled, uncombed, unsightly, untidy, straggly, unwashed, stained, tarnished, spotted, smudged, foul, fouled, grimy, greasy, muddy, mucky, sooty, smoked, slimy, rusty, unlaundered, unswept, *crummy, grubby, scummy.—*Ant.* pure, unspotted, sanitary. **2.** [Without honor or decency] base, low, filthy; see **lewd 2, mean 3.**

dirty, *v.* soil, sully, defile, pollute, foul, tarnish, spot, smear, blot, blur, smudge, smoke, botch, spoil, sweat up, blotch, spatter, splash, stain, debase, corrupt, taint, contaminate.—*Ant.* **clean,** cleanse, rinse.

disability, *n.* feebleness, inability, incapacity; see **injury, weakness 1.**

disable, *v.* cripple, impair, put out of action; see **damage, weaken 2.**

disabled, *a.* crippled, helpless, useless, wrecked, stalled, maimed, wounded, mangled, lame, mutilated, run-down, worn-out, weakened, impotent, castrated, paralyzed, handicapped, senile, decrepit, *laid up, *done up *or* for *or* in, *cracked up, *counted out; see also **hurt, useless 1, weak 1.**—*Ant.* **healthy,** strong, capable.

disadvantage, *n.* **1.** [Loss] damage, harm, deprivation; see **loss 3. 2.** [A position involving difficulties] bar, obstacle, handicap; see **restraint 2. 3.** [Unfavorable details or prospects; *often plural*] inconvenience, obstacle, drawbacks; see **weakness 1.**

disagree, *v.* **1.** [To differ] dissent, object, oppose; see **differ 1. 2.** [To have uncomfortable effect] nauseate, make ill, go against the grain; see **bother 2.**

disagreeable, *a.* **1.** [Having an unpleasant disposition] difficult, obnoxious, offensive; see **irritable, rude 2. 2.** [Irritating; *said of things and conditions*] bothersome, unpleasant, upsetting; see **disturbing, offensive 2.**

disagreement, *n.* **1.** [Discord] contention, strife, conflict, controversy, wrangle, dissension, animosity, ill feeling, ill will, misunderstanding, division, opposition, hostility, breach, discord, feud, clashing, antagonism, bickering, squabble, tension, split, quarreling, falling out, break, rupture, quarrel, clash, opposition, contest, friction; see also **battle, competition, fight. 2.** [Inconsistency] discrepancy, dissimilarity, disparity; see **difference 1. 3.** [A quarrel] fight, argument, feud; see **dispute.**

disappear, *v.* cease, fade, die; see **escape, evaporate, vanish.**

disappearance, *n.* vanishing, fading, departure, ebbing away, removal, dissipation, ceasing to exist *or* appear, desertion, flight, retirement, escape, exodus, vanishing point, going, disintegration, exit, withdrawal, decline and fall, eclipse; see also **escape, evaporation.**

disappoint, *v.* fail, delude, deceive, dissatisfy, disillusion, harass, embitter, chagrin, dumbfound, fall short of, cast down, frustrate, torment, tease, miscarry, abort, thwart, foil, baffle, balk, mislead, bungle, let down, *leave in the lurch, *fizzle out.

disappointed, *a.* dissatisfied, discouraged, unsatisfied, despondent, depressed, objecting, complaining, distressed, hopeless, balked, disconcerted, aghast, disgruntled, disillusioned; see also **sad.**—*Ant.* satisfied, pleased, content.

disappointing, *a.* unsatisfactory, ineffective, uninteresting, discouraging, unpleasant, inferior, unlooked for, lame, insufficient, failing, at fault, limited, second-rate, mediocre, ordinary, unexpected, unhappy, depressing, disconcerting, disagreeable, irritating, annoying, troublesome, disheartening, unlucky, uncomfortable, bitter, distasteful, disgusting, deplorable, short of expectations; see also **inadequate.**

disappointment, *n.* **1.** [The state of being disappointed] dissatisfaction, frustration, chagrin, lack of success, despondency, displeasure, distress, discouragement, disillusionment, check, disillusion, setback, adversity, hard fortune; see also **defeat, failure 1, regret 1.**—*Ant.* **success,** fulfillment, realization. **2.** [A person *or* thing that disappoints] miscarriage, misfortune, calamity, blunder, bad luck, setback, downfall, slip, defeat, mishap, error, mistake, discouragement, obstacle, cold comfort, miscalculation,

fiasco, *no go, *blind alley, *washout, *lemon, *dud, letdown, *bust, *false alarm; see also sense 1; **failure 2.**—*Ant.* **achievement,** successful venture, success.

disapproval, *n.* criticism, censure, disparagement; see **objection.**

disapprove, *v.* blame, chastise, reprove; see **denounce.**

disapprove of, *v.* object to, dislike, deplore; see **complain, oppose 1.**

disarm, *v.* demobilize, disable, unarm, weaken, debilitate, incapacitate, muzzle, deprive of weapons *or* means of defense, subdue, strip, tie the hands, *clip the wings of; see also **defeat 2, 3.**—*Ant.* **arm,** outfit, equip.

disarmament, *n.* arms reduction, de-escalation, cease fire; see **peace 1.**

disaster, *n.* accident, calamity, mishap, debacle, casualty, emergency, adversity, harm, misadventure, collapse, slip, fall, collision, crash, hazard, setback, defeat, failure, woe, trouble, scourge, grief, undoing, curse, tragedy, blight, cataclysm, downfall, rainy day, bankruptcy, upset, blast, blow, wreck, bad luck, comedown, *pile-up, smash-up, *washout, *flop, *bust; see also **catastrophe, misfortune.**

disastrous, *a.* calamitous, ruinous, unfortunate; see **harmful, unfavorable.**

disband, *v.* scatter, disperse, dismiss; see **leave 1.**

disbelief, *n.* unbelief, skepticism, mistrust; see **doubt.**

disbeliever, *n.* doubter, skeptic, agnostic; see **critic 1.**

disburse, *v.* expend, use, contribute; see **pay 1, spend 1.**

discard, *v.* reject, expel, repudiate, protest, cast aside *or* away *or* out *or* off, throw away *or* aside *or* overboard *or* out, get rid of, give up, renounce, have done with, make away with, dismantle, discharge, write off, banish, eject, divorce, dispossess, dispense with, shake off, pass up, free oneself from, free of, give away, part with, dispose of, do away with, dispense with, shed, relinquish, thrust *or* cast *or* lay aside, sweep away, cancel, abandon, forsake, desert, cut, have nothing to do with, brush away, *scotch, *chuck, drop, wash one's hands of, *junk; see also **abandon 1, dismiss.**—*Ant.* **save,** retain, preserve.

discarded, *a.* rejected, repudiated, cast off, thrown away, dismantled, dismissed, useless, damaged, outworn, worn out, done with, run down, not worth saving, abandoned, obsolete, shelved, neglected, deserted, forsaken, outmoded, out of date, out of style *or* fashion, old-fashioned, *junked, *old hat, ancient.—*Ant.* **kept,** worthwhile, modern.

discern, *v.* find out, determine, discriminate; see **discover.**

discerning, *a.* discriminating, perceptive, penetrating; see **discreet.**

discharge, *v.* 1. [To unload] unpack, release, remove cargo; see **empty, unload.** 2. [To remove] take off, send, carry *or* take away; see **remove 1.** 3. [To cause to fire] blast, shoot off, fire; see **shoot 1.** 4. [To release] emancipate, liberate, let go; see **free.**

discharged, *a.* mustered out, sent home, recalled, freed, liberated, released, let go, sent away, emancipated, expelled, ejected, fired, ousted, *canned, scrapped; see also **free 2, 3.**

disciple, *n.* 1. [A follower] adherent, pupil, believer; see **follower.** 2. [A follower of Christ; *usually capitalized*] apostle, witness, revealer. Christ's disciples mentioned in the New Testament include—Matthew, John, Peter, James, Philip, Andrew, Thaddaeus, Thomas, Judas Iscariot, Simon the Canaanean.

discipline, *n.* 1. [Mental self-training] preparation, development, exercise, drilling, training, regulation, self-disciplining; see also **drill 3, education 1.** 2. [A system of obedience] conduct, regulation, drill, orderliness, restraint, limitation, curb, indoctrination, brainwashing; see also **training.**

discipline, *v.* chastise, correct, limit; see **punish.**

disc jockey, *n.* radio announcer, commentator, *DJ; see **announcer, reporter.**

disclose, *v.* make known, confess, publish; see **reveal.**

disclosure, *n.* exposé, acknowledgment, confession; see **admission 3, declaration.**

discolor, *v.* stain, rust, tarnish; see **color, dirty.**

discoloration, *n.* blot, blotch, splotch; see **blemish, stain.**

discomfort, *n.* trouble, displeasure, uneasiness; see **annoyance, embarrassment.**

disconnect, *v.* separate, detach, disengage; see **cut 1, divide.**

disconnected, *a.* broken off, detached, switched off; see **separated.**

discontent, *n.* envy, uneasiness, depression; see **regret 1.**

discontented, *a.* unhappy, disgruntled, malcontented; see **sad 1.**

discontinue, *v.* finish, close, cease; see **end 1, stop 2.**

discontinued, *a.* ended, terminated, given up *or* over; see **abandoned.**

discord, *n.* 1. [Conflict] strife, contention, dissension; see **disagreement 1.** 2. [Noise] din, tumult, racket; see **noise 2.**

discount, *n.* deduction, allowance, rebate, decrease, markdown, concession, per-

centage, premium, subtraction, commission, exemption, modification, qualification, drawback, depreciation, cut, cut rate; see also **reduction 1.**—*Ant.* increase, markup, surcharge. —**at a discount,** discounted, cheap, depreciated; see **reduced 2.**

discount, *v.* reduce, remove, redeem, diminish, depreciate, deduct from, lower, make allowance (for), allow, take off, charge *or* strike off, rebate, mark down, anticipate, discredit, *rake off; see also **decrease 2.**—*Ant.* raise, mark up, advance.

discourage, *v.* repress, appall, intimidate, break one's heart, deject, unnerve, scare, confuse, dampen, dismay, daunt, bully, demoralize, *throw a wet blanket on, *throw cold water on, *dampen the spirits; see also **depress 2, frighten.**—*Ant.* encourage, cheer, inspire.

discouraged, *a.* downcast, pessimistic, depressed; see **sad 1.**

discouragement, *n.* 1. [Dejection] melancholy, despair, the blues; see **depression 2, sadness.** 2. [A restriction] constraint, hindrance, deterrent; see **impediment 1.**

discouraging, *a.* 1. [Acting to discourage one] depressing, disheartening, repressing; see **dismal 1.** 2. [Suggesting an unwelcome future] inopportune, disadvantageous, dissuading; see **unfavorable 2.**

discourteous, *a.* boorish, crude, impolite; see **rude 2.**

discourtesy, *n.* impudence, impoliteness, vulgarity; see **rudeness.**

discover, *v.* invent, find out, ascertain, detect, discern, recognize, distinguish, determine, observe, explore, hear of *or* about, awake to, bring to light, uncover, ferret *or* root *or* trace out, unearth, look up, light *or* stumble *or* come on *or* upon, run across, fall *or* strike *or* light upon, think of, perceive, glimpse, identify, devise, catch, spot, create, make out, sense, feel, sight, smell, hear, spy, bring out, find a clue, put a *or* one's finger on, *get wise to, *dig out *or* up, turn up, smell *or* sniff out, come up with, hit *or* happen upon, get wind of, *hit upon, run down, put *or* lay one's hands on; see also **find, learn 1.**—*Ant.* miss, pass by, omit.

discovered, *a.* found, searched out, come on, happened on *or* upon, unearthed, ascertained, detected, revealed, disclosed, unveiled, observed, sighted, shown, exposed, traced out, made out, met with, come across, recognized, identified, laid bare, opened, presented, spotted, perceived, learned; see also **real 2.**—*Ant.* hidden, unfound, lost.

discovery, *n.* invention, detection, exploration, identification, discernment, distinction, determination, calculation, experimentation, feeling, hearing, sighting, strike, results, findings, formula, device, find, contrivance, design, machine, invention, process, breakthrough, data, principle, law, theorem, innovation, conclusion, method, way; see also **result**.

discredit, v. question, disbelieve, distrust; see **doubt**.

discreet, a. cautious, prudent, discerning, discriminating, not rash, strategic, noncommittal, heedful, vigilant, civil, sensible, reserved, alert, awake, wary, watchful, wise, circumspect, attentive, considerate, intelligent, guarded, politic, diplomatic, tight-lipped, *cagey; see also **careful, thoughtful** 2.—Ant. **rash**, indiscreet, imprudent.

discretion, n. caution, foresight, carefulness, wariness, sound judgment, thoughtfulness, attention, heed, concern, consideration, observation, watchfulness, precaution, good sense, providence, maturity, discernment, forethought, calculation, deliberation, vigilance, discrimination, responsibility, presence of mind; see also **care** 1, **prudence, tact**.—Ant. **carelessness**, thoughtlessness, rashness. —**at one's discretion**, as one wishes, whenever appropriate, discreetly; see **appropriately**.

discriminate, v. 1. [To differentiate] specify, separate, tell apart; see **distinguish** 1. 2. [To be (racially) prejudiced] be a bigot, set apart, segregate; see also **hate, separate** 1.

discrimination, n. 1. [The power to make distinctions] perception, acuteness, understanding; see **intelligence** 1. 2. [The act of drawing a distinction] separation, differentiation, difference; see **judgment** 2. 3. [Partiality] unfairness, bias, bigotry; see **hatred, prejudice**.

discuss, v. argue, debate, dispute, talk of or about, explain, contest, confer, deal or advise or reason with, take up, look over, consider, talk over or out, take up in conference, engage in conversation, go into, think over, telephone about, have a conference on or upon, take into consideration or account, reason or discourse about, argue for and against, canvass, consider, handle, present, review, recite, treat or speak of, converse, discourse, take under advisement, comment upon, have out, speak on, *kick about or around, *toss or bat around, *chew the fat, *jaw, *air out, *knock around, put heads together, *compare notes, *chew the rag; see also **talk** 1.—Ant. **delay**, table, postpone.

discussed, a. talked over, debated, argued; see **considered** 1.

discussion, n. conversation, exchange, consultation, interview, deliberation, argumentation, contention, (meaningful)

dialogue, talk, conference, argument(s), dialogue, debate, panel discussion, summit meeting, dealing with the agenda, controversy, altercation, review, reasons, dispute, symposium, quarrel, pros and cons, *powwow, *bull session; see also **conversation, dispute**.—Ant. **agreement**, decision, conclusion.

disease, n. 1. [A bodily infirmity] sickness, malady, ailment; see **illness** 1. 2. [Loosely used term for any ailment] condition, defect, infirmity; see **illness** 2.

diseased, a. unhealthy, unsound, ailing; see **sick**.

disengage, v. loose, undo, disentangle; see **free**.

disengaged, a. detached, unattached, disjoined; see **separated**.

disentangle, v. disengage, untangle, untwist; see **free**.

disfavor, n. displeasure, disapproval, disrespect; see **disappointment** 1.

disfigure, v. deface, mar, mutilate; see **damage, hurt**.

disgrace, n. scandal, shame, stain, slur, slight, stigma, brand, spot, slander, dishonor, infamy, reproach, disrepute, humiliation, degradation, taint, tarnish, *mark of Cain, scarlet letter; see also **insult**.—Ant. **pride**, praise, credit.

disgrace, v. debase, shame, degrade, abase, dishonor, disparage, discredit, deride, disregard, strip of honors, dismiss from favor, disrespect, mock, humble, reduce, put to shame, tarnish, stain, blot, sully, taint, defile, stigmatize, brand, *tar and feather, *put down, snub, derogate, *belittle, *take down a peg; see also **humiliate, ridicule, slander**.—Ant. **praise**, honor, exalt.

disgraced, a. discredited, in disgrace, dishonored; see **ashamed**.

disgraceful, a. dishonorable, disreputable, shocking; see **offensive, shameful** 1, 2.

disguise, n. mask, deceptive covering, make-up, faking, (false) front, deception, (smoke) screen, blind, concealment, counterfeit, pseudonym, costume, masquerade, veil, cover, façade, *put-on; see also **camouflage** 1.

disguise, v. mask, conceal, camouflage, pretend, screen, cloak, shroud, cover, veil, alter, obscure, feign, counterfeit, varnish, age, redo, make up, simulate, muffle, dress or touch or doctor up; see also **change** 2, **deceive, hide**.—Ant. **reveal**, open, strip.

disguised, a. cloaked, masked, camouflaged; see **changed** 2, **covered** 1, **hidden**.

disgust, n. loathing, abhorrence, aversion; see **hatred, objection**.

disgust, v. repel, revolt, offend, displease, nauseate, sicken, make one sick, fill with loathing, cause aversion, be repulsive, irk, scandalize, shock, upset, *turn one's stomach; see also **disturb, insult.**

disgusted, *a.* overwrought, offended, sickened, displeased, repelled, unhappy, revolted, appalled, outraged, *had a bellyful, *fed up, *had it, *had enough; see also **insulted, shocked.**

disgusted with (someone or something), *a.* repelled by, *sick of, *fed up with; see **insulted, shocked.**

disgusting, *a.* repugnant, revolting, sickening; see **offensive 2.**

dish, *n.* 1. [Plate] vessel, pottery, ceramic; see also **plate 4.** Table dishes include the following—dinner plate, luncheon plate, salad plate, bread and butter plate, platter, casserole, cake plate, coffee cup, coffee mug, espresso cup, demitasse, teacup, egg cup, saucer, beer mug, cereal bowl, soup bowl or plate, gravy bowl or boat, relish tray, cruet, teapot, coffeepot, chocolate pot, cream pitcher, water pitcher, lemonade pitcher, sugar bowl, butter dish, salt cellar; see also **container, cup, pottery. 2.** [Meal] course, serving, helping; see **meal 2.**

dishonest, *a.* deceiving, fraudulent, double-dealing, backbiting, treacherous, deceitful, cunning, sneaky, tricky, wily, crooked, deceptive, misleading, elusive, slippery, shady, swindling, cheating, sneaking, traitorous, villainous, sinister, lying, underhanded, *two-timing, *two-faced, *double-crossing, unprincipled, shiftless, unscrupulous, undependable, disreputable, questionable, dishonorable, counterfeit, infamous, corrupt, immoral, discredited, unworthy, shabby, mean, low, venial, self-serving, contemptible, *rotten, *fishy, crooked; see also **false 1, lying 1.**—*Ant.* honest, irreproachable, scrupulous.

dishonesty, *n.* infidelity, faithlessness, falsity, falsehood, deceit, trickery, duplicity, insidiousness, cunning, guile, slyness, double-dealing, trickiness, treachery, crookedness, corruption, cheating, stealing, lying, swindle, fraud, fraudulence, forgery, perjury, treason, flimflam, *hocus-pocus, *hanky-panky; see also **deception, hypocrisy, lie 1.**—*Ant.* honesty, virtue, integrity.

dishonor, *n.* shame, ignominy, abasement; see **disgrace.**

dish out, *v.* give or hand out, serve (up), deliver; see **distribute, give 1.**

dish towel, *n.* tea towel, kitchen towel, drying towel; see **towel.**

disillusion, *v.* disenchant, let down easy, *bring down; see **disappoint.**

disinfect, *v.* purify, fumigate, use disinfectant on; see **clean.**

disinherit, *v.* disown, evict, dispossess; see **dismiss, neglect 2.**

disintegrate, *v.* break down, separate, divide, dismantle, break into pieces, disunite, disperse, crumble, disband, take apart, disorganize, detach, break or come or fall apart, sever, disconnect, *fall to pieces, *fade away, *reduce to ashes; see also **dissolve.**—*Ant.* unite, put together, combine.

disinterested, *a.* impartial, not involved, unconcerned; see **indifferent.**

disjoint, *v.* dismember, cut up, carve; see **cut 1, divide, separate 1.**

disjointed, *a.* disconnected, divided, unattached; see **separated.**

dislike, *n.* opposition, offense, distaste; see **hate, hatred, objection.**

dislike, *v.* detest, condemn, deplore, regret, lose interest in, speak down to, have hard feelings toward, not take kindly to, not be able to say much for, not have the stomach or taste for, not speak well of, not have any part of, not care for, bear or carry a grudge, have nothing to do with, keep one's distance (from), care nothing for, resent, not appreciate, not endure, be averse to, abhor, hate, abominate, disapprove, loathe, despise, object to, shun, shrink or recoil from, mind, shudder at, scorn, avoid, be displeased by, turn up the nose at, look on with aversion, not be able to stomach, regard with displeasure or disfavor, not like, *take a dim view of, *have it in for, *be down on, *look down one's nose, have a bone to pick with; see also **hate.**

dislocate, *v.* disjoint, disunite, disengage; see **break 1, divide, separate 1.**

dislocation, *n.* displacement, discontinuity, luxation; see **break 1, division 1.**

dislodge, *v.* eject, evict, uproot; see **oust, remove 1.**

disloyalty, *n.* treason, betrayal, bad faith; see **dishonesty, treason.**

dismal, *a.* gloomy, monotonous, dim, melancholy, desolate, dreary, sorrowful, morbid, troublesome, horrid, shadowy, overcast, cloudy, unhappy, discouraging, hopeless, black, unfortunate, ghastly, horrible, boring, gruesome, tedious, mournful, dull, disheartening, regrettable, cheerless, dusky, dingy, sepulchral, joyless, funereal, comfortless, murky, wan, bleak, somber, disagreeable, creepy, *spooky, blue; see also **dark 1.**—*Ant.* happy, joyful, cheerful.

dismantle, *v.* take apart, disassemble, break up or down, take or tear or pull or break or knock down, undo, demolish, level, ruin, unrig, subvert, raze, take to pieces, fell, take apart; see also **destroy.**

dismay, *n.* terror, dread, anxiety; see fear.

dismember, *v.* dissect, disjoint, amputate; see cut 1, divide.

dismiss, *v.* discard, reject, decline, repel, let out, repudiate, disband, detach, send *or* lay *or* pack off, cast off *or* forth *or* out, relinquish, dispense with, disperse, push *or* put back, remove, expel, abolish, relegate, push aside, shed, do without, have done with, dispose of, sweep away, clear, rid, chase, dispossess, boycott, exile, expatriate, banish, outlaw, deport, excommunicate, get rid of, *send packing, drop, *brush off, *kick out, blackball, write off; see also oust, refuse.—*Ant.* maintain, retain, keep.

dismissal, *n.* deposition, displacement, expulsion; see removal.

dismissed, *a.* sent away, ousted, removed; see discharged, free 2, 3.

disobedience, *n.* insubordination, defiance, insurgence, disregard, violation, neglect, mutiny, revolt, nonobservance, strike, stubbornness, noncompliance, infraction (of the rules), unruliness, sedition, rebellion, sabotage, riot; see also revolution 2.

disobedient, *a.* insubordinate, refractory, defiant; see rebellious, unruly.

disobey, *v.* balk, decline, neglect, desert, be remiss, ignore (the commands of), refuse (submission to), disagree, differ, evade, disregard (the authority of), break rules, object, defy, resist, revolt, strike, violate, infringe, transgress, shirk, misbehave, withstand, counteract, take the law into one's own hands, *not mind, pay no attention to, go counter to, *not listen to; see also dare 2, oppose 1, rebel.—*Ant.* obey, follow, fulfill.

disorder, *n.* tumult, discord, turmoil, complication, chaos, mayhem, terrorism, rioting, mob rule, anarchy, anarchism, lawlessness, entanglement, commotion, agitation, insurrection, revolution, rebellion, strike, disorganization, riot, reign of terror, uproar, dither, *static; see also disturbance 2, trouble 1.—*Ant.* order, peace, tranquillity.

disorder, *v.* disarrange, clutter, scatter; see confuse, disorganize.

disordered, *a.* displaced, misplaced, dislocated, mislaid, out of place, deranged, in disorder, out of kilter, out of hand, in confusion, in a mess, all over the place, in a mess *or* muddle *or* jumble, upset, unsettled, disorganized, disarranged, moved, removed, shifted, tampered with, tumbled, ruffled, rumpled, jumbled, jarred, tossed, stirred (up), rolled, jolted, muddled; see also confused 2, tangled.—*Ant.* ordered, arranged, settled.

disorderly, *a.* 1. [Lacking orderly arrangement] confused, jumbled, undisciplined, unrestrained, scattered, dislocated, unsystematic, messy, slovenly, untidy, cluttered, unkempt, scrambled, uncombed, badly managed, in confusion, disorganized, untrained, out of control, topsy-turvy, *all over the place, mixed up; see also disordered.—*Ant.* regular, neat, trim. 2. [Creating a disturbance] intemperate, drunk, rowdy; see unruly.

disorganization, *n.* disunion, dissolution, derangement; see confusion 2.

disorganize, *v.* break up, disperse, destroy, scatter, litter, clutter, break down, put out of order, disarrange, disorder, upset, disrupt, derange, dislocate, disband, jumble, muddle, unsettle, disturb, perturb, shuffle, toss, turn topsy-turvy, complicate, confound, overthrow, overturn, scramble; see also confuse.—*Ant.* systematize, order, distribute.

disown, *v.* repudiate, deny, retract; see discard.

dispatch, *v.* 1. [To send something on its way] transmit, express, forward; see send 1. 2. [To make an end] finish, conclude, perform; see achieve.

dispel, *v.* disperse, deploy, dissipate; see distribute, scatter.

dispensable, *a.* removable, excessive, unnecessary; see useless 1.

dispense, *v.* apportion, assign, allocate; see distribute, give 1.

dispenser, *n.* vendor, tap, vending machine. spray can, spray gun, cigarette machine, Coke machine (trademark), automat, squeeze bottle, tapper, bubblegum, coffee, cold drink, etc., machine.

dispense with, *v.* ignore, pass over, brush aside; see disregard, neglect 2.

disperse, *v.* break up, separate, disband; see scatter.

displace, *v.* 1. [To remove] replace, transpose, dislodge; see remove 1. 2. [To put in the wrong place] mislay, misplace, disarrange; see lose 2.

display, *n.* exhibition, exhibit, presentation, representation, exposition, arrangement, demonstration, performance, revelation, procession, parade, pageant, example, appearance, waxworks, fireworks, tinsel, carnival, fair, pomp, splendor, unfolding; see also show 1.

display, *v.* show (off), exhibit, uncover, open (up), unfold, spread, parade, unmask, present, represent, perform, flaunt, lay *or* put *or* set out, disclose, unveil, arrange, make known; see also expose.—*Ant.* hide, conceal, veil.

displayed, *a.* presented, visible, on display; see advertised, shown 1.

displease, *v.* vex, provoke, enrage; see anger 1.

displeasure, n. disapproval, annoyance, resentment; see **anger.**

disposal, n. action, provision(s), determination, disposition, distribution, arrangement(s), conclusion, assortment, settlement, control, winding up; see also **result. —at one's disposal,** ready, prepared, usable; see **available.**

dispose, v. settle, adapt, condition; see **adjust 1, prepare 1.**

disposed, a. inclined, prone, apt; see **likely 4.**

dispose of, v. relinquish, throw away, part with; see **discard, sell.**

disposition, n. 1. [Arrangement] decision, method, distribution; see **organization 1, plan 2.** 2. [Temperament] character, nature, temper; see **mood, temperament.**

disproportionate, a. unsymmetrical, incommensurate, excessive; see **irregular 4.**

disprove, v. prove false, throw out, set aside, find fault in, invalidate, weaken, overthrow, tear down, confound, expose, take or cut the ground from under, *poke holes in; see also **deny.**

disputable, a. debatable, doubtful, dubious; see **questionable 1, uncertain 2.**

dispute, n. argument, quarrel, debate, misunderstanding, conflict, strife, discussion, polemic, bickering, squabble, disturbance, feud, commotion, tiff, fracas, controversy, altercation, dissension, squall, difference of opinion, *rumpus, row, flare-up, fuss, *fire-works; see also **disagreement 1.**

dispute, v. debate, contradict, quarrel; see **argue, discuss.**

disqualify, v. preclude, disentitle, disbar; see **bar 2.**

disregard, v. ignore, pass over, let (it) go or pass, make light of, have no use for, laugh off, take no account of, brush aside, turn a deaf ear to, be blind to, shut one's eyes to; see also **neglect 1.**

disrepair, n. decrepitude, deterioration, dilapidation; see **decay.**

disreputable, a. low, objectionable, discreditable; see **offensive 2, shameful 1, 2.**

disrespect, n. discourtesy, coarseness, irreverence; see **rudeness.**

disrespectful, a. ill-bred, discourteous, impolite; see **rude 2.**

disrobe, v. strip, divest, unclothe; see **undress.**

disrupt, v. fracture, intrude, obstruct; see **break 1, interrupt.**

disruption, n. debacle, disturbance, agitation; see **confusion.**

dissatisfaction, n. dislike, displeasure, disapproval; see **objection.**

dissatisfied, a. displeased, unsatisfied, *fed up; see **disappointed.**

dissect, v. dismember, quarter, operate; see **cut 1, divide.**

disseminate, v. sow, propagate, broadcast; see **distribute.**

dissension, n. difference, quarrel, trouble; see **disagreement 1, dispute.**

dissent, n. nonconformity, difference, heresy; see **disagreement 1, objection, protest.**

dissent, v. disagree, refuse, contradict; see **differ 1, oppose 1.**

dissenter, n. disputant, dissentient, demonstrator; see **nonconformist, radical, rebel 1.**

disservice, n. wrong, injury, outrage; see **damage 1, injustice, insult.**

dissipate, v. 1. [To dispel] spread, diffuse, disseminate; see **scatter 2.** 2. [To squander] use up, consume, misuse; see **spend 2, waste 2.**

dissipated, a. 1. [Scattered] dispersed, strewn, disseminated; see **scattered.** 2. [Wasted] squandered, spent, consumed; see **empty, wasted.**

dissipation, n. scattering, dispersal, spread; see **distribution.**

dissolve, v. liquefy, melt (away), thaw, soften, run, defrost, waste away, cause to become liquid or fluid; see also **evaporate, melt 1.—Ant.** harden, freeze, solidify.

distance, n. 1. [A degree or quantity of space] reach, span, range; see **expanse, extent, length 1, 2.** 2. [A place or places far away] background, horizon, as far as the eye can reach, sky, heavens, outskirts, foreign countries, new or other or different world(s), strange place(s), distant or strange or foreign or unknown terrain, objective, where one is or is not going, the country, beyond the horizon.—Ant. **neighborhood,** surroundings, neighbors. 3. [A measure of space] statute mile, rod, yard, foot, kilometer, meter, centimeter, millimeter, micrometer, league, fathom, span, hand, cubit, furlong, a stone's throw, as the crow flies, *down the road apiece. **—go the distance,** finish, bring to an end, see through; see **complete. —keep at a distance,** ignore, reject, shun; see **avoid. —keep one's distance,** be aloof or indifferent, ignore, shun; see **avoid.**

distant, a. afar, far (back or off), abroad, not (at) home, faraway, yonder, backwoods, removed, abstracted, inaccessible, unapproachable, out of the way, at arm's length, stretching to, out of range or reach, out of earshot, out of sight, in the background, in the distance, separate, farther, further, far away, at a distance, abroad, different; see also **separated.—Ant.** close, near, next.

distaste, *n.* aversion, dislike, abhorrence; see **hatred.**

distasteful, *a.* disagreeable, repugnant, undesirable; see **offensive 2.**

distend, *v.* enlarge, widen, inflate; see **distort 2, increase, stretch 1, 2.**

distill, *v.* vaporize and condense, steam, press; see **concentrate 1, evaporate.**

distinct, *a.* 1. [Having sharp outlines] lucid, plain, obvious; see **clear 2, definite 2.** 2. [Not connected with another] discrete, separate, disunited; see **separated.** 3. [Clearly heard] clear, sharp, enunciated; see **audible.**

distinction, *n.* 1. [The act or quality of noticing differences] separation, difference, refinement; see **definition.** 2. [A difference used for distinction, sense 1] distinctive feature, particular, qualification; see **characteristic, detail.** 3. [A mark of personal achievement] repute, renown, prominence; see **fame 1.**

distinctive, *a.* peculiar, unique, distinguishing; see **characteristic.**

distinctly, *a.* precisely, sharply, plainly; see **clearly 1, 2, surely.**

distinctness, *n.* sharpness, lucidity, explicitness; see **clarity.**

distinguish, *v.* 1. [To make distinctions] discriminate (between), differentiate, classify, specify, identify, individualize, characterize, separate, divide, collate, sort out *or* into, set apart, mark off, criticize, select, draw the line, tell from, pick and choose, *separate the wheat from the chaff *or* the sheep from the goats; see also **define 2.** 2. [To discern] detect, discriminate, notice; see **discover, see 1.** 3. [To bestow honor upon] pay tribute to, honor, celebrate; see **acknowledge 2, admire, praise 1.**

distinguishable, *a.* separable, perceptible, discernible; see **audible, obvious, tangible.**

distinguished, *a.* 1. [Made recognizable by markings] characterized, labeled, marked, stamped, signed, signified, identified, made certain, obvious, set apart, branded, earmarked, separate, unique, differentiated, observed, distinct, conspicuous; see also **separated.**—*Ant.* typical, unidentified, indistinct. 2. [Notable for excellence] eminent, illustrious, venerable, renowned, honored, memorable, celebrated, well-known, noted, noteworthy, highly regarded, well thought of, esteemed, prominent, reputable, superior, outstanding, brilliant, glorious, extraordinary, singular, great, special, striking, unforgettable, shining, foremost, dignified, famed, talked of, first-rate, *big-name, *headline; see also **famous.**—*Ant.* **obscure,** insignificant, unimportant.

distinguishing, *a.* distinctive, differentiating, different; see **characteristic.**

distort, *v.* 1. [To alter the meaning] pervert, misinterpret, misconstrue; see **deceive.** 2. [To change shape] contort, sag, twist, slump, knot, get out of shape, buckle, writhe, melt, warp, deform, collapse; see also **change 2.**

distortion, *n.* 1. [Deformity] twist, malformation, mutilation; see **contortion.** 2. [Misrepresentation] perversion, misinterpretation, misuse; see **lie 1.**

distract, *v.* detract, occupy, amuse, entertain, draw away (from), call away, take *or* draw one's attention from, lead astray, attract from; see also **mislead.**

distracted, *a.* distraught, panicked, frenzied; see **troubled.**

distraction, *n.* 1. [Confusion] perplexity, abstraction, complication; see **confusion.** 2. [Diversion] amusement, pastime, preoccupation; see **entertainment, game 1.**

distress, *n.* worry, anxiety, misery, sorrow, wretchedness, pain, dejection, irritation, suffering, ache, heartache, ordeal, desolation, anguish, affliction, woe, torment, shame, embarrassment, disappointment, tribulation, pang; see also **grief, trouble 1.**—*Ant.* joy, happiness, jollity.

distress, *v.* irritate, disturb, upset; see **bother 1, 2.**

distribute, *v.* dispense, divide, share, deal, bestow, issue, dispose, disperse, mete *or* pass *or* parcel *or* dole *or* hand *or* pay out, give away, assign, allocate, ration, appropriate, pay dividends, dish out, *divvy up; see also **give 1.**—*Ant.* hold, keep, preserve.

distributed, *a.* delivered, scattered, shared, dealt, divided, apportioned, assigned, awarded, peddled from door to door, sowed, dispensed, dispersed, appropriated, budgeted, made individually available, equally divided, spread evenly, returned, rationed, given away, handed *or* parceled out, spread.

distribution, *n.* dispersal, allotment, partitioning, partition, dividing (up), deal, circulation, disposal, apportioning, prorating, arrangement, scattering, dissemination, sorting, spreading, parceling *or* dealing *or* handing out, peddling, assorting, frequency, occurrence, ordering, pattern, combination, relationship(s), appearance, configuration, scarcity, number, plenty, saturation, population, spread, concentration; see also **division 1, 2, order 3.**—*Ant.* **collection,** retention, storage.

distributor, *n.* wholesaler, jobber, merchant; see **businessman.**

district, *a.* community, provincial, territorial; see **local 1.**

district, *n.* neighborhood, community, vicinity; see **area.**

distrust, *v.* mistrust, suspect, disbelieve; see **doubt.**

distrustful, *a.* distrusting, doubting, fearful; see **suspicious 1.**

disturb, *v.* trouble, worry, agitate, perplex, rattle, startle, shake, amaze, astound, alarm, excite, arouse, badger, plague, fuss, perturb, vex, upset, outrage, molest, grieve, depress, distress, irk, ail, tire, provoke, afflict, irritate, pain, make uneasy, harass, exasperate, pique, gall, displease, complicate, involve, astonish, fluster, ruffle, *burn up; see also **bother 2, confuse.**–*Ant.* quiet, calm, soothe.

disturbance, *n.* 1. [Interpersonal disruption] quarrel, brawl, fisticuffs; see **fight 1.** 2. [Physical disruption] turmoil, rampage, tumult, clamor, violence, restlessness, uproar, riot, disruption, agitation, turbulence, change, bother, stir, racket, ferment, spasm, convulsion, tremor, shock, explosion, eruption, earthquake, flood, shock wave, storm, whirlwind, hurricane, tornado, twister, avalanche, whirlpool, whirl; see also **trouble.** 3. [A political or social uprising] revolt, insurrection, riot; see **revolution 2.**

disturbed, *a.* 1. [Disturbed physically] upset, disorganized, confused; see **disordered.** 2. [Disturbed mentally] agitated, disquieted, upset; see **troubled 1.**

disturbing, *a.* disquieting, upsetting, tiresome, perturbing, bothersome, unpleasant, provoking, annoying, alarming, painful, discomforting, inauspicious, foreboding, aggravating, disagreeable, troublesome, worrisome, burdensome, trying, frightening, startling, perplexing, threatening, distressing, galling, difficult, severe, hard, inconvenient, discouraging, pessimistic, gloomy, depressing, irritating, harassing, unpropitious, unlikely, embarassing, ruffling, agitating; see also **ominous.**

disunite, *v.* dissociate, disjoin, separate; see **divide.**

ditch, *n.* canal, moat, furrow; see **channel, trench.**

***ditch,** *v.* desert, forsake, leave; see **abandon 2, discard.**

ditto, *n.* ditto mark ("), the (very) same, as is; see **alike.**

dive, *n.* 1. [A sudden motion downward] plunge, leap, spring, nosedive, headlong leap *or* jump, pitch, ducking, swim, swoop, dip; see also **fall 1, jump 1.** 2. [*An establishment offering accommodation] saloon, tavern, cafe; see **bar 2, restaurant.**

dive, *v.* plunge, spring, jump, vault, leap,

go headfirst, plummet, sink, dip, duck, submerge, nose-dive; see also **fall 1, jump 1.**

diver, *n.* high diver, fancy diver, submarine diver, deep-sea diver, aquanaut, pearl diver, skin diver, scuba diver, swimmer, athlete, frog man; see also **athlete.**

diverge, *v.* radiate, veer, swerve; see **deviate.**

diverse, *a.* different, assorted, distinct; see **various.**

diversify, *v.* vary, expand, alter; see **change 2, increase 1.**

diversion, *n.* 1. [The act of changing a course] detour, alteration, deviation; see **change 1.** 2. [Entertainment] amusement, recreation, play; see **entertainment, sport 1.**

divert, *v.* 1. [To deflect] turn aside, redirect, avert; see **turn 3.** 2. [To distract] attract the attention of, lead away from, disturb; see **distract 1.**

diverted, *a.* deflected, turned aside, redirected, perverted, averted, turned into other channels, rechanneled, taken, adopted, used, made use of, taken over; see also **changed 2.**–*Ant.* untouched, undiverted, left.

divide, *v.* part, cut up, fence off, detach, disengage, dissolve, sever, rupture, dismember, sunder, split, unravel, carve, cleave, intersect, cross, bisect, rend, tear, segment, halve, quarter, third, break down, divorce, dissociate, isolate, count off, pull away, chop, slash, gash, carve, splinter, pull to pieces, tear *or* break apart, segregate, fork, branch, *tear limb from limb, split off *or* up; see also **break 1, cut 1, separate 1.**–*Ant.* unite, combine, connect.

dividend, *n.* pay, check, coupon, proceeds, returns, quarterly *or* annual dividend, share, allotment, appropriation, remittance, allowance, *cut, *rake-off; see also **profit 2.**

divine, *a.* sacred, hallowed, spiritual, sacramental, ceremonial, ritualistic, consecrated, dedicated, devoted, venerable, pious, religious, anointed, sanctified, ordained, sanctioned, set apart, sacrosanct, scriptural, blessed, worshiped, revered, venerated, mystical, adored, solemn, faithful; see also **holy.**

divinity, *n.* deity, godhead, higher power; see **god.**

divisible, *a.* separable, distinguishable, distinct, divided, fractional, fragmentary, detachable; see also **separated.**–*Ant.* inseparable, indivisible, fast.

division, *n.* 1. [The act or result of dividing] separation, detachment, apportionment, partition, parting, distribution, severance, cutting, subdivision, dismemberment, distinction, distinguishing, selection, analysis, diagnosis, reduction, splitting, breakdown, fracture, disjuncture.—*Ant.* union, joining, glueing. 2. [A part produced by dividing] section, kind, sort, portion, compartment, share, split, member, subdivision, parcel, segment, fragment, department, category, branch, fraction, dividend, degree, piece, slice, lump, wedge, cut, book, chapter, verse, class, race, clan, tribe, caste; see also **part** 1. 3. [Discord *or* disunion] trouble, words, difficulty; see **disagreement** 1, **dispute**. 4. [An organic military unit] armored division, airborne division, infantry division; see **army** 2. 5. [An organized area] state, government, range; see **nation**.

divorce, *n.* separation, partition, divorcement, bill of divorce *or* divorcement, annulment, separate maintenance, parting of the ways, dissolution, *split-up, *the cure.—*Ant.* **marriage,** betrothal, wedding.

divorce, *v.* separate, annul, release from *or* put out of wedlock *or* matrimony, nullify, put away, *split up; see also **cancel** 2.

divorced, *a.* dissolved, parted, disunited, divided, *split, *washed up; see also **separated.**—*Ant.* **married,** joined, mated.

divulge, *v.* disclose, impart, confess; see **admit** 2, **expose** 1.

dizzy, *a.* confused, lightheaded, giddy, bemused, staggering, upset, dazzled, dazed, dumb, faint, with spots before one's eyes, out of control, weak-kneed, wobbly; see also **unstable** 1.

do, *v.* 1. [To discharge one's responsibilities] effect, execute, achieve, act, perform, finish, complete, work, labor, produce, create, effect, accomplish; see also **achieve, perform** 1, **succeed** 1. 2. [To execute commands or instructions] carry out, complete, fulfill; see **obey.** 3. [To suffice] serve, be sufficient, give satisfaction; see **satisfy** 3. 4. [To solve] figure *or* work out, decipher, decode; see **solve.** 5. [To present a play, etc.] give, put on, produce; see **perform** 2. 6. [To act] perform, portray, render the role of; see **act** 3. 7. [To conduct oneself] behave *or* comport *or* acquit oneself, seem, appear; see **behave. —have to do with,** related, connected, concerning; see **about** 2. **—make do,** get by *or* along, manage, survive; see **endure** 2.

do about, *v.* assist, take care of, correct; see **help, improve** 1, **repair.**

do away with, *v.* 1. [To eliminate] get rid of, cancel, take away; see **eliminate, remove** 1. 2. [To kill] slay, execute, put to death; see **kill** 1.

do by, *v.* handle, act toward, deal with; see **treat** 1.

docile, *a.* meek, mild, tractable, pliant, submissive, accommodating, adaptable,

resigned, agreeable, willing, obliging, well-behaved, manageable, tame, yielding, teachable, easily influenced, easygoing, usable, soft, childlike; see also **gentle** 3, **humble** 1, **obedient** 1.

docility, *n.* obedience, gentleness, adaptability; see **humility, shyness.**

dock, *n.* landing pier, wharf, lock, (boat) landing, marina, dry dock, embarcadero, waterfront.

dock, *v.* lessen, withhold, deduct; see **decrease** 2.

doctor, *n.* Doctor of Medicine (M.D), physician, general practitioner (G.P.), surgeon, medical attendant, consultant, specialist, interne, house physician, veterinarian, chiropractor, homeopath, osteopath, (faith) healer, witch doctor, shaman, medicine man, quack, *doc, *sawbones. Types of doctors include the following—heart specialist; eye, ear, nose, and throat specialist; inhalation therapist, anesthetist, dentist, pediatrician, gynecologist, oculist, obstetrician, psychiatrist, psychoanalyst, orthopedist, neurologist, cardiologist, pathologist, dermatologist, endocrinologist, opthamologist, urologist, hematologist; see also **medicine** 3.

doctor, *v.* attend, administer, supply professional services; see **treat** 3.

doctrine, *n.* principle, proposition, precept, article, concept, conviction, opinion, convention, attitude, tradition, unwritten law, universal *or* natural *or* common law, teachings, accepted belief, article of faith *or* belief, canon, regulation, rule, pronouncement, declaration; see also **law** 2, 4.

document, *n.* paper, diary, report; see **record** 1.

dodge, *v.* duck, elude, evade; see **avoid.**

***do dirt to,** *v.* hurt, mistreat, injure; see **abuse, slander.**

doer, *n.* actor, performer, instrument; see **means** 1.

do for, *v.* provide *or* care for, assist, look after; see **help** 1, **support** 5.

dog, *n.* hound, bitch, puppy, pup, *mongrel, *stray, *canine, *cur, *pooch, *mutt. Types and breeds of dogs include the following—hunting dog, field dog, racing dog, boxer, shepherd dog, bloodhound, wolfhound, greyhound, whippet, St. Bernard, Great Dane, German shepherd, Doberman (pinscher), Afghan (hound), Irish wolfhound, Labrador retriever, Chesapeake Bay retriever, malamute, husky, collie, Old English sheep dog, Irish setter, pointer, spaniel, cocker (spaniel), basset, beagle, dachshund, Dalmatian, poodle, French poodle, Pekingese, Chihuahua, Airedale, schnauzer, fox terrier, wirehaired terrier, Scottie, bull terrier, Boston terrier. **—a dog's life,** wretched existence, bad luck, trouble; see **poverty** 1. —*go to the dogs, deteriorate, degenerate, weaken; see **weaken** 1, 2. —let sleeping dogs lie, ignore, leave well enough alone, pass over; see **neglect** 1. —*put on the dog, show off, entertain lavishly, exhibit; see **display**. —teach an old dog new tricks, influence, convince, change; see **persuade**.

dog eat dog, *a.* vicious, ferocious, brutal; see **cruel, ruthless**.

dogged, *a.* stubborn, obstinate, firm; see **stubborn**.

dogmatic, *a.* 1. [Based on an assumption of absolute truth] authoritarian, on faith, by nature; see **absolute** 1, 2. 2. [Acting as though one possessed absolute truth] dictatorial, stubborn, egotistical, bigoted, fanatical, intolerant, opinionated, overbearing, magisterial, arrogant, domineering, tyrannical, obstinate, confident, downright, arbitrary, unequivocal, definite, formal, stubborn, determined, emphatic, narrow-minded, one-sided, hidebound, *high and mighty, pigheaded, bullheaded, *stubborn as a mule; see also **absolute** 2.—*Ant.* liberal, tolerant, dubious.

do in, *v.* eliminate, slay, murder; see **destroy, kill** 1.

doing, *n.* performing, accomplishing, achieving; see **performance**.

doings, *n.* activities, conduct, dealings; see **action** 1.

do justice to, *v.* esteem, pay tribute, honor; see **admire, consider, respect** 2.

dole (out), *v.* share, assign, parcel; see **distribute**.

doll, *n.* baby, figurine, manikin, model, dolly, *doll baby; see also **toy** 1.

dollar, *n.* coin, legal tender, dollar bill, silver dollar, Eisenhower dollar, currency, bank note, greenback, *folding money, *buck; see also **money** 1.

doll up, *v.* fix up, put on one's best clothes, primp; see **dress** 1.

dolt, *n.* simpleton, nitwit, blockhead; see **fool**.

domain, *n.* dominion, field, specialty; see **area**.

dome, *n.* ceiling, top, vault; see **roof**.

domestic, *a.* 1. [Home-loving] houseloving, domesticated, stay-at-home, household, family, quiet, sedentary, indoor, tame, settled; see also **calm** 1, 2, tranquil 2.—*Ant.* unruly, roving, restless. 2. [Home-grown] indigenous, handcrafted, native; see **homemade**.

domesticate, *v.* tame, breed, housebreak; see **teach, train** 2.

domesticated, *a.* tamed, trained, housebroken; see **tame** 1.

dominant, *a.* commanding, authoritative, assertive; see **aggressive, powerful** 1.

dominate, *v.* rule, manage, control, dictate (to), subject, subjugate, tyrannize, have one's (own) way, have influence over, domineer, lead by the nose, *boss, keep under one's thumb; see also **govern**.

domination, *n.* rule, control, mastery; see **command, power** 2.

domineering, *a.* despotic, imperious, oppressive; see **egotistic**.

dominion, *n.* region, district, state; see **area, nation** 1.

donate, *v.* grant, bestow, bequeath; see **distribute, give** 1, **provide** 1.

donation, *n.* contribution, offering, present; see **gift** 1.

done, *a.* 1. [Accomplished] over, through, completed, realized, effected, executed, performed, fulfilled, brought to pass, brought about, succeeded, perfected; see also "finished 1.—*Ant.* unfinished, unrealized, failed. 2. [Cooked] brewed, stewed, broiled, boiled, crisped, crusted, fried, browned, done to a turn; see also **baked**.—*Ant.* raw, burned, uncooked.

*done for, *a.* defeated, conquered, vanquished; see **beaten** 1.

*done in, *a.* exhausted, worn out, weary; see **tired**.

*done out of, *a.* defrauded, bilked, *taken; see **cheated**, deceived 1.

*done up, *a.* prepared, packaged, finished; see **wrapped**.

*done with, *a.* finished with, dispatched, no longer needing *or* in need of; see **finished** 1.

donkey, *n.* burrow, ass, jackass; see **horse** 1.

donor, *n.* benefactor, contributor, patron, philanthropist, giver, subscriber, altruist, Good Samaritan, *fairy godmother; see also **patron**.

doom, *n.* fate, lot, destination, predestination, future, fortune, ruin, goal.

doomed, *a.* ruined, cursed, sentenced, lost, condemned, unfortunate, (ill) fated, foreordained, predestined, threatened, menaced, suppressed, wrecked; see also **destroyed, fated**.

do one proud, *v.* entertain lavishly *or* handsomely *or* well, feast, provide for; see **entertain** 2.

door, *n.* entry, portal, hatchway, doorway, gateway, opening; see also **entrance** 2, **gate**. —out of doors, outside, in the air, out; see **outdoors**. —show (someone) the door, show out, ask to leave, eject; see **oust**.

do out of, *v.* cheat, trick, *beat out of; see **deceive, steal**.

do over, *v.* redo, do again, rework; see **repeat** 1.

dope, *n.* 1. [*A drug] narcotic, stimulant, opiate; see **drug** 2. 2. [*Pertinent information] details, account, developments; see **information 1, knowledge 1, news 1. 3.** [*A dull-witted person] dunce, dolt, simpleton; see **fool.**

dope, *v.* anesthetize, drug, put to sleep; see **deaden.**

dormitory, *n.* barracks, residence hall or house, *dorm; see **hotel.**

***dos and don'ts,** *n.* rules, regulations, instruction(s); see **advice, command, directions.**

dose, *n.* prescription, dosage, treatment, spoonful, portion, *doctor's orders; see also **quantity, share.**

dot, *n.* point, spot, speck; see **mark 1.** — *on the dot,** precisely, accurately, punctually; see **punctual.**

dote, *v.* adore, pet, admire; see **love 1.**

***do time,** *v.* serve (out) a sentence, be in jail, pay one's debt to society; see **serve time.**

double, *a.* twofold, two times, paired, coupled, binary, doubled, redoubled, duplex, renewed, dual, both one and the other, repeated, second, increased, as much again, duplicated; see also **twice, twin.**—*Ant.* single, **alone, apart.** —*on (or at) the double,** hastily, rapidly, hurriedly; see **quickly.**

double, *v.* **1.** [To make or become double] make twice as much, duplicate, multiply; see **grow 1, increase 1. 2.** [To replace] substitute for, stand in, act for; see **substitute.**

double back, *v.* backtrack, reverse, circle; see **return 1, turn 2, 6.**

double-cross, *v.* cheat, defraud, trick; see **deceive.**

double-dealing, *n.* deceit, cheating, trickery; see **dishonesty, hypocrisy 2.**

double meaning, *n.* play on words, innuendo, pun; see **joke.**

double up, *v.* combine, join, share; see **join 1, 2, unite 1.**

doubly, *a.* twofold, redoubled, increased; see **again, double, twice.**

doubt, *n.* distrust, mistrust, disbelief, suspicion, misgiving, skepticism, apprehension, agnosticism, incredulity, lack of faith *or* confidence *or* certainty, jealousy, rejection, scruple, misgiving, indecision, lack of conviction, ambiguity, dilemma, reluctance, quandary, feeling of inferiority; see also **uncertainty 1, 2.** —*Ant.* **belief, conviction, certainty.** — **beyond (or without) doubt,** doubtless, sure, unquestionable; see **certain 2.** — **no doubt,** doubtless, in all likelihood, certainly; see **probably, surely.**

doubt, *v.* wonder, imagine, question, query, ponder, dispute, be dubious *or* uncertain *or* curious *or* puzzled *or* doubtful, refuse to believe, demur, have doubts about, have one's doubts, stop

to consider, have qualms, call in question, give no credit to, throw doubt upon, have no conception, not know which way to turn, not know what to make of, close one's mind, not admit, not believe, refuse to believe, *not buy; see also **ask, deny, question 1.**—*Ant.* believe, **trust, confide.**

doubter, *n.* questioner, unbeliever, agnostic; see **cynic.**

doubtful, *a.* **1.** [Uncertain in mind] dubious, doubting, questioning, undecided, unsure, wavering, hesitating, undetermined, uncertain, unsettled, confused, disturbed, lost, puzzled, perplexed, flustered, baffled, distracted, unresolved, in a quandary, of two minds, unable to make up one's mind, troubled with doubt, having *or* of little faith, in question, not knowing what's what, not following, *up a tree, not able to make head or tail of, *going around in circles, out of focus, up in the air, *wishy-washy, iffy; see also **suspicious 1. 2.** [Improbable] probably wrong, questionable, unconvincing; see **obscure 1, uncertain 1.**

doubting, *a.* questioning, dubious, skeptical; see **doubtful 1, suspicious 1.**

doubtless, *a.* positively, certainly, unquestionably; see **surely.**

dough, *n.* **1.** [A soft mixture] paste (especially of flour), pulp, mash; see **batter 2, mixture 1. 2.** [*Money] dollars, change, silver; see **money 1, wealth.**

doughnut, *n.* jelly doughnut, powdered doughnut, chocolate doughnut, etc.; see **cake 2, pastry.**

douse, *v.* submerge, splash, drench; see **immerse, soak 1.**

dove, *n.* peacemaker, activist, pacifier; see **pacifist.**

dowdy, *a.* untidy, slovenly, plain; see **shabby.**

do well by, *v.* aid, favor, treat well; see **help 1.**

do with, *v.* get on, manage, get along with; see **endure 2.**

do without, *v.* manage, get along without, forego; see **endure 1, 2, need.**

down, *a.* and *prep.* forward, headlong, bottomward, downhill, on a downward course, from higher to lower, to the bottom, to a lower position, declining, falling, descending, gravitating, slipping, sliding, sagging, slumping, dropping, sinking, earthward, groundward, downward; see also **backward 1.**—*Ant.* up, upward, rising.

down, *n.* feathers, fluff, fur; see **hair 1.**

down, *v.* put *or* throw *or* pull *or* knock down, throw, fell, subdue, tackle, trip, overthrow, overpower, upset, overturn; see also **defeat 3, hit 1.**—*Ant.* raise, lift, elevate.

down and out, *a.* ruined, defeated, finished; see **beaten.**

downcast, *a.* discouraged, dejected, unhappy; see **sad 1.**

downfall, *n.* drop, comedown, ruin; see **destruction 2.**

downgrade, *v.* minimize, deprecate, lower; see **decrease 2.**

downhearted, *a.* dejected, despondent, downcast; see **sad 1.**

***down on,** *a.* against, disillusioned (about), furious (with); see **opposed.**

downpour, *n.* rain, deluge, flood, monsoon; see **storm.**

downright, *a.* total, complete, utter; see **absolute 1, whole 1.**

downstairs, *a.* underneath, below decks, on the floor below; see **below 4, under 1.**

downstairs, *n.* first floor, ground floor, cellar; see **basement.**

down-to-earth, *a.* sensible, mundane, practicable; see **common 1, practical, rational 1.**

downtown, *a.* city, central, inner-city, main, midtown, in the business district, on the main street, metropolitan, business, shopping; see also **urban.—*Ant.*** suburban, residential, **rural.**

downtown, *n.* hub, crossroads, inner city; see **center 2, city.**

downtrodden, *a.* tyrannized, subjugated, overcome; see **oppressed.**

downward, *a.* earthward, descending, downwards; see **down.**

downy, *a.* woolly, fuzzy, fluffy; see **light 5, soft 2.**

doze, *v.* nap, drowse, slumber; see **sleep.**

dozen, *a.* twelve, baker's dozen, long dozen, handful, pocketful.

drab, *a.* **1.** [Dismal] dingy, colorless, dreary; see **dull 2, 4. 2.** [Dun-colored] yellowish brown, brownish, dull brown *or* gray, grayish; see **brown, gray.**

draft, *n.* **1.** [A preliminary sketch] plans, blueprint, sketch; see **design. 2.** [A breeze] current of air, gust, puff; see **wind 1. 3.** [An order for payment] cashier's check, bank draft, (money) order; see **check 1. 4.** [The selection of troops] conscription, induction, recruiting; see **selection 1.**

draft, *v.* **1.** [Make a rough plan] outline, delineate, sketch; see **plan 1, 2. 2.** [Select for military service] select, conscript, choose; see **recruit 1.**

draftsman, *n.* sketcher, designer, drawer; see **architect, artist.**

drag, *n.* **1.** [A restraint] hindrance, burden, impediment; see **barrier. 2.** [*An annoying person, thing, or situation] bother, annoyance, *hang-up; see **nuisance 3.**

drag, *v.* **1.** [To go slowly; *said of animate beings*] lag, straggle, dawdle; see **loiter, pause. 2.** [To go slowly; *said of*

an activity] slow down, be delayed, fail to show progress, *crawl; see also **delay.—*Ant.*** improve, progress, pick up. **3.** [To pull an object] haul, move, transport; see **draw 1.**

drag on, *v.* go on slowly *or* badly, keep going, persist; see **continue 1, endure 1.**

dragon, *n.* mythical beast, serpent, hydra; see **monster 1, snake.**

drag one's feet, *v.* lag behind, obstruct, hold back; see **hesitate, hinder, pause, resist.**

drain, *n.* duct, channel, sewer; see **conduit, pipe 1. —down the drain,** wasted, ruined, gone; see **lost 1.**

drain, *v.* **1.** [To withdraw fluid] tap, draw off, remove; see **empty 2. 2.** [To withdraw strength] exhaust, weary, tire (out); see **spend 1, weaken 2. 3.** [To seep away] run *or* flow *or* seep away *or* out *or* off, exude, trickle (out), filter (off), ooze, find an opening, decline, diminish, leave (something) dry; see also **flow.**

drama, *n.* play, (theatrical) piece *or* production, dramatization, (stage) show, theatre. Types of drama include the following—melodrama, tragicomedy, comedy of manners, burlesque, pantomime, mime, (grand) opera, operetta, light opera, musical comedy, musical, mystery, murder mystery, farce, classical drama, historical drama, theater of the absurd, epic, pageant, miracle play, revival; see also **acting, comedy, performance.**

dramatic, *a.* tense, climactic, moving; see **exciting.**

dramatist, *n.* playwright, script writer, scenario writer, *scripter, *the brains; see also **author, writer.** Major dramatists include the following—Great Britain: Christopher Marlowe, Ben Jonson, William Shakespeare, Oscar Wilde, George Bernard Shaw, Sean O'Casey; United States: Thornton Wilder, Eugene O'Neill, William Inge, Tennessee Williams, Arthur Miller, Edward Albee; Greece: Aeschylus, Sophocles, Euripides; France: Molière, Pierre Corneille, Jean Racine, Jean Anouilh, Eugéne Ionesco, Jean Genêt, Jean Cocteau; Germany: Wolfgang von Goethe, Friedrich Schiller, Bertolt Brecht; other: Maxim Gorky, Anton Chekov, Henrik Ibsen, August Strindberg, Samuel Beckett, Karel Capek.

dramatize, *v.* enact, produce, execute; see **perform 2.**

drape, *v.* clothe, wrap, model; see **dress.**

drapes, *n.* window covering, drapery, hanging; see **curtain.**

drastic, *a.* extravagant, exorbitant, radical; see **extreme.**

draw, *v.* **1.** [To move an object] pull, drag, attract, move, bring, tug, lug, tow, take in tow, carry, jerk, wrench, yank, haul, extract.—*Ant.* repel, repulse, reject. 2. [To make a likeness by drawing] sketch, describe, etch, pencil, outline, trace (out), make a picture of, depict, model, portray, engrave, chart, map; see also **paint 1.** —beat to the draw, be quicker than another, forestall, stop; see **anticipate, prevent.**

draw away, *v.* pull away (from), gain on, increase a lead; see **advance 1, defeat, leave 1.**

drawback, *n.* detriment, hindrance, check; see **lack 1.**

draw back, *v.* withdraw, recede, draw in; see **retreat.**

drawing, *n.* sketching, designing, illustrating, tracing, etching, design, illustration, commercial designing; see **picture 3, representation.**

draw on, *v.* take from, extract, employ; see **use 1.**

draw out, *v.* 1. [To induce to talk] talk, lead on, extract; see **discover 2.** 2. [To pull] drag, tug, attract; see **draw 1.**

draw up, *v.* draft, execute, prepare (a statement); see **write 1.**

draw upon, *v.* rely upon, employ, make use of; see **use 1.**

dread, *n.* awe, horror, terror; see **fear.**

dreadful, *a.* hideous, fearful, shameful; see **frightful 1.**

dream, *n.* nightmare, apparition, hallucination, image, trance, idea, impression, emotion, romance, daydream, castle in the air, chimera; see also **fantasy, illusion 1, thought 2, vision 3, 4.**—*Ant.* reality, verity, truth.

dream, *v.* 1. [To have visions, usually during sleep or fever] hallucinate, fancy, visualize; see **imagine.** 2. [To entertain or delude oneself with imagined things] fancy, imagine, conceive, have notions, conjure up, create, picture, idealize, daydream, be up in the clouds, *pipedream, *blow bubbles; see also **invent 1.**

dreamer, *n.* visionary, utopist, theorizer; see **radical.**

dreaming, *a.* thinking, daydreaming, in a reverie; see also **thoughtful 1.**

dream up, *v.* devise, contrive, concoct; see **imagine.**

dreamy, *a.* whimsical, fanciful, daydreaming, visionary, given to reverie, illusory, introspective, otherworldly, idealistic, mythical, utopian, romantic; see also **imaginary, impractical.**—*Ant.* practical, active, real.

dreary, *a.* damp, raw, windy; see **cold 1, dismal.**

dregs, *n.* scum, grounds, slag; see **residue.**

drench, *v.* wet, saturate, flood; see **immerse, soak 1.**

dress, *n.* 1. [Clothing] ensemble, attire, garment(s), garb, apparel, array, costume, wardrobe, uniform, habit, livery, formal dress, evening clothes, trappings, things, *get-up, *threads, *rags, *duds; see also **clothes, coat 1, pants 1, shirt, suit 3, underwear.** 2. [A woman's outer garment] frock, gown, wedding dress, evening gown *or *formal, cocktail gown, suit, skirt, robe, shift, strapless, wraparound, housedress, smock; see also **clothes.**

dress, *v.* 1. [To put on clothes] don, wear, garb, clothe, robe, attire, drape, array, cover, spruce *or* dress *or* bundle up, *get *or* pile into, *fix *or* doll up, *put on the dog; see also **wear 1.** 2. [To provide with clothes] costume, outfit, clothe; see **support 5.** 3. [To give medical treatment] treat, bandage, give first aid; see **heal.**

dressed up, *a.* dressed formally, in full dress, *dolled up; see **fancy, fashionable, ornate 1.**

dresser, *n.* dressing table, chest of drawers, bureau; see **furniture, table 1.**

dressing, *n.* 1. [A food mixture] stuffing, filling. Dressings include the following—bread, giblet, oyster, chestnut, potato, prune, plum, apple, duck, turkey, chicken, fish, clam, wild rice. 2. [A flavoring sauce] Salad dressings include the following—mayonnaise, French, Russian, thousand island, blue cheese, Roquefort, Italian, Caesar, oil and vinegar; see also **sauce 1.** 3. [An external medical application] bandage, plaster cast, adhesive tape, Bandaid (trademark), compress, gauze, tourniquet, pack; see also **cast 4.**

dressmaker, *n.* seamstress, designer, (dress) fitter; see **tailor.**

dress up, *v.* primp, dress for dinner, *put on the dog; see **dress 1.**

dressy, *a.* dressed up, elegant, elaborate; see **fancy, fashionable, ornate 1.**

dribble, *v.* trickle, spout, squirt; see **drop 1.**

dried, *a.* drained, dehydrated, desiccated; see **dry 1, preserved 2.**

drift, *n.* 1. [A tendency in movement] bent, trend, tendency, end, inclination, impulse, propulsion, aim, scope, goal, push, bias, set, leaning, progress, disposition, bearing, line, set; see also **direction 1, way 2.**—*Ant.* indifference, aimlessness, inertia. 2. [The measure or character of movement] current, diversion, digression, departure; see **flow.**

drift, *v.* float, ride, sail, wander at random, move with the current, gravitate, tend, be carried along (by the current), move toward, go with the tide, be caught in the current, move without ef-

fort, move slowly; see also **flow 1,
move 1.**–*Ant.* steer, **lead,** pull.

drill, *n.* **1.** [Practice] preparation, repetition, learning by doing; see **practice 3.**
2. [A tool for boring holes] borer, wood bit, steel drill, steam drill, diamond drill, compressed-air drill, boring tool, tap-borer, auger, corkscrew, awl, riveter, jackhammer; see also **tool 1. 3.** [Exercise, especially in military formation] training, maneuvers, marching, close-order drill, open-order drill, conditioning, survival training, guerilla training; see also **parade 1. 4.** [Device for planting seed in holes] planter, seeder, implement; see **tool 1.**

drill, *v.* **1.** [To bore] pierce, sink (in), puncture; see **dig 1, penetrate. 2.** [To train] practice, rehearse, discipline; see **teach.**

drink, *n.* **1.** [A draft] gulp, sip, potion, drop, bottle, glass, refreshment, tall drink, mouthwash, *shot, *stiff one, *slug, *nip, *swig, *spot, *short one, *nightcap, *one for the road. **2.** [Something drunk] rye, Bourbon, Scotch, Irish whiskey, ale, stout, rum, liqueur, tequila, vodka, distilled water, mineral water, carbonated water, mixer, tonic, quinine, Seltzer, cocoa, (hot) chocolate, chocolate milk, milkshake *or* frappé, lemonade, orangeade, punch, soft drink, soda (water), ginger ale, ice-cream soda, fountain drink, bottled drink, orange *or* tomato *or* grapefruit, etc., juice; pop, soda pop; see also **beer, coffee, milk, water 1, whiskey, wine.**

drink, *v.* **1.** [To swallow liquid] gulp (down), take (in), sip, suck (in), guzzle, imbibe, wash down, gargle; see also **swallow. 2.** [To consume alcoholic liquor] tipple, swill, swig, guzzle, *take a drop *or* nip, *wet one's whistle, *down, *booze, *hit the bottle, *go on a drunk *or* a binge.

drinker, *n.* tippler, guzzler, alcoholic, *lush; see **drunkard.**

drip, *v.* dribble, trickle, plop; see **drop 1.**

drive, *n.* **1.** [A ride in a vehicle] ride, trip, outing, airing, tour, excursion, jaunt, spin, *Sunday drive; see also **journey. 2.** [A driveway] approach, avenue, boulevard; see **driveway, road 1.
3.** [Impelling force] energy, effort, impulse; see **force 2.**

drive, *v.* **1.** [To urge on] impel, propel, instigate, incite, animate, hasten, egg *or* urge on, compel, coerce, induce, force, press, stimulate, hurry, provoke, arouse, make, put up to, inspire, prompt, rouse, work on, act upon; see also sense 2; **encourage, push 2.**–*Ant.* stop, hinder, drag. **2.** [To manage a propelled vehicle] direct, manage, handle, run, wheel, bicy-cle *or* *bike, cycle, transport, float, drift, dash, put in motion, start, set going, speed, roll, coast, get under way, keep going, back in *or* up, *burn up the road, *go like hell, *step on it, *give it the gun *or* the gas; see also **ride 1.**–*Ant.* **walk,** crawl, stay.

*drive a bargain, *v.* deal, close a deal, bargain; see **buy, sell.**

drive at, *v.* allude, indicate, signify; see **mean 1.**

drive away, *v.* drive off, disperse, banish; see **scatter 2.**

drive crazy *or* **mad,** *v.* anger, perplex, infuriate; see **bother 2.**

driven, *a.* blown, drifted, herded, pushed, pounded, washed, guided, steered, directed, urged (on), forced, shoved, sent, hard pressed, impelled, unable to help oneself, *with (one's) back (up) to the wall.

driver, *n.* chauffeur, motorist, (licensed) operator, bus driver, truck driver, cab driver, person in the driver's seat, *cab-bie, *hack.

driveway, *n.* drive, entrance, street, avenue, roadway, parkway, boulevard, approach, lane, track, path, pavement; see also **road 1.**

drizzle, *v.* spray, shower, sprinkle; see **drop 1, rain.**

drool, *v.* drivel, drip, salivate, spit, dribble, trickle, ooze, run (out); see also **drop 1.**

droop, *v.* settle, sink, hang down; see **lean 1.**

drop, *n.* **1.** [Enough fluid to fall] drip, trickle, droplet, bead, tear(drop), dew-drop, raindrop; see also **tear. 2.** [A lowering or falling] fall, tumble, reduction, decrease, slide, descent, slump, lapse, slip, decline, downfall, upset; see also **fall 1. 3.** [A small quantity] speck, dash, dab; see **bit 1.** –*at the drop of a hat,* without warning, at the slightest provocation, quickly; see **immediately.**

drop, *v.* **1.** [To fall in drops] drip, fall, dribble, trickle, descend, leak, ooze, seep, drain, filter, sink, bleed, bead, splash, hail; see also **rain.**–*Ant.* rise, spurt, squirt. **2.** [To cause or to permit to fall] let go, give up, release, shed, relinquish, abandon, loosen, lower, floor, ground, shoot, knock (down), fell, topple; see also **dump.**–*Ant.* raise, elevate, send up. **3.** [To discontinue] give up, quit, leave; see **stop 2. 4.** [*To break off an acquaintance] break (with), part from *or* with, cast off; see **abandon 1.**

drop a hint, *v.* suggest, intimate, imply; see **hint, propose 1.**

drop a line, *v.* write (to), post, communicate with; see **communicate, write 1.**

drop back, *v.* lag, fall back, retire; see **recede 2, retreat.**

drop behind, v. slow down, worsen, decline; see **fail 1, lose 3.**

*drop dead,** v. expire, collapse, succumb; see **die.**

drop in, v. call, stop, look in on; see **visit 1.**

drop off, v. 1. [To sleep] fall asleep, doze, drowse; see **sleep. 2.** [To deliver] leave, hand over, present; see **give 1.**

dropout, n. failing student, truant, quitter; see **failure 1.**

drop out, v. withdraw, cease, quit; see **abandon 1, retreat 1.**

dropped, a. discontinued, released, expelled; see **abandoned.**

drought, n. dry season, dehydration, dry spell; see **weather.**

drove, n. flock, pack, rout; see **crowd, herd 1.**

drown, v. 1. [To cover with liquid] swamp, inundate, overflow; see **flood 2.** [To lower into a liquid] dip, plunge, submerge; see **immerse, sink 2.** 3. [To kill *or* to die by drowning] go down three times, suffocate, asphyxiate; see **die, kill 1.**

drowned, a. suffocated, sunk, foundered; see **dead 1, gone 2.**

drown out, v. silence, hush, muffle; see **quiet 2.**

drowsy, a. sleepy, languid, indolent; see **lazy 1.**

drudge, n. slave, menial, hard worker; see also **laborer, workman.**

drug, n. sedative, potion, essence, smelling salts, powder, tonic, opiate, *ups and downs, pills, *downers. Kinds of drugs include the following—general: caffeine, coffee, alcohol, quinine, tea, salts, adrenalin, amphetamine, nicotine; hallucinogens: marijuana, *pot, *grass, *weed; peyote, mescaline, psilocybin; D-lysergic acid diethylamide *or* LSD, *acid; stimulants: cocain *or* *coke, *snow; benzedrine *or* *bennies, *pep pills; dexedrine *or* dex, *dexies; methedrine *or* *meth, *crystal, *speed; amyl nitrate *or* *poppers; narcotics: opium; morphine *or* heroin *or* *H, *horse, *junk, *smack, codeine; see **medicine 2.**

drug, v. anesthetize, desensitize, *dope; see also **deaden.**

drugged, a. comatose, doped, stupified; see **unconscious.**

druggist, n. apothecary, chemist, (registered *or* licensed) pharmacist, manufacturing pharmacist, proprietor, drugstore owner, merchant; see also **doctor.**

drum, n. snare drum, tabla, *traps; see also **musical instrument.**

drum up, v. attract, provide, succeed in finding; see **discover, find.**

drunk, a. intoxicated, inebriated, befuddled, tipsy, overcome, sottish, drunken, *stoned, *feeling no pain, *out of it, *seeing double, *smashed, *blotto, *canned, *gassed, *plowed, *under the table, *tanked, *wiped out, *soused, *high, *pickled, *stewed, *boozed up, *tight, *higher than a kite; see also **dizzy.—Ant. sober,** steady, temperate.

drunkard, n. sot, inebriate, (heavy) drinker, tippler, alcoholic, drunken sot, *drunk, *sponge, *boozer, *barfly, *pub-crawler, *wino; see also **addict.**

drunkenness, n. inebriety, intoxication, intemperance, insobriety, alcoholism, *jag.—Ant. abstinence,** sobriety, temperance.

dry, a. 1. [Having little or no moisture] arid, parched, waterless, hard, dried (up), evaporated, desiccated, barren, dehydrated, drained, rainless, not irrigated, bare, thirsty, waterproof, rainproof, baked, shriveled, desert, dusty, depleted, *dry as a bone; see also **sterile 2.—Ant. wet,** moist, damp. 2. [Thirsty] parched, dehydrated, athirst; see **thirsty. 3.** [Lacking in interest] boring, uninteresting, tedious; see **dull 4. 4.** [Possessed of intellectual humor] sarcastic, cynical, biting; see **funny 1.**

dry, v. 1. [To become dry] dry up *or* out, shrivel, wilt; see **evaporate, wither. 2.** [To cause to become dry] air dry, condense, concentrate, dehydrate, freeze dry, blot, sponge, parch, scorch, dry up, exhaust; see also **drain 1, empty 2.**

dry goods, n. cloth, yard goods, yardage; see **cotton, linen, silk, wool 2.**

dryness, n. aridity, lack of moisture, drought; see also **thirst.**

dry out *or* **up,** v. drain, dehydrate, undergo evaporation; see **dry 1, 2.**

dual, a. binary, twofold, coupled; see **double, twin.**

dubious, a. 1. [Doubtful] indecisive, perplexed, hesitant; see **doubtful, uncertain 1. 2.** [Vague] ambiguous, indefinite, unclear; see **obscure 1.**

dubiously, a. doubtfully, doubtingly, indecisively; see **suspiciously.**

duck, n. teal, mallard, fresh water *or* sea duck; see **bird. –like water off a duck's back,** ineffective, ineffectual, weak; see **useless 1.**

duck, v. 1. [To immerse quickly] plunge, submerge, drop; see **dip 1, immerse. 2.** [To avoid] dodge, escape, elude; see **avoid, evade.**

duct, n. tube, canal, channel; see **pipe 1.**

*duds,** n. garb, garments, gear; see **clothes.**

due, a. payable, owed, owing, overdue, collectable, unsatisfied, unsettled, not met, receivable, to be paid, chargeable, outstanding, in arrears; see also **unpaid 1, 2. –become (or fall) due,** be owed, payable, remain unsettled *or* unsatisfied; see **mature 1.**

duel, *n.* combat, engagement, contest; see **fight 1.**

dues, *n.* contribution, obligation, toll, duty, levy, collection, fee, annual assessment, tax, rates; see also **pay 1, tax 1.**

due to, *a.* and *conj.* because *or* as a result of, resulting from, accordingly; see **because.**

dull, *a.* 1. [Without point or edge] blunt, blunted, unsharpened, pointless, unpointed, round, square, flat, nicked, broken, toothless.—*Ant.* **sharp,** sharpened, keen. 2. [Lacking brightness or color] gloomy, sober, somber, drab, dismal, dark, dingy, dim, dusky, colorless, plain, obscure, tarnished, opaque, leaden, grave, grimy, pitchy, sooty, inky, dead, black, coal-black, unlighted, sordid, dirty, muddy, gray, lifeless, rusty, flat.—*Ant.* **bright,** colorful, gleaming. 3. [Lacking intelligence; *said usually of living beings*] slow, retarded, witless; see **stupid 1.** 4. [Lacking interest; *said usually of writing, speaking, or inanimate things*] heavy, prosaic, trite, hackneyed, monotonous, humdrum, tedious, dreary, dismal, dry, arid, colorless, insipid, boring, vapid, flat, senseless, longwinded, stupid, commonplace, ordinary, common, usual, old, ancient, stale, moth-eaten, out of date, archaic, worn out, tiring, banal, tired, uninteresting, driveling, pointless, uninspiring, piddling, senile, proverbial, lame, routine, familiar, known, well-known, conventional, depressing, sluggish, repetitious, boresome, repetitive, soporific, tiresome, lifeless, wearying, unexciting, flat, stereotyped, stock, the usual thing, the same old thing, the same thing day after day, slow, *dry as a bone, cut and dried, *dead as a doornail.—*Ant.* **exciting,** fascinating, exhilarating. 5. [Not loud or distinct] low, soft, softened; see **faint 3.** 6. [Showing little activity] still, routine, regular; see **slow 1.** 7. [Gloomy] cloudy, dim, unlit; see **dark 1.**

dullness, *n.* 1. [Quality of being boring] flatness, sameness, routine, evenness, aridity, depression, dimness, commonplaceness, mediocrity, tedium, tameness, familiarity; see also **boredom, monotony.**—*Ant.* **action,** liveliness, interest. 2. [Stupidity] stupidness, insensibility, slow-wittedness; see **stupidity 1.**

duly, *a.* rightfully, properly, decorously; see **justly 1.**

dumb, *a.* 1. [Unable to speak] silent, inarticulate, deaf and dumb, voiceless, speechless, having a speech impediment *or* problem *or* difficulty; see also **mute 1, quiet.** 2. [Slow of wit] simpleminded, feeble-minded, moronic; see **dull 3, stupid 1.**

dummy, *n.* 1. [Fool] dolt, blockhead, oaf; see **fool.** 2. [Imitation] sham, counterfeit, duplicate; see **copy, imitation 2.**

dump, *n.* refuse *or* ash heap, junk pile, garbage dump, city dump, dumping ground, swamp, garbage lot.

dump, *v.* empty, unload, deposit, unpack, discharge, evacuate, drain, eject, exude, expel, throw out *or* over *or* overboard; see also **discard.**—*Ant.* **load,** fill, pack.

dumps, *n.* despondency, dejection, despair; see **desperation 1, gloom 2.**

dunce, *n.* dolt, lout, moron; see **fool.**

dune, *n.* rise, knoll, ridge; see **hill.**

dung, *n.* offal, defecation, compost, manure, guano, fertilizer, excreta, horse dung, cow dung, etc.; chips, pellets, spoor, tracks, leavings, muck, feces, filth, garbage, sludge, slop, sewage; see also **excrement, fertilizer.**

duplicate, *n.* 1. [A second object like the first] double, second, mate, facsimile, replica, carbon (copy), likeness, counterpart, analogue, parallel, correlate, repetition, duplication, recurrence, match, twin, Xerox (trademark), chip off the old block; see also **copy, imitation. —in duplicate,** duplicated, doubled, copied; see **reproduced.**

duplicate, *v.* 1. [To copy] reproduce, counterfeit, make a replica of; see **copy.** 2. [To double] make twofold, multiply, make twice as much; see **increase.** 3. [To repeat] redo, remake, rework; see **repeat 1.**

durability, *n.* durableness, stamina, persistence; see **endurance.**

durable, *a.* strong, firm, enduring; see **permanent 2.**

duration, *n.* span, continuation, continuance; see **term 2.**

duress, *n.* compulsion, discipline, control; see **pressure 2, restraint 2.**

during, *a.* and *prep.* as, at the time, at the same time as, the whole time, the time between, in the course of, in the middle of, when, all along, pending, throughout, in the meanwhile, in the interim, all the while, for the time being; see also **meanwhile, while 1.**

dusk, *n.* gloom, twilight, dawn; see **night 1.**

dust, *n.* dirt, lint, soil, sand, flakes, ashes, cinders, grime, soot, grit, filings, sawdust; see also **earth 2, filth. —bite the dust,** be killed, fall in battle, succumb; see **die. —make the dust fly,** move swiftly, work hard, be active *or* energetic; see **act 1, move 1.**

dust, *v.* sprinkle, sift, powder; see **scatter 2.**

dusty, *a.* undusted, unused, untouched; see **dirty 1.**

dutiful, *a.* devoted, respectful, conscientious; see **faithful, obedient 1.**

duty, *n.* 1. [A personal sense of what one should do] (moral) obligation, conscience, liability, charge, accountability, faithfulness, pledge, burden, good faith, honesty, integrity, sense of duty, call of duty; see also **responsibility 1, 2.**—*Ant.* **dishonesty**, irresponsibility, disloyalty. **2.** [Whatever one has to do] work, task, occupation, function, business, province, part, calling, charge, office, service, mission, obligation, contract, station, trust, burden, undertaking, commission, engagement, assignment, routine, chore, pains, responsibility; see also **job 2.**— *Ant.* **entertainment**, amusement, sport. **3.** [A levy, especially on goods] charge, revenue, custom; see **tax 1.** —**off duty**, not engaged, free, inactive; see **unemployed.** —**on duty**, employed, engaged, at work; see **busy 1.**

dwarf, *a.* dwarfed, low, diminutive; see **little 1.**

dwarf, *v.* minimize, overshadow, dominate, predominate over, tower over, detract from, belittle, rise over *or* above, look down upon.—*Ant.* **increase**, magnify, enhance.

dwell, *v.* live, inhabit, stay, lodge, stop, settle, remain, live in *or* at, continue, go on living, rent, tenant, have a lease on, make one's home at, have one's address at, keep house, be at home, room, *bunk; see also **occupy 2.**

dweller, *n.* tenant, inhabitant, occupant; see **resident.**

dwelling, *n.* house, establishment, lodging; see **home 1.**

dwell on, *v.* involve (oneself) in, think about, be engrossed in; see **consider, emphasize.**

dye, *n.* tinge, stain, tint; see **color.**

dye, *v.* tint, stain, impregnate with color; see **color.**

dying, *a.* **1.** [Losing life] sickening, sinking, passing (away), fated, going, perishing, failing, expiring, moribund, withering away, *at death's door, *done for, *cashing in (one's checks), with one foot in the grave; see also **weak 2. 2.** [Becoming worse or less] declining, going down, receding, retarding, decreasing, disappearing, dissolving, disintegrating, vanishing, failing, fading, ebbing, decaying, overripe, decadent, passé, doomed, neglected; see also **sick, weak 2.**

dynamic, *a.* energetic, potent, compelling, forceful, changing, progressive, productive, vigorous, magnetic, electric, effective, influential, charismatic, high-powered, *peppy, *hopped *or* hyped up; see also **active 2, powerful 1.**

dynamite, *n.* trinitrotoluene *or* TNT, detonator, blasting powder; see **explosive.**

dynasty, *n.* sovereignty, empire, absolutism; see **nation 1.**

E

each, *a.* 1. [Every] all, any, one by one, separate, particular, specific, private, several, respective, various, piece by piece, individual, personal, without exception. 2. [For each time, person, or the like] individually, proportionately, respectively, for one, per unit, singly, per capita, apiece, separately, every, without exception, by the, per, *a whack, *a throw, *a shot.

each, *pron.* each one, one, each for himself, each in his own way, every last one, one another, each other.

eager, *a.* anxious, keen, fervent; see **zealous.**

eagerly, *a.* zealously, intently, anxiously, sincerely, vigorously, readily, earnestly, willingly, heartily, strenuously, fiercely, rapidly, hungrily, thirstily, fervently, actively, with enthusiasm, gladly, lovingly, with zeal, with heart in hand, with open arms, with all the heart, from the bottom of one's heart, with delight.—*Ant.* unwillingly, slowly, grudgingly.

eagerness, *n.* zest, anticipation, excitement; see **zeal.**

eagle, *n.* hawk, falcon, bird of prey; see **bird.**

eagle-eyed, *a.* discerning, keen-sighted, clear-sighted; see **observant.**

ear, *n.* outer ear, middle ear, inner ear, eardrum, labyrinth, acoustic organ, auditory apparatus. —**all ears,** attentive, hearing, paying attention; see **listening.** —*bend someone's ear,** jabber, chatter, gossip; see **talk** 1. —**fall on deaf ears,** be ignored, fail to attract notice, be received with indifference; see **fail** 1, **wait** 1. —*have (or keep) an ear to the ground,** be aware (of), observe, keep one's eyes open; see **listen** 1, **mind** 3. —**in one ear and out the other,** ignored, forgotten, unnoticed; see **neglected.** —*play it by ear,** improvise, concoct, go along; see **make up** 2. —*set on its ear,** stir up, agitate, arouse; see **excite.** —**turn a deaf ear (to),** disregard, ignore, shun; see **neglect** 2.

earlier, *a.* former, previous, prior; see **preceding.**

early, *a.* 1. [Near the beginning] recent, primitive, prime, new, brand-new, fresh, budding.—*Ant.* late, old, superannuated. 2. [Sooner than might have been expected] quick, premature, in advance, far ahead, in the bud, preceding, advanced, immediate, unexpected, speedy, ahead of time, direct, prompt, punctual, briefly, shortly, presently, beforehand,

*on short notice, *on the dot, with time to spare.—*Ant.* late, slow, tardy.

earn, *v.* 1. [To deserve as reward] win, merit, gain; see **deserve.** 2. [To receive in payment] obtain, attain, get, procure, realize, obtain a return, make money by, acquire, profit, net, clear, score, draw, gather, secure, derive, make money, bring home, bring in, collect, pick up, *scrape together.—*Ant.* spend, consume, exhaust.

earnest, *a.* ardent, zealous, warm; see **enthusiastic.**

earnestly, *a.* solemnly, soberly, thoughtfully; see **seriously** 2.

earnings, *n.* net proceeds, balance, receipts; see **pay** 2.

earring, *n.* pendant, ornament, jewel; see **jewelry.**

earth, *n.* 1. [The world] globe, sphere, planet, *terra* (Latin), mundane world, creation, terrestrial sphere, orb, cosmos, universe, star. 2. [The earthly crust] dirt, clean dirt, loam, humus, clay, gravel, sand, land, dry land, terrain, mud, muck, soil, ground, fill, compost, topsoil, alluvium, terrane, surface, shore, coast, deposit. —**come back (or down) to earth,** be practical *or* sensible, return to one's senses, quit dreaming; see **calm down, work** 1. —**down to earth,** earthly, realistic, mundane; see **practical.** —**on earth,** of all things, of everything, what; see **whatever.**

earthen, *a.* clay, stone, mud, dirt, rock, fictile, made of earth, made of baked *or* burnt clay.

earthenware, *n.* crockery, ceramics, china; see **pottery.**

earthly, *a.* human, mortal, global, mundane, worldly, under the sun, in all creation.—*Ant.* unearthly, superhuman, unnatural.

earthquake, *n.* tremor, temblor *or* tremblor *or* trembler, earthquake shock, shock, quake, fault, slip, movement of the earth's surface *or* crust, earth tremor, earth shock, an earthquake *or* a quake registering *or* reading one *or* two, etc., points on the Richter scale, volcanic quake.

earthy, *a.* 1. [Characteristic of earth] dusty, made of earth, muddy; see **earthen.** 2. [Unrefined] coarse, dull, unrefined; see **crude.**

ease, *n.* 1. [Freedom from pain] comfort, rest, quietness, peace, prosperity, leisure, repose, satisfaction, calm, calmness, restfulness, tranquility, solace, consolation.—*Ant.* pain, discomfort, unrest. 2.

[Freedom from difficulty] expertness, facility, efficiency, knack, readiness, quickness, skillfulness, dexterity, cleverness, smoothness; child's play, *clear sailing, *snap, *breeze, *cinch, *push-over.—*Ant.* difficulty, trouble, clumsiness. —at ease, relaxed, collected, resting; see calm 1.

ease, v. 1. [To relieve of pain] alleviate, allay, drug, keep under sedation or tranquilizers, tranquilize, sedate, anesthetize, give relief, comfort, relieve pressure, cure, attend to, doctor, nurse, relieve, soothe, set at ease, cheer.—*Ant.* hurt, injure, pain. 2. [To lessen pressure or tension] prop up, lift, bear, hold up, make comfortable, raise, unburden, release, soften, relieve one's mind, lighten, let up on, give rest to, relax, quiet, calm, pacify. 3. [To move carefully] induce, remove, extricate, set right, right, insert, join, slide, maneuver, handle.—*Ant.* rush, **hurry**, blunder.

easily, a. readily, with ease, in an easy manner, effortlessly, simply, with no effort, without trouble, evenly, regularly, steadily, efficiently, smoothly, plainly, comfortably, calmly, coolly, surely, *just like that, *with one hand tied behind one's back.

easiness, n. carelessness, nonchalance, facility; see **ability.**

east, a. 1. [Situated to the east] eastward, in the east, on the east side of, toward the sunrise, east side, eastern, lying or situated toward the east, easterly, easternmost. 2. [Going toward the east] eastbound, eastward, to or toward the east, headed east, in an easterly direction. 3. [Coming from the east] westbound, headed west, out of the east, westward, westerly, tending to or toward the west.

East, n. 1. [The eastern part of the United States] (the) eastern states, the Atlantic or Eastern seaboard, land east of the Alleghenies or Allegheny Mountains or Appalachians or Appalachian Mountains or the Mississippi valley, older sections of the country. Areas in the East include the following—East Coast, Atlantic Coast, Boston to Washington megalopolis, Appalachia, Middle Atlantic States, Maine, New England, down East, the Thirteen Colonies; see also **America 2, United States.** 2. [The eastern part of Eurasia] Asia, Asia Minor, Near East, Far East, Middle East, Siberia, Mongolia, southeast Asia, Arabia, Mesopotamia, Orient, Levant, Mohammedan peoples; for countries in the East see **Asia.**

eastern, a. 1. [Concerning the direction to the east] easterly, eastward, on the east side of; see **east** 1. 2. [Concerning the eastern part of the United States]

East, Atlantic, Atlantic Seaboard, east of the Appalachian Mountains, Allegheny, Appalachian, New England, Middle Atlantic, South Atlantic. 3. [Concerning the Near East or Middle East] Southwest Asian, Egyptian, of the Holy Land, Arabic, Hellenic, Hebraic, in Asia Minor. 4. [Concerning the Orient] Far Eastern, East Asian, Asian; see **Oriental.**

easy, a. 1. [Free from constraint] secure, at ease, prosperous, leisurely, unembarrassed, spontaneous, calm, peaceful, tranquil, careless, content(ed), carefree, untroubled, moderate, hospitable, *soft.—*Ant.* difficult, impoverished, hard. 2. [Providing no difficulty] simple, facile, obvious, apparent, yielding, easily done, smooth, manageable, accessible, wieldy, slight, little, paltry, inconsiderable, *nothing to it, *simple as ABC, *pushover, *easy as pie, *like taking candy from a baby.—*Ant.* difficult, complicated, **hard.** 3. [Lax] lenient, indulgent, easygoing; see **kind.** —take it easy, relax, rest, slow down; see **calm down.**

easygoing, a. tranquil, carefree, patient; see **calm** 1.

eat, v. 1. [To take as food] consume, bite, chew, devour, swallow, fatten or feast upon or on, dine out, get away with, peck at, gorge, gobble up or down, eat up, digest, masticate, feed on, breakfast, dine, eat out, sup, lunch, feed, feast, banquet, fall to, live or feed on, take in, enjoy a meal, *have a bite, *pack or put away, *make a pig of oneself, *eat out of house and home.—*Ant.* fast, starve, vomit. 2. [To reduce gradually] eat up or away, liquefy, melt, disappear, vanish, waste, rust (away), spill, dissipate, squander, drain, spill, fool away, run through.—*Ant.* increase, swell, build.

eatable, a. digestible, nutritious, delicious; see **edible.**

eating, n. consuming, consumption, devouring, feasting or gorging or feeding (on or upon), biting, chewing, dining, breakfasting, lunching, eating or dining out, eating up, having a coffee or lunch break, having a bite or a snack, breaking bread, making a hog or a pig of oneself, bolting, swallowing, gulping (down), gobbling (up or down), *putting on the feed bag, *eating out of house and home.

eat one's heart out, v. fret, pine, grieve; see **worry** 2.

eat one's words, v. retract (a statement), take back, rescind; see **abandon** 1.

eat out of house and home, v. devour, be ravenous, have a huge appetite; see **eat** 1.

eat out of one's hand, v. be tame, submit, acquiesce; see **yield 1.**

eavesdrop, v. overhear, wiretap, listen, listen in (on), try to overhear, *bend an ear, *bug, tap.

ebb, n. recession, decline, outward flow or sweep, shrinkage, wane, waste, depreciation, reduction, lessening, ebb tide, regression, withdrawal, decrease, depreciation.—*Ant.* flow, **increase, rise.**

ebb, v. recede, subside, retire, flow back, sink, decline, decrease, drop off, melt, fall away, peter out, wane, fall off, decay.—*Ant.* flow, rise, **increase.**

eccentric, a. odd, queer, strange; see **unusual 2.**

eccentricity, n. peculiarity, abnormality, idiosyncrasy; see **characteristic.**

echo, n. repetition, imitation, reply; see **answer 1.**

echo, v. repeat, mimic, impersonate; see **imitate 1.**

eclipse, n. solar eclipse, lunar eclipse, total eclipse; see **darkness 1.**

ecologist, n. environmentalist, conservationist, naturalist, ecological engineer, oceanographer, biologist, botanist; see also **scientist.**

ecology, n. ecological engineering, human environment, anti-pollution project(s), pollution control, survival studies, study of ecosystems, conservation (of natural resources); see also **science 1, zoology.**

economic, a. industrial, business, financial; see **commercial.**

economical, a. 1. [Careful of expenditures] saving, sparing, careful, economizing, thrifty, prudent, miserly, stingy, mean, close, watchful, *tight, closefisted, *penny-pinching; see also **stingy.**—*Ant.* liberal, **generous,** wasteful. 2. [Advantageously priced] cheap, sound, low, reasonable, fair, moderate, inexpensive, marked down, on sale. 3. [Making good use of materials] practical, efficient, methodical; see **efficient 1.**

economics, n. commerce, finance, public economy, political economy, science of wealth, economic theory, commercial theory, theory of business or finance, principles of business or finance or industry, study of industry, study of production and distribution, theory of trade, financial or economic principles; see also **law 4, science 1.**

economist, n. statistician, business analyst, efficiency expert; see **scientist.**

economize, v. husband, manage, stint, conserve, scrimp, skimp, be frugal or prudent, pinch, cut costs or corners, meet expenses, keep within one's means, cut down, meet a budget, make both ends meet, *tighten one's belt, *save for a rainy day, pinch pennies;

see also **accumulate, maintain 3, save 2.**—*Ant.* **spend,** waste, splurge.

economy, n. curtailment, cutback, business recession, reduction, layoff, wage decrease, cut in wages, lowered materials cost or contract price or piece rate, etc..—*Ant.* **increase,** outlay, raise.

ecstasy, n. joy, rapture, delight; see **happiness.**

edge, n. 1. [The outer portion] border, frontier, extremity, threshold, brink, boundary, end, limit, brim, rim, margin, ring, frame, side, corner, point, bend, peak, turn, crust, verge, bound, ledge, skirt, outskirt, lip, limb, hem, seam, fringe, frill, mouth, shore, strand, bank, beach, curb, periphery, circumference.—*Ant.* surface, **center,** interior. 2. [Anything linear and sharp] blade, cutting edge, razor edge; see **knife.** 3. [*Advantage] upper hand, handicap, head start; see **advantage.** —**on edge,** nervous, tense, *uptight; see **irritable.** —**set one's teeth on edge,** irritate, annoy, provoke; see **bother 2.** —**take the edge off,** weaken, subdue, dull; see **soften 2.**

edgy, a. irritable, touchy, excitable; see **nervous.**

edible, a. palatable, good, delicious, satisfying, fit to eat, savory, tasty, culinary, *yummy, nutritious, digestible; see **delicious 1.**

edifice, n. structure, architectural monument, pile; see **building.**

edit, v. revise, alter, rewrite, arrange materials for publication, prepare for the press, compose, compile, select, arrange, set up, censor, polish, finish, analyze, revise and correct, delete, condense, discard, strike out, write, proofread, cut, trim, blue-pencil, *doctor up.

edition, n. printing, reprint, revision; see **book.**

editor, n. reviser, copyreader, supervisor, director, manager, editor-in-chief, proofreader, reader, editorial writer, desk man, newspaper man, *bluepenciler; see also **author, writer.**

editorial, n. essay, article, column; see **composition.**

educate, v. tutor, instruct, train; see **teach.**

educated, a. trained, accomplished, skilled, well-taught, scientific, scholarly, intelligent, learned, well-informed, well-read, well-versed, well-grounded, disciplined, prepared, instructed, developed, civilized, fitted, versed in, informed in, acquainted with, professional, expert, polished, cultured, finished, initiated, enlightened, literate, lettered, tutored, schooled.—*Ant.* illiterate, **ignorant,** unlettered.

education, n. 1. [The process of directing learning] schooling, study, training, direction, instruction, guidance, apprenticeship, teaching, tutelage, learning, reading, discipline, preparation, adult education, book learning, information, indoctrination, brainwashing, cultivation, background, rearing, *reading, 'riting, and 'rithmetic, the three R's. 2. [Knowledge acquired through education] learning, wisdom, scholarship; see **knowledge** 1. 3. [The teaching profession] teaching, tutoring, pedagogy, instruction, training, the field of education, the educational profession, progressive education, lecturing.

educational, a. enlightening, instructive, enriching; see **cultural**.

educator, n. pedagogue, instructor, tutor; see **teacher**.

eerie, a. strange, ghostly, weird; see **frightful** 1.

effect, n. conclusion, consequence, outcome; see **result**. —**in effect**, as a result, in fact, actually; see **really** 1. —**take effect**, work, produce results, become operative; see **act** 1. —**to the effect (that)**, as a result, so that, therefore; see **for**.

effect, v. produce, cause, make; see **begin** 1, **cause** 2.

effective, a. efficient, serviceable, useful, operative, effectual, sufficient, adequate, productive, capable, competent, yielding, practical, valid, resultant.—*Ant.* inoperative, **useless**, inefficient.

effectively, a. efficiently, completely, finally, expertly, conclusively, definitely, persuasively, adequately, capably, productively; see also **well** 2.

effects, n. personal property, baggage, possessions; see **property** 1.

effectual, a. adequate, efficient, qualified; see **effective**.

efficiency, n. productivity, capability, capableness; see **ability**.

efficient, a. 1. [*Said of persons*] competent, businesslike, good at, apt, adequate, fitted, able, capable, qualified, skillful, clever, talented, energetic, skilled, adapted, familiar with, deft, adept, expert, experienced, equal to, practiced, practical, proficient, accomplished, active, productive, dynamic, decisive, tough, shrewd.—*Ant.* incompetent, inefficient, incapable. 2. [*Said of things*] economical, fitting, suitable, suited, effectual, effective, adequate, serviceable, useful, saving, profitable, valuable, expedient, handy, conducive, well-designed, streamlined, good for.—*Ant.* **inadequate**, unsuitable, ineffectual.

effluent, a. emanating, issuing forth, seeping; see **flowing**.

effort, n. attempt, enterprise, undertaking, struggle, battle, try, trial, work, venture, aim, aspiration, purpose, intention, resolution, exercise, discipline, drill,

training, *crack, *go, *whirl; see also **action** 1, 2.

effortless, a. simple, offhand, smooth; see **easy** 2.

egg, n. ovum, seed, germ, spawn, bud, embryo, nucleus, cell. Prepared eggs include the following—fried, scrambled, poached, deviled, hard boiled, soft boiled, soufflé, raw, buttered, on toast, egg salad, ham *or* bacon and eggs, over easy, sunnyside up. —*lay an egg, be unsuccessful, err, make a mistake; see **fail** 1. —**put (*or* have) all one's eggs in one basket**, chance, gamble, bet; see **risk**.

egg on, v. encourage, goad, incite; see **drive** 1, 2, **urge** 2, 3.

egg-shaped, a. rounded, oval, pear-shaped; see **round** 1.

ego, n. personality, individuality, self; see **character** 1, 2.

egotism, n. egoism, conceit, vanity, pride, assurance, self-love, self-confidence, self-glorification, self-worship, arrogance, insolence, overconfidence, haughtiness.—*Ant.* humility, **modesty**, meekness.

egotist, n. conceited *or* proud person, boaster, egoist; see **braggart**.

egotistic, a. conceited, vain, boastful, inflated, pompous, arrogant, insolent, puffed up, affected, self-centered, self-glorifying, presumptuous, blustering, showy, boisterous, haughty, snobbish, contemptuous, proud, bullying, sneering, aloof, pretentious, assuming, *cocky, brazen, impertinent, selfish, bragging, insulting, theatrical, garish, gaudy, spectacular, reckless, impudent, inflated, stiff, overbearing, domineering, bold, rash, overconfident, self-satisfied, *stuck up, *too big for one's boots, *looking down one's nose, *snooty, uppity, *wrapped up in oneself, *on one's high horse, *high and mighty, *too big for one's breeches, *big as you please.—*Ant.* **humble**, meek, modest.

egotistically, a. vainly, boastfully, arrogantly, haughtily, pretentiously, loftily.

either, a. and *conj.* on the one hand, whether or not, unless, it could be that, it might be that.

either, *pron.* one, one or the other, this one, either/or, each of two, as soon one as the other, one of two.

eject, v. dislodge, discard, reject, run *or* kick *or* throw *or* put *or* force *or* spit *or* turn *or* squeeze out, oust, do away with, evict, banish, throw off, vomit, excrete, dump, get rid of, send packing, *give the boot, *ditch, *bounce.

ejection, n. eviction, expulsion, dismissal; see **removal**.

elaborate, a. 1. [Ornamented] gaudy, decorated, garnished, showy, fussy, dressy, refined, flowery, flashy; see also **ornate** 1.—*Ant.* **common**, ordinary, unpolished. 2. [Detailed] complicated, extensive, laborious, minute, intricate, involved, many-faceted, complex, a great many, painstaking, studied.—*Ant.* general, usual, unified.

elaborate, *v.* embellish, bedeck, deck; see **decorate.**

elaborate upon, *v.* expand, discuss, comment upon; see **explain.**

elapse, *v.* transpire, pass away, slip by; see **pass 2.**

elastic, *a.* plastic, tempered, pliant; see **flexible 1.**

elasticity, *n.* resiliency, buoyancy, pliability; see **flexibility 1.**

elbow, *n.* joint, angle, funny bone; see **bone. —rub elbows with,** mingle (with), associate, be friends (with); see **join 2. —up to the elbows (in),** engaged, employed, working at; see **busy 1.**

elbowroom, *n.* sweep, range, margin; see **space 2.**

elder, *n.* veteran, old lady, old man, old woman, superior, old timer, senior, one of the old folk(s) *or* older generation, patriarch, chief, tribal head, dignitary, counselor, father, uncle, grandfather, ancestor.

elderly, *a.* declining, retired, venerable; see **old 1.**

elect, *v.* choose, name, select; see **choose.**

elected, *a.* chosen, duly elected, picked; see **named 2.**

election, *n.* poll, polls, ballot, balloting, ticket, vote, voting, vote-casting, primaries, suffrage, referendum, franchise, constitutional right.

elective, *a.* voluntary, selective, not compulsory; see **optional.**

electric, *a.* electrical, magnetic, galvanic, electronic, power (driven), telegraphic, electrified, pulsing, vibrating, dynamic, energetic.—*Ant.* old-fashioned, manual, steam.

electricity, *n.* power, current, service, heat, light, ignition, spark, utilities, alternating current (A.C.), direct current (D.C.), voltage, 110 volts, 220 volts, high voltage, high tension, kilowatts, kilowatt hours, kilocycles, megacycles.

electrify, *v.* wire, charge, power, heat, light, equip, lay wires *or* cables, provide service, magnetize, galvanize, energize, subject to electricity, pass an electric current through, give an electric shock to, charge with electricity.

electrocute, *v.* execute, put to death, kill by electric shock, put in the electric chair, *send to the hot seat, *fry, *burn.

electron, *n.* (negative) particle, negatron, electrically charged element; see **atom.**

electronic, *a.* photoelectric, cathodic, anodic, voltaic, photoelectronic, autoelectronic, computerized, automatic, automated; see also **electric.**

electronics, *n.* radionics, electron physics, radar, physics, photoelectronics, automatics, cybernetics, computer electronics; see also **science 1.**

elegance, *n.* culture, tastefulness, taste, cultivation, politeness, polish, grace, delicacy, splendor, beauty, balance, purity, grace, gracefulness, delicacy, magnificence, courtliness, nobility, charm, sophistication, propriety, style.

elegant, *a.* ornate, polished, perfected, elaborate, finished, ornamented, adorned, embellished, embroidered, flowing, artistic, fancy, rich, pure, fluent, neat.—*Ant.* dull, ill-chosen, inarticulate.

element, *n.* 1. [A constitution] portion, particle, detail; see **part 1. 2.** [A form of matter] The older sciences determined the following elements—earth, air, fire, water; modern chemistry and physics identify the following elements—actinium (Ac), aluminum (Al), americium (Am), antimony (Sb), argon (A), arsenic (As), astatine (At), barium (Ba), berkelium (Bk), beryllium (Be), bismuth (Bi), boron (B), bromine (Br), cadmium (Cd), calcium (Ca), californium (Cf), carbon (C), cerium (Ce), cesium (Cs), chlorine (Cl), chromium (Cr), cobalt (Co), copper (Cu), curium (Cm), dysprosium (Dy), einsteinium (E), erbium (Er), europium (Eu), fermium (Fm), fluorine (F), francium (Fr), gadolinium (Gd), gallium (Ga), germanium (Ge), gold (Au), hafnium (Hf), helium (He), holmium (Ho), hydrogen (H), indium (In), iodine (I), iridium (Ir), iron (Fe), krypton (Kr), lanthanum (La), lawrencium (Lw), lead (Pb), lithium (Li), lutetium (Lu), magnesium (Mg), manganese (Mn), mendelevium (Mv), mercury (Hg), molybdenum (Mo), neodymium (Nd), neon (Ne), neptunium (Np), nickel (Ni), niobium *or* columbium (Nb), nitrogen (N), nobelium (No), osmium (Os), oxygen (O), palladium (Pd), phosphorus (P), platinum (Pt), plutonium (Pu), polonium (Po), potassium (K), praseodymium (Pr), promethium (Pm), protoactinium (Pa), radium (Ra), radon (Rn), rhenium (Re), rhodium (Rh), rubidium (Rb), ruthenium (Ru), samarium (Sm), scandium (Sc), selenium (Se), silicon (Si), silver (Ag), sodium (Na), strontium (Sr), sulphur (S), tantalum (Ta), technetium (Tc), tellurium (Te), terbium (Tb), thallium (Tl), thorium (Th), thulium (Tm), tin (Sn), titanium (Ti), tungsten (W), uranium (U), vanadium (V), xenon (Xe), ytterbium (Yb), yttrium (Y), zinc (Zn), zirconium (Zr).

elementary, *a.* 1. [Suited to beginners] primary, introductory, rudimentary; see

easy 2. **2.** [Fundamental] foundational, essential, basic; see **fundamental** 1.

elements, *n.* basic material, fundamentals, grammar, ABC's, initial stage, basis, beginning, first step, principles, rudiments, groundwork.

elevate, *v.* **1.** [To lift bodily] hoist, heave, tilt; see **raise** 1. **2.** [To promote] advance, appoint, further; see **promote** 1.

elevated, *a.* aerial, towering, tall; see **high** 2, **raised** 1.

elevation, *n.* top, roof, platform; see **height**.

elevator, *n.* **1.** [Machine for lifting] lift, escalator, conveyor, elevator stack, chair lift, passenger elevator, freight elevator, automatic elevator, hoist, chute. **2.** [A building handling grain] bin, storage plant, silo; see **barn**.

elf, *n.* brownie, sprite, leprechaun; see **fairy** 1.

eligibility, *n.* fitness, acceptability, capability; see **ability**.

eligible, *a.* qualified, fit, suitable, suited, equal to, worthy of being chosen, capable of, fitted for, satisfactory, trained, employable, usable, becoming, likely, in the running, in line for, *up to.—Ant.* **unfit,** ineligible, disqualified.

eliminate, *v.* take *or* wipe *or* clean *or* throw *or* weed *or* stamp *or* blot *or* cut *or* phase *or* drive out, dispose *or* get rid of, do away with, put *or* set aside, exclude, eject, cast off, disqualify, oust, evict, cancel, eradicate, erase, expel, discharge, dislodge, put out of doors, reduce, invalidate, abolish, repeal, exterminate, annihilate, kill, murder, throw overboard, be done with, discard, dismiss, blot out, obliterate, discount, exile, banish, deport, expatriate, maroon, blackball, ostracize, fire, *dump, *ditch, scrap, *bounce, *sack, root out, drop.—*Ant.* **accept,** include, welcome.

elimination, *n.* **1.** [The act of removing] dismissal, expulsion, exclusion; see **removal.** **2.** [The act of declining to consider] rejection, repudiation, denial, disqualification, avoidance.

elite, *n.* society, nobility, celebrities; see **aristocracy.**

ellipse, *n.* oval, conic section, curve; see **circle** 1.

elongate, *v.* prolong, lengthen, extend; see **stretch** 1.

eloquence, *n.* fluency, wit, wittiness, expression, expressiveness, appeal, ability, diction, articulation, delivery, power, force, vigor, facility, style, poise, expressiveness, flow, command of language, *gift of gab.

eloquent, *a.* vocal, articulate, outspoken; see **fluent** 2.

elsewhere, *a.* gone, somewhere (else), not here, in another place, in *or* to some other place, away, absent, abroad, hence, removed, remote, outside, formerly, subsequently.—*Ant.* **here,** at this point, in this spot.

elude, *v.* dodge, shun, escape; see **avoid.**

elusive, *a.* slippery, fleeting, fugitive; see **temporary.**

emaciated, *a.* gaunt, famished, wasted; see **thin** 2.

emanate, *v.* exude, radiate, exhale; see **emit** 1.

emancipate, *v.* release, liberate, deliver; see **free** 1.

emancipation, *n.* liberty, release, liberation; see **freedom.**

emasculate, *v.* geld, unman, mutilate; see **castrate.**

embalm, *v.* preserve, process, freeze, anoint, wrap, mummify, prepare for burial, lay out.

embankment, *n.* dike, breakwater, pier; see **dam.**

embargo, *n.* restriction, prohibition, impediment; see **restraint** 2.

embark, *v.* set out, leave port, set sail; see **leave** 1.

embarrass, *v.* perplex, annoy, puzzle, vex, distress, disconcert, agitate, bewilder, confuse, chagrin, confound, upset, bother, plague, tease, worry, trouble, distract, discomfort, disturb, let down, perturb, fluster, irk, shame, stun, rattle, *put on the spot, *make a monkey of.—*Ant.* **encourage,** cheer, please.

embarrassed, *a.* abashed, perplexed, disconcerted; see **ashamed.**

embarrassing, *a.* difficult, disturbing, confusing, distracting, bewildering, puzzling, rattling, perplexing, delicate, unbearable, distressing, disconcerting, upsetting, discomforting, ticklish, flustering, troublesome, worrisome, uncomfortable, awkward, disagreeable, helpless, unseemly, impossible, uneasy, mortifying, shameful, annoying, irksome, exasperating, inconvenient, unmanageable, *sticky.—*Ant.* **comfortable,** easy, agreeable.

embarrassment *n.* confusion, chagrin, mortification, discomfiture, shame, humiliation, shyness, timidity, inhibition, dilemma, puzzle, perplexity, tangle, strait, pinch, quandary, mistake, blunder, clumsiness, indebtedness, uncertainty, hindrance, poverty, destitution, distress, difficulties, involvement, obligation, indiscretion, awkward situation, predicament, plight, *pinch, *fix, *snag, *hitch, hot seat, hot water, pickle, stew.

embassy, *n.* commission, mission, delegation; see **committee, diplomat.**

embed, *v.* plant, implant, secure; see **fasten** 1.

embezzle, v. thieve, forge, pilfer; see **steal.**

embezzlement, n. fraud, misappropriation, stealing; see **theft.**

embezzler, n. thief, robber, defaulter; see **criminal.**

embitter, v. irritate, aggravate, annoy; see **bother 2.**

emblem, n. symbol, figure, image, design, token, sign, insignia, banner, seal, colors, crest, coat of arms, representation, effigy, reminder, mark, badge, souvenir, keepsake, medal, character, motto, hallmark, flag, pennant, banner, standard.

embodiment, n. incarnation, matter, structure; see **characteristic, essence 1, image 2.**

emboss, v. raise, design, enchase; see **decorate.**

embrace, v. enfold, squeeze, grip; see **hug.**

embroider, v. stitch, knit, quilt; see **sew.**

embryo, n. fetus, incipient organism, nucleus; see **egg.**

embryonic, a. incipient, immature, undeveloped; see **early 1.**

emerald, n. rare green beryl, valuable gem, precious stone; see **jewel.**

emerge, v. rise, arrive, come out; see **appear 1.**

emergence, n. rise, evolution, visibility; see **view.**

emergency, n. accident, unforeseen occurrence, misadventure, strait, urgency, necessity, pressure, tension, distress, turn of events, obligation, pass, crisis, predicament, turning point, impasse, dilemma, quandary, pinch, *fix, *hole; see also **difficulty 1, 2.**

emigrant, n. exile, expatriate, colonist, migrant, displaced person (D.P.), traveler, foreigner, pilgrim, refugee, fugitive, wayfarer, wanderer, immigrant, alien, outcast, man without a country.

emigrate, v. migrate, immigrate, quit; see **leave 1.**

emigration, n. re-establishing, departure, removal, leaving, expatriation, displacement, moving (away), crossing, migrating, exodus, exile, trek, journey, movement, trend, march, travel, voyage, wayfaring, wandering, migration, shift, settling, homesteading.—*Ant.* immigration, arriving, remaining.

eminence, n. standing, prominence, distinction; see **fame 1.**

eminent, a. renowned, celebrated, prominent; see **dignified, distinguished 2.**

emissary, n. intermediary, ambassador, consul; see **agent.**

emission, n. ejection, effusion, eruption; see **radiation 1.**

emit, v. give or let off or out, send forth or out, throw up or out, spill or pour out, pour or give forth, eject, blow, hurl, gush, secrete, spurt, shoot, erupt,

squirt, shed, expel, expend, vomit, belch, excrete, issue, perspire, spew (forth), spit, ooze, exhale, emanate; see **empty 2.**

emotion, n. agitation, tremor, commotion, excitement, disturbance, sentiment, feeling(s), tumult, turmoil, sensation. Emotions include the following—love, passion, ecstasy, fire, warmth, glow, fervor, ardor, zeal, thrill, elation, joy, satisfaction, happiness, sympathy, tenderness, concern, grief, remorse, sorrow, sadness, melancholy, despondency, despair, depression, worry, disquiet, uneasiness, dread, fear, apprehension, hate, resentment, conflict, jealousy, greed, anger, rage, ire, shame, pride, sensuality, lust, desire.

emotional, a. hysterical, demonstrative, fiery, warm, zealous, sensuous, fervent, ardent, enthusiastic, passionate, excitable, impulsive, spontaneous, ecstatic, impetuous, nervous, wrought up, overwrought, temperamental, irrational, sensitive, oversensitive, hypersensitive, sentimental, maudlin, overflowing, affectionate, loving, feminine, neurotic, fickle, with or wearing one's heart on one's sleeve, high-strung, *mushy.—*Ant.* rational, cold, hard.

emotionalism, n. hysteria, sentimentality, excitement; see **emotion.**

empathy, n. vicarious emotion, insight, understanding; see **pity 1.**

emperor, n. monarch, sovereign, dictator; see **ruler 1.**

emphasis, n. stress, accent, weight; see **importance.**

emphasize, v. make clear or emphatic, underline, underscore, highlight, dramatize, pronounce, enunciate, articulate, accentuate, accent, stress, point up or out, strike, call to the attention of, reiterate, repeat, insist, maintain, impress, affirm, indicate, lay stress on, *rub in, *pound or drum into one's head, make much of, make a fuss about.

emphatic, a. assured, strong, determined, forceful, forcible, earnest, positive, energetic, potent, powerful, dynamic, stressed, pointed, flat, definitive, categorical, dogmatic, explicit.

emphatically, a. definitely, certainly, of course, undoubtedly, decidedly, decisively, absolutely, entirely, flatly, distinctly.—*Ant.* slowly, hesitantly, indistinctly.

empire, n. union, people, federation; see **nation 1.**

employ, v. 1. [To make use of] operate, manipulate, apply; see **use 1. 2.** [To obtain services for pay] engage, contract, procure; see **hire.**

employed, a. working, occupied, busy, laboring, gainfully employed, not out of work, in one's employ, on the job, hired, operating, active, engaged, on duty, on the payroll.—*Ant.* out of work, unemployed, jobless.

employee, *n.* worker, laborer, servant, domestic, agent, representative, (hired) hand, salesman, assistant, attendant, apprentice, operator, workman, laboring man, workingman, breadwinner, craftsman, wage earner, hireling, lackey, flunky.

employer, *n.* owner, manager, proprietor, management, head, director, executive, superintendent, supervisor, president, chief, businessman, manufacturer, corporation, company, boss, front office, *big shot.

employment, *n.* job, profession, vocation; see **business 1, trade 2, work 2.**

emptiness, *n.* void, vacuum, vacancy, gap, chasm, blankness, blank, exhaustion, hollowness.

empty, *a.* hollow, bare, clear, blank, unfilled, unfurnished, unoccupied, vacated, vacant, void, vacuous, void of, devoid, lacking, wanting, barren, emptied, abandoned, exhausted, depleted, deserted, stark, deprived of, dry, destitute, negative, deflated, evacuated.—*Ant.* full, filled, occupied.

empty, *v.* 1. [To become empty] discharge, leave, pour, flow (out), ebb, run (out), open into, be discharged, void, release, exhaust, leak, drain (off), rush out, escape.—*Ant.* flow in, enter, absorb. 2. [To cause to become empty] dump, dip, ladle, tap, void, pour, spill or let out, deplete, exhaust, deflate, drain, bail (out), clean or clear out, evacuate, eject, expel, draw off or out, disgorge, suck dry, drink.—*Ant.* pack, fill, stuff.

emulate, *v.* challenge, contend, imitate; see **compete, follow 2.**

enable, *v.* make possible, sanction, give power or authority (to or for), invest, endow, authorize, allow, let, permit, license, set up; see also **approve.**

enact, *v.* decree, sanction, ordain, order, dictate, make into law, legislate, pass, establish, ratify, vote in, proclaim, vote favorably, determine, authorize, appoint, institute, railroad through, get the floor, put in force, make laws, put through, constitute, fix, set, formulate.

enactment, *n.* edict, decree, statute; see **law 3.**

enamel, *n.* lacquer, coating, finish, polish, gloss, top coat, varnish, glaze, veneer.

enamel, *v.* lacquer, glaze, gloss, paint, veneer, coat, varnish, finish, paint.

encampment, *n.* village, campsite, bivouac; see **camp 1.**

enchant, *v.* entrance, entice, allure; see **fascinate.**

enchanted, *a.* enraptured, entranced, captivated; see **fascinated.**

encircle, *v.* encompass, circle, throw a cordon about; see **surround 1.**

enclose, *v.* insert, jail, corral, impound, confine, blockade, imprison, block or fence off, set apart, lock up or in, keep or box or close or hem or shut or wall in, box off or up.—*Ant.* free, liberate, open.

enclosed, *a.* stuffed or locked or penned in, jailed, packed or wrapped or shut up, buried, encased, imprisoned.

enclosure, *n.* 1. [A space enclosed] pen, sty, yard, jail, garden, corral, cage, asylum, pound, park, zone, precinct, plot, court, patch, coop, den, cell, dungeon, vault, paddock, stockade, concentration camp, prison; see also **building, place 2, room 2.** 2. [Something inserted] information, check, money, circular, copy, questionnaire, forms, documents, printed matter.

encompass, *v.* encircle, compass, gird; see **surround 1.**

encounter, *n.* 1. [A coming together] interview, rendezvous, appointment; see **meeting 1.** 2. [Physical violence] conflict, clash, collision; see **fight 1.**

encounter, *v.* 1. [To meet unexpectedly] meet, confront, come across; see **find. 2.** [To meet in conflict] battle, attack, struggle; see **fight.**

encourage, *v.* cheer, refresh, enliven, exhilarate, inspire, cheer up, praise, restore, revitalize, gladden, fortify, console, ease, relieve, help, aid, comfort, approve, reassure, assist, befriend, uphold, reinforce, back, bolster, brace, further, favor, strengthen, side with, back up, *lead or egg on, *root for, pat on the back.—*Ant.* restrain, discourage, caution.

encouraged, *a.* inspired, enlivened, renewed, aided, supported, hopeful, confident, enthusiastic, roused, cheered; see also **helped.**—*Ant.* sad, discouraged, disheartened.

encouragement, *n.* aid, faith, help, assistance, support, cheer, confidence, trust, advance, promotion, reward, reassurance, incentive, backing, optimism, comfort, consolation, hope, relief, pat on the back, lift, shot in the arm.

encouraging, *a.* bright, good, promising; see **hopeful 1, 2.**

encyclopedia, *n.* book of facts, thesaurus, book of knowledge, compilation, general or encyclopedic reference work, cyclopedia.

end, *n.* 1. [Purpose] aim, object, intention; see **purpose 1.** 2. [The close of an action] expiration, completion, target date, termination, adjournment, final event, ending, close, finish, conclusion, finis, finale, retirement, accomplishment, attainment, determination, achievement, fulfillment, pay-off, realization, period, consummation, culmination, execution, performance, last line, curtain, terminus, *last word, *wrap-up, windup, cutoff, *end of the line.—*Ant.* beginning, origin, opening. 3. [A result] conclusion, effect, outcome; see **result** 4. [The extremity] terminal, termination, terminus, boundary, limit, borderline, point, stub, stump, tail (end), edge, tip, top, head, butt end.—*Ant.* center, middle, hub. 5. [The close of life] demise, passing, doom; see **death**.

end, *v.* 1. [To bring to a halt] stop, finish, quit, close, halt, shut (down), settle (up), bring to an end, make an end of, break off *or* up, put an end to, discontinue, postpone, delay, conclude, interrupt, dispose of, drop, *call it a day, cut short, wind up, *get done, call off, give up, *wrap up.—*Ant.* begin, initiate, start. 2. [To bring to a conclusion] settle, conclude, terminate; see **achieve** 3. [To come to an end] desist, cease, die; see **stop** 2. 4. [To die] expire, depart, pass away; see **die**. —*keep one's end up, do one's share, join, participate; see **share** 1. —make (both) ends meet, manage, get along *or* by, survive; see **endure** 2. —*no end, very much, extremely, greatly; see **much, very.** —on end, 1. [Endless] ceaseless, without interruption, constant; see **endless.** 2. [Upright] erect, vertical, standing up; see **straight** 1. —put an end to, stop, finish, cease; see **end** 1.

endanger, *v.* imperil, jeopardize, expose to danger, expose to hazard *or* peril, be careless with, lay open, *put on the spot, leave in the middle.—*Ant.* save, protect, preserve.

endangered, *a.* exposed, imperiled, in a dilemma, in a predicament, jeopardized, in danger, (put) in jeopardy, *in a bad way, *on thin ice, *hanging by a thread.

endeavor, *v.* attempt, aim, essay; see **try** 1.

ended, *a.* done, completed, concluded; see **finished** 1.

ending, *n.* finish, closing, terminus; see **end** 2.

endless, *a.* infinite, interminable, untold, without end, unbounded, unlimited, immeasurable, limitless, boundless, incalculable, unfathomable.

endorse, *v.* 1. [To inscribe one's name] sign, put one's signature to *or* on, countersign, underwrite, sign one's name on, subscribe, notarize, add one's name to, *sign on the dotted line. 2. [To indicate one's active support of] approve, confirm, sanction, ratify, guarantee, underwrite, support, stand up for, stand *or*

be behind, vouch for, ·uphold, recommend, praise, give one's word for, O.K., back up, *go to bat for.—*Ant.* censure, condemn, **blame.**

endorsed, *a.* signed, notarized, legalized, ratified, sealed, settled, approved, upheld, supported, recommended, sanctioned, advocated, *backed, O.K.'d.

endorsement, *n.* support, sanction, permission; see **signature.**

endow, *v.* enrich, provide, supply; see **give** 1.

endowment, *n.* benefit, provision, bequest, gratuity, grant, pension, stipend, legacy, inheritance, subsidy, revenue, trust, nest egg.

end up, *v.* finish, cease, come to a close; see **end** 1, **stop** 2.

endurable, *a.* sustainable, tolerable, supportable; see **bearable.**

endurance, *n.* sufferance, fortitude, long-suffering, capacity to endure, resignation, patience, tolerance, courage, perseverance, stamina, restraint, resistance, will, backbone, *guts, *spunk.—*Ant.* weakness, feebleness, infirmity.

endure, *v.* 1. [To continue] persist, remain, last, continue, exist, be, stay, prevail, wear, sustain, survive, outlast, carry *or* stay *or* live *or* go *or* hold *or* hang *or* keep on, linger, outlive, hold out, *never say die, *wear on, *stick to *or* at, ride out.—*Ant.* die, cease, end. 2. [To sustain adversity] suffer, tolerate, bear with *or* up, allow, permit, support, undergo, sit through, take, withstand, bear up under, stand, accustom oneself to, submit to, sustain, go *or* pass through, encounter, be patient with, keep up, resign oneself, weather, brave, face, put up with, live through, *stand for, swallow, stomach, *never say die, grin and bear it, brace oneself, *like it or lump it, hang on, keep one's chin up.—*Ant.* avoid, resist, refuse.

enduring, *a.* lasting, abiding, surviving; see **permanent** 2.

enemy, *n.* foe, rival, assailant, competitor, attacker, antagonist, opponent, adversary, public enemy, criminal, opposition, guerrilla(s), guerrilla force *or* army *or* band, fifth column, saboteur, spy, foreign agent, assassin, murderer, betrayer, traitor, terrorist, revolutionary, rebel, invader.—*Ant.* ally, **friend,** supporter.

energetic, *a.* industrious, vigorous, forcible; see **active.**

energy, *n.* 1. [One's internal powers] force, power, virility; see **strength.** 2. [Power developed or released by a device] horsepower, power, pressure, potential energy, kinetic energy, atomic energy, solar energy, high pressure, foot pounds, magnetism, friction, voltage, kilowatt hours, current, electricity, gravity, heat, friction, suction, radioactivity, potential, fuel consumption.

enfold, v. envelop, encase, enclose; see **surround 1, wrap.**

enforce, v. urge, compel, incite, exert, drive, demand, carry out vigorously, put in force, dictate, exact, require, execute, coerce, oblige, insist (upon), emphasize, necessitate, press, impel, make, sanction, force (upon), goad, stress, spur, hound, crack down.—*Ant.* **abandon,** neglect, evade.

enforced, a. compelled, established, demanded, exacted, required, executed, pressed, sanctioned, forced upon, kept, dictated, admonished, advocated, charged, meted out, cracked down.

enforcement, n. requirement, enforcing, prescription, compulsion, constraint, coercion, pressure, duress, obligation, necessity, insistence, carrying out, fulfilling.

engage, v. 1. [To hire] employ, contract, retain; see **hire 1.** 2. [To engross] absorb, captivate, bewitch; see **fascinate.** 3. [To enmesh, especially gears] interlock, mesh, interlace; see **fasten 1.**

engaged, a. 1. [Promised in marriage] bound, pledged, betrothed, matched, *hooked.—Ant.* **free,** unpledged, unbetrothed. 2. [Not at liberty] working, occupied, employed; see **busy 1.** 3. [In a profession, business, or the like] employed, practicing, performing, dealing in, doing, interested, absorbed in, pursuing, at work, involved *or* engaged with *or* in, working (at), connected with; see also **employed.—Ant. unemployed,** out of a job, without connection.

engage in, v. take part in, attack, undertake; see **perform 1.**

engagement, n. 1. [A predetermined action] meeting, rendezvous, errand; see **appointment 2.** 2. [The state of being betrothed] contract, promise, match, betrothal, espousal, betrothing.

engine, n. motor, power plant, dynamo, generator, turbine, diesel engine, traction engine, source of power, diesel.

engineer, n. 1. [A professional engineer] surveyor, designer, planner, builder. Types of engineers include the following—mining, civil, metallurgical, geological, electrical, architectural, chemical, construction, military, naval, flight, industrial. 2. [The operator of a locomotive] motorman, brakeman, stoker; see **driver.**

engineering, n. design, planning, blueprinting, structure *or* structures, surveying, metallurgy, architecture, shipbuilding, installations, stresses, communications.

England, n. Britain, Great Britain, Brit-

ish Isles, Britannia, member of the British Commonwealth of Nations, Albion, the mother country, *John Bull.

English, a. British, Britannic, Anglian, Anglican, Anglo-, England's, His *or* Her Majesty's, Commonwealth, anglicized, English-speaking, Norman.

engrave, v. etch, bite, stipple, lithograph, cut, burn, incise, grave, chisel, crosshatch.

engraved, a. carved, decorated, etched, scratched, bitten into, embossed, furrowed, incised, deepened, marked deeply, lithographed.

engraving, n. print, wood engraving, etching, aquatint, graphotype, rotogravure, lithograph, cut, woodcut, illustration, impression, copy, proof.

engross, v. absorb, busy, fill; see **occupy 3.**

engulf, v. swallow up, submerge, inundate; see **sink 2.**

enhance, v. heighten, magnify, amplify; see **increase.**

enigma, n. problem, riddle, parable; see **puzzle 3.**

enjoy, v. relish, luxuriate in, delight in; see **like 1.**

enjoyable, a. agreeable, welcome, genial; see **pleasant 1, 2.**

enjoying, a. gratified, refreshed, experiencing, partaking of, tasting, savoring, feeling, sensing, sharing, undergoing, delighting *or* basking in, relishing, using, making use of, exercising, *getting a kick out of.

enjoyment, n. satisfaction, gratification, triumph, loving, enjoying, rejoicing, having, using, occupation, use, diversion, entertainment, luxury, sensuality, indulgence, self-indulgence, hedonism.—*Ant.* dislike, displeasure, abuse.

enjoy oneself, v. take pleasure, celebrate, have a good time, revel *or* delight *or* luxuriate in, be pleased with; see also **play 1.**

enlarge, v. 1. [To increase] expand, spread, swell; see **grow 1.** 2. [To cause to increase] extend, augment, expand; see **increase.**

enlarged, a. increased, augmented, expanded, developed, exaggerated, extended, amplified, spread, added to, lengthened, broadened, widened, thickened, magnified, filled out, inflated, stretched, heightened, intensified, *blown up.

enlargement, n. 1. [Growth or extension] augmentation, amplification, expansion; see **increase 1.** 2. [An enlarged photograph] view, enlarged print, blow up; see **photograph, picture 2.**

enlighten, v. inform, divulge, acquaint; see **teach, tell 1.**

enlightened, *a.* instructed, learned, informed; see **educated.**

enlightenment, *n.* wisdom, culture, education; see **knowledge 1.**

enlist, *v.* 1. [To enroll others] engage, hire, retain, call up, recruit, mobilize, induct, register, list, initiate, employ, place, admit, draft, conscribe, muster, call to arms.—*Ant.* **refuse,** neglect, turn away. 2. [To enroll oneself] enter, sign up, serve; see **join 2, register 4.**

enlisted, *a.* recruited, commissioned, engaged; see **enrolled.**

enlistment, *n.* conscription, levy, recruitment; see **enrollment 1, induction 3.**

en masse, *a.* bodily, ensemble, together; see **together 2, unified.**

enmity, *n.* animosity, malice, rancor; see **hatred.**

enormous, *a.* monstrous, immense, huge; see **large 1.**

enough, *a.* 1. [Sufficient] plenty, abundant, adequate, acceptable, ample, satisfactory, complete, plentiful, satisfying, unlimited, suitable.—*Ant.* **inadequate,** deficient, insufficient. 2. [Sufficiently] satisfactorily, amply, abundantly; see **adequately.** 3. [Fully] quite, rather, just; see **very.** 4. [Just adequately] tolerably, fairly, barely; see **adequately.**

enough, *n.* abundance, sufficiency, adequacy; see **plenty.**

enrage, *v.* anger, incite, provoke, irk, bother, annoy, tease, pester, agitate, arouse, stir, goad, bait, inflame, incense, infuriate, madden; see **incite.**

enrich, *v.* adorn, better, decorate; see **improve 1.**

enriched, *a.* improved, bettered, embellished; see **improved.**

enrichment, *n.* advancement, promotion, endowment; see **improvement 1.**

enroll, *v.* 1. [To obtain for service] recruit, obtain, employ; see **hire.** 2. [To register oneself] enter, sign up, enlist; see **join 2, register 4.**

enrolled, *a.* joined, inducted, registered, installed, settled, pledged, enlisted, commissioned, employed, recruited, signed up.—*Ant.* **separated,** mustered out, discharged.

enrollment, *n.* 1. [The act of enrolling] registering, listing, record, enlistment, matriculation, induction, entry, enlisting, selecting, registration. 2. [The persons enrolled] group, students, conscript, volunteers, number enrolled, response, registration, entrance, subscription.

en route, *a.* on the way, flying, driving, traveling, midway, in passage, on the road (to), making headway toward, bound, heading toward.—*Ant.* **motionless,** delayed, stalled.

enslave, *v.* bind, imprison, incarcerate, shut in, enclose, confine, hold under, subjugate, restrain, oppress, restrict, co-

erce, check, subdue, capture, suppress, make a slave of, hold in bondage, compel, chain, jail, deprive, tie, shackle.

enslavement, *n.* oppression, subjection, servitude; see **slavery 1.**

ensnare, *v.* entrap, trap, snare; see **catch 1.**

ensure, *v.* secure, assure, warrant; see **guarantee 1.**

entail, *v.* occasion, necessitate, evoke; see **cause.**

entangle, *v.* ensnare, entrap, trap, involve, complicate, snarl, corner, catch, tangle, ravel, unsettle, *foul or mess up, *goof.—*Ant.* **liberate,** disentangle, free.

entanglement, *n.* complexity, intricacy, complication; see **difficulty 1, 2.**

enter, *v.* invade, set foot in, pass or come or drive or burst or rush or go or break or get or go in or into, penetrate, intrude, re-enter, slip, sneak, infiltrate, insert, *horn or butt or pile or move or edge in, *fall into, crowd or push in, worm oneself into.—*Ant.* **leave,** depart, exit.

entered, *a.* filed, listed, posted; see **recorded.**

enter into, *v.* engage in, take part (in), become part of; see **join 2.**

enter on or **upon,** *v.* start, take up, make a beginning; see **begin 2.**

enterprise, *n.* undertaking, endeavor, affair; see **business.**

entertain, *v.* 1. [To keep others amused] amuse, cheer, please, interest, enliven, delight, divert, beguile, charm, captivate, inspire, stimulate, satisfy, humor, distract, indulge, flatter, relax, make merry, comfort.—*Ant.* **tire,** bore, weary. 2. [To act as host or hostess] receive, invite, treat, charm, feed, dine, wine, give a party, do the honors, welcome, give a warm reception (to), receive with open arms.—*Ant.* **bore,** keep aloof, neglect, ignore.

entertained, *a.* amused, diverted, pleased, occupied, charmed, cheered, interested, relaxed, delighted, enjoying oneself, happy, in good humor, in good company.—*Ant.* **bored,** depressed, irritated.

entertainer, *n.* performer, player, artist; see **actor.**

entertaining, *a.* diverting, amusing, engaging, enchanting, sprightly, lively, witty, clever, interesting, gay, charming, enjoyable, delightful, funny, pleasing, cheerful, relaxing, moving, inspiring, captivating, thrilling, entrancing, stirring, poignant, impressive, soul-stirring, stimulating, absorbing, exciting, provocative, fascinating, ravishing, satisfying, seductive; see also **funny 1.**—*Ant.* **boring,** irritating, **dull.**

entertainment, *n.* amusement, enjoyment, merriment, fun, pleasure, sport, recreation, pastime, diversion, relaxation, distraction, play, feast, banquet, picnic, show, television, the movies, treat, game, party, spree.

*enthuse, v. applaud, admire, be enthusiastic about; see praise 1.

*enthused, a. excited, approving, eager; see enthusiastic.

enthusiasm, n. fervor, ardor, eagerness; see zeal.

enthusiast, n. 1. [An impetuous, zealous person] zealot, fanatic, fan; see believer 2. [One who has warm personal interest] partisan, supporter, participant; see follower.

enthusiastic, a. interested, fascinated, willing, thrilled, fevered, concerned, pleased, excited, attracted, exhilarated, anxious, eager, *dying to, inflamed, absorbed, devoted, diligent, ardent, fiery, longing, desiring, spirited, zestful, fervent, ecstatic, impatient, delighted, enraptured, avid, *wild or crazy or mad about, *hot for, gung-ho, *aching to, *hyped on.—Ant. opposed, reluctant, apathetic.

entice, v. lure, allure, attract; see fascinate.

enticement, n. lure, bait, promise; see attraction.

entire, a. complete, untouched, undamaged; see whole 1, 2.

entirely, a. 1. [Completely] totally, fully, wholly; see completely. 2. [Exclusively] uniquely, solely, undividedly; see only 1.

entirety, n. total, aggregate, sum; see whole.

entitle, v. authorize, empower, qualify; see allow.

entity, n. existence, substance, actuality; see reality.

entourage, n. retinue, associates, followers; see following.

entrails, n. viscera, guts, insides; see intestines.

entrance, n. 1. [The act of coming in] ingress, progress, incoming, ingoing, arrival, access, entry, passage, approach, induction, initiation, admission, admittance, appearance, introduction, penetration, trespass, debut, enrollment, invasion, immigration.—Ant. escape, exit, issue. 2. [The opening that permits entry] gate, door, doorway, entry, gateway, portal, opening, passage, staircase, porch, hall, hallway, path, way, entrance or passageway, threshold, lobby, corridor, approach.

entrap, v. catch, ensnare, decoy; see catch 1.

entrapment, n. snare, ambush, ruse; see trap 1.

entree, n. main course, main dish, meat dish; see meal.

entrepreneur, n. manager, contractor, producer; see businessman.

entrust, v. deposit with, trust to, leave with; see trust 4.

entry, n. approach, hall, lobby, foyer, door, gate; see entrance 2.

enumerate, v. list, mention, identify; see record 1.

enumeration, n. inventory, catalogue, register; see record 1.

envelop, v. encompass, contain, hide; see surround 1, wrap.

envelope, n. receptacle, pouch, pocket, bag, container, box, covering, case, wrapper, wrapping, enclosure, cover, casing.

enviable, a. welcome, good, superior; see excellent.

envious, a. covetous, desirous, resentful, desiring, wishful, longing for, aspiring, greedy, grasping, craving, begrudging, green-eyed, green with envy; see also jealous.—Ant. generous, trustful, charitable.

environment, n. conditions, living conditions, circumstances, surroundings, scene, external conditions, background, setting, habitat, situation.

envoy, n. emissary, medium, intermediary; see agent.

envy, n. jealousy, ill-will, spite, rivalry, opposition, grudge, malice, prejudice, malevolence, the evil eye, enviousness, jealous competition, backbiting, maliciousness, bad sportsmanship, *the green-eyed monster.

envy, v. grudge, begrudge, covet, lust after, crave, be envious of, feel ill toward, feel resentful toward, have a grudge against, object to.

eon, n. eternity, cycle, time; see age 3.

epic, a. heroic, classic, grand; see important 1.

epic, n. narrative or heroic poem or story, saga, legend; see poem, story.

epidemic, n. plague, scourge, pestilence; see illness 1.

epidermis, n. cuticle, dermis, hide; see skin.

episode, n. happening, occurrence, interlude; see event 1, 2.

epoch, n. era, period, time; see age 3.

equal, a. even, regular, like, same, identical, similar, uniform, invariable, fair, just, impartial, unbiased, to the same degree, on a footing with, without distinction, equitable, identical in size or value or quantity, one and the same, of a piece, level, parallel, corresponding, equivalent, according, proportionate, comparable, tantamount.—Ant. irregular, unequal, uneven.

equal, n. parallel, match, counterpart, complement, peer, fellow, twin, double, likeness, companion, copy, duplicate, rival, competitor.

equal, *v.* match, equalize, make equal *or* alike, rank with, be the same in quantity *or* value *or* number *or* degree, rival, touch, equate, co-ordinate, approach, live *or* come up to, amount to, consist of, comprise, be made *or* composed of, measure up (to), check with, even off, break even, come to, compare, accord *or* square *or* tally with, agree, correspond, be tantamount to, be identical, meet, rise to (meet).

equality, *n.* balance, parity, uniformity, sameness, likeness, identity, evenness, equilization, equilibrium, impartiality, fairness, civil rights, equivalence, lack of distinction, tolerance, *all for one and one for all, *six of one and half a dozen of the other, *even Stephen.—*Ant.* injustice, inequality, unfairness.

equalize, *v.* make even *or* equal, balance, equate, match, level, adjust, establish equilibrium, socialize, even up.

equally, *a.* evenly, symmetrically, proportionately, co-ordinately, equivalently, on a level, both, either...or, impartially, justly, fairly, across the board, on even terms, as well as, the same for one as for another.

equal to, *a.* adequate (for), capable, qualified; see **able.**

equate, *v.* 1. [To equalize] make equal, average, balance; see **equalize.** 2. [To compare] liken, associate, relate; see **compare 1.**

equation, *n.* mathematical statement, formal statement of equivalence, chemical statement. Kinds of equations include the following—linear, quadratic, conic, cubic.

equator, *n.* middle, circumference of the earth, tropics; see **jungle.**

equatorial, *a.* tropical, mediterranean, central, see **hot 1.**

equilibrium, *n.* stability, center of gravity, equipoise; see **balance 2.**

equip, *v.* furnish, outfit, implement; see **provide 1.**

equipment, *n.* material, materiel, tools, facilities, implements, utensils, apparatus, furnishings, appliances, paraphernalia, belongings, devices, outfit, accessories, attachments, extras, conveniences, articles, tackle, rig, machinery, fittings, trappings, fixtures, supplies, accompaniments, gear, fixings, gadgets, things; see also **machine, part 3.**

equipped, *a.* outfitted, furnished, supplied, rigged (up), fitted (out), arrayed, dressed, accoutered, assembled, readied, provided, implemented, decked, completed, supplemented, set up.

equitable, *a.* impartial, just, moral; see **fair 1.**

equity, *n.* investment, money, outlay; see **property 1.**

equivalent, *a.* commensurate, comparable, similar; see **equal.**

era, *n.* epoch, period, date; see **age 3, time 2.**

eradicate, *v.* eliminate, exterminate, annihilate; see **destroy.**

eradication, *n.* extermination, annihilation, elimination; see **destruction 2.**

erase, *v.* delete, efface, omit, obliterate, cut, clean, nullify, eradicate; see **cancel.**

erect, *a.* upright, vertical, perpendicular; see **straight 1.**

erect, *v.* construct, raise, fabricate; see **build.**

erected, *a.* constructed, completed, raised; see **built.**

erection, *n.* building, erecting, constructing; see **construction 2.**

erode, *v.* disintegrate, corrode, consume; see **disintegrate.**

erosion, *n.* wearing away, decrease, carrying *or* eating away; see **destruction 1, 2.**

erotic, *a.* amorous, lecherous, carnal; see **sensual 1, 2.**

err, *v.* misjudge, blunder, be mistaken; see **fail 1.**

errand, *n.* mission, task, commission; see **duty 1.**

erratic, *a.* 1. [Wandering] nomadic, rambling, roving; see **wandering 1.** 2. [Strange] eccentric, queer, irregular; see **unusual 2.** 3. [Variable] inconsistent, unpredictable, variable; see **irregular 1.**

erring, *a.* mistaken, faulty, delinquent; see **wrong 1.**

erroneous, *a.* untrue, inaccurate, incorrect; see **false 1.**

error, *n.* blunder, mistake, fault, oversight, inaccuracy, omission, deviation, fall, slip, wrong, lapse, miss, failure, slight, misunderstanding, flaw, *boner, bad job, *blooper, botch.

erupt, *v.* eruct, eject, emit; see **explode 1.**

eruption, *n.* burst, outburst, flow; see **explosion 1.**

escalate, *v.* heighten, intensify, make worse; see **increase.**

escalation, *n.* intensification, growth, acceleration; see **increase, rise 2.**

escapade, *n.* caper, adventure, prank; see **joke.**

escape, *n.* flight, retreat, disappearance, evasion, avoidance, leave, departure, withdrawal, liberation, deliverance, rescue, freedom, release.—*Ant.* **imprisonment,** retention, grasp.

escape, *v.* flee, fly, leave, depart, elude, avoid, evade, shun, run off *or* away, make off, disappear, vanish, steal off *or* away, flow out, get away (from), break out or away, desert, slip away, elope, *run out (on), go scot-free, decamp, *duck out, get clear of, break loose; cut and run, worm out (of), *cut loose, *clear out, *make oneself scarce, *bail out, crawl out of, save one's neck, *scram, *make a break.—Ant. return, come back, remain.

escaped, a. out, at liberty, liberated; see **free 2.**

escort, n. guide, attendant, guard; see **companion.**

escort, v. go with, attend, take out; see **accompany, date 2.**

esophagus, n. trachea, jugular region, gullet; see **throat.**

especially, a. 1. [To an unusual degree] particularly, unusually, abnormally, extraordinarily, uncommonly, peculiarly, pre-eminently, eminently, supremely, remarkably, strangely, curiously, notably, uniquely, singularly, to a special or marked or notable degree, in particular, above all. 2. [For one more than for others] chiefly, mainly, primarily; see **principally.**

espionage, n. undercover work, reconnaissance, watching; see **intrusion.**

espouse, v. advocate, adopt, uphold; see **support 2.**

essay, n. dissertation, treatise, tract; see **writing 2.**

essence, n. 1. [Basic material] pith, core, kernel, vein, gist, root, nature, basis, being, essential quality, reality, constitution, substance, nucleus, vital part, base, primary element, germ, heart, marrow, backbone, soul, bottom, life, grain, structure, principle, character, fundamentals. 2. [Distinctive quality] principle, nature, essential quality; see **characteristic.**

essential, a. 1. [Necessary] imperative, required, indispensable; see **necessary 1.** 2. [Rooted in the basis or essence] basic, primary, quintessential; see **fundamental 1.**

essentially, a. basically, fundamentally, radically, at bottom, at heart, centrally, originally, intimately, chiefly, naturally, inherently, permanently, necessarily, primarily, significantly, importantly, at the heart of, in effect, in essence, materially, in the main, at first, characteristically, intrinsically, substantially, typically, approximately, precisely, exactly, actually, truly, really; see also **principally.**

establish, v. 1. [To set up in a formal manner] institute, found, authorize; see **organize 2.** 2. [To work or settle in a permanent place] build or set up, install, build, erect, set, plant, root, build, place, settle (in), practice, live, ground.—Ant. unsettle, **leave,** break up. 3. [To prove] verify, authenticate, con-

firm; see **prove. 4.** [To make secure] fix, secure, stabilize; see **fasten 1.**

established, a. 1. [Set up to endure] endowed, founded, organized, instituted, set up, originated, chartered, incorporated, settled, begun, initiated, completed, finished; see also **finished 1, certain 2.**—Ant. **temporary,** unsound, insolvent. 2. [Conclusively proved] approved, verified, guaranteed, endorsed, demonstrated, determined, confirmed, substantiated, assured, concluded, authenticated, found out, achieved, upheld, certain, validated, identified, proved, undeniable.—Ant. **false,** invalidated, untrue.

establishing, n. verifying, demonstrating, confirming; see **proof 1.**

establishment, n. 1. [A business, organization, or the like] company, corporation, enterprise; see **business 4.** 2. [The act of proving] verification, substantiation, demonstration; see **proof 1.**

estate, n. property, bequest, inheritance, fortune, endowment, wealth, legacy, heritage, belongings, effects, earthly possessions, personal property, private property.

esteem, n. regard, respect, appreciation; see **admiration.**

esteem, v. prize, respect, appreciate; see **admire.**

esthetic, a. creative, appreciative, emotional; see **artistic, beautiful.**

estimate, n. evaluation, assessment, guess, appraisal, estimation, calculation, gauging, rating, survey, measure, reckoning; see **judgment 2.**

estimate, v. rate, value, measure, calculate, appraise, assess, account, compute, evaluate, count, number, reckon, guess, judge, figure, plan, outline, run over, rank, furnish an estimate, set a value on, appraise, assay, consider, predict, suppose, reason, think through, surmise, determine, decide, budget.

estimated, a. supposed, approximated, guessed at; see **likely 1.**

estimation, n. opinion, appraisal, valuation; see **judgment 2.**

et cetera (etc.), a. and so forth, and so on, and others; see **and.**

etching, n. print, colored print, colored etching; see **engraving.**

eternal, a. endless, interminable, continual, unbroken, continuous, continued, unceasing, ceaseless, constant, unending, undying, enduring, persistent, always, uninterrupted, everlasting, perpetual, never-ending, indefinite, permanent, ageless, boundless, timeless, eternal, immortal, forever, indeterminable, immeasurable, having no limit, enduring, imperishable, illimitable, to one's dying day, *for ever and ever.—Ant. finite, **temporary,** ending.

eternally, *a.* endlessly, continually, perpetually; see **regularly.**

eternity, *n.* endlessness, forever, endless *or* infinite duration, timelessness, *forever and a day, world without end, the future, infinity, all eternity, *for ever and ever.—*Ant.* moment, instant, second:

ethical, *a.* humane, moral, respectable; see **decent** 2, **honest, noble** 1, 2.

ethics, *n.* conduct, morality, mores, decency, integrity, moral conduct, social values, moral code, right and wrong, natural law, honesty, goodness, honor, social laws, human nature, the Golden Rule.

etiquette, *n.* conduct, manners, social graces; see **behavior.**

Eucharist, *n.* sacrament, Mass, communion; see **sacrament.**

eulogize, *v.* laud, extol, applaud; see **praise** 1.

eulogy, *n.* elegy, glorification, commendation; see **praise** 2.

euphoria, *n.* relaxation, health, wellbeing; see **happiness.**

Europe, *n.* the Continent, continental Europe, part of Eurasia *or* the Eurasian landmass. Terms associated with countries, areas, and political divisions in Europe include the following—western, northern, southern, central, eastern, etc. Europe; (the) Mediterranean world, the Low Countries, Balkan states, Adriatic states, Baltic states, Slavic countries, Scandinavian peninsula, Holy Roman Empire, Hellenic *or* Balkan peninsula, Albania, Austria, Austria-Hungary, Bulgaria, Czechoslovakia, Denmark, Norway, Sweden, Iceland, Finland, France, Provence, Normandy, Brittany, Germany, West Germany, East Germany, Prussia, Bavaria, Greece, Hungary, Iceland, Republic of Ireland, Eire, Ulster, Italy, San Marino, Sicily, Liechtenstein, Luxemborg, Malta, Monaco, (The) Netherlands, Holland, Norway, Poland, Portugal, Romania, Spain, Switzerland, Turkey, Union of Soviet Socialist Republics, USSR, Russia, the Ukraine, Lithuania, Latvia, Estonia, Georgia, United Kingdom of Great Britain and Northern Ireland, England, Britain, Scotland, Wales, the British Isles, the Vatican, Yugoslavia, Serbia, Croatia, Montenegro; see also **England, France, Germany, Italy, Spain.**

European, *a.* Continental, Old Country *or* World, Eurasian, Caucasian, Indo-European, Motherland, Western, West European, East European. Terms associated with particular areas include the following—Anglo-Saxon, British, English, Irish, Scottish, Scots, Welsh, Cornish, Kentish, French, Norman, Gallic, German, Germanic, Dutch, Netherlandish, Belgian, Flemish, Low German, Saxon, Bavarian, Prussian, Gothic, Teutonic, Nordic, Scandinavian, Danish, Swedish, Norwegian, Icelandic, Swiss, Greek, Hellenic, Athenian, Corinthian, Spartan, Peloponnesian, Mycenean, Cretan, Thracian, Ionian, Corinthian, Slovak(ian), Rumanian, Bulgarian, Slav(ic), Aegean, Balkan, Adriatic, Yugoslavian, Serbian, Croatian, Austro-Hungarian, Czechoslovak(ian), Czech, Bohemian, Turk, Turkish, Russian, Polish, Baltic, Latvian, Lithuanian, Ukranian, Finnish, Lap, Italian, Latin, Roman, Venetian, Florentine, Neapolitan, Sicilian, Maltese, Sardinian, Tyrolese, Apennine, Spanish, Hispanic, Iberian, Portuguese, Catalan, Basque, Majorcan, Castilian, Andalusian, Jewish, Yiddish; see also **English, German, Greek, Italian, Roman, Spanish.**

European, *n.* Terms associated with Europeans from particular areas include the following—Englishman, Briton, Scotsman, Scot, Highlander, Lowlander, Welshman, Irishman, Ulsterman, Cornishman, Celt, Anglo-Saxon; Frenchman, Norman, Basque; German, Teuton, Prussian, Bavarian, Saxon, Swiss; Dutchman, Hollander, Belgian, Scandinavian, Dane, Norwegian, Swede, Icelander, Finn, Lap; Italian; Roman, Sicilian, Venetian, Florentine; Spaniard, Castilian, Andalusian, Portuguese; Austrian, Hungarian, Czechoslovak(ian), Czech, Bohemian, Slovak, Slav, Russian, Pole, Lithuanian, Latvian, Estonian, Ukrainian, White Russian, Yugoslav(ian), Bulgarian, Rumanian, Balkan, Greek, Turk, Jew, Gipsy; see also **European, a.** French, German, Greek.

evacuate, *v.* 1. [To empty] void, exhaust, deplete; see **remove** 1. 2. [To abandon] vacate, desert, leave; see **abandon** 1.

evacuation, *n.* 1. [Removal] draining, depletion, exhaustion; see **removal.** 2. [Withdrawal] abandonment, removal, retreat; see **departure.**

evade, *v.* lie, prevaricate, dodge, shun, put off, avoid, elude, baffle, quibble, shift, mystify, cloak, cover, conceal, deceive, screen, veil, hide, drop the subject, *pretend, confuse, dodge the issue, beat around the bush, *give (someone) the run-around, *throw off the scent, lead one a merry chase, pass up, put off, get around, lie out of; see also **avoid.**—*Ant.* **explain,** make clear, elucidate.

evaluate, *v.* appraise, judge, assess; see **decide, estimate.**

evangelical, *a.* pious, fervent, spiritual; see **religious** 2.

evangelist, *n.* preacher, missionary, revivalist; see **minister 1.**

evangelize, *v.* proselytize, instruct, convert; see **preach.**

evaporate, *v.* diffuse, vanish, fade, dissolve, dissipate, steam, steam *or* boil away, fume, distill, turn to steam, rise in a fog *or* mist.

evaporation, *n.* drying, dehydration, vanishing, steaming *or* boiling away, vaporization, distillation, dissipation, disappearance, vanishing into thin air.

evasion, *n.* quibble, subterfuge, equivocation; see **lie 1, trick 1.**

evasive, *a.* elusory, fugitive, shifty; see **sly 1.**

eve, *n.* night *or* evening before, night preceding, evening; see **night 1.**

even, *a.* 1. [Lying in a smooth plane] smooth, level, surfaced; see **flat 1. 2.** [Similar] uniform, unbroken, homogeneous; see **alike, regular 3. 3.** [Equal] commensurate, coterminous, equivalent; see **equal 4.** [In addition] also, too, as well; see **and.** —**break even,** make nothing, tie, neither win nor lose; see **balance 2.**

evening, *n.* twilight, dusk, late afternoon; see **night 1.**

evenly, *a.* 1. [On an even plane] smoothly, regularly, without bumps *or* lumps, uniformly, placidly, unvaryingly, steadily, constantly, fluently, on an even keel, without variation, neither up nor down. **2.** [Equally proportioned or distributed] exactly, justly, fairly, precisely, equally, impartially, identically, equitably, symmetrically, proportionately, synonymously, analogously, correspondingly, tied, alike, *fifty-fifty, *squarely.—*Ant.* wrongly, unfairly.

evenness, *n.* smoothness, similarity, likeness; see **regularity.**

event, *n.* occurrence, happening, episode, incident, circumstance, affair, phenomenon, development, function, transaction, experience, appearance, turn, tide, shift, phase, accident, chance, pass, situation, story, case, matter, occasion, catastrophe, mishap, mistake, experience, parade, triumph, coincidence, miracle, adventure, holiday, wonder, marvel, celebration, crisis, predicament, misfortune, situation, calamity, emergency, *something to write home about; see **also disaster, holiday, wonder 2.** —**in any event,** anyway, no matter what happens, however; see **anyhow.** —**in the event of** (*or* that), in case of, if it should happen that, if there should happen to be; see **if.**

eventful, *a.* momentous, memorable, signal; see **important 1.**

eventual, *a.* inevitable, ultimate, consequent; see **last 1.**

eventually, *a.* in the end, at last, ultimately; see **finally 2.**

ever, *a.* eternally, always, at all times; see **regularly.** —*for ever and a day,** always, for ever and ever, perpetually; see **forever 1.**

evergreen, *n.* coniferous tree, ornamental shrub, fir; see **pine, tree.**

everlasting, *a.* permanent, unending, perpetual; see **eternal.**

every, *a.* each one, all, without exception; see **each 1.**

everybody, *n.* each one, every one, all, the public, old and young; men, women, and children; the people, the populace, the voters; the buying *or* voting, etc., public; generality, anybody, all sorts, the masses, *the man on *or* in the street, you and I; see also **man 1.**—*Ant.* **nobody,** no one, not a one.

everyday, *a.* commonplace, normal, plain; see **common 1.**

every day, *a.* always, all the time, frequently; see **regularly.**

every now and then *or* *every so often,** *a.* sometimes, occasionally, once in a while; see **frequently.**

everyone, *pron.* all, each person, whoever; see **everybody.**

everything, *pron.* all, all things, the universe, the whole complex, the whole, many things, all that, every little thing, the whole kit and kaboodle; lock stock and barrel; the works, the lot.

everywhere, *a.* everyplace, here and there, at all points *or* places, wherever (one turns), at each point, without exception, universally, at all times and places; here, there and everywhere; in every quarter *or* direction, on all hands, all over the place, throughout, *to the four winds, *in all creation, *to hell and back, *inside and out, *from beginning to end, high and low, all around, the world over.

evict, *v.* remove, expel, oust; see **dismiss.**

eviction, *n.* ouster, ejection, dispossession; see **removal.**

evidence, *n.* testimony, data, confirmation; see **proof 1.** —**in evidence,** evident, visible, manifest; see **obvious 1, 2.**

evident, *a.* apparent, visible, manifest; see **obvious 1.**

evidently, *a.* seemingly, obviously, so far as one can see; see **apparently.**

evil, *a.* immoral, sinful, corrupt; see **bad.**

evil, *n.* 1. [The quality of being evil] sin, wickedness, depravity, crime, sinfulness, corruption, vice, immorality, iniquity, perversity, badness, vileness, baseness, meanness, malevolence, indecency, hatred, viciousness, wrong, debauchery, lewdness, wantonness, grossness, foulness, degradation, obscenity.—*Ant.* **virtue**, good, goodness. 2. [A harmful or malicious action] ill, harm, mischief, misfortune, scandal, calamity, pollution, contamination, catastrophe, blow, disaster, plague, outrage, foul play, *ill wind, *crying shame, *double cross, *raw deal.

evildoer, *n.* malefactor, sinner, wrongdoer; see **criminal**.

evoke, *v.* summon forth, call out, invoke; see **summon**.

evolution, *n.* growth, unfolding, natural process; see **development**.

evolve, *v.* result, unfold, emerge; see **develop 3, grow 2**.

exact, *a.* 1. [Accurate] precise, correct, perfect; see **accurate 2, definite 1**. 2. [Clear] sharp, distinct, clear-cut; see **definite 2**.

exacting, *a.* precise, careful, critical; see **difficult 1, 2**.

exactly, *a.* precisely, specifically, correctly; see **detailed**.

exactness, *n.* precision, nicety, scrupulousness; see **accuracy**.

exaggerate, *v.* overestimate, overstate, misrepresent, falsify, magnify, expand, amplify, pile up, heighten, intensify, distort, enlarge (on), stretch, overdo, misquote, go to extremes, give color to, misjudge, elaborate, romance, embroider, color, make too much of, lie, fabricate, corrupt, *paint in glowing colors, *carry too far, lay it on (thick), make a mountain out of a molehill, *cook up, build up, make much of, make the most of—*Ant.* **underestimate**, tell the truth, minimize.

exaggerated, *a.* colored, magnified, overwrought, extravagant, preposterous, impossible, fabulous, sensational, spectacular, melodramatic, out of proportion, fantastic, high-flown, farfetched, false, distorted, fabricated, strained, artificial, glaring, pronounced, unrealistic, *whopping, too much—*Ant.* **accurate**, exact, precise.

exaggeration, *n.* overestimation, misrepresentation, extravagance, elaboration, coloring, flight of fancy, fantasy, fancy, stretch of the imagination, figure of speech, yarn, making a mountain out of a molehill, *tall story, *whopper, *playup.—*Ant.* **truth**, accuracy, understatement.

exalt, *v.* commend, glorify, laud; see **praise 1**.

exaltation, *n.* rapture, elation, rhapsody; see **happiness**.

examination, *n.* 1. [The act of seeking evidence] search, research, survey, scrutiny, investigation, inquiry (into), inspection, observation, checking, exploration, analysis, audit, study, questioning, testing program, inquest, test,

trial, cross-examination, *third degree. 2. [A formal test] experiment, review, questionnaire, battery, quiz, *exam, *make-up, *midterm, final, blue book, orals, *writtens; see **test**. 3. [A medical checkup] checkup, (physical) examination, physical; see **test**.

examine, *v.* 1. [To inspect with care] inspect, analyze, criticize, scrutinize, investigate, go *or* inquire into, scan, probe, sift, explore, reconnoitor, audit, take stock *or* note of, make an inventory of, consider, canvass, find *or* search out, review, assay, check, check out, check up on, re-examine, go back over, concentrate on, give one's attention to, look at *or* into *or* over, conduct research on, run checks on, put to the test, sound *or* feel out, probe, subject to scrutiny, peer *or* look *or* pry into, hold up to the light, finger, pick over, sample, experiment with, *give the once-over, *size up, smell out *or* around, see about *or* into, poke into, nose around, look up and down, *go over with a fine-toothed comb, *dig into. 2. [To test] question, interrogate, cross-examine; see **test**.

examined, *a.* checked, tested, inspected; see **investigated**.

examiner, *n.* tester, questioner, observer; see **inspector**.

example, *n.* 1. [A representative] illustration, representation, warning, sample, citation, case in point, concrete example, case, prototype, archetype, stereotype, original, copy, instance, quotation. 2. [Something to be imitated] standard, pattern, sample; see **model 2**. —**set an example**, instruct, behave as a model, set a pattern; see **teach 1**.

excavate, *v.* shovel, empty, hollow out; see **dig 1**.

excavation, *n.* cavity, hollow, pit; see **hole 1, tunnel**.

exceed, *v.* excel, outdo, overdo, outdistance, pass, overstop, outrun, beat, get *or* have the better of, go by *or* beyond, surpass, transcend, eclipse, rise above, pass over, *run circles around, *get *or* have the edge on, excel in, *have it all over (someone), *get the drop on, *beat to the draw, *break the record, have the best of, *have the jump on, be ahead of the game, get *or* have the advantage, gain the upper hand.

exceedingly, *a.* greatly, remarkably, in a marked degree; see **very**.

excel, *v.* surpass, transcend, improve upon; see **exceed**.

excellence, *n.* superiority, worth, distinction; see **perfection**.

excellent, *a.* first-class, premium, choice, first, choicest, prime, high, picked, the best obtainable, select, exquisite, highgrade, (very) fine, finest, good, desirable, admirable, distinctive, attractive, great, highest, superior, exceptional, superb, striking, supreme, unique, custom made, incomparable, surprising, transcendent, priceless, rare, invaluable, highest priced, magnificent, wonderful, skillfull, above par, superlative, worthy, refined, well-done, cultivated, to be desired, competent, skilled, notable, first-rate, *terrific, *sensational, *sharp, *groovy, all right, *A-1, *grade A, *classy, *top-notch, *cream, *tops.—*Ant.* poor, inferior, imperfect.

excellently, *a.* perfectly, exquisitely, splendidly; see **well 2.**

except, *prep.* excepting, excluding, rejecting, omitting, barring, save, but, with the exclusion *or* exception of, other than, if not, not for, without, outside of, aside from, leaving out, exempting, minus.

except, *v.* exclude, reject, leave out; see **bar 1.**

exception, *n.* exclusion, omission, making an exception of *or* for, rejection, barring, reservation, leaving out, segregation, limitation, exemption, elimination, expulsion, excusing. —**take exception (to),** 1. [To differ] object, disagree, demur; see **differ 1. 2.** [To dislike] resent, be offended, take offense; see **dislike.**

exceptional, *a.* uncommon, extraordinary, rare; see **unusual 1, 2.**

exceptionally, *a.* unusually, particularly, abnormally; see **especially 1.**

excerpt, *n.* selection, extract, citation; see **quotation.**

excess, *n.* **1.** [More than is needed] profusion, abundance, surplus, remainder, too much *or* many, exorbitance, waste, wastefulness, luxuriance, lavishness, over-supply, plenty, *bellyful, *too much of a good thing.—*Ant.* lack, dearth, deficiency. **2.** [Conduct that is not temperate] prodigality, dissipation, intemperance; see **greed, waste 1.** —**in excess of,** additional, surplus, more than; see **extra.** —**to excess,** too much, excessively, extravagantly; see **extreme.**

excessive, *a.* immoderate, extravagant, exhorbitant; see **extreme.**

excessively, *a.* extravagantly, extremely, unreasonably; see **very.**

exchange, *n.* **1.** [The act of replacing one thing with another] transfer, substitution, replacement, change, rearrangement, shift, revision, sleight-of-hand, reciprocity, barter, correspondence, interdependence, buying and selling, negotiation, transaction, commerce, trade, give and take. **2.** [A substitution] change, shift, *swap, trade, interchange, replacing, shuffle, reciprocation, replacement, switch.

exchange, *v.* substitute, transfer, replace, go over to, give in exchange, remove,

pass to, reverse, provide a substitute *or* replacement, shuffle, shift, revise, rearrange, change, interchange, transact, reset, change hands, borrow from Peter to pay Paul, *swap. **2.** [To give and receive reciprocally] reciprocate, barter, trade with, buy and sell, deal *or* do business with, correspond, *swap.

exchanged, *a.* restored, traded, brought *or* sent back; see **returned.**

excitable, *a.* sensitive, high-strung, impatient; see **nervous.**

excite, *v.* stimulate, inflame, arouse, anger, delight, move, tease, worry, infuriate, madden, stir (up), fire (up), work up (to), goad, taunt, mock, provoke, incite, astound, amaze, annoy, jolt, fan the flames, carry away, warm, irritate, offend, bother.

excited, *a.* aroused, stimulated, inflamed, agitated, hot, annoyed, seething, wrought up, frantic, flushed, overwrought, restless, feverish, apprehensive, roused, disturbed, perturbed, flustered, upset, angry, tense, discomposed, embarrassed, hurt, angered, distracted, distraught, edgy, furious, beside oneself, delighted, eager, enthusiastic, frenzied, troubled, ruffled, moved, avid, hysterical, passionate, provoked, quickened, inspired, wild, nervous, animated, ill at ease, jumpy, *jittery, *turned on, *hyped up, *hopped up, *worked up, *in a tizzy, *up tight, *all nerves, *blue in the face, *on fire.—*Ant.* calm, reserved, self-confident.

excitedly, *a.* tensely, apprehensively, hysterically; see **excited.**

excitement, *n.* confusion, disturbance, tumult, enthusiasm, rage, turmoil, stir, excitation, agitation, movement, feeling, exhilaration, emotion, stimulation, drama, melodrama, activity, commotion, *fuss, hullabaloo, bother, dither, hubbub, bustle, *to-do.—*Ant.* peace, calm, quiet.

exciting, *a.* stimulating, moving, animating, provocative, arousing, arresting, stirring, thrilling, dangerous, breathtaking, overwhelming, interesting, new, mysterious, overpowering, inspiring, impressive, soul-stirring, sensational, astonishing, bracing, appealing, blood-curdling, racy, *hair-raising, *mind-blowing. —*Ant.* dull, pacifying, tranquilizing.

exclaim, *v.* cry *or* call out, burst out, assert, shout, call aloud, say loudly; see also **yell.**

exclamation, *n.* yell, clamor, vociferation; see **cry 1.**

exclude, *v.* shut out, reject, ban; see **bar 1, 2.**

exclusion, *n.* keeping out, rejection, elimination, prohibition, nonadmission, omission, segregation, isolation, blockade, repudiation, separation, eviction, dismissal, suspension, refusal, expulsion, barring.—*Ant.* welcome, invitation, inclusion.

exclusive, *a.* restricted, restrictive, fashionable, aristocratic, preferential, privileged, particular, licensed, select, private, segregated, prohibitive, clannish, independent, *swank.—*Ant.* free, inclusive, unrestricted.

exclusively, *a.* particularly, solely, completely; see **only 1.**

excommunicate, *v.* expel, curse, oust; see **dismiss.**

excommunication, *n.* expulsion, dismissal, suspension; see **removal.**

excrement, *n.* excretion, stool, fecal matter, offal, droppings, discharge, dung, manure, urine, effluvium, feces, sweat, perspiration, excreta.

excrete, *v.* remove, eliminate, eject, defecate, urinate, discharge, secrete, go to the bathroom *or* the toilet, answer a call of nature, pass, expel, exude, perspire, sweat, squeeze out, give off.

excretion, *n.* eliminating, elimination, urinating, discharging, secreting, secretion, defecation, ejecting, ejection, passing off.

excruciating, *a.* torturing, intense, agonizing; see **painful 1.**

excursion, *n.* jaunt, ramble, tour; see **journey.**

excusable, *a.* pardonable, forgivable, understandable, justifiable, reasonable, defensible, permissible, trivial, passable, slight, plausible, allowable, explainable, not excessive *or* fatal *or* too bad *or* inexcusable *or* injurious, moderate, temperate, all right, fair, within limits, O.K.

excuse, *n.* apology, reason, defense; see **explanation.** —a poor excuse for, inferior, poor, unsatisfactory; see **inadequate.** —make one's excuses (for), regret, apologize (for), offer an explanation (of); see **apologize, explain.**

excuse, *v.* pardon, forgive, justify, discharge, vindicate, apologize (for), release (from), dispense with *or* for, free, set free, overlook, purge, exempt (from), rationalize, acquit, condone, appease, reprieve, absolve, exonerate, clear (of), give absolution (to), pass over, give as an excuse, make excuses *or* allowances *or* apologies (for), grant amnesty (to), provide with an alibi (for), plead ignorance (of), whitewash, let off (easy), let go (Scot free), wink at, wipe the slate clean, shrug off, *take the rap for.

excused, *a.* forgiven, freed, permitted; see **pardoned.**

excuse me, *interj.* pardon me, forgive me, begging your pardon, I'm sorry.

execute, *v.* 1. [To carry out instructions] act, do, effect; see **perform 1.** 2. [To put to death] electrocute, hang, behead; see **kill 1.**

executed, *a.* 1. [Performed] completed, done, carried out; see **finished 1.** 2. [Formally put to death] killed, hanged, electrocuted, gassed, shot (at sunrise), sent before a firing squad, beheaded, guillotined, crucified, *sent to the chair, *fried, *cooked.

execution, *n.* punishment, capital punishment, killing, electrocution, hanging, gassing, beheading, decapitation, guillotining, crucifixion, martyrdom.

executive, *a.* administrative, governing, ruling; see **managing.**

executive, *n.* businessman, president, vice-president, secretary, treasurer, supervisor, chairman, dean, head, chief, superintendent, bureaucrat, leader, governor, controller, organizer, commander, director, boss, big shot, official, manager; see also **businessman, leader 2.**

exemplify, *v.* illustrate, give an example, represent; see **explain.**

exempt, *a.* free(d), clear(ed), liberated, privileged, excused, absolved, not subject to, released from, not responsible (to *or* for), set apart, excluded, released, not liable, unrestrained, unbound, uncontrolled, unrestricted, free(d) from, not restricted by *or* to, outside.—*Ant.* responsible, liable, subject.

exempt, *v.* free, liberate, pass by; see **excuse.**

exemption, *n.* exception, immunity, privilege; see **freedom.**

exercise, *n.* 1. [Action, undertaken for training] practice, exertion, drill, drilling, gymnastics, sports, calisthenics, workout. 2. [The means by which training is promoted] performance, action, activity; see **action.** 3. [Use] application, employment, operation; see **use 1.**

exercise, *v.* 1. [To move the body] stretch, bend, pull, tug, hike, work, promote muscle tone, labor, strain, loosen up, discipline, drill, execute, perform exercises, practice, take a walk, work out, limber *or* warm up; see also **train 1.** 2. [To use] employ, practice, exert, apply, operate, execute, sharpen, handle, utilize, devote, put in practice; see also **use 1.** 3. [To train] drill, discipline, give training to; see **teach, train 1.**

exert, *v.* put forth, bring to bear, exercise; see **use 1.**

exertion, *n.* struggle, attempt, endeavor; see **effort.**

exert oneself, *v.* strive, attempt, endeavor; see **try 1.**

exhalation, *n.* emanation, vapor, air; see **breath.**

exhaust, *v.* 1. [To consume strength] debilitate, tire, wear out *or* down; see

weaken 1, 2, **weary** 1, 2. 2. [To use entirely] use up, take the last of, deplete; see **wear 3.**

exhausted, *a.* 1. [Without further physical resources] debilitated, wearied, worn; see **tired, weak 1.** 2. [Having nothing remaining] all gone, consumed, used; see **empty.**

exhaustion, *n.* weariness, fatigue, depletion; see **fatigue.**

exhibit, *n.* show, performance, presentation; see **display.**

exhibit, *v.* show, present, manifest; see **display.**

exhibited, *a.* shown, presented, advertised; see **shown 1.**

exhibition, *n.* exposition, fair, carnival; see **show 1.**

exile, *n.* 1. [Banishment] expulsion, deportation, expatriation, ostracism, displacement, separation. 2. [An outcast] fugitive, outlaw, man without a country; see **refugee.**

exile, *v.* ostracize, outlaw, cast out; see **banish.**

exist, *v.* 1. [To have being] breathe, live, survive; see **be 1.** 2. [To carry on life] be alive, endure, go on; see **survive 1.**

existence, *n.* 1. [The carrying on of life] being, actuality, reality; see **life 1.** 2. [The state of being] presence, actuality, permanence; see **reality.**

existing, *a.* for the time being, temporary, just now; see **present 1.**

exit, *n.* 1. [A means of egress] way *or* passage out, outlet, opening; see **door.** 2. [The act of leaving] going, farewell, exodus; see **departure.**

exorbitant, *a.* excessive, extravagant, too much; see **wasteful.**

exotic, *a.* 1. [Foreign] imported, not local *or* native, extrinsic; see **foreign 1, 2.** [Peculiar] strange, fascinating, different; see **foreign 2, unusual 2.**

expand, *v.* extend, augment, dilate; see **grow 1.**

expanse, *n.* breadth, width, length, extent, reach, stretch, distance, area, belt, space, field, territory, span, spread, room, scope, range, compass, sphere, margin, sweep, radius, wilderness, region, immensity.

expansion, *n.* enlargement, augmentation, extension; see **increase 1.**

expatriate, *n.* exile, emigrant, outcast; see **refugee.**

expatriate, *v.* exile, ostracize, deport; see **banish.**

expect, *v.* 1. [To anticipate] await, look for, look forward to, count *or* plan on, assume, suppose, lean on, *feel it in one's bones, wait for, hope for; see also **anticipate.** 2. [To require] demand, insist upon, exact; see **require 2. 3.** [To assume] presume, suppose, suspect; see **assume.**

expectancy, *n.* hope, prospect, likelihood; see **anticipation.**

expectant, *a.* 1. [Characterized by anticipation] expecting, hoping, hopeful, waiting, awaiting, in anticipation, watchful, vigilant, eager, ready, prepared, in suspense, gaping, wide-eyed, on edge, itching, *raring, wild, *with bated breath.– *Ant.* **indifferent,** nonchalant, **unprepared.** 2. [Anticipating birth] pregnant, parturient, expecting; see **pregnant.**

expectation, *n.* hope, belief, prospect; see **anticipation.**

expected, *a.* looked for, counted upon, contemplated, looked forward to, hoped for, relied upon, foreseen, predictable, predetermined, foretold, prophesied, planned *or* prepared for, budgeted, (included) within (normal) expectations, *in the works *or* the cards, coming up, *in the bag; see also **likely.**

expecting, *a.* expectant, due, about to become a mother; see **pregnant.**

expediency, *n.* advantageousness, efficiency, profitableness; see **usefulness.**

expedient, *a.* profitable, useful, convenient; see **practical.**

expedition, *n.* 1. [Travel undertaken] excursion, voyage, campaign; see **journey.** 2. [That which undertakes travel] party, hunters, explorers, pioneers, traders, soldiers, scouts, archaeologists, tourists, sightseers, caravan, posse; see also **crowd 1.**

expel, *v.* 1. [To eject] get rid of, cast out, dislodge; see **eject. 2.** [To dismiss] suspend, discharge, oust; see **dismiss.**

expend, *v.* pay (out), write checks for, lay out; see **spend 1.**

expenditure, *n.* outgo, investment, payment; see **expense 1.**

expense, *n.* expenditure, responsibility, obligation, loan, mortgage, lien, debt, liability, investment, insurance, upkeep, alimony, debit, account, cost, price, outlay, charge, payment, outgo, value, worth, sum, amount, risk, capital, rate, tax, carrying charges, budgeted items, cost of materials, overhead, time, payroll, investment.–*Ant.* **profit,** income, receipts. –**at the expense of,** paid by, at the cost of, charged to; see **owed.**

expenses, *n.* expense, living, cost of living, damages, outlay, overhead, expense account, traveling expenses, living expenses, costs, lodging, room and board, incidentals, carrying charge.

expensive, *a.* dear, precious, valuable, invaluable, rare, high-priced, costly, prized, choice, rich, priceless, high, too high, unreasonable, exorbitant, extravagant, at a premium, *out of sight, at great cost, sky-high, *steep, *stiff.–*Ant.* inexpensive, **cheap,** low.

experience, *n.* background, skill, knowledge, wisdom, practice, maturity, judgment, practical knowledge, sense, patience, caution, *know-how; see also **background** 2.

experience, v. undergo, feel, live through; see **endure 2, feel 2**.

experienced, a. skilled, practiced, instructed, accomplished, versed, qualified, able, skillful, knowing, trained, wise, expert, veteran, mature, with a good background, rounded, *knowing the score *or* the ropes *or* all the answers, *having been around *or* through the mill, *broken in.—*Ant.* new, apprentice, beginning.

experiment, n. analysis, essay, examination, trial, inspection, search, organized observation, research, scrutiny, speculation, check, proof, operation, test, exercise, quiz, investigation.

experiment, v. analyze, investigate, probe, search, venture, explore, test, rehearse, try out, sample, subject to discipline, prove, conduct an experiment, research, study, examine, scrutinize, weigh, play around with, *fool with.

experimental, a. tentative, trial, temporary, test, provisional, preliminary, preparatory, under probation, on approval *or* trial, pending verification, momentary, primary, beginning, laboratory, in its first stage.—*Ant.* permanent, tried, tested.

expert, a. skillful, practiced, proficient; see **able**.

expert, n. graduate, master, trained personnel; see **specialist**.

expiration, n. close, closing, finish; see **end** 2.

expire, v. stop, finish, quit; see **end 1**.

explain, v. interpret, explicate, account for, elucidate, illustrate, clarify, illuminate, make clear, describe, expound, teach, reveal, point up *or* out, demonstrate, tell, read, translate, paraphrase, put in other words, define, justify, untangle, unravel, make plain, come to the point, put across, throw light upon, comment *or* remark upon *or* on, make *or* prepare *or* offer an explanation *or* an exposition (of), resolve, clear up, get right, set right, put (someone) on the right track, spell out, go into detail, get to the bottom of, figure out, cast light upon, get across *or* through, bring out, work out, solve, *put in plain English.—*Ant.* puzzle, confuse, confound.

explainable, a. explicable, accountable, intelligible; see **understandable**.

explained, a. made clear, interpreted, elucidated; see **known 2, obvious 2**.

explanation, n. information, answer, account, reason, illustration, description, comment, justification, narrative, story, tale, footnote, anecdote, example, analysis, criticism, exegesis, key, commentary, note, summary, report, brief, the details, budget, breakdown; see also **proof 1**.

explanatory, a. expository, illustrative, informative, allegorical, interpretative, instructive, guiding, descriptive, analytical, graphic, critical.

explicit, a. express, sure, plain; see **definite 1, understandable**.

explode, v. blow up, blow out, blow a fuse, break out, erupt, go off, detonate, discharge, backfire, shatter, fracture, split, collapse, blow off, blast, *blow to smithereens.

exploit, n. deed, venture, escapade; see **achievement**.

exploit, v. utilize, take advantage of, employ; see **use 1**.

exploited, a. taken advantage of, utilized, worked; see **used**.

exploration, n. investigation, research, search; see **examination 1**.

explore, v. search, investigate, hunt, seek; see **examine**.

explorer, n. adventurer, traveler, pioneer, wayfarer, pilgrim, voyager, space traveler, astronaut, cosmonaut, deep-sea diver, seafarer, mountaineer, mountain climber, scientist, navigator, colonist.

explosion, n. detonation, blast, burst, discharge, blowout, blowup, eruption, combustion, outburst, firing, ignition, backfire.

explosive, a. stormy, fiery, forceful, raging, wild, violent, uncontrollable, vehement, sharp, hysterical, frenzied, savage. —*Ant.* gentle, mild, uneventful.

explosive, n. mine, gunpowder, ammunition, TNT, plastic, dynamite, nitroglycerine, bomb, missile, grenade, charge, shell, Molotov cocktail; see also **ammunition, weapon**.

export, n. shipping, trading, overseas shipment, commodity, international trade, foreign trade.

export, v. send out, sell *or* trade abroad, ship (across), transport, consign, *dump.

expose, v. 1. [To uncover] disclose, smoke out, show up, present, prove, reveal, air, exhibit, unmask, lay open *or* bare, bring to light, open, dig up, give away, bring into view, unfold, let the cat out of the bag, *paint in its true color, *put the finger on. 2. [To endeavor to attract attention] show, show off, bare; see **display**. 3. [To open to danger] lay open to, subject to, imperil; see **endanger**.

exposed, a. disclosed, defined, revealed, divulged, made public, laid bare, dug up, brought to light *or* the light of day, solved, resolved, discovered, found out, seen through.—*Ant.* hidden, concealed, disguised.

exposition, n. 1. [The process of making clear] elucidation, delineation, explication; see **explanation**. 2. [A popular exhibition] exhibit, showing, performance; see **display**.

ex post facto, *a.* subsequently, retroactively, retrospectively; see **finally 2**.

exposure, *n.* disclosure, betrayal, display, exhibition, publication, showing, revelation, confession, unveiling, acknowledgment, exposé, *giveaway, bombshell, *stink.—*Ant.* protection, concealment, secrecy.

express, *v.* declare, tell, signify; see **utter**.

expression, *n.* 1. [Significant appearance] look, cast, character; see **looks**. 2. [Putting into understandable form] representation, art product, utterance, narration, interpretation, invention, creation, declaration, commentary, diagnosis, definition, explanation, illustration; see also **composition, writing 1. 3.** [A traditional form of speech] locution, idiom, speech pattern; see **phrase, word 1. 4.** [Facial cast] grimace, smile, smirk, mug, sneer, pout, grin, wry face; see also **smile**.

expressionless, *a.* wooden, dull, vacuous; see **blank**.

expressive, *a.* eloquent, demonstrative, revealing, indicative, representative, dramatic, stirring, sympathetic, articulate, touching, significant, meaningful, pathetic, spirited, emphatic, strong, forcible, energetic, lively, tender, passionate, warm, colorful, vivid, picturesque, brilliant, stimulating.—*Ant.* **indifferent**, impassive, dead.

express oneself, *v.* communicate, declare, enunciate; see **utter**.

expulsion, *n.* ejection, suspension, purge; see **removal 1**.

exquisite, *a.* fine, scrupulous, precise; see **dainty**.

extemporaneous, *a.* spontaneous, impromptu, unprepared; see **automatic, immediate, immediately**.

extend, *v.* 1. [To make larger] lengthen, enlarge, prolong; see **increase**. 2. [To occupy space to a given point] continue, go as far as, spread; see **reach 1**.

extended, *a.* 1. [Outspread] spread, widespread, expansive; see **widespread**. 2. [Very long] elongated, drawn out, lengthened; see **long 1**.

extending, *a.* reaching, continuing, continual, perpetual, ranging, stretching, spreading, spanning, going on, running to, drawn out (to), lengthening; see also **endless**.

extension, *n.* section, branch, additional *or* second telephone; see **addition 2**.

extensive, *a.* wide, broad, long; see **large 1**.

extensively, *a.* widely, broadly, greatly; see **widely**.

extent, *n.* degree, limit, span, space, area,

measure, size, bulk, length, compass, scope, reach, sweep, wideness, width, range, amount, expanse, magnitude, intensity; see also **expanse**.

exterior, *a.* outer, outlying, outermost; see **outside**.

exterior, *n.* surface, covering, visible portion; see **outside 1**.

exterminate, *v.* annihilate, eradicate, abolish; see **destroy**.

external, *a.* surface, visible, open to the air; see **obvious 1**.

extinct, *a.* dead, ended, terminated, exterminated, deceased, lost, unknown, no longer known.

extinction, *n.* abolition, extermination, extirpation; see **destruction 1, murder**.

extinguish, *v.* smother, choke, quench, douse, put *or* snuff *or* drown *or* blow out, stifle, suffocate.

extort, *v.* extract, wrench, force; see **steal**.

extortion, *n.* fraud, stealing, blackmail; see **theft**.

extortionist, *n.* thief, blackmailer, oppressor; see **criminal**.

extra, *a.* additional, in addition, other, one more, spare, reserve, supplemental, increased, another, new, auxiliary, added, besides, also, further, more, beyond, plus, supplementary, accessory, unused.—*Ant.* **less**, short, subtracted.

extract, *n.* distillation, infusion, concentration; see **essence 1**.

extract, *v.* evoke, derive, secure; see **obtain 1**.

extradite, *v.* obtain, apprehend, bring to justice *or* to trial; see **arrest 1**.

extraordinarily, *a.* remarkably, notably, peculiarly; see **very**.

extraordinary, *a.* remarkable, curious, amazing; see **unusual 1**.

extravagance, *n.* lavishness, expenditures, improvidence; see **waste 1**.

extravagant, *a.* lavish, prodigal, immoderate; see **wasteful**.

extravagantly, *a.* expensively, beyond one's means, without restraint; see **rashly, wastefully**.

extreme, *a.* radical, intemperate, immoderate, imprudent, excessive, inordinate, extravagant, flagrant, outrageous, unreasonable, irrational, improper, preposterous, thorough, far, fanatical, desperate, severe, intense, drastic, sheer, total, advanced, violent, sharp, acute, unseemly, beyond control, fantastic, to the extreme, absurd, foolish, monstrous, exaggerated.—*Ant.* cautious, **restrained**, moderate.

extreme, *n.* height, apogee, apex; see **end 4, limit 2. —go to extremes**, be excessive *or* immoderate *or* careless, act rashly, fly apart; see **exceed. —in the extreme**, extremely, to the highest degree, inordinately; see **much**.

extremely, *a.* greatly, remarkably, notably; see **much.**

extremist, *n.* zealot, fanatic, die-hard; see **radical.**

exuberance, *n.* fervor, eagerness, exhilaration; see **zeal.**

exuberant, *a.* ardent, vivacious, passionate; see **zealous.**

eye, *n.* 1. [The organ of sight] instrument of vision, compound eye, simple eye, naked eye, optic, orb, *peeper, *lamp. Parts of the eye include the following—eyeball *or* ball, pupil, retina, iris, cornea, eye muscles, optic nerve, white, lens. 2. [Appreciation] perception, taste, discrimination; see **taste** 1, 3. 3. [A center] focus, core, heart, kernel, nub; see **center** 1. —*private eye, detective, investigator, *gumshoe; see **policeman.** —all eyes, attentive, aware, perceptive; see **observant.** —an eye for an eye, punishment, retaliation, vengeance; see **revenge** 1. —catch one's eye, attract one's attention, cause notice, stand out; see **fascinate.** —*easy on the eyes, attractive, appealing, pleasant to look at; see **beautiful.** —*give a person the eye, attract, charm, invite; see **seduce.** —have an eye for, appreciate, be interested in, desire; see **want** 1. —have an eye to, watch (out) for, be mindful of, attend to; see **watch out.** —*have eyes for, appreciate, be interested in, desire; see **want** 1. —*in a pig's eye, under no circumstances, impossible, no way; see **never.** —in the public eye, well-known, renowned, celebrated, see **famous.** —keep an eye on, look after, watch over, protect; see **guard** 2. —keep an eye out for, watch for, be mindful of, attend to; see **watch out.** —keep one's eyes open (*or* peeled *or* skinned), be aware, regard, look out; see **watch.** —lay eyes on, look at, stare, survey; see **see** 1. —make eyes at, attract, charm, invite; see **seduce.** —open one's eyes, make aware, inform, apprise; see **tell** 1. —shut one's eyes to, refuse, reject, ignore; see **refuse.** —with an eye to, considering, mindful of, aware of; see **observant.**

eyesight, *n.* vision, sense of seeing, visual perception; see **sight** 1.

eyesore, *n.* ugly thing, distortion, deformity; see **ugliness.**

eyewitness, *n.* onlooker, passer-by, observer; see **witness.**

F

fable, *n.* allegory, tale, parable; see **story**.

fabric, *n.* textile, stuff, material; see **goods**.

fabricate, *v.* 1. [To construct] erect, make, form; see **build, manufacture 1**. 2. [To misrepresent] make up, contrive, prevaricate; see **lie 1**.

fabulous, *a.* remarkable, amazing, immense; see **unusual 1**.

façade, *n.* face, appearance, look; see **front 4**.

face, *n.* 1. [The front of the head] visage, countenance, appearance, feature, silhouette, profile, front, *mug. 2. [A plane surface] front, surface, finish; see **plane 1**. 3. [Prestige] status, standing, social position; see **reputation 2**. — **make a face**, distort one's face, grimace, scowl; see **frown**. —**on the face of it**, to all appearances, seemingly, according to the evidence; see **apparently**. —**pull (or wear) a long face**, look sad, scowl, pout; see **frown**. — **show one's face**, be seen, show up, come; see **appear 1**. —**to one's face**, candidly, openly, frankly, see **boldly 1**.

face, *v.* 1. [To confront conflict or trouble] confront, oppose, defy, meet, dare, brave, challenge, withstand, encounter, risk, tolerate, endure, sustain, suffer, bear, tell to one's face, make a stand, meet face to face, cope with, allow, stand, submit, abide, take (it).—*Ant.* evade, elude, shun. 2. [To put a face on a building] refinish, front, redecorate; see **cover 1, paint 2**. 3. [To look out on] front (toward), border, be turned toward; see **lie 2**.

facet, *n.* aspect, face, side; see **plane 1**.

facetious, *a.* humorous, whimsical, ridiculous; see **funny 1**.

face to face, *a.* eye to eye, cheek by jowl, facing; see **opposite 3**.

facile, *a.* simple, obvious, apparent; see **easy 1**.

facilitate, *v.* promote, aid, make easy, simplify; see **help**.

facility, *n.* 1. [Material; *usually plural*] tools, plant, buildings; see **equipment**. 2. [Agency; *usually plural*] department, bureau, company; see **office 3**.

facsimile, *n.* duplicate, reproduction, mirror; see **copy**.

fact, *n.* 1. [A reliable generality] certainty, truth, appearance, experience, matter, the very thing, not an illusion, what has really happened, something concrete, what is the case, matter of fact, hard evidence, actuality, naked truth, gospel, reality, law, basis, state of being, *hard facts.—*Ant.* fancy, fiction, imagination. 2. [An individual reality] circumstance, detail, factor, case, evidence, event, action, deed, happening, occurrence, creation, conception, manifestation, being, entity, experience, affair, act, episode, performance, proceeding, phenomenon, incident, thing done, plain fact, accomplishment, accomplished fact; *fait accompli* (French).—*Ant.* error, illusion, untruth. —**as a matter of fact**, in reality, in fact, actually; see **really 1**.

faction, *n.* cabal, combine, party, conspiracy, plot, gang, crew, wing, block, junta, clique, splinter party, set, clan, club, lobby, camp, inner circle, sect, coterie, partnership, cell, unit, mob, side, machine, tong, band, team, machine ring, knot, circle, concern, guild, schism, outfit, *crowd, *bunch.

factor, *n.* portion, constituent, determinant; see **part 1, 3**.

factory, *n.* manufactory, plant, branch, shop, industry, workshop, machine shop, mill, laboratory, assembly plant, foundry, forge, loom, mint, carpenter shop, brewery, sawmill, supply house, warehouse, processing plant, works, workroom, firm, packing plant.

facts, *n.* reality, certainty, information; see **fact 1**.

factual, *a.* exact, specific, descriptive; see **accurate 1**.

faculty, *n.* 1. [A peculiar aptitude] peculiarity, strength, forte; see **ability 1. 2. [A group of specialists, usually engaged in instruction or research] staff, teachers, research workers, personnel, instructors, university, college, institute, teaching *or* instructional *or* research staff *or* personnel, teaching assistants, professorate, society, body, organization, mentors, professors, assistant professors, associate professors, docents, tutors, foundation, department, pedagogues, lecturers, advisers, masters, scholars, fellows.

fad, *n.* fancy, style, craze, fashion, humor, fit, prank, quirk, kink, eccentricity, popular innovation, vogue, fantasy, whimsy, passing fancy, latest word, (all the) rage, (the latest) thing, the last word; see **fashion 2**.—*Ant.* custom, convention, practice.

fade, *v.* 1. [To lose color or light] bleach,

tone down, wash out, blanch, tarnish, dim, discolor, pale, grow dim, neutralize, become dull, lose brightness *or* luster *or* color.—*Ant.* color, brighten, glow. 2. [To diminish in sound] hush, quiet, sink; see **decrease 1.**

faded, *a.* used, bleached, shopworn; see **dull 2.**

fail, *v.* 1. [To be unsuccessful] fall short, miss, back out, abandon, desert, neglect, slip, lose ground, come to naught *or* nothing, falter, flounder, blunder, break down, come to grief, get into trouble, abort, fault, come down, fall flat, go amiss, go astray, fall down *or* away, get left, be found lacking, go down, go under, not hold a candle to, fold up, go on the rocks, not have it in one, *miss the boat, not measure up (to expectation), lose out, give out, fall short of, *not make the grade, miss the mark, lose control, fall down on the job, go wrong, be out of it, *blow the chance, *fizzle out, hit (rock) bottom, go up in smoke, *bomb, *not get to first base, *get hung up *or* bogged down, *flunk (out), *flop, *conk out, *peter out.—*Ant.* succeed, **win**, triumph. 2. [To prove unsatisfactory] lose out, come short of, displease; see **disappoint.** 3. [To grow less] lessen, worsen, sink; see **decrease 1.** 4. [To become insolvent] go bankrupt, go out of business, *go broke; see sense 1.—**without fail**, constantly, dependably, reliably; see **regularly.**

failing, *a.* declining, feeble, faint; see **weak 1.**

failure, *n.* 1. [An unsuccessful attempt] fiasco, misadventure, abortion, bankruptcy, miscarriage, frustration, misstep, faux pas, breakdown, checkmate, stoppage, collapse, defeat, overthrow, downfall, total loss, stalemate, *flop, *bust, dud, *washout, botch, losing game, sinking ship, mess.—*Ant.* **success**, accomplishment, triumph. 2. [An unsuccessful person] no-good, incompetent, underachiever, bankrupt, derelict, dropout, *lemon, bum, dud.—*Ant.* **success**, veteran, star.

faint, *a.* 1. [Having little physical strength] shaky, faltering, dizzy; see **weak 1.** 2. [Having little light or color] vague, thin, hazy; see **dull 2.** 3. [Having little volume of sound] whispered, breathless, murmuring, inaudible, indistinct, low, stifled, dull, hoarse, soft, heard in the distance, quiet, low-pitched, muffled, hushed, padded, distant, subdued, gentle, softened, deep, rumbling, far-off, out of earshot.—*Ant.* **loud**, audible, raucous.

faint, *v.* lose consciousness, become unconscious, fall, go into a coma, drop, collapse, succumb, pass out, *go out like

a light, *keel over, black out.—*Ant.* **recover**, awaken, come to.

fair, *a.* 1. [Just] forthright, impartial, plain, scrupulous, upright, candid, generous, frank, open, sincere, straightforward, honest, lawful, clean, legitimate, decent, honorable, virtuous, righteous, temperate, unbiased, reasonable, civil, courteous, blameless, uncorrupted, square, equitable, fair-minded, dispassionate, uncolored, objective, unprejudiced, evenhanded, good, principled, moderate, praiseworthy, aboveboard, trustworthy, due, fit, appropriate, *on the level, *on the up-and-up, *fair and square, straight.—*Ant.* **unfair**, unjust, biased. 2. [Moderately satisfactory] average, pretty good, not bad, up to standard, ordinary, mediocre, usual, common, all right, commonplace, *fair to middling, so-so, O.K.; see also **common 1.**—*Ant.* **poor**, bad, unsatisfactory. 3. [Not stormy or likely to storm] clear, pleasant, sunny, bright, calm, placid, tranquil, favorable, balmy, mild.—*Ant.* **stormy**, threatening, overcast. 4. [Of light complexion] blond, light colored *or* complexioned, pale, white, bleached, white-skinned, flaxen, fair-haired, snow-white, snowy, whitish, light, lily-white, faded, neutral, platinum blonde, peroxide blonde, *bleached blonde, pale-faced, *white as a sheet *or* as the driven snow.—*Ant.* **dark**, brunet, black.

fair, *n.* exposition, county *or* state *or* world fair, carnival, bazaar, exhibition, display, festival, market, exchange, centennial, observance, celebration.

fairground, *n.* enclosure, coliseum, race track, racecourse, exhibition place, fairway, concourse, rink, midway, exposition.

fairly, *a.* 1. [In a just manner] honestly, reasonably, honorably; see **justly 1.** 2. [A qualifying word] somewhat, moderately, reasonably; see **adequately.**

fairness, *n.* decency, honesty, uprightness, truth, integrity, charity, impartiality, justice, tolerance, honor, moderation, consideration, good faith, decorum, propriety, courtesy, reasonableness, rationality, humanity, equity, justness, goodness, measure for measure, give and take, fair-mindedness, open-mindedness, just dealing, good sense, fair treatment, even-handed justice, due, accuracy, scrupulousness, correctness, virtue, duty, dutifulness, legality, rightfulness, lawfulness, *square deal, fair play, *fair shake, *doing right by.—*Ant.* **injustice**, unfairness, partiality.

fairy, *n.* 1. [A minor supernatural being] spirit, sprite, good fairy, elf, goblin, hobgoblin, nymph, pixy, mermaid, siren, bogie, genie, imp, enchantress, witch, warlock, banshee, werewolf, ogre, demon, succubus, devil, ghoul, harpy, poltergeist, troll, gnome, coltpixie, leprechaun, satyr, fiend, Fate, Weird Sister. 2. [A homosexual] *queer, not a heterosexual, pervert; see **homosexual.**

fairy tale, *n.* folk tale, children's story, romance; see **story.**

faith, *n.* 1. [Complete trust] confidence, trust, credence, credit, assurance, acceptance, troth, dependence, conviction, sureness, fidelity, loyalty, certainty, allegiance, reliance.—*Ant.* doubt, suspicion, distrust. 2. [A formal system of beliefs] creed, doctrine, dogma, tenet, revelation, credo, gospel, profession, conviction, canon, principle, church, worship, teaching, theology, denomination, cult, sect. —**bad faith,** insincerity, duplicity, infidelity; see **dishonesty.** —**break faith,** be disloyal, abandon, fail; see **deceive.** —**good faith,** sincerity, honor, trustworthiness; see **honest.** —**in faith,** indeed, in fact, in reality; see **really 1.** —**keep faith,** be loyal, adhere, follow; see **support 2.**

faithful, *a.* reliable, genuine, dependable, incorruptible, straight, honest, upright, honorable, scrupulous, firm, sure, unswerving, conscientious, enduring, unchanging, steady, staunch, attached, obedient, steadfast, sincere, resolute, *on the level, devoted (to), true, dutiful; see also **loyal.**—*Ant.* fickle, **false,** faithless.

faithfully, *a.* 1. [Loyally] trustingly, conscientiously, truly; see **loyally.**

faithfulness, *n.* trustworthiness, care, duty; see **devotion.**

fake, *a.* pretended, fraudulent, bogus; see **false 3.**

fake, *n.* deception, counterfeit, sham, copy, cheat, imitation, charlatan, fraud, make-believe, pretense, fabrication, forgery, cheat, humbug, trick, swindle, *phony, *gyp, *put-on, flimflam.—*Ant.* fact, original, reality.

fake, *v.* feign, simulate, disguise; see **pretend 1.**

fall, *n.* 1. [The act of falling] drop, decline, lapse, collapse, breakdown, tumble, spill, downfall, overthrow, defeat, degradation, humiliation, descent, plunge, slump, recession, ebb.—*Ant.* rise, elevation, ascent. 2. [That which falls] rainfall, snowfall, precipitation; see **rain 1, snow.** 3. [The season after summer] autumn, the fall of the year, harvest, September, October, November, harvest time.—**ride for a fall,** endanger oneself, take risks *or* chances, act indiscreetly; see **risk.**

fall, *v.* 1. [To pass quickly downward] sink, topple, drop, settle, droop, stumble, trip, plunge, tumble, descend, totter, break down, cave in, make a forced

landing, decline, subside, collapse, drop down, pitch, be precipitated, fall down *or* flat, fall in, fold up, keel over, tip over, slip, recede, ebb, diminish, flop.—*Ant.* rise, ascend, climb. 2. [To be overthrown] submit, yield, surrender, succumb, be destroyed, be taken, bend, defer to, obey, resign, capitulate, back down, fall to pieces, break up.—*Ant.* prevail, **endure,** resist. —**fall in love (with),** *v.* lose one's heart (to), take a fancy *or* liking to, become attached to *or* fond of; see **fall in love.**

fallacy, *n.* inconsistency, quibbling, evasion, fallacious *or* illogical reasoning, mistake, deceit, deception, subterfuge, inexactness, perversion, bias, prejudice, preconception, ambiguity, paradox, miscalculation, quirk, flaw, irrelevancy, erratum, heresy; see also **error.**—*Ant.* theory, reason, **law.**

fall asleep, *v.* go to sleep, doze, *drop off; see **sleep.**

fallen, *a.* sinful, shamed, shameless; see **corrupt.**

***fall for,** *v.* become infatuated, desire, *flip over; see **fall in love.**

fallibility, *n.* imperfection, misjudgment, frailty; see **uncertainty 2.**

fallible, *a.* deceptive, frail, imperfect, ignorant, uncertain, erring, unpredictable, unreliable, in question, prone to error, untrustworthy, questionable; see also **wrong 2.**

fall in, *v.* get into line, form ranks, take a place; see **line up.**

falling, *a.* dropping, sinking, descending, plunging, slipping, sliding, declining, settling, toppling, tumbling, tottering, diminishing, weakening, decreasing, ebbing, subsiding, collapsing, crumbling, dying.—*Ant.* **increasing,** improving, mounting.

fall in love, *v.* become enamoured, lose one's heart, take a fancy to, have eyes for, take a liking to, become attached to, become fond of (someone), fancy.

fall off, *v.* decline, lessen, wane; see **decrease 1.**

fall out, *v.* argue, disagree, fight; see **quarrel.**

fallow, *a.* unplowed, unplanted, unproductive; see **vacant 2.**

fall short, *v.* fail, be deficient, be lacking; see **need.**

false, *a.* 1. [Said of persons] faithless, treacherous, unfaithful, disloyal, dishonest, lying, foul, hypocritical, double-dealing, malevolent, mean, malicious, deceitful, underhanded, corrupt, wicked, unscrupulous, untrustworthy, dishonorable, two-faced.—*Ant.* **faithful,** true, honorable. 2. [Said of statements *or* supposed facts] untrue, spurious, fanciful, lying, untruthful, fictitious, deceptive, fallacious, incorrect, misleading, delusive, imaginary, illusive, erroneous, invalid, inaccurate, deceiving, misrepresentative, fraudulent, trumped up.—*Ant.* accurate, correct, established. 3. [*Said of things*] sham, counterfeit, fabricated, manufactured, synthetic, bogus, spurious, make-believe, assumed, unreal, copied, forged, pretended, faked, made-up, simulated, pseudo, hollow, mock, feigned, bastard, alloyed, artificial, contrived, colored, disguised, deceptive, adulterated, so-called, fake, *phony, *gyp, *bum, shoddy, *not what it's cracked up to be.—*Ant.* real, genuine, authentic.

falsehood, *n.* deception, prevarication, story; see lie 1.

falsely, *a.* traitorously, treacherously, deceitfully, foully, faithlessly, behind one's back, disloyally, underhandedly, maliciously, malevolently, unfaithfully, dishonestly, unscrupulously, dishonorably.—*Ant.* truly, justly, honorably.

falsify, *v.* adulterate, counterfeit, misrepresent; see deceive.

falter, *v.* waver, fluctuate, be undecided; see hesitate.

fame, *n.* renown, glory, distinction, eminence, honor, celebrity, esteem, name, estimation, public esteem, credit, note, greatness, dignity, rank, splendor, position, standing, pre-eminence, superiority, regard, character, station, place, degree, popularity.

familiar, *a.* everyday, well-known, customary, frequent, homely, humble, usual, intimate, habitual, accustomed, common, ordinary, informal, unceremonious, plain, simple, matter-of-fact, workaday, prosaic, commonplace, homespun, natural, native, unsophisticated, *old hat, *garden variety.—*Ant.* unusual, exotic, strange.

familiarity, *n.* 1. [Acquaintance with people] friendliness, acquaintanceship, fellowship; see friendship 1, 2. 2. [Acquaintance with things] the feel of, being at home with, comprehension; see awareness, experience.

familiarize (oneself with), *v.* acquaint, accustom, habituate, make the acquaintance of, get acquainted (with), gain the friendship of, make friends (with), awaken to, come to know, become aware of.

familiar with, *a.* well-acquainted with, acquainted with, aware of, introduced, informed of, on speaking terms (with), having some connections, cognizant of, attuned to.—*Ant.* unacquainted, unaware, unknown.

family, *n.* kin, folk, clan, relationship, relations, tribe, dynasty, breed, house,

kith and kin, blood, blood tie, progeny, offspring, descendants, forbears, heirs, race, ancestry, pedigree, genealogy, descent, parentage, extraction, paternity, inheritance, kinship, lineage, line, one's own flesh and blood, strain, siblings, in-laws, people.

famine, *n.* starvation, want, misery; see hunger.

famished, *a.* starving, hungering, starved; see hungry.

famous, *a.* eminent, foremost, famed, pre-eminent, acclaimed, illustrious, celebrated, noted, conspicuous, far-famed, prominent, honored, reputable, renowned, recognized, notable, important, well-known, of note, notorious, exalted, remarkable, extraordinary, great, powerful, noble, grand, mighty, imposing, towering, influential, leading, noteworthy, talked of, outstanding, distinguished, excellent, memorable, elevated, in the spotlight, in the limelight.—*Ant.* unknown, obscure, humble.

fan, *n.* 1. [An instrument for creating currents of air] ventilator, agitator, blower, forced draft, vane, air conditioner, propeller, electric fan, Japanese fan, windmill. 2. [*Supporter] follower, amateur, devotee; see follower.

fanatic, *n.* devotee, bigot, enthusiast; see zealot.

fanatical, *a.* obsessed, passionate, devoted; see zealous.

fanaticism, *n.* bigotry, intolerance, obsession, prejudice, hatred, superstition, narrow-mindedness, injustice, obstinacy, stubbornness, bias, unfairness, partiality, devotion, violence, immoderation, zeal, single-mindedness, willfulness, infatuation, dogma, arbitrariness, unruliness, enthusiasm, frenzy, passion, rage.—*Ant.* tolerance, indifference, moderation.

fanciful, *a.* unreal, incredible, whimsical; see fantastic.

fancy, *a.* elegant, embellished, rich, adorned, ostentatious, gaudy, showy, intricate, baroque, lavish; see also elaborate, ornate 1.

fancy, *n.* 1. [The mind at play] whimsy, frolic, caprice, banter, sport, diversion, whim, notion, quip, prank, wit, buffoonery, fooling, facetiousness, merriment, levity, humor. 2. [The product of a playful mind] whim, notion, impulse; see idea. 3. [Inclination] wishes, will, preference; see desire 1.

fang, *n.* tusk, prong, duct; see tooth.

fantastic, *a.* whimsical, capricious, extravagant, freakish, strange, odd, queer, quaint, peculiar, outlandish, farfetched, wonderful, comical, humorous, foreign, exotic, extreme, ludicrous, ridiculous, preposterous, grotesque, frenzied, absurd, vague, hallucinatory, high-flown, affected, artificial, *out of sight.—*Ant.* conventional, routine, common.

fantasy, *n.* vision, appearance, illusion, flight, figment, fiction, romance, mirage, nightmare, fairyland.

far, *a.* 1. [Distant from the speaker] removed, faraway, remote; see **distant**. 2. [To a considerable degree] extremely, incomparably, notably; see **very. —by far,** very much, considerably, to a great degree; see **much 1, very. —few and far between,** scarce, sparse, in short supply; see **rare 2. —(in) so far as,** to the extent that, in spite of, within limits; see **considering. —so far,** thus far, until now, (up) to this point; see **now 1. —so far, so good,** all right, favorable, going well; see **successful**.

farce, *n.* travesty, burlesque, horseplay; see **fun 1**.

fare, *n.* 1. [A fee paid, usually for transportation] ticket, charge, passage, passage money, toll, tariff, expense(s), transportation, check, token. 2. [Served food] menu, rations, meals; see **food**.

fare, *v.* prosper, prove, turn out; see **happen 2**.

farewell, *n.* goodbye, valediction, parting; see **departure 1**.

farfetched, *a.* forced, strained, unbelievable; see **fantastic**.

farm, *n.* plantation, ranch, homestead, claim, holding, field, kibbutz, pasture, meadow, grassland, truck farm, estate, land, acres, freehold, cropland, soil, acreage, garden, patch, vegetable garden, orchard, nursery, vineyard.

farm, *v.* cultivate land, produce crops, cultivate, till, garden, work, run, ranch, crop, graze, homestead, produce, pasture, till the soil.

farmer, *n.* planter, grower, (livestock) breeder, stockman, feeder, agriculturalist, rancher, dirt farmer, lessee, homesteader, producer, tiller of the soil, peasant, peon, herdsman, plowman, sharecropper, hired man, cropper, grazer, cattleman, sheepman, harvester, truck gardener, gardener, nurseryman, horticulturist, settler, *sodbuster, farm hand, hired hand, help.

farming, *n.* agriculture, tillage, cultivation, husbandry, farm management, soil culture, ranching, sharecropping, homesteading, plantation, horticulture, agronomy, grazing, livestock raising, taking up a claim, hydroponics, growing, cropraising.

farm out, *v.* lease, rent, allot; see **distribute, rent 1**.

farmyard, *n.* barnyard, yard, farmstead; see **farm**.

far-off, *a.* far, remote, strange; see **distant 1**.

farsighted, *a.* aware, perceptive, sagacious; see **intelligent**.

farther, *a.* at a greater distance, more distant, beyond, further, more remote, remoter, longer.

farthest, *a.* remotest, ultimate, last; see **furthest**.

fascinate, *v.* charm, entrance, captivate, enchant, bewitch, ravish, enrapture, delight, overpower, please, attract, compel, lure, seduce, entice, tempt, draw, engage, excite, stimulate, overwhelm, provoke, arouse, intoxicate, thrill, stir, kindle, absorb, tantalize, win, interest, enthrall, influence, capture, coax, tease, lead on, *knock dead, *cast a spell over, catch one's eye, carry away, invite attention.—*Ant.* disgust, repel, horrify.

fascinated, *a.* enchanted, bewitched, dazzled, captivated, attracted, seduced, enraptured, charmed, hypnotized, delighted, infatuated, thrilled, spellbound; see also **charmed.—*Ant.* disgusted, repelled, disenchanted.

fascinating, *a.* engaging, attractive, delightful; see **charming**.

fascination, *n.* charm, power, enchantment; see **attraction**.

fascism, *n.* dictatorship, totalitarianism, Nazism; see **government 2.—*Ant.* democracy,** self-government, socialism.

fascist, *n.* reactionary, Nazi *or* nazi, rightist; see **dictator**.

fashion, *n.* 1. [The manner of behavior] way, custom, convention, style, vogue, mode, tendency, trend, formality, formula, procedure, practice, device, usage, observance, new look. 2. [Whatever is temporarily in vogue] craze, sport, caprice, whim, hobby, innovation, custom, amusement, eccentricity, rage, cry. — **after (or in) a fashion,** somewhat, to some extent, in a way; see **moderately**.

fashion, *v.* model, shape, form; see **create**.

fashionable, *a.* in fashion *or* style *or* vogue, being done, well-liked, favored, smart, stylish, chic, *hot, *in, up to the minute.

fashioned, *a.* molded, shaped, intended; see **formed**.

fast, *a.* 1. [Rapid] swift, fleet, quick, speedy, brisk, accelerated, hasty, nimble, active, electric, agile, ready, quick as lightning, like a flash, racing, *like a bat out of hell, *like a house afire.—*Ant.* slow, sluggish, tardy. 2. [Firmly fixed] adherent, attached, immovable; see **firm 1**.

fast, *n.* abstinence (especially from food), day of fasting, Lent; see **abstinence**.

fast, *v.* not eat, go hungry, observe a fast; see **abstain.**

fasten, *v.* lock, fix, tie, lace, close, bind, tighten, make firm, attach, secure, anchor, grip, zip (up), hold, screw up *or* down, clasp, clamp, pin, nail, tack, bolt, rivet, set, weld, cement, glue, hold fast, make secure *or* fast, cinch, catch, buckle, bolt, bar, seal up.—*Ant.* **release,** loosen, unfasten.

fastened, *a.* locked, fixed, tied; see **tight 2.**

fastener, *n.* buckle, hook, hasp, lock, clamp, tie, stud, vise, grip, grappling iron, clasp, snap, bolt, bar, lace, cinch, grip, pin, safety pin, nail, rivet, tack, thumbtack, screw, dowel, hook, brake, binder, binding, button, padlock, catch, bond, band, mooring, rope, cable, anchor, chain, harness, strap, thong, girdle, latch, staple, zipper.

fastening, *n.* catch, clasp, hook; see **fastener.**

fat, *a.* portly, stout, obese, corpulent, fleshy, potbellied, beefy, brawny, solid, plumpish, plump, burly, bulky, unwieldy, heavy, husky, puffy, on the heavy *or* plump, etc., side, in need of dieting *or* reducing, swollen, inflated, ponderous, lumpish, fat as a pig, *tubby.—*Ant.* **thin,** lean, skinny. —*chew the fat,* chat, gossip, confer; see **talk 1.**

fat, *n.* blubber, lard, oil; see **grease.**

fatal, *a.* inevitable, mortal, lethal; see **deadly.**

fatality, *n.* casualty, dying, accident; see **death.**

fate, *n.* fortune, destination, luck; see **doom.**

fated, *a.* lost, destined, elected; see **doomed.**

fateful, *a.* **1.** [Momentous] portentous, critical, decisive; see **crucial 1. 2.** [Fatal] destructive, ruinous, lethal; see **deadly.**

father, *n.* **1.** [A male parent] sire, progenitor, procreator, forebear, ancestor, head of the house(hold), papa, *dad, *daddy, *pa, *the old man, *pappy, *pop. **2.** [An originator] founder, inventor, promoter; see **author. 3.** [A priest, especially a Catholic priest] pastor, ecclesiastic, parson; see **priest.**

Father, *n.* Supreme Being, Creator, Author; see **God 1.**

father-in-law, *n.* spouse's father, parent, in-law; see **relative.**

fatherland, *n.* mother country, homeland, native land; see **nation 1.**

fatherly, *a.* paternal, patriarchal, benevolent; see **kind.**

fatigue, *n.* weariness, lassitude, exhaustion, weakness, feebleness, faintness, battle fatigue, nervous exhaustion, dullness, heaviness, listlessness, tiredness.

fatness, *n.* plumpness, obesity, weight, flesh, heaviness, grossness, corpulence, bulkiness, girth, breadth, largeness, protuberance, inflation, fleshiness, stoutness, *heftiness.

fatten *v.* feed, stuff, prepare for market, plump, cram, fill, round one out.—*Ant.* **starve,** reduce, constrict.

fatty, *a.* greasy, blubbery, containing fat; see **oily 1.**

faucet, *n.* tap, fixture, petcock, drain, spigot, plumbing, hot-water faucet, cold-water faucet.

fault, *n.* **1.** [A moral delinquency] misdemeanor, weakness, offense, wrongdoing, transgression, crime, sin, impropriety, juvenile delinquency, misconduct, malpractice, failing; see also **mistake. 2.** [An error] blunder, mistake, misdeed; see **error 1. 3.** [Responsibility] liability, accountability, blame; see **responsibility 2.** —**at** *or* **in fault,** culpable, blamable, in the wrong; see **guilty 2.** —**find fault (with),** complain (about), carp (at), criticize; see **blame.**

faulty, *a.* imperfect, flawed, blemished, deficient, distorted, weak, tainted, leaky, defective, damaged, unsound, spotted, cracked, warped, injured, broken, wounded, hurt, impaired, worn, battered, frail, crude, botched, insufficient, inadequate, incomplete, out of order, below par, incorrect, unfit; see also **unsatisfactory.—*Ant.* **whole,** perfect, complete.

favor, *n.* **1.** [Preference] help, support, encouragement; see **encouragement 2.** [Kindness] service, courtesy, boon; see **kindness 2.** —**find favor,** please, suit, become welcome; see **satisfy 1.** —**in favor,** liked, esteemed, wanted; see **favorite.** —**in favor of,** approving, endorsing, condoning; see **for.** —**in one's favor,** to one's advantage *or* credit, on one's side, creditable; see **favorable 3.**

favor, *v.* prefer, like, approve, sanction, praise, regard with favor *or* favorably, be in favor of, pick, choose, lean toward, incline toward, value, prize, esteem, think well of, set great store by, look up to, *think the world of, be partial to, grant favors to, promote, play favorites, show consideration for, spare, make an exception for, pull strings for; see also **promote 1.—*Ant.* dislike, **hate,** disesteem.

favorable, *a.* **1.** [Friendly] well-disposed, kind, well-intentioned; see **friendly. 2.** [Displaying suitable *or* promising qualities] propitious, convenient, beneficial; see **hopeful 2. 3.** [Commendatory] approving, commending, assenting, complimentary, well-disposed (toward), in favor of, agreeable, in one's favor.

favorably, *a.* approvingly, agreeably,

kindly, helpfully, fairly, willingly, heartily, cordially, genially, graciously, courteously, receptively, in an approving or encouraging or cordial, etc., manner, positively, in the budget, without prejudice.—*Ant.* **unfavorably**, adversely, discouragingly.

favorite, *a.* liked, beloved, personal, favored, intimate, to one's taste or liking, choice, pet, desired, wished-for, preferred, adored.—*Ant.* **unpopular**, unwanted, unwelcome.

favorite, *n.* darling, pet, idol, ideal, favored or adored or beloved one, mistress, love, favorite son, favorite child, fair-haired boy, teacher's pet, odds-on favorite, apple of one's eye.

favoritism, *n.* bias, partiality, inequity; see **inclination 1**.

fawn, *n.* baby deer, baby doe, baby buck; see **deer**.

faze, *v.* bother, intimidate, worry; see **disturb**.

fear, *n.* fright, terror, horror, panic, dread, dismay, awe, scare, revulsion, aversion, tremor, mortal terror, cowardice, dread, timidity, misgiving, trembling, anxiety, phobia, foreboding, despair, agitation, hesitation, worry, concern, suspicion, doubt, qualm, funk, cold feet, cold sweat.—*Ant.* **courage**, intrepidity, dash. **—for fear of**, avoiding, lest, in order to prevent; see **or 1**.

fear, *v.* be afraid, shun, avoid, falter, lose courage, be alarmed or frightened or scared, live in terror, dare not, have qualms (about), cower, flinch, shrink, quail, cringe, turn pale, tremble, *break out in a sweat.—*Ant.* **outface**, withstand, dare.

fearful, *a.* timid, shy, apprehensive; see **cowardly**.

fearfully, *a.* apprehensively, shyly, with fear and trembling, for fear of, in fear or terror or fright or trepidation.

fearless, *a.* bold, daring, courageous, dashing; see **brave**.

feasible, *a.* 1. [Suitable] fit, expedient, worthwhile; see **convenient 1.** 2. [Likely] probable, practicable, attainable; see **likely 1**.

feast, *n.* banquet, entertainment, festival, treat, merrymaking, fiesta, barbecue, picnic; see also **dinner**.

feat, *n.* act, effort, deed; see **achievement**.

feather, *n.* quill, plume, plumage, down, wing, tuft, crest, fringe. **—in fine or high or good feather**, gay, well, in good humor or health; see **happy**.

feature, *n.* 1. [*Anything calculated to attract interest] innovation, highlight, prominent part, drawing card, main bout, specialty, special or featured attraction. 2. [Matter other than news

published in a newspaper] article, editorial, feature story; see **story. 3.** [A salient quality] point, pecularity, notability; see **characteristic**.

features, *n.* lineaments, looks, appearance; see **face 1**.

featuring, *a.* presenting, showing, recommending, calling attention to, giving prominence to, emphasizing, making much of, pointing up, drawing attention to, turning the spotlight on, centering attention on or upon, *starring.

February, *n.* winter (month), second month of the year, shortest month (of the year); see **month, winter**.

feces, *n.* excretion, waste, dung; see **excrement**.

federal, *a.* general, central, governmental; see **national 1**.

federation, *n.* confederacy, alliance, combination; see **organization 2**.

fee, *n.* remuneration, salary, charge; see **pay 2**.

feeble, *a.* fragile, puny, strengthless; see **weak 1, 2**.

feeble-minded, *a.* foolish, retarded, senile; see **dull 3**.

feed, *n.* provisions, supplies, fodder, food for animals, pasture, forage, roughage. Common feeds include the following—grain, small grain, corn, oats, barley, rye, wheat, peanuts, hay, clover, sweet clover, alfalfa, sorghum, kale, soybeans, beets, straw.

feed, *v.* feast, give food to, satisfy hunger of, nourish, supply, support, satisfy, fill, stuff, cram, gorge, banquet, dine, nurse, maintain, fatten, provide, cater to, stock, furnish, nurture, sustain, encourage, serve.—*Ant.* **starve**, deprive, quench.

feel, *n.* touch, quality, air; see **feeling 2**.

feel, *v.* 1. [To examine by touch] finger, explore, stroke, palm, caress, handle, manipulate, press, squeeze, fondle, tickle, paw, feel for, fumble, grope, grasp, grapple, grip, clutch, clasp, run the fingers over, pinch, poke, contact. 2. [To experience] sense, perceive, receive, be aware of, observe, be moved by, respond, know, acknowledge, appreciate, accept, be affected or impressed or excited by, have the experience of, take to heart.—*Ant.* **ignore**, be insensitive to, be unaware of. 3. [To believe] consider, hold, sense, know; see **think 1. 4.** [To give an impression through touch] appear, exhibit, suggest; see **seem**.

feeler, *n.* hint, tentative proposal, trial balloon; see **test**.

feeling, *n.* 1. [The sense of touch] tactile sensation, tactility, power of perceiving by touch, tangibility. 2. [State of the body, or of a part of it] sense, sensation, sensibility, feel, sensitiveness, sensory response, perception, perceptivity, susceptibility, consciousness, receptivity, responsiveness, excitability, excitement, awareness, activity, enjoyment, sensuality, pain, pleasure, reaction, motor response, reflex, excitation.—*Ant.* indifference, apathy, numbness. 3. [A personal reaction] opinion, thought, outlook; see **attitude.** 4. [Sensitivity] taste, emotion, passion, tenderness, discrimination, delicacy, discernment, sentiment, sentimentality, refinement, culture, cultivation, capacity, faculty, judgment, affection, sympathy, imagination, intelligence, intuition, spirit, soul, appreciation, response.—*Ant.* rudeness, crudeness, coldness.

feign, *v.* simulate, imagine, fabricate; see **pretend** 1.

feigned, *a.* imagined, fictitious, simulated; see **imaginary.**

fell, *v.* mow *or* pull *or* knock *or* bring down, cause to fall, ground; see **cut** 1.

fellow, *n.* 1. [A young man] youth, lad, boy, person, teen-ager, stripling, novice, cadet, apprentice, adolescent, juvenile, youngster, *guy, *kid, *squirt. 2. [An associate] peer, associate, colleague; see **friend.**

fellowship, *n.* 1. [Congenial social feeling] comradeship, conviviality, sociality, sociability, intimacy, acquaintance, friendliness, familiarity, good-fellowship, amity, affability, camaraderie, togetherness.—*Ant.* rudeness, unsociability, surliness. 2. [Subsistence payment to encourage study] stipend, scholarship, honorarium, subsidy, teaching fellowship, assistantship.

felon, *n.* outlaw, delinquent, convict; see **criminal.**

felony, *n.* misconduct, offense, transgression; see **crime.**

female, *a.* reproductive, fertile, childbearing, of the female gender.—*Ant.* masculine, male, virile.

feminine, *a.* soft, womanly, delicate, gentle, ladylike, female, matronly, maidenly, tender, womanish, fair; see also **womanly.**—*Ant.* male, masculine, virile.

fence, *n.* 1. [That which surrounds an enclosure] picket fence, wire fence, board fence, barbed-wire fence, rail fence, chain fence, iron fence, hedge, backstop, rail, railing, barricade, net, barrier, wall, dike. 2. [A receiver of stolen goods] accomplice, *front (man), *uncle; see **criminal.** —**mend one's fences,** renew contacts, look after one's political interests, solicit votes; see **campaign.** —**on the fence,** undecided, uncommitted, indifferent; see **uncertain.**

fender, *n.* guard, mudguard, shield, apron, buffer, mask, cover, frame, cushion, protector, bumper.

fend for oneself, *v.* take care of oneself, stay alive, eke out an existence; see **survive** 1.

fend off, *v.* keep off, ward away, repel; see **defend** 1.

ferment, *v.* effervesce, sour, foam, froth, bubble, seethe, fizz, sparkle, boil, work, ripen, dissolve, evaporate, rise.

fermentation, *n.* souring, foaming, seething; see **decay.**

fern, *n.* greenery, bracken, lacy plant; see **plant.**

ferocious, *a.* fierce, savage, wild; see **fierce.**—*Ant.* gentle, meek, mild.

ferocity, *n.* fierceness, brutality, barbarity; see **cruelty.**

ferry, *n.* passage boat, barge, packet; see **boat.**

fertile, *a.* fruitful, rich, productive, fat, teeming, yielding, arable, flowering.—*Ant.* sterile, barren, desert.

fertility, *n.* fecundity, richness, fruitfulness, potency, virility, pregnancy, productiveness, productivity, generative capacity.

fertilization, *n.* 1. [The enrichment of land] manuring, dressing, mulching; see **preparation** 1. 2. [Impregnation of the ovum] insemination, impregnation, pollination, implantation, breeding, propagation, generation, procreation.

fertilize, *v.* 1. [To enrich land] manure, dress, spread, lime, mulch, cover, treat. 2. [To impregnate] breed, make pregnant, generate, germinate, pollinate, inseminate, propagate, procreate, get with child, beget, *knock up.

fertilizer, *n.* manure, commercial *or* chemical fertilizer, plant food, compost, humus, mulch. Common fertilizers include the following—barnyard manure, guano, sphagnum, peat moss, phosphate, dung, litter, crushed limestone, bone dust, kelp, bone meal, nitrogen, ammonium sulphate, potash.

fervent, *a.* zealous, eager, ardent; see **enthusiastic.**

fervor, *n.* fervency, ardor, enthusiasm; see **zeal.**

fester, *v.* rankle, putrefy, rot; see **spoil.**

festival, *n.* festivity, feast, competition; see **celebration.**

festive, *a.* merry, gay, joyful; see **happy.**

festivity, *n.* revelry, pleasure, amusement; see **entertainment.**

fetch, *v.* bring to, get, retrieve; see **carry** 1.

fetish, *n.* fixation, craze, mania; see **obsession.**

fetus, *n.* organism, embryo, the young of an animal in the womb; see **child.**

feud, *n.* quarrel, strife, bickering; see **fight.**

fever, *n.* abnormal temperature and

pulse, febrile disease, high body temperature; see **illness** 1.

feverish, *a*. burning, above normal, running a temperature; see **hot** 1.

few, *a*. not many, minority, scarcely any or anything, less, sparse, scanty, thin, scattering, widely spaced, inconsiderable, negligible, infrequent, not too many, a few, some, any, scarce, rare, seldom, few and far between.—*Ant.* **many**, numerous, innumerable.

few, *pron*. not many, a small number, a handful, scarcely any, not too many, several, a scattering, three or four, a sprinkling.—*Ant.* **many**, a multitude, a great many. —**quite a few**, several, some, a large number; see **many**.

fiancé, *n*. intended, betrothed, person engaged to be married; see **lover**.

fib, *n*. prevarication, fabrication, misrepresentation; see **lie** 1.

fiber, *n*. thread, cord, string, strand, tissue, filament, vein, hair, strip, shred. Some common fibers include the following—vegetable fiber, animal fiber, synthetic fiber, silk, linen, hemp, cotton, wool, jute, rayon, nylon, orlon, polyester, acetate.

fibrous, *a*. veined, hairy, coarse; see **stringy**.

fickle, *a*. capricious, whimsical, mercurial; see **changing**.

fiction, *n*. novel, tale, romance; see **story**.

fictitious, *a*. made-up, untrue, counterfeit; see **false** 1, 2.

fiddle, *n*. violin, stringed instrument, cornstalk fiddle; see **musical instrument**. —**fit as a fiddle**, healthy, strong, sound; see **well** 1.

fidelity, *n*. fealty, loyalty, devotion; see **loyalty**.

fidget, *v*. stir, twitch, worry; see **wiggle**.

fidgety, *a*. nervous, uneasy, apprehensive; see **restless**.

field, *n*. 1. [Open land] grainfield, hayfield, meadow, pasture, range, acreage, plot, patch, garden, cultivated ground, grassland, green, ranchland(s), arable land, plowed or cultivated land, cleared land, cropland, tract, vineyard. 2. [An area devoted to sport] diamond, gridiron, track, rink, court, course, racecourse, golf course, race track, arena, stadium, theater, amphitheater, playground, park, turf, green, fairground. 3. [An area devoted to a specialized activity] airfield, airport, flying field, terminal, battlefield, battleground, sector, field of fire, terrain, no man's land, theater of war, field of battle, field of honor, parade ground, range, parking lot. —**play the field**, experiment, explore, look elsewhere; see **discover, examine, try** 1.

fielder, *n*. infielder, outfielder, right or left or center fielder; see **baseball player**.

fiend, *n*. 1. [A wicked or cruel person] monster, barbarian, brute; see **beast** 2. 2. [An addict] fan, aficionado, monomaniac; see **addict**.

fiendish, *a*. diabolical, demoniac, infernal; see **bad**.

fierce, *a*. ferocious, wild, furious, enraged, raging, impetuous, untamed, angry, passionate, savage, primitive, brutish, animal, raving, outrageous, terrible, vehement, frightening, awful, horrible, venomous, bold, malevolent, malign, brutal, monstrous, severe, rough, rude, vicious, dangerous, frenzied, mad, insane, desperate, ravening, frantic, wrathful, irate, fanatical, bestial, boisterous, violent, threatening, stormy, thunderous, howling, tumultuous, turbulent, uncontrolled, raging, storming, blustering, cyclonic, torrential, frightful, fearful, devastating, hellish, *rip-roaring.—*Ant.* **mild**, moderate, calm.

fiercely, *a*. ferociously, violently, wildly, terribly, vehemently, angrily, threateningly, frighteningly, awfully, horribly, mightily, passionately, impetuously, boldly, irresistibly, furiously, riotously, brutally, monstrously, forcibly, forcefully, convulsively, hysterically, severely, roughly, rudely, viciously, dangerously, madly, insanely, desperately, outrageously, savagely, frantically, wrathfully, irately, virulently, relentlessly, turbulently, overpoweringly, strongly, deliriously, fanatically, with rage, in a frenzy, tooth and nail.—*Ant.* mildly, reasonably, **peacefully**.

fiesta, *n*. festival, holiday, feast; see **celebration**.

fifty, *a*. half a hundred, half a century, two score and ten, many, five times ten, a considerable number.

fight, *n*. 1. [A violent physical struggle] strife, contention, feud, quarrel, contest, encounter, row, dispute, disagreement, battle, confrontation, controversy, brawl, bout, match, fisticuffs, round, fracas, difficulty, altercation, bickering, wrangling, riot, argument, debate, competition, rivalry, conflict, skirmish, clash, scuffle, collision, brush, action, engagement, combat, blow, exchange of blows, wrestling match, squabble, game, discord, estrangement, *fuss, tussle, *scrap, free-for-all, *ruckus, *run-in, tiff, flareup, *go, row, *set-to, difference of opinion. 2. [Willingness or eagerness to fight] mettle, hardihood, boldness; see **courage** 1.

fight, *v*. strive, war, struggle, resist, assert oneself, challenge, meet, contend, attack, carry on war, withstand, give blow for blow, do battle, war against, persevere, force, go to war, exchange shots or blows, encounter, oppose, tussle, grapple, brush with, flare up, engage with, combat, wrestle, box, spar, skirmish, quarrel, bicker, dispute, have it out, squabble, come to grips with, row, *light or tear at or into, *mix it up with.—Ant. retreat, submit, yield.

fight back, v. defend oneself, resist, retaliate; see **oppose 2.**

fighter, n. 1. [One who fights] contestant, disputant, contender, party to a quarrel, warrior, soldier, combatant, belligerent, assailant, aggressor, antagonist, rival, opponent, champion, bully, competitor, controversialist. 2. [A professional pugilist] boxer, prize fighter, *pug, *bruiser; see sense 1.

fighting, a. combative, battling, brawling, unbeatable, resolute, argumentative, angry, ferocious, quarrelsome, ready to fight, belligerent, boxing, wrestling, warlike, contending, up in arms.

fighting, n. combat, struggle, strife; see **fight.**

fight off, v. defend from, hold back, resist; see **defend 1.**

figurative, a. not literal, metaphorical, allegorical; see **illustrative.**

figure, n. 1. [A form] shape, mass, structure; see **form 1.** 2. [The human torso] body, frame, torso, shape, form, development, configuration, build, appearance, outline, posture, attitude, pose, carriage. 3. [A representation of quantity] sum, total, symbol; see **number.** 4. [Price] value, worth, terms; see **price.**

figure, v. 1. [To compute] reckon, number, count; see **calculate.** 2. [To estimate] set a figure, guess, fix a price; see **estimate.** 3. [*To come to a conclusion] suppose, think, opine; see **decide.** 4. [Figure out] comprehend, master, reason; see **discover.**

figure of speech, n. Varieties include the following—image, comparison, metaphor, simile, epic, personification, hyperbole, allegory, parable, allusion, euphemism, analogue, parallel, irony, satire, understatement, paradox.

file, n. 1. [An orderly collection of papers] card index, card file, portfolio, record, classified index, list, register, dossier, notebook. 2. [Steel abrasive] rasp, steel, sharpener. Types of files include the following—flat, round or rat-tail, ignition, triangular or saw, fingernail, (wood) rasp, 10-inch, 12-inch, etc. 3. [A line] rank, row, column; see **line 1. —on file**, filed, catalogued, registered; see **recorded.**

file, v. 1. [To arrange in order] classify, index, deposit, categorize, catalogue, record, register, list, arrange. 2. [To use an abrasive] abrade, rasp, scrape, smooth, rub down, level off, finish, sharpen.

fill, n. enough, capacity, satiety; see **plenty.**

fill, v. 1. [To pour to the capacity of the container] pack, stuff, replenish, furnish, supply, satisfy, blow or fill or pump or puff up, fill to capacity, fill to overflowing, brim over, swell, charge, inflate.—Ant. empty, exhaust, drain. 2. [To occupy available space] take up, pervade, overflow, stretch, bulge or curve out, distend, brim over, stretch, swell, blow up, run over at the top, permeate, take over.

filled, a. finished, completed, done; see **full 1.**

fill in, v. 1. [To insert] write in, answer, sign; see **answer.** 2. [To substitute] replace, act for, represent; see **substitute 2.**

filling, n. stuffing, dressing, contents, mixture, center, layer, filler, fill, sauce, insides, lining, wadding, padding, cement, *innards, guts.

fill out, v. 1. [To enlarge] swell out, expand, overgrow; see **grow 1.** 2. [To insert] write or fill in, sign, apply; see **answer.**

fill up, v. saturate, pack, stuff; see **fill 1.**

film, n. 1. [Thin, membranous matter] gauze, tissue, fabric, sheet, membrane, layer, transparency, foil, fold, skin, coat, coating, scum, veil, cobweb, web, mist, cloud. 2. [A preparation containing a light-sensitive emulsion] negative, positive, Kodachrome (trademark), microfilm, color film. 3. [A moving picture film] motion picture, cinema, photoplay; see **movie.**

film, v. record, take, shoot; see **photograph.**

filter, v. 1. [To soak slowly] seep, penetrate, percolate; see **soak 1.** 2. [To clean by filtering] strain, purify, sift, sieve, refine, clarify, clean, separate.

filth, n. dirt, dung, feces, contamination, corruption, pollution, foul matter, sewage, muck, manure, slop, squalor, trash, grime, mud, smudge, silt, garbage, carrion, slush, slime, sludge, foulness, filthiness, excrement, dregs, lees, sediment, rottenness, impurity.—Ant. cleanliness, purity, spotlessness.

filthy, a. foul, squalid, nasty; see **dirty 1.**

fin, n. membrane, paddle, propeller, balance, guide, blade, ridge, organ, spine, pectoral fin, ventral fin, dorsal fin, caudal fin, flipper, fishtail.

final, a. terminal, concluding, ultimate; see **last 1**.

finalized, a. concluded, decided, completed; see **finished 1**.

finally, a. **1.** [As though a matter were settled] with finality or conviction, settled, in a final manner, certainly, officially, irrevocably, decisively, definitely, beyond recall, permanently, for all time, conclusively, assuredly, done with, once and for all, for good, beyond the shadow of a doubt.—Ant. **temporarily,** momentarily, for the time being. **2.** [After a long period] at length, at last, in or at the end, subsequently, in conclusion, lastly, after all, after a time or a while, eventually, ultimately, at long last, at the final point, at the last moment, at the end, tardily, belatedly, when all is said and done, in spite of all.

finance, n. business, commerce, financial affairs; see **economics**.

finance, v. fund, pay for, provide funds (for); see **pay for**.

finances, n. revenue, capital, funds; see **wealth**.

financial, a. economic, business, monetary; see **commercial**.

financier, n. capitalist, banker, merchant; see **executive**.

find, n. (fortunate) discovery, findings, acquisition; see **discovery**.

find, v. discover, detect, notice, observe, perceive, arrive at, discern, hit upon, encounter, uncover, recover, expose, stumble or happen or come on or upon or across, track down, dig or turn or *scare up, run across or into, lay one's finger or hand on, bring to light, spot; see also **see 1**.—Ant. lose, mislay, miss.

finder, n. acquirer, discoverer, search party; see **owner**.—Ant. loser, seeker, failure.

find fault, v. blame, criticize, condemn; see **blame**.

finding, n. verdict, decision, sentence; see **judgement 3**.

findings, n. data, discoveries, conclusions; see **summary**.

find out, v. recognize, learn, identify; see **discover**.

fine, a. **1.** [Not coarse] light, powdery, granular; see **little 1**. **2.** [Of superior quality] well-made, supreme, fashionable; see **excellent**. **3.** [Exact] precise, distinct, strict; see **accurate 2**, **definite 2**.

fine, n. penalty, damage, forfeit; see **punishment**.

fine, v. penalize, exact, tax, confiscate, levy, seize, extort, alienate, make pay; see also **punish**.

finger, n. digit, organ of touch, tactile member, forefinger, thumb, index finger,

extremity, pointer, feeler, tentacle, *pinky. —have (or keep) one's fingers crossed, wish, aspire to, pray for; see hope. —lift a finger, make an effort, attempt, endeavor; see try 1. —put one's fing.r on, indicate, ascertain, detect; see **discover**. —*put the finger on, inform on, turn in, spy on; see **tell 1**.

finger, v. **1.** [To feel] handle, touch, manipulate; see feel **1**. **2.** [*To choose or specify] appoint, point out, name; see **choose**.

fingernail, n. nail, talon, matrix; see **claw**.

finish, n. **1.** [The end] close, termination, ending; see end **2**. **2.** [An applied surface] shine, polish, glaze, surface. Finishes include the following—shellac or shellack, oil, plastic, turpentine, lacquer, stain, varnish, polish, wall paper, wash, whitewash, paint, casein paint, enamel, gold leaf, wax, veneer, cement, stucco, luster.

finish, v. **1.** [To bring to an end] complete, end, perfect; see **achieve**. **2.** [To develop a surface] polish, wax, stain; see **cover 1**, **paint 2**. **3.** [To come to an end] cease, close, end; see **stop**.

finished, a. **1.** [Completed] done, accomplished, perfected, achieved, ended, performed, executed, dispatched, concluded, complete, through, fulfilled, closed, over, decided, brought about, ceased, stopped, resolved, settled, made, worked out, rounded out, discharged, satisfied, disposed of, realized, finalized, effected, put into effect, all over with, attained, turned or shut off, done with, made an end of, brought to a conclusion or a close, said and done, *sewed up, wound up.—Ant. **unfinished,** imperfect, incomplete. **2.** [Given a finish] polished, coated, varnished; see **painted 2**.

fire, n. **1.** [Burning] flame, conflagration, burning, blaze, campfire, coals, flame and smoke, blazing fire, hearth, burning coals, tinder, bonfire, bed of coals, embers, source of heat, sparks, heat, glow, warmth, luminosity, combustion. **2.** [The discharge of ordinance] artillery attack, bombardment, rounds, barrage, explosions, bombings, curtain (of fire), volley, sniping, mortar attack, salvos, shells, pattern of fire, fire superiority, cross fire, machine-gun or automatic fire, rifle or small-arms fire, antiaircraft fire; see also **attack**. —catch (on) fire, begin burning, ignite, flare up; see **burn**. —on fire, **1.** [Burning] flaming, fiery, hot; see **burning**. **2.** [Excited] full of ardor, enthusiastic, zealous; see **excited**. —open fire, start shooting, shoot (at), attack; see **shoot 1**. —play with fire, gamble, endanger oneself or one's interests, do something dangerous; see **risk.** —**set fire to**, ignite, oxidize, make burn; see **burn.** —**set the world on fire**, achieve, become famous, excel; see **succeed 1.** —**under fire**, criticized, censured, under attack; see **questionable 1, 2.**

fire, *v.* 1. [To set on fire] kindle, enkindle, ignite, inflame, light, burn, set fire to, put a match to, start a fire, set burning, touch off, rekindle, relight.— *Ant.* **extinguish**, smother, quench. 2. [To shoot] discharge, shoot *or* set off, hurl; see **shoot 1.** 3. [To dismiss] discharge, let go, eject; see **dismiss.**

fired, *a.* 1. [Subjected to fire] set on fire, burned, baked, ablaze, afire, on fire, aflame, burning, incandescent, scorched, glowing, kindled, enkindled, smoking, smoldering, heated. 2. [Discharged] dropped, let out, *given one's walking papers; see **discharged.**

fireman, *n.* 1. [One who extinguishes fires] fire-fighter, engineman, ladderman, fire chief. 2. [One who fuels engines *or* furnaces] stoker, engineer's helper, railroad man, trainman, attendant, oil feeder, *cinder monkey, *hellholer, *boy in the hot spot.

fireplace, *n.* hearth, chimney, hearthside, stove, furnace, blaze, bed of coals, grate.

fireproof, *a.* noninflammable, noncombustible, nonflammable, fire-resistant, incombustible, concrete and steel, asbestos.

fireworks, *n. pl.* rockets, Roman candles, sparklers; see **explosive.**

firm, *a.* 1. [Stable] fixed, solid, rooted, immovable, fastened, motionless, secured, steady, substantial, durable, rigid, bolted, welded, riveted, soldered, imbedded, nailed, tightened, fast, secure, sound, immobile, unmovable, mounted, stationary, set, settled.—*Ant.* **loose,** movable, mobile. 2. [Firm in texture] solid, dense, compact, hard, stiff, impenetrable, impervious, rigid, hardened, inflexible, unyielding, thick, compressed, substantial, heavy, close, condensed, impermeable.—*Ant.* **soft,** porous, flabby. 3. [Settled in purpose] determined, steadfast, resolute; see **constant.** —**stand** *or* **hold firm,** be steadfast, endure, maintain one's resolution; see **fight, resolve.**

firmly, *a.* 1. [Not easily moved] immovably, solidly, rigidly, stably, durably, enduringly, substantially, securely, heavily, stiffly, inflexibly, soundly, strongly, thoroughly.—*Ant.* **lightly,** tenuously, insecurely. 2. [Showing determination] resolutely, steadfastly, doggedly, stolidly, tenaciously, determinedly, staunchly, constantly, intently, purposefully, persistently, obstinately, stubbornly, un-

waveringly, unchangeably, through thick and thin.

firmness, *n.* stiffness, hardness, toughness, solidity, impenetrability, durability, imperviousness, temper, impermeability, inflexibility.

first, *a.* beginning, original, primary, prime, primal, antecedent, initial, virgin, earliest, opening, introductory, primeval, leading, in the beginning, front, head, rudimentary.—*Ant.* **last,** ultimate, final. —**in the first place,** firstly, initially, to begin with; see **first.**

first aid, *n.* emergency medical aid, Red Cross, emergency relief; see **medicine 2, treatment 2.**

first-class, *a.* superior, supreme, choice; see **excellent.**

first-rate, *a.* prime, very good, choice; see **excellent.**

fish, *n.* seafood, panfish, denizen of the deep. Types of fish include the following—catfish, pickerel, pike, perch, trout, flounder, sucker, sunfish, bass, crappy, mackerel, cod, salmon, carp, minnow, eel, bullhead, herring, shad, barracuda, swordfish, goldfish, gar, octopus, dogfish, flying fish, whitefish, tuna, pompano, haddock, hake, halibut, mullet, loach, muskellunge, sardine, smelt; see also **shellfish.** —**drink like a fish,** imbibe, get drunk, become inebriated; see **drink 2.** —**like a fish out of water,** out of place, alien, displaced; see **unfamiliar 1.**

fish, *v.* go fishing, troll (for), net, bob (for), shrimp, bait the hook, trawl, angle, cast one's net.

fisherman, *n.* angler, fisher, harpooner, sailor, seaman, whaler, fish catcher.

fish for, *v.* hint at, elicit, try to evoke; see **hint.**

fishing, *n.* angling, casting, trawling; see **sport 1.**

fishy, *a.* improbable, dubious, implausible; see **unlikely.**

fist, *n.* clenched hand, clenched fist, hand, clutch, clasp, grasp, grip, hold.

fit, *a.* 1. [Appropriate by nature] suitable, proper, fitting, fit, likely, expedient, appropriate, convenient, timely, opportune, feasible, practicable, wise, advantageous, favorable, preferable, beneficial, desirable, adequate, tasteful, becoming, agreeable, seasonable, due, rightful, equitable, legimate, decent, harmonious, pertinent, according, relevant, in keeping, consistent, applicable, compatible, admissible, concurrent, to the point *or* purpose, answerable *or* agreeable *or* adapted to, fitted, suited, calculated, prepared, qualified, competent, matched, ready-made, accomodated, right, happy, lucky, cut out for.—*Ant.* **unfit,** unseemly, inappropriate. 2. [In good physical condition] trim, competent, robust; see **healthy 1.**

fit, n. 1. [Sudden attack of disease] (muscular) convulsion, rage, spasm, seizure, stroke, epileptic attack, paroxysm, *jumps; see also **illness 1.** 2. [Transitory spell of action or feeling] impulsive action, burst, rush, outbreak, torrent, tantrum, mood, outburst, whimsy, huff, rage, spell. —**have (or throw) a fit,** become angry or excited, lose one's temper, give vent to emotion; see **rage 1.**

fit, v. 1. [To be suitable in character] agree, suit, accord, harmonize, apply, belong, conform, consist, fit (right) in, be in keeping, parallel, relate, concur, match, correspond, be comfortable, respond, have its place, answer the purpose, meet, *click.—Ant. disagree, **oppose,** clash. 2. [To make suitable] arrange, alter, adapt; see **adjust 1.**

fitness, n. appropriateness, suitability, propriety, expediency, convenience, adequacy, correspondence, decency, decorum, harmony, keeping, consistency, applicability, compatibility, rightness, timeliness, adaptation, qualification, accommodation, competence.

fit out, v. supply, equip, outfit; see **provide 1.**

fitted, a. suited, proper, adapted; see **fit 1.**

fix, v. 1. [To make firm] plant, implant, secure; see **fasten.** 2. [To prepare a meal] prepare, heat, get ready; see **cook.** 3. [To put in order] correct, improve, settle, put into shape, reform, patch, rejuvenate, touch up, revive, refresh, renew, renovate, rebuild, make compatible, clean, align, adapt, mend, adjust.

fixed, a. [Firm] solid, rigid, immovable; see **firm 1.** 2. [Repaired] rebuilt, in order, timed, synchronized, adjusted, settled, mended, rearranged, adapted, corrected, restored, renewed, improved, patched up, put together, in working order. 3. [*Prearranged] predesigned, *put-up, *set-up; see **planned.**

fixings, n. parts, components, constituents; see **ingredients.**

fixture, n. convenience, gas or electric appliance or fixture or machine or devices or equipment; see **appliance.**

*fix up, v. fix, mend, rehabilitate; see **repair.**

fizz, n. hissing, sputtering, bubbling; see **noise 1.**

*fizzle, n. disappointment, fiasco, defeat; see **failure 1.**

flabby, a. limp, tender, soft; see **fat.**

flag, n. banner, standard, colors; see **emblem.**

flagrant, a. notorious, disgraceful, infamous; see **outrageous.**

flair, n. talent, aptitude, gift; see **ability.**

flake, n. scale, cell, sheet, wafer, peel, skin, slice, sliver, layer, sheet, leaf, shaving, plate, section, scab.

flake, v. scale, peel, sliver, shed, drop, chip, scab, slice, pare, trim, wear away.

flamboyant, a. baroque, bombastic, ostentatious; see **ornate 1.**

flame, n. blaze, flare, flash; see **fire 1.**

flame, v. blaze, oxidize, flare up; see **burn.**

flaming, a. blazing, ablaze, fiery; see **burning.**

flannel, n. woolen, cotton flannel, flannelette; see **wool.**

flap, n. fold, tab, lapel, fly, cover, pendant, drop, tail, appendage, tag, accessory, apron, skirt, strip, wing.

flap, v. flutter, flash, swing; see **wave 1.**

flare, n. glare, brief blaze, spark; see **flash.**

flare, v. blaze, glow, burn; see **flash.**

flare out, v. widen out, spread out, splay; see **grow 1.**

flare up,/ v. 1. [Said of persons] lose one's temper, rant, seethe; see **rage 1.** 2. [Said of fire] glow, burst into flame, blaze; see **burn.**

flash, n. glimmer, sparkle, glitter, glisten, gleam, beam, blaze, flicker, flame, glare, burst, impulse, vision, dazzle, shimmer, shine, glow, twinkle, twinkling, phosphorescence, reflection, radiation, ray, luster, spark, streak, stream, illumination, incandescence.

flash, v. glimmer, sparkle, glitter, glisten, gleam, beam, blaze, flame, glare, dazzle, shimmer, shine, glow, twinkle, reflect, radiate, shoot out beams, flicker; see **shine 1, 2.**

·**flashlight,** n. flash lamp, spotlight, torch; see **light 1.**

flashy, a. gaudy, showy, ostentatious; see **ornate 1.**

flask, n. decanter, jug, canteen; see **bottle.**

flat, a. 1. [Lying in a smooth plane] level, even, smooth, spread out, extended, prostrate, horizontal, low, on a level, fallen, level with the ground, prone.—Ant. rough, raised, uneven. 2. [Lacking savor] unseasoned, insipid, flavorless; see **tasteless 1.**

flatten, v. level (off), even out, smooth (off), spread out, depress, squash, smash, level, even, knock or wear or beat down, fell, floor, ground, smooth, roll out, straighten, deflate.—Ant. **raise,** elevate, inflate.

flattened, *a.* leveled, depressed, planed, smoothed; see **flat 1.**

flatter, *v.* overpraise, adulate, glorify; see **praise 1.**

flattered, *a.* praised, lauded, exalted; see **praised.**

flatterer, *n.* parasite, lickspittle, flunky, slave, puppet, groveler, sniveler, *apple-polisher, *doormat.

flattering, *a.* pleasing, favorable, unduly favorable; see **complimentary.**

flattery, *n.* adulation, compliments, excessive compliment, applause, false praise, commendation, tribute, gratification, pretty speeches, soft words, fawning, blarney, *applesauce, *soft soap, *hokum, *mush.–*Ant.* criticism, censure, hatred.

flaunt, *v.* vaunt, display, brandish; see **boast.**

flaunting, *a.* gaudy, ostentatious, pretentious; see **ornate 1.**

flavor, *n.* taste, savor, tang, relish, smack, twang, gusto. Individual flavors include the following–tartness, sweetness, acidity, saltiness, spiciness, piquancy, astringency, bitterness, sourness, pepperiness, hotness, gaminess, greasiness, fishy taste.

flavor, *v.* season, salt, pepper, spice (up), give a tang to, make tasty, bring out a flavor in, put in flavoring.

flavoring, *n.* essence, extract, seasoning, spice, additive, condiment, sauce, relish; see also **herb, spice.**

flavorless, *a.* insipid, vapid, mawkish; see **tasteless 1.**

flaw, *n.* defect, imperfection, stain; see **blemish.**

flawless, *a.* faultless, sound, impeccable; see **perfect.**

flea, *n.* dog flea, sand flea, flea louse; see **insect.**

fleck, *n.* mite, speck, dot; see **bit 1.**

flee, *v.* desert, escape, run; see **retreat 1.**

fleet, *n.* armada, naval force, task force; see **navy.**

flesh, *n.* meat, fat, muscle, brawn, tissue, cells, flesh and blood, protoplasm, plasm, plasma, body parts, heart, *insides. –one's (own) flesh and blood, family, kindred, kin; see **relative.**

fleshy, *a.* obese, plump, corpulent; see **fat.**

flexibility, *n.* pliancy, plasticity, flexibleness, pliableness, suppleness, elasticity, extensibility, limberness, litheness.

flexible, *a.* limber, lithe, supple, plastic, elastic, bending, malleable, pliable, soft, extensile, spongy, tractable, moldable, yielding, formable, bendable, formative, impressionable, like putty *or* wax, adjustable, stretchable.–*Ant.* stiff, hard, rigid.

flicker, *v.* sparkle, twinkle, glitter; see **flash, shine 1.**

flight, *n.* 1. [Act of remaining aloft] soaring, winging, flying, journey by air, aviation. 2. [Travel by air] aerial navigation, aeronautics, flying, gliding, space flight, air transport, aviation. 3. [Act of fleeing] fleeing, running away, retreating; see **retreat 1.** 4. [Stairs] steps, staircase, ascent; see **stairs.**

flighty, *a.* capricious, fickle, whimsical; see **changing.**

flimsy, *a.* slight, infirm, frail, weak, unsubstantial, inadequate, defective, wobbly, fragile, makeshift, decrepit; see also **poor 2.**

flinch, *v.* start, shrink back, blench; see **wince.**

fling, *n.* indulgence, party, good time; see **celebration.**

fling, *v.* toss, sling, dump; see **throw 1.**

flippancy, *n.* impertinence, impudence, sauciness; see **rudeness.**

flippant, *a.* impudent, saucy, smart; see **rude 2.**

flirt, *n.* coquette, tease, siren; see **lover.**

flirt, *v.* make advances, tease, make eyes at; see **seduce.**

float, *n.* buoy, air cell, air cushion, lifesaver, bobber, cork, raft, diving platform, life preserver.

float, *v.* waft, stay afloat, swim; see **drift.**

floating, *a.* buoyant, hollow, unsinkable, lighter-than-water, light, swimming, inflated, sailing, soaring, volatile, loose, free.–*Ant.* heavy, submerged, sunk.

flock, *n.* group, pack, litter; see **herd 1.**

flock, *v.* throng, congregate, crowd; see **gather 1.**

flood, *n.* deluge, surge, tide, high tide, overflow, torrent, wave, flood tide, tidal flood *or* flow, inundation.

flood, *v.* inundate, swamp, overflow, deluge, submerge, immerse, brim over.

floor, *n.* 1. [The lower limit of a room] floorboards, deck, flagstones, tiles, planking, ground, carpet, rug, linoleum. 2. [The space in a building between two floors] story, stage, landing, level, flat, basement, cellar, ground floor *or* story, lower story, first floor, mezzanine, upper story, downstairs, upstairs, loft, attic, garret, penthouse.

flooring, *n.* floors, woodwork, oak flooring, hardwood flooring, tile, flagstones, boards, cement, floor covering, linoleum.

flop, *v.* 1. [To move with little control] wobble, teeter, stagger, flounder, wriggle, squirm, stumble, tumble, totter, flounce, quiver, flap, wiggle, spin, *jitter, jerk. 2. [To fall without restraint] tumble, slump, drop; see **fall 1.** 3. [*To be a complete failure] miscarry, founder, fall short; see **fail 1.**

flounder, v. struggle, wallow, blunder; see **flop 1, toss 2.**

flour, n. meal, pulp, powder, grit, bran, starch, wheat germ, white flour, (whole) wheat flour, rye flour, potato flour, barley meal, corn meal, oatmeal, rolled oats, cake flour, pancake flour, soybean *or* soyabean *or* soyflour.

flourish, v. thrive, increase, wax; see **succeed 1.**

flourishing, a. thriving, doing well, growing; see **rich 1, successful.**

flow, n. current, movement, progress, stream, tide, run, river, flood, ebb, gush, spurt, spout, leakage, dribble, oozing, flux, overflow, issue, discharge, drift, course, draft, down-draft, up-current, wind, breeze.

flow, v. stream, course, slide, slip, glide, move, progress, run, pass, float, sweep, rush, whirl, surge, roll, swell, ebb, pour out, spurt, squirt, flood, jet, spout, rush, gush, well (up), drop, drip, seep, trickle, overflow, spill, run, spew, stream, brim, surge, leak, run out, ooze, splash, pour forth, bubble.

flower, n. blossom, bud, spray, cluster, shoot, posy, herb, vine, annual, perennial, flowering shrub, potted plant. Common flowers include the following—daisy, violet, cowslip, jack-in-the-pulpit, goldenrod, orchid, primrose, bluebell, salvia, geranium, begonia, pansy, calendula, forsythia, daffodil, jonquil, crocus, dahlia, cosmos, zinnia, tulip, iris, lily, petunia, gladiolus, aster, rose, peony, nasturtium, chrysanthemum, poppy, morning-glory, lily-of-the-valley, clematis, buttercup, bougainvillaea, dandelion, fuchsia, bridal wreath, lilac, stock, sweet William, bachelor's button, tuberose, bleeding heart, phlox; see also **fruit.**

flower, v. open, blossom, blow; see **bloom.**

flowery, a. elaborate, ornamented, rococo; see **ornate 1.**

flowing, a. sweeping, sinuous, spouting, running, gushing, pouring out, rippling, issuing, fluid, tidal, liquid.

fluctuate, v. vacillate, waver, falter; see **hesitate.**

fluctuation, n. vacillation, variation, inconstancy; see **change 1.**

fluency, n. facility of speech, volubility, multiloquence; see **eloquence.**

fluent, a. eloquent, voluble, glib, wordy, smooth, talkative, smooth-spoken, garrulous, verbose, chatty, argumentative, articulate, vocal, cogent, persuasive, *silver-tongued or* -throated, *having or* with the gift of gab.—*Ant.* dumb, tongue-tied, stammering.

fluffy, a. fleecy, fuzzy, lacy; see **soft 2.**

fluid, a. liquid, fluent, flowing, running, watery, molten, liquefied, juicy.—*Ant.* stiff, solid, frozen.

fluid, n. liquor, vapor, solution; see **liquid.**

*****flunk,** v. miss, drop, have to repeat; see **fail 1.**

flute, n. pipe, piccolo, wind instrument, fife, recorder; see **musical instrument.**

flutter, v. flap, ripple, wiggle; see **wave 1, 3.**

fly, n. 1. [An insect] housefly, bluebottle, bug, winged insect, gnat, horsefly, fruit fly, tsetse fly. 2. [A ball batted into the air] infield, fly, high fly, fly ball, *aerial, *pop fly. 3. [A hook baited artificially] lure, fish lure, dry fly, wet fly, spinner, trout fly, bass fly, minnow.

fly, v. 1. [To pass through the air] wing, soar, float, glide, remain aloft, take flight, take wing, hover, sail, swoop, dart, drift, flutter, circle. 2. [To move swiftly] rush, dart, flee away; see **speed.** 3. [To flee from danger] retreat, hide, withdraw; see **escape.** 4. [To manage a plane in the air] pilot, navigate, control, jet, take off, operate, glide, climb, dive, manipulate, maneuver.

flyer, n. aviator, navigator, airman; see **pilot 1.**

flying, a. floating, making flight, passing through the air, on the wing, soaring, gliding, winging, swooping, darting, plummeting, drifting, rising, air-borne, in mid-air.

foam, n. fluff, bubbles, lather; see **froth.**

focus, n. focal point, locus, point of convergence; see **center 1. —in focus,** distinct, obvious, sharply defined; see **clear 2. —out of focus,** indistinct, unclear, blurred; see **obscure 1.**

focus, v. 1. [To draw toward a center] attract, converge, convene; see **center.** 2. [To make an image clear] adjust, bring out, get detail; see **sharpen 2.**

foe, n. opponent, antagonist, adversary; see **enemy.**

fog, n. mist, haze, cloud, film, steam, wisp, smoke, *soup, *pea soup, smog.

foggy, a. dull, misty, gray; see **hazy 1.**

fold, n. lap, pleat, lapel, tuck, folded portion, part turned over, part turned back, doubled material, crease, turn, folded edge, crimp, wrinkle.

fold, v. 1. [To place together, or lay in folds] double, crease, curl, crimp, wrinkle, ruffle, pucker, gather, double over, lap, overlap, overlay.—*Ant.* unfold, straighten, expand. 2. [*To fail] become insolvent, declare oneself bankrupt, close; see **fail 4.**

folder, n. circular, pamphlet, paper, bulletin, advertisement, enclosure, brochure, throwaway, sheath, envelope, binder, portfolio.

folk, *n.* race, nation, community, tribe, society, nationality, population, state, settlement, culture, (ethnic) group, clan, confederation.

folklore, *n.* traditions, (folk) tales, oral tradition, folk wisdom, oral literature, ballad lore, customs, superstitions, legends, folkways, folk wisdom, traditional lore; see also **myth.**

folks, *n.* relatives, relations, kin; see **family.**

follow, *v.* 1. [To be later in time] come next, ensue, postdate; see **succeed 2.** 2. [To regulate one's action] conform, observe, imitate, copy, take after, match, mirror, reflect, follow the example of, do as, mimic, follow suit, do like, tag along, obey, abide by, adhere to, comply, be in keeping, be consistent with.—*Ant.* disregard, **neglect,** depart from. 3. [To observe] heed, regard, keep an eye on; see **watch. 4.** [To understand] comprehend, catch, realize; see **understand 1. 5.** [To result] proceed *or* spring *or* come from, happen, ensue; see **begin 2.** —**as follows,** the following, next, succeeding; see **following.**

follower, *n.* henchman, attendant, hanger-on, companion, lackey, helper, partisan, recruit, disciple, pupil, protegé, imitator, apostle, adherent, supporter, zealot, backer, participant, sponsor, witness, devotee, believer, advocate, member, admirer, patron, promoter, upholder, copycat, *yes man.—*Ant.* **opponent,** deserter, heretic.

following, *a.* succeeding, next, ensuing, subsequent, later, after a while, by and by, when, later on, a while later, then, henceforth, afterwards, presently, afterward, coming after, directly after, in the wake of, pursuing, in pursuit (of), in search (of), resulting, latter, rear, back.—*Ant.* **preceding,** former, earlier.

following, *n.* group, clientele, public, audience, train, adherents, supporters, hangers-on, patrons.

fond, *a.* enamored, attached, affectionate; see **loving.**

fondness, *n.* partiality, attachment, kindness; see **affection.**

food, *n.* victuals, foodstuffs, meat and drink, meat, nutriment, refreshment, edibles, table, comestibles, provisions, stores, sustenance, subsistence, rations, board, cooking, cookery, cuisine, nourishment, fare, *grub, *vittles, *eats, *chow; see also **meal 2.** For food in the menu, see **bread, butter, cake 2, candy, cheese, delicatessen 1, dessert, drink 2, egg, fish, flavoring, fowl, fruit, jam 1, jelly, meat, milk, nut 1, pastry, salad, soup, spice, stew, vegetable.**

fool, *n.* nitwit, simpleton, dunce, oaf, ninny, cretin, nincompoop, bore, dolt, idiot, jackass, ass, buffoon, blockhead, numskull, booby, boob, goose, ignoramus, imbecile, moron, clown, loon, dullard, *fathead, halfwit, *lightweight, babbler, *bonehead, dope, *sap, *crackpot.—*Ant.* philosopher, sage, scholar. — **no** (*or* nobody's) **fool,** shrewd, calculating, capable; see **able, intelligent.** — **play the fool,** be silly, show off, clown; see **joke.**

fool, *v.* trick, dupe, mislead; see **deceive.**

fool around, *v.* waste time, idle, dawdle; see **play 1, 2, waste 1, 2.**

fooled, *a.* tricked, duped, deluded; see **deceived.**

fooling, *a.* joking, jesting, humorous, deceitful, gay, witty, smart, frivolous, flippant, laughable, insincere, misleading, absurd, clever, playful, merry, *kidding, *spoofing.—*Ant.* **serious,** grave, earnest.

foolish, *a.* silly, simple, half-witted; see **stupid 1.**

foolishly, *a.* stupidly, irrationally, idiotically, insanely, imprudently, ineptly, mistakenly, illogically, unwisely, illadvisedly, crazily, thoughtlessly, carelessly, irresponsibly, absurdly, preposterously, ridiculously, with bad judgment, without good sense.

foolishness, *n.* folly, weakness, silliness; see **stupidity 1.**

foot, *n.* 1. [A unit of measurement] twelve inches, running foot, front foot, board foot, square foot, cubic foot. 2. [End of the leg] (pedal) extremity, hoof, paw, pad, dog, *tootsie. 3. [A foundation] footing, base, pier; see **foundation 2. 4.** [A metrical unit in verse] measure, accent, interval, meter, duple meter, triple meter. Metrical feet include the following—iamb, dactyl, spondee, trochee, anapest. —**on foot,** running, hiking, moving; see **walking.** —**on one's feet,** 1. [Upright] standing, erect, vertical; see **straight.** 2. [Established] sound, settled, secure; see **established 1.** —**on the wrong foot,** unfavorably, ineptly, incapably; see **wrongly 2.** —*put one's best foot forward,** do one's best, appear at one's best, try hard; see **display.** —*put one's foot down,** be firm, act decisively, determine; see **resolve.** —**under foot,** on the ground *or* the floor, at one's feet, in one's way; see **under 1.**

football, *n.* 1. [A sport] American football, Association football, soccer, the pigskin sport. 2. [The ball used in football, sense 1] leather oval, pigskin, sphere; see **ball 1.**

football player, *n.* In the United States, football players include the following— right end, left end, right tackle, left tackle, right guard, left guard, center, quarterback, left halfback, right halfback, fullback.

foothold, *n.* ledge, footing, niche; see **step 2.**

footing, *n.* basis, resting place, foot; see **step 2.**

footprint, *n.* trace, trail, footstep; see **track 2.**

footstep, *n.* trace, trail, evidence; see **track 2.** —follow in (someone's) footsteps, emulate, succeed, resemble a predecessor; see **imitate 1.**

for, *conj.* as, since, in consequence of the fact that; see **because.**

for, *prep.* toward, to, in favor of, intended to be given to, in order to get, under the authority of, in the interest of, during, in order to, in the direction of, to go to, to the amount of, in place of, in exchange for, as, in spite of, supposing, concerning, with respect *or* regard to, notwithstanding, with a view to, for the sake of, in consideration of, in the name of, on the part of.

forasmuch as, *conj.* since, inasmuch as, whereas; see **because.**

for a while, *a.* for a short time, for a few minutes, briefly; see **awhile.**

forbid, *v.* prohibit, debar, embargo, restrain, inhibit, preclude, oppose, cancel, hinder, obstruct, bar, prevent, censor, outlaw, declare illegal, withhold, restrict, deny, block, check, disallow, deprive, exclude, ban, taboo, say no to, put under an injunction.—*Ant.* **approve,** recommend, authorize.

forbidden, *a.* denied, taboo, kept back; see **refused.**

forbidding, *a.* unpleasant, offensive, repulsive; see **grim 1.**

force, *n.* **1.** [Force conceived as a physical property] power, might, energy; see **strength. 2.** [Force conceived as part of one's personality] forcefulness, dominance, competence, energy, persistence, willpower, drive, determination, effectiveness, efficiency, energy, impressiveness, ability, capability, potency, sapience, guts.—*Ant.* **indifference,** impotence, incompetence. **3.** [An organization] group, band, unit; see **organization 2,** police. —in force, **1.** [Powerfully] in full strength, totally, all together; see **all 2. 2.** [In operation] operative, valid, in effect; see **working.**

force, *v.* compel, coerce, press, drive, make, impel, constrain, oblige, obligate, necessitate, require, enforce, demand, order, command, inflict, burden, impose, insist, exact, put under obligation, contract, charge, restrict, limit, pin down, bring pressure to bear upon, bear down

(against *or* upon), ram down one's throat, high-pressure, strong-arm.

forced, *a.* compelled, coerced, constrained; see **bound 2.**

forceful, *a.* commanding, dominant, electric; see **powerful 1.**

forcefully, *a.* forcibly, stubbornly, willfully; see **vigorously.**

foreboding, *n.* premonition, dread, presentiment; see **anticipation.**

forecast, *n.* prediction, guess, estimate, prognosis, divination, forethought, foresight, prescience, foreknowledge, conjecture, prophecy, calculation, foreseeing.

forecast, *v.* predetermine, reason, guess; see **foretell.**

forefather, *n.* ancestor, progenitor, forebear, father, parent, sire, forerunner, author, predecessor, originator, precursor, grandfather, procreator, patriarch, relative, begetter, founder, kinsman.

for effect, *a.* artificially, hypocritically, ostentatiously; see **deliberately.**

foregoing, *a.* prior, former, previous; see **preceding.**

foreground, *n.* face, forefront, frontage, façade, neighborhood, proximity, nearness, adjacency, range, reach, view.—*Ant.* **background,** shadow, perspective.

forehead, *n.* brow, countenance, temples; see **face 1.**

foreign, *a.* remote, exotic, strange, far, distant, inaccessible, unaccustomed, different, unknown, alien, imported, borrowed, immigrant, outside, expatriate, exiled, from abroad, coming from another land, not native, not domestic, nonresident, alienated, faraway, far-off, outlandish.—*Ant.* **local,** national, indigenous.

foreigner, *n.* stranger, immigrant, newcomer; see **alien.**

foreknowledge, *n.* foresight, prescience, premonition; see **feeling 4, forecast.**

foreman, *n.* overseer, manager, supervisor, superintendent, head, head man, shop foreman, boss, slavedriver.

foremost, *a.* fore, original, primary; see **first.**

forerunner, *n.* herald, harbinger, precursor; see **forefather, messenger.**

foresee, *v.* prophesy, understand, predict; see **foretell.**

foreseen, *a.* anticipated, predictable, prepared for; see **expected, likely 1.**

foreshadow, *v.* imply, presage, suggest; see **foretell.**

foresight, *n.* economy, carefulness, husbandry; see **prudence.**

forest, *n.* wood, jungle, timber, growth, stand of trees, grove, woodland, park, greenwood, cover, clump, timbered *or* forested land *or* area, shelter, brake, backwoods, tall timber; see also **tree.**

forestall, v. thwart, prevent, preclude; see **hinder**.

forestry, n. forest service, horticulture, dendrology, woodcraft, forestation, reclamation, woodmanship; see **conservation**.

foretell, v. predict, prophesy, divine, foresee, announce in advance, foreknow, forebode, augur, portend, foreshadow.—Ant. record, confirm, recount.

forethought, n. provision, planning, foresight; see **prudence**.

forever, a. everlastingly, permanently, immortally, on and on, ever, perpetually, always, in perpetuity, world without end, eternally, interminably, enduringly, unchangingly, durably, ever and again, indestructibly, endlessly, forevermore, for good (and all), *till hell freezes over, *for keeps, for always, now and forever, till death do us part.—Ant. temporarily, for a time, at present.

forewarn, v. premonish, admonish, alarm; see **warn 1**.

for example, a. for instance, as a model, as an example, to illustrate, to cite an instance, to give or offer or provide an illustration, a case in point.

forfeit, v. sacrifice, give up, give over, relinquish; see **abandon 1**.

for fun, a. for no reason, for the fun of it, in fun; see **happily**.

forge, v. falsify, counterfeit, fabricate, trump up, coin, invent, frame, feign, make, fashion, design, imitate, copy, duplicate, reproduce, trace.

forger, n. falsifier, counterfeiter, coiner; see **criminal**.

forgery, n. imitation, copy, cheat, counterfeit, fake, fabrication, sham, bogus, phoney, pseudo.—Ant. real article, real thing, **original**.

forget, v. lose consciousness of, put out of one's head, fail to remember, be forgetful, have a short memory, overlook, ignore, omit, neglect, slight, disregard, pass over, skip, think no more of, close one's eyes to, not give another thought, *draw a blank, dismiss from the mind, *kiss off, *laugh off or away.—Ant. remember, recall, recollect.

forget about, v. omit, let slip one's memory, miss; see **forget, neglect 2**.

forgetful, a. inattentive, neglectful, heedless; see **careless**.

forgetfulness, n. negligence, heedlessness, inattention; see **carelessness**.

forget oneself, v. offend, trespass, daydream; see **misbehave**.

forgivable, a. venial, trivial, pardonable; see **excusable**.

forgive, v. pardon, forgive and forget, let pass, excuse, condone, remit, forget, relent, bear no malice, exonerate, exculpate, let bygones be bygones, laugh it

off, let up on, let it go, kiss and make up, bury the hatchet, turn the other cheek, make allowance, write off.—Ant. hate, resent, retaliate.

forgiven, a. reinstated, taken back, welcomed home; see **pardoned**.

forgiveness, n. absolution, pardon, acquittal, exoneration, remission, dispensation, reprieve, justification, amnesty, respite.

forgiving, a. noble, open-hearted, free; see **kind 1**.

forgo, v. quit, relinquish, waive; see **abandon 1**.

for good, a. permanently, for all time, henceforth; see **forever**.

forgotten, a. not remembered or recalled or recollected, lost, (clear or clean) out of one's mind, gone out of or erased from one's mind or recollection or consciousness, beyond or past recollection or recall, not recoverable, blotted or blanked out; see also **abandoned**.

fork, n. 1. [A furcated implement] table fork, hay fork, pitchfork, manure fork, trident, prong, spear, scepter. 2. [A branch of a road or river] bend, turn, crossroad, tributary, byway, junction, branch, stream, creek.

form, n. 1. [Shape] figure, appearance, plan, arrangement, design, outline, conformation, configuration, formation, structure, style, construction, fashion, mode, scheme, framework, contour, profile, silhouette, skeleton, anatomy. 2. [The human form] body, frame, torso; see **figure 2**. 3. [The approved procedure] manner, mode, custom; see **method 2**. 4. [Anything intended to give form] pattern, model, die; see **mold 1**. 5. [A standard letter or blank] mimeographed letter, duplicate, routine letter, form letter, data sheet, information blank, chart, card, reference form, order form, questionnaire, application; see also **copy**.

form, v. 1. [To give shape to a thing] mold, pattern, model, arrange, make, block out, fashion, construct, devise, plan, design, contrive, produce, invent, frame, scheme, plot, compose, erect, build, cast, cut, carve, chisel, hammer out, put together, whittle, assemble, conceive, create, outline, trace, develop, cultivate, work, complete, finish, perfect, fix, regulate, establish, sculpture, bend, twist, knead, set, determine, arrive at, reach.—Ant. destroy, demolish, shatter. 2. [To give character to a person] instruct, rear, breed; see **teach**. 3. [To comprise] constitute, figure in, act as; see **compose 1**. 4. [To take form] accumulate, condense, harden, set, settle, rise, appear, take shape, grow, develop, unfold, mature, materialize, become a reality, take on character, become visible, *shape up, *fall into place, *get into shape or shaped up.—Ant. **disappear**, dissolve, waste away.

formal, a. 1. [Notable for arrangement] orderly, precise, set; see **regular 3. 2.** [Concerned with etiquette and behavior] reserved, distant, stiff; see **conventional 3, polite. 3.** [Official] confirmed, directed, lawful; see **approved, legal 1. 4.** [In evening clothes] full dress, black tie, dressed up; see **social.**

formality, n. decorum, etiquette, correctness; see **behavior.**

format, n. make-up, arrangement, construction; see **form 1.**

formation, n. arrangement, crystallization, accumulation, production, composition, development, fabrication, generation, creation, genesis, constitution.— Ant. **destruction**, dissolution, annihilation.

formed, a. shaped, molded, patterned, modeled, carved, outlined, developed, cultivated, completed, finished, built, created, invented, concocted, designed, accomplished, manufactured, produced, born, perfected, fixed, established, solidified, hardened, set, determined.—Ant. **shapeless**, formless, nebulous.

former, a. earlier, previous, foregoing; see **preceding.**

formerly, a. before now, some time ago, once, once upon a time, already, in former times, previously, earlier, time out of mind, in the early days, eons or centuries ago, in the past, in the olden days, used to be, long ago, earlier, before this, in time past, heretofore, *a while back.—Ant. **recently**, subsequently, immediately.

formula, n. direction, description, recipe; see also **method 2.**

formulate, v. express, give form to, set down; see **form 1.**

fornication, n. adultery, incontinence, carnality, lechery, improper or illicit intercourse, lewdness, licentiousness, venery, unfaithfulness, promiscuousness, coitus, debauchery, libertinism.

for rent, a. on the market, renting, selling, for hire, available, offered, advertised, to let.

forsake, v. desert, leave, quit; see **abandon 2.**

forsaken, a. destitute, deserted, left; see **abandoned.**

for sale, a. selling, saleable, on the market, on auction, advertised, listed, up (for sale), *to be cleared (out) or knocked down.

fort, n. fortress, citadel, acropolis; see **fortification.**

forth, a. first, out, into; see **ahead. —and so forth**, and so on, similarly, and other; see **other.**

forthcoming, a. expected, inevitable, anticipated, future, impending, pending, awaited, destined, fated, predestined, approaching, in store, at hand, inescapable, imminent, in prospect, prospective, in the wind, in preparation, in the cards.

for the time being, a. at the moment, for now, for the present; see **temporarily.**

forthright, a. at once, straight away, forthwith; see **immediately.**

fortification, n. fort, fortress, defense, dugout, trench, entrenchment, gun emplacement, barricade, battlement, stockade, outpost, citadel, support, wall, barrier, earthwork, castle, pillbox, bastion, bulwark, defense in depth, hill position.

fortified, a. defended, guarded, safeguarded, protected, manned, garrisoned, barricaded, armed, barbed, secured, strong, covered, strengthened, supported, surrounded, fortressed, walled, enclosed, stockaded, armored, dug in, hidden, camouflaged.—Ant. **open**, unprotected, unguarded.

fortify, v. barricade, entrench, buttress; see **defend 1.**

fortitude, n. firmness, valor, fearlessness; see **determination.**

fortunate, a. lucky, blessed, prosperous, successful, having a charmed life, in luck, favored, well-to-do, happy, triumphant, victorious, overcoming, affluent, thriving, flourishing, healthy, wealthy, *well-fixed, *well-heeled, *born with a silver spoon in one's mouth.—Ant. **unfortunate**, unlucky, cursed.

fortunately, a. luckily, happily, seasonably, in good time, auspiciously, favorably, prosperously, in the nick of time.— Ant. **unfortunately**, unluckily, unhappily.

fortune, n. 1. [Chance] luck, fate, uncertainty; see **chance 1. 2.** [Great riches] possessions, inheritance, estate; see **wealth. —a small fortune**, a high price or cost, a great expense, a large amount of money; see **price.**

forward, a. 1. [Going forward] advancing, progressing, leading, on, ahead, progressive, onward, propulsive, in advance.—Ant. **backward**, retreating, regressive. **2.** [Bold] presumptuous, impertinent, fresh; see **rude 2.**

forwarded, a. shipped, expressed, dispatched; see **delivered.**

fossil, n. (organic) remains, reconstruction, specimen, skeleton, relic, impression, trace, petrified deposit, petrifaction; see **relic.**

foster, *v.* cherish, nurse, nourish; see **raise** 2.

foul, *a.* 1. [Disgusting] nasty, vulgar, coarse; see **offensive** 2. 2. [Unfair] vicious, inequitable, unjust; see **dishonest.**

foul, *v.* 1. [To make dirty] defile, pollute, sully; see **dirty.** 2. [To become dirty] soil, spot, stain; see **dirty.**

found, *a.* unearthed, described, detected; see **discovered.**

found, *v.* establish, endow, set up; see **establish** 2.

foundation, *n.* 1. [An intellectual basis] reason, justification, authority; see **basis** 1. 2. [A physical basis] footing, base, foot, basement, pier, groundwork, bed, ground, resting place, bottom, substructure, wall, underpinning, solid rock, rest, roadbed, support, prop, stand, shore, post, pillar, skeleton, column, shaft, pedestal, buttress, framework, scaffold, beam. 3. [That which has been founded] institution, organization, endowment, institute, society, plantation, establishment, company, guild, corporation, company, association, charity.

founded, *a.* organized, endowed, set up; see **established** 2.

founder, *n.* originator, patron, prime mover; see **author, forefather.**

fountain, *n.* 1. [A jet of water] jet stream, gush, bubbler, spout, geyser, pump, spurt, play; see **water** 1, 2. 2. [A soda-water dispensary] soda fountain, ice-cream parlor, drugstore fountain; see **bar** 2.

fowl, *n.* barnyard fowl, wild fowl, poultry, chicken, duck, goose, turkey, cock, hen, Cornish hen, pheasant, partridge, prairie chicken, grouse, ptarmigan, swan; see also **bird.**

fox, *n.* 1. [A clever person] cheat, trickster, *con man; see **rascal.** 2. [An animal] red fox, gray fox, silver fox; see **dog.**

fraction, *n.* section, portion, part; see **division** 2.

fractional, *a.* partial, sectional, fragmentary; see **unfinished** 1.

fracture, *n.* rupture, wound, crack, shattering, breach, fragmentation, displacement, dislocation, shearing, severing, separating, dismembering.

fragile, *a.* brittle, frail, delicate; see **dainty** 1, **weak** 1, 2.

fragment, *n.* piece, scrap, remnant; see **bit** 1.

fragrance, *n.* perfume, aroma, redolence; see **smell** 1.

fragrant, *a.* aromatic, sweet, perfumed; see **sweet** 3.

frail, *a.* feeble, breakable, tender; see **dainty.**

frailty, *n.* fragility, delicacy, feebleness; see **weakness** 1.

frame, *n.* 1. [The structural portion] skeleton, scaffold, framework, scaffolding, casing, framing, support, stage, groundwork, organization, anatomy, fabric, architecture, enclosure, support, shutter, girdle, span, clasp, block, window frame, doorjamb. 2. [A border intended as an ornament] margin, verge, fringe, hem, flounce, trim, trimming, outline, mounting.

frame, *v.* 1. [To make] construct, erect, raise; see **build.** 2. [To enclose in a frame] mount, border, enclose; see **support** 1. 3. [To act as a frame] encircle, confine, enclose; see **surround** 1. 4. [*To cause a miscarriage of justice] conspire against, double-cross, fix; see **deceive.**

framed, *a.* 1. [Surrounded by a frame] mounted, enclosed, bordered, encircled, fringed, enveloped, outlined, confined, enclosed, wrapped, clasped. 2. [*Arranged beforehand] faked, *fixed, *planted; see **false** 3.

*****frame-up,** *n.* hoax, dodge, frame; see **trick** 1.

framework, *n.* skeleton, structure, core; see **frame.**

France, *n.* French nation, French people, French Republic, Fourth Republic, French Union, French empire, Franks, Gaul; see also **Europe.**

frank, *a.* artless, candid, sincere, free, easy, familiar, open, direct, unreserved, uninhibited, downright, ingenuous, unsophisticated, unaffected, plain, aboveboard, forthright, outspoken, straightforward, plain-spoken, natural, blunt, matter-of-fact.—*Ant.* secretive, **dishonest,** insincere.

frankfurter, *n.* wiener, wiener sausage, *weenie, *(hot) dog, *frank, dog, link.

frankly, *a.* freely, honestly, candidly; see **openly** 1.

frankness, *n.* openness, sincerity, ingenuousness; see **honesty** 1.

frantic, *a.* distracted, mad, wild, frenetic, furious, raging, raving, frenzied, violent, deranged, crazy, delirious, insane, angry; see also **excited.**—*Ant.* calm, composed, subdued.

fraternity, *n.* brotherhood, Greek letter society, fellowship; see **organization** 2.

fraud, *n.* 1. [Deceit] trickery, duplicity, guile; see **deception.** 2. [An imposter] pretender, charlatan, quack; see **cheat.**

fraudulent, *a.* deceitful, tricky, swindling; see **dishonest.**

freak, *n.* monstrosity, monster, rarity, malformation, freak of nature, oddity, aberration, curiosity, hybrid; see also **monster**.

freckle, *n.* mole, patch, blotch; see **blemish**.

free, *a.* **1.** [Not restricted politically] sovereign, independent, released, autonomous, autarchic, freed, liberated, self-governing, democratic, at liberty, unconstrained.—*Ant.* restricted, enslaved, subject. **2.** [Not restricted in space; *said of persons*] unconfined, at large, cast loose, escaped, let out *or* off, scot-free, free as air, free to come and go, foot-loose and fancy-free, *freewheeling, *on the loose.—*Ant.* confined, imprisoned, restrained. **3.** [Not restricted in space; *said of things*] unimpeded, unobstructed, unhampered, unattached, loose, not attached, clear of *or* from, unentangled, unengaged, disengaged, untrammeled, unfastened.—*Ant.* fixed, fastened, rooted. **4.** [Given without charge] gratuitous, gratis, for nothing, for love, without charge, free of cost, complimentary, *for free, on the house, *free for nothing.—*Ant.* paid, charged, costly. — **for free**, without cost, gratis, unencumbered; see **free 4.** —**set free**, release, liberate, discharge, emancipate; see **free 1.**

free, *v.* release, discharge, deliver, save, emancipate, rescue, extricate, loosen, unbind, disengage, undo, set free, let out *or* loose, bail out, cut loose, relieve, absolve, acquit, dismiss, pardon, clear, ransom, redeem, unbind, unchain, disentangle, untie, let go, unlock, unhand, let out of prison, open the cage, turn loose. —*Ant.* seize, capture, incarcerate.

freedom, *n.* **1.** [Political liberty] independence, sovereignty, autonomy, democracy, self-government, citizenship, self-determination, representative government; see also **liberty 4.**—*Ant.* slavery, bondage, regimentation. **2.** [Exemption from necessity] privilege, immunity, license, indulgence, facility, range, latitude, scope, play, own accord, free rein, leeway, *plenty of rope.—*Ant.* restraint, constraint, hindrance. **3.** [Natural ease and facility] readiness, forthrightness, spontaneity; see **ease 2.**

freeing, *n.* emancipation, releasing, salvation; see **rescue**.

freely, *a.* **1.** [Without physical restriction] loosely, without encumbrance, unhindered, without restraint, as one pleases, easily, without stint.—*Ant.* with difficulty, under obstacles, in clogs. **2.** [Without mental restriction] voluntarily, willingly, fancy-free, of one's own accord, at will, at pleasure, of one's own free will, purposely, deliberately, intentionally, advisedly, spontaneously,

frankly, openly.—*Ant.* unwillingly, under compulsion, hesitantly.

freeway, *n.* turnpike, superhighway, toll road; see **highway**, **road 1.**

free will, *n.* willingness, volition, intention, purpose, choice, free choice, power of choice, will and pleasure, freedom, pleasure, discretion, inclination, desire, wish, intent, option, determination, mind, consent, assent.—*Ant.* restraint, pre-destination, unwillingness.

freeze, *v.* **1.** [To change to a solid state] congeal, harden, solidify, ice, quick-freeze, glaciate, chill, benumb, cool, *ice up.—*Ant.* melt, thaw, liquefy. **2.** [To control] seal, terminate, immobilize; see **control**.

freezing, *a.* frosty, wintry, frigid; see **cold 1.**

freight, *n.* burden, load, contents, weight, bulk, encumbrance, lading, cargo, shipping, consignment, goods, tonnage, packages, ware.

freighter, *n.* tanker, tramp, cargo ship; see **ship**.

French, *a.* **1.** [Referring to the French culture or people] Gallic, Latin, Frenchified, Parisian. **2.** [Referring to the French language] Romance, Romantic, Romanic, Parisian, Gallic.

French, *n.* **1.** [The French people] Gallic nation, Parisians, Frenchmen, Latins, Basques, Gauls, Normans, Provençals, French provincials. **2.** [The French tongue] Romance language, modern French, Middle French, Old French, Norman, Anglo-Norman, French of Paris.

frenzy, *n.* rage, craze, furor; see **excitement**, **insanity**.

frequency, *n.* recurrence, number, reiteration; see **regularity**.

frequent, *a.* **1.** [Happening often] many, repeated, numerous, common, habitual, thick, monotonous, profuse, incessant, continual, customary, intermittent, familiar, commonplace, expected, various, a good many.—*Ant.* rare, infrequent, occasional. **2.** [Happening regularly] recurrent, usual, periodic; see **regular 3.**

frequent, *v.* visit often, go to, be seen at daily, attend regularly, be at home in, be often in, be accustomed to, *hang around, *hang out; see also **visit 1.**

frequently, *a.* often, regularly, usually, commonly, successively, many times, in many instances, all the time, notably, repeatedly, intermittently, generally, every now and then, at times, not infrequently, often enough, not seldom, periodically, at regular intervals; see also **regularly.**—*Ant.* seldom, infrequently, rarely.

fresh, *a.* **1.** [Newly produced] new, green,

crisp, raw, recent, current, late, this season's, factory-fresh, garden-fresh, farm-fresh, brand-new, newborn, immature, young, beginning, *hot off the press, just out, newfangled.—*Ant.* old, stale, musty. 2. [Not preserved] unsalted, uncured, unsmoked; see sense 1. 3. [Unspoiled] uncontaminated, green, not stale, good, undecayed, well-preserved, odor-free, in good condition, preserved, new, virgin, unimpaired.—*Ant.* decayed, spoiled, contaminated. 4. [Not faded] colorful, vivid, sharp; see **bright 1, definite 2.** 5. [Not salt; *said of water*] potable, drinkable, cool, clear, pure, clean, sweet, fit to drink, safe.—*Ant.* dirty, brackish, briny. 6. [Refreshed] rested, restored, rehabilitated, like new, unused, new, relaxed, stimulated, relieved, freshened, reinvigorated, revived.—*Ant.* tired, exhausted, worn-out. 7. [Inexperienced] untrained, untried, unskilled; see **inexperienced.**

freshman, *n.* first-year man, novice, probationer, *frosh; see **amateur.**

fret, *v.* disturb, agitate, vex; see **bother 2.**

friar, *n.* brother, father; see **monk.**

friction, *n.* 1. [The rubbing of two bodies] attrition, abrasion, erosion; see **grinding.** 2. [Trouble between individuals or groups] animosity, quarrel, discontent; see **hatred 1, 2.**

fried, *a.* grilled, cooked, rendered; see **done 2.**

friend, *n.* familiar, schoolmate, playmate, best friend, roommate, companion, intimate, confidant, comrade, fellow, *pal, birds of a feather, *chum, *crony, *buddy, *side-kick.—*Ant.* foe, enemy, stranger. —**make** *or* **be friends (with),** befriend, stand by, become familiar (with); see **associate 1.**

friendless, *a.* deserted, alone, forlorn; see **abandoned 1.**

friendliness, *n.* kindness, amiability, geniality; see **friendship 2.**

friendly, *a.* kind, kindly, helpful, sympathetic, amiable, well-disposed, neighborly, sociable, civil, peaceful, loving, affectionate, fond, warm-hearted, attentive, brotherly, agreeable, genial, benevolent, accommodating, unoffensive, pleasant, tender, companionable, with open arms, cordial, familiar, intimate, close, devoted, dear, attached, loyal, faithful, steadfast, true, responsive, understanding, congenial, approachable, cheerful, convivial, good-humored, good-natured, generous, gracious, cooperative, whole-hearted, *big-hearted, *chummy, *thick, arm in arm.—*Ant.* **unfriendly,** antagonistic, spiteful.

friendship, *n.* harmony, friendliness, brotherly love; see **fellowship 1.**

fright, *n.* panic, terror, dread, horror; see **fear.**

frighten, *v.* scare, scare away *or* off, dismay, terrify, cow, shock, intimidate, threaten, badger, petrify, panic, demoralize, disrupt, give cause for alarm, terrorize, horrify, astound, awe, perturb, disturb, startle, frighten one out of one's wits, take one's breath away, chill to the bone, make one's hair stand on end, make one's blood run cold, *make one's flesh creep, put one's heart in his mouth, scare one stiff, freeze *or* curdle the blood.

frightened, *a.* terrorized, affrighted, startled; see **afraid.**

frightful, *a.* 1. [Causing fright] fearful, awful, dreadful; see **terrible 1, 2.** 2. [Very unpleasant] calamitous, shocking, terrible; see **offensive 2.**

frigid, *a.* 1. [Thermally cold] freezing, frosty, refrigerated; see **cold 1, 2.** 2. [Unresponsive] unloving, undersexed, chilly; see **cold 2, indifferent.**

fringe, *n.* hem, trimming, border; see **edge 1.**

frisky, *a.* spirited, dashing, playful; see **active.**

frivolity, *n.* silliness, levity, folly; see **fun.**

frivolous, *a.* superficial, petty, trifling; see **trivial.**

frog, *n.* amphibian, spring peeper, tree frog *or* toad, bullfrog, horned frog *or* toad, batrachian, polliwog.

from, *prep.* in distinction to, out of possession of, outside of; see **of.**

from side to side, *a.* back and forth, wobbly, unstable; see **irregular 1.**

front, *a.* fore, forward, frontal, foremost, head, headmost, leading, in the foreground.—*Ant.* rear, back, hindmost.

front, *n.* 1. [The forward part or surface] exterior, fore part, anterior, bow, foreground, face, head, breast, frontal area.—*Ant.* posterior, back, rear. 2. [The fighting line] front line, no man's land, advance position, line of battle, vanguard, outpost, field of fire, advance guard. 3. [The appearance one presents before others] port, demeanor, aspect, countenance, face, presence, expression, figure, exterior. —**in front of,** before, preceding, leading; see **ahead.**

frontier, *n.* hinterland, remote districts, outskirts; see **country 1.**

frost, *n.* black frost, white frost, rime; see **ice.**

frosting, *n.* finish, covering, coating; see **icing.**

frosty, *a.* frigid, freezing, chilly; see **cold 1**.

froth, *n.* bubbles, scum, fizz, effervescence, foam, ferment, head, lather, suds, spray.

frothy, *a.* fizzing, bubbling, foaming, soapy, sudsy, bubbly, fizzy, foamy, with a head on.

frown, *n.* scowl, grimace, wry face, gloomy countenance, forbidding aspect, *dirty look.

frown, *v.* scowl, grimace, pout, glare, sulk, glower, gloom, look stern.—*Ant.* smile, laugh, grin.

frozen, *a.* chilled, frosted, iced; see **cold 1, 2**.

frugal, *a.* thrifty, saving, prudent, parsimonious; see **careful**.

frugality, *n.* carefulness, conservation, management; see **economy**, **saving**.

fruit, *n.* berry, grain, nut, root; see also **vegetable**. Common fruits include the following—apple, pear, peach, plum, nectarine, orange, grapefruit, banana, pineapple, watermelon, cantaloupe, honeydew melon, papaya, mango, guava, grape, lime, lemon, persimmon, pomegranate, raspberry, blackberry, blueberry, huckleberry, olive, date, fig, apricot, cherry, raisin, avocado, gooseberry, strawberry.

fruitful, *a.* prolific, productive, fecund; see **fertile**.

fruitless, *a.* vain, unprofitable, empty; see **futile**.

frustrate, *v.* defeat, foil, balk; see **prevent**.

frustration, *n.* disappointment, impediment, failure; see **defeat 3**.

fry, *v.* sauté, sear, singe, brown, grill, pan-fry, deep-fry *or* French fry, sizzle; see also **cook**. —**small fry**, children, infant(s), toddler(s); see **baby**, **child**.

fudge, *n.* penuche, chocolate fudge, divinity fudge; see **candy**.

fuel, *n.* Fuels include the following—coal, gas, oil, coke, charcoal, anthracite, propane, bituminous coal, peat, slack, stoker coal, lignite, carbon, turf, cordwood, firewood, log, kindling, timber, diesel oil, crude oil, fuel oil, natural gas, gasoline, kerosene, wax.

fuel, *v.* fill up, *tank up, *gas up; see **fill 1**.

fugitive, *n.* outlaw, refugee, truant, runaway, exile, vagabond, waif, stray, derelict, outcast, recluse, hermit.

fulfill, *v.* accomplish, effect, complete; see **achieve**.

fulfilled, *a.* accomplished, completed, achieved, realized, effected, finished, obtained, perfected, attained, reached, actualized, executed, concluded, brought about, performed, carried out, put into effect, made good, brought to a close.—*Ant.* **disappointed**, unfulfilled, unrealized.

fulfillment, *n.* attainment, accomplishment, realization; see **achievement**.

full, *a.* **1.** [Filled] running over, abundant, weighted, satisfied, saturated, crammed, packed, stuffed, jammed, glutted, gorged, loaded, chock-full, stocked, satiated, crowded, *stuffed to the gills, jam-packed, *crawling (with), up to the brim, *packed like sardines. —*Ant.* **empty**, exhausted, void. **2.** [Well supplied] abundant, complete, copious, ample, plentiful, sufficient, adequate, competent, lavish, extravagant, profuse.—*Ant.* **inadequate**, scanty, insufficient. **3.** [Not limited] broad, unlimited, extensive; see **absolute 1, 2**. —**in full**, for the entire amount *or* value, fully, thoroughly; see **completely**.

full blast, *a.* wide open, full throttle, to the hilt; see **fast 1**.

full-grown, *a.* adult, prime, grown-up; see **mature 1**.

fully, *a.* entirely, thoroughly, wholly; see **completely**.

fumble, *n.* mistake, blunder, dropped ball; see **error**.

fumble, *v.* mishandle, bungle, mismanage; see **botch**.

fun, *n.* play, game, sport, jest, amusement, relaxation, pastime, diversion, frolic, mirth, entertainment, solace, merriment, pleasure, caper, foolery, romping, joke, absurdity, playfulness, laughter, festivity, carnival, tomfoolery, *ball, escapade, antic, romp, prank, comedy, teasing, celebration, holiday, rejoicing, good humor, joking, enjoyment, gladness, good cheer, delight, glee, treat, lark, recreation, joy, time of one's life, *blast, *big time, *picnic, *riot.—*Ant.* **unhappiness**, tedium, sorrow. —**for** *or* **in fun**, for amusement, not seriously, playfully; see **happily 2**. —**make fun of**, mock, satirize, poke fun at; see **ridicule**.

function, *n.* employment, capacity, faculty; see **use 1**.

function, *v.* perform, run, work; see **operate 2**.

functional, *a.* occupational, utilitarian, anatomic; see **practical**.

fund, *n.* endowment, matching *or* trust *or* endowment fund, capital; see **gift 1**.

fundamental, *n.* buttocks, bottom, rear, seat; see **rump**.

fundamental, *a.* basic, underlying, primary, first, rudimentary, elemental, supporting, elementary, cardinal, organic, theoretical, structural, sustaining, central, original.—*Ant.* **superficial**, incidental, consequent.

fundamentally, *a.* basically, radically, centrally; see **essentially**.

fundamentals, *n.* .essentials, basics, foundation; see **basis 1**.

funds, *n.* capital, wealth, cash, collateral, money, assets, currency, savings, revenue, wherewithal, proceeds, hard cash, stocks and bonds, money in *or* on hand *or* in the bank, accounts receivable, property, means, affluence, belongings, resources, securities, stakes, earnings, winnings, possessions, profits, stocks, nest egg; see **money**.

funeral, *n.* interment, last rites, burial, burial ceremony, entombment, requiem, cremation.

fungus, *n.* mushroom, mold, rust; see **decay, parasite 1**.

funnel, *n.* duct, shaft, conduit; see **pipe 1**.

funny, *a.* 1. [Stirring to laughter] laughable, comic, comical, whimsical, amusing, entertaining, diverting, humorous, witty, jesting, jocular, waggish, droll, facetious, clever, mirthful, ludicrous, jolly, absurd, ridiculous, gay, sly, sportive, playful, merry, joyful, joyous, good-humored, glad, gleeful, hilarious, jovial, farcical, joking, side-splitting, *a laugh.—Ant.* sad, serious, melancholy. 2. [Likely to arouse suspicion] curious, unusual, odd; see **suspicious 2**.

fur, *n.* pelt, hide, hair, coat, brush. Types of fur include the following—sable, mink, chinchilla, karakul, seal, muskrat, ermine, monkey, beaver, skunk, otter, marten, stone marten, weasel, squirrel, leopard, raccoon, wolverine, white fox, blue fox, red fox, etc.; sheepskin, bearskin, calfskin, rabbit, cony. —**make the fur fly**, fight, bicker, stir up trouble; see **excite**.

furious, *a.* enraged, raging, fierce; see **angry**.

furnace, *n.* heater, heating system, boiler, (forced draft) hot-air furnace, steam furnace, hot-water furnace, oil burner, gas furnace, electric furnace, kiln, blast furnace, open-hearth furnace, stove, forge.

furnish, *v.* fit out, equip, stock; see **provide 1**.

furnished, *a.* supplied, provided, fitted out; see **equipped**.

furniture, *n.* movables, household goods, home furnishings. Furniture includes the following—*home*: table, chair, rug, carpet(ing), drapes, sofa, davenport, couch, cabinet, picture, chest, bureau, buffet, cupboard, stove, washing machine *or* washer, (clothes) dryer, dishwasher, refrigerator, bed, dresser, mirror, commode, chiffonier, tapestry, footstool, secretary, sideboard, clock, bookcase; *office*: desk, filing cabinet, stool, chair, table, counter, typewriter table.

furor, *n.* tumult, excitement, stir; see **disturbance 2**.

further, *a.* more, to *or* at a greater distance, in addition; see **distant**.

furthermore, *a.* moreover, too, in addition; see **besides**.

furthest, *a.* most remote, most distant, remotest, farthest, uttermost, outermost, ultimate, extreme, outmost.

fury, *n.* wrath, fire, rage; see **anger**.

fuse, *n.* wick, tinder, kindling; see **fuel**. —*blow a fuse*, become angry, lose one's temper, rant; see **rage 1**.

fuss, *n.* trouble, complaint, bother; see **disturbance 2**.

fuss, *v.* whine, whimper, object; see **complain**.

fussy, *a.* fastidious, particular, meticulous; see **careful**.

futile, *a.* vain, useless, in vain, fruitless, hopeless, impractical, worthless, unprofitable, to no effect, not successful, to no purpose, unneeded, unsatisfactory, unsatisfying, ineffective, ineffectual, unproductive, idle, empty, hollow, unreal.—*Ant.* hopeful, practical, effective.

futility, *n.* uselessness, falseness, hollowness, frivolity, idleness, emptiness, fruitlessness, hopelessness, worthlessness, illusion, folly, unimportance, *carrying water in a sieve*, *wild-goose chase*, *running around in circles*, *carrying coals to Newcastle.—Ant.* **importance**, fruitfulness, significance.

future, *a.* coming, impending, imminent, destined, fated, prospective, to come, in the course of time, expected, inevitable, approaching, eventual, ultimate, planned, scheduled, budgeted, booked, looked toward, likely, *up, *coming up, in the cards.—*Ant.* **past**, completed, recorded.

future, *n.* infinity, eternity, world to come, subsequent time, coming time, events to come, prospect, tomorrow, (the) hereafter, by and by.—*Ant.* **past**, historic ages, recorded time.

fuzz, *n.* nap, fluff, fur; see **hair 1**.

fuzzy, *a.* hairy, woolly, furry; see **hairy**.

G

*gab, n. gossip, idle talk, prattle; see nonsense 1. —*gift of (the) gab, loquacity, volubility, verbal ability; see eloquence.

*gab, v. gossip, jabber, chatter; see babble.

gadget, n. mechanical contrivance, object, contraption; see device 1.

gag, v. 1. [To stop the mouth] choke, muzzle, muffle, obstruct, stifle, throttle, tape (up), deaden. 2. [To retch] be nauseated, sicken, choke; see vomit.

gaiety, n. jollity, mirth, exhilaration; see happiness 1.

gaily, a. showily, brightly, vivaciously, spiritedly, brilliantly, splendidly, gaudily, expensively, colorfully, extravagantly, in a bright or vivacious or sprightly manner.—Ant. quietly, modestly, peacefully.

gain, n. increase, accrual, accumulation; see addition 1.

gain, v. 1. [To increase] augment, expand, enlarge; see grow 1, increase. 2. [To advance] progress, overtake, move forward; see advance 1. 3. [To achieve] attain, realize, reach; see succeed 1.

gainful, a. lucrative, productive, useful; see profitable.

gait, n. walk, run, motion, step, tread, stride, pace, tramp, march, carriage, movements.

galaxy, n. cosmic system, star cluster, nebula; see star.

gale, n. hurricane, blow, typhoon; see storm, wind 1.

gallant, a. bold, courageous, intrepid; see brave.

gallantry, n. heroism, valor, bravery; see courage.

gallery, n. 1. [An elevated section of seats] arcade, upstairs, balcony; see upstairs. 2. [Onlookers, especially from the gallery] spectators, audience, public; see listener. 3. [A room for showing works of art] salon, museum, exhibition room, studio, hall, exhibit, showroom.

gallon, n. 231 cubic inches, 3.7853 liters, liquid measure, four quarts, eight pints.

gallop, v. run, spring, leap, jump, go at a gallop, bound, hurdle, swing, stride, lope, amble, trot.

galoshes, n. overshoes, rubbers, boots; see shoe.

gamble, n. chance, lot, hazard; see chance 1.

gamble, v. game, wager, bet, play, plunge, play at dice, cut the cards, bet against, speculate, back, lay money or odds on, try one's luck, *go for broke, shoot craps; see also risk.

gambler, n. backer, sharper, card-sharp, speculator, confidence man, bettor, bookmaker, croupier, banker, player, *sport, *highroller, *shark, *shill, *bookie, *con man.

gambling, n. betting, staking, venturing, gaming, laying money on, speculating.

game, a. spirited, hardy, resolute; see brave.

game, n. 1. [Entertainment] Card games include the following—poker, bridge, contract bridge, duplicate bridge, five hundred, casino, war, seven-up, cribbage, solitaire, hearts, twenty-one or blackjack, baccarat. Children's games include—hide-and-go-seek, tag, hopscotch, jacks, ball, fox and geese, marbles, crack the whip, statues, London Bridge, ring around the roses, drop the handkerchief, blindman's buff, follow the leader, Simon says, catch, post office, favors, musical chairs, streets and alleys, cops and robbers, soldier, Indian, mother-may-I. Board games include—chess, (Chinese) checkers, backgammon, go; Monopoly, Sorry, Clue, Parcheesi, Mah-Jongg (all trademarks). 2. [Sport] play, recreation, merrymaking; see sport 1. 3. [Wild meat, fish, or fowl] quarry, prey, wildlife; see fish, fowl, meat. —*ahead of the game, winning, doing well, thriving; see successful. —*play the game, behave (properly), act according to custom, do what is expected; see behave.

gang, n. horde, band, troop; see organization 2.

gangster, n. gunman, underworld leader, racketeer; see criminal.

*gang up on or against, v. combat, overwhelm, fight with; see attack.

gap, n. 1. [A breach] cleft, cleavage, rift; see hole 1. 2. [A break in continuity] hiatus, recess, lull; see pause. 3. [A mountain pass] chasm, hollow, cleft, ravine, gorge, arroyo, canyon, passageway, notch, gully, gulch.

garage, n. car stall, parking space, parking garage, parking, parking lot, carport.

garbage, n. refuse, waste, table scrapings; see trash 1, 3.

garden, n. vegetable patch, melon or berry or potato, etc., patch; cultivated area, truck garden, enclosure, field, plot, bed, herb garden, rock garden, rose garden, formal garden, kitchen garden, hotbed, cold frame, greenhouse, patio, terrace, back yard, nursery, flower garden, garden spot, oasis.

gardener, *n.* vegetable grower, caretaker, landscaper; see **farmer.**

gardening, *n.* truck farming, vegetable raising, tillage; see **farming.**

gargle, *v.* swash, rinse the mouth, use a mouthwash; see **clean.**

garish, *a.* showy, gaudy, ostentatious; see **ornate 1.**

garment, *n.* dress, attire, apparel; see **clothes.**

garnish, *v.* embellish, beautify, deck; see **decorate.**

gas, *n.* 1. [A state of matter] vapor, volatile substance, fumes, aeriform fluid, gaseous mixture. 2. [Gasoline] propellant, petrol (British), motor fuel; see **gasoline.** 3. [Poisonous gas] systemic poison, mustard gas, tear gas; see **poison.** 4. [An anesthetic] ether, general anesthetic, chloroform, nitrous oxide, laughing gas. 5. [A fuel] natural gas, propane, bottled gas, acetylene, coal gas; see also **fuel.** —*step on the gas,** rush, hasten, move fast; see **hurry 1.**

gaseous, *a.* vaporous, effervescent, aeriform; see **light 5.**

gash, *n.* slash, slice, wound; see **cut.**

gasoline, *n.* petrol (British), motor fuel, propellant, gas, juice, low octane gasoline, high octane gasoline, ethyl gasoline.

gasp, *v.* labor for breath, gulp, have difficulty in breathing, pant, puff, wheeze, blow, snort.

gate, *n.* entrance, ingress, passage, way, bar, turnstile, revolving door, barrier; see also **door.**

gather, *v.* 1. [To come together] assemble, meet, gather around, congregate, flock *or* pour in, rally, crowd, throng, come together, convene, collect, unite, reunite, associate, hold a meeting *or* convention *or* reunion, swarm, huddle, draw in, group, converge, concentrate.—*Ant.* scatter, disperse, part. 2. [To bring together] collect, aggregate, amass; see **accumulate 1, assemble 2.** 3. [To conclude] infer, deduce, find; see **assume.**

gathered, *a.* assembled, met, congregated, joined, rallied, crowded together, thronged, collected, united, associated, swarmed, huddled, grouped, massed, amassed, accumulated, picked, garnered, harvested, stored, combined, brought together, convened, convoked, summoned, compiled, mobilized, lumped together, raked up, concentrated, heaped, stacked, piled, stowed away.—*Ant.* scattered, dispersed, separated.

gathering, *n.* assembly, meeting, conclave, caucus, parley, council, conference, band, congregation, company, rally, crowd, throng, bunch, collection, union, association, society, committee, legislature, house, senate, parliament, swarm, huddle, group, body, mass, herd, turnout, flock, combination, convention, discussion, panel, reunion, meet, congress, attendance, multitude, audience, horde, mob, crush, party, social gathering, crew, gang, school, bevy, troop, drove, concentration, convocation, get-together, *bull session.

gaudy, *a.* showy, flashy, tawdry; see **ornate 1.**

gauge, *n.* scale, criterion, standard; see **measure 2.**

gauge, *v.* check, weigh, calibrate, calculate; see **measure 1.**

gaunt, *a.* emaciated, scraggy, skinny; see **thin 2.**

gauze, *n.* veil, bandage, dressings; see **dressing 3.**

gawk, *v.* stare, ogle, gaze; see **look 2.**

gay, *a.* cheerful, merry, vivacious; see **happy 1.**

gaze, *v.* stare, watch, gape; see **look 2.**

gear, *n.* 1. [Equipment] material, tackle, things; see **equipment.** 2. [A geared wheel] cog, cogwheel, pinion, toothed wheel, sprocket. Driving gears include: first *or* low, second *or* intermediate, third *or* high, fourth, reverse, overdrive. —*in gear,* usable, efficient, productive; see **working 1.** —*out of gear,* inefficient, not working, broken; see **useless 1.**

gem, *n.* 1. [A jewel] precious stone, bauble, ornament; see **jewel.** Types of gems include the following—diamond, emerald, ruby, pearl, brilliant, aquamarine, amethyst, topaz, turquoise, jade, opal, sapphire, garnet, carnelian, jacinth, beryl, cat's eye, chrysoprase, chalcedony, agate, bloodstone, moonstone, onyx, sard, lapis lazuli, chrysolite, carbuncle, coral. 2. [Anything excellent, especially if small and beautiful] jewel, pearl of great price, paragon, ace, nonpareil, perfection, ideal.

gender, *n.* sexuality, sort, variety; see **kind 2, sex 3.**

genealogy, *n.* derivation, lineage, extraction; see **family.**

general, *a.* 1. [Having wide application] comprehensive, -comprehending, widespread, universal, limitless, unlimited, extensive, ecumenical, all-embracing, ubiquitous, unconfined, broad, taken as a whole, not particular, not specific, blanket, inclusive, wide, infinite, worldwide, endless.—*Ant.* particular, special, limited. 2. [Of common occurrence] usual, customary, prevailing; see **common 1.** 3. [Not specific] indefinite, uncertain, imprecise; see **vague 2.** —in

general, generally, usually, ordinarily; see **regularly.**

generality, n. abstraction, universality, principle; see **law 4.**

generalize, v. theorize, speculate, postulate; see **understand.**

generally, a. usually, commonly, ordinarily; see **regularly 1.**

generate, v. form, make, beget, create; see **produce 1.**

generation, n. 1. [The act of producing offspring] procreation, reproduction, breeding; see **birth.** 2. [One cycle in the succession of parents and children] age, crop, rank, step in continuous generation, age group. 3. [The time required for a generation, sense 2] span, 20 to 30 years, period; see **age 3.**

generosity, n. hospitality, benevolence, charity, liberality, philanthropy, altruism, unselfishness; see also **kindness 2.**—Ant. **greed,** miserliness, stinginess.

generous, a. 1. [Open-handed] bountiful, liberal, charitable, altruistic, free-handed, beneficent, lavish, profuse, unselfish, hospitable, philanthropic, prodigal, unsparing, unstinting.—Ant. **stingy,** close, tight-fisted. 2. [Considerate] kindly, magnanimous, reasonable; see **kind.**

generously, a. 1. [With a free hand] bountifully, liberally, lavishly, unsparingly, unstintingly, in full measure, handsomely, freely, profusely, with open hands, abundantly, munificently, charitably, copiously.—Ant. **selfishly,** grudgingly, sparingly. 2. [With an open heart] charitably, liberally, magnanimously, wholeheartedly, unreservedly, nobly, majestically, royally, genially, honestly, candidly, enthusiastically, unselfishly, disinterestedly, chivalrously, benevolently, warmly.—Ant. **selfishly,** coldly, heartlessly.

genetic, a. sporogenous, hereditary, matriclinous, patrimonial; see also **historical.**

genetics, n. heredity, genesiology, eugenics; see **heredity.**

genial, a. cordial, kind, warmhearted; see **friendly.**

genitals, n. organs, sexual organs, genitalia, private parts, reproductory organs, pudenda, gonads, testicles, testes, privates.

genius, n. 1. [The highest degree of intellectual capacity] ability, talent, intellect, brains, intelligence, inspiration, imagination, gift, aptitude, wisdom, astuteness, penetration, grasp, discernment, acumen, acuteness, power, capability, accomplishment, sagacity, understanding, reach, enthusiasm, creative gift, knack, bent, turn. 2. [One having genius, sense 1] gifted person, prodigy,

adept; see **artist, author, doctor, philosopher, poet, writer.**

gentility, n. decorum, propriety, refinement; see **behavior.**

gentle, a. 1. [Soft] tender, smooth, sensitive; see **faint 3, soft 2, 3.** 2. [Kind] tender, considerate, benign; see **kind.** 3. [Tamed] domesticated, housebroken, disciplined, educated, trained, civilized, tractable, pliable, taught, cultivated, tame.—Ant. **wild,** savage, untamed.

gentleman, n. man of honor, man of his word, sir, gentleman and a scholar.

gentlemanly, a. polite, polished, gallant; see **refined 2.**

gentleness, n. tenderness, softness, delicacy, smoothness, fragility, sweetness.—Ant. **roughness,** hardness, imperviousness.

gently, a. considerately, tenderly, benevolently; see **generously 2.**

genuine, a. 1. [Authentic; said of things] real, true, actual, original, veritable, unadulterated, official, whole, accurate, proved, tested, good, natural, unimpeachable, pure, unquestionable, authenticated, existent, essential, substantial, factual, palpable, exact, precise, positive, valid, literal, sound, plain, certain, legitimate, *legit, *for real, *honest-to-goodness, *in the flesh.—Ant. **vulgar,** spurious, sham. 2. [Sincere] real, actual, unaffected, unquestionable, certain, absolute, unimpeachable, definite, incontrovertible, well-established, known, reliable, bona fide, staunch, trustworthy, certain, valid, positive, frank.

geographical, a. terrestrial, geographic, earthly; see **physical 1, worldly.**

geography, n. earth science, geology, topography, economic geography, political geography, geopolitics, geopolitical study, physiography, cartography; see also **science 1.**

geology, n. applied geology, mineral or mining geology, paleontology; see **geography, science 1.**

geometrical, a. square, many-sided, multilateral, bilateral, triangular, trilateral, quadrilateral.

germ, n. microbe, antibody, bacteria, disease germ, micro-organism, virus, parasite, *bug.

German, a. Germanic, Teutonic, Prussian, Saxon, Bavarian.

German, n. 1. [The German language] Teutonic language, Proto-Germanic, High German, Low German, Old High German, Middle High German, Modern German, New High German, Deutsch (German); see also **language.** 2. [A German person] East German, West German, Teuton, Berliner, East Berliner, West Berliner, Bavarian, Hanoverian, Prussian, Franconian,

Rhinelander, Saxon, Swabian, Hitlerite, Nazi, Aryan.

Germany, *n.* German nation, German Reich, German people, West Germany, East Germany, Communist Germany, Axis power, Third Reich, German Empire, Nazi state; see also **Europe**.

germinate, *v.* generate, live, develop; see **grow 1**.

gestation, *n.* reproduction, gravidity, fecundation; see **pregnancy**.

gesture, *n.* gesticulation, indication, intimation; see **sign 1**.

gesture, *v.* make a sign, motion, signal, pantomime, act out, use sign language, use one's hands, indicate, signalize, point, nod; see also **move 1**.

get, *v.* 1. [To obtain] gain, procure, occupy, reach, capture, recover, take, grab, accomplish, attain, gain, win, secure, achieve, collect, purchase, earn, receive, realize, possess, get possession of, take title to, acquire. 2. [To become] grow, develop into, go; see **become**. 3. [To receive] be given, take, accept; see **receive 1**. 4. [To induce] persuade, talk into, compel; see **urge 2**. 5. [To overcome] beat, vanquish, overpower; see **defeat 2, 3**. 6. [To prepare] make, arrange, dress; see **prepare 1**. 7. [To contract; *said of bodily disorders*] fall victim to, succumb (to), get sick; see **catch 4**. 8. [To learn] acquire, gain, receive; see **learn 1**. 9. [To understand] comprehend, perceive, know; see **understand 1**. 10. [*To irritate*] annoy, provoke, vex; see **bother 2**. 11. [To arrive] come to, reach, land; see **arrive**.

****get across**, *v.* impart, convey, pass on; see **communicate 1**.

get ahead, *v.* climb, prosper, thrive; see **succeed 1**.

get along, *v.* 1. [To be successful] thrive, prosper, flourish; see **succeed 1**. 2. [To proceed] progress, move on, push ahead; see **advance 1**.

get angry, *v.* become enraged or infuriated or furious, etc.; lose one's temper or self-control, ***get mad or sore, ***blow up, ***blow or lose one's cool, ***get hot under the collar, ***get steamed up, ***fly off the handle, ***blow a fuse.

get at, *v.* 1. [To arrive at] achieve, reach, ascertain; see **arrive**. 2. [To intend] mean, aim, purpose; see **intend 1**.

get away (from), *v.* flee, run away, elude; see **escape**.

****get away with**, *v.* escape notice, manage (to), succeed (in); see also **achieve**, **satisfy 3**.

get back, *v.* retrieve, reclaim, salvage; see **recover 1**.

****get back at**, *v.* get even with, pay back, retaliate; see **revenge**.

get behind, *v.* loiter, fall behind, hesitate; see **lag 1**.

get by, *v.* manage, get along, do well enough; see **survive 1**.

get down, *v.* dismount, come down, alight; see **descend**.

get even with, *v.* settle a score, avenge, pay back; see **revenge**.

****get going**, *v.* start, progress, move; see **begin 1, 2**.

get in, *v.* 1. [To arrive] come, land, reach the airport or dock or hotel, etc.; see **arrive**. 2. [To enter] get inside, find a way in, gain ingress; see **enter**.

get or be in touch (with), *v.* call, telephone, write (to), contact, wire, telegraph, correspond (with), communicate (with), reach, keep in touch or in contact (with), make overtures (to).

****get it**, *v.* 1. [To understand] comprehend, perceive, know; see **understand 1**. 2. [To be punished] suffer, get what is coming to one, be scolded or reprimanded, suffer for, ***catch it, get in trouble.

****get mad**, *v.* lose one's self-control or temper, become angry or infuriated or irate, rant and rave; see **get angry**.

get off, *v.* 1. [To go away] depart, escape, go; see **leave 1**. 2. [To dismount] alight, light, disembark; see **descend**.

get on, *v.* 1. [To mount] go up, ascend, scale; see **climb**. 2. [To succeed] manage, do well enough, get along; see **succeed 1**. 3. [To age] grow old(er), advance in years, approach retirement; see **age**.

get out, *interj.* leave, begone, be off, go away, get away, ***scram! ***clear out, ***split, ***beat it, ***get the hell out.

get out, *v.* 1. [To leave] go, depart, take one's departure; see **leave 1**. 2. [To escape] break out, run away, flee; see **escape**.

get out of, *v.* 1. [To obtain] get (from), secure, gain; see **get 1**. 2. [To escape] flee, fly, run away; see **escape**. 3. [To leave] depart, go away, withdraw; see **leave 1**.

get over, *v.* overcome, recuperate, survive; see **recover 3**.

get ready, *v.* make preparations, arrange, plan; see **prepare 1**.

get rid of, *v.* eject, expel, remove; see **eliminate**.

get set, *v.* be on the alert, be ready, consolidate one's position; see **prepare 1**.

get sick, *v.* become sick or ill, contract a disease, take sick; see **sicken 1**.

****get the hang of**, *v.* comprehend, become acquainted with, grasp; see **understand 1**.

get to, *v.* 1. [To arrive] reach, approach,

land at; see **arrive. 2.** [To make listen or understand] reach, talk to, approach; see **influence.**

get through, *v.* **1.** [To complete] discharge, enact, finish; see **achieve. 2.** [To endure] live *or* come through, survive, subsist; see **endure 1, 2.**

get through to, *v.* make understand *or* listen, reach, come to an agreement (with); see **influence.**

getting, *n.* taking, obtaining, gaining, catching, earning, winning, seizing, securing, capturing, mastering, confiscating, appropriating.

get together, *v.* **1.** [To gather] collect, accumulate, congregate; see **assemble 2. 2.** [To reach an agreement] come to terms, settle, make a bargain; see **agree.**

get up, *v.* **1.** [To climb] ascend, mount, go up; see **climb. 2.** [To arise] get out of bed, rise, turn out; see **arise 1.**

ghastly, *a.* **1.** [Terrifying] hideous, horrible, frightening; see **frightful. 2.** [*Unpleasant] repulsive, disgusting, abhorrent; see **offensive 2.**

ghost, *n.* vision, specter, apparition, spirit, demon, shade, phantom, appearance, spook; see also **devil.**

giant, *a.* monstrous, colossal, enormous; see **large 1.**

giant, *n.* ogre, Cyclops, Titan, colossus, Goliath, Hercules, Atlas, mammoth, behemoth, monster, whale, elephant, leviathan, mountain, hulk, lump, bulk; see also **monster 1.**

gibberish, *n.* jargon, chatter, claptrap; see **nonsense 1.**

giddy, *a.* high, towering, lofty; see **steep.**

gift, *n.* **1.** [A present] presentation, donation, grant, gratuity, alms, endowment, bequest, bounty, charity, favor, legacy, award, reward, offering, souvenir, token, remembrance, courtesy, bonus, subsidy, tribute, subvention, contribution, subscription, relief, ration, benefit, tip, allowance, handout, hand-me-down. **2.** [An aptitude] faculty, capacity, capability; see **ability. —look a gift horse in the mouth,** carp, criticize, be ungrateful; see **judge.**

gifted, *a.* smart, skilled, talented; see **able.**

gigantic, *a.* massive, huge, immense; see **large 1.**

giggle, *n.* titter, chuckle, snicker; see **laugh.**

gild, *v.* varnish, whitewash, paint in rosy colors; see **paint 2.**

***gimmick,** *n.* catch, secret device, method; see **trick 1.**

girder, *n.* truss, rafter, mainstay; see **beam 1.**

girdle, *n.* belt, cinch(er), sash; see **underwear.**

girdle, *v.* encircle, enclose, clasp; see **surround 1.**

girl, *n.* schoolgirl, miss, lass, young woman, coed, lassie, damsel, maid, maiden, tomboy, teen-ager, *chick, *skirt, *dame, *babe.

girlish, *a.* juvenile, naive, unsophisticated, fresh, unaffected, teenage; see also **young 1.—Ant.** mature, matronly, sophisticated.

girth, *n.* circumference, distance around, bigness; see **size 2.**

gist, *n.* substance, essence, significance; see **basis, summary.**

give, *v.* **1.** [To transfer] grant, bestow, confer, impart, present, endow, bequeath, award, dispense, subsidize, contribute, parcel *or* hand *or* dole *or* give out, pass *or* hand *or* throw in, hand down *or* over, deliver, let have, tip, pass down, convey, deed, sell, will, give *or* make over (to), put into the hands of, contribute to, consign, relinquish, cede, lease, invest, dispose of, part with, lay upon, turn over, *come through *or* across with, *shell out, *fork over, *kick in, *palm off.—Ant. **maintain,** withhold, take. **2.** [To yield under pressure] give way, retreat, collapse, fall, contract, shrink, recede, open, relax, sag, bend, flex, crumble, yield.—Ant. **resist,** remain rigid, stand firm. **3.** [To allot] assign, dispense, deal; see **distribute. 4.** [To pass on] communicate, transmit, transfer; see **send 1. 5.** [To administer] minister, provide with, dispense; see **provide 1.**

***give away,** *v.* **1.** [To reveal] betray, divulge, disclose; see **reveal. 2.** [To give] bestow, award, present; see **give 1.**

give back, *v.* return, refund, reimburse; see **repay 1.**

give in, *v.* capitulate, submit, surrender; see **admit 2, yield 1.**

given, *a.* granted, supplied, donated, bestowed, presented, awarded, bequeathed, dispensed, doled *or* handed out, contributed, offered.—Ant. **kept,** taken, withheld.

give out, *v.* **1.** [To emit] emanate, expend, exude; see **emit, smell 1. 2.** [To deliver] deal, dole, hand *or* pass out; see **distribute. 3.** [To publish] proclaim, make known, announce; see **advertise, declare. 4.** [To weaken] faint, fail, break down; see **tire 1, weaken 1.**

give over, *v.* give up, deliver, relinquish; see **give 1.**

giver, *n.* provider, supplier, donator; see **donor.**

give up, *v.* **1.** [To surrender] stop fighting, cede, hand over; see **yield 1. 2.** [To stop] quit, halt, cease; see **end 1.**

give way, *v.* 1. [To collapse] sag, fall, crumble; see **give** 2. 2. [To concede] yield, accede, grant; see **admit** 2, 3.

giving, *n.* donating, granting, supplying, awarding, presenting, dispensing, doling *or* passing *or* handing out, contributing, conferring (on *or* upon), distributing, remitting, transferring, consigning, yielding, giving up, furnishing, allowing, expending, offering, tipping, parting with, pouring forth, discharging, emitting.— *Ant.* getting, taking, appropriating.

giving up, *n.* quitting, losing, giving in; see **end** 2.

glacial, *a.* icy, frozen, polar; see **cold** 1.

glacier, *n.* ice floe, floe, iceberg, berg, glacial mass, snow slide, icecap, ice field, ice stream, glacial table.

glad, *a.* exhilarated, animated, jovial; see **happy** 1.

gladly, *a.* joyously, happily, gaily, blithely, cheerfully, ecstatically, blissfully, contentedly, readily, gratefully, enthusiastically, merrily, heartily, willingly, zealously, pleasantly, pleasurably, zestfully, complacently, delightfully, gleefully, cheerily, warmly, passionately, ardently, lovingly, cordially, genially, sweetly, joyfully, with relish, with (deep) satisfaction, with full agreement, with (full) approval, with delight.—*Ant.* unwillingly, sadly, gloomily.

gladness, *n.* cheer, mirth, delight; see **happiness** 1.

glamour, *n.* allurement, charm, attraction; see **beauty** 1.

glance, *n.* glimpse, sight, fleeting impression; see **look** 3.

glance, *v.* 1. [To look] see, peep, glimpse; see **look** 2. 2. [To ricochet] skip, slide, rebound; see **bounce**.

gland, *n.* (endocrine) organ, pancreas, kidney, liver, testicle, spleen, epithelial cells. Kinds of glands include the following—simple, compound, tubular, saccular, ductless, adrenal, carotid, endocrine, lymphatic, parathyroid, parotid, pineal, pituitary, thyroid, thymus, sweat, lacrimal, salivary, mammary, seminal, prostrate, urethral, vaginal.

glare, *v.* 1. [To shine fiercely] beam, glow, radiate; see **shine** 1, 2. 2. [To stare fiercely] pierce, glower, scowl; see **frown, look** 2.

glaring, *a.* 1. [Shining] blinding, dazzling, blazing; see **bright** 1. 2. [Obvious] evident, conspicuous, obtrusive; see **obvious** 2.

glass, *n.* Objects referred to as *glass* include the following—tumbler, goblet, beaker, chalice, cup, looking glass, mirror, barometer, thermometer, hourglass, windowpane, watch crystal, monocle, telescope, microscope, spyglass, burning glass, eyeglass, lens, optical glass.

glasses, *n.* spectacles, eyeglasses, bifocals, trifocals, goggles, field glasses, opera glasses, contact lenses, *specs.

glassware, *n.* crystal, glasswork, glass. Types of common glassware include the following—tumbler, jug, decanter, bottle, fruit jar, tableware, glass ovenware, vase, flower bowl, goblet, sherbet glass, wine glass, liqueur glass, champagne glass, cocktail glass, highball glass, old-fashioned glass, brandy snifter, shot glass, cake tray, parfait glass, beer mug.

glassy, *a.* vitreous, lustrous, polished; see **smooth** 1.

glaze, *n.* enamel, polish, varnish; see **finish** 2.

glaze, *v.* coat, enamel, gloss (over); see **shine** 3.

glazed, *a.* glassy, translucent, transparent, enameled, varnished, filmed over, shiny, incrusted, burnished, lustrous, smooth.—*Ant.* fresh, **rough,** unglazed.

glee, *n.* joviality, merriment, mirth; see **happiness** 1.

gleeful, *a.* joyous, jolly, merry; see **happy** 1.

glide, *n.* floating, continuous motion, smooth movement, flowing, slide, drift, swoop, skimming, flight, soaring, slither.

glide, *v.* float, slide, drift, waft, skim, skip, trip, fly, coast, flit, wing, soar, coast *or* slide *or* skim along.—*Ant.* **hit,** rattle, lurch.

glimmer, *n.* gleam, flash, flicker; see **light** 1.

glimpse, *n.* flash, impression, sight; see **look** 3.

glisten, *v.* sparkle, shimmer, flicker; see **shine** 1.

glitter, *n.* sparkle, shimmer, gleam; see **light** 1.

glitter, *v.* glare, shimmer, sparkle; see **shine** 1.

globe, *n.* balloon, orb, spheroid; see **ball** 1.

gloom, *n.* woe, sadness, depression, dejection, melancholy, melancholia, dullness, despondency, misery, sorrow, morbidity, pessimism, foreboding, low spirits, cheerlessness, heaviness of mind, weariness, apprehension, misgiving, distress, affliction, despair, anguish, grief, horror, mourning, bitterness, chagrin, discouragement, the blues, the dumps.—*Ant.* **happiness,** optimism, gaiety.

gloomy, *a.* dreary, depressing, discouraging; see **dismal**.

glorify, *v.* laud, commend, acclaim; see **praise** 1.

glorious, *a.* famous, renowned, famed, well-known, distinguished, splendid, excellent, noble, exalted, grand, illustrious, notable, celebrated, esteemed, honored, eminent, remarkable, brilliant, great, heroic, memorable, immortal, time-honored, admirable, praiseworthy, remarkable; see also **famous.**—*Ant.* unimportant, inglorious, ignominious.

glory, *n.* 1. [Renown] honor, distinction, reputation; see **fame.** 2. [Splendor] grandeur, radiance, majesty, brilliance, richness, beauty, fineness.—*Ant.* tawdriness, meanness, baseness.

glossy, *a.* shining, reflecting, lustrous; see **bright 1.**

glove, *n.* mitten, mitt, finger mitten; see **clothes.**

glow, *n.* warmth, shine, ray; see **heat 1, light 1.**

glow, *v.* gleam, redden, radiate; see **burn, shine 1.**

glowing, *a.* gleaming, lustrous, phosphorescent; see **bright 1.**

glue, *n.* paste, mucilage, cement; see **adhesive.**

glue, *v.* paste, gum, cement; see **repair 1.**

glum, *a.* moody, morose, sullen; see **sad 1.**

glut, *v.* 1. [To oversupply] overwhelm, overstock, fill; see **flood 1.** 2. [To eat to satiety] stuff, cram, gorge, overeat, hog, eat one's fill, gobble up, eat out of house and home, fill, feast, wolf, bolt, devour, *eat like a horse.*—*Ant.* starve, diet, fast.

glutton, *n.* greedy person, hog, pig; see **beast 2.**

gluttony, *n.* voracity, edacity, intemperance; see **greed.**

gnarled, *a.* knotted, twisted, contorted; see **bent.**

gnaw, *v.* crunch, champ, masticate; see **bite, chew.**

go, *v.* 1. [To leave] quit, withdraw, take leave, depart, move, set out, go away, take off, start, leave, vanish, retire, vacate, flee, get out, fly, run along, say goodby, escape, run away, *clear or pull out,* *push or cast off,* *scram,* *split,* *blow,* *ditch,* *beat it,* *take a powder,* *get along,* fade away; see also **leave 1.** 2. [To proceed] travel, progress, proceed; see **advance 1, move 1.** 3. [To function] work, run, perform; see **operate 2.** 4. [To fit or suit] conform, accord, harmonize; see **agree, fit 1.** 5. [To extend] stretch, cover, spread; see **reach 1.** 6. [To elapse] be spent, waste away, transpire; see **pass 2.** 7. [To fail] miss, flunk, fall short; see **fail 1.** 8. [To continue] maintain, carry on, persist; see **continue 1.** 9. [To die] pass on, depart, succumb; see **die.** 10. [To end] terminate, finish, conclude; see **stop 2.** 11. [To endure] persevere, go on, persist; see **endure 1.** —**as people (or things)** go, in comparison with other people or things, by all standards, according to certain criteria; see **according to.** —

from the word "go", from the outset, at the start, beginning with; see **first.** —*have a go at,* attempt, endeavor, try one's hand at; see **try 1.** —*let go,* let free, give up, release; see **abandon 1.** —*let oneself go,* be unrestrained or uninhibited, free oneself, have fun; see **relax.** —*no go,* impossible, worthless, without value; see **useless 1.** —*on the go,* in constant motion, moving, busy; see **active.**

go about, *v.* engage in, busy oneself with, be employed; see **work 1, 2.**

goad, *v.* prod, urge, prick, prompt, spur, drive, whip, press, push, impel, force, stimulate, provoke, tease, excite, needle, instigate, arouse, animate, encourage, bully, coerce; see **urge 2.**—*Ant.* restrain, curb, rein in.

go after, *v.* 1. [To chase] seek, run or go after, hunt; see **pursue 1.** 2. [To follow in time] come after, supersede, supplant; see **succeed 2.**

go against, *v.* be opposed to, contradict, counteract; see **oppose 1, 2.**

go ahead, *v.* move on, proceed, progress; see **advance 1.**

goal, *n.* object, aim, intent; see **end 2, purpose 1.**

go all out, *v.* attempt, make a (great) effort, strive; see **try 1.**

go along, *v.* carry on, keep up, go; see **continue 1.**

go along with, *v.* 1. [To agree with] concur, conspire, collaborate; see **agree.** 2. [To cooperate] work together, act jointly, share in; see **cooperate.** 3. [To accompany] escort, squire, go with; see **accompany.**

goat, *n.* nanny goat, buck, kid; see **animal.** —*get one's goat,* annoy, irritate, anger; see **bother 2.**

go back on, *v.* desert, be unfaithful, forsake; see **abandon 2.**

go bad, *v.* degenerate, deteriorate, rot; see **spoil.**

go badly, *v.* miscarry, fall short, dissatisfy; see **disappoint, fail 1.**

gobble, *v.* bolt, cram, stuff; see **eat 1.**

go-between, *n.* middleman, referee, mediator; see **agent, messenger.**

go between, *v.* intervene, mediate, arbitrate; see **meddle 1, reconcile 2.**

go beyond, *v.* overdo, distance, surpass; see **exceed.**

go by, *v.* move onward, make one's way, proceed; see **pass 1.**

go crazy, *v.* become insane, lose one's wits, get angry; see **rage 1.**

god, *n.* 1. [A supernatural being] deity, divinity, divine or superhuman being, spirit, numen, power, demigod, oversoul, prime mover, godhead, omnipotence, world spirit or soul, universal life force, infinite spirit. Greek gods and their Roman counterparts include—Zeus *or* Jupiter *or* Jove, Phoebus (Apollo) *or* Apollo, Ares *or* Mars, Hermes *or* Mercury, Poseidon *or* Neptune, Hephaestus *or* Vulcan, Dionysius *or* Bacchus, Hades *or* Pluto, Kronos *or* Saturn, Eros *or* Cupid. Norse gods include—Balder, Frey, Loki, Odin *or* Woden *or* Wotan, Thor. For specific female deities see also **goddess**. 2. [Capitalized, the Judeo-Christian deity] Lord, Jehovah, Yahweh, the Almighty, the King of Kings, the Godhead, the Creator, the Maker, the Supreme Being, the Ruler of Heaven, Our Father in Heaven, Almighty God, God Almighty, the Deity, the Divinity, Providence, the All-knowing, the Infinite Spirit, the First Cause, the Lord of Lords, the Supreme Soul, the All-wise, the All-merciful, the All-powerful; the Trinity, the Holy Trinity, Threefold Unity, Father, Son, and Holy Ghost; God the Son, Jesus Christ, Christ, Jesus, Jesus of Nazareth, the Nazarene, the Messiah, the Savior, the Redeemer, the Son of God, the Son of Man, the Son of Mary, the Lamb (of God), Immanuel *or* Emmanuel, the King of the Jews, the Prince of Peace, the Good Shepherd, the Way, the Door, the Truth, the Life, the Light, the Christ Child, the Holy Spirit, the Spirit of God. 3. [Capitalized, the supreme deity of other religions] Allah (Mohammedanism); Khuda (Hinduism); Brahma *or* the Supreme Soul, Atman *or* the Universal Ego, Vishnu *or* the Preserver, Shiva *or* the Destroyer (all Brahamanism); (the Lord) Buddha *or* the Blessed One (Buddhism); Mazda *or* Ormazd (Zoroastrianism).

goddess, *n*. female deity, she-god; see also **god**. Greek goddesses and their Roman counterparts include the following—Hera *or* Juno, Ceres *or* Demeter, Proserpina *or* Persephone, Artemis *or* Diana, Minerva, *or* Athena, Aphrodite *or* Venus. Hindu and Brahmanic goddesses include—Chandi, Devi, Kali, Parvati, Sarasvati.

godly, *a*. righteous, devout, pious; see **holy** 1, 3.

go down, *v*. 1. [To sink] descend, decline, submerge; see **sink** 1. 2. [To lose] be defeated, submit, succumb; see **fail** 1, **lose** 3. 3. [To decrease] reduce, make less, lessen; see **decrease** 1.

go easy, *v*. skimp, be sparing *or* careful, reprieve; see **pity** 2, **save** 2.

go far, *v*. 1. [To extend] reach, buy, reinforce; see **increase** 1. 2. [To succeed] rise, achieve, rise in the world; see **succeed** 1.

go for, *v*. 1. [To reach for] stretch out for, outreach, clutch at; see **reach** 2. 2.

[*To attack] rush upon, run at, spring; see **attack**. 3. [*To like] be fond of, fancy, care for; see **like** 2.

go in for, *v*. 1. [To advocate] endorse, favor, back; see **promote** 1. 2. [To like] care for, be fond of, fancy; see **like** 1.

going, *a*. flourishing, thriving, profitable; see **successful**. —**be going to**, shall, be intending to, be prepared to; see **will** 1. 3. —*get one going, annoy, excite, enrage; see **bother** 2. —**have (something) going for one**, have an advantage, be successful *or* able *or* talented, have opportunity; see **succeed** 1. —*going strong, flourishing, surviving, thriving; see **successful**.

go into, *v*. 1. [To investigate] analyze, probe, look into; see **examine**. 2. [To take up an occupation, hobby, etc.] develop, undertake, enter into, participate in, take upon oneself, engage in, take up *or* on, get involved with, be absorbed in.

go in with, *v*. form a partnership, join forces, consolidate; see **unite**.

gold, *a*. yellow, gold-colored, red-gold, greenish gold, flaxen, wheat-colored, deep tan, tawny.

gold, *n*. 1. [A color] dark *or* deep yellow, ochroid, tawny; see **color**, **gold**, *a*. 2. [A precious metal] green gold, white gold, red gold, gold foil, gold leaf, gold plate, filled gold, commercial gold, gold alloy, cloth of gold *or* gold cloth, gold thread, gold wire; see **metal**. —*as good as gold, very good, well behaved, obedient; see **excellent**.

golf, *n*. match play, medal play, nine holes, eighteen holes, game, *pasture pool; see also **sport** 1.

gone, *a*. 1. [Having left] gone out *or* away, moved, removed, traveling, transferred, displaced, shifted, withdrawn, retired, left, taken leave, departed, deserted, abandoned, quit, disappeared, not here, not a sign of, no more, flown, run off, decamped.—*Ant.* returned, remained, **here**. 2. [Being no longer in existence] dead, vanished, dissipated, disappeared, dissolved, burned up, disintegrated, decayed, rotted away, extinct. —**far gone**, 1. advanced, deeply involved, absorbed; see **interested** 2. 2. crazy, mad, eccentric; see **insane**.

good, *a*. 1. [Moral] upright, just, honest, worthy, respectable, noble, ethical, fair, guiltless, blameless, pure, truthful, decent, kind, conscientious, as honest as the day is long, honorable, charitable. 2. [Kind] considerate, tolerant, generous; see **kind** 3. 3. [Proper] suitable, becoming, desirable; see **fit** 1. 4. [Reliable] trustworthy, dependable, loyal; see **reliable**. 5. [Sound] safe, solid, stable; see **reliable**. 6. [Pleasant] agreeable, satisfying, enjoyable; see **pleasant** 1, 2. 7. [Qualified] suited, competent, suitable; see **able**. 8. [Of approved quality] choice, select, high-grade; see **excellent**. 9. [Healthy] sound, normal, vigorous; see **healthy**. 10. [Obedient] dutiful, tractable, well-behaved; see **obedient** 1. 11. [Genuine] valid, real, sound; see **genuine** 1. 12. [Delicious] tasty, flavorful, tasteful; see **delicious**. 13. [Considerable] great, big, immeasurable; see **large** 1, **much**. 14. [Favorable] approving, commendatory, commending; see **favorable** 3. —**as good as**, in effect, virtually, nearly; see **almost**. —**come to no good**, come to a bad end, get into trouble, have difficulty; see **fail** 1. —**make good**, fulfill, satisfy the requirement(s), accomplish; see **satisfy** 3. —**no good**, useless, valueless, unserviceable; see **worthless**. —**to the good**, favorable, advantageous, beneficial; see **profitable**.

good, *n.* 1. [A benefit] welfare, gain, asset; see **advantage**. 2. [That which is morally approved] ethic, merit, ideal; see **virtue** 1.

good-by, *interj.* farewell, fare you well, God bless you and keep you, God be with you, adieu, *adios* (Spanish), so long, bye-bye, see you later, take it easy, have a good day *or* weekend.

good for, *a.* 1. [Helpful] useful, beneficial, salubrious; see **helpful** 1. 2. [Financially sound] safe, competent, worth it; see **valid** 2.

good-for-nothing, *n.* loafer, vagabond, bum; see **vagrant**.

good humor, *n.* cordiality, levity, geniality; see **happiness**.

good-looking, *a.* clean-cut, attractive, impressive; see **beautiful**, **handsome**.

good luck, *interj.* cheers, best wishes, God bless you, peace be with you.

good luck, *n.* prosperity, fortune, affluence; see **success** 2.

good morning, *interj.* good day, good morrow, greetings; see **hello**.

good-natured, *a.* cordial, kindly, amiable; see **friendly**.

goodness, *n.* decency, morality, honesty; see **virtue** 1, 2.

good night, *interj.* sleep well, see you in the morning, nighty-night; see **good-by**.

goods, *n. pl.* 1. [Effects] equipment, personal property, possessions; see **property** 1. 2. [Dress goods] fabric, material, textile, cloth, dry goods, weave, twill, synthetics, double-knit, nylon, rayon, acetate.

good will, *n.* benevolence, charity, kindness, cordiality, sympathy, tolerance, helpfulness, altruism.—*Ant.* **hatred**, malevolence, animosity.

goof, *v.* err, make a mistake, flub; see **fail 1.

go off, *v.* 1. [To leave] quit, depart, part; see **leave** 1. 2. [To explode] blow up, detonate, discharge; see **explode**.

go on, *v.* 1. [To act] execute, behave, conduct; see **act** 1, 2. 2. [To happen] occur, come about, take place; see **happen** 2. 3. [To persevere] persist, continue, bear; see **endure** 1. 4. [*To talk] chatter, converse, speak; see **talk** 1.

goose, *n.* gray goose, snow goose, Canada goose, Canadian honker; see **bird**.

go out, *v.* cease, die, darken, flicker (out), flash out, become dark *or* black, burn out, stop shining.

go over, *v.* 1. [To rehearse] repeat, say something repeatedly, practice; see **rehearse** 3. 2. [To examine] look at, investigate, analyze; see **examine**, **study**.

gorge, *n.* chasm, abyss, crevasse; see **ravine**.

gorge, *v.* glut, surfeit, stuff oneself; see **eat** 1, **fill** 1.

gorgeous, *a.* superb, sumptuous, impressive; see **beautiful**, **grand**.

gory, *a.* blood-soaked, bloodstained, bloody; see **offensive** 2.

gospel, *n.* 1. [A record of Christ] New Testament, Christian Scripture, Evangelist; see **Bible**. 2. [Belief or statement supposedly infallible] creed, certainty, dogma; see **doctrine**, **faith** 2, **truth**.

gossip, *n.* 1. [Local, petty talk] babble, chatter, meddling, small talk, malicious talk, hearsay, rumor, scandal, news, slander, defamation, injury, blackening, *the grapevine. 2. [One who indulges in gossip, sense 1] snoop, meddler, tattler, newsmonger, scandalmonger, muckraker, backbiter, chatterbox, talkative person, babbler.

gossip, *v.* tattle, prattle, tell tales, talk idly, chat, chatter, rumor, report, tell secrets, blab, babble, repeat.

go through, *v.* 1. [To inspect] search, audit, investigate; see **examine**. 2. [To undergo] withstand, survive, suffer; see **endure** 2. 3. [To spend] consume, deplete, pay, expend; see **spend** 1.

go through with, *v.* fulfill, finish, follow through (with); see **achieve**, **complete**.

go together, *v.* 1. [To harmonize] be suitable, match, fit; see **agree**. 2. [To keep company] go steady, escort, go with; see **date** 2, **keep company with**.

go to the dogs, *v.* deteriorate, backslide, decline; see **spoil.

gouge, *v.* scoop, chisel, channel; see **dig** 1.

go under, *v.* 1. [To drown] sink, drown, suffocate; see **die**. 2. [To become bankrupt] default, go broke, (go) bankrupt; see **lose** 2.

go up, v. increase, rise, double; see **grow 1.**

govern, v. command, administer, reign, legislate, oversee, assume (the) command, hold office, administer (the laws), exercise authority, be in power, supervise, direct, dictate, tyrannize.

governed, a. commanded, administered, under authority, supervised, directed, dictated to, conducted, guided, piloted, mastered, led, driven, subjugated, subordinate, determined, guided, influenced, swayed, inclined, regulated, directed, ordered, dependent, obedient, under one's jurisdiction.—*Ant.* **unruly,** self-determined, capricious.

governing, a. commanding, administrative, executive, authoritative, supervisory, regulatory, controlling, directing, overseeing, dictatorial, conducting, guiding, mastering, dominating, dominant, determining, supreme, influential, presidential, absolute, ruling, checking, curbing, inhibiting, limiting.—*Ant.* **subordinate,** powerless, tributary.

government, n. 1. [The process of governing] rule, control, command, regulation, bureaucracy, direction, dominion, sway, authority, jurisdiction, sovereignty, direction, power, management, authorization, mastery, supervision, superintendance, supremacy, domination, influence, politics, state, statecraft, political practice; see also **administration 2. 2.** [The instrument of governing] administration, assembly, legislature, congress, cabinet, executive power, authority, party, council, parliament, senate, department of justice, soviet, synod, convocation, convention, court, house. Types of government include the following—absolute monarchy, dictatorship, empire, tyranny, fascism, imperialism, colonialism, despotism, limited monarchy, constitutional monarchy, oligarchy, aristocracy, democracy, popular government, representative government, democratic socialism, communism, socialism, party government. Divisions of government include—state, province, kingdom, territory, colony, dominion, commonwealth, soviet, republic, shire, city, county, town, village, township, municipality, borough, commune, ward, district, department.

governmental, a. political, administrative, executive, regulatory, bureaucratic, legal, supervisory, sovereign, presidential, official, gubernatorial, national.

governor, n. director, leader, head, presiding officer, ruler; see **leader 2.**

go with, v. 1. [*To keep company with] escort, attend, be with; see **accompany,** date 2, keep company with. 2. [To be appropriate to] match, correspond, not clash, go well with, harmonize, complement, fit; see also **agree.**

go without, v. lack, fall short, want; see **need.**

gown, n. garb, garment, clothes; see **dress 2.**

go wrong, v. slip, break down, go amiss; see **fail 1.**

grab, v. clutch, grasp, take; see **seize 1, 2.**

grace, n. 1. [The quality of being graceful] suppleness, ease (of movement), nimbleness, agility, pliancy, smoothness, form, poise, dexterity, symmetry, balance, style, harmony.—*Ant.* **awkwardness,** stiffness, maladroitness. 2. [Mercy] forgiveness, love, charity; see **mercy 1. —in the bad graces of,** in disfavor, rejected, disapproved; see **hated. —in the good graces of,** favored, accepted, admired; see **approved.**

graceful, a. 1. [*Said of movement*] supple, agile, lithe, pliant, nimble, elastic, springy, easy, dexterous, adroit, smooth, controlled, light-footed, willowy, poised, practiced, skilled, rhythmic, sprightly, elegant.—*Ant.* **awkward,** fumbling, stiff. 2. [*Said of objects*] elegant, neat, well-proportioned, trim, balanced, symmetrical, dainty, pretty, harmonious, beautiful, comely, seemly, handsome, fair, delicate, tasteful, slender, decorative, artistic, exquisite, statuesque.—*Ant.* **ugly,** shapeless, cumbersome. 3. [*Said of conduct*] cultured, seemly, becoming; see **polite.**

gracefully, a. lithely, agilely, harmoniously, daintily, nimbly, elegantly, trimly, symmetrically, beautifully, delicately, tastefully, artistically, easily, dexterously, smoothly, skillfully, fairly, adroitly, handsomely, rhythmically, exquisitely, neatly, delightfully, charmingly, imaginatively, becomingly, suitably, pleasingly, appropriately, happily, decoratively, prettily.—*Ant.* **awkwardly,** insipidly, grotesquely.

gracious, a. 1. [Genial] amiable, courteous, condescending; see **polite.** 2. [Merciful] tender, loving, charitable; see **kind.**

grade, n. 1. [An incline] slope, inclined plane, gradient, slant, inclination, pitch, ascent, descent, ramp, upgrade, downgrade, climb, elevation, height; see also **hill.** 2. [An embankment] fill, causeway, dike; see **dam.** 3. [Rank or degree] class, category, classification; see **degree** 2 4. [A division of a school] standard, form, rank; see **gathering. —make the grade,** win, prosper, achieve; see **succeed 1.**

grade, *v.* rate, give a grade *or* grades (to), assort; see **rank 2.**

gradual, *a.* creeping, regular, continuous; see **regulated.**

gradually, *a.* step by step, by degrees, steadily, increasingly, slowly, regularly, a little at a time, little by little, bit by bit, inch by inch, by installments, in small doses, continuously, progressively, successively, sequentially, constantly, unceasingly, imperceptibly, deliberately.—*Ant.* quickly, haphazardly, by leaps and bounds.

graduate, *n.* recipient of a degree *or* certificate, alumnus, alumna, former student, holder *or* bearer of a degree *or* certificate, baccalaureate, *grad, *alum.

graduate, *v.* receive *or* be awarded *or* win *or* earn *or* take a degree *or* certificate *or* diploma, become an alumna *or* alumnus, get out, finish (up), become qualified, *get a B.A., M.A., Ph.D., M.D., etc.; *get a sheepskin.

graduated, *a.* 1. [Granted a degree] certified, ordained, passed; see **official 1.** 2. [Arranged *or* marked according to a scale] graded, sequential, progressive; see **organized.**

graduation, *n.* commencement, convocation, granting of diplomas, promotion, bestowal of honors, commissioning.

grain, *n.* 1. [Seeds of domesticated grasses] cereal(s), corn (British), small grain, seed. Varieties of grain include the following—rice, wheat, oats, barley, maize *or* corn, rye, millet, Indian corn, hybrid corn, pop corn. 2. [Character imparted by fiber] texture, warp and woof, tendency, fabric, tissue, current, direction, tooth, nap. —**against the grain,** disturbing, irritating, bothersome; see **offensive 2.**

grammar, *n.* syntax, morphology, structure, syntactic structure, sentence structure, language *or* sentence pattern, linguistic science, generative grammar, stratificational grammar, transformational grammar, universal grammar, tagmemics, synthetic *or* inflectional grammar, analytic *or* distributive grammar, traditional grammar, the new grammar. Terms in grammar include the following—tense, mood, aspect, case, modification, incorporation, inflection, concord *or* agreement, sentence, nexus, coordination, subordination, structure, phrase structure, structural linguistics, phoneme, phonemics, string, head word, morpheme, transform; see also **language.**

grammatical, *a.* 1. [Having to do with grammar] linguistic, syntactic, morphological, logical, philological, analytic. 2. [Conforming to rules of grammar] grammatically correct, conventional, accepted; see **conventional 1.**

grand, *a.* lofty, stately, dignified, elevated, high, regal, noble, illustrious, sublime, great, ambitious, august, majestic, solemn, grave, pre-eminent, extraordinary, monumental, stupendous, huge, chief, commanding, towering, overwhelming, impressive, imposing, awe-inspiring, mighty, *terrific.—*Ant.* poor, low, mediocre.

grandeur, *n.* splendor, magnificence, pomp, circumstance, impressiveness, eminence, distinction, fame, glory, brilliancy, richness, luxury, stateliness, beauty, ceremony, importance, celebrity, solemnity, fineness, majesty, sublimity, nobility, scope, dignity, elevation, preeminence, height, greatness, might, breadth, immensity, amplitude, vastness.

grandfather, *n.* grandsire, elder, forefather, ancestor, patriarch, *grandpa, *granddaddy, *grandpappy.

grandmother, *n.* grandam, matriarch, dowager, ancestor, *grandma, *gram, *granny.

grant, *n.* gift, boon, reward, present, allowance, stipend, donation, matching grant, benefaction, gratuity, endowment, concession, bequest, privilege, federal grant.—*Ant.* deprivation, deduction, detriment.

grant, *v.* 1. [To permit] yield, cede, impart; see **allow.** 2. [To accept as true] concede, accede, acquiesce; see **acknowledge 2.**

granted, *a.* 1. [Awarded] conferred, bestowed, awarded; see **given.** 2. [Allowed] accepted, admitted, acknowledged; see **assumed.** —**take for granted,** accept, presume, consider true *or* settled; see **assume.**

grape, *n.* wine grapes, raisin grapes, Concord grapes; see **fruit.**

graph, *n.* diagram, chart, linear representation; see **design, plan 1.**

graphic, *a.* 1. [Pictorial] visible, illustrated, descriptive, photographic, visual, depicted, seen, drawn, portrayed, traced, sketched, outlined, pictured, painted, engraved, etched, chiseled, penciled, printed.—*Ant.* unreal, imagined, chimerical. 2. [Vivid] forcible, telling, picturesque, intelligible, comprehensible, clear, explicit, striking, definite, distinct, precise, expressive, eloquent, moving, stirring, concrete, energetic, colorful, strong, figurative, poetic.—*Ant.* obscure, ambiguous, abstract.

grasp, *v.* 1. [To clutch] grip, enclose, clasp; see **seize 1, 2.** 2. [To comprehend] perceive, apprehend, follow; see **understand 1.**

grasp, *n.* hold, clutch, cinch; see **grip 2.**

grass, *n.* 1. Wild grasses include the following—Johnson grass, salt grass, blue grass, foxtail, buffalo grass, sand-bur, crab grass, deer grass, bunch grass, meadow grass, fescue, orchard grass, pampas grass, June grass, redtop, river grass, ribbon grass, sweet grass, cat-tail, wild rice. 2. [Grassed area] grassland, meadow, lawn, turf, pasture, prairie(s), bottomland, hayfield; see also **field 1, yard 1.** 3. [*A drug] marijuana, cannabis, *pot; see **drug.**

grassland, *n.* plains, meadow, prairie; see **field 1.**

grassy, *a.* grass-grown, verdant, green, reedy, lush, matted, tangled, carpeted, sowed, luxurious, deep.

grate, *v.* rasp, grind, abrade; see **rub 1.**

grateful, *a.* appreciative, pleased, obliged; see **thankful.**

gratefully, *a.* appreciatively, thankfully, with a sense of obligation, delightedly, responsively, admiringly.—*Ant.* **rudely,** ungratefully, thanklessly.

gratitude, *n.* thankfulness, appreciation, acknowledgment, response, sense of obligation *or* indebtedness, feeling of obligation, responsiveness, thanks, praise, recognition, honor, thanksgiving, grace.—*Ant.* ingratitude, **indifference,** thanklessness.

grave, *a.* 1. [Important] momentous, weighty, consequential; see **important 1.** 2. [Dangerous] critical, serious, ominous; see **dangerous.** 3. [Solemn] serious, sober, earnest; see **solemn 1.**

grave, *n.* vault, sepulcher, tomb, pit, crypt, mausoleum, catacomb, long home, six feet of earth, last resting place, place of interment, mound, burial place, charnel house, *last home. —**make one turn (over) in one's grave,** do something shocking *or* disrespectful, sin, err; see **misbehave.** —**one foot in the grave,** old, infirm, near death; see **dying 2.**

gravel, *n.* sand, pebbles, shale, macadam, screenings, crushed rock, washings, alluvium, tailing.

graveyard, *n.* burial ground, necropolis, God's acre; see **cemetery.**

gravity, *n.* 1. [Weight] heaviness, pressure, force; see **pressure 1.** 2. [Importance] seriousness, concern, significance; see **importance.**

gravy, *n.* sauce, dressing, brown gravy, white gravy, milk gravy, pan gravy, meat gravy.

gray, *a.* neutral, dusky, silvery, dingy, somber, shaded, drab, leaden, grayish, ashen, grizzled. Shades of gray include the following—blue-gray, silver-gray, smoke-gray, slate, bat, mouse-colored, iron-gray, lead, ash-gray, pepper and salt, dusty, smoky.

gray, *n.* shade, drabness, dusk; see **color.**

graze, *v.* 1. [To touch or score lightly] brush, scrape, rub; see **touch 1.** 2. [To pasture] browse, feed, crop, gnaw, nibble, bite, uproot, pull grass, forage, eat, munch, ruminate.

grazing, *a.* cropping, feeding, gnawing, nibbling, biting, uprooting, pasturing, pulling grass, foraging, eating, munching, ruminating.

grease, *n.* oil, wax, fat, lubricant, salve, Vaseline (trademark), axle grease, olive oil, cottonseed oil, peanut oil; see also **oil 1.**

grease, *v.* oil, lubricate, smear, salve, coat *or* rub with oil, cream, pomade, grease the wheels, anoint, swab, *give a grease job.

greasy, *a.* creamy, fat, oleaginous, fatty; see **oily 1.**

great, *a.* 1. [Eminent] noble, grand, majestic, dignified, exalted, commanding, famous, renowned, widely acclaimed, famed, celebrated, distinguished, noted, conspicuous, elevated, prominent, high, stately, honorable, magnificent, glorious, regal, royal, kingly, imposing, preeminent, unrivaled, fabulous, fabled, storied.—*Ant.* **obscure,** retired, anonymous. 2. [Large] numerous, big, vast; see **large 1.** 3. [*Excellent] exceptional, surpassing, transcendant; see **excellent.**

greatly, *a.* exceedingly, considerably, hugely; see **very.**

greatness, *n.* 1. [Eminence] prominence, renown, importance; see **fame.** 2. [Size] bulk, extent, largeness; see **size 2.**

Greece, *n.* Hellas, Greek peninsula, Hellenic peoples; see **Europe.**

greed, *n.* greediness, selfishness, eagerness, voracity, excess, gluttony, piggishness, indulgence, hoggishness, niggardliness, acquisitiveness, intemperance, covetousness, desire, grabbiness, an itching palm.—*Ant.* **generosity,** liberality, kindness.

greedy, *a.* avid, grasping, rapacious, selfish, miserly, parsimonious, close, closefisted, tight, tight-fisted, niggardly, exploitative, grudging, devouring, ravenous, omnivorous, carnivorous, intemperate, gobbling, indulging one's appetites, mercenary, stingy, covetous, pennypinching.—*Ant.* **generous,** munificent, bountiful.

Greek, *a.* Hellenic, Hellenistic, Minoan, Dorian, Attic, Athenian, Spartan, Peloponnesian, Ionian, Corinthian, Thessalian, ancient, classic; see also **classical 2.**

Greek, *n.* 1. [A citizen of Greece] Hellene, Athenian, Spartan; see **European.** 2. [The Greek language] Hellenic, Ionic, New Ionic; see **language 1.**

Greeks, *n.* Greek culture, Hellenes, the Ancients, Hellenism, classical times, Athens, the glory that was Greece, the Golden Age.

green, *a.* 1. [Of the color green] Tints and shades of green include the following—emerald, blue-green, sage, aquamarine, chartreuse, lime, kelly, bronze-green, yellow-green, bottle-green, pea-green, sea-green, apple-green, grass-green, forest-green, spinach-green, moss-green, pine-green, olive-green, jade. 2. [Verdant] growing, leafy, sprouting, grassy, grass-grown, flourishing, lush. 3. [Immature] young, growing, unripe, maturing, developing, half-formed, fresh.—*Ant.* mature, ripe, gone to seed. 4. [Inexperienced] youthful, callow, raw; see **inexperienced.**

green, *n.* greenness, verdure, emerald, chlorophyl; see also **color.**

greet, *v.* welcome, speak to, salute, address, hail, recognize, embrace, shake hands, nod, receive, call to, stop, acknowledge, bow (to), approach, give one's love, extend the right of friendship, bid good day *or* hello *or* welcome, exchange greetings, usher in, attend, pay one's respects.—*Ant.* ignore, snub, slight.

greeting, *n.* welcome, address, notice, speaking to, ushering in, acknowledgment, one's compliments, regards. Common greetings include the following—hello, how do you do? how are you? good morning, good day, good afternoon, good evening, hi, *hey, you; *say.

grey, *a.* dun, drab, grayish; see **gray.**

grief, *n.* sorrow, sadness, regret, melancholy, mourning, misery, trouble, anguish, despondency, pain, worry, harassment, anxiety, woe, heartache, malaise, disquiet, discomfort, affliction, gloom, unhappiness, desolation, despair, agony, torture, purgatory.—*Ant.* happiness, exhilaration, pleasure.

grievance, *n.* complaint, injury, case; see **objection.**

grieve, *v.* lament, bewail, regret, sorrow (for); see **mourn 1.**

grill, *v.* roast, sauté, barbecue; see **cook.**

grim, *a.* 1. [Sullen] sour, crusty, gloomy, sulky, morose, churlish, forbidding, glum, grumpy, scowling, grouchy, crabbed, glowering, stubborn, cantankerous.—*Ant.* happy, cheerful, gay. 2. [Stern] austere, strict, harsh; see **severe 1.** 3. [Relentless] unrelenting, implacable, inexorable; see **severe 2.**

grimace, *n.* smirk, smile, sneer; see **expression 4.**

grime, *n.* soil, smudge, dirt; see **filth.**

grimy, *a.* begrimed, dingy, soiled; see **dirty 1.**

grin, *n.* smirk, simper, wry face; see **smile.**

grin, *v.* smirk, simper, beam; see **smile.**

grind, *v.* crush, powder, mill, grate, granulate, disintegrate, rasp, scrape, file, abrade, pound, reduce to powder *or* fine particles, crunch, roll *or* pound out, chop up, crumble.—*Ant.* organize, mold, solidify.

grinding, *a.* abrasive, crushing, pulverizing, grating, rasping, rubbing, milling, powdering, cracking, bone-crushing, crunching, splintering, shivering, smashing, crumbling, scraping, chopping, wearing away, eroding.

grip, *n.* 1. [The power and the application of the power to grip] grasp, hold, manual *or* digital strength, clutch, clasp, catch, cinch, vise, clench, clinch, embrace, handhold, fist, handshake, anchor, squeeze, wrench, grab, enclosure, fixing, fastening, crushing, clamp, hoops of steel, vicelike grip, jaws. 2. [Something suited to grasping] knocker, knob, ear; see **handle 1.** 3. [A traveling bag] valise, suitcase, satchel; see **bag.**

grip, *v.* clutch, grasp, clasp; see **seize 1.** —**come to grips,** engage, encounter, cope with; see **fight, try 1.**

***gripe,** *n.* complaint, grievance, *beef; see **objection.**

***gripe,** *v.* grumble, mutter, fuss; see **complain.**

gristle, *n.* ossein, cartilage, osseous matter; see **bone.**

grit, *n.* sand, dust, crushed rock; see **gravel.**

gritty, *a.* rough, abrasive, sandy, rasping, lumpy, gravelly, muddy, dusty, powdery, granular, crumbly, loose, scratchy.

groan, *n.* moan, sob, grunt; see **cry 1.**

groan, *v.* moan, murmur, keen; see **cry 1.**

groceries, *n.* food, edibles, produce, comestibles, foodstuffs, perishables, vegetables, staples, green groceries, fruits, dairy products, processed foods, frozen foods, freeze-dried foods, dried *or* desiccated foods, packaged foods, canned foods.

grocery, *n.* food store, vegetable market, corner store; see **market 1.**

groggy, *a.* sleepy, dizzy, reeling; see **tired.**

groom, *n.* bridegroom, married man, successful suitor; see **husband.**

groom, *v.* rub down, comb, brush; see **prepare 1.**

groove, *n.* channel, trench, gouge, depression, scratch, canal, valley, notch, furrow, rut, incision, slit, gutter, ditch, crease. —***in the groove,** efficient, skillful, operative; see **working 1.**

grope, v. fumble, touch, feel blindly; see feel 1.

gross, a. 1. [Fat] corpulent, obese, huge; see fat 2. 2. [Obscene] foul, swinish, indecent; see **lewd** 1, 2. 3. [Without deduction] in sum, total, entire; see **whole** 1.

grotesque, a. malformed, ugly, distorted; see deformed.

grouch, n. complainer, grumbler, growler, *bear, *sourpuss, *sorehead, *crab, *crank, *bellyacher.

grouch, v. mutter, grumble, *gripe; see complain.

grouchy, a. surly, ill-tempered, crusty; see irritable.

ground, n. 1. [Soil] sand, dirt, soil; see earth 2. 2. [An area] spot, terrain, territory; see area. —**break ground,** start, initiate, commence; see **begin** 1. —**cover ground,** move, go on, progress; see **advance** 1. —**from the ground up,** thoroughly, wholly, entirely; see completely. —**gain ground,** move, go on, progress; see **advance** 1. —**get off the ground,** start, commence, come into being; see **begin** 2. —**hold** (or **stand**) **one's ground,** maintain one's position, defend, sustain; see **endure** 2. —**lose ground,** withdraw, fall behind, drop back; see **lag** 1. —*run into the ground,** exaggerate, do too much, press; see **overdo** 1.

ground, v. 1. [To bring to the ground] floor, bring down, prostrate; see **trip** 2. 2. [To restrict] cause to remain on the ground, confine, prevent from driving; see **restrict.** 3. [To instruct in essentials] train, indoctrinate, educate; see teach.

grounds, n. 1. [Real estate] lot, environs, territory; see **property** 2. 2. [Basis] reasons, arguments, proof; see **basis.** 3. [Sediment] dregs, lees, leavings; see residue.

groundwork, n. background, base, origin; see **basis, foundation** 2.

group, n. 1. [A gathering of persons] assembly, assemblage, crowd; see **gathering.** 2. [Collected things] accumulation, assortment, combination; see **collection.** 3. [An organized body of people] association, club, society; see **organization** 3.

group, v. file, assort, arrange; see **classify.**

grovel, v. crawl, beg, sneak, stoop, kneel, crouch (before), kowtow (to), sponge, cower, snivel, beseech, wheedle, flatter, cater to, humor, pamper, curry favor with, court, act up to, play up to, beg for mercy, prostrate oneself, soft-soap, *butter up, make up to, *kiss one's feet, *lick another's boots, knuckle under, *polish the apple, *eat dirt, *brown-nose.—*Ant.* hate, spurn, scorn.

grow, v. 1. [To become larger] increase, expand (in size), swell, wax, thrive, gain, enlarge, advance, dilate, stretch, mount, build, burst forth, spread, multiply, develop, mature, flourish, grow up, rise, sprout, shoot or jump or start or spring up, spread like wildfire.—*Ant.* lessen, shrink, wither. 2. [To change slowly] become, develop, alter, tend, pass, evolve, flower, shift, flow, progress, advance, get bigger, larger, etc.; wax, turn into, improve, mellow, age, better, ripen (into), blossom, open out, resolve itself into, mature. 3. [To cultivate] raise, nurture, tend, nurse, foster, produce, plant, breed.—*Ant.* harm, impede, neglect.

growing, a. increasing, ever-widening, expanding, budding, germinating, maturing, waxing, enlarging, amplifying, swelling, developing, mushrooming, spreading, thriving, flourishing, stretching, living, sprouting, viable, organic, animate, spreading like wildfire.—*Ant.* contraction, withering, shrinking.

growl, n. snarl, gnarl, moan, bark, bellow, rumble, roar, howl, grumble, grunt.

growl, v. snarl, bark, gnarl; see **cry** 2.

grown, a. of age, adult, grown up; see **mature** 1.

growth, n. 1. [The process of growing] extension, (organic) development, germination; see **increase.** 2. [The result of growing] completion, adulthood, fullness; see **majority** 2. 3. [An organic excrescence] tumor, cancer, swelling, mole, fungus, parasite, outgrowth, thickening.

grudge, n. spite, rancor, animosity; see hatred.

grudge, v. begrudge, covet, be reluctant; see envy.

gruesome, a. grim, grisly, fearful; see **frightful, offensive** 2.

gruff, a. harsh, grating, rough; see hoarse.

grumble, v. whine, protest, fuss; see **complain** 1.

grumpy, a. sullen, grouchy, cantankerous; see **irritable.**

grunt, v. snort, squawk, squeak; see **cry** 2.

guarantee, v. attest, testify, vouch for, declare, assure, answer for, be responsible for, pledge, give bond, go bail, wager, stake, give a guarantee, stand good for, back, sign for, become surety for, endorse, secure, make sure or certain, warrant, insure, witness, prove, reassure, support, affirm, confirm, cross one's heart.

guaranteed, a. warranted, certified, bonded, secured, endorsed, insured, pledged, confirmed, assured, approved, attested, sealed, certificated, protected, affirmed, *sure-fire.—*Ant.* unsupported, anonymous, unendorsed.

guaranty, n. warrant, warranty, bond, contract, certificate, charter, testament, security.

guard, n. sentry, sentinel, protector; see **watchman.** —off one's guard, unaware, unprotected, defenseless; see **unprepared.** —on one's guard, alert, mindful, vigilant; see **ready 2.**

guard, v. watch, observe, superintend, patrol, picket, police, look out or after, see after, supervise, tend, keep in view, keep an eye on, attend, overlook, hold in custody, stand over, babysit, care for, look or see to, chaperone, oversee, *ride herd on, *keep tab(s) (on).—*Ant.* disregard, **neglect,** forsake.

guarded, a. 1. [Protected] safeguarded, secured, defended; see **safe 1.** 2. [Cautious] circumspect, attentive, overcautious; see **careful.**

guardian, n. 1. [One who regulates or protects] overseer, safeguard, curator, guard, protector, preserver, trustee, custodian, keeper, patrol, warden, defender, supervisor, babysitter, sponsor, superintendent, sentinel. 2. [A foster parent] adoptive parent, foster mother, foster father; see **father, mother.**

guerrilla, a. auxiliary, independent, predatory; see **fighting.**

guerrilla, n. irregular soldier, saboteur, independent; see **soldier.**

guess, n. conjecture, surmise, supposition, theory, hypothesis, presumption, opinion, postulate, estimate, suspicion, hypothesis, guesswork, view, belief, assumption, speculation, fancy, inference, conclusion, deduction, induction, shot in the dark.

guess, v. conjecture, presume, infer, suspect, speculate, imagine, surmise, theorize, hazard a supposition or conjecture, suggest, figure, venture, suppose, presume, imagine, think likely, reckon, calculate.

guess at, v. reckon, calculate, survey; see **estimate.**

guessing, n. guesswork, supposition, imagination, fancy, inference, deduction, presupposition, reckoning, surmise, theorizing, taking for granted, postulating, assuming, presuming, *leaping to conclusions.

guest, n. visitor, caller, house guest, dinner guest, luncheon guest, etc.; visitant, confidant or confidante, friend.

guidance, n. direction, leadership, supervision; see **administration 2.**

guide, n. pilot, captain, pathfinder, scout, escort, courier, director, explorer, lead, guru, conductor, pioneer, leader, superintendent.

guide, v. conduct, escort, show the way; see **lead 1.**

guilt, n. culpability, blame, error, fault, crime, sin, offence, liability, criminality, sinfulness, misconduct, misbehavior, malpractice, delinquency, transgression, indiscretion, weakness, failing, felonious conduct.—*Ant.* innocence, freedom from fault, blamelessness.

guilty, a. found guilty, guilty as charged, condemned, sentenced, criminal, censured, impeached, incriminated, indicted, liable, condemned, convictable, judged, damned, doomed, in or at fault, sinful, to blame, in the wrong, in error, wrong, blameable, reproachable, chargeable.—*Ant.* blameless, **innocent,** right.

gulch, n. gully, ditch, gorge; see **ravine.**

gulf, n. 1. [Chasm] abyss, abysm, depth; see **ravine.** 2. [An arm of the sea] inlet, sound, cove; see **bay.**

gullible, a. innocent, trustful, simple; see **naïve.**

gully, n. ditch, chasm, crevasse; see **ravine.**

gulp, v. swig, choke down, *toss off; see **swallow.**

gum, n. resin, glue, pitch, tar, pine tar, amber, wax. Commercial gums include the following—chewing gum, sealing wax, rosin, mucilage, chicle, latex, gum arabic.

gummy, a. sticky, cohesive, viscid; see **sticky.**

gun, n. Types include the following—rifle, automatic rifle, repeating rifle, repeater, recoilless rifle, air rifle, shotgun, sawed-off shotgun, musket, hand gun, automatic, semiautomatic pistol or rifle, squirrel gun, carbine, long rifle, laser gun, revolver, pistol, *rod; see also **machine gun.** —*jump the gun, start too soon, act inappropriately, give oneself away; see **begin 1, hurry 1.**

gunfire, n. bombardment, fire to pin down someone, artillery support, air support, air strike, mortar fire, heavy arms attack, explosion, shooting, shot, report, artillery, volley, discharge, detonation, blast, firing, burst, (creeping) barrage, curtain of fire, cannonade, fire superiority, salvo, fire power.

gunman, n. killer, thug, gangster; see **criminal.**

gunner, n. machine gunner, rocketeer, missile launcher, bazooka carrier or launcher, sniper, sharpshooter, aerial gunner, artilleryman, cannoneer.

gurgle, v. ripple, murmur, pour; see **flow.**

gush, v. pour, well, spew; see **flow.**

gust, n. blast, blow, breeze; see **wind 1.**

gusto, n. zeal, fervor, ardor; see **zeal.**

gut, *n.* small intestine, large intestine, duodenum; see **intestines.**

guts, *n.* **1.** [Bowels] viscera, insides, belly; see **intestines. 2.** [*Fortitude] pluck, hardihood, effrontery; see **courage.** —*hate someone's guts, detest, dislike, despise; see **hate.**

gutter, *n.* canal, gully, sewer, watercourse, channel, dike, drain, moat, trough; see also **trench.**

guttural, *a.* throaty, gruff, deep; see **hoarse.**

guy, *n.* chap, lad, person; see **fellow 1.**

guzzle, *v.* swill, quaff, swig; see **drink 1.**

gymnasium, *n.* health or recreation center, playing floor, exercise room, sports center, field house, court, athletic club, arena, coliseum, theater, circus, stadium, ring, rink, pit, *gym.

gymnast, *n.* acrobat, tumbler, jumper; see **athlete.**

gymnastics, *n.* trapeze performance, health exercises, acrobatics, aerobatics, therapeutics, body-building exercises, tumbling, vaulting, work on the rings, bars, balance beam, horizontal bars, horse, etc.; *slimnastics.

gypsy, *n.* tramp, Bohemian, vagrant; see **traveler.**

H

habit, *n.* 1. [A customary action] mode, wont, routine, rule, characteristic, practice, disposition, way, fashion, manner, propensity, bent, turn, proclivity, addiction, predisposition, susceptibility, weakness, bias, persuasion, second nature; see **custom** 1. 2. [An obsession] addiction, fixation, hang-up; see **obsession.**

habitat, *n.* locality, territory, (natural) surroundings; see **environment, home** 1, **position** 1.

habitual, *a.* ingrained, confirmed, frequent, periodic, continual, routine, mechanical, automatic, seasoned, permanent, perpetual, fixed, rooted, systematic, recurrent, periodical, methodical, repeated, disciplined, practiced, accustomed, established, set, repetitious, cyclic, reiterated, settled, trite, stereotyped, in a groove *or* rut.—*Ant.* different, exceptional, departing.

hack, *n.* 1. [A literary drudge] pulp-story writer, ghost writer, propagandist, commercial writer, popular novelist; see **writer.** 2. [A cut] notch, nick, cleavage; see **cut** 1. 3. [*Commercial driver, especially of a taxicab] taxi *or* cab driver, chauffeur, *cabbie; see **driver.**

hack, *v.* chop, whack, mangle; see **cut** 1.

hag, *n.* crone, virago, withered old woman, shrew, ogress, hellcat, fishwife, harridan, old witch, *battle-ax; see also **witch.**

haggle, *v.* deal, wrangle, argue; see **buy, sell.**

hail, *n.* hailstorm, sleet, icy particles, ice; see also **rain** 1.

hail, *v.* cheer, welcome, honor; see **greet.**

hail from, *v.* come from, be born in, be a native of; see **begin** 2.

hair, *n.* 1. [Threadlike growth] locks, wig, moustache, whiskers, eyebrow, eyelash, sideburn, mane, fluff; see also **beard, fur.** 2. [Anything suggesting the thickness of a hair] a hairbreadth, a narrow margin, hair trigger, hairspring, splinter, shaving, sliver; see also bit 1. —*get in one's hair,** irritate, annoy, disturb; see **bother** 2. —*let one's hair down,** be informal, have fun, let oneself go; see **relax.** —**make one's hair stand on end,** terrify, scare, horrify; see **frighten.**

haircut, *n.* trim, trimming, shingling, bob, crew cut, *flat-top, Beatle, page boy, pigtails, French roll, bun, ponytail, braid, feather cut, bangs, *butch, *D.A., *ducktail.

hair-do, *n.* coiffure, hairdressing, hair style; see **haircut.**

hairless, *a.* clean-shaven, beardless, smooth-faced; see **bald, smooth** 3.

hairpin, *n.* bobby pin, hair clip, barrette; see **fastener.**

hair style, *n.* hair-do, coiffure, haircut; see **haircut.**

hairy, *a.* bristly, shaggy, wooly, unshorn, downy, fleecy, whiskered, tufted, unshaven, bearded, bewhiskered, furry, fuzzy, hirsute, fluffy.—*Ant.* hairless, bald, smooth.

half, *a.* partial, divided by two, equally distributed in halves, mixed, divided, halved, bisected; see also **halfway.**—*Ant.* all, full, whole. —**by half,** considerably, many, very much; see **much.** —**in half,** into halves, split, divided; see **half.** —**not the half of it,** not all of it, partial, incomplete; see **unfinished.**

halfback, *n.* right halfback, left halfback, back; see **football player.**

half-baked, *a.* senseless, brainless, indiscreet; see **stupid** 1.

half-breed, *n.* half-caste, crossbreed, half-blood; see also **hybrid.**

half dollar, *n.* fifty cents, fifty-cent piece, *four bits; see **money** 1.

halfhearted, *a.* lukewarm, indecisive, irresolute; see **indifferent.**

halfway, *a.* midway, half the distance, in the middle, incomplete, unsatisfactory, partially, fairly, imperfectly, in part, partly, nearly, insufficiently, to a degree, to some extent, comparatively, moderately, to *or* at half the distance, in some measure, *middling; see also **half.**—*Ant.* wholly, **completely,** entirely.

halfway house, *n.* alcoholic *or* addiction facility, referral center, (rest) home; see **hospital.**

hall, *n.* 1. [A large public or semi-public building or room] legislative chamber, assembly (room), meeting place, banquet hall, town hall, concert hall, dance hall, music hall, arena, ballroom, clubroom, church, salon, lounge, chamber, stateroom, gymnasium, dining hall, armory, amphitheater, council chamber, reception room, waiting room, lecture room, gallery, *gym, mess hall. 2. [An entrance way] foyer, corridor, hallway; see **entrance** 2, **room** 2.

hallelujah, *interj.* praise God, praise the Lord, glory be; see **yell.**

hallmark, *n.* endorsement, seal (of approval), mark of acceptance; see **emblem.**

hallowed, *a.* sacred, sacrosanct, consecrated; see **divine.**

hallway, *n.* foyer, entrance way, corridor; see **entrance 2.**

halt, *v.* pull up, check, terminate, suspend, put an end to, interrupt, break into, block, cut short, adjourn, hold off, cause to halt, stem, deter, bring to a stand *or* standstill, stall, bring to an end, curb, stop, restrict, arrest, hold (in check), defeat, thwart, hamper, frustrate, suppress, clog, intercept, extinguish, blockade, obstruct, repress, inhibit, hinder, barricade, impede, overthrow, vanquish, override, dam, upset, stand in the way of, baffle, contravene, overturn, reduce, counteract, quell, prohibit, outdo, put down, finish, forbid, oppose, crush, *nip in the bud, break (it) up, *freeze, *put on the brakes, *hold on, *throw a wet blanket on, *throw a (monkey) wrench in the works, *clip one's wings, *tie one's hands, take the wind out of one's sails, *squelch.—*Ant.* begin, start, instigate.

halter, *n.* leash, bridle, rein; see **bit 4, rope.**

halve, *v.* split, bisect, cut in two; see **divide.**

ham, *n.* **1.** [Smoked pork thigh] sugarcured ham, Virginia ham, picnic ham; see **meat. 2.** [An incompetent actor] inferior player, nonprofessional, *ham actor; see **amateur.**

hamburger, *n.* ground round, ground beef, burger; see **meat.**

hammer, *n.* maul, mallet, mace, club, gavel, steam hammer, triphammer, jackhammer, sledge; see also **stick, tool 1.**

hammer, *v.* strike, bang, pound (away at); see **beat 2, hit.**

hammer out, *v.* work out, fight through, get settled; see **decide.**

hammock, *n.* (porch) swing, hanging bed, bunk; see **bed 1.**

hamper, *v.* impede, thwart, embarrass; see **hinder.**

hand, *n.* **1.** [The termination of the arm] fingers, palm, grip, grasp, hold, knuckles; see also **fist. 2.** [A workman] helper, worker, hired hand; see **laborer. 3.** [Handwriting] chirography, script, penmanship; see **handwriting. 4.** [Aid] help, guidance, instruction; see **help 1. 5.** [Applause] (standing) ovation, thunderous reception, handclapping; see **praise 2. 6.** [Round of cards] good *or* poor *or* strong, etc., hand; deal, round; see **game 1.** —**at hand,** immediate, approximate, close by; see **near 1.** —**by hand,** handcrafted, handmade, manual; see **homemade.** —**change hands,** transfer, pass on, shift; see **give 1.** —**from**

hand to hand, shifted, given over, changed; see **transferred.** —**from hand to mouth,** from day to day *or* paycheck to paycheck, by necessity, in poverty; see **poor 1.** —**hold hands,** touch, press, squeeze; see **hold 1.** —**in hand,** under control, in order, all right; see **managed 2.** —**join hands,** unite, associate, agree; see **join 1.** —**keep one's hand in,** carry on, continue, make a practice of; see **practice 1.** —**not lift a hand,** do nothing, be lazy, not try; see **neglect 1, 2.** —**off one's hands,** out of one's responsibility, no longer one's concern, not accountable for; see **irresponsible.** —**on hand,** ready, close by, usable; see **available.** —**on one's hands,** in one's care or responsibility, chargeable to one, accountable to; see **responsible 1.** —**on the other hand,** otherwise, conversely, from the opposite position; see **otherwise 1, 2.** —**out of hand,** out of control, wild, unmanageable; see **unruly.** —**take in hand,** take control of *or* responsibility for, take over, handle; see **try 1.** —**throw up one's hands,** give up, resign, quit; see **yield 1.** —**wash one's hands of,** deny, reject, refuse; see **denounce.**

hand, *v.* deliver, give to, return; see **give 1.**

hand around, *v.* hand out, pass out *or* around, allot; see **distribute, give 1.**

handbag, *n.* lady's pocketbook, bag, clutch purse; see **purse.**

handbook, *n.* textbook, directory, guidebook; see **book.**

hand down, *v.* pass on, bequeath, grant; see **give 1.**

handed, *a.* given to, conveyed, bestowed; see **given.**

handful, *n.* a small quantity, some, a sprinkling; see **few.**

handicap, *n.* **1.** [A disadvantage] hindrance, obstacle, block; see **barrier. 2.** [A physical injury] impairment, affliction, chronic disorder; see **impediment 2, injury.**

handicapped, *a.* thwarted, crippled, impeded, burdened, hampered, obstructed, encumbered, put at a disadvantage, checked, blocked, limited, restrained, wounded, curbed, put behind; see also **disabled, restricted.—*Ant.* aided, helped, supported.

handily, *a.* skillfully, intelligently, smoothly; see **cleverly, easily.**

hand in, *v.* deliver, submit, return; see **give 1, offer 1.**

hand in hand, *a.* (closely) associated, working together, related; see **together 2, united.**

handiwork, *n.* handicraft, creation, handwork; see **workmanship.**

handkerchief, n. napkin, *rag, *hanky; see **towel**.

handle, n. 1. [A holder] handhold, hilt, grasp, crank, knob, stem, grip, arm; see also **holder**. 2. [*A title] nickname, designation, *moniker; see **name 1, title 3**. —**fly off the handle**, become angry, lose one's temper, *blow off steam; see **rage 1**.

handle, v. 1. [To deal in] retail, market, offer for sale; see **sell**. 2. [To touch] finger, check, examine; see **feel 2, touch 1**. 3. [To do whatever is necessary] manipulate, operate, work; see **manage 1**.

handling, n. treatment, approach, styling; see **management**.

handmade, a. made by hand, handicraft, handcrafted; see **homemade**.

hand-me-down, n. secondhand article, discard(s), old clothes or articles or utensils, etc.; see **secondhand**.

handout, n. contribution, donation, free meal; see **gift 1, grant**.

hand out, v. give to, deliver, distribute; see **give 1, provide 1**.

hand over, v. deliver, surrender, give up; see **give 1, yield 1**.

hands off, interj. keep away, leave me alone, stay back; see **avoid**.

handsome, a. smart, impressive, stately, good-looking, attractive, athletic, personable, strong, muscular, robust, well-dressed, *slick; see also **beautiful**.—Ant. homely, ugly, unsightly.

hand-to-hand, a. face-to-face, facing, close; see **near 1**.

handwriting, n. penmanship, hand, writing, script, longhand, scrawl, scribble, manuscript, a kind or style of writing, calligraphy, *scratching, *chicken tracks.

handwritten, a. in manuscript or writing, in long hand, not typed; see **reproduced, written 2**.

handy, a. 1. [Near] nearby, at hand, close by; see **near 1, 2**. 2. [Useful] beneficial, advantageous, gainful; see **helpful 1, profitable, usable**.

hang, v. 1. [To suspend] dangle, attach, drape, hook (up), hang up, nail on the wall, put on a clothesline, fix, pin or tack up, drape on the wall, fasten up; see also **fasten 1**.—Ant. drop, throw down, let fall. 2. [To be suspended] overhang, wave, flap, be loose, droop, flop, be in mid-air, swing, dangle, be fastened, hover, stay up.—Ant. fall, come down, drop. 3. [To kill by hanging] execute, lynch, hang by the neck until dead; see **kill 1**. —**get** (or **have**) **the hang of**, have the knack of, comprehend, lynch; see **understand 1**. —**not care** (or **give**) **a hang about**, be indifferent toward, not care about, ignore; see **neglect 2**.

hang around, v. associate (with), get along with, have relations with; see **keep company with**.

hanged, a. lynched, strung up, brought to the gallows; see **executed 2**.

hanger, n. (coat) hook, nail, peg, coat hanger, clothes hanger, holder, clothes rod, wire hanger, collapsible hanger; see also **holder**.

hanger-on, n. leech, nuisance, parasite; see **dependent 2, a**.

hanging, a. dangling, swaying, swinging, overhanging, projecting, suspended, fastened to, pendulous, drooping.

hang on, v. persist, remain, continue; see **endure 1, 2**.

hang-out, n. bar, *joint, *hole; see **bar 2, headquarters, room 2**.

hang out, v. loiter, spend time, haunt; see **visit 1**.

hangover, n. nausea, sickness, headache; see **drunkenness, illness 1**.

hang-up, n. problem, predicament, disturbance; see **difficulty 1, 2**.

hang up, v. finish a telephone call, ring off, hang up the phone; see **end 1**.

haphazard, a. offhand, casual, random, careless, slipshod, incidental, unthinking, unconscious, uncoordinated, reckless, unconcerned, unpremeditated, loose, indiscriminate, unrestricted, irregular, blind, purposeless, unplanned, hit-or-miss, willy-nilly; see also **aimless**.—Ant. careful, studied, planned.

haphazardly, a. unexpectedly, casually, every now and then; see **accidentally, carelessly**.

happen, v. 1. [To be by chance] come up or about, turn or crop up, chance, occur unexpectedly, come face to face with, befall, *hit one like a ton of bricks, be one's luck. 2. [To occur] take place, (come to) pass, arrive, ensue, befall, come after, arise, take effect, come into existence, recur, come into being, spring, proceed, follow, come about, fall, repeat, appear, go on, become a fact, turn out, become known, be found, come to mind, transpire, come off; see also **result**.

happening, n. incident, affair, accident; see **event 1**.

happily, a. joyously, gladly, joyfully, cheerily, gaily, laughingly, smilingly, jovially, merrily, brightly, vivaciously, hilariously, with pleasure, peacefully, blissfully, cheerfully, gleefully, playfully, heartily, lightheartedly, lightly, to one's delight, optimistically, with all one's heart, with relish, with good will, in a happy manner, with zeal, with good grace, zestfully, with open arms, sincerely, willingly, with right good will, freely, graciously, tactfully, lovingly, agreeably.—*Ant.* morosely, sadly, dejectedly.

happiness, *n.* mirth, merrymaking, cheer, merriment, joyousness, vivacity, laughter, delight, gladness, good spirits, hilarity, playfulness, exuberance, gaiety, cheerfulness, good will, rejoicing, exhilaration, glee, geniality, good cheer, light-heartedness, joy; see also **joy.**

happy, *a.* joyous, joyful, merry, mirthful, glad, gleeful, delighted, cheerful, gay, laughing, contented, genial, satisfied, enraptured, congenial, cheery, jolly, hilarious, sparkling, enchanted, transported, rejoicing, blissful, jovial, delightful, delirious, exhilarated, pleased, gratified, peaceful, comfortable, intoxicated, debonair, light, bright, ecstatic, charmed, pleasant, hearty, overjoyed, lighthearted, radiant, vivacious, sunny, smiling, content, animated, lively, spirited, exuberant, good-humored, elated, jubilant, rollicking, playful, thrilled, fun-loving, carefree, at peace, in good *or* high spirits, happy as a lark *or* a king *or* as the day is long, in ecstasies, beside oneself, *jazzed up, bubbling over, tickled (*pink *or* *to death *or* silly), happy-go-lucky, *in seventh heaven.—*Ant.* sorrowful, sad, melancholy.

happy-go-lucky, *a.* cheerful, easygoing, unconcerned; see **irresponsible.**

harass, *v.* tease, vex, irritate; see **bother 2.**

harbor, *n.* port, pier, inlet, wharf; see **dock.**

harbor, *v.* 1. [To protect] shelter, provide refuge, secure; see **defend 2.** 2. [To consider] entertain, cherish, regard; see **consider.**

hard, *a.* 1. [Compact] unyielding, thick, solid, heavy, strong, impermeable, tough, tempered, hardened, dense; see **firm 2.** 2. [Difficult] arduous, tricky, impossible, trying, tedious, complex, abstract, puzzling, troublesome, laborious; see also **difficult 1, 2.** 3. [Cruel] perverse, unrelenting, vengeful; see **cruel.** 4. [Severe] harsh, exacting, grim; see **severe 1, 2.** 5. [Alcoholic] intoxicating, inebriating, stimulating; see **strong 8.** 6. [With difficulty] strenuously, laboriously, with great effort; see **carefully 1, vigorously.** —be hard on, treat severely, be harsh toward, be painful to; see **abuse.**

hard-core, *a.* dedicated, steadfast, unwavering; see **faithful.**

harden, *v.* steel, temper, solidify, precipitate, crystallize, freeze, coagulate, clot, granulate, make callous *or* firm *or* compact *or* tight *or* hard, petrify, starch, cure, bake, dry, flatten, cement, compact, concentrate, sun, fire, fossilize, vulcanize, toughen, concrete, encrust; see also **stiffen.**—*Ant.* **soften,** unloose, melt.

hardened, *a.* 1. [Made hard] compacted, stiffened, stiff; see **firm 2.** 2. [Inured to labor or hardship] accustomed, conditioned, tough; see **habitual.**

hardening, *n.* thickening, crystallization, setting; see **solidification.**

hard going, *n.* trouble, emergency, competition; see **difficulty 2.**

hardheaded, *a.* willful, stubborn, headstrong; see **stubborn.**

hardhearted, *a.* cold, unfeeling, heartless; see **cruel.**

hardly, *a.* scarcely, barely, just, merely, imperceptibly, not noticeably, gradually, not markedly *or* notably *or* mainly, etc.; no more than, not likely, not a bit, almost not, only just, with difficulty *or* trouble, by a narrow margin, not by a great deal, seldom, almost not at all, but just, in no manner, by no means, little, infrequently, somewhat, not quite, here and there, simply, not much, rarely, slightly, sparsely, not often, *once in a blue moon, *by the skin of one's teeth; see also **only.**—*Ant.* **easily,** without difficulty, readily.

hard of hearing, *a.* almost deaf, having a hearing problem, in need of a hearing device; see **deaf.**

hard on, *a.* unjust *or* unkind *or* cruel to, brutal, inclined to blame; see **cruel, harmful.**

hardship, *n.* trial, sorrow, worry; see **difficulty 2, grief.**

hard up, *a.* in trouble, poverty-stricken, in the lower income brackets; see **poor 1.**

hardware, *n.* domestic appliances, fixtures, metal manufactures, casting, plumbing, metalware, implements, tools, housewares, fittings, aluminum ware, cutlery, house furnishings, kitchenware, household utensils, equipment.

hardy, *a.* tough, toughened, in good shape *or* condition, hardened, resistant, solid, staunch, seasoned, capable of endurance, able-bodied, physically fit, well-equipped, acclimatized, rugged, mighty, well, fit, robust, hearty, sound, fresh, hale, brawny, able, vigorous, powerful, firm, sturdy, solid, substantial; see also **strong.**—*Ant.* **weak,** unaccustomed, unhabituated.

harm, *n.* 1. [Injury] hurt, infliction, impairment; see **injury.** 2. [Evil] wickedness, outrage, foul play; see **abuse, evil 2, wrong 2.**

harm, *v.* injure, wreck, cripple; see **hurt.**

harmed, *a.* damaged, injured, wounded; see **hurt.**

harmful, *a.* injurious, detrimental, hurtful, noxious, evil, mischievous, ruinous, adverse, sinister, subversive, incendiary, virulent, cataclysmic, corroding, toxic, baleful, painful, wounding, crippling, bad, malicious, malignant, sinful, pernicious, unwholesome, corrupting, menacing, dire, prejudicial, damaging, corrupt, vicious, insidious, treacherous, catastrophic, disastrous, wild, murderous, destructive, unhealthy, killing, fatal, mortal, serious, fraught with *or* doing harm *or* evil, painful, sore, distressing, diabolic, brutal, unhealthful, satanic, grievous, mortal, lethal, venomous, cruel, unfortunate, disadvantageous, felonious, objectionable, fiendish, unlucky, malign, devilish, corrosive.

harmless, *a.* pure, innocent, painless, powerless, controllable, manageable, safe, sure, reliable, trustworthy, sanitary, germproof, sound, sterile, disarmed.—*Ant.* injurious, harmful, poisonous.

harmonica, *n.* mouth organ, harmonicon, mouth harp; see **musical instrument.**

harmonious, *a.* 1. [Harmonic] melodious, tuneful, musical, rhythmical, melodic, symphonic, in tune, in unison. 2. [Congruous] agreeable (to), corresponding, suitable, adapted, similar, like, peaceful, cooperative, in step, in accordance with, in concord *or* favor *or* harmony (with), on a footing with, friendly, conforming, well-matched, evenly balanced, symmetrical, congruent; see also **fit.**—*Ant.* incongruous, incompatible, **opposed.**

harmonize, *v.* blend, arrange, put to harmony, adapt, set, orchestrate, tune, sing a duet.

harmony, *n.* 1. [Musical concord] chord, consonance, accord, symphony, harmonics, counterpoint, concert, music, chorus, blending, unity, accordance, chime, unison, overtone, musical pattern, musical blend. 2. [Social concord] compatibility, equanimity, unanimity; see **agreement 1, peace 2.** 3. [Musical composition] melody, piece, arrangement; see **composition, music 1.**

harness, *n.* tackle, gear, yoke, apparatus, bridle, rigging, fittings; see also **equipment.**

harness, *v.* fetter, saddle, yoke, outfit, bridle, hold in leash, hitch up, control, limit, cinch, strap, collar, put in harness, rig up *or* out, tie, secure, rein in, curb, check, constrain.

harp, *n.* lyre, multi-stringed instrument, claviharp; see also **musical instrument.**

harp on, *v.* repeat, pester, nag; see **complain, talk 1.**

harsh, *a.* discordant, jangling, cacophonous, grating, rusty, dissonant, assonant, strident, creaking, clashing, sharp, jarring, jangled, clamorous, cracked, hoarse, out of tune, unmelodious, rasping, screeching, earsplitting, disturbing,

off balance, noisy, flat, sour, out of key, tuneless, unmusical, off key; see also **shrill.**

harshly, *a.* sternly, powerfully, grimly; see **brutally, firmly 2, loudly, seriously 1, 2.**

harshness, *n.* crudity, brutality, roughness; see **anger, cruelty, tyranny.**

harvest, *n.* reaping, yield, crop; see **crop, fruit, grain 1, produce, vegetable.**

harvest, *v.* gather (in), accumulate, pile up, collect, garner, crop, cut, pluck, pick, cull, take *or* draw in, glean, gather the harvest, hoard, mow.—*Ant.* **sow,** plant, seed.

hash, *n.* ground meat and vegetables, leftovers, casserole; see **meat, stew.**

hash over, *v.* debate, argue about, review; see **discuss.**

haste, *n.* hurry, scramble, bustle, scurry, precipitation, flurry, hurly-burly, impetuosity, rashness, dispatch, impetuousness, foolhardiness, want of caution, hustling, press, recklessness, rush, hastiness, carelessness, irrationality, rashness, giddiness, impatience, heedlessness, plunge, testiness, excitation, outburst, abruptness, anticipation.—*Ant.* **prudence,** caution, attention. **—in haste,** hastening, in a hurry, moving fast; see **fast.** **—make haste,** hurry, move *or* act quickly, speed up; see **hasten 2.**

hasten, *v.* 1. [To make haste] rush, fly, sprint; see **hurry.** 2. [To expedite] accelerate, speed up, advance, move up, quicken, stimulate, hurry (up), push, make short work of, urge, goad, press, whip on, agitate, push forward *or* ahead, put into action, get started, give a start, drive on, set in motion, take in hand, *put on wheels, blast off, gear up; see also **speed.**—*Ant.* defer, **delay,** put off.

hastily, *a.* 1. [Rapidly] hurriedly, speedily, nimbly; see **quickly.** 2. [Carelessly] thoughtlessly, recklessly, rashly; see **carelessly.**

hasty, *a.* 1. [Hurried] quick, speedy, swift; see **fast 1.** 2. [Careless] ill-advised, precipitate, foolhardy; see **careless, rash.**

hat, *n.* headgear, millinery, headpiece, helmet, chapeau, bonnet. Hatlike coverings include the following—for men: cap, skullcap, derby, straw hat, felt hat, sombrero, cowboy's hat, top hat, topper, bowler, panama, fedora, beret, turban; for women: hood, cowl, kerchief, beret, bandanna, cloche, sailor, bonnet, turban, Breton, pillbox, scarf, babushka. **—take one's hat off to,** salute, cheer, congratulate; see **praise 1.** **—*talk through one's hat,** chatter, talk nonsense, make foolish statements; see **babble.** **—throw one's hat into the ring,** enter a contest, file or run for office, enter politics; see **campaign**. —*under one's hat, confidential, private, hidden; see **secret 1**.

hatch, v. bear, lay eggs, give birth; see **produce 1**.

hate, n. ill will, animosity, enmity; see **hatred**.

hate, v. 1. [To detest] abhor, abominate, loathe, scorn, despise, have an aversion (toward), look at with loathing, spit upon, curse, dislike intensely, shudder at, not care for, have enough of, be repelled by, feel repulsion for, have no use for, object to, bear a grudge against, shun, denounce, resent, curse, be sick or tired of, reject, revolt against, deride, have no taste or stomach for, disfavor, look down upon, hold in contempt, have no use for, be disgusted with, view with horror, *be down on, *have it in for, hate like poison.—*Ant.* love, adore, worship. 2. [To dislike; *often used with infinitive or participle*] object to, shudder at, not like; see **dislike**.

hated, a. despised, loathed, abhorred, detested, disliked, cursed, unpopular, avoided, shunned, out of favor, condemned; see also **undesirable**.

hateful, a. odious, detestable, repugnant; see **offensive 2, undesirable**.

hater, n. enemy of, racist, antagonist; see **bigot, enemy**.

hatred, n. abhorrence, loathing, rancor, detestation, antipathy, repugnance, repulsion, disgust, contempt, (intense) dislike, scorn, abomination, distaste, disapproval, horror, hard feelings, displeasure, ill will, bitterness, antagonism, animosity, pique, grudge, malice, malevolence, revulsion, militancy, prejudice, spite, revenge, hate, venom, envy, spleen, coldness, distaste, contempt, hostility, alienation, bad blood, *chip on one's shoulder, grudge; see also **anger**.—*Ant.* friendship, devotion, affection.

haughty, a. arrogant, disdainful, proud; see **egotistic**.

haul, n. 1. [A pull] tug, lift, wrench; see **pull 1**. 2. [The distance something is hauled] trip, voyage, yards; see **distance 3**. 3. [*Something obtained, especially loot*] find, spoils, take; see **booty**. —in (or over) the long haul, over a long period of time, for a long time, in the end; see **finally 2**.

haul, v. pull, drag, bring; see **draw 1**.

haunt, v. 1. [To frequent persistently] habituate, visit often, resort to; see **loiter**. 2. [To prey upon] recur in one's mind, obsess, torment, beset, possess, trouble, weigh on one's mind, craze, madden, hound, terrify, plague, vex, harass, weigh or prey on, pester, worry, tease, terrorize, frighten, annoy, cause regret or sorrow, molest, appall, agitate, *drive one nuts; see also **bother 2, disturb**.

haunted, a. frequented, visited by, preyed upon; see **troubled**.

haunting, a. eerie, unforgettable, seductive; see **frightful, remembered**.

have, v. 1. [To be in possession of] own, possess, keep, retain, guard, use, maintain, control, treasure, keep title to, hold; see also **own 1**. 2. [To be obliged; *used with infinitive*] be compelled or forced to, should, ought, be one's duty to, fall on, be up to, have got to; see also **must**. 3. [To bear] beget, give birth to, bring forth; see **produce 1**. 4. [To have sexual intercourse with] seduce, sleep with, deflower; see **copulate**.

*have a ball, v. revel, have fun, celebrate; see **play 1**.

have a heart, v. take pity on, be merciful (to), be considerate (of); see **pity 1, 2**.

*have had it, v. be out, be defeated, come to the end of things or everything; see **lose 3, suffer 1**.

have in mind, v. expect, foresee, hope; see **anticipate, think 1**.

*have it good, v. do well, thrive, have it easy; see **succeed 1**.

haven, n. port, harbor, roadstead; see **refuge 1, shelter**.

have on, v. be clothed in, be wearing, try on; see **wear 1**.

have something on one, v. be able to expose, have special knowledge of, be able to control; see **convict, know 1**.

*have something on the ball, v. be alert, be quick, be in tune, have a keen mind, be industrious, *be with it; see **succeed 1**.

have the law on one, v. bring court action, file or bring suit, take it to court; see **sue**.

having, a. owning, possessing, enjoying, commanding, holding, controlling; see also **commanding**.

havoc, n. devastation, plunder, ruin; see **destruction 2**.

hawk, n. 1. [A member of the Accipitridae] bird of prey, osprey, falcon; see **bird**. 2. [A warlike person] militarist, chauvinist, warmonger; see **conservative, radical**.

hay, n. fodder, roughage, forage, feed; see also **grass 1**. Hay includes the following—red clover, wild hay, timothy, sweetgrass, alsike, sweet clover, soybeans, swamp hay, alfalfa, oat hay, millet. —*hit the hay, go to bed, rest, recline; see **sleep**.

hazard, n. risk, peril, jeopardy; see **danger.**

hazard, v. stake, try, guess; see **chance, gamble, risk.**

hazardous, a. perilous, uncertain, precarious; see **dangerous.**

haze, n. mist, smog, cloudiness; see **fog.**

hazy, a. cloudy, foggy, murky, misty, unclear, overcast, steaming, screened, filmy, gauzy, vaporous, smoky, dim, dull, indistinct, nebulous, shadowy, dusky, obscure, thick, opaque, frosty, veiled, blurred, semitransparent, blurry, faint; see also **dark 1.**–*Ant.* bright, clear, cloudless.

he, *pron.* this one, the male, the above-named, the man, the boy, third person, masculine singular.

head, n. 1. [The skull] brainpan, scalp, crown, headpiece, *bean, *noggin, *noodle. 2. [A leader or supervisor] commander, commanding officer, ruler; see **leader 2.** 3. [The top] summit, peak, crest; see **top 1.** 4. [The beginning] front, start, source; see **origin 2.** 5. [An attachment] cap, bottle top, cork; see **cover 1.** 6. [Intelligence] brains, foresight, ingenuity; see **judgment 1.** 7. [Drug addict] victim of drug abuse, habitual user of drugs, one subject to addiction; see **addict.** —**come to a head**, culminate, reach a crisis, come to a climax; see **climax.** —**get it through one's head**, learn, comprehend, see; see **understand 1.** —**go to one's head**, stir mentally, stimulate, intoxicate; see **excite.** —**hang** (or **hide**) **one's head**, repent, be sorry, grieve; see **regret 1.** —**keep one's head**, remain calm, keep one's self-control, hold one's emotions in check; see **restrain.** —**lose one's head**, become excited or angry, go mad, rave; see **rage 1.** —**make head or tail of**, comprehend, apprehend, see; see **understand 1.** —**one's head off**, greatly, extremely, considerably; see **much.** —**on** (or **upon**) **one's head**, burdensome, taxing, strenuous; see **difficult 1.** —**out of** (or **off**) **one's head**, crazy, delirious, raving; see **insane.** —**over one's head**, incomprehensible, not understandable, hard; see **difficult 2.**

head, v. direct, oversee, supervise; see **command 2, manage 1.**

headache, n. 1. [A pain in the head] migraine, sick headache, neuralgia; see **pain 2.** 2. [*A source of vexation and difficulty] problem, jumble, mess; see **difficulty 1, 2, trouble 1.**

headed, a. in transit, in motion, en route, going, directed, started, aimed, slated for, on the way to, pointed toward, consigned or on the road to.

heading, n. headline, subtitle, address, caption, legend, head, banner head, subject, capital, superscription, ticket, headnote, display line, preface, prologue, streamer, preamble, topic, designation, specification.

headless, a. 1. [Unthinking] witless, fatuous, brainless; see **dull 3, stupid 1.** 2. [Without a head] decapitated, lifeless, truncated; see **dead 1.**

headlight, n. searchlight, beacon, spotlight; see **light 3.**

headline, n. heading, caption, title; see **heading.**

head off, v. block (off), interfere (with), intervene; see **stop 1.**

head over heels, a. entirely, precipitately, unreservedly; see **completely.**

headquarters, n. main or home or chief office, (central) station or place, distributing center, police station, meeting place or house, manager's office, quarters, base, military station or town, post, center or base of operation, H.Q..

headstone, n. gravestone, marker, stone; see **grave.**

headstrong, a. determined, strong-minded, stubborn; see **stubborn.**

headway, n. advance, increase, promotion; see **progress 1.**

heal, v. restore, renew, treat, attend, make healthy, return to health, fix, repair, regenerate, bring around, remedy, purify, rejuvenate, medicate, make clean, dress (a wound), rebuild, revive, rehabilitate, work a cure, cause to heal (up), resuscitate, salve, help (to) get well, ameliorate, *doctor, put one on his feet again, *breathe new life into.–*Ant.* make ill, expose, infect.

healing, a. restorative, invigorating, medicinal; see **healthful.**

health, n. vigor, wholeness, good condition, healthfulness, good health, fitness, bloom, soundness of body, physical fitness, tone, hardiness, well-being, stamina, energy, full bloom, *rosy cheeks, good shape, *clean bill of health; see also **strength.**

healthful, a. nutritious, restorative, body-building, sanitary, hygienic, salutary, invigorating, tonic, stimulating, bracing, salubrious, wholesome, beneficial, health-giving, nutritive, nourishing, energy-giving, fresh, pure, clean, corrective, cathartic, sedative, regenerative, substantial, sustaining, benign, good for one, desirable, harmless, innocuous, healing, preventive, disease-free, unpolluted, unadulterated, favorable.–*Ant.* sickly, unwholesome, **unhealthy.**

healthy, a. sound, trim, all right, normal, robust, vigorous, well, hearty, athletic, rosy-cheeked, hardy, able-bodied, virile, muscular, blooming, sturdy, safe and sound, in good condition, in full possession of one's faculties, in good health, *full of pep, never feeling better, fresh, whole, firm, lively, undecayed, flourishing, good, (physically) fit, clear-eyed, in fine fettle, youthful, free from disease *or* infirmity, fine, *fine and dandy, *hunky-dory, *in the pink (of condition), rugged, fit as a fiddle, *feeling one's oats; see also **sane 1, strong 1.**—*Ant.* **unhealthy,** ill, diseased.

heap, *n.* pile, mass, stack; see **quantity.**

heap, *v.* pile, add, lump; see **load 1, pack 2.**

hear, *v.* 1. [To perceive by ear] listen to, give attention, attend to, make out, become aware of, catch, apprehend *or* take in, eavesdrop, detect, perceive by the ear, overhear, take cognizance of, keep one's ears open, have the sense of hearing, read (loud and clear), strain one's ears, listen in, *get (an earful). 2. [To receive information aurally] overhear, eavesdrop, find out; see **listen 1.** 3. [To hold a hearing] preside over, put on trial, summon to court; see **judge.** —**not hear of,** not allow, refuse to consider, reject; see **forbid.**

heard, *a.* perceived, listened to, witnessed, caught, made out, understood, heeded, noted, made clear.

hearer, *n.* listener, witness, bystander; see **listener.**

hear from, *v.* have *or* get *or* receive word (from), be informed, learn through; see **receive 1.**

hearing, *n.* 1. [An opportunity to be heard] audition, interview, test, fair hearing, tryout, attendance, conference, audit, notice, performance, consultation, council, reception, presentation, audience, attention; see also **trial 2.** 2. [The act of hearing] detecting, recording, distinguishing; see **listening.** 3. [The faculty for hearing] ear, auditory faculty, perception, listening ear, sense of hearing, audition, act of perceiving sound, acoustic sensation. 4. [Range of hearing] earshot, hearing distance, reach, sound, carrying distance, range, auditory range; see also **extent.**

hear of, *v.* hear *or* know about, be *or* become aware of, discover; see **know 1, 3.**

hear out, *v.* listen to, yield (the floor) to, remain silent; see **listen 1.**

hearsay, *n.* noise, scandal, report; see **gossip 1, rumor 1.**

heart, *n.* 1. [The pump in the circulatory system] vital organ, vascular organ, blood pump, cardiac organ, right *or* left ventricle, *ticker, *clock; see also **organ 2.** 2. [Feeling] response, sympathy, sensitivity; see **emotion, feeling 4, pity 1.** 3. [The center] core, middle, pith; see **center 1.** 4. [The most important por-

tion] gist, essence, root; see **soul 2. 5.** [Courage] fortitude, gallantry, spirit; see **courage, mind 1, soul 4.** —**after one's own heart,** suitable, pleasing, lovable; see **pleasant 2.** —**break one's heart,** grieve, disappoint, pain; see **hurt.** —**by heart,** from memory, memorized, learned; see **remembered.** —**change of heart,** change of mind, reversal, alteration; see **change 1.** —**do one's heart good,** please, make content, delight; see **satisfy 1.** —**eat one's heart out,** worry, regret, nurse one's troubles; see **brood 2.** —**from the bottom of one's heart,** deeply, honestly, frankly; see **sincerely.** —**have a heart,** be kind, empathize, take pity; see **sympathize.** —**lose one's heart to,** love, cherish, adore; see **fall in love.** —**set one's heart at rest,** calm, placate, soothe; see **comfort 1.** —**set one's heart on,** long for, need, desire; see **want 1.** —**take to heart,** think about, take into account, believe; see **consider.** —**wear one's heart on one's sleeve,** disclose, divulge, confess; see **reveal.** —**with all one's heart,** honestly, deeply, frankly; see **sincerely.**

heartache, *n.* sorrow, despair, anguish; see **grief, regret.**

heartbeat, *n.* pulsation, throb of the heart, cardio-vascular activity; see **beat 1.**

heartbreaking, *a.* cheerless, deplorable, joyless; see **pitiful 1, tragic.**

heartbroken, *a.* melancholy, sorrowful, doleful; see **sad 1.**

heartburn, *n.* indigestion, nervous stomach, stomach upset; see **illness 2.**

heart disease, *n.* heart failure, coronary illness, thrombosis; see **illness 2.**

hearth, *n.* 1. [A fireplace] grate, fireside, hearthstone; see **fireplace.** 2. [Home] dwelling, abode, residence; see **home 1.**

heartily, *a.* enthusiastically, earnestly, cordially; see **seriously 2, sincerely.**

heartless, *a.* unkind, unthinking, insensitive; see **cruel, ruthless.**

hearty, *a.* warm, zealous, sincere, cheery, cheerful, jovial, wholehearted, neighborly, well-meant, animated, jolly, ardent, genial, glowing, enthusiastic, genuine, avid, deepest, passionate, deep, intense, exuberant, profuse, eager, devout, deep-felt, unfeigned, fervent, warmhearted, authentic, impassioned, heartfelt, responsive; see also **friendly.**—*Ant.* false, mock, sham.

heat, *n.* 1. [Warmth] torridity, high temperature, hot wind, heat wave, fever, hot weather, temperature, hotness, warmness, sultriness, red *or* white heat, torridness, tropical heat, dog days; see also **warmth.**—*Ant.* cold, frost, frigidity. 2. [Fervor] ardor, passion, excitement; see **desire 2. 3.** [Sources of heat] flame, radiation, solar energy; see **energy 2, fire 1, 2.**

heat, *v.* 1. [To make hot] warm, fire, heat up, inflame, kindle, enkindle, subject to heat, put on the fire, make hot *or* warm, scald, thaw, boil, char, roast, chafe, seethe, toast, oxidize, set fire to, melt, cauterize, reheat, steam, incinerate, sear, singe, scorch, fry, turn on the heat; see also **burn, cook, ignite.—***Ant.* **cool, freeze, reduce the temperature.** 2. [To become hot] glow, warm (up), rise in temperature, grow hot, blaze, flame, seethe, burst into flame, kindle, ignite, thaw, swelter, perspire, begin to pant, record a higher temperature.

heated, *a.* 1. [Warmed] cooked, fried, burnt; see **baked, burned.** 2. [Fervent] fiery, ardent, avid; see **excited, passionate 2.**

heater, *n.* radiator, auto heater, oil *or* gas *or* electric heater; see **furnace.**

heathen, *n.* infidel, non-Christian, atheist; see **barbarian.**

heating, *n.* boiling, warming, cooking; see **heat.**

heave, *n.* throw, hurl, fling, cast, wing, toss; see also **pitch 2.**

heave, *v.* rock, bob, pitch, go up and down, lurch, roll, reel, sway, swell, dilate, expand, be raised, swirl, throb, waft, ebb and flow, wax and wane, puff, slosh, wash; see also **wave 3.—***Ant.* **rest, lie still, quiet.**

heaven, *n.* 1. [The sky: *often plural*] firmament, stratosphere, heights, atmosphere, azure, beyond, heavenly spheres, upstairs. 2. [The abode of the blessed] Paradise, (Great) Beyond, Abode of the Dead, Home of the Gods, Heavenly Home, God's Kingdom, Valhalla, Holy City, Nirvana, throne of God, the New Jerusalem, afterworld, heavenly city, the city of God, our eternal home, Kingdom of Heaven, next world, world to come, our Father's house, life *or* world beyond the grave, *happy hunting grounds, *the eternal rest, Kingdom Come, the hereafter.—***Ant.* **hell, underworld, inferno.** 3. [A state of great comfort] bliss, felicity, harmony; see **happiness 2.**

heavenly, *a.* 1. [Concerning heaven] divine, celestial, supernal; see **angelic, divine, holy 1.** 2. [*Much approved of or liked*] blissful, sweet, enjoyable; see **excellent, pleasant 1, 2.**

heavily, *a.* laboriously, tediously, weightily, massively, ponderously, gloomily, with difficulty, wearily, profoundly, with force *or* energy, densely; see also **gradually.—***Ant.* **lightly,** gently, easily.

heaviness, *n.* burden, denseness, ballast; see **density, mass 1, weight 1.**

heavy, *a.* 1. [Weighty] bulky, massive, unwieldy, ponderous, huge, overweight, top-heavy, of great weight, burdensome, weighty, stout, big, hard to lift *or* carry, dense, fat, substantial, ample, *hefty, *chunky; see also **large 1.—***Ant.* **light,** buoyant, feather-light. 2. [Burdensome] troublesome, oppressive, vexatious; see **difficult 1, disturbing, onerous 1.** 3. [Dull] listless, slow, apathetic; see **dull 4, indifferent.** 4. [Gloomy] dejected, cloudy, overcast; see **dark 1, dismal, sad 1.**

heavy-handed, *a.* oppressive, harsh, coercive; see **cruel, severe 2.**

heckle, *v.* torment, disturb, pester; see **bother 2, ridicule.**

hectic, *a.* unsettled, boisterous, restless; see **confused 2, disordered.**

hedge, *n.* shrubbery, bushes, thicket; see **plant.**

heed, *v.* pay attention (to), notice, be aware; see **look out.**

heel, *n.* 1. [Hind part of the foot] hock, hind toe, Achilles' tendon; see also **foot 2.** 2. [The portion of the shoe under the heel, sense 1] low, spring, wedge sole; see **bottom, foundation 2, shoe.** 3. [*A worthless individual*] scamp, skunk, trickster; see **rascal. —down at (the) heel(s),** shabby, seedy, rundown; see **worn 2. —kick up one's heels,** be lively, have fun, enjoy oneself; see **play 1, 2. —on (or upon) the heels of,** close behind, in back of, behind; see **following. —take to one's heels,** run (away), flee, take flight; see **escape.**

heel, *v.* follow, stay by one's heel, attend; see **obey.**

heifer, *n.* yearling, baby cow, calf; see **animal, cow.**

height, *n.* elevation, extent upward, prominence, loftiness, highness, perpendicular distance, upright distance, tallness, stature; see also **expanse, extent, length 1.—***Ant.* **depth,** breadth, width.

heighten, *v.* 1. [Increase] sharpen, redouble, emphasize; see **increase, strengthen.** 2. [Raise] uplift, elevate, lift; see **raise 1.**

heir, *n.* future possessor, legal heir, heir apparent, successor, descendent, one who inherits, heiress, beneficiary, inheritor, crown prince.

heiress, *n.* female inheritor, crown princess, inheritress; see **heir.**

heirloom, *n.* inheritance, legacy, bequest; see **gift 1.**

held, *a.* grasped, controlled, occupied, guarded, taken, gripped, clutched, defended, stuck, detained, sustained, believed.—*Ant.* released, freed, lost.

held over, v. returned, presented again, retold; see **repeated 1**.

held up, a. 1. [Robbed] assaulted, shot at, beaten; see **attacked 2**. 2. [Postponed] withheld, put off, delayed; see **postponed**.

hell, n. 1. [Place of the dead, especially of the wicked dead; *often capital H*] underworld, inferno, place of departed spirits, the lower world, the grave, infernal regions, abyss, Satan's Kingdom, everlasting fire, purgatory, nether world, hell-fire, Hades, bottomless pit, perdition, place of the lost, place of torment, limbo, *hot place, *you-know-where, the hereafter.–*Ant.* heaven, earth, paradise. 2. [A condition of torment] trial, agony, ordeal; see **crisis, difficulty 1, 2, emergency**. –*catch (or get) hell, get into trouble, be scolded, receive punishment; see **get it 2**. –*for the hell of it, for no reason, for the fun of it, playfully; see **lightly 1**.

hellish, a. diabolical, fiendish, destructive; see **bad 1**.

hello, *interj.* how do you do, greetings, welcome, how are you, good morning, good day, hi, *howdy, *lo, *hyah, how goes it.–*Ant.* goodbye, farewell, so long.

***hell of a**, a. *helluva, bad, awful; see **faulty, poor 2**.

***hell on**, a. hard on, prejudiced (against), strict *or* firm with; see **cruel, harmful**.

helmet, n. football helmet, diver's helmet, hard hat; see **hat**.

help, n. 1. [Assistance] advice, comfort, aid, favor, support, gift, reward, charity, encouragement, advancement, advice, aid, subsidy, service, relief, care, endowment, cooperation, guidance. 2. [Employees] aides, representatives, hired help; see **assistant, faculty 2, staff 2**. 3. [Physical relief] maintenance, sustenance, nourishment; see **relief 4, remedy**. –cannot help but, be compelled *or* obliged to, cannot fail to, have to; see **must**. –cannot help oneself, be compelled to, have a need to, be the victim of circumstance *or* habit; see **must**. –so help me (God), as God is my witness, by God, I swear; see **oath**.

help, v. assist, uphold, advise, encourage, stand by, co-operate, intercede for, befriend, accommodate, work for, back up, maintain, sustain, benefit, bolster, lend a hand, do a service, see through, do one's part, give a hand, be of use, come to the aid of, be of some help, help along, do a favor, promote, back, advocate, abet, stimulate, uphold, further, work for, *stick up for, take under one's wing, *go to bat for, side with, give a

lift, boost, *pitch in; see also **support 2**.–*Ant.* oppose, rival, combat.

helped, a. aided, maintained, supported, advised, befriended, relieved, sustained, nursed, encouraged, assisted, accompanied, taken care of, subsidized, upheld.–*Ant.* impeded, hurt, harmed.

helper, n. apprentice, aide, secretary; see **assistant**.

helpful, a. 1. [Useful] valuable, important, significant, crucial, essential, co-operative, symbiotic, serviceable, profitable, advantageous, favorable, convenient, suitable, practical, operative, usable, applicable, conducive, improving, bettering, of service, all-purpose, desirable, instrumental, contributive, good for, to (one's) advantage, at one's command; see also **convenient 1**.–*Ant.* useless, ineffective, impractical. 2. [Curative] healthy, salutary, restorative; see **healthful**. 3. [Obliging] accommodating, considerate, neighborly; see **kind**.

helpfully, a. usefully, constructively, advantageously; see **effectively**.

helpfulness, n. assistance, convenience, help; see **use 2, usefulness**.

helping, a. aiding, assisting, co-operating, collaborating, synergistic, working *or* co-operating *or* collaborating (with), being assistant *or* consultant to, in co-operation *or* combination (with), contributing (to), accessory (to), going along (with), *in cahoots (with), *thick as thieves, in the same boat (with); see **helpful 1**.

helping, n. serving, plateful, portion; see **food, meal 2, share**.

helpless, a. 1. [Dependent] feeble, unable, invalid; see **dependent 2, disabled, weak 1, 5**. 2. [Incompetent] incapable, unfit, inexpert; see **incompetent**.

helplessness, n. 1. [Disability] poor health, disorder, convalescence; see **illness 1, weakness 1**. 2. [Incompetence] incapacity, weakness, failure; see **weakness 1**.

help oneself, v. aid *or* promote *or* further, etc., oneself, live by one's own efforts, get on *or* along; see **help**.

help oneself to, v. take, grab, pick (up); see **seize 1, 2, steal**.

hem, n. border, skirting, edging; see **edge 1, fringe, rim**.

hemisphere, n. half of the globe, Western *or* Eastern *or* Northern *or* Southern Hemisphere, territory; see **earth 1**.

hemorrhage, n. discharge, bleeding, bloody flux; see **illness 1, injury**.

hen, n. female chicken, pullet, *egger; see **bird, fowl**.

hence, a. 1. [Therefore] consequently, for that reason, on that account; see **so 2, therefore**. 2. [From now] henceforth, henceforward, from here; see **hereafter**.

henpeck, v. bully, suppress, intimidate; see **bother 2, threaten.**

henpecked, a. dominated by a wife, subjected to nagging, browbeaten, intimidated, passive, constrained, compliant, in bondage, yielding, without freedom or independence, acquiescent, in subjection, subject, obedient, resigned, submissive, docile, meek, cringing, unresisting, unassertive, led by the nose, under one's thumb, at one's beck and call, tied to one's apron strings, nagged, in harness; see also **obedient 1.**

herb, n. Herbs include the following—ginger, peppermint, thyme, savory, mustard, chicory, chives, cardamom, coriander, sweet basil, parsley, anise, cumin, fennel, caraway, rosemary, tarragon, oregano, wintergreen; see also **spice.**

herd, n. flock, drove, pack, brood, swarm, lot, bevy, covey, gaggle, nest, brood, flight, school, clan; see also **gathering.**

herdsman, n. shepherd, herder, sheepherder; see **cowboy, rancher.**

here, a. in this place, hereabout(s), in this direction, on this spot over here, up here, down here, right here, on hand or board or *deck, in the face of, within reach or call.

hereafter, a. hence, henceforth, from now on, after this, in the future, hereupon, in the course of time.

hereafter, n. underworld, abode of the dead, the great beyond; see **heaven 2, hell 1.**

here and there, a. often, patchily, sometimes; see **everywhere, scattered.**

hereby, a. at this moment, with these means, with this, thus, herewith.

hereditary, a. inherited, genetic, paternal; see **genetic.**

heredity, n. inheritance, ancestry, hereditary transmission, genetics, eugenics.

heresy, n. nonconformity, dissidence, protestantism, dissent, heterodoxy, sectarianism, agnosticism, schism, unorthodoxy, secularism.

heretic, n. schismatic, apostate, sectarian; see **cynic.**

heritage, n. **1.** [Inheritance] legacy, birthright, heirship, ancestry, right, dowry; see also **division 2, heredity, share. 2.** [Tradition] convention, endowment, cultural inheritance; see **culture 1, custom 2, fashion 2, method 2, system 2.**

hermit, n. holy man, ascetic, anchorite, solitary, recluse, solitarian, anchoress, pillar saint.

hero, n. **1.** [One distinguished for action] brave man, model, conqueror, victorious general, god, martyr, champion, prize athlete, master, brave, warrior, saint, man of courage, star, popular figure, great man, knight-errant, a man among men, man of the hour or day; see also **heroine 1. 2.** [Principal male character in a literary composition] protagonist, male lead, leading man; see **actor.**

heroic, a. valiant, valorous, fearless; see **brave, noble 1, 2.**

heroine, n. **1.** [A female hero] courageous woman, champion, goddess, ideal, intrepid or resourceful or supremely courageous woman, woman of heroic character, woman of the hour or day; see also **hero 1. 2.** [Leading female character in a literary composition] protagonist, leading lady, prima donna; see **actor.**

heroism, n. rare fortitude, valor, bravery; see **courage, strength.**

hesitancy, n. wavering, delaying, procrastination; see **delay, pause.**

hesitant, a. **1.** [Doubtful] skeptical, unpredictable, irresolute; see **doubtful, uncertain 2. 2.** [Slow] delaying, wavering, dawdling; see **lazy 1, slow 2.**

hesitantly, a. dubiously, falteringly, shyly; see **cautiously.**

hesitate, v. falter, fluctuate, vacillate, pause, stop, hold off or back, be dubious or uncertain, flounder, alternate, ponder, think about, defer, delay, think it over, change one's mind, recoil, not know what to do, be uncertain or irresolute, pull back, catch one's breath, weigh, consider, hang back, swerve, debate, shift, wait, deliberate, linger, balance, think twice, drag one's feet, hem and haw, blow hot and cold, dillydally, straddle the fence, leave up in the air.—*Ant.* decide, resolve, conclude.

hesitation, n. **1.** [Doubt] equivocation, skepticism, irresolution; see **doubt, uncertainty 2. 2.** [Delay] wavering, delaying, dawdling; see **delay, pause.**

hey, interj. you there, say, hey there; see **halt, hello, stop 1.**

heyday, n. adolescence, bloom, prime (of life); see **youth 1.**

hibernate, v. sleep through the winter, lie dormant, *hole up; see **sleep.**

hidden, a. secluded, out of sight, private, covert, concealed, undercover, occult, in the dark, in a haze or fog, in darkness, masked, screened, veiled, cloaked, obscured, disguised, invisible, clouded, sealed, unobserved, blotted, impenetrable, unseen, eclipsed, camouflaged, shrouded, shadowy, unknown, buried, undetected, deep, unsuspected, inscrutable, illegible, puzzling, unobserved, out of view, dim, clandestine, subterranean, cloistered, suppressed, dark, inward, underground, unrevealed, withheld, surreptitious, underhand, kept (in the) dark, under wraps; see also **private.**—*Ant.* obvious, open, apparent.

hide, n. pelt, rawhide, pigskin, chamois,

bearskin, goatskin, jacket, sheepskin, sealskin, snakeskin, alligator skin, calfskin; see also **fur, leather, skin**. — **neither hide nor hair**, nothing whatsoever, no indication, not at all; see **nothing**.

hide, v. 1. [To conceal] shroud, curtain, veil, camouflage, cover, mask, cloak, not give away, screen, blot out, bury, suppress, withhold, keep underground, stifle, keep secret, hush up, shield, eclipse, not tell, lock up, confuse, put out of sight, put out of the way, hold back, keep from, secrete, smuggle, shadow, conceal from sight, keep out of sight, stow away, protect, hoard, store, seclude, closet, conceal, hush, obscure, wrap, shelter, throw a veil over, keep in the dark, *keep under one's hat, *seal one's lips, *put the lid on, *salt away; see also **disguise**.—*Ant.* **expose**, lay bare, uncover. 2. [To keep oneself concealed] disguise oneself, change one's identity, cover one's traces, keep out of sight, go underground, lie in ambush, sneak, prowl, burrow, skulk, avoid notice, lie in wait, hibernate, lie *or* be concealed, lie low, conceal oneself, lurk, shut oneself up, seclude oneself, lie hidden, keep out of the way, go *or* stay in hiding, hide out, cover up, *duck, *keep in the background; see also **deceive**.

hide-and-seek, n. evasion, mystification, elusiveness; see **game 1**.

hideous, a. ghastly, grisly, frightful; see **ugly 1**.

hideout, n. lair, den, hermitage; see **refuge 1, retreat 2, shelter**.

hiding, a. concealing, in concealment, out of sight; see **hidden**.

hierarchy, n. ministry, regime, theocracy; see **government 1, 2**.

high, a. 1. [Tall] towering, gigantic, big, colossal, tremendous, great, giant, huge, formidable, immense, long, sky-scraping, steep, sky-high; see also **large 1**.—*Ant.* **short**, diminutive, undersized. 2. [Elevated] lofty, uplifted, soaring, aerial, high-reaching, flying, hovering, overtopping, jutting; see also **raised 1**.—*Ant.* **low**, depressed, underground. 3. [Exalted] eminent, leading, powerful; see **distinguished 2, noble 1, 2**. 4. [Expensive] high-priced, costly, precious; see **expensive**. 5. [To an unusual degree] great, extraordinary, special; see **unusual 1, 2**. 6. [Shrill] piercing, sharp, penetrating; see **loud 1, shrill**. 7. [*Drunk] intoxicated, tipsy, inebriated; see **drunk**. 8. [Under the influence of drugs] stoned, freaked-out, wasted, turned-on, on a trip, tripping, hyped-up, psyched.

high and low, a. in every nook and corner, in all possible places, exhaustively; see **completely, everywhere**.

high and mighty, a. pompous, vain, conceited; see **egotistic**.

higher, a. taller, more advanced, superior to, over, larger than, ahead, surpassing, bigger, greater; see also **above 1, beyond**.—*Ant.* smaller, **shorter**, inferior.

highest, a. topmost, superlative, supreme, maximal, most, top, maximum, head, pre-eminent, capital, chief, paramount, tiptop, crown.

highly, a. extremely, profoundly, deeply; see **very**.

highness, n. 1. [Quality of being high] length, tallness, loftiness; see **height**. 2. [Term of respect, usually to royalty; *often* *capital*] majesty, lordship, ladyship; see **royalty**.

high-pressure, a. forceful, potent, compelling; see **powerful 1**.

high-priced, a. costly, precious, extravagant; see **expensive**.

high school, n. public school, secondary school, preparatory school, private academy, military school, upper grades, trade school, seminary, junior high school, vocational school; see also **school 1**.

high-speed, a. swift, rapid, quick; see **fast 1**.

high-spirited, a. daring, dauntless, reckless; see **brave**.

high-strung, a. nervous, tense, impatient; see **restless**.

highway, n. roadway, parkway, superhighway, freeway, turnpike, toll road, state *or* national highway, two-lane highway, four-lane highway, six-lane highway, etc.; see also **road 1**.

***hijack**, v. highjack, privateer, capture; see **seize 2**.

hike, n. trip, backpack, tour; see also **journey, walk 3**.

hike, v. 1. [To tramp] take a hike, tour, explore; see **travel, walk 1**. 2. [*To raise] lift, advance, pull up; see **increase**.

hiking, a. hitchhiking, backpacking, exploring; see **walking**.

hilarious, a. amusing, lively, witty; see **entertaining, funny 1**.

hill, n. mound, knoll, butte, bluff, promontory, precipice, cliff, range, rising ground, headland, upland, downgrade, inclination, descent, slope, ascent, slant, grade, incline, height, highland, rise, foothill, dune, climb, elevation, ridge, heap, hillside, upgrade, hilltop, vantage point *or* ground, gradient, summit; see also **mountain 1**.

hillside, n. grade, gradient, acclivity; see **hill**.

hilltop, *n.* peak, height, elevation; see **hill, top 1.**

hilly, *a.* steep, sloping, rugged; see **mountainous, rough 1, steep.**—*Ant.* **level,** even, regular.

hinder, *v.* impede, obstruct, interfere with, check, retard, fetter, block, thwart, bar, clog, encumber, burden, cripple, handicap, cramp, preclude, inhibit, shackle, interrupt, arrest, curb, resist, oppose, baffle, deter, hamper, frustrate, outwit, stop, counteract, offset, neutralize, tie *or* hold up, embarrass, delay, postpone, keep *or* set back, dam, close, box in, end, terminate, shut out, choke, intercept, bottleneck, defeat, trap, control, conflict with, deadlock, hold from *or* back, clash with, be an obstacle *or* impediment to, cross, exclude, limit, shorten, go against, prohibit, withhold, slow down, stall, bring to a standstill, smother, disappoint, spoil, gag, annul, silence, invalidate, detain, stalemate, taboo, suspend, set *or* pit against, *clip one's wings, tie one's hands, get in the way of, hold up, *throw a monkey wrench into the works, *put the lid on, *knock the props from under.—*Ant.* **help,** assist, aid.

hindrance, *n.* obstacle, intervention, trammel; see **barrier, interference 1.**

hinge, *n.* hook, pivot, juncture, articulation, link, elbow, ball-and-socket, knee, butt, strap, articulated joint, flap; see also **joint 1.**

hinge, *v.* connect, add, couple; see **join 1.**

hint, *n.* allusion, inkling, insinuation, implication, reference, advice, observation, reminder, communication, notice, information, announcement, inside information, tip, clue, token, idea, omen, scent, cue, trace, notion, whisper, taste, suspicion, evidence, reminder, innuendo, symptom, sign, bare suggestion, impression, supposition, inference, premonition, broad *or* gentle hint, word to the wise, indication, tip-off, *pointer; see also **suggestion 1.**

hint, *v.* touch on, refer *or* allude to, intimate, inform, hint at, imply, infer, acquaint, remind, impart, bring up, recall, cue, prompt, insinuate, indicate, wink, advise, cause to remember, make an allusion to, jog the memory, give a hint of, suggest, make mention of, remark in passing, drop a hint, whisper, give an inkling of, tip-off.—*Ant.* hide, conceal, cover.

hinted at, *a.* signified, intimated, referred to; see **implied, suggested.**

hip, *a.* aware, informed, enlightened; see **modern 1, observant.**

hip, *n.* side, hipbone, pelvis; see **bone.**

hippie, *n.* dissenter, Bohemian, nonconformist; see **radical.**

hire, *v.* engage, sign up, draft, obtain, secure, enlist, give a job to, put *or* set to work, bring in, occupy, use, fill a position, appoint, delegate, authorize, retain, commission, empower, book, utilize, select, pick, contract (for), procure, fill an opening, find help, find a place for, exploit, make use of, use another's services, add to the payroll.—*Ant.* discharge, **dismiss,** fire.

hired, *a.* contracted, signed up, given work; see **busy, employed, engaged 3.**

hiring, *n.* engaging, contracting, employing; see **employer.**

hiss, *n.* buzz, sibilance, escape of air; see **noise 1.**

hiss, *v.* sibilate, fizz, seethe; see **sound 1.**

historical, *a.* factual, traditional, chronicled; see **old 3, past 1.**

history, *n.* annals, records, archives, recorded history, chronicle, historical knowledge, historical writings, historical evidence, historical development; see also **record 1, social science.** —make **history,** accomplish, do something important, achieve; see **succeed 1.**

hit, *a.* shot, struck, slugged, cuffed, slapped, smacked, clouted, punched, boxed, slammed, knocked, beat, pounded, thrashed, spanked, banged, smashed, tapped, rapped, whacked, thwacked, thumped, kicked, *swatted, mugged, *pasted, knocked out; see also **hurt.**—*Ant.* unhurt, unscathed, untouched.

hit, *n.* 1. [A blow] slap, rap, punch; see **blow.** 2. [A popular success] favorite, *sellout, knockout; see **success 2.** 3. [In baseball, a batted ball that cannot be fielded] base hit *or* single, two-base hit *or* double, three-base hit *or* triple, home run, *wallop, *blow.

hit, *v.* 1. [To strike] knock, beat, sock, slap, jostle, butt, knock against, scrape, bump, run against, thump, collide (with), bump into, punch, punish, hammer, strike down, bang, whack, thwack, jab, tap, smack, kick at, pelt, flail, thrash, cuff, kick, rap, clout, club, bat *or* kick around, lash out at, not hold one's punches, hit at, hit out (at), let have it, crack, *pop, *bash, *box the ears; see also **beat 1.** 2. [To fire in time; *said of an internal combustion motor*] catch, go, run; see **operate 2.** 3. [In baseball, to hit safely] make a hit, make a two-base *or* three-base hit *or* a home run, get on (base).

hit-and-run, *a.* leaving illegally *or* without offering assistance, fugitive, illegally departed; see **illegal.**

hitch, *n.* 1. [A knot] loop, noose, yoke;

see **knot** 1, **tie** 1. **2.** [A difficulty] block, obstacle, tangle; see **difficulty**.

hitch, v. tie up, strap, hook; see **fasten, join** 1.

hitchhike, v. take a lift, hitch or bum or catch or thumb a ride, *thumb; see **ride** 1, **travel**.

hit it off, v. get on or along (well), become friends or acquaintances, become friendly; see **agree, like** 1, 2.

hit on or **upon,** v. realize, come upon, stumble on; see **discover, find, recognize** 1.

hit or miss, a. at random, uncertainly, sometimes; see **scattered**.

*hit the jackpot, v. be lucky, be well paid, strike it rich; see **win** 1.

hitting, a. slapping, beating, punishing; see **hit** 1, v.

hive, n. apiary, swarm, colony; see **colony**.

hoard, v. store up, acquire, keep; see **accumulate, save** 2.

hoarse, a. grating, rough, uneven, harsh, raucous, discordant, gruff, husky, thick, growling, croaking, cracked, guttural, dry, piercing, scratching, indistinct, squawking, jarring, rasping.—Ant. sweet, pure, mellifluous.

hoax, n. falsification, fabrication, deceit; see **deception, lie** 1.

hobby, n. avocation, pastime, diversion, side interest, leisure-time activity, specialty, whim, favorite occupation or pursuit, fancy, whimsy, labor of love, play, craze, sport, amusement, craft, fun, art, game, sideline; see also **entertainment**.

hobo, n. vagrant, vagabond, wanderer; see **beggar**.

*hock, v. sell temporarily, pledge, deposit; see **pawn, sell**.

hockey, n. ice hockey, field hockey, hockey game; see **game** 1, **sport** 3.

hodgepodge, n. jumble, combination, mess; see **mixture** 1.

hoe, n. digger, scraper, garden hoe; see **tool** 1.

hog, n. **1.** [A pig] swine, sow, boar, shoat, razorback, wild boar, wart hog, peccary, porker, piggy, pork; see also **animal** 2. **2.** [A person whose habits resemble a pig's] glutton, filthy person; see **slob**.

hogtie, v. fetter, shackle, tie up; see **bind**.

hogwash, n. foolishness, absurdity, ridiculousness; see **nonsense** 1.

hoist, n. crane, lift, derrick; see **elevator** 1.

hold, v. **1.** [To have in one's grasp] grasp, grip, clutch, carry, embrace, cling to, detain, enclose, restrain, confine, check, take hold of, contain, hold down or onto, not let go, hang on, squeeze, press, hug, handle, fondle, have or keep

in hand, get a grip (on), retain, keep, clasp, hold fast or tight, keep a firm hold on, tie, take, catch; see also **seize** 1.—Ant. let fall, release, drop. **2.** [To have in one's possession] keep, retain, possess; see **have** 1. **3.** [To remain firm] resist, persevere, keep staunch; see **continue** 1, **endure** 2. **4.** [To adhere] attach, cling, take hold; see **fasten, stick** 1. **5.** [To be valid] exist, continue, operate; see **be** 1.—Ant. stop, expire, be out-of-date. **6.** [To contain] have capacity for, carry, be equipped for; see **include** 1. **7.** [To support; often used with up] sustain, brace, buttress, prop, lock, stay, shoulder, uphold, bear or bolster up; see also **support** 1.

hold back, v. **1.** [To restrain] inhibit, control, curb; see **check** 2, **prevent, restrain**. **2.** [To refrain] desist, hesitate, forbear; see **abstain, avoid**.

holder, n. **1.** [An instrument used in holding] sheathe, container, holster, bag, sack, fastener, clip, handle, rack, knob, stem; see also **container, fastener**. **2.** [An owner or occupant] leaseholder, renter, dweller; see **owner, resident, tenant**.

hold fast, v. clasp, lock, clamp; see **fasten, stick** 1.

holdings, n. lands, possessions, security; see **estate, property** 1.

hold off, v. be above, keep aloof, stave off; see **avoid, prevent**.

hold office, v. be in (office), direct, rule; see **govern, manage** 1.

hold on, v. hang on, attach oneself to, cling (to); see **seize** 1.

hold one's own. v. keep one's advantage, stand one's ground, do well, keep up; see also **succeed** 1.

hold one's tongue or **one's peace,** v. be silent, conceal, keep secret, not say a word; see also **hide** 1.

holdout, n. die-hard, objector, resister; see **resistance** 4.

hold out, v. **1.** [To offer] proffer, tempt (with), grant; see **give** 1, **offer** 1. **2.** [To endure] suffer, hold on, withstand; see **continue** 1, **endure** 2.

hold out for, v. persist, go on supporting, stand firmly for; see **continue** 1.

holdover, n. remnant, relic, surplus; see **remainder**.

hold over, v. do again or over, show again, play over; see **repeat** 1.

holdup, n. robbery, burglary, stick-up; see **crime, theft**.

hold up, v. **1.** [To show] exhibit, raise high, elevate; see **display** 2. **2.** [To delay] stop, pause, interfere with; see **delay** 1, **hinder, interrupt**. **3.** [To rob at gunpoint] waylay, burglarize, steal from; see **rob** 4. **4.** [To support] brace, prop, shoulder; see **hold** 7, **support** 1.

hole, *n.* 1. [A perforation or cavity] notch, puncture, slot, eyelet, keyhole, porthole, buttonhole, peephole, loophole, air hole, window, crack, rent, split, tear, cleft, opening, fissure, gap, gash, rift, rupture, fracture, break, leak, aperture, space, chasm, breach, slit, nick, cut, chink, incision, orifice, eye, acupuncture, crater, mouth, gorge, throat, gullet, cranny, dent, opening, depression, indentation, impression, corner, pockmark, pocket, dimple, dip, drop, gulf, depth, pit, abyss, hollow, chasm, crevasse, mine, shaft, chamber, valley, ravine, burrow, rift, cell, niche. 2. [A cave] burrow, den, lair; see sense 1. 3. [*Serious difficulty*] impasse, tangle, mess; see **crisis, difficulty 1, emergency. —in a hole,** in trouble, suffering, caught; see **abandoned. —in the hole,** broke, without money, in debt; see **poor 1.**

holiday, *n.* feast day, fiesta, legal holiday, holy day, festival, centennial, carnival, jubilee, red-letter day; see also **anniversary, celebration.** Common holidays include the following—Sunday, Independence Day, Veterans Day, Memorial Day, Mardi Gras, New Year's Day, Saint Valentine's Day, Christmas, Easter Sunday, Lincoln's Birthday, Thanksgiving Day, Washington's Birthday, Columbus Day, Labor Day, Halloween, Election Day, Good Friday.

holiness, *n.* devoutness, humility, saintliness; see **devotion, worship 1.**

hollow, *a.* 1. [Concave] rounded *or* curving inward, bellshaped, curved, carved out, sunken, depressed, arched, vaulted, cup-shaped, excavated, hollowed out, indented, cupped; see also **bent, round 3.** —*Ant.* convex, **raised,** elevated. 2. [Sounding as though from a cave] cavernous, echoing, deep, resonant, booming, roaring, rumbling, reverberating, muffled, dull, resounding, sepulchral, vibrating, low, ringing, deep-toned, thunderous; see also **loud 1.**—*Ant.* dead, mute, silent.

hollow, *n.* dale, bowl, basin; see **valley.**

hollow (out), *v.* excavate, indent, remove earth; see **dig 1, shovel.**

holy, *a.* 1. [Sinless] devout, pious, blessed, righteous, moral, just, good, angelic, godly, reverent, venerable, immaculate, pure, spotless, clean, humble, saintly, innocent, godlike, saintlike, perfect, faultless, undefiled, untainted, chaste, upright, virtuous, revered, dedicated *or* devoted, sainted, heavensent, pious, believing, profoundly good, sanctified, devotional, reverent, spiritual, unstained, pure in heart, dedicated, unspotted; see also **faithful, religious 2.**—*Ant.* **bad,** wicked, sinful. 2. [Concerned

with worship] devotional, religious, ceremonial; see **divine 2.**

Holy Ghost, *n.* Holy Spirit, the Dove, third person of the Holy Trinity; see **God.**

homage, *n.* respect, adoration, deference; see **devotion, reverence, worship 1.**

home, *a.* in one's home *or* house, at ease, at rest, homely, domestic, familiar, being oneself, homey, in the bosom of one's family, down home, in one's element; see also **comfortable 1.**

home, *n.* 1. [A dwelling place] house, dwelling, residence, habitation, tenement, abode, lodging, quarters, homestead, domicile, dormitory, apartment house, flat, living quarters, chalet, shelter, asylum, hut, cabin, cottage, mansion, castle, summer home, rooming house, place, address, hovel, lodge, hotel, inn, farmhouse, tavern, tent, *pad, *dump, *hang-out; see also **apartment. 2.** [An asylum] orphanage, sanatorium, mental hospital; see **hospital. —at home,** relaxed, at ease, familiar; see **comfortable 1, home 1. —come home,** come or go back, return home, regress; see **return 1.**

homecoming, *n.* homecoming celebration, entry, revisitation; see **arrival 1.**

homeless, *a.* desolate, outcast, destitute, vagrant, wandering, itinerant, friendless, banished, derelict, without a country, exiled, having no home, vagabond, forsaken, friendless, unsettled, unwelcome, dispossessed, disinherited, *left to shift for oneself, *without a roof over one's head: see also **abandoned, poor 1.**—*Ant.* at home, **established,** settled.

homely, *a.* 1. [Unpretentious] snug, simple, cozy; see **modest 2. 2.** [Ill-favored] plain, unattractive, uncomely; see **ugly 1.**

homemade, *a.* homespun, domestic, do-it-yourself, self-made, made at home, home, not foreign.

home run, *n.* four-base hit, run, *homer; see **score 1.**

homesick, *a.* nostalgic, pining, yearning for home, ill with longing, unhappy, alienated, rootless; see also **lonely 1.**

homesickness, *n.* nostalgia, isolation, unhappiness; see **loneliness.**

homespun, *a.* handicrafted, domestic, handspun; see **homemade.**

homestead, *n.* house, ranch, estate; see **home 1, property 2.**

homeward, *a.* toward home, back home, on the way home, homewards, home, homeward bound, to one's family *or* native land.

homework, *n.* outside assignment, library assignment, preparation; see **education 1.**

homey, *a.* enjoyable, livable, familiar; see **comfortable 2, pleasant 2.**

honest, *a.* 1. [Truthful] true, trustworthy, correct, exact, verifiable, undisguised, candid, straightforward, aboveboard, just, frank, impartial, respectful, factual, sound, unimpeachable, legitimate, unquestionable, realistic, true-to-life, reasonable, naked, plain, *square, honest as the day is long, on the level, *kosher, *fair and square, straight.—*Ant.* deceptive, false, misleading. 2. [Frank] candid, straightforward, aboveboard; see sense 1; see **frank.** 3. [Fair] just, equitable, impartial; see **fair 1.**

honestly, *a.* 1. [In an honest manner] uprightly, fairly, genuinely; see **justly 1, sincerely.** 2. [Really] indeed, truly, naturally; see **really 1.**

honesty, *n.* honor, fidelity, scrupulousness, self-respect, straightforwardness, trustworthiness, confidence, soundness, right, principle, truthfulness, candor, frankness, openness, morality, goodness, responsibility, loyalty, faithfulness, good faith, probity, courage, moral strength, virtue, reliability, character, conscience, worth, conscientiousness, trustiness, faith, justice, respectability.—*Ant.* dishonesty, deception, deceit.

honey, *n.* comb honey, extracted honey, wild honey; see **food.**

honk, *n.* croak, quack, blare; see **noise 1.**

honk, *v.* blare, trumpet, bellow; see **sound 1.**

honor, *n.* 1. [Respect] reverence, esteem, worship, adoration, veneration, high regard, trust, faith, confidence, righteousness, recognition, praise, attention, deference, notice, consideration, renown, reputation, elevation, credit, tribute, popularity; see also **admiration 1.**—*Ant.* opprobrium, **disgrace,** disrepute. 2. [Integrity] courage, character, truthfulness; see **honesty.** —**do the honors,** act as host or hostess, present, host; see **serve.** —**on** (or upon) **one's honor,** by one's faith, on one's word, staking one's good name; see **sincerely.**

honor, *v.* 1. [To treat with respect] worship, sanctify, venerate; see **praise 1.** 2. [To recognize worth] esteem, value, look up to; see **admire.** 3. [To recognize as valid] clear, pass, accept; see **acknowledge 2.**

honorable, *a.* proud, reputable, creditable; see **distinguished 2, famous, noble 2, 3.**

honorably, *a.* nobly, fairly, virtuously; see **justly 1.**

honorary, *a.* titular, nominal, privileged; see **complimentary.**

honored, *a.* respected, revered, decorated, privileged, celebrated, reputable, well-known, esteemed, eminent, distinguished, dignified, noble, recognized, highly regarded, venerated; see also **famous.**—*Ant.* **corrupt,** disgraced, shamed.

honors, *n.* 1. [Courtesies] ceremony, privilege, duties; see **duty 2.** 2. [Distinction] high honors, award, prize, medal; see **fame.**

hood, *n.* 1. [Covering worn over the head] cowl, shawl, bonnet, protector, veil, capuchin, kerchief, mantle; see also **hat.** 2. [A covering for vehicles and the like] canopy, awning, auto top; see **cover 1.** 3. [*A criminal] gangster, hoodlum, crook; see **criminal.**

hoodlum, *n.* outlaw, gangster, crook; see **criminal.**

hoof, *n.* ungula, animal foot, paw; see **foot 2.**

hook, *n.* lock, catch, clasp; see **fastener.**

hook, *v.* 1. [To curve in the shape of a hook] angle, crook, curve; see **arch.** 2. [To catch on a hook] pin, catch, secure; see **fasten.**

hooked up, *a.* connected, circuited, attached; see **joined.**

hookup, *n.* attachment, connection, consolidation; see **link, union 1.**

hook up, *v.* combine, connect, attach; see **join 1, unite.**

hoop, *n.* wooden wheel, band, circlet; see **circle 1.**

hoot, *n.* howl, whoo, boo; see **cry 2.**

hop, *n.* spring, bounce, leap; see **jump 1.**

hop, *v.* leap, skip, jump on one leg; see **bounce, jump 1.**

hope, *n.* 1. [Reliance upon the future] faith, expectation, confidence; see **anticipation, optimism 2.** 2. [The object of hope] wish, goal, dream; see **desire 1, end 2, purpose 1.**

hope, *v.* be hopeful, lean on or upon, wish, desire, live in hope, rely or depend or count on, aspire to, doubt not, keep one's fingers crossed, hope for the best, be of good cheer, pray, cherish the hope, look forward to, await, dream, presume, watch for, bank or reckon on, foresee, think to, promise oneself, suppose, deem likely, believe, suspect, surmise, hold, be assured, be or feel confident, anticipate, be prepared for, make plans for, have faith, rest assured, feel confident, be sure of, be reassured, take heart, *hope to hell, *knock on wood; see also **expect 1, trust 1.**

hopeful, *a.* 1. [Optimistic] expectant, assured, sanguine, buoyant, enthusiastic, trustful, reassured, emboldened, full of hope, cheerful, anticipating, trusting, expecting, in hopes of, forward-looking, lighthearted, serene, calm, poised, comfortable, eager, elated, looking through rose-colored glasses; see also **confident, trusting.** 2. [Encouraging] promising, reassuring, favorable, bright, cheering, flattering, gracious, opportune, timely, fortunate, propitious, auspicious, well-timed, fit, suitable, convenient, beneficial, fair, uplifting, heartening, inspiring, exciting, pleasing, fine, lucky, stirring, making glad, helpful, rose-colored, rosy, animating, attractive, satisfactory, refreshing, probable, good, conducive, advantageous, pleasant, of promise, happy, cheerful.—*Ant.* discouraging, **unfortunate**, unfavorable.

hopefully, *a.* 1. [Optimistically] confidently, expectantly, with confidence *or* with (good) hope, trustingly, naively, with some reassurance, trustfully; see also **boldly** 1, **positively** 1, **surely**.—*Ant.* doubtfully, **hopelessly**, gloomily. 2. [Probably] expectedly, conceivably, feasibly; see **probably**.

hopeless, *a.* unfortunate, threatening, bad, sinister, unyielding, incurable, past hope *or* cure, vain, irreversible, irreparable, without hope, with no hope, impracticable, ill-fated, disastrous, menacing, foreboding, unfavorable, dying, worsening, past recall *or* saving, tragic, fatal, desperate, helpless, lost, to no avail, gone, empty, idle, useless, pointless, worthless; see **abandoned, impossible**.—*Ant.* **favorable**, heartening, cheering.

hopelessly, *a.* cynically, pessimistically, despondently, dejectedly, desperately, mechanically, automatically, emptily, darkly, gloomily, dismally, desolately, *down in the mouth; see also **sadly**.—*Ant.* confidently, **hopefully**, expectantly.

hoping, *a.* believing, expecting, wishing; see **trusting**.

horde, *n.* pack, throng, swarm; see **crowd, gathering**.

horizon, *n.* range, border, limit; see **boundary, extent**.

horizontal, *a.* 1. [Level] plane, aligned, parallel; see **flat** 1, **level** 3, **straight** 1. 2. [Even] flush, uniform, regular; see **flat** 1, **smooth** 1.

horn, *n.* 1. [A hornlike sounding instrument] Horns include the following—bugle, trombone, saxophone, cornet, clarinet, bassoon, pipe, fife, flute, piccolo, oboe, English horn, French horn, tuba; see also **musical instrument**. 2. [Hard process protruding from the head of certain animals] tusk, antler, outgrowth, pronghorn, frontal bone, spine, spike, point; see also **bone, tooth**. — **lock horns**, disagree, conflict, defy; see **oppose** 1.

horn in (on), *v.* intrude, impose (upon), get in on; see **enter, meddle** 1.

horny, *a.* 1. [Callous] hard, firm, bony; see **tough** 2. 2. [*Sexually excited] sensual, aroused, lecherous; see **excited**, lewd 2.

horrible, *a.* 1. [Offensive] repulsive, dreadful, disgusting; see **offensive** 2. 2. [Frightful] shameful, shocking, awful; see **frightful, terrible** 1.

horrid, *a.* hideous, disturbing, shameful; see **offensive** 2, **pitiful** 1.

horror, *n.* awe, terror, fright; see **fear**.

horse, *n.* nag, draft animal, plow horse, racer, saddlehorse, steed, mount, charger, hunter, cutting horse, stallion, gelding, hack, mare, thoroughbred, pacer, trotter, courser; see also **animal**. —*from the horse's mouth, originally, from an authority, according to the source of the information; see **officially** 1. —*hold one's horses, curb one's impatience, slow down, relax; see **restrain**. —*on one's high horse, arrogant, haughty, disdainful; see **egotistic**.

horse around, *v.* fool around, cavort, cause trouble; see **misbehave, play** 2.

horseman, *n.* equestrian, rider, jockey; see **cowboy, rider** 1.

horseplay, *n.* clowning, play, fooling around; see **fun, joke** 1.

horsepower, *n.* strength, pull, power; see **energy** 2.

hose, *n.* 1. [Stocking] men's *or* women's hose, tights, panty hose; see **hosiery**. 2. [A flexible conduit] garden hose, fire hose, line, tubing; see also **pipe** 1, **tube** 1.

hosiery, *n.* silk *or* rayon *or* nylon *or* woolen stockings, full-fashioned hose, seamless hose, socks, anklets, tights, panty hose, leotards, knee socks, knitted *or* crocheted *or* bulky stockings, body stocking.

hospitable, *a.* cordial, courteous, open; see **friendly**.

hospital, *n.* clinic, infirmary, sanatorium, sanitarium, dispensary, mental hospital, army hospital, city hospital, public hospital, veteran's hospital, medical center, lying-in hospital, health service, outpatient ward, sick bay, rest home.

hospitality, *n.* good cheer, companionship, good fellowship; see **entertainment** 1, **welcome**.

host, *n.* 1. [A man who entertains] man of the house, entertainer, toastmaster, master, master of ceremonies. 2. [A large group] throng, multitude, army; see **crowd, gathering**. 3. [Organism on which a parasite subsists] host mother, host body, animal; see **parasite** 1.

host, *v.* receive, treat, wine and dine; see **entertain** 2.

hostage, *n.* security, captive, victim of a kidnapping; see **prisoner**.

hostess, *n.* society lady, socialite, clubwoman, social leader, social climber, entertainer, lady of the house, mistress of the household, toastmistress, mistress of ceremonies.

hostile, *a.* antagonistic, hateful, opposed; see **unfriendly**.

hostility, *n.* abhorrence, aversion, bitterness; see **hatred**.

hot, *a.* 1. [Having a high temperature] torrid, burning, fiery, flaming, blazing, very warm, baking, roasting, smoking, scorching, blistering, searing, sizzling, tropical, warm, broiling, red-hot, grilling, piping-hot, white-hot, scalding, parching, sultry, on fire, at high temperature, incandescent, smoldering, thermal, toasting, simmering, *blazing hot, *boiling hot, *like an oven, *hotter than blazes; see also **boiling, cooking, molten.**—*Ant.* **cold**, frigid, chilly. 2. [Aroused] furious, ill-tempered, indignant; see **angry**. 3. [*Erotic] spicy, salacious, carnal; see **sensual** 2. —*get hot, become excited or enthusiastic, burn with fervor or anger, rave; see **rage** 1. —*make it hot for, create discomfort for, cause trouble for, vex; see **disturb**.

hotel, *n.* stopping place, inn, (lodging) house, halfway house, boarding house, hostel, motel, motor hotel, resort (hotel), country or health or mountain resort, tavern, spa, rooming house, *flophouse, *bughouse, *dump.

hotheaded, *a.* unmanageable, wild, reckless; see **rash, unruly**.

hot under the collar, *a.* furious, mad, resentful; see **angry**.

hound, *n.* greyhound, bloodhound, beagle; see **animal, dog**.

hound, *v.* badger, provoke, annoy; see **bother** 2, 3.

hour, *n.* time unit, sixty minutes, man-hour, planetary hour, horsepower hour, class hour, supper hour, study hour, rush hour; see also **time** 1.

hour after hour, *a.* continually, steadily, on and on; see **regularly**.

hourly, *a.* each hour, every hour, every sixty minutes; see **frequently** 1, **regularly**.

house, *n.* 1. [A habitation] dwelling, apartment house, residence; see **apartment, home** 1. 2. [A family] line, family tradition, ancestry; see **family**. 3. [A legislative body] congress, council, parliament; see **legislature**. —*bring down the house, receive applause, create enthusiasm, please; see **excite**. —**clean house**, arrange, put in order, tidy up; see **clean**. —**keep house**, manage a home, run a house, be a housekeeper; see **manage** 1. —**like a house on fire**, actively, vigorously, energetically; see **quickly**. —**on the house**, without expense, gratis, for nothing; see **free** 4.

household, *n.* family unit, house, domestic establishment; see **family, home** 1.

housekeeper, *n.* wife and mother, caretaker, serving woman; see **servant**.

housekeeping, *n.* household management, domestic science, home economy; see **housework**.

housewife, *n.* mistress or lady of the house, housekeeper, mother of one's children, home economist, home-maker, family manager, wife and mother, *stay-at-home; see also **wife**.

housework, *n.* house cleaning, spring cleaning, window-washing, sweeping, cooking, baking, dusting, mopping, washing, laundering, bed-making, sewing, ironing, mending; see also **job** 2.

housing, *n.* habitation, home construction, housing development, low-cost housing, house-building program, sheltering, installation, abode, domicile, house, accommodations, quarters, roof, dwelling, lodging, residence, headquarters; see also **home** 1, **shelter**.

hover, *v.* float, flutter, waver; see **fly** 1, **hang** 2.

how, *a. and conj.* in what way, to what degree, by what method, in what manner, according to what specifications, from what source, by whose help, whence, wherewith, by virtue of what, whereby, through what agency or medium, by what means or aid.

however, *a. and conj.* 1. [But] still, though, nevertheless; see **but** 1, **yet** 1. 2. [In spite of] despite, without regard to, nonetheless; see **notwithstanding**.

howl, *n.* moan, wail, lament; see **cry** 2, **yell**.

howl, *v.* bawl, wail, lament; see **cry** 2, **yell**.

hub, *n.* core, heart, middle; see **center** 1.

hubbub, *n.* turmoil, fuss, disorder; see **confusion** 2, **noise** 2, **uproar**.

huddle, *v.* crouch, press close, crowd, bunch, draw together, mass, cluster, throng, nestle, cuddle, hug, curl up, snuggle.

hue, *n.* hue, value, dye; see **tint**.

huff, *n.* annoyance, offense, perturbation; see **anger, rage** 2.

huffy, *a.* offended, piqued, huffish; see **angry, insulted, irritable**.

hug, *n.* embrace, squeeze, tight grip, caress, clinch, bear hug; see also **touch** 2.

hug, *v.* embrace, squeeze, clasp, press (close), love, catch hold of, be near to, cling, fold in the arms, clutch, seize, envelop, enfold, nestle, welcome, cuddle, lock, press to the bosom, snuggle.

huge, *a.* tremendous, enormous, immense; see **large** 1.

hulk, *n.* bulk, hunk, lump; see **mass 1, part 1.**

hult, *n.* **1.** [The body of a vessel] framework, skeleton, main structure; see **frame 1. 2.** [A shell] peeling, husk, shuck; see **shell 1.**

hullabaloo, *n.* tumult, chaos, clamor; see **confusion 2, noise 2, uproar.**

hum, *v.* buzz, drone, murmur, sing low, hum a tune, croon, whisper, moan, make a buzzing sound, whir, vibrate, purr.

human, *a.* anthropoid, animal, biped, civilized, man-made, anthropomorphic, manlike, of man, belonging to man, humanistic, individual, man's, personal, humane; see also **animal.**—*Ant.* divine, bestial, nonhuman.

human being, *n.* being, mortal, individual; see **man 1, 2, person 1, woman 1.**

humane, *a.* benevolent, sympathetic, understanding, pitying, compassionate, kindhearted, human, tenderhearted, forgiving, gracious, charitable, gentle, tender, friendly, generous, lenient, tolerant, democratic, good-natured, liberal, open-minded, broad-minded, altruistic, philanthropic, helpful, magnanimous, amiable, genial, cordial, unselfish, warmhearted, big-hearted, soft-hearted, good, soft, easy; see also **kind.**—*Ant.* cruel, barbaric, inhuman.

humanitarian, *n.* altruist, helper, benefactor; see **patron.**

humanity, *n.* **1.** [The human race] man, mankind, men; see **man 1. 2.** [An ideal of human behavior] tolerance, sympathy, understanding; see **kindness 1, virtue 1, 2.**

humble, *a.* **1.** [Meek] lowly, submissive, gentle, quiet, unassuming, diffident, simple, retiring, bashful, shy, timid, reserved, deferential, self-conscious, soft-spoken, sheepish, mild, withdrawn, unpretentious, hesitant, fearful, tentative, poor in spirit, sedate, unpresuming, manageable, ordinary, unambitious, commonplace, free from pride, peaceful, without arrogance, peaceable, obedient, passive, tame, restrained, unostentatious, unimportant, gentle as a lamb, resigned, subdued, tolerant, content, eating humble pie; see also **modest 2.**—*Ant.* proud, haughty, conceited. **2.** [Lowly] unpretentious, unassuming, modest, seemly, becoming, homespun, natural, low, proletarian, servile, undistinguished, pitiful, sordid, shabby, underprivileged, meager, beggarly, commonplace, unimportant, insignificant, small, poor, rough, hard, base, meek, little, of low birth, obscure, inferior, plain, common, homely, simple, uncouth, miserable, scrubby, ordinary, humdrum,

trivial, vulgar.—*Ant.* upper-class, **noble,** privileged.

humble, *v.* shame, mortify, chasten, demean (oneself), demote, lower, crush, hide one's face, bring low, put to shame, silence, reduce, humiliate, degrade, overcome, strike dumb, take *or* put *or* pull *or* bring down, snub, discredit, deflate, upset, make ashamed, take down a peg, *pull rank, *squelch, *squash.—*Ant.* exalt, **praise,** glorify.

humbly, *a.* meekly, submissively, simply, obscurely, apologetically.

humbug, *n.* lie, fraud, faker; see **deception, nonsense 1.**

humdrum, *a.* monotonous, common, uninteresting; see **dull 4.**

humid, *a.* stuffy, sticky, muggy; see **close 5, wet 1.**

humidity, *n.* moisture, wetness, dampness, mugginess, dankness, heaviness, sogginess, thickness, fogginess, wet, sultriness, steaminess, steam, evaporation, dewiness, stickiness, moistness; see also **rain 1.**

humiliate, *v.* debase, chasten, mortify, make a fool of, put to shame, humble, degrade, crush, shame, confuse, snub, confound, lower, dishonor, depress, fill with shame, break, demean, bring low, conquer, make ashamed, vanquish, take down a peg; see also **disgrace, embarrass.**

humiliation, *n.* chagrin, mortification, mental pain; see **disgrace 1, embarrassment 1, shame 2.**

humility, *n.* meekness, timidity, submissiveness, servility, reserve, subservience, subjection, humbleness, submission, obedience, passiveness, nonresistance, resignation, bashfulness, shyness, inferiority complex.—*Ant.* pride, vainglory, conceit.

humor, *n.* **1.** [Comedy] amusement, jesting, raillery, joking, merriment, clowning, farce, facetiousness, black humor, *comedy; see also **entertainment 1, fun. 2.** [An example of humor] witticism, pleasantry, banter; see **joke 1, 2. 3.** [The ability to appreciate comedy] good humor, sense of humor, wittiness, high spirits, jolliness, gaiety, joyfulness, playfulness, happy frame of mind.

humor, *v.* indulge, pamper, baby, play up to, gratify, please, pet, coddle, spoil, comply with, appease, placate, soften, be playful with; see also **comfort 1.**—*Ant.* provoke, **anger,** enrage.

humorous, *a.* comical, comic, entertaining; see **funny 1.**

humorously, *a.* comically, ridiculously, playfully, absurdly, ludicrously, amusingly, jokingly, ironically, satirically, facetiously, merrily, genially, jovially, in a comical *or* amusing *or* ridiculous, etc., manner, just for fun, *like or as if he was crazy or nuts or off his rocker, etc.

hump, n. protuberance, mound, bump, swelling, camel hump, humpback, hunchback, hummock, protrusion, knob, prominence, eminence, projection, swell, hunch, lump, dune.

hunch, n. idea, notion, feeling, premonition, forecast, presentiment, instinct, expectation, anticipation, precognition, prescience, forewarning, clue, foreboding, hint, portent, apprehension, misgiving, qualm, suspicion, inkling, glimmer; see also **thought** 2.

hundred, n. ten tens, five score, century; see **number**.

hung, a. suspended, swaying, dangling; see **hanging**.

hunger, n. craving, longing, yearning, mania, lust, desire for food, famine, gluttony, hungriness, panting, drought, want, vacancy, void, greed, *sweet tooth.—Ant. satisfaction, satiety, glut.

hungry, a. starved, famished, ravenous, desirous, hankering, unsatisfied, unfilled, starving, insatiate, voracious, half-starved, omnivorous, piggish, hoggish, *on an empty stomach, *hungry as a wolf, *empty.—Ant. satisfied, full, fed.

***hung up**, v. 1. [Troubled] disturbed, psychotic, psychopathic; see **troubled**. 2. [Intent] absorbed, engrossed, preoccupied; see **thoughtful** 1.

hunk, n. lump, large piece, good-sized bit, portion, a fair quantity, a good bit, chunk, bunch, mass, clod, a pile, thick slice, morsel, a lot, slice, gob, loaf, wad; see also **piece** 1.

hunt, n. chase, shooting, game, field sport; see **hunting**, **sport** 3.

hunt, v. 1. [To pursue with intent to kill] follow, give chase, stalk, hound, trail, dog, seek, capture, kill, shoot, track, heel, shadow, chase (after), hunt out, snare, look for, fish, fish for, poach, *gun for, *go gunning for; see also **track** 1. 2. [To try to find] investigate, probe, look for; see **seek**.

hunted, a. pursued, followed, tracked, sought (for), trailed, chased, stalked, hounded, tailed, wanted, driven out, searched for.

hunter, n. huntsman, stalker, chaser, sportsman, pursuer, big-game hunter, gunner, poacher, horsewoman, huntress, horseman, archer, deerstalker, angler, fisherman, bowman, shooter.

hunting, a. looking for or around, seeking, in search (of); see **searching**.

hunting, n. the chase, the hunt, sporting, shooting, stalking, trapping, big-game hunting, deer hunting, fox hunting, pheasant shooting, angling, fishing, steeplechase, riding to hounds, gunning; see also **sport** 3.

hurdle, n. barricade, earthwork, blockade; see **barrier**.

hurdle, v. jump over or across, scale, leap over; see **jump** 1.

hurl, v. cast, fling, heave; see **throw** 1.

hurrah, interj. three cheers, hurray, yippee; see **cheer** 2, **cry** 1, **encouragement**, yell 1.

hurricane, n. typhoon, tempest, monsoon; see **storm**.

hurry, interj. run, hasten, speed, move, get on it, hustle, gain time, look alive, get a move on, bear down on it, on the double.

hurry, n. dispatch, expedition, rush; see **speed** 1.

hurry, v. 1. [To act hastily] hasten, be quick, make haste, scurry, scuttle, fly, tear, dash, sprint, be in a hurry, waste or lose no time, move quickly or rapidly, bolt, bustle, rush, make short work of, scoot, work at high speed, dash on, hurry about or off or up, run (off), lose no time, plunge, skip, gallop, zoom, dart, spring, press (on), make haste or (good) time, whip off or away, go by forced marches, speed (up), work under pressure, run like mad, go at full blast or tilt, put on (more) speed, make strides, run wide open, act on a moment's notice, *turn on the steam, *get cracking, *step on it, *shake a leg.—Ant. delay, lose time, procrastinate. 2. [To move rapidly] fly, bustle, dash off; see **race** 1, **run** 1. 3. [To urge others] push, spur, goad on; see **drive** 1, **urge** 2.

hurrying, a. speeding, in a hurry, running; see **fast**.

hurt, a. injured, damaged, harmed, marred, (slightly or severely) wounded, in critical condition, impaired, shot, warped, bolt, bruised, stricken, battered, mauled, hit, stabbed, mutilated, disfigured, in pain, suffering, distressed, tortured, unhappy, grazed, scratched, nicked, *winged; see also **wounded**.

hurt, n. 1. [A wound] blow, gash, ache; see **injury**, **pain** 1. 2. [Damage] illtreatment, harm, persecution; see **damage** 1, **disaster**, **misfortune**.

hurt, v. 1. [To cause pain] cramp, squeeze, cut, bruise, tear, torment, afflict, kick, puncture, do violence to, slap, abuse, flog, whip, torture, gnaw, stab, pierce, maul, cut up, harm, injure, wound, lacerate, sting, bite, inflict pain, burn, crucify, tweak, thrash, punch, pinch, spank, punish, trounce, scourge, lash, cane, switch, *work over, *lay or wrack up, *wallop, slug.—Ant. comfort, ease, soothe. 2. [To harm] maltreat, injure, spoil; see **damage** 1, **destroy**. 3. [To give a feeling of pain] ache, throb, sting; see **sense** 1.

hurtful, *a.* aching, injurious, bad; see **dangerous, deadly, harmful.**

husband, *n.* spouse, married man, mate, bedmate, helpmate, consort, bridegroom, breadwinner, provider, man, common-law husband *or* spouse, *hubby, *lord and master, *the man of the house, *old man; see also **man 2.**

hush, *interj.* quiet, be quiet, *pipe down; see **shut up 1.**

hush, *n.* peace, stillness, quiet; see **silence 1.**

hush, *v.* silence, gag, stifle; see **quiet 2.**

hush (up), *v.* cover, conceal, suppress (mention of); see **hide 1.**

husk, *n.* shuck, covering, outside; see **cover 1, shell 1.**

husky, *a.* 1. [Hoarse] throaty, growling, gruff; see **hoarse.** 2. [Strong] muscular, sinewy, strapping; see **strong 1.**

hustle, *v.* act quickly, rush, push; see **hurry 1, race 1, run 1, speed.**

***hustler,** *n.* 1. [A professional gambler] gamester, bookmaker, plunger; see **gambler.** 2. [A prostitute] whore, harlot, call girl; see **prostitute.** 3. [A fast worker] man of action, enthusiast, worker; see **executive, zealot.**

hut, *n.* shanty, lean-to, shack, bungalow, bunkhouse, refuge, lodge, dugout, hovel, cottage, cabin, hogan, tepee, log house *or* cabin, wigwam, *dump, *rathole; see also **home 1, shelter.**

hybrid, *a.* crossed, alloyed, crossbred, cross, half-blooded, half-breed, half-caste, heterogeneous, intermingled, half-and-half.

hybrid, *n.* crossbreed, cross, mixture, composite, half-breed, half-blood, half-caste, combination, mestizo, mulatto, outcross; see also **mixture 1.**

hydraulics, *n.* science of liquids in motion, hydrodynamics, hydrology; see **science 1.**

hygiene, *n.* cleanliness, hygienics, preventive medicine, public health, hygiantics, sanitary measures *or* provisions; see also **health.**

hygienic, *a.* healthful, sanitary, clean; see **pure 2, sterile 3.**

hymn, *n.* chant, psalm, carol; see **song.**

hypnosis, *n.* trance, anesthesia, lethargy; see **sleep.**

hypnotic, *a.* sleep-inducing, opiate, narcotic, anesthetic, soporific, sleep-producing, soothing, calmative, trance-inducing.

hypnotism, *n.* bewitchment, suggestion,

hypnotherapy, deep sleep, self-hypnosis, autohypnosis, hypnotic suggestion, induction of hypnosis, fascination, psychokinesis.

hypnotize, *v.* mesmerize, put *or* lull to sleep, dull the will, hold under a spell, bring under one's control, stupefy, drug, soothe, anesthetize, subject to suggestion, make drowsy or sleepy.

hypnotized, *a.* entranced, mesmerized, enchanted; see **charmed.**

hypochondria, *n.* depression, imagined ill-health, anxiety neurosis; see **pretense 1.**

hypochondriac, *n.* malingerer, masochist, self-tormentor; see **fake.**

hypocrisy, *n.* quackery, affectation, bad faith, hollowness, display, lip service, bigotry, sham, fraud, pretense of virtue *or* piety, empty ceremony, sanctimony, cant; see also **dishonesty, lie 1.**—*Ant.* **virtue,** devotion, piety.

hypocrite, *n.* pretender, fraud, faker, fake, deceiver, charlatan, bigot, quack, pharisee, sham, actor, cheat, informer, trickster, one given to hypocrisy, confidence man, malingerer, humbug, swindler, informer, rascal, traitor, wolf in sheep's clothing, masquerader, *four-flusher, *two-timer, *two-face; see also **fake.**

hypocritical, *a.* deceptive, double-dealing, insincere; see **dishonest.**

hypothesis, *n.* supposition, theory, assumption; see **guess, opinion 1.**

hypothetical, *a.* 1. [Supposed] imagined, uncertain, vague; see **assumed, likely 1.** 2. [Characterized by hypothesis] postulated, academic, philosophical; see **logical 1.**

hysteria, *n.* delirium, agitation, feverishness; see **confusion, excitement, nervousness.**

hysterical, *a.* convulsed, uncontrolled, raving, delirious, wildly emotional, unnerved, neurotic, spasmodic, emotional, rabid, emotionally disordered, distracted, fuming, distraught, unrestrained, possessed, fanatical, irrepressible, convulsive, carried away, seething, beside oneself, rampant, out of one's wits, mad, uncontrollable, agitated, raging, frenzied, confused, tempestuous, maddened, crazy, impetuous, crazed, furious, violent, impassioned, panic-stricken, nervous, vehement, overwrought, fiery, passionate, *jittery, *wild-eyed, *on a laughing *or* crying jag; see also **angry, excited, troubled.**

I

I, *pron.* myself, *ego* (Latin), self; see **character 2.**

ICBM, *n.* Intercontinental Ballistic Missile, guided missile, strategic deterrent; see **rocket, weapon.**

ice, *n.* crystal, hail, floe, glacier, icicle, ice cube, cube ice, dry ice, black ice, white ice, chunk ice, iceberg, permafrost; see also **frost. —break the ice,** make a start, initiate, commence; see **begin 1.** **—*on ice,** in reserve, held, in abeyance; see **saved 2. —*on thin ice,** in a dangerous situation, imperiled, insecure; see **endangered.**

ice, *v.* frost, coat, mist; see **freeze 1.**

iceberg, *n.* ice field, berg, icecap; see **ice.**

icebox, *n.* cooler, quick *or* fast freezer, ***fridge; see **refrigerator.**

ice cream, *n.* mousse, spumoni, *glacé* (French), sherbet, ice, parfait, frozen dessert; see **dessert.**

icy, *a.* frozen over, iced, glaring, freezing, glacial, frostbound, frosted, frosty, smooth as glass; see also **slippery.**

idea, *n.* 1. [A concept] conception, plan(s), view, fancy, impression, image, understanding, conception, observation, belief, feeling, opinion, guess, inference, theory, hypothesis, supposition, assumption, intuition, conjecture, design, approach, mental impression, notion. 2. [Fancy] whimsy, whim, fantasy; see **fancy 1, imagination.** 3. [Meaning] sense, import, purport; see **meaning.**

ideal, *a.* 1. [Typical] prototypical, model, archetypical; see **typical.** 2. [Perfect] supreme, fitting, exemplary; see **excellent, perfect.**

ideal, *n.* paragon, goal, prototype; see **model 1.**

idealism, *n.* principle, conscience, philosophy; see **ethics.**

idealistic, *a.* lofty, noble, exalted; see **impractical, noble 1.**

idealize, *v.* romanticize, glorify, build castles in the air; see **dream 2, invent 1.**

ideals, *n.* standards, principles, goals; see **ethics, morals.**

identical, *a.* like, twin, indistinguishable; see **alike.**

identification, *n.* 1. [The act of identifying] classifying, naming, cataloguing; see **classification, description.** 2. [Means of identifying] credentials, letter of introduction, testimony, letter of credit, badge, papers, ID; see also **passport.**

identify, *v.* classify, catalogue, analyze; see **describe, name 1, 2.**

identity, *n.* identification, character, individuality, uniqueness, antecedents, true circumstances, parentage, status, citizenship, nationality, connections; see also **name 1.**

ideology, *n.* belief(s), ideas, philosophy; see **culture 2, ethics.**

idiot, *n.* simpleton, nincompoop, booby; see **fool.**

idiotic, *a.* thickwitted, dull, moronic; see **stupid 1.**

idle, *a.* unoccupied, workless, uncultivated, fallow, vacant, deserted, not in use *or* operation, barren, void, empty, abandoned, still, quiet, motionless, inert, dead, rusty, dusty, out of action, out of a job, resting; see also **unemployed.— *Ant.* active, busy, engaged.

idle, *v.* slack, shirk, slow down; see **loaf 2.**

idleness, *n.* loitering, time-killing, dawdling, inertia, inactivity, indolence, sluggishness, unemployment, dormancy, lethargy, stupor, loafing.—*Ant.* industry, action, occupation.

idol, *n.* icon, graven image, god, Buddha, false god, figurine, fetish, totem, golden calf, pagan deity.

idolatry, *n.* infatuation, fervor, transport; see **zeal.**

idolize, *v.* glorify, adore, canonize; see **worship 2.**

I don't know, *interj.* (It) beats me! Who knows? How should I know? You've got me! Ask me another!

if, *conj.* provided that, with the condition that, supposing that, conceding that, on the assumption that, granted that, assuming (that), whenever, wherever. **—as if,** as though, assuming that, in a way; see **as if.**

ignite, *v.* enkindle, light, strike a light, start up, burst into flames, touch off, touch a match to, set off; see also **burn.**

ignition, *n.* 1. [Igniting] combustion, bursting into flame, kindling; see **fire 1.** 2. [A system for igniting] distributor, firing system, wiring system; see **engine, machine, motor.**

ignorance, *n.* unconsciousness, incomprehension, bewilderment, incapacity, inexperience, disregard, illiteracy, denseness, dumbness, empty-headedness, unintelligence, rawness, blindness, simplicity, lack of learning *or* education *or* erudition *or* background, insensitivity, shallowness, fog, vagueness, half-knowledge, a little learning.—*Ant.* ability, learning, erudition.

ignorant, *a.* 1. [Unaware] unconscious (of), uninformed (about), unknowing, uninitiated, inexperienced, unwitting, unmindful, disregarding, misinformed, unsuspecting, unaware (of), unmindful *or* unconscious (of), mindless, witless, not conversant (with), unintelligent, obtuse, thick, dense, unscientific, *bird-brained, *lowbrow, *sappy, green; see also sense 2, **dull** 3, **shallow** 2, **stupid** 1.—*Ant.* **intelligent,** alert, aware. 2. [Untrained] illiterate, uneducated, unlettered, untaught, uninstructed, uncultivated, unenlightened, untutored, unread, unschooled, benighted, shallow, superficial, gross, coarse, vulgar, crude, green, knowing nothing, misinformed, misguided, just beginning, apprenticed, unbriefed; see also **inexperienced, naïve, unaware.**—*Ant.* **learned,** cognizant, tutored.

ignore, *v.* disregard, overlook, pass over; see **discard, neglect** 2.

ill, *a.* 1. [Bad] harmful, evil, noxious; see **bad** 1. 2. [Sick] unwell, unhealthy, ailing; see **sick.**

ill, *n.* depravity, misfortune, mischief; see **evil** 2, **insult, wrong** 1, 2.

ill at ease, *a.* anxious, uneasy, uncomfortable; see **doubtful, restless, suspicious** 1, 2.

illegal, *a.* illicit, unlawful, contraband, unwarranted, banned, unconstitutional, outside the law, extralegal, outlawed, not legal, unauthorized, unlicensed, lawless, actionable, illegitimate, prohibited, forbidden, criminal, against the law, not approved, uncertified, unlicensed, smuggled, bootlegged, *hot.—*Ant.* lawful, legal, authorized.

illegible, *a.* faint, unintelligible, difficult to read; see also **confused** 2, **obscure** 1.

illegibly, *a.* faintly, unintelligibly, indistinctly; see **confused** 2.

illegitimate, *a.* 1. [Unlawful] contraband, wrong, illicit; see **bad** 1, **illegal.** 2. [Misbegotten] born out of wedlock, unlawfully begotten, unfathered; see **bastard** 1.

illicit, *a.* unlawful, prohibited, unauthorized; see **bad** 1, **illegal, wrong** 1.

illiteracy, *n.* lack of education, stupidity, idiocy; see **ignorance.**

illiterate, *a.* uneducated, unenlightened, *dumb; see **ignorant** 2.

ill-mannered, *a.* impolite, uncouth, rough; see **rude** 2.

illness, *n.* 1. [Poor health] sickness, failing health, seizure, ailing, infirmity, disorder, relapse, attack, fit, convalescence, complaint, delicate health, collapse,

breakdown, confinement, disturbance, ill health; see also **weakness** 1. 2. [A particular disease] sickness, ailment, malady, ache, infection, stroke, allergy; see also **cold** 2, **impediment** 2, **insanity, pain** 2.

illogical, *a.* irrational, unreasonable, absurd, fallacious, unsubstantial, incorrect, inconsistent, false, unscientific, contradictory, untenable, unsound, preposterous, invalid, self-contradictory, unproved, groundless, implausible, hollow, irrelevant, inconclusive, prejudiced, biased, unconnected, without foundation, not following, without rhyme or reason; see also **wrong** 2.—*Ant.* sound, reasonable, **logical.**

ill-tempered, *a.* cross, touchy, querulous; see **irritable, sullen.**

illuminate, *v.* 1. [To make light(er)] lighten, irradiate, illume; see **brighten** 1, **light** 1. 2. [To explain] interpret, elucidate, clarify; see **explain.**

illumination, *n.* 1. [A light] gleam, flame, brilliance, lighting; see also **flash, light** 1, 3. 2. [Instruction] teaching, education, information; see **knowledge** 1.

illusion, *n.* fancy, hallucination, mirage, apparition, ghost, delusion, figment of the imagination, image, trick of vision, myth, make-believe; see also **dream.**

illustrate, *v.* picture, represent, portray, depict, imitate; see also **draw** 2, **paint** 1.

illustrated, *a.* engraved, decorated, portrayed; see **descriptive.**

illustration, *n.* engraving, tailpiece, cartoon, vignette, etching, inset picture, newsphoto; see also **picture** 3.

illustrative, *a.* symbolic, representative, pictorial; see **descriptive, explanatory, graphic** 1, 2.

ill will, *n.* malevolence, dislike, hostility; see **blame, hatred, objection.**

image, *n.* 1. [Mental impression] concept, conception, perception; see **idea** 1, **thought** 2. 2. [Representation] idol, carved figure, effigy, form, drawing, model, illustration, portrait, photograph, reproduction, copy, likeness, facsimile, counterpart, replica; see also **picture** 2.

imagery, *n.* illustration, metaphor, representation; see **comparison.**

imaginable, *a.* conceivable, comprehensible, credible, thinkable, sensible, possible, plausible, believable, reasonable; see also **likely** 1.—*Ant.* unimaginable, **unbelievable,** inconceivable.

imaginary, *a.* fancied, illusory, visionary, shadowy, dreamy, dreamlike, hypothetical, theoretical, deceptive, imagined, hallucinatory, ideal, whimsical, fabulous, nonexistent, apocryphal, fantastic, mythological, legendary, fictitious, imaginative; see also **unreal.**—*Ant.* real, factual, existing.

imagination, *n.* intelligence, thoughtfulness, inventiveness, conception, mental agility, wit, sensitivity, fancy, visualization, realization, cognition, awareness, dramatization, pictorialization, insight; see also **mind 1.**

imaginative, *a.* creative, inventive, originative; see **artistic, original 2.**

imagine, *v.* conceive, picture, conjure up, envisage, envision, see in one's mind, invent, fabricate, formulate, devise, think of, make up, conceptualize, dream, perceive, dramatize, create.

imagined, *a.* not real, insubstantial, thought up; see **false 1, 2, 3, imaginary.**

imbalance, *n.* lack of balance, unevenness, inequality; see **irregularity 1.**

imbibe, *v.* ingest, gorge, guzzle; see **drink 1, swallow.**

imitate, *v.* 1. [To mimic] impersonate, mirror, copy, mime, ape, simulate, duplicate, act, repeat, echo, parody, do like, reflect, pretend, play a part, *take off. 2. [To copy] duplicate, counterfeit, falsify; see **copy, reproduce 2.** 3. [To resemble] look *or* be like, simulate, parallel; see **resemble.**

imitated, *a.* copied, duplicated, mimicked, mocked, aped, counterfeited, caricatured, parodied.

imitation, *a.* copied, feigned, bogus; see **false 3.**

imitation, *n.* 1. [The act of imitating] simulation, counterfeiting, copying, duplication, patterning (after), picturing, representing, mimicry, aping, impersonation, echoing, matching, mirroring, paralleling; see also **copy. 2.** [An object made by imitating] counterfeit, mime, sham, fake, picture, replica, echo, reflection, match, parallel, resemblance, transcription, image, mockery, take-off, parody, satire (upon), substitution, forgery; see also **copy.**—*Ant.* original, novelty, pattern.

imitative, *a.* forged, sham, deceptive; see **false 2, 3.**

imitator, *n.* follower, copier, impersonator, mime, mimic, pretender, counterfeiter, forger.

immaculate, *a.* unsullied, spotless, stainless; see **bright 1, clean 1.**

immature, *a.* youthful, sophomoric, half-grown; see **naive.**

immaturity, *n.* imperfection, incompleteness, childlike behavior; see also **instability.**

immediate, *a.* at once, instant, now, on the moment, at this moment, at the present time, next, prompt; see also **following.**—*Ant.* someday, later, any time.

immediately, *a.* at once, without delay, instantly, directly, right away, at the first opportunity, at short notice, now, this instant, speedily, quickly, promptly, on the spot *or* dot, rapidly, instantaneously, shortly, *in a jiffy; see also **urgently 1.**—*Ant.* in the future, later, in a while.

immense, *a.* gigantic, tremendous, enormous; see **large 1.**

immensity, *n.* infinity, vastness, greatness; see **extent.**

immerse, *v.* submerge, dip, douse, plunge, duck, cover with water, drown, bathe, steep, soak, drench, dunk, souse; see also **soak 1.**

immersed, *a.* drowned, plunged, bathed; see **dipped, soaked, wet 1.**

immigrant, *n.* newcomer, naturalized citizen, adoptive citizen; see **alien, emigrant.**

immigrate, *v.* be smuggled in, come in under the quota, seek (political) asylum; see **enter.**

immigration, *n.* colonization, settlement, migration; see **entrance 1.**

imminent, *a.* approaching, in store, about to happen; see **coming 1, destined 1.**

immodest, *a.* brazen, shameless, bold; see **egotistic, rude 2.**

immoral, *a.* sinful, corrupt, shameless; see **bad 1.**

immorality, *n.* vice, depravity, dissoluteness; see **evil 1.**

immorally, *a.* sinfully, wickedly, unrighteously; see **wrongly 1.**

immortal, *a.* 1. [Deathless] undying, permanent, imperishable, endless, timeless, everlasting, death-defying, unfading, never-ending, perennial, constant, ceaseless, indestructible, enduring; see also **eternal.**—*Ant.* mortal, perishable, corrupt. 2. [Illustrious] celebrated, eminent, glorious; see **famous.**

immortality, *n.* deathlessness, everlasting life, permanence, endlessness, timelessness, divinity, indestructibility, continuity, perpetuation, endless life, unlimited existence, perpetuity; see also **eternity.**—*Ant.* mortality, death, decease.

immovable, *a.* solid, stable, fixed; see **firm 1.**

immune, *a.* free, unaffected by, hardened to, unsusceptible, privileged, not liable, excused; see also **safe 1.**

immunity, *n.* 1. [Exemption] favor, privilege, license; see **freedom 2. 2.** [Freedom from disease] resistance, immunization, protection, active immunity, passive immunity; see also **safety 1.**

impact, *n.* shock, impression, contact; see **collision.**

impair, *v.* spoil, injure, hurt; see **break 2, damage, destroy.**

impart, *v.* 1. [To give] bestow, grant, present; see **allow, give 1.** 2. [To inform] tell, announce, divulge; see **admit 2, reveal.**

impartial, *a.* unbiased, unprejudiced, disinterested; see **equal, fair 1.**

impartiality, *n.* objectivity, candor, justice; see **equality, fairness.**

impasse, *n.* deadlock, standstill, cessation; see **pause.**

impatience, *n.* agitation, restlessness, anxiety; see **excitement, nervousness.**

impatient, *a.* anxious, eager, feverish; see **restless.**

impeach, *v.* criticize, charge, arraign, denounce, indict, discredit, reprimand, blame, incriminate, try, bring charges against, question; see also **blame.**—*Ant.* free, acquit, absolve.

impediment, *n.* 1. [An obstruction] hindrance, obstacle, difficulty; see **barrier.** 2. [An obstruction in speech] speech impediment *or* difficulty *or* block *or* trouble, stutter, stammer, lisp, halting, hairlip, cleft palate.

impending, *a.* in the offing, threatening, menacing; see **ominous.**

impenetrable, *a.* 1. [Dense] impervious, hard, compact; see **firm 2, thick 3.** 2. [Incomprehensible] unintelligible, inscrutable, unfathomable; see **obscure 1.**

imperative, *a.* 1. [Necessary] inescapable, immediate, crucial; see **important 1, necessary 1, urgent 1.** 2. [Authoritative] masterful, commanding, dominant; see **aggressive, powerful 1.**

imperfect, *a.* flawed, incomplete, deficient; see **faulty.**

imperfection, *n.* fault, flaw, stain; see **blemish.**

imperialism, *n.* empire, international domination, power politics; see **power 2.**

impersonal, *a.* detached, disinterested, cold; see **indifferent.**

impersonate, *v.* mimic, portray, act out, pose as, pass *or* double for, put on an act, pretend to be, act *or* take the part of, act a part, dress as, represent; see also **imitate 1.**

impersonation, *n.* imitation, role, enactment; see **performance.**

impertinence, *n.* impudence, insolence, disrespectfulness; see **rudeness.**

impertinent, *a.* saucy, insolent, impudent; see **rude 2.**

impervious, *a.* impenetrable, watertight, hermetic; see **tight 2.**

impetus, *n.* force, cause, stimulus; see **incentive, purpose 1, reason 3.**

impious, *a.* sinful, profane, blasphemous; see **bad 1.**

implant, *v.* stick in, insert, root; see **plant.**

implement, *n.* utensil, device, instrument; see **equipment, machine, tool 1.**

implicate, *v.* connect, cite, associate, tie up with, charge, link, catch up in, relate, compromise; see also **blame.**

implicated, *a.* under suspicion, suspected, known to have been associated (with); see **guilty, involved, suspicious 1, 2.**

implication, *n.* 1. [Assumption] reference, indication, inference; see **assumption 1, guess.** 2. [A link] connection, involvement, entanglement; see **joint 1, link, union 1.**

implicit, *a.* unquestionable, certain, absolute; see **accurate 2, definite 1, inevitable.**

implied, *a.* implicit, indicated, foreshadowed, involved, tacit, signified, figured, intended, meant, alluded to, latent, hidden, insinuated, hinted at, understood, symbolized, indicative, potential, indirectly meant, inferred, inferential, undeclared; see also **suggested.**

imply, *v.* 1. [To indicate] intimate, hint at, suggest; see **hint, mention, refer 2.** 2. [To mean] import, indicate, signify; see **intend 2, mean 1.**

impolite, *a.* discourteous, moody, churlish; see **irritable, rude 2, sullen.**

import, *v.* introduce, ship *or* carry *or* transport *or* ferry *or* truck *or* freight in, buy abroad; see **carry 1, send 2.**

importance, *n.* import, force, sense, consequence, bearing, denotation, gist, effect, distinction, influence, usefulness, moment, weightiness, momentousness, emphasis, standing, stress, accent, weight, concern, attention, interest, seriousness, point, substance, relevance, sum and substance; see also **meaning.**—*Ant.* insignificance, triviality, emptiness.

important, *a.* 1. [Weighty; *said usually of things*] significant, considerable, momentous, essential, great, decisive, critical, determining, chief, paramount, primary, foremost, principal, influential, marked, of great consequence, ponderous, of importance, never to be forgotten *or* overlooked, of note, valuable, crucial, substantial, vital, serious, grave, relevant, pressing, far-reaching, extensive, conspicuous, heavy, front-page, *big-league, *big; see also **necessary 1.**—*Ant.* trivial, inconsequential, unimportant. 2. [Eminent; *said usually of persons*] illustrious, well-known, influential; see **famous.** 3. [Relevant] material, influential, significant; see **fit 1, related 2, relevant.**

imported, *a.* shipped in, produced

abroad, exotic, alien; see also **foreign.—** *Ant.* **native,** domestic, made in America.

impose, *v.* force upon, compel, fix; see **force.**

impose on *or* **upon,** *v.* intrude, interrupt, presume; see **bother 2, disturb.**

imposing, *a.* stirring, exciting, overwhelming; see **impressive.**

imposition, *n.* demand, restraint, encumbrance; see **command, pressure 2.**

impossibility, *n.* hopelessness, impracticality, impracticability, difficulty, unlikelihood, failure, unworkability; see also **futility.**

impossible, *a.* inconceivable, vain, unachievable, unattainable, out of the question, too much (for), insurmountable, useless, inaccessible, unworkable, preposterous, unimaginable, unobtainable, not to be thought of, hardly possible, *like finding a needle in a haystack, *a hundred to one, out of the question; see also **futile, hopeless.—***Ant.* possible, likely, **reasonable.**

impostor, *n.* pretender, charlatan, quack; see **cheat.**

impotence, *n.* 1. [Sterility] unproductiveness, frigidity, infecundity; see **emptiness.** 2. [Weakness] inability, feebleness, infirmity; see **weakness 1.**

impotent, *a.* 1, [Weak] powerless, inept, infirm; see **unable, weak 1. 2.** [Sterile] barren, frigid, unproductive; see **sterile 1.**

impound, *v.* appropriate, take, usurp; see **seize 2.**

impounded, *a.* kept, seized, confiscated; see **held, retained 1.**

impoverish, *v.* make poor, bankrupt, exhaust; see **destroy.**

impoverished, *a.* poverty-stricken, bankrupt, *broke; see **poor 1, ruined 4.**

impractical, *a.* unreal, unrealistic, unworkable, improbable, illogical, unreasonable, absurd, wild, abstract, impossible, idealistic, unfeasible, out of the question.—*Ant.* practical, logical, reasonable.

impregnate, *v.* 1. [To permeate] fill up, pervade, overflow; see **fill 2, soak 1. 2.** [To beget] procreate, conceive, reproduce; see **fertilize 2.**

impregnated, *a.* 1. [Full] saturated, shot through and through, full of; see **full 1. 2.** [Pregnant] bred, *in a family way, with child; see **pregnant.**

impress, *v.* 1. [To make an impression] indent, emboss, imprint; see **dent, mark 1, print 2. 2.** [To attract attention] stand out, be conspicuous, cause a stir, create *or* make an impression, direct attention to, make an impact upon, engage the thoughts, engage attention,

be listened to, find favor with, *make a hit, make a dent in; see also **fascinate.**

impressed, *a.* aroused, awakened, awed; see **affected 1, excited.**

impression, *n.* 1. [An imprint] print, footprint, fingerprint, dent, mold, indentation, depression, cast, form, track, pattern; see also **mark 1. 2.** [An effect] response, consequence, reaction; see **result. 3.** [A notion based on scanty evidence] theory, conjecture, supposition; see **guess, opinion 1.**

impressionable, *a.* perceptive, impressible, receptive; see **affected 1.**

impressive, *a.* stirring, moving, inspiring, effective, affecting, eloquent, impassioned, thrilling, excited, intense, well-done, dramatic, absorbing, deep, profound, penetrating, remarkable, extraordinary, notable, important, momentous, vital; see also **profound.—***Ant.* **dull,** uninteresting, common.

imprint, *n.* 1. [A printed identification] firm name, banner, trademark, direction, heading; see **emblem, signature. 2.** [An impression] dent, indentation, print; see **mark 1.**

imprint, *v.* print, stamp, designate; see **mark 1, 2.**

imprison, *v.* jail, lock *or* bottle up, confine, incarcerate, immure, impound, detain, keep (in), hold, intern, shut *or* lock *or* box *or* fence in, cage, send to prison, keep as captive, hold captive *or* as hostage, enclose, keep in custody, put behind bars, *put away, send up.—*Ant.* free, liberate, release.

imprisoned, *a.* arrested, jailed, incarcerated; see **confined 3.**

imprisonment, *n.* captivity, isolation, incarceration, duress, bondage; see also **confinement.—***Ant.* freedom, liberty, enlargement.

improbable, *a.* not likely, doubtful, not to be expected; see **unlikely.**

improper, *a.* at odds, ill-advised, unsuited, incongruous, out of place, ludicrous, incorrect, preposterous, unwarranted, undue, imprudent, abnormal, irregular, inexpedient, unseasonable, inadvisable, untimely, inopportune, unfit, malapropos, unfitting, inappropriate, unbefitting, ill-timed, awkward, inharmonious, inapplicable, odd; see also **unsuitable.**

improperly, *a.* poorly, inappropriately, clumsily; see **awkwardly, badly 1, inadequately.**

improve, *v.* 1. [To make better] mend, update, refine; see also **change 1, repair. 2.** [To become better] regenerate, advance, progress, renew, enrich, enhance, augment, gain strength, develop, get *or* grow better, grow, make progress, widen, increase, mellow, mature, come *or* get along *or* on, look up, *shape *or* pick *or* perk up, come around, make headway, *snap out of; see also **change 2**, **recover 3**.—*Ant.* weaken, worsen, grow worse.

improved, *a.* corrected, bettered, amended, mended, reformed, elaborated, refined, modernized, brought up-to-date, enhanced, repaired, bolstered up, rectified, remodeled, reorganized, made over, better for, *doctored up, *polished up; see also **changed 2**.

improvement, *n.* 1. [The process of becoming better] amelioration, betterment, rectification, change, alteration, reformation, progression, advance, advancement, development, growth, rise, civilization, gain, cultivation, increase, enrichment, promotion, elevation, recovery, regeneration, renovation, reorganization, amendment, reform, revision, elaboration, refinement, modernization, enhancement, remodeling.—*Ant.* decay, deterioration, retrogression. 2. [That which has been improved] addition, supplement, repair, extra, attachment, correction, reform, remodeling, repairing, refinement, luxury, advance, latest thing, last word; see also **change 1**.

improve *on or* **upon**, *v.* make better, develop, refine; see **correct**, **repair**.

improving, *a.* reconstructing, repairing, elaborating, bettering, correcting, developing, fixing, remodeling, on the mend.

impudence, *n.* insolence, impertinence, effrontery; see **rudeness**.

impudent, *a.* forward, insolent, shameless; see **rude 2**.

impulse, *n.* 1. [A throb] surge, pulse, pulsation; see **beat 2**. 2. [A sudden urge] fancy, whim, caprice, motive, motivation, spontaneity, drive, appeal, notion, inclination, disposition, wish, whimsy, inspiration, hunch, flash, thought.

impulsive, *a.* offhand, unpremeditated, extemporaneous; see **automatic**, **spontaneous**.

impulsively, *a.* imprudently, hastily, abruptly; see **carelessly**, **rashly**.

impure, *a.* 1. [Adulterated] not pure, loaded, weighted, salted, diluted, debased, contaminated, mixed, watered (down), polluted, corrupted, raw, tainted, cut, adulterated, *doctored, tampered with; see also **unclean**. 2. [Not chaste] unclean, unchaste, corrupt; see **bad 1**, **lewd 2**.

impurity, *n.* 1. [Lewdness] indecency, profligacy, pornography; see **lewdness**. 2. [Filth] dirt, defilement, excrement; see **filth**, **pollution 1**.

in, *prep.* 1. [Within] surrounded by, in the midst of, within the boundaries of, in the area of, within the time of, concerning the subject of, as a part of, inside of, enclosed in, not out of; see also **within**. 2. [Into] to the center *or* midst of, in the direction of, within the extent of, under, near, against; see also **into**, **toward**. 3. [While engaged in] in the act of, during the process of, while occupied with; see **during**, **meanwhile**, **while** 1. —*have it in for, wish to harm, be out to destroy, detest; see **hate 1**.

inability, *n.* 1. [Lack of competence] incapacity, incompetence, shortcoming; see **failure 1**, **weakness 1**. 2. [A temporary lack] disability, failure, frailty; see **lack 2**, **necessity 2**.

inaccessible, *a.* unobtainable, unworkable, out of reach; see **away 1**, **beyond**, **difficult 2**, **distant**, **rare 2**, **remote 1**, **separated**.

inaccuracy, *n.* exaggeration, mistake, deception; see **error**.

inaccurate, *a.* fallacious, in error, incorrect; see **mistaken 1**, **wrong 2**.

inactive, *a.* dormant, stable, still; see **idle**, **motionless**.

inadequacy, *n.* 1. [Inferiority] ineptitude, incompetence, insufficiency; see **weakness 1**. 2. [A defect] flaw, drawback, shortcoming; see **blemish**, **defect**, **lack 2**.

inadequate, *a.* lacking, scanty, short, meager, failing, unequal, not enough, sparing, stinted, stunted, feeble, sparse, (too) little, small, thin, deficient, incomplete, inconsiderable, spare, bare, niggardly, miserly, scarce, barren, depleted, low, weak, impotent, unproductive, dry, sterile, imperfect, defective, lame; *skimpy; see also **unsatisfactory**.—*Ant.* **enough**, adequate, sufficent.

inadequately, *a.* insufficiently, not enough, partly, partially, incompletely, scantily, deficiently, perfunctorily, ineffectively, inefficiently, ineptly, not up to standard(s) *or* specifications *or* requirements, meagerly, not in sufficient quantity *or* quality, in a limited manner, to a limited degree, *not up to snuff; see also **badly 1**.

in advance, *a.* ahead (of), earlier, in time; see **before**.

inadvisable, *a.* unsuitable, inappropriate, inconvenient; see **improper 1**, **wrong 2**.

inadvisedly, *a.* impulsively, regrettably, unwisely; see **foolishly**, **rashly**.

in all respects, *a.* entirely, altogether, totally; see **completely**.

in a minute, *a.* before long, shortly, presently; see **soon 1**.

in and about *or* around, *a.* close to, there, approximately; see **about 2**, **near 1**.

inane, *a.* pointless, foolish, ridiculous; see **illogical, silly, stupid 1.**

inanimate, *a.* dull, inert, inoperative; see **idle, motionless 1.**

in any case, *a.* regardless, nonetheless, no matter what; see **anyhow.**

in a pinch, *a.* in an emergency, if necessary, under pressure; see also **in trouble.**

inappropriate, *a.* improper, irrelevant, inapplicable; see **unsuitable.**

inarticulate, *a.* 1. [Mute] reticent, wordless, mute; see **dumb 1.** 2. [Indistinct] unintelligible, inaudible, vague; see **obscure 1.**

inasmuch as, *conj.* in view of (the fact that), making allowance for (the fact that), while; see **because, since 1.**

inattentive, *a.* preoccupied, indifferent, negligent; see **careless, diverted.**

inaudible, *a.* low, indistinct, silent; see **obscure 1, vague.**

inaugurate, *v.* introduce, initiate, originate; see **begin 1.**

inauguration, *n.* initiation, commencement, installment; see **installation 1.**

inborn, *a.* essential, intrinsic, inbred; see **native 1.**

in brief, *a.* concisely, to the point, cut short, abbreviated; see also **briefly.**

incalculable, *a.* unpredictable, unforeseen, unfixed; see **uncertain 2.**

incandescent, *a.* radiant, glowing, brilliant; see **bright 1.**

incapable, *a.* unsuited, poor, inadequate; see **incompetent, inexperienced, naive.**

incapable of, *a.* ineffective, inadequate, unsuited; see **incompetent.**

incapacity, *n.* inadequacy, insufficiency, uselessness; see **weakness 1.**

in case, *a.* in the event that, provided, if it should happen (that); see **if.**

in case of, *a.* in the event of, in order to be prepared for, as a provision against; see **if.**

incense, *n.* scent, fragrance, essence; see **perfume.**

incentive, *n.* spur, inducement, motive, stimulus, stimulation, impetus, provocation, enticement, temptation, bait, consideration, excuse, rationale, urge, influence, lure, persuasion, inspiration, encouragement, insistence, instigation, incitement, reason why; see also **purpose 1.**

incessant, *a.* ceaseless, continuous, monotonous; see **constant.**

incessantly, *a.* steadily, monotonously, perpetually; see **regularly.**

inch, *n.* 1. [Twelfth of a foot] fingerbreadth, measurement, 1/36 yard; see **measure 1.** 2. [Small degree] jot, little bit, iota; see **bit 2.** —**every inch,** in all

respects, thoroughly, entirely; see **completely.** —**by inches,** slowly, by degrees, step by step; see **gradually.**

inch, *v.* creep, barely move, make some progress; see **crawl.**

incident, *n.* episode, happening, occurrence; see **event.**

incidental, *a.* subsidiary, relative to, contributing to; see **related 2, subordinate.**

incidentally, *a.* subordinately, by chance, by the way, as a side effect, as a by-product, unexpectedly, not by design, remotely; see also **accidentally.**

incidentals, *n.* (minor) needs *or* requirements *or* necessities, incidental expenses, per diem; see **expenses, necessity 2.**

incinerate, *v.* cremate, parch, burn up; see **burn.**

incise, *v.* dissect, chop, split; see **cut 1, divide.**

incision, *n.* gash, slash, surgery; see **cut 1, hole 1.**

incite, *v.* arouse, rouse, impel, stimulate, instigate, provoke, excite, spur, goad (on), persuade, influence, induce, taunt, activate, animate, inspirit, coax, stir up, motivate, prompt, urge on, inspire, force, *work up, *talk into, whip *or* egg on, *fan the flame; see also **urge 2.—***Ant.* discourage, dissuade, check.

incited, *a.* driven, pushed, motivated; see **urged 2.**

inclination, *n.* 1. [A tendency] bias, bent, propensity, predilection, penchant, attachment, capability, capacity, aptness, leaning, fondness, disposition, liking, preference, movement, susceptibility, weakness, drift, trend, turn, slant, impulse, attraction, affection, desire, temperament, whim, idiosyncrasy, urge, persuasion. 2. [A slant] pitch, slope, incline, angle, ramp, bank, lean, list; see also **grade 1.**

incline, *n.* slope, inclined plane, approach; see **grade 1, inclination 2.**

incline, *v.* 1. [To lean] bow, nod, cock; see **lean 1.** 2. [To tend toward] prefer, be disposed, be predisposed; see **favor 1.**

inclined, *a.* prone, slanted, willing; see **likely 4.**

include, *v.* 1. [To contain] hold, admit, cover, embrace, involve, consist of, take in, entail, incorporate, constitute, accommodate, be comprised *or* composed of, embody, be made up of, number among, carry, bear; see also **compose 1.—***Ant.* omit, bar, stand outside of. 2. [To place into or among] enter, introduce, take in, incorporate, make room for, build, work in, inject, interject, add on, insert, combine, make a part of, make allowance for, give consideration to, count in.—*Ant.* **discard**, exclude, reject.

included, *a.* counted, numbered, admitted, covered, involved, constituted, embodied, inserted, entered, incorporated, combined, placed, fused, merged; see also **within**.—*Ant.* excluded, left out, refused.

including, *a.* together *or* along *or* coupled with, as well as, in conjunction with, not to mention, to say nothing of, among other things, with the addition of, in addition to, counting, made up of; see also **plus**.—*Ant.* **besides**, not counting, aside from.

incoherence, *n.* disagreement, dissimilarity, incongruity; see **inconsistency**.

incoherent, *a.* mumbling, stammering, confused, speechless, puzzling, indistinct, faltering, stuttering, unintelligible, muttered, mumbled, jumbled, gasping, breathless, disconnected, tongue-tied, muffled, indistinguishable, incomprehensible, muddled.—*Ant.* clear, eloquent, distinct.

incoherently, *a.* frantically, drunkenly, confusedly, spasmodically, chaotically, randomly, ineptly, unsystematically, aimlessly, casually, sloppily, ambiguously, equivocally, illegibly, incomprehensibly, unrecognizably, uncertainly, inaudibly; see also **wildly**.

in cold blood, *a.* heartlessly, ruthlessly, unmercifully; see **brutally**.

income, *n.* earnings, salary, wages, returns, profit, dividends, assets, proceeds, benefits, receipts, gains, commission, drawings, rent, royalty, honorarium, net income, gross income, taxable income, cash, take; see also **pay** 2.—*Ant.* expense, expenditures, outgo.

incomparable, *a.* unequaled, exceptional, superior; see **excellent**, **perfect**.

incompatibility, *n.* variance, conflict, animosity; see **disagreement** 1.

incompatible, *a.* inconsistent, contrary, clashing, inappropriate, contradictory, disagreeing, inconstant, unadapted, opposite, jarring, discordant, incoherent, inadmissible; see also **opposed**, **unsuitable**.

incompetence, *n.* inadequacy, inexperience, worthlessness; see **weakness** 1.

incompetent, *a.* incapable, inefficient, unskillful, not qualified, inadequate, unfit, unskilled, bungling, inexpert, ineffectual, unsuitable, untrained, clumsy, awkward, uninitiated, raw, inexperienced, unadapted, not equal to, amateurish; see also **unable**.—*Ant.* able, fit, qualified.

in competition with, *a.* opposed to, competing, against; see **opposed**.

incomplete, *a.* rough, half-done, under construction; see **unfinished** 1.

inconceivable, *a.* fantastic, unimaginable, incredible; see **impossible**.

inconclusive, *a.* indecisive, deficient, lacking; see **faulty**, **inadequate**, **unsatisfactory**.

in condition, *a.* physically fit, conditioned, *in the pink; see **healthy**, **strong** 1.

incongruous, *a.* uncoordinated, unconnected, contradictory; see **illogical**, **unsuitable**.

in consequence of, *a.* because of, owing to, consequently; see **because**.

inconsequential, *a.* unimportant, immaterial, insignificant; see **irrelevant**, **trivial**, **unnecessary**.

inconsiderate, *a.* boorish, impolite, discourteous; see **rude** 2, **thoughtless** 2.

inconsistency, *n.* discrepancy, disagreement, dissimilarity, disparity, variance, incongruity, inequality, divergence, deviation, disproportion, paradox; see also **difference** 1.—*Ant.* consistency, congruity, similarity.

inconsistent, *a.* contradictory, illogical, incoherent; see **illogical**.

inconspicuous, *a.* concealed, indistinct, retiring; see **hidden**, **obscure** 1, 3, **secretive**.

inconspicuously, *a.* slyly, surreptitiously, not openly *or* noticeably; see **slyly**.

in contact with, *a.* 1. [Contiguous] meeting, joining, connecting, bordering, adjacent, close; see also **near** 1.—*Ant.* distant, out of contact, far. 2. [Communicating with] in touch (with), writing (to), corresponding (with), in communication.

in contrast to *or* **with**, *a.* as against, opposed to, contrasting; see **against** 1, **opposed**.

inconvenience, *n.* bother, trouble, awkward detail; see **difficulty** 1.

inconvenient, *a.* bothersome, awkward, badly arranged; see **disturbing**.

in cooperation (with), *a.* cooperating, collaborating, assisting; see **helping**.

incorporate, *v.* add to, combine, fuse; see **include** 2, **join** 1.

incorporated, *a.* entered, placed, fused; see **included**, **joined**.

incorporation, *n.* embodiment, adding, fusion; see **addition** 1.

incorrect, *a.* inaccurate, not trustworthy, false; see **mistaken** 1, **unreliable** 1, **wrong** 2.

incorrectly, *a.* mistakenly, inaccurately, clumsily; see **badly** 1, **wrongly** 1, 2.

increase, *n.* development, spread, enlargement, expansion, escalation, elaboration, swelling, addition, incorporation, merger, inflation, heightening, extension, dilation, multiplication, rise, broadening, advance, intensification, deepening, swell, amplification, progression, improvement, boost, *hike, jump, boom; see also **progress** 1.—*Ant.* **reduction**, decline, decrease. —**on the increase,** growing, developing, spreading; see **increasing.**

increase, *v.* extend, enlarge, expand, dilate, broaden, widen, thicken, deepen, heighten, build, lengthen, magnify, add on, augment, escalate, let out, branch *or* open out, further, mark up, sharpen, build up, raise, enhance, amplify, reinforce, supplement, annex, double, triple, stretch, multiply, intensify, exaggerate, prolong, redouble, boost, step up, *rev up.—*Ant.* decrease, reduce, abridge.

increased, *a.* marked up, raised, heightened, elevated, added on, doubled.

increasing, *a.* developing, maturing, multiplying, broadening, widening, intensifying, heightening, growing, dominant, advancing, growing louder, sharpening, accentuating, aggravating, emphasizing, accelerating, deepening, flourishing, rising, expanding, enlarging, accumulating, piling up, shooting up, getting big, swelling, on the rise, on the increase, booming; see also **growing.**

increasingly, *a.* with (continual) acceleration, more and more, with (steady) increase *or* build-up; see **more** 1, 2.

incredible, *a.* unbelievable, improbable, ridiculous; see **impossible.**

incriminate, *v.* implicate, blame, charge; see **implicate.**

incriminating, *a.* damning, damaging, accusatory; see **suspicious** 2.

incurable, *a.* fatal, serious, hopeless; see **deadly.**

in danger, *a.* imperiled, threatened, in jeopardy; see **endangered.**

indebted, *a.* obligated, grateful, appreciative; see **responsible** 1, **thankful.**

indebtedness, *n.* deficit, responsibility, obligation; see **debt.**

indecency, *n.* impurity, immodesty, vulgarity, impropriety, obscenity, raciness, four-letter word, lewdness, foulness; see also **evil** 1.—*Ant.* **chastity**, purity, delicacy.

indecent, *a.* immoral, shocking, shameless; see **bad** 1, **lewd** 2, **shameful** 1, 2.

indecision, *n.* hesitation, question, irresolution; see **doubt, uncertainty** 2.

indecisive, *a.* irresolute, unstable, *wishy-washy; see **doubtful.**

indeed, *a.* 1. [Surely] naturally, of course, certainly; see **really** 1, **surely.** 2. [Really] For sure? Honestly? So?; see **oh.**

indefensible, *a.* bad, unforgivable, unpardonable; see **wrong** 1.

indefinite, *a.* unsure, unsettled, loose; see **uncertain** 2, **vague** 2.

indefinitely, *a.* 1. [Vaguely] loosely, unclearly, ambiguously, indistinctly, incoherently, obscurely, indecisively, incompletely, lightly, briefly, momentarily, generally; see also **vaguely.**—*Ant.* **positively,** clearly, exactly. 2. [Without stated limit] endlessly, continually, considerably; see **frequently** 1, **regularly.**

indelible, *a.* ingrained, enduring, strong; see **permanent** 2.

in demand, *a.* desired, requisite, on the market; see **wanted.**

indent, *v.* make a margin, range, space inward; see **order** 3.

indentation, *n.* imprint, recession, depression; see **dent.**

independence, *n.* sovereignty, autonomy, license; see **freedom** 2.

independent, *a.* self-ruling, autonomous, unregimented; see **free** 1.

independently, *a.* alone, autonomously, unilaterally, without support, separately, exclusive of, without regard to, by oneself, *on one's own; see also **freely** 2.

indestructible, *a.* durable, unchangeable, immortal; see **permanent** 2.

in detail, *a.* minutely, item by item, part by part, step by step, inch by inch, systematically, intimately.—*Ant.* **vaguely,** generally, indefinitely.

index, *n.* 1. [An indicator] formula, rule, average (rate *or* price); see **model** 2. 2. [An alphabetic arrangement] tabular matter, book index, guide to publications, bibliography, bibliographical work, card file, book list, appendix, end list, directory, dictionary; see also **file** 1, **list, record** 1.

index, *v.* alphabetize, arrange, tabulate; see **file** 1, **list** 1, **record** 1.

India, *n.* The Indian Empire, Southern Asia, The Orient, The East, The Fabulous East, British India, Crown Jewel, Mother India, Hindustan; see also **Asia.**

Indian, *a.* native American, pre-Columbian, Amerindian; see **Indian,** *n.* 1.

Indian, *n.* 1. [American native] American aborigine, American Indian, Amerindian, red man. Terms for Indian groups having had historical or social importance include the following—*United States and Canada: Arctic Indians*: Eskimo, Aleut; *eastern or Woods Indians*: Iroquois *or* Six Nations, Mohawk, Oneida, Seneca, Cayuga, Huron, Algonkin, Mohican, Delaware, Ojibway *or* Chippewa, Sauk, Fox, Pottawattamic, Seminole, Chérokee, Choctaw, Chicasaw, Creek, Natchez, Winnebago; *Plains Indians*:

Sioux, Oglala, Mandan, Iowa, Omaha, Comanche, Dakota, Crow, Osage, Apache, Kiowa, Arapahoe, Cheyenne, Pawnee; *Great Basin Indians*: Blackfoot, Ute, Paiute, Shoshone, Bannock, Modoc, Digger, Pueblo, Hopi, Navaho, Zuni; *west coast Indians*; Athabascan, Costanoa, Chinook, Nez Perce, Tlingit, Flathead, Kwakiutl, Bella Coola, Klamath, Luiseno, Pomo; *Mexico and Central America*: Maya, Aztec, Toltec, Nahuatl, Zacateca, Quiche; *South America*: Inca, Quechua, Carib, Tupi, Arawak. 2. [A native of India] Hindu, Muslim, Brahmin; see **Oriental**.

indicate, *v.* 1. [To signify] symbolize, betoken, intimate; see **mean 1.** 2. [To designate] show, point out *or* to, register; see **name 2**.

indication, *n.* evidence, sign, implication; see **hint, suggestion 1**.

indicator, *n.* notice, pointer, symbol; see **sign 1**.

indict, *v.* charge, face with charges, arraign; see **blame**.

indictment, *n.* detention, censure, incrimination; see **blame**.

indifference, *n.* unconcern, nonchalance, aloofness, coldness, insensitivity, callousness, alienation, disregard, neutrality, isolationism, heedlessness, detachment, dullness, sluggishness, stupor, coldbloodedness, disdain, *cool.

indifferent, *a.* listless, cold, cool, unemotional, unsympathetic, heartless, unresponsive, unfeeling, uncommunicative, nonchalant, impassive, detached, callous, uninterested, stony, reticent, remote, reserved, distant, unsocial, scornful, apathetic, heedless, unmoved, not inclined toward, neutral, uncaring, aloof, silent, disdainful, haughty, superior, condescending, snobbish, arrogant, not caring (about); see also **unmoved 2**.—*Ant.* excited, aroused, warm.

indifferently, *a.* 1. [Rather badly] poorly, not (very) well (done), in a mediocre *or* ordinary *or* routine manner; see **badly 1, inadequately**. 2. [In an indifferent manner] nonchalantly, coolly, detached; see **calmly**.

indigestible, *a.* inedible, rough, hard, unripe, green, tasteless, unhealthy, undercooked, raw, poisonous, toxic, moldy, bad-smelling, rotten, uneatable—*Ant.* appetizing, tasty, **delicious**.

indigestion, *n.* heartburn, nausea, acid indigestion; see **illness 1, pain 2**.

indignant, *a.* upset, displeased, piqued; see **angry**.

indirect, *a.* roundabout, out-of-the-way, tortuous, twisting, long, complicated, devious, erratic, sidelong, zigzag,

crooked, backhanded, obscure, sinister, rambling, long-winded, secondary, implied, oblique.—*Ant.* **direct**, straight, immediate.

indirectly, *a.* by implication *or* indirection, in a roundabout way, from a secondary source, secondhand, not immediately, discursively, obliquely.—*Ant.* **immediately**, directly, primarily.

indiscreet, *a.* naïve, inopportune, misguided; see **rash, tactless**.

indiscretion, *n.* recklessness, tactlessness, rashness; see **carelessness**.

indiscriminate, *a.* random, confused, chaotic; see **aimless**.

indispensable, *a.* required, needed, essential; see **necessary 1**.

indisputable, *a.* undeniable, undoubted, unquestionable; see **certain 2**.

indistinct, *a.* vague, confused, indefinite; see **obscure 1**.

indistinguishable, *a.* 1. [Identical] like, same, equivalent; see **alike, equal**. 2. [Indistinct] vague, invisible, dull; see **obscure 1, uncertain 2**.

individual, *a.* specific, personal, special, proper, own, particular, definite, lone, alone, solitary, secluded, original, distinct, distinctive, personalized, individualized, exclusive, select, single, only, reserved, separate, sole; see also **private, special 1**.—*Ant.* collective, **public**, social.

individual, *n.* human being, self, somebody; see **child, man 2, person 1, woman 1**.

individuality, *n.* peculiarity, distinctiveness, particularity, separateness, dissimilarity, singularity, idiosyncrasy, air, manner, habit, eccentricity, oddity, rarity, way of doing things; see also **originality**.

individually, *a.* separately, severally, one by one, one at a time, personally, exclusively, singly, by oneself, alone, independently, without help, distinctively, apart; see also **only 1**.—*Ant.* **together**, collectively, co-operatively.

indoctrinate, *v.* inculcate, imbue, implant; see **convince, influence, teach**.

indoctrination, *n.* propagandism, instruction, brainwashing; see **education 1, training**.

indoors, *a.* in the house, at home, under a roof; see **inside 2, within**.

in doubt, *a.* unsure, dubious, perplexed; see **doubtful, questionable 1, uncertain 2**.

induce, *v.* produce, effect, make; see **begin 1**.

induced, *a.* 1. [Brought about] effected, achieved, caused; see **finished 1.** 2. [Inferred] thought, concluded, reasoned; see **assumed, considered, determined 1**.

induct, v. conscript, initiate, draft; see **enlist 1, recruit 1.**

inducted, a. conscripted, called up, drafted; see **initiated 2.**

induction, n. 1. [Logical reasoning] inference, rationalization, generalization, conclusion, judgment, conjecture; see also **reason 2.** 2. [The process of electrical attraction] electric induction, magnetic induction, electromagnetic action; see **electricity. 3.** [The process of being initiated] initiation, introduction, ordination, consecration, entrance into service.

in due time, a. eventually, at an appropriate time, in the natural course of events; see **finally 2, ultimately.**

indulge, v. 1. [To humor] tickle, nourish, coddle; see **entertain 1, humor. 2.** [To take part in] go in for, revel, give way to; see **join 2.**

indulgence, n. 1. [Humoring] coddling, pampering, petting, fondling, babying, spoiling, placating, pleasing, toadying, favoring, kowtowing, gratifying. 2. [Revelry] intemperance, overindulgence, self-indulgence; see **greed, waste 1.**

indulgent, a. fond, considerate, tolerant; see **kind.**

industrial, a. manufacturing, manufactured, mechanized, automated, industrialized, factory-made, machine-made, modern, streamlined, in industry, technical; see also **mechanical 1.—Ant.** handmade, domestic, **homemade.**

industrious, a. intent, involved, diligent; see **active, busy 1.**

industriously, a. diligently, energetically, busily; see **carefully 1, vigorously.**

industry, n. 1. [Attention to work] activity, persistence, application, patience, intentness, perseverance, enterprise, hard work, zeal, energy, dynamism, pains, inventiveness; see also **attention.—Ant.** laziness, lethargy, idleness. 2. [Business as a division of society] big business, management, corporation officers, shareholders, high finance, entrepreneurs, capital, private enterprise, monied interests, stockholders.

inebriated, a. intoxicated, tipsy, *plastered; see **drunk.**

in effect, a. in reality, in fact, absolutely; see **really 1.**

ineffective, a. not effective, worthless, neutralized; see **incompetent, weak 1, 2.**

inefficiency, n. incompetence, incapability, incapacity; see **failure 1, weakness 1.**

inefficient, a. extravagant, prodigal, improvident; see **wasteful.**

ineligible, a. inappropriate, unavailable, unsuitable; see **incompetent, unfit.**

inept, a. clumsy, gauche, ungraceful; see **awkward.**

inequality, n. disparity, dissimilarity, irregularity; see **contrast, difference 1, variation 2.**

in error, a. mistaken(ly), inaccurate(ly), by mistake; see **badly 1, wrong 2, wrongly 1.**

inert, a. still, dormant, inactive; see **idle.**

inertia, n. passivity, indolence, inactivity; see **laziness.**

in essence, a. ultimately, fundamentally, basically; see **essentially.**

inevitable, a. fated, sure, unavoidable, impending, inescapable, necessary, unpreventable, irresistible, destined, assured, unalterable, compulsory, obligatory, binding, irrevocable, inexorable, without fail, undeniable, fateful, doomed, determined, decreed, fixed, ordained, foreordained, decided, *sure as shooting, in the cards, *come rain or shine.—Ant. doubtful, contingent, indeterminate.

inevitably, a. unavoidably, inescapably, surely; see **necessarily.**

inexcusable, a. unpardonable, reprehensible, indefensible; see **wrong 1.**

inexpensive, a. thrifty, low-priced, modest; see **cheap 1, economical 2.**

inexperience, n. naïveté, inability, incompetence; see **ignorance.**

inexperienced, a. unused, unaccustomed, unadapted, unskilled, common, ordinary, unlicensed, untried, youthful, undeveloped, naïve, amateur, untrained, untutored, inefficient, fresh, ignorant, innocent, uninformed, unacquainted, undisciplined, new, immature, tender, not dry behind the ears, soft, raw, green.—Ant. experienced, seasoned, hardened.

in fact, a. certainly, in truth, truly; see **really 1.**

infallibility, n. supremacy, impeccability, consummation; see **perfection.**

infallible, a. perfect, reliable, unquestionable; see **accurate 1, 2, certain 3.**

infamous, a. shocking, disgraceful, heinous; see **offensive 2, shameful 2.**

infancy, n. cradle, babyhood, early childhood; see **childhood.**

infant, n. small child, tot, little one; see **baby, child.**

infantile, a. babyish, childlike, juvenile; see **childish, naïve.**

infantry, n. foot soldiers, infantrymen, combat troops; see **army 1, 2.**

in fashion, a. stylish, modish, à la mode; see **fashionable, popular 1.**

in favor, favored, feted, honored; see **approved, popular 1.**

in favor of, a. approving, supporting, encouraging; see **enthusiastic.**

infect, v. defile, taint, spoil; see **poison.**

infection, n. 1. [The spread of a disease]

contagion, communicability, epidemic; see **catching**, a. 2. [Disease] virus, impurity, germs; see **germ**.

infectious, a. transferable, diseased, communicable; see **catching**, **contagious**, **dangerous**.

infer, v. deduce, gather, come or reach the conclusion that; see **assume**, **understand** 1.

inference, n. deduction, conclusion, answer; see **judgment** 3, **result**.

inferior, a. mediocre, common, second-rate; see **poor** 2.

inferiority, n. deficiency, mediocrity, inadequacy; see **failure** 1, **weakness** 1.

infest, v. 1. [To contaminate] pollute, infect, defile; see **corrupt**, **dirty**. 2. [To swarm] overrun, swarm about, crowd, press, harass, jam, pack, teem, fill, flood, throng, flock, *be thick as flies; see also **swarm**.

infested, a. 1. [Overrun] swarming or thick with, full of, overwhelmed; see **full** 1. 2. [Diseased] wormy, lousy, grubby; see **sick**.

infielder, n. first baseman or first, second baseman or second, third baseman or third; see **baseball player**.

infiltrate, v. permeate, pervade, penetrate; see **join** 2.

infinite, a. unlimited, incalculable, boundless, unconfined, countless, interminable, measureless, inexhaustible, bottomless, unfathomable, without number or end or limit, limitless, tremendous, immense, having no limit or end, never-ending, immeasurable; see also **endless**, **unlimited**.—*Ant.* limited, bounded, restricted.

infinite, n. boundlessness, infinity, the unknown; see **eternity**, **space** 1.

infinitely, a. extremely, very much, unbelievably; see **very**.

infinity, n. boundlessness, endlessness, the beyond, limitlessness, expanse, extent, continuum, continuity, infinite space; see also **space** 1.

infirmary, n. clinic, sickroom, sick bay; see **hospital**.

infirmity, n. frailty, deficiency, debility; see **weakness** 1.

inflame, v. 1. [To arouse emotions] incense, aggravate, disturb; see **excite**. 2. [To cause physical soreness] redden, break into a rash, swell; see **hurt** 1. 3. [To burn] kindle, set on fire, scorch; see **burn**, **ignite**.

inflamed, a. 1. [Stirred to anger] aroused, incited, angered; see **angry**. 2. [Congested] raw, blistered, swollen; see **hurt**, **painful** 1, **sore** 1.

inflammable, a. combustible, burnable, liable to burn, risky, hazardous, dangerous, unsafe, flammable.—*Ant.* safe, fireproof, non-flammable.

inflammation, n. congestion, soreness, infection; see **pain** 2, **sore**.

inflate, v. 1. [To fill with air or gas] blow or pump or puff out or up, expand, swell; see **fill** 1. 2. [To distend] exaggerate, bloat, cram, expand, balloon, swell up, widen, augment, spread out, enlarge, magnify, exalt, build up, raise, maximize, overestimate; see also **stretch** 1, **swell**.

inflated, a. distended, swollen, extended, puffed, filled, grown, stretched, spread, enlarged, amplified, augmented, pumped up, exaggerated, bloated, crammed, magnified, overestimated, bombastic, flatulent, pretentious, pompous, verbose.—*Ant.* reduced, deflated, minimized.

inflation, n. 1. [Increase] expansion, extension, build-up; see **increase**. 2. [General rise in price levels] financial crisis, inflationary pattern or trend or cycle, move toward higher price levels or structures; see **rise** 3.

inflection, n. pronunciation, enunciation, intonation; see **accent**, **sound** 2.

inflexibility, n. stability, toughness, rigidity, stiffness, petrifaction, fossilization, glaciation, crystallization; see also **firmness**.

inflexible, a. rigid, hardened, taut; see **firm** 2, **stiff** 1.

inflict, v. deliver, strike, do to; see **cause**.

influence, n. control, weight, authority, supremacy, command, domination, esteem, (political) influence, monopoly, rule, fame, prominence, prestige, character, reputation, force, importance, money, *power behind the throne, *clout; see **leadership**, **power** 2.

influence, v. sway, affect, impress, carry weight, count, be influential, determine, make oneself felt, have influence over, lead to believe, bring (pressure) to bear, bribe, seduce, talk (one) into, alter, change, act upon or on, lead, brainwash, direct, modify, regulate, rule, compel, urge, incite, bias, prejudice, train, channel, mold, form, shape, carry weight, exercise or exert influence, get at, be recognized, induce, convince, persuade, motivate, *have an in, pull strings, *have a finger in the pie, lead by the nose.

influenced, a. changed, swayed, persuaded; see **affected** 1.

influential, a. prominent, substantial, powerful; see **famous**.

influx, n. introduction, penetration, coming in; see **entrance** 1.

inform, v. instruct, relate, teach; see **tell** 1.

informal, a. intimate, relaxed, frank, open, straightforward, ordinary, every-

informality, n. casualness, familiarity, ease; see **comfort 1**.

information, n. 1. [Derived knowledge] acquired facts, evidence, knowledge, reports, details, results, notes, documents, testimony, facts, figures, statistics, measurements, conclusions, deductions, plans, field or laboratory notes, learning, erudition; see also **knowledge 1**. 2. [News] report, notice, message; see **news 1, 2**.

informative, a. instructive, informing, advisory; see **detailed**.

informed, a. versed, knowledgeable, well-read; see **educated, learned 1**.

infrequent, a. sparse, occasional, scarce; see **rare 2**.

infrequently, a. occasionally, rarely, hardly ever; see **seldom**.

infringe, v. transgress, violate, trespass; see **meddle 1**.

in full, a. complete, entire, inclusive; see **whole 1**.

in full measure, a. completely, sufficiently, amply; see **adequately**.

infuriate, v. aggravate, enrage, provoke; see **anger**.

infuriated, a. furious, enraged, incensed; see **angry**.

in general, a. on the whole, usually, generally; see **regularly**.

ingenious, a. original, skillful, gifted; see **able, intelligent**.

ingenuity, n. inventiveness, imagination, productiveness; see **originality**.

ingrain, v. imbue, fix, instill; see **teach**.

ingrained, a. congenital, inborn, indelible; see **native 1**.

ingratitude, n. thanklessness, ungratefulness, callousness, boorishness, disloyalty, lack of appreciation, inconsiderateness, thoughtlessness; see also **rudeness**.—*Ant.* gratitude, appreciation, consideration.

ingredient, n. constituent, component, element; see **fundamental**.

ingredients, n. parts, elements, additives, constituents, pieces, components, makings, *fixings, *innards.

inhabit, v. occupy, stay, live in; see **dwell**.

inhabitant, n. occupant, dweller, settler, lodger, permanent resident, roomer, boarder, occupier, householder, addressee, inmate, tenant, settler, colonist, native; see also **citizen, resident**.—*Ant.* alien, transient, nonresident.

inhabited, a. settled, owned, lived or dwelt in, sustaining human life, peopled, occupied, colonized, developed, pioneered.

inhale, v. gasp, smell, sniff; see **breathe**.

inherent, a. innate, inborn, inbred; see **natural 1, native 1**.—*Ant.* incidental, extrinsic, superficial.

inherently, a. naturally, intrinsically, by birth; see **essentially**.

inherit, v. succeed to, acquire, receive, get one's inheritance, fall heir to, come into, take over, receive an endowment, *come in for; see also **get 1**.—*Ant.* lose, be disowned, miss.

inheritance, n. bequest, legacy, heritage; see **gift 1**.

inhibit, v. repress, frustrate, hold back; see **hinder, restrain**.

inhibition, n. prevention, restraint, hindrance; see **barrier, interference 1**.

inhuman, a. mean, heartless, coldblooded; see **cruel, fierce, ruthless**.

inhumanity, n. savagery, barbarity, brutality; see **cruelty, evil 1, tyranny**.

initial, a. basic, primary, elementary; see **first, fundamental**.

initially, a. at first, in or at the beginning, originally; see **first**.

initiate, v. open, start, inaugurate; see **begin 1**.

initiated, a. 1. [Introduced into] proposed, sponsored, originated, entered, brought into, admitted, inserted, put into, instituted; see also **proposed**. 2. [Having undergone initiation] installed, inducted, instructed, grounded, passed, admitted, approved, made part of, made a member of, received, acknowledged, accepted, introduced, drafted, called up, levied, confirmed, approved.

initiation, n. investment, induction, indoctrination; see **introduction 3**.

initiative, n. action, enterprise, first step; see **responsibility 1**.

inject, v. inoculate, shoot, *mainline; see **vaccinate**.

injection, n. dose, vaccination, inoculation; see also **treatment 2**.

injure, v. harm, damage, wound; see **hurt 1**.

injured, a. spoiled, damaged, harmed; see **hurt, wounded**.

injurious, a. detrimental, damaging, bad; see **dangerous, deadly, harmful, poisonous**.

injury, n. harm, sprain, damage, mutilation, blemish, cut, gash, scratch, stab, bite, fracture, hemorrhage, sting, bruise, sore, cramp, trauma, abrasion, burn, swelling, wound, scar, laceration, affliction; see also **pain 1**.

injustice, n. wrongdoing, malpractice, offense, crime, villainy, injury, infringement, violation, abuse, criminal negligence, transgression, grievance, breach, damage, infraction, *a crying shame;

see also **evil 1**, **wrong 2**.—*Ant*. **right**, just decision, honest verdict.

ink, *n*. tusche, paint, watercolor; see **color**.

inkling, *n*. indication, innuendo, suspicion; see **hint**, **suggestion 1**.

inland, *a*. toward the interior, backcountry, backland, hinterland, interior, midland, provincial, domestic, inward; see also **central**.—*Ant*. **foreign**, international, frontier.

in light of, *a*. in view of, since, taking into account; see **considering**.

in line, *a*. even, regular, balanced; see **flat 1**.

in line with, *a*. similar to, in accord or agreeing with, consonant; see **harmonious 2**, **fit 1**.

inmate, *n*. patient, convict, internee; see **patient**, **prisoner**.

in memory, *a*. for, in honor of, in memoriam; see **remembered**.

in motion, *a*. traveling, going, under way; see **moving 1**.

inn, *n*. tavern, hostel, saloon; see **bar 2**, **hotel**, **motel**, **resort 2**.

inner, *a*. innate, inherent, essential, inward, internal, interior, inside, nuclear, central, spiritual, private, subconscious, intrinsic, deep seated or rooted, intuitive.—*Ant*. **outer**, surface, external.

innocence, *n*. 1. [Freedom from guilt] guiltlessness, blamelessness, integrity, clear conscience, faultlessness, clean hands; see also **honesty**.—*Ant*. **guilt**, culpability, dishonesty. 2. [Freedom from guile] frankness, candidness, simple-mindedness, plainness, forthrightness, inoffensiveness; see also **simplicity 1**. 3. [Lack of experience] purity, virginity, naïveté; see **chastity**, **ignorance**, **virtue 1**.

innocent, *a*. 1. [Guiltless] not guilty, blameless, impeccable, faultless, safe, free of, uninvolved, above suspicion, *clean; see also **honest 1**.—*Ant*. **guilty**, culpable, blameworthy. 2. [Without guile] open, fresh, guileless; see **frank**, **childish**, **naïve**, **natural 3**, **simple 1**. 3. [Morally pure] sinless, unblemished, pure, unsullied, undefiled, spotless, wholesome, upright, unimpeachable, clean, virtuous, virginal, immaculate, impeccable, righteous, uncorrupted, irreproachable, unstained, stainless, moral, angelic.—*Ant*. **dishonest**, sinful, corrupt. 4. [Harmless] innocuous, free, inoffensive; see **harmless**, **safe 1**.

innocently, *a*. without guilt, with good or the best of intentions, ignorantly; see **nicely 1**, **politely**.

innovation, *n*. change, newness, addition; see **change 1**.

innuendo, *n*. aside, intimation, insinuation; see **hint**, **suggestion 1**.

inoculate, *v*. immunize, shoot, vaccinate; see **treat 3**.

inoculation, *n*. hypodermic, injection, shot; see **treatment 2**.

inoffensive, *a*. innocuous, pleasant, peaceable; see **calm 1**, **friendly 1**.

in part, *a*. partially, somewhat, to some extent or degree; see **partly**, **unfinished 1**.

in particular, *a*. especially, particularly, mainly; see **principally**.

in pieces, *a*. shattered, damaged, *busted; see **broken 1**, **destroyed**, **ruined 1**, **2**.

input, *n*. information, knowledge, facts; see **data**.

in question, *a*. up or open for discussion, in debate, at issue; see **controversial**, **questionable 1**, **uncertain 2**.

inquire, *v*. make an inquiry, probe, interrogate; see **ask**, **question**.

inquiry, *n*. probe, analysis, hearing; see **examination**.

inquisitive, *a*. curious, inquiring, speculative, questioning, meddling, searching, challenging, analytical, scrutinizing, prying, forward, presumptuous, impertinent, *snoopy, *nosey; see also **interested 1**.—*Ant*. **indifferent**, unconcerned, aloof.

in reality, *a*. in truth, truly, honestly; see **really 1**.

in regard or **respect to**, *a*. as to, concerning, with regard to; see **about 2**, **regarding**.

in reserve, *a*. withheld, out of circulation, stored away; see **kept 2**, **retained 1**, **saved 2**.

insane, *a*. 1. [Deranged] crazy, crazed, deranged, wild, raging, frenzied, lunatic, balmy, schizophrenic, psychotic, psychopathic, paranoid, *non compos mentis* (Latin), maniacal, raving, demented, rabid, unhinged, mentally unsound or diseased, suffering from hallucinations, deluded, possessed, stark mad, out of one's head or mind, obsessed, touched, *cracked, *screwy, *nutty, *nuts, *haywire, *batty, *off the beam, *unglued, *off one's nut or rocker, *not all there; see also **sick**.—*Ant*. **sane**, rational, sensible. 2. [Utterly foolish] madcap, daft, idiotic; see **stupid 1**.

insanely, *a*. furiously, psychopathically, fiercely; see **crazily**, **violently**, **wildly**.

insanity, *n*. mental derangement or abnormality or unbalance, delusions, hysteria, anxiety, obsession, compulsion, madness, dementia, lunacy, psychosis, alienation, neurosis, phobia, mania. —*Ant*. **sanity**, reason, normality.

inscription, *n.* engraving, saying, legend; see **writing 2.**

in season, *a.* legal to hunt *or* take, ready to pick, mature; see **legal 1, ready 2, ripe 1, 3.**

insect, *n.* bug, beetle, mite, vermin, *cootie; see also **pest 1.** Creatures commonly called insects include the following—spider, ant, bee, flea, fly, mosquito, gnat, silver fish, hornet, leaf hopper, squash bug, earwig, May fly, dragonfly, termite, cicada, aphid, aphis, mantis, beetle, butterfly, moth, wasp, locust, bedbug, moth, caterpillar, grasshopper, cricket, bumblebee, honeybee, cockroach, potato bug, corn borer, boll weevil, stinkbug, firefly, Japanese beetle, yellow jacket; see **fly 1, spider.**

insecticide, *n.* DDT, insect poison, pesticide; see **poison.**

insecure, *a.* anxious, vague, uncertain; see **troubled.**

insecurity, *n.* 1. [Anxiety] vacillation, indecision, instability; see **doubt, uncertainty 2.** 2. [Danger] risk, hazard, vulnerability; see **chance 1, danger.**

inseparable, *a.* indivisible, as one, tied up, intertwined, integrated, integral, whole, connected, attached, conjoined, united; see also **joined, unified.**—*Ant.* separable, divisible, apart.

insert, *n.* inclusion, introduction, new material; see **addition 2.**

insert, *v.* enter, interpolate, inject; see **include 2.**

inserted, *a.* introduced, added, stuck in; see **included.**

insertion, *n.* insert, introduction, inclusion; see **addition 2.**

in short, *a.* in summary, to put it briefly, (and) so; see **briefly.**

inside, *a.* 1. [Within] inner, in, within the boundaries *or* circumference of, bounded, surrounded by; see also **inner, under.**—*Ant.* after, **beyond,** outside. 2. [Within doors] indoors, under a roof, in a house, out of the open, behind closed doors, under a shelter, in the interior; see also **within.**—*Ant.* **outside,** out-of-doors, in the open.

inside, *n.* inner wall, sheathing, plaster, facing, wadding, inlayer; see also **lining.**

insides, *n.* interior, inner portion, bowels, recesses, inland, middle, belly, womb, heart, soul, breast; see also **center 1, stomach.**

insight, *n.* penetration, perspicacity, shrewdness; see **intelligence 1.**

insignia, *n.* ensign, coat of arms, symbol; see **decoration 2, emblem.**

insignificance, *n.* unimportance, worthlessness, indifference, triviality, nothingness, smallness, pettiness, matter of no consequence, nothing to speak of, nothing particular, *drop in the bucket, *molehill.

insignificant, *a.* irrelevant, petty, trifling; see **trivial, unimportant.**

insincere, *a.* deceitful, pretentious, shifty; see **dishonest, false 1, hypocritical, sly.**

insincerity, *n.* distortion, falsity, lies; see **deception, dishonesty, hypocrisy.**

insinuate, *v.* imply, suggest, purport; see **hint, mention, propose 1, refer 2.**

insinuation, *n.* implication, veiled remark *or* observation, innuendo; see **hint, suggestion 1.**

insistence, *n.* demand, perseverance, determination; see **determination.**

insistent, *a.* persistent, reiterative, continuous; see **stubborn.**

insist (that) *or* **upon,** *v.* expect, request, order; see **ask.**

insolvent, *a.* bankrupt, failed, *broke; see **ruined 4.**—*Ant.* solvent, **running,** in good condition.

inspect, *v.* scrutinize, probe, investigate; see **examine.**

inspected, *a.* tried, checked, authorized; see **approved, investigated.**

inspection, *n.* inventory, investigation, inquiry; see **examination 1.**

inspector, *n.* police inspector, chief detective, investigating officer, customs officer, immigration inspector, government inspector, checker; see also **policeman.**

inspiration, *n.* 1. [An idea] notion, hunch, whim; see **fancy 1, impulse 2, thought 2.** 2. [A stimulant to creative activity] stimulus, spur, influence; see **incentive.**

inspire, *v.* fire, be the cause of, start off, put one in the mood, give one the idea for, motivate, give an impetus.

inspired, *a.* roused, animated, motivated, stirred, excited, exhilarated, influenced, set going, started, activated, moved; see also **encouraged.**

inspiring, *a.* encouraging, exhilarating, revealing; see also **exciting, stimulating.**

in spite of, *a.* nevertheless, in defiance of, despite; see **regardless 2.**

instability, *n.* inconstancy, changeability, immaturity, variability, inconsistency, irregularity, imbalance, unsteadiness, restlessness, disquiet, anxiety, fluctuation, alternation, fitfulness, impermanence, transience, vacillation, hesitation, wavering, fickleness; see also **change 1, uncertainty 2.**

install, *v.* set up, establish, build *or* put in, place, invest, introduce, inaugurate, furnish with, put *or* fix up, line.

installation, *n.* 1. [The act of installing] placing, induction, ordination, inauguration, launching, investment, establishment. 2. [That which has been installed] machinery, wiring, lighting, insulation, power, power plant, heating system, furnishings, foundation, base.

installed, *a.* set *or* put up, started, put in; see **established 2, finished 1.**

installment, *n.* partial payment, periodic payment, down payment; see **part 1, payment 1.**

instance, *n.* case, situation, occurrence; see **example.** —**for instance**, as an example, by way of illustration, in this fashion; see **for example.**

instant, *n.* short while, second, flash, split second, wink *or* bat of the eye, *jiffy; see also **moment 1.** —**on the instant**, instantly, without delay, simultaneously; see **immediately.**

instantly, *a.* directly, at once, without delay; see **immediately.**

instead, *a.* in place of, as a substitute, alternative, on second thought, in lieu of, on behalf of, alternatively; see also **rather 2.**

instead of, *prep.* rather than, in place *or* lieu of, as a substitute *or* alternative *or* proxy for.

instill, *v.* inject, infiltrate, inoculate, impregnate, implant, inspire, impress, catechize, brainwash, introduce, inculcate, indoctrinate, impart, insert, force in, *put into someone's head; see also **teach.**—*Ant.* remove, draw out, extract.

instinct, *n.* drive, sense, intuition; see **feeling 4.**

instinctive, *a.* spontaneous, accustomed, normal; see **natural 2.**

instinctively, *a.* inherently, intuitively, by *or* on instinct; see **naturally 2.**

institute, *v.* found, establish, launch; see **establish 2.**

institution, *n.* system, company, association; see **business 4, office 3, university.**

institutionalize, *v.* standardize, incorporate into a system, make official; see **order 3, regulate 2, systematize.**

instruct, *v.* educate, give lessons, direct; see **teach.**

instructed, *a.* told, advised, informed; see **educated 1, learned 1.**

instruction, *n.* guidance, preparation, direction; see **education 1.**

instructions, *n.* orders, plans, directive; see **advice, directions.**

instructor, *n.* professor, tutor, lecturer; see **teacher.**

instrument, *n.* means, apparatus, implement; see **device 1, machine, tool 1.**

instrumental, *a.* partly responsible for, contributory, conducive; see **effective, helpful 1, necessary 1.**

in style, *a.* current, modish, stylish; see **fashionable, popular 1.**

insubordinate, *a.* disobedient, treacherous, defiant; see **rebellious.**

insubordination, *n.* mutiny, treason, rebellion; see **revolution 2.**

insubstantial, *a.* petty, slight, inadequate; see **flimsy 1, poor 2.**

insufficient, *a.* skimpy, meager, thin; see **inadequate, unsatisfactory.**

insufficiently, *a.* barely, incompletely, partly; see **badly 1, inadequately.**

insulate, *v.* protect, coat, inlay, treat, apply insulation, tape up, glass in.

insulation, *n.* nonconductor, protector, covering, packing, lining, resistant material.

insult, *n.* indignity, offense, affront, abuse, outrage, impudence, insolence, blasphemy, mockery, derision, impertinence, discourtesy, invective, disrespect, slander, libel, slap in the face, *black eye; see also **rudeness.**—*Ant.* praise, tribute, homage.

insult, *v.* revile, libel, offend, outrage, humiliate, mock, vex, tease, irritate, annoy, aggravate, provoke, taunt, ridicule, jeer, step on one's toes; see also **curse, slander.**

insulted, *a.* slandered, libeled, reviled, cursed, dishonored, mocked, ridiculed, jeered at, humiliated, mistreated, offended, hurt, outraged, affronted, slighted, shamed; see also **hurt.**—*Ant.* praised, admired, extolled.

insulting, *a.* outrageous, offensive, degrading, humiliating, humbling, deriding, contemptuous.—*Ant.* **respectful,** complimentary, honoring.

in support of, *a.* for, condoning, approving; see **for.**

insurance, *n.* indemnity, assurance, warrant, backing, allowance, safeguard, support, *something to fall back on; see also **security 2.**

insure, *v.* register, warrant, protect; see **guarantee.**

insured, *a.* safeguarded, defended, warranteed; see **guaranteed, protected.**

insurrection, *n.* insurgence, revolt, rebellion; see **disorder 2, revolution 2.**

intact, *a.* together, entire, uninjured; see **whole 2.**

intake, *n.* 1. [Contraction] alteration, shortening, constriction; see **abbreviation, reduction 1.** 2. [Profit] harvest, gain, accumulation; see **profit 2.**

intangible, *a.* indefinite, unsure, hypothetical; see **uncertain 2, vague 2.**

integrated, *a.* nonsegregated, not segregated, (for) both black and white, interracial, nonracial, for all races, nonsectarian, without restriction (as to race, creed or color), combined; see also **free 1, 2, open 3.**

integration, *n.* unification, combination,

co-operation; see **alliance 1, mixture 1, union 1.**

integrity, *n.* uprightness, honor, probity; see **honesty.**

intellect, *n.* intelligence, brain, mentality; see **mind 1.**

intellectual, *a.* mental, inventive, creative; see **intelligent, learned 1.**

intellectual, *n.* genius, philosopher, academician, highbrow, member of the intelligentsia, *egghead, *brain, *Einstein; see also **artist, philosopher, scientist, writer.**

intelligence, *n.* 1. [Understanding] perspicacity, discernment, comprehension; see **judgment 1.** 2. [Secret information] report, statistics, facts, inside information, account, *info, *the dope; see also **knowledge 1, news 1, secret.** 3. [The mind] intellect, brain, mentality; see **mind 1.**

intelligent, *a.* clever, bright, exceptional, astute, smart, brilliant, perceptive, well-informed, resourceful, profound, penetrating, original, keen, imaginative, inventive, reasonable, capable, able, ingenious, knowledgeable, creative, responsible, understanding, alert, quick-witted, clear-headed, quick, sharp, witty, ready, calculating, comprehending, discerning, discriminating, knowing, intellectual, studious, contemplative, having a head on one's shoulders, talented, apt, wise, shrewd, *smart as a whip, *on the ball or beam, *not born yesterday.—*Ant.* dull, slow-minded, shallow.

intelligently, *a.* skillfully, admirably, reasonably, logically, judiciously, capably, diligently, sharply, astutely, discerningly, knowingly, knowledgeably, farsightedly, sensibly, prudently, alertly, keenly, resourcefully, aptly, discriminatingly; see also **effectively.**—*Ant.* badly, foolishly, stupidly.

intelligible, *a.* plain, clear, obvious; see **understandable.**

intend, *v.* 1. [To propose] plan, purpose, aim, expect, be resolved *or* determined (to), aspire to, have in mind *or* view, hope to, contemplate, think, aim at, take into one's head. 2. [To destine for] design, mean, devote to, reserve, appoint, set apart, aim at *or* for, have in view; see also **assign, dedicate.** 3. [To mean] indicate, signify, denote; see **mean 1.**

intended, *a.* designed, advised, expected, predetermined, calculated, prearranged, predestined, meant; see also **planned, proposed.**

intense, *a.* intensified, deep, profound, extraordinary, exceptional, heightened, marked, vivid, ardent, powerful, passionate, impassioned, diligent, hard, full, great, exaggerated, violent, excessive, acute, keen, piercing, cutting, bitter, severe, concentrated, intensive, forceful, sharp, biting, stinging, shrill, high pitched, strenuous, fervent, earnest, zealous, vehement, harsh, strong, brilliant.

intensely, *a.* deeply, profoundly, strongly; see **very.**

intensify, *v.* heighten, sharpen, emphasize; see **increase, strengthen.**

intensity, *n.* strain, force, concentration, power, vehemence, passion, fervor, ardor, severity, acuteness, depth, deepness, forcefulness, high pitch, sharpness, emphasis, magnitude.

intensive, *a.* accelerated, speeded up, hard; see **fast 1, severe 1, 2.**

intention, *n.* aim, end, plan; see **purpose 1.**

intentional, *a.* intended, meditated, prearranged; see **deliberate.**

intentionally, *a.* specifically, with malice aforethought, in cold blood; see **deliberately.**

intently, *a.* hard, with concentration, keenly; see **closely.**

intercept, *v.* cut off, stop, ambush, block, catch, take away, appropriate, *hijack, head off; see also **prevent.**

interception, *n.* blocking, interfering (with), interposing; see **interference 1.**

interchange, *n.* 1. [The act of giving and receiving reciprocally] barter, trade, reciprocation; see **exchange 2.** 2. [A highway intersection] cloverleaf, intersection, off-ramp; see **highway, road 1.**

intercourse, *n.* 1. [Communication] association, dealings, interchange; see **communication.** 2. [Sex act] coitus, coition, sexual relations; see **copulation, sex 4.**

interest, *n.* 1. [Concern] attention, curiosity, excitement; see **attention.** 2. [Advantage] profit, benefit, gain; see **advantage.** 3. [Premium] credit, gain, earnings; see **addition 2, profit 2.** —**in the interest(s) of,** for the sake of, on behalf of, in order to promote; see **for.**

interest, *v.* intrigue, amuse, please; see **entertain 1, fascinate.**

interested, *a.* 1. [Having one's interest aroused] stimulated, attentive, curious, drawn, touched, moved, affected, inspired, sympathetic (to), responsive, struck, impressed, roused, awakened, stirred, open to suggestion, all for, all wrapped up in.—*Ant.* bored, tired, annoyed. 2. [Concerned with or engaged in] occupied, engrossed, partial, prejudiced, biased, taken, obsessed with, absorbed in; see also **involved.**—*Ant.* indifferent, impartial, disinterested.

interesting, *a.* pleasing, pleasurable, fine, satisfying, fascinating, arresting, engaging, readable, absorbing, stirring, affecting, exotic, unusual, lovely, gracious, impressive, attractive, captivating, enchanting, beautiful, inviting, winning, magnetic, delightful, amusing, genial, refreshing; see also exciting.—*Ant.* dull, shallow, boring.

interfere, *v.* intervene, interpose, interlope; see **meddle 1.**

interference, *n.* 1. [Taking forcible part in the affairs of others] meddling, interruption, prying, trespassing, tampering, barging in, back-seat driving; see also **interruption**. 2. [That which obstructs] obstruction, check, obstacle; see **barrier, restraint 2.**

interior, *a.* inner, internal, inward; see **central, inside 2.**

interior, *n.* 1. [Inside] inner part, lining, heart; see **center 1, inside.** 2. [The inside of a building] rooms, hall(s), stairway, vestibule, lobby, chapel, choir, gallery, basement.

interjection, *n.* 1. [Insertion] interpolation, insinuation, inclusion; see **addition 1.** 2. [Exclamation] utterance, ejaculation, exclamation; see **cry 1.**

intermediate, *a.* mean, between, medium, half-way, compromising, intermediary, neutral, standard, median, moderate, average; see also **central, common 1, middle.**

intermission, *n.* interim, wait, respite; see **pause, recess 1.**

intermittent, *a.* periodic, coming and going, recurrent; see **changing, irregular 1.**

internal, *a.* 1. [Within] inside, inward, interior, private, intrinsic, innate, inherent, under the surface, intimate, subjective, enclosed, circumscribed; see also **inner.**—*Ant.* external, outer, outward. 2. [Within the body] intestinal, physiological, physical, neurological, abdominal, visceral.—*Ant.* foreign, alien, external.

internally, *a.* within the body, beneath or below the surface, inwardly, deep down, spiritually, mentally, invisibly, by injection, out of sight; see also **inside 1, within.**

international, *a.* world-wide, worldly, world, intercontinental, between nations, all over the world, universal, all-embracing, foreign, cosmopolitan; see also **universal 3.**—*Ant.* domestic, national, internal.

internationally, *a.* interculturally, interracially, co-operatively, globally, universally, concerning the intercourse of nations or peoples, not provincial or bigoted; see also **abroad, everywhere.**

interpret, *v.* give one's impressions of, render, play, perform, depict, delineate, enact, portray, make sense of, read (into), improvise on, re-enact, mimic, gather from, view as, give one an idea about, *make something of; see also **define, describe.**

interpretation, *n.* account, rendition, exposition, statement, diagnosis, description, representation, definition, presentation, argument, answer, solution; see also **explanation.**

interpreter, *n.* commentator, writer, artist, editor, reviewer, biographer, analyst, scholar, spokesman, delegate, speaker, exponent, demonstrator, philosopher, professor, translator, linguist, language expert.

interrogate, *v.* cross-examine, ask, give the third degree; see **examine, question.**

interrogation, *n.* inquiry, query, investigation; see **examination 1.**

interrupt, *v.* intrude, intervene, cut in on, break in or into, interfere, infringe, cut off, break someone's train of thought, come between, *worm or muscle or butt or horn or barge or burst in, *crash.

interrupted, *a.* stopped, checked, held up, obstructed, delayed, interfered or meddled with, disordered, hindered, suspended, cut short.

interruption, *n.* check, break, suspension, intrusion, obstruction, holding over; see also **delay, interference 1.**

intersect, *v.* cut across, break in two, intercross; see **divide.**

interstate, *a.* internal, interior, domestic; see **local 1.**

interval, *n.* period, interlude, interim; see **pause.**

intervene, *v.* step in, intercede, mediate; see **negotiate 1, reconcile 2.**

intervention, *n.* 1. [The act of intervening] intercession, interruption, breaking in; see **interference 1, intrusion 2.** 2. [Armed interference] invasion, military occupation, (armed) aggression; see **attack.**

interview, *n.* meeting, audience, conference; see **communication, conversation.**

interview, *v.* converse with, get one's opinion, consult with, interrogate, hold an inquiry, give (one) an oral examination, get something for the record.

intestines, *n.* entrails, bowels, viscera, vitals, digestive organs, *guts; see also **insides.**

in the air, *a.* prevalent, abroad, current; see **fashionable, popular 1.**

in the background, *a.* retiring, unseen, out of sight; see **obscure 3, unnoticed, withdrawn.**

*in the bag, *a.* assured, definite, clinched; see **definite 1.**

in the dark, *a.* uninformed, uninstructed, confused; see **deceived, ignorant 1.**

in the end, *a.* at length, in conclusion, as a result; see **finally 2.**

in the future, *a.* eventually, sometime, in due time; see **finally 2, someday.**

in the lead, *a.* ahead, winning, leading; see **triumphant.**

in the market, *a.* negotiating, purchasing, prepared to buy; see **buying,** *n.*

in the meantime, *a.* in anticipation, at the same time, meanwhile; see **during, while 1.**

in the way, *a.* bothersome, nagging, obstructing; see **disturbing.**

intimacy, *n.* closeness, familiarity, confidence; see **affection, friendship.**

intimate, *a.* close, near, trusted; see **private, secret 1, special 1.**

intimate, *n.* associate, (constant) companion, close friend; see **friend, lover 1.**

intimately, *a.* closely, personally, informally, familiarly, confidentially, without reserve, privately; see also **lovingly, secretly.—Ant.** openly, reservedly, publicly.

in time, *a.* eventually, in the end, at the last; see **finally 2, ultimately.**

into, *prep.* inside, in, in the direction of, through, to, to the middle of; see also **in 1, 2, toward, within.**

intolerable, *a.* insufferable, unendurable, unbearable; see **impossible, offensive 2, painful 1, undesirable.**

intolerance, *n.* racism, chauvinism, nationalism; see **fanaticism, prejudice.**

intolerant, *a.* dogmatic, narrow, bigoted; see **prejudiced, stupid 1.**

in touch, *a.* knowing, acquainted with, in communication; see **familiar with.**

intoxicant, *n.* 1. [Alcohol] alcoholic drink, liquor, *booze; see **drink 2.** 2. [Drug] narcotic, hallucinogen, *dope; see **drug.**

intoxicate, *v.* befuddle, inebriate, muddle; see **confuse.**

intoxicated, *a.* inebriated, *high, *stoned; see **dizzy 1, drunk.**

intoxication, *n.* infatuation, inebriation, intemperance; see **drunkenness.**

intricacy, *n.* complication, elaborateness, complexity; see **confusion, difficulty 1, 2.**

intricate, *a.* involved, tricky, abstruse; see **complex 2, difficult 1, 2, obscure 1.**

intrigue, *n.* scheme, conspiracy, ruse; see **trick 1.**

intrigue, *v.* delight, please, attract; see **charm 1, entertain 1, fascinate.**

intrigued, *a.* attracted, delighted, pleased; see **charmed, entertained 2, fascinated.**

intriguing, *a.* engaging, attractive, delightful; see **beautiful, charming, handsome, pleasant 1.**

introduce, *v.* 1. [To bring in] freight, carry in, transport; see **carry, send 1. 2.** [To present] set forth, submit, advance; see **offer 1, propose 1. 3.** [To make strangers acquainted] present, give an introduction, make known, put on speaking terms with, do the honors, break the ice. 4. [To insert] put in, add, enter; see **include 2.**

introduced, *a.* 1. [Brought in] made current *or* known, put on the market, advanced, proposed, offered, imported, popularized; see also **received. 2.** [Made acquainted] acquainted with, befriended, acknowledged, recognized, on speaking terms, not unknown to each other *or* one another; see **familiar with.**

introduction, *n.* 1. [The act of bringing in] admittance, initiation, installation; see **entrance 1. 2.** [The act of making strangers acquainted] presentation, debut, meeting, formal acquaintance, preliminary encounter. 3. [Introductory knowledge] first acquaintance, elementary statement, first contact, start, awakening, first taste, baptism, preliminary training, basic principles; see also **knowledge 1. 4.** [An introductory explanation] preface, preamble, foreword, prologue, prelude, overture; see also **explanation. 5.** [A work supplying introductory knowledge] primer, manual, handbook; see **book.**

introductory, *a.* initial, opening, early, prior, starting, beginning, preparatory, primary, original, provisional.—*Ant.* principal, substantial, secondary.

in trouble, *a.* in a quandary, never free from, *in bad, *in hot water, *in for it, *in the doghouse, *in a jam, *out on a limb; see also **troubled.**

intrude, *v.* interfere, interrupt, interpose; see **meddle 1.**

intruder, *n.* prowler, thief, unwelcome guest, meddler, invader, snooper, unwanted person, interferer, interrupter, trespasser; see also **robber, trouble 1.**

intrusion, *n.* interruption, forced entrance, trespass, intervention, meddling, encroachment, invasion, infraction, overstepping, transgression, *nose-in, *horn-in, *muscle-in; see also **interference 1.**

in trust, *a.* in escrow, on deposit, held; see also **retained 1.**

intuition, *n.* presentiment, foreknowledge, inspiration; see **feeling 4.**

intuitive, *a.* instantaneously apprehended, emotional, instinctive; see **automatic, natural 1, spontaneous.**

invade, *v.* 1. [To enter with armed force] force a landing, penetrate, fall on; see **attack. 2.** [To encroach upon] infringe on, trespass, interfere with; see **meddle 1.**

invader, *n.* trespasser, alien, attacking force; see **attacker, enemy.**

in vain, *a.* futilely, purposelessly, unprofitably; see **useless.**

invalid, *a.* irrational, unreasonable, fallacious; see **illogical, wrong 2.**

invalid, *n.* disabled person, incurable, paralytic, cripple, tubercular, leper, inmate; see also **patient.**

invalidate, *v.* annul, refute, nullify; see **cancel 2.**

invaluable, *a.* priceless, expensive, dear; see **valuable.**

invariable, *a.* unchanging, uniform, static; see **constant, regular 3.**

invariably, *a.* perpetually, constantly, habitually; see **customarily, regularly.**

invasion, *n.* forced entrance, intrusion, aggression; see **attack.**

invent, *v.* 1. [To create or discover] originate, devise, fashion, form, project, design, find, improvise, contrive, execute, come upon, conceive, author, plan, think *or* make up, bear, turn out, forge, make, hatch, *dream *or* cook up. 2. [To fabricate] misrepresent, fake, make believe; see **lie 1.**

invention, *n.* contrivance, contraption, design; see **discovery.**

inventive, *a.* productive, imaginative, fertile; see **artistic, original 2.**

inventor, *n.* author, originator, creator; see **architect, artist.**

inventory, *n.* 1. [A list] stock book, itemization, register; see **index 2, list, record 1.** 2. [The act of taking stock] inspection, examination, investigation; see **summary.**

inventory, *v.* take stock of, count, audit; see **file 1, list 1, record 1.**

invert, *v.* 1. [To upset] overturn, turn upside-down, tip; see **upset 1.** 2. [To reverse] change, rearrange, transpose; see **exchange.**

invest, *v.* lay out, spend, put one's money into, lend (on security), advance, give money over, buy stocks, make an investment, loan, buy into, *sink money in, *put up the dough; see also **buy.**

investigate, *v.* look over *or* into, interrogate, review; see **examine, study.**

investigated, *a.* examined, tried, tested, inspected, searched, questioned, probed, considered, measured, checked, studied, researched, made the subject of an investigation *or* hearing *or* trial *or* probe, worked on, thought out *or* through, scrutinized, put to the test, gone over *or* into, cross-examined.

investigation, *n.* inquiry, search, research; see **examination 1.**

investigator, *n.* reviewer, spy, auditor; see **detective, inspector.**

investment, *n.* grant, loan, expenditure, expense, backing, speculation, financing, finance, purchase, advance, bail, interest. Types of investment include the following—stocks, bonds, shares, securities, property, real estate, mortgage, capital, goods, insurance liens, debentures, futures, gold, grain, bonded liquor.

in view of, *a.* in consideration of, because, taking into consideration; see **considering.**

invigorate, *v.* stimulate, freshen, exhilarate; see **animate, excite.**

invigorating, *a.* refreshing, exhilarating, bracing; see **stimulating.**

invincible, *a.* unconquerable, insuperable, impregnable; see **powerful 1, strong 1, 2.**

invisibility, *n.* obscurity, concealment, camouflage, indefiniteness, seclusion, cloudiness, haziness, fogginess, mistiness, duskiness, darkness, gloom, intangibility, disappearance, vagueness, indefiniteness.

invisible, *a.* intangible, out of sight, microscopic, beyond the visual range, unseen, undisclosed, occult, ideal, unreal, vaporous, gaseous.—*Ant.* real, substantial, material.

invisibly, *a.* imperceptibly, undetectibly, out of sight; see **vaguely.**

invitation, *n.* note, card, message, encouragement, proposition, proposal, call, petition, overture, offer, temptation, attraction, lure, prompting, urge, pressure, reason, motive, ground.

invite, *v.* bid, request, beg, suggest, encourage, entice, solicit, pray, petition, persuade, insist, press, ply, propose, appeal to, implore, call upon, ask, have over *or* out *or* in, formally invite, issue *or* send *or* give an invitation (to); see also **ask.**

invited, *a.* asked, requested, solicited, persuaded, bade, summoned; see **welcome.**

inviting, *a.* appealing, alluring, tempting, attractive, captivating, agreeable, open, encouraging, delightful, pleasing, persuasive, magnetic, fascinating, provocative, bewitching.—*Ant.* painful, unbearable, insufferable.

invoice, *n.* bill of lading, receipt, bill of shipment; see **statement 2.**

involuntary, *a.* unintentional, uncontrolled, instinctive; see **automatic, habitual.**

involve, *v.* draw into, compromise, implicate, entangle, link, connect, incriminate, associate, relate, suggest, prove, comprise, point to, commit, bring up.

involved, *a.* brought into difficulties, entangled in a crime, incriminated, embarrassed, embroiled, caught *or* wrapped up *or* immersed in; see also **included.**

involvement, *n.* 1. [Difficulty] quandary, crisis, embarrassment; see **difficulty 1, 2. 2.** [Engrossment] intentness, study, preoccupation; see **reflection 1.**

invulnerable, *a.* strong, invincible, secure; see **safe 1.**

inward, *a.* 1. [Moving into] penetrating, ingoing, through, incoming, entering, inbound, infiltrating, inflowing; see also **through 4. 2.** [Placed within] inside, internal, interior; see **in 1, within. 3.** [Private] spiritual, intellectual, intimate; see **private, religious 2.**

inwardly, *a.* from within *or* the inside, fundamentally, basically; see **naturally 2, within.**

iota, *n.* grain, particle, speck; see **bit 1.**

irate, *a.* enraged, furious, incensed; see **angry.**

Irish, *a.* Celtic, Gaelic, *from the old sod; see **European.**

irk, *v.* annoy, harass, disturb; see **bother 1, 2.**

iron, *a.* ferrous, ironclad, hard, robust, strong, unyielding, dense, inflexible, heavy; see also **firm 2, thick 3.**

iron, *n.* 1. [A metallic element] pig iron, cast iron, wrought iron, sheet iron, coke; see also **metal. 2.** [An appliance] pressing device, presser, steam iron; see **appliance.**

iron, *v.* use a flatiron *or* steam iron (on), press, mangle, roll, finish, smooth (out); see also **smooth.**

ironical, *a.* contradictory, twisted, ridiculous, mocking, satiric, paradoxical, critical, derisive, exaggerated, caustic, biting, incisive, scathing, satirical, bitter; see also sense 2, **sarcastic.**

iron out, *v.* compromise, settle differences, reach an agreement about; see **agree, negotiate 1.**

irony, *n.* satire, wit, ridicule, mockery, quip, banter, derision, criticism, paradox, twist, humor, reproach, repartee, back-handed compliment; see also **sarcasm.**

irrational, *a.* 1. [Illogical] unreasonable, specious, fallacious; see **illogical, wrong 2. 2.** [Stupid] senseless, silly, ridiculous; see **stupid 1.**

irrationally, *a.* illogically, unreasonably, stupidly; see **foolishly.**

irregular, *a.* 1. [Not even] uneven, spasmodic, fitful, uncertain, random, unsettled, inconstant, unsteady, fragmentary, unsystematic, occasional, infrequent, fluctuating, wavering, intermittent, sporadic, changeable, capricious, variable, shifting, unmethodical, jerky, up and down.–*Ant.* **regular,** even, punctual. 2. [Not customary] unique,

extraordinary, abnormal; see **unusual 2. 3.** [Questionable] strange, overt, debatable; see **questionable 2, suspicious 2. 4.** [Not regular in form or in outline] not uniform, unsymmetrical, uneven, unequal, craggy, hilly, broken, jagged, notched, eccentric, bumpy, meandering, variable, wobbly, lumpy, off balance, off center, lopsided, pock-marked, scarred, bumpy, sprawling, out of proportion; see also **bent.**

irregularity, *n.* peculiarity, singularity, abnormality, strangeness, uniqueness, exception, excess, malformation, deviation, allowance, exemption, privilege, nonconformity, innovation, oddity, eccentricity, rarity; see also **characteristic.**–*Ant.* custom, regularity, rule.

irregularly, *a.* periodically, at (irregular) intervals, intermittently, fitfully, off and on; see **unexpectedly.**

irrelevant, *a.* inapplicable, impertinent, off the topic, inappropriate, unrelated, extraneous, unconnected, off the point, foreign, outside *or* beside the question, out of order *or* place, pointless, beside the point, not pertaining to, without reference to, out of the way, remote, neither here nor there; see also **trivial, unnecessary.**

irreparable, *a.* incurable, hopeless, irreversible; see also **broken 1, destroyed, ruined 1.**

irresistible, *a.* compelling, overpowering, invincible; see **overwhelming, powerful 1.**

irresponsible, *a.* untrustworthy, capricious, flighty, fickle, thoughtless, rash, undependable, unstable, loose, lax, immoral, shiftless, unpredictable, wild, devil-may-care; see also **unreliable 1**–*Ant.* **responsible,** trustworthy, dependable.

irrevocable, *a.* permanent, indelible, lost; see **certain 2, inevitable.**

irrigate, *v.* water, pass water through, inundate; see **flood.**

irrigation, *n.* watering, flooding, inundation; see **flood.**

irritability, *n.* anger, peevishness, impatience; see **anger, annoyance.**

irritable, *a.* sensitive, touchy, testy, ill-tempered, huffy, peevish, petulant, tense, resentful, fretting, carping, crabbed, hypercritical, quick-tempered, easily offended, glum, complaining, brooding, dissatisfied, snarling, grumbling, surly, gloomy, ill-natured, morose, moody, snappish, waspish, in bad humor, cantankerous, fretful, hypersensitive, annoyed, cross, churlish, grouchy, sulky, sullen, high-strung, thin-skinned, grumpy; see also **angry.**–*Ant.* **pleasant,** agreeable, good-natured.

irritant, *n.* bother, burden, nuisance; see **annoyance**.

irritate, *v.* 1. [To bother] provoke, exasperate, pester; see **bother 2, confuse, disturb**. 2. [To inflame] redden, chafe, swell, erupt, pain, sting; see also **burn, hurt 1, itch**.

irritated, *a.* disturbed, upset, bothered; see **troubled**.

irritating, *a.* annoying, bothersome, trying; see **disturbing**.

irritation, *n.* 1. [The result of irritating] soreness, tenderness, rawness; see **feeling 4**. 2. [A disturbed mental state] excitement, upset, provocation; see **anger, annoyance**.

is, *v.* lives, breathes, transpires, happens, amounts to, equals, comprises, signifies, means.

island, *n.* isle, bar, archipelago; see **land 1**.

isolate, *v.* confine, detach, seclude; see **divide**.

isolated, *a.* secluded, apart, backwoods, insular, segregated, confined, withdrawn, rustic, separate, lonely, forsaken, hidden, remote, out-of-the-way, lonesome, Godforsaken; see also **alone, private, solitary**.

isolation, *n.* detachment, solitude, loneliness, seclusion, segregation, confinement, separation, self-sufficiency, obscurity, retreat, privacy; see also **withdrawal**.

Israel, *n.* Palestine, Judea, Canaan, the State of Isreal, the Promised Land; see also **Asia**.

issue, *n.* 1. [Question] point, matter, problem, concern, point in question, argument; see also **matter**. 2. [Result] upshot, culmination, effect; see **result**. 3. [Edition] number, copy, impression; see **copy**. —**at issue**, in dispute, unsettled, controversial; see **controversial**. —**take issue**, differ, disagree, take a stand against; see **oppose 1**.

issue, *v.* 1. [To emerge] flow out, proceed, come forth; see **appear 1**. 2. [To be a result of] rise from, spring, originate; see **begin 2, result**. 3. [To release] circulate, send out, announce; see **advertise, declare, publish 1**.

issued, *a.* circulated, broadcast, televised, made public, announced, published, sent out, spread; see also **distributed**.

it, *pron.* such a thing, that which, that object, this thing, the subject; see also **that, this**. —*with it**, alert, aware, up-to-date; see **ready 2**.

Italian, *a.* Latin, Etruscan, Florentine, Milanese, Venetian, Neapolitan, Sicilian.

italicize, *v.* stress, underline, print in italic type, draw attention to; see also **distinguish 1, emphasize**.

Italy, *n.* Italia, Italian peninsula, Italian people, Italian Republic, Rome.

itch, *n.* tingling, prickling, crawling, creeping sensation, rawness, psoriasis, scabbiness.

itch, *v.* creep, prickle, be irritated, crawl, tickle; see also **tingle**.

item, *n.* piece, article, matter; see **detail, part 1**.

itemize, *v.* inventory, enumerate, number; see **detail, list 1**.

itemized, *a.* counted, particularized, enumerated; see **detailed**.

itinerant, *a.* roving, nomadic, peripatetic; see **vagrant, wandering 1**.

itinerant, *n.* nomad, wanderer, vagrant; see **tramp 1**.

itinerary, *n.* course, travel plans, route; see **path, plan 2, program 2, way 2**.

ivory, *a.* creamy, cream-colored, off-white; see **white 1**.

ivy, *n.* climber, creeper, plant; see **vine**.

J

jab, n. poke, punch, hit; see blow.

jabber, v. gibber, babble, mutter; see murmur 1, sound 1.

jack, n. automobile jack, pneumatic jack, hydraulic jack; see device 1, tool 1.

jacket, n. tunic, jerkin, parka; see cape 2, clothes, coat 1.

jackknife, n. clasp knife, case knife, Barlow knife; see knife.

jack-of-all-trades, n. handy man, factotum, versatile person; see laborer, workman.

jackpot, n. bonanza, find, winnings; see luck 1, profit 2, success 2. —*hit the jackpot, succeed, achieve, attain; see win 1. —*jack up, lift, add to, accelerate; see increase 1, raise 1.

jaded, a. cold, nonchalant, impassive; see indifferent.

jagged, a. serrated, ragged, rugged; see irregular 4, rough 1.

jail, n. penitentiary, cage, cell, dungeon, bastille, pound, reformatory, stockade, detention camp, gaol, concentration camp, penal institution, house of detention, prison, lockup, death house, *pen, *stir, *clink, *jug, *can; see also prison.

jail, v. confine, lock up, incarcerate, sentence, impound, detain, put behind bars, *put in the clink, *throw away the keys; see also imprison.—Ant. liberate, discharge, free.

jailed, a. arrested, incarcerated, in jail; see confined 3, held, under arrest.

jam, n. 1. [Preserves] conserve, fruit butter, spread, marmalade, candied fruit, blackberry jam, plum jam, strawberry jam, etc.; see also jelly 1. 2. [*A troublesome situation] dilemma, problem, trouble; see difficulty 1.

jam, v. 1. [To force one's way] jostle, squeeze, crowd, throng, press, thrust, pack; see also push 1 2. [To compress] bind, squeeze, push; see compress, pack 2, press 1.

jammed, a. 1. [Stuck fast] wedged, caught, frozen; see tight 2. 2. [Thronged] crowded, busy, congested; see full 1.

janitor, n. cleaning man, watchman, doorman; see attendant, custodian.

January, n. New Year(s), the new year, first month of the year; see month, winter.

Japan, n. the Japanese Empire, Nippon, the Land of the Rising Sun; see Asia.

Japanese, a. Ainu, Nipponese, East Asiatic; see Oriental.

jar, n. 1. [A glass or earthen container] crock, pot, fruit jar, can, vessel, basin, beaker, jug, cruet, vat, decanter, pitcher, bottle, flagon, flask, phial, vase, chalice, urn; see also container. 2. [A jolt] jounce, thud, thump; see bump 1.

jar, v. jolt, bounce, bump; see crash 4, hit 1.

jargon, n. 1. [Trite speech] banality, patter, hackneyed term, overused words, commonplace term or phrase, shopworn language, trite vocabulary, hocus-pocus; see also language 1. 2. [Specialized vocabulary or pronunciation, etc.] argot, patois, lingo, broken English, idiom, pidgin English, vernacular, colloquialism, coined word(s), dog or pig Latin, localism, rhyming slang, doubletalk, officialese, newspeak, journalese; see also dialect, slang.

jarring, a. 1. [Discordant] unharmonious, grating, rasping; see harsh, loud 1, 2, shrill. 2. [Jolting] bumpy, rough, uneven; see unstable 1.

jaunt, n. excursion, trip, tour; see journey, walk 3.

jaw, n. jawbone, muzzle, jowl, mandible, maxilla, chops; see also bone.

jaywalk, v. cross (a street) obliquely, walk in a forbidden traffic zone, walk or cross against a light, cut across, cross illegally.

jazz, n. Dixieland, ragtime, modern jazz, improvisation, *hot music, bop, swing, jive; see also music 1.

jealous, a. possessive, demanding, monopolizing, envious, watchful, resentful, mistrustful, doubting, apprehensive; see also suspicious 1.—Ant. trusting, confiding, believing.

jealousy, n. resentment, possessiveness, suspicion; see doubt, envy.

jeep, n. four-wheel drive vehicle, general purpose or G. P. vehicle, army car; see automobile, vehicle. Jeeplike vehicles include the following—Jeep, Jeepster, Scout, Land Rover, Land Cruiser, Bronco (all trade marks).

jell, v. set, crystallize, condense; see also freeze 1, harden, stiffen, thicken.

jelly, n. 1. [Jam] jell, extract. preserve, gelatin, apple jelly, currant jelly, raspberry jelly, etc.; see also jam 1.

jellyfish, n. medusa, coelenterate, hydrozoan; see fish.

jeopardize, v. imperil, expose, venture; see **endanger, risk**.

jeopardy, n. risk, peril, exposure; see **chance 1, danger 1**.

jerk, n. 1. [A twitch] tic, shrug, wiggle, shake, quiver, flick, jiggle; see also **bump 1**. 2. [*A detested person] scamp, scoundrel, *rat; see **fool, rascal**.

jerk, v. 1. [To undergo a spasm] have a convulsion, quiver, shiver; see **shake 1, twitch 2**. 2. [To move an object with a quick tug] snatch, grab, flick; see **seize 1, 2**.

jester, n. comedian, buffoon, joker; see **actor, clown, fool**.

Jesus, n. Saviour, Redeemer, the Son of God; see **Christ, God 2**.

jet, n. jet-propelled ship *or* aircraft *or* vehicle, jet plane, twin jet, strato-jet; jet bomber *or* fighter, etc.; supersonic *or* jet-age plane *or* airplane *or* aircraft, etc.; see also **plane 3**.

Jew, n. Hebrew, Israelite, Semite.

jewel, n. bauble, gem, trinket. Jewels include the following—emerald, amethyst, sapphire, opal, pearl, jade, aquamarine, moonstone, agate, ruby, turquoise, topaz, garnet, jasper, coral, peridot, lapis lazuli, bloodstone, onyx, zircon; see also **diamond**.

jeweler, n. goldsmith, diamond setter, lapidary; see **artist, craftsman, specialist**.

jewelry, n. gems, jewels, baubles, trinkets, adornments, frippery, ornaments, costume jewelry, bangles; see also **jewel**.

Jewish, a. Hebrew, Semitic, Yiddish.

jiggle, v. shake, twitch, wiggle; see **jerk 2**.

jingle, n. tinkle, jangle, clank; see **noise 1**.

jingle, v. tinkle, clink, rattle; see **sound 1**.

jinx, n. evil eye, hex, spell; see **chance 1**.

job, n. 1. [Gainful employment] situation, place, position, appointment, operation, task, line, calling, vocation, handicraft, career, craft, pursuit, office, function, means of livelihood; see also **business 1, profession 1, trade 2, work 2**. 2. [Something to be done] task, business, action, act, mission, assignment, affair, concern, obligation, enterprise, undertaking, project, chore, errand, care, matter (in hand), commission, function, responsibility, office, tour of duty, operation; see also **duty 1**. 3. [The amount of work done] assignment, day's work, output; see **duty 1**. —**odd jobs**, miscellaneous duties, chores, occasional labor; see **work 2**. —**on the job**, busy, engaged, occupied; see **busy 1**.

jog, n. 1. [A slow run] trot, amble, pace;

see **run 1**. 2. [A bump] jiggle, whack, hit; see **blow, bump 1**.

jog, v. jog along, take one's exercise, trot; see **run 1**.

jog (someone's) memory, v. bring up, recall, suggest; see **remind**.

John Doe, n. the average citizen, John Q. Public, anyone; see **mister**.

join, v. 1. [To unite] put *or* piece together, blend, combine, bring in contact with, touch, connect (up), couple, mix, assemble, stick *or* bind *or* lump together, fasten, attach, annex, cross *or* pair with, link, yoke, marry, wed, copulate, cement, weld, clasp, fuse, lock, grapple, clamp, entwine; see also **unite**. —*Ant.* separate, sunder, sever. 2. [To enter the company of] go to, seek, associate with, join forces, go to the aid of, place by the side of, follow, register, team *or* take *or* tie *or* line up with, be in, sign on *or* up, go *or* fall in with, consort, enlist, fraternize, throw in with, pair with, affiliate, act *or* side *or* align with, make one of, take part in, seek a place among, advance toward, seek reception, go to meet. —*Ant.* leave, desert, abandon. 3. [To adjoin] lie next to, neighbor, border, fringe, verge upon, be adjacent to, open into, be close to, bound, lie beside *or* near, be at hand, touch, skirt, parallel, rim, hem.

joined, a. linked, yoked, coupled, allied, akin, intertwined, blended, connected, united, federated, banded, wedded, married, mixed, put *or* tied together, combined, touching, cemented, welded, fused, locked, grappled, clipped together, accompanying, associated, confederated, mingled, spliced, affixed, attached, joint, incorporated, involved, inseparable, affiliated, related, pieced *or* fastened *or* stuck together, coupled with, bound up with *or* in; see also **unified**.—*Ant.* separated, disparate, apart.

joint, n. 1. [A juncture] union, coupling, hinge, tie, swivel, link, connection, point of union, bond, splice, bend, hyphen, junction, bridge; see also **bond 1**. 2. [A section] piece, unit, portion; see **link, part 3**. 3. [*An establishment, particularly one providing entertainment] *hangout, *dive, *hole in the wall; see **bar 2, restaurant**. 4. [*A marijuana cigarette] hemp, cannabis, *grass; see **drug**. —**out of joint**, dislocated, disjointed, wrong; see **disordered**.

jointly, a. conjointly, mutually, combined; see **together**.

joke, n. prank, put-on, game, sport, frolic, practical joke, jest, pun, witticism, play on words, quip, pleasantry, banter, drollery, retort, repartee, *crack, *wisecrack, clowning, caper, mischief, escapade, tomfoolery, play, antic, spree, farce, *monkeyshine, *shenanigan, horseplay, stunt, *gag; see also **trick 1**.

joke, v. jest, quip, banter, laugh, raise laughter, poke fun, play, frolic, play tricks, pun, twit, trick, fool, make merry (with), play the fool *or* the clown, *wisecrack, *pull one's leg.

joking, a. humorous, facetious, not serious; see **funny 1**.

jokingly, a. facetiously, amusingly, not seriously; see **humorously**.

jolly, a. gay, merry, joyful; see **happy**.

jolt, n. 1. [A bump] jar, punch, bounce; see **blow, bump 1**. 2. [A surprise] jar, start, shock; see **surprise 2, wonder 1**.

jostle, v. nudge, elbow, shoulder; see **press 1, push 1**.

jot, v. scribble (down), indicate, list; see **record 1, write 1**.

journal, n. 1. [A daily record] diary, almanac, chronicle; see **record 1**. 2. [A periodical] publication, annual, daily; see **magazine, newspaper**.

journalism, n. reportage, news coverage, the fourth estate; see **writing 3**.

journalist, n. commentator, publicist, member of the fourth estate; see **announcer, reporter, writer**.

journey, n. trip, visit, run, passage, tour, excursion, jaunt, pilgrimage, voyage, crossing, expedition, patrol, beat, venture, adventure, drive, flight, cruise, course, route, sojourn, traveling, travels, trek, migration, caravan, roaming, quest, safari, exploration, hike, airing, outing, march, picnic, survey, mission, ride.

journey, v. tour, jaunt, take a trip; see **travel**.

jovial, a. affable, amiable, merry; see **happy**.

jowl, n. mandible, chin, cheek; see **jaw**.

joy, n. mirth, cheerfulness, delight, pleasure, gratification, treat, diversion, sport, refreshment, revelry, frolic, playfulness, gaiety, geniality, good *or* high humor, merriment, merrymaking, levity, rejoicing, liveliness, high *or* good spirits, jubilation, celebration, game; see also **laughter**.—*Ant.* weeping, wailing, **complaining**.

joyful, a. joyous, cheery, glad; see **happy**.

joyous, a. blithe, glad, gay; see **happy**.

*joy ride, n. dangerous *or* reckless trip *or* travel, car theft, pleasure trip; see **drive 1, race 3**.

Judaism, n. Jewish religion, Hebraism, Zionism; see **religion 2**.

Judas, n. betrayer, fraud, informer; see **hypocrite, traitor**.

judge, n. 1. [A legal official] justice, executive judge, magistrate, justice of the peace, chief justice, associate justice, judiciary, circuit judge, county judge, judge of the district court, appeal judge. 2. [A connoisseur] expert, man of taste, professional; see **critic 2, specialist**.

judge, v. adjudge, adjudicate, rule *or* act *or* pass on, sit in judgment, sentence, give a hearing to, hold the scales; see also **condemn, convict**.

judged, a. found guilty *or* innocent, convicted, settled; see **determined 1, guilty**.

judgment, n. 1. [Discernment] discrimination, taste, shrewdness, sapience, understanding, knowledge, wit, keenness, sharpness, critical *or* rational faculty, reason, rationality, intuition, mentality, acuteness, intelligence, awareness, experience, profundity, depth, brilliance, mentality, intellectual power, capacity, comprehension, sanity, mother wit, quickness, readiness, grasp, apprehension, perspicacity, soundness, genius, (good) sense, breadth, astuteness, prudence, wisdom, gray matter, brains, a good head, horse sense.—*Ant.* **stupidity**, simplicity, naïveté. 2. [The act of judging] decision, consideration, appraisal, examination, weighing, sifting (evidence), determination, inspection, assessment, estimate, estimation, probing, appreciation, evaluation, review, contemplation, analysis, inquiry, inquisition, inquest, search, quest, pursuit, scrutiny, exploration, close study, observation, exhaustive inquiry; see also **examination 1**. 3. [A pronouncement] conclusion, appraisal, estimate, opinion, report, view, summary, belief, idea, conviction, inference, resolution, deduction, induction, determination, decree, opinion, supposition, commentary, finding, recommendation; see also **verdict**.

Judgment Day, n. doomsday, day of judgment, retribution, visitation, chastisement, correction, castigation, mortification, end of the world, last day, private *or* particular judgment; see also **judgment 1, 2**.

judicial, a. legalistic, authoritative, administrative; see **lawful 1**.

judiciary, n. justices, bench, bar; see **court 2**.

judicious, a. well-advised, prudent, sensible; see also **discreet, intelligent, rational 1**.—*Ant.* **rash**, ill-advised, hasty.

jug, n. crock, flask, pitcher; see **container**.

juggle, v. 1. [To keep in the air by tossing] toss, keep in motion, perform sleight of hand; see also **balance 2**. 2. [To alter, usually to deceive] shuffle, trick, delude; see **deceive**.

juice, n. sap, extract, fluid; see **liquid**.

juicy, a. succulent, moist, wet, watery, humid, dewy, sappy, dank, dripping, sodden, soaked, liquid, oily, sirupy; see also **wet.**—*Ant.* **dry**, dehydrated, bone-dry.

July, *n.* summer month, midsummer, baseball season; see **month, summer.**

jumble, *n.* clutter, mess, hodgepodge; see **confusion, mixture 1.**

jump, *n.* 1. [A leap up or across] skip, hop, rise, pounce, lunge, jumping, skip, broad jump, high jump, vault, bounce, hurdle, spring, bound, caper. 2. [A leap down] plunge, plummet, fall; see **dive, drop 2.** 3. [Distance jumped] leap, stretch, vault; see **height, length 1.** 4. [*An advantage] upper hand, handicap, head start; see **advantage.** 5. [A sudden rise] ascent, spurt, inflation; see **increase, rise 3.**

jump, *v.* 1. [To leap across or up] vault, leap (over), spring, lurch, lunge, pop up *or* out, bound, hop, skip, high-jump, broad-jump, hurdle, top. 2. [To leap down] drop, plummet, plunge; see **dive, fall 1.** 3. [To pass over] cover, take, skip, traverse, remove, nullify; see also **cancel, cross 1.** 4. [To vibrate] jiggle, wobble, rattle; see **bounce.** 5. [*To accost belligerently] halt, hold up, approach; see **attack.**

jumping, *a.* vaulting, hopping, skipping; see **active.**

jumpy, *a.* sensitive, restless, nervous; see **excited.**

junction, *n.* 1. [A meeting] joining, coupling, reunion; see **joint 1, union 1.** 2. [A place of meeting, especially of roads] crossroads, crossing, intersection; see **road 1.**

June, *n.* spring *or* summer (month), month of brides *or* graduation *or* roses, beginning of summer; see also **month, summer.**

jungle, *n.* wilderness, undergrowth, wood; see **forest.**

junk, *n.* waste, garbage, filth; see **trash 1.**

junk, *v.* dump, (sell for) scrap, wreck; see **discard.

junkie, *n.* dope addict, *mainliner, *monkey; see **addict.

jurisdiction, *n.* authority, range, supervision, control, discretion, province, commission, inquisition, scope, arbitration, reign, domain, extent, empire, sovereignty.

jurist, *n.* attorney, judge, legal adviser; see **lawyer.**

juror, *n.* juryman, peer, hearer; see **witness.**

jury, *n.* tribunal, panel, board; see **court 2.**

just, *a.* 1. [Precisely] exactly, correctly, perfectly; see **accurate.** 2. [Hardly] barely, scarcely, by very little; see **hardly.** 3. [Only] merely, simply, plainly; see **simply 1.** 4. [Recently] just a while ago, lately, a moment ago; see **recently.** 5. [Fair] impartial, equal, righteous; see **fair 1.**

justice, *n.* 1. [Fairness] right, truth, equity; see **fairness.** 2. [Lawfulness] legality, equity, prescriptive *or* statutory *or* established right, legitimacy, sanction, legalization, constitutionality, authority, code, charter, decree, rule, legal process, authorization; see also **custom 2, law 2, power 2.**—*Ant.* illegality, illegitimacy, **wrong.** 3. [The administration of law] adjudication, settlement, arbitration, hearing, legal process, due process, judicial procedure, jury trial, trial by law *or* jury, regulation, decision, pronouncement, review, appeal, sentence, consideration, taking evidence, litigation, prosecution; see also **judgment 1, law 3, trial 2.**—*Ant.* lawlessness, **disorder,** despotism. 4. [A judge] magistrate, umpire, chancellor; see **judge 1.** —**do justice to,** treat fairly, do right by, help; see **treat 1.** —**do oneself justice,** be fair to oneself, give oneself credit, be fair; see **approve.**

justifiable, *a.* proper, suitable, probable; see **fit 1, logical.**

justification, *n.* excuse, defense, reason; see **appeal 1, explanation.**

justify, *v.* 1. [To vindicate] absolve, acquit, clear; see **excuse.** 2. [To give reasons for] support, apologize (for), excuse; see **defend, explain.**

justly, *a.* 1. [Honorably] impartially, honestly, frankly, candidly, fairly, straightforwardly, reasonably, moderately, temperately, even-handedly, rightly, equitably, equably, tolerantly, charitably, respectably, lawfully, legally, legitimately, rightfully, properly, duly, in justice, as it ought to be. 2. [Exactly] properly, precisely, rationally; see **accurately.**

just the same, *a.* and *prep.* nevertheless, just the same, in spite of that; see **but 1.**

jut, *v.* extend, bulge, stick out; see **project 1.**

juvenile, *a.* youthful, adolescent, teenage; see **young 1.**

K

keen, a. 1. [Sharp] pointed, edged, acute; see **sharp** 1. 2. [Astute] bright, clever, shrewd; see **intelligent.** 3. [Eager] ardent, interested, intent; see **zealous.**

keenly, a. acutely, sharply, penetratingly; see **clearly** 1, 2, very, **vigorously.**

keep, v. 1. [To hold] retain, grip, own, possess, have, take, seize, save, grasp; see also **hold** 1. 2. [To maintain] preserve, conserve, care for; see **maintain** 3. 3. [To continue] keep going, carry on, sustain; see **continue** 1, **endure** 1. 4. [To operate] administer, run, direct; see **manage** 1. 5. [To tend] care for, minister to, attend; see **tend** 1. 6. [To remain] stay, continue, abide; see **settle** 7, 8. 7. [To store] deposit, hoard, retain, store, preserve, reserve, put away, conserve, warehouse, *stash (away), put (away or back), cache; see also **save** 2, **store** 2. 8. [To prevent; used with from] stop, block, avert; see **hinder, prevent.** 9. [Retain] not spoil, season, put up; see **preserve** 3. —*for keeps,* permanently, changelessly, perpetually; see **forever.**

keep after, v. 1. [To pursue] track, trail, follow; see **pursue** 1. 2. [To nag] push, remind, pester; see **bother** 2, **disturb.**

keep an appointment, v. show up, be on time, be there; see **arrive.**

keep an eye on, v. observe, investigate, look after; see **guard, watch.**

keep at, v. persist, persevere, endure; see **continue** 1.

keep away, v. 1. [To remain] stay away, hold back, not come or appear; see **wait** 1. 2. [To restrain] keep off, hold back, defend oneself (from); see **hinder, prevent, restrict.**

keep back, v. 1. [To delay] check, hold, postpone; see **delay, hinder, suspend** 2. 2. [To restrict] inclose, inhibit, oppose; see **forbid, restrict.**

keep calm, v. take (one's) time, keep cool, be patient; see **calm down, relax.**

keep company with, v. fraternize, accompany, associate, go together, date, go with, *take up with, *hang around with, *pal around with.

keep down, v. reduce, deaden, muffle; see **decrease** 2, **soften** 2.

keeper, n. guard, official, attendant; see **warden, watchman.**

keep from, v. 1. [To abstain] desist, refrain, avoid; see **abstain.** 2. [To prevent] prohibit, forestall, impede; see **hinder, prevent.**

keep going, v. progress, promote, proceed; see **advance** 1, **improve** 2.

keeping, n. care, custody, guard; see **protection** 2. —*in keeping with,* similar to, much the same, in conformity with; see **alike.**

keep in line, v. 1. [To behave] obey, be good, restrain oneself; see **behave.** 2. [To manage] check, watch over, be responsible for; see **restrain.**

keep off or out, interj. Hands off! Stay away! Stop! Keep off, the grass! No trespassing! No hunting or fishing! Private property!

keep on, v. finish, repeat, pursue; see **continue** 1, **endure** 1.

keep safe, v. care for, chaperone, protect; see **guard, watch.**

keepsake, n. memento, token, remembrance; see **reminder.**

keep to oneself, v. be a recluse or a hermit, cultivate solitude, avoid human companionship, stay away, keep one's own counsel; see also **hide.**

keep up, v. support, care for, safeguard; see **sustain** 2.

keep up with, v. keep pace or step, pace, run with; see **compete.**

keg, n. cask, drum, vat; see **barrel, container.**

kennel, n. doghouse, den, pound; see **enclosure** 1, **pen** 1.

kept, a. 1. [Preserved] put up, pickled, stored; see **preserved** 2. 2. [Retained] maintained, withheld, held, guarded, watched over, reserved, on file, at hand; see also **saved** 2. 3. [Observed] obeyed, honored, continued, discharged, maintained, carried on; see also **fulfilled.**— Ant. **abandoned,** dishonored, forgotten.

kernel, n. nut, core, germ; see **grain** 1, **seed.**

ketchup, n. tomato sauce, mushroom sauce, condiment; see **relish.**

kettle, n. cauldron, saucepan, stewpot; see **pot** 1.

key, n. 1. [Instrument to open a lock] latchkey, opener, master key, passkey, skeleton key. 2. [A means of solution] clue, code, indicator; see **answer** 2.

keyed up, a. stimulated, spurred on, nervous; see **excited.**

keynote, a. main, leading, official; see **important** 1, **principal.**

kick, n. 1. [A blow with the foot] boot, swift kick, jolt, jar, hit; see also **blow.** 2. [In sports, a kicked ball] punt, drop kick, place kick; see **kick** 1. 3. [*Pleasant reaction] joy, pleasant sensation, refreshment; see **enjoyment**.

kick, v. 1. [To give a blow with the foot] boot, jolt, punt, dropkick, place kick, kick off; see also **beat 1**, **hit 1**. 2. [*To object] make a complaint, criticize, carp; see **complain**, **oppose 1**.

kick about or **around**, v. mistreat, treat badly, misuse; see **abuse**.

kickoff, n. opening, beginning, launching; see **origin 2**.

kick off, v. start, open, get under way; see **begin 1**.

*****kick out**, v. reject, throw out, eject; see **dismiss**, **remove 1**.

kid, n. 1. [The young of certain animals] lamb, lambkin, fawn, calf, yearling; see also **animal**. 2. [*A child] son, daughter, tot; see **boy**, **child**, **girl**.

*****kid**, v. tease, pretend, fool; see **bother 2**, **joke**.

kidnap, v. abduct, ravish, capture, steal, rape, carry away, hold for ransom, shanghai, carry off, make off or away with, grab, spirit away, pirate, snatch, bundle off.—*Ant.* ransom, rescue, release.

kidnapped, a. made off with, abducted, ravished, stolen, carried away, held for ransom, shanghaied, waylaid, manhandled, seized, held under illegal restraint; see also **captured**.—*Ant.* free, rescued, freed.

kidney, n. excretory organ, urinary organ, abdominal gland; see **organ 2**.

kill, v. 1. [To deprive of life] slay, slaughter, murder, assassinate, massacre, butcher, hang, lynch, electrocute, dispatch, execute, knife, sacrifice, shoot, strangle, poison, choke, smother, suffocate, asphyxiate, drown, behead, guillotine, crucify, dismember, decapitate, disembowel, quarter, tear limb from limb, destroy, give the death blow, give the *coup de grâce*, put to death, deprive of life, put an end to, exterminate, stab, cut the throat, shoot down, mangle, cut or bring or mow down, machine gun, pick off, liquidate, put one out of his misery, starve, do away with, commit murder, *bump off, *rub or wipe out, *do in, *knock off, *finish off, *blow one's brains out, *put to sleep, *brain, *zap.—*Ant.* rescue, resuscitate, animate. 2. [To cancel] annul, nullify, counteract; see **cancel**. 3. [To turn off] turn out, shut off, stop; see **halt**, **turn off**. 4. [To veto] cancel, prohibit, refuse; see **forbid**.

killer, n. murderer, manslayer, gunman, gangster, shooter, butcher, hangman, assassin, slayer, sniper, cutthroat, thug, Cain; see also **criminal**.

killing, a. mortal, lethal, fatal; see **deadly**.

killing, n. slaying, assassination, slaughter; see **crime**.

kin, n. (blood) relation or relative, member of the family, sibling; see **family**, **relative**.

kind, a. tender, well-meaning, considerate, charitable, loving, pleasant, amiable, soft, softhearted, compassionate, sympathetic, understanding, solicitous, sweet, generous, helpful, obliging, neighborly, accommodating, indulgent, delicate, tactful, gentle, tenderhearted, kindhearted, good-natured, inoffensive, benevolent, altruistic, other-directed, lenient, easy-going, patient, tolerant, mellow, genial, sensitive, courteous, agreeable, thoughtful, well-disposed.—*Ant.* rough, brutal, harsh.

kind, n. 1. [Class] classification, species, genus; see **class 1**. 2. [Type] sort, variety, description, stamp, character, tendency, gender, habit, breed, set, tribe, denomination, persuasion, manner, connection, designation.

kindergarten, n. class for small children, pre-elementary grade, preschool training; see **school 1**.

kindhearted, a. amiable, generous, good; see **humane**, **kind**.

kindle, v. light, catch fire, set fire; see **burn 2**, **ignite**.

kindling, n. firewood, tinder, coals; see **fuel**, **wood 2**.

kindly, a. generous, helpful, good; see **humane**, **kind**.

kindness, n. 1. [The quality of being kind] tenderness, good intention, consideration, sympathy, sweetness, helpfulness, tact, benignity, mildness, courtesy, thoughtfulness, humanity, courteousness, understanding, compassion, unselfishness, altruism, warmheartedness, softheartedness, politeness, kindliness, clemency, benevolence, goodness, philanthropy, charity, friendliness, mercy, affection, loving kindness, cordiality, amiability, forbearance, graciousness, kindheartedness, virtue.—*Ant.* brutality, **cruelty**, selfishness. 2. [A kindly act] (good) service, relief, charity, benevolence, philanthropy, favor, good deed, good turn, self-sacrifice, mercy, lift, boost; see also **help 1**.—*Ant.* transgression, **injury**, wrong.

*****kind of**, a. somewhat, having the nature of, *sort of; see **moderately**.

kindred, n. kinship, connection, blood relationship; see **relationship**.

king, n. 1. [A male sovereign] monarch, tyrant, prince, autocrat, czar, caesar, lord (temporal), emperor, overlord, crowned head, imperator, majesty, regal personage, sultan, caliph, shah, rajah, maharajah; see also **ruler** 1.—*Ant.* servant, slave, subordinate. 2. [A very superior being] lord, chief, head; see **leader** 2.

kingdom, *n.* realm, domain, country, empire, lands, possessions, principality, state, dominions, sway, rule, crown, throne, subject territory.

kingship, *n.* supremacy, divinity, majesty; see **power** 2, **royalty.**

king-size, *a.* big, large-size, giant; see **broad** 1, **large** 1.

kinky, *a.* fuzzy, curled, crimped; see **curly.**

kinship, *n.* affiliation, kindred, relationship, affinity, cohesion, unity, familiarity, intimacy, connection, alliance; see also **family, relationship.**

kiss, *n.* embrace, endearment, touch of the lips, butterfly kiss, caress, *smack, *peck; see also **touch** 2.

kiss, *v.* salute, osculate, make love, *play post office, *smack, *smooch, *pet, *neck, *make out, *blow a kiss; see also **love** 2.

kit, *n.* 1. [Equipment] material, tools, outfit; see **equipment.** 2. [A pack] poke, knapsack, satchel; see **bag, container.**

kitchen, *n.* scullery, galley, canteen, cook's room, kitchenette, mess.

kite, *n.* box kite, Chinese kite, tailless kite; see **toy** 1.

kitten, *n.* pussy, kitty, baby cat; see **animal, cat.**

knack, *n.* trick, skill, faculty; see **ability.**

knapsack, *n.* (back)pack, kit, rucksack; see **bag, container.**

knead, *v.* work, shape, twist; see **press** 1.

knee, *n.* (knee) joint, crook, bend, hinge, kneecap, articulation of the femur and the tibia; see also **bone.**

kneel, *v.* bend the knee, rest on the knees, genuflect, bend, stoop, bow down, curtsey.

knickknack, *n.* gadget, bric-a-brac, curio, ornament, trifle, bauble, trinket, toy, plaything, showpiece, *gewgaw; see also **toy** 1.

knife, *n.* blade, cutter, sword, bayonet, cutting edge, dagger, stiletto, lance, machete, poniard, scalpel, edge, dirk, sickle, scythe, sabre, scimitar, broadsword, point, *pigsticker, *toad-stabber, *shiv; see also **razor.** Knives include the following—carving, chopping, table, dinner, breakfast, dessert, grapefruit, fish, pocket, hunting, Bowie, cane, butcher, skinning, surgical, paper, pruning, oyster, putty, palette, bread, cake, serving, Boy Scout, Swiss Army.

knife, *v.* 1. [To stab] spit, lance, thrust through; see **hurt** 1, **kill** 1, **stab.** 2. [To injure in an underhanded way] trick,

give a coward's blow, strike below the belt; see **deceive.**

knight, *n.* cavalier, champion, knighterrant; see **aristocrat.**

knit, *v.* 1. [To form by knitting] spin, crochet, web, cable, net; see also **sew, weave** 1. 2. [To combine or join closely] intermingle, connect, affiliate; see **join** 1.

knitted, *a.* knit, crocheted, stitched; see also **woven.**

knob, *n.* 1. [A projection] hump, bulge, knot, node, bend, bump, protuberance; see also **lump.** 2. [A door handle] doorknob, latch, door latch; see **handle** 1.

knobby, *a.* knobbed, lumpy, bumpy; see **bent, crooked** 1.

knock, *n.* rap, thump, whack; see **beat** 1, **blow** 1, **injury** 1.

knock, *v.* tap, rap, thump; see **beat** 2, **hit** 1, **hurt** 1.

knock down, *v.* thrash, drub, kayo; see **beat** 1, **hit** 1, **knock out** 2.

*knock off, *v.* 1. [To kill] murder, stab, shoot; see **kill** 1. 2. [To accomplish] complete, finish, eliminate; see **achieve, succeed** 1. 3. [To stop] quit, leave, halt; see **stop** 2.

knock oneself out, *v.* slave, labor, do one's utmost; see **work** 1.

knockout, *n.* 1. [A blow that knocks unconscious] knockout blow, finishing or final blow, *kayo; see **blow.** 2. [A success] excellent thing, sensation, perfection; see **success** 1.

knock out, *v.* 1. [To anesthetize] etherize, put to sleep, stupefy; see **deaden.** 2. [To strike down] strike senseless, render unconscious, knock a person out of his senses, *knock cold, *kayo, *knock for a loop, *put out like a light.

*knock up, *v.* impregnate, make pregnant, inseminate; see **fertilize** 2.

knot, *n.* 1. [An arrangement of strands] tie, clinch, hitch, splice, ligature, bond. 2. [A hard or twisted portion] snarl, gnarl, snag, bunch, coil, entanglement, tangle, twist, twirl, whirl.

knot, *v.* bind, tie, cord; see **fasten.**

knotted, *a.* tied, twisted, tangled, snarled, entangled, bunched, clustered, whirled, looped, hitched, spliced, fastened, bent, warped, clinched, banded, lassoed, braided, linked, involved.—*Ant.* free, loose, separate.

know, *v.* 1. [To possess information] be cognizant *or* acquainted *or* informed, be in possession of the facts, have something cold, have knowledge of, be schooled *or* read *or* learned *or* versed in, be conversant with, recognize, know full well, have at one's fingertips, be master of, know by heart, know inside and out, be instructed, awaken to, keep up on, have information about, know what's what, know all the answers, *have one's number, *have the jump on, *have down cold, *know one's stuff, *know the score *or* the ropes.—*Ant.* be oblivious of, **neglect**, overlook. **2.** [To understand] comprehend, apprehend, see into; see **understand 1. 3.** [To recognize] perceive, discern, be familiar with, have the friendship of, acknowledge, be accustomed to, associate with, be *or* get acquainted.

*know-how, *n.* skill, background, wisdom; see **ability, experience, knowledge 1.**

*know how, *v.* be able, have the (necessary) background *or* training, be trained in *or* for; see **understand 1.**

knowing, *a.* sharp, clever, acute; see **intelligent, reasonable 1.**

knowingly, *a.* intentionally, purposely, consciously; see **deliberately.**

knowledge, *n.* **1.** [Information] learning, lore, scholarship, facts, wisdom, instruction, book-learning, enlightenment, expertise, intelligence, light, theory, science, principles, philosophy, awareness, insight, education, substance, store of learning, *know-how; see also **information 1.**—*Ant.* emptiness, **ignorance**, pretension. **2.** [Culture] dexterity, cultivation, learning; see **experience, refinement 2.**

known, *a.* **1.** [Open] discovered, disclosed, revealed; see **obvious 1, public 1. 2.** [Established] well-known, published, recognized, notorious, received, accepted, noted, proverbial, hackneyed, certified, *down pat; see also **familiar.**

know-nothing, *n.* imbecile, clod, illiterate; see **fool.**

knuckle under, *v.* give in, give up, acquiesce; see **yield 1.**

L

label, *n.* tag, marker, mark, stamp, hallmark, insignia, design, number, identification, description, classification; see also **name 1.**

label, *v.* specify, mark, identify; see **name 1, 2.**

labeled, *a.* identified, provided with identification, stamped; see **marked 1, 2.**

labor, *n.* 1. [The act of doing work] activity, toil, operation; see **work 2.** 2. [Work to be done] task, employment, undertaking; see **job 2.** 3. [Exertion required in work] exertion, energy, industry, diligence, strain, stress, drudgery; see also **effort, exercise 1.** 4. [The body of workers] laborers, workers, working-men, proletariat, work *or* labor force, working people, employee(s).—*Ant.* **employer,** capitalist, businessman. 5. [Childbirth] parturition, giving birth, labor pains; see **birth.**

labor, *v.* toil, strive, *get cracking; see **work 1.**

laboratory, *n.* workroom, *lab, research room, testing room; see **office 3.**

laborer, *n.* day laborer, (unskilled) worker, hand, manual laborer, ranch *or* farm hand, apprentice, (hired) man, transient worker, toiler, seasonal laborer, ditch-digger, pick and shovel man, roust-about, stevedore, miner, street cleaner, instrument, peon, flunky, lackey, hireling, hack, *beast of burden, *doormat.

labor union, *n.* organized labor, American Federation of Labor and Congress of Industrial Organizations (AFL-CIO), (independent) union, local, labor party; see also **organization 2.**

lace, *n.* 1. [Ornamental threadwork] border, tissue, net; see **decoration 2.** 2. [Material for binding through openings] thong, cord, band; see **rope.**

lace, *v.* strap, bind, close; see **fasten, tie 2.**

lacing, *n.* bond, hitch, tie; see **fastener, knot 1.**

lack, *n.* 1. [The state of being lacking] destitution, absence, need, shortage, paucity, deprivation, deficiency, scarcity, insufficiency, inadequacy, privation, poverty, distress, scantiness. —*Ant.* **plenty,** sufficiency, abundance. 2. [That which is lacking] need, decrease, want, loss, depletion, shrinkage, shortage, defect, inferiority, paucity, stint, curtailment, reduction; see also **necessity 2.**—*Ant.* **wealth,** overflow, satisfaction.

lack, *v.* want, require, have need (of); see **need.**

lacking, *a.* needed, deprived of, missing; see **wanting.**

lacy, *a.* sheer, thin, gauzy; see **transparent 1.**

lad, *n.* fellow, youth, stripling; see **boy, child.**

ladder, *n.* stairway, step-stool, scale; see **stairs.** Ladders include the following—stepladder, rope ladder, ship's ladder, fireman's scaling (extension) ladder, gangway, fire escape.

ladle, *n.* skimmer, scoop, vessel; see **silverware.**

lady, *n.* 1. [A woman] female, adult, matron; see **woman 1.** 2. [A woman of gentle breeding] gentlewoman, well-bred woman, woman of good taste *or* breeding *or* quality, woman of education, cultured woman, high-born lady, mistress of a manor *or* estate, noblewoman, titled lady; see also **woman.**

ladylike, *a.* womanly, cultured, well-bred; see **polite, refined 2.**

lag, *n.* slack, slowness, tardiness, falling behind, sluggishness, backwardness.—*Ant.* **progress,** progression, advance.

lag, *v.* dawdle, linger, fall *or* hold back, loiter, tarry, straggle, get behind, slacken, slow up, fall *or* lag behind, procrastinate, plod, trudge, lounge, shuffle, falter, stagger, limp, *get no place fast; see also **delay.**—*Ant.* **hasten,** hurry, keep pace with.

lagoon, *n.* inlet, sound, pool; see **bay, lake.**

lair, *n.* cave, home, den; see **pen 1.**

lake, *n.* pond, creek, loch, pool, inland sea; see also **sea.** Famous lakes include the following—Titicaca, Yellowstone, Geneva *or* Leman, Lucerne, Arrowhead, Great Salt, Superior, Huron, Michigan, Erie, Ontario, Champlain, Tahoe, Tanganyika, Nyasa, Como, Windermere, Derwentwater, Lake of the Woods, Loch Lomond.

lamb, *n.* young sheep, young one, yeanling; see **animal.**

lame, *a.* 1. [Forced to limp] crippled, unable to walk, halt, weak, paralyzed, impaired, handicapped, defective, limping; see also **deformed, disabled.** 2. [Weak; *usually used figuratively*] inefficient, ineffective, faltering; see **unsatisfactory, wanting.**

lamp, *n.* light, light bulb, lighting device; see **light 3.** Types and forms of lamps include the following—wick, oil, gas, electric, sun, hanging, bracket, portable, table, standing, floor, miner's, street, arc, incandescent, gasoline, night, chandelier, lantern, torch.

lance, *n.* lancet, foil, point; see **spear, weapon 1.**

land, *n.* **1.** [The solid surface of the earth] ground, soil, dirt, clay, loam, gravel, subsoil, clod, sand, rock, mineral, metal, pebble, stone, dry land, valley, desert, hill, bank, seaside, shore, beach, crag, cliff, boulder, ledge, peninsula, delta, promontory; see also **earth 2, mountain 1, plain.**—*Ant.* **sea,** stream, ocean. **2.** [Land as property] estate, tract, ranch, farm, home, lot, real estate; see **area, property 2. 3.** [A country] continent, province, region; see **nation 1.**

land, *v.* **1.** [To bring a boat to shore] dock, set on shore, set down, bring in, come to land, pilot, steer, drop *or* cast anchor, put in.—*Ant.* **leave,** weigh anchor, cast off. **2.** [To come into port] dock, berth, come to berth; see **arrive. 3.** [To go ashore] disembark, come ashore, arrive, alight, leave the boat *or* ship, go down the gangplank, *hit the beach.—*Ant.* **leave,** go on shipboard, go up the gangplank. **4.** [To bring an airplane to earth] touch *or* get down, ground, take down, alight, come in, settle, level off, come down, descend upon, make a forced landing, crash-land, *nose over, overshoot, splash down, check in, undershoot, pancake, *settle her down hot, fishtail down; see also **arrive.**

landing, *n.* **1.** [The act of reaching shore] arriving, docking, making port, steering, anchoring, dropping anchor; see also **arrival 1. 2.** [The place where landing, sense 1, is possible] marina, pier, wharf; see **dock. 3.** [The act of reaching the earth] setting down, grounding, getting in, arriving, deplaning, reaching an airport, splashing down, completing a mission, settling, splashdown.

landlady, *n.* homeowner, apartment manager, innkeeper; see **owner.**

landlord, *n.* homeowner, apartment manager, realtor, landowner, lessor, property *or* house *or* condominium owner, innkeeper; see also **owner.**

landmark, *n.* **1.** [A notable relic] remnant, vestige, souvenir; see **monument 1, relic. 2.** [A point from which a course may be taken] vantage point, mark, blaze, guide, marker, stone, tree, hill, mountain, bend, promontory, *duck on a rock.

landscape, *n.* scene, scenery, panorama; see **view 1, 2.**

landscape, *v.* provide *or* do the landscap-

ing, finish off *or* up, put in the lawn and shrubbery; see **decorate.**

landscaping, *n.* lawn, shrubbery, garden; see **decoration 2.**

landslide, *n.* slide, avalanche, rock slide; see **descent 2.**

lane, *n.* way, alley, passage; see **path, road 1.**

language, *n.* **1.** [A means of communication] voice, utterance, expression, vocalization, sound, phonation, (native *or* mother) tongue, articulation, metalanguage, physical language; language of diplomacy, language of chemistry, language of flowers, etc.; accent, word, sign, signal, pantomine, (facial) gesture, vocabulary, diction, dialect, idiom, local speech, broken *or* pidgin English, polyglot, patios *or* venacular, lingua franca *or* trade language, gibberish, pig Latin, debased speech; see also **dialect, jargon 2, writing 1, 2. 2.** [The study of language, sense 1] morphology, phonology, phonemics, morphemics, morphophonemics, phonics, phonetics, criticism, letters, linguistic studies, history of language, etymology, dialectology, linguistic geography; see also **grammar, linguistics, literature 1.** Types of languages include the following—synthetic *or* inflectional, analytic *or* isolating *or* distributive, incorporating, agglutinative, computer, artificial, polysynthetic. Indo-European languages include the following—Germanic: Gothic, Old Saxon, Old English *or* Anglo-Saxon, English, Frisian, Old High German, German, Yiddish, Dutch, Afrikaans, Flemish, Old Norse, Danish, Swedish, Norwegian, Icelandic; Celtic: Breton, Welsh *or* Cymric, Cornish, Irish *or* Erse, Scots Gaelic, Manx; Italic: Oscan, Umbrian, Venetic, Latin; Romance: Portuguese, Galician, Spanish, Catalan, Provençal, French, Haitian Creole, Walloon, Italian, Sardinian, Romanian, Rhaeto-Romantic *or* Romansh *or* Ladin; Greek: Attic, Ionic, Doric, Koine; Slavic: Old Church Slavonic, Russian, Byelorussian, Ukrainian, Polish, Czech, Slovak, Slovene, Serbo-Croatian, Bulgarian; Baltic: Old Prussian, Lithuanian, Latvian *or* Lettish; Albanian; Armenian; Iranian: Old Persian, Avestan, Pahlavi, Kurdish, Persian, Pushtu *or* Afghan; Indic: Sanskrit, Pali, Prakrit, Hindi, Urdu; Tocharian; Hittite. Other Eurasian languages include the following—Uralic: Finnish, Estonian, Hungarian, Samoyed; Altaic: Turkish, Mongolian; Georgian; Abkhasian, Kabardian, Chechen; Basque; Etruscan. For terms applying to African, Asian and Oceanic languages see **Africa, Asia, Oceania.** North American languages include the following—

Algonquian: Massachusetts, Delaware, Mohegan, Penobscot, Pasamaquoddy, Fox-Sauk-Kickapoo, Cree, Menomini, Shawnee, Blackfoot, Arapaho, Cheyenne; Wiyot, Yurok; Kutenai; Salishan: Tillamook, Lillooet; Wakashan: Nootka, Kwakiutl; Muskogean: Creek, Choctaw-Chickasaw, Seminole; Natchez, Chitimacha; Iroquoian: Cherokee, Huron or Wayondot, Erie, Oneida, Mohawk, Seneca, Cayuga, Susquehanna or Conestoga; Siouan: Biloxi, Dakota, Mandan, Winnebago, Hidatsa, Crow; Caddoan: Caddo, Wichita, Pawnee; Yuchi; Aleut, Eskimo; Penutian: Tsimshian, Maidu, Miwok, Klamath-Modoc; Zuni; Hokan: Karok, Shasta, Washo, Pomo; Mayan: Kekchi, Quiche, Yucatec; Totonac; Mixe, Zoque, Vera Cruz; Huave; Zapotec, Chatino; Mixtec; Pueblo or Popoluca; Otomi, Pame; Tarascan; Uto-Aztecan: Tubatulabal, Luiseño, Tepehuan, Pima-Papago, Hopi, Huichol, Nahuatl or Aztec, Northern Paiute or Paviotso, Mono, Shoshoni-Comanche, Southern Paiute-Ute, Chemehuevi; Kiowa-Tanoan; Keresan; Na-Dené: Haida, Tlingit, Athabaskan; Chippewayan, Apachean, Navaho, Hupa. —speak the same language, understand one another, communicate, get along; see agree.

lantern, *n.* torch, lamp, lighting device; see light 3.

lap, *n.* 1. [That portion of the body that is formed when one sits down] knees, legs, thighs, front. 2. [The portion that overlaps] extension, projection, fold; see flap. 3. [Part of a race] circuit, round, course; see distance 3, race 3. —drop into someone's lap, transfer responsibility, shift blame, *pass the buck; see give 1. —in the lap of luxury, surrounded by luxury, living elegantly, prospering; see rich 1.

lapse, *n.* slip, mistake, failure; see error.

lapse, *v.* slip, deteriorate, decline; see weaken 1.

larceny, *n.* burglary, thievery, robbery; see crime, theft.

large, *a.* 1. [Of great size] huge, big, wide, grand, great, considerable, substantial, vast, massive, immense, spacious, bulky, colossal, gigantic, mountainous, immeasurable, extensive, plentiful, copious, populous, ample, abundant, liberal, comprehensive, lavish, swollen, bloated, puffy, obese, monstrous, towering, mighty, magnificent, enormous, giant, tremendous, monumental, stupendous, voluminous, cumbersome, ponderous, gross, immoderate, extravagant, super, *booming, *bumper, *whopping; see also big 1, broad 1, deep 2, extensive, high 1.—*Ant.* little, small, tiny. 2. [Involving great plans] extensive, extended, considerable; see general 1.

largely, *a.* 1. [In large measure] mostly, mainly, chiefly; see principally 1. 2. [In a large way] extensively, abundantly, comprehensively; see widely.

largeness, *n.* magnitude, proportion, breadth; see measure 1, measurement 2, quantity, size.

lariat, *n.* lasso, tether, line; see rope.

lark, *n.* songbird, warbler, philomel; see bird.

larva, *n.* maggot, grub, caterpillar; see worm.

lash (out), *v.* strike, thrash, scourge; see beat 1, hit 1.

lass, *n.* young woman or lady, damsel, maiden; see girl, woman.

lasso, *n.* tether, lariat, noose; see rope.

last, *a.* 1. [Final] ultimate, utmost, lowest, meanest, least, latest, end, extreme, remotest, furthest, outermost, farthest, uttermost, concluding, hindmost, far, far-off, ulterior, once and for all, definitive, after all others, ending, at the end, terminal, eventual, settling, resolving, decisive, crowning, climactic, closing, ending, finishing, irrefutable—*Ant.* first, foremost, beginning. 2. [Most recent] latest, newest, current, freshest, immediate, in the fashion, modish, *the last word; see also fashionable, modern 1.—*Ant.* old, stale, outmoded.

last, *n.* tail end, last or terminal or final one, ending; see end 4. —at (long) last, after a long time, in the end, ultimately; see finally 2. —see the last of, see for the last time or never again, dispose of, get rid of; see end 1.

last, *v.* 1. [To endure] remain, carry on, survive, hold out, suffer, stay, overcome, persist, sustain, maintain, *stick it out or with it, go on; see also continue 1, endure 1, 2. 2. [To be sufficient] hold out, be adequate or enough or ample or satisfactory, serve, do, accomplish the purpose, answer; see also satisfy 3.

lasting, *a.* enduring, abiding, constant; see permanent 2.

latch, *n.* catch, hook, bar; see fastener, lock 1.

latch, *v.* lock, cinch, close up; see close 4, fasten.

late, *a.* 1. [Tardy] too late, held up, overdue, stayed, postponed, put off, not on time, belated, behind time, lagging, delayed, backward, not in time; see also slow 2, 3.—*Ant.* early, punctual, on time. 2. [Recently dead] defunct, deceased, departed; see dead 1. 3. [Recent] new, just out, recently published; see fresh 1. 4. [Far into the night] nocturnal, night-loving, advanced, tardy, toward morning, after midnight. —of late, lately, in recent times, a short time ago; see **recently**.

lately, a. a short time ago, in recent times, of late; see **recently**.

lateness, n. belatedness, procrastination, hesitation, tardiness, retardation, protraction, prolongation, slowness, backwardness, advanced hour, late date.— Ant. anticipation, earliness, promptness.

latent, a. underdeveloped, potential, inactive; see **dormant**.

later, a. succeeding, next, more recent; see **following**.

lateral, a. oblique, sidelong, side by side; see **side**.

latest, a. most recent, immediately prior (to), just done or finished or completed; see **last** 1, 2.

lather, n. suds, foam, bubbles; see **froth**.

Latin, a. 1. [Pertaining to ancient Rome or to its language] Roman, Romanic, Latinic; see **language** 2, n. 2. [Pertaining to southwestern Europe] Roman, Mediterranean, Italian; see **European**.

Latin, n. Romance language, Classical Latin, Vulgar or Late Latin; see **language** 2.

latitude, n. (meridional) distance, degree, measure, degrees of latitude; see also **measure** 1.

latter, a. late, last, recent; see **following**, **last** 1.

latter, n. the nearest or most recent or subsequent or second, third, etc., person referred to; the last named; see **end** 4.

laugh, n. mirth, merriment, amusement, rejoicing, gesture, crow, shout, chuckle, chortle, cackle, fit or peal of laughter, horselaugh, guffaw, titter, snicker, giggle, roar, snort; see also **laughter**.—Ant. sob, cry, whimper. —have the last laugh, defeat (finally), beat in the end, overcome all obstacles; see **win** 1. —no laughing matter, serious, grave, significant; see **important** 1.

laugh, v. chuckle, chortle, guffaw, laugh off, snicker, titter, giggle, burst out (laughing), shriek, roar, beam, grin, smile, smirk, shout, *die laughing, *break or crack up, *howl, *roll in the aisles, be in stitches; see also **smile**.— Ant. cry, sob, weep.

laughable, a. ludicrous, comic, comical; see **funny** 1.

laugh at, v. deride, taunt, make fun of; see **ridicule**.

laughing, a. chortling, giggling, chuckling; see **happy**.

laughter, n. chortling, chuckling, guffawing, tittering, giggling, shouting, roaring, howling, snorting; see also **laugh**.—Ant. cry, weeping, wailing.

launch, v. 1. [To initiate] originate, start, set going; see **begin** 1. 2. [To send off] set in motion, propel, drive, thrust, fire off, send forth, eject; see also **drive** 1, 2, **propel**.

launched, a. started, sent, set in motion; see **begun**, **driven**, **sent**.

launder, v. cleanse, do the wash, wash and iron; see **clean**, **wash** 2.

laundry, n. ironing, washing, clothes; see **wash** 1.

lavatory, n. privy, bathroom, washroom; see **bath** 2, **toilet**.

lavender, a. or n. lilac, lilac-purple, bluish-red; see **color**, **purple**.

lavish, a. generous, unstinted, unsparing; see **plentiful** 1, 2.

lavish, v. scatter freely, give generously, squander; see **spend** 1, **waste** 2.

lavishly, a. profusely, richly, expensively; see **carelessly**, **foolishly**, **wastefully**.

law, n. 1. [The judicial system] judicial procedure, legal process, the (legal) authorities, the police, (due) process, precept, summons, notice, (bench) warrant, search warrant, warrant of arrest, subpoena. 2. [Bodies of law] code, constitution, criminal law, statute law, civil law, martial law, military law, private law, public law, commercial law, probate law, statutory law, statutes, civil code, ordinances, equity, cases, common law, canon law, decisions, unwritten law, natural law. 3. [An enactment] statute, edict, decree, order, ordinance, judicial decision, ruling, injunction, summons, act, enactment, requirement, demand, canon, regulation, commandment, mandate, dictate, instruction, bidding, legislation; see also **command**, **order** 1. 4. [A principle] foundation, fundamental, origin, source, (ultimate) cause, truth, axiom, maxim, ground, base, reason, rule (of action), theorem, guide, precept, usage, postulate, proposition, generalization, assumption, hard and fast rule; see also **reason** 3. 5. [Officers appointed to enforce the law] sheriff, state police, city police; see **judge** 1, **lawyer**, **police**. —lay down the law, establish rules, order, prohibit; see **order** 1.

lawbreaker, n. felon, offender, violator; see **criminal**.

lawful, a. legalized, legitimate, statutory, passed, decreed, judged, judicial, juridical, commanded, ruled, ordered, constitutional, legislated, enacted, official, enforced, protected, vested, within the law, legitimatized, established; see also **legal**, **permitted**. —Ant. **illegal**, unlawful, illegitimate.

lawfully, a. licitly, in accordance with the law, by law; see **legally**.

lawless, a. 1. [Without law] wild, untamed, uncivilized, savage, native, uncultivated, barbarous, fierce, violent, tempestuous, disordered, agitated, dis-

turbed, warlike; see also **uncontrolled.**
—*Ant.* **cultured,** cultivated, controlled.
2. [Not restrained by law] riotous, insubordinate, disobedient; see **unruly.**

lawlessness, *n.* irresponsibility, terrorism, chaos; see **disorder 2, disturbance 2.**

lawmaker, *n.* lawgiver, congressman, councilman; see **governor.**

lawn, *n.* green, grassplot, grassland; see **grass 2, yard 1.**

lawsuit, *n.* action, prosecution, suit; see **claim, trial 2.**

lawyer, *n.* professional man, legal adviser *or* practitioner, jurist, defender, prosecuting attorney, prosecutor, attorney, counsel, counselor, counselor at law, solicitor, barrister, advocate, professor of law, attorney at law, public attorney, private attorney, attorney general, district attorney (D.A.), federal attorney, *Philadelphia lawyer, *legal eagle.

lax, *a.* slack, remiss, soft; see **careless, indifferent.**

laxative, *n.* physic, purgative, diuretic, cathartic, purge, remedy, cure, dose; see also **medicine 2.** Common laxatives include the following—castor oil, mineral oil, agar-agar, cascara sagrada, flaxseed, milk of magnesia, croton oil, epsom salts, cascarin compound, psyllium seeds.

lay, *v.* **1.** [To knock down] trounce, defeat, club; see **beat 1, hit 1. 2.** [To place] put, locate, settle, deposit, plant, lodge, store, stow, situate, deposit, set; see also **set 1. 3.** [To put in order] arrange, organize, systematize; see **order 3.**

lay aside, *v.* **1.** [To place] deposit, put, set; see **set 1. 2.** [To save] lay away, collect, keep; see **save 2, store.**

lay away, *v.* lay aside, keep, collect; see **store.**

lay claim to, *v.* appropriate, demand, take; see **seize 2.**

lay down, *v.* **1.** [To declare] assert, state, affirm; see **declare, report 1, say. 2.** [To bet] game, put up, wager; see **bet, gamble 1.**

lay down the law, *v.* demand, stress, emphasize; see **order 1.**

layer, *n.* thickness, fold, band, overlay, lap, overlap, seam, floor, story, tier, zone, stripe, coating, flap, panel.

lay eyes on, *v.* stare, view, notice; see **see 1.**

lay hands on, *v.* get, acquire, grasp; see **seize 1, 2.**

lay into, *v.* battle, invade, fire at; see **attack, fight.**

***lay low,** *v.* go underground, disappear, hide out; see **hide 2, sneak.**

layman, *n.* nonprofessional, novice, dilettante; see **amateur, recruit.**

laymen, *n.* laity, converts, congregation, neophytes, parish, parishioners, the faithful, communicants, members, believers; see also **following.**

lay off, *v.* **1.** [To discharge employees, usually temporarily] fire, discharge, let go; see **dismiss, oust. 2.** [*To stop] cease, halt, desist; see **end 1, stop 2.**

layout, *n.* arrangement, design, draft; see **organization 2, plan 1, purpose 1.**

lay out, *v.* lend, put out (at interest), put up; see **invest, spend 1.**

layover, *n.* break, stop, rest; see **delay, pause.**

lay over, *v.* delay, stay over, break a journey; see **stop 1.**

lay plans (for), *v.* draft, design, think out; see **form 1, intend 1, plan 2.**

lay to rest, *v.* inter, give burial (to), take to a last resting place; see **bury 1.**

lay up, *v.* **1.** [To save] conserve, preserve, hoard; see **save 2, store. 2.** [To disable] injure, harm, beat up; see **hurt.**

lazily, *a.* indolently, nonchalantly, slackly; see **gradually, slowly.**

laziness, *n.* indolence, sloth, lethargy, inactivity, slackness, sluggishness, dullness, heaviness, inertia, drowsiness, passivity, listlessness, laxness, negligence, sleepiness, dullness, stupidity, dreaminess, weariness, apathy, indifference, tardiness, shiftlessness, procrastination; see also **idleness.**—*Ant.* action, promptitude, agility.

lazy, *a.* **1.** [Indolent] indolent, idle, remiss, sluggish, lagging, apathetic, loafing, dallying, passive, asleep on the job, procrastinating, neglectful, indifferent, dilatory, tardy, slack, inattentive, careless, flagging, weary, tired.—*Ant.* active, businesslike, indefatigable. **2.** [Slow] slothful, inactive, lethargic; see **slow 1, 2.**

lead, *a.* leading, head, foremost; see **best, first 1, principal.**

lead, *n.* **1.** [The position at the front] head, advance, first place, point, edge, front rank, first line, scout, outpost, scouting party, patrol, advance position, forerunner; see also **front.**—*Ant.* end, rear, last place. **2.** [Leadership] direction, guidance, headship; see **leadership. 3.** [A clue] evidence, trace, hint; see **proof 1, sign 1. 4.** [A leading role] principal part, important role, chief character; see **role.**

lead, *n.* metallic lead, galena, blue lead; see **element 2, metal.**

lead, *v.* **1.** [To conduct] guide, steer, pilot, show *or* point (the way), show in *or* around, point out, escort, accompany, protect, guard, safeguard, watch over, go along with, drive, discover the way, find

a way through, be responsible for.—*Ant.*
follow, be conveyed, be piloted. 2. [To
exercise leadership] direct, manage, supervise; see **manage** 1. 3. [To extend]
traverse, pass along, span; see **reach** 1.

leaden, *a.* 1. [Made of lead] metal, pewter, galena; see also **metallic** 1. 2.
[Heavy] burdensome, oppressive,
weighty; see **heavy** 1. 3. [Lead-colored]
dull, pewter, blue-gray; see **gray.**

leader, *n.* 1. [A guide] conductor, lead,
pilot; see **guide.** 2. [One who provides
leadership] general, commander, director, manager, head, officer, captain,
master, chieftain, governor, ruler, executor, boss (man), *brains; see also **executive.**

leadership, *n.* authority, control, administration, effectiveness, superiority,
supremacy, skill, initiative, foresight,
energy, capacity; see also **influence,
power** 2.

leading, *a.* foremost, chief, dominating;
see **best, principal.**

lead on, *v.* lure, entice, intrigue; see **deceive.**

lead up to, *v.* prepare (for), introduce,
make preparations for; see **begin** 2,
propose 1.

leaf, *n.* leaflet, needle, blade, stalk, scale,
floral leaf, seed leaf, sepal, petal. —**turn
over a new leaf,** make a new start,
redo, begin again; see **change** 2.

leaflet, *n.* handbill, circular; see **pamphlet, sheet** 2.

leafy, *a.* leafed (out), in leaf, shaded; see
shady.

league, *n.* band, group, unit; see **organization** 2.

leak, *n.* 1. [Loss through leakage] leakage, loss, flow, seepage, escape, falling
off, expenditure, decrease; see also
waste 1. 2. [An aperture through which
a leak may take place] puncture, chink,
crevice; see **hole** 1. 3. [Surreptitious
news] news leak, exposé, slip; see **news**
1, 2.

leak, *v.* 1. [To escape by leaking] drip,
ooze, drool; see **flow.** 2. [To permit
leakage] be cracked *or* broken *or* split,
have a fissure *or* hole, be out of order
or in disrepair, have a slow leak.

leakproof, *a.* watertight, impervious,
waterproof; see **tight** 2.

leaky, *a.* punctured, cracked, split; see
broken 1, **open** 4.

lean, *a.* 1. [Thin] lank, meager, slim; see
thin 2. 2. [Containing little fat] fibrous,
muscular, sinewy, meaty, free from fat,
all-meat, protein-rich.

lean, *v.* 1. [To incline] slope, slant, sag,
sink, decline, list, tip, bow, roll, veer,
droop, drift, pitch, bend, be slanting *or*
slanted, be off; see also **bend, tilt** 1. 2.

[To tend] favor, be disposed, incline;
see **tend** 2.

leaning, *a.* inclining, tilting, out of perpendicular; see **oblique.**

lean on *or* **upon,** *v.* 1. [To be supported
by] rest on, be upheld by, bear on, put
one's weight on, hang on *or* upon, fasten on; see also **lean** 1. 2. [To rely
upon] believe in, count on, put faith in;
see **trust** 1.

lean-to, *n.* shelter, shanty, cabin; see
hut.

leap, *v.* spring, vault, bound; see **bounce**
2, **jump** 1.

learn, *v.* acquire, receive, get, take *or*
drink in, pick up, read, master, ground
oneself in, pore over, gain (information),
ascertain, determine, unearth, hear, find
out, learn by heart, memorize, be
taught a lesson, collect one's knowledge,
improve one's mind, build one's background, *get up on, *get the signal; see
also **study.**

learned, *a.* 1. [Having great learning;
said of people] scholarly, erudite,
academic, accomplished, conversant
with, lettered, instructed, collegiate,
well-informed, bookish, pedantic, profes-
sorial; see also **cultured, educated** 1.—
Ant. ignorant, incapable, illiterate. 2.
[Showing evidence of learning: *said of
productions*] deep, sound, solemn; see
profound.

learned, *a.* memorized, word for word,
by heart; see **known** 2.

learning, *n.* lore, scholarship, training;
see **education** 1, **knowledge** 1.

lease, *n.* document of use, permission to
rent, charter; see **contract, record** 1.

lease, *v.* let, charter, rent out; see **rent**
1.

leash, *n.* cord, chain, strap; see **rope.**

least, *a.* 1. [Smallest] tiniest, infinitesimal, microscopic; see **minute** 1. 2.
[Least important] slightest, piddling,
next to nothing; see **trivial, unimportant.** 3. [In the lowest degree] minimal,
most inferior, bottom; see also **lowest,
minimum.** —**at (the) least,** in any
event, with no less than, at any rate;
see **anyhow.** —**not in the least,** not at
all, in no way, not in the slightest degree; see **never.**

leather, *n.* tanned hide, parchment, calfskin, horsehide, buckskin, deerskin, elk
hide, goatskin, sheepskin, rawhide, cow-
hide, buffalo hide *or* robe, snakeskin,
sharkskin, lizard, shoe leather, glove
leather, chamois skin, sole leather, alligator hide; see also **hide, skin.**

leave, *n.* 1. [Permission] consent, dispensation, allowance; see **permission.** 2.
[Authorized absence] leave of absence,
holiday, furlough; see **vacation.** —**on
leave,** away, gone, on a vacation; see

absent. —**take one's leave,** go away, depart, remove oneself; see **leave** 1.

leave, v. 1. [To go away] go, depart, take leave, withdraw, move, set out, come away, go forth, take off, start, step down, quit (a place), part (company), defect, vanish, walk or get or slip or break or ride or go or move out or off or away, vacate, abscond, flee, get out, flit, migrate, fly, run along, embark, say good-by, emigrate, *clear or pull or cut out, *push or cast off, *scram, *split, *sign or check out, *beat it, *take a powder, *pull up stakes.— *Ant.* arrive, get to, reach. 2. [To abandon] back out, forsake, desert; see **abandon** 2. 3. [To allow to remain] let be or stay, leave behind, let continue, let go, drop, lay down, omit, forget; see also **neglect** 1, 2.—*Ant.* seize, take away, keep. 4. [To allow to fall to another] bequeath, hand down, transmit; see **give** 1.

leave home, v. run away or off, play or become truant, depart; see **leave** 1.

leave out, v. cast aside, reject, dispose of; see **discard, eliminate.**

leave out in the cold, v. ignore, slight, neglect; see **abandon** 2.

leave to, v. bequeath, hand down, pass on; see **give** 1.

leave word, v. inform, let know, report; see **tell** 1.

leavings, n. remains, residue, garbage; see **trash** 1.

lecture, n. discourse, instruction, lesson; see **education** 1, **speech** 3.

lecture, v. talk, instruct, teach; see **address** 2, **teach.**

led, a. taken, escorted, guided; see **accompanied.**

ledge, n. shelf, mantle, strip, bar, step, ridge, reef, rim, bench, edge, path, route, way, walk, track, trail.

leech, n. 1. [A parasite] tapeworm, hookworm, bloodsucker; see **parasite** 1. 2. [Dependent] parasite, hanger-on, *sponger; see **weakling.**

leeward, a. protected, screened, safe; see also **calm** 2.

leeway, n. space, margin, latitude; see **extent.**

left, a. 1. [Opposite to right] leftward, left-hand, near, sinister, larboard, port, portside.—*Ant.* right, right-hand, starboard. 2. [Remaining] staying, continuing, over; see **extra.** 3. [Radical] leftwing, liberal, progressive; see **radical** 2, **revolutionary** 1. 4. [Departed] gone out, absent, lacking; see **gone** 1.

left, n. left hand or side or direction or part, port, not the right or center; see **position** 1.

leftist, n. socialist, anarchist, communist; see **liberal, radical.**

left out, a. lost, neglected, removed; see **lost** 1.

leftover, a. remaining, unwanted, unused, residual, uneaten, unconsumed, untouched, (perfectly) good; see also **extra.**

leftovers, n. leavings, scraps, debris; see **food, gathering.**

left-wing, a. leftist, not conservative, reform; see **liberal, radical** 2.

leg, n. part, member, lower appendage, hind leg, foreleg, back leg, front leg, left leg, right leg, shank; see also **limb** 2. —*not have a leg to stand on,** be illogical or unreasonable, make rash statements, have no defense or excuse or justification; see **mistake.** —*on one's (or its) last legs,** decaying, not far from exhaustion or death or breakdown, old; see **dying** 2, **worn** 2. —*pull someone's leg,** make fun of, fool, play a trick on; see **deceive.**

legal, a. lawful, constitutional, permissible, allowable, allowed, proper, legalized, sanctioned, legitimate, right, just, justifiable, justified, fair, authorized, accustomed, due, rightful, warranted, admitted, sound, granted, acknowledged, equitable, within the law, protected, enforced, judged, decreed, statutory, contractual, customary, chartered, *clean, *legit, *straight, *on the up and up; see also **lawful, permitted.**—*Ant.* illegal, unlawful, prohibited.

legality, n. legitimacy, lawfulness, authority; see **law** 1.

legalize, v. authorize, formulate, sanction; see **approve.**

legally, a. lawfully, legitimately, permissibly, authorized, warranted, allowably, admittedly, constitutionally, with due process of law, by statute or law, in the eyes of the law, in accordance with law or the statute or the constitution or the ordinance; see also **rightfully.**—*Ant.* illegal, unauthorized, illicitly.

legend, n. folk tale, saga, fable; see **myth, story.**

legendary, a. fabulous, mythical, mythological, fanciful, imaginative, created, invented, allegorical, apocryphal, improbable, imaginary, dubious, not historical or verified, doubtful, romantic, storied, unverifiable; see also **imaginary.**

legible, a. distinct, plain, sharp; see **clear** 2.

legion, n. multitude, body, group; see **crowd, gathering.**

legislate, v. make or enforce laws, pass, constitute; see **enact.**

legislation, *n.* bill, enactment, act; see **law 3**.

legislative, *a.* lawmaking, enacting, decreeing, ordaining, lawgiving, congressional, parliamentarian, senatorial, parliamentary, from *or* by the legislature.

legislator, *n.* lawmaker, lawgiver, assemblyman, representative, congressman, senator, member of parliament, floor leader, councilman, alderman; see also **executive**.

legislature, *n.* lawmakers, congress, parliament, chamber, assembly, senate, house, congress, (elected) representatives, soviet, plenum, law-making body, voice of the people.

legitimate, *a.* **1.** [In accordance with legal provisions] licit, statutory, authorized; see **lawful, legal. 2.** [Logical] reasonable, probable, consistent; see **logical, understandable. 3.** [Authentic] verifiable, valid, reliable; see **genuine 1, 2**.

leisure, *n.* freedom, (free) time, spare time *or* moments, relaxation, recreation, ease, recess, holiday, leave of absence, convenience, idle hours, opportunity; see also **rest 1, vacation.** *–Ant.* work, toil, travail. **–at leisure,** idle, resting, not busy; see **resting 1. –at one's leisure,** when one has time, at one's convenience, at an early opportunity; see **whenever**.

leisurely, *a.* slowly, unhurriedly, lazily, deliberately, calmly, inactively, taking one's time, gradually, sluggishly, lethargically, indolently, listlessly.*–Ant.* quickly, rapidly, hastily.

lemon, *n.* citrus fruit, citron, food; see **fruit**.

lend, *v.* advance, provide with, let out, furnish, permit to borrow, allow, trust with, lend on security, extend credit, entrust, place *or* put (out) at interest, accomodate.*–Ant.* borrow, repay, pay back.

lend a hand, *v.* assist, aid, succor; see **help**.

lender, *n.* moneylender, bank, loan company; see **banker, donor**.

length, *n.* **1.** [Linear distance] space, measure, span, reach, range, longitude, remoteness, magnitude, compass, portion, dimension, unit, radius, diameter, longness, mileage, stretch, extensiveness, spaciousness, tallness, height, expansion; see also **expanse, extent.***–Ant.* shortness, **nearness,** closeness. **2.** [Duration] period, interval, season, year, month, week, day, minute, limit; see also **time 1**.

lengthen, *v.* **1.** [To make longer] extend, stretch, protract; see **increase. 2.** [To

grow longer] produce, increase, expand; see **grow 1**.

lengthwise, *a.* longitudinally, the long way, along, endlong, from end to end, from stem to stern, overall, from head to foot, from top to toe *or* bottom; see also **alongside**.

lengthy, *a.* tedious, not brief, long; see **dull 4**.

lenient, *a.* soft, mild, tolerant; see **kind**.

lens, *n.* microscope, camera, spectacles; see **glass**.

leopard, *n.* panther, hunting leopard, jaguar; see **animal, cat 2**.

less, *a.* smaller, lower, not so much as, not as much, lesser, minor, fewer, reduced, declined, in decline, depressed, inferior, secondary, subordinate, beneath, minus, deficient, diminished, shortened, limited; see also **shorter.**
–Ant. more, more than, longer.

lessen, *v.* **1.** [To grow less] diminish, dwindle, decline; see **decrease 1. 2.** [To make less] reduce, diminish, slack up; see **decrease 2**.

lessening, *a.* decreasing, declining, waning, dropping, diminishing, abating, slowing (down), dwindling, sinking, sagging, subsiding, moderating, slackening, ebbing, lowering, shrinking *or* drying *or* shriveling (up), softening, weakening, decaying, narrowing (down), drooping, wasting, running low *or* down, dying away *or* down, wearing off *or* out *or* away *or* down, falling *or* slacking (away *or* off *or* down), growing less (and less), losing momentum *or* impetus *or* spirit, etc., slumping, plunging, plummeting, going down *or* back *or* backward, in reverse, getting worse *or* lower *or* slower, etc.

lesser, *a.* inferior, minor, secondary; see **subordinate**.

lesson, *n.* drill, assignment, reading; see **job 2**.

let, *v.* **1.** [To permit] suffer, give *or* grant permission, allow, condone, approve, authorize, consent, permit, tolerate; see also **allow. 2.** [To rent] lease, hire, sublet; see **rent 1**.

let alone, *v.* ignore, leave (to oneself *or* itself), abandon; see **leave 3, neglect 2**.

letdown, *n.* frustration, setback, disillusionment; see **disappointment 1**.

let down, *v.* disappoint, disillusion, not support; see **abandon 2, fail 1**.

let go, *v.* relinquish, dismiss, release, part with; see **abandon 1**.

lethal, *a.* fatal, mortal, malignant; see **deadly, harmful, poisonous**.

let in, *v.* admit, allow to enter, give admission to; see **receive 4**.

let off, *v.* leave, excuse, let go, remove; see **abandon 1, drop 1**.

*let on, v. imply, indicate, suggest; see hint.

let out, v. liberate, let go, eject; see free.

letter, n. 1. [A unit of the alphabet] capital, upper case, lower case, small letter, vowel, consonant, digraph, rune, stop or plosive, fricative, diphthong, nasal, dental, glottal, gutteral; see also consonant, vowel 2. [A written communication] note, epistle, missive, message, memorandum, report, line. Types of letters include the following—business, form, circular, drop, open, personal; billet-doux, postcard, postal, direct mail advertising, *junk mail. —to the letter, just as written or directed, perfectly, precisely; see perfectly 1.

let the cat out of the bag, v. divulge, let out; see reveal, tell 1.

letup, n. interval, recess, respite; see pause 1, 2.

let up, v. cease, release, slow down; see slow 1, stop 2.

level, a. 1. [Smooth] polished, rolled, planed; see flat 1, smooth 1. 2. [Of an even height] regular, equal, uniform, flush, of the same height, same, constant, straight, balanced, steady, stable, trim, precise, exact, matched, unbroken, on a line, lined up, aligned, uninterrupted, continuous; see also smooth 1.—Ant. irregular, uneven, crooked. 3. [Horizontal] plane, leveled, lying prone, in the same plane, on one plane; see also flat 1. —*one's level best, one's best, the best one can do, all one's effort; see best. —*on the level, fair, sincere, truthful; see honest 1.

level, v. 1. [To straighten] surface, bulldoze, equalize; see smooth, straighten. 2. [To demolish] ruin, waste, wreck; see destroy. 3. [*To be honest with] be frank or straight (with), come to terms, be open and aboveboard; see declare.

level-headed, a. wise, practical, prudent; see rational 1, reasonable 1.

level off, v. level out, find a level, reach an equilibrium; see decrease 1, straighten.

lever, n. lifter, pry, leverage, (prying or pinch) bar, crowbar, handspike, arm, advantage; see leverage.

leverage, n. purchase, lift, hold; see support 2.

levied, a. exacted, taken, collected; see taxed 1.

levy, n. toll, duty, custom; see tax 1.

lewd, a. 1. [Suggestive of lewdness] ribald, smutty, indecent; see sense 2; sensual 2. 2. [Inclined to lewdness] lustful, wanton, lascivious, libidinous, licentious, lecherous, profligate, dissolute, carnal, sensual, debauched, corrupt, unchaste, depraved, unbridled, ruttish, nymphomaniacal, prurient, concupiscent, in-

continent, incestuous, goatish, *horny, *in heat; see also vulgar.—Ant. chaste, pure, modest.

lewdly, a. wantonly, shockingly, indecently, lasciviously, lecherously, libidinously, unchastely, carnally, dissolutely, immodestly, voluptuously, sensually, incontinently, indelicately, in a lewd manner, with lewd gestures, in a suggestive manner, with phallic implications.

lewdness, n. indecency, unchastity, incontinence, vulgarity, lechery, wantonness, lasciviousness, sensuality, licentiousness, voluptuousness, lecherousness, profligacy, dissoluteness, obscenity, scurrility, coarseness, carnal passion, grossness, sensuous desire, salaciousness, pornography, lust, depravity, carnality, nymphomania, corruption, raunchiness, dirtiness, incest, indelicacy, eroticism, erotism, smut, impurity, debauchery.—Ant. modesty, decency, continency.

liability, n. obligation, indebtedness, answerability; see responsibility 2.

liable, a. 1. [Responsible] answerable, subject, accountable; see responsible 1. 2. [Likely] tending, apt, inclined; see likely 4.

liar, n. prevaricator, false witness, deceiver, perjurer, trickster, cheat, misleader, falsifier, story-teller, equivocator, fibber, fabricator; see also cheat.

libel, n. calumny, slander, lying; see lie.

liberal, a. tolerant, receptive, nonconformist, progressive, advanced, left, radical, interested, wide-awake, broadminded, understanding, permissive, indulgent, unprejudiced, impartial, reasonable, rational, unbiased, detached, dispassionate, unconventional, avant-garde, left-wing, objective, magnanimous; see also fair 1.—Ant. prejudiced, intolerant, biased.

liberal, n. individualist, insurgent, rebel, revolutionary, nonconformist, nonpartisan, independent; believer in civil rights, welfare, reform, etc.; socialist, eccentric, freethinker, left-winger; see also radical.

liberate, v. set free, loose, release; see free.

liberation, n. rescue, freedom, deliverance; see rescue 1.

liberty, n. 1. [Freedom from bondage] deliverance, emancipation, enfranchisement; see rescue 1. 2. [Freedom from occupation] rest, leave, relaxation; see freedom 2, leisure, recreation. 3. [Freedom to choose] permission, alternative, decision; see choice, selection 1. 4. [The rights supposedly natural to man] freedom, independence, power of choice; see democracy. —at liberty, unrestricted, unlimited, not confined; see free 1, 2. —take liberties, be too familiar *or* impertinent, act too freely, use carelessly; see **abuse**.

librarian, *n.* keeper, caretaker, curator; see **executive**.

library, *n.* books, book collection, manuscripts, manuscript collection, institution, public library, private library, book room, lending library, reference library *or* collection, archives, museum, treasury, memorabilia, rare books, reading room.

license, *n.* 1. [Unbridled use of freedom] looseness, excess, immoderation; see **freedom 2.** 2. [A formal permission] permit, form, identification, tag, card, consent, grant; see also **permission**.

license, *v.* permit, authorize, privilege; see **allow**.

lick, *v.* 1. [To pass the tongue over] stroke, rub, touch, pass over *or* across, caress, wash, graze, brush, glance, tongue, fondle, soothe, tranquilize, calm, quiet. 2. [To play over; *said of flames*] rise and fall, fluctuate, leap; see **burn, dart 1, wave 3.** 3. [*To beat] whip, trim, thrash; see **beat 1.** 4. [*To defeat] overcome, vanquish, frustrate; see **defeat 3.**

lid, *n.* cap, top, roof; see **cover 1, hood 1.**

lie, *n.* falsehood, untruth, fiction, inaccuracy, misstatement, myth, fable, deceptiveness, misrepresentation, lying, prevarication, falsification, falseness, defamation, tall story, fabrication, deception, slander, aspersion, tale, perjury, libel, forgery, distortion, fib, white lie, *fish story, *whopper.—*Ant.* truth, veracity, truthfulness.

lie, *v.* 1. [To utter an untruth] falsify, prevaricate, tell a lie, lie out of, deceive, mislead, misinform, exaggerate, distort, concoct, equivocate, be untruthful, be a liar, break one's word, bear false witness, go back on, say one thing and mean another, misrepresent, dissemble, perjure oneself, delude, invent.—*Ant.* **declare,** tell the truth, be honest. 2. [To be situated] extend, be (on), be beside, be located *or* fixed *or* established *or* placed *or* seated *or* set, be level *or* smooth *or* even *or* plane, exist in space, stretch *or* reach *or* spread along. 3. [To be prostrate] be flat *or* prone, sprawl, loll, be stretched out; see also **rest 1.**—*Ant.* **stand,** be upright, sit. 4. [To assume a prostrate position] lie down, recline, stretch out, go to bed, turn in, retire, take a nap *or* siesta, *hit the sack *or* hay; see also **rest 1, sleep.**—*Ant.* **rise,** get up, arise. —**take lying down,** submit, surrender, be passive; see **yield 1.**

lie down on the job, *v.* dawdle, slack off, fool around; see **loiter.**

lie low, *v.* keep out of sight, conceal oneself, go underground; see **hide 2, sneak.**

life, *n.* 1. [The fact or act of living] being, entity, growth, animation, endurance, survival, presence, living, consciousness, breath, continuance, flesh and blood, viability, metabolism, vitality, vital spark; see also **experience.**—*Ant.* **death,** discontinuance, nonexistence. 2. [The sum of one's experiences] life experience, conduct, behavior, way *or* manner of life, reaction, response, participation, enjoyment, joy, suffering, happiness, tide of events, circumstances, realization, knowledge, enlightenment, attainment, development, growth, personality. 3. [A biography] life story, memoir, memorial; see **biography, story.** 4. [Duration] lifetime, one's natural life, period of existence, duration of life, endurance, continuance, span, history, career, course, era, epoch, century, decade, days, generation, time, period, life span, season, cycle, record; see also **time 1.** 5. [One who promotes gaiety] animator, entertainer, *life of the party; see **host 1, hostess.** 6. [Vital spirit] vital force, vital principle, *élan vital* (French); see **excitement, zeal. —as large** (*or* **big**) **as life,** actually, truly, in (actual) fact; see **truly. —for dear life,** intensely, desperately, for all one is worth; see **strongly. —for life,** for the duration of one's life, for a long time, as long as one lives; see **forever. —*for the life of me,** by any means, as if one's life were at stake, whatever happens; see **anyhow. —matter of life and death,** crisis, grave concern, something vitally important; see **importance. —*not on your life,** by no means, certainly not, never; see **no. —take one's own life,** kill oneself, die by one's own hand, murder; see **commit suicide. —true to life,** true to reality, realistic, representational; see **genuine 1.**

life-giving, *a.* invigorating, animating, productive; see **stimulating.**

lifeless, *a.* 1. [Without life] inert, inanimate, departed; see **dead 1.** 2. [Lacking spirit] lackluster, listless, heavy; see **dull 3, 4, slow 2.**

lifelike, *a.* simulated, exact, imitative; see **graphic 1, 2.**

life or death, *a.* decisive, necessary, critical; see **important 1.**

lifetime, *a.* lifelong, continuing, enduring; see **permanent 2.**

lifetime, *n.* existence, endurance, continuance; see **life 4, record 2.**

lift, *n.* 1. [The work of lifting] pull, lifting, ascension, raising, weight, foot pounds, elevation, escalation, ascent, mounting. 2. [A ride] transportation, drive, passage; see **journey**. 3. [Aid] help, assistance, support; see **help 1**.

lift, v. hoist, elevate, upheave; see **raise 1**.

light, a. 1. [Having illumination] illuminated, radiant, luminous; see **bright 1**. 2. [Having color] vivid, rich, clear; see **clear 2**. 3. [Having little content] superficial, slight, frivolous; see **trivial, unimportant**. 4. [Having gaiety and spirit] lively, merry, animated; see **active**. 5. [Having little weight] airy, fluffy, feathery, slender, downy, floating, lighter than air, light as air, floatable, light as a feather, frothy, buoyant, dainty, thin, sheer, insubstantial, ethereal, graceful, weightless, atmospheric.—Ant. heavy, ponderous, weighty. 6. [Digestible] slight, edible, moderate; see **eatable**. 7. [Small in quantity or number] wee, small, tiny, minute, thin, inadequate, insufficient, hardly enough, not much, hardly or scarcely any, not many, slender, scanty, slight, sparse, fragmentary, fractional; see also **few**.—Ant. large, great, immense.

light, n. 1. [The condition opposed to darkness] radiance, brilliance, splendor, glare, brightness, clearness, lightness, incandescence, shine, luster, sheen, sparkle, glitter, glimmer, flood of light, blare, radiation, gleam.—Ant. **darkness**, blackness, blankness. 2. [Emanations from a source of light] radiation, stream, blaze; see **flash, ray**. 3. [A source of light] match, wick, sun, planet, star, moon, lightning, torch, flashlight, chandelier, spotlight, halo, corona. 4. [Day] daylight, sun, sunrise; see **day 1**. 5. [Aspect] point of view, condition, standing; see **circumstances 2**. **—in (the) light of**, with knowledge of, because of, in view or consideration of; see **considering**. **—see the light (of day)**, 1. come into being, exist, begin; see **be**. 2. comprehend, realize, be aware; see **understand 1**.

light, v. 1. [To provide light] illuminate, illumine, lighten, give light to, shine upon, furnish with light, light up, turn on the electricity, make a light, make visible, provide adequate illumination, turn or switch on a light, floodlight, make bright, flood with light, fill with light; see also **brighten 1**.—Ant. shade, put out, darken. 2. [To cause to ignite] inflame, spark, kindle; see **burn, ignite**. 3. [To become ignited] take fire, become inflamed, flame; see **burn, ignite**. 4. [To come to rest from flight or travel] rest, fly or come down, stop; see **arrive 1**. **—make light of**, make fun of, mock, belittle; see **neglect 1, ridicule**.

lighted, a. 1. [Illuminated] brilliant, alight, glowing; see **bright 1**. 2. [Burning] blazing, flaming, aflame; see **burning**.

lighten, v. unburden, make lighter, reduce the load of, lessen (the weight of), uplift, buoy up, alleviate, take off a load, remove, take from, pour out, throw overboard, reduce, cut down, put off, make buoyant, take off weight, eradicate, shift, change; see also **unload**.—Ant. load, burden, overload.

lighter, a. smaller, thinner, more buoyant; see **less**.

lighter, n. cigar or cigarette or pipe lighter, igniter, flame; see **light 3, match 1**.

lightheaded, a. 1. [Giddy] inane, fickle, frivolous; see **silly**. 2. [Faint] tired, delirious, dizzy; see **weak 1**.

lighthearted, a. gay, joyous, cheerful; see **happy**.

lighting, n. brilliance, flame, brightness; see **flash, light 1, 3**.

light into, v. rebuke, blame, assault; see **scold**.

lightly, a. delicately, airily, buoyantly, daintily, readily, gently, subtly, mildly, softly, tenderly, carefully, leniently, effortlessly, smoothly, blandly, sweetly, comfortably, restfully, peacefully, quietly; see also **easily**.—Ant. heavily, ponderously, roughly.

lightness, n. 1. [Illumination] sparkle, blaze, shine; see **flash, light 1, 3**. 2. [The state of being light] airiness, volatileness, etherealness, downiness, thinness, sheerness, fluffiness, featheriness. 3. [Agility] balance, deftness, nimbleness; see **agility, grace 1**.

lightning, n. electrical discharge, bolt, streak of lightning, thunderstroke, firebolt, fireball, thunderbolt; see also **electricity 2**.

likable, a. agreeable, amiable, attractive; see **friendly**.

like, a. similar, same, alike, near, resembling, close, not far from, according to, conforming with, matching, equaling, not unlike, akin, related, analogous, twin, corresponding, allied to, much the same, the same form, comparable, identical, in the manner of, parallel, homologous, to the effect that, consistent, approximating.—Ant. unlike, different, unrelated.

like, prep. similar (to), same, near to; see **alike, like**.

like, n. counterpart, resemblance, parallelism; see **similarity**. **—and the like**, and so forth, etc., similar kinds; see **others, same**. **—*more like it**, acceptable, good, improved; see **better 1**. **—nothing like**, dissimilar, contrasting, opposed; see **unlike**. —something like, similar, resembling, akin; see **like** *a*.

like, *v*. **1**. [To enjoy] take delight in, relish, take *or* derive pleasure in *or* from, be pleased by, revel *or* indulge *or* rejoice in, find agreeable *or* congenial *or* appealing, be gratified by, take satisfaction in, savor, fancy, dote on, take an interest in, develop interest for *or* in, delight *or* bask *or* luxuriate in, regard with favor, have a liking for, love, have a taste for, care to, *get a kick out of, be tickled by, eat up, go in for.—*Ant*. **endure**, detest, dislike. **2**. [To be fond of] have a fondness for, admire, take a fancy to, feel warmly *or* affectionately toward, prize, esteem, hold dear, care about *or* for, approve, be pleased with, take to, have a soft spot in one's heart for, hanker for, *have a yen for, become attached to, be sweet on, have eyes for; see also **love** 1.—*Ant*. **hate**, disapprove, dislike. **3**. [To be inclined] choose, feel disposed, wish, desire, have a preference for, prefer, fancy, feel like, incline toward.

liked, *a*. popular, loved, admired; see **beloved**, honored.

likely, *a*. **1**. [Probable] apparent, probable, seeming, credible, possible, feasible, presumable, conceivable, reasonable, workable, attainable, achievable, believable, rational, thinkable, imaginable, plausible, anticipated, expected, imminent.—*Ant*. **impossible**, doubtful, questionable. **2**. [Promising] suitable, apt, assuring; see **fit** 1, **hopeful** 2. **3**. [Believable] plausible, true, acceptable; see **convincing**. **4**. [Apt] inclined, tending, disposed, predisposed, prone, liable, subject to, on the verge *or* point of, in the habit of, given to, in favor of, having a weakness for.

likeness, *n*. **1**. [Similarity] resemblance, correspondence, affinity; see **similarity**. **2**. [A representation] image, effigy, portrait; see **copy**, picture 3.

likewise, *a*. in like manner, furthermore, moreover; see **also**, besides.

liking *n*. desire, fondness, devotion; see **affection**, love 1.

limb, *n*. **1**. [A tree branch] arm, bough, offshoot; see **branch** 2. **2**. [A bodily appendage] arm, leg, appendage, part, wing, pinion, fin, flipper; see also **arm** 1, leg.

limber, *a*. nimble, spry, deft; see **agile**, graceful 1.

limit, *n*. **1**. [The boundary] end, frontier, border; see **boundary**. **2**. [The ultimate] utmost, ultimate, farthest point, farthest reach, destination, goal, conclusion, extremity, eventuality, termination, absolute, *the bitter end, deadline, cut-off

point; see also **end** 4.—*Ant*. **origin**, incipience, start.

limit, *v*. bound, confine, curb; see **define** 1, restrict.

limitation, *n*. **1**. [The act of limiting] restriction, restraint, control; see **arrest**, interference 1, interruption, prevention. **2**. [That which limits] condition, definition, qualification, reservation, control, curb, check, injunction, bar, obstruction, stricture, taboo, inhibition, modification; see also **arrest**, barrier, boundary, refusal, restraint 2.—*Ant*. **freedom**, latitude, liberty. **3**. [A shortcoming] inadequacy, insufficiency, deficiency, shortcoming, weakness, want, imperfection, failing, fault, frailty, flaw; see also **fault** 1.—*Ant*. **strength**, perfection, ability.

limited, *a*. **1**. [Restricted] confined, checked, curbed; see **bound** 1, 2, restricted. **2**. [Having only moderate capacity] cramped, insufficient, short; see **faulty**, inadequate, poor 2, unsatisfactory.

limitless, *a*. unending, boundless, immeasurable; see **endless**, infinite, unlimited.

limp, *a*. pliant, soft, flaccid, flabby, supple, pliable, limber, relaxed, bending readily, plastic, yielding, lax, slack, loose, flimsy.—*Ant*. **stiff**, rigid, wooden.

limp, *v*. halt, walk lamely, proceed slowly, shuffle, lag, stagger, totter, dodder, hobble, falter.

line, *n*. **1**. [A row] length, list, rank, file, catalogue, order, group, arrangement, ridge, range, seam, band, border, block, series, sequence, succession, chain, train, string, column, formation, division, queue, channel, groove, mark, thread, fissure, crack, straight line. **2**. [A mark] outline, tracing, stroke; see **mark** 1. **3**. [A rope] cord, filament, steel tape; see **rope**, wire 1. **4**. [Lineal descent] descent, pedigree, lineage; see **family**, heredity. **5**. [A border line] border, mark, limit; see **boundary**, edge 1. **6**. [Matter printed in a row of type] row, words, letters; see **copy**. **7**. [A military front] disposition, formation, position; see **front** 2. **8**. [A railroad] trunk line, sideline, mainline; see **railroad**. **9**. [Goods handled by a given house] wares, merchandise, produce; see **material** 2. **10**. [Talk intended to influence another] prepared speech, patter, persuasion; see **conversation**, speech 3. —all along the line, at every turn, completely, constantly; see **everywhere**. —bring (*or* come *or* get) into line, align, make uniform, regulate; see **order** 3. —down the line, entirely, thoroughly, wholly; see **completely**. —draw the (*or* a) line, set a limit, prohibit, restrain; see **restrict.** —**get a line on,** find out about, investigate, expose; see **discover.** —**in line,** agreeing, conforming, uniform; see **regular 3.** —**in line for,** being considered for, ready, thought about; see **considered.** —**lay (or put) it on the line,** elucidate, define, clarify; see **explain.** —**on a line,** linear, lined, level; see **direct 1, straight 1.** —**out of line,** misdirected, not uniform, not even; see **irregular 1, 4.** —**read between the lines,** read meaning into, discover a hidden meaning, expose; see **understand 1.**

line, v. 1. [To provide a lining] interline, stuff, wad, panel, pad, quilt, fill. 2. [To provide lines] trace, delineate, outline; see **draw 2, mark 1.** 3. [To be in a line] border, edge, outline, rim, bound, fall in, fall into line, fringe, follow. 4. [To arrange in a line] align, queue (up), marshal, dress (up), face in, arrange, range, array, group, set out, bring into a line with others, fix, place, line right or left, draw up; see also **line up.** —Ant. disarrange, disperse, **scatter.**

linear, a. lined, elongated, successive; see **direct 1, straight 1.**

lined, a. interlined, stuffed, faced; see **full 1.**

linen, n. material, sheeting, linen cloth; see **goods.** Articles called linens include the following—handkerchiefs, towels, bedding, sheets, pillowcases, underwear, shirts, dishtowels, tablecloths, napkins, doilies.

lineup, n. starters, entrants, first string; see **list.**

line up, v. fall in, form in or into (a) line, take one's proper place in line, queue up, form ranks, get in line or formation.

linger, v. tarry, saunter, lag, hesitate, delay, plod, trudge, falter, dawdle, procrastinate, slouch, shuffle, crawl, loll, take one's time, wait, putter, be tardy, be long, sit around, *hang around; see also **loiter.**—Ant. hasten, **hurry,** speed.

lingerie, n. women's underwear, *dainties, unmentionables; see **clothes, underwear.**

linguist, n. student of language or languages, language expert, philologist, lexicographer, polyglot, translator, grammarian; see also **scientist.**

linguistics, n. pl. grammar, semantics, phonology, etymology, prosody, morphology, syntax, philology; see also **grammar, language 2.**

liniment, n. ointment, cream, lotion; see **balm 1, medicine 2,** salve.

lining, a. edging, outlining, rimming; see **bordering.**

lining, n. interlining, inner coating or

layer or surface, filling, quilting, stuffing, wadding, padding, sheathing, covering, wall, reinforcement, partition, paneling.

link, n. ring, loop, coupling, section, seam, weld, hitch, intersection, copula, connection, fastening, splice, interconnection, junction, joining, articulation; see also **joint 1.**

link, v. connect, associate, combine; see **join 1.**

linked, a. connected, combined, associated; see **joined.**

linking, a. combining, joining, associating; see **connecting.**

lint, n. raveling, fluff, fiber; see **dust.**

lion, n. king of beasts or the jungle, African or Asian cat, lioness; see **animal, cat 2.**

lip, n. speech organ, fold of flesh, edge or border of the mouth, liplike part, labium; see also **mouth 1.** —**keep a stiff upper lip,** take heart, be encouraged, remain strong; see **endure 2.**

liquid, a. 1. [In a state neither solid nor gaseous] watery, fluidic, liquiform, molten, damp, moist, aqueous, liquefied, dissolved, melted, thawed; see also **fluid, wet 1.** 2. [Having qualities suggestive of fluids] flowing, running, splashing, thin, moving, viscous, diluting; see also **fluid, juicy.**

liquid, n. liquor, fluid, juice, sap, extract, secretion, flow; see also **water 1.**

liquidate, v. 1. [To change into money] sell, convert, change; see **exchange. 2.** [To abolish] annul, cancel, destroy; see **abolish, eliminate.**

liquor, n. whiskey, *booze, alcohol; see **cocktail, drink 2.**

lisp, v. mispronounce, sputter, stutter; see also **utter.**

list, n. roll, record, schedule, agenda, arrangement, enrollment, slate, draft, panel, brief, invoice, register, memorandum, inventory, account, outline, tally, bulletin, directory, roster, subscribers, subscription list, muster, poll, ballot, table of contents, menu, dictionary, glossary, vocabulary, docket.

list, v. 1. [To enter in a list] set down, arrange, bill, catalogue, schedule, enter, note, post, insert, enroll, register, tally, inventory, index, calendar, tabulate, book, take a census, poll, slate, keep count of, run down, call the roll.—Ant. remove, wipe out, obliterate. 2. [To lean] pitch, slant, incline; see **lean 1.**

listed, a. filed, catalogued, indexed; see **recorded.**

listen, v. attend, keep one's ears open, be attentive, listen in, pick up, overhear, give attention or a hearing to, give ear, listen to, pay or give attention, hear, *tune in, *lend an ear, *strain one's ears, *prick up *or* cock one's ears.—*Ant.* ignore, be deaf to, turn a deaf ear to.

listener, *n.* auditor, hearer, spectator, audience, eavesdropper, witness.

listening, *a.* hearing, paying attention, heeding, attending, overhearing, straining to hear, receiving, *lending an ear, *pricking up one's ears.—*Ant.* indifferent, giving no attention, inattentive.

listless, *a.* passive, sluggish, indolent; see indifferent, slow 2.

lit, *a.* illuminated, lighted, resplendent; see bright 1, burning.

literacy, *n.* scholarship, ability to read and write, verbal competence; see education 1, knowledge 1.

literal, *a.* true, verbatim, methodical; see accurate 2.

literally, *a.* really, actually, precisely, exactly, completely, indisputably, correctly, strictly, to the letter, faithfully, rigorously, straight, unmistakably, truly, not metaphorically *or* figuratively, word for word, verbatim, letter by letter.—*Ant.* freely, figuratively, fancifully.

literary, *a.* arcane, bookish, literate; see learned 1.

literate, *a.* informed, scholarly, able to read and write; see educated, intelligent, learned 1.

literature, *n.* 1. [Artistic production in language] letters, lore, belles lettres, literary works, literary productions, the humanities, classics, books, republic of letters, writings. 2. [Written matter treating a given subject] discourse, composition, treatise, dissertation, thesis, paper, treatment, essay, discussion, research, observation, comment, findings, abstract, report, summary.

litter, *n.* 1. [A mess] scattering, jumble, hodgepodge; see trash 1. 2. [The young of certain animals] piglets, puppies, kittens; see offspring.

litter, *v.* scatter, confuse, jumble; see dirty.

litterbug, *n.* delinquent, offender, *slob; see slob.

little, *a.* 1. [Small in size] diminutive, small, tiny, wee, undersized, not big *or* large, stunted, limited, cramped, imperceptible, light, slight, microscopic, short, runty, shriveled, toy, miniature, puny, pygmy, dwarfed, bantam, *half-pint, *pocket-sized, *pint-sized.—*Ant.* large, big, huge. 2. [Small in quantity] inappreciable, inconsiderable, insufficient; see inadequate. 3. [Few in number] scarce, not many, hardly any; see few. 4. [Brief] concise, succinct, abrupt; see short 2. 5. [Small in importance] trifling, shallow, petty, superficial, frivolous, irrelevant, meaningless, slight,

paltry, insignificant, inconsiderable; see also trivial, unimportant. 6. [Small in character] base, weak, shallow, small-minded, prejudiced, bigoted, low, sneaky, mean, petty; see also vulgar. 7. [Weak] stunted, runty, undersized; see weak 1. —make little of, make fun of, mock, abuse; see ridicule.

little, *n.* trifle, modicum, whit; see bit 1.

livable, *a.* habitable, tenantable, inhabitable; see bearable, comfortable 2.

live, *a.* 1. [Active] energetic, vital, vivid; see active. 2. [Not dead] aware, conscious, existing; see alive. 3. [Not taped or filmed] broadcast direct, unrehearsed; see real 2.

live, *v.* 1. [To have life] exist, continue, subsist, prevail, survive, breathe, be alive; see also be 1. 2. [To enjoy life] relish, savor, experience, love, make every moment count, experience life to the full, *live it up, make the most of life, take pleasure in, get a great deal from life.—*Ant.* suffer, endure pain, be discouraged. 3. [To dwell] live in, inhabit, abide; see dwell. 4. [To gain subsistence] remain, continue, earn a living, support oneself, earn money, get ahead, provide for one's needs, maintain oneself; see also survive 1. 5. [To persist in human memory] remain, last, be remembered; see endure 1. —*where one lives, personally, in a sensitive *or* vulnerable area, at one's heart; see personally 2.

live and let live, *v.* be tolerant *or* broadminded, accept, ignore; see allow.

live at, *v.* inhabit, tenant, occupy; see dwell.

live by, *v.* survive, maintain life, acquire a livelihood; see live 4.

live down, *v.* overcome, survive, outgrow; see endure 2.

*live it up, *v.* have fun, enjoy, paint the town red; see celebrate 2.

livelihood, *n.* means, circumstances, resources; see subsistence 2.

lively, *a.* vigorous, brisk, industrious; see active.

live on, *v.* be supported, earn, subsist (on); see live 4.

livestock, *n.* cows, sheep, domestic animals; see cattle, herd.

live up to, *v.* meet (expectations), do well, give satisfaction; see satisfy 3.

living, *a.* 1. [Alive] existing, breathing, (having) being; see alive. 2. [Vigorous] awake, brisk, alert; see active 2.

living, *n.* 1. [A means of survival] existence, sustenance, maintenance; see subsistence 2. 2. [Those not dead; *usually used with* the] the quick, real people, flesh and blood; see animal, person, plant.

living room, *n.* lounge, front room, den; see **room** 2.

load, *n.* 1. [A physical burden] weight, truckload, carload, wagonload, shipload, cargo, haul, lading, charge, pack, mass, payload, shipment, contents, capacity, bundle, base load, peak load. —*Ant.* lightness, buoyancy, weightlessness. 2. [Responsibility] charge, obligation, trust; see **duty** 1. 3. [A charge; *said especially of firearms*] shot, clip, round; see **ammunition.** 4. [A measure] shot, amount, part; see **measurement** 2, **quantity.**

load, *v.* 1. [To place a load] place, arrange, stow (away), store, burden, stuff, put goods in *or* on, freight, weight, pile, heap, fill (up), cram, put aboard, stack, pour in, take on cargo; see also **pack** 1.—*Ant.* unload, unpack, take off cargo. 2. [To overload] encumber, saddle, weigh down; see **burden.** 3. [To charge; *said especially of firearms*] prime, ready, make ready to fire; see **shoot** 1.

loaded, *a.* 1. [Supplied with a load] laden, burdened, weighted; see **full** 1. 2. [Ready to discharge; *said of firearms*] charged, primed, ready to shoot. 3. [*Intoxicated] inebriated, drunken, *gassed; see **drunk.**

loaf, *n.* roll, bun, pastry; see **bread, cake** 2.

loaf, *v.* idle, trifle, lounge, kill time, be inactive *or* unoccupied *or* slothful *or* indolent *or* lazy, take it easy, not lift a finger, potter, drift, relax, slack, shirk, waste time, slow down, evade, dilly-dally, sit *or* stand around, dream, *goof off, *bum, stall, piddle.

loafer, *n.* idler, lounger, lazy person, ne'er-do-well, good-for-nothing, lazy-bones, malingerer, waster, slacker, shirker, wanderer, *bum, *goldbrick, *deadbeat.

loafing, *a.* dawdling, wasting time, shirking; see **lazy** 1.

loan, *n.* lending, trust, advance, investment, giving credit, mortgage, time payment, *touch, *bite.

loan, *v.* provide with, advance, let out; see **lend** 1.

loaned, *a.* lent, advanced, invested, granted, furnished, put out at interest, let, risked, leased; see also **given.**—*Ant.* borrowed, pledged, pawned.

lobby, *n.* vestibule, entryway, antechamber; see **hall** 1, **room** 2.

lobby, *v.* induce, put pressure on, promote; see **influence.**

local, *a.* 1. [Associated with a locality] sectional, divisional, territorial, district, provincial, neighborhood, town, civic, geographical, descriptive, historical, legendary, small town, parochial, social, rural, urban, economic; see also re-

gional, traditional. 2. [Restricted to a locality] limited, confined, bounded; see **restricted.**

locale, *n.* vicinity, territory, district; see **area, region** 1.

locality, *n.* 1. [Area] district, section, sector; see **area, region** 1. 2. [Position] spot, location, site; see **position** 1. 3. [Neighborhood] block, vicinity, district; see **neighborhood.**

locally, *a.* regionally, sectionally, provincially, in the neighborhood, in the town, nearby, narrowly.

locate, *v.* 1. [To determine a location] discover, search out, find, come on *or* across, position, ferret out, stumble on, discover the location *or* place of, get at, hit *or* light *or* come *or* happen *or* fix upon, lay one's fingers *or* hands on, track down, establish, determine, station, place; see also **find.** 2. [To take up residence] settle down, establish oneself, inhabit; see **dwell, settle** 7.

located, *a.* 1. [Determined in space] traced, found, happened on; see **discovered.** 2. [Situated] positioned, seated, fixed; see **placed.**

location, *n.* 1. [A position] place, spot, section; see **position** 1. 2. [A site] situation, place, scene; see **area** 2, **neighborhood.**

lock, *n.* 1. [A device for locking] hook, catch, latch, bolt, bar, hasp, clinch, bond, fastening, padlock, safety catch, clamp, clasp, link, tumblers, barrier, device, fixture, grip; see also **fastener.** 2. [A tuft *or* ringlet of hair] tress, ringlet, curl; see **hair** 1. —**under lock and key,** locked up, imprisoned, in jail; see **confined** 3.

lock, *v.* bolt, bar, turn the key; see **fasten.**

locked, *a.* secured, padlocked, cinched; see **tight** 2.

locker, *n.* cabinet, wardrobe, cupboard; see **closet, furniture.**

locket, *n.* miniature case, memento case, pendant; see **jewelry, necklace.**

lock up, *v.* confine, put behind bars, shut up; see **imprison.**

lodge, *n.* inn, hostel, chalet; see **hotel, motel, resort** 2.

lodge, *v.* 1. [To become fixed] catch, stay, abide; see **stick** 1. 2. [To take (temporary) residence] room, stay *or* stop over, board; see **dwell.**

lodger, *n.* guest, roomer, resident; see **tenant.**

lodging, *n.* 1. [Personal accommodation] harbor, protection, roof over one's head; see **refuge** 1, **shelter.** 2. [A (temporary) living place; *usually plural*] address, residence, home; see **hotel, motel, resort** 2.

lofty, *a.* tall, elevated, towering; see **high 2, raised 1.**

log, *n.* 1. [The main stem of a fallen or cut tree] timber, stick, length; see also **wood 2.** 2. [The record of a voyage] journal, account, diary; see **record 1.**

logic, *n.* reasoning, deduction, induction; see **philosophy 1, thought 1.**

logical, *a.* coherent, consistent, probable, sound, pertinent, germane, legitimate, relevant, congruent *or* consistent with, as it ought to be; see also **reasonable 1.**

logically, *a.* rationally, by logic *or* reason, inevitably; see **reasonably 1, 2.**

loiter, *v.* saunter, stroll, dawdle, delay, lag, shuffle, waste time, potter, procrastinate, tarry, fritter away time, loll, dabble, wait, pause, dillydally, hang back, trail, drag, ramble, idle; see also **linger.**—*Ant.* **hurry,** hasten, stride along.

lone, *a.* solitary, lonesome, deserted; see **alone.**

loneliness, *n.* detachment, separation, solitude, desolation, isolation, aloneness, lonesomeness, forlornness.

lonely, *a.* abandoned, homesick, forlorn, forsaken, friendless, deserted, desolate, homeless, left, lone, lonesome, solitary, withdrawn, secluded, unattended, by oneself, apart, reclusive, single, rejected, unaccompanied; see also **alone.**—*Ant.* **accompanied,** joined, associated.

lonesome, *a.* solitary, forlorn, alone; see **homesick, lonely.**

long, *a.* 1. [Extended in space] lengthy, extended, outstretched, elongated, interminable, boundless, endless, unending, limitless, stretching, great, high, deep, drawn out, enlarged, expanded, spread, tall, lofty, towering, lengthened, stringy, rangy, lanky, gangling, far-reaching, distant, running, faraway, far-off, remote; see also **large 1.**—*Ant.* **short,** small, stubby. 2. [Extended in time] protracted, prolonged, enduring, unending, meandering, long-winded, spun out, lengthy, for ages, without end, forever and a day, day after day, hour after hour, etc.; lasting, continued, long-lived, sustained, lingering.—*Ant.* **short,** brief, uncontinued. 3. [Tedious] hard, long-spun, long-drawn; see **dull 4.** 4. [Having (a certain commodity) in excess] rich, profuse, abundant; see **plentiful 1.** —**as (*or* so) long as,** seeing that, provided, since; see **because.** —**before long,** in the near future, immediately, shortly; see **soon 1.**

long, *v.* desire, yearn for, wish; see **want 1.**

long and short of it, *n.* conclusion, totality, upshot; see **result, whole.**

longing, *n.* yearning, pining, hunger; see **desire 1, wish.**

long-lived, long-lasting, perpetual, enduring; see **permanent 2.**

look, *n.* 1. [Appearance] aspect, presence, mien; see **expression 4, looks.** 2. [An effort to see] gaze, stare, scrutiny, inspection, examination, contemplation, speculation, attending, noticing, regarding, marking, observation, keeping watch; see also **attention.** 3. [A quick use of the eyes] glance, survey, squint, glimpse, peek, peep, leer.

look, *v.* 1. [To appear] seem to be, look like, resemble; see **seem 2.** 2. [To endeavor to see] view, gaze, glance (at), scan, stare, behold, contemplate, watch, survey, scrutinize, regard, inspect, discern, spy, observe, attend, examine, mark, gape, give attention, peer, have an eye on, study, peep, look on *or* at *or* upon *or* through, *take a gander at, *get a load of; see also **see 1.** —*it **looks like,** probably, it seems that there will be, it seems as if; see **seem.**

look after, *v.* look out for, support, watch; see **guard.**

look for, *v.* research, pry, follow; see **search, seek.**

look into, *v.* investigate, study, probe; see **examine.**

lookout, *n.* 1. [A place of vantage] outlook, view, prospect, panorama, scene, watchtower, observatory, patrol station. 2. [One stationed at a lookout, sense 1] watcher, sentinel, scout; see **watchman.**

look out, *interj.* be careful, pay attention, listen, notice, have a care, heads up; see also **watch out.**

looks, *n.* appearance, countenance, aspect, manner, demeanor, face, expression, features, form, shape, posture, bearing, presence.

***look up,** *v.* 1. [To improve] get better, advance, progress; see **improve 2.** 2. [To find by search] come upon, research, find; see **discover, search, seek.**

look up to, *v.* respect, adulate, honor; see **admire.**

loom, *v.* 1. [To appear] come into view, come on the scene, rise; see **appear 1.** 2. [To appear large *or* imposing] menace, overshadow, hulk, figure, tower, impress, hang over, rise gradually, seem large *or* huge, be coming *or* near *or* imminent, hover, approach, come forth; see also **threaten.**

loop, *n.* ring, eye, circuit; see **circle 1.** —***knock (*or* throw) for a loop,** confuse, disturb, startle; see **shock 2.**

loop, v. curve, connect, tie together; see bend.

loophole, n. avoidance, means of escape, deception; see lie, trick 1.

loose, a. 1. [Unbound] unfastened, undone, untied, insecure, relaxed, unattached, unconnected, disconnected, untethered, unbuttoned, unclasped, unhooked, unsewed, unstuck, slack, loosened, baggy, unconfined, unlatched, unlocked, unbolted, unscrewed, unhinged, worked free; see also free 3.—Ant. tight, confined, bound. 2. [Movable] unattached, free, wobbly; see movable. 3. [Vague] disconnected, detached, random; see obscure 1, vague 2. 4. [Wanton] unrestrained, dissolute, disreputable; see lewd 2. —*on the loose, unconfined, unrestrained, wild; see free. —set (or turn) loose, set free, release, untie; see free.

loosen, v. 1. [To make loose] extricate, untie, unbind, undo, disentangle, let go, unlock, release, unfix; see also free 1. 2. [To become loose] relax, slacken, work loose or free, break up, let go, become unstuck.—Ant. tighten, tighten up, become rigid.

loot, n. spoils, plunder, *take; see booty.

loot, v. plunder, thieve, rifle; see rob, steal.

lop, v. trim, prune, chop; see cut 1.

lopsided, a. uneven, unbalanced, crooked; see irregular 4.

Lord, n. Divinity, the Supreme Being, Jehovah; see God 1, 2.

lord, n. 1. [A master] ruler, governor, prince; see leader 2. 2. [A member of the nobility] nobleman, count, titled person; see aristocrat, royalty.

lordly, a. grand, dignified, honorable; see noble 1, 2, 3.

lore, n. enlightenment, wisdom, learning; see knowledge 1.

lose, v. 1. [To bring about a loss] mislay, misplace, misfile, disturb, disorder, confuse, mix, scatter, mess, muss, disorganize, forget, be careless with. 2. [To incur loss] suffer, miss, be deprived of, fail to keep, suffer loss, be impoverished from, become poorer by, *let slip through the fingers; see also waste 1.—Ant. profit, gain, improve. 3. [To fail to win] be defeated, suffer defeat, go down in defeat, succumb, fall, be the loser, miss, have the worst of it, be humbled, take defeat at the hands of, *drop, *go down for the count, *be sunk; see also fail 1.—Ant. win, triumph, be victorious. 4. [To suffer financially] squander, expend, dissipate; see spend 1, waste 2.

loser, n. sufferer, victim, prey, failure, defeated, forfeiter, dispossessed, underdog, disadvantaged, underprivileged, fallen.—Ant. winner, gainer, conqueror.

losing, a. 1. [Said of one who loses] failing, having the worst of it, on the way out; see ruined 1. 2. [Said of an activity in which one must lose] futile, desperate, lost; see hopeless.

loss, n. 1. [The act or fact of losing] ruin, destruction, mishap, misfortune, giving up, ill fortune, accident, calamity, trouble, disaster, sacrifice, catastrophe, trial, failure. 2. [Damage suffered by loss, sense 1] hurt, injury, wound; see damage 1, 2, 3. [The result of unprofitable activity] privation, want, bereavement, deprivation, need, destitution, being without, lack, waste, deterioration, impairment, degeneration, decline, disadvantage, wreck, wreckage, undoing, annihilation, bane, end, undoing, disorganization, breaking up, suppression, relapse.—Ant. advantage, advancement, supply. —at a loss, confused, puzzled, unsure; see uncertain 1, 2.

losses, n. casualties, damage, deaths; see destruction 2.

lost, a. 1. [Not to be found] misplaced, mislaid, missing, hidden, obscured, (gone) astray, nowhere to be found, strayed, lacking, wandered off, absent, forfeited, vanished, wandering, without, gone out of one's possession.—Ant. found, come back, returned. 2. [Ignorant of the way] perplexed, bewildered, ignorant; see doubtful 2. 3. [Destroyed] demolished, devastated, wasted; see destroyed, ruined 1. 4. [No longer to be gained] gone, passed, costly; see unprofitable. 5. [Helpless] feeble, sickly, disabled; see weak 1, 3. —*get lost, go away, leave, begone; see get out.

lot, n. 1. [A small parcel of land] parcel, part, division, patch, clearing, piece of ground, plat, plot, field, tract, block, portion, parking lot, piece, property, acreage. 2. [A number of individual items, usually alike] consignment, requisition; see load 1. 3. [Destiny] doom, portion, fate; see chance 1. 4. [*A great quantity] large amount, abundance, plenty, considerable amount, great numbers, bundle, bunch, cluster, group, pack, batch, large numbers, (very) much or many, quite a lot or bit, a good deal, a whole bunch, *loads, *oodles; see also plenty.

lotion, n. liniment, hand lotion, cream, wash, unguent; see also balm 1, cosmetic, medicine 2, salve.

loud, a. 1. [Having volume of sound] deafening, ringing, ear-piercing, ear-splitting, booming, intense, resounding, piercing, blaring, sonorous, resonant, crashing, deep, full, powerful, emphatic, thundering, heavy, big, deep-toned, full-tongued, roaring, *enough to wake the dead; see also shrill.—Ant. soft, faint, feeble. 2. [Producing loud sounds] clamorous, noisy, uproarious, blatant, vociferous, turbulent, tumultuous, blustering, lusty, loud-voiced, boisterous, cacophonous, raucous; see also harsh.—Ant. quiet, soft-voiced, calm. 3. [*Lacking manners and refinement] loud-mouthed, brash, offensive; see rude 2, vulgar. 4. [*Lacking good taste, especially in colors] garish, flashy, tawdry; see ornate 1.

loudly, a. 1. [With loud sound] audibly, fully, powerfully, crashingly, shrilly, deafeningly, piercingly, resonantly, emphatically, vehemently, thunderingly, in full cry, clamorously, noisily, uproariously, blatantly, at the top of one's lungs. 2. [Rudely] boorishly, crudely, gaudily; see rudely.

loud-speaker, n. speaker, amplifier, public address system, high-fidelity speaker, full- or high-frequency speaker, low-frequency speaker, bullhorn.

lounge, v. idle, repose, kill time; see loaf, rest 1.

lousy, a. 1. [Having lice] infected or crawling with lice, pediculous, pedicular; see creeping. 2. [*Bad] horrible, disliked, unwelcome; see offensive 2.

lovable, a. winning, winsome, lovely; see friendly.

love, n. 1. [Passionate and tender devotion] attachment, devotedness, passion, infatuation, yearning, flame, rapture, enchantment, ardor, emotion, sentiment, fondness, tenderness, adoration, *crush; see also affection.—Ant. hate, aversion, antipathy. 2. [Affection based on esteem] respect, regard, appreciation; see admiration. 3. [A lively and enduring interest] involvement, concern, enjoyment; see devotion. 4. [A beloved] dear one, loved one, cherished one; see lover 1. —fall in love (with), begin to feel love (for), adore, be infatuated; see fall in love. —for the love of, for the sake of, with fond concern for, because of; see for. —in love, enamored, infatuated, charmed; see loving. —make love, fondle, embrace, sleep with; see copulate, love 2. —not for love or money, under no conditions, by no means, no; see never.

love, v. 1. [To be passionately devoted] adore, be in love with, care for, hold dear, choose, fancy, be enchanted by, be passionately attached to, have affection for, dote on, glorify, idolize, prize, be fascinated by, hold high, think the world of, treasure, prefer, yearn for, be fond of, admire, long for, *flip over, *fall for, *be nuts or crazy about, *go for, *have it bad.—Ant. hate, detest, loathe. 2. [To express love by caresses]

cherish, fondle, kiss, make love to, embrace, cling to, clasp, hug, take into one's arms, hold, pet, stroke, draw close, bring to one's side, *make a play for, *make it; see also kiss.—Ant. exclude, spurn, refuse. 3. [To possess a deep and abiding interest] enjoy, delight in, relish; see admire, like 1.

loved, a. desired, cherished, well beloved; see beloved.

loveliness, n. appeal, charm, fairness; see beauty 1.

lovely, a. 1. [Beautiful] attractive, comely, fair; see sense 2, beautiful, handsome. 2. [Charming] engaging, enchanting, captivating; see charming. 3. [*Very pleasing] nice, splendid, delightful; see pleasant 1, 2.

lover, n. 1. [A suitor] sweetheart, admirer, escort, paramour, fiancé, gentleman friend, *boyfriend, *girlfriend, steady. 2. [A willing student or practitioner; used only in phrases] practitioner, fan, hobbyist; see zealot. 3. [An epithet for a beloved] beloved, sweetheart, dear; see darling.

loving, a. admiring, respecting, valuing, liking, fond, tender, kind, enamored, attached, devoted, appreciative, attentive, thoughtful, passionate, ardent, amiable, warm, amorous, affectionate, anxious, concerned, sentimental, earnest, benevolent, cordial, caring, considerate, loyal, generous.

lovingly, a. tenderly, devotedly, adoringly, warmly, ardently, fervently, zealously, earnestly, loyally, generously, kindly thoughtfully, dotingly, fondly, affectionately, passionately, longingly, rapturously, admiringly, respectfully, reverently, with love, attentively.

low, a. 1. [Close to the earth] squat, flat, level, low-lying, prostrate, crouched, below, not far above the horizon, low-hanging, knee-high, beneath, under, depressed, sunken, nether, inferior, lying under.—Ant. high, lofty, elevated. 2. [Far down on a scale] muffled, hushed, quiet; see faint 3. 3. [Low in spirits] dejected, moody, *blue; see sad 1. 4. [Vulgar] base, mean, coarse; see vulgar. 5. [Faint] ill, dizzy, feeble; see sick, weak 1. 6. [Simple] economical, moderate, inexpensive; see cheap 1. —lay low, bring to ruin, overcome, kill; see destroy. —lie low, wait, conceal oneself, take cover; see hide 2.

lower, a. beneath, inferior, under; see low 1.

lower, v. bring low, set or let or cast down, depress; see decrease 1, 2, drop 2.

lowest, a. shortest, littlest, smallest, slightest, least, rock-bottom, ground, base; see also smallest.

lowly, *a.* unpretentious, cast down, meek; see **humble** 2.

loyal, *a.* true, dependable, firm; see **faithful.**

loyally, *a.* faithfully, conscientiously, truly, devotedly, constantly, sincerely, obediently, resolutely, earnestly, steadfastly, with fidelity *or* fealty *or* allegiance *or* constancy, in good faith.

loyalty, *n.* allegiance, faithfulness, fidelity, trustworthiness, constancy, integrity, attachment, sincerity, adherence, bond, tie, honor, reliability, (good) faith, conscientiousness, dependability, devotedness, support, zeal, ardor, earnestness, resolution, obedience, duty, honesty, truthfulness; see also **devotion.**—*Ant.* disloyalty, **dishonesty,** faithlessness.

lubricant, *n.* cream, ointment, oil; see **grease.**

lubricate, *v.* oil, anoint, cream; see **grease.**

luck, *n.* 1. [Good fortune] good luck, prosperity, wealth, run *or* piece *or* streak of luck, windfall, advantage, profit, triumph, victory, win, happiness, blessings, opportunity, lucky break, *break, *the breaks.—*Ant.* failure, ill-fortune, bad luck. 2. [Chance] unforeseen occurrence, hap, fate; see **accident, chance** 1. *crowd (*or* push) **one's luck,** gamble, take risks, chance; see **risk.** —**in luck,** lucky, successful, prosperous; see **fortunate.** —**out of luck,** unlucky, in misfortune, in trouble; see **unfortunate.** —**try one's luck,** attempt, risk, endeavor; see **try** 1.

luckily, *a.* opportunely, happily, favorably; see **fortunately.**

lucky, *a.* 1. [Enjoying good luck] blessed, wealthy, victorious, happy, favored, winning, in luck, successful, prosperous; see **fortunate.** 2. [Supposed to bring good luck] providential, propitious, auspicious; see **magic** 1.

lucrative, *a.* fruitful, productive, gainful; see **profitable.**

ludicrous, *a.* comical, odd, farcical; see **funny** 1.

lug, *v.* carry, tug, lift; see **draw** 1.

luggage, *n.* trunks, bags, valises; see **baggage.**

lukewarm, *a.* cool, tepid, chilly; see **warm** 1.

lull, *n.* quiet, stillness, hush; see **silence** 1.

lull, *v.* calm, quiet down, bring *or* encourage repose; see **quiet** 1, 2.

lullaby, *n.* good-night song, bedtime song, sleep-song; see **song.**

lumber, *n.* cut timber, logs, sawed timber, forest products, boards, hardwood, softwood, lumbering products; see also **wood** 2.

luminescence, *n.* fluorescence, fire, radiance; see **light** 1.

luminous, *a.* lighted, glowing, radiant; see **bright** 1.

lump, *n.* handful, protuberance, bunch, bump, block, bulk, chunk, piece, portion, section; see **hunk.**

lumpy, *a.* knotty, clotty, uneven; see **irregular** 4, **thick** 1, 3.

lunacy, *n.* madness, dementia, mania; see **insanity.**

lunatic, *a.* 1. [Insane] demented, deranged, psychotic; see **insane.** 2. [Foolish] irrational, idiotic, daft; see **stupid** 1.

lunatic, *n.* crazy person, demoniac, insane person; see **madman.**

lunch, *n.* meal, luncheon, refreshment, sandwich, snack, (high) tea.

lunch, *v.* dine, have lunch, take a (lunch) break; see **eat** 1.

lunge, *v.* surge, lurch, bound; see **jump** 1.

lurch, *v.* stagger, weave, sway; see **totter.**

lure, *n.* bait, decoy, fake; see **camouflage** 1, **trick** 1.

lure, *v.* enchant, bewitch, allure; see **charm, fascinate.**

lurk, *v.* wait, crouch, conceal oneself; see **hide** 2.

lurking, *a.* hiding out, sneaking, hidden; see **hidden.**

luscious, *a.* sweet, toothsome, palatable; see **delicious.**

lush, *a.* 1. [Green] verdant, dense, grassy; see **green** 2. 2. [Delicious] rich, juicy, succulent; see **delicious.** 3. [Elaborate] extensive, luxurious, ornamental; see **elaborate** 1, **ornate** 1.

lust, *n.* appetite, passion, sensuality; see **desire** 2.

lust (after), *v.* long (for), desire, hunger *or* wish for; see **want** 1.

luster, *n.* glow, brilliance, radiance; see **light** 1.

lusty, *a.* hearty, robust, vigorous; see **healthy.**

luxurious, *a.* comfortable, easy, affluent; see **expensive, rich** 2.

luxury, *n.* 1. [Indulgence of the senses, regardless of the cost] gratification, costliness, expensiveness, richness, idleness, leisure, high-living, lavishness; see also **indulgence** 1.—*Ant.* poverty, poorness, lack. 2. [An indulgence beyond one's means] extravagance, exorbitance, wastefulness; see **excess** 1, **waste** 1.

lying, *a.* 1. [In the act of lying] falsifying, prevaricating, swearing falsely, committing perjury, fibbing, misrepresenting, inventing.—*Ant.* **frank,** truthful, veracious. 2. [Given to lying] deceitful, unreliable, double-dealing; see **dishonest.** 3. [Not reliable] unsound, tricky,

treacherous; see **false 2, unreliable 2.**
4. [Prostrate] supine, reclining, resting, horizontal, reposing, recumbent, flat, fallen, prone, crashed, powerless.

lying down, *a.* reclining, reposing, sleeping; see **asleep, resting 1.**

lynch, *v.* hang, mob, murder; see **kill 1.**

lyric, *n.* 1. [Verses set to music] (the) words, (the) poem, (the) verse; see **poem. 2.** [A short, songlike poem] lyrical poem, ode, sonnet, hymn, roundel; see also **poetry, song, verse 1.**

lyrical, *a.* melodious, sweet, rhythmical; see **musical 1, poetic.**

M

*ma, n. mama, *mommy, *mom; see
mother 1.

machine, n. instrument, appliance, vehicle, tool, implement, gadget; see device
1, engine, motor, tool 1.

machine gun, n. automatic rifle, semiautomatic rifle, automatic arms, light
ordnance, *Tommy gun, *burp gun,
*squirt gun; see also gun, weapon.

machinery, n. appliances, implements,
tools; see appliance, device 1, engine,
machine, motor.

machinist, n. machine operator, engineer,
skilled workman; see workman.

mad, a. 1. [Insane] demented, deranged,
psychotic; see insane. 2. [Angry]
provoked, enraged, exasperated; see angry. 3. [Afflicted with rabies] frenzied,
raging, foaming at the mouth; see sick.

madden, v. craze, infuriate, enrage; see
anger.

maddening, a. annoying, infuriating, offensive; see disturbing.

made, a. fashioned, shaped, finished; see
built, formed, manufactured. —*have
(or get) it made, prosper, win, do well;
see succeed 1.

made easy, a. reduced, made plain, uncomplicated; see easy 2, simplified.

made-up, a. 1. [False] invented, concocted, devised, fabricated, exaggerated,
prepared, fictitious; see also false 2, 3,
unreal. 2. [Marked by the use of
make-up] rouged, powdered, colored,
freshened, reddened, cosmeticized.

madhouse, n. mental hospital, asylum,
bedlam; see hospital.

madly, a. rashly, crazily, hastily; see violently, wildly.

madman, n. lunatic, maniac, raver, insane or deranged person, psychiatric patient; *nut, *screwball, *oddball, *psycho.

madness, n. derangement, aberration,
delusion; see insanity.

magazine, n. publication, broadside,
pamphlet, booklet, manual, circular,
periodical, weekly, monthly, quarterly,
annual, bulletin, transactions, review,
supplement, gazette, report, brochure.

maggot, n. grub, slug, larva; see parasite 1, worm 1.

magic, a. magical, mystic, diabolic, Satanic, necromantic, fiendish, demoniac,
malevolent, shamanist, voodooistic, conjuring, spellbinding, enchanting, fascinating, cryptic, transcendental, supernatural, alchemistic, spooky, ghostly,
haunted, weird, uncanny, eerie, disembodied, immaterial, astral, spiritualistic,
psychic, supersensory, otherworldly,
fairylike, mythical, mythic, charmed, enchanted, bewitched, entranced, spellbound, under a spell or charm, cursed,
prophetic, telepathic, clairvoyant, telekinetic, parapsychological; see also mysterious 2.

magic, n. 1. [The controlling of supernatural powers] occultism, legerdemain,
necromancy, incantation, spell, wizardry,
alchemy, superstition, enchantment, sorcery, supersensory power, prophecy,
divination, astrology, taboo, witchcraft,
black magic, voodooism, fire worship;
see also witchcraft. 2. [An example of
magic] incantation, prediction, soothsaying, fortunetelling, foreboding, exorcism,
ghost dance.

magical, a. occult, enchanting, mystic;
see magic 1, mysterious 2.

magician, n. enchanter, necromancer,
conjurer, seer, soothsayer, diviner, sorceror, wizard, warlock, medicine man,
shaman, exorcist; see also prophet,
witch.

magnet, n. lodestone, magnetite, magnetic iron ore, natural magnet, artificial
magnet, bar magnet, electromagnet,
horseshoe magnet.

magnetic, a. irresistible, captivating, fascinating; see charming.

magnetism, n. lure, influence, charm; see
attraction.

magnificence, n. grandeur, majesty,
stateliness, nobleness, glory, radiance,
grace, beauty, style, flourish, luxuriousness, glitter, nobility, greatness, lavishness, brilliance, splendor, richness,
pomp, *swank, *posh; see also grandeur.—Ant. dullness, simplicity, unostentatiousness.

magnificent, a. exalted, great, majestic;
see grand.

magnify, v. amplify, blow up, expand;
see increase.

magnitude, n. 1. [Size] extent, breadth,
dimension; see measure 1, measurement 2, quantity, size. 2. [Importance]
greatness, consequence, significance; see
degree 2, importance.

maid, n. 1. [A female servant] maidservant, nursemaid, housemaid, chambermaid, barmaid; see also servant. 2. [A
girl] child, virgin, *kid; see girl,
woman 1.

maiden, *a.* earliest, beginning, virgin; see **first**.

maiden name, *n.* family *or* inherited name, surname, cognomen; see **name 1**.

mail, *n.* letter, post, communication, airmail letter(s), postal, junk mail, post card, printed matter; see also **letter 2**.

mail, *v.* post, send by post *or* mail, drop into a letter box; see **send 1**.

mailed, *a.* posted, sent by post, transmitted by post, in the mail, shipped, consigned, dispatched, sent by mail, dropped in the post office; see also **sent**.

maim, *v.* mutilate, disable, disfigure; see **damage, hurt 1**.

main, *a.* 1. [Principal] chief, dominant, first, authoritative, significant, most important, superior, foremost, leading; see also **major 1**. 2. [Only] utter, pure, simple; see **absolute**.

mainland, *n.* shore, beach, dry land; see **land 1, region 1**.

mainly, *a.* chiefly, largely, essentially; see **principally**.

maintain, *v.* 1. [To uphold] hold up, advance, keep; see **support 2, sustain 1**. 2. [To assert] state, affirm, attest; see **declare, report 1, say**. 3. [To keep ready for use] preserve, keep, conserve, repair, withhold, renew, reserve, defer, hold back, have in store, care for, save, put away, set aside, store up, keep for, lay aside *or* away, set by, keep on hand, keep in reserve, set apart, keep up, keep aside, control, hold over, manage, direct, have, own, sustain, secure, stick to, stand by; see also **keep 1.—** *Ant.* waste, neglect, consume. 4. [To continue] carry on, persevere, keep up *or* on; see **continue 1**. 5. [To support] provide *or* care for, take care of, keep; see **support 5, sustain 2**.

maintenance, *n.* sustenance, livelihood, resources; see **pay 1, 2, subsistence 2**.

majestic, *a.* dignified, sumptuous, exalted; see **grand, noble 1, 3**.

majesty, *n.* 1. [Grandeur] nobility, illustriousness, greatness; see **grandeur**. 2. [A form of address; *usually capital*] Lord, King, Emperor, Prince, Royal Highness, Highness, Sire, Eminence, Queen.

major, *a.* 1. [Greater] higher, larger, dominant, primary, upper, exceeding, extreme, ultra, over, above; see also **superior**. 2. [Important] significant, main, influential; see **important 1, principal**.

majority, *n.* 1. [The larger part] more than half, preponderance, most, best, gross, *lion's share, greater number. 2. [Legal maturity] full age, adulthood, voting age; see **manhood 1**.

make, *v.* 1. [To manufacture] construct, fabricate, assemble, fashion, compose, compile, create, effect, produce; see also **build, manufacture**. 2. [To total] add up to, come to, equal; see **amount to**. 3. [To create] originate, actualize, effect, generate, compose, plan, devise, construct, cause, conceive; see also **compose 2, create, invent 1, produce 2**. 4. [To acquire] gain, get, secure; see **get 1**. 5. [To force] constrain, compel, coerce; see **force**. 6. [To cause] start, effect, initiate; see **begin 1, cause**. 7. [To wage] carry on, conduct, engage in; see **act 2**. 8. [To prepare] get ready, arrange, adjust; see **cook, prepare 1**.

make amends, *v.* atone, make up for, compensate; see **reconcile 2, repay 1, settle 9**.

make as if *or* **as though,** *v.* make believe, simulate, affect; see **pretend 1**.

make-believe, *a.* pretended, fraudulent, acted; see **false 3, fantastic, unreal**.

make-believe, *n.* sham, unreality, fairy tale; see **fantasy, pretense 2**.

make believe, *v.* feign, simulate, counterfeit; see **dream 2, pretend 1**.

make certain (of), *v.* make sure of, check into, find out, investigate; see also **examine, guarantee**.

make do, *v.* employ, suffice, accept; see **endure 2, survive 1, use 1**.

make ends meet, *v.* survive, subsist, get along; see **budget, estimate, manage 1**.

make fun of, *v.* tease, embarrass, mimic; see **bother 2, imitate 1**.

make good, *v.* 1. [To repay] compensate, adjust, reimburse; see **pay 1, repay 1**. 2. [To justify] maintain, support, uphold; see **support 2**. 3. [To succeed] arrive, pay off, prove oneself; see **pay 2, succeed 1**.

make headway, *v.* progress, achieve, become better; see **advance 1, improve 2**.

*make it,** *v.* achieve, triumph, accomplish; see **succeed 1**.

make known, *v.* tell, advise, announce; see **advertise, declare**.

make love, *v.* fondle, sleep with, *pet; see **copulate, join 1, love 2**.

make merry, *v.* frolic, revel, enjoy; see **play 1**.

make of, *v.* interpret, translate, understand; see **think 1**.

make off with, *v.* abduct, rob, kidnap; see **steal**.

make out, *v.* 1. [To understand] perceive, recognize, see; see **understand 1**. 2. [To succeed] accomplish, achieve, prosper; see **succeed 1**. 3. [To see] discern, perceive, detect; see **discover, see 1**.

make over, *v.* 1. [To improve] amend, correct, restore; see **improve 1, redecorate, remodel**. 2. [To rebuild] renovate, refashion, refurbish; see **repair 1, restore 3.**

make peace, v. propitiate, negotiate, make up; see **reconcile 2.**

make progress, v. go forward, progress, proceed; see **advance 1, improve 2.**

make ready, v. arrange, get ready, prearrange; see **cook, prepare 1.**

make sense, v. be reasonable or intelligible or clear or understandable or logical or coherent, articulate, add up, follow, infer, deduce, *hang together, *hold water, put two and two together, straighten up or out, stand to reason.

makeshift, a. substitute, alternative, stopgap; see **temporary.**

make sure of, v. ensure, determine, review; see **check 2, discover.**

make the most of, v. take advantage (of), employ, promote; see **use 1.**

make the rounds, v. inspect, scrutinize, check-up (on); see **examine 1.**

make time, v. gain, speed up, make good or fast or quick or rapid time; see **speed, travel.**

make-up, n. 1. [Cosmetics] grease paint, mascara, (eye) liner, powder, pomade. 2. [*Anything offered to make good a shortage] atonement, compensation, conciliation; see **payment.** 3. [Composition] scheme, structure, arrangement; see **composition, design, formation.**

make up, v. 1. [To compose] compound, combine, mingle; see **join 1, mix 1.** 2. [To constitute] comprise, belong to, go into the making of, be contained in, be an element or portion of, include, consist of; see **compose 1.** 3. [To invent] fabricate, devise, fashion; see **compose 2, create, invent 1.** 4. [To reconcile] conciliate, pacify, accommodate; see **reconcile 2.** 5. [To apply cosmetics] powder, rouge; apply face powder or lipstick or eyeshadow or eye make-up, etc.; beautify, *do up.

make up for, v. compensate, balance, counterbalance; see **balance 2.**

make up (one's) mind, v. choose, pick, elect; see **decide, resolve.**

make use of, v. need, employ, utilize; see **use 1.**

make war, v. battle, combat, encounter; see **fight.**

make way, v. progress, proceed, break ground or trail; see **advance 1.** —*on the make, zealous, belligerent, ruthless; see **aggressive 2.**

making, n. imagination, conception, formulation, devising, producing, constituting, causation, fashioning, building, origination, shaping, forging, designing, planning, fabrication, composition; see also **production 1.**

male, a. manlike, virile, powerful; see **masculine.**

male, n. male sex, man-child, he; see **boy, father 1.**

malformed, a. distorted, grotesque, abnormal; see **deformed, twisted 1.**

malfunction, n. slip, bad or faulty performance, failure to work or function or perform, etc.; see **failure 1.**

malice, n. spite, animosity, resentment; see **evil 1, hatred.**

malicious, a. ill-disposed, spiteful, hateful; see **bad 1.**

malignant, a. 1. [Diseased] cancerous, lethal, poisonous; see **deadly.** 2. [Harmful] deleterious, corrupt, sapping; see **dangerous, harmful.**

malpractice, n. negligence, misbehaviour, neglect; see **carelessness, violation.**

mama, n. female progenitor, mamma, parent; see **mother 1.**

mammal, n. vertebrate, creature, beast; see **animal.**

man, n. 1. [The human race] mankind, human beings, race, humanity, human species, human nature, persons, mortals, individuals, earthlings, civilized society, creatures, fellow creatures, people, folk, society, *Homo sapiens* (Latin). 2. [An adult male] he, gentleman, Sir, Mr., fellow, mister, master, *chap, *guy; see also **boy.** 3. [Anyone] human being, an individual, fellow creature; see **person 1.** 4. [An employee] hand, worker, representative; see **employee.** 5. [Husband] married man, spouse, partner; see **husband.** —**as a man,** in unison, united, all together; see **unanimously.** —**be one's own man,** be independent, stand alone, be free; see **endure 1.** —**to a man,** all, everyone, with no exception; see **everybody.**

man, v. garrison, protect, fortify; see **defend 1, guard.**

manage, v. 1. [To direct] lead, oversee, indicate, designate, instruct, mastermind, engineer, show, disburse, distribute, execute, handle, watch, guide, supervise, conduct, engage in, officiate, pilot, steer, minister, regulate, administer, manipulate, officiate, superintend, preside, suggest, advocate, counsel, request, call upon, maintain, care for, take over, take care of, carry on, watch over, have in one's charge, look after, see to, *run the show, *hold down, call the shots, *run a tight ship.—*Ant.* obey, follow, take orders. 2. [To contrive] accomplish, bring about, effect; see **achieve, succeed 1.** 3. [To get along] bear up, survive, scrape or get by; see **endure 2.**

manageable, a. controllable, docile, compliant, governable, teachable, tractable, willing, obedient, submissive, yielding, adaptable, flexible, dutiful, humble, meek, easy; see also **gentle 3, obedient 1, willing.**—*Ant.* **rebellious,** ungovernable, unruly.

managed, *a.* 1. [Trained] handled, guided, persuaded, influenced, driven, counselled, urged, taught, instructed, coached, groomed, primed, given a workout; see **educated, trained.**—*Ant.* **wild,** undisciplined, uneducated. 2. [Governed] ruled, controlled, dominated, commanded, directed, swayed, mastered, run, regulated, ordered, compelled, supervised, piloted, cared for, taken care of; see also **governed.**—*Ant.* ungoverned, **free,** unsupervised.

management, *n.* 1. [Direction] supervision, superintendence, government, command, guidance, conduct, organization, handling, policy, order, power, control; see also **command.** 2. [Those who undertake management; *usually preceded by* the] directors, administrators, executives; see **administration 2.**

manager, *n.* director, handler, superintendent, supervisor; see also **executive.**

managing, *n.* directing, supervising, superintending, advising, overseeing, controlling, taking charge of, caring for, administering, executing, organizing, regulating, leading, piloting, steering, handling, charging, manipulating; see **operating.**

mandate, *n.* command, decree, order; see **command.**

mandatory, *a.* compulsory, forced, obligatory; see **necessary.**

man-eating, *a.* cannibal, carnivorous, omnivorous; see **dangerous, deadly.**

maneuver, *n.* 1. [A movement, usually military] stratagem, movement, procedure; see **plan 2, tactics.** 2. [A trick] subterfuge, finesse, ruse; see **trick 1.** 3. [Extensive practice in arms; *plural*] imitation war, exercises, war games; see **drill 3, exercise 1, parade 1.**

maneuver, *v.* plot, scheme, move, manage, contrive, design, devise, trick, cheat, conspire, sham, *angle for; see also **plan 1.**

mangle, *v.* 1. [To mutilate] tear, lacerate, wound, injure, cripple, maim, rend, disfigure, cut, slit, butcher, slash, slice, carve, bruise, mutilate; see also **hurt 1.** 2. [To iron with a power roller] steam press, smooth, iron; see **iron.**

manhandle, *v.* damage, maul, mistreat; see **abuse, beat 1.**

manhood, *n.* 1. [Male maturity] postpubescence, coming of age, full age, prime of life, middle age, voting age, adulthood. 2. [Manly qualities] virility, resoluteness, honor, gallantry, nobility, forcefulness, daring, boldness, tenacity, potency, self-reliance.

mania, *n.* craze, lunacy, madness; see **desire 1, insanity, obsession.**

maniac, *n.* lunatic, insane person, crazy man; see **madman.**

manipulate, *v.* handle, shape, mold; see **form 1, manage 1, plan 1.**

manipulation, *n.* guidance, use, direction; see **management 1.**

mankind, *n.* humanity, human race, society; see **man 1.**

manlike, *a.* anthropoid, simian, anthropomorphic; see **human.**

manly, *a.* masculine, courageous, fearless, firm, noble, valiant, high-spirited, intrepid, gallant, resolute, bold, confident, dauntless, self-reliant; see also **masculine.**—*Ant.* **cowardly,** timid, effeminate.

man-made, *a.* manufactured, artificial, unnatural, counterfeit, not organic, ersatz, not genuine.

manner, *n.* 1. [Personal conduct] mien, deportment, demeanor; see **behavior.** 2. [Customary action] use, way, practice; see **custom 1, 2, habit 1.** 3. [Method] mode, fashion, style; see **method.** —**in a manner of speaking,** in a way, so to speak, so to say; see **rather.**

mannerism, *n.* idiosyncrasy, pretension, peculiarity; see **characteristic, quirk.**

mannerly, *a.* polished, considerate, charming; see **polite.**

manners, *n.* 1. [Personal behavior] conduct, deportment, bearing; see **behavior 1.** 2. [Culture] urbanity, taste, refinement; see **courtesy 1, culture 2, elegance.**

manpower, *n.* youth, men of military age, males; see **labor 4.**

mansion, *n.* villa, house, hall; see **estate, home 1.**

manslaughter, *n.* killing, homicide, assassination; see **crime, murder.**

mantle, *n.* fireplace, mantlepiece, chimney piece; see **shelf 2.**

manual, *a.* hand-operated, not automatic, standard; see **old-fashioned.**

manual, *n.* guidebook, reference book, textbook; see **book.**

manufacture, *n.* fashioning, forming, assembling; see **production 1.**

manufacture, *v.* make, construct, fabricate, produce, form, fashion, carve, mold, cast, frame, put together, turn out, stamp *or* print *or* cut out, have in production *or* on the assembly line, print, erect, shape, execute, accomplish, complete, tool, machine, mill, make up; see also **build 1.**—*Ant.* **destroy,** demolish, tear down.

manufactured, *a.* made, produced, constructed, fabricated, erected, fashioned, shaped, forged, turned out, tooled, executed, done, assembled, ready for (the) market, in shape, complete, completed; see also **built, formed.**

manufacturer, *n.* maker, producer, fabricator, constructor, builder, operator, craftsman, corporation, entrepreneur, company.

manufacturing, *a.* producing, industrial, fabricative; see **making.**

manufacturing, *n.* fabrication, building, construction, assembling, preparing for market, putting in production, continuing *or* keeping in production *or* on the assembly line, forging, formation, erection, composition, accomplishment, completion, finishing, doing, turning out; see also **production** 1.—*Ant.* destruction, wreck, demolition.

manure, *n.* guano, plant-food, compost; see **dung, fertilizer.**

manuscript, *n.* composition, parchment, tablet, paper, document, original, copy, letterpress, autograph, translation, facsimile, book, script; see also **writing** 2.

many, *a.* numerous, multiplied, manifold, multitudinous, multifarious, diverse, sundry, profuse, innumerable, not a few, numberless, a world of, countless, uncounted, alive with, teeming, in heaps, several, of every description, prevalent, no end of *or* to, everywhere, crowded, common, usual, plentiful, abundant, galore; see also **various.**—*Ant.* few, meager, scanty.

many, *n.* a great number, abundance, *thousands; see **plenty.** —a good *or* (great) many,** a great number, abundance, thousands; see **plenty.** —as **many (as),** as much (as), an equal number, a similar amount; see **same.**

many-sided, *a.* 1. [Multilateral] polyhedral, geometric, bilateral, dihedral, trilateral, quadrilateral, tetrahedral; see also **geometrical.** 2. [Gifted] endowed, talented, adaptable; see **able, versatile.**

map, *n.* chart, graph, plat, sketch, delineation, drawing, picture, portrayal, draft, tracing, outline, ground plan. —**put on the map,** make famous, bring fame to, glorify; see **establish** 2. —**wipe off the map,** eliminate, put out of existence, ruin; see **destroy.**

map, *v.* outline, draft, chart; see **plan** 2.

mar, *v.* 1. [To damage slightly] harm, bruise, scratch; see **break** 2, **damage.** 2. [To impair] deform, deface, warp; see **destroy.**

marble, *a.* petrified, granitelike, unyielding; see **rock** 1, **stone.**

marble, *n.* 1. [Metamorphic limestone] Marbles include the following—Parian, Pentelic, Carrian, Serpentine, Algerian, Tecali (onyx marbles), Tuscan, Gibraltar, Vermont, Georgia, fire, black, ophicalcite; see also **stone.** 2. [A piece of

carved marble] carving, figurine, figure; see **art** 2, **sculpture, statue.** 3. [A ball used in marbles] *marb, *nib, *shooter; see **toy** 1.

March, *n.* spring month, beginning of spring, month that comes in like a lion and goes out like a lamb; see **month, spring** 2.

march, *n.* 1. [The act of marching] progression, movement, advancing, advancement, countermarch, goose step, military parade; see also **step** 1, **walk** 3. 2. [The distance or route marched] walk, trek, hike; see **journey.** 3. [Music for marching] martial music, wedding march, processional; see **music.**

march, *v.* move, advance, step out, go on, proceed, step, tread, tramp, patrol, prowl, parade, goose step, file, range, strut, proceed, progress, go ahead, forge ahead.—*Ant.* pause, halt, retreat. —**on the march,** proceeding, advancing, tramping; see **moving** 1.

marching, *a.* advancing, parading, pacing; see **moving** 1, **traveling, walking.**

mare, *n.* female horse, brood mare, breeding stock; see **animal, horse.**

margin, *n.* border, lip, shore; see **boundary, edge** 1.

marginal, *a.* rimming, edging, verging; see **bordering.**

marijuana, *n. cannibis sativa,* *grass, *pot; see **drug.**

marine, *a.* maritime, of the sea, oceanic; see **maritime, nautical.**

marital, *a.* conjugal, connubial, nuptial; see **married.**

maritime, *a.* naval, marine, oceanic, seagoing, hydrographic, seafaring, aquatic, natatorial, Neptunian; see also **nautical.**

mark, *n.* 1. [The physical result of marking] brand, stamp, blaze, imprint, impression, line, trace, check, stroke, streak, dot, point, nick. 2. [A target] butt, prey, bull's eye. 3. [Effect] manifestation, consequence, value; see **result.** —**hit the mark,** achieve, accomplish, do right *or* well; see **succeed** 1. —**make one's mark,** accomplish, prosper, become famous; see **succeed** 1. —**miss the mark,** be unsuccessful, err, mistake; see **fail** 1.

mark, *v.* 1. [To make a mark] brand, stamp, imprint, blaze, print, check, chalk, label, sign, identify, check off, trace, stroke, streak, dot, point, nick, underline. 2. [To designate] earmark, point out, stake out, indicate, check *or* mark off, signify, denote; see also **mean** 1. 3. [To distinguish] characterize, signalize, qualify; see **distinguish** 1. 4. [To put prices upon] ticket, label, tag; see **price.**

mark down, v. reduce, put on sale, cut the price (of), see **price**.

marked, a. 1. [Carrying a mark] branded, signed, sealed, stamped, imprinted, inscribed, characterized by, distinguished by, recognized or identified by. 2. [Priced] labeled, trade-marked, price-marked, marked down, marked up, ticketed, priced, tagged; see also **costing**.

marked down, a. lowered, priced lower, discounted; see **reduced 2**.

marked up, a. added on, more expensive, raised; see **raised 1**.

marker, n. ticket, price mark, trademark, seal, brand, stamp, pencil, pen, boundary mark, inscription; see also **label**.

market, n. 1. [A place devoted to sale] trading post, mart, shopping mall, shopper's square, emporium, exchange, city market, public market, supermarket, meat market, fish market, curb market, stock market, stock exchange, fair, dime store, drug store, department store, variety store, bazaar, warehouse, business, delicatessen; see also **shop**, **store**. 2. [The state of trade] supply and demand, sale, run; see **business 1, 4, demand 2**. —**be in the market (for)**, want (to buy), be willing to purchase, need; see **want 1**. —**on the market**, saleable, ready for purchase, available; see **for sale**.

market, v. vend, exchange, barter; see **sell**.

mark off, v. segregate, separate, indicate; see **mark 2**.

mark out, v. delete, omit, erase; see **eliminate**.

mark time, v. put off, postpone, kill time; see **delay**, **wait 1**.

mark up, n. raise, margin, gross profit; see **increase**, **profit 2**.

markup, v. raise the price, adjust, add to; see **increase**.

marriage, n. wedding, espousal, spousal, nuptials, pledging, mating, matrimony, conjugality, union, match, wedlock, wedded state, wedded bliss, holy matrimony.

married, a. wedded, mated, espoused, united, given or pledged in marriage, living in the married state, in the state of matrimony. —*Ant*. single, unwedded, unmarried.

marry, v. 1. [To take a spouse] wed, espouse, enter the matrimonial state, take wedding vows, promise or pledge in marriage, mate, lead to the altar, *tie the knot, *get hooked.—*Ant*. divorce, put away, reject. 2. [To join in wedlock] unite, give, join in matrimony,

pronounce man and wife; see also **join 1**.—*Ant*. divorce, annul, separate.

marsh, n. morass, bog, quagmire; see **swamp**.

marshy, a. swampy, wet, sloppy; see also **muddy 1, 2**.

martial, a. warlike, soldierly, combative; see **aggressive**.

martyr, n. sufferer, offering, scapegoat; see **saint 1, victim**.

martyrdom, n. agony, suffering, devotion; see **torture**.

marvel, n. miracle, phenomenon, curiosity; see **wonder 2**.

marvel, v. stare, stand in awe, stare with open mouth; see **wonder 1**.

marvelous, a. fabulous, astonishing, spectacular; see **unusual 1**.

masculine, a. courageous, male, virile, potent, vigorous, forceful, aggressive, adult, honorable; see also **manly**.

masculinity, n. virility, power, manliness; see **manhood 2, strength**.

mash, n. mix, pulp, paste; see **feed**, **mixture 1**.

mash, v. crush, bruise, squash, chew, masticate, smash, pound, reduce, squeeze, brew, pulverize; see also **grind**, **press 1**.

mashed, a. crushed, pressed, mixed, pulpy, battered, pounded, smashed, squashed, softened, reduced, spongy, pasty, pulverized, masticated, chewed, bruised; made into a powder or a paste, etc. —*Ant*. whole, hard, uncrushed.

mask, n. 1. [A disguise] cover, false face, veil, hood, costume, theater device; see also **camouflage**, **disguise**. 2. [A protection] gas mask, catcher's mask, fencing mask, fireman's mask, respirator; see also **protection 2**. 3. [A masquerade] revel, party, carnival; see **party 1**.

mask, v. cloak, conceal, veil; see **disguise**, **hide 1**.

masquerade, n. Mardi Gras, masked ball, pretense; see **dance 2**, entertainment, **party 1**.

mass, n. 1. [A body of matter] lump, bulk, piece, portion, section, batch, block, body, core, clot, coagulation, *wad, *gob; see **hunk**. 2. [A considerable quantity] heap, volume, crowd; see **quantity**, **size 2**. 3. [Size] magnitude, volume, span; see **extent**, **size 2**.

mass, n. eucharistic rite, Catholic service, Eucharist, Lord's Supper, Holy Communion, ceremony, observance; see also **celebration**, **worship 1**. Masses include the following—High Mass, Low Mass, Solemn High Mass, Requiem Mass, Votive Mass.

massacre, n. butchering, killing, slaughter; see **murder**.

massacre, v. exterminate, mass murder, annihilate; see **kill 1**.

massage, v. stimulate, caress, press; see **rub 1**.

masses, n. proletariat, the rank and file, multitude; see **people 3**.

massive, a. huge, heavy, cumbersome; see **large 1**.

mass production, n. mass producing, assemblyline methods, automation; see **manufacturing, production 1**.

mast, n. spar, pole, post, timber, trunk, Maypole; see also **post 1**.

master, a. leading, supreme, main; see **excellent, major 1, principal**.

master, n. 1. [One who directs others] chief, director, boss; see **executive, leader 2**. 2. [A teacher] instructor, preceptor, mentor; see **teacher**. 3. [One who possesses great skill] genius, maestro, sage, scientist, past master, champion, prima donna, connoisseur, fellow, doctor; see also **artist**.—Ant. **disciple**, beginner, undergraduate.

master, v. 1. [To conquer] subdue, rule, humble; see **succeed 1**. 2. [To become proficient in] gain mastery in, understand, comprehend; see **learn, study**.

masterful, a. commanding, expert, skillful; see **excellent**.

masterpiece, n. perfection, model, standard, cream of the crop, masterwork, *magnum opus* (Latin).

mastery, n. 1. [Control] dominance, sovereignty, government; see **command, power 2**. 2. [Ability to use to the full] skill, capacity, proficiency; see **ability, education 1**.

masturbation, n. sexual self-gratification, onanism, self-love; see **sex 1, 4**.

mat, n. covering, floor covering, doormat, place mat, network, table mat, place setting, web, mesh, cloth, straw mat; see also **cover 1, rug**.

mat, v. braid, tangle, snarl; see **twist, weave 1**.

match, n. 1. [An instrument to produce fire] safety match, sulphur match, matchstick, fuse; see also **light 3**. 2. [An article that is like another] peer, equivalent, mate, analogue, counterpart, approximation; see also **equal 3**. 3. [A formal contest] race, event, rivalry; see **competition, sport 3**.

match, v. 1. [To find or make equals] equalize, liken, equate, make equal, pair, coordinate, level, even, match up, balance, mate, marry, unite; see also **equal 2**. 2. [To be alike] harmonize, suit, be twins, be counterparts, be doubles, match *or* check with, go together, go with, rhyme with, take after; see also **agree, resemble**.—Ant. **differ**, be unlike, bear no resemblance. 3. [To meet

in contest] equal, meet, compete with; see **compete**.

matched, a. doubled, similar, equated, evened, coordinated, harmonized, paired, mated; see also **alike, balanced 1**.—Ant. **unlike**, unequal, different.

matching, a. comparable, analogous, parallel; see **equal**.

mate, n. 1. [One of a pair] complement, analog, counterpart; see **match 2**. 2. [A companion] playmate, classmate, buddy; see **friend**. 3. [A marriage partner] spouse, bride, groom, bedmate, *(the) old man, *(the) old lady; see also **husband, wife**.

material, a. palpable, sensible, corporeal; see **physical 1, real 2, tangible**.

material, n. 1. [Matter] body, corporeality, substance; see **element 2, matter 1**. 2. [Unfinished matter; *often plural*] raw material, stuff, stock, staple, ore, stockpile, crop, supply, accumulation; see also **alloy, element 2, goods, metal, mineral, plastic, rock 1, wool**.

materialistic, a. possessive, acquisitive, opportunistic; see also **greedy, worldly**.

materialize, v. 1. [To become matter] be realized, take (on) form, become real, actualize, become concrete, metamorphose, reintegrate; see also **become**.—Ant. **dissolve**, disintegrate, disperse.

maternal, a. parental, sympathetic, protective; see **motherly**.

maternity, n. parenthood, mothership, motherliness; see **parent**.

mathematical, a. arithmetical, numerical, computative; see **numerical**.

mathematics, n. science of (real) (positive) numbers, language of numbers, computation, reckoning, calculation, new math, math. Types of mathematics include the following—arithmetic, algebra, plane *and* spherical geometry, trigonometry *or* *trig, analytic(al) geometry, differential *and* intregral calculus, programming, applied mathematics, probability, statistics, topology, transforms, logarithms.

matriarch, n. female ruler, dowager, matron; see **queen**.

matrimony, n. conjugality, wedlock, union; see **marriage**.

matron, n. lady, wife, mother; see **woman 1**.

matronly, a. middle-aged, grave, sedate; see **mature, motherly**.

matted, a. snarled, rumpled, disordered; see **tangled, twisted 1**.

matter, n. 1. [Substance] body, material, substantiality, corporeality, constituents, stuff, object, thing, physical world; see also **element 2**.—Ant. **nothing**, nihility, immateriality. 2. [Subject] interest, focus, resolution; see **subject, theme 1**. 3. [An affair] undertaking, circumstance, concern; see **affair 1.** —**as a matter of fact**, in fact, in actuality, truly; see **really 1.** —**for that matter**, in regard to that, as far as that is concerned, concerning that; see **and.** —**no matter**, it doesn't matter, it is of no concern, regardless of; see **regardless 2.**

matter, v. value, carry weight, weigh, signify, be substantive or important, have influence, imply, express, be of consequence, involve, be worthy of notice, *cut ice; see also **mean 1.**

matter of course, n. expected or anticipated result, routine event or happening, the usual thing; see **event, result.**

matter-of-fact, a. objective, prosaic, feasible; see **practical.**

matter of life or death, n. significance, seriousness, concern; see **importance.**

mattress, n. innerspring, springs, box spring, bedding, cushion, crib mattress; see also **bed.**

mature, a. full-grown, middle-aged, grown, grown-up, of age, in full bloom, womanly, manly, matronly, developed, prepared, settled, cultivated, cultured, sophisticated; see also **experienced.**—Ant. adolescent, **young**, immature.

mature, v. grow up, become a man or woman, come of age, become experienced, settle down, ripen (into), reach perfection, attain majority, culminate, become wise, become perfected, grow skilled, fill out; see also **age, develop 1.**

matured, a. grown, full-grown, aged; see **finished.**

maturity, n. 1. [Mental competence] development, sophistication, cultivation, culture, civilization, advancement, mental power, capability. 2. [Physical development] prime of life, postpubescence, adulthood; see **majority 2.** 3. [Ripeness] readiness, mellowness, sweetness; see **development.**

maul, v. pound, whip, trample; see **beat 1, hit 1.**

maxim, n. aphorism, adage, epithet; see **proverb, saying.**

maximum, a. supreme, highest, greatest; see **best.**

maximum, n. supremacy, height, pinnacle, pre-eminence, culmination, matchlessness, preponderance, apex, peak, greatest number, highest degree, summit; see also **climax.**—Ant. minimum, foot, bottom.

May, n. spring month, baseball season, fifth month; see **month, spring 2.**

may, v. 1. [Grant permission] be permitted, be allowed, can, be privileged to, be authorized, be at liberty to. 2. [Concede possibility] will, shall, be going to, should, be conceivable, be possible, be

practicable, be within reach, be obtainable; see also **will 3.**

maybe, a. perhaps, possibly, can be, might be, could be, maybe so, as it may be, conceivable, weather permitting, God willing. —Ant. **hardly**, scarcely, probably not.

mayor, n. magistrate, Lord Mayor, burgomaster, chairman or president of a city council, civil administrator, civil judge, Burgermeister (German), city father; see also **executive.**

maze, n. tangle, entanglement, twist, winding, convolution, intricacy, confusion, meandering, puzzle.—Ant. order, disentanglement, simplicity.

meadow, n. grass, pasture, mountain meadow, upland pasture, alp, meadow land, bottom land, bottoms, pasturage; hay meadow, clover meadow, bluegrass meadow, etc.; salt marsh, steppe, heath, pampa, savanna; see also **field 1.**

meager, a. lank, lanky, gaunt, starved, emaciated, lean, bony, slender, slim, spare, little, bare, scant, stinted, lacking, wanting, scrawny, withered, lithe, narrow, tenuous, slightly-made, skinny; see also **thin 2.**—Ant. fat, plump, stout.

meal, n. 1. [Ground feed] bran, farina, grits, fodder, provender, forage; see also **feed, flour, grain 1.** Types of meal include the following—corn meal, corn grits, hominy (grits), corn starch, barley meal, oatmeal, soybean meal, soybean flour. 2. [The quantity of food taken at one time] repast, feast, refreshment, mess, *feed (bag), *eats, *grub, *chow, *spread, *square meal, snack. Meals include the following—breakfast, dinner, lunch, banquet, brunch, snack, tea, picnic, luncheon, dessert, midnight supper; see also **breakfast, dinner, lunch.**

mean, a. 1. [Small-minded] base, low, debased; see **vulgar 2.** [Of low estate] servile, pitiful, shabby; see **humble 2.** 3. [Vicious] shameless, dishonorable, degraded, contemptible, evil, infamous, treacherous, crooked, fraudulent, faithless, unfaithful, ill-tempered, dangerous, despicable, degenerate, knavish, unscrupulous, hard as nails. 4. [Average] mediocre, middling, halfway; see **common 1.**

mean, n. middle, median, midpoint; see **average, center 1.**

mean, v. 1. [To have as meaning] indicate, spell, denote, signify, add up, determine, symbolize, imply, involve, speak of, touch on, stand for, drive at, point to, connote, suggest, express, designate, intimate, tell the meaning of, purport 2. [To have in mind] anticipate, propose, expect; see **intend 1.** 3. [To design for] destine for, aim at, set apart; see **intend 2.**

meander, v. twist and turn, roam, flow; see **ramble 2, run 1, walk 1.**

meaning, n. sense, import, purport, purpose, definition, object, implication, application, intent, suggestion, connotation, aim, drift, context, significance, essence, worth, intrinsic value, interest.— Ant. **nonsense,** aimlessness, absurdity.

meaningful, a. significant, exact, essential; see **important 1.**

meaningless, a. vague, absurd, insignificant; see **trivial, unimportant.**

meanness, n. 1. [The quality of being mean] small-mindedness, debasement, degradation, degeneracy, unscrupulousness, stinginess, disrepute, malice, unworthiness, ill-temper, unkindness, covetousness, avarice, miserliness; see also **greed.**—Ant. **generosity,** nobility, worthiness. 2. [A mean action] belittling, defaming, groveling, cheating, sneaking, quarreling, scolding, taking advantage of, deceiving, coveting, grudging, dishonoring, defrauding, shaming, degrading, stealing.

means, n. 1. [An instrumentality or instrumentalities] machinery, mechanism, agency, organ, channel, medium, factor, agent, power, organization; see also **method, system 2.** 2. [Wealth] resources, substance, property; see **wealth.** —**by all means,** of course, certainly, yes indeed; see **surely, yes.** —**by any means,** in any way, at all, somehow; see **anyhow.** —**by means of,** with the aid of, somehow, through; see **by 2.** —**by no (manner of) means,** in no way, not possible, (definitely) not; see **never, no.**

meanwhile, a. meantime, during the interval, in the interim, at interim, for the time being, until, till, up to, in the meantime, when; see also **during, while 1.**

measurable, a. weighable, definite, limited, determinable, knowable, recognizable, detectable, calculable, real, present, fathomable, assessible.

measure, n. 1. [A unit of measurement] dimension, capacity, weight, volume, distance, degree, quantity, area, mass, frequency, density, intensity, rapidity, speed, caliber, bulk, sum, duration, magnitude, amplitude, size, pitch, ratio, depth, scope, height, strength, breadth, amplification. Common units of measure include the following—*linear:* inch, foot, yard, rod, mile, millimeter, centimeter, decimeter, meter, kilometer; *surface:* square inch, square foot, square yard, acre, square rod, square mile; *volume:* dram, pint, quart, gallon, centiliter, liter; *weight:* gram, ounce, pound; milligram, gram, kilogram; *relationship:* revolutions per minute (r.p.m.), miles

per hour (m.p.h.), feet per second (f.p.s.), per second per second, erg, footpound, kilowatt-hour, acre-foot, decibel, man-hour, frequency modulation (FM), ohm, watt, volt, octane number *or* rating, percentage. 2. [Anything used as a standard] rule, test, trial, example, standard, yardstick, norm, pattern, type, model; see also **criterion.** 3. [A beat] rhythm, tempo, time, step, throb, stroke, accent, meter, cadence, tune, melody, stress, vibration, division; see also **beat 2.** —**for good measure,** added, as a bonus, additionally; see **extra.** —**take measures,** take action, do things to accomplish a purpose, employ; see **act 1.**

measure, v. 1. [To apply a standard of measurement] rule, weigh, mark, lay off *or* out, grade, graduate, gauge, sound, pitch, beat, stroke, time, mark off, scale, rank, even, level, gradate, line, align, line out, regulate, portion, set a criterion *or* standard, average, equate, square, calibrate, block in, survey, map. 2. [To contain by measurement] hold, cover, contain; see **include 1.**

measured, a. 1. [Steady] steady, systematic, deliberate; see **regular 3.** 2. [Determined] checked, evaluated, calculated; see **determined 1.**

measurement, n. 1. [The act of measuring] estimation, analysis, computation; see also **judgment 2.** 2. [The result of measuring] distance, dimension, weight, degree, pitch, time, height, depth, density, volume, area, length, measure, thickness, quantity, magnitude, extent, range, scope, reach, amount, capacity, frequency, intensity, pressure, speed, caliber, grade, span, step, strength, mass. 3. [A set of measures] inch, foot, yard; see **measure 1.**

measuring, n. weighing, grading, gauging; see **judgment 1.**

meat, n. veal, mutton, lamb, chicken, turkey, goose, duck, rabbit, venison, horsemeat; see also **food.** Cuts and forms of meat include the following— roast, cutlet, steak, filet, leg, shoulder, loin, tenderloin, rib, round, rump, flank, chop, liver, brains, kidneys, heart, bacon, tripe, shank, sausage, frankfurter, ground meat, chipped meat, dried meat, salt *or* pickled meat.

mechanic, n. machinist, repair man, skilled workman; see **workman.**

mechanical, a. 1. [Concerning machinery] engineering, production, manufacturing, tooling, tuning, implementing, fabricating, forging, machining, building, construction, constructing. 2. [Like a machine] made to a pattern, machinelike, stereotyped, standardized, without variation, unchanging, monotonous.—

Ant. **original,** varied, changing. **3.** [Operated by the use of machinery] power-driven, involuntary, programmed; see **automated, automatic.**

mechanically, *a.* automatically, unreasoningly, unchangeably; see **regularly.**

mechanism, *n.* working parts, mechanical action, system of parts; see **device 1, tool 1.**

mechanize, *v.* equip, computerize, industrialize, motorize, automate, put on the assembly line, make mechanical, introduce machinery into.

medal, *n.* reward, commemoration, badge; see **decoration 2.**

medallion, *n.* ornament, emblem, necklace; see **jewelry.**

meddle, *n.* **1.** [To interfere in others' affairs] interfere, obtrude, interlope, intervene, pry, snoop, impose oneself, infringe, break in upon, make it one's business, abuse one's rights, push in, chime in, force an entrance, encroach, intrude, be officious, obstruct, impede, hinder, encumber, busy oneself with, come uninvited, tamper with, inquire, be curious, *stick one's nose in, *monkey with, *bust in, *muscle in, barge in, *have a finger in, *butt in, *horn in; see also **interrupt.**—*Ant.* **neglect,** ignore, let alone. **2.** [To handle others' things] tamper, molest, pry, fool with, trespass, snoop, nose, use improperly.

meddlesome, *a.* obtrusive, interfering, officious, meddling, intrusive, impertinent, interposing, interrupting, obstructive, impeding, hindering, encumbering, curious, tampering, prying, snooping, troublesome, *snoopy, *nosy, *kibitzing, *chiseling.

meddling, *n.* interfering, interrupting, snooping; see **interference 1, rudeness.**

media, *n. pl.* radio, television, newspaper, journalism, news, reporters, reportage, programming, audiovisual devices.

*medic,** *n.* physician, practitioner, surgeon; see **doctor.**

medical, *a.* healing, medicinal, curative, therapeutic, restorative, prophylactic, preventive, alleviating, medicating, pharmaceutical, sedative, narcotic, tonic, disinfectant, corrective, pathological, cathartic, health-bringing, demulcent, balsamic, emollient.—*Ant.* destructive, disease-giving, harmful.

medication, *n.* remedy, pill, vaccination; see **medicine 2.**

medicinal, *a.* curative, healing, therapeutic; see **healthful.**

medicine, *n.* **1.** [The healing profession] medical men, healers, practitioners, doctors, physicians, surgeons, osteopaths, chiropractors, the profession, American Medical Association (A.M.A.). **2.** [A medical preparation] drug, dose, potion,

prescription, pill(s), tablet, capsule, draft, patent medicine, remedy, cure, antipoison, antibiotic, medication, vaccination, inoculation, injection, draught, herb, specific, nostrum, elixir, tonic, balm, salve, lotion, ointment, emetic, shot. **3.** [The study and practice of medicine] medical science, physic, healing art, medical profession. Branches of medicine include the following—surgery, therapy, therapeutics, anesthesiology, internal medicine, general practice, psychiatry, psychotherapy, psychoanalysis, ophthalmology, obstetrics, gynecology, pediatrics, orthopedics, neurology, cardiology, dermatology, pathology, endocrinology, immunology, urology, hematology, inhalation therapy, diagnostics, radiotherapy, geriatrics, veterinary medicine.

medieval, *a.* pertaining to the Middle Ages, feudal, antiquated; see **old 3.**

mediocre, *a.* average, ordinary, standard; see **common 1, dull 4.**

mediocrity, *n.* commonplaceness, commonness, normality; see **regularity.**

meditate, *v.* **1.** [To muse] ponder, study, contemplate, muse (on *or* over *or* upon), revolve, say to oneself, reflect, view, brood over, dream; see also **think 1. 2.** [To think over] weigh, consider, speculate; see **think 1.**

meditation, *n.* examination, contemplation, speculation; see **reflection 1, thought 1.**

medium, *a.* commonplace, mediocre, ordinary; see **common 1.**

medium, *n.* **1.** [A means] mechanism, tool, factor; see **means 1, part 3. 2.** [A means of expression] symbol, sign, token, interpretation, manifestation, revelation, evidence, mark, statement; see also **communication, speech 2. 3.** [A supposed channel of supernatural knowledge] oracle, seer, spiritualist; see **prophet.**

medley, *n.* mingling, melee, conglomeration; see **mixture 1, variety 1.**

meek, *a.* **1.** [Humble] unassuming, plain, mild; see **humble 1, modest 2. 2.** [Long-suffering] passive, resigned, serene; see **patient 1. 3.** [Lacking spirit] submissive, compliant, subdued; see **docile, resigned.**

meekness, *n.* submission, mildness, timidity; see **humility.**

meet, *n.* match, athletic event, tournament; see **competition, event.**

meet, *v.* **1.** [To come together] converge, assemble, crowd, rally, convene, collect, associate, unite, swarm, get together, enter in; see **gather 1. 2.** [To go to a place of meeting] resort, be present at, gather together, convene, congregate, muster, appear, go to the meeting; see also **assemble 2, attend.**—*Ant.* leave, disperse, scatter. **3.** [To touch] reach, coincide, adhere; see **join 1. 4.** [To become acquainted] make the acquaintance of, be presented to, be introduced, present oneself, make oneself known, *get next to, *get to know; see also **familiarize (oneself with). 5.** [To fulfill] answer, fit, suffice; see **satisfy 3. 6.** [To encounter] fall in with, come on or upon, meet by accident, come across, meet face to face, face up to, bump into, touch shoulders with, meet at every turn, engage, join issue with, battle, match, push, brush against, shove; see also **face 1, fight.**—*Ant.* abandon, turn one's back on, leave.

meeting, *n.* **1.** [The act of coming together] encounter, juxtaposition, joining, juncture, unifying, unification, adherence, convergence, confrontation, contacting, connection, conflict, contention, accord, agreement, compromising.—*Ant.* departure, **separation,** dispersal. **2.** [A gathering, usually of people] conference, assemblage, rally; see **gathering.**

meet (up) with, *v.* encounter, become acquainted (with), be introduced; see **meet 4.**

meet with, *v.* observe, experience, suffer; see **find.**

melancholy, *a.* depressed, unhappy, dispirited; see **sad 1.**

melancholy, *n.* wistfulness, despair, unhappiness; see **depression 2, grief, sadness.**

mellow, *a.* **1.** [Ripe] sweet, soft, perfected; see **ripe 1. 2.** [Culturally mature] cultured, fully developed, broadminded; see **mature.**

mellowed, *a.* mature, ripened, softened; see **ripe 1, soft 2, 3.**

melodious, *a.* agreeable, pleasing, resonant; see **harmonious 1, musical 1.**

melodrama, *n.* play, opera, theater; see **drama.**

melodramatic, *a.* artificial, spectacular, sensational; see **exaggerated.**

melody, *n.* **1.** [The quality of being melodious] concord, unison, chime; see **harmony 1. 2.** [A melodious arrangement] air, lyric, strain; see **song.**

melon, *n.* watermelon, cantaloupe, muskmelon; see also **food, fruit.**

melt, *v.* **1.** [To liquefy] thaw, fuse, blend, merge, soften, flow, run, disintegrate, waste away; see also **dissolve.**—*Ant.* freeze, harden, coagulate. **2.** [To relent] forgive, show mercy, become lenient; see **yield 1. 3.** [To decrease] vanish, pass away, go; see **decrease 1.**

melted, *a.* softened, thawed, liquefied, dwindled, blended, merged, wasted

away, disintegrated, vanished, decreased, diminished, tempered, relaxed.

melting, *a.* softening, liquefying, reducing; see **soft 2.**

member, *n.* **1.** [A person or group] constituent, charter member, active member, member in good standing, honorary member, affiliate, brother, sister, comrade, chapter, post, branch, lodge, district, county, town, township, state, country, countries, company, battalion, regiment, division. **2.** [A part] portion, segment, fragment; see **division 2, part 1. 3.** [A part of the body] organ, arm, leg; see also **limb 2.**

membership, *n.* club, society, association; see **member 1.**

memorable, *a.* **1.** [Historic] momentous, critical, unforgettable, crucial, famous, illustrious, distinguished, great, notable, significant, decisive, enduring, lasting, monumental, eventful, interesting; see **famous. 2.** [Unusual] remarkable, exceptional, singular; see sense 1, **unusual 1.**

memorandum, *n.* notice, record, jotting; see **note 2, reminder.**

memorial, *a.* dedicatory, commemorative, remembering; see **remembered.**

memorial, *n.* remembrance, testimonial, tablet, slab, pillar, tombstone, headstone, column, monolith, mausoleum, record, inscription, memento, statue; see also **celebration, ceremony 2, monument.**

memorize, *v.* fix in the memory, make memorable, record, commemorate, memorialize, retain, commit to memory, imprint in one's mind, bear in mind, give word for word, *get down pat, *have in one's head, *have at one's fingertips, learn by heart; see also **learn, remember 2.**—*Ant.* neglect, forget, fail to remember.

memory, *n.* **1.** [The power to call up the past] recollection, retrospection, reminiscence, thought, consciousness, subconsciousness, unconscious memory, retentive memory, exact *or* photographic memory, visual memory, auditory memory; see also **mind 1. 2.** [That which can be recalled] (mental) image, picture, vision; see **thought 2.**

menace, *n.* **1.** [A threat] caution, intimidation, foretelling; see **warning. 2.** [An imminent danger] hazard, peril, threat; see **danger.**

menace, *v.* intimidate, portend, loom; see **threaten.**

menacing, *a.* imminent, impending, threatening; see **dangerous, ominous.**

mend, *v.* **1.** [To repair] heal, patch, fix; see **repair. 2.** [To improve] aid, remedy, cure; see **correct.**

mended, *a.* restored, put in shape,

patched up, renovated, refreshed, renewed, corrected, helped, bettered, lessened, remedied, cured, relieved, rectified, rejuvenated, remodeled, altered, changed, fixed, regulated, rebuilt, regenerated, reorganized, revived, touched up, *gone over, *doctored; see also **repaired.**

menial, n. domestic, maid, lackey; see **servant.**

menstruation, n. menses, lady's time, time of the month, *monthlies, *the curse; see also **flow.**

mental, a. 1. [Concerning the mind] reasoning, cerebral, thinking; see **rational 1, thoughtful 1.** 2. [Existing only in the mind] subjective, subliminal, subconscious, telepathic, psychic, clairvoyant, imaginative; see also **imaginary.** —*Ant.* objective, bodily, sensual.

mentality, n. intellect, comprehension, reasoning; see **mind 1.**

mentally, a. rationally, psychically, intellectually; see **reasonably 1.**

mention, n. notice, naming, specifying; see **remark.** —**not to mention,** in addition, too, without even mentioning; see **also.**

mention, v. notice, specify, cite, introduce, state, declare, quote, refer to, discuss, touch on, instance, infer, intimate, notify, communicate, suggest, make known, point out, speak of, *throw out; see also **tell 1.**—*Ant.* overlook, take no notice of, disregard.

mentioned, a. noticed, cited, specified, named, quoted, introduced, referred to, discussed, declared, revealed, brought up, considered, communicated, made known, spoken of; see also **told.**

menu, n. bill of fare, cuisine, table; see **list.**

merchandise, n. wares, commodities, stock; see **goods 1.**

merchant, n. trader, storekeeper, retailer, shopkeeper, wholesaler, exporter, shipper, dealer, jobber, tradesman; see also **businessman.**

merciful, a. lenient, feeling, compassionate, pitiful, softhearted, mild, tolerant, kindly, indulgent; see also **kind.**—*Ant.* cruel, pitiless, unsparing.

merciless, a. pitiless, unsparing, relentless; see **cruel, fierce, ruthless.**

mercy, n. leniency, soft-heartedness, mildness, clemency, tenderness, gentleness, compassion; see also **generosity, tolerance 1.**—*Ant.* intolerance, indifference, selfishness. —**at the mercy of,** in the power of, vulnerable to, controlled by; see **subject.**

mere, a. small, minor, insignificant; see **little 1, poor 2.**

merely, a. slightly, solely, simply; see **hardly, only 3.**

merge, v. fuse, join, blend; see **mix 1, unite.**

merger, n. pool, consolidation, alliance; see **organization 1.**

merit, n. 1. [Worth] credit, benefit, advantage; see **quality 3, value 3.** 2. [A creditable quality] worthiness, excellence, honor; see **character 2, virtue 1.**

merit, v. be worth, warrant, justify; see **deserve.**

merited, a. earned, proper, fitting; see **deserved, fit.**

merrily, a. joyfully, gleefully, genially; see **cheerfully, happily.**

merriment, n. joy, cheerfulness, gaiety; see **happiness, humor 3.**

merry, a. gay, joyous, mirthful; see **happy.**

mesa, n. plateau, table, tableland, butte, table mountain; see also **hill, mountain 1.**

mesh, v. coincide, suit, be in gear; see **agree, fit 1.**

mess, n. 1. [A mixture] combination, compound, blend; see **mixture 1.** 2. [A confusion] jumble, muss, chaos, clutter, clog, congestion, snag, scramble, complexity, mayhem, hodgepodge; see also **confusion, disorder 2.**

message, n. tidings, information, intelligence; see **advice, broadcast, communication, directions.** —*get the message,** get the hint, comprehend, perceive; see **understand 1.**

mess around or **about (with),** v. dawdle, fool around, play the fool (with); see **loiter, play 1, 2.**

messenger, n. bearer, minister, dispatcher, herald, carrier, courier, runner, crier, errand boy, intermediary, envoy, emissary, agent, prophet, go-between; see also **agent.**

Messiah, n. Saviour, Redeemer, Jesus Christ; see **Christ, god.**

mess up, v. spoil, ruin, foul up, damage; see **botch, destroy.**

messy, a. rumpled, untidy, slovenly; see **dirty, disordered.**

metal, n. element, native rock, ore deposit, free metal, refined ore, smelted ore. Types of metal include the following—gold, silver, copper, iron, steel, aluminum, manganese, nickel, lead, cobalt, platinum, zinc, tin, barium, cadmium, chromium, tungsten, mercury, molybdenum, sodium, potassium, radium, magnesium, calcium, titanium, arsenic, uranium.

metallic, a. 1. [Made of metal] hard, rocklike, iron, leaden, silvery, golden, metallurgic, mineral, geologic. 2. [Suggestive of metal; *said especially of* _sound_] ringing, resounding, resonant, bell-like, clanging.

metaphor, _n._ trope, simile, implied comparison; see **comparison.** —**mix metaphors,** be inconsistent, garble, talk illogically; see **confuse.**

metaphorical, _a._ symbolical, allegorical, figurative; see **descriptive, graphic 1, 2.**

metaphysical, _a._ mystical, abstract, spiritual; see **difficult 2.**

meteor, _n._ falling star, shooting star, meteorite, fireball, meteroid.

meteorology, _n._ climate science, climatology, aerology; see **science 1, weather.**

meter, _n._ measure, rhythm, metrical feet, common meter, long meter, ballad meter, tetrameter, pentameter, sprung rhythm, dipodic rhythm.

method, _n._ mode, style, standard procedure, fashion, way, means, process, proceeding, adjustment, disposition, practice, routine, technic _or_ technique, attack, mode of operation, manner of working, ways and means, habit, custom, manner, formula, process, course, rule; see also **system 2.**

methodical, _a._ well-regulated, systematic, exact; see **orderly 2, regular 3.**

metropolis, _n._ capital, megalopolis, municipality; see **center 2, city.**

metropolitan, _a._ city, municipal, cosmopolitan; see **modern 2, urban.**

Mexican, _a._ Latin American, (from) south of the border, Hispanic; see **American 1.**

Mexico, _n._ the other side of the Rio Grande, land south of the border, the republic to the south; see **America 1.**

*__mickey mouse,__ _a._ trite, platitudinous, simplistic; see **dull 4, easy 2,** naïve.

microbe, _n._ microorganism, bacterium, bacillus; see **germ.**

microphone, _n._ sound transmitter, receiver, pickup instrument, *__mike,__ *__bug,__ walkie-talkie.

microscope, _n._ lens, magnifying glass, optical instrument, scope. Microscopes include the following—high-powered, compound, photographic, electron, electronic.

microscopic, _a._ diminutive, tiny, infinitesimal; see **little 1, minute 1.**

middle, _a._ between, mean, midway, medial, average, equidistant; see also **central, halfway, intermediate.**

middle, _n._ mean, focus, core, nucleus, heart, navel, midst, marrow, pivot, axis, media, midpoint; see also **center 1.**

middle age, _n._ adulthood, prime, maturity; see **majority 2.**

middle-aged, _a._ adult, in one's prime, matronly; see **mature.**

middle-class, _a._ white-collar, bourgeois, substantial; see **common 1, popular 1, 3.**

midget, _n._ pygmy, dwarf, mannikin; see **person.**

midnight, _n._ dead of night, stroke of midnight, 12:00 P.M., noon of night, witching hour; see also **night 1.** —**burn the midnight oil,** stay up late, work _or_ study (late), keep late hours; see **study, work 1.**

midst, _n._ midpoint, nucleus, middle; see **center 1.** —**in our** (_or your or their_) **midst,** between us, with, accompanying; see **among.** —**in the midst of,** in the course of, engaged in, in the middle of; see **central.**

midway, _a._ in the thick of, between, in the middle; see **central, halfway, intermediate, middle.**

might, _n._ strength, force, sway; see **strength 1.**

mightily, _a._ energetically, strongly, forcibly; see **powerfully, vigorously.**

mighty, _a._ 1. [Strong] powerful, stalwart, muscular; see **strong 1.** 2. [Powerful through influence] great, all-powerful, omnipotent; see **powerful 1.** 3. [Imposing] great, extensive, impressive, gigantic, magnificent, towering, dynamic, notable, extraordinary, grand, considerable, monumental, tremendous; see also **large 1.**—_Ant._ plain, unimpressive, ordinary.

*__mighty,__ _a._ great, exceedingly, extremely; see **very.**

migrate, _v._ move, emigrate, immigrate; see **leave 1.**

migration, _n._ emigration, immigration, voyage; see **departure, journey, movement 2.**

migratory, _a._ wandering, migrant, vagrant; see **temporary.**

mild, _a._ 1. [Gentle; _said especially of persons_] meek, easy going, patient; see **kind.** 2. [Temperate; _said especially of weather_] bland, untroubled, tropical, peaceful, summery, tepid, cool, balmy, breezy, gentle, soft, lukewarm, clear, moderate, mellow, fine, uncloudy, sunny, warm.—_Ant._ **rough, cold, stormy.** 3. [Easy; _said especially of burdens or punishment_] soft, light, tempered; see **moderate 4.** 4. [Not irritating] bland, soothing, soft, smooth, gentle, moderate, easy, mellow, delicate, temperate.

mildly, _a._ gently, meekly, calmly, genially, tranquilly, softly, lightly, moderately, tenderly, compassionately, tolerantly, patiently, temperately, indifferently, quietly.—_Ant._ **violently,** harshly, roughly.

mildness, *n.* tolerance, tenderness, gentleness; see **kindness 1.**

mile, *n.* 5,280 feet, statute mile, geographical mile, nautical mile, Admiralty mile; see also **distance 3, measure 1.**

mileage, *n.* rate, space, measure; see **distance 3, length 1.**

militant, *a.* combative, belligerent, offensive; see **aggressive.**

militant, *n.* rioter, violent objector, demonstrator; see **radical.**

military, *a.* armed, militant, combative; see **aggressive.**

militia, *n.* military force, civilian army, National Guard; see **army 1.**

milk, *n.* fluid, juice, sap; see also **liquid.** Types of milk include the following—whole, skim, raw, pasteurized, homogenized, certified; grade-A, grade-B, etc.; loose, condensed, dried, evaporated, powdered, two-percent, four-percent, etc.; goat's, mare's, mother's; cream, half-and-half, buttermilk, kefir. —**cry over spilt milk,** mourn, lament, sulk; see **regret.**

milky, *a.* opaque, pearly, cloudy; see **white 1.**

mill, *n.* **1.** [A factory] manufactory, plant, millhouse; see **factory. 2.** [A machine for grinding, crushing, pressing, etc.] Types of mills include the following—flour, coffee, cotton, weaving, spinning, powder, rolling, cider, cane, lapidary; sawmill, coin press.

millionaire, *n.* man of wealth *or* means, capitalist, tycoon, rich man, moneyed man, man of substance, Midas, *big-money man, robber baron, *bankroll.—*Ant.* beggar, poor man, pauper.

mimic, *n.* mime, impersonator, comedian; see **actor, imitator.**

mimic, *v.* **1.** [To imitate] copy, simulate, impersonate; see **imitate. 2.** [To mock] make fun of, burlesque, caricature; see **ridicule.**

mimicry, *n.* mime, pretense, mockery; see **imitation 2.**

mind, *n.* **1.** [Intellectual potentiality] soul, spirit, intellect, brain, consciousness, thought, mentality, intuition, perception, conception, intelligence, intellectuality, capacity, judgment, understanding, wisdom, genius, talent, reasoning, instinct, wit, mental *or* intellectual faculties, creativity, ingenuity, intellectual powers *or* processes, *gray matter, *brainpower. **2.** [Purpose] intention, inclination, determination; see **purpose 1.** —**bear** (*or* **keep**) **in mind,** heed, recollect, recall; see **remember 1.** —**be in one's right mind,** be mentally well, be rational, be sane; see **reason 2.** —**be of one mind,** have the same opinion *or* desire, concur, be in accord; see **agree.** —**call to mind,** recall, recollect, bring to

mind; see **remember 1.** —**change one's mind,** alter one's opinion, change one's views, disagree with oneself; see **change one's mind.** —**give someone a piece of one's mind,** rebuke, confute, criticize; see **scold.** —**have a good mind to,** be inclined to, propose, tend to; see **intend 1.** —**have half a mind to,** be inclined to, propose, tend to; see **intend 1.** —**have in mind, 1.** recall, recollect, think of; see **remember 1. 2.** purpose, propose, be inclined to; see **intend 1.** —**know one's own mind,** know oneself, be deliberate, have a plan; see **know 1.** —**make up one's mind,** form a definite opinion, choose, finalize; see **decide.** —**meeting of the minds,** concurrence, unity, harmony; see **agreement 1.** —**never mind,** don't be concerned, it doesn't matter, it is of no importance; see **never mind.** —**on one's mind,** occupying one's thoughts, causing concern, worrying one; see **important 1.** —**out of one's mind,** mentally ill, raving, mad; see **insane.** —**take one's mind off,** turn one's attention from, divert, change; see **distract.**

mind, *v.* **1.** [To obey] be under the authority of, heed, do as told; see **behave, obey. 2.** [To give one's attention] heed, regard, be attentive to; see **attend. 3.** [To be careful] tend, watch out for, take care, trouble, be wary, be concerned for, object, *mind one's *p*'s and *q*'s; see also **consider.**—*Ant.* neglect, ignore, be careless. **4.** [To remember] recollect, recall, bring to mind; see **remember 1. 5.** [To object to] complain, deplore, be opposed to; see **dislike.**

minded, *a.* disposed, inclined, turned *or* leaning toward; see also **willing.**

mindful, *a.* attentive, heedful, watchful; see **careful.**

mindless, *a.* **1.** [Careless] inattentive, oblivious, neglectful; see **careless, indifferent, rash. 2.** [Stupid] foolish, senseless, unintelligent; see **stupid 1.**

mine, *a.* my own, belonging to me, possessed by me, mine by right, owned by me, left to me, from me, by me; see also **our.**

mine, *n.* **1.** [A source of natural wealth] pit, well, shaft, diggings, excavation, workings, quarry, deposit, vein, lode, ore bed, placer (deposit), pay dirt, bonanza, strip mine, open-pit mine, surface mine, hard-rock mine. **2.** [An explosive charge] landmine, ambush, trap; see **bomb, explosive, weapon.**

mine, *v.* **1.** [To dig for minerals] excavate, work, quarry; see also **dig 1. 2.** [To lay mines] sow with mines, prepare mine fields, set booby traps; see **defend 1.**

miner, *n.* excavator, digger, driller, dredger, mine worker, prospector, mucker, driller, placer miner, hard-rock miner, mine superintendent, mining *or* geological engineer, *desert rat, *sourdough, *forty-niner; see also **laborer, workman**.

mineral, *a.* geologic, rock, metallurgic; see **metallic 1**.

mineral, *n.* earth's crust, geologic formation, geologic rock, rock deposit, ore deposit, igneous rock, metamorphic rock, magma, petroleums, crystal; see also **metal**.

mingle, *v.* combine, blend, admix; see **mix 1**.

miniature, *a.* diminutive, small, tiny; see **little 1, minute 1**.

minimize, *v.* lessen, depreciate, reduce; see **decrease 2**.

minimum, *a.* smallest, tiniest, merest; see **smallest**.

minimum, *n.* smallest, least, lowest, narrowest, atom, molecule, particle, dot, jot, iota, spark, shadow, gleam, grain, scruple.

mining, *n.* excavating, hollowing, opening, digging, boring, drilling, delving, burrowing, tunneling, honeycombing, placer mining, hard-rock mining, prospecting.

minister, *n.* 1. [One authorized to conduct Christian worship] pastor, parson, preacher, clergyman, rector, monk, abbot, prelate, curate, vicar, deacon, chaplain, servant of God, shepherd, churchman, cleric, padre, ecclesiastic, bishop, archbishop, confessor, reverend, diocesan, divine, missionary; see also **priest**. —*Ant.* **layman**, church member, parishioner. 2. [A high servant of the state] ambassador, consul, liaison officer; see **diplomat, representative 2, statesman**.

minister, *v.* administer to, tend, wait on; see **help**.

ministry, *n.* 1. [The functions of the clergy] preaching, prayer, spiritual leadership; see **religion 2**. 2. [The clergy] the cloth, clergymen, ecclesiastics, clerics, the clerical order, priesthood, clericals, prelacy, vicarage, clergy. 3. [A department of state] bureau, administrative agency, executive branch; see **department**.

minor, *a.* secondary, lesser, insignificant; see **trivial, unimportant**.

minor, *n.* person under eighteen *or* twenty-one, underage person, boy, girl, child, infant, little one, lad, schoolboy, schoolgirl; see also **youth 3**.

minority, *n.* 1. [An outnumbered group] opposition, less than half, the outvoted, the few, the outnumbered, the losing side, splinter group. 2. [The time before one is of legal age] childhood, immaturity, adolescence; see **youth 1**.

mint, *v.* strike, coin, issue; see **print 2**.

minus, *a.* diminished, short of, deficient; see **less**.

minute, *a.* 1. [Extremely small] microscopic, diminutive, wee, tiny, atomic, miniature, puny, microbic, molecular, exact, precise, fine, inconsiderable, *teeny, weeny, invisible; see also **little 1**. —*Ant.* **large**, huge, immense. 2. [Trivial] immaterial, nonessential, paltry; see **trivial, unimportant**. 3. [Exact] particular, circumstantial, specialized; see **detailed, elaborate 2**.

minute, *n.* 1. [The sixtieth part of an hour] sixty seconds, unit *or* measure of time, moment, space of time; see also **time 1**. 2. [A brief time] short time, second, flash, twinkling, breath, *jiffy, *bat of an eye.—*Ant.* **eternity**, long time, forever. —**up to the minute**, modern, contemporary, in the latest style; see **fashionable**.

(the) minute that, *conj.* as soon as, the second that, at the time that; see **when 1, 2, whenever**.

miracle, *n.* marvel, revelation, supernatural occurrence; see **wonder 2**.

miraculous, *a.* 1. [Caused by divine intervention] supernatural, marvelous, superhuman, beyond understanding, phenomenal, unimaginable, stupendous, awesome, monstrous; see also **mysterious 2**.—*Ant.* **natural**, familiar, imaginable. 2. [So unusual as to suggest a miracle] extraordinary, freakish, wondrous; see **unusual 1, 2**.

mirage, *n.* phantasm, delusion, hallucination; see **fantasy, illusion**.

mirror, *n.* looking glass, speculum, reflector, polished metal, hand glass, pier glass, mirroring surface, camera finder, hand mirror, full-length mirror; see also **glass**.

mirth, *n.* frolic, jollity, entertainment; see **fun**.

misbehave, *v.* do wrong *or* evil, sin, fail, trip, blunder, offend, trespass, behave badly, misdo, err, lapse, be delinquent, be at fault, be culpable *or* blameworthy *or* guilty *or* censurable, be bad, forget oneself, be immoral *or* dissolute *or* disreputable *or* indecorous, carry on, be naughty, go astray, *sow one's wild oats, *cut up.—*Ant.* **behave**, be good, do well.

misbehaved, *a.* uncivil, discorteous, ill-mannered; see **naughty, rude 2**.

miscalculate, *v.* blunder, miscount, err; see **mistake**.

miscarriage, *n.* 1. [Failure] malfunction, defeat, mistake; see **failure 1**. 2. [A too premature delivery] unnatural birth, untimely delivery, birth interruption; see **abortion**.

miscellaneous, *a*. 1. [Lacking unity] diverse, disparate, unmatched; see **unlike**. 2. [Lacking order] mixed, muddled, scattered; see **confused 2, disordered**.

mischief, *n*. troublesomeness, harmfulness, prankishness, playfulness, acting like a brat, impishness, misbehavior, misconduct, fault, transgression, wrongdoing, misdoing, naughtiness, mischiefmaking, friskiness.—*Ant*. **dignity**, demureness, sedateness.

mischievous, *a*. playful, roguish, prankish; see **naughty, rude 2**.

misconception, *n*. delusion, blunder, fault; see **error, mistake 2, misunderstanding 1**.

misconduct, *n*. misbehavior, offense, wrongdoing; see **evil 2, mischief**.

misdemeanor, *n*. misconduct, misbehavior, misdeed; see **crime**.

miser, *n*. extortioner, usurer, misanthropist, stingy *or* grasping person, *skinflint, *Scrooge, *money-grubber.—*Ant*. **beggar**, spendthrift, waster.

miserable, *a*. distressed, afflicted, sickly, ill, wretched, sick, ailing, unfortunate, uncomfortable, suffering, hurt, wounded, tormented, tortured, in pain, strained, injured, convulsed; see also **troubled**.—*Ant*. helped, aided, comfortable.

miserably, *a*. poorly, unsatisfactorily, imperfectly; see **badly 1, inadequately**.

miserly, *a*. covetous, parsimonious, close-fisted; see **stingy**.

misery, *n*. 1. [Pain] distress, suffering, agony; see **pain 2**. 2. [Dejection] worry, despair, desolation; see **depression 2, grief, sadness**. 3. [Trouble] grief, anxiety, problem; see **difficulty 2**.

misfit, *n*. paranoid, psychotic, maladjusted *or* disoriented person; see **pervert**.

misfortune, *n*. misadventure, ill luck, ill *or* bad *or* adverse chance *or* fortune, disadvantage, mischance, disappointment, adversity, discomfort, burden, annoyance, nuisance, unpleasantness, inconvenience, worry, anxiety; see **difficulty 1**.—*Ant*. **advantage**, good fortune, stroke of fortune.

misgiving, *n*. distrust, mistrust, unbelief; see **doubt, uncertainty 2**.

misguided, *a*. misled, deceived, confused; see **mistaken 1**.

mishap, *n*. accident, mischance, misadventure; see **catastrophe, disaster, misfortune**.

misinform, *v*. mislead, report inaccurately (to), misstate; see **deceive, lie**.

misinterpret, *v*. falsify, distort, miscalculate; see **mistake, misunderstand**.

misinterpretation, *n*. distortion, misreckoning, delusion; see **mistake 2, misunderstanding 1**.

misjudge, *v*. 1. [To make a wrong judgement, usually of a person] be overcritical, be unfair, come to a hasty conclusion; see **misunderstand**. 2. [To make an inaccurate estimate] miss, miscalculate, misconceive, misthink, misconstrue, overestimate, underestimate, bark up the wrong tree; see also **mistake**.—*Ant*. **estimate, understand**, calculate.

misjudgment, *n*. distortion, misinterpretation, misconception; see **mistake 2**.

mislead, *v*. delude, cheat, defraud, bilk, take in, outwit, trick, entangle, advise badly, victimize, lure, beguile, hoax, dupe, bait, misrepresent, bluff, *give a bum steer, *throw off the scent, *bamboozle, *hoodwink, *put (someone) on; see also **deceive**.

misled, *a*. misguided, deluded, wronged; see **deceived, mistaken 1**.

mismanage, *v*. bungle, blunder, *mess *or* foul up; see **fail 1**.

mismatched, *a*. incompatible, discordant, inconsistent; see **unfit**.

misplace, *v*. mislay, displace, shuffle, disarrange, remove, disturb, take out of its place, disorder, tumble, confuse, mix, scatter, unsettle, muss, disorganize; see also **lose 2**.—*Ant*. find, locate, place.

misplaced, *a*. displaced, mislaid, out of place; see **lost 1**.

mispronounce, *v*. falter, misspeak, mouth; see **hesitate, stammer**.

misrepresent, *v*. distort, falsify, understate; see **deceive, lie 1, mislead**.

misrepresentation, *n*. untruth, deceit, disguise; see **deception, lie**.

miss, *n*. 1. [A failure] slip, blunder, mishap; see **mistake 2**. 2. [A young woman] lass, maid, female; see **girl**.

miss, *v*. 1. [To feel a want] desire, crave, yearn; see **need, want 1**. 2. [To fail to catch] snatch at, drop, *fumble the ball, *blow, *have butterfingers, *muff, *boot.—*Ant*. catch, grab, hold. 3. [To fail to hit] miss one's aim, miss the mark, be wide of the mark, overshoot, undershoot, go above *or* below *or* to the side, *fan the air.—*Ant*. hit, shoot, get.

missed, *a*. 1. [Not found *or* noticed] gone, misplaced, mislaid, forgotten, unrecalled, unnoticed, not in sight, put away, in hiding, hidden, strayed, moved, removed, unseen; see also **lost 1**.—*Ant*. remembered, found, located. 2. [Longed for] needed, desired, wished for, pined for, wanted, yearned for, clung to, craved, hungered *or* thirsted for.—*Ant*. hated, disliked, unwanted.

missile, *n*. cartridge, projectile, ammunition; see **bullet, shot 1, weapon**. Terms for types of missiles include the following—Polaris, Poseidon, RPV *or* remotely piloted vehicle, Minuteman, ICBM *or* intercontinental ballistic missile, ABM *or* anti-ballistic missile, ASW *or* anti-submarine warfare, MERV *or* multiple independently targetable reentry vehicle.

missing, *a.* disappeared, lacking, removed; see **absent, lost 1.**

mission, *n.* charge, sortie, commission; see **purpose 1.**

missionary, *n.* apostle, evangelist, preacher; see **messenger, minister 1.**

mist, *n.* cloud, rain, haze; see **fog.**

mistake, *n.* 1. [A blunder] false step, blunder, slip, error, omission, failure, confusion, wrongdoing, sin, crime, *goof; see also **error.** 2. [A misunderstanding] misapprehension, confusion, misconception, delusion, illusion, overestimation, underestimation, impression, muddle, confounding, misinterpretation, perversion, perplexity, bewilderment, misjudgment; see also **exaggeration, misunderstanding 1.**—*Ant.* knowledge, certainty, interpretation.

mistake, *v.* err, blunder, slip, lapse, miss, overlook, omit, underestimate, overestimate, substitute, misjudge, misapprehend, misconceive, misunderstand, confound, misinterpret, confuse, botch, bungle, have the wrong impression, tangle, snarl, slip up, *make a mess of (it), *miss the boat, *open one's mouth and put one's foot in it.—*Ant.* succeed, be accurate, explain.

mistaken, *a.* 1. [In error] misinformed, deceived, confounded, confused, having the wrong impression, deluded, misinformed, misguided, at fault, off the track; see also **wrong 2.** 2. [Ill-advised] unadvised, duped, fooled, misled, tricked, unwarranted; see also **deceived.** 3. [Taken for another] improperly *or* wrongly identified, unrecognized, confused with, taken for, in a case of mistaken identity, misnamed, misconstrued.

mistakenly, *a.* badly, falsely, inadvisedly; see **wrongly 1, 2.**

mister, *n.* Mr., man, sir, *monsieur* (French), *Herr* (German), *signor* (Italian), *señor* (Spanish).

mistreat, *v.* harm, injure, wrong; see **abuse 1.**

mistress, *n.* 1. [A woman in authority] housekeeper, chaperone, housemother; see **lady 2.** 2. [An illegitimate consort] courtesan, paramour, kept woman; see **prostitute.**

mistrust, *v.* suspect, distrust, scruple; see **doubt.**

misty, *a.* dim, foggy, hazy, murky, shrouded, obscure; see also **dark 1.**

misunderstand, *v.* err, misconceive, misinterpret, misapprehend, misjudge, miscalculate, misconstrue, be perplexed,

be bewildered, confuse, confound, have the wrong impression, fail to understand, misapprehend, overestimate, underestimate, be misled, be unfamiliar with, *have the wrong slant on, not register; see also **mistake.** —*Ant.* understand, grasp, apprehend.

misunderstanding, *n.* 1. [Misapprehension] delusion, miscalculation, confusion, misinterpretation, confounding; see also **mistake 2.**—*Ant.* conception, understanding, apprehension. 2. [Mutual difficulty] debate, dissension, quarrel; see **disagreement 1, dispute.**

misunderstood, *a.* misinterpreted, badly *or* falsely interpreted, misconceived; see **mistaken 1, wrong 2.**

mitt, *n.* baseball glove, catcher's mitt, first baseman's mitt; see **equipment.**

mitten, *n.* mitt, gauntlet, glove; see **clothes.**

mix, *v.* 1. [To blend] fuse, merge, coalesce, brew, unite, combine, cross, interbreed, amalgamate, incorporate, alloy, mingle, compound, intermingle, weave, interweave, throw together, adulterate, infiltrate, twine, knead, stir, suffuse, instill, transfuse, synthesize, stir around, infuse, saturate, dye, season. 2. [To confuse] mix up, jumble, tangle; see **confuse.** 3. [To associate] fraternize, get along, consort with; see **join 2.**

mixed, *a.* 1. [Commingled] blended, fused, mingled, compounded, combined, amalgamated, united, brewed, merged, transfused, crossed, assimilated, married, woven, kneaded, incorporated.—*Ant.* **separated,** severed, raveled. 2. [Various] miscellaneous, unselected, diverse; see **various.** 3. [Confused] mixed up, jumbled, disordered; see **confused 2.**

mixer, *n.* 1. [An instrument used to mix materials] blender, Osterizer (trademark), juicer, egg beater, cake mixer, food mixer, cocktail shaker, converter, carburetor, concrete *or* cement mixer, paint mixer; see also **machine.** 2. [A substance used in a mixture] ingredient, component, combining element; see **part 1.**

mixture, *n.* 1. [A combination] blend, compound, composite, amalgam, miscellany, mishmash, mingling, medley, mix, potpourri, alloy, fusion, jumble, brew, merger, hybrid, crossing, infiltration, transfusion, infusion, mélange, saturation, assimilation, incorporation, hodgepodge. 2. [A mess] mix-up, muddle, disorder; see **confusion.**

mix-up, *n.* turmoil, chaos, commotion; see **confusion, disorder 2.**

moan, *n.* plaint, groan, wail; see **cry 1.**

moan, *v.* groan, wail, whine; see **cry 1.**

mob, *n.* 1. [A disorderly crowd of people] swarm, rabble, throng, press, multitude, populace, horde, riot, host, lawless element; see also **crowd**, **gathering**. 2. [The lower classes] burgeoisie, plebeians, proletariat; see **people** 3.

mob, *v.* hustle, crowd, swarm; see **attack**, **rebel**.

mobile, *a.* unstationary, loose, free; see **movable**.

mobility, *n.* changeability, versatility, flow; see **movement** 1.

mobilize, *v.* assemble, prepare, gather; see **enlist** 1.

moccasin, *n.* heelless shoe, slipper, sandal; see **shoe**.

mock, *a.* counterfeit, sham, pretended; see **false** 3, **unreal**.

mock, *v.* 1. [To ridicule] deride, scorn, taunt; see **ridicule**. 2. [To mimic] mime, burlesque, caricature; see **imitate**.

mockery, *n.* disparagement, imitation, sham; see **ridicule**.

model, *n.* 1. [A person worthy of imitation] archetype, prototype, exemplar, paradigm, ideal, good man, good woman, good example, hero, demigod, saint. 2. [Anything that serves as a copy] original, text, guide, copy, tracing, facsimile, duplicate, pattern, design, gauge, ideal, shape, form, specimen, mold, principle, basis, standard, sketch, painting, precedent, archetype, prototype; see also **criterion**. 3. [A duplicate on a small scale] miniature, image, illustration, representation, reduction, statue, figure, figurine, effigy, mock-up, skeleton, portrait, photograph, relief, print, engraving; see also **copy**, **duplicate**. 4. [One who poses professionally] poser, sitter, mannequin; see **nude**.

model, *v.* 1. [To form] shape, mold, fashion; see **create**, **form** 1. 2. [To imitate a model] trace, duplicate, sketch, reduce, represent, print, counterfeit, caricature, parody; see also **illustrate**, **paint** 1. 3. [To serve as a model] sit, act as model, set an example; see also **pose** 2. 4. [To demonstrate] show (off), wear, parade *or* pose in; see **display**.

moderate, *a.* 1. [Not expensive] inexpensive, low-priced, reasonable; see **cheap** 1, **economical** 2. 2. [Not violent] modest, cool, tranquil; see **calm** 1, **reserved** 3. 3. [Not radical] tolerant, judicious, nonpartisan, liberal, middle-of-the-road, unopinionated, not given to extremes, measured, low-key, evenly balanced, neutral, impartial, straight, midway, in the mean, average, restrained, sound, cautious, considered, considerate, respectable, middle-class, compromising; see also **conservative**. –*Ant.* radical, unbalanced, partial. 4. [Not intemper-

ate] pleasant, gentle, soft, balmy, inexcessive, tepid, easy, not rigorous *or* severe, temperate, favorable, tolerable, bearable, tame, untroubled, unruffled, monotonous, even; see also **fair** 3, **mild** 2.–*Ant.* **severe**, rigorous, bitter. 5. [Not indulgent] sparing, frugal, regulated, self-denying, abstinent, non-indulgent, self-controlled, disciplined, careful, *on the wagon, *sworn off, teetotalling; see also **sober** 2.–*Ant.* **wasteful**, excessive, self-indulgent.

moderate, *v.* abate, modify, decline; see **decrease** 1.

moderately, *a.* tolerantly, tolerably, temperately, somewhat, to a degree, enough, to some *or* a certain extent, a little, to some degree, fairly, not exactly, in moderation, within reason *or* bounds *or* restrictions *or* reasonable limits, as far as could be expected, within the bounds of reason, in reason; see also **reasonably** 2, **slightly**.–*Ant.* **much**, extremely, remarkably.

moderation, *n.* 1. [Restraint] toleration, steadiness, sobriety, coolness, the golden mean, quiet, temperance, patience, fairness, justice, constraint, forbearance, poise, balance; see also **restraint** 1. 2. [The act of moderating] settlement, regulation, limitation; see **restraint** 2.

modern, *a.* 1. [Up to date] stylish, modish, chic, smart, up-to-the-minute, late, current, recent, of the present, prevailing, prevalent, avant-garde, present-day, latest, most recent, advanced, streamlined, breaking with tradition, new, newest, untraditional, contemporary, in vogue, in use, common, newfangled, *cool, *sharp, *smooth, just out, *mod, jet-age; see also **fashionable**.–*Ant.* **old-fashioned**, out-of-date, out-of-style. 2. [Having the comforts of modern life] modernistic, modernized, renovated, functional, with modern conveniences, done over, having modern improvements; see also **convenient** 1, **improved**. 3. [Concerning recent times] contemporary, contemporaneous, recent, concurrent, present-day, coincident, twentieth-century, latter-day, mechanical, of the Machine Age, automated, of modern times, modernist; see also **new** 1, 2, **now** 1.–*Ant.* old, medieval, primordial.

modest, *a.* 1. [Humble] unassuming, meek, diffident; see **humble** 1, **resigned**. 2. [Not showy] unpretentious, plain, unostentatious, unobtrusive, demure, quiet, seemly, proper, decorous, simple, natural, unassuming, humble, tasteful, unadorned, unaffected, homely. 3. [Moderate] reasonable, inexpensive, average; see **cheap** 1, **economical** 2. 4. [Proper] pure, chaste, seemly; see decent 2, honest 1. 5. [Lowly] plain, simple, unaffected; see **humble 2.**

modestly, *a.* unobtrusively, retiringly, quietly, unpretentiously, diffidently, bashfully, unassumingly, chastely, virtuously, purely, shyly, demurely.—*Ant.* **boldly,** boastfully, pretentiously.

modesty, *n.* 1. [The attitude that leads one to make a modest self-estimate] humility, delicacy, reticence, constraint, unobtrusiveness, meekness; see also **courtesy 1, dignity, restraint 1.**—*Ant.* **vanity,** conceit, egotism. 2. [Shyness] inhibition, timidity, diffidence; see **shyness. 3.** [Chastity] decency, innocence, celibacy; see **chastity, virtue 1.**

modification, *n.* qualification, alteration, correction; see **adjustment, change 2.**

modified, *a.* varied, mutated, adjusted; see **changed 2.**

modify, *v.* 1. [To change] alter, modify, vary; see **become, change 2.** 2. [To moderate] mitigate, restrain, curb; see **decrease 2,** restrict.

moist, *a.* humid, dank, moistened; see **wet 1.**

moisten, *v.* sprinkle, dampen, saturate, drench, waterlog, steep, sog, sop, dip, rinse, wash (over), wet (down), water (down), squirt, shower, rain on, splash, splatter, bathe, steam, spray, sponge.

moisture, *n.* precipitation, mist, drizzle; see **fog, water 1.**

mold, *n.* 1. [A form] matrix, womb, cavity, shape, frame, pattern, design, die, cast, cup, image, kind, molding, casting, reproduction, form, pottery, shell, core. 2. [A parasitic growth] rust, (blue *or* black) mold, parasite, fungus, lichen; see also **decay.**

mold, *v.* 1. [To give physical shape to] make, round into, fashion; see **form 1.** 2. [To decay through the action of mold] molder, mildew, rust; see **spoil.**

moldy, *a.* musty, mildewed, dank; see **rotten 1.**

mole, *n.* flaw, birthmark, blotch; see **blemish.**

molecular, *a.* miniature, microscopic, atomic; see **little 1, minute 1.**

molecule, *n.* 1. [Unit] particle, fragment, unit; see **bit 1.** 2. [Atom] electron, ion, particle; see **atom.**

molest, *v.* 1. [To disturb objects] displace, meddle, disorganize; see **disturb.** 2. [To disturb people] bother, interrupt, break in upon, intrude, encroach upon, annoy, worry, irritate, plague, badger, bait, pester, hinder, tease, irk, vex, trouble, confuse, perturb, frighten, terrify, scare; see also **bother 2.**

molten, *a.* heated, melted, fused, liquefied, running, fluid, seething; see also **hot 1.**—*Ant.* **cold,** cool, solid.

moment, *n.* 1. [A brief time] minute, instant, millisecond, trice, second, bit, while, flash, *jiffy; see also **minute 2.** 2. [Importance] significance, note, consequence; see **importance.**

momentarily, *a.* immediately, right now, instantly; see **now 1.**

momentary, *a.* fleeting, quick, passing, flitting, flashing, transient, impermanent, shifting, ephemeral, vanishing, cursory, temporary, dreamlike, *in the bat *or* wink of an eye, *quicker than one can say Jack Robinson.—*Ant.* **eternal,** continual, ceaseless.

momentum, *n.* impulse, force, drive; see **energy 3.**

***mommy,** *n.* *mom, female parent, mama; see **mother 1,** parent.

monarch, *n.* despot, sovereign, autocrat; see **king 1.**

monarchy, *n.* kingship, sovereignty, command; see **power 2.**

monastery, *n.* abbey, priory, religious community; see **church 1.**

monetary, *a.* pecuniary, financial, fiscal; see **commercial.**

money, *n.* 1. [A medium of exchange] gold, silver, cash, currency, check, bills, notes, specie, legal tender, *Almighty Dollar, *gravy, *wampum, *shekels, *dough, *long green, *coins, lucre, *folding money, *wad, *bucks, *hard cash, *bread. Money includes the following— cent, dollar, penny, pound, *centime, franc, centesimo, lira, centavo, peso, kopek, ruble, ore, krone, yuan, sen, yen, Pfennig, Mark.* 2. [Wealth] funds, capital, property; see **wealth.** 3. [Merged interests] financiers, corporate interests, capitalists; see **business 4.** 4. [Pay] payment, salary, wages; see **pay 2.** — *for one's money, for one's choice, in one's opinion, to one's mind; see **personally 2.** —*in the money, wealthy, *flush, *loaded; see **rich 1.** —**make money,** gain profits, become wealthy, earn; see **profit 2.** —**one's money's worth,** full value, gain, benefit; see **value 1, 3.** —**put money into,** invest (money) in, support, underwrite; see **invest.**

monk, *n.* hermit, religious, ascetic, solitary, recluse, abbot, prior; see also **priest.**

monkey, *n.* primate, lemur, anthropoid ape; see also **animal.** Monkeys include the following—chimpanzee, orangutan, baboon, marmoset, gibbon, gorilla, mandrill; spider, squirrel, capuchin.

***monkey,** *v.* pry, fool around, tamper with; see **meddle 2.**

***monkey business,** *n.* deceit, conniving, misconduct; see **deception, lie.**

monologue, *n.* talk, speech, discourse; see **address 2.**

monopolize, *v.* engross, acquire, exclude, own exclusively, absorb, consume, manage, have, hold, corner, restrain, patent, copyright, *corner the market.—Ant.* include, give, invite.

monopoly, *n.* trust, syndicate, cartel; see **business 1.**

monotonous, *a.* 1. [Tiresome] tedious, wearisome, wearying; see **dull 4.** 2. [Having but one tone] monotonic, monotonical, unvarying, lacking variety, in one key, unchanged, reiterated, recurrent, single, uniform.—*Ant.* varying, **various**, multiple.

monotony, *n.* invariability, likeness, tediousness, similarity, continuity, continuance, oneness, evenness, levelness, flatness, the same old thing; see also **boredom.—Ant.** difference, variability, **variety**.

monster, *n.* 1. [A great beast] beastlike creature, centaur, monstrosity, sphinx, chimera, unicorn, dragon, griffin, cyclops, phoenix, mermaid, sea serpent, rhinoceros, elephant, werewolf. 2. [An unnatural creation] abnormality, abnormity, monstrosity; see **freak.** 3. [An inhuman person] brute, beast, cruel *or* brutish person; see **criminal, rascal.**

monstrous, *a.* 1. [Huge] stupendous, prodigious, enormous; see **large 1.** 2. [Unnatural] abnormal, preposterous, uncanny; see **unnatural 1, unusual 2.**

month, *n.* measure of time, thirty days, one-twelfth of a year, four weeks, moon, period. Months of the year are the following—January, February, March, April, May, June, July, August, September, October, November, December.

monthly, *a.* once a month, every month, menstrual, punctually, steadily, recurrent, cyclic, cyclical, repeated, rhythmic, methodically, periodically, from month to month; see also **regularly.**

monument, *n.* 1. [Anything erected to preserve a memory] tomb, shaft, column, pillar, headstone, tombstone, gravestone, mausoleum, obelisk, shrine, statue, building, tower, monolith, tablet, slab, stone; see also **memorial.** 2. [A landmark in the history of creative work] work of art, magnum opus, permanent contribution; see **achievement, masterpiece.**

monumental, *a.* lofty, impressive, majestic; see **grand, great 1.**

mood, *n.* 1. [A state of mind] state, condition, frame of mind, temper, humor, disposition, inclination, caprice, whim, fancy, pleasure, freak, wish, desire. 2. [A quality of mind] bent, propensity, tendency; see **attitude.** 3. [Grammatical mode] aspect, inflection, mode. Moods in English grammar include the following—indicative, subjunctive, imperative, interrogative, conditional, potential.

moody, *a.* pensive, unhappy, low-spirited; see **sad 1.**

moon, *n.* celestial body, heavenly body, planet, planetoid, crescent, new moon, half-moon, full moon, old moon, Luna, moon goddess, dry moon, wet moon, *sailor's friend.*

moonlight, *n.* effulgence, radiance, luminescence; see **light 3.**

moonshine, *n.* 1. [Moonlight] effulgence, radiance, luminosity; see **light 3.** 2. [Whisky distilled illicitly] *mountain dew, *mule, *white lightning; see **whiskey.**

mop, *n.* swab, duster, sweeper; see also **broom.**

mop, *v.* swab, wipe, rub, dab, pat, polish, wash, dust, wipe up; see also **clean.**

mope, *v.* fret, pine away, grieve, sorrow, sink, lose heart, brood, pine, yearn, despair, grumble, chafe, lament, regret, look glum, sulk, *pull a long face.—Ant.* revive, **celebrate**, cheer up.

mopped, *a.* swabbed, washed, polished; see **clean.**

mop up, *v.* finish off, dispatch, clean (up); see **defeat 2, eliminate.**

moral, *a.* 1. [Characterized by conventional virtues] trustworthy, kindly, courteous, respectable, proper, scrupulous, conscientious, good, truthful, decent, just, honorable, honest, high-minded, saintly, pure, worthy, correct, seemly, aboveboard, dutiful, principled, conscientious, chaste, ethical; see also **noble 1, 2, reliable.—Ant.** unscrupulous, **lying, dishonest.** 2. [Having to do with approved relationships between the sexes] virtuous, immaculate, decent; see **chaste, innocent 2.**

morale, *n.* assurance, resolve, spirit; see **confidence 1.**

morality, *n.* righteousness, uprightness, honesty; see **virtue 1.**

morally, *a.* 1. [In accordance with accepted standards of conduct] conscientiously, truthfully, honestly, honorably, appropriately, respectably, courteously, scrupulously, uprightly, righteously, trustworthily, decently, properly, in a manner approved by society; see also **justly 1, sincerely.—Ant.** wrongly, worthlessly, dishonorably. 2. [In a chaste manner] chastely, virtuously, purely; see **modestly.**

morals, *n.* ideals, customs, standards, mores, policies, beliefs, dogmas, social standards, principles; see also **ethics.**

morbid, *a.* 1. [Diseased] sickly, unhealthy, ailing; see **sick.** 2. [Pathological] gloomy, melancholic, depressed; see also **insane, sad 1.**

more, *a.* 1. [Additional] also, likewise, and, over and above, more than that, further, in addition, beside(s), added; see also **extra**.—*Ant.* less than, **less**, subtracted from. 2. [Greater in quantity, amount, degree, or quality] numerous, many, exceeding, extra, expanded, increased, major, augmented, extended, enhanced, added to, larger, higher, wider, deeper, heavier, solider, stronger, over *or* above the mark.—*Ant.* lessened, weaker, decreased.

more and more, *a.* increasingly, more frequently; increasing in weight *or* size *or* number, etc.; see **frequently, increasing**.

more or less, *a.* about, somewhat, in general; see **approximate, approximately**.

moreover, *a.* further, by the same token, furthermore; see **besides**.

morning, *n.* 1. [Dawn] the East, morn, daybreak, break of day, first blush *or* flush of morning, daylight, cockcrow, sun-up, *the wee small hours, *crack of dawn. 2. [The time before noon] forenoon, morningtide, after midnight, before noon, breakfast time, before lunch.

mornings, *a.* in the morning(s), every morning, before noon; see **daily, regularly**.

moron, *n.* feeble-minded person, imbecile, idiot, simpleton, goose, addlepate, dullard, dunce, blockhead, cretin, dunce, *dunderhead, numskull, *loony; see also **fool**.—*Ant.* philosopher, sage, scientist.

moronic, *a.* foolish, mentally retarded, *dumb; see **stupid** 1.

morsel, *n.* bite, chunk, piece; see **bit** 1, **part** 1.

mortal, *a.* 1. [Causing death] malignant, fatal, lethal; see **deadly, poisonous**. 2. [Subject to death] human, transient, temporal, passing, frail, impermanent, perishable, fading, passing away, momentary; see also **temporary**.—*Ant.* eternal, perpetual, everlasting.

mortal, *n.* creature, being, human; see **animal, man** 1.

mortality, *n.* dying, extinction, fatality; see **death, destruction** 1.

mortgage, *n.* lease, title, debt; see also **contract**.

mortuary, *n.* charnel house, funeral parlor, funeral home; see **funeral**.

mosaic, *a.* diapered, varied, inlaid; see **ornate** 1.

moss, *n.* lichen, Iceland moss, rock moss; see **plant**.

mossy, *a.* tufted, velvety, plushy, downy, smooth, fresh, damp, moist, resilient, soft, covered, overgrown.—*Ant.* dry, bare, prickly.

most, *a.* nearly all, all but, not quite all, close upon all, in the majority. —**at the most**, in toto, not more than, at the outside; see **most**. —**make the most of**, exploit, utilize, take advantage of; see **use** 1.

mostly, *a.* 1. [Frequently] often, many times, in many instances; see **frequently, regularly**. 2. [Largely] chiefly, essentially, for the most part; see **principally**.

motel, *n.* motor hotel, inn, cabins, stopping place, road house, court, motor court; see also **hotel, resort** 2.

moth, *n.* (moth) miller, tineid, *Heterocera* (Latin); see **insect**.

mother, *n.* 1. [A female parent] parent, matriarch, dam, mama, *mammy, *mum, *ma, *mom, *mommy, *maw, mater; see also **parent, relative**. 2. [A matron] superintendent, mother superior, housemother; see **executive**. 3. [The source] fountainhead, source, beginning; see **origin** 2.

mother-in-law, *n.* husband's *or* wife's mother, mother by marriage; see **relative**.

motherly, *a.* maternal, devoted, careful, watchful, kind, warm, gentle, tender, sympathetic, supporting, protective; see also **loving**.

motion, *n.* 1. [A movement] change, act, action; see **movement** 2. 2. [The state of moving] passage, translating, changing; see **movement** 1. 3. [An act formally proposed] suggestion, consideration, proposition; see **plan** 2.

motionless, *a.* 1. [Not moving] still, unmoving, dead, deathly still, inert, stock-still, stagnant, quiet.—*Ant.* **moving**, shifting, **changing**. 2. [Firm] unmovable, fixed, stationary; see **firm** 1.

motion picture, *n.* moving picture, cinema, (the silver) screen; see **movie**.

motivate, *v.* impel, inspire hope, stimulate, incite, propel, spur, goad, move, induce, prompt, arouse, whet, instigate, fire, provoke, cause, *touch off, *egg on, *trigger; see also **drive** 1, **excite**, urge 2.

motive, *n.* cause, purpose, idea; see **reason** 3.

motor, *n.* machine, device, instrument; see also **engine**. Types of motors include the following—internal combustion, diesel, spark diesel, compound, steam, external combustion, Wankel, piston, turbine, gas turbine, jet, rotary, radial, airplane, automobile, truck, A.C. *or* D.C. electric, high compression, low compression.

motorboat, *n.* speedboat, putt-putt, hop-up, skip-jack; see also **boat**. Types of motorboats include the following—open, outboard, electric-powered, gasoline-powered; cruiser, runabout.

motorcycle, *n.* motorized two-wheeled vehicle, cycle, *pig, *hog, *bike, *chopper; see also **vehicle**.

motorist, *n.* automobile operator, autoist, gear grinder; see **driver**.

motorized, *a.* motor-driven, motor-powered, electric-driven, gasoline-driven, oil-driven, motor-equipped, motor-operated.

motto, *n.* maxim, adage, saw, epigram, aphorism, (pretty) sentiment, slogan, catchword, axiom; see also **proverb**, **saying**. Familiar mottoes include the following—in God we trust, *e pluribus unum* (Latin), time flies, rest in peace *or* R.I.P., peace be with you, peace on earth, good will toward men, one for all and all for one, home sweet home, God bless our home, don't tread on me, give me liberty *or* give me death, all or nothing, you can't take it with you; all men are created free and equal; liberty, equality, fraternity; for God and country, what's worth doing is worth doing well, don't give up the ship; don't fire until you see the whites of their eyes; remember the Alamo *or* the Maine *or* Pearl Harbor, etc.; our Country, right or wrong; hew to the line and let the chips fall where they may; praise the Lord and pass the ammunition; put your trust in God and keep your powder dry, abandon hope, all ye who enter here, to err is human, to forgive divine; make hay while the sun shines, *Pike's Peak or bust.

mound, *n.* pile, heap, knoll; see **hill**.

mount, *v.* 1. [To rise] ascend, arise, uprise; see **rise** 1. 2. [To climb (until one can stand or sit on the top)] ascend, scale, clamber; see **climb**.

mountain, *a.* towering, steep, lofty; see **mountainous**.

mountain, *n.* 1. [A lofty land mass] mount, elevation, peak, sierra, butte, hill, alp, range, ridge, pike, bluff, headland, volcano, crater, tableland, mesa, plateau, height, crag, precipice, cliff, earth mass.—*Ant.* valley, ravine, flatland. Famous chains of mountains include the following—Alps, Himalayas, Caucasus, Urals, Pyrenees, Andes, Rockies, Canadian Rockies, Appalachians, Cascades, Adirondacks, White Mountains, Sierra Nevada, Sierra Madre, Cordillera, Apennine chain. Famous peaks include the following—Mont Blanc, Mt. Aetna, Vesuvius, the Matterhorn, Pike's Peak, Mt. Whitney, Mt. Shasta, Mt. Washington, the Jungfrau, the Grand Teton, Mt. McKinley, Krakatoa, Pelee, Popocatepetl, Mt. Cook, Mt. Everest, Annapurna, Mount of Olives, Mt. Sinai, Fujiyama, Mt.

Kenya, Mt. Kilimanjaro. 2. [A pile] mass, mound, glob; see **heap**.

mountaineer, *n.* mountain man, mountain dweller, hillman, highlander, uplander, native of mountains, mountain climber, rock climber, mountain guide, mountain scaler, *hillbilly.

mountainous, *a.* mountainlike, mountain, with mountains, difficult, barbarous, wild, untamed, strange, remote, uncivilized, rude, unpopulated, solitary, unfamiliar, isolated, steep, lofty, hilly, alpine, upland, elevated, volcanic, towering, craggy, cliffy, rugged. —*Ant.* low, small, flat.

mounted, *a.* 1. [On horseback] seated, riding, in the saddle, cavalry, *horsed, up.—*Ant.* afoot, unhorsed, dismounted. 2. [Firmly fixed] supported, set, attached; see **firm** 1. 3. [Backed] pasted on, set off, strengthened; see **reinforced**.

mourn, *v.* deplore, grieve, fret, sorrow, rue, regret, bemoan, sigh, long for, miss, droop, languish, yearn, pine, anguish, complain, agonize, weep (over), suffer, wring one's hands, be brokenhearted, be in distress, be sad.—*Ant.* celebrate, rejoice, be happy.

mourner, *n.* lamenter, griever, keener, weeper, wailer, sorrower, pallbearer, friend of the deceased, member of the family.

mournful, *a.* sorrowful, mourning, unhappy; see **sad** 1.

mourning, *n.* 1. [The act of expressing grief] sorrowing, grieving, yearning, sorrow, lamentation, pining, sighing, regretting, deploring, weeping over, wailing, crying, moaning, murmuring, complaining, sobbing; see also **depression** 2, **grief**, **sadness**.—*Ant.* celebration, rejoicing, being glad. 2. [Symbols of mourning] black, mourning coach, arm band, mourning veil, widow's weeds, black suit, black tie.

mouse, *n.* rodent, vermin, rat; see **animal**.

mouth, *n.* 1. [The principal facial opening] Parts of the mouth include the following—lips, roof, floor, tongue, jaws, gums, teeth, soft palate, alveolar ridge, hard palate, uvula. 2. [Any opening resembling a mouth] orifice, entrance, aperture; see **entrance** 2. 3. [The end of a river] estuary, firth, delta, portal, harbor, roads, sound, tidewater. — *down in (or at) the mouth*, depressed, discouraged, unhappy; see **sad** 1. —*have a big mouth*, talk loudly, exaggerate, brag; see **talk** 1.

mouthful, *n.* portion, piece, morsel; see **bite** 1.

movable, *a.* not fastened, portable, adjustable, adaptable, not fixed, unstationary, mobile, demountable, detachable, turnable, removable, separable, transferable, loose, unfastened, free, unattached, in parts, in sections, knocked down, on wheels.—*Ant.* fixed, fastened, stationary.

move, *n.* motility, transit, progress; see **movement** 1, 2. —*get a move on,* go faster, start moving, *get cracking; *get hurry 1. —on the move, moving, busy, acting; see **active 2.**

move, *v.* 1. [To be in motion] go, walk, run, glide, travel, drift, budge, stir, shift, pass, cross, roll, flow, march, travel, progress, proceed, traverse, drive, ride, fly, hurry, head for, bustle, climb, crawl, leap, hop to it, *get a move on, get going or *cracking; see also advance 1.—*Ant.* stop, remain stationary, stay quiet. 2. [To set in motion] impel, actuate, propel; see **push 2.** 3. [To arouse the emotions of] influence, stir, instigate, stimulate, touch, play on, sway, induce, rouse, prevail upon, work upon, *touch a (sympathetic) chord; see also **drive 1, encourage, excite.**—*Ant.* quiet, lull, pacify. 4. [To take up another residence] pack up, move out or in, be transferred; see **leave 1.** 5. [To propose an action formally] suggest, introduce, submit; see **propose 1.**

moved, *a.* 1. [Transported] conveyed, carried, sent, taken, shifted, transferred, reassigned, changed, flown, driven, drawn, pushed, lifted, elevated, lowered, let down, displaced, withdrawn, replaced, sent abroad, trucked, hauled, dragged; see also **sent. 2.** [Gone to a different residence] emigrated, migrated, vacated, removed, at a new or different address, departed, gone away, changed residences, left, gone for good, see also **gone 1.**—*Ant.* resident, remaining, still there or here. 3. [Proposed] recommended, submitted, introduced; see **proposed. 4.** [Excited] disturbed, stimulated, upset; see **excited.**

movement, *n.* 1. [The state of moving] move, transit, passage, progress, journey, advance, mobility, change, shift, alteration, ascension, descension, propulsion, flow, flux, action, flight, wandering, journeying, voyaging, migration, emigration, transplanting, evolving, shifting, changing, locomotion, drive, evolution, undertaking, regression.—*Ant.* rest, quiet, fixity. 2. [An example of movement] journey, trip, immigration, migration, march, crusade, patrol, sweep, emigration, evolution, unrest, transition, change, transfer, displacement, withdrawal, ascension, descension, progression, regression, transportation, removal, departure, shift, flight, slip, slide, step, footfall, stride, gesture, act, action, pilgrimage, expedition, locomo-

tion. 3. [A trend] drift, tendency, bent; see **inclination 1.**

movie, *n.* moving or motion picture, photoplay, cinema, film, show, screenplay, photodrama, cinematograph, cartoon, animated cartoon, serial, comedy, foreign film, travelogue, short, documentary, videotape, *flick, *flicker; see also **drama.**

movies, *n.* 1. [A showing of a moving picture] motion picture, film, photoplay; see **movie. 2.** [The motion picture industry] moving pictures, screen pictures, the cinematic industry, Hollywood, the screen world, *the silver screen, *the industry, *pictures, *the flicks, *celluloids.

move in, *v.* take up residence, take occupancy (of), get a home; see **arrive, establish 2.**

move off, *v.* depart, be in motion, go; see **leave 1.**

move on, *v.* keep moving or going, continue, go; see **travel, walk 1.**

move up, *v.* go forward, do well, go or get ahead; see **advance 1, rise 1.**

moving, *a.* 1. [In motion] going, changing, progressing, advancing, shifting, evolving, withdrawing, rising, going down, descending, ascending, getting up, traveling, journeying, on the march, moving up, starting, proceeding, flying, climbing, *up-tempo, *on the jump, *going great guns. 2. [Going to another residence] migrating, emigrating, vacating, removing, departing, leaving, going away, changing residences. 3. [Exciting] affecting, emotional, touching; see **exciting.**

mow, *v.* scythe, reap, lay in swaths; see **harvest.**

much, *a.* 1. [To a great degree or extent] important, weighty, notable, considerable, prominent, memorable, momentous, stirring, eventful, serious, urgent, pressing, critical, paramount, principal, leading, significant, telling, *first-rate, *in the front rank.—*Ant.* little, inconsiderable, trivial. 2. [In great quantity] full, many, very many, abundant, satisfying, enough, sufficient, adequate, considerable, substantial, ample, everywhere, copious, voluminous, plentiful, profuse, complete, lavish, generous, immeasurable, endless, countless, extravagant, *hell of a lot, *all over the place, *no end.—*Ant.* inadequate, insufficient, limited. 3. [Very] greatly, enormously, extremely; see **very.**

much, *pron.* a great quantity, abundance, quantities, a great deal, riches, wealth, volume, very much, breadth, plentifulness, fullness, completeness, lavishness, *lot, *great lot, *quite a bit, *gobs, *thousands, *tons, *oodles; see also **plenty.**—*Ant.* penury, scarcity, little. —

as much as, practically, virtually, in effect; see **almost, equal. —make much of**, treat with importance, expand, exaggerate; see **overdo** 1. **—not much of a**, inferior, mediocre, unsatisfactory; see **poor** 2.

muck, *n.* refuse, dung, waste; see **trash** 1.

mud, *n.* dirt, muck, clay, mire, slush, silt, muddiness, stickiness, ooze, bog, marsh, swamp, soup, axle grease.

muddle, *n.* trouble, disarrangement, disarray; see **confusion, disorder** 2.

muddle, *v.* stir up, disarrange, entangle, foul, mix, jumble, derange, shake up, mess, botch, clutter, snarl, complicate, disorder; see also **confuse**.

muddled, *a.* uncertain, addled, stupid; see **confused** 2.

muddy, *a.* 1. [Containing sediment] stirred, dull, dark, cloudy, murky, indistinct, roiled, roily, confused, obscure, opaque; see also **dirty** 1.—*Ant.* clear, translucent, pellucid. 2. [Deep with mud] sloppy, swampy, soggy, sodden, slushy, watery, boggy, soaked.—*Ant.* dry, barren, parched.

muffle, *v.* deaden, mute, stifle; see **decrease** 2, **soften** 2.

muffled, *a.* suppressed, stifled, indistinct; see **obscure** 1.

muffler, *n.* chest protector, neckpiece, babushka, neckerchief, kerchief, neckband, neck cloth, Ascot, choker, mantle, stole; see also **clothes**.

mug, *n.* vessel, stein, flagon; see **cup**.

muggy, *a.* damp, humid, moist; see **wet** 1.

mule, *n.* hinney, army mule, Missouri mule; see **animal**.

mull, *v.* reflect, meditate, ponder; see **think** 1.

multicolored, *a.* dappled, motley, spotted; see **colored** 1.

multiple, *a.* 1. [Various] complicated, more than one, many, manifold, compound, having many uses, multifold, multitudinous, aggregated, many-sided, versatile, increased, varied, compound, added; see also **various**.—*Ant.* simple, united, centralized. 2. [Repeated] reoccurring, repetitious, duplicated; see **multiplied**.

multiplication, *n.* duplication, reproduction, addition, increase, repetition, compounding, recurrence, amplification, making more, reproducing, repeating, augmenting; see also **mathematics**.—*Ant.* reduction, subtraction, decrease.

multiplied, *a.* compounded, added, reproduced, amplified, repeated, augmented, duplicated, reduplicated, made many.—*Ant.* reduced, divided, decreased.

multiply, *v.* 1. [To increase] add, augment, double; see **increase**. 2. [To bring forth young] generate, produce, populate; see **reproduce** 3. 3. [To employ multiplication as an arithmetical process] square, cube, raise to a higher power; see **increase**.

multitude, *n.* throng, drove, mob; see **crowd, gathering, people** 3.

mumble, *v.* mutter, utter, whine, whimper, grumble, murmur, maunder, ramble on, whisper, speak indistinctly, say to oneself; see also **hesitate, stammer**.—*Ant.* say, articulate, enunciate.

mumbo jumbo, *n.* gibberish, double talk, drivel; see **nonsense** 1.

munch, *v.* crunch, bite, crush; see **chew, eat**.

mundane, *a.* normal, ordinary, everyday; see **wordly** 1.

municipal, *a.* self-governing, metropolitan, city, town, community, local, civil, incorporated, corporate; see also **public**.—*Ant.* national, state, **private**.

municipality, *n.* district, village, borough; see **city, town** 1.

munitions, *n.* materiel, weapons, war material, ordnance; see **ammunition, bomb, bullet, cannon, explosive, gun, machine gun, rocket, shot** 1.

murder, *n.* killing, homicide, death, destruction, annihilation, carnage, putting an end to, slaying, shooting, knifing, assassination, lynching, crime, felony, killing with malice aforethought, murder in the first degree, first degree murder, contract killing, murder in the second degree, murder in the third degree, massacre, genocide, butchery, patricide, matricide, infanticide, fratricide, genocide, suicide, foul play. **—get away with murder**, escape (punishment), take flight, avoid prosecution *or* punishment; see **evade** 1.

murder, *v.* 1. [To kill unlawfully] slay, assassinate, butcher; see **kill** 1. 2. [*To ruin, especially by incompetence] spoil, mar, misuse; see **botch, destroy, fail** 1.

murdered, *a.* killed, assassinated, massacred; see **dead** 1.

murderer, *n.* slayer, assassin, butcher; see **criminal, killer**.

murderous, *a.* killing, cruel, criminal; see **deadly**.

murky, *a.* dim, dusky, dingy; see **dark** 1, **dirty** 1.

murmur, *v.* 1. [To make a low, continuous sound] ripple, moan, trickle, burble, babble, tinkle, gurgle, meander, flow gently; see also **hum, whisper**.—*Ant.* sound, peal, clang. 2. [To mutter] mumble, rumble, growl; see **mutter** 2.

muscle, *n.* fiber, flesh, protoplasm, meat, brawn; *beef, *horseflesh.

muscular, *a.* brawny, powerful, husky; see **strong 1.**

museum, *n.* institution, building, hall, place of exhibition, foundation, art gallery, library, picture gallery, archives, treasury, storehouse, depository, vault, aquarium, menagerie, zoological garden *or* park, zoo, botanical garden, herbarium, arboretum.

mush, *n.* 1. [Boiled meal] Indian meal, hasty pudding, hominy, cereal, grain; see also **food.** 2. [*Sentimentality] sentimentalism, excessive sentiment, mawkishness, affectation, superficiality, romanticism, puppy love, *hearts and flowers, *sob story.

mushroom, *n.* toadstool, fungus, *champignon* (French); see **food, plant.**

mushroom, *v.* augment, spread, sprout; see **grow 1, increase.**

mushy, *a.* 1. [Soft] pulpy, mashy, muddy; see **soft 2.** 2. [Sentimental] romantic, maudlin, effusive; see **emotional, sentimental.**

music, *n.* 1. [A combination of tone and rhythm] harmony, melody, tune, air, strain, harmonics, song, measure, refrain, phrasing; see **beat 2, harmony 1.** Terms used in music include the following—scale, clef, note, tone, pitch, sharp, flat, major, minor, key, mode, bridge, theme, movement, orchestration, instrumentation, variation, improvisation, rhythm, accent, beat, down-beat, upbeat, off-beat, chord, counterpoint, timbre, volume, resonance; see **song.** Musical forms for instruments include the following—symphony (the conventional four movements of a symphony are sonata, andante, scherzo, finale), concerto, suite, trio *or* quartet *or* quintet, etc., for strings *or* woodwinds, etc.; overture, prelude, sonata, mass, scherzo, nocturne, fugue, étude, tone poem, variations, rhapsody, serenade, ballade, march, rhythm and blues, dance; see **overture 2, symphony.** Musical dance forms include the following—waltz, tango, polka; see **dance 1.** General styles of music include the following—classical *or* *long-hair, serious, medieval, modern, folk, primitive, popular, national, sacred, baroque, modernistic, formal, romantic, jazz, blues, boogiewoogie, folk rock, *acid rock, rock-and-roll, *bebop *or* bop, *soul rock, soul, ragtime, swing; see **jazz.** 2. [Responsiveness to music] musical appreciation, sensitivity, aesthetic sense; see **appreciation 2, feeling 4.** —*face the music, accept the consequences (of one's actions), suffer, undergo; see **endure 2.**

musical, *a.* 1. [Having the qualities of music] tuneful, sweet, pleasing, agreeable, symphonic, lyric, mellow, vocal, choral, consonant, rhythmical; see also **harmonious 1.**—*Ant.* tuneless, discordant, **harsh.** 2. [Having aptitude for music] gifted, talented, musically inclined; see **artistic.**

musical, *n.* musicale, musical comedy, burlesque; see **performance, show 1.**

musical instrument, *n.* Types of musical instruments include the following—recorder, grand piano, concert piano, lyre, bell, flute, piccolo, violin *or* fiddle, oboe, clarinet, bassoon, fife, bagpipe, trombone, French horn, tuba, cornet, trumpet, saxophone, dulcimer, harpsichord, harmonica, organ, harp, tambourine, ukelele, guitar, electric guitar, banjo, mandolin, lute, viola, cello, xylophone, marimba, cymbal, (kettle) drum, accordion, concertina, tom-tom, sitar, calliope.

musician, *n.* player, performer, composer; see **artist 1.** Musicians include the following—singer, instrumentalist, soloist, soprano, alto, contralto, tenor, baritone, bass, conductor *or* director *or* leader, basso profundo, folk singer, drummer, pianist, violinist, cellist; performer on a woodwind instrument, performer on a brass instrument, percussion performer, etc.; jazzmen, blues men.

***muss**, *n.* chaos, disarrangement, turmoil; see **confusion, disorder 2.**

muss, *v.* rumble, tousle, dishevel, ruffle, crumple, jumble, disarrange, disturb, mess up; see also **tangle.**

mussey, *a.* messy, chaotic, rumpled; see **tangled.**

***must**, *n.* requirement, need, obligation; see **necessity 2.**

must, *v.* ought, should, have, have (got) (to), be compelled (to), be obliged *or* required, be doomed *or* destined, be ordered *or* directed, be made *or* driven, have no choice, be one's fate; see also **need.**

mustache, *n.* moustachio, handlebars, *soup-strainer; see **beard, whiskers.**

musty, *a.* dusty, moth-eaten, crumbling; see **wasted.**

mutation, *n.* modification, deviation, variation; see **change 1, variety 1, 2.**

mute, *a.* 1. [Without power of speech] tongueless, deaf and dumb, inarticulate, voiceless, tongue-tied; see also **dumb 1, quiet.**—*Ant.* vocal, noisy, unimpaired. 2. [Suddenly deprived of speech] speechless, wordless, silent; see **bewildered, surprised.**

mutilate, *v.* 1. [To maim] cut, batter, scratch; see **weaken 2.** 2. [To damage] injure, deface, ravage; see **damage, hurt 1.**

mutilated, *a.* disfigured, distorted, maimed; see **deformed.**

mutiny, *n.* insurrection, revolt, resistance; see **revolution 2.**

mutter, *v.* 1. [To make a low, mumbling sound] rumble, growl, snarl; see **sound 1.** 2. [To speak as if to oneself] murmur, grunt, grumble, sputter, whisper, speak inarticulately *or* indistinctly, speak in an undertone, *swallow one's words; see also **mumble, murmur 1.** 3. [To complain] grumble, moan, groan; see **complain.**

mutual, *a.* 1. [Reciprocal] interchangeable, two-sided, given and taken; see **complementary.** 2. [Common] joint, shared, belonging equally to; see **common 1.**

mutually, *a.* commonly, co-operatively, jointly, reciprocally, in cooperation *or* collaboration *or* combination, by common consent *or* agreement *or* contract, in conjunction (with); see also **together 2.**

muzzle, *v.* 1. [To fasten a muzzle upon] wrap, muffle, deaden; see **bind 1, gag 1.** 2. [To silence] gag, restrain, restrict, repress, suppress, check, stop, stop one's mouth, hush, still, *shush; see also **quiet 2.**

myriad, *a.* variable, infinite, innumerable; see **endless, multiple 1.**

myself, *pron.* me, personally, I *or* me personally; the speaker *or* author *or* writer, etc.; on my own authority *or* responsibility, *yours truly, your humble servant, me myself; see also **I.**

mysterious, *a.* 1. [Puzzling] enigmatic, enigmatical, strange; see **difficult 2, unnatural 1.** 2. [Concerning powers beyond those supposedly natural] mystic, occult, dark, mystifying, transcendental, spiritual, symbolic, subjective, mystical, magical, dark, veiled, strange, astrological, unknowable, unfathomable, esoteric, cryptic, oracular, unrevealed, incredible; see also **magic.** 3. [Not generally known] obscure, hidden, ambiguous; see **secret 1.**

mystery, *n.* 1. [The quality of being mysterious] inscrutability, occultism, cabalism; see **magic 1, 2, strangeness.** 2. [Something difficult to know] riddle, conundrum, enigma; see **difficulty 2, puzzle 2.** 3. [A trick] sleight-of-hand, trick of magic, juggle; see **trick 1.** 4. [A mystery story] detective story, mystery play, mystery movie; see **story.**

mystic, *a.* occult, transcendental, spiritual; see **mysterious 2, secret 1.**

mystify, *v.* perplex, trick, hoodwink; see **deceive, lie 1.**

mystique, *n.* attitude, complex, nature; see **character 1, temperament.**

myth, *n.* fable, folk tale, legend, lore, saga, folk ballad, allegory, parable, tale; see also **story.**

mythical, *a.* mythological, fabricated, fictitious; see **false 3, unreal.**

mythological, *a.* whimsical, fictitious, chimerical; see **fantastic, imaginary.**

mythology, *n.* belief, conviction, mythicism; see **faith 2, religion 1.**

N

nab, *v.* grab, take, snatch; see **seize 2**.

nag, *v.* vex, annoy, pester; see **bother 3**.

nail, *n.* brad, pin, peg, hob, stud; see also **tack 1**.

nail, *v.* **1.** [To hammer] drive, pound, spike; see **hit 1**. **2.** [To fasten with nails] secure, hold, bind; see **fasten**. **3.** [*To arrest] capture, detain, apprehend; see **arrest, seize 2**. —**hard as nails**, callous, unfeeling, remorseless; see **cruel**. —**hit the nail on the head**, do *or* say what is exactly right, be accurate, come to the point; see **define 2**.

naive, *a.* unaffected, childish, plain, artless, innocent, untrained, countrified, callow, natural, unschooled, ignorant, untaught, provincial, unsophisticated, unworldly, guileless, spontaneous, instinctive, impulsive, simple-minded, innocuous, unsuspecting, harmless, gullible, credulous, trusting, original, unpolished, rude, primitive, ingenuous, sincere, open, candid, forthright, aboveboard, romantic, fanciful, unpretentious, transparent, straightforward, uncomplicated, easily imposed upon; see also **inexperienced**.—*Ant.* experienced, sophisticated, complicated.

naively, *a.* childishly, ingenuously, stupidly; see **foolishly, openly 1**.

naiveté, *n.* ingenuousness, childishness, inexperience; see **innocence 2**.

naked, *a.* **1.** [Nude] unclothed, undressed, stripped, unclad, unrobed, disrobed, threadbare, leafless, hairless, bare, undraped, exposed, having nothing on, unapparaled, denuded, unveiled, uncovered, uncloaked, stark naked, bald, *in the altogether, *in one's birthday suit, in the buff, *peeled, without a stitch, in the raw, *in a state of nature. **2.** [Unadorned] plain, simple, artless; see **modest 2, natural 3**.

nakedness, *n.* nudity, bareness, nature in the raw, undress, exposure, *state of nature, the raw.

name, *n.* **1.** [A title] proper name, Christian name, given name, cognomen, appellation, designation, first name, compellation, title, prenomen, denomination, surname, sign, *moniker, *handle. **2.** [Reputation] renown, honor, repute; see **fame 1**. **3.** [An epithet] nickname, pen name, pseudonym, sobriquet, stage name, *nom de plume, nom de guerre* (both French), pet name, fictitious name. Insulting names include the following—devil, imbecile, idiot, blackguard, rat, skunk, dog, pig, fool, moron, brute, *cochon, canaille* (both French), *ladrón, galopin* (both Spanish), *Schweinhund, Schweinigel, Lausejunge, Lausehund* (all German); bum, boob, oaf, goon, sourpuss, dumb Dora, specks, four-eyes, skinny, fatty, windbag, buttinski, meshugana; see also **insult**. **4.** [A famous person] star, hero, lion, a person of renown; see **celebrity**. —**call names**, swear at, castigate, slander; see **scold 1**. —**in the name of**, by authority of, in reference to, as representative of; see **for**. —**know only by name**, be familiar with, not know personally, have heard of; see **know 3**. —**to one's name**, belonging to one, in one's possession, possessed by; see **owned**.

name, *v.* **1.** [To give a name] call, christen, baptize, style, term, label, identify, provide with nomenclature, classify, denominate, title, entitle, nickname, characterize, label, ticket, *dub; see also **describe, define**. **2.** [To indicate by name] refer to, specify, signify, denote, single out, mark, suggest, connote, point to, note, remark, index, list, cite; see also **mention**. **3.** [To appoint] elect, nominate, select; see **delegate 1**.

name calling, *n.* insulting, abusing, derogating; see **insult**.

named, *a.* **1.** [Having as a name] called, designated, entitled, titled, termed, specified, styled, appellatea, denominated, christened, baptized, nicknamed, labeled, *tagged, *dubbed. **2.** [Chosen] appointed, commissioned, delegated, deputed, authorized, nominated, returned, elected, invested, vested, assigned, ordained, entrusted, picked, selected, chosen, decided *or* fixed upon, determined *or* settled on, picked out, preferred, favored, supported, approved, certified, called, anointed, consecrated, sanctioned, drafted, opted, declared, announced, singled out.

nameless, *a.* inconspicuous, undistinguished, obscure; see **unknown 2**.

namely, *a.* specifically, to wit, that is to say, particularly, by way of explanation, strictly speaking, in other words, in plain English.

naming, *n.* identifying, giving a name (to), finding a name (for); see **classification, description**.

nap, *n.* **1.** [A short sleep] siesta, cat nap, doze; see **rest 1, sleep**. **2.** [The finish of certain goods, especially fabric] pile, shag, surface; see **grain 2, outside 1, texture 1**.

napkin, *n.* serviette, paper napkin, (table) linen; see **towel**.

narcotic, *n.* stupefacient, anodyne, opiate; see **drug**.

narrate, *v.* recite, describe, reveal; see **report 1, tell 1**.

narrative, *a.* fictional, historical, reported; see **chronological**.

narrow, *a.* 1. [Lacking breadth] close, cramped, tight, confined, shrunken, compressed, slender, thin, fine, linear, threadlike, tapering, slim, spare, scant, scanty, lanky, small, meager; see also **thin 1.**—*Ant.* broad, wide, extensive. 2. [Lacking tolerance] dogmatic, narrow-minded, parochial; see **conservative, conventional 3, prejudiced**. 3. [Lacking a comfortable margin] close, near, precarious; see **dangerous, endangered, unsafe**.

narrowly, *a.* nearly, close(ly), by a (narrow) margin; see **almost**.

narrow-minded, *a.* bigoted, biased, provincial; see **conservative, conventional 3, prejudiced**.

narrowness, *n.* 1. [A physical restriction] confinement, slimness, restriction; see **barrier, interference 1**. 2. [A mental restriction] intolerance, bigotry, bias; see **prejudice, stubborness**.

nasty, *a.* 1. [Offensive to the senses] foul, gross, revolting; see **offensive 2, vulgar**. 2. [Indecent] immoral, immodest, smutty; see **lewd 2, shameful 1**. 3. [Unkind] sarcastic, critical, mean; see **cruel, fierce, ruthless 1**.

nation, *n.* 1. [An organized state] realm, country, commonwealth, republic, state, monarchy, dominion, body politic, land, domain, empire, kingdom, principality, sovereignty, colony; see also **government 1**. 2. [A people having some unity] populace, community, public; see **population, race 2, society 2**.

national, *a.* 1. [Concerning a nation] racial, political, sovereign, state, social, politic, civic, civil, communal, royal, imperial, federal; see also **governmental, public 2**. 2. [Operative throughout a nation] nation-wide, country-wide, inter-state, social, widespread, sweeping; see also **general 1**.

nationalism, *n.* provincialism, chauvinism, jingoism; see **loyalty, patriotism**.

nationality, *n.* native land, adopted country, political home; see **origin 2**.

nationally, *a.* politically, governmentally, as a state, as a country, publicly, of the people, throughout the country, transcending state boundaries, for the general welfare.

native, *a.* 1. [Natural] innate, inherent, inborn, implanted, inbred, ingrained, congenital, fundamental, hereditary, inherited, essential, constitutional; see also

natural 1.—*Ant.* unnatural, foreign, alien. 2. [Characteristic of a region] aboriginal, indigenous, original, primitive, primary, primeval, vernacular, domestic, local, found locally; see also **regional.**—*Ant.* imported, brought in, transplanted.

native, *n.* 1. [Aborigine] primitive, ancient, man of old; see **man 1**, 2. [Citizen] national, inhabitant, indigene; see **citizen, resident**.

natural, *a.* 1. [Rooted in nature] intrinsic, original, essential, true, fundamental, inborn, ingrained, inherent, instinctive, implanted, innate, inbred, subjective, inherited, congenital, genetic; see also **native 1.**—*Ant.* foreign, alien, acquired. 2. [To be expected] normal, typical, characteristic, usual, customary, habitual, accustomed, involuntary, spontaneous, uncontrolled, uncontrollable, familiar, common, universal, prevailing, prevalent, general, uniform, constant, consistent, ordinary, logical, reasonable, anticipated, looked for, hoped for, counted on, relied on; see also **regular 3.**—*Ant.* unknown, unexpected, unheard of. 3. [Not affected] ingenuous, simple, artless, innocent, unstudied, spontaneous, impulsive, childlike, unfeigned, open, frank, candid, unsophisticated, homey, unpretentious, forthright, sincere, straightforward, being oneself, unsuspecting, credulous, trusting, plain, direct, rustic; see also **naive.**—*Ant.* or-nate, pretentious, affected. 4. [Concerning the physical universe] actual, tangible, according to nature; see **physical 1, real**.

naturalist, *n.* botanist, zoologist, biologist; see **scientist**.

naturally, *interj.* certainly, absolutely, of course; see **surely, yes**.

naturally, *a.* 1. [In an unaffected manner] artlessly, spontaneously, innocently, candidly, openly, impulsively, freely, readily, easily, without restraint, directly; see also **simply, sincerely.**—*Ant.* awkwardly, restrainedly, clumsily. 2. [As a matter of course] casually, according to expectation, as anticipated, characteristically, typically, normally, commonly, usually, ordinarily, habitually, by nature, by birth, uniformly, generally, consistently; see also **regularly.**—*Ant.* strangely, astonishingly, amazingly.

nature, *n.* 1. [The external universe] cosmos, creation, macrocosm; see **universe**. 2. [The complex of essential qualities] characteristics, quality, constitution; see **character 1, essence 1**. 3. [Natural surroundings] outside world, out-of-doors, scenery, rural *or* natural setting, view, seascape, landscape, (the) outdoors, natural scenery, recreational facilities, the great outdoors; see also **environment, reality. 4.** [Natural forces] natural law, natural order, underlying cause, cosmic process, physical energy, kinetic energy, potential energy, water power, fission, fusion, atomic power, the sun, radiation, rays; see also **energy** 2. **5.** [Vital forces in an organism] creation, generation, regeneration; see **life** 1, 2, **strength. 6.** [Kind] species, sort, type; see **kind** 2, **variety** 1, 2. **—by nature,** inherently, by birth, as a matter of course; see **naturally** 2. **—of** (or **in**) **the nature of,** similar to, having the essential character of, as compared to; see **like.**

naughty, *a.* wayward, disobedient, mischievous, impish, fiendish, badly behaved, roguish, bad, unmanageable, ungovernable, insubordinate; see also **rude** 2, **unruly.**

nausea, *n.* motion sickness, queasiness, vomiting; see **illness** 1.

nauseate, *v.* sicken, offend, repulse; see **bother** 2, **disgust, disturb.**

nauseous, *a.* queasy, ill, squeamish; see **sick.**

nautical, *a.* ocean-going, marine, naval, oceanic, deep-sea, aquatic, sailing, seafaring, seaworthy, sea-going, boating, rowing, navigating; see also **maritime.**

naval, *a.* seagoing, marine, aquatic; see **maritime, nautical.**

navel, *n.* omphalos, depression, umbilicus; see **center** 1.

navigable, *a.* passable, deep enough, open; see **safe** 1.

navigate, *v.* pilot, steer, lie to, head out for, ride out, lay the course, operate; see also **drive** 2.

navigation, *n.* navigating, seamanship, piloting, aeronautics, flying, sailing, seafaring, ocean travel, exploration, voyaging, shipping, cruising, plotting a course, boating, coasting, spherical navigation.

navigator, *n.* seaman, explorer, mariner; see **pilot** 1, **sailor.**

navy, *n.* fleet, first line of defense, squadron, flotilla, armada, task force, submarine force, amphibious force, marine air arm, coast guard.

near, *a.* **1.** [Not distant in space] nigh, adjacent, adjoining, neighboring, not remote, close at hand, contiguous, handy, near *or* hard by, next door to, at close quarters, beside, side by side, in close proximity; see also **bordering.**— *Ant.* **distant,** removed, far off. **2.** [Not distant in relationship] touching, affecting, akin; see **friendly, related** 3. **3.** [Not distant in time] at hand, approaching, next; see **coming** 1, **expected.**

nearly, *a.* within a little, all but, approximately; see **almost.**

nearness, *n.* **1.** [Nearness in time or space] closeness, contiguity, proximity, vicinity, approximation, approach, intimacy, resemblance, likeness, handiness, close quarters, imminence, immediacy, loom, threat, menace, prospectiveness.— *Ant.* **distance,** remoteness, difference. **2.** [Nearness in feeling] familiarity, affection, intimacy; see **admiration, friendship.**

neat, *a.* **1.** [Clean and orderly] tidy, trim, prim, spruce, dapper, smart, correct, shipshape, methodical, regular, orderly, systematic, spotless, nice, dainty, elegant, spick-and-span, immaculate, chic, well-groomed, exact, precise, proper, neat as a pin, in good order, spruced up; see also **clean** 1.—*Ant.* unkempt, **disordered,** slovenly. **2.** [Clever; *said of something done*] dexterous, skillful, expert, proficient, handy, apt, ready, artful, nimble, agile, adept, speedy, finished, practiced, easy, effortless; see also **able.**—*Ant.* awkward, clumsy, fumbling.

neatly, *a.* **1.** [Arranged so as to present a neat appearance] tidily, orderly, systematically, methodically, correctly, exactly, uniformly, levelly, flatly, smoothly, regularly, precisely; see also **evenly** 1, **organized. 2.** [In an adroit manner] skillfully, deftly, agilely; see **cleverly, easily.**

neatness, *n.* cleanness, tidiness, orderliness; see **cleanliness.**

necessarily, *a.* vitally, fundamentally, importantly, indispensably, unavoidably, undeniably, certainly, as a matter of course, inescapably, irresistibly, inevitably, assuredly, significantly, undoubtedly, indubitably, positively, unquestionably, no doubt, without fail, of necessity, of course, by force, come what may, without recourse, beyond one's control, by its own nature, from within, by definition; see also **surely.**

necessary, *a.* important, (badly) needed, requisite, expedient, needful, indispensable, required, urgent, wanted, imperative, prerequisite, pressing, vital, fundamental, significant, momentous, compulsory, mandatory, basic, paramount, obligatory, essential, compelling, incumbent on *or* upon, all-important, binding, specified, unavoidable, decisive, crucial, elementary, chief, principal, prime, intrinsic, fixed, constant, permanent, inherent, ingrained, innate, without choice *or* appeal.

necessitate, *v.* compel, constrain, oblige; see **force.**

necessity, *n.* **1.** [The state of being required] need, essentiality, indispensability; see **requirement** 2. **2.** [That which is needed] need, want, requisite, vital part, essential, demand, imperative, fundamental, claim; see also **lack 2. 3.** [The state of being forced by circumstances] exigency, pinch, stress, urgency, extremity, privation, obligation, case of life or death; see also **emergency, poverty 1. —of necessity,** inevitably, importantly, surely; see **necessarily.**

neck, *n.* 1. [The juncture of the head and the trunk] cervical vertebræ, nape, scruff; see **throat.** 2. [The part of a dress at the neck, sense 1] neckband, neckline, collar line; see **dress 1, 2. —risk one's neck,** endanger oneself, gamble, take a chance; see **risk. —stick one's neck out,** endanger oneself, take a chance, gamble; see **risk.**

necklace, *n.* ornament, accessory, (string of) beads, jewels, chain, neckband, necklet, pearls, diamonds, choker; see also **jewelry.**

necktie, *n.* neckwear, knot, ascot; see **tie 2.**

need, *n.* 1. [Poverty] indigence, penury, pennilessness; see **poverty 1.** 2. [Lack] insufficiency, shortage, inadequacy; see **lack 1, 2. 3.** [A requirement] obligation, necessity, urgency; see **requirement 2. —if need be,** if it is required, if the occasion demands, if necessary; see **if.**

need, *v.* lack, require, feel the necessity for, be in need (of), suffer privation, be in want, be destitute, be short, be inadequate, have occasion for, have use *or* need for, miss, be *or* do without, be needy *or* poor, be deficient (in), go hungry, live from hand to mouth, *feel the pinch, *be down and out, be hard up, be up against it, do with; see also **want 1.—Ant. own,** have, hold.

needed, *a.* wanted, required, desired; see **necessary.**

needle, *n.* awl, spike, hypodermic (needle), syringe, phonograph needle, stylus, electric needle, electrolytic needle, probe, skewer, pin, darner.

*needle, *v.* quiz, question, nag; see **bother 2, examine.**

needless, *a.* unwanted, excessive, groundless; see **unnecessary, useless 1.**

need to, *v.* have to, be obligated to, have reason to; see **must.**

needy, *a.* destitute, indigent, penniless; see **poor 1.**

negate, *v.* repeal, retract, neutralize; see **cancel.**

negation, *n.* opposition, contradiction, repudiation; see **denial, refusal.**

negative, *a.* 1. [Involving a refusal] denying, contradictory, contrary, repugnant, contravening, rejecting, disallowing.—*Ant.* **favorable,** encouraging. 2. [Lacking positive qualities] absent, removed, neutralizing, counteractive, an-

nulling, invalidating.—*Ant.* **emphatic,** validating, affirmative.

negative, *n.* 1. [A refusal] contradiction, disavowal, refutation; see **denial, refusal.** 2. [A negative image] film, plate, developed film; see **image 2, picture 2.**

neglect, *n.* 1. [The act of showing indifference to a person] slight, disregard, thoughtlessness, disrespect, carelessness, scorn, oversight, heedlessness, inattention, unconcern, inconsideration, disdain, coolness; see also **indifference.** 2. [The act of neglecting duties or charges] negligence, slovenliness, neglectfulness; see **carelessness.**

neglect, *v.* 1. [To treat with indifference] slight, scorn, overlook, disregard, disdain, detest, rebuff, affront, despise, ignore, depreciate, spurn, underestimate, undervalue, shake off, make light of, laugh off, keep one's distance, pass over *or* up *or* by, have nothing to do with, let alone, let go, not care for, pay no attention to, leave alone, *not give a hoot *or* darn *or* damn, let the grass grow under one's feet, leave well enough alone, let (it) ride, *play possum, keep at arms length.—*Ant.* **consider,** appreciate, value. 2. [To fail to attend to responsibilities] pass over, defer, procrastinate, suspend, dismiss, discard, let pass *or* slip, miss, skip, let go, ignore, trifle, postpone, lose sight of, look the other way, let (it) go, not trouble oneself with, evade, be careless *or* irresponsible.—*Ant.* **watch,** care for, attend.

neglected, *a.* slighted, disregarded, scorned, disdained, despised, affronted, overlooked, ignored, spurned, omitted, undervalued, deferred, dismissed, passed over, postponed, evaded, deteriorated, underestimated, declined, lapsed, uncared for, unwatched, depreciated, unconsidered, shaken off, unused, unwanted, tossed aside, abandoned, forgotten, (out) in the cold, dropped, put on the shelf.—*Ant.* **considered,** cared for, heeded.

negligence, *n.* remissness, oversight, heedlessness; see **carelessness, indifference, neglect 1.**

negligent, *a.* indifferent, inattentive, neglectful; see **careless.**

negotiate, *v.* 1. [To make arrangements for] arrange, bargain, confer, consult, parley, transact, mediate, make peace, contract, settle, adjust, conciliate, accommodate, arbitrate, compromise, bring to terms, make terms, make the best of, treat with, moderate, work out, *dicker, haggle, bury the hatchet. 2. [To transfer] barter, allocate, transmit; see **assign, sell.**

negotiation, *n.* compromise, intervention, mediation; see **agreement.**

negro, *a.* black, negroid, African, black-skinned, dark-skinned, Afro-American, Afro-Asian, Ethiopian, brown; see also **black 2.**

Negro, *n.* black, Ethiopian, African, Afro-American, Afro-Asian, colored *or* Negroid person, black man, Black Panther, Black Muslim.

neighbor, *n.* acquaintance, bystander, next-door-neighbor, nearby resident; see also **friend.**

neighborhood, *n.* environs, block, vicinity, locality, proximity, district, closeness, nearness, precinct, community, region, zone, section, suburb, part, tract. —*in the neighborhood of, about, approximately, close to; see **near 1.**

neighboring, *a.* adjacent, adjoining, contiguous; see **bordering, near 1.**

neighborly, *a.* sociable, hospitable, helpful; see **friendly.**

neither, *a. and conj.* nor yet, also not, not either, not, not at all.

neither, *pron.* no one, nobody, neither one, not this one, nor this nor that, no one of two, not the one, not any one; see also **none 1, nothing.**

nephew, *n.* brother's *or* sister's son, grandnephew, son of a brother-in-law *or* sister-in-law, nephew by marriage; see also **niece, relative.**

nerve, *n.* 1. [The path of nervous impulses] nerve fiber, nerve tissue, nerve filament, nerve cord, nervure, venation. Types of nerves include the following—motor, sensory, efferent, afferent, effectors, receptors. 2. [Courage] resolution, spirit, mettle; see **courage.** 3. [Impudence] temerity, audacity, effrontery; see **rudeness.**

nerve-racking, *a.* exhausting, horrible, wearisome; see **difficult 1, painful 1.**

nerves, *n.* strain, tension, hysteria, emotional stress, sleeplessness; see **nervousness.** —*get on one's nerves, exasperate, irritate, annoy; see **bother 2.**

nervous, *a.* 1. [Excitable] sensitive, excitable, irritable, impatient, moody, peevish, restless, uneasy, impulsive, rash, hasty, reckless, touchy, readily upset, high-strung, neurotic; see also **unstable 2.** 2. [Excited] agitated, bothered, annoyed; see **excited.**

nervousness, *n.* stimulation, agitation, animation, intoxication, sensitivity, delirium, excitability, irascibility, impulsiveness, impetuosity, moodiness, hastiness, vehemence, impatience, feverishness, *the jerks, stage fright, *butterflies in the stomach, *the jitters, the shakes; see also **embarrassment, excitement.**—*Ant.* rest, calm, relaxation.

nest, *n.* den, cradle, incubator; see **retreat 2.**

nest egg, *n.* personal *or* accumulated savings, real *or* personal property, *something for a rainy day; see **money 1, savings.**

nestle, *v.* cuddle, snuggle, settle down, take shelter, lie close, make oneself snug, huddle, move close to, lie against, curl up (to).

net, *a.* clear, pure, remaining, exclusive, gross, excluding, irreducible, undeductible.

net, *n.* screen, mesh, fabric; see also **web.** Varieties of nets include the following—hair, mosquito, tennis, ping-pong, bird, butterfly, fish, draw, drag, drop, hand, landing, scoop, bag, purse.

net, *v.* make, clear, gain above expenses; see **profit 2.**

network, *n.* 1. [System of channels] tracks, circuitry, channels, system, labyrinth, artery, arrangement; see also **chain, wiring.** 2. [Netting] fiber, weave, mesh; see **goods, web.**

neurosis, *n.* compulsion, instability, mental disorder; see **insanity 1, nervousness, obsession.**

neurotic, *a.* disturbed, unstable, sick; see **insane, troubled.**

neurotic, *n.* paranoid, sick person, psychotic; see **madman.**

neutral, *a.* 1. [Not fighting] noncombatant, nonpartisan, on the side lines, nonparticipating, inactive, disengaged, uninvolved, bystanding, standing by, inert, on the fence.—*Ant.* engaged, involved, active. 2. [Without opinion] nonchalant, disinterested, impartial; see **indifferent.** 3. [Without distinctive color] drab, indeterminate, vague; see **dull 2.**

never, *a.* not ever, at no time, not at any time, not in the least, not in any way, in no way, not at all, not under any condition, nevermore, never again.

never-ending, *a.* timeless, endless, persistent; see **constant, eternal.**

never mind, *interj.* forget it, it doesn't matter, ignore it, don't bother, let it go, *drop it; see also **stop 2.**

nevertheless, *a.* not the less, nonetheless, notwithstanding; see **although, but 1.**

new, *a.* 1. [Recent] current, brand-new, newborn, young, new-fangled, late, just out; see also **fresh 1.** 2. [Modern] modish, popular, faddish, up to the minute, contemporary, latest; see also **fashionable, modern 1.** 3. [Novel] unique, original, bizarre; see **unusual 1, 2. 4.** [Different] unlike, dissimilar, distinct; see **unlike.** 5. [Additional] further, increased, supplementary; see **extra. 6.** [Inexperienced] unseasoned, unskilled, untrained; see **incompetent, inex-**

perienced. **7.** [Recently] newly, freshly, lately; see **recently.**

newcomer, *n.* immigrant, outsider, foreigner, tenderfoot, *maverick, *Johnny-come-lately; see also **alien, stranger.**

newfangled, *a.* novel, unique, new; see **fashionable, modern 1.**

newly, *a.* lately, anew, afresh; see **recently.**

newlywed, *n.* bride, bridegroom, honeymooner; see **husband, wife.**

newness, *n.* uniqueness, modernity, recentness; see **originality.**

news, *n.* **1.** [Information] intelligence, tidings, advice, discovery, recognition, *the scoop, *the goods, headlines, front-page news; see also **data, knowledge 1. 2.** [A specific report] telling, narration, recital, account, description, message, copy, communication, release, communiqué, telegram, cable, radiogram, broadcast, telecast, bulletin, dispatch, (news) story, *scoop, big news, *eye opener; see also **announcement.** —**make news,** become famous or notorious, accomplish, create events; see **expose, reveal.**

newspaper, *n.* publication, (daily) paper, journal, press, fourth estate, public press, sheet, tabloid, gazette; see also **record 1.** Varieties of newspapers include the following—daily, weekly, biweekly, metropolitan, rural, county, country, trade, provincial, community. Parts of newspapers include the following—front page section, news section, foreign news section, editorial page, state or city or local news section, domestic news section, magazine, business section, society section, women's section, sports section, entertainment or amusement section, comics or comic page, advertising section, syndicated section or *boiler plate.

newspaperman, *n.* newsman, journalist, member of the editorial department; see **author, editor, reporter, writer.**

New York, *n.* Manhattan, Greater New York, Metropolitan New York, Gotham, little old New York, Brooklyn, the Bronx, the Town, the (Big) City, the Garment Capital, Metropolis of America, Wall Street, Financial Capital; see also **city.**

next, *a.* **1.** [Following in order] succeeding, later, afterwards, presently, resulting, subsequent, ensuing; see also **following. 2.** [Adjacent] beside, close, alongside, on one or the side, adjoining, neighboring, meeting, touching, bordering (on), cheek by jowl, side by side, attached, abutting, back to back, to the left or right; see also **near 1.**

nibble, *n.* morsel, peck, cautious bite; see **bit 1, bite 1.**

nibble, *v.* nip, gnaw, snack; see **bite 1, eat 1.**

nice, *a.* **1.** [Approved] likable, superior, admirable; see **excellent. 2.** [Behaving in a becoming manner] pleasing, agreeable, winning, refined, cultured, amiable, delightful, charming, inviting, pleasant, cordial, courteous, considerate, kind, kindly, helpful, gracious, obliging, genial, gentle, becoming, unassuming, modest, demure; see also **friendly.**—*Ant.* **rude,** indecorous, crude.

nicely, *a.* **1.** [In a welcome manner] pleasantly, perfectly, pleasingly, amiably, winningly, creditably, acceptably, excellently, distinctively, happily, triumphantly, admirably, desirably, pleasurably, attractively, likably, enjoyably, beautifully, graciously, finely; see also **agreeably.**—*Ant.* **badly,** unfortunately, unsuccessfully. **2.** [In a becoming manner] winsomely, invitingly, charmingly; see **modestly, politely.**

niceness, *n.* discernment, taste, refinement; see **care 1, discretion, kindness 1.**

niche, *n.* cranny, corner, cubbyhole; see **hole 1.**

nick, *n.* indentation, notch, slit; see **cut 1, dent.**

nick, *v.* indent, notch, slit; see **cut 1, dent.**

nickel, *n.* **1.** [A mineral] *Ni,* metallic or chemical element, plating material; see **element 2, metal, mineral. 2.** [A coin made of nickel, sense 1] five-cent piece, coin, five cents, *five-center, *jitney; see also **money 1.**

niece, *n.* sister's or brother's daughter, niece by marriage, grandniece, daughter of a brother-in-law or sister-in-law; see also **nephew, relative.**

night, *n.* **1.** [The diurnal dark period] after dark, evening, from dusk to dawn, nightfall, after nightfall, twilight, nighttime, bedtime, midnight, before dawn, the dark hours, dead of night. **2.** [The dark] blackness, duskiness, gloom; see **darkness 1.**

night club, *n.* casino, discotheque, cabaret; see **bar 2, restaurant.**

nightly, *a.* nocturnal, in the hours of night, every twenty-four hours, during the hours of darkness, at night, each night, every night, by night; see also **regularly.**—*Ant.* **daily,** by day, diurnal.

nightmare, *n.* bad dream, horror, incubus; see **dream.**

nighttime, *n.* darkness, bedtime, dark of night; see **night 1.**

nimble, *a.* **1.** [Agile] quick, spry, active; see **agile, graceful 1. 2.** [Alert] quick-witted, bright, clever; see **intelligent.**

nip, *v.* nibble, snap, munch; see **bite 1, pinch.**

nipple, *n.* mamilla, mammary gland, teat; see **breast 2.**

no, *a.* and *interj.* (absolutely) not, not at all, by no means, the answer is in the negative, not by any means, none, *nyet* (Russian), *nix; see also **negative 2, neither, never.**

nobility, *n.* ruling class, gentry, peerage; see **aristocracy, royalty.**

noble, *a.* 1. [Possessing an exalted mind and character] generous, princely, magnanimous, magnificent, courtly, lofty, elevated, splendid, excellent, supreme, eminent, lordly, dignified, great, good, superior, great-hearted, high-minded, honorable, distinguished, liberal, tolerant, gracious, humane, benevolent, charitable, sympathetic, bounteous, brilliant, extraordinary, remarkable, devoted, heroic, resolute, valorous; see also **worthy.**—*Ant.* corrupt, low, ignoble. 2. [Possessing excellent qualities or properties] meritorious, virtuous, worthy, valuable, useful, first-rate, refined, cultivated, chivalrous, trustworthy, candid, liberal, gracious, princely, magnanimous, generous, sincere, truthful, constant, faithful, upright, honest, warmhearted, true, incorruptible, distinctive, reputable, respectable, admirable, good, aboveboard, fair, just, estimable; see also **excellent, perfect 2.**—*Ant.* poor, inferior, second-rate. 3. [Belonging to the nobility] titled, aristocratic, patrician, highborn, wellborn, blue-blooded, of gentle birth *or* blood, imperial, lordly, highbred, princely, of good breed, kingly; see also **royal.**—*Ant.* common, plebeian, lowborn. 4. [Grand] stately, impressive, imposing; see **grand.**

nobly, *a.* 1. [Majestically] aristocratically, illustriously, royally; see **generously 2, politely.** 2. [Honorably] fairly, respectably, honestly; see **justly 1.**

nobody, *a.* 1. [No one at all] no person, no one, not anybody; see **none 1.** 2. [A person of little importance] upstart, cipher, nonentity, whippersnapper, *no great shakes, *nix, zero.

nocturnal, *a.* at night, night-loving, nighttime; see **late 4, nightly.**

nod, *n.* dip, inclination, greeting; see **greeting.**

nod, *v.* 1. [To make a nodding movement] assent, sign, signal, greet, bend, curtsy, incline the head, bow, nod yes, acquiesce, consent, respond, fall in with, concur, acknowledge, recognize; see also **agree, approve.**—*Ant.* deny, dissent, disagree. 2. [To become sleepy or inattentive] drowse, nap, drift (off); see **sleep.**

noise, *n.* 1. [A sound] sound, something

heard *or* audible, impact of sound waves. Kinds of noises include the following—brief, loud noises: bang, boom, crash, thud, blast, blast off, roar, bellow, blat, shout, peal, cry, yelp, squawk, blare, clang, ring, shot, sonic boom, jangle, eruption, explosion, detonation; brief faint noises: peep, squeak, squawk, cackle, cluck, tweet, clink, tinkle, pop, whisper, stage whisper, sigh, splash, swish, note, sob, whine, whimper, plunk, plop, pat, ping, rustle, murmur, beat, stir, purr; soft *or* stifled *or* dulled *or* suppressed, etc. sound, still small voice; continuing noises: reverberation, ringing, tone, tune, clanging, tinkling, resonance, cacophony, rattle, whir, whistle, dissonance, discord, shouting, roaring, bellowing, rumble, rumbling, grunting, murmuring, drone, droning, thunder(ing), whine, screech(ing), scream(ing), banging, clanging, hum, humming, laugh(ing), chuckle, swishing, rustling, ripple, strumming, beating, patter(ing), clatter(ing), trill(ing), whinney(ing), neigh(ing), caw(ing), cackling. 2. [Clamor] racket, fracas, din; see **uproar.**

noiseless, *a.* 1. [Containing no noise] silent, still, soundless; see **quiet.** 2. [Making no noise] voiceless, speechless, wordless; see **dumb 1, mute 1.**

noiselessly, *a.* inaudibly, quietly, without a sound; see **silently.**

noisy, *a.* clamorous, vociferous, boisterous; see **loud 1, 2.**

nomad, *n.* wanderer, migrant, vagabond; see **traveler.**

nominal, *a.* professed, pretended, in effect only; see **given, named 1.**

nominate, *v.* propose as a candidate, designate for election, put up; see **choose, decide.**

nominated, *a.* designated, called, suggested; see **approved, named 2.**

nomination, *n.* naming, designation, proposal; see **appointment 1.**

nonchalance, *n.* apathy, disregard, insouciance; see **indifference.**

nonchalant, *a.* 1. [Cool and casual] uncaring, unconcerned, untroubled, apathetic, cold, frigid, unfeeling, impassive, imperturbable, easygoing, listless, lackadaisical, unruffled, lukewarm, composed, collected, aloof, detached, calm, serene, placid, disinterested, easy, effortless, light, smooth, neutral; see also **indifferent.**—*Ant.* warm, ardent, enthusiastic. 2. [Careless] negligent, neglectful, trifling; see **careless.**

nonchalantly, *a.* coolly, indifferently, casually; see **calmly.**

nonconformist, *n.* rebel, eccentric, maverick, malcontent, dissenter, demonstrator, hippie, protester, dissident, a different breed of cat; see also **radical.**

nonconformity, *n.* dissent, opposition, difference; see **individuality** 1.

none, *pron.* 1. [No person] no one, not one, not anyone, no one at all, not a person, not a soul, neither one (nor the other); see also **neither.—***Ant.* many, some, a few. 2. [No thing] not a thing, not anything, not any; see **nothing.**

nonetheless, *a.* nevertheless, in spite of that, anyway; see **although, but** 1.

nonexistent, *a.* missing, unsubstantial, fictitious; see **imaginary, unreal.**

nonpartisan, *a.* unprejudiced, unbiased, independent; see **neutral** 1.

nonpayment, *n.* failure, delinquency, bankruptcy; see **default.**

nonproductive, *a.* unproductive, waste, not producing; see **idle** 1, **useless** 1.

nonprofit, *a.* charitable, altruistic, humane; see **generous.**

nonresident, *a.* absentee, out-of-state, living abroad; see **foreign.**

nonsense, *n.* 1. [Matter that has no meaning] balderdash, rubbish, trash, scrawl, inanity, senselessness, buncombe, idle chatter, prattle, rant, bombast, claptrap, *bull, *baloney, *hooey, *bunk, *poppycock, *guff, *hot air. 2. [Frivolous behavior] unsteadiness, flightiness, stupidity, thoughtlessness, fickleness, foolishness, giddiness, rashness, infatuation, extravagance, imprudence, irrationality, madness, senselessness, inconsistency, shallowness.—*Ant.* consideration, steadiness, thoughtfulness. 3. [Pure fun] absurdity, jest, joke; see **fun.**

nonviolent, *a.* passive, passively, resistant, without violence; see **calm** 1, quiet.

nook, *n.* niche, cubbyhole, cranny; see **hole** 1.

noon, *n.* noontime, noontide, noonday, midday, twelve noon, meridian, noon hour; see also **time** 1, 2.

no one, *pron.* no man, not one, nobody; see **neither, none** 1.

noose, *n.* hitch, running knot, lasso; see **knot** 1, **rope.**

nor, *conj.* and not, not any, not either, not one, nor yet; see also **neither.**

normal, *a.* 1. [Usual] ordinary, run-of-the-mill, typical; see **common** 1, **conventional** 1, 3. 2. [Regular] routine, orderly, methodical; see **regular** 3. 3. [Sane] lucid, wholesome, right-minded; see **rational, reasonable, sane** 1. 4. [Showing no abnormal bodily condition] in good health, whole, sound; see **healthy.**

normality, *n.* 1. [Mediocrity] ordinariness, uniformity, commonness; see **regularity** 2. [Sanity] normalcy, mental balance, reason; see **sanity** 1.

normally, *a.* usually, commonly, in accordance with the *or* a norm; see **frequently, regularly** 1, 2.

north, *a.* 1. [Situated to the north] northward, northern, in the north, on the north side of, northerly, northmost, northernmost. 2. [Moving toward the north] northerly, northbound, northward, to the north, headed north, toward the North Pole, in a northerly direction; see also **south** 4. 3. [Coming from the north] northerly, southbound, headed south, out of the north, moving toward the equator, moving toward the South Pole; see also **south** 3. 4. [Associated with the north] polar, frozen, boreal; see **cold** 1.

north, *n.* the Barrens, tundra, northern section, northland, Northern Hemisphere, the north country, the north woods, Arctic regions, polar regions, the frozen north, land of ice and snow; see also **direction** 1.

northeast, *a.* NE, northeastern, northeasterly, northeastward(s), north-north-east (NNE), northeast by east (NEbE), northeast by north (NEbN); see also **direction** 1.

northerly, *a.* boreal, northern, polar; see **north** 2.

northern, *a.* northerly, arctic, polar; see **north** 1.

northwest, *a.* NW, nor'west, northwestern, northwesterly, northwestward(s), north-north-west (NNW), northwest by west (NWbW), northwest by north (NWbN); see also **direction** 1.

nose, *n.* 1. [The organ of smell] nasal organ, nasal cavity, nares, nasal passages, nostrils, olfactory nerves, *snoot, beak, bill; see also **organ** 2. 2. [A projection] snout, nozzle, muzzle; see **beak.** —by a nose, by a very small margin, too close for comfort, barely; see **almost.** —*look down one's nose at, disdain, snub, be disgusted by; see **abuse.** —*on the nose, precisely, to the point, correctly; see **accurate.** —turn up one's nose at, sneer at, refuse, scorn; see **abuse.** —under one's very nose, in plain sight, visible, at one's fingertips; see **obvious** 1.

nostalgia, *n.* remorse, wistfulness, sentimentality; see **loneliness.**

nostalgic, *a.* lonesome, regretful, sentimental; see **homesick, lonely.**

nosy, *a.* *snoopy, *snooping, unduly curious; see **inquisitive, interested** 2.

not, *a.* no, non-, un-, in-; see also **negative** 2.

notable, *a.* distinguished, important, striking; see **famous, unusual** 1.

not a little, *a.* great, large, copious; see **many, much** 1, 2.

not always, *a.* not usually, sometimes, occasionally; see **seldom.**

not at all, *a.* by no (manner of) means, definitely not, in no way; see **negative 2, no.**

notch, *n.* nock, nick, indent; see **cut 1, dent, groove.**

notch, *v.* indent, nick, chisel; see **cut 1, dent.**

notched, *a.* nicked, jagged, saw-toothed; see **irregular 4, rough 1.**

note, *n.* 1. [A representation] sign, figure, mark; see **representation.** 2. [A brief record] notation, jotting, scribble, reminder, scrawl, annotation, agenda, entry, memorandum, journal, inscription, calendar, diary; see also **notes, summary.** 3. [A brief communication] dispatch, epistle, announcement; see **letter 2.** 4. [A musical tone, or its symbol] tone, key, scale, shape note, interval, degree, step, sharp, flat, natural; see also **music 1.**

note, *v.* 1. [To notice] remark, heed, perceive; see **regard 1, see 1.** 2. [To record] write down, enter, transcribe; see **record 1, write.**

notebook, *n.* memorandum book, record book, diary; see **journal 1, record 1.**

noted, *a.* well-known, celebrated, notorious; see **famous.**

notes, *n.* commentary, interpretation, explanation, findings, recordings, field notes, observations; see also **data, records.** —**compare notes,** exchange views, confer, go over; see **discuss.** —**take notes,** write down, keep a record, enter; see **record 1.**

nothing, *n.* not anything, no thing, trifle, blank, emptiness, nothingness, nonexistence, inexistence, nonbeing, nullity, zero, extinction, oblivion, obliteration, annihilation, nonentity, neither hide nor hair. —**for nothing,** 1. gratis, without cost, unencumbered; see **free 4.** 2. in vain, for naught, emptily; see **unnecessary.** —**have nothing on,** have no evidence, be without proof, be only guessing; see **guess.** —**in nothing flat,** in almost no time at all, speedily, rapidly; see **quickly 1.** —**think nothing of,** minimize, underplay, disregard; see **neglect 1.**

nothing but, *a.* and *prep.* only that, nothing else, without exception; see **only 1, 3.**

*****nothing doing,** *interj.* certainly not, by no means, the reply is in the negative; see **no.**

nothingness, *n.* 1. [Void] vacuum, blank, hollowness; see **emptiness, nothing.** 2. [Worthlessness] pettiness, unimportance, smallness; see **insignificance.**

nothing to it, *a.* facile, slight, like taking candy from a baby; see **easy 2.**

notice, *n.* 1. [A warning] note, notification, intimation; see **sign 1, warning.** 2. [An announcement] comments, remark, enlightenment; see **announcement, declaration, report 1.** —**serve notice,** give warning, notify, announce; see **declare.** —**take notice,** become aware, pay attention, observe; see **see 1.**

notice, *v.* mark, remark, look at; see **see 1.**

noticeable, *a.* observable, appreciable, conspicuous; see **obvious 1.**

noticed, *a.* seen, remarked, observed; see **recorded.**

notify, *v.* declare, announce, inform; see **advertise, communicate, tell 1.**

notion, *n.* 1. [Opinion] idea, assumption, sentiment; see **opinion 1, thought 2.** 2. [Conception] whim, fancy, imagination; see **awareness, knowledge 1.**

not now, *a.* sometime, later, at another time; see **someday.**

notoriety, *n.* repute, renown, name; see **fame.**

notorious, *a.* ill-famed, infamous, disreputable; see **bad 1.**

not really, *a.* not entirely, doubtful, uncertain; see **questionable 1.**

notwithstanding, *a.* and *prep.* despite, in spite of, in any case *or* event; see also **although, but 1.**

not worth it, *a.* not good enough, too poor, inadequate; see **poor 2, worthless.**

noun, *n.* substantive, common noun, proper noun; see **label, name 1.**

nourish, *v.* feed, supply, sustain; see **provide 1, support 5.**

nourishing, *a.* healthy, nutritious, full of vitamins, proteins, etc.; see **healthful.**

nourishment, *n.* nurture, nutriment, provender; see **food.**

novel, *a.* new, odd, strange; see **unique, unusual 1, 2.**

novel, *n.* paperback, best-seller, fiction; see also **book, story.** Types of novels include the following—romance, detective story, love story, novella, adventure story, ghost story, mystery, western, science fiction *or* fantasy; historical, sectional, regional, naturalistic, Gothic, biographical, psychological, pornographic, satirical, adventure, supernatural, etc., novel; thriller, *****porn.**

novelist, *n.* fiction writer, fictionist, story-teller, narrative writer, writer of novels, writer of prose fiction; see also **author 2, writer.**

novelty, *n.* 1. [The quality of being novel] recentness, modernity, freshness; see **originality.** 2. [Something popular because it is new] innovation, origination, creation; see **fad**.

November, *n.* fall *or* autumn (month), Thanksgiving (season), hunting season; see also **month**.

novice, *n.* beginner, learner, neophyte; see **amateur**.

now, *a.* 1. [At the present] at this time, right now, at this *or* the moment, just now, momentarily, this day, these days, here and now, for the nonce. 2. [In the immediate future] promptly, in a moment, in a minute; see **soon** 1. 3. [Immediately] at once, forthwith, instantly; see **immediately**.

nowadays, *a.* in these days, in this age, in the present age; see **now** 1.

now and then, *a.* sometimes, infrequently, occasionally; see **seldom**.

no way, *a.* not at all, on no account, by no means, not a bit of it, nowhere(s) near, in no case *or* respect.

nowhere, *a.* not anywhere, not in any place, not at any place, nowhere at all, in no place, to no place.

nozzle, *n.* spout, outlet, vent; see also **end** 4.

nuance, *n.* subtlety, refinement, distinction; see **difference** 1.

nuclear bomb, *n.* nuclear armament *or* warhead; hydrogen bomb *or* H-bomb, atomic bomb *or* A-bomb, cobalt bomb *or* C-bomb, etc.; atomic *or* nuclear weapon; see also **arms**.

nucleus, *n.* 1. [Essence] core, gist, kernel; see **essence** 1, **matter** 1. 2. [Center] hub, focus, pivot; see **center** 1.

nude, *a.* stripped, unclothed, bare; see **naked** 1.

nude, *n.* naked body *or* man *or* woman, nudist, pin-up, model, *stripper, *peeler.

nudge, *n.* tap, poke, shove; see **bump** 1, **push, touch** 2.

nudge, *v.* poke, bump, tap; see **push** 1, **touch** 1.

nudity, *n.* bareness, nudeness, undress; see **nakedness**.

nugget, *n.* ingot, bullion, chunk; see **gold, rock** 1.

nuisance, *n.* 1. [A bother] annoyance, vexation, bore; see **trouble** 2. 2. [An offense against the public] breach, infraction, affront; see **crime** 1. 3. [An unpleasant *or* unwelcome person] problem (child), frump, bother, *holy terror, *bad egg, *insect, *louse, *pain in the neck, *poor excuse, *bum; see also **trouble** 1.

null, *a.* invalid, vain, unsanctioned; see **void**.

numb, *a.* 1. [Insensible] deadened, dead, unfeeling, (be)numbed, asleep, senseless, anesthetized, comatose; see also **paralyzed**. 2. [Insensitive] apathetic, lethargic, phlegmatic; see **indifferent**.

numb, *v.* paralyze, stun, dull; see **deaden** 1.

number, *n.* amount, sum total, totality, aggregate, whole, whole number, product, measurable quantity, estimate, the lot, plenty, abundance; see also **quantity**. —*get (*or* have) one's number,* discover one's true character, find out about, know; see **understand** 1. —*one's number is up,* one's time to die has arrived, one's time has come, one's destiny is fulfilled; see **doomed**. —*without number,* too numerous to be counted, innumerable, countless; see **many**.

number, *v.* count, calculate, enumerate; see **add** 1, **total**.

numbered, *a.* designated, told, enumerated, checked, specified, indicated; see also **marked** 1.

numbness, *n.* deadness, anesthesia, dullness, insensitivity, insensibility, paralysis, loss of motion *or* sensation.

numeral, *n.* character, cipher, digit; see **number**.

numerical, *a.* arithmetical, statistical, fractional, exponential, logarithmic, differential, integral, digital, mathematical, binary.

numerous, *a.* copious, various, diverse; see **infinite, many**.

nun, *n.* sister, religious woman, one who has taken vows, anchorite, prioress, mother superior, ecclesiastic; see also **ministry**.

nuptials, *n.* wedding, matrimony, marriage ceremony; see **marriage**.

nurse, *n.* 1. [One who cares for the sick] attendant, male nurse, practical nurse, private nurse, registered nurse (R.N.), floor nurse, night nurse, day nurse, doctor's assistant, student nurse, nurse's aide, therapist, Red Cross nurse, *Florence Nightingale. 2. [One who cares for the young] nursemaid, babysitter, tutor; see **attendant**.

nurse, *v.* attend *or* minister (to), aid, medicate; see **heal, sustain** 2, **tend** 1, **treat** 3.

nursery, *n.* 1. [A place for children] child's room, playroom, nursery school; see **school** 1. 2. [A place for plants] hothouse, hotbed, green house; see **building**.

nurture, *v.* nourish, care for, provide (for); see **feed, sustain** 2.

nut, *n.* 1. [A dry fruit] seed, kernel, stone; see also **fruit**. Common nuts include the following—acorn, beechnut, peanut, hazelnut, black walnut, English walnut, almond, nutmeg, pecan, filbert, coconut, pistachio, cashew, pignut, chestnut, butternut, (swamp *or* shellbank) hickory, kola nut, Brazil nut, betel nut. 2. [A threaded metal block] bur, lock nut, cap, ratchet nut; see **bolt**. 3. [*An eccentric or insane person] eccentric, fanatic, maniac; see **zealot**.

nutriment, *n.* nourishment, provisions, sustenance; see **food**.

nutrition, *n.* diet, nourishment, victuals; see **food**, **subsistence** 1.

nutritive. *a.* edible, wholesome, nutritious; see **healthful**.

*****nuts**, *a.* crazy, deranged, ridiculous; see **insane**, **unusual** 2.

nuzzle, *v.* caress, cuddle, snuggle; see **nestle**.

nylon, *n.* synthetic(s), polyamide product; synthetic fiber *or* cloth *or* plastic, etc.; see **plastic**.

nymph, *n.* nature goddess, sprite, mermaid; see **fairy**.

O

oak, *n.* **1.** [An oak tree] willow, laurel, casuarina; see also **tree**. **2.** [Oak woods] hardwood, oaken wood, oak paneling; see also **wood 2**.

oar, *n.* pole, sweep, scull; see **tool 1**.

oasis, *n.* green *or* fertile area, irrigated land(s), watered tract, garden spot, desert garden, water hole, watering place, desert resting place; see also **refuge 1**, **retreat 2**.

oath, *n.* **1.** [An attestation of the truth] affirmation, declaration, affidavit, vow, sworn statement, testimony, word, contract, pledge; see also **promise 1.**—*Ant.* denial, disavowal, lie. **2.** [The name of the Lord taken in vain] malediction, swearword, blasphemy; see **curse 1**.

obedience, *n.* docility, submission, compliance; see **willingness**.

obedient, *a.* **1.** [Dutiful] loyal, lawabiding, governable, resigned, devoted, respectful, controllable, attentive, obliging, willing, tractable, deferential, under the control of, at one's command *or* nod, at one's beck and call, *on a string, *wrapped around one's (little) finger; see also **faithful.**—*Ant.* **unruly**, disobedient, undutiful. **2.** [Docile] pliant, acquiescent, compliant; see **docile**.

obediently, *a.* dutifully, submissively, loyally; see **willingly**.

obese, *a.* corpulent, plump, stout; see **fat**.

obey, *v.* submit, answer (to), respond, act (upon *or* on), bow to, surrender, yield, perform, do, carry out, attend to orders, do what one is told, accept, consent, do what is expected of one, do one's duty, do as one says, come at call, serve, concur, assent, conform, acquiesce, mind, take orders, do one's bidding, comply, fulfill; see also **agree.**—*Ant.* **rebel**, disobey, mutiny.

object, *n.* **1.** [A corporeal body] article, something, gadget; see **thing 1**. **2.** [A purpose] objective, aim, wish; see **purpose 1**. **3.** [One who receives] recipient, target, victim; see **receiver**.

object, *v.* protest, take exception (to), dispute; see **complain 1**.

objection, *n.* disapproval, scruple, hesitation, question, criticism, complaint, charge, accusation, reprimand, exception, admonition, reproach, dispute, opposition, adverse comment, rejection, ban, countercharge, grievance, contradiction, censure, abuse, scolding, denunciation, lecture, disagreement, difference, disdain, insistence, condemnation, grumbling, faultfinding, reproof, dissent, insinuation, complaining, frown, blame, sarcasm, wail, groan, murmur, lament, regret, aspersion, *beef, *gripe, *kick, demurring, reluctance, unwillingness, rejection, dislike, dissatisfaction, discontent, displeasure, low opinion, abhorrence, dubiousness; see also **doubt.**—*Ant.* **permission**, acceptance, desire.

objectionable, *a.* **1.** [Revolting] gross, repugnant, abhorrent; see **offensive 2**. **2.** [Undesirable] unacceptable, unsatisfactory, inexpedient; see **undesirable**.

objective, *a.* **1.** [Existing independently of the mind] actual, external, material, scientific, sure, extrinsic, measurable, extraneous, reified, tactile, corporeal, bodily, palpable, physical, sensible, outward, outside, determinable, unchangeable, invariable; see also **real 2.**—*Ant.* **mental**, subjective, introspective. **2.** [Free from personal bias] detached, impersonal, unbiased; see **accurate 2**, **fair 1**.

objective, *n.* goal, aim, aspiration; see **purpose 1**.

objectively, *a.* impartially, indifferently, neutrally, open-mindedly, dispassionately, justly, equitably, detachedly, soberly, accurately, candidly, considerately, not subjectively, with objectivity *or* impartiality *or* (due) consideration *or* (good) judgment, etc.; without prejudice *or* bias *or* partiality *or* passion, etc.

object to, *v.* disapprove, doubt, question; see **oppose 1**.

obligate, *v.* bind, restrict, constrain; see **force**.

obligation, *n.* responsibility, burden, debt; see **duty 1**.

obligatory, *a.* required, essential, binding; see **necessary**.

oblige, *v.* **1.** [To accommodate] assist, aid, contribute; see **accommodate 1**, **help**. **2.** [To require] compel, coerce, bind; see **force**, **require 2**.

obliged, *a.* compelled, obligated, required; see **bound 2**.

obliging, *a.* amiable, accommodating, helpful; see **kind**.

obligingly, *a.* helpfully, thoughtfully, graciously; see **agreeably**.

oblique, *a.* **1.** [Slanting] inclined, inclining, diverging, leaning, sloping, angled, askew, asymmetrical, turned, twisted, awry, strained, askance, distorted, off level, sideways, slanted, tipping, tipped, at an angle, on the bias; see also **bent**, crooked 1.—*Ant.* vertical, perpendicular, straight.

oblivion, *n.* nonexistence, obscurity, void; see **emptiness, nothing.**

oblivious, *a.* abstracted, preoccupied, absorbed; see **absent-minded, dreamy.**

oblong, *a.* elongated, rectangular, oval, elliptical, egg-shaped. —*Ant.* **square,** circle, circular.

obnoxious, *a.* annoying, disagreeable, displeasing; see **offensive 2.**

obscene, *a.* wanton, lustful, lascivious; see **lewd 2.**

obscenity, *n.* vulgarity, impropriety, smut; see **indecency, lewdness.**

obscure, *a.* 1. [Vague] indistinct, ambiguous, indefinite, indecisive, unintelligible, impenetrable, inscrutable, unfathomable, unclear, vague, involved, undecisive, undefined, intricate, illegible, incomprehensible, hazy, dark, dim, inexplicable, inconceivable, unbelievable, incredible, complicated, illogical, unreasoned, mixed up, doubtful, questionable, dubious, inexact, unreasoned, loose, ill-defined, unidentified, invisible, undisclosed, perplexing, cryptic, escaping notice, mystical, secret, enigmatic, concealed, mysterious, esoteric, puzzling, lacking clarity, unreadable, contradictory, out of focus, unrelated, *clear as mud, over one's head, deep, *far out; see also **complex 2, confused 2, confusing, difficult 2.**—*Ant.* clear, definite, distinct. 2. [Dark] cloudy, dense, hazy; see **dark 1.** 3. [Little known] unknown, rare, hidden, covered, remote, reticent, secretive, seldom seen, unseen, inconspicuous, humble, invisible, mysterious, deep, cryptic, enigmatic, esoteric, arcane, undisclosed, dark; see also **distant, irrelevant, profound.**

obscure, *v.* 1. [To dim] shadow, cloud, screen; see **shade 2.** 2. [To conceal] cover, veil, wrap (up); see **disguise, hide 1.**

obscurely, *a.* dimly, darkly, thickly; see **vaguely.**

obscurity, *n.* vagueness, dimness, fuzziness; see **uncertainty 1, 2.**

observable, *a.* perceptible, noticeable, discernible; see **obvious 1.**

observance, *n.* 1. [A custom] ritual, practice, rite; see **custom 2.** 2. [Attention] awareness, observation, notice; see **attention 1.**

observant, *a.* keen, alert, penetrating, wide-awake, discerning, perceptive, sharp, eager, interested, discovering, detecting, discriminating, judicious, searching, understanding, questioning, deducing, surveying, considering, sensitive, clear-sighted, comprehending, bright, intelligent, *on the ball *or* beam, *on one's toes; see also **intelligent 1.**—

Ant. **thoughtless,** unobservant, insensitive.

observation, *n.* 1. [The power of observing] seeing, recognizing, perception; see **sight 1.** 2. [A remark] comment, note, commentary; see **remark, speech 3.**

observe, *v.* 1. [To watch] scrutinize, inspect, examine; see **see, watch.** 2. [To comment] note, remark, mention; see **comment.** 3. [To commemorate] dedicate, solemnize, keep; see **celebrate 1.** 4. [To abide by] conform to, comply, adopt; see **follow 2, obey.**

observed, *a.* 1. [Noticed] seen, noted, marked; see **recognized.** 2. [Commemorated] kept, celebrated, recalled; see **remembered.**

observer, *n.* watcher, watchman, sentinel, lookout, sentry, guard, detective, policeman, spy, spectator, eyewitness, beholder, onlooker, bystander, passer-by, meddler, peeper, voyeur, prying person, *peeping Tom; see also **witness.**

obsess, *v.* dominate, possess, hound; see **haunt 2.**

obsessed, *a.* haunted, beset, controlled; see **troubled 1, 2.**

obsession, *n.* fixation, fascination, passion, fancy, phantom, craze, delusion, mania, infatuation, fixed idea, compulsion, *bee in one's bonnet, *hang-up; see also **fantasy.**

obsolete, *a.* antiquated, archaic, out-of-date; see **old 2, 3, old-fashioned.**

obstacle, *n.* restriction, obstruction, hindrance; see **barrier.**

obstinate, *a.* firm, headstrong, opinionated; see **stubborn.**

obstinately, *a.* doggedly, bullheadedly, persistently; see **stubbornly.**

obstruct, *v.* stop, interfere, bar; see **hinder, prevent.**

obstruction, *n.* difficulty, trouble, roadblock; see **barrier, impediment 1.**

obtain, *v.* 1. [To gain possession] take, acquire, seize; see **get 1.** 2. [Pertain] be pertinent to, appertain to, bear upon; see **concern 1.**

obtainable, *a.* ready, attainable, achievable; see **available.**

obvious, *a.* 1. [Clearly apparent to the eye] clear, visible, apparent, public, transparent, observable, perceptible, exposed, noticeable, plain, conspicuous, overt, glaring, prominent, standing out, light, bright, open, unmistakable, evident, recognizable, discernible, in evidence, in view *or* sight, perceivable, discoverable, distinguishable, palpable, distinct, *clear as a bell *or* day, *hitting one in the face; see also **definite 2.**—*Ant.* **obscure,** hidden, indistinct. 2. [Clearly apparent to the mind] lucid, apparent, conclusive, explicit, understood, intelligible, comprehensible, self-evident, indisputable, unquestionable, undeniable, proverbial, aphoristic, reasonable, broad, unambiguous, on the surface, *as plain as the nose on one's face, *going without saying, *staring one in the face, *open and shut; see also **understandable.**—*Ant.* profound, ambiguous, equivocal.

obviously, *a.* without doubt, unmistakably, certainly; see **clearly 1, 2.**

obviously, *interj.* of course, yes, evidently; see **surely.**

occasion, *n.* 1. [An event] occurrence, incident, happening; see **event 1, 2. 2.** [An opportunity] chance, excuse, opening; see **opportunity 1, possibility 2.** —**on occasion,** once in a while, sometimes, occasionally; see **hardly, seldom.**

occasional, *a.* 1. [Occurring at odd times] sporadic, random, infrequent; see **irregular 1. 2.** [Intended for special use] especial, particular, specific; see **exclusive, special 1.**

occasionally, *a.* infrequently, at random, irregularly; see **hardly, seldom.**

occult, *a.* secret, magical, supernatural; see **mysterious 2.**

occupancy, *n.* possession, occupation, inhabitance; see **deed 2, ownership.**

occupant, *n.* lessee, inhabitant, renter; see **resident, tenant.**

occupation, *n.* 1. [The act of occupying] seizure, entering, invasion; see **attack, capture. 2.** [A vocation] calling, affair, chosen work; see **job 1, profession 1, trade 2.**

occupational, *a.* professional, career, vocational, technical, workaday, official, industrial.

occupied, *a.* 1. [Busy] engaged, working, engrossed; see **busy 1. 2.** [Full] in use, leased, taken; see **rented.**

occupy, *v.* 1. [To take possession] conquer, take over, invade; see **get 1, seize 2. 2.** [To fill space] remain, tenant, reside, live in, hold, take up, pervade, keep, own, (be in) command, extend, control, maintain, involve, permeate; see also **fill 2.**—*Ant.* empty, remove, move. 3. [To absorb attention] engage, engross, attend, monopolize, interest, immerse, arrest, absorb, take up, utilize, involve, keep busy, busy, be active with, be concerned with; see also **fascinate.**

occupying, *a.* 1. [Filling a place] holding, remaining, situated, posted, assigned to, tenanting, residing, living in, taking up, possessing, pervading, covering, settled on, controlling, maintaining, commanding, sitting, staying, established in or at, owning, *set up, *running; see also **placed.**—*Ant.* gone, leaving, removing. 2. [Engaging attention] absorbing, engrossing, concerned with, monopolizing,

engaging, arresting, working at, attracting, focusing, drawing, exacting, requiring; see also **exciting, interesting.**

occur, *v.* take place, transpire, befall; see **happen 1, 2.**

occurrence, *n.* happening, incident, episode; see **event.**

occur to, *v.* come to mind, present or offer or suggest itself, spring, issue, rise, appear, catch one's attention, strike one, pass through one's mind, impress one, enter or cross one's mind, crop up.

ocean, *n.* great sea, high seas, salt water, seashore, seaside, shores, the mighty deep, the main, the great waters, the Seven Seas; see also **sea.** Oceans include the following—Atlantic, Pacific, Arctic, Antarctic, Indian, North Atlantic, South Atlantic, North Pacific, South Pacific.—*Ant.* earth, lake, river.

ocean floor, *n.* sea bed, bottom of the sea, offshore lands; see **sea bottom.**

Oceania, *n.* islands, South Sea Islands, Pacific Islands, Hawaii, Polynesia, Samoa, desert islands, tropics.

oceanic, *a.* marine, aquatic, pelagic; see **maritime, nautical.**

October, *n.* fall or autumn or harvest month, Indian summer, hunting season; see also **autumn, month.**

odd, *a.* 1. [Unusual] queer, unique, strange; see **unusual 2. 2.** [Miscellaneous] fragmentary, odd-lot, varied; see **various. 3.** [Single] sole, unpaired, unmatched; see **alone. 4.** [Not even] remaining, over and above, leftover; see **irregular 1, 4.**

oddly, *a.* curiously, ridiculously, inexplicably; see **foolishly, strangely.**

odds, *n.* 1. [An advantage] allowance, edge, benefit, difference, superiority, *place money, *show money; see also **advantage. 2.** [A probability] favor, superiority, chances; see **chance 1.**

odds and ends, *n.* miscellany, scraps, particles; see **remnants, rummage 2.**

odor, *n.* perfume, fragrance, bouquet; see **smell 1, 2.**

odorless, *a.* flat, scentless, unaromatic, unperfumed, unsmelling, unscented, without odor, odor-free, unfragrant, lacking fragrance.

odorous, *a.* 1. [Having an offensive odor] smelly, stinking, putrid; see **offensive 2, rotten 1. 2.** [Having a pleasant odor] spicy, sweet-smelling, fragrant; see **sweet 3.**

of, *prep.* from, out of or from, away from, proceeding or coming or going from, about, concerning, as concerns, appropriate or pertaining or appertaining or peculiar or attributed to, characterized by, regarding, as regards, in regard to, referring to, with or in reference to, like, belonging or related to, having relation to, native to, consequent to, based on, akin to, connected with; see also **about** 2.

off, *a.* and *prep.* 1. [Situated at a distance] ahead, behind, up front, to one side, divergent, beside, aside, below, beneath, above, far, absent, not here, removed, apart, in the distance, at a distance, gone, away; see also **distant.–Ant.** here, at hand, present. 2. [Moving away] into the distance, away from, farther away, disappearing, vanishing, removing, turning aside; see also **away** 1.–*Ant.* returning, coming, approaching. 3. [Started] initiated, commenced, originated; see **begun.** 4. [Mistaken] erring, in error, confused; see **mistaken** 1, **wrong** 2. 5. [*Crazy] odd, peculiar, queer; see **insane.** 6. [*Not employed] not on duty, on vacation, gone; see **unemployed.**

off and on, *a.* now and again *or* then, sometimes, occasionally; see **seldom.**

off balance, *a.* unbalanced, tipsy, eccentric; see **irregular** 1, **unstable.**

off base, *a.* incorrect, faulty, erroneous; see **mistaken** 1, **wrong** 2.

off center, *a.* off-centered, not centered, eccentric; see **irregular** 1, **unstable.**

off course, *a.* strayed, drifting, misguided; see **lost** 1.

offend, *v.* annoy, affront, outrage; see **bother** 2.

offended, *a.* vexed, provoked, exasperated; see **angry, insulted.**

offense, *n.* 1. [A misdeed] misdemeanor, malfeasance, transgression; see **crime, sin.** 2. [An attack] assault, aggression, battery; see **attack.** Styles of offense in football include the following–running *or* rushing *or* ground attack, passing *or* aerial attack, straight football, power plays, flying wedge, razzle-dazzle. Styles of offense in basketball include the following–five-man attack, four-man offense, slow-breaking attack, fast-breaking attack. 3. [Resentment] umbrage, pique, indignation; see **anger.**

offensive. *a.* 1. [Concerned with an attack] assaulting, attacking, invading; see **aggressive.** 2. [Revolting] disgusting, horrid, repulsive, shocking, dreadful, detestable, repugnant, obnoxious, hideous, horrible, displeasing, disagreeable, repellent, nauseating, invidious, nauseous, revolting, distasteful, unspeakable, accursed, unutterable, terrible, grisly, ghastly, filthy, bloody, gory, hateful, low, foul, corrupt, bad, indecent, nasty, dirty, unclean, filthy, sickening, malignant, rancid, putrid, vile, impure, beastly, monstrous, coarse, loathsome, abominable, stinking, reeking, obscene, smutty, damnable, distressing, irritating, unpleasant, contaminated, frightful, unattractive, forbidding, repelling, incompatible, unsavory, intolerable, unpalatable, dissatisfactory, unpleasing, unsuited, objectionable, to one's disgust, beneath contempt, *(giving) bad vibes, *gosh-awful, *icky, *lousy; see also **revolting.–Ant.** pleasant, agreeable, likable. 3. [Insolent] impertinent, impudent, insulting; see **rude** 2.

offensive, *n.* position of attack, invasion, assault; see **attack.**

offer, *n.* proposal, presentation, proposition; see **suggestion** 1.

offer, *v.* 1. [To present] proffer, tender, administer, donate, put forth, advance, extend, submit, hold out, grant, allow, award, volunteer, accord, place at one's disposal, lay at one's feet, put up; see also **contribute, give** 1.–*Ant.* refuse, withhold, keep. 2. [To propose] suggest, submit, advise; see **propose** 1.

offering, *n.* contribution, donation, present; see **gift** 1.

offhand, *a.* at the moment, unprepared, impromptu, informal, extemporary, unpremeditated, spontaneous, unstudied, unrehearsed, improvised, by ear.

office, *n.* 1. [A position involving responsibility] employment, business, occupation; see **job** 1, **profession** 1, **trade** 2. 2. [A function] performance, province, service; see **duty** 1. 3. [A place in which office work is done] room, office building, factory, bureau, agency, warehouse, facility, school building; see also **building, department.** Types of offices include the following–governmental, school principal's, counseling, secretarial, stenographic, filing, typing, insurance, data processing, real estate, brokerage, law, bank, foreign, consular, doctor's, dentist's, advertising agency, booking office, box office.

officer, *n.* 1. [An executive] manager, director, president; see **executive, leader** 2. 2. [One who enforces civil law] magistrate, military police, deputy; see **policeman.** 3. [One holding a responsible post in the armed forces] American officers include the following–*Army commissioned and special officers:* Commander in Chief, Five-star General, Four-star General, Three-star General, Two-star General, General of the Army, Lieutenant General, Major General, Brigadier General, Colonel, Lieutenant Colonel, Major, Captain, First Lieutenant, Second Lieutenant, Chief of Staff; *Navy commissioned officers:* Admiral of the Fleet *or* Fleet Admiral, Admiral, Rear Admiral, Vice Admiral, Captain, Commander, Lieutenant Commander, Lieutenant, Lieutenant, junior grade; Ensign; *Army noncommissioned officers:* Chief Warrant Officer; Warrant Officer, junior grade; Master Sergeant, First Sergeant, Technical Sergeant, Staff Sergeant, Sergeant, Corporal.

official, *a.* **1.** [Having to do with one's office] formal, fitting, suitable, precise, established, according to precedent *or* protocol, proper, correct, accepted, recognized, customary; see also **conventional 1, 3, fit 1.**—*Ant.* informal, unceremonious, ill-fitting. **2.** [Authorized] ordered, endorsed, sanctioned; see **approved. 3.** [Reliable] authoritative, authentic, trustworthy; see **certain 3, genuine 1, reliable 2.**

official, *n.* **1.** [Administrator] comptroller, director, administrator; see **executive, leader 2. 2.** [A sports official] referee, umpire, linesman; see **umpire.**

officially, *a.* **1.** [In an official manner] regularly, formally, orderly, suitably, according to form, ceremoniously, in set form, precisely, according to precedent, conventionally, in an established manner, as prescribed, according to protocol, all in order, correctly, properly, customarily. **2.** [With official approval] authoritatively, authorized, sanctioned; see **approved.**

offset, *v.* counterbalance, compensate, allow for; see **balance 2.**

offspring, *n.* progeny, issue, descendant(s), children, sibling(s), lineage, generation, brood, seed, family, heirs, offshoot(s), heredity, succession, successor(s), next generation; see also **baby, child.**

off the record, *a.* not for publication, restricted, confidential; see **secret 1, 3.**

off work, *a.* not on duty *or* working, gone (home), not employed; see **unemployed.**

often, *a.* usually, many times, oftentimes; see **frequently.**

oh, *interj.* indeed! oh-oh! oh, no! oh, yes! oops; see also **no, yes.**

oil, *n.* **1.** [Liquid, greasy substance] melted fat, unction, lubricant; see **grease.** Common oils include the following—vegetable, animal, mineral, saturated, poly-unsaturated, fatty, volatile, essential, machine, crude, lubricating, cottonseed, olive, castor, palm, corn, safflower, whale, cocoa, linseed, drying, nondrying, soybean, sesame, cod-liver, fish; lard, tallow, oleo, Vaseline (trademark), turpentine. **2.** [Liquid substance used for power or illumination] petroleum, kerosene, coal oil, crude oil, liquid coal, rock *or* fossil oil; see also **fuel.**

oil, *v.* lubricate, smear, coat with oil; see **grease.**

oily, *a.* **1.** [Rich with oil] fatty, greasy, buttery, oil-soaked, rich, lardy, bland, oleaginous, soapy, soothing, creamy, oil-bearing. —*Ant.* **dry,** dried, gritty. **2.** [Having a surface suggestive of oil] oiled, waxy, sleek, slippery, smooth, polished, lustrous, bright, brilliant, gleaming, glistening, shining; see also **smooth 1, 2.**—*Ant.* **rough,** dull, unpolished. **3.** [Unctuous] fulsome, sauve, flattering; see **affected 2, treacherous.**

ointment, *n.* unguent, lotion, cream; see **balm 1, medicine 2.**

O.K., *interj.* all right, correct, surely; see **yes.**

O.K., *n.* approval, endorsement, affirmation; see **permission.**

O.K., *v.* confirm, condone, notarize; see **approve, endorse 2.**

old, *a.* **1.** [No longer vigorous] aged, elderly, partriarchal, gray, venerable, not young, of long life, past one's prime, far advanced in years, matured, having lived long, full of years, seasoned, infirm, inactive, enfeebled, decrepit, superannuated, exhausted, tired, impaired, broken down, wasted, doddering, senile, on the shelf, ancient, gone to seed.—*Ant.* **young,** fresh, youthful. **2.** [Worn] time-worn, worn-out, thin, patched, ragged, faded, used, in holes, rubbed off, mended, broken-down, fallen to pieces, fallen in, given way, out of use, rusted, crumbled, dilapidated, battered, shattered, shabby, castoff, decayed, decaying, stale, useless, tattered, in rags, torn, moth-eaten.—*Ant.* **fresh,** new, unused. **3.** [Ancient] archaic, time-honored, prehistoric, bygone, early, antique, forgotten, immemorial, antediluvian, olden, remote, past, distant, former, of old, gone by, classic, medieval, in the Middle Ages, out of the dim past, primordial, primeval, before history, dateless, unrecorded, handed down, of earliest time, of the old order, ancestral, traditional, time out of mind, in the dawn of history, old as the hills: see also senses 1, 2.—*Ant.* **modern,** recent, late.

old age, *n.* seniority, dotage, infirmity; see **age 2.**

older, *a.* elder, senior, sooner, former, preceding, prior, more aged, less young, not so new, earlier, first, first-born, having come before, more ancient, lower, of an earlier time, of an earlier vintage, of a former period; see also **old 3.**—*Ant.* **young,** newer, of a later vintage.

oldest, *a.* most aged, initial, primeval; see **first, original 1.**

old-fashioned, *a.* antiquated, out-of-date, obsolete, obsolescent, outmoded, demoded, unfashionable, traditional, unstylish, passé, before the War, Victorian, not modern, old-time, time-honored, not current, antique, ancient, no longer prevailing, bygone, archaic, grown old, primitive, quaint, amusing, odd, neglected, outworn, of long standing, unused, past, behind the times, gone by, of the old school, extinct, out, gone out, *out of it; see also old 3.—*Ant.* modern, fashionable, stylish.

*old lady, *n.* female parent *or* spouse, woman, female member of the family; see mother 1, parent, wife.

*old man, *n.* head of the house, male parent *or* spouse, man; see father 1, husband, parent.

Old Testament, *n.* the Covenant, Hebrew Scripture, Jewish *or* Mosaic Law; see Bible.

old-time, *a.* outmoded, ancient, obsolete; see old-fashioned.

Old World, *n.* Europe, Asia, mother country; see East 2, Europe.

Olympics, *n.* Olympian *or* Olympic Games, world championships, international amateur athletic competition; see competition, sport 3.

omen, *n.* portent, augury, indication; see sign 1.

ominous, *a.* threatening, forbidding, foreboding, menacing, dark, suggestive, fateful, premonitory, dire, grim, gloomy, haunting, perilous, ill-starred, ill-fated, impending, fearful, prophetic; see also dangerous, dismal, doomed.—*Ant.* favorable, encouraging, auspicious.

omission, *n.* 1. [The act of omitting] overlooking, missing, leaving out; see carelessness, exclusion, neglect 1.—*Ant.* addition, mentioning, inserting. 2. [Something omitted] need, want, imperfection; see lack 2.

omit, *v.* 1. [To fail to include] leave out, reject, exclude; see bar 2, dismiss 1, eliminate. 2. [To neglect] ignore, slight, overlook; see disregard, neglect 2.

omitted, *a.* left out, overlooked, unmentioned; see missed 1, neglected.

on, *a.* and *prep.* 1. [Upon] above, in contact with, touching, supported by, situated upon, resting upon, on top of, about, held by, moving across *or* over, covering; see also upon 1.—*Ant.* under, underneath, below. 2. [Against] in contact with, close to, leaning on; see next 2. 3. [Toward] proceeding, at, moving; see approaching, toward. 4. [Forward] onward, ahead, advancing; see forward 1. 5. [Near] beside, close to, adjacent to; see bordering, near 1. —and so on, and so forth, also, in addition; see and.

on account, *a.* on credit, payable, credited; see bought, charged 1, due.

on account of, *a.* since, for the sake of, for the reason that; see because.

on and off, *a.* now and then, sometimes, infrequently; see seldom.

on board, *a.* loaded, shipped, in transit; see aboard.

on call, *a.* alerted, ready, handy; see available.

once, *a.* 1. [One time] this time, but once, once only, before, one time before, already, one, just this once, not more than once, never again, a single time, one time previously, on one occasion, only one time.—*Ant.* twice, many times, frequently. 2. [Formerly] long ago, previously, earlier; see formerly. —all at once, simultaneously, all at the same time, unanimously; see together 2. —at once, now, quickly, this moment; see immediately. —for once, for at least one time, once only, uniquely; see once 1.

once and for all, *a.* with finality, permanently, unalterably; see finally 1.

once in a while, *a.* sometimes, occasionally, on occasion; see seldom.

once or twice, *a.* a few times, infrequently, not much; see seldom.

*once-over, *n.* look, inspection, checkup; see examination 1.

oncoming, *a.* impending, expected, imminent; see approaching.

one, *a.* individual, peculiar, special, specific, separate, single, singular, odd, one and only, precise, definite, sole, uncommon; see also special 1, unique, unusual 2.—*Ant.* common, several, imprecise.

one, *n.* unit, 1, whole, person, thing, identity, ace, integer, item, example, digit, singleness, individual, individuality, individuation.—*Ant.* plural, many, several. —all one, making no difference, (be) insignificant, of no importance; see unimportant. —at one, in accord, agreeing, of the same opinion; see united. —*tie one on, go on a drinking spree, get drunk, imbibe; see drink 2.

one another, *pron.* each other, reciprocally, each to the other; see each.

oneness, *n.* integrity, harmony, indivisibility; see unity 1.

one-sided, *a.* 1. [Unilateral] single, uneven, partial; see irregular 4. 2. [Prejudiced] biased, partial, narrow-minded; see prejudiced, unfair.

one-time, *a.* prior, former, previous; see past 1.

one-way, *a.* directional, with no return, restricted; see narrow 1.

on file, *a.* preserved, at hand, filed; see recorded.

on fire, *a.* aflame, blazing, afire; see burning.

ongoing, *a.* open-ended, continuous, in process; see regular 3.

on hand, *a.* in stock, stocked, present; see **available.**

only, *a.* 1. [Solely] exclusively, uniquely, wholly, entirely, particularly, and no other, and no more, and nothing else, nothing but, totally, utterly, first and last, one and only; see also **singly.** 2. [Merely] just, simply, plainly, barely, solely; see also **hardly.** 3. [Sole] single, without another, companionless, by oneself, isolated, apart, unaccompanied, exclusive, unique; see also **alone 1.**

on occasion, *a.* occasionally, at certain *or* appropriate times, sometimes; see **seldom.**

on one hand, *a.* on one side of the question, from one viewpoint, from one direction.

on one's hands, *a.* in one's care, charged with, responsible for; see **responsible 1.**

on or about, *prep.* at about, approximately, in the vicinity (of); see **at.**

on or before, *prep.* at about the time (of), prior to; in anticipation of; see **before.**

on purpose, *a.* knowingly, meaningfully, consciously; see **deliberately.**

on sale, *a.* marked down, reduced, cut, at a bargain, at a cut rate, on the bargain counter, in the bargain basement, among the remnants; see also **reduced 2.**

on second thought, *a.* on mature consideration, as afterthought, in reality; see **incidentally.**

onset, *n.* incipience, opening, start; see **origin 2.**

on the air, *a.* broadcasting, going on, televising, in progress, speaking, performing, telecasting, being telecast, live.

***on the ball,** *a.* competent, qualified, alert; see **able.**

on the contrary, *a.* conversely, antithetically, inversely, contrasting, on the other hand, at the opposite pole, on the other side; see also **not.**

on time, *a.* prompt, on schedule, dependable; see **punctual.**

onto, *a.* and *prep.* 1. [To] toward, in contact with, adjacent; see **against 1.** 2. [Upon] over, out upon, above; see **upon 1.**

on trial, *a.* 1. [In court] in litigation, up for investigation *or* hearing, at the bar, before the bar, before a judge *or* jury, being tried *or* judged, contested, appealed, indicted; see also **accused 2.** 2. [Experimental] on a trial basis, for a trial period, on approval; see **uncertain 1, 2.**

onward, *a.* on ahead, beyond, in front of; see **forward 1, moving 1.**

ooze, *n.* slime, fluid, mire; see **mud.**

ooze, *v.* seep, exude, leak; see **flow.**

opaque, *a.* not transparent, dim, dusky, darkened, murky, gloomy, smoky, thick, misty, cloudy, clouded, shady, muddy, dull, blurred, frosty, filmy, foggy, sooty, dirty, dusty, coated over, covered. —*Ant.* **clear,** transparent, translucent.

open, *a.* 1. [Not closed] unclosed, accessible, clear, open to view, uncovered, disclosed, divulged, introduced, initiated, begun, full-blown, unfurled, susceptible, ajar, gaping, wide, rent, torn, spacious, unshut, expansive, extensive, spread out, revealed; see also senses 2, 4.—*Ant.* tight, **closed,** shut. 2. [Not obstructed] unlocked, unbarred, unbolted, unblocked, unfastened, cleared (away), removed, made passable, unsealed, unobstructed, unoccupied, vacated, unburdened, emptied; see also sense 1.—*Ant.* **taken,** barred, blocked. 3. [Not forbidden] free (of entrance), unrestricted, permitted, allowable, free of access, public, welcoming, not posted; see also **permitted.**—*Ant.* refused, restricted, forbidden. 4. [Not protected] unguarded, unsecluded, liable, exposed, out in the weather, uncovered, apart, unshut, unroofed, insecure, unsafe, conspicuous, unhidden, unconcealed, subject, sensitive; see also sense 1, **unsafe.**—*Ant.* safe, secluded, secure. 5. [Not decided] in question, up for discussion, debatable; see **questionable 1, uncertain 2.** 6. [Frank] plain, candid, straightforward; see **frank.**

open, *v.* 1. [To begin] start, inaugurate, initiate; see **begin 1, 2.** 2. [To move aside a prepared obstruction] unbar, unlock, unclose, clear, admit, reopen, open the lock, lift the latch, free, loosen, disengage, unfasten, undo, unbolt, turn the key *or* knob.—*Ant.* **close,** shut, lock. 3. [To make an opening] force an entrance, breach, cut in, tear down, push in, shatter, destroy, burst in, break open, cave in, burst out from, penetrate, pierce, force one's way into, smash, punch a hole into, slit, puncture, crack, ***muscle in, ***jimmy; see also **force,** remove 1.—*Ant.* repair, seal, mend. 4. [To make available] make accessible, put on sale *or* view, open to the public, make public, put forward, free, make usable, prepare, present, make ready.—*Ant.* remove, put away, lock up. 5. [To expose to fuller view] unroll, unfold, uncover; see **expose 1, reveal 1.**

open-door, *a.* unrestricted, unlimited, hospitable; see **free 1, 2, 3.**

opened, *a.* unlocked, made *or* thrown open, not closed; see **free 3, open 2.**

open-ended, *a.* going on, without specified limits, optional; see **constant, uncertain.**

opening, *a.* initial, beginning, primary; see **first.**

opening, *n.* 1. [A hole] break, crack, tear; see **hole** 1. 2. [An opportunity] chance, availability, occasion; see **opportunity 1, possibility 2.**

openly, *a.* 1. [Frankly] naturally, simply, artlessly, naively, unsophisticatedly, (out) in the open, candidly, aboveboard, straightforwardly, honestly, unreservedly, fully, readily, willingly, without restraint, plainly, without reserve, to one's face, in public, face to face; see also **sincerely.**—*Ant.* **secretly,** furtively, surreptitiously. 2. [Shamelessly] immodestly, brazenly, not caring, regardlessly, insensibly, unconcernedly, crassly, insolently, flagrantly, wantonly, unblushingly, notoriously, without pretense, in defiance of the law; see also **carelessly, lewdly.**—*Ant.* **carefully,** prudently, discreetly.

open-minded, *a.* tolerant, fair-minded, just; see **fair 1, liberal.**

open out, *v.* fan (out), diverge, enlarge; see **grow 1, spread 2.**

open up, *v.* enlarge, grow, start; see **begin 1, 2, spread 2.**

opera, *n.* musical drama, libretto, score, operetta, grand *or* light opera, opera performance; see also **performance.**

operate, *v.* 1. [To keep in operation] manipulate, conduct, administer; see **manage 1.** 2. [To be in operation] function, work, serve, carry on, run, revolve, act, behave, fulfill, turn, roll, spin, pump, lift, spark, burn, move, progress, advance, proceed, go, contact, hit, engage, transport, convey, contain, *click, *tick, *percolate.—*Ant.* **stop,** stall, break down. 3. [To produce an effect] react, act on, influence, bring about, determine, turn, bend, contrive, work, accomplish, fulfill, finish, complete, benefit, compel, promote, concern, enforce, take *or* have effect, work on, succeed, get results, get across, *turn the trick; see also **achieve, produce 1.** 4. [To perform a surgical operation] remove diseased tissue, amputate, transplant (an organ); see **treat 3.**

operated, *a.* conducted, handled, run, carried on, regulated, ordered, maintained, supervised, superintended, governed, *administered, transacted, performed, conveyed, transported, moved, determined, achieved, contrived, accomplished, fulfilled, promoted, enforced, worked, served, guided, executed, sustained, used, practiced, put into effect, finished, driven, brought about, bent, manipulated, negotiated; see also **directed, managed 2.**

operating, *a.* managing, conducting, directing, executing, manipulating, administering, ordering, regulating, supervising, running, wielding, transacting, guiding, putting into effect, sustaining, maintaining, performing, practicing, revolving, promoting, determining, moving, turning, spinning, driving, contriving, fulfilling, accomplishing, finishing, effecting, bringing about, serving, enforcing, in operation, at work; see **using.**

operation, *n.* 1. [The act of causing to function] execution, guidance, superintendence, carrying out, ordering, order, maintenance, handling, manipulating, manipulation, supervision, control, conduct, agency, enforcement, advancement, regulating, running, supervising, directing, transacting, conducting; see also **management 1, regulation 1.** 2. [An action] performance, act, employment, labor, service, carrying on, transaction, deed, doing, proceeding, handiwork, workmanship, enterprise, movement, progress, development, engagement, undertaking; see also **action 1, work 2.** 3. [A method] process, formula, procedure; see **method, plan 2.** 4. [Surgical treatment] surgery, transplant, amputation, dismemberment, vivisection, dissection, biopsy, emergency operation, acupuncture, exploratory operation, section, excision, removal, tonsillectomy, appendectomy, open-heart surgery, abortion, autopsy, *the knife; see also **medicine 3.**

operator, *n.* 1. [One who operates a machine] engineer, operative, skilled *or* trained employe(e); see **laborer, workman.** Kinds of operators include the following—telephone, computer, switchboard, PBX, long-distance, information, emergency. 2. [One who operates workable property] executive, supervisor, director; see **executive.** 3. [*Manipulator] speculator, scoundrel, fraud; see **rascal.**

opinion, *n.* 1. [A belief] notion, view, sentiment, conception, idea, surmise, impression, inference, conjecture, inclination, fancy, imagining, supposition, suspicion, notion, assumption, guess, theory, thesis, theorem, postulate, hypothesis, point of view, presumption, presupposition, persuasion, mind; see also **belief.** 2. [A considered judgment] estimation, estimate, view, summary, belief, idea, resolution, determination, recommendation, finding, conviction, conclusion; see also **judgment 3, verdict.**

opinionated, *a.* bigoted, stubborn, unyielding; see **obstinate, prejudiced.**

opium, *n.* opiate, soporific, *dope; see **drug 2.**

opponent, *n.* 1. [A rival] competitor, contender, challenger, candidate, equal, entrant, the opposition, aspirant, bidder.—*Ant.* supporter, defender, abettor. 2. [An opposing contestant] antagonist, contestant, litigant; see **player** 1. 3. [An enemy] foe, adversary, assailant; see **enemy**.

opportunity, *n.* 1. [Favorable circumstances] chance, occasion, suitable circumstance, excuse, happening, event, probability, good fortune, luck, (even) break; see also **possibility** 2. 2. [A suitable time] occasion, moment, time and tide; see **time** 2.

oppose, *v.* 1. [To hold a contrary opinion] object, disapprove, debate, dispute, contradict, argue, deny, run counter to, protest, defy, cross, speak against, confront, thwart, neutralize, reverse, turn the tables, be opposed to, oppose change, not have any part of, face down, interfere with, disapprove of, cry out against, disagree (with), not conform, run against or counter to, come in conflict with, go contrary to, frown at, not be good for, not accept, call in question, conflict or grapple with, doubt, be reluctant or against or unwilling, reject, dislike, take exception, repudiate, question, probe, resist, confound, confute, refute, *buck, *turn thumbs down (on); see also sense 2, **dare** 2, **face** 1.—*Ant.* agree, approve, accept. 2. [To fight] resist, battle, encounter, assault, attack, assail, storm, protest, clash, meet, skirmish, engage, contest, face, restrain, go or match or turn or count or mark against, uphold, defend, rebel, revolt, mutiny, strike back, combat, run counter to, defy, snub, grapple with, fight off, withstand, repel, guard, counter-attack, struggle, outflank, antagonize, retaliate, impede, overpower, *take on all comers, lock horns (with); see **fight**.

opposed, *a.* antagonistic (to), averse, opposite, contrary, hostile to, at odds, disputed, counter (to), at cross-purposes, up against, against the grain; see also **opposite** 2.

opposing, *a.* 1. [In the act of opposition] conflicting, clashing, unfriendly; see **opposed**. 2. [Situated opposite] contrary, facing, fronting; see **opposite** 3.

opposite, *a.* 1. [Contrary] antithetical, diametric, reversed; see **unlike**. 2. [In conflict] adverse, inimical, antagonistic, rival, unfavorable, averse, argumentative, contradictory, hostile; see **against** 1. 3. [So situated as to seem to oppose] facing, fronting, in front of, on different sides of, on opposite sides, in opposition to, contrasting, on the other side of, contrary, (over) against, front to front, back to back, nose to nose, on the far-

ther side, opposing, diametrical, *eyeball to eyeball.—*Ant.* **matched**, on the same side, side by side.

opposite, *n.* contradiction, contrary, converse, direct opposite, opposition, vice versa, antithesis, antonym, counter term, counterpart, inverse, reverse, adverse, the opposite pole, the other extreme, the other side, the opposite term or force or idea, etc. —*Ant.* alike, same, a related or similar thing.

opposition, *n.* 1. [The act of opposing] hostilities, conflict, combat; see **battle**, **fight** 1. 2. [The attitude suggestive of opposition] dislike, disagreement, hostility, antagonism, defiance, antipathy, abhorrence, aversion, constraint, restriction, restraint, hindrance, discord, distaste, disfavor, dissatisfaction, discontent, displeasure, irritation, offense, chagrin, humiliation, anger, loathing, disapproval, complaint, repugnance; see also **hatred**, **resentment**.—*Ant.* support, enthusiasm, accord. 3. [The individual or group that opposes] antagonist, disputant, adversary; see **enemy**, **opponent** 1.

oppress, *v.* suppress, harass, maltreat; see **abuse** 1, **bother** 2.

oppressed, *a.* misused, downtrodden, enslaved; see **hurt** 1.

oppression, *n.* tyranny, hardness, domination, coercion, dictatorship, fascism, persecution, severity, harshness, abuse, conquering, overthrowing, compulsion, force, torment, martial law; see also **cruelty**.—*Ant.* freedom, liberalism, voluntary control.

optical, *a.* ocular, seeing, visible; see **visual**.

optimism, *n.* 1. [Belief in the essential goodness of the universe] mysticism, philosophy of goodness, belief in progress; see **faith** 1. 2. [An inclination to expect or to hope for the best] cheerfulness, hopefulness, confidence, assurance, encouragement, happiness, brightness, enthusiasm, good cheer, trust, calmness, elation, expectancy, expectation, anticipation, certainty.—*Ant.* gloom, despair, melancholy.

optimist, *n.* Pollyanna, dreamer, positivist.

optimistic, *a.* cheerful, sanguine, assured; see **confident**, **hopeful** 1, **trusting**.

option, *n.* 1. [A choice] selection, alternative, dilemma; see **choice**. 2. [A privilege to purchase] right, prerogative, grant, claim, license, lease, franchise, advantage, security, immunity, benefit, title, prior claim, *dibs.

optional, *a.* discretionary, elective, noncompulsory, free, unrestricted, arbitrary, not required, *with no strings attached, *take it or leave it; see also **volun-**

tary.–*Ant.* necessary, compulsory, enforced.

or, *conj.* 1. [A suggestion of choice] or only, or but, as an alternative *or* choice *or* substitute, on the other hand, in turn, conversely, in other words, or else, in preference to; see also either.–*Ant.* neither, nor, without choice. 2. [A suggestion of correction] or not, or not exactly, in reverse, reversing it, on the contrary, contrary to, oppositely, or rather, instead of, correctly speaking; see also **instead.** 3. [A suggestion of approximation] roughly, about, practically; see **approximately.**

oral, *a.* vocal, verbal, uttered, voiced, unwritten, phonetic, sounded, from the lips *or* mouth, in the mouth, not written, by word of mouth; see also **spoken.**–*Ant.* written, unspoken, printed.

orange, *a.* reddish, ocherous, glowing; see **orange,** *n.* 1.

orange, *n.* 1. [Color] red-yellow, apricot, tangerine, burnt orange, peach, coral, salmon; see also **color.** 2. [Fruit] citrus fruit, tropical fruit, sour orange; see also **food, fruit.**

orbit, *n.* 1. [Path described by one body revolving around another] ellipse, circle, ring, circuit, apogee, course, perigee, lap, round, cycle, curve, flight path; see also **revolution** 1. 2. [Range of activity or influence] range, field, boundary; see **area.**

orbit, *v.* 1. [To revolve around another body] encircle, (en)compass, ring, move in a circuit, go around, revolve; see also **circle.** 2. [To put into orbit] fire, blast *or* lift off, project; see **launch** 2.

orbited, *a.* put *or* placed *or* lofted *or* sent into orbit, put *or* sent up, rocketed; see **driven, sent.**

orchard, *n.* fruit *or* nut trees, fruit plantation *or* farm; apple orchard, peach orchard, etc.; see **farm.**

orchestra, *n.* musical ensemble, symphony, trio, quartet, quintet, etc.; see also **band.**

ordain, *v.* 1. [To establish] install, institute, appoint; see **enact.** 2. [To destine] determine, foreordain, intend; see **intend** 2. 3. [To invest with priestly functions] install, confer holy orders upon, consecrate, frock, delegate, invest; see also **bless.**

ordained, *a.* 1. [Ordered] commanded, determined, established by law *or* ordinance *or* edict *or* declaration, etc.; see **established** 2, **ordered** 2. 2. [Invested into the ministry] consecrated, anointed, received into the ministry; see **named** 2.

ordeal, *n.* tribulation, distress, calamity; see **difficulty** 1, 2.

order, *n.* 1. [A command] direction, demand, decree, rule, edict, charge, requirement, ordinance, act, warrant, mandate, injunction; see also **command, law** 3. 2. [Sequence] progression, succession, procession; see **line** 1, **sequence** 1, **series.** 3. [Orderly arrangement] regulation, plan, disposition, management, establishment, method, distribution, placement, scale, rule, computation, adjustment, adaptation, ordering, ranging, standardizing, lining up, trimming, grouping, composition, cast, assortment, disposal, scheme, form, routine, array, procedure, method, index, regularity, uniformity, symmetry, harmony, placement, layout, line-up, setup; see also **classification, system** 1.–*Ant.* confusion, disarray, displacement. 4. [Organization] society, sect, company; see **organization** 3. 5. [A formal agreement to purchase] engagement, reserve, application, requisition, request, stipulation, booking, arrangement; see also **buying, reservation** 1. 6. [Kind] hierarchy, rank, degree; see **class** 1, **classification.** 7. [Customary method] ritual, rite, plan; see **custom** 2. **–in order,** working, efficient, operative; see **effective. –in order to,** for the purpose of, as a means to, so that; see **for. –in short order,** rapidly, without delay, soon; see **quickly. –on order,** requested, on the way, sent for; see **ordered** 1.

order, *v.* 1. [To give a command] direct, command, instruct, bid, tell, demand, impose, give orders *or* directions, dictate, decree; see also **require** 2. 2. [To authorize a purchase] secure, reserve, request; see **buy** 1, **obtain** 1. 3. [To put in order] arrange, plan, furnish, regulate, establish, manage, systematize, space, file, put away, classify, distribute, alphabetize, regularize, pattern, formalize, settle, fix, locate, dress up, sort out, index, put to rights, set *or* establish *or* lay down guide lines *or* parameters (for), adjust, adapt, set in order, assign, place, align, standardize, plan, group; see also **organize** 1.–*Ant.* confuse, disarrange, disarray.

ordered, *a.* 1. [On order] requested, requisitioned, applied *or* sent for, spoken for, engaged, booked, arranged for, retained, written for, telephoned for; see also **reserved** 1. 2. [Commanded] directed, ordained, commanded, charged, dictated, regulated, decreed, ruled, enjoined, stipulated, bidden, imposed, authorized, exacted, forbidden, required, announced, by order *or* command, as ordered, under one's jurisdiction; see also **approved, requested.**—*Ant.* omitted, revoked, **neglected. 3.** [Put in order] arranged, regulated, placed; see **classified, organized.**

orderly, *a.* **1.** [Ordered; *said of objects and places*] neat, tidy, arranged; see **clean 1, neat 1. 2.** [Methodical; *said of persons*] systematic, correct, formal, businesslike, systematical, exact, tidy, neat, thorough, precise; see also **careful.**—*Ant.* **irregular,** inaccurate, unmethodical.

ordinance, *n.* direction, mandate, authorization; see **law 3.**

ordinarily, *a.* usually, generally, habitually; see **frequently, regularly 1.**

ordinary, *a.* **1.** [In accordance with a regular order or sequence] customary, normal, regular, constant, usual, habitual, routine, mundane, everyday; see also **common 1, popular 1, 3, traditional. 2.** [Lacking distinction] average, mediocre, familiar, natural, everyday, accepted, typical, commonplace, characteristic, prosaic, simple, banal, bland, trite, monotonous, stale, tedious, plain, normal; see also **common 1, conventional 3, dull 4.** —**out of the ordinary,** extraordinary, uncommon, special; see **unusual 2.**

ore, *n.* unrefined earth or rock, ore bed, native mineral; see **mineral.**

organ, *n.* **1.** [An instrument] medium, means, way; see **tool 1. 2.** [A part of an organism having a specialized use] vital part or structure, functional division, process; see **gland.** Human organs include the following—brain, heart, eye, ear, nose, tongue, lung, kidney, stomach, intestine, pancreas, gall bladder, liver, penis, womb. **3.** [A musical instrument] wind instrument, keyboard instrument, calliope, hurdy-gurdy, accordion; see also **musical instrument.** Types of organs include the following— choir, orchestral, solo, pipe, echo, pedal, reed, electric, hand.

organic, *a.* basic, vital, essential; see **fundamental, natural 1.**

organically, *a.* by nature, inevitably, wholly; see **essentially, naturally 2.**

organism, *n.* person, organic structure, physiological individual; see **animal, body 1, plant.**

organization, *n.* **1.** [The process or manner of organizing] establishment, plan, planning, ordering, creation, grouping, design, provision, working out, assembling, construction, regulation, systematization, system, method, co-ordination, adjustment, harmony, unity, correlation, standard, standardization, settlement, arrangement, disposition, classification, alignment, institution, foundation, preparation, rehearsal, direction, struc-

ture, situation, formation, association, uniformity; see also **classification 1, order 3.**—*Ant.* **confusion,** bedlam, chance. **2.** [An organized body] aggregation, association, federation, combine, corporation, union, institute, trust, cartel, confederation, monopoly, combination, machine, business, industry, company, society, league, club, fraternity, house, order, alliance, party, cooperative, guild, profession, trade, coalition, syndicate, fellowship, lodge, brotherhood, confederacy, affiliation, body, band, team, squad, crew, clique, circle, set, troupe, group; see also **system 1.**

organize, *v.* **1.** [To put in order] arrange, fix, straighten, standardize, compose, combine, systematize, methodize, coordinate, adjust, put in order, line up, regulate; see also **classify, order 3. 2.** [To form an organization] establish, build, found; see **plan 2.**

organized, *a.* established, methodized, co-ordinated, systematized, systematic, constituted, directed, adjusted, assigned, distributed, grouped, fixed up, standardized, in place or order, in turn or succession, in good form, placed, put away, orderly, in series or sequence, arranged, prepared, made ready, constructed, settled, composed, framed, planned, ranked, put in order, ordered, regulated, ranged, disposed, formulated, formed, fashioned, shaped, made, projected, designed, harmonized, related, correlated, founded, associated; see also **classified.**

Orient, *n.* **1.** [Eastern Asia] Far East, Asia, China, India, Japan, Vietnam, Siam or Thailand, Laos, Indo-China, Cambodia, Korea, Burma, the mysterious East, land of the rising sun; see also **Asia, east 2.**—*Ant.* Europe, Occident, Western World. **2.** [Southwestern Asia] Near East, Middle East, Levant, Egypt, Mohammedan world, Turkey, Syria, Lebanon, Israel, Jordan, Iraq, Iran, Persia, Moslem world, Arabia, the Golden or Fertile Crescent, the cradle of mankind; see also **east 2.**

Oriental, *a.* (Far) Eastern, Near Eastern, Asian, Chinese, Indian, Japanese, Vietnamese, Cambodian, Laotian, Thai, Korean, Burmese, Siberian, Arabic, Jewish, Iraqi, Iranian, Malaysian, Hindustani, Ceylonese.

orientation, *n.* familiarization, bearings, introduction; see **adjustment, introduction 3, 4.**

origin, *n.* **1.** [The act of beginning] rise, start, foundation; see **birth. 2.** [The place or time of beginning] source, spring, issue, fountain, inlet, derivation, root, stem, shoot, twig, sapling, portal, door, gate, gateway, fountainhead, wellspring, font, fount, birthplace, cradle, nest, womb, reservoir, infancy, babyhood, childhood, youth.—*Ant.* result, outcome, issue. 3. [Cause] seed, germ, stock, parentage, ancestry, parent, ancestor, egg, sperm, embryo, principle, element, nucleus, first cause, author, creator, prime mover, producer, causation, source, influence, generator, occasion, root, spring, antecedent, motive, inspiration; see also **cause**.—*Ant.* result, consequence, conclusion.

original, *a.* 1. [Pertaining to the source] primary, primeval, primordial, rudimentary, elementary, inceptive, in embryo, fundamental, primitive, initial, beginning, commencing, starting, opening, dawning, incipient; see also **first**.—*Ant.* late, recent, developed. 2. [Creative] originative, productive, causal, causative, generative, imaginative, inventive, formative, resourceful, ready, quick, seminal, envisioning, sensitive, archetypal, inspiring, devising, conceiving, fertile, fashioning, molding.—*Ant.* stupid, imitative, unproductive. 3. [Not copied] primary, principal, first, genuine, new, firsthand, uncopied, fresh, novel, independent, one, sole, lone, single, solitary, authentic, unique, pure, rare, unusual, not translated *or* copied *or* imitated, real, absolute, sheer.—*Ant.* imitated, copied, repeated.

originality, *n.* creativeness, inventiveness, invention, ingenuity, conception, authenticity, novelty, freshness, newness, individuality, brilliance; see also **imagination**.

originally, *a.* 1. [In an original manner] imaginatively, creatively, ingeniously, inventively, freshly, startlingly, in a new fashion, independently, artistically. 2. [In the beginning] first, incipiently, basically; see **formerly**.

originate, *v.* start, introduce, found; see **begin 1**.

originated, *a.* introduced, started, commenced; see **begun**.

ornament, *n.* embellishment, adornment, beautification; see **decoration 2**.

ornamental, *a.* 1. [Intended for ornament] fancy, luxurious, showy; see **elaborate 1, ornate**. 2. [Beautiful] delicate, exquisite, spiritual; see **beautiful**.

ornate, *a.* showy, gaudy, sumptuous, lavish, bright, colored, tinseled, jeweled, embroidered, glossy, burnished, polished, gorgeous, pompous, stylish, magnificent, adorned, trimmed, gilded, embellished, inlaid, garnished, flowered, glowing, vivid, radiant, fine, gay, alluring, dazzling, sparkling, shining, flashing, glistening, glamorous, artificial, pretentious, baroque, rococo, tawdry, flashy; see also **elaborate 1**.

orphan, *n.* foundling, ragamuffin, parentless child, orphaned child, waif, stray; see also **child**.

orphanage, *n.* orphans' home, institution, foundling home; see **school 1**.

other, *a.* one of two, the remaining one, another, one beside, some beside, additional, different, separate, distinct, opposite, across from, lately, recently, not long ago, other than; see also **extra**.

other, *pron.* the one remaining, the part remaining, the alternate, the alternative; see also **another**.—*Ant.* this, that, the first choice.

others, *n.* unnamed persons, the remainder, some, a few, any others, a number, a handful, a small number, not many, hardly any, two or three, more than one, many, a great number, a great many, they, folks, the rest; see also **everybody**.—*Ant.* no one, **none**, not any.

otherwise, *a.* 1. [In another way] in a different way, contrarily, in an opposed way, under other conditions, in different circumstances, on the other hand, in other respects, in other ways.—*Ant.* like, so, in like manner. 2. [Introducing an alternative threat] unless you do, with this exception, except on these conditions, barring this, in any other circumstances, except that, without this, unless...then, other than; see also **unless**.—*Ant.* therefore, hence, as a result.

ought (to), *v.* should, have to, is necessary *or* fitting *or* becoming *or* expedient, behooves, is reasonable *or* logical *or* natural, requires, is in need of, is responsible for; see also **must**.

ounce, *n.* measure, troy ounce, avoirdupois ounce, fluid ounce, one sixteenth of a pound (avoirdupois), one sixteenth of a pint, one twelfth of a pound (troy); see also **measure 1**.

our, *a.* ours, our own, belonging to us, owned *or* used by us, due to us, a part of us, of interest to us, done *or* accomplished by us, in our employ, with *or* near *or* of us.

ourselves, *pron.* us, our own selves, the speakers, individually, personally, privately, without help, *our own selves; see also **we**.

oust, *v.* eject, discharge, dispossess, evict, dislodge, remove, deprive, expel, drive *or* force out, show the door, chase out, cast out, depose, dethrone, disinherit, banish, *boot out, *bundle off, *send packing, *give the gate, *pack off.

out, *a.* and *prep.* 1. [In motion from within] out of, away from, from, from within, out from, out toward, outward, on the way.—*Ant.* in from, in, into. 2. [Not situated within] on the outer side, on the surface, external, extrinsic, outer, outdoors, out-of-doors, unconcealed, open, exposed, in the open; see also **outside, without.–***Ant.* within, inside, on the inner side. 3. [Beyond] distant, removed, removed from; see **away 1, beyond.** 4. [Continued to the limit or near it] ended, accomplished, fulfilled; see **done 1, finished 1. 5.** [Not at home or at one's office] not in, away, busy, on vacation, at lunch, gone, left; see also **absent.–***Ant.* in, receiving, not busy. 6. [*Unconscious] insensible, out cold, *blotto; see **unconscious. 7.** [Wanting] lacking, missing, without; see **wanting 1. –*all out,** wholeheartedly, with great effort, entirely; see **completely.**

*out, *n.* means of escape, way out, excuse; see **escape, explanation.**

outage, *n.* interruption of service, blackout, dimout, brownout; failure of electrical service *or* electricity *or* gas *or* utilities, etc.; see also **interruption.**

out-and-out, *a.* complete, entire, total; see **completely.**

outbid, *v.* bid *or* offer higher *or* more (than), raise the price, bid something up; see **pay 1.**

outbreak, *n.* 1. [A sudden violent appearance] eruption, explosion, outburst, disruption, burst, bursting (forth), detonation, thunder, commotion, rending, break, breaking out, breaking forth, gush, gushing forth, outpouring, pouring forth, tumult, discharge, blast, blowup, crash, roar, earthquake, squall, paroxysm, spasm, convulsion, fit, effervescence, boiling, flash, flare, crack.–*Ant.* peace, tranquillity, quiet. 2. [Sudden violence] fury, mutiny, brawl; see **disorder 2, revolution 2.**

outburst, *n.* discharge, upheaval, eruption; see **disturbance 2, outbreak 1.**

outcast, *a.* vagabond, driven out, hounded, untouchable, rejected, thrown aside, pushed out, disgraced, hunted, not accepted by society, cast out, degraded, expelled, outlawed, cast away, exiled, expatriated, serving a life sentence, having a price on one's head.

outcast, *n.* fugitive, pariah, untouchable; see **refugee.**

outcome, *n.* issue, upshot, consequence; see **end 2, result.**

outcrop, *n.* bared rock *or* soil, exposed surface, projecting land mass; see **earth 2, land 1.**

outcry, *n.* complaint, clamor, scream; see **objection.**

outdated, *a.* outmoded, out of fashion, antiquated; see **old 3.**

outdo, *v.* surpass, best, beat; see **exceed.**

outdone, *a.* defeated, bettered, improved upon; see **beaten 1.**

outdoor, *a.* outside, airy, out-of-doors, open-air, out of the house, out in the open, free, unrestricted, rustic, free and easy, healthful; see also **outdoors.–***Ant.* interior, indoor, in the house.

outdoors, *a.* out-of-doors, outdoor, without, out of the house, outside, on the outside, in the yard, in the open, in the garden *or* patio, into the street.

outdoors, *n.* the out-of-doors, natural scenery, fresh air, garden, patio, woods, hills, mountains, streams, Mother Nature, the great outdoors, countryside, the country.–*Ant.* **inside,** domestic matters, household concerns.

outer, *a.* outward, without, external, exterior, foreign *or* alien to, beyond, exposed; see also **outside.–***Ant.* inner, inward, inside.

outer space, *n.* infinity, (the) heavens, (the) universe; see **space 1.**

outfield, *n.* left field, deep left, over third (base) *or* short stop, center field, deep center, over second (base), right field, deep right, over first (base), down the left *or* right foul line; *pasture, *garden; see also **baseball, field 2.**

outfielder, *n.* fielder, *gardener, *fly chaser; see **baseball player.**

outfit, *n.* trappings, outlay, gear; see **equipment.**

outfit, *v.* equip, fit out, supply, see **provide 1.**

outflank, *v.* bypass, surround, outmaneuver; see **defeat 2, pass 1.**

outgo, *n.* costs, losses, outflow; see **expenses.**

outgoing, *a.* sociable, civil, kind; see **friendly 1.**

outgrowth, *n.* end result, outcome, effect; see **end 2, result.**

outing, *n.* excursion, airing, drive; see **vacation.**

outlast, *v.* outlive, outwear, remain; see **endure 1, survive 1.**

outlaw, *n.* fugitive, bandit, badman; see **criminal.**

outlaw, *v.* make illegal, stop, ban; see **banish, condemn.**

outlawed, *a.* stopped, banned, made illegal; see **illegal.**

outlet, *n.* 1. [An opening] break, crack, tear; see **hole 1. 2.** [An electric terminal] plug-in, socket, double *or* triple socket, wall *or* floor plug, electric service connection.

outline, *n.* 1. [A skeletonized plan] frame, skeleton, framework; see **plan 1. 2.** [The line surrounding an object; *often plural*] contour, side, boundary; see **edge 1, frame 2. 3.** [A shape seen in outline] silhouette, profile, configuration, shape, figure, formation, aspect, appearance; see also **form 1.**

outline, v. 1. [To draw] sketch, paint, describe; see **draw 2.** 2. [To plan] rough or block out, draft, sketch; see **plan 2.**

outlined, a. 1. [Marked in outline] bounded, edged, bordered, circumscribed, marked, zoned, girdled, banded, configurated. 2. [Given in summary] charted, summarized, surveyed; see **planned.**

outlive, v. live longer (than), outlast, last; see **endure 1.**

outlook, n. 1. [Point of view] scope, vision, standpoint; see **viewpoint.** 2. [Apparent future] probability, prospect(s), likelihood, possibility, chance(s), opportunity, appearances, probable future, openings, normal course of events, probabilities, risk, law of averages.

out loud, a. aloud, above a whisper, audible; see **heard, loud 1, loudly.**

outlying, a. afar, far-off, external; see **distant.**

outnumbered, a. exceeded, bested, overcome; see **beaten 1.**

out of, a. 1. [Having none in stock] all out of stock, not in stock, gone; see **sold out.** 2. [From] out from, away from, from within; see **from.** 3. [Beyond] outside of, on the border of, in the outskirts; see **beyond.**

out of bounds, a. outlawed, forbidden, controlled; see **illegal.**

out of breath, a. exhausted, gasping, winded; see **breathless.**

out of control, a. gone, doomed, uncontrolled; see **lost 1, unruly.**

out-of-date, a. obsolete, passé, antiquated; see **old-fashioned.**

out of hand, a. beyond control, out of control, unchecked; see **uncontrolled, unruly.**

*****out of it,** a. uninformed, behind the times, *square; see **ignorant 1, old-fashioned.**

out of line, a. 1. [Crooked] not lined up, uneven, devious; see **crooked, irregular 4.** 2. [Disrespectful] outspoken, dissident, insolent; see **radical 2, rebellious 2, unruly.**

out of one's mind or **head,** a. crazy, deranged, irresponsible; see **insane.**

out of order, a. broken down, defective, faulty; see **broken 2.**

out of place, a. mislaid, displaced, gone; see **lost 1.**

out of print, a. sold out, not available, (all) gone; see **sold.**

out-of-the-way, a. far-off, secluded, isolated; see **distant.**

out of work, a. out of a job or employment, dismissed, without work or job; see **unemployed.**

outplay, v. overcome, surpass, beat; see **defeat 3.**

outpost, n. advance(d) or forward post or position or station, listening post, point of attack; see **boundary, position 1.**

output, n. yield, amount, crop; see **produce.**

outrage, n. indignity, abuse, affront; see **insult.**

outrage, v. offend, wrong, affront; see **abuse, insult.**

outrageous, a. wanton, notorious, shameless, disgraceful, brazen, barefaced, gross, scandalous, disorderly, insulting, affronting, abusive, oppressive, dishonorable, injurious, glaring, immoderate, extreme, flagrant, glaring, contemptible, ignoble, malevolent, odious, monstrous, atrocious, nefarious, vicious, iniquitous, wicked, shocking, violent, unbearable, villainous, infamous, corrupt, degenerate, criminal, sinful, abandoned, vile, abominable.—*Ant.* **excellent,** laudable, honorable.

outright, a. out-and-out, unmitigated, unconditional; see **completely, obvious 1.**

outset, n. start, beginning, source; see **origin 2.**

outside, a. extreme, outermost, farthest, apart from, external, away from, farther; see also **outer.**—*Ant.* **inner,** inside, interior.

outside, n. 1. [An outer surface] exterior, outer side, surface, skin, cover, covering, topside, upper side, front side, face, appearance, outer aspect, seeming.—*Ant.* interior, **inside,** inner side. 2. [The limit] outline, border, bounds; see **boundary, edge 1, end 4.** —**at the outside,** at the most, at the absolute limit, no or not more than; see **most.**

outsider, n. foreigner, stranger, refugee; see **alien.**

outskirts, n. border, suburbs, limits; see **boundary, edge 1.**

outspoken, a. blunt, candid, artless; see **frank.**

outspread, a. spread (out or wide), expanded, extended; see **widespread.**

outstanding, a. conspicuous, leading, notable; see **distinguished 2.**

outward, a. 1. [In an outwardly direction] out, toward the edge, from within; see **outer, outside.** 2. [To outward appearance] on the surface, visible, to the eye; see **obvious 1, open 1.**

outwear, v. sustain, last longer than, outlast; see **continue 1, endure 1, survive 1.**

outweigh, v. 1. [To exceed in weight] overbalance, overweigh, weigh more (than), go beyond; see also **burden 2.** 2. [To exceed in importance] excel, surpass, outrun; see **exceed.**

outwit, v. baffle, trick, bewilder; see **confuse, deceive.**

outwitted, a. tricked, outsmarted, taken; see **deceived.**

oval, a. egg-shaped, elliptical, ellipsoidal; see **oblong.**

oven, n. hot-air chamber, oil burner, broiler; see **furnace, stove.**

over, a. and prep. 1. [Situated above] aloft, overhead, up beyond, covering, roofing, protecting, upper, higher than, farther up, upstairs, in the sky, straight or high up, up there, in the clouds, among the stars, in heaven, just over, up from, outer, on top of; see also **above.**—Ant. under, below, beneath. 2. [Passing above] overhead, aloft, up high; see **across.** 3. [Again] once more, afresh, another time; see **again.** 4. [Beyond] past, farther on, out of sight; see **beyond.** 5. [Done] accomplished, ended, completed; see **done 2, finished 1. 6.** [*In addition] over and above, extra, additionally; see **besides.** 7. [Having authority] superior to, in authority, above; see **higher, superior.**

over-all, a. complete, thorough, comprehensive; see **general 1.**

overalls, n. an over-all garment, jump suit, coveralls; see **clothes, pants 1.**

overbearing, a. despotic, tyrannical, dictatorial; see **absolute 3.**

overboard, a. over the side, out of the boat, into the water; see **wet 1.**

overcast, a. cloudy, gloomy, not clear or fair; see **dark 1.**

overcoat, n. greatcoat, topcoat, raincoat; see **clothes, coat 1.**

overcome, a. conquered, overwhelmed, overthrown; see **beaten 1.**

overcome, v. overwhelm, best, vanquish, conquer, outdo, surpass, overpower, overwhelm, beat, trounce, subdue, master; see also **defeat 2, 3, win 1.**

overconfident, a. reckless, impudent, heedless; see **careless, rash.**

overcritical, a. domineering, harsh, hypercritical; see **severe 1, 2.**

overcrowd, v. crowd, stuff, fill; see **pack 2, press 1.**

overcrowded, a. congested, overbuilt, overpopulated; see **full 1.**

overdo, v. 1. [To do too much] magnify, pile up or on, amplify, overestimate, overreach, stretch, go or carry too far, overrate, exaggerate, go to extremes, overstate, enlarge, enhance, exalt, *bite off more than one can chew, *run into the ground, *do to death, *go overboard, burn the candle at both ends, *lay it on, have too many irons in the fire, *have one's cake and eat it too; see also **exceed.**—Ant. neglect, underdo, slack. 2. [To overtax oneself physically] tire, fatigue, exhaust; see **weary 2.**

overdone, a. excessive, too much, pushed too far; see **exaggerated.**

overdose, n. excessive or heavy dose or dosage, too much, overtreatment; see **excess 1.**

overdrawn, a. exhausted, depleted, (all) paid out; see **gone 2.**

overdue, a. delayed, belated, tardy; see **late 1.**

overeat, v. overindulge, stuff, gorge; see **eat 1.**

overemphasize, v. stress, *make a big thing of, *make something out of (nothing); see **emphasize, exceed.**

overestimate, v. overvalue, overprice, overrate; see **exaggerate, exceed.**

overflow, n. 1. [The act of overflowing] redundancy, inundation, overproduction; see **flood.** 2. [That which overflows] superfluity, surplus, surplusage; see **excess 1.**

overflow, v. 1. [To flow over the top, or out at a vent] spill over, fall, run or pour (out or over), waste, shed, cascade, spout (forth), jet, squirt, drain, leak, squirt, spray, shower, gush, shoot, issue, rush, wave, surge, overtop, brim or lap or bubble or flow over; see also **leak 1.** 2. [To flow out upon] inundate, water, wet; see **flood.**

overflowing, a. abundant, in (God's) plenty, bountiful; see **plentiful 2.**

overfly, v. survey, fly across or over, inspect; see **fly 1, 4.**

overgrown, a. disproportionate, excessive, huge; see **large 1.**

overgrowth, n. growth, abundance, luxuriance; see **excess 1.**

overhang, v. jut, be suspended, swing or dangle or droop or flap over; see **project 1.**

overhaul, v. modernize, fix, renew; see **repair 1.**

overhead, a. above, aloft, hanging; see **over 1.**

overhear, v. hear intentionally, listen in on, catch; see **eavesdrop, hear 1.**

overheard, a. listened to, recorded, *bugged; see **heard.**

overheat, v. heat (up) too much, bake, blister; see **heat 2.**

overindulgence, n. overeating, overdrinking, eating or drinking too much; see **drunkenness, eating, greed.**

overlap, n. extension, overlay, addition; see **flap.**

overlap, v. overlie, overhang, lap or fold over, extend (alongside), flap, extend or project or fold upon, overlay; see also **project 1.**

overload, v. oppress, weigh down, encumber; see **burden, load 1.**

overlook, v. 1. [To occupy a commanding height] look over, top, survey, inspect, watch over, look out, view, give upon *or* on, front on, have a prospect of. 2. [To ignore deliberately] slight, make light of, disdain; see **neglect 1**. 3. [To fail to see] miss, leave out, neglect; see **neglect 2**.

overlooked, *a.* missed, left out, forgotten; see **neglected**.

overlooking, *a.* 1. [Providing a view] looking over, looking out on, commanding; see **seeing**. 2. [Disregarding] missing, neglecting, forgetting.

overnight, *a.* one night, lasting one night, during one *or* the night; see **late 4**.

****over (one's) dead body**, *a.* not if one can help it, (only) with (great) difficulty, by no means; see **never**.

overpass, *n.* span, footbridge, walkway; see **bridge 1**.

overpower, *v.* overwhelm, master, subjugate; see **defeat 2, 3**.

overpowering, *a.* irresistible, uncontrollable, overwhelming; see **intense**.

overproduction, *n.* excess, excessive production, overstock; see **production 1**.

overrate, *v.* build up, magnify, overestimate; see **exaggerate, exceed**.

overrated, *a.* not (very) good, overblown, not satisfactory; see **poor 2, unsatisfactory**.

override, *v.* 1. [To dismiss] pass over, not heed, take no account of; see **disregard, neglect 1**. 2. [To thwart] make void, reverse, annul; see **cancel, revoke**.

overrule, *v.* 1. [To nullify] invalidate, rule against, override; see **cancel, revoke**. 2. [To rule] direct, control, manage; see **govern**.

overrun, *v.* 1. [To defeat] overwhelm, invade, occupy; see **defeat 2**. 2. [To infest] ravage, invade, overwhelm; see **infest 2**.

overseas, *a.* away, across, in foreign countries; see **abroad**.

oversee, *v.* superintend, supervise, look after; see **manage 1**.

overseer, *n.* supervisor, manager, superintendent; see **foreman**.

overshoes, *n.* rubber shoes, galoshes, rubbers; see **shoe**.

overshoot, *v.* overreach, overdo, overact; see **exceed**.

oversight, *n.* failure, overlooking, mistake; see **error**.

oversleep, *v.* sleep late *or* in, miss the alarm (clock), stay in bed; see **sleep**.

overspecialize, *v.* limit (oneself), specialize too much, be a specialist; see **restrain 1, restrict 2**.

overstay, *v.* stay (too long), stop, outstay one's welcome; see **remain 1**.

overstep, *v.* violate, encroach, trespass; see **exceed, meddle 1**.

overtake, *v.* overhaul, catch up with, get to; see **reach 1**.

overtaken, *a.* caught (up with *or* to), reached, apprehended; see **beaten 1, captured**.

overthrow, *v.* overcome, overrun, overpower; see **defeat 2**.

overthrown, *a.* overcome, overwhelmed, vanquished; see **beaten 1**.

overtime, *n.* extra *or* additional pay *or* wages, late hours, larger *or* bigger check; see **pay 2**.

overtone, *n.* tone, inference, hint; see **meaning, suggestion 1**.

overture, *n.* 1. [Preliminary negotiations; *sometimes plural*] approach, advance, tender; see **suggestion 1**. 2. [A musical introduction] prelude, prologue, *Vorspiel* (German), voluntary, proem, preface; see also **introduction 3**.

overturn, *v.* reverse, upturn, overthrow; see **upset 1**.

overwhelm, *v.* 1. [To defeat] overcome, overthrow, conquer; see **defeat 2, 3, win 1**. 2. [To astonish] puzzle, bewilder, confound; see **confuse, surprise**.

overwhelmed, *a.* beaten, worsted, submerged; see **beaten 2**.

overwhelming, *a.* overpowering, ruinous, overthrowing, crushing, smashing, extinguishing, invading, ravaging, overriding, upsetting, inundating, drowning, deluging, surging, obliterating, dissolving, blotting out, wrecking, erasing, effacing, expunging, burying, immersing, engulfing, engrossing, covering; see also **harmful, triumphant**.

overwork, *n.* extra work, overtime, exhaustion; see **abuse**.

overwork, *v.* overdo, exhaust, wear out; see **burden, weary 2**.

overworked, *a.* too busy, overburdened, worked too hard; see **tired**.

owe, *v.* be under obligation, be indebted *or* obligated to *or* for, have an obligation, ought to, be bound, get on credit, feel bound, be bound to pay, be contracted to, be in debt for, have signed a note for, have borrowed, have lost.

owed, *a.* owing, becoming due, indebted; see **due, unpaid 1**.

owl, *n.* bird of prey, night bird, nocturnal bird; see also **bird**.

own, *a.* mine, yours, his, hers, its, theirs, personal, individual, owned, *very own; see also **private**.

own, *v.* 1. [To possess] hold, have, enjoy, fall heir to, have title to, have rights to, be master of, occupy, control, dominate, have claim upon, reserve, retain, keep, have in hand, have a deed for. —*Ant.* **lack**, want, need. 2. [To acknowledge] assent to, grant, recognize; see **admit 2,**

declare. —**come into one's own**, receive what one deserves, gain proper credit or recognition, thrive; see **profit 2**. —**of one's own**, personal, private, belonging to one; see **owned**. —**on one's own**, by oneself, acted independently, singly; see **independently**.

owned, *a*. possessed, had, bought, purchased, kept, inherited, enjoyed, in or on hand, bound over, in the possession of, among the possessions of, the property of.

owner, *n*. one who has or retains, keeper, buyer, purchaser, heir, heiress, proprietor, landlord, landlady, sharer, partner, title holder, master, heir-apparent.

ownership, *n*. possession, having, holding, claim, deed, title, control, buying, purchasing, heirship, proprietorship, occupancy, use, residence, tenancy, dominion.

own up, *v*. be honest, admit error, confess; see **admit 2**.

oyster, *n*. bivalve, mollusk, sea food; see also **fish, shellfish**.

P

*pa, n. sire, paterfamilias, *dad; see father 1, parent.

pace, n. step, velocity, movement; see speed 1. —change of pace, variation, alteration, diversity; see change 1. —keep pace (with), go at the same speed, maintain the same rate of progress, keep up with; see equal. —set the pace, begin, initiate, establish criteria; see lead 1.

pace, v. determine, pace off, step off; see measure 1.

Pacific, n. North Pacific, South Pacific, South Seas; see ocean.

pacifist, n. man of peace, peace-lover, CO or conscientious objector; see radical, resister.

pacify, v. conciliate, appease, placate; see quiet 1.

pack, n. 1. [A package] bundle, parcel, load; see package. 2. [Kit] outfit, baggage, luggage; see equipment. 3. [A group] number, gang, mob; see crowd. 4. [A medical dressing] application, hot pack, ice pack; see dressing 3. 5. [A set of cards] canasta or poker or rummy or bridge or pinochle deck, set, assortment; see deck 2.

pack, v. 1. [To prepare for transportation] prepare, gather, collect, (make) ready, get ready, put in (order), stow away, dispose, sock up, tie, bind, brace, fasten.—Ant. undo, untie, take out. 2. [To stow compactly] stuff, squeeze, bind, compress, condense, arrange, ram, cram, jam, insert, press, contract, put away.—Ant. scatter, loosen, fluff up.

package, n. parcel, packet, burden, load, kit, bunch, sheaf, pack, batch, baggage, luggage, grip, suitcase, bag, handbag, valise, trunk, box, carton, crate, bundle, bale, can, tin, sack, bottle; see also container.

packed, a. 1. [Ready for storage or shipment] prepared, bundled, wrapped; see also ready 2. 2. [Pressed together] compact, compressed, pressed down; see full 1.

packet, n. pack, receptacle, parcel; see container, package.

packing, n. preparation, arrangement, compression, consignment, disposal, disposition, sorting, grading, laying away.

pact, n. settlement, compact, bargain; see treaty.

pad, n. 1. [Material for writing] note paper or pad, stationery, notebook, parchment; see also paper 5, tablet 2. 2.

[Material for padding] stuffing, wadding, waste; see filing. 3. [*A residence] room, apartment, living quarters; see home.

pad, v. 1. [To stuff] pack, fill out, pad out; see fill 1. 2. [To increase] inflate, build up, falsify; see deceive, increase.

padded, a. stuffed, filled, quilted; see full 1.

padding, n. stuffing, wadding, waste; see filing.

paddle, n. oar, pole, paddle wheel; see tool 1.

paddle, v. 1. [To propel by paddling] scull, boat, cruise, drift, navigate, cut water, run rapids; see also drive 2. 2. [To beat, usually rather lightly] spank, thrash, rap; see beat 1, punish.

padlock, n. latch, fastener, catch; see lock 1.

pagan, a. unchristian, idolatrous, heathenish.

pagan, n. gentile, pantheist, heathen, doubter, scoffer, unbeliever, infidel.

paganism, n. heathenism, agnosticism, idolatry; see atheism.

page, n. leaf, sheet, folio, side, surface, recto, verso.

page, v. 1. [To call] hunt for, seek for, call the name of; see summon. 2. [To mark the pages] number, check, paginate; see check 2.

pageant, n. exhibition, celebration, pomp; see parade 1.

paid, a. rewarded, paid off, reimbursed, indemnified, remunerated, solvent, unindebted, unowed, recompensed, salaried, hired, out of debt, refunded; see also repaid.

paid for, a. purchased, bought and paid for, owned; see bought.

paid off, a. out of debt, solvent, (in the) clear; see bought.

pail, n. pot, receptacle, jug; see container.

pain, n. 1. [Suffering, physical or mental] hurt, anguish, distress, discomfort, disorder, agony, misery, martyrdom, wretchedness, shock, torture, torment, passion; see also injury.—Ant. health, wellbeing, ease. 2. [Suffering, usually physical] ache, twinge, catch, throe, spasm, cramp, torture, malady, sickness, laceration, soreness, fever, burning, torment, distress, agony, affliction, discomfort, hurt, wound, strain, sting, burn, crick; see also illness 1, injury. 3. [Suffering, usually mental] despondency, worry, anxiety; see depression 2, grief, sadness. —*feeling no pain, intoxicated, inebriated, *stoned; see drunk.

pain, v. distress, grieve, trouble; see hurt 1.

painful, a. 1. [Referring to physical anguish] raw, aching, throbbing, burning, torturing, hurtful, biting, piercing, sharp, severe, caustic, tormenting, smarting, extreme, grievous, stinging, bruised, sensitive, tender, irritated, distressing, inflamed, burned, unpleasant, ulcerated, abscessed, uncomfortable; see also sore 2.—Ant. healthy, comfortable, well. 2. [Referring to mental anguish] worrying, depressing, saddening; see disturbing.

paint, n. 1. [Pigment] coloring material, chroma, chlorophyll; see color. Paints and colorings include the following—artist's materials: oil, acrylic, pastel, crayon, charcoal, water color, tempera; architectural finishes: house paint, enamel, varnish, (redwood) stain, oil, wax, whitewash, tempera, fresco, luminous or plastic or cold-water or flat or high-gloss or metallic paint, barn paint, inside paint, outside paint, white lead. 2. [Covering] overlay, varnish, veneer; see finish 2.

paint, v., 1. [To represent by painting] portray, paint in oils, sketch, outline, picture, depict, catch a likeness, design, shade, tint, compose, fresco, wash; see also draw 2. 2. [To protect, or decorate by painting] coat, decorate, apply, brush, tint, touch up, ornament, gloss over, swab, daub, slap on; see also cover 1, spread 3.

painted, a. 1. [Portrayed] outlined, pictured, drawn, sketched, composed, designed, depicted, washed on; see also colored 1. 2. [Finished] coated, covered, enameled, decorated, ornamented, brushed over, tinted, washed, daubed, touched up, smeared; see also finished 1.

painter, n. 1. [House painter] interior decorator, dauber, paint-slinger; see workman. 2. [An artist] craftsman, artisan, illustrator, draftsman, etcher, sketcher, cartoonist, animator; see also artist. Major painters include the following—Giotto, Sandro Botticelli, Jan van Eyck, Albrecht Dürer, Hieronymus Bosch, Pieter Breughel (the elder and the younger), Leonardo da Vinci, Raphael, Titian, Tintoretto, El Gréco, Peter Paul Rubens, Anthony Van Dyck, Rembrandt van Rijn, Jan Vermeer, Sir Joshua Reynolds, Thomas Gainsborough, Diego Velázquez, Francisco Goya, Eugène Delacroix, Auguste Renoir, Edgar Degas, James Whistler, Winslow Homer, Edouard Manet, Claude Monet, Paul Cézanne, Vincent van Gogh, Paul Gauguin, Henri de Toulouse-Lautrec, Pablo Picasso, Henri Matisse, Paul Klee, Salvador Dali, Jackson Pollock.

painting, n. 1. [A work of art] oil painting, water color, abstract design, landscape, composition, sketch, picture, likeness, art work, canvas, mural, depiction, delineation; see also art. 2. [The act of applying paint] enameling, covering, coating; see art.

pair, n. couple, mates, two, two of a kind, twins, deuce, fellows, duality, biformation; see also both.

pair, v. combine (with), match, balance (off); see join 1, 2.

pajamas, n. nightwear, lounging pajamas, lounging robe, *PJ's, *jamas, *nightie; see also clothes.

*pal, n. companion, bosom friend, *buddy; see friend.

palace, n. royal residence, manor, mansion; see castle.

pale, a. 1. [Wan] pallid, sickly, anemic, bloodless, ghastly, cadaverous, haggard, deathlike, ghostly; see also dull 2. 2. [Lacking color] white, colorless, bleached; see dull 2.

pale, v. grow pale, lose color, blanch; see whiten 1.

paleness, n. whiteness, anemia, colorlessness; see illness 1.

palmy, a. prosperous, glorious, delightful; see happy, pleasant 2.

paltry, a. small, insignificant, trifling; see unimportant.

pamper, v. spoil, indulge, pet, cater to, humor, gratify, yield to, coddle, overindulge, please, *spare the rod and spoil the child.

pamphlet, n. booklet, brochure, pocketbook, chapbook, leaflet, bulletin, circular, broadside, handbill; see also announcement.

pan, n. vessel, kettle, container, pail, bucket, baking pan, gold pan; see also container. Kitchen pans include the following—kettle, stew pan, sauce pan, double boiler, roaster, casserole, cake pan, bread pan, pie pan, cookie sheet, frying pan or skillet or spider, dishpan.

*pan, v. criticize, review unfavorably, jeer at; see blame. —*pan out, pay (off), be a success, work; see succeed 1.

pancake, n. flapjack, hot cake, cake; see food.

pandemonium, n. uproar, anarchy, riot; see confusion.

pane, n. window glass, stained glass, mirror; see glass.

panel, n. ornament, tablet, inset; see decoration 2.

pang, n. throb, sting, bite; see pain 1.

*panhandle, *v.* solicit, ask alms, **bum; see beg.

*panhandler, *n.* vagrant, **bum, mendicant; see beggar.

panic, *n.* dread, alarm, fright; see fear.

panic-stricken, *a.* terrified, hysterical, fearful; see afraid.

panorama, *n.* spectacle, scenery, prospect; see view 2.

*pan out, *v.* yield, net, come *or* work out; see result.

pant, *v.* wheeze, throb, palpitate; see breathe, gasp.

panties, *n.* pants, underpants, briefs; see underwear.

pantomime, *n.* sign, sign language, dumb show, mimicry, play without words, acting without speech, charade, mime.

pantry, *n.* storeroom, larder, cupboard; see closet, room 2.

pants, *n.* 1. [Trousers] breeches, slacks, jeans, overalls, cords, shorts, corduroys, pantaloons, bell bottoms, toreador pants, riding breeches, chaps, short pants, knee pants, knickers, bloomers, rompers, sun suit; see also clothes. 2. [Underclothing, especially women's] shorts, briefs, panties; see clothes, underwear.

papa, *n.* dad, daddy, male parent; see father 1, parent.

paper, *n.* 1. [A piece of legal *or* official writing] document, official document, legal paper; see record 1. Papers, sense 1, include the following–abstract, affidavit, bill, certificate, citation, contract, credentials, data, deed, diploma, indictment, grant, order(s), passport, visa, plea, records, safe-conduct, subpoena, summons, testimony, voucher, warrant, will. 2. [A newspaper] journal, daily, daily journal; see newspaper. 3. [A piece of writing] essay, article, theme; see writing 2. 4. [A manufactured product] Paper, sense 5, includes the following– *writing material*: typing *or* typewriter paper, stationery, bond paper, letterhead, personal stationery, ruled paper, second sheet, onion skin, carbon paper, note pad, note card, filing card. —**on paper,** 1. recorded, signed, official; see written 2. 2. in theory, assumed to be feasible, not yet in practice; see theoretical.

paper, *v.* hang, paste up, plaster; see cover 1.

paperback, *n.* paperbacked *or* paperbound book, paperback original, reprint; see book.

papers, *n.* 1. [Evidence of identity or authorization] naturalization papers, identification card, ID; see identification 2, passport. 2. [Documentary materials]

writings, documents, effects; see record 1.

paper work, *n.* office *or* desk *or* inside work, keeping up with *or* handling the correspondence, keeping one's desk clear, doing the office chores, keeping records, filing, preparing *or* getting up reports, taking dictation, typing, keeping books.

papery, *a.* flimsy, insubstantial, slight; see poor 2.

*pappy, *n.* *papa, *daddy, *pa; see father 1, parent.

par, *n.* standard, level, norm; see model 2.

parable, *n.* fable, moral story, tale; see story.

parachute, *n.* chute, seat pack parachute, lap pack parachute, harness and pack, *umbrella, *bailer, *silk.

parachute, *v.* fall, bail out, hit the silk; see jump 1.

parade, *n.* 1. [A procession] spectacle, ceremony, demonstration, review, line of floats, line of march, pageant, ritual. 2. [An ostentatious show] show, ostentation, ceremony; see display.

parade, *v.* demonstrate, display, exhibit; see march.

paradise, *n.* 1. [Heaven] Kingdom Come, Celestial Home, (the) other world; see heaven. 2. [The home of Adam and Eve] Garden of Eden, Eden, the Garden.

paradox, *n.* mystery, enigma, ambiguity; see puzzle 2.

paragon, *n.* ideal, perfection, best; see model 1.

paragraph, *n.* passage, section, division of thought, topic, statement, verse, article, item, notice.

parallel, *a.* 1. [Equidistant at all points] side by side, never meeting, running parallel, co-ordinate, co-extending, lateral, laterally, in the same direction, extending equally. 2. [Similar in kind, position, or the like] identical, equal, conforming; see alike.

parallel, *n.* resemblance, likeness, correspondence; see similarity.

parallel, *v.* match, correspond, correlate; see equal.

paralysis, *n.* insensibility, loss of motion, loss of sensation; see illness 2.

paralytic, *a.* inactive, paralyzed, crippled; see disabled, sick.

paralytic, *n.* paralysis victim, cripple, paralyzed person; see patient.

paralyze, *v.* strike with paralysis, make inert, render nerveless; see deaden.

paralyzed, *a.* insensible, nerveless, benumbed, stupefied, inert, inactive, unmoving, helpless, torpid; see also disabled.

paraphernalia, *n.* gear, material, apparatus; see **equipment**.

parasite, *n.* 1. [A plant or animal living on another] bacteria, parasitoid, saprophyte, epiphyte. 2. [A hanger-on] dependent, slave, sponger; see **slave**.

parcel, *n.* bundle, packet, carton; see **package**.

parch, *v.* dessicate, dehydrate, brown; see **dry 1**.

parched, *a.* burned, withered, dried; see **dry 1**.

parchment, *n.* vellum, goatskin, sheepskin; see **paper 5**.

pardon, *n.* 1. [The reduction or removal of punishment] absolution, grace, remission, amnesty, exoneration, discharge; see also **mercy 1**.—*Ant.* punishment, condemnation, conviction. 2. [Forgiveness] excuse, forbearance, conciliation; see **forgiveness, kindness 1**.

pardon, *v.* 1. [To reduce punishment] exonerate, clear, absolve, reprieve, acquit, set free, liberate, discharge, rescue, justify, suspend charges, put on probation, grant amnesty to; see also **free, release**.—*Ant.* punish, chastise, sentence. 2. [To forgive] condone, overlook, exculpate; see **excuse, forgive**.

pardoned, *a.* forgiven, freed, excused, released, granted amnesty, given a pardon, reprieved, granted a reprieve, acquitted, let off, sprung, back in circulation; see also **discharged, free 1**.—*Ant.* accused, convicted, condemned.

pare, *v.* scalp, strip, flay; see **cut 1, shave, skin**.

parent, *n.* immediate forebear, procreator, progenitor, sire, he *or* she from whom one has one's being; see also **father 1, mother 1**.

parental, *a.* paternal, maternal, familial; see **genetic**.

parenthesis, *n.* brackets, enclosure, punctuation marks; see **punctuation**.

parish, *n.* archdiocese, congregation, diocese; see **area, church 3**.

park, *n.* 1. [A place designated for outdoor recreation] square, plaza, lawn, green, village green, promenade, boulevard, tract, recreational area, pleasure ground, national park *or* forest, national monument, enclosure, woodland, meadow. 2. [A place designed for outdoor storage] parking lot, parking space, lot; see **garage 1, parking lot**.

park, *v.* mass, collect, order, place in order, station, place in rows, leave, store, impound, deposit; see also **line up**.

parked, *a.* stationed, standing, left, put, lined up, in rows, by the curb, in the parking lot, stored, halted, unmoving.

parking lot, *n.* lot, parking, space, parking space *or* garage *or* area *or* facility *or* slot, pigeonhole parking, off-street parking, parking area.

Parliament, *n.* national legislative body of Great Britain, House of Commons, House of Lords; see **government 2, legislature**.

parliamentary, *a.* congressional, administrative, lawmaking; see **governmental, legislative**.

parochial, *a.* provincial, insular, sectional; see **local 1, regional**.

parody, *n.* travesty, burlesque, mimicry; see **joke**.

parody, *v.* mimic, copy, caricature; see **imitate 1, joke**.

parole, *v.* discharge, pardon, liberate; see **free, release**.

parrot, *n.* 1. [A bird] parakeet, lovebird, cockatoo; see **bird**. 2. [One who copies others] plagiarist, mimic, mimicker, ape, impersonator, imposter, mocker, *copycat; see also **imitator**.

parson, *n.* clergyman, cleric, preacher; see **minister 1**.

part, *n.* 1. [A portion] piece, fragment, fraction, section, sector, member, segment, division, allotment, apportionment, ingredient, element, slab, subdivision, partition, particle, installment, component, constituent, bit, slice, scrap, chip, chunk, lump, sliver, splinter, shaving, molecule, atom, electron, proton, neutron; see also **share**.—*Ant.* whole, total, aggregate. 2. [A part of speech] modifier, preposition, conjunction; see **noun, verb**. 3. [A machine part] molding, casting, fitting, lever, shaft, cam, spring, band, belt, chain, pulley, clutch, spare part, replacement; see also **bolt, gear, machine, wheel 1**. 4. [A character in a drama] hero, heroine, character; see **role**. —**for the most part**, mainly, mostly, to the greatest part *or* extent; see **most**. —**in part**, to a certain extent, somewhat, slightly; see **partly**. —**on one's part**, privately, as far as one is concerned, coming from one; see **personally 2**. —**play a part**, share, join, take part; see **participate 1**.

part, *v.* 1. [To put apart] separate, break, sever; see **divide**. 2. [To depart] withdraw, take leave, part company; see **leave 1**.

partake, *v.* participate, divide, take; see **share 2**.

parted, *a.* divided, severed, sundered; see **separated**.

part from, *v.* separate, part, break up with; see **leave 1**.

partial, *a.* 1. [Not complete] unperformed, incomplete, half done; see **unfinished 1**. 2. [Showing favoritism] unfair, influenced, biased; see **prejudiced**.

partiality, *n.* fondness, inclination, preference; see **affection.**

participant, *n.* co-operator, partner, sharer; see **associate.**

participate, *v.* 1. [To take part in] share, partake, aid, co-operate, join in, come in, associate with, be a party to, have a finger *or* hand in, concur, take an interest in, take part in, enter into, have to do with, get in the act, go into, *chip in; see also **join** 2.—*Ant.* retire, withdraw, refuse. 2. [To engage in a contest] play, strive, engage; see **compete.**

participation, *n.* partnership, joining in, sharing, support, aid, assistance, help, encouragement, seconding, standing by, taking part; see also **partnership.**

particle, *n.* jot, scrap, atom, molecule, fragment, piece, shred; see also **bit** 1.

particular, *a.* 1. [Specific] distinct, singular, appropriate; see **special** 1. 2. [Accurate] precise, minute, exact; see **accurate** 2. —**in particular,** expressly, particularly, individually; see **especially** 1.

particular, *n.* fact, specification, item; see **detail.**

particularly, *a.* unusually, expressly, individually; see **especially** 1.

parting, *n.* leavetaking, good-bye, farewell; see **departure.**

partisan, *n.* adherent, supporter, disciple; see **follower.**

partition, *n.* 1. [Division] apportionment, separation, severance; see **distribution.** 2. [That which divides or separates] bar, obstruction, hindrance; see **barrier, wall** 1.

partly, *a.* in part, partially, to a degree, in some degree *or* measure, measurably, somewhat, noticeably, notably, in some part, incompletely, insufficiently, inadequately, up to a certain point, so far as possible, not wholly *or* entirely, as much as could be expected, to some *or* a certain extent, within limits, slightly, to a slight degree, in a portion only, in some ways, in certain particulars, only in details, in a general way, not strictly speaking, in bits and pieces, by fits and starts, carelessly, with large omissions, short of the end, at best *or* worst *or* most *or* least, at the outside.—*Ant.* completely, wholly, entirely.

partner, *n.* co-worker, ally, comrade; see **associate.**

partnership, *n.* alliance, union, co-operation, company, combination, corporation, connection, brotherhood, society, lodge, club, fellowship, fraternity, confederation, band, body, crew, clique, gang, ring, faction, party, community, conjunction, joining, companionship, friendship, help; see also **alliance** 1, **union** 1.

part of, *pron.* portion, section, division; see **some.**

part of speech, *n.* grammatical unit *or* construction, word *or* phrase, lexeme; see **adjective, grammar, pronoun, verb, word** 1.

partway, *a.* started, toward the middle, somewhat; see **begun, some** 1.

part with, *v.* let go (of), suffer loss, give up; see **lose** 2.

party, *n.* 1. [A social affair] at-home, tea, luncheon, dinner party, dinner, cocktail hour, surprise party, house party, social, bee, reception, banquet, feast, affair, gathering, function, fete, ball, recreation, fun, cheer, amusement, entertainment, festive occasion, carousal, diversion, performance, high tea, *binge, *spree, *blowout, *bash. 2. [A group of people] multitude, mob, company; see **crowd, gathering.** 3. [A political organization] organized group, body, electorate, combine, combination, bloc, ring, junta, partisans, cabal; see also **faction** 1. 4. [A specified but unnamed individual] party of the first, second, third, etc., part; someone, individual; see **person** 1, **somebody.**

pass, *n.* 1. [An opening through mountains] gorge, ravine, crossing, track, way, path, passageway; see also **gap** 3. 2. [A document assuring permission to pass] ticket, permit, passport, visa, order, admission, furlough, permission, right, license. 3. [In sports, the passing of the ball from one player to another] toss, throw, fling; see **pitch** 2. 4. [An advance] approach, sexual overture, proposition; see **suggestion** 1.

pass, *v.* 1. [To move past] go *or* run by *or* past, flit by, come by, shoot ahead of, catch, come to the front, go beyond, roll on, fly past, reach, roll by, cross, flow past, glide by, go in opposite directions; see also **move** 1. 2. [To elapse] transpire, slip *or* pass away *or* by, fly, fly by, linger, glide by, run out, drag, crawl. 3. [To complete a course successfully] matriculate, be graduated, pass with honors; see **succeed** 1. 4. [To hand to others] transfer, relinquish, hand over; see **give** 1. 5. [To enact] legislate, establish, vote in; see **enact.** 6. [To become enacted] carry, become law, become valid, be ratified, be established, be ordained, be sanctioned. 7. [To exceed] excel, transcend, go beyond; see **exceed.** 8. [To spend time] fill, occupy oneself, while away; see **spend** 2. 9 [To proceed] progress, get ahead, move *or* go on; see **advance** 1. 10. [To emit] give off, send forth, exude; see **emit.** —**bring to pass,** bring about, initiate, start; see **cause.** —**come to pass,** occur, develop, come about; see **happen** 2.

passable, *a.* open, fair, penetrable, navigable, accessible, traveled, easy, broad, graded; see also **available, fair 2.**

passage, *n.* 1. [A journey] voyage, crossing, trek; see **journey. 2.** [A passageway] way, exit, entrance; see **entrance 2. 3.** [A reading] section, portion, paragraph; see **reading 3.**

pass away, *v.* depart, expire, pass on; see **die.**

pass by, *v.* 1. [To go past] travel, move past, depart from; see **leave 1, pass 1. 2.** [To neglect] pass over, not choose, omit; see **abandon 1, neglect 1.**

passed, *a.* missed, forgotten, gone by; see **forgotten.**

passenger, *n.* commuter, tourist, wanderer; see **rider 1.**

passer-by, *n.* witness, traveler, bystander; see **observer.**

passing, *a.* 1. [In the act of going past] departing, crossing, going by, gliding by, flashing by, speeding by, going in opposite directions, passing in the night; see also **moving 1. 2.** [Of brief duration] fleeting, transitory, transient; see **temporary.**

passion, *n.* lust, craving, sexual excitement; see **desire 2, emotion.**

passionate, *a.* 1. [Excitable] vehement, hotheaded, tempestuous; see **sense 2. 2.** [Ardent] intense, impassioned, loving, fervent, moving, inspiring, dramatic, melodramatic, romantic, poignant, swelling, enthusiastic, tragic, stimulating, wistful, stirring, thrilling, warm, burning, glowing, vehement, deep, affecting, eloquent, spirited, fiery, expressive, forceful, heated, hot. 3. [Intense] strong, vehement, violent; see **intense.**

passive, *a.* 1. [Being acted upon] receptive, stirred, influenced; see **affected 1. 2.** [Not active] inactive, inert, lifeless; see **idle.**

pass off, *v.* 1. [To pretend] pass for, make a pretense of, *palm off;* see **pretend 1. 2.** [To emit] give off, send forth, eject; see **emit.**

pass on, *v.* 1. [To decide] determine, conclude, make a judgment; see **decide, judge. 2.** [To die] expire, depart, succumb; see **die.**

pass out, *v.* 1. [To faint] swoon, lose consciousness, black out; see **faint. 2.** [To distribute] hand out, circulate, deal out; see **distribute, give 1.**

pass over, *v.* 1. [To traverse] travel through, go or move over, go across; see **cross 1. 2.** [To ignore] dismiss, overlook, neglect; see **disregard.**

passport, *n.* pass, license, permit, safe-conduct, visa, travel permit, authorization, warrant, credentials; see also **identification 2.**

*****pass the buck,** *v.* transfer responsibility, assign, refer; see **avoid, delegate 1.**

pass up, *v.* dismiss, send away, reject; see **deny, refuse.**

password, *n.* countersign, signal, phrase, secret word, watchword, identification, open sesame.

past, *a.* 1. [Having occurred previously] former, preceding, gone by, foregoing, elapsed, anterior, antecedent, prior. 2. [No longer serving] ex-, retired, earlier; see **preceding.**

past, *n.* 1. [Past time] antiquity, long ago, the past, past times, old times, years ago, good old days or times, ancient times, former times, days gone by, (auld) lang-syne, yore, days of old or yore, yesterday.—*Ant.* future, the present, tomorrow. 2. [Past events] knowledge, happenings, events; see **history.**

past, *prep.* through, farther than, behind; see **beyond.**

paste, *n.* cement, glue, mucilage; see **cement.**

paste, *v.* glue, fix, affix, repair, patch; see also **stick 1.**

pastime, *n.* recreation, amusement, sport; see **entertainment, hobby.**

pastor, *n.* priest, rector, clergyman; see **minister 1.**

pastry, *n.* baked goods, dainty, delicacy, bread, goodies, fixings, trimmings; see also **bread.** Pastries include the following—French, Danish; tart, turnover, oatcake, shortbread, pudding, eclair, cakes, sweet roll.

pasture, *n.* grazing land, pasturage, hayfield; see **field 1, meadow.**

pat, *v.* 1. [To strike lightly] tap, beat, punch; see **hit 1. 2.** [To strike lightly and affectionately] stroke, pet, rub; see **touch 2.**

patch, *n.* piece, mend, bit, scrap, spot, application.

patch, *v.* darn, mend, cover; see **repair.**

patch up, *v.* appease, adjust, compensate; see **settle 7.**

patent, *n.* patent right, protection, concession, control, limitation, license, copyright, privilege; see also **right 1.**

patent, *v.* license, secure, control, limit, monopolize, safeguard, exclude, copyright.

patented, *a.* copyright(ed), patent applied for, trade-marked, under patent or copyright, patent pending; see also **restricted.**

paternal, *a.* patrimonial, fatherly, protective; see **protective.**

paternity, *n.* progenitorship, paternal parentage, fathership; see **father 1.**

path, *n.* trail, way, track, short cut, footpath, crosscut, footway, roadway, cinder track, byway; see also **route 1.**

pathetic, *a.* touching, affecting, moving; see **pitiful.**

patience, *n.* 1. [Willingness to endure] forbearance, fortitude, composure, submission, endurance, nonresistance, self-control, passiveness, bearing, serenity, humility, yielding, poise, sufferance, long-suffering, moderation, leniency; see also **resignation 1.**—*Ant.* **nervousness,** fretfulness, restlessness. 2. [Ability to continue] submission, perseverance, persistence; see **endurance.**

patient, *a.* 1. [Enduring without complaint] submissive, meek, forbearing, mild-tempered, composed, tranquil, serene, long-suffering, unruffled, imperturbable, passive, cold-blooded, easygoing, tolerant, gentle, unresentful; see also **resigned.**—*Ant.* **irritable,** violent, resentful. 2. [Quietly persistent in an activity] steady, dependable, calm, reliable, stable, composed, unwavering, quiet, serene, unimpassioned, enduring; see also **reliable.**—*Ant.* **restless,** irrepressible, feverish.

patient, *n.* case, inmate, victim, sufferer, sick *or* ill individual, medical *or* surgical *or* psychiatric *or* dental, etc., case *or* patient, outpatient, bed patient, emergency (ward) patient, convalescent, hospital case, hospitalized person, subject.

patiently, *a.* 1. [Suffering without complaint] enduringly, bravely, impassively, resignedly, numbly, forbearingly, tolerantly, submissively, meekly; see also **calmly.** 2. [Continuing without impatience] steadily, firmly, unabatingly; see **regularly 2.**

patio, *n.* porch, courtyard, square; see **yard 1.**

patriarch, *n.* master, head of family, ancestor; see **chief 2.**

patriot, *n.* lover of his country, good citizen, statesman, nationalist, volunteer, loyalist, jingoist, chauvinist.

patriotic, *a.* devoted, zealous, public-spirited, consecrated, dedicated, jingoistic, chauvinistic.

patriotism, *n.* love of country, public spirit, good citizenship, nationality, nationalism; see also **loyalty.**

patrol, *n.* guard, watch, protection; see **army 2.**

patrol, *v.* watch, walk, inspect; see **guard.**

patrolman, *n.* police, police officer, constable; see **policeman.**

patron, *n.* philanthropist, benefactor, helper, protector, encourager, champion, backer, advocate, defender, guide, leader, friend, ally, sympathizer, well-wisher, partisan, buyer, *angel, *sugar daddy, booster.—*Ant.* **enemy,** obstructionist, adversary.

patronage, *n.* 1. [Trade] commerce, trading, shopping; see **business 1. 2.** [Condescension] deference, patronization, toleration; see **pride 2.**

patronize, *v.* 1. [To trade with] habituate, buy *or* purchase from, shop with; see **buy, sell.** 2. [To assume a condescending attitude] talk down to, be overbearing, stoop, be gracious to, favor, pat on the back, play the snob, snub, lord it over; see also **condescend.**

patronizing, *a.* condescending, gracious, stooping; see **egotistic, polite.**

pattern, *n.* original, guide, copy; see **model 2.**

pauper, *n.* dependent, indigent, destitute person; see **beggar.**

pause, *n.* lull, rest, stop, halt, truce, stay, respite, standstill, stand, deadlock, stillness, intermission, suspension, discontinuance, breathing space, hitch, hesitancy, interlude, hiatus, interim, lapse, cessation, stopover, interval, rest period, gap, stoppage.

pause, *v.* delay, halt, rest, catch (one's) breath, cease, hold back, reflect, deliberate, suspend, think twice, discontinue, interrupt; see also **hesitate.**

pave, *v.* lay concrete, asphalt, gravel; see **cover 1.**

paved, *a.* hard-surfaced, flagged, cobblestone, asphalt, concrete, brick, bricked, surfaced with wood blocks; see also **covered 1.**

pavement, *n.* hard surface, paving, paving stone, paving tile, flagging, pave. Road surfaces include the following—concrete, asphalt, black top, stone, brick, tile, macadam, gravel, cobblestone, wood blocks, flagstone.

paving, *n.* hard surface, concrete, paved highway; see **pavement.**

paw, *n.* forefoot, talon, hand; see **claw.**

paw, *v.* 1. [To strike wildly] clutch, grasp, smite; see **hit 1.** 2. [To scrape with the front foot] scratch, rake, claw; see **dig 1.**

pawn, *v.* deposit, pledge, hock, hang up, *soak, *pop; see also **sell.**

pawned, *a.* deposited, pledged, hocked; see **sold out.**

pay, *n.* 1. [Monetary return] profit, proceeds, interest, return, recompense, indemnity, reparation, rake-off, reward, consideration, defrayment.—*Ant.* **expense,** disbursement, outlay. 2. [Wages] compensation, salary, payment, hire, remuneration, commission, redress, fee, stipend, earnings, settlement, consideration, reimbursement, satisfaction, reward, time, time and a half, double time, overtime.

pay, *v.* 1. [To give payment] pay up, compensate, recompense, make payment, reward, remunerate, charge, discharge, pay *or* *foot a bill, refund, settle, get even with, reckon with, lay *or* put down, make restitution *or* reparation, hand over, repay, liquidate, handle, take care of, give, confer, bequeath, defray, meet, disburse, clear, adjust, satisfy, reimburse, *kick in, *dig up, *plank down, *put up, pay as you go, *fork out *or* over, *even the score, *chip in. —*Ant.* deceive, swindle, victimize. 2. [To produce a profit] return, pay off, pay out, show *or* yield profit, yield excess, show gain, pay dividends.—*Ant.* fail, lose, become bankrupt. 3. [To retaliate] repay, punish, requite; see revenge.

pay back, *v.* discharge a responsibility, even up, compound (for); see return 2.

pay down on, *v.* make a payment on, pay in on, start (the) purchase (of); see pay 1.

pay for, *v.* atone for, make amends for, do penance for, compensate for, make up for, make satisfaction for, expiate, make reparation for, give satisfaction for, pay the penalty for, make compensation for.

payment, *n.* 1. [The act of paying] recompense, reimbursement, restitution, subsidy, return, redress, refund, remittance, reparation, disbursement, down, amends, cash, salary, wage, sum, payoff, repayment, defrayment, retaliation; see also pay 1. 2. [An installment] portion, part, amount; see debt.

pay-off, *n.* settlement, conclusion, reward; see pay, 1, payment 1.

pay off, *v.* discharge, let go, drop (from the payroll); see dismiss.

payroll, *n.* employees, workers, pay list; see faculty 2, staff 2.

peace, *n.* 1. [The state of being without war] armistice, pacification, conciliation, order, concord, amity, union, unity, reconciliation, brotherhood, love, unanimity; see also agreement 1, friendship.—*Ant.* war, warfare, battle. 2. [State of being without disturbance] calm, repose, quiet, tranquillity, harmony, lull, hush, congeniality, equanimity, silence, stillness; see also rest 1.—*Ant.* fight, noisiness, quarrel. 3. [Mental or emotional calm] calmness, repose, harmony, concord, contentment, sympathy; see also composure, reserve 2, tranquillity.—*Ant.* distress, disturbance, agitation. —at peace, peaceful, quiet, tranquil; see calm 1. —hold (*or* keep) one's peace, be silent, keep quiet, not speak; see shut up 1. —make peace, end hostilities, settle, reconcile; see quiet 1.

peaceable, *a.* conciliatory, pacific, peaceful; see friendly.

peaceful, *a.* 1. [At peace] quiet, tranquil, serene; see calm 1, 2. 2. [Inclined to

peace] well-disposed, sociable, amiable; see friendly.

peacefully, *a.* 1. [Calmly] tranquilly, quietly, composedly; see calmly. 2. [Without making trouble] harmoniously, placatingly, inoffensively, temperately, civilly; see also modestly.

peak, *n.* 1. [A mountain] summit, top, crown; see mountain 1. 2. [The maximum] zenith, highest point, greatest quantity; see height, tip 1, top 1.

peaked, *a.* pointed, topped, triangletopped; see sharp 1.

pearl, *n.* nacre, margarite, cultured pearl; see jewel.

peasant, *n.* small farmer, farm laborer, farm worker; see farmer, laborer, workman.

pebble, *n.* pebblestone, gravel, cobblestone; see also rock 1, stone.

peck, *n.* 1. [A slight, sharp blow] pinch, tap, rap; see blow 1. 2. [One fourth of a bushel] eight quarts, quarter-bushel, large amount; see measure 1, quantity.

peck, *v.* nip, pick, tap; see bite 1, pinch.

peculiar, *a.* 1. [Unusual] wonderful, singular, outlandish; see strange, unusual 2. 2. [Characteristic of only one] strange, uncommon, eccentric; see characteristic, unique.

peculiarity, *n.* distinctiveness, unusualness, singularity; see characteristic.

pedal, *n.* treadle, foot lever, accelerator; see lever.

pedal, *v.* treadle, operate, work; see drive 2.

peddle, *v.* hawk, vend, trade; see sell.

peddler, *n.* hawker, vender, seller; see businessman.

pedestal, *n.* stand, foundation, footstall, plinth; see also column 1, support 2.

pedestrian, *n.* foot-traveler, one who walks, hiker; see walking, a.

peek, *n.* sight, glimpse, glance; see look 3.

peek, *v.* glance, peep, glimpse; see see 1.

peel, *n.* husk, bark, shell; see skin.

peel, *v.* pare, strip, tear *or* pull off, flay, uncover; see also skin.

peeling, *n.* paring, strip, sliver; see skin.

peep, *n.* 1. [A peek] glimpse, glance, sight; see look 3. 2. [A peeping sound] cheep, chirp, hoot; see cry 2.

peep, *v.* 1. [To look cautiously] peek, glimpse, glance; see see 1. 2. [To make a peeping sound] cheep, chirp, squeak; see cry 2.

peer, *n.* match, rival, companion; see equal.

peer, *v.* gaze, inspect, scrutinize; see see 1.

peer group, *n.* equals, age *or* social group *or* class, one's peers; see associate, equal.

peeve, v. irritate, annoy, anger; see bother 2.

peeved, a. sullen, irritated, upset; see angry.

peevish, a. cross, fretful, fretting; see angry.

peg, n. pin, tack, fastener; see nail. — take down a peg, humiliate, criticize, diminish; see humble.

pellet, n. pill, bead, grain; see stone.

pell-mell, a. impetuously, hurriedly, indiscreetly; see foolishly.

pelt, n. fell, hair, wool; see hide 1.

pen, n. 1. [An enclosed place] coop, cage, corral, sty, close, concentration camp, penitentiary; see also enclosure 1. 2. [A writing instrument] Pens and pen points include the following —fountain, desk, drawing, ruling, artist's, reed, quill, steel, ball point pen.

pen, v. 1. [To enclose] close or fence in, confine, *coop up; see enclose 1. 2. [To write] compose, indict, commit to writing; see write 1, 2.

penalize, v. scold, chasten, castigate; see punish.

penalty, n. fine, mortification, discipline; see punishment.

penance, n. mortification, purgation, repentance, retribution, compensation, self-imposed atonement, fasting, suffering, sackcloth and ashes, hair shirt, reparation; see also punishment.

pencil, n. Types of pencils include the following—lead, mechanical, colored, drawing, slate, indelible, charcoal, eyebrow, cosmetic, drafting; chalk, crayon, stylus.

pendant, n. earring, locket, lavalière; see decoration 2, jewelry.

pending, a. continuing, indeterminate, awaiting; see ominous.

pendulum, n. swing, pendant, suspended body; see device, machine.

penetrable, a. permeable, receptive, open, passable, accessible; see porous.

penetrate, v. bore, perforate, enter, insert, go through, make an entrance, stick into, jab, thrust, stab, force (a way), make a hole, run into, run through, punch, puncture, drive into, stick, drill, eat through, spear, impale, wound, gore, sting, sink into, knife, go or pass through.—Ant. leave, withdraw, turn aside.

penetrating, a. 1. [Entering] piercing, going through, puncturing; see sharp 1. 2. [Mentally keen] astute, shrewd, sharp; see intelligent.

penetration, n. 1. [Act of entering] insertion, invasion, perforation; see entrance 1. 2. [Mental acuteness] discernment, perception, keen sightedness; see intelligence 1.

peninsula, n. point, promontory, cape; see land 1.

penitentiary, n. reformatory, penal institution, *pen; see jail, prison.

penniless, a. poverty-stricken, lacking means, indigent; see poor 1.

penny, n. cent, copper, red cent; see money 1.

pension, n. annuity, premium, payment, grant, social security, gift, reward; see also allowance.

people, n. 1. [Humankind] humanity, mankind, the human race; see man 1. 2. [A body of persons having racial or social ties] nationality, tribe, community; see race 2. 3. [The humbler portions of society] mass, folk, proletariat, rabble, masses, the multitude, the majority, democracy, crowd, common people, common herd, rank and file, the underprivileged, the public, the man in the street, *bourgeoisie* (French), *riffraff; *the herd, *the horde, the many, the great unwashed, John or Jane Q. Public. 4. [Family] close relatives, kinsmen, siblings; see family. 5. [Society in general] they, anybody, the public; see everybody.

peopled, a. lived in, dwelt in, sustaining human life; see inhabited.

per, prep. to each, for each, contained in each, according to, through, by, by means of.

perceive, v. 1. [See] observe, note, notice; see look 2, see 1. 2. [Understand] comprehend, sense, grasp; see understand 1.

perceived, a. seen, felt, touched; see understood 1.

per cent, a. by the hundred, reckoned on the basis of a hundred, percentaged, in a hundred, percentile.

percentage, n. per cent, rate, rate per cent, portion, section, allotment, duty, discount, commission, winnings, cut, *rake-off, *holdout, *corner, pay-off, *slice; see also division 2.

perceptible, a. perceivable, discernible, cognizable; see obvious 1.

perception, n. 1. [The act of perceiving] realizing, understanding, apprehending; see attention, judgment 2. 2. [The result of perceiving] insight, knowledge, observation; see attitude, opinion 1, viewpoint.

perceptive, a. alert, incisive, keen; see conscious 1, observant 1.

perch, n. seat, pole, landing place; see roost.

perch, v. roost, settle down, land; see rest 1, sit.

perfect, a. 1. [Having all necessary qualities] complete, sound, entire; see absolute 1; whole 1. 2. 2. [Without defect] excelling, faultless, flawless, impeccable, immaculate, unblemished, foolproof, untainted, unspotted, absolute, classical, stainless, spotless, crowning, culminating, supreme, ideal, sublime, beyond all praise, beyond compare; see also excellent, pure 2, whole 2.—*Ant.* ruined, damaged, faulty. 3. [Exact] precise, sharp, distinct; see accurate 2.

perfect, *v.* fulfill, realize, develop; see achieve, complete.

perfected; *a.* completed, developed, mature, conclusive, full, elaborate, thorough; see also finished 1, fulfilled.

perfection, *n.* completion, fulfillment, finishing, consummation, supremacy, ideal, ending, realization; see also achievement.—*Ant.* ruin, destruction, neglect.

perfectly, *a.* excellently, fitly, correctly, flawlessly, faultlessly, supremely, ideally.—*Ant.* badly, poorly, incorrectly.

perforate, *v.* drill, slit, stab; see penetrate.

perforation, *n.* break, aperture, slit; see hole 1.

perform, *v.* 1. [To accomplish an action] do, make, achieve, rehearse, accomplish, fulfill, execute, transact, carry out *or* off *or* through, discharge, effect, enforce, administer, complete, consummate, operate, finish, realize, go about *or* through (with), discharge the duties of, put through, work out, devote oneself to, come through (with), be engrossed *or* engaged in, see to (it), bring off *or* about *or* through, engage in, concern oneself with, have effect, fall to, do justice to, do one's part, make a move, follow through, apply oneself to, put across, deal with, do something, look to, take measures, act on, lose oneself in, make it one's own business, dispose of, bring to pass, do what is expected of one, put into effect, occupy oneself with, take action, address oneself to, put in action, *lift a finger, *keep one's hand in, *go in for, *pull off. 2. [To present a performance] give, present, enact, play, offer, impersonate, show, exhibit, display, act out, dramatize, execute, put on the stage, produce, act the part of, put on an act, act one's part.

performance, *n.* appearance, rehearsal, exhibition, offering, representation, spectacle, review, revue, opera, play, concert, exhibit, display, special; see also drama.

perfume, *n.* scent, fragrance, aroma, odor, sweetness, bouquet, incense; see also smell 1. Perfumes include the following—attar of roses, sandalwood, bay, rosemary, palm oil, frankincense, myrrh, Eau de Cologne (trademark), musk, orange-flowers, spice, sachet, lavender, rose geranium.

perhaps, *a.* conceivably, possibly, reasonably; see maybe.

perilous, *a.* precarious, unsafe, uncertain; see dangerous.

perimeter, *n.* margin, outline, border; see boundary, edge 1.

period, *n.* 1. [A measure of time] epoch, time, era; see age 3. 2. [An end] limit, conclusion, close; see end 2. 3. [A mark of punctuation] point, full stop, full pause, dot, ending-pitch; see also punctuation.

periodical, *a.* rhythmic, regular, recurrent; see also regular 3.

periodical, *n.* review, number, publication; see magazine 2, newspaper.

periodically, *a.* rhythmically, systematically, annually; see regularly 2.

peripheral, *a.* external, outer, surface; see outside.

periphery, *n.* covering, perimeter, border; see outside 1.

perish, *v.* pass away, be lost, depart; see die.

perjure, *v.* prevaricate, swear falsely, falsify; see lie 1.

perjury, *n.* false statement, violation of an oath, willful falsehood; see lie.

perk (up), *v.* 1. [Be refreshed] revive, recuperate, liven up; see recover 3. 2. [Cheer or refresh] invigorate, shake, enliven; see renew 1, revive 1.

permanence, *n.* continuity, dependability, durability; see stability 1.

permanent, *a.* durable, enduring, abiding, uninterrupted, stable, continuing, lasting, firm, hard, tough, strong, hardy, robust, sound, sturdy, steadfast, imperishable, surviving, living, long-lived, long-standing, invariable, persisting, tenacious, persevering, unyielding, resisting, resistant, impenetrable, recurring, wearing, constant, changeless, persistent, perennial.

permanently, *a.* for all time, enduringly, lastingly; see forever.

permeate, *v.* pervade, saturate, fill; see filter 1.

permissible, *a.* allowable, sanctioned, to be permitted; see permitted.

permission, *n.* leave, liberty, consent, assent, acceptance, letting, approbation, agreement, license, permit, allowance, authority, tolerance, toleration, authorization, approval, acknowledgment, admission, verification, recognition, concurrence, promise, avowal, support, corroboration, guarantee, guaranty, visa, encouragement, ratification, grace, authority, sanction, confirmation, endorsement, affirmation, assurance, empowering, legalization, grant, indulgence, trust, concession, adjustment, settlement, accord, *nod, O.K., *rubber stamp, *the go-ahead, *high-sign, *green light. —*Ant.* denial, injunction, interdiction.

permissive, *a.* authorizing, allowing, agreeable; see **permitted**.

permit, *n.* license, grant, consent; see **permission**.

permit, *v.* sanction, tolerate, let; see **allow**.

permitted, *a.* granted, allowed, licensed, authorized, legalized, tolerated, empowered, sanctioned, conceded, consented, favored, suffered, chartered, accorded, let, indulged, privileged; see also **approved.**—*Ant.* refused, denied, prohibited.

perpendicular, *a.* vertical, plumb, straight; see **straight 1**.

perpetrate, *v.* commit, act, do; see **perform 1**.

perpetual, *a.* 1. [Never stopping] continual, unceasing, constant; see **endless 1**. 2. [Continually repeating] repetitious, repeating, recurrent; see also **constant**.

perpetually, *a.* enduringly, unceasingly, permanently; see **forever**.

perplex, *v.* puzzle, confound, bewilder; see **confuse**.

perplexed, *a.* troubled, uncertain, bewildered; see **doubtful**.

perplexing, *a.* bewildering, confusing, mystifying; see **difficult 2**.

per se, *a.* as such, intrinsically, alone, singularly, fundamentally, in essence, in or by itself, virtually; see also **essentially**.

persecute, *v.* afflict, harass, victimize; see **abuse**.

persecution, *n.* torture, torment, teasing, provoking; see **abuse**.

perseverance, *n.* grit, resolution, pluck; see **determination**.

persevere, *v.* persist, remain, pursue; see **endure 1**.

persist, *v.* persevere, pursue, strive; see **continue 1, endure 1**.

persistence, *n.* constancy, resolution, stamina; see **endurance**.

persistent, *a.* tenacious, steadfast, determined; see **resolute 2**.

person, *n.* 1. [An individual] (human) being, child, somebody, self, oneself, I, me, soul, spirit, character, individuality, personage, personality, (personal) identity; see also **man 2, woman 1**. 2. [An individual enjoying distinction] distinguished person, personality, success; see **character 4**. 3. [Bodily form] physique, frame, form; see **body 1**. —**in person**, personally, in the flesh, present; see **near 1**.

personable, *a.* agreeable, pleasant, attractive; see **charming**.

personage, *n.* human being, someone, individual; see **man 2, person 1**.

personal, *a.* 1. [Private] secluded, secret, retired; see **private**. 2. [Individual] claimed, peculiar, particular; see **individual, special 1**. 3. [Pertaining to one's person] fleshly, corporeal, corporal; see **bodily**.

personality, *n.* 1. [The total of one's nature] self, oneself, being; see **character 2**. 2. [Individual characteristics] disposition, nature, temper; see **character 1**. 3. [A notable person] celebrity, star, cynosure; see **character 4**.

personally, *a.* 1. [Viewed in a personal manner] narrowly, selfishly, with concern for self; see **selfishly**. 2. [From the point of view of the speaker] for me, myself, by or for myself, for my part, as I see it, according to my opinion; see also **individually.**—*Ant.* certainly, objectively, scientifically.

personify, *v.* 1. [To impersonate] represent, live as, act out; see **impersonate**. 2. [To represent] copy, symbolize, exemplify; see **represent 3**.

personnel, *n.* workers, employees, group; see **staff 2**.

perspective, *n.* aspect, attitude, outlook; see **viewpoint**.

perspiration, *n.* water, exudation, beads of moisture; see **sweat**.

perspire, *v.* secrete, exude, lather; see **sweat**.

persuade, *v.* convince, move, induce, assure, cajole, incline, talk (someone) into something, win over, bring around or over, lead to believe or to act or to do something, gain the confidence of, prevail on or upon, overcome another's resistence, wear down, bring a person to his senses, win an argument, make or carry one's point, gain the confidence of, make (someone) see the light; see also **influence.**—*Ant.* dissuade, **neglect,** dampen.

persuaded, *a.* convinced, won over, moved (to), led, influenced, motivated, attracted (to), brought to see the light, turned on (to).

persuasion, *n.* 1. [The act of persuading] inducing, influencing, enticing; see **influence**. 2. [A belief] creed, tenet, religion; see **faith**.

persuasive, *a.* convincing, alluring, luring, seductive, influential, winning, enticing, impelling, moving, actuating, efficient, effective, effectual, compelling, touching, forceful, potent, powerful, swaying, pointed, strong, energetic, forcible, plausible, inveigling; see also **convincing**.

pertain, *v.* relate to, belong to, refer to; see **concern** 1.

pertaining, *a.* belonging to, appropriate to, connected with; see **referring.**

pertinence, *n.* consistency, congruity, relevance; see **importance.**

pertinent, *a.* appropriate, suitable, related; see **relevant.**

perturb, *v.* pester, worry, irritate; see **bother** 2.

perturbed, *a.* uneasy, anxious, restless; see **troubled** 1.

pervade, *v.* suffuse, permeate, spread through; see **penetrate** 1.

perverse, *a.* wayward, delinquent, capricious; see **bad** 1.

perversion, *n.* 1. [A distortion] involution, regression, abuse; see **contortion.** 2. [Sexual deviation] corruption, debasement, depravity, wickedness, depredation, degeneration, prostitution, masturbation, degradation, impairment, self-defilement, vice, narcissism, sodomy, bestiality; see also **lewdness.**

pervert, *n.* sex maniac, sex criminal, sodomist, transvestite, rapist, autoeroticist, lecher, seducer, Don Juan, nymphomaniac, pederast, the third sex; see also **prostitute.**

pervert, *v.* ruin, vitiate, divert; see **corrupt.**

perverted, *a.* distorted, deviating, corrupt; see **bad** 1.

pessimism, *n.* unhappiness, gloom, low spirits; see **depression** 2, **grief, sadness.**

pessimistic, *a.* 1. [Discouraging] worrisome, troublesome, troubling; see **dismal.** 2. [Inclined to a discouraging view] hopeless, gloomy, cynical; see **sad** 1.

pest, *n.* 1. [Anything destructive] virus, germ, insect pest, bug, harmful bird, bird of prey, destructive animal. Common pests include the following—house fly, mosquito, flea, louse, mite, bedbug, tick, aphid, Japanese beetle, corn borer, boll weevil, squash bug, peach moth, gypsy moth, cutworm, pear slug, mouse, rat, gopher, prairie dog, woodchuck, groundhog, rabbit, mole, weasel, coyote, hawk. 2. [A nuisance] bore, tease, annoyance; see **trouble** 2.

pester, *v.* annoy, harass, provoke; see **bother** 2.

pestilence, *n.* epidemic, endemic, sickness; see **illness** 1.

pet, *n.* 1. [A term of endearment] lover, dear, love; see **darling.** 2. [Favorite] darling, idol, adored one; see **favorite.** 3. [A creature kept as an object of affection] Common pets include the following—pony, dog, cat, horse, goldfish, rabbit, hamster, guinea pig, lamb, mouse, white rat, chicken, pigeon, canary, parrot.

pet, *v.* 1. [To caress] fondle, cuddle, kiss; see **touch** 2. 2. [*To make love] embrace, hug, *neck; see **caress, kiss, love** 2.

petal, *n.* floral leaf, flower part, leaf; see **flower.**

petition, *n.* prayer, request, supplication; see **appeal** 1.

petrified, *a.* stone, hardened, mineralized; see **firm** 2.

petrify, *v.* mineralize, clarify, solidify; see **harden.**

petroleum, *n.* crude oil, fuel, coal oil; see **oil.**

petty, *a.* small, insignificant, frivolous; see **trivial, unimportant.**

phantom, *n.* apparition, specter, shade; see **ghost.**

phase, *n.* condition, stage, appearance, point, aspect; see also **state** 2.

phase out, *v.* slowly get rid of, gradually dispose of, *weed out; see **eliminate.**

phenomenal, *a.* extraordinary, unique, remarkable; see **unusual** 1.

phenomenon, *n.* aspect, appearance, happening; see **event.**

philanthropic, *a.* kindhearted, benevolent, humanitarian; see **humane, kind.**

philospher, *n.* logician, wise man, sage, savant, Sophist, Solon. Major philosophers include the following—Epicurus, Plato, Aristotle, Marcus Aurelius, St. Augustine, St. Thomas Aquinas, Thomas Hobbes, John Locke, Immanuel Kant, John Stuart Mill, Friedrich Schiller, Jean Jacques Rousseau, Arthur Schopenhauer, G. W. F. Hegel, Soren Kierkegaard, Friedrich Nietzsche, William James, Karl Marx, Ernst Cassirer, Jean-Paul Sartre.

philosophical, *a.* 1. [Given to thought] reflective, cogitative, rational; see **thoughtful** 1. 2. [Embodying deep thought] erudite, thoughtful, deep; see **learned** 1, **profound.**

philosophize, *v.* ponder, weigh, deliberate (upon); see **think** 1.

philosophy, *n.* 1. [The study of knowledge] theory, reasoned doctrine, explanation of phenomena, logical concept, systematic view, theory of knowledge, early science, natural philosophy; see also **knowledge** 1. Fields of philosophy include the following—aesthetics, logic, ethics, metaphysics, epistemology, psychology, axiology, ontology, teleology. Philosophic attitudes include the following—idealism, realism, existentialism, nihilism, mechanism, naturalism, determinism, natural realism, intuitionism, utilitarianism, nominalism, conceptualism, pragmatism, Kantianism, Hegelianism, logical empiricism, absolutism, transcendentalism, logical positivism. 2. [A fundamental principle] truth, axiom, conception; see **basis, law 4, theory 1.** 3. [A personal attitude or belief] outlook, view, position; see **belief, opinion 1, viewpoint.**

phlegm, *n.* spittle, discharge, spit; see **saliva.**

phobia, *n.* disgust, avoidance, aversion; see **hatred, resentment 2.**

phone, *n.* wireless, radiophone, private phone; see **telephone.**

phonograph, *n.* graphophone, gramophone, juke box; see **record player.**

*phony, *a.* affected, imitation, artificial; see **false 3.**

photograph, *n.* photo, print, portrait, image, likeness, snapshot, microcopy, microfilm, radiograph, photomontage, photomural, snap, shot, *pic, close-up, candid (photo); see also **picture 2, 3.**

photograph, *v.* take a picture, get a likeness, film, snapshot, copy, reproduce, illustrate, make an exposure, make a picture, catch a likeness, get a film, make a moving picture, of microfilm, snap, shoot, get a close-up.

photographer, *n.* picture-taker, cameraman, cinematographer; see **artist.**

photographic, *a.* accurate, detailed, exact; see **graphic 1.**

photography, *n.* picture-taking, portrait photography, view photography, aerial photography, tactical photography, candid camera photography, snapshooting.

phrase, *n.* group of words, expression, slogan, catchword, maxim, wordgroup. Grammatical phrases include the following—prepositional, gerund, gerundive, participial, infinitive, noun, adjective *or* adjectival, adverbial, conjunctive, absolute, attributive, headed, nonheaded, exocentric, endocentric.

phraseology, *n.* style, manner, idiom; see **diction.**

physical, *a.* 1. [Concerning matter] material, corporeal, visible, tangible, environmental, palpable, substantial, natural, sensible, concrete, materialistic; see also **real 2.** 2. [Concerning the body] corporal, corporeal, fleshly; see **bodily.** 3. [Concerning physics] mechanical, motive, electrical, sonic, vibratory, thermal, radioactive, radiational, atomic, relating to matter, dynamic.

physical, *n.* medical checkup, health examination, *exam; see **examination 2.**

physically, *a.* corporally, really, actually; see **bodily.**

physician, *n.* practitioner, doctor of medicine, surgeon; see **doctor.**

physicist, *n.* biophysicist, geophysicist, nuclear physicist; see **scientist.**

physics, *n.* natural philosophy, science of the material world, science of matter and motion; see **science 1.** Divisions of physics include the following—heat, light, electricity, sound, mechanics, dynamics, kinetics, atomic structure, radiant energy, supersonics, hydraulics, pneumatics, aerodynamics, engineering.

physiology, *n.* study of living organisms, study of organic functions, biology; see **science 1.**

physique, *n.* build, structure, constitution; see **body 1.**

pianist, *n.* performer, piano player, virtuoso; see **musician.**

piano, *n.* grand, baby grand, upright, square, concert grand, spinet, clavichord, electric piano, player piano; see also **musical instrument.**

pick, *n.* 1. [An implement for picking] pickax, mattock, ice pick; see **tool 1.** 2. [A blow with a pointed instrument] peck, nip, dent; see **blow 3.** 3. [A choice selection] best, elect, select; see **best.**

pick, *v.* 1. [To choose] select, pick out, separate; see **choose.** 2. [To gather] pluck, pull, choose; see **accumulate.** 3. [To use a pointed instrument] dent, indent, strike; see **hit 1.**

pick a fight, *v.* provoke, start, foment; see **fight.**

pick apart, *v* dissect, break up *or* down, pick to pieces; see **break 2, cut 1.**

picked, *a.* elite, special, exclusive; see **excellent.**

picket, *n.* 1. [A stake] stake, pole, pillar; see **post 1.** 2. [A watchman] patrolman, guard, union member, vedette, sentry, inlying picket.

picket, *v.* 1. [To strike] walk out, blockade, boycott; see **strike 2.** 2. [To enclose] imprison, fence, corral; see **enclose 1.**

picking, *n.* gathering, culling, separating; see **choice 3, preference.**

pickings, *n.* profits, earnings, proceeds; see **booty.**

pickle, *n.* 1. [A relish] Varieties of pickles include the following—cucumber, beet, green tomato, dill, bread-and-butter, sweet, mustard, garlic, half-sour, pickled peppers, pickled beans, pickled apricots, pickled cherries, pickled peaches, pickled pears, piccalilli, chutney, cranberry-orange relish, spiced currants, spiced gooseberries, beet relish, chili sauce, catsup. 2. [*A troublesome situation] disorder, dilemma, evil plight; see **difficulty 2.**

pick off, *v.* snipe, get, shoot; see **kill 1.**

pick out, *v.* select, make a choice of, notice; see **choose.**

pickpocket, *n.* cutpurse, thief, purse snatcher; see **criminal, robber.**

pick up, *v.* 1. [To acquire incidentally] happen upon, find, secure; see **get 1.** 2. [To take up in the hand or arms] lift, uplift, cuddle; see **raise** 1. 3. [To receive] get, take, acquire; see **receive** 1. 4. [To increase] pay better, swell, swell out; see **increase**. 5. [To improve] get better, get well, recover health; see **recover** 3. 6. [*To call for] call *or* go *or* stop *or* drop in for, bring (along), go to get, accompany, get, invite; see also **invite**.

picnic, *n.* barbecue, cookout, fish fry; see **meal** 2.

pictorial, *a.* 1. [Having the quality of a picture] graphic, scenic, striking; see **graphic** 1. 2. [Making use of pictures] decorated, embellished, adorned.

picture, *n.* 1. [A scene before the eye or the imagination] spectacle, panorama, pageant; see **view** 1. 2. [A human likeness] portrait, representation, photo, photograph, snapshot, cartoon, image, effigy, statue, statuette, figure, figurine, close-up. 3. [A pictorial representation] illustration, engraving, etching, woodcut, cut, outline, cartoon, draft, crayon sketch, pastel, water color, poster, oil, chart, map, plot, mosaic, blueprint, advertisement, facsimile, animation, tracing, photograph, lithograph, print; see also **design**, **drawing**, **painting** 1. Types of pictures, as works of art, include the following—landscape, seascape, genre painting, madonna, ascension, annunciation, Last Judgment, crucifixion; St. Anthony, St. Anne, etc.; birth of Christ, battle scene, triumphal entry, detail, icon, illumination, miniature, portrait, self-portrait, illustration, nude, fresco, mural, collage, pin-up, figure, still life, center spread, animal picture, hunting print, fashion plate, photomural, photomontage. 4. [A motion picture] cinema, cinerama, cartoon; see **movie**. 5. [A description] depiction, delineation, portrayal; see **description**. 6. [Adequate comprehension; *usually with* the] (the) idea, understanding, survey; see **knowledge** 1.

picture, *v.* 1. [To depict] sketch, delineate, portray; see **draw** 2. 2. [To imagine] portray, create, conceive; see **imagine**.

picturesque, *a.* pictorial, scenic, graphic, striking, arresting.

pie, *n.* Varieties of pies include the following—*meat pies*: fish, chicken, lamb, pork, beef, steak-and-kidney, cottage; *dessert pies*: apple, banana, banana cream, chiffon, apricot, peach, pear, raisin, custard, coconut cream, rice custard, fig and pecan, caramel, caramel nut, chocolate, lemon, cranberry and raisin, orange, mince, prune, cherry, gooseberry, huckleberry, blueberry, strawberry, strawberry cream, Washington; see also **dessert**. —*as easy as pie,* not difficult, simple, uncomplicated; see **easy** 2.

piece, *n.* 1. [Part] portion, share, section; see **part** 1. 2. [Work of art] study, composition, creation; see **art** 3. [Musical, literary, or theatrical composition] suite, orchestration, production, opus, study, arrangement, treatise, dissertation, sketch, play, novel, thesis, dissertation, discourse, discussion, treatment, essay, article, paper, memoir, homily, poem, theme, monograph, commentary, review, paragraph, criticism, play, drama, melodrama, pageant, monologue, opera, ballet. —**go to pieces,** 1. come *or* fall apart, break (up), fail; see **break down** 2. 2. quit, collapse, lose control; see **cry** 1, **worry** 2. —**speak one's piece,** air one's opinions, talk, reveal; see **tell** 1.

piece together, *v.* combine, make, create; see **assemble** 2.

pier, *n.* wharf, landing, quay; see **dock**.

pierce, *v.* go *or* pass *or* break through *or* into, stab, intrude; see **penetrate**.

piercing, *a.* 1. [Shrill] deafening, earsplitting, sharp; see **loud** 1, **shrill**. 2. [Penetrating] entering, boring, puncturing; see **sharp** 1.

piety, *n.* reverence, duty, zeal; see **devotion**.

pig, *n.* piglet, swine, shoat; see **animal**, **hog** 1.

pigeon, *n.* dove, culver, squab; see **bird**.

piggish, *a.* selfish, dirty, ravenous; see **greedy**.

pigheaded, *a.* recalcitrant, insistent, stubborn; see **stubborn**.

pigment, *n.* paint, oil paint, dye; see **color**.

***pigskin,** *n.* regulation football, (the) ball, (the) *oval*; see **football** 2.

pigtail, *n.* plait, hairdo, twine; see **hair** 1.

pile, *n.* 1. [A heap] collection, mass, quantity; see **collection**. 2. [*Money] affluence, riches, *dough*; see **wealth**.

pile, *v.* rank, stack, gather; see **accumulate**, **store**.

pilgrim, *n.* wayfarer, wanderer, sojourner; see **traveler**.

pilgrimage, *n.* travel, wayfaring, trip; see **journey**.

pill, *n.* 1. [A tablet] capsule, pilule, pellet; see **medicine** 2. 2. [*A contraceptive tablet: *usually with* the] contraceptive drug, oral contraceptive, prophylactic; see **drug**.

pillage, *v.* plunder, loot, rob; see **destroy**, **steal**.

pillar, *n.* 1. [A column] pedestal, mast, shaft; see **column** 1, **post** 1. 2. [A support] mainstay, dependence, guider; see **support** 2.

pillow, *n.* feather pillow, down pillow,

foam rubber cushion, pad, padding, rest, bag, support, headrest.

pillowcase, *n.* pillow slip, pillow casing, pillow cover; see **cover 1.**

pilot, *n.* 1. [Flier] airman, fighter pilot, commercial pilot, bomber pilot, automatic pilot, mechanical pilot, aeronaut, aerial navigator, navigator, aerialist. 2. [Guide] scout, leader, director; see **guide.**

pilot, *v.* guide, conduct, manage; see **lead 1.**

pimp, *n.* procurer, whoremonger, pander; see **criminal.**

pimple, *n.* pustule, swelling, acne, white-head, blackhead, inflammation, bump, lump, boil, carbuncle, blister, *zit; see also **blemish.**

pin, *n.* 1. [A device to fasten goods by piercing or clasping] clip, catch, needle, bodkin, quill, clasp, nail; see also **fastener.** Pins include the following—common, safety, hat, knitting, hair, clothes, bobby, cotter, push. 2. [A piece of jewelry] tiepin, stickpin, brooch, badge, stud, sorority *or* fraternity *or* school pin; see also **jewelry.**

pin, *v.* close, clasp, bind; see **fasten.**

pinch, *n.* squeeze, compression, nip, grasp, grasping, pressure, cramp, contraction, confinement, limitation, hurt, torment. —**in a pinch,** if necessary, in an emergency, under stress; see **hardly.**

pinch, *v.* nip, grasp, squeeze, compress, press, cramp, grab, contract, confine, limit, torment; see also **hurt 1.**

pinchers, *n.* pliers, pair of pincers, wrench; see **tool 1.**

pinch-hit, *v.* replace, act for, succeed; see **substitute.**

pine, *n.* Pines include the following—white, stone, whitebark, foxtail, bristle-cone, nut, singleleaf, piñon, sugar, long-leaf, western yellow, lodge-pole, Georgia pitch *or* yellow, Scotch fir; see also **tree, wood 2.**

pink, *a.* rosy, reddish, pinkish, flushed, dawn-tinted.

pink, *n.* rose, red, roseate, blush-rose, salmon, shocking pink, blushing pink; see also **color.**

pinnacle, *n.* zenith, crest, summit; see **climax.**

pioneer, *a.* pioneering, initial, untried; see **brave, early 1, experimental.**

pioneer, *n.* 1. [One who prepared the way] pathfinder, scout, explorer; see **guide 1.** 2. [One in the vanguard of civilization] early settler, colonist, pilgrim, immigrant, colonizer, homesteader, squatter.

pioneer, *v.* discover, explore, found; see **colonize, establish 2, settle 1.**

pious, *a.* divine, holy, devout; see **religious 2.**

pipe, *n.* 1. [A tube] pipeline, (drain) pipe, sewer, conduit, culvert, waterpipe, aqueduct, trough, passage, duct, tubular runway, canal, vessel. 2. [A device for smoking] Varieties of smoking pipes include the following—meerschaum, corn-cob (Missouri meerschaum); bulldog pipe, brierwood pipe, clay pipe, hookah, Turkish pipe, opium pipe, water pipe, hashish pipe *or* *hash pipe. 3. [A musical instrument] wind instrument, flageolet, piccolo; see **musical instrument.**

***pipe down,** *v.* become quiet, hush, speak lower; see **stop 2.**

piracy, *n.* pillage, holdup, robbery; see **crime, theft.**

pirate, *n.* thief, freebooter, plunderer, marauder, conduit, privateer, soldier of fortune, buccaneer, searobber; see also **criminal, robber.**

piss, *v.* pass *or* make water, go to the bathroom, *pee; see **urinate.**

pistol, *n.* revolver, automatic (pistol), six-shooter, *rod, *cannon, *six-gun, *iron, *forty-five, *thirty-eight; see also **gun, weapon.**

pit, *n.* abyss, cavity, depression; see **hole 1.**

pitch, *n.* 1. [Slope] slant, incline, angle; see **grade 1, inclination 2.** 2. [A throw] toss, fling, hurl, heave, cast, pitched ball, ball, strike, delivery, offering, the old apple. 3. [Musical frequency] frequency of vibration, rate of vibration, tone; see **sound 2.** 4. [A viscous liquid] resin, gum resin, rosin; see **gum, tar 1.**

pitch, *v.* 1. [To throw] hurl, fling, toss; see **throw 1.** 2. [To fall forward] plunge, flop, vault; see **dive, fall 1.** 3. [To slope abruptly] rise, fall, ascend; see **bend, lean 1.**

pitcher, *n.* 1. [A utensil for pouring liquid] cream pitcher, milk pitcher, water pitcher, jug, vessel, amphora; see also **container.** 2. [In baseball, one who pitches to the batter] right-hand pitcher *or* right-hander, left-hand pitcher *or* left-hander, *hurler, *ace hurler, twirler, *chucker.

pitchfork, *n.* fork, hayfork, three-tined fork; see **tool 1.**

pitch in, *v.* volunteer, work, aid; see **help.**

pitch into, *v.* assault, blame, scold; see **attack, fight.**

pitfall, *n.* snare, meshes, deadfall; see **trap 1.**

pitiful, *a.* miserable, mournful, sorrowful, woeful, distressed, distressing, cheerless, comfortless, deplorable, joyless, dismal, touching, pathetic, affecting, stirring, arousing, tender, heart-warming, human, dramatic, impressive, pitiable, tearful, gratifying, heart-rending, depressing, afflicted, suffering, moving, vile; see also **sad** 1.—*Ant.* happy, cheerful, joyful.

pitiless, *a.* unfeeling, heartless, cold; see **indifferent**.

pitter-patter, *n.* thump, patter, tap; see **noise** 1.

pity, *n.* sympathy, compassion, charity, softheartedness, tenderness, goodness, understanding, mercy, soft-heartedness, warm-heartedness, kindliness, brotherly love, unselfishness, benevolence, favor, condolence, fellow feeling, commiseration, large-heartedness, clemency, humanity.—*Ant.* hatred, severity, ferocity. —**have** (*or* **take**) **pity on**, show pity to, spare, pardon; see **forgive, pity** 2.

pity, *v.* 1. [To feel pity for] feel for, sympathize with, commiserate, be sorry for, condole, be sympathetic to, show sympathy, express sympathy for, feel with *or* for, grieve with, weep for; see also **comfort, sympathize**. 2. [To be merciful to] spare, take pity on, show pity to, show forgiveness to, be merciful to, pardon, reprieve, grant amnesty to; see also **forgive**.—*Ant.* destroy, condemn, accuse.

pivot, *v.* whirl, swivel, rotate; see **turn** 1.

place, *n.* 1. [Position] station, point, spot; see **position** 1. 2. [Space] room, compass, stead, void, distance, area, seat, volume, berth, reservation, accommodation; see also **extent**. 3. [Locality] spot, locus, site, community, district, suburb, country, section, habitat, home, residence, abode, house, quarters; see also **area, neighborhood, region** 1. 4. [Rank] status, position, station; see **rank** 3. —*go places, attain success, achieve, advance; see **succeed** 1. —**in place**, fitting, timely, appropriate; see **fit** 1. —**in place of**, as a substitute for, instead (of), taking the place of; see **instead**. —**out of place**, inappropriate, unsuitable, not fitting; see **improper**. —**put someone in his place**, humiliate, reprimand, derogate; see **humble**. —**take place**, occur, come into being, be; see **happen** 2. —**take the place of**, replace, act in one's stead, serve as proxy for; see **substitute**.

place, *v.* 1. [To put in a place] locate, assign, deposit; see **put** 1. 2. [To put in order] fix, arrange, group; see **order** 3.

placed, *a.* established, settled, fixed, located, rated, deposited, lodged, quartered, planted, set, arranged, stowed, stored, installed, situated, implanted, set up, ordered.

placement, *n.* situation, position, arrangement; see **organization** 1.

plagiarism, *n.* literary theft, cheating, fraud; see **theft**.

plague, *n.* epidemic, pestilence, influenza; see **illness** 2.

plague, *v.* disturb, trouble, irk; see **bother** 2.

plain, *a.* 1. [Obvious] open, manifest, clear; see **obvious** 1, 2, **understandable**. 2. [Simple] unadorned, unostentatious, unpretentious; see **modest** 2. 3. [Ordinary] everyday, average, commonplace; see **common** 1. 4. [Homely] plain-featured, coarse-featured, unattractive; see **ugly** 1. 5. [In blunt language] outspoken, candid, impolite; see **rude** 2.

plain, *n.* prairie, steppe, pampas, reach, expanse, open country, lowland, flat, level land, mesa, savanna, moorland, moor, heath, tundra, veldt, downs, the High Plains; see also **field** 1, **meadow**.

plainly, *a.* manifestly, evidently, visibly; see **clearly** 1, 2.

plan, *n.* 1. [A preliminary sketch] draft, diagram, map, time line, design, outline, representation, form, drawing, view, projection, rough draft, road map. 2. [A proposed sequence of action] plans, scheme, project, scope, outline, idea, handling, manipulating, projection, undertaking, method, design, tactics, procedure, treatment, intention, policy, course of action, plot, conspiracy, expedient, strategy, stratagem, arrangement, way of doing things, *angle, the picture; see also **program** 2, **purpose** 1. 3. [Arrangement] layout, method, disposition; see **order** 3.

plan, *v.* 1. [To plot an action in advance] prepare, scheme, devise, invent, outline, project, contrive, shape, design, map, plot (a course), form (a plan), think out, engineer, figure on *or* for, intrigue, conspire, frame, steer one's course, establish *or* set guidelines *or* parameters (for), work up *or* out, line up, plan an attack, come through, calculate on, make arrangements, take measures, bargain for, *cook up, *dope out, *put on ice. 2. [To arrange in a preliminary way] outline, draft, sketch, lay out, map out, organize, prepare a sketch, chart, map, draw, trace, design, illustrate, depict, delineate, represent, shape, chalk out, rough in, block out, block in. 3. [To have in mind] propose, think, purpose; see **intend** 1.

plane, *n.* 1. [A plane surface] level, extension, horizontal, flat, sphere, face, stratum. 2. [A tool for smoothing wood] Types include the following—jack, smoothing, jointing, block, circular, rabbet, grooving, routing, scraper, dado, trying, chamfer: electric planer, jointer, foreplane; see also **tool** 1. 3. [An airplane] aircraft, airliner, aeroplane, airship, heavier-than-air craft, ship, boat, crate, heap, hack, taxi, bus. Kinds of planes include the following—propeller, jet, rocket, scout, observation, reconnaissance, transport, pursuit, passenger; biplane, triplane, monoplane, racer, glider, bomber, clipper, seaplane, hydroplane, fighter, fighter-bomber, interceptor, turbojet, stratojet, helicopter, gyroplane, amphibian, sailplane.

plane, v. finish, smooth, level; see **flatten.**

planet, n. celestial body, heavenly body, luminous body, wandering star, planetoid, asteroid, star. The known planets are as follows—Mercury, Venus, Earth, Mars, Jupiter, Saturn, Uranus, Neptune, Pluto, the planetoids *or* asteroids.

plank, n. board, planking, 2-inch piece; see **lumber.**

planned, a. projected, budgeted, in the budget, provided for, included in the plans *or* provisions, on the drawing board, programmed, in the making, under consideration, on the docket, prospective, cut out, cut and dried, under advisement, prepared.

planning, n. preparation, devising, outlining; see **plan** 2.

plans, n. outline, expectations, planned procedure(s); see **plan** 1, 2, **program** 2, sketch.

plant, n. shrub, weed, corn, bush, slip, shoot, cutting, sprout, seedling, plantlet.

plant, v. put in the ground, sow, set (out), pot, start, transplant, seed, stock, colonize, settle, establish, locate.

plantation, n. acreage, estate, ranch; see **farm.**

planted, a. cultivated, sown, seeded, stocked, implanted, strewn, drilled.

planting, n. sowing, seeding, drilling; see **farming.**

plaster, n. mortar, binding, plaster of Paris; see **cement.**

plaster, v. coat, bind, cement; see **cover** 1.

plastic, a. substitute, synthetic, cellulose; see **synthetic** 2.

plastic, n. synthetic, synthetic *or* artificial product, substitute, plastic material, processed material, polymerized substance.

plate, n. 1. [A flat surface] lamina, slice, stratum; see **plane** 1. 2. [A full-page illustration] photography, lithograph, etching; see also **illustration**, **picture** 3. 3. [A flattish dish] dinner plate, soup plate, salad plate, casserole, dessert plate, platter, trencher; see also **dish** 1. 4. [Food served on a plate, sense 4]

helping, serving, course; see **meal** 2. 5. [In baseball, the base immediately before the **catcher**] home base, home plate, home; see **base** 4.

plate, v. laminate, stratify, layer, scale, flake, overlay, gild, nickel, bronze, chrome, silver, enamel, encrust, platinize.

plateau, n. tableland, mesa, elevation; see **hill**, **plain.**

platform, n. 1. [A stage] dais, pulpit, speaker's platform, rostrum, stand, floor, staging, terrace. 2. [A program] principles, policies, *the party planks; see **program** 2.

platoon, n. detachment, military unit, company; see **army** 2.

platter, n. tray, serving platter, meat platter; see **dish** 1, **plate** 3.

plausible, a. probable, credible, supposable; see **likely** 1.

play, n. 1. [Amusement] enjoyment, diversion, pleasure; see **entertainment**. 2. [Recreation] relaxation, game, sport; see **entertainment**. 3. [Fun] frolic, happiness, sportiveness; see **fun**. 4. [A drama] piece, musical, theatrical; see **drama**. 5. [Sport] exhibition, match, tryout; see **sport** 1, 3. 6. [Action] activity, movement, working; see **action** 1. —*make a play for, make advances to, court, try for; see **try** 1.

play, v. 1. [To amuse oneself] entertain oneself, revel, make merry, carouse, play games, rejoice, have a good time, idle away, *horse around.—*Ant.* mourn, grieve, sulk. 2. [To gambol] frisk, sport, cavort, joke, dance, play games, make jokes, be a practical joker, jump (about), skip, frolic, caper.—*Ant.* drag, mope, droop. 3. [To produce music] perform, execute, work, cause to sound, finger, pedal, bow, plunk, tinkle, pipe, toot, mouth, pump, fiddle, sound, strike, saw, scrape, twang, pound, thump, tickle. 4. [To engage in sport] participate, engage, rival; see **compete**. 5. [To pretend] imagine, suppose, think; see **pretend** 1.

play down, v. belittle, hold down *or* back, minimize; see **restrain** 1.

player, n. 1. [One who takes part in a game] member, athlete, sportsman, sportswoman, amateur, professional, gymnast, acrobat, swimmer, diver, trackman, *champ, *pro, *semipro, *nonpro; see also **contestant**. 2. [An actor] performer, vaudeville performer, ham; see **actor**, **actress.**

playful, a. joking, whimsical, comical; see **funny** 1.

playground, n. playing field, park, school ground, municipal playground, yard, school yard, diamond, gridiron.

playing, *a.* sportive, sporting, gamboling; see **active.**

playmate, *n.* comrade, neighbor, companion; see **friend.**

plaything, *n.* gadget, amusement, trinket; see **doll, game 1, toy 1.**

playwright, *n.* scripter, scenarist, tragedian; see **author, writer.**

plea, *n.* 1. [An appeal] overture, request, supplication; see **appeal 1. 2.** [A form of legal defense] pleading, argument, case; see **defense 2.**

plead, *v.* 1. [To beg] implore, beseech, solicit; see **ask, beg 2.** 2. [To enter a plea] present, allege, cite; see **declare.**

plead guilty, *v.* confess, repent, concede; see **admit 2.**

pleading, *a.* imploring, supplicating, desirous.

pleasant, *a.* 1. [Affable] agreeable, attractive, obliging, charming, mild, amusing, kindly, mild-mannered, gracious, genial, amiable, polite, urbane, cheerful, sympathetic, civil, cordial, engaging, social, bland, diplomatic, civilized, good-humored, good-natured, soft, fun, delightful, jovial, jolly.—*Ant.* **sullen,** unsympathetic, unkind. 2. [Giving pleasure; *said of occasions, experiences, and the like*] gratifying, pleasurable, agreeable, cheering, amusing, welcome, refreshing, satisfying, all right, satisfactory, adequate, acceptable, comfortable, diverting, fascinating, adorable, enjoyable, delightful, sociable, lively, exciting, glad, festive, cheerful, entertaining, relaxing, joyous, joyful, merry, happy, pleasing, favorable, bright, sunny, brisk, catchy, sparkling, enlivening, colorful, light, humorous, laughable, comforting.—*Ant.* **sad,** unhappy, disagreeable.

pleasantly, *a.* pleasingly, charmingly, welcomely; see **agreeably.**

please, *interj.* if you please, if it please you, may it please you, by your leave.

please, *v.* 1. [To give pleasure] gratify, satisfy, make up to; see **entertain. 2.** [To desire] wish, demand, command; see **want 1.**—**if you please,** if you will, if I may, by your leave; see **please.**

pleased, *a.* gratified, satisfied, charmed; see **happy.**

pleasing, *a.* charming, agreeable, delightful; see **pleasant 1.**

pleasure, *n.* 1. [Enjoyment] bliss, delight, ease; see **happiness. 2.** [Will] want, preference, wish; see **desire 1.**

pleat, *n.* pleating, tuck, crease; see **fold.**

pleat, *v.* ruffle, crease, gather; see **fold.**

pledge, *n.* guarantee, token, agreement; see **promise 1.**

pledge, *v.* swear, vow, vouch; see **promise 1.**

plentiful, *a.* 1. [Bountiful] prolific, fruitful, profuse, lavish, liberal, unsparing, inexhaustible, replete, generous, abundant, liberal, extravagant, improvident, excessive, copious, superabundant, overliberal, superfluous, overflowing, flowing. —*Ant.* **stingy,** niggardly, skimpy. 2. [Existing in plenty] sufficient, abundant, copious, ample, overflowing, large, chock-full, teeming, unlimited, well-provided, flowing, full, flush, lush with, pouring, fruitful, swarming, swimming, abounding.—*Ant.* **poor,** scant, scanty.

plenty, *n.* abundance, fruitfulness, fullness, lavishness, deluge, torrent, sufficient, bounty, profusion, adequacy, flood, avalanche, good store, limit, capacity, adequate stock, enough and to spare, everything, all kinds of, all one wants, all one can eat *or* drink, more than one knows what to do with, too much of a good thing, a good bit, all one needs, all one can use, a great deal, *a lot *or* lots, *oodles.

pliable, *a.* limber, supple, plastic; see **flexible.**

pliant, *a.* limber, supple, plastic; see **flexible.**

pliers, *n.* pinchers, wrench, pincers, tongs, forceps, tweezers.

plod, *v.* trudge, hike, plug; see **walk 1.**

plop, *v.* thump, thud, bump; see **sound 1.**

plot, *n.* 1. [An intrigue] conspiracy, scheme, artifice; see **trick 1. 2.** [The action of a story] plan, scheme, outline, design, development, progress, unfolding, movement, climax, events, incidents, enactment, suspense, structure, build-up, scenario. 3. [A piece of ground] parcel, land, division; see **area, lot 1.**

plot, *v.* 1. [To devise an intrigue] frame, contrive, scheme; see **plan 1. 2.** [To plan] sketch, outline, draft; see **plan 2.**

plow, *n.* Plows include the following—moldboard, gang, steam, tractor, double, straddle, sulky, wheel, shovel, hand; lister, hoe plow *or* horse-hoe, garden plow *or* wheel hoe, (corn) cultivator; see also **tool 1.**

plow, *v.* 1. [To use a plow] break, furrow, cultivate, turn, plow up, turn over, till, list, ridge, break ground, do the plowing; see also **farm. 2.** [To act like a plow] smash into, rush through, shove apart; see **dig 1, push 1.**

plug, *n.* 1. [An implement to stop an opening] cork, stopper, stopple, filling, stoppage, spigot, wedge. 2. [An electrical fitting] attachment plug, fitting, connection, wall plug, floor plug, plug fuse. 3. [A large pipe with a discharge valve] water plug, fire hydrant, fire plug; see **pipe 1.**

plug, *v.* stop, fill, obstruct, secure, ram, make tight, drive in; see also **stop 2.**

plug in, *v.* connect, make a connection, bring in electricity; see **join 1, 3.**

plum, *n.* Plums and plumlike fruits include the following—freestone, Damson, Satsuma, Green Gage, Reine Claude, Sugar plum; French prune, improved French prune, Stanley prune; see also **fruit.**

plumber, *n.* tradesman, metal worker, handy man; see also **workman.**

plumbing, *n.* pipes, water pipes, sewage pipes, heating pipes, bathroom fixtures, sanitary provisions; see also **pipe 1.**

plump, *a.* obese, stout, fleshy; see **fat.**

plunder, *v.* burn, steal, lay waste; see **raid, ravage.**

plunge, *v.* fall, throw oneself, rush; see **dive, jump 1.**

plural, *a.* few, a number of, abundant; see **many.**

plurality, *n.* majority, advantage or lead in votes cast, favorable returns; see **lead 1, majority 1.**

plus, *a.* and *prep.* added to, additional, additionally, increased by, with the addition of, surplus, positive; see also **extra.**—*Ant.* **less,** minus, subtracted from.

pneumonia, *n.* pneumonitis, lobar pneumonia, croupous pneumonia; see **illness 2.**

poach, *v.* filch, pilfer, smuggle; see **steal.**

pock, *n.* flaw, hole, mark; see **blemish, scar.**

pocket, *a.* small, tiny, miniature; see **little 1, minute 1.**

pocket, *n.* **1.** [A cavity] hollow, opening, airpocket; see **hole 1. 2.** [A pouch sewed into a garment] pouch, poke, sac, pod. Kinds of pockets include the following—patch, slash, inset, watch, coin, invisible, pants, jacket, coat, vest, inner, outer, inside, outside. **3.** [Small area] isolated or separated group, enclave, survival; see **area.**

pocket, *v.* conceal, hide, enclose; see **steal.**

pocketbook, *n.* wallet, pouch, coin purse; see **bag, purse.**

pod, *n.* seed vessel, bean pod, pea pod; see **seed.**

poem, *n.* poetry, lyric, sonnet, edda, ballad, quatrain, blank verse, free verse, song, composition, creation; see also **writing 2.**

poet, *n.* writer, poemwriter, bard, versifier, minstrel, troubadour, verse maker, maker of verses, lyrist, author of the lyric or the book, dramatic poet, dramatist, lyric poet, writer of lyrics, poetaster; see also **artist, writer.** Major poets include the following—*British*: Geoffrey Chaucer, Edmund Spenser, William Shakespeare, John Donne, John Milton, John Dryden, Alexander Pope, Samuel Johnson, Robert Burns, William Blake, William Wordsworth, Samuel Taylor Coleridge, Lord Byron, John Keats, Percy Bysshe Shelly, Alfred Lord Tennyson, Robert Browning, Gerard Manley Hopkins, William Butler Yeats, Thomas Stearns Eliot, Dylan Thomas; *American*: Edgar Allan Poe, Walt Whitman, Emily Dickinson, Edwin Arlington Robinson, Robert Frost, Carl Sandburg, Edna St. Vincent Millay, Ezra Pound, Wallace Stevens, E. E. Cummings; *Classical Greek*: Homer, Pindar, Aeschylus, Sophocles, Euripides; *Latin*: Virgil, Lucretius, Ovid, Horace, Catullus, Juvenal; *European*: Dante Alighieri, Petrarch, Ludovico Ariosto, François Villon, Jean de La Fontaine, Charles Baudelaire, Stéphane Mallarmé, Paul Verlaine, Arthur Rimbaud, Victor Hugo, Pedro Calderón, Federico García Lorca, Luis Vaz de Camões, Wolfgang von Goethe, Friedrich Schiller, Heinrich Heine, Rainer Maria Rilke, Bertolt Brecht, Alexander Pushkin, Boris Pasternak, Yevgeni Yevtushenko.

poetic, *a.* poetical, lyric, lyrical, metrical, tuneful, elegiac, romantic, dramatic, iambic, dactylic, spondaic, trochaic, anapestic, imaginative.

poetry, *n.* poem, song, versification, metrical composition, rime, rhyme, poesy, stanza, rhythmical composition, poetical writings. Forms of verse include the following—sonnet, Shakespearean sonnet, Italian sonnet, Miltonic sonnet, Wordsworthian sonnet, Chaucerian stanza, Spenserian stanza, heroic couplet, Alexandrine, iambic pentameter, rhyme royal, ottava rima, couplet, distich, ode, epode, triolet, rondeau, rondel, rondelet, tanka, haiku, kyrielle, ballade, sestine, sloka, triad, villanelle, limerick, blank verse, free verse, stop-short, strophic verse, stanzaic verse, assonance, accentual verse, alliterative verse.

pogrom, *n.* slaughter, mass murder, massacre, genocide; see also **murder.**

point, *n.* **1.** [A position having no extent] location, spot, locality; see **position 1. 2.** [A sharp, tapered end] end, pointed end, needle point, pin point, barb, prick, spur, spike, snag, spine, claw, tooth, calk, sticker; see also **tip 1. 3.** [Anything having a point, sense 2] sword, dagger, stiletto; see **knife, needle. 4.** [Purpose] aim, object, intent; see **purpose 1. 5.** [Meaning] force, drift, import; see **meaning. 6.** [A detail] case, feature, point at issue; see **circumstance 1, detail.** —**at** or **on the point of,** on the verge of, close to, almost; see **near 1.** —**beside the point,** immaterial, not pertinent, not germane; see **irrele-**

vant. —**make a point of**, stress, emphasize, make an issue of; see **declare**. —**to the point**, pertinent, apt, exact; see **relevant**.

point, *v*. 1. [To indicate] show, name, denote; see **name** 2. 2. [To direct] guide, steer, influence; see **lead** 1.

pointed, *a*. 1. [Sharp] fine, keen, spiked; see **sharp** 1. 2. [Biting or insinuating] caustic, tart, trenchant; see **sarcastic**.

pointer, *n*. 1. [A pointing instrument] hand, rod, indicator, dial, gauge, director, index, mark, signal-needle, register. 2. [A variety of dog] hunting dog, gun dog, game dog; see **dog**. 3. [*A hint] clue, tip, warning; see **hint**.

pointing, *a*. showing, signifying, denoting; see **shown** 1.

pointless, *a*. 1. [Dull] uninteresting, prosaic, not pertinent; see **irrelevant**, **trivial**, **unnecessary**. 2. [Blunt] worn, obtuse, rounded; see **dull** 1. 3. [Ineffective] useless, powerless, impotent; see **incompetent**, **weak** 1, 2.

point of view, *n*. outlook, position, approach; see **attitude**.

point out, *v*. indicate, show, denote; see **name** 2.

poise, *n*. balance, gravity, equilibrium; see **composure**, **dignity** 1.

poison, *n*. virus, bane, toxin, infection, germ, bacteria, oil, vapor, gas. Poisons include the following—rattlesnake, copperhead, black-widow-spider, tarantula venom; smallpox, yellow-fever, common-cold, flu virus; poison oak, poison ivy, carbon monoxide gas, cooking gas, arsenic, lead, strychnine, oxalic, sulphuric, hydrochloric, nitric, carbolic, prussic, hydrocyanic acid; cantharides, caustic soda, lye, belladonna, aconite, lead arsenate, blue vitriol *or* copper sulfate, nicotine.

poison, *v*. infect, injure, kill, murder, destroy, corrupt, pervert, undermine, defile, harm, taint, make ill, cause violent illness.—*Ant*. **benefit**, **help**, purify.

poisoned, *a*. 1. [Suffering from poisoning] infected, indisposed, diseased; see **sick**. 2. [Dying of poison] fatally poisoned, beyond recovery, succumbing; see **dying** 1. 3. [Polluted with poison] contaminated, tainted, defiled, corrupted, venomous, virulent, impure, malignant, noxious, deadly, toxic; see also **poisonous**.—*Ant*. **pure**, fresh, untainted.

poisonous, *a*. bad, noxious, hurtful, dangerous, malignant, infective, venomous, virulent, vicious, corrupt, morbid, fatal, pestilential, toxic, deadly, destructive; see also **harmful**.—*Ant*. **healthy**, wholesome, nourishing.

poke, *n*. jab, thrust, punch; see **blow** 1.

poke, *v*. jab, punch, crowd; see **push** 1.

polar, *a*. glacial, frozen, frigid; see **cold** 1.

pole, *n*. shaft, flagpole, flagstaff; see **post** 1.

police, *n*. arm of the law, law enforcement body, FBI, police officers, policemen, police force, detective force, military police, Royal Canadian Mounted Police, *New York's Finest.

police, *v*. watch, control, patrol; see **guard**.

policeman, *n*. patrolman, officer (of the law), magistrate, process server, constable, *cop, *copper, *flatfoot, *fuzz, *the Man, *speed cop, *bobby, *pig. Policemen include the following—man on a beat, mounted police, motorcycle police, traffic police, squad-car police, municipal police, state police, highway patrol, detective, federal agent *or* investigator, *fed, *narc, F.B.I. man, prefect, inspector, member of the homicide squad *or* vice ³quad *or* drug patrol, etc.

police state, *n*. dictatorship, autocracy, authoritarian *or* fascist *or* rightest government; see **tyranny**.

policy, *n*. course, procedure, method, system, strategy, tactics, administration, management, theory, doctrine, behavior, scheme, design, arrangement, organization, plan, order.

polish, *n*. shine, burnish, glaze; see **finish** 2.

polish, *v*. burnish, furbish, finish; see **shine** 3.

polished, *a*. 1. [Bright] glossy, shining, gleaming; see **bright** 1. 2. [Refined] polite, well-bred, cultured; see **refined** 2.

polite, *a*. obliging, thoughtful, mannerly, attentive, pleasant, gentle, mild, nice, concerned, considerate, solicitous, bland, condescending, honey-tongued, amiable, gracious, cordial, considerate, good-natured, sympathetic, interested, smooth, diplomatic, kindly, kind, kindly-disposed, affable, agreeable, civil, complacent, respectful, amenable, gallant, genteel, gentlemanly, mannered, sociable, ingratiating, neighborly, friendly, respectful.—*Ant*. **egotistic**, insolent, pompous.

politely, *a*. thoughtfully, considerately, attentively, solicitously, cordially, graciously, amiably, kindheartedly, compassionately, gently, urbanely, affably, agreeably, civilly, gallantly, complacently, sociably, elegantly, gracefully, charmingly, ingratiatingly, winningly, tactfully, in good humor, with good grace; see also **respectfully**.

politeness, *n*. refinement, culture, civility; see **courtesy** 1.

political, *a.* legislative, executive, administrative; see **governmental**.

politician, *n.* officeholder, office seeker, party man, partisan, legislator, congressman, member of parliament, politico.

politics, *n.* practical government, functional government, systematic government, domestic affairs, internal affairs, foreign affairs, matters of state, campaigning, getting votes, seeking nomination, electioneering, being up for election, running for office.

poll, *n.* 1. [A census] vote, consensus, ballot; see **census**. 2. [A voting place; *usually plural*] ballot box(es), voting machines, polling place *or* area; see **voting**.

poll, *v.* question, register, enroll; see **examine, list** 1.

pollute, *v.* deprave, soil, stain; see **dirty, poison**.

polluted, *a.* corrupted, defiled, poisoned; see **dirty** 1.

pollution, *n.* corruption, defilement, adulteration, blight, soiling, fouling, foulness, taint, tainting, polluting, decomposition, desecration, profanation, abuse, deterioration, rottenness, impairment, misuse, infection, besmearing, besmirching, smirching. Some common pollutants of the air and water include the following —sewage, soapsuds, garbage, factory waste, detergent, carbon monoxide, automobile *or* bus *or* truck exhaust, pesticides, factory smoke.

poltergeist, *n.* spirit, spook, supernatural visitant; see **ghost**.

polygamy, *n.* (fraternal) polyandry, plural marriage, bigamy; see also **marriage**.

pomp, *n.* magnificence, affectation, splendor; see **magnificence**.

pompous, *a.* arrogant, haughty, proud; see **egotistic**.

pond, *n.* fishpond, millpond, lily pond; see **lake, pool** 1.

ponder, *v.* meditate, deliberate, consider; see **think** 1.

ponderous, *a.* dull, weighty, lifeless; see **heavy**.

pony, *n.* Shetland pony, bronco, mustang; see **horse**.

poodle, *n.* French poodle, French barbet, fancy dog; see **dog**.

pool, *n.* 1. [Small body of liquid, usually water] puddle, mudpuddle, pond, fishpond, millpond; see also **lake**. 2. [Supply] funds, provisions, amount available; see **equipment**. 3. [Game] snooker, 8-ball, billiards; see **game** 1.

pool, *v.* combine, merge, blend; see **join** 1.

poor, *a.* 1. [Lacking worldly goods] indigent, penniless, moneyless, impecunious, destitute, needy, poverty-stricken, un-

derprivileged, fortuneless, starved, pinched, reduced, beggared, empty-handed, meager, scanty, insolvent, ill-provided, ill-furnished, in want, suffering privation, in need, poor as a church mouse, broke, hard up, down and out.—*Ant.* **wealthy**, well-to-do, affluent. 2. [Lacking excellences] pitiful, paltry, contemptible, miserable, pitiable, dwarfed, insignificant, diminutive, ordinary, common, mediocre, trashy, shoddy, worthless, sorry, base, mean, coarse, vulgar, inferior, imperfect, smaller, lesser, below par, subnormal, under average, second-rate, third-rate, fourth-rate, etc.; reduced, defective, deficient, lower, subordinate, minor, secondary, humble, second-hand, pedestrian, beggarly, tawdry, petty, unimportant, bad, cheap, flimsy, threadbare, badly made, less than good, unwholesome, lacking in quality, dowdy, second-class, shabby, gaudy, mass-produced, squalid, trivial, sleazy, trifling, unsuccessful, second-best, tasteless, insipid, rustic, crude, odd, rock-bottom, garish, flashy, showy, loud, unsightly, affected, ramshackle, tumble-down, glaring, artificial, newfangled, out-of-date, *crummy, *junky, *two-bit, *raunchy, *corny, *cheesy; see also **inadequate, unsatisfactory**. 3. [Lacking strength] puny, feeble, infirm; see **weak** 1. 4. [Lacking vigor *or* health] indisposed, impaired, imperfect; see **sick** 1. 5. [Lacking fertility] infertile, unproductive, barren; see **sterile** 1, 2, **worthless**.

poor, *n.* needy, forgotten man, the unemployed, underdogs, the underprivileged, beggars, the impoverished masses, second-class citizen, have-nots; see also **people** 3.

poorly, *a.* defectively, crudely, unsuccessfully; see **badly** 1, **inadequately**.

pop, *n.* 1. [A slight explosive sound] report, burst, shot; see **noise** 1. 2. [A carbonated drink] soda pop, ginger pop, soda water, beverage, soft drink; see also **drink** 2.

pop, *v.* dart, leap, protrude; see **jump** 1.

Pope, *n.* head of the Roman Catholic Church, bishop of Rome, the Holy Father; see **priest**.

poppy, *n.* bloom, blossom, herb; see also **drug, flower**.

populace, *n.* masses, commonality, multitude; see **man** 1, **people** 3.

popular, *a.* 1. [Generally liked] favorite, well-liked, approved, pleasing, suitable, well-received, sought, fashionable, stylish, beloved, likable, lovable, attractive, praised, promoted, recommended, in the public eye, celebrated, noted, admired, famous, *run after.—*Ant.* **unknown**, in disrepute, out of favor. 2. [Cheap] low-priced, popular-priced, marked down;

see **cheap 1, economical 2. 3.** [Commonly accepted] general, familiar, demanded, in demand, prevalent, prevailing, current, in use, widespread, ordinary, adopted, embraced, having caught on, in the majority; see also **fashionable, modern 1. 4.** [Pertaining to the common people] proletarian, accessible, neighborly; see **democratic, republican.**

popularity, *n.* approval, general esteem, widespread acceptance, following, prevalence, universality, demand, fashionableness, *the rage.

popularly, *a.* commonly, usually, ordinarily; see **regularly 1.**

populated, *a.* crowded, teeming, populous, peopled, urban, inhabited; see also **inhabited.**

population, *n.* inhabitants, dwellers, number *or* group of people, citizenry, natives, group, residents, culture, community, state, populace; see also **society 2.**

porch, *n.* entrance, doorstep, stoop; see **entrance 2.**

pore, *n.* opening, foramen, orifice, vesicle; see also **hole 1.**

pork, *n.* ham, bacon, chops; see **meat.**

pornographic, *a.* immoral, dirty, obscene; see **lewd 2.**

pornography, *n.* vulgarity, obscenity, smut; see **lewdness.**

porous, *a.* pervious, permeable, acceptable; see **open 1.**

port, *n.* haven, anchorage, gate; see **dock.**

portable, *a.* transportable, transferable, manageable; see **movable.**

portal, *n.* gateway, opening, ingress; see **door, entrance 2, gate.**

portfolio, *n.* **1.** [A flat container] briefcase, attaché case, folder; see **bag, container. 2.** [Assets, especially stocks and bonds] holdings, selection, documents; see **wealth.**

portion, *n.* section, piece, part; see **division 2, share.**

portrait, *n.* likeness, portraiture, representation; see **painting 1, picture 2.**

portray, *v.* depict, characterize, reproduce; see **describe, represent 2.**

portrayal, *n.* depiction, replica, likeness; see **description, imitation 2.**

pose, *n.* artificial position, affectation, attitudinizing; see **fake, pretense 1.**

pose, *v.* **1.** [To pretend] profess, feign, make believe; see **act 1, pretend 1. 2.** [To assume a pose for a picture] model, adopt a position, posture; see **sit.**

position, *n.* **1.** [A physical position] location, locality, spot, seat, ground, environment, post, whereabouts, bearings, station, point, place, stand, space, sur-

roundings, situation, site, geography, region, tract, district, scene, setting; see also **area, place 3. 2.** [An intellectual position] view, belief, attitude; see **judgment 3, opinion 1. 3.** [An occupational position] office, employment, occupation; see **job 1, profession 1. 4.** [A social position] station, state, status; see **rank 3. 5.** [Posture] pose, carriage, bearing; see also **posture 1.**

positive, *a.* **1.** [Definite] decisive, actual, concrete; see **definite 1, real 2. 2.** [Emphatic] peremptory, assertive, obstinate; see **emphatic, resolute 2. 3.** [Certain] sure, convinced, confident; see **certain 1.**

positively, *a.* **1.** [In a positive manner] assertively, uncompromisingly, dogmatically, arbitrarily, stubbornly, obstinately, emphatically, dictatorially, imperatively, decidedly, absolutely, insistently, authoritatively, assuredly, confidently, unhesitatingly, with conviction *or* emphasis. **2.** [Without doubt] undoubtedly, unmistakably, undeniably; see **surely.**

posse, *n.* lynch mob, armed band, police force; see **police.**

possess, *v.* hold, occupy, control; see **maintain 3, own 1.**

possessed, *a.* **1.** [Insane] mad, crazed, violent; see **insane. 2.** [Owned] kept, enjoyed, in one's possession; see **held, owned.**

possession, *n.* **1.** [Ownership] proprietary rights, hold, mastery; see **ownership. 2.** [Property] personal property, real estate, something possessed; see **property 1, 2.**

possessions, *n.* belongings, goods, effects; see **estate, property 1.**

possessor, *n.* holder, proprietor, occupant; see **owner.**

possibility, *n.* **1.** [The condition of being possible] plausibility, feasibility, workableness; see **chance 1. 2.** [A possible happening] hazard, chance, occasion, circumstance, hope, occurrence, hap, happening, outside chance, incident, instance; see also **event, opportunity 1.**

possible, *a.* **1.** [Within the realm of possibility] conceivable, imaginable, thinkable; see **likely 1. 2.** [Acceptable] expedient, desirable, welcome; see **pleasant 2. 3.** [Contingent upon the future] indeterminate, fortuitous, adventitious; see **likely 1, uncertain 2.**

possibly, *a.* perhaps, by chance, potentially; see **likely 1, maybe, probably.**

post, *n.* **1.** [An upright in the ground] prop, support, pillar, pedestal, stake, stud, upright, doorpost; see also **column 1, mast. 2.** [The mails] mail *or* postal service, post office, P.O.; see **mail.**

postcard, n. postal card, note, letter card; see **letter 2**.

poster, n. placard, bill, sign, banner, sheet, billboard, handbill, broadside; see also **advertisement**.

posterior, a. 1. [Subsequent] coming after, succeeding, next; see **following**. 2. [Behind] in back of, last, after; see **back**.

posterity, n. descendants, breed, children; see **family, offspring**.

postman, n. mailman, mail or letter carrier, postal employee; see **workman**.

post office, n. mail office, postal service, P.O.; see **mail**.

postpone, v. defer, put off, hold over; see **delay 1, suspend 2**.

postponed, a. deferred, delayed, retarded, put off, set for a later time, to be done later, withheld, shelved, tabled, adjourned, suspended; see also **late 1**.

postponement, n. respite, suspension, adjournment; see **delay 1, pause**.

posture, n. 1. [Stance] pose, carriage, demeanor, aspect, presence, condition. 2. [Attitude] way of thinking, feeling, sentiment; see **attitude**.

postwar, a. peacetime, post-bellum, after the war, peaceful.

pot, n. 1. [Container] vessel, kettle, pan, jug, jar, mug, tankard, cup, can, crock, canister, receptacle, bucket, urn, pitcher, bowl, cauldron, melting pot; see also **container**. 2. [*Marijuana] *cannabis sativa* (Latin), *grass, *weed; see **drug**. —go to pot, deteriorate, go to ruin, fall apart; see **spoil**.

potato, n. tuber, white potato, sweet potato, yam, *spud, *tater.

potency, n. 1. [Strength] power, energy, vigor; see **manhood 2, strength**. 2. [Authority] influence, control, dominion; see **command, power 2**.

potent, a. 1. [Strong] vigorous, robust, sturdy; see **strong 1, 2**. 2. [Powerful] mighty, great, influential; see **powerful 1**.

potential, a. implied, inherent, dormant; see **likely 1**.

potentially, a. conceivably, imaginably, possibly; see **likely 1, maybe, probably**.

potion, n. dose, draft, liquor; see **drink 2, liquid, medicine 2**.

pottery, n. ceramics, porcelain, crockery, earthenware, clay ware; see also **utensils**.

pouch, n. sack, receptacle, poke; see **bag, container**.

poultry, n. domesticated birds, pullets, barnyard fowls; see **fowl**.

pounce, v. bound, surge, dart; see **dive, jump 1**.

pound, n. 1. [Measure of weight] sixteen ounces, Troy pound, avoirdupois pound,

commercial pound, pint; see also **measure 1, weight 1**. 2. [Kennel] coop, doghouse, cage; see **pen 1**.

pound, v. strike, crush, pulverize; see **beat 1, hit 1**.

pour, v. 1. [To flow] discharge, emit, issue; see **drain 3, flow**. 2. [To allow to flow] replenish with, spill, splash; see **empty 2**. 3. [To rain heavily] stream, flood, drench; see **rain**.

pouring, a. streaming, gushing, spouting, rushing, raining, flooding, showering, discharging, emitting, issuing, escaping, emanating, welling out, spurting, spilling, shedding, draining, running (down or away or out); see also **flowing**.

pout, v. make a long face, protrude the lips, be sullen; see **frown**.

poverty, n. 1. [Want of earthly goods] destitution, pennilessness, indigence, pauperism, want, need, insufficiency, starvation, famine, privation, insolvency, broken fortune, straits, scantiness, deficiency, meagerness, aridity, sparingness, stint, depletion, reduction, emptiness, vacancy, deficit, debt, *wolf at the door, *deep water, *hard spot, *pinch, *tough going; see also **lack 1**.—Ant. **wealth**, prosperity, comfort. 2. [Want of any desirable thing] shortage, inadequacy, scarcity; see **lack 2**.

poverty-stricken, a. penniless, broke, bankrupt; see **poor 1, wanting 1**.

powder, n. particles, film, powderiness, explosive powder, medicinal powder, cosmetic powder; see also **cosmetic, explosive, medicine 2**.

powdery, a. sandy, gravelly, dusty; see **gritty**.

power, n. 1. [Strength] vigor, energy, stamina; see **strength**. 2. [Controlling sway] authority, command, jurisdiction, dominion, ascendency, superiority, domination, dominance, mastery, preponderance, control, sway, sovereignty, prerogative, prestige, omnipotence, puissance, supreme authority, the last word, rule, law, first strike capability, warrant, supremacy, legal sanction, government, *say-so; see also **influence, leadership**. 3. [Ability; *often plural*] skill, endowment, capability; see **ability**. 4. [Force] compulsion, coercion, duress; see **pressure 2, restraint 2**. 5. [Energy] horsepower, potential, dynamism; see **energy 2**. —in power, ruling, authoritative, commanding; see **powerful 1**.

powerful, a. 1. [Wielding power] mighty, all-powerful, almighty, superhuman, omnipotent, overpowering, great, invincible, dominant, influential, authoritative, overruling, potent, forceful, forcible, compelling, ruling, prevailing, preeminent, commanding, supreme, highest, important, authoritarian, ruthless, having the upper hand, in control.—*Ant.* weak, incompetent, impotent. 2. [Strong] robust, stalwart, sturdy; see **strong 1, 2. 3.** [Effective] efficacious, effectual, convincing; see **persuasive.**

powerfully, *a.* forcibly, forcefully, effectively, severely, intensely, with authority; see also **vigorously.**

powerless, *a.* impotent, feeble, infirm; see **weak 1, 2.**

(the) powers that be, *n.* boss(es), higher authorities, higher-ups; see **administration 2.**

practical, *a.* matter-of-fact, pragmatical, unimaginative, practicable, feasible, workable, functional, useful, sound, sound-thinking, down-to-earth, unromantic, realistic, sensible, sane, reasonable, rational, to (one's) advantage, operative, utilitarian, possible, usable, serviceable, efficient, effective, working, in action, in operation, with both feet on the ground.—*Ant.* unreal, imaginative, unserviceable.

practically, *a.* 1. [In a practical manner] unimaginatively, pragmatically, efficiently, functionally, sensibly, rationally, reasonably, realistically, with regard to use, from a workable standpoint; see also **effectively.** 2. [Virtually] for ordinary purposes, nearly, just about; see **almost.**

practice, *n.* 1. [A customary action] usage, use, wont; see **custom 2. 2.** [A method] mode, manner, fashion; see **method, system 2. 3.** [Educational repetition] exercise, drill, repetition, iteration, rehearsal, recitation, recounting, relating, *tune-up, *prepping. 4. [A practitioner's custom] work, patients, clients; see **business 4.**

practice, *v.* 1. [To seek improvement through repetition] drill, train, exercise, study, rehearse, repeat, recite, iterate, put in practice, make it one's business, work at, accustom oneself, act up to, *polish up, *sharpen up, build up. 2. [To employ one's professional skill] function, work at, employ oneself in; see **work 2.**

practiced, *a.* trained, expert, exercised; see **able.**

pragmatic, *a.* realistic, utilitarian, logical; see **practical.**

prairie, *n.* steppe, savanna, grassland; see **field 1, meadow, plain.**

praise, *n.* 1. [The act of praising] applause, approval, appreciation; see **admiration.** 2. [An expression of praise] laudation, eulogy, regard, applause, recommendation, hand-clapping, hurrahs, bravos, ovation, cheers, cries, whistling, tribute, compliment, acclaim, flattery, blessing, benediction, boost, rave.—*Ant.* censure, **blame,** condemnation.

praise, *v.* 1. [To commend] recommend, applaud, cheer, acclaim, endorse, sanction, admire, eulogize, adulate, elevate, smile on, cajole, give an ovation to, clap, pay tribute to, do credit to, have a good word for, make much of, extend credit, advocate, compliment, appreciate, admire, celebrate, honor, congratulate, flatter, rave over, boost, give a big hand, raise the roof; see also **approve.** 2. [To speak or sing in worship] glorify, adore, reverence; see **worship.**

praised, *a.* admired, aided, helped, flattered, worshiped, glorified, exalted, blessed, celebrated, paid tribute to, magnified.

prance, *v.* cavort, frisk, gambol; see **dance.**

prank, *n.* game, escapade, caper; see **joke.**

pranks, *n.* antics, capers, frolics; see **trick 1.**

pray, *v.* 1. [To ask or beg] importune, petition, plead; see **ask, beg. 2.** [To call upon God] hold communion (with God), supplicate, implore, petition, entreat, commend someone to God.

prayer, *n.* 1. [An earnest request] entreaty, request, petition; see **appeal 1. 2.** [An address to the deity] invocation, act of devotion, supplication, (private) devotions, benediction, litany. Prayers include the following—Lord's Prayer, Pater Noster, Ave Maria, grace (at meals), *Kaddish* (Hebrew), matins, vespers, Angelus, general confession, Miserere, collects, hours, stations of the cross, evensong.

prayer book, *n.* liturgy, mass book, missal, hymnal, holy text, guide; see also **bible.**

preach, *v.* exhort, discourse, moralize, teach, lecture, talk, harangue, inform, address.

preacher, *n.* missionary, parson, evangelist; see **minister 1.**

preamble, *n.* prelude, preface, introductory part; see **introduction 4.**

precarious, *a.* doubtful, uncertain, dubious; see **dangerous.**

precaution, *n.* anticipation, forethought, regard; see **care 1.**

precede, *v.* go before, come first, be *or* move ahead of, take precedence over, preface, introduce, usher *or* ring in, herald, forerun, head, lead, run *or* go ahead, scout, light the way, go in advance, come before, come to the front, forge ahead, *head up. —*Ant.* succeed, come after, come last.

precedence, *n.* preference, precession, the lead; see **advantage**.

precedent, *n.* authoritative example, exemplar, pattern; see **example 1, model 2.**

preceding, *a.* antecedent, precedent, previous, other, prior, aforesaid, ahead of, earlier, former, forerunning, past, foregoing, above-mentioned, above-named, above-cited, afore-mentioned, before-mentioned, above, before, prefatory, front, forward, anterior, preliminary, preparatory, introductory, afore-known, already indicated, previously mentioned.

precious, *a.* 1. [Valuable] high-priced, costly, dear; see **expensive, valuable.** 2. [Beloved] cherished, inestimable, prized; see **beloved, favorite.** 3. [Refined and delicate] overrefined, overnice, fragile; see **dainty.**

precipice, *n.* crag, cliff, bluff; see **hill, mountain 1.**

precipitate, *v.* accelerate, press, hurry; see **hasten 2, speed.**

precipitation, *n.* 1. [Carelessness] rashness, presumption, impetuosity; see **carelessness, rudeness.** 2. [Condensation]·hail, rain, snow; see **storm.**

precise, *a.* 1. [Exact] decisive, well-defined, strict; see **accurate 2, definite 1, 2.** 2. [Fussily or prudishly careful] rigid, inflexible, uncompromising; see **careful, severe 1.**

precisely, *a.* correctly, exactly, definitely; see **accurate 2.**

precision, *n.* exactness, correctness, sureness; see **accuracy.**

preconception, *n.* prejudice, bias, assumption; see **inclination 1.**

predatory, *a.* voracious, carnivorous, bloodthirsty; see **greedy, hungry.**

predecessor, *n.* antecedent, forerunner, ancestor; see **parent.**

predicament, *n.* strait, quandary, plight, puzzle, perplexity, dilemma, scrape, corner, hole, impasse, tight situation, state, condition, position, lot, circumstance, mess, muddle, deadlock, pinch, crisis, *fix, *pickle, *hot water, *jam; see also **difficulty 1, 2.**

predicate, *n.* verbal phrase, part of speech, word; see **verb.**

predicate, *v.* assert, declare, state; see **mean 1.**

predict, *v.* prophesy, prognosticate, divine; see **foretell.**

predictable, *a.* anticipated, foreseen, prepared for; see **expected, likely 1.**

prediction, *n.* prophecy, foresight, prognostication; see **guess.**

predominance, *n.* reign, supremacy, control; see **command, power 2.**

predominant, *a.* 1. [Supreme in power] mighty, almighty, supreme; see **power**-ful 1. 2. [Of first importance] transcendent, surpassing, superlative; see **principal.**

predominate, *v.* dominate, prevail, rule; see **govern, manage 1.**

***prefab**, *n.* prefabricated *or* mass-produced building, (temporary) structure, standardized housing; see **building.**

prefabricate, *v.* fabricate, preform, set up, co-ordinate, pre-assemble; see also **assemble 2.**

preface, *n.* prelude, prelogomenon, preliminary; see **explanation, introduction 4.**

preface, *v.* introduce, commence, precede; see **begin 1.**

prefer, *v.* single out, fix upon, fancy; see **favor.**

preferable, *a.* more eligible, more desirable, good; see **excellent.**

preferably, *a.* by preference, by *or* at choice, by selection, in preference, first, sooner, before, optionally, at pleasure, willingly, at will; see also **rather 2.**

preference, *n.* favorite, election, option, decision, selection, pick; see also **choice.**

preferred, *a.* chosen, selected, fancied, adopted, picked out, taken, elected, liked, favored, set apart, handpicked, singled out, endorsed, settled upon, sanctioned, decided upon.—*Ant.* neglected, unpreferred, overlooked.

prefix, *n.* 1. [An addition] affix, adjunct, preflex, prefixture. 2. [A designation] title, cognomen, designation; see **name 1.**

pregnancy, *n.* reproduction, fertilization, gestation; see **birth.**

pregnant, *a.* gestating, gravid, fruitful, with child, big with child, hopeful, anticipating, *in a family way, *expecting.

prehistoric, *a.* preceding history, very early, unknown; see **old 3.**

prejudge, *v.* presuppose, forejudge, presume; see **decide.**

prejudice, *n.* partiality, unfairness, spleen, bias, detriment, enmity, prejudgment, dislike, disgust, aversion, antipathy, race prejudice, apartheid, misjudgment, pique, coolness, animosity, contemptuousness, bad opinion, displeasure, repugnance, revulsion, preconception, foregone conclusion, quirk, warp, twist.—*Ant.* admiration, appreciation, good opinion.

prejudiced, *a.* preconceived, prepossessed, biased, directed against, influenced, inclined, leaning, conditioned, presupposing, predisposed, dogmatic, opinionated, partisan, extreme, hidebound, narrow, intolerant, canting, blind, partial, narrow-minded, parochial, provincial, one-sided, not seeing an inch beyond one's nose, squint-eyed, intolerant of, disliking, having a predilection, closed against, judging on slight knowledge, smug.—*Ant.* **generous,** open-minded, receptive.

preliminary, *a.* preparatory, preceding, prefatory; see **introductory.**

prelude, *n.* preface, preliminary preparation, prelusion; see **introduction 3.**

premarital, *a.* before the vows, before marriage, during courtship; see **before.**

premature, *a.* unanticipated, precipitate, rash; see **early 2, untimely.**

prematurely, *a.* too early, rash, precipitately; see **early 2, untimely.**

premiere, *n.* first night, beginning, opening; see **performance.**

premise, *n.* proposition, evidence, assumption; see **basis, proof 1.**

premises, *n.* 1. [Evidence] testimony, reason, support; see **basis, proof 1. 2.** [Real estate] bounds, limits, land; see **property 2.**

premium, *a.* prime, superior, select(ed); see **excellent.**

premium, *n.* remuneration, bonus, annual installment; see **prize.**

premonition, *n.* omen, portent, forewarning; see **sign 1, warning.**

preoccupation, *n.* absorption, daydreaming, amusement; see **fantasy, thought 1.**

preoccupied, *a.* removed, absorbed, distracted; see **rapt 2.**

preparation, *n.* 1. [The act of preparing] preparing, fitting, making ready, manufacture, readying, putting in order, establishment, compounding, adapting, rehearsal, incubation, gestation, building, construction, formation, maturing, anticipation, development, evolution, furnishing, *build-up. 2.** [The state of being prepared] preparedness, readiness, fitness, adaptation, suitability, capacity, qualification, background, ripeness, mellowness, maturity, training, education, equipment. 3. [Something that is prepared] arrangement, product, compound; see **mixture 1.**

prepare, *v.* 1. [To make oneself ready] get ready, foresee, arrange, make preparations *or* arrangements, fit, adapt, qualify, put in order, adjust, set one's house in order, prime, fix, settle, fabricate, appoint, furnish, elaborate, perfect, develop, prepare the ground, lay the foundations, block out, smooth the way, man, arm, set for, cut out, warm up, lay the groundwork, contrive, devise, make provision, put in readiness, build up (for), provide (for *or* against), make snug, be prepared, be ready; see also **anticipate, plan 1. 2.** [To make other persons *or* things ready] outfit, equip, fit out; see **provide 1. 3.** [To cook and serve] concoct, dress, brew; see **cook, serve.**

prepared, *a.* 1. [Fitted] adapted, qualified, adjusted; see **able, fit 1. 2.** [Subjected to a special process or treatment] frozen, pre-cooked, processed; see **preserved 2. 3.** [Ready] available, on hand, in order; see **ready 2.**

preposition, *n.* part of speech, function word, form word; see also **grammar, word 1.**

prepossessing, *a.* handsome, captivating, attractive; see **charming, pleasant 1.**

prerequisite, *n.* essential, necessity, need; see **requirement 1.**

prerogative, *n.* privilege, advantage, exemption; see **right 1.**

prescribe, *v.* guide, order, give directions; see **order 1.**

prescription, *n.* direction, medical recipe, formula; see **medicine 2.**

presence, *n.* 1. [The fact of being present] occupancy, occupation, residence, inhabitance, habitancy; see also **attendance 1. 2.** [The vicinity of a person] propinquity, nearness, closeness; see **neighborhood. 3.** [One's appearance and behavior] carriage, port, demeanor; see **appearance 1, behavior.**

presence of mind, *n.* sensibility, alertness, acumen; see **attention.**

present, *a.* 1. [Near in time] existing, being, in process, in duration, begun, started, commenced, going on, under consideration, at this time, contemporary, immediate, instant, prompt, at this moment, at present, today, nowadays, already, even now, but now, just now, for the time being, for the occasion; see also **now 1.** —*Ant.* **past,** over, completed. 2. [Near in space] in view, at hand, within reach; see **near 1.**

present, *n.* 1. [The present time] instant, this time, present moment; see **today. 2.** [A gift] grant, donation, offering; see **gift 1.**

present, *v.* 1. [To introduce] make known, acquaint with, give an introduction; see **introduce 3. 2.** [To submit] donate, proffer, put forth; see **offer 1. 3.** [To give] grant, bestow, confer; see **give 1. 4.** [To give a play, etc.] put on, do, impersonate; see **act 3, perform 2.**

presentable, *a.* attractive, prepared, satisfactory; see **fit 1.**

presentation, *n.* 1. [The act of presenting] bestowal, donation, delivering; see **giving. 2.** [Something presented] present, offering, remembrance; see **gift 1.**

presented, *a.* bestowed, granted, conferred; see **given.**

presently, *a.* directly, without delay, shortly; see **immediately, soon 1.**

preservation, *n.* security, safety, protection, conservation, maintenance, saving, keeping, storage, curing, tanning, freezing, sugaring, pickling, evaporation, canning, refrigeration.

preserve, v. 1. [To guard] protect, shield, save; see **defend 2.** 2. [To maintain] keep up, care for, conserve; see **maintain 3.** 3. [To keep] can, conserve, process, save, put up, put down, store, cure, bottle, do up, season, salt, pickle, put in brine, put in vinegar, pot, tin, dry, smoke, corn, dry-cure, smoke-cure, freeze, quick freeze, keep up, cold-pack, refrigerate, dehydrate, seal up, kipper, marinate, evaporate, embalm, mummify, mothball, fill.—*Ant.* **waste,** allow to spoil, let spoil.

preserved, a. 1. [Saved] rescued, guarded, secured; see **saved 1.** 2. [Prepared for preservation] canned, corned, dried, freeze-dried, dehydrated, evaporated, smoked, seasoned, pickled, salted, brined, put up, conserved, cured, marinated, tinned, potted, bottled, embalmed, mummified.

preserves, n. spread, sweet, jell; see **jam 1, jelly.**

preside, v. direct, lead, control; see **advise, manage 1.**

presidency, n. office of the president, chairmanship, position; see **administration 2.**

president, n. presiding officer, chief director, *great White Father; see **executive.**

presidential, a. official, regulatory, of the chief executive; see **managing.**

press, n. 1. [The pressure of circumstances] rush, confusion, strain; see **haste. 2.** [Publishing as a social institution] the Fourth Estate, publishers, publicists, newsmen, newspapermen, journalists, journalistic writers, editors, correspondents, political writers, columnists, periodicals, periodical press, papers, newspapers.

press, v. 1. [To subject to pressure] thrust, crowd, bear upon, bear down on *or* upon, squeeze, hold *or* pin *or* screw *or* force down, crush, drive, weight, urge; see also **push 1.**—*Ant.* **raise,** release, relieve. **2.** [To smooth, usually by heat and pressure] finish, mangle, roll; see also **iron, smooth.**

press conference, n. interview, public report *or* statement, briefing; see **announcement, hearing 1.**

pressing, a. importunate, constraining, distressing; see **important 1, urgent 1.**

pressure, n. 1. [Physical pressure] force, burden, mass, load, encumbrance, stress, thrust, tension, squeeze; see also **weight 1.** —*Ant.* **release,** relief, deliverance. **2.** [Some form of social pressure] compulsion, constraint, urgency, persuasion, stress, affliction, coercion, trouble, hardship, humiliation, misfortune, necessity, repression, confinement, unnaturalness, obligation, discipline.—*Ant.* **aid,** assistance, encouragement.

pressure, v. press, compel, constrain; see **urge 2, 3.**

prestige, n. renown, effect, influence; see **fame.**

presumably, a. in all probability *or* likelihood, credibly, likely; see **probably.**

presume, v. consider, suppose, take for granted; see **assume.**

presumption, n. 1. [An assumption] conjecture, guess, hypothesis; see **assumption 1.** 2. [Impudence] arrogance, audacity, effrontery; see **rudeness.**

pretend, v. 1. [To feign] affect, simulate, claim falsely, imitate, counterfeit, sham, make as if *or* though, mislead, beguile, delude, pass (off) for, cheat, dupe, hoodwink, be deceitful, bluff, falsify, be hypocritical, fake, *put on, *let on, go through the motions, keep up appearances; see also **deceive. 2.** [To make believe] mimic, fill a role, take a part, represent, portray, put on a front, play, make believe, act the part of, *put on (an act), act a part, *put on airs, playact.

pretended, a. feigned, counterfeit, assumed, affected, shammed, bluffing, simulated, lying, falsified, put on, concealed, covered, masked, cheating; see also **false 3.**

pretense, n. 1. [The act of pretending] affectation, misrepresentation, falsification, act, deceit, fabrication, trickery, double-dealing, misstatement, falsifying, simulation, excuse, insincerity, profession, ostentation, assumption, dissimulation, evasion, equivocation, prevarication, egotism, brazenness, arrogance, dandyism, foppery, servility, complacency, smugness, prudishness, coyness, formality, stiffness, *blind, *smoke screen; see also **dishonesty, imitation 1.**—*Ant.* honesty, candor, sincerity. **2.** [Something pretended] falsehood, lie, falseness, affectation, mask, cloak, show, excuse, subterfuge, pretext, fraud, appearance, seeming, semblance, wile, ruse, sham, airs, claim, mannerism; see also **deception, imitation 2.**

prettily, a. pleasingly, gently, quietly; see **politely.**

pretty, a. 1. [Attractive] comely, lovely, good-looking; see **beautiful. 2.** [Pleasant] delightful, cheerful, pleasing; see **pleasant 2.** 3. [*Considerable] ample, sizeable, notable; see **large 1, much 1, 2.** 4. [Somewhat] rather, tolerably, a little; see **moderately.**

prevalence, *n*. dissemination, occurrence, currency; see **regularity**.

prevalent, *a*. widespread, accepted, frequently met; see **common 1**.

prevent, *v*. preclude, obviate, forestall, anticipate, block, arrest, stop, thwart, repress, interrupt, halt, impede, check, avert, frustrate, balk, foil, retard, obstruct, counter, countercheck, counteract, inhibit, restrict, block off, limit, hold back *or* off, stop from, deter, intercept, override, circumvent, bar, ward off, keep from happening, nip in the bud, put a stop *or* an end to, stave *or* keep *or* draw off, turn aside; see also **hinder, restrain 1**. *—Ant*. help, aid, encourage.

prevented, *a*. obviated, stopped, interfered with; see **interrupted**.

prevention, *n*. anticipation, forestalling, arresting, obviating, bar, debarring, halt, impeding, retardation, repression, restraint, restriction, inhibition, interception, overriding, circumvention, hindering, counteraction, obstruction, opposition, warding *or* staving *or* drawing *or* keeping off, stopping, thwarting, blocking; see also **refusal**.*—Ant*. aid, encouragement, help.

preventive, *a*. deterrent, precautionary, tending to prevent; see **cautiously**.

previous, *a*. antecedent, prior, former; see **preceding**.

previously, *a*. long ago, earlier, beforehand; see **before**.

prey, *n*. spoil, pillage, loot; see **victim**.

prey on, *v*. 1. [To destroy] seize, raid, pillage; see **destroy**. 2. [To eat] feed on, devour, consume; see **eat 1**.

price, *n*. expenditure, outlay, expense, cost, value, worth, figure, dues, tariff, valuation, quotation, fare, hire, wages, return, disbursement, rate, appraisal, reckoning, equivalent, payment, demand, barter, consideration, amount, marked price, asking price, estimate, output, ransom, reward, carry charge, pay, prize, return, par value, money's worth, price ceiling, ceiling; see also **value 1**. *—at any price*, whatever the cost, expense no object, anyhow; see **regardless 2**.

price, *v*. fix the price of, appraise, assess; see **rate, value 2**.

priced, *a*. valued, estimated, worth; see **costing**.

priceless, *a*. invaluable, inestimable, without price; see **valuable**.

prick, *n*. tap, stab, stick; see **cut**.

prick, *v*. pierce, puncture, stick; see **cut, hurt 1**.

prickly, *a*. thorny, pointed, spiny; see **sharp 1**.

pride, *n*. 1. [The quality of being vain] vainglory, egoism, egotism, self-esteem, self-love, self-exaltation, self-glorification, self-admiration, pretension.*—Ant*. humility, self-effacement, unpretentiousness. 2. [Conduct growing from pride, sense 1] haughtiness, vanity, disdain, condescension, patronizing, patronage, superiority; see **sense 1**. 3. [Sense of personal satisfaction] self-respect, self-satisfaction, self-sufficiency; see **happiness**. 4. [A source of satisfaction] enjoyment, repletion, sufficiency; see **satisfaction 2**.

pride oneself on, *v*. take pride in, flatter oneself, be proud of; see **boast**.

priest, *n*. Names for priests in various sects include the following—father confessor, spiritual father, priest-vicar, high priest, minor canon, pontiff, vicar, care of souls, clergyman, rector, preacher, presbyter, elder, rabbi, lama, monk, friar; see also **minister 1**.

priesthood, *n*. clergy, Holy Orders, monasticism; see **ministry 2**.

priestly, *a*. ecclesiastic, episcopal, ministerial; see **clerical 2**.

prim, *a*. stiff, formal, precise, demure, decorous, nice, orderly, tidy, cleanly, trim, spruce, pat; see also **polite**.

primarily, *a*. originally, fundamentally, in the first place; see **principally**.

primary, *a*. 1. [Earliest] primitive, initial, first; see **original 1**. 2. [Fundamental] elemental, basic, central; see **fundamental**. 3. [Principal] chief, prime, main; see **principal**.

primate, *n*. gorilla, chimpanzee, orangutan, gibbon, great ape; see **man 1, monkey**.

prime, *a*. 1. [Principal] earliest, beginning, original; see **principal**. 2. [Excellent] top, choice, superior; see **excellent**.

primitive, *a*. 1. [Simple] rudimentary, first; see **fundamental**. 2. [Ancient] primeval, archaic, primordial; see **old 3**. 3. [Uncivilized] crude, rough, simple, rude, atavistic, uncivilized, savage, uncultured, natural, barbaric, barbarous, barbarian, fierce, untamed, uncouth, ignorant, undomesticated, wild, animal, brutish, raw, untaught, green, unlearned, untutored, underdeveloped.

primp, *v*. make one's toilet, paint and powder, get (all) dressed up; see **dress, prepare 1**.

prince, *n*. sovereign, ruler, monarch, potentate; see also **royalty**.

princely, *a*. 1. [Royal] sovereign, regal, august; see **royal**. 2. [Suited to a prince] lavish, sumptuous, luxurious; see **expensive, handsome, rich 1, 2**.

princess, *n*. sovereign, monarch, infanta; see **royalty**.

Princeton, *n*. Princeton University,

Princeton College, Orange and Black, Old Nassau, Tiger; see also **university**.

principal, *a.* leading, chief, first, head, prime, main, foremost, cardinal, essential, capital, important, preeminent, highest, supreme, prominent, dominant, predominant, controlling, superior, prevailing, paramount, greatest, incomparable, unapproachable, peerless, matchless, unequaled, unrivaled, maximum, crowning, unparalleled, sovereign, second to none.—*Ant.* unimportant, secondary, accessory.

principal, *n.* chief, head, chief party, master; see also **executive**.

principally, *a.* chiefly, mainly, essentially, substantially, materially, eminently, pre-eminently, superlatively, supremely, vitally, especially, particularly, peculiarly, notably, importantly, fundamentally, dominantly, predominantly, basically, largely, first and foremost, in large measure, first of all, to a great degree, prevalently, generally, universally, mostly, above all, in the first place, for the most part, for the greatest part, before anything else, in the main.—*Ant.* **slightly**, somewhat, tolerably.

principle, *n.* 1. [A fundamental law] origin, source, postulate; see **law** 4. 2. [A belief or set of beliefs; *often plural*] system, opinion, teaching; see **belief, faith** 2, **policy**.

principles, *n.* ideals, standard of conduct, beliefs; see **attitude, character** 1, 2.

print, *n.* 1. [Printed matter] impression, reprint, issue; see **copy**. 2. [A printed picture] engraving, lithograph, photograph; see **picture** 3, **sketch**. —in print, printed, available, obtainable; see **published**. —out of print, O.P., unavailable, remaindered; see **sold out**.

print, *v.* 1. [To make an impression] impress, imprint, indent; see **mark** 1. 2. [To reproduce by printing] run off, print up, issue, reissue, reprint, bring out, go to press, set type, compose, start the presses; see also **publish** 1.—*Ant.* talk, write, inscribe. 3. [To simulate printing] letter, do lettering, calligraph; see **write** 2.

printed, *a.* impressed, imprinted, engraved, stamped, lithographed, multilithed, Xeroxed (trademark), printed by (photo-)offset, silkscreened; see also **reproduced**.

printer, *n.* typesetter, compositor, linotype operator; see **workman**.

printing, *n.* 1. [A process of reproduction] typography, composition, typesetting, presswork. 2. [Printed matter] line, page, sheet; see **page**. 3. [Publication] issuing, issuance, distribution; see **publication** 1.

prior, *a.* antecedent, above-mentioned, foregoing; see **preceding**.

priority, *n.* superiority, preference, precedence; see **advantage**.

prison, *n.* penitentiary, reformatory, prison house, guardhouse, stockade; see also **jail**.

prisoner, *n.* captive, convict, culprit, jailbird, detainee, the legally retarded, escapee, hostage, *con; see also **defendant**.

prisoner of war, *n.* captive *or* captured *or* interned person *or* personnel, person in captivity, POW; see **prisoner**.

privacy, *n.* seclusion, solitude, retreat, isolation, separateness, aloofness, separation, concealment; see also **secrecy**.

private, *a.* special, separate, retired, secluded, withdrawn, removed, not open, behind the scenes, off the record, privy, clandestine, single; see also **individual, own**.—*Ant.* public, open, exposed. —in private, privately, personally, not public; see **secretly**.

private, *n.* enlisted man, infantryman; private first class, second class, etc.; see **sailor, soldier**.

privately, *a.* confidentially, clandestinely, alone; see **personally** 1, **secretly**.

private parts, *n.* (genital) organs, organs of reproduction, privates; see **genitals**.

privilege, *n.* 1. [A customary concession] due, perquisite, prerogative; see **right** 1. 2. [An opportunity] chance, fortunate happening, event; see **opportunity** 1.

privileged, *a.* free, vested, furnished; see **exempt**.

prize, *n.* reward, advantage, privilege, possession, honor, inducement, premium, meed, bounty, bonus, spoil, booty, plunder, pillage, loot, award, accolade, recompense, requital, acquisitions, laurel, decoration, medal, trophy, palm, crown, citation, scholarship, fellowship, feather in one's cap, title, championship, first place, pay-off, cake, plum.

prize, *v.* guess, count, esteem; see **estimate, value** 2.

probability, *n.* likelihood, possibility, chance; see **chance** 1, **possibility** 2.

probable, *a.* seeming, presumable, feasible; see **likely** 1.

probably, *a.* presumably, seemingly, apparently, believably, reasonably, imaginably, feasibly, practicably, expediently, plausibly, most likely, everything being equal, as like as not, as the case may be, one can assume, like enough, no doubt, to all appearance, in all probability.—*Ant.* unlikely, doubtfully, questionably.

problem, *n.* 1. [A difficulty] dilemma, quandary, obstacle; see **difficulty** 1, 2. 2. [A question to be solved] query, intricacy, enigma; see **puzzle** 2.

procedure, *n.* fashion, style, mode; see method, system 2.

proceed, *v.* move, progress, continue; see advance 1.

proceeding, *n.* [*Often plural*] process, transaction, deed, experiment, performance, measure, step, course, undertaking, venture, adventure, occurrence, incident, circumstance, happening, movement, operation, procedure, exercise, maneuver; see also action 1.

proceeds, *n.* gain, interest, yield; see return 3.

process, *n.* means, rule, manner; see method. —in (the) process of, while, when, in the course of; see during.

process, *v.* treat, make ready, concoct; see prepare 1.

processed, *a.* treated, handled, fixed; see preserved 2.

prod, *v.* provoke, crowd, shove; see push 1.

prodigy, *n.* marvel, portent, miracle, monster, enormity, spectacle, freak, curiosity; see also wonder 2. —(child) prodigy, genius, gifted child, boy *or* girl wonder; see artist, musician, scientist, writer.

produce, *n.* product, harvest, result, crop, return, effect, consequence, amount, profit, outcome, outgrowth, aftermath, gain, realization; see also butter, cheese, cream 1, food, fruit, grain 1, milk, vegetable.

produce, *v.* 1. [To bear] yield, bring *or* give forth, give birth (to), propagate, bring out, come through, blossom, flower, deliver, generate, engender, breed, contribute, give, afford, furnish, return, render, show fruit, fetch, bring in, present, offer, provide, contribute, sell for, bear (fruit), accrue, allow, admit, proliferate, be delivered of, bring to birth, reproduce, foal, lamb, drop, calve, fawn, whelp, cub, kitten, hatch, usher into the world, spawn. 2. [To create by mental effort] originate, author, procreate, bring forth, conceive, engender, write, design, fabricate, imagine, turn out, devise; see also compose 2, create, invent 1. 3. [To cause] effect, occasion, bring about; see begin 1. 4. [To show] exhibit, present, unfold; see display 5. 5. [To make] assemble, build, construct; see manufacture. 6. [To present a performance] present, play, put on the stage; see act 3, perform 2.

produced, *a.* 1. [Created] originated, composed, made; see formed 2. 2. [Presented] performed, acted, put on; see shown 1. 3. [Caused] occasioned, propagated, begot, bred, engendered, generated, hatched, induced.

product, *n.* 1. [A result] output, outcome, produce; see result. 2. [Often

plural; goods produced] stock, goods, merchandise; see goods 1.

production, *n.* 1. [The act of producing] origination, creation, authoring, reproduction, yielding, giving, bearing, rendering, giving forth, increasing, return, procreation, generation, engendering, blooming, blossoming; see also making. 2. [The amount produced] crop, result, stock; see quantity.

productive, *a.* rich, fruitful, prolific; see fertile.

productivity, *n.* richness, potency, fecundity; see fertility.

profanity, *n.* abuse, cursing, swearing; see curse 1.

profession, *n.* 1. [A skilled or learned occupation] calling, business, avocation, vocation, employment, occupation, engagement, office, situation, position, lifework, chosen work, role, service, pursuit, undertaking, concern, post, berth, craft, sphere, field, walk of life; see also church 3, education 3, judiciary, medicine 3, trade 2, writing 3. 2. [A declaration] pretense, avowal, vow; see declaration, oath 1.

professional, *a.* 1. [Skillful] expert, learned, adept; see able. 2. [Well-qualified] acknowledged, known, licensed; see able.

professional, *n.* expert, trained *or* experienced personnel, specially trained person; see specialist.

professor, *n.* educator, faculty member, sage; see teacher 2. Teachers popularly called professors include the following—full professor, associate professor, assistant professor, instructor, lecturer, graduate assistant, teaching assistant *or* T.A., tutor, school principal, fellow, teaching fellow, master docent.

proficiency, *n.* learning, skill, knowledge; see ability.

proficient, *a.* skilled, expert, skillful; see able.

profile, *n.* silhouette, shape, figure; see form 1, outline 4.

profit, *n.* 1. [Advantage] avail, good, value; see advantage. 2. [Excess of receipts over expenditures] gain, return(s), proceeds, receipts, take, gate, acquisition, rake-off, accumulation, saving, interest, remuneration, earnings.—*Ant.* loss, debits, costs.

profit, *v.* 1. [To be of benefit] benefit, assist, avail; see help. 2. [To derive gain] benefit, capitalize on, cash in on, realize, clear, gain, reap profits, make a profit, recover, thrive, prosper, harvest, make money.—*Ant.* lose, lose out on, miss out on.

profitable, *a.* lucrative, useful, sustaining, aiding, remunerative, beneficial, gainful, advantageous, paying, successful, favorable, assisting, productive, serviceable, valuable, instrumental, practical, pragmatic, effective, to advantage, effectual, sufficient, paying its way, bringing in returns, making money, paying well, paying out, in the black; see also **helpful 1.**—*Ant.* **unprofitable, unsuccessful,** unproductive.

profitably, *a.* lucratively, remuneratively, gainfully, usefully, advantageously, successfully, favorably, for money, productively, practically, effectively, effectually, sufficiently, sustainingly.

profiteer, *n.* exploiter, chiseler, cheater; see **cheat.**

profound, *a.* 1. [Physically deep] fathomless, bottomless, subterranean; see **deep 1. 2.** [Intellectually deep] heavy, erudite, scholarly, mysterious, sage, serious, sagacious, penetrating, discerning, knowing, wise, knowledgeable, intellectual, enlightened, thorough, informed; see also **learned 1, solemn 1.**—*Ant.* **superficial,** shallow, flighty. 3. [Emotionally deep] heartfelt, deep-felt, great; see **intense.**

profoundly, *a.* deeply, extremely, thoroughly; see **very.**

program, *n.* 1. [A list of subjects] schedule, memoranda, printed program; see **list.** 2. [A sequence of events] happenings, schedule, agenda, order of business, calendar, plans, business, affairs, details, arrangements, catalogue, curriculum, order of the day, series of events, appointments, things to do, chores, preparations, meetings, getting and spending, all the thousand and one things; see also **plan 2.** 3. [An entertainment] performance, show, presentation; see **performance 2.**

program, *v.* 1. [To schedule] slate, book, bill; see sense 2. 2. [To work out a sequence to be performed] feed through *or* in, activate a computer, compute, reckon, figure, calculate, estimate, enter, compile, feed, edit, process, extend, delete, add.

programmed, *a.* scheduled, slated, lined up; see **planned.**

progress, *n.* 1. [Movement forward] progression, advance, headway, impetus, velocity, pace, momentum, motion, rate, step, stride, current, flow, tour, circuit, transit, journey, voyage, march, expedition, locomotion, ongoing, passage, course, procession, process, lapse of time, march of events, course of life, movement of the stars, motion through space.—*Ant.* **stop,** stay, stand. 2. [Improvement] advancement, development, growth; see **improvement 1.** —**in progress,** advancing, going on, continuing; see **moving 1.**

progress, *v.* proceed, move onward, move on; see **advance 1.**

progressive, *a.* 1. [In mounting sequence] advancing, mounting, rising; see **moving 1.** 2. [Receptive to new ideas] tolerant, lenient, open-minded; see **liberal.**

prohibit, *v.* interdict, put under the ban, obstruct; see **forbid, prevent.**

prohibited, *a.* forbidden, restricted, not approved; see **illegal, refused.**

project, *n.* outline, design, scheme; see **plan 2.**

project, *v.* 1. [To thrust out] protrude, hang over, extend, jut, bulge, stretch *or* push *or* stand *or* stick *or* hang *or* jut out, be prominent, be conspicuous.—*Ant.* **withdraw,** regress, revert. 2. [To throw] pitch, heave, propel; see **throw 1.**

projection, *n.* 1. [Bulge] prominence, jut, protuberance, step, ridge, rim; see also **bulge.** 2. [Forecast] prognostication, prediction, guess; see **guess.**

prolong, *v.* continue, hold, draw out; see **increase.**

prolonged, *a.* extended, lengthened, continued; see **dull 4.**

prominence, *n.* 1. [A projection] jut, protrusion, bump; see **bulge, projection 1.** 2. [Notability] reknown, influence, distinction; see **fame.**

prominent, *a.* 1. [Physically prominent] protuberant, extended, jutting, conspicuous, protruding, projecting, noticeable, rugged, rough, obtrusive, shooting out, hilly, raised, relieved, rounded. —*Ant.* **hollow,** depressed, sunken. 2. [Socially prominent] notable, pre-eminent, leading; see **famous.** 3. [Conspicuous] remarkable, striking, noticeable; see **conspicuous.**

promiscuity, *n.* lechery, looseness, indiscrimination; see **lewdness.**

promiscuous, *a.* indiscriminate, indiscriminative, unrestricted; see **lewd 2.**

promise, *n.* 1. [A pledge] assurance, agreement, pact, oath, engagement, covenant, consent, warrant, affirmation, swearing, plight, word, troth, vow, profession, guarantee, insurance, obligation, commitment, betrothal, espousal, plighted faith, marriage contract, giving one's word, gentleman's agreement, word of honor, parole, foretaste. 2. [Hope] outlook, good omen, good appearance; see **encouragement.**

promise, *v.* 1. [To give one's word] engage, declare, agree, vow, swear, consent, affirm, profess, undertake, pledge, covenant, contract, bargain, espouse, betroth, assure, guarantee, warrant, give assurance *or* warranty, insure, cross one's heart, keep a promise, live up to, plight faith *or* troth, bind *or* commit *or* obligate oneself, make oneself answerable (for), give security, underwrite, subscribe, lead one to expect, answer for, pledge one's honor.–*Ant.* deceive, deny, break faith. 2. [To appear promising] ensure, insure, assure; see encourage.

promised, *a.* pledged, sworn, vowed, agreed, covenanted, as agreed upon, undertaken, professed, consented, affirmed, insured, warranted, vouched for, underwritten, subscribed, stipulated, assured, ensured; see also guaranteed.

promising, *a.* likely, assuring, encouraging; see hopeful 2.

promote, *v.* 1. [To further] forward, urge, encourage, profit, patronize, help, aid, assist, develop, support, boom, back, uphold, champion, advertise, advocate, cultivate, improve, push, bolster, develop, speed, foster, nourish, nurture, subsidize, befriend, benefit, subscribe to, favor, expand, improve, better, cooperate, get behind, boost.–*Ant.* discourage, weaken, enfeeble. 2. [To advance in rank] raise, advance, elevate, graduate, move up, exalt, aggrandize, magnify, prefer, favor, increase, ascend, better, dignify.–*Ant.* humble, demote, reduce.

promotion, *n.* 1. [Advancement in rank] preferment, elevation, raise, improvement, advance, lift, betterment, favoring.–*Ant.* removal, demotion, lowering. 2. [Improvement] advancement, progression, development; see improvement 1, increase.

prompt, *a.* early, timely, precise; see punctual.

prompt, *v.* 1. [To instigate] arouse, provoke, inspire; see incite, urge 2. 2. [To suggest] bring up, indicate, imply; see propose 1.

promptly, *a.* on time, punctually, hastily; see immediately, quickly.

prone, *a.* inclined, predisposed, devoted; see likely 4.

prong, *n.* spine, spur, spike; see fastener.

pronoun, *n.* Pronouns include the following—personal, possessive, demonstrative, relative, definite, indefinite, interrogative, intensive, reflexive, reciprocal.

pronounce, *v.* 1. [To speak formally] proclaim, say, assert; see declare 2. 2. [To articulate] enunciate, phonate, vocalize; see utter.

pronounced, *a.* notable, noticeable, clear; see definite 2, obvious 1, 2, strong 8, unusual 1.

pronouncement, *n.* report, declaration, statement; see announcement 1.

pronunciation, *n.* articulation, utterance, voicing; see diction.

proof, *n.* 1. [Evidence] demonstration,

verification, case, reasons, exhibits, credentials, data, warrant, confirmation, substantiation, attestation, corroboration, affidavit, facts, witness, testimony, deposition, trace, record, criterion. 2. [Process of proving] test, attempt, assay; see trial 2.

prop, *n.* aid, assistance, strengthener; see post 1.

propaganda, *n.* promotion, publicity, advertisement, *plug, *publication, announcement, ballyhoo, handout.

propel, *v.* impel forward, move, press onward; see drive 2.

propellant, *n.* charge, gunpowder, combustible; see explosive, fuel.

propeller, *n.* Propellers include the following—screw, Archimedean, fishtail, variable-pitch, feathering, marine, airplane, two-bladed, three-bladed, fourbladed, weedless, pusher, pulling.

propensity, *n.* talent, capacity, competence; see ability 1, 2.

proper, *a.* 1. [Suitable] just, decent, fitting; see fit 1. 2. [Conventional] customary, usual, decorous; see conventional 1, 3. 3. [Prudish] prim, precise, strait-laced; see prudish.

properly, *a.* correctly, fitly, suitably; see well 3.

property, *n.* 1. [Possession] belongings, lands, assets, holdings, inheritance, capital, equity, investment(s), goods (and) chattels), earthly possessions, real property, personal property, taxable property, resources, private property, public property, wealth; see also business 4, estate, farm, home 1. 2. [A piece of land] section, quarter section, estate, tract, part, real estate, farm, park, ranch, homestead, yard, grounds, frontage, acres, acreage, premises, campus, grant, landed property, field, claim, holding, plot; see also lot 1.

prophesy, *n.* prediction, prognostication, augury; see idea 1.

prophesy, *v.* predict, prognosticate, divine; see foretell.

prophet, *n.* seer, oracle, soothsayer, prophetess, seeress, clairvoyant, wizard, augur, sibyl, sorcerer, predictor, forecaster, prognosticator, diviner, medium, witch, palmist, fortuneteller, weather forecaster, meteorologist, magus, astrologer, horoscopist.

prophetic, *a.* predictive, occult, veiled.

propitious, *a.* 1. [Favorable] auspicious, encouraging, promising; see hopeful 2. 2. [Kindly] benignant, helpful, generous; see kind.

proponent, *n.* defender, advocate, champion; see protector.

proportion, *n.* relationship, dimension, share; see balance 2, part 1.

proportional, *a.* proportionate, equivalent, comparable; see **equal**.

proposal, *n.* 1. [Offer] overture, recommendation, proposition; see **suggestion** 1. 2. [Plan] scheme, program, prospectus; see **plan** 2.

propose, *v.* 1. [To make a suggestion] suggest, offer, put forward, move, set forth, come up with, state, proffer, advance, propound, introduce, put to, contend, assert, tender, recommend, advise, counsel, lay before, submit, affirm, volunteer, press, urge (upon), hold out, make a motion, lay (something) on the line.—*Ant.* oppose, dissent, protest. 2. [To mean] purpose, intend, aim; see **mean** 1. 3. [To propose marriage] offer marriage, ask in marriage, make a proposal, ask for the hand of, *pop the question.

proposed, *a.* projected, prospective, advised, scheduled, expected, arranged, advanced, suggested, moved, put forward, submitted, recommended, urged, volunteered, pressed, intended, determined, anticipated, designed, schemed, purposed, considered, referred to, contingent; see also **planned**.

proposition, *n.* proposal, scheme, project; see **plan** 1.

proposition, *v.* ask, accost, approach; see **ask**.

proprietor, *n.* heritor, master, proprietary; see **owner**, **possessor**.

propriety, *n.* aptness, suitability, advisability, accordance, agreeableness, compatibility, correspondence, consonance, appropriateness, congruity, modesty, good breeding, dignity, concord, harmony, expedience, convenience, pleasantness, welcomeness; see also **fitness**.—*Ant.* **inconsistency**, incongruity, inappropriateness.

prose, *n.* fiction, non-fiction, composition; see **literature** 1, **story**, **writing** 2.

prosecute, *v.* contest, indict, involve in litigation; see **sue**.

prosecution, *n.* state, government, prosecuting attorney, state's attorney; see also **lawyer**.

prospect, *n.* 1. [A view] sight, landscape, vista; see **view** 1. 2. [A probable future] expectancy, promise, hope; see **outlook** 2. 3. [A possible candidate] possibility, likely person, interested party; see **candidate**.

prospective, *a.* considered, hoped for, promised; see **planned**, **proposed**.

prosper, *v.* become rich *or* wealthy, be enriched, thrive, turn out well, fare *or* do well, be fortunate, have good fortune, flourish, get on, rise (in the world), fatten, increase, bear fruit, bloom, blossom, flower, make money, make a fortune, benefit, advance, gain,

*make good, *do well by oneself, make one's mark, *roll in the lap of luxury, *come along, *do wonders; see also **succeed** 1.

prosperity, *n.* accomplishment, victory, successfulness; see **success** 2.

prosperous, *a.* flourishing, well-off, well-to-do; see **rich** 1.

prostitute, *n.* harlot, strumpet, lewd woman, whore, bawd, streetwalker, loose woman, fallen woman, courtesan, abandoned woman, concubine, vice girl, hustler, call girl, tramp, slut, *tart, *hooker; see also **criminal**.

prostitution, *n.* hustling, harlotry, *hooking; see **lewdness**.

protagonist, *n.* leading character, lead, combatant; see **hero** 1, **idol**.

protect, *v.* shield, guard, preserve; see **defend** 1, 2.

protected, *a.* shielded, safeguarded, cared for, watched over, preserved, defended, guarded, secured, kept safe, sheltered, harbored, screened, fostered, cherished, curtained, shaded, disguised, camouflaged; see also **covered** 1, **safe** 1.—*Ant.* weak, insecure, unsheltered.

protection, *n.* 1. [A covering] shield, screen, camouflage; see **shelter**. 2. [A surety] certainty, safeguard, safekeeping, assurance, invulnerability, reassurance, security, stability, strength; see also **guaranty** 2.—*Ant.* insecurity, **weakness**, frailty.

protector, *n.* champion, defender, patron, sponsor, safeguard, benefactor, supporter, advocate, guardian angel, guard, shield, savior, stand-by, promoter, mediator, counsel, second, backer, upholder, sympathizer, *big brother, *big sister, *angel, *cover, *front; see also **guardian**.

protest, *n.* mass meeting, rally, demonstration, peace demonstration, draft demonstration, peace rally, race riot, clamor, tumult, turmoil, student *or* campus revolt, moratorium, sit-in, *love-in.

protest, *v.* demur, disagree, object; see **oppose** 1.

Protestant, *n.* Some Protestant sects include the following —Evangelist, Adventist, Baptist, Congregational, Episcopal, Lutheran, Methodist, Presbyterian.

protestant, *a.* non-Catholic, new; Adventist, Baptist, Congregational *or* Congregationalist, etc.; see also **Protestant**.

protester, *n.* demonstrator, dissident, rebel; see **radical**.

protrude, *v.* come through, stick out, jut out; see **project** 1.

proud, *a.* 1. [Having a creditable self-respect] self-respecting, self-sufficient, self-satisfied, ambitious, spirited, vigorous, high-spirited, honorable, great-hearted, fiery, dignified, stately, lordly, lofty-minded, high-minded, impressive, imposing, fine, splendid, looking one in the face *or* eye, on one's high horse, high and mighty, holding up one's head.— *Ant.* humble, unpretentious, unassuming. 2. [Egoistic] egotistical, vain, vainglorious; see egotistic.—*do oneself proud, achieve, prosper, advance; see succeed 1.

proudly, *a.* boastfully, haughtily, insolently; see arrogantly.

prove, *v.* justify, substantiate, authenticate, corroborate, testify, explain, attest, show, warrant, uphold, determine, settle, fix, certify, back, sustain, validate, bear out, affirm, confirm, make evident, convince, evidence, be evidence of, witness, declare, testify, have a case, manifest, demonstrate, document, establish, settle once and for all.

proved, *a.* confirmed, established, demonstrated; see establish 3.

proverb, *n.* maxim, adage, aphorism, precept, saw, saying, motto, dictum, text, witticism, repartee, axiom, truism, byword, epigram, moral, folk wisdom, platitude.

proverbial, *a.* current, general, unquestioned; see common 1, dull 4.

provide, *v.* 1. [To supply] furnish, equip, grant, replenish, provide with, accommodate, care for, indulge *or* favor with, contribute, give, outfit, fit, stock, store, minister, administer, render, procure, afford, present, bestow, cater, rig (up), fit out *or* up, provision, ration, implement.—*Ant.* refuse, take away, deny. 2. [To yield] render, afford, give; see produce 1.

provided, *conj.* on the assumption (that), in the event, in the case that; see if, supposing.

provided that, *conj.* on condition, in the event, with that understood; see if, supposing.

provide for *or* **against**, *v.* prepare for, arrange, care for, plan ahead; see prepare 1.

providence, *n.* divine government, divine superintendence, Deity; see god.

providing, *conj.* provided, in the event *or* the case that, on the assumption (that); see if, supposing.

providing, *n.* provision, supplying, furnishing, equipping, replenishing, replenishment, contributing, outfitting, stocking, filling, procurement, affording, presenting, preparing, preparation, arrangement, planning, putting by, laying by *or* in, putting in readiness, granting, bestowing, giving, offering, tendering, accumulating, storing, saving.

province, *n.* area, region, dependency; see territory 2.

provincial, *a.* rude, unpolished, countrified; see rural.

provision, *n.* 1. [Arrangement] preparation, outline, procurement; see plan 2. 2. [Supplies; *usually plural*] stock, store, emergency; see equipment. 3. [A proviso] stipulation, prerequisite, terms; see requirement 1.

provisional, *a.* transient, passing, ephemeral; see temporary.

provisionally, *a.* conditionally, on these *or* certain conditions, for the time being; see temporarily.

provocation, *n.* incitement, stimulus, inducement; see incentive.

provocative, *a.* alluring, arousing, intriguing; see interesting.

provoke, *v.* 1. [To vex] irritate, put out, aggravate; see bother 2. 2. [To incite] stir, rouse, arouse; see incite. 3. [To cause] make, produce, bring about; see begin 1.

provoked, *a.* exasperated, incensed, enraged; see angry.

prowl, *v.* slink, lurk, rove; see sneak.

proxy, *n.* substitute, broker, representative; see agent, delegate.

prude, *n.* prig, puritan, old maid, prudish person, *prune, *priss, *sourpuss, *stick-in-the-mud, spoilsport, *wet blanket, *goody-goody.

prudence, *n.* caution, circumspection, judgment, providence, considerateness, judiciousness, deliberation, wisdom, foresight, forethought, care, carefulness, frugality, watchfulness, precaution, heedfulness, heed, economy, husbandry, concern, conservatism, conservation, discrimination, cunning, vigilance, coolness, calculation, presence of mind.—*Ant.* carelessness, imprudence, rashness.

prudent, *a.* 1. [Cautious and careful] cautious, circumspect, wary; see careful, discreet. 2. [Sensible and wise] discerning, sound, reasonable; see careful.

prudish, *a.* overnice, mincing, precise, narrow-minded, illiberal, bigoted, prissy, priggish, over-refined, fastidious, stuffy, conventional, offish, stiff, smug, straitlaced, demure, narrow, puritanical, affected, artificial, scrupulous, overexact, pedantic, pretentious, strict, rigid, rigorous, simpering, finical, finicking, finicky, squeamish, like a maiden aunt *or* old maid; see also prim.—*Ant.* sociable, broad-minded, genial.

pry, *v.* 1. [To move, with a lever] push, lift, raise, pull, move, tilt, hoist, heave, uplift, upraise, elevate, turn out, *jimmy; see also force, open 2. 2. [To endeavor to discover; *often used with* into] search, ferret out, seek, ransack, reconnoiter, peep, peer, peek, snoop, gaze, look closely, spy, stare, gape, nose, be curious, inquire; see also **meddle 1.**

pseudo, *a.* imitation, quasi, sham; see **false 3.**

psyche, *n.* subconscious, mind, ego; see **character 2.**

psychiatrist, *n.* analyst, therapist, shrink; see **doctor.**

psychiatry, *n.* psychopathology, psychotherapy, psychoanalysis; see **medicine 1, science 1.**

psychic, *a.* 1. [Mental] analytic, intellectual, psychological; see **mental 2.** 2. [Spiritual] telepathic, mystic, immaterial; see **supernatural.**

psycho, *a.* mad, crazy, psychopathic; see **insane.**

psychological, *a.* directly experimental, subjective, experimental; see **mental 2.**

psychologist, *n.* psychiatrist, analyst, clinician; see **doctor, scientist.**

psychology, *n.* science of mind, study of personality, medicine, therapy; see also **science 1, social science.** Divisions and varieties of psychology include the following—rational, existential, functional, structural, self, dynamic, motor, physiological, abnormal, differential, Gestalt, Freudian, Adlerian, Jungian, genetic, applied, popular, analytical, comparative, child, animal, mass, individual, social, behaviorism, parapsychology.

psychopath, *n.* lunatic, psychopathic or unstable or aggressive or antisocial personality, sociopath; see **madman.**

puberty, *n.* boyhood, pubescence, adolescence; see **youth 1.**

public, *a.* 1. [Available to the public] free to all, without charge, open (to the public), unrestricted, not private, known; see also **free 4.** 2. [Owned by the public] governmental, government, civil, civic, common, communal, publicly owned, municipal, metropolitan, state, federal, county, city, township.—*Ant.* private, personal, restricted.

public, *n.* men, society, the community; see **people 3.** —**in public,** candidly, plainly, above board; see **openly 1.**

publication, *n.* 1. [The act of making public] writing, printing, broadcasting, announcement, notification, promulgation, issuing, statement, acquaintance, advisement, advertisement, communication, revelation, disclosure, discovery, making current, making available. 2. [Something published] news, tidings, information; see **book, magazine 2, newspaper.**

publicity, *n.* 1. [Public distribution] notoriety, currency, publicness; see **distribution.** 2. [Free advertising] public relations copy, release, report; see **propaganda, reporting.** 3. [Activity in-

tended to advertise] promotion, publicizing, advertising; see also **advertisement.**

publicize, *v.* announce, broadcast, promulgate; see **advertise.**

publicly, *a.* candidly, plainly, aboveboard; see **openly 1.**

public opinion, *n.* public pressure, power of the press, popular pressure; see **influence, opinion 1.**

public relations, *n.* promotion, public image, favorable climate (of opinion); see **advertisement, propaganda.**

public-spirited, *a.* altruistic, humanitarian, openhanded; see **generous 1.**

public utility, *n.* (public) service(s), natural monopoly, light and power; see **utilities.**

publish, *v.* 1. [To print and distribute] reprint, issue, reissue, distribute, bring out, write, do publishing, become a publisher, get off or out, put to press, put forth or about, be in the newspaper or magazine or book business, own a publishing house, send forth, give out or forth; see also **print 2.** 2. [To make known] announce, promulgate, proclaim; see **advertise.**

published, *a.* written, printed, made public, circulated, proclaimed, promulgated, propagated, pronounced, ventilated, divulged, made current, made known, broadcast, circulated, spread abroad, disseminated, got out, appeared, released, coming forth, seeing the light, presented, offered, voiced, noised abroad, given publicity, brought before the public; see also **advertised, issued.**—*Ant.* unknown, unpublished, unwritten.

publisher, *n.* publicist, businessman, administrator; see **editor.**

pudding, *n.* mousse, custard, tapioca; see also **dessert.**

puddle, *n.* plash, mud puddle, rut; see **pool 1.**

pudgy, *a.* chubby, chunky, stout; see **fat.**

puff, *n.* whiff, sudden gust, quick blast; see **wind 1.**

puff, *v.* distend, enlarge, swell; see **fill 1.**

puffy, *a.* 1. [Windy] airy, gusty, breezy; see **windy.** 2. [Swollen] distended, expanded, blown; see **full 1.**

puke, *v.* throw up, retch, *upchuck; see **vomit.**

pull, *n.* 1. [The act of pulling] tow, drag, haul, jerk, twitch, wrench, extraction, drawing, rending, tearing, uprooting, weeding, row, paddle. 2. [Exerted force] work, strain, tug; see **strength.** 3. [*Influence] inclination, inducement, weight; see **influence.**

pull, *v.* 1. [To exert force] tug, pull at, draw in; see **work 1.** 2. [To move by pulling] draw, ease, drag, lift, stretch, move, jerk, haul, tear, rend, gather; see also **draw 1. 3.** [To incline] slope, tend, move toward; see **lean 1.**

pull apart, v. separate, split, force apart; see **divide.**

pull away, v. depart, pull off, go; see **leave 1.**

pull down, v. raze, wreck, remove; see **destroy.**

pulley, n. sheave, block, lift, lifter, crowbar, crow, pry; see also **tool 1.**

pull into, v. come in, land, make a landing; see **arrive.**

Pullman, n. (railroad or railway) sleeping car, chair car, sleeper, first-class coach or accomodation, wagon-lit.

pull off, v. **1.** [To remove] detach, separate, yank or wrench off; see **remove 1. 2.** [*To achieve] accomplish, manage, succeed; see **achieve.**

pull oneself together, v. recover, revive, get on one's feet; see **improve 2.**

pull out, v. go, depart, stop participating; see **leave 1, stop 2.**

pull over, v. drive or turn to the side, pull up, park; see **stop 1.**

***pull through,** v. get better, get over something, triumph; see **survive 1.**

pull up, v. **1.** [To remove] dislodge, elevate, pull or dig out; see **remove 1. 2.** [To stop] arrive, come to a halt or a stop, get there; see **stop 1.**

pulp, n. pap, mash, sponge, paste, dough, batter, curd, jam, poultice.

pulpit, n. **1.** [The ministry] priesthood, clergy, ecclesiastics; see **ministry 2. 2.** [A platform in a church] desk, rostrum, stage; see **platform 1.**

pulpy, a. smooth, thick, fleshy; see **soft 2.**

pulse, n. pulsation, vibration, throb; see also **beat 1.**

pump, n. air pump, suction or vacuum pump, jet (pump); see also **machine 1, tool 1.**

pump, v. elevate, draw out or up, tap; see **draw 1.**

pun, n. witticism, quip, play upon words; see **joke.**

punch, n. thrust, knock, stroke; see **blow.**

punch, v. **1.** [To hit] strike, knock, thrust against; see **hit. 2.** [To perforate] pierce, puncture, bore; see **penetrate 1.**

punched, a. perforated, dented, pierced, punctured, needled, stamped, imprinted, bored, wounded, bitten, tapped, impaled, spiked, gored, speared, stabbed, stuck.

punctual, a. prompt, precise, particular, on time, on schedule, exact, timely, seasonable, regular, cyclic, dependable, recurrent, constant, steady, scrupulous, punctilious, meticulous, on the nose. — Ant. unreliable, **careless,** desultory.

punctuation, n. Marks of punctuation include the following —period, colon, semicolon, comma, interrogation, exclamation, parentheses, dash, brackets, apostrophe, hyphen, quotation marks, brace, ellipsis.

puncture, n. punctured tire, flat tire, flat; see **hole, trouble 1.**

puncture, v. prick, perforate, pierce; see **penetrate.**

punish, v. correct, discipline, chasten, chastise, sentence, train, reprove, lecture, penalize, fine, incarcerate, expel, execute, exile, behead, hang, electrocute, dismiss, debar, whip, spank, paddle, trounce, switch, cuff, inflict penalty, *come down (upon), attend to, *crack down on, *make it hot for, *pitch into, *give a dressing-down, *lower the boom (on), *ground, *throw the book at, *blacklist, *blackball; see also **beat 1, imprison, kill 1, scold.**

punished, a. corrected, disciplined, chastened, penalized, sentenced, trained, reproved, chastised, castigated, lectured, scolded, imprisoned, incarcerated, expelled, exiled, transported, dismissed, disbarred, defrocked, whipped, spanked, trounced, flogged, birched, switched, cuffed, cracked down on, pitched into, grounded; see also **beaten 1, confined 3, executed 2.**—Ant. cleared, exonerated, released.

punishment, n. correction, discipline, reproof, penalty, infliction, suffering, deprivation, unhappiness, trial, penance, retribution, mortification, disciplinary action, fine, reparation, forfeiture, forfeit, confiscation, *bit of one's mind, *rap on the knuckles. —Ant. **freedom,** exoneration, release.

puny, a. feeble, inferior, diminutive; see **weak 1.**

pup, n. puppy, whelp, young dog; see **animal, dog.**

pupil, n. schoolboy, schoolgirl, learner; see **student.**

puppet, n. manikin, figurine, moppet; see **doll.**

puppy, n. pup, whelp, young dog; see **animal, dog.**

purchase, n. **1.** [The act of buying] procurement, getting, obtaining, shopping, installment plan or buying, bargaining, marketing, investing; see also **buying. 2.** [Something bought] buy, order, goods, shipment, acquisition, invoice, package(s), delivery, article(s), property, possession, gain, booty, acquirement, investment; see also **bargain, goods.**

purchase, v. obtain, acquire, buy up; see **buy.**

purchaser, *n.* shopper, obtainer, procurer; see **buyer.**

pure, *a.* 1. [Not mixed] unmixed, unadulterated, unalloyed, unmingled, simple, clear, genuine, undiluted, classic, real, true, fair, bright, unclouded, transparent, lucid, straight, neat; see also **clear 2, genuine 1, simple 1.**—*Ant.* mixed, mingled, blended. 2. [Clean] immaculate, spotless, stainless, unspotted, germ-free, unstained, unadulterated, unblemished, untarnished, unsoiled, disinfected, sterilized, uncontaminated, sanitary, unpolluted, purified, refined.—*Ant.* dirty, sullied, contaminated. 3. [Chaste] virgin, continent, celibate; see **chaste.** 4. [Absolute] sheer, utter, complete; see **absolute 1.**

purely, *a.* entirely, totally, essentially; see **completely.**

purification, *n.* purifying, cleansing, purgation; see **cleaning.** —*Ant.* pollution, defilement, contamination.

purify, *v.* cleanse, clear, refine, wash, disinfect, fumigate, deodorize, clarify, sublimate, purge, filter; see also **clean.**

purity, *n.* 1. [The state of being pure] pureness, cleanness, cleanliness, immaculateness, stainlessness, whiteness, clearness. 2. [Innocence] artlessness, guilelessness, blamelessness; see **innocence 2.** 3. [Chastity] abstemiousness, continence, self-command; see **chastity, virtue 1.**

purple, *a.* purpled, reddish blue, bluish red; see **color.** Tints and shades of purple include the following—lilac, violet, mauve, heliotrope, magenta, plum, lavender, pomegranate, royal purple, Tyrian purple, wine.

purpose, *n.* 1. [Aim] intention, end, goal, mission, objective, object, idea, design, hope, resolve, meaning, view, scope, desire, dream, expectation, ambition, intent, destination, direction, scheme, prospective, proposal, target, aspiration; see also **plan 2.** 2. [Resolution] tenacity, constancy, persistence; see **confidence 1, determination, faith 1.** —**on purpose,** purposefully, intentionally, designedly; see **deliberately.** —**to the purpose,** to the point, pertinent, apt; see **relevant.**

purpose, *v.* aim, plan, propose; see **intend 1.**

purposeful, *a.* obstinate, stubborn, persistent; see **resolute 2.**

purr, *v.* hum, drone, sigh; see **sound 1.**

purse, *n.* pouch, pocketbook, receptacle, moneybag, wallet, pocket, coin purse, billfold, money belt, sack, vanity case, vanity bag.

pursue, *v.* 1. [To chase] seek, hound, track (down), dog, shadow, search for or out, give chase (to), drive out or away, stalk, run or search or get or go or make or send or prowl or look for or after, gun or hunt down, trail, tag with, camp on the trail of, follow close upon, move behind, hunt or fish or scout out, nose or poke around, keep on foot, follow up. 2. [To seek] strive or try for, aspire to, attempt; see **try 1 3.** 3. [To continue] persevere, proceed, carry on; see **continue 1.**

pursuit, *n.* chase, race, pursuance; see **hunt 1.**

pus, *n.* infection, discharge, mucus; see **matter 2.**

push, *n.* shove, force, bearing, propulsion, drive, exertion, weight, straining, putting forth one's strength, shoving, thrusting, forcing, driving, inducement, mass, potential, reserve, impact, blow; see also **pressure.**

push, *v.* 1. [To press against] thrust, shove, butt, crowd, gore, ram, shove or crush or bear against, jostle, push out of one's way, bear or lie on, shoulder, elbow, struggle, strain, exert, set one's shoulder to, rest one's weight on, put forth one's strength; see also **force.** 2. [To move by pushing] impel, accelerate, drive onward, launch, start, set or put in motion, push forward, shift, start going or rolling, budge, stir, inch or shove along; see also **drive 2.** 3. [To promote] advance, expedite, urge; see **promote 1.** 4. [*To sell illegally] sell under the counter, black-market, bootleg, moonshine; see also **sell.**

push off, *v.* depart, start, take off; see **leave 1.**

push on, *v.* keep going, go, make progress; see **continue 1, 2.**

pushover, *n.* sucker, easy pickings, fool; see **victim.**

put, *v.* 1. [To place] set, locate, deposit, plant, lodge, store, situate, fix, put in a place, lay, pin down, seat, settle. 2. [To establish] install, quarter, fix; see **establish 2.** 3. [To deposit] invest in, insert, embed; see **plant.**

put across or **over,** *v.* succeed, fulfill, complete; see **achieve.**

put aside, *v.* deposit, save, put out of the way; see **store.**

put away, *v.* deposit, save, put out of the way; see **store.**

put back, *v.* bring back, make restitution (for), put in (its) place; see **replace 1, return 2.**

put-down, *n.* suppression, indignity, ‡cut; see **insult.**

put down, *v.* silence, repress, crush; see **defeat 2, 3.**

put in, *v.* sail for, move toward, land; see **approach 2.**

put (someone) in his place, v. reprimand, censure, correct; see **scold.**

put off, v. postpone, defer, retard; see **delay.**

put-on, a. feigned, simulated, calculated; see **pretended.**

***put-on,** n. deception, device, *job; see **trick** 1.

put on, v. 1. [To pretend] feign, sham, make believe; see **pretend** 1. 2. [*To deceive] trick, confuse, confound; see **deceive.**

put on airs, v. brag, show off, make pretensions; see **boast.**

put or lay one's cards on the table, v. say, display, show; see **reveal, tell** 1.

put out, v. discard, throw away, turn adrift; see **eject.**

***put over,** v. manage, do, get done; see **achieve.**

putrid, a. corrupt, putrified, decayed; see **rotten** 1.

putter, v. dawdle, fritter, poke; see **loiter.**

put through, v. do, manage, finish; see **achieve.**

***put to sleep,** v. knock out, subject to euthanasia, murder; see **kill** 1.

put up, a. canned, pickled, tinned; see **preserved** 2.

put up, v. 1. [To preserve] can, smoke, pickle; see **preserve** 2. 2. [To build] erect, fabricate, construct; see **build.** 3. [To bet] speculate. wager, put one's money on; see **gamble.** 4. [To enter-tain] house, provide or give bed and board, make welcome; see **entertain** 2.

put up with, v. undergo, tolerate, stand; see **endure** 2.

puzzle, n. 1. [The state of being puzzled] uncertainty, hardship, vexation; see **confusion.** 2. [A problem] tangle, bafflement, question, frustration, intricacy, maze, issue, enigma, proposition, mystification, bewilderment, query, mystery, dilemma, muddle, secret, riddle, ambiguity, difficulty, perplexity, confusion, entanglement, stickler, paradox.—*Ant.* **answer,** solution, development. 3. [A problem to be worked for amusement] Varieties include the following—riddle, cryptogram, logogram, crossword puzzle, jigsaw puzzle, anagram, acrostic, charade, rebus, puzzle-ring, Chinese puzzle.

puzzle, v. 1. [To perplex] obscure, bewilder, complicate; see **confuse.** 2. [To wonder] marvel, be surprised, be astonished; see **wonder** 1.

puzzled, a. perplexed, bewildered, mystified; see **doubtful.**

puzzle out, v. figure out, work out, decipher; see **solve.**

puzzle over, v. think about, consider, debate; see **think.**

puzzling, a. 1. [Obscure] uncertain, ambiguous, mystifying; see **obscure** 1. 2. [Difficult] perplexing, abstruse, hard; see **difficult** 2.

pyramid, n. tomb, shrine, remains; see **monument** 1.

Q

quack, *a.* unprincipled, pretentious, dissembling; see **dishonest**.

quack, *n.* rogue, charlatan, humbug; see **cheat, impostor**.

quadrangle, *n.* geometrical four-sided figure, parallelogram, rhombus; see **rectangle**.

quadrangular, *a.* rectangular, quadrilateral, plane; see **angular, square**.

quadruped, *n.* four-legged animal, domestic beast, mammal; see **animal**.

quadruple, *a.* fourfold, four-way, four times as great, consisting of four parts, quadruplex, four-cycle, quadruplicate.

quaint, *a.* fanciful, cute, pleasing, captivating, curious, ancient, antique, whimsical, affected, enchanting, baroque, Victorian, French Provincial, Early American, Colonial; see also **charming**. *—Ant.* modern, up-to-date, fashionable.

quake, *n.* temblor, tremor, shock; see **earthquake**.

quake, *v.* tremble, shrink, cower; see **shake 1**.

qualification, *n.* need, requisite, essential; see **requirement 1**.

qualifications, *n.* endowments, acquirements, attainments; see **experience**.

qualified, *a.* 1. [Limited] conditional, modified, confined; see **restricted**. 2. [Competent] adequate, equipped, fitted; see **able**.

qualify, *v.* 1. [To limit] reduce, restrain, temper; see **alter 1**. 2. [To fulfill requirements] fit, suit, pass, be capacitated for, have the requisites, meet the demands, be endowed by nature for, measure up, meet the specifications.*—Ant.* fail, become unfit, be unsuited.

quality, *n.* 1. [A characteristic] attribute, trait, endowment; see **characteristic**. 2. [Essential character] nature, essence, genius; see **character 2**. 3. [Grade] class, kind, state, condition, merit, worth, excellence, stage, step, variety, standing, rank, group, place, position, repute.

qualm, *n.* indecision, scruple, suspicion; see **doubt, uncertainty 2**.

quantity, *n.* amount, number, bulk, mass, measure, extent, abundance, volume, capacity, lot, deal, pile, multitude, portion, carload, sum, profusion, mountain, load, barrel, shipment, consignment, bushel, supply, ton, ocean, flood, sea, flock, the amount of, score, swarm, quite a few, army, host, pack, crowd, *bunch, *heap, *mess, *gob, batch, *all kinds of, *all sorts of; see also **size 2**.

quarantined, *a.* shut up *or* away, in *or* under quarantine, hospitalized, restrained, separated; see also **isolated**.

quarrel, *n.* 1. [An angry dispute] wrangle, squabble, dissension; see **disagreement 1, dispute**. 2. [Objection] complaint, disapproval, disagreement; see **objection**.

quarrel, *v.* wrangle, dispute, contend, fight, squabble, clash, altercate, dissent, bicker, struggle, strive, contest, object, complain, disagree, argue, charge, allegate, feud, strike, engage in blows, come to an encounter, pick a bone with, tread on one's toes, *get tough with, lock horns, have words with, *have a brush with, *have it out, *fall out (with), *break with; see also **oppose 1**.*—Ant.* agree, accord, harmonize.

quarrelsome, *a.* factious, irritable, combative, pugnacious, turbulent, unruly, passionate, violent, contentious, disputatious, dissentious, fiery, cross, cross-grained, irascible, snappish, waspish, peevish, petulant, churlish, cantankerous, thin-skinned, touchy, huffy, pettish, peppery, impassioned, hotheaded, excitable, hasty, tempestuous, *with a chip on one's shoulder.*—Ant.* calm, peaceful, agreeable.

quart, *n.* two pints, thirty-two ounces, one-fourth gallon; see **measure 1**.

quarter, *n.* 1. [One of four equal parts] fourth, one-fourth part, portion, farthing, division, three months, semester, school term, quarter of an hour, quarter section; see also **part 1**. 2. [One quarter of a dollar; *United States*] twenty-five cents, one-fourth of a dollar, coin, *two bits; see also **money 1**. 3. [A section of a community] neighborhood, district, section; see **area**. —**at close quarters**, at close range, cramped, restricted; see **near 1**.

quarter, *v.* 1. [To divide into quarters] cleave, dismember, cut up; see **cut 1, divide**. 2. [To provide living quarters] lodge, shelter, house; see **shelter**.

quarterback, *n.* back, Q.B., quarter; see **football player**.

quarterly, *a.* by quarters, once every three months, periodically; see **regularly 1**.

quarters, *n.* house, apartment, room, barracks, tent, lodge, cabins, cottage, car trailer.

quartet, *n.* four persons, four voices, four musicians, string quartet, principals, four-voice parts.

quartz, *n.* Types of quartz include the following—amethyst, false topaz, rock crystal, rose quartz, smoky quartz, blood-stone, agate, onyx, sardonyx, carnelian, chrysoprase, prase, flint, jasper; see also **rock** 1.

quasi, *a.* supposedly, to a certain extent, apparently; see **almost.**

queasy, *a.* squeamish, sick, uneasy; see **uncomfortable** 1.

queen, *n.* ruler, female ruler, female sovereign, woman monarch, queen mother, regent, wife of a king, consort, queen consort, queen dowager, queen regent, fairy queen, May Queen, matriarch.

*queen-size, *a.* medium large, outsize, not king-size; see **broad** 1, **large** 1.

queer, *a.* 1. [Odd] odd, peculiar, uncommon; see **unusual** 2. 2. [*Suspicious] strange, questionable, curious; see **suspicious** 2. 3. [*Homosexual] *butch, *gay, *nellie.

quench, *v.* 1. [To satisfy] slake, glut, gorge; see **drink** 1. 2. [To smother] stifle, dampen, *douse; see **moisten.**

quest, *n.* journey, search, crusade; see **examination** 1.

question, *n.* 1. [A query] inquiry, interrogatory, interrogation, inquisition, feeler, catechism, inquest, rhetorical question, burning question, crucial question, leading question, catch question, academic question, vexed question, *sixty-four dollar question.—*Ant.* answer, solution, reply. 2. [A puzzle] enigma, mystery, problem; see **puzzle** 2. 3. [A subject] proposal, topic, discussion; see **subject.** —**beside the question,** not germane, beside the point, unnecessary; see **irrelevant.** —**beyond question,** beyond dispute, without any doubt, sure; see **certain** 2. —**in question,** being considered, under discussion, controversial; see **considered.** —**out of the question,** not to be considered, by no means, no; see **impossible** 1.

question, *v.* 1. [To ask] inquire, interrogate, query, quest, seek, search, sound out, petition, solicit, ask about, catechize, show curiosity, pry into, ask a leading question, challenge, raise a question, make inquiry, quiz, cross-examine, probe, investigate, put to the question, bring into question; see also **ask.** 2. [To doubt] distrust, suspect, dispute; see **doubt.**

questionable, *a.* 1. [Justifying doubt] doubtful, undefined, equivocal, disputable, obscure, occult, indecisive, controversial, vague, unsettled, open to doubt, indeterminate, debatable, uncon-

firmed, problematical, cryptic, apocryphal, hypothetical, mysterious, enigmatic, ambiguous, indefinite, contingent, provisional, paradoxical, under advisement *or* examination, open to question, up for discussion, in question, to be voted on, to be decided, hard to prove, incredible; see also **uncertain** 2.—*Ant.* definite, undoubted, credible. 2. [Having a poor appearance *or* reputation] dubious, disreputable, notorious, opprobrious, obnoxious, of ill repute, unsatisfactory, of little account, thought ill of, under a cloud, ill-favored, unpopular, unpleasing, ugly, unattractive, offensive, disagreeable, evil-looking, illegitimate, discreditable, unhonored, unliked, unloved; see also **suspicious** 2.—*Ant.* honored, esteemed, liked.

questionnaire, *n.* set of questions, inquiry, survey; see **census.**

quick, *a.* 1. [Rapid] swift, expeditious, fleet; see **fast** 1. 2. [Almost immediate] posthaste, prompt, instantaneous; see **immediate** 3. 3. [Hasty] impetuous, mercurial, quick-tempered; see **rash** 4. 4. [Alert] ready, sharp, vigorous; see **active.**

quicken, *v.* 1. [To hasten] speed, hurry, make haste; see **hasten** 2. 2. [To cause to hasten] expedite, urge, promote; see **hasten** 2.

quickly, *a.* speedily, swiftly, fleetly, flying, wingedly, with dispatch, scurrying, hurrying, rushing, shooting, bolting, darting, flashing, dashing, suddenly, in (great) haste, in a hurry, just now, this minute, in a moment, on the instant, in an instant, right away, by forced marches, at a greater rate, without delay, against the clock, racing, galloping, loping, sweeping, light-footedly, briskly, at once, *like a bat out of hell, *on the double, *in a flash *or* jiffy, *to beat the band, *on the nail, *at full blast, *hellbent for leather, *hand over fist, *like mad, *at one jump, by leaps and bounds, *like a house afire.—*Ant.* slowly, sluggishly, creepingly.

quickness, *n.* swiftness, haste, agility; see **speed** 1.

quick-tempered, *a.* temperamental, quarrelsome, sensitive; see **irritable.**

quiet, *a.* calm, peaceful, hushed, muffled, noiseless, still, stilled, mute, muted, soundless, dumb, quieted, speechless, unspeaking, quiescent, taciturn, reserved, reticent, not excited *or* anxious *or* disturbed *or* perturbed *or* troubled, silent, unexpressed, close-mouthed, close, tight-lipped, uncommunicative, secretive.

quiet, *n.* 1. [Rest] calm, tranquillity, relaxation; see **peace** 2. 2. [Silence] hush, stillness, speechlessness; see **silence** 1.

quiet, *v.* 1. [To make calm] calm, cool,

relax, compose, tranquilize, satisfy, please, pacify, mollify, console, subdue, reconcile, gratify, calm down, soften, moderate, smooth, ameliorate, lull, appease, restrain, sober, slacken, soothe.—*Ant.* excite, increase, agitate. 2. [To make silent] noiselessly, deaden, silence, reduce *or* lower the sound level, muffle, mute, stop, check, restrain, suppress, break in, confute, eliminate, repress, refute, confound, answer, quell, *to stop the mouth, *floor, *put the lid on, *button up, *choke off, *put the stopper on.—*Ant.* sound, ring, cause to sound.

quiet down, *v.* grow silent, be hushed, hush, be subdued, be suppressed, become speechless, fall quiet, break off, be answered.

quietly, *a.* 1. [Calmly] peacefully, unconcernedly, confidently; see calmly. 2. [Almost silently] still, deaden, silence, speechlessly, as quietly as possible; see silently. 3. [Without attracting attention] humbly, unostentatiously, simply; see modestly.

quilt, *n.* bed covering, coverlet, comforter, feather bed, puff, down puff, batt, bed quilt, patchwork quilt, pieced quilt, bedspread, pad; see also cover 1.

quip, *n.* jest, repartee, banter; see language 1.

quirk, *n.* vagary, whim, caprice, fancy, whimsy, conceit, humor, turn, twist, knack, peculiarity, idiosyncrasy, quibble, equivocation, subterfuge, *bee in the bonnet; see also characteristic, irregularity 1.

quit, *v.* 1. [Abandon] surrender, renounce, relinquish; see abandon 1. 2. [To cease] discontinue, cease, halt, pause, stop, end, desist; see stop 2. 3.

[To leave] go away from, depart, vacate; see leave 1. 4. [To resign] leave, resign, leave *or* stop work, walk out, quit, change jobs, cease work, give notice; see resign 2.

quite, *a.* 1. [Completely] entirely, wholly, totally; see completely. 2. [Really] truly, positively, actually; see really 1. 3. [To a considerable degree] pretty, more or less, considerably; see very.

quitter, *n.* shirker, dropout, deserter, *goldbricker, *piker, *ratter, *striker, *slacker.

quiver, *n.* shudder, shiver, tremble; see vibration.

quiver, *v.* vibrate, shudder, shiver; see wave 3.

quiz, *n.* test, questioning, query; see examination 2.

quiz, *v.* question, test, cross-examine; see examine.

quorum, *n.* enough to transact business, majority of the membership, legal minimum; see member.

quota, *n.* portion, part, division; see share.

quotation, *n.* 1. [Quoted matter] excerpt, passage, citation, citing, extract, recitation, repetition, sentence, quote, plagiarism. 2. [A quoted price] market price, current price, published price; see price.

quote, *v.* 1. [To repeat verbatim] recite, excerpt, extract; see say. 2. [To state a price] give *or* name a price, request, demand; see price, value 2.

quoted, *a.* 1. [Repeated from another] recited, excerpted, extracted, cited, instanced, copied. 2. [Offered or mentioned at a stated price] asked, stated, announced, published, named, marked, given, priced, price-marked, ticketed, tagged.

R

rabbi, *n.* Jewish teacher *or* minister, teacher, Hebrew theologian; see also **priest.**

rabbit, *n.* hare, pika, bunny, Easter bunny; see also **animal, rodent.** Kinds of rabbits include the following—jack, cottontail, snowshoe, Chinchilla hare, tapeti.

rabble, *n.* mob, masses, riffraff; see **crowd, people 3.**

rabid, *a.* 1. [Fanatical] obsessed, zealous, keen; see **radical 2.** 2. [Insane] mad, raging, deranged; see **insane 3.** 3. [Affected with rabies] attacked by a mad dog, hydrophobic, frothing *or* foaming at the mouth; see **sick.**

rabies, *n.* canine madness, hydrophobia, lyssa; see **illness 2.**

race, *n.* 1. [A major division of mankind] species, culture, variety, type, kind, strain, breed, family, cultural group, color; see also **man 1.** The supposed races, sense 1, include the following—Caucasian *or* white, Mongolian *or* yellow, Ethiopian *or* black, American *or* red, Malay *or* brown. 2. [Roughly, people united by blood or custom] nationality, caste, variety, type, (the) people, mankind, tribe, group, ethnic stock, human race, class, kind, nation, folk, gene pool, pedigree, lineage, community, inhabitants, population, populace, public, clan, breeding population; see also **heredity, society 2.** 3. [A contest, usually in speed] competition, run, sprint, clash, meet, event, engagement, competitive trial of speed, competitive action, pursuit, rush, steeplechase, handicap, chase, match, derby, regatta, sweepstakes, turf, marathon, heat, *grind; see also **sport 3.**

race, *v.* 1. [To move at great speed] speed, hurry, run, pursue, chase, tear (around), bustle, spurt, post, press *or* dash on, run swiftly, hasten, trip, fly, hustle, dash, rush, sprint, swoop, scuttle, dart, scamper, haste, plunge ahead, whiz, bolt, scramble, whisk, shoot, run like mad, *burn up the road, *gun the motor, *skedaddle. 2. [To compete] run a race, compete in a race, contend in running, follow a course, engage in a contest of speed, try to beat in a contest of speed, contend, enter a competition.

race prejudice, *n.* race hatred, bigotry, intolerance; see **prejudice.**

race riot, *n.* civil disturbance, color riot, demonstration; see **fight, protest.**

racial, *a.* lineal, hereditary, ancestral, genetic, ethnic, genealogical, ethnological, patriarchal, paternal, parental.

racist, *a.* white supremacist, favoring racism, bigoted; see **conservative, prejudiced.**

racist, *n.* white supremacist, believer in racism, supporter of the color line; see **bigot, conservative.**

rack, *n.* holder, receptacle, framework, stand, shelf, ledge, perch, frame, bracket, whatnot, arbor, box, counter, trestle, hat *or* clothes *or* cake *or* bottle *or* pen *or* gun *or* tie *or* feed rack; see also **frame 1.**

racket, *n.* 1. [Disturbing noise] uproar, clatter, din; see **disturbance 2, noise 2.** 2. [Confusion accompanied by noise] squabble, scuffle, fracas, clash, row, wrangle, agitation, babel, pandemonium, turbulence, clamor, outcry, hullabaloo, tumult, hubbub, commotion, blare, turmoil, stir, noisy fuss, uproar, clatter, charivari, babble, roar, shouting, rumpus, riot, squall, brawl, fight, pitched battle, free-for-all, *(great) to-do, *fuss. 3. [*A means of extortion] illegitimate business, confidence game *or* *con game, conspiracy; see **corruption 2, crime, theft.**

racketeer, *n.* gang leader, trickster, dealer in illicit goods; see **criminal.**

racy, *a.* 1. [Full of zest] spicy, sharp, spirited; see **exciting.** 2. [Not quite respectable] indecent, erotic, indelicate; see **lewd 2, sensual 2.**

radar, *n.* radio detecting *and* ranging, radar principle, Missile Site Radar (MSR); see **electronics.**

radial, *a.* branched, outspread, radiated; see **spiral, spreading.**

radiance, *n.* brightness, brilliance, effulgence; see **light 1.**

radiant, *a.* shining, luminous, radiating; see **bright 1.**

radiate, *v.* 1. [To send forth from a center] shed, diffuse, spread, disperse, shoot in all directions, irradiate, emit (in straight lines), transmit, disseminate, broadcast, dispel, strew, sprinkle, circulate, send out in rays from a point, throw out. 2. [To shed light or heat] beam, light up, illumine, heat, warm, circulate, expand, widen, brighten, illuminate, irradiate, glitter, glisten, glow, glare, gleam, glimmer, flare, blaze, flicker, sparkle, flash, shimmer, reflect.

radiation, *n.* 1. [Dissemination] propagation, dissipation, polarization, scattering, spread, diffraction, transmission, broadcast, emission, diffusion, dispersion, circulation, divergence, dispersal; see also **distribution, extent.** 2. [Fallout] nuclear *or* radioactive particles, pollution, radioactivity, radiant energy; see **energy** 2.

radical, *a.* 1. [Fundamental] original, primitive, native; see **fundamental, organic.** 2. [Advocating violent change] extreme, thorough, complete, insurgent, revolutionary, iconoclastic, advanced, forward, progressive, abolitionist, militant, ·uncompromising, recalcitrant, mutinous, seditious, riotous, lawless, racist, insubordinate, anarchistic, unruly, nihilistic, communistic, liberal, leftist, immoderate, freethinking, *ultra, *red; see also **rebellious.**—*Ant.* conservative, reformist, gradualist. 3. [Believing in violent political and social change] leftist, communistic, heretical; see **revolutionary** 1.

radical, *n.* insurgent, objector, revolutionist, revolutionary, insurrectionist, leftist, Bolshevist, anarchist, socialist, communist, pacifist, nihilist, traitor, revolter, mutineer, firebrand, renegade, extremist, crusader, individualist, fascist, Nazi, misfit, iconoclast, eccentric, freethinker, rightist, yippie, hippie, fanatic, Black nationalist, demonstrator, peace marcher, rioter, fifth columnist, nonconformist, left-winger, right-winger, *(John) Bircher, *pinko, *red.

radically, *a.* 1. [Completely] wholly, thoroughly, entirely; see **completely.** 2. [Originally] basically, primitively, firstly; see **essentially, formerly.**

radio, *n.* 1. [The study and practice of wireless communication] radio transmission, radio reception, signaling; see **broadcasting, communication.** 2. [A receiving device] wireless, ship's radio, radio set, home radio, transistor radio *or* transistor, portable radio, pocket radio, auto radio, walkie-talkie, *squawk box; see also **electronics.**

radioactive, *a.* active, energetic, radiating poison, dangerous, *hot; see also **poisonous.**

radioactivity, *n.* radiant energy *or* heat, radioactive particles, Roentgen rays; see **energy** 2.

radius, *n.* space, sweep, range; see **boundary, expanse.**

raffle, *n.* sweepstakes, pool, lottery; see **gambling.**

raft, *n.* flatboat, barge, float, catamaran, life raft, swimming raft, rubber raft; see also **boat.**

rag, *n.* remnant, wiper, dishrag, discarded material, hand rag, tatter, shred; see

also **goods** 1. —*chew the fat or the rag,** chat, converse, have a talk; see **talk** 1.

rage, *n.* 1. [A fit of anger] frenzy, tantrum, uproar, hysterics, explosion, storm, outburst, spasm, convulsion, eruption, furor, excitement, extreme agitation, madness, vehemence, fury, rampage, huff, wrath, raving, violent anger, ire, resentment, bitterness, gall, irritation, animosity, exasperation, passion, indignation, apoplexy, heat, temper, *blowup, *fireworks, *hemorrhage. 2. [The object of enthusiasm and imitation] style, mode, fashion, vogue, craze, mania, the last word, the latest; see also **fad.**

rage, *v.* 1. [To give vent to anger] rant, fume, rave, foam, splutter, yell, scream, roar, rail at, boil (over), shake, quiver, seethe, shout, scold, go into a tantrum, have a fit, run amok, run riot, fly apart, flare *or* blaze *or* flame *or* fire *or* bristle up, carry *or* go on, show violent anger, bluster, storm, be furious, fret, lose one's temper, *work oneself into a sweat, go berserk, go into a tailspin, *go up in the air, *blow one's top, gnash one's teeth, *raise Cain *or* the devil, *take on, *throw a fit, *fly off the handle, explode, vent one's spleen, snap at, *blow up, *blow a fuse, *fly *or* go off at a tangent, *cut loose, *have a hemorrhage, *make a fuss over, *kick up a row, have a nervous breakdown, *let off steam, *get oneself into a lather, *lose one's head.—*Ant.* cry, be calm, pout. 2. [To be out of control] explode, flare, roar; see **burn, run** 1.

ragged, *a.* tattered, in shreds, patched, badly worn, rough, worn out, broken, worn to rags, frayed, frazzled, threadbare, shoddy, out at the seams, shredded, battered, the worse for wear, worn to a thread, down at the heels, motheaten, full of holes, torn, badly dressed; see also **shabby, worn** 2.—*Ant.* whole, new, unworn.

raging, *a.* furious, irate, enraged; see **angry.**

rags, *n.* old clothes, patched clothing, tatters, torn garments, shreds and patches, scraps, castoff clothes, shreds, patches, remnants; see also **clothes.**

raid, *n.* 1. [A predatory attack] invasion, assault, forced entrance; see **attack.** 2. [An armed investigation] seizure, surprise entrance, police raid, roundup, *bust; see also **arrest, capture.**

raid, *v.* bomb, shell, bombard; see **attack.**

raider, *n.* bandit, thief, plunderer; see **criminal, pirate, robber.**

rail, *n.* 1. [A polelike structure] post, railing, barrier, picket, rail fence, siding, banister, paling, rest, hand rail, guard rail, brass rail; see also **bar 1, fence. 2.** [A track; *often plural*] railway, monorail, railroad track; see **railroad.**

railroad, *n.* track, line, railway, trains, rails, elevated, underground, subway, commuter line, sidetrack, siding, passing track, loading track, feeder line, main line, double track, single track, trunk line, transcontinental railroad; see also **train.**

railway, *n.* track, line, route; see **railroad.**

rain, *n.* **1.** [Water falling in drops] drizzle, mist, sprinkle, sprinkling, damp day, spring rain, rainfall, shower, precipitation, wet weather. **2.** [A rainstorm] thunderstorm, tempest, cloudburst; see **storm.**

rain, *v.* pour, drizzle, drop, fall, shower, sprinkle, mist, mizzle, spit, lay the dust, patter, rain cats and dogs, come down in bucketfuls; see also **storm.**

raincoat, *n.* oilskin, canvas *or* reversible *or* rubber coat, mackintosh *or* *mac; see **coat 1, clothes.**

rainy, *a.* moist, coastal, drizzly; see **stormy 1, wet 2.**

raise, *n.* raising, salary increment, advance; see **promotion 1.**

raise, *v.* **1.** [To lift] uplift, upraise, upheave, elevate, hoist, run *or* pull *or* set *or* lift *or* tilt *or* throw *or* take *or* bring *or* move *or* put *or* hold *or* block *or* stand up, heave, set upright, put on its end, shove, boost, rear, mount, pry.—*Ant.* lower, bring down, take down. **2.** [To nurture] bring up, rear, nurse, suckle, nourish, wean, breed, cultivate, train, foster; see also **provide 1, support 5. 3.** [To collect or make available] gather, borrow, have ready; see **accumulate, appropriate 2. 4.** [To erect] construct, establish, put up; see **build. 5.** [To ask] bring up, suggest, put; see **ask, propose 1. 6.** [To advance in rank] exalt, dignify, honor; see **promote 2.**

raised, *a.* **1.** [Elevated] lifted, hoisted, built high, heightened, set high, in relief, erected, constructed, set up; see also **built.** —*Ant.* reduced, lowered, taken down. **2.** [*Nurtured] reared, brought up, trained, prepared, educated, fostered, bred, nourished, nursed. **3.** [Produced] harvested, cultivated, mass-produced; see **made.**

***raise hell,** *v.* carry on, celebrate, carouse; see **drink 2.**

raise money, *v.* make money (by), collect, procure; see **earn 2.**

rake, *n.* **1.** [A debauched person] lecher, libertine, profligate; see **drunkard, rascal. 2.** [A pronged implement] Rakes include the following—clam, lawn, garden, moss, hay, stubble, weeding, oyster, horse, revolving, leaf sweeper; see also **tool 1.**

rake, *v.* **1.** [To use a rake] clear up, collect, scratch, gather, scrape, clean up, weed, clear, grade, level. **2.** [To sweep with gunfire] strafe, machine-gun, blister; see **shoot 1.**

rally, *n.* celebration, mass meeting, session; see **gathering.**

rally, *v.* unite against, renew, redouble; see **return 1, revenge.**

ram, *n.* **1.** [An object used to deliver a thrust] plunger, pump, beam, prow, hammerhead, weight, pole, shaft, lever, spike, battering-ram, pile driver, tamping iron, punch, sledge hammer, rammer, tamper, monkey, bat, maul, hydraulic ram, spar, piston, drop weight, bow; see also **bar 1, hammer. 2.** [A male sheep] buck, bucksheep, bighorn (sheep); see **animal.**

ram, *v.* **1.** [To strike head-on] bump, collide, hook; see **butt, hit 1. 2.** [To pack forcibly] cram, jam, stuff; see **pack 2.**

ramble, *v.* **1.** [To saunter] stroll, promenade, roam; see **walk 1. 2.** [To speak or write aimlessly] drift, stray, diverge, meander, gossip, talk nonsense, chatter, babble, digress, maunder, get off the point *or* subject, go on and on, expatiate, protract, enlarge, be diffuse, dwell on, amplify, go astray, drivel, rant and rave, talk off the top of one's head, go off on a tangent, beat around the bush.

rambling, *a.* **1.** [Strolling] hiking, roaming, roving; see **walking, wandering 1. 2.** [Incoherent] discursive, disconnected, confused; see **incoherent. 3.** [Covering considerable territory without much plan] spread out, strewn, straggling, trailing, random, here and there, at length, widely thrown, unplanned, sprawling, gangling; see also **scattered.** —*Ant.* closely formed, **planned,** compact.

ramp, *n.* incline, slope, grade; see **hill, inclination 2.**

rampant, *a.* raging, uncontrolled, growing (without check), violent, vehement, impetuous, rank, turbulent, wild, luxuriant, tumultuous, profuse, plentiful, unruly, wanton, rife, prevalent, dominant, predominant, excessive, impulsive, impassioned, intolerant, unrestrained, extravagant, overabundant, sweeping the country, *like wildfire.—*Ant.* modest, mild, meek.

ranch, *n.* plantation, grange, farmstead, ranchland(s), ranch house, ranch buildings; poultry, fruit, cattle, etc., ranch; Western cattle farm, horse *or* sheep *or* cattle spread; see also **farm, property 2.**

rancher, *n.* ranch-owner, ranchman, stockman, breeder, cattle farmer, cowherder, shepherd, drover, stock breeder, horse trainer, herdsman, herder, ranchero, *broncobuster, granger, cattleman, owner of a cow *or* horse spread, cowboy, *cowpoke, ranch hand, cattle baron *or* king; see also **farmer.**

rancid, *a.* tainted, stale, bad; see **rotten 1.**

random, *a.* haphazard, chance, purposeless, thoughtless, careless, blind, casual, fickle, eccentric, unpredictable, accidental; see also **aimless, irregular 1. —at random,** haphazardly, by chance, aimlessly; see **accidentally.**

range, *n.* 1. [Distance] reach, span, horizontal projection; see **expanse.** 2. [Extent] length, area, expanse; see **extent.** 3. [A series of mountains] highlands, alps, sierras; see **mountain 1.** 4. [Land open to grazing] pasture, grazing land, field; see **country 1.** 5. [A kitchen stove] gas range, electric range, portable range; see **appliance, stove.**

range, *v.* 1. [To vary] differ, fluctuate, diverge from; see **vary.** 2. [To traverse wide areas] encompass, reach, spread *or* sweep *or* pass over, cover, stray, stroll, wander, ramble, explore, scour, search, traverse, *roam, rove; see also **cross 1, travel.** 3. [To place in order] line up, classify, arrange; see **order 3.**

rank, *a.* 1. [Having luxurious growth] wild, dense, lush; see **green 2, thick 1.** 2. [Having a foul odor] smelly, fetid, putrid, stinking, rancid, disagreeable, smelling, offensive, sour, foul, noxious, stale, tainted, gamy, musty, strong, rotten, moldy, high, ill-smelling, turned, nauseating, obnoxious, disgusting, reeking, malodorous, nasty, strong-smelling.—*Ant.* fragrant, **sweet,** fresh.

rank, *n.* 1. [A row] column, file, string; see **line 1.** 2. [Degree] seniority, standing, station; see **degree 2.** 3. [Social eminence] station, position, distinction, note, nobility, caste, privilege, standing, reputation, quality, situation, esteem, condition, state, place (in society), status, circumstance, footing, grade, blood, family, pedigree, ancestry, stock, parentage, birth. —***pull (one's) rank on,** take advantage (of), exploit, abuse subordinates; see **govern, humiliate.**

rank, *v.* 1. [To arrange in a row, or rows] put in line, line up, place in formation; see **order 3.** 2. [To evaluate comparatively] place, put, regard, judge, assign, give precedence to, fix, establish, settle, estimate, value, valuate, include, list, rate; see also **classify.** 3. [To possess relative evaluation] be worth, stand, be at the head, have a place, go ahead of *or* before, come first, forerun,

antecede, have supremacy (over) *or* the advantage (of), precede, outrank, take the lead, take precedence (over), belong, count among, be classed, stand in relationship.

ranked, *a.* ordered, piled, (neatly) stacked; see also **organized.**

ransack, *v.* 1. [To search thoroughly] rummage, explore, turn upside down, look all over for, look high and low for, leave no stone unturned, scour, seek everywhere, sound, spy, peer, look around, pry, scan, probe, look into, investigate, scrutinize; see also **search.** 2. [To loot] pillage, plunder, ravish, rape, strip, rifle, forage, maraud, make off with, take away, seize, appropriate, spoil, poach, gut, rustle, lift, thieve, ravage, pilfer, bag, rob, steal, filch, *pinch.

ransom, *n.* redemption (money), compensation, expiation; see **bribe.**

ransom, *v.* release, rescue, deliver; see **free.**

rant, *v.* rave, fume, rail; see **rage 1, yell.**

rap, *n.* knock, thump, slap; see **blow.** — ***beat the rap,** avoid punishment, evade, be acquitted; see **escape.** —***bum rap,** unfair sentence, blame, *frame; see **punishment.** —***take your rap,** be punished, suffer, take the blame; see **pay for.**

rap, *v.* 1. [To tap sharply] knock, strike, whack; see **beat 1, hit 1.** 2. [To talk, often compulsively] chatter, jabber, discuss; see **babble, talk 1.**

rape, *n.* seduction, violation, deflowering, criminal attack, assault, abduction, statutory offense, defilement, abuse, molestation, maltreatment, forcible violation of a woman, *(gang) bang; se also **crime.**

rape, *v.* violate, seize, compromise, force a woman, molest, ravish, attack, assault, defile, wrong, debauch, ruin, corrupt, seduce, maltreat, abuse.

rapid, *a.* speedy, accelerated, hurried; see **fast 1.**

rapidly, *a.* fast, swiftly, posthaste; see **immediately, quickly.**

rapist, *n.* raper, ravager, ravisher; see **rascal.**

rapt, *a.* transported, entranced, enchanted; see **happy.**

rapture, *n.* pleasure, cheer, satisfaction; see **happiness.**

rare, *a.* 1. [Uncommon] exceptional, singular, extraordinary; see **unusual 1, 2.** 2. [Scarce] sparse, few, scanty, meager, limited, short, expensive, precious, out of circulation, off the market, in great demand, occasional, uncommon, isolated, scattered, infrequent, deficient, almost unobtainable, few and far between; see also **unique.**—*Ant.* profuse, **cheap,** tawdry. 3. [Choice] select, matchless, superlative; see **excellent**. 4. [Lightly cooked] not cooked or done, seared, braised, not overdone, nearly raw, underdone, red, rarely or moderately done, not thoroughly cooked; see also **raw 1**.

rarely, a. unusually, occasionally, once in a great while; see **seldom**.

rascal, n. scoundrel, rogue, rake, knave, villain, robber, fraud, scamp, hypocrite, sneak, shyster, cad, trickster, charlatan, swindler, grafter, cheat, black sheep, ruffian, tough, rowdy, bully, scalawag, mountebank, liar, blackguard, wretch, quack, fellow, tramp, beggar, bum, idler, wastrel, prodigal, hooligan, ne'er-do-well, reprobate, misdoer, felon, sinner, delinquent, recreant, malefactor, profligate, loafer, renegade, imposter, opportunist, vagrant, pretender, gambler, mischief-maker, sharper, faker, *skunk, bastard, *fink, *rat, *rotten or bad egg, *con man, *con artist, *flimflammer, *dirty dog, good-for-nothing, worm, *two-timer, *stool pigeon, *case, *double-dealer, *phony, *four-flusher, *slicker; see also **criminal.**—*Ant.* hero, gentleman, philanthropist.

rash, a. impetuous, impulsive, foolish, hotheaded, thoughtless, reckless, headstrong, bold, careless, determined, audacious, heedless, madcap, unthinking, headlong, incautious, wild, precipitant, overhasty, unwary, injudicious, venturous, foolhardy, imprudent, venturesome, adventurous, daring, jumping to conclusions, insuppressible, breakneck, irrational, fiery, furious, frenzied, passionate, immature, hurried, aimless, excited, feverish, tenacious, frantic, indiscreet, quixotic, ill-advised, unconsidered, without thinking, imprudent, unadvised, irresponsible, brash, precipitous, premature, sudden, harebrained, harum-scarum, *devil-may-care, daredevil; see also **rude 1.**—*Ant.* calm, cool, level-headed.

rashly, a. brashly, impulsively, unwisely, abruptly, foolishly, impetuously, incautiously, carelessly, precipitately, imprudently, recklessly, boldly, indiscreetly, inadvisedly, ill-advisedly, thoughtlessly, unthinkingly, furiously, hurriedly, heedlessly, boldly, unpreparedly, excitedly, overhastily, wildly, frantically, irrepressibly, without (due) consideration or thinking (about it) or forethought or planning or investigation or research; in a hasty or rash or thoughtless, etc., manner; passionately, fiercely, feverishly, headily; see also **rudely.**

rashness, n. frenzy, recklessness, foolhardiness; see **carelessness.**

rasping, a. hoarse, grating, grinding; see **harsh.**

rat, n. 1. [A rodent] mouse, muskrat, vermin; see **pest 1, rodent.** 2. [A deserter] informer, turncoat, *fink; see **deserter, traitor.**

rate, n. 1. [Ratio] proportion, degree, standard, scale, fixed amount, quota, relation, relationship, comparison, relative, weight, percentage, numerical progression; see also **measure 1, 2.** 2. [Price] valuation, allowance, estimate; see **price.** 3. [Speed] velocity, pace, time; see **speed.**

rate, v. 1. [To rank] judge, estimate, evaluate, grade, relate to a standard, fix, tag, calculate, assess, class, determine, apprise, guess at; see also **measure 1, price, rank 2.** 2. [*To be well-thought-of] be a favorite or accepted or welcome, etc.; triumph, succeed; see **succeed 1.**

rated, a. ranked, classified, graded, classed, put, thought of, given a rating, weighted, measured; see also **placed.**

rather, *interj.* I should say, certainly, of course, by all means, most assuredly, no doubt about it, *and how! *you're telling me.

rather, a. 1. [To some degree] fairly, somewhat, a little; see **moderately, reasonably 2.** 2. [By preference] first, by choice, in preference, sooner, more readily, willingly, much sooner, just as soon, as a matter of choice; see also **preferably.**

ratification, n. acceptance, confirmation, sanction; see **permission.**

ratify, v. sanction, establish, substantiate; see **approve, endorse 2.**

rating, n. grade, commission, number; see **class 1, degree 2, rank 2.**

ratio, n. proportion, quota, quotient; see **degree 1, rate 1.**

ration, n. allotment, portion, quota; see **division 2, share.**

ration, v. proportion, allot, apportion; see **distribute.**

rational, a. 1. [Acting in accordance with reason] stable, calm, cool, deliberate, discerning, discriminating, level-headed, collected, logical, thoughtful, knowing, sensible, of sound judgment or good sense, impartial, exercising reason, intelligent, wise, reasoning, prudent, circumspect, intellectual, reflective, philosophic, objective, far-sighted, enlightened, well-advised, judicious, analytical, deductive, synthetic, conscious, balanced, sober, systematic; see also **reasonable 1.**—*Ant.* rash, reckless, wild. 2. [Of a nature that appeals to reason] intelligent, sensible, wise; see **reasonable 1.** 3. [Sane] normal, lucid, responsible; see **sane 1.**

rationalize, v. explain away, vindicate, reconcile; see **explain**.

rationally, a. sensibly, normally, intelligently; see **reasonably 1**.

rattle, n. clatter, noise, racket; see **noise 1**.

rattle, v. 1. [To make a rattling sound] drum, clack, knock; see **sound 1**. 2. [To talk with little meaning] chatter, gush, prattle; see **babble**. 3. [To disconcert] bother, put out, unnerve; see **confuse**, **disturb**, **embarrass**.

raucous, a. hoarse, loud, gruff; see **harsh**.

raunchy, a. indelicate, *sexy, suggestive; see **lewd 2**.

ravage, v. pillage, overrun, devastate, destroy, crush, desolate, despoil, overspread, wreck, waste, disrupt, disorganize, demolish, annihilate, overthrow, overwhelm, break up, pull down, smash, shatter, scatter, batter down, exterminate, extinguish, trample (down), dismantle, stamp out, lay waste, lay in ruins, sweep away, raze, ruin, plunder, strip, impair, sack, consume, spoil, harry, ransack, maraud, prey, crush, rape, rob, raid, pirate, seize, capture, gut, loot; see also **damage**.—*Ant.* build, improve, rehabilitate.

rave, v. 1. [To babble] gabble, jabber, rattle on; see **babble**. 2. [To rage] storm, splutter, rail; see **rage 1**.

ravel, v. untwist, come apart, wind or weave or smooth out, untangle, disentangle, unsnarl, unbraid, untwine, unweave, unravel, make plain; see also **free**, **loosen 2**.

ravenous, a. voracious, omnivorous, starved; see **hungry**.

ravine, n. gully, gorge, canyon, gulch, arroyo, valley, gap, chasm, abyss, break, crevice, crevasse, coulee.

raving, a. violent, shouting, fuming;* see **insane**.

raw, a. 1. [Uncooked] fresh, rare, hard, unprepared, undercooked, fibrous, coarse-grained, unpasteurized, unbaked, unfried; see also **rare 5**.—*Ant.* cooked, baked, fried. 2. [Unfinished] natural, untreated, crude, rough, newly cut, unprocessed, unrefined, untanned, coarse, newly mined, uncut, virgin; see also **unfinished 2**.—*Ant.* manufactured, refined, processed. 3. [Untrained] immature, new, fresh; see **inexperienced**. 4. [Cold] biting, windy, bleak; see **cold 1**. 5. [Without skin] peeled, skinned, dressed, galled, scraped, blistered, cut, wounded, pared, uncovered, chafed, bruised.—*Ant.* coated, **covered**, healed. 6. [*Nasty] low, dirty, unscrupulous; see **mean 3**, **vulgar 1**. —**in the raw**, nude, bare, unclothed; see **naked 1**.

ray, n. beam, flash, light, stream, gleam, blaze, sunbeam, wave, moonbeam, radiation, flicker, spark, emanation, radiance, streak, shaft, pencil, patch, blink, glimmer, glitter, glint, sparkle.

razor, n. shaving instrument, cutting edge, blade, *scraper, *mower or mowing machine; see also **knife**. Razors include the following—double-edged, single-edged, straight-back, safety, hollowground, electric, electric shaver, dryshave, blade.

reach, n. compass, range, scope, grasp, stretch, extension, orbit, horizon, gamut; see also **ability**.

reach, v. 1. [To extend to] touch, span, encompass, pass along, continue or get or go to, roll or go on, stretch, go as far as, attain, equal, approach, lead, stand, terminate, end, overtake, join, come up (to), sweep; see also **spread 2**. 2. [To extend a part of the body to] lunge, strain, move, reach out, feel for, come at, make contact with, shake hands, throw out a limb, make for, put out, touch, strike, seize, grasp; see also **stretch 1**. 3. [To arrive] get to, come to, enter; see **arrive**.

reaching, a. 1. [Extending to a point] going up to, ending at, stretching, encompassing, taking in, spanning, spreading to, embracing, joining, sweeping on to. 2. [Arriving] coming to, landing, touching·down; see **landing 1**. 3. [Extending a part of the body] stretching, straining, lunging; see **extending**.

react, v. 1. [To act in response] reciprocate, respond, act; see **answer 1**. 2. [To feel in response] be affected, be impressed, be involved; see **feel 2**.

reaction, n. reply, rejoinder, reception, receptivity, response, return, feeling, opinion, reflection, backlash, attitude, retort, reciprocation, repercussion, reflex; see also **answer 1**, **opinion 1**. Reactions to stimuli include the following—contraction, expansion, jerk, knee jerk, cognition, shock, relapse, exhaustion, stupor, anger, disgust, revulsion, fear, illness, joy, laughter, wonder.

reactionary, a. rigid, retrogressive, regressive; see **conservative**.

reactionary, n. die-hard, reactionist, conservative; see **radical**.

read, a. examined, gone or checked over, scanned; see **understood 1**.

read, v. 1. [To understand by reading] comprehend, go through, peruse, scan, glance or go over, gather, see, know, skim, perceive, apprehend, grasp, learn, flip through the pages, dip into, scratch the surface, bury oneself in; see also **understand 1**. 2. [To interpret] view, render, translate, decipher, make out, unravel, express, explain, expound, con-

strue, paraphrase, restate, put; see also
- **interpret.**
readable, *a.* 1. [Capable of being read]
clear, legible, coherent, distinct, intelligible, lucid, comprehensible, plain, unmistakable, decipherable, regular, orderly,
fluent, tidy, flowing, precise, graphic,
understandable, unequivocal, explicit,
straightforward, simple. 2. [Likely to be
read with pleasure] interesting, absorbing, fascinating, pleasurable, engrossing,
satisfying, amusing, entertaining, enjoyable, rewarding, gratifying, pleasing,
worth reading, pleasant, inviting, engaging, eloquent, well-written, smooth, exciting, attractive, clever, brilliant, ingenious, relaxing, stimulating, appealing.
—Ant. dreary, depressing, **dull.**
read between the lines, *v.* surmise, conclude, suspect; see **guess.**
reader, *n.* 1. [One who reads habitually]
editor, literary critic, proofreader; see
writer. 2. [A book intended for the
study of reading] primer, graded text,
selected readings; see **book.**
readily, *a.* quickly, promptly, immediately; see **eagerly, easily 1, willingly.**
readiness, *n.* aptness, predisposition, eagerness; see **willingness, zeal.**
reading, *n.* 1. [Interpretation] version,
treatment, commentary; see **interpretation, translation.** 2. [A selection from
written matter] excerpt, passage, section; see **quotation.** 3. [A version] account, paraphrase, rendering; see **interpretation.**
read up on, *v.* prepare, investigate, research; see **study.**
ready, *a.* 1. [Prompt] quick, spontaneous,
alert, wide-awake, swift, fleet, fast,
sharp, immediate, instant, animated; see
also **active, observant, punctual.**—*Ant.*
slow, dull, dilatory. 2. [Prepared] fit,
apt, skillful, ripe, handy, in readiness,
waiting, on call, in line for, in position,
on the brink of, equipped to do the job
or perform the services, open to, fixed
for, on the mark, equal to, expectant,
available, at hand, anticipating, in order, *all systems go, *(all) squared
away, *in a go condition. *—Ant.* unprepared, unready, unavailable. 3. [Enthusiastic] eager, willing, ardent; see
zealous. —make ready, order, prepare
for something, equip; see **prepare 1.**
ready-made, *a.* instant, prefabricated,
built; see **preserved 2.**
real, *a.* 1. [Genuine] true, authentic,
original; see **genuine 1.** 2. [Having
physical existence] actual, solid, firm,
substantive, material, live, substantial,
existent, tangible, existing, present, palpable, factual, sound, concrete, corporal,
corporeal, bodily, incarnate, embodied,
physical, sensible, stable, in existence,

perceptible, evident, undeniable, irrefutable, practical, true, true to life.*—Ant.*
unreal, unsubstantial, hypothetical. 3.
[*Very much] exceedingly, exceptionally,
uncommonly; see **very. —for real,** actually, in fact, certainly; see **really 1.**
real estate, *n.* land, property, realty; see
building, estate, farm, home 1.
realism, *n.* authenticity, naturalness, actuality; see **reality.**
realist, *n.* pragmatist, naturalist, scientist; see **philosopher.**
realistic, *a.* authentic, original, representative; see **genuine 1.**
reality, *n.* authenticity, factual basis,
truth, actuality, realness, substantiality,
existence, substance, materiality, being,
presence, actual existence, sensibility,
corporeality, solidity, perceptibility, true
being, absoluteness, tangibility, palpability.
realization, *n.* understanding, comprehension, consciousness; see **awareness.**
realize, *v.* 1. [To bring to fulfillment]
perfect, make good, actualize; see **complete.** 2. [To understand] recognize, apprehend, discern; see **understand 1.** 3.
[To receive] get clear, make a profit
from, obtain; see **earn 2, profit 2, receive 1.**
realized, *a.* 1. [Fulfilled] completed, accomplished, done; see **finished 1.** 2.
[Earned] gained, gotten, acquired, received, accrued, made, reaped, harvested, gathered, inherited, taken,
cleared, obtained, gleaned, netted.
really, *a.* 1. [In fact] actually, indeed,
genuinely, certainly, surely, absolutely,
in effect, positively, veritably, in fact *or*
reality, authentically, upon my honor,
legitimately, precisely, literally, indubitably, unmistakably, undoubtedly, in
point of fact, I assure you, I'll answer
for it, be assured, believe me, as a matter of fact, of course, honestly, truly,
admittedly, nothing else but, beyond
(any) doubt, in actuality, unquestionably, *as sure as you're alive, *no buts
about it, without the shadow of a
doubt, you said it. 2. [To a remarkable
degree] surprisingly, remarkably, extraordinarily; see **very.**
really, *interj.* indeed? honestly? for a
fact? yes? is that so? are you sure? no
fooling? cross your heart and hope to
die? on your honor? *you don't say?
*ain't it the truth? *you said it! *do
tell? *no kidding?
realm, *n.* domain, area, sphere; see
department, expanse, region 1.
reappear, *v.* come again, re-enter, crop
up again; see **appear 1, repeat 2.**
rear, *n.* hind part, back seat, rear end,
rumble seat, tail end, posterior, rump,
*butt; see also **back 1.**

rear, v. lift, elevate, turn or bring up; see **raise 1, support 5**.

rearrange, v. do over, reconstruct, rework; see **order 3, prepare 1**.

reason, n. 1. [The power of reasoning] intelligence, mind, sanity; see **judgment 1**. 2. [A process of reasoning] logic, intellection, dialectics, speculation, generalization, rationalism, argumentation, inference, induction, deduction, analysis, rationalization. 3. [A basis for rational action] end, object, rationale, intention, (ulterior) motive, basis, wherefore, aim, intent, cause, design, ground, impetus, idea, motivation, root, incentive, goal, purpose, the why and wherefore; see also **purpose 1**. 4. [The mind] brain, mentality, intellect; see **mind 1**. —**by reason of**, because of, for, by way of; see **because**. —**in or within reason**, in accord with what is reasonable, rationally, understandably; see **reasonably 1**. —**stand to reason**, be plausible or logical or feasible or practical, etc.; seem all right, appeal; see **convince**. —**with reason**, understandably, soundly, plausibly; see **reasonably 1**.

reason, v. 1. [To think logically] reflect, deliberate, contemplate; see **think 1**. 2. [To seek a reasonable explanation] suppose, gather, conclude; see **assume**. 3. [To discuss persuasively] argue, contend, debate; see **discuss**.

reasonable, a. 1. [Amenable to reason] rational, sane, level-headed, intelligent, clear-cut, tolerant, endowed with reason, conscious, cerebral, capable of reason, reasoning, cognitive, perceiving, consistent, broad-minded, liberal, generous, sensible, unprejudiced, unbiased, persuasible, flexible, agreeable; see **rational 1**.—Ant. prejudiced, intolerant, biased. 2. [Characterized by justice] fair, right, just; see **honest 1**. 3. [Likely to appeal to the reason] feasible, sound, plausible; see **understandable 4**. 4. [Moderate in price] inexpensive, reduced, fair; see **cheap 1**.

reasonably, a. 1. [In a reasonable manner] rationally, sanely, logically, understandably, plausibly, sensibly, soundly, persuasively, fairly, justly, honestly, wisely, judiciously, plainly, intelligently, soberly, agreeably, in or within (all) reason, within the limits or bounds of reason, as far as possible, as far as could be expected, as much as good sense dictates, within reasonable limitations or the bounds of possibility, with due restraint. 2. [To a moderate degree] mildly, prudently, fairly, moderately, inexpensively, temperately, evenly, calmly, gently, leniently, sparingly, frugally, indulgently, tolerantly, within bounds.

reasoning, n. thinking, rationalizing, drawing conclusions; see **thought 1**.

reassure, v. convince, console, give confidence; see **comfort 1, encourage, guarantee**.

rebel, n. insurrectionist, revolutionist, revolutionary, agitator, insurgent, traitor, seditionist, mutineer, subverter, anarchist, overthrower, nihilist, guerrilla, member of the uprising, rioter, demagogue, revolter, separatist, malcontent, schismatic, deserter, dissenter, apostate, turncoat, counter-revolutionary, renegade, secessionist, underground worker, *Third Worlder; see also **radical.**.

rebel, v. rise (up), resist, revolt, turn against, defy, resist lawful authority, fight in the streets, strike, boycott, break with, overturn, mutiny, riot (against), take up arms (against), start a confrontation, secede, renounce, combat, oppose, be insubordinate, be treasonable, upset, overthrow, dethrone, disobey, *raise hell, *kick up a row, *run amok.—Ant. submit, obey, be contented.

rebellion, n. insurrection, revolt, defiance; see **disobedience, revolution 2**.

rebellious, a. revolutionary, insurgent, counterrevolutionary, warring, stubborn, contemptuous, insolent, scornful, intractable, unyielding, recalcitrant, insurrectionary, attacking, rioting, mutinous, dissident, factious, seditious, disobedient, treasonable, refractory, defiant, resistant, restless, riotous, insubordinate, sabotaging, disloyal, disaffected, alienated, ungovernable, threatening, anarchistic, iconoclastic, individualistic, radical, quarrelsome, independent-minded.—Ant. calm, docile, peaceful.

rebirth, n. resurrection, rejuvenation, rehabilitation; see **revival 1**.

rebound, v. reflect, ricochet, repercuss; see **bounce**.

rebuild, v. touch up, patch, build up; see **repair**.

rebuke, n. condemnation, reproof, reprimand; see **insult**.

rebuke, v. reprove, reprimand, censure; see **oppose 1**.

recall, v. 1. [To call to mind] recollect, think of, revive; see **remember 1**. 2. [To remove from office] discharge, disqualify, suspend; see **dismiss**. 3. [To summon again] call back, reconvene, reassemble; see **summon**.

recalled, a. 1. [Remembered] recollected, brought to mind, summoned up; see **remembered**. 2. [Relieved of responsibility] brought back, stripped of office, dismissed, cast out, displaced, fired, replaced, ousted, suspended, pensioned, let out, let go, removed (from office), retired, replaced, *kicked upstairs, *canned, *busted, washed out; see also **discharged**.

recapture, v. regain, reobtain, reacquire; see **recover 1**.

recede, v. 1. [To go backward] fall or draw back, shrink (from), withdraw; see **retreat 1**. 2. [To sink] ebb, drift away, lower, turn down, abate, decline, die or move or go away, drop, fall off, lessen; see also **decrease 1, fall 2.**–*Ant.* rise, flow, increase.

receipt, n. 1. [The act of receiving] receiving, acquisition, accession, acceptance, taking, arrival, recipience, getting, admitting, reception; see also **admission 2.**–*Ant.* shipment, **delivery,** giving. 2. [An acknowledgement of receipt, sense 1] letter, voucher, release, cancellation, slip, signed notice, stub, discharge, declaration, paid bill; see also **certificate**.

receive, v. 1. [To take into one's charge] accept, be given, admit, get, gain, inherit, acquire, gather up, collect, obtain, reap, procure, derive, appropriate, seize, take possession, redeem, pocket, pick up, hold, come by, earn, take (in), assume, draw, arrogate, win, secure, come into, come in for, catch, get from; see also **get 1.** –*Ant.* discard, abandon, refuse. 2. [To endure] undergo, experience, suffer; see **endure 2**. 3. [To support] bear, sustain, prop; see **support 1**. 4. [To make welcome] accommodate, initiate, induct, install, make welcome, shake hands with, admit, permit, welcome (home), accept, entertain, invite or let or show or bring or usher in, let through, make comfortable, bring as a guest into, introduce, give a party, give access to, allow entrance to, *roll out the red carpet (for), *give the red-carpet treatment (to), *get out the welcome mat (for); see also **greet.**–*Ant.* visit, be a guest, call.

received, a. taken, gotten, acquired, obtained, honored, brought in, signed for, admitted, collected, gathered; see also **accepted, acknowledged.**–*Ant.* given, disbursed, delivered.

receiver, n. 1. [One who receives] customer, recipient; see **heir**. 2. [A device for receiving] telephone, television, radio, receiving set, mission control, control center, detection or detecting or listening device, transceiver.

recent, a. 1. [Lately brought into being] fresh, novel, newly born; see **modern 1, unusual 1, 2.** 2. [Associated with modern times] contemporary, up-to-date, streamlined; see **modern 1, 3**.

recently, a. lately, in recent times, just now, just a while ago, not long ago, a short while ago, of late, newly, freshly,

new, the other day, within the recent past.–*Ant.* once, long ago, formerly.

receptacle, n. box, wastebasket, holder; see **container**.

reception, n. 1. [The act of receiving] acquisition, acceptance, accession; see **receipt 2.** 2. [The manner of receiving] meeting, encounter, introduction, gathering, welcome, salutation, induction, admission, disposition; see also **greeting**. 3. [A social function] tea, party, soiree; see **gathering**.

receptive, a. alert, sensitive, perceptive; see **observant, sympathetic**.

recess, n. 1. [An intermission] respite, rest, pause, interlude, break, cessation, stop, suspension, interval, intervening period, halt. 2. [An indentation] break, dent, corner; see **hole 1**. 3. [A recessed space] cell, cubicle, nook; see **room 2**.

recession, n. unemployment, inflation, decline; see **depression 3**.

recipe, n. formula, compound, receipt, instructions, prescription, cookery formula, directions, method.

recipient, n. receiver, object, legatee; see **heir**.

recital, n. presentation, portrayal, musical; see **performance**.

recitation, n. 1. [The act of reciting] delivery, speaking, playing, narrating, recounting, declaiming, discoursing, soliloquizing, discussion, holding forth, performance, recital, rehearsal, monologue, discourse. 2. [A composition used for recitation, sense 1] address, talk, reading selection; see **speech 3, writing 2**.

recite, v. 1. [To repeat formally] declaim, address, read, render, discourse, hold forth, enact, dramatize, deliver from memory, interpret, soliloquize. 2. [To report on a lesson] answer, give a report, explain; see also **discuss, report 1**. 3. [To relate in detail] enumerate, enlarge, report, account for, give an account of, impart, chant, convey, quote, communicate, utter, describe, relate, state, tell, mention, narrate, recount, retell, picture, delineate, portray; see also **explain, tell 1**.

reckless, a. thoughtless, breakneck, wild; see **rash**.

recklessly, a. dangerously, heedlessly, with abandon; see **bravely, carelessly**.

reckon, v. consider, evaluate, judge; see **estimate**.

reclaim, v. 1. [To bring into usable condition] rescue, regenerate, redeem; see **recover 1**. 2. [To reform] resolve, mend, improve; see **reform 3**.

reclamation, n. redemption, repair, repossession; see **recovery 3**.

recognition, n. 1. [The act of recognizing] recalling, remembering, identifying, perceiving, verifying, apprehending, acknowledging, noticing, recollection, memory, identification, recall, reidentification, recognizance, remembrance, mental reproduction *or* recurrence, cognizance. **2.** [Tangible evidence of recognition, sense 1] greeting, acknowledgment, identification, perception, admission, verification, comprehension, appreciation, renown, esteem, notice, attention, acceptance, regard, honor.

recognize, *v.* **1.** [To know again] be familiar, make out, distinguish, verify, recollect, sight, diagnose, place, espy, descry, recall, remember, see, perceive, admit knowledge of, notice; see also **know 1. 2.** [To acknowledge] assent, appreciate, realize; see **allow 3.** [To acknowledge the legality of a government] exchange diplomatic representatives, have diplomatic relations with, sanction, approve, extend formal recognition to; see also **acknowledge 2.**

recognized, *a.* sighted, caught, perceived, realized, acknowledged, known, appreciated, admitted, recalled, remembered.

recoil, *v.* turn away, shrink (from), draw *or* step *or* pull back; see **retreat.**

recollect, *v.* recall, bring to mind, look back on; see **remember 1.**

recollection, *n.* remembrance, reminiscence, retrospection; see **memory 1.**

recommend, *v.* **1.** [To lend support or approval] agree to, sanction, hold up, commend, extol, compliment, applaud, celebrate, praise, speak well *or* highly of, acclaim, eulogize, confirm, laud, second, favor, back, stand by, magnify, glorify, exalt, think highly of, be satisfied with, esteem, value, prize, uphold, justify, endorse, go on record for, be all for, front for, *go to bat for. —Ant.* censure, disesteem, **denounce. 2.** [To make a suggestion or prescription] prescribe, suggest, counsel; see **advise, urge 2.**

recommendation, *n.* **1.** [The act of recommending] guidance, counsel, direction; see **advice, suggestion 1. 2.** [A document that vouches for character or ability] certificate, testimonial, reference, character, character reference, letter of recommendation, letter in support; see also **letter 2.**

recommended, *a.* urged, endorsed, suggested; see also **approved.**

reconcile, *v.* **1.** [To adjust] adapt, arrange, regulate; see **adjust 1, 2. 2.** [To bring into harmony] conciliate, assuage, pacify, propitiate, mitigate, make up, mediate, arbitrate, intercede, bring together, accustom oneself to, harmonize, accord, dictate peace, accomodate, appease, reunite, make peace between,

bring to terms, bring into one's camp, win over, bury the hatchet, patch up, kiss and make up; see also **settle 7.— Ant.** bother, irritate, alienate.

reconciled, *a.* settled, regulated, arranged; see **determined 1.**

reconciliation, *n.* conciliation, settlement, payment; see **adjustment, agreement 1.**

reconsider, *v.* re-evaluate, think *or* go *or* work over, rearrange, consider again, recheck, re-examine, correct, amend, revise, retrace, emend, rework, replan, review, withdraw for consideration, reweigh, amend one's judgment; see also **consider.**

reconstruct, *v.* rebuild, remodel, construct again, make over, revamp, recondition, reconstitute, re-establish, restore, refashion, reorganize, replace, overhaul, renovate, modernize, rework, construct from the original, copy, remake; see also **build, repair.**

reconstruction, *n.* reorganization, rehabilitation, restoration; see **repair.**

record, *n.* **1.** [Documentary evidence] manuscript, inscription, transcription, account, history, legend, story, writing, written material, document. Types of records include the following:—register, catalogue, list, inventory, memo, memorandum, registry, schedule, chronicle, docket, scroll, archive, note, contract, statement, will, testament, petition, calendar, log(book), letter, memoir, reminiscence, dictation, confession, deposition, inscription, official record, sworn document, evidence, license, bulletin, gazette, newspaper, magazine, annual report, journal, Congressional Record, transactions, debates, bill, annals, presidential order, state paper, white paper, blue book, budget, report, entry, book, publication, autograph, signature, vital statistics, deed, paper, diary, stenographic notes, ledger, daybook, almanac, proceedings, minutes, description, affidavit, certificate, transcript, dossier, roll. **2.** [One's past] career, experience, work; see **life 2. 3.** [A device for the reproduction of sound] recording, disk, phonograph record, wax plate, steel plate, recording wire, transcription, *canned music, cut, take, *platter. —go on record, assert, attest, state; see **declare. —off the record,** confidential, unofficial, secret; see **private. —on the record,** recorded, stated, official; see **public 1.**

record, *v.* **1.** [To write down] register, write (in), put *or* mark *or* jot *or* set *or* note *or* write *or* take down, put on record, transcribe, list, note, file, mark, inscribe, log, catalogue, tabulate, put in writing, put in black and white, chronicle, keep accounts, keep an account of, spill ink, make a written account of, put on paper, preserve, make an entry in, chalk up, write (up), enter, report, book, post, copy, document, insert, enumerate; see also **write 1. 2.** [To indicate] point out or to, explain, show; see **name 2. 3.** [To record electronically] tape, cut, photograph, make a record of, make a tape, tape-record, film, cut a record.

recorded, a. listed, filed, on file, in black and white, in writing, inscribed, put down, registered, documented, entered, written, published, noted down, described, reported, catalogued, mentioned, certified, kept, chronicled, booked.

recorder, n. dictaphone, recording instrument, stereophonic recorder; see **tape recorder**.

recording, n. documentation, recounting, self-debriefing; see **record 1.**

record player, n. phonograph, stereo, high fidelity set, hi-fi, component set, sound system, victrola, talking machine, music box, juke box, gramophone; see also **tape recorder**. Record player parts include the following—changer, turntable, tone arm, amplifier, speakers, stylus, cartridge, woofer, tweeter, spindle, needle.

records, n. documents, chronicles, archives, public papers, registers, annals, memorabilia, memoranda, lists, return, diaries, accounts.

recover, v. 1. [To obtain again] redeem, salvage, retrieve, rescue, reclaim, recoup, find again, recapture, repossess, bring or get or win back, regain, rediscover, resume, catch up; see also **get 1.**—*Ant.* lose, let slip, fall behind. **2.** [To improve one's condition] gain, increase, collect; see **improve 2, profit 2.**—*Ant.* fail, go bankrupt, give up. **3.** [To regain health] rally, come around or back or up or to or out of it, get out of danger, improve, convalesce, heal, get the better of, overcome, start anew, be restored, mend, revive, be oneself again, perk up, gain (strength), recuperate, get well or back or over or better, *make a comeback, *get back in shape, *snap out of, sober up.—*Ant.* die, fail, become worse.

recovered, a. renewed, found, replaced, reborn, rediscovered, reawakened, retrieved, redeemed, reclaimed, regained, revived, returned, resumed; see also **discovered.**—*Ant.* lost, missed, dropped.

recovery, n. 1. [The act of returning to normal] re-establishment, resumption, restoration, reinstatement, rehabilitation, reconstruction, return, reformation, recreation, replacement, readjustment, improving, getting back to normal or normalcy; see also sense 2, **improvement 1. 2.** [The process of regaining

health] convalescence, recuperation, revival, rebirth, renaissance, resurgence, resurrection, regeneration, cure, improvement, reawakening, renewal, resuscitation, rejuvenation, rehabilitation, return of health, bodily or physical improvement, healing, betterment. **3.** [The act of regaining possession] repossession, retrieval, reclamation, redemption, indemnification, reparation, compensation, recapture, return, restoration, remuneration, reimbursement, retaking, recall.

recreation, n. amusement, relaxation, diversion, play, fun, entertainment, enjoyment, festivity, hobby, holiday, vacation, pastime, pleasure, game, avocation, refreshment; see also **sport 1.**

recruit, n. new man, novice, tyro, beginner, selectee, draftee, trainee, volunteer, enlisted man, serviceman, soldier, sailor, marine; see also **soldier.**

recruit, v. 1. [To raise troops] draft, call up, select, supply, muster, deliver, sign up, induct, take in, find manpower, call to arms or colors, bring into service; see also **enlist 1. 2.** [To gather needed resources] restore, store up, replenish; see also **get 1.**

rectangle, n. geometrical figure, square, box, oblong, four-sided figure, right-angled parallelogram; see also **form 1.**

rectangular, a. square, four-sided, right-angled; see **angular.**

recuperate, v. heal, pull through, get back on one's feet; see **recover 3.**

recur, v. return, reappear, crop up again; see **happen 2, repeat 1.**

recurrent, a. reoccurring, repetitive, habitual; see **repeated 1.**

recycle, v. start or do over, start again, restart; see **begin 1, resume.**

red, n. Tints and shades of red include the following—scarlet, carmine, vermilion, crimson, cerise, cherry-red, ruby, garnet, maroon, brick-red, infrared, claret, rust, red-gold, magenta, pink, coral-red, blood-red, russet, terra cotta, bittersweet, hyacinth red, Chinese red, Morocco red or caldron, Turkey red, aniline red, chrome-red, rose, rose blush, old rose; see also **color.** –**in the red,** in debt, losing money, *going broke; see **ruined 3.** –*see red, become angry, lose one's temper, get mad; see **rage 1.**

redden, v. color, tint, dye; see **color.**

reddish, a. flushed, somewhat red, rose; see **red, n.**

redecorate, v. refurbish, refresh, renew, paint, restore, recondition, remodel, renovate, revamp, rearrange, touch or patch up, plaster, refurnish, wallpaper, clean (up), carpet, do over, *fix (up); see also **decorate.**

redeem, v. 1. [To recover through a payment] buy back, repay, purchase; see get 1. 2. [To save] liberate, set free, deliver; see **rescue 1**.

redeemer, *n.* rescuer, deliverer, liberator; see **protector**.

redeem oneself, *v.* atone, give satisfaction, make amends; see also **pay for**.

redemption, *n.* regeneration, salvation, rebirth; see **rescue 1**.

redheaded, *a.* auburn-haired, red-haired, sandy-haired, titian-haired, strawberry blonde, carrot-topped, brick-topped.

red-hot, *a.* 1. [Burning] heated, sizzling, scorching; see **burning, hot 1**. 2. [Raging] excessive, rabid, very; see **extreme**. 3. [Newest] latest, recent, *hippest; see **modern 1**.

redo, *v.* start over, redesign, rethink, go back to the drawing board, revamp, do over again; see also **repeat 1**.

redone, *a.* done over, refinished, fixed up; see **improved**.

redress, *n.* compensation, satisfaction, payment; see **pay 2, prize**.

red tape, *n.* 1. [Delay] wait, roadblock, impediment; see **delay**. 2. [Bureaucracy] officialism, inflexible routine, officialdom; see **government 1, 2**.

reduce, *v.* 1. [To make less] lessen, diminish, cut down; see **decrease 2**. 2. [To defeat] conquer, overcome, subdue; see **defeat 2, 3**. 3. [To humble] degrade, demote, abase; see **humble, humiliate**.

reduced, *a.* 1. [Made smaller] lessened, decreased, diminished, shortened, abridged, abbreviated, condensed, miniaturized, transistorized, compressed, economized, cut down, shrunk, subtracted, contracted, melted, boiled down.—*Ant.* enlarged, stretched, **spread**. 2. [Made lower] lowered, abated, sunk, deflated, leveled, cheapened, marked *or* taken down, discounted, weakened, debilitated, humbled, demoted, degraded.—*Ant.* heightened, **raised**, elevated.

reduction, *n.* 1. [The process of making smaller] conversion, contraction, abatement, reducing, refinement, diminution, lowering, lessening, shortening, condensation, decrease, loss, compression, depression, subtraction, discount, shrinkage, constriction, modification, curtailment, abbreviation, miniaturization, abridgment, modulation, moderation, mitigation, remission, decline. —*Ant.* **increase**, increasing, enlargement. 2. [An amount that constitutes reduction, sense 1] decrease, rebate, cut; see **discount**.

redundant, *a.* wordy, bombastic, verbose; see **dull 3, 4**.

re-educate, *v.* reinstruct, readjust, rehabilitate; see **teach**.

reef, *n.* ridge, shoal, (sand) bar; see **rock 2**.

reek, *v.* smell of, give off (an odor), emit stench; see **smell 1**.

reel, *n.* spool, bobbin, spindle; see **roll 2**.

re-examine, *v.* go back over, review, check thoroughly; see **examine**.

refer, *v.* 1. [To concern] regard, relate, have relation, have to do with, apply, be about, answer (to), involve, connect, be a matter of, have a bearing on, correspond with, bear upon, comprise, include, belong, pertain, have reference, take in, cover, point, hold, encompass, incorporate, touch, deal with; see also **concern 1**. 2. [To mention] allude to, bring up, direct a remark *or* mention, make reference *or* allusion, ascribe, direct attention, attribute, cite, quote, hint at, point to, notice, indicate, speak about, suggest, touch on, give as example, associate, exemplify, instance, excerpt, extract; see also **mention**. 3. [To direct] send to, put in touch with, relegate, commit, submit to, assign, give a recommendation to, introduce; see also **lead 1**.

referee, *n.* arbitrator, conciliator, judge; see **umpire**.

reference, *n.* 1. [An allusion] mention, relation, implication; see **hint**. 2. [A book of reference] original (text), source, informant; see **book, dictionary**. 3. [A person vouching for another] associate, employer, patron; see **friend**.

referred (to), *a.* 1. [Mentioned] brought up, alluded to, spoken about; see **mentioned, suggested**. 2. [Directed] recommended, sent on, introduced; see **proposed**.

refine, *v.* 1. [To purify] rarefy, strain, filter; see **clean, purify**. 2. [To improve] make clear, better, clarify; see **explain**.

refined, *a.* 1. [Purified] cleaned, cleansed, aerated, strained, washed, clean, rarefied, boiled down, distilled, clarified, tried, drained; see also **pure**.—*Ant.* raw, crude, unrefined. 2. [Genteel] cultivated, civilized, polished, elegant, well-bred, gracious, enlightened, gentlemanly, ladylike, restrained, gentle, mannerly, highminded, subtle, courteous; see also **polite**.

refinement, *n.* 1. [The act of refining] cleansing, clearing, purification; see **cleaning**. 2. [Culture] civilization, cultivation, sophistication, breeding, enlightenment, wide knowledge, lore, subtlety, science, scholarship, learning; see also **culture 1**. 3. [Genteel feelings and behavior] elegance, politeness, polish, good manners, suavity, courtesy, grace, gentleness, tact, cultivation, graciousness, civility, affability, taste, discrimination, fineness, delicacy, dignity, urbanity; see also **culture 2.**

refinished. *a.* redone, remodeled, fixed up; see **changed 2, repaired.**

reflect, *v.* **1.** [To contemplate] speculate, concentrate, weigh; see **consider, think 1. 2.** [To throw back] echo, re-echo, repeat, match, take after, return, resonate, reverberate, copy, resound, reproduce, reply, be resonant, emulate, imitate, follow, catch, rebound. **3.** [To throw back an image] mirror, shine, reproduce, show up on, flash, cast *or* give back, return, give forth.

reflection, *n.* **1.** [Thought] consideration, absorption, imagination, observation, thinking, contemplation, rumination, speculation, musing, deliberation, study, pondering, meditation, concentration, cogitation; see also **thought 2. 2.** [An image] impression, rays, light, shine, glitter, appearance, idea, reflected image, likeness, shadow, duplicate, picture, echo, representation, reproduction; see also **copy, image 2**:

reflector, *n.* shiny metal, glass, reverberator; see **mirror.**

reflex, *a.* mechanical, unthinking, habitual; see **automatic, spontaneous.**

reform, *n.* reformation, betterment, new law; see **improvement 2.**

reform, *v.* **1.** [To change into a new form] reorganize, remodel, revise, repair, reconstruct, rearrange, transform, ameliorate, redeem, rectify, better, rehabilitate, improve, correct, cure, remedy, convert, mend, amend, restore, rebuild, reclaim, revolutionize, regenerate, refashion, renovate, renew, rework, reconstitute, make over, remake; see also **correct, repair.—***Ant.* degrade, corrupt, botch. **2.** [To correct evils] amend, clean out, give a new basis, abolish, repeal, uplift, ameliorate, rectify, regenerate, give new life to, remedy, stamp out, make better, standardize, bring up to code; see also **improve 1. 3.** [To change one's conduct for the better] resolve, mend, regenerate, uplift, make amends, make a new start, make (New Year) resolutions, turn over a new leaf, *go straight, swear off; see also **sense 2.**

Reformation, *n.* Renaissance, Lutheranism, Protestantism, Puritanism, Calvinism, Anglicanism, Unitarianism, Counter Reformation, Protestant Movement; see also **revolution 2.**

reformation, *n.* repeal, remaking, reestablishment; see **recovery 1.**

reformatory, *n.* house of correction, penal institution, boys' *or* girls' reformatory; see **jail, school 1.**

reformed, *a.* **1.** [Changed] altered, transformed, shifted, reconstituted, reorganized, shuffled, re-established, revolutionized, rectified, amended, reset, reworked, renewed, regenerated; see also **changed 2, improved.—***Ant.* degenerated, vicious, corrupt.

refrain, *n.* undersong, theme, strain; see **music 1, song.**

refrain, *v.* cease, avoid, forbear; see **abstain.**

refresh, *v.* invigorate, animate, exhilarate; see **renew 1.**

refreshing, *a.* invigorating, rousing, exhilarating; see **stimulating.**

refreshment, *n.* tidbit, ice cream, cakes; see **drink 1, food.**

refrigerate, *v.* chill, make cold, freeze; see **cool.**

refrigeration, *n.* cooling, chilling, freezing; see **preservation.**

refrigerator, *n.* icebox, Frigidaire (trademark) (*or* *fridge), automatic cooler, cold-storage box, refrigerator car, electric refrigerator, cooling apparatus, refrigeration equipment, quick *or* deep freezer.

refuge, *n.* **1.** [A place of protection] shelter, asylum, ambush, sanctuary, covert, home, retreat, anchorage, nunnery, convent, monastery, poorhouse, safe place, hiding place, game farm *or* refuge *or* preserve, harbor (of refuge), haven, fortress, stronghold. **2.** [A means of resort] alternative, resource, last resort; see **escape.**

refugee, *n.* exile, expatriate, fugitive, emigrant, renegade, foreigner, castaway, derelict, foundling, homeless person, leper, pariah, outlaw, prodigal, displaced person (*or* DP), alien, outcast.

refund, *n.* return, reimbursement, repayment, remuneration, compensation, allowance, payment for expenses, rebate, discount, settlement, discharge, acquittance, retribution, satisfaction, consolation, money back; see also **payment 1.**

refund, *v.* pay back, reimburse, remit, repay, relinquish, make good, balance, recoup, adjust, reward, restore, redeem, make repayment (to), compensate, recompense, make amends, redress, remunerate, give back, settle, honor a claim, *kick back, *make good, make up for; see **pay 1.**

refunded. *a.* acquitted, reimbursed, discharged; see **paid, returned.**

refusal, *n.* repudiation, renunciation, rebuff, snub, rejection, nonacceptance, denial, disavowal, noncompliance, opposition, forbidding, veto, interdiction, proscription, ban, writ, exclusion, negation, repulse, withholding, disclaimer, nonconsent, unwillingness, regrets, declination, repulsion, reversal, dissent, prohibition, disfavor, disapproval, curb, restraint.

refuse, *n.* leavings, remains, residue; see **trash** 1.

refuse, *v.* dissent, desist, repel, rebuff, scorn, pass up, reject, disallow, have no plans to *or* for, not anticipate, demur, protest, withdraw, hold back, withhold, shun, turn thumbs down (on), evade, dodge, ignore, spurn, regret, turn down, turn from, beg to be excused, send regrets, not budge, cut out of the budget, not budget, not care to, refuse to receive, dispense with, not be at home to, say no, make excuses, disapprove, set aside, turn away, beg off, *brush off, not buy, hold out *or* off, turn one's back on, turn a deaf ear to; see also **deny.**—*Ant.* **allow,** admit, consent.

refused, *a.* declined, rejected, rebuffed, vetoed, repudiated, forbidden, denied (to), disowned, disavowed, forsaken, blocked, repelled, closed to, dismissed, turned down, not budgeted, not in *or* cut from *or* removed from the budget.—*Ant.* **permitted,** allowed, consented to.

refute, *v.* disprove, answer, prove false; see **deny** 1.

regain, *v.* recapture, retrieve, reacquire; see **recover** 1.

regard, *n.* 1. [A look] gaze, glance, *once-over; see **look** 3. 2. [A favorable opinion] esteem, respect, honor, favor, liking, interest, fondness, attachment, deference, opinion, sympathy, estimation, appreciation, reverence, consideration, love, affection, value, devotion; see also **admiration.**

regard, *v.* 1. [To look at] observe, notice, mark; see **see** 1. 2. [To have an attitude] surmise, look upon, view; see **consider,** **think** 1. 3. [To hold in esteem] respect, esteem, value; see **admire.**

regarding, *a.* and *prep.* concerning, with respect *or* reference *or* regard to, in relation to, as regards; see also **about** 2.

regardless, *a.* 1. [Heedless] negligent, careless, unobservant, unheeding, inattentive, reckless, inconsiderate, inadvertent, blind, unfeeling, deaf, coarse, crude, neglectful, mindless, insensitive, lax, indifferent, listless, uninterested, unconcerned.—*Ant.* **observant,** alert, watchful, vigilant. 2. [In spite of; *usually used with* of] despite, aside from, distinct from, without regard to, without considering, notwithstanding, at any cost, leaving aside; see also **although,** **but** 1.

regards, *n.* best wishes, compliments, greetings, salutations, remembrances, respects, love, deference, commendation, *love and kisses; see also **greeting.**

regenerate, *v.* raise from the dead, recreate, exhilarate; see **produce** 2, **revive** 1.

regeneration, *n.* rebuilding, rehabilitation, renovation; see **repair.**

regime, *n.* administration, management, political system; see **government** 2.

regiment, *n.* corps, soldiers, military organization; see **army** 2.

regimentation, *n.* massing, collectivization, organization, planned economy, standardization, methodization, regulation, uniformity, arrangement, mechanization, institutionalization, classification, division, lining up, adjustment, harmonization, grouping, ordering; see also **restraint** 2.

region, *n.* 1. [An indefinite area] country, district, territory, section, sector, province, zone, realm, vicinity, quarter, locale, locality, environs, precinct, county, neighborhood, terrain, domain, range. 2. [A limited area] precinct, ward, block; see **area** 3. 3. [Scope] sphere, province, realm; see **field** 3.

regional, *a.* provincial, territorial, local, environmental, positional, geographical, parochial, sectional, topical, locational, insular, topographic.

register, *n.* 1. [A list] file, registry, roll; see **list, record** 1. 2. [A heating regulator] grate, hot-air opening, radiator; see **appliance.**

register, *v.* 1. [To record] check in, enroll, file; see **list** 1, **record** 1. 2. [To indicate] point out *or* to, designate, record; see **name** 2. 3. [To show] express, disclose, manifest; see **display.** 4. [To enlist or enroll] go through registration, check into, make an entry, sign up for, check in, sign in, join.

registration, *n.* 1. [The act of registering] enrolling, signing up, certification, matriculation, recording, listing, filing, cataloguing, booking, noting down, stamping, authorizing, notarization; see also **enrollment** 1. 2. [Those who have registered] enrollment, turnout, registrants, voters, hotel guests, students, student body, delegation.

regress, *v.* backslide, relapse, revert; see **retreat** 1, **sink** 1.

regressive, *a.* conservative, reverse, reactionary; see **backward** 1.

regret, *n.* 1. [Remorse] concern, compunction, worry, repentance, self-reproach, self-condemnation, self-disgust, misgiving, regretfulness, nostalgia, self-accusation, contrition, qualm, scruple, penitence, bitterness, disappointment, dissatisfaction, uneasiness, conscience, discomfort, annoyance, spiritual disturbance; see also **care** 2.—*Ant.* **comfort,** satisfaction, ease. 2. [Grief] sorrow, pain, anxiety; see **grief.**

regret, *v.* 1. [To be sorry for] mourn, bewail, lament, cry over, rue, grieve, repent, have compunctions about, look back upon, feel conscience-stricken, moan, have a bad conscience, have qualms about, weep over, be disturbed over, feel uneasy about, *laugh out of the other side of one's mouth, *kick oneself, *bite one's tongue, *cry over spilled milk.—*Ant.* celebrate, be satisfied with, be happy. **2.** [To disapprove of] deplore, be averse *or* opposed to, deprecate; see **denounce, dislike.**

regular, *a.* **1.** [In accordance with custom] customary, usual, routine; see **conventional 1, 3. 2.** [In accordance with law] normal, legitimate, lawful; see **legal. 3.** [In accordance with an observable pattern] orderly, methodical, routine, symmetrical, precise, exact, systematic, arranged, organized, patterned, constant, congruous, consonant, accordant, consistent, invariable, formal, regulated, rational, steady, rhythmic, periodic, measured, classified, in order, unconfused, harmonious, systematic, normal, natural, cyclic, successive, momentary, alternating, probable, recurrent, general, usual, expected, serial, automatic, mechanical, alternate, hourly, daily, monthly, weekly, annual, seasonal, yearly, pulsating, diurnal, quotidian, tertian, menstrual, anticipated, looked *or* hoped for, counted *or* relied on *or* upon, generally occurring, in the natural course of events, punctual, steady, uniform, *regular as clockwork.—*Ant.* irregular, sporadic, erratic.

regularity, *n.* evenness, steadiness, uniformity, routine, constancy, consistency, invariability, rhythm, recurrence, system, congruity, homogeneity, punctuality, periodicity, swing, rotation, conformity, proportion, symmetry, balance, cadence, harmony.

regularly, *a.* customarily, habitually, punctually, systematically, unchangingly, right along, as a rule, usually, commonly, as a matter of course, tirelessly, conventionally, ordinarily, repeatedly, frequently, faithfully, religiously, mechanically, automatically, without once missing, normally, periodically, evenly, methodically, exactly, monotonously, rhythmically, steadily, unbrokenly, typically, continually, like clockwork, cyclically, day in and day out, constantly, always, ceaselessly, time and time again, invariably, redundantly, hourly, incessantly, daily, perpetually, over and over again, weekly, monthly, annually, exactly.—*Ant.* irregularly, unevenly, brokenly.

regulate, *v.* **1.** [To control] rule, legislate, direct; see **govern, manage 1. 2.** [To adjust] arrange, methodize, dispose,

classify, systematize, put in order, fix, settle, adapt, standardize, co-ordinate, allocate, readjust, reconcile, rectify, correct, improve, temper, set; see also **adjust 1.**

regulated, *a.* fixed, adjusted, arranged, directed, controlled, supervised, methodized, systematized, settled, adapted, coordinated, reconciled, improved, standardized, tempered, ruled; see also **classified, managed 2, organized.—*Ant.* confused, disarranged, upset.

regulation, *n.* **1.** [The act of regulating] handling, direction, control; see **management 1. 2.** [A rule] law, statute, ordinance; see **command, law 3.**

regulator, *n.* adjuster, thermostat, valve; see **machine.**

rehabilitate, *v.* restore, change, reestablish; see **renew 1.**

rehabilitation, *n.* rebuilding, reestablishment, remaking; see **improvement 1, repair.**

rehearsal, *n.* recitation, recital, trial *or* practice performance, experiment, test flight, reading, dress rehearsal, *call; see also **performance, practice 3.**

rehearse, *v.* **1.** [To tell] describe, recount, relate; see **tell 1. 2.** [To repeat] tell again, retell, do over, recapitulate, re-enact; see also **repeat 3. 3.** [To practice for a performance] drill, test, experiment, hold rehearsals, speak from a script, go *or* run through, hold a reading, learn one's part; see also **practice 1.**

reign, *v.* hold power *or* sovereignty, sit on the throne, wear the crown; see **govern, manage 1.**

reimburse, *v.* repay, compensate, make reparations; see **pay 1, refund 1.**

reimbursement, *n.* compensation, restitution, recompense; see **payment 1.**

rein, *n.* bridle strap, line, control; see **rope.** —**give (free) rein to,** authorize, permit, condone; see **allow.** —**keep a rein on,** control, check, have authority over; see **manage 1.**

reincarnation, *n.* incarnation, reanimation, rebirth; see **birth, return 2.**

reinforce, *v.* buttress, pillar, add to; see **strengthen.**

reinforced, *a.* supported, assisted, strengthened, augmented, buttressed, fortified, pillowed, banded, backed, built-up, stiffened, thickened, cushioned, lined; see also **strong 2.**

reinforcement, *n.* **1.** [Support] coating, concrete block, pillar; see **support 2. 2.** [Military aid; *usually plural*] fresh troops, additional matériel, new ordnance; see **help 1.**

reject, *v.* **1.** [To refuse] repudiate, decline, renounce; see **deny, refuse. 2.**

[To discard] cast off *or* out, throw out, expel; see **discard**.

rejected, *a.* returned, given back, denied; see **refused**.

rejection, *n.* repudiation, denial, dismissal; see **refusal**.

rejoice, *v.* exult, enjoy, revel; see **celebrate 2**.

rejuvenate, *v.* reinvigorate, exhilarate, refresh; see **strengthen**.

rejuvenation, *n.* reinvigoration, stimulation, revivification; see **revival 1**.

relapse, *n.* reversion, recidivation, return; see **loss 3**.

relapse, *v.* lapse, retrogress, fall, backslide, revert, regress, suffer a relapse, deteriorate, degenerate, fall from grace, fall back *or* off, weaken, sink back, fall into again, slide *or* slip back, be overcome *or* overtaken, give in to again.

relate, *v.* **1.** [Tell] recount, recite, retell; see **describe**, **report 1**. **2.** [Connect] bring into relation, associate, correlate; see **compare 1**.

related, *a.* **1.** [Told] narrated, described, recounted; see **told**. **2.** [Connected] associated, in touch with, linked, tied up, knit together, allied, affiliated, complementary, analogous, correspondent, akin, alike, like, parallel, correlated, intertwined, interrelated, similar, mutual, dependent, interdependent, interwoven, of that ilk, in the same category, reciprocal, interchangeable. **3.** [Akin] kindred, of the same family, germane, fraternal, cognate, consanguine, of one blood; see also **sense 2**.

relate to, *v.* be associated to, be connected with, affect; see **concern 1**, **refer 1**.

relation, *n.* **1.** [Relationship] connection, association, similarity; see **relationship**. **2.** [A relative] family connection, sibling, kinsman; see **relative**. —**in relation to**, concerning, with reference to, about; see **regarding**.

relationship, *n.* relation, connection, tie, association, affinity, likeness, link, kinship, bond, dependence, relativity, proportion, rapport, analogy, homogeneity, interrelation, correlation, nearness, alliance, relevance, accord, *hookup, contact; see also **similarity**.—*Ant.* **difference**, dissimilarity, oppositeness.

relative, *a.* **1.** [Pertinent] dependent, contingent, applicable; see **related 2**, **relevant**. **2.** [In regard to] with respect to, concerning, relating to; see **about 2**.

relative, *n.* kin, family connection, relation, member of the family, blood relation, next of kin, sibling *or* sib, kinsman. Relatives include the following—mother, father, parent, grandmother, grandfather, great-grandmother, great-grandfather, ancestor, aunt, uncle, great-aunt, great-uncle, (first) cousin, second cousin, third cousin, fourth cousin, distant cousin, wife, husband, spouse, daughter, son, nephew, niece, brother, sister, kinsman, kinswoman, mother-in-law, father-in-law, brother-in-law, sister-in-law, aunt by marriage, cousin by marriage, *in-law.

relatively, *a.* comparatively, approximately, nearly; see **almost**.

relax, *v.* repose, recline, settle back, make oneself at home, breathe easy, take one's time, take a break, sit around *or* back, stop work, lie down, unbend, be at ease, *take a breather; see also **rest 1**.

relaxation, *n.* repose, reclining, loosening; see **rest 1**.

relaxed, *a.* untroubled, carefree, at ease; see **comfortable 1**.

relay, *v.* communicate, transfer, send forth, transmit, hand over *or* on *or* down, turn over, deliver, communicate, pass on; see also **carry 1**, **send 1**.

release, *n.* **1.** [Freedom] liberation, discharge, freeing; see **freedom 2**. **2.** [That which has been released; *usually, printed matter*] news story, publicity, news flash; see **propaganda**, **story**.

release, *v.* liberate, let go, acquit; see **free**.

released, *a.* **1.** [Freed] discharged, dismissed, liberated; see **free 1**, **2**. **2.** [Announced] broadcast, stated, made public; see **published**.

relent, *v.* soften, comply, relax; see **yield 1**.

relentless, *a.* unmerciful, vindictive, hard; see **ruthless**.

relevance, *n.* connection, significance, pertinence; see **importance**.

relevant, *a.* suitable, appropriate, fit, proper, pertinent (to), becoming, pertaining to, apt, applicable, important, fitting, congruous, cognate, related, conforming, concerning, suitable, conformant, compatible, accordant, referring, harmonious, correspondent, consonant, congruent, consistent, correlated, associated, allied, relative, connected, to the point, bearing on the question, having direct bearing, having to do with, related to, on the nose.—*Ant.* **irrelevant**, not pertinent, **wrong**.

reliability, *n.* dependability, trustworthiness, constancy, loyalty, faithfulness, sincerity, devotion, honesty, authenticity, steadfastness, fidelity, safety, security.

reliable, *a.* firm, unimpeachable, sterling, strong, positive, stable, dependable, sure, solid, staunch, decisive, unequivocal, steadfast, definite, conscientious, constant, steady, trustworthy, faithful, loyal, good, true, sure, devoted, tried, trusty, honest, honorable, candid, true-hearted, high-principled, responsible, sincere, altruistic, determined, reputable, careful, proved, respectable, righteous, decent, incorrupt, truthful, upright, regular, all right, *kosher, O.K., *on the up and up, trueblue, safe, honest, sound, stable, solid, steady, guaranteed, sure, certain, substantial, secure, unquestionable, conclusive, irrefutable, incontestable, dependable, good, firm, strong, unfailing, infallible, authentic, competent, assured, workable, foolproof, sure-fire.—*Ant.* **dangerous**, insecure, undependable.

reliably, *a.* assuredly, presumably, certainly; see **probably**, **surely**.

reliance, *n.* confidence, trust, hope; see **faith 1**.

relic, *n.* **1**. [Something left from an earlier time] vestige, trace, survival, heirloom, antique, keepsake, memento, curio, curiosity, token, souvenir, testimonial, evidence, monument, trophy, remain(s), artifact, remembrance, bric-a-brac. **2**. [A ruin] remnant, residue, remains, broken stone; see also **destruction 2, ruin 2**.

relief, *n.* **1**. [The act of bringing succor] alleviation, softening, comforting; see **comfort 1**. **2**. [Aid] assistance, support, maintenance; see **help 1**. **3**. [A relieved state of mind] satisfaction, relaxation, ease, comfort, release, happiness, contentment, cheer, restfulness, a load off one's mind; see also **comfort 1**. **4**. [The person or thing that brings relief] diversion, relaxation, consolation, solace, reinforcement, supplies, food, shelter, clothing, release, respite, remedy, nursing, medicine, medical care, redress, reparations, indemnities, variety, change, cure; see also **help 1**. **5**. [The raised portions of a sculptural decoration or map] projection, contour, configuration; see **decoration 1**.

relieve, *v.* **1**. [To replace] discharge, throw out, force to resign; see **dismiss**. **2**. [To lessen; *said especially of pain*] assuage, alleviate, soothe, comfort, allay, divert, free, ease, lighten, soften, diminish, mitigate, console, cure, aid, assist; see also **decrease 2, help**.

relieved, *a.* **1**. [Eased in mind] comforted, solaced, consoled, reassured, satisfied, soothed, relaxed, put at ease, restored, reconciled, appeased, placated, alleviated, mollified, disarmed, pacified, adjusted, propitiated, *breathing easy; see also **comfortable 1**.—*Ant.* sad, worried, distraught. **2**. [Deprived of something, or freed from it] replaced, dismissed, separated (from), disengaged, released, made free of, rescued, delivered, supplanted, superseded, succeeded,

substituted, interchanged, exchanged. **3**. [Lessened; *said especially of pain*] mitigated, palliated, softened, assuaged, eased, abated, diminished, salved, soothed, lightened, alleviated, drugged, anesthetized.

religion, *n.* **1**. [All that centers about man's belief in or relationship to a superior being or beings] belief, devotion, piety, spirituality, persuasion, godliness, sense of righteousness, morality, theology, faithfulness, devoutness, creed, myth, superstition, doctrine, cult, denomination, mythology, communion, religious conscience, fidelity, conscientiousness, religious bent, ethical standard; see also **faith 2**. **2**. [Organized worship or service of a deity] veneration, adoration, consecration, sanctification, prayer, rites, ceremonials, holy sacrifice, incantation, holiday, observance, orthodoxy, reformism; see also **ceremony 2**. Religions include the following—Christianity, (Zen) Buddhism, Hinduism, Islam, Judaism, Zoroastrianism, Shintoism, Taoism, deism, theism, polytheism, dualism; see also **church 3**. —**get religion**, become converted, believe, change; see **reform 2, 3**.

religious, *a.* **1**. [Pertaining to religion] ethical, spiritual, moral, ecclesiastical, clerical, theological, canonical, divine, supernatural, holy, sacred, churchly, theistic, deistic, priestly, pontifical, ministerial.—*Ant.* secular, **worldly**, earthly. **2**. [Devout] pious, puritanical, sanctimonious, pietistic, godly, god-fearing, orthodox, reverend, reverential, believing, faithful, Christian, fanatic, evangelistic, revivalistic, church-going; see also **holy 1**. **3**. [Scrupulous] methodical, minute, thorough; see **careful**.

relish, *n.* **1**. [A condiment] seasoning, herb, savor. Relishes include the following—catsup *or* ketchup, piccalilli, Indian *or* corn *or* beet *or* horseradish *or* cucumber *or* pepper *or* pickle *or* tomato *or* green bean *or* orange *or* mango *or* pear relish, chowchow, spiced currants *or* gooseberries *or* grapes, ginger tomatoes, (pear) mincemeat, pickled pears *or* peaches *or* apricots *or* pineapple, chili *or* chutney *or* hot *or* cranberry sauce. **2**. [Obvious delight] gusto, joy, great satisfaction; see **zeal**.

relish, *v.* enjoy, fancy, be fond of; see **like 1, 2**.

reluctance, *n.* disinclination, qualm, hesitation; see **doubt 2**.

reluctant, *a.* disinclined, loath, unwilling, averse, opposed, tardy, backward, adverse, laggard, remiss, slack, squeamish, demurring, grudging, involuntary, uncertain, hanging back, hesitant, hesitating, diffident, with bad grace, indisposed, disheartened, discouraged, queasy.—*Ant.* willing, eager, disposed.

rely on *or* **upon**, *v.* hope, have faith in, count on; see **trust 1.**

remade, *a.* rebuilt, redone, made over; see **improved.**

remain, *v.* 1. [To stay] inhabit, stop, stay in; see **settle 7.** 2. [To endure] keep on, go on, prevail; see **continue 1, endure 1.** 3. [To be left] remain standing, outlive, outlast; see **survive 1.**

remainder, *n.* remaining portion, leftover, residue, remains, relic, remnant, dregs, surplus, leavings, balance, residuum, excess, overplus, scrap, fragment, small piece, carry-over, rest, residual portion, whatever is left, salvage.

remains, *n.* corpse, cadaver, relics; see **body 2.**

remake, *v.* change, revise, alter; see **correct.**

remark, *n.* statement, saying, utterance, annotation, note, mention, reflection, illustration, point, conclusion, consideration, talk, observation, expression, comment, assertion, witticism.

remark, *v.* speak, mention, observe; see **say, talk 1.**

remarkable, *a.* exceptional, extraordinary, uncommon; see **unusual 1.**

remarkably, *a.* exceptionally, singularly, notably; see **especially, very.**

remedy, *n.* 1. [A medicine] antidote, pill, drug; see **medicine 2, treatment 2.** 2. [Effective help] relief, cure, redress, support, improvement, solution, plan, panacea, cure-all, assistance, counteraction; see also **relief 4.**

remedy, *v.* cure, help, aid; see **heal.**

remember, *v.* 1. [To recall] recollect, recognize, summon up, relive, dig into the past, refresh one's memory, be reminded of, think of, revive, bring *or* call to mind, think *or* look *or* go back, brood over, conjure up, call in *or* back *or* up, carry one's thoughts back, look back upon, have memories of, commemorate, memorialize, reminisce, carry in one's thoughts, keep a memory alive, enshrine in the memory.—*Ant.* lose, forget, neglect. 2. [To bear in mind] keep in mind, memorize, know by heart, learn, master, get, be impressed on one's mind, fix in the mind, retain, treasure, hold dear, dwell upon, brood over, keep forever. —*Ant.* neglect, ignore, disregard.

remembered, *a.* thought of, recalled, recollected, rewarded, summoned up, brought to mind, memorialized, haunting one's thoughts, commemorated, dug up.—*Ant.* forgotten, lost, overlooked.

remembrance, *n.* 1. [Memory] recall, recollection, recognition; see **memory 1.**

2. [A gift] reward, token, keepsake; see **gift 1.**

remind, *v.* 1. [To bring into the memory] bring back, make one think of, intimate; see **hint.** 2. [To call the attention of another] caution, point out, jog *or* refresh the memory, remind one of, mention to, call attention to, bring up, prompt, prod, stress, emphasize, note, stir up, put a flea *or* a bug in one's ear, give a cue; see also **warn.**

reminded, *a.* warned, cautioned, prompted, put in mind (of), made aware, advised, forewarned, notified, awakened, prodded.

reminder, *n.* warning, notice, admonition, note, memorandum, memo, hint, suggestion, memento, token, keepsake, trinket, remembrance, souvenir.

remit, *v.* make payment, forward, dispatch; see **pay 1.**

remittance, *n.* transmittal, money sent, enclosure; see **payment 1.**

remnant, *n.* residue, leavings, dregs; see **excess 1, remainder.**

remnants, *n.* scraps, odds and ends, leftovers, particles, surplus, endpieces, remains, leavings; see also **excess 1, remainder.**

remodel, *v.* renovate, refurnish, refurbish, readjust, reconstruct, readapt, rearrange, redecorate, refashion, improve, reshape, recast, rebuild, repair, modernize, repaint; see also **repair.**

remodeled, *a.* refurnished, redecorated, rebuilt; see **changed 2.**

remorse, *n.* compunction, contrition, self-reproach; see **grief, regret 1.** — **without remorse,** cruel, pitiless, relentless; see **ruthless.**

remorseful, *a.* contrite, penitent, repentant; see **sorry 1.**

remorseless, *a.* unyielding, unforgiving, vindictive; see **severe 1, 2.**

remote, *a.* 1. [Distant] far-off, faraway, out-of-the-way, removed, beyond, secluded, inaccessible, isolated, unknown, alien, foreign, undiscovered, off the beaten track, over the hills and far away, godforsaken; see also **distant.**—*Ant.* near, close, accessible. 2. [Ancient] forgotten, past, aged; see **old 3.** 3. [Separated] unrelated, irrelevant, unconnected; see **separated.**

removal, *n.* dismissal, discharge, expulsion, exile, deportation, banishment, elimination, extraction, dislodgement, evacuation, ejection, transference, eradication, extermination, replacement, translocation, *the can *or* chuck *or* gate *or* bounce. —*Ant.* entrance, induction, introduction.

remove, *v.* 1. [To move physically] take away from, cart *or* clear *or* carry *or* take *or* tear *or* brush away, transfer, transport, dislodge, uproot, excavate, displace, unload, discharge, lift up, doff, raise, evacuate, shift, switch, lift, push, draw away or in, withdraw, separate, extract, cut or dig or dip or tear or pull or take or burn or smoke or rip out, take down, tear or draw or take or skip or carry or cart or clear or strike or cut or rub or scrape off, take or pull in. 2. [To eliminate] get rid of, do away with, exclude; see **eliminate**. 3. [To dismiss] discharge, displace, discard; see **dismiss**.

removed, a. 1. [Taken out] extracted, eliminated, withdrawn, evacuated, dislodged, ejected, pulled out, amputated, excised, expunged, extirpated.—*Ant*. left, ignored, established. 2. [Distant] faraway, out-of-the-way, far-off; see **distant** 1. 3. [Dismissed] banished, relieved of office, retired; see **discharged, recalled** 2.

rend, v. rip, sever, sunder; see **break** 1.

render, v. 1. [To give] present, hand over, especially distribute; see **give** 1. 2. [To perform, especially a service] do, act, execute; see **perform** 1. 3. [To interpret; *said especially of music*] play, perform, depict; see **interpret**.

rendition, n. interpretation, version, reading; see **translation**.

renew, v. 1. [To refresh] revive, reawaken, regenerate, re-establish, rehabilitate, reinvigorate, replace, revive, rebuild, reconstitute, remake, refinish, refurbish, redo, repeat, invigorate, exhilarate, restore, resuscitate, recondition, overhaul, replenish, go over, cool, brace, freshen, stimulate, recreate, remodel, revamp, redesign, modernize, rejuvenate, give new life to, recover, renovate, reintegrate, make a new beginning, bring up or down to date, do over, make like new; see also **revive** 1. 2. [To repeat] resume, reiterate, recommence; see **repeat** 1. 3. [To replace] resume, supplant, take over; see **substitute**.

renewal, n. resurrection, new start, renovation; see **revival** 1.

renewed, a. revived, readapted, refitted; see **repaired**.

renounce, v. disown, disavow, give up; see **deny, discard**.

renovate, v. make over, remake, rehabilitate; see **renew** 1.

renovated, a. renewed, remodeled, redone; see **clean** 1, **repaired**.

renovation, n. reform, revision, change; see **improvement** 1.

rent, v. 1. [To sell the use of property] lease, lend, let, make available, allow the use of, take in roomers, sublet, put on loan. 2. [To obtain use by payment] hire, pay rent for, charter, contract, sign

a contract for, engage, borrow, pay for services; see also **pay** 1.

rented, a. leased, lent, hired, contracted, engaged, let, chartered, taken, on lease, out of the market.

reopen, v. revive, re-establish, begin again; see **open** 2, **renew** 1.

reorganization, n. re-establishment, reconstitution, reorientation; see **change** 2, **improvement** 1.

reorganize, v. rebuild, renovate, regenerate; see **reconstruct**.

repaid, a. paid back, reimbursed, refunded; see **paid**.

repair, n. reconstruction, substitution, reformation, rehabilitation, new part, patch, restoration, restored portion, replacement; see also **improvement** 1, 2.—*Ant*. break, tear, fracture.

repair, v. fix, adjust, improve, correct, settle, put into shape, reform, patch, rejuvenate, refurbish, retread, touch up, put in order, revive, refresh, renew, mend, darn, sew, revamp, rectify, right, ameliorate, renovate, reshape, rebuild, *work over, fix up.—*Ant*. wreck, damage, smash.

repaired, a. fixed, adjusted, rearranged, adapted, settled, remodeled, rectified, mended, corrected, righted, restored, renewed, remedied, improved, renovated, retouched, in (working) order, patched up, put together, put back into shape, sewn, reset, stitched up.—*Ant*. damaged, worn, torn.

reparation, n. indemnity, retribution, amends; see **payment** 1.

repay, v. 1. [To pay back] reimburse, recompense, refund, return, indemnify, give back, make amends, requite, compensate, *square oneself, settle up; see also **pay** 1. 2. [To retaliate] get even with, square accounts, reciprocate; see **revenge**.

repayment, n. compensation, indemnity, restitution; see **payment** 1.

repeal, n. annulment, cancellation, abolition; see **withdrawal**.

repeal, v. annul, abolish, abrogate; see **cancel**.

repeat, v. 1. [To do again] redo, remake, do or play over, recur, rehash, reciprocate, return, rework, reform, refashion, recast, (re)duplicate, renew, reconstruct, reerect, revert, hold over, go over again and again. 2. [To happen again] reoccur, recur, revolve, reappear, occur again, come again, return; see also **happen** 2. 3. [To say again] (re)iterate, restate, reissue, republish, reutter, echo, recite, re-echo, rehearse, retell, go over, play or read back, recapitulate, name over, drum into, rehash, come again; see also **say**.

repeated, a. 1. [Done again] redone,

remade, copied, imitated, reworked, refashioned, recast, done over, reciprocated, returned, reverted, (re)duplicated. 2. [Said again] reiterated, restated, reannounced, reuttered, recited, reproduced, seconded, paraphrased, reworded, retold.

repeatedly, *a.* again and again, many times, time and again; see **frequently**, **regularly**.

repel, *v.* 1. [To throw back] rebuff, resist, stand up against, oppose, check, repulse, put to flight, keep at bay, knock down, drive *or* chase away, drive *or* beat *or* hold *or* force *or* push back, beat *or* ward *or* chase *or* stave *or* fight off.—*Ant.* **fall**, fail, retreat. 2. [To cause aversion] nauseate, offend, revolt; see **disgust**. 3. [To reject] disown, dismiss, cast aside; see **refuse**.

repent, *v.* be sorry, have qualms, be penitent; see **apologize**, **regret** 1.

repentance, *n.* sorrow, remorse, self-reproach; see **regret** 1.

repentant, *a.* penitent, regretful, contrite; see **sorry** 1.

repetition, *n.* recurrence, reoccurrence, reappearance, reproduction, copy, rote, duplication, renewal, recapitulation, reiteration, return; see also **wordiness**.

repetitious, *a.* boring, wordy, repeating; see **dull** 4.

replace, *v.* 1. [To supply an equivalent] repay, compensate, mend; see **reconstruct**, **renew** 1, **repair** 2. 2. [To take the place of] take over, supplant, displace; see **substitute**. 3. [To put back in the same place] restore, reinstate, put back; see **return** 2.

replaced, *a.* 1. [Returned to the same place] restored, reinstated, reintegrated, recovered, recouped, reacquired, regained, repossessed, resumed, rewon, retrieved. 2. [Having another in one's place; *said of persons*] dismissed, cashiered, dislodged; see **recalled** 2. 3. [Having another in its place; *said of things*] renewed, interchanged, replenished; see **changed** 1.

replica, *n.* copy, likeness, model; see **duplicate**, **imitation** 2.

reply, *n.* response, return, retort; see **answer** 1.

reply, *v.* retort, rejoin, return; see **answer** 1.

report, *n.* 1. [A transmitted account] tale, narrative, description; see **news** 1, 2, **story**. 2. [An official summary] proclamation, outline, release; see **record** 1, **summary**. 3. [A loud, explosive sound] detonation, bang, blast; see **noise** 1.

report, *v.* 1. [To deliver information] describe, recount, narrate, provide (the) details (of *or* for), give an account (of),

set forth, inform, advise, communicate, retail, wire, cable, telephone, radio, broadcast, notify, relate, state; see also **tell** 1. 2. [To make a summary statement] summarize, publish, proclaim; see sense 1. 3. [To present oneself] be at hand, reach, come; see **arrive**. 4. [To record] take minutes, inscribe, note down; see **record** 1.

reported, *a.* stated, recited, recounted, narrated, described, set forth, announced, broadcast, rumored, noted, expressed, proclaimed, made known, according to rumor, revealed, communicated, disclosed, imparted, divulged, recorded, in the air, all over town.—*Ant.* **unknown**, verified, certain.

reporter, *n.* newspaperman, news writer, columnist, journalist, newsman, correspondent, interviewer, cub reporter, star reporter, newsgatherer; see also **writer**.

represent, *v.* 1. [To act as a delegate] be an agent for, serve, hold office, be deputy for, be attorney for, steward, act as broker, sell for, buy for, do business for, be spokesman for, be ambassador for, exercise power of attorney for. 2. [To present as a true interpretation] render, depict, portray; see **enact** 3. [To serve as an equivalent] copy, imitate, reproduce, symbolize, exemplify, typify, signify, substitute, stand for, impersonate, personify.

representation, *n.* description, narration, delineation; see **copy**.

representative, *n.* 1. [An emissary] deputy, salesman, messenger; see **agent**, **delegate**. 2. [One who is elected to the lower legislative body] congressman, assemblyman, councilman, member of parliament, deputy, legislator, senator, councilor; see also **diplomat**.

represented, *a.* 1. [Depicted] portrayed, interpreted, pictured; see **made**. 2. [Presented] rendered, exhibited, enacted; see **shown** 1.

repress, *v.* control, curb, check; see **hinder**, **restrain**.

reprimand, *v.* reproach, denounce, criticize; see **scold**.

reproach, *n.* discredit, censure, rebuke; see **blame**.

reproach, *v.* condemn, censure, scold; see **blame**.

reproduce, *v.* 1. [To make an exact copy] photograph, print, mimeograph; see **copy**. 2. [To make a second time] repeat, duplicate, recreate, recount, revive, re-enact, redo, reawaken, relive, remake, reflect, follow, mirror, echo, re-echo, represent. 3. [To multiply] procreate, engender, breed, generate, propagate, fecundate, hatch, father, beget, impregnate, progenerate, sire, repopulate, multiply, give birth.

reproduced, *a.* copied, printed, traced, duplicated, transcribed, dittoed, recorded, multiplied, Xeroxed (trademark), repeated, made identical, typed, set up, set in type, in facsimile, transferred, photographed, blueprinted, photostated, mimeographed, electrotyped, electroplated, engraved, photoengraved; reproduced in facsimile, in duplicate, in triplicate, etc.; see also **manufactured.**

reproduction, *n.* 1. [A copy] imitation, print, offprint; see **copy.** 2. [A photographic reproduction] photostat, photoengraving, rotograph, photogram, rotogravure, telephoto, wirephoto, X-ray, radiograph, radiogram, candid photo, closeup, pic, pix, blowup, flash-photo.

reproductive, *a.* generative, creative, conceptive; see **genetic.**

reptile, *n.* serpent, amphibian, one of the reptilia; see **snake.**

republic, *n.* democracy, democratic state, constitutional government, commonwealth, self-government, representative government, government by popular sovereignty; see also **government 2.**

Republican, *n.* registered Republican, G.O.P., Old Guard, Young Republican, Old Line Republican; see **conservative.**

republican, *a.* democratic, constitutional, popular; see **conservative, democratic.**

repudiate, *v.* retract, repeal, revoke; see **abandon 1.**

repulse, *v.* 1. [To throw back] set back, overthrow, resist; see **repel 1.** 2. [To rebuff] spurn, repel, snub; see **refuse.**

repulsion, *n.* 1. [Rejection] rebuff, denial, snub; see **refusal.** 2. [Aversion] hate, disgust, resentment; see **hatred.**

repulsive, *a.* 1. [Capable of repelling] offensive, resistant, unyielding, stubborn, opposing, retaliating, insurgent, counteracting, attacking, counterattacking, defensive, combative, aggressive, pugnacious; see also **stubborn.**—*Ant.* yielding, surrendering, capitulating. 2. [Disgusting] odious, forbidding, horrid; see **offensive 2.**

reputable, *a.* 1. [Enjoying a good reputation] distinguished, celebrated, honored; see **important 2.** 2. [Honorable] trustworthy, honest, worthy; see **brave, noble 1, 2.**

reputation, *n.* 1. [Supposed character] reliability, trustworthiness, respectability, dependability, credit, esteem, estimation; see also **character 2.** 2. [Good name] standing, prestige, regard, favor, account, respect, privilege, acceptability, social approval; see also **honor 1.** 3. [Fame] prominence, eminence, notoriety; see **fame 1.**

request, *n.* call, inquiry, petition, question, invitation, offer, solicitation, supplication, prayer, requisition, recourse, suit, entreaty, demand; see also **appeal 1.** —by request, asked for, sought for, wanted; see **requested.**

request, *v.* 1. [To ask] demand, inquire, call for; see **ask.** 2. [To solicit] beseech, entreat, sue; see **beg.**

requested, *a.* asked, demanded, popular, wished, desired, sought, hunted, needed, solicited, petitioned, appealed, requisitioned, in demand; see also **wanted.**

require, *v.* 1. [To need] want, feel the necessity for, have need for; see **need.** 2. [To demand] exact, insist upon, expect; see **ask.**

required, *a.* requisite, imperative, essential; see **necessary.**

requirement, *n.* 1. [A prerequisite] (preliminary) condition, essential, imperative, element, requisite, provision, terms, necessity, stipulation, fundamental, first principle, precondition, reservation, specification, proviso, fulfillment, qualification, vital part, *sine qua non* (Latin); see also **basis.** 2. [A need] necessity, necessary, lack, want, demand, claim, obsession, preoccupation, prepossession, engrossment, stress, extremity, exigency, pinch, obligation, pressing concern, urgency, compulsion, exaction.

rescue, *n.* 1. [The act of rescuing] deliverance, saving, release, extrication, liberation, ransom, redemption, freeing, salvation, reclamation, reclaiming, emancipation, disentanglement, disembarrassment, recovering, heroism. 2. [An instance of rescue] action, deed, feat, performance, exploit, accomplishment, heroics; see also **achievement.**

rescue, *v.* 1. [To save] preserve, recover, redeem, recapture, salvage, retain, hold over, keep (back), safeguard, ransom, protect, retrieve, withdraw, take to safety; see also **save 1.**—*Ant.* lose, slip from one's hands, relinquish. 2. [To free] deliver, liberate, release; see **free.**

research, *n.* investigation, analysis, experimentation; see **examination 1, study.**

research, *v.* get *or* read up on, do research, look into *or* up; see **examine, study 1.**

resemblance, *n.* likeness, correspondence, coincidence; see **similarity.**

resemble, *v.* be *or* look *or* seem *or* sound like, follow, take after, parallel, match, coincide, relate, mirror, approximate, give indication *or* remind one of, bring to mind, catch a likeness, have all the signs of, be the very image of, be similar to, come close to, appear like, bear a resemblance to, come near, pass for, have all the earmarks of, echo, compare with, be comparable to, *smack of, *be the spit and image of, *be a dead-ringer for; see also **agree.**— *Ant.* **differ,** contradict, oppose.

resent, *v.* frown at, be vexed, be insulted; see **dislike.**

resentment, *n.* exasperation, annoyance, irritation; see also **anger.**

reservation, *n.* 1. [The act of reserving] restriction, limitation, withholding; see **restraint** 2. 2. [An instrument for reserving] card, pass, license; see **ticket** 1. 3. [The space reserved] seat, car, room, bus, train, box, stall, place, parking spot, table, berth, compartment.

reserve, *n.* 1. [A portion kept against emergencies] savings, insurance, resources, reserved funds, store, provisions, assets, supply, hoard, backlog, nest egg, something in the sock, something for a rainy day; see also **security** 2. 2. [Calmness] backwardness, restraint, reticence, modesty, unresponsiveness, uncommunicativeness, caution, inhibition, coyness, demureness, aloofness.— **in reserve,** withheld, kept back *or* aside, saved; see **reserved** 2.

reserve, *v.* 1. [To save] store up, set aside, put away; see **maintain** 3, **save** 2. 2. [To retain] keep, possess, have; see **hold** 1, **own** 1.

reserved, *a.* 1. [Held on reservation] pre-empted, claimed, booked; see **saved** 2. 2. [Held in reserve] saved, withheld, kept aside, preserved, conserved, stored away, funded, put in a safe, *on ice.— Ant.* **used,** spent, exhausted. 3. [Restrained] shy, modest, backward, reticent, secretive, quiet, composed, retiring, controlling oneself, mild, gentle, peaceful, soft-spoken, sedate, collected, serene, placid.—*Ant.* **loud,** ostentatious, boisterous.

reserves, *n.* reinforcements, enlisted reserves, volunteers; see **army** 2.

reservoir, *n.* storage (place), tank, reserve, store, pool, cistern, water supply.

reside, *v.* dwell, stay, lodge; see **occupy** 2.

residence, *n.* house, habitation, living quarters; see **apartment, home** 1.

resident, *n.* house-dweller, citizen, suburbanite, tenant, inhabitant, native, denizen, occupant, inmate, householder, boxholder, dweller.

residue, *n.* residual, residuum, remainder, leavings, scraps, scourings, scobs, parings, raspings, shavings, debris, sewage, silt, slag, soot, scum; see also **trash** 1.

resign, *v.* 1. [To relinquish] surrender, capitulate, give up; see **abandon** 1, **yield** 1. 2. [To leave one's employment] quit, separate oneself from, retire, step down, drop out, stand down *or* aside,

sign off, end one's services, leave, hand in one's resignation, cease work, give notice, ask for one's time, walk out of *or* off the job.

resignation, *n.* 1. [Mental preparation for something unwelcome] submission, humility, passivity, patience, deference, docility, submissiveness, abandonment, renunciation, self-abnegation, acquiescence, endurance, compliance.—*Ant.* **resistance,** unsubmissiveness, unwillingness. 2. [The act of resigning] retirement, departure, leaving, quitting, giving up, abdication, surrender, withdrawal, relinquishment, vacating, tendering one's resignation, giving up office, termination of one's connection.

resigned, *a.* quiet, peaceable, docile, tractable, submissive, yielding, relinquishing, gentle, obedient, manageable, willing, agreeable, ready, amenable, pliant, compliant, easily managed, genial, cordial, well-disposed, satisfied, patient, unresisting, tolerant, calm, reconciled, adjusted, adapted, accommodated, tame, nonresisting, passive, philosophical, renouncing, unassertive, subservient, deferential.—*Ant.* **rebellious,** recalcitrant, resistant.

resilience, *n.* elasticity, snap, recoil; see **flexibility.**

resilient, *a.* rebounding, elastic, springy; see **flexible.**

resin, *n.* copal, pitch, gum; see **gum.**

resist, *v.* hold, remain, maintain, endure, bear, continue, persist, obtain, occur, repeat, stay, retain, brook, suffer, abide, tolerate, persevere, last, oppose change, bear up against, stand up to, put up a struggle, hold off, repel, remain firm, die hard. —*Ant.* **stop,** desist, cease.

resistance, *n.* 1. [A defense] parrying, stand, holding, withstanding, warding off, rebuff, obstruction, defiance, striking back, coping, check, halting, protecting, protection, safeguard, shield, screen, cover, watch, support, fight, impeding, blocking, opposition; see also **defense** 1.—*Ant.* retirement, **withdrawal,** withdrawing. 2. [The power of remaining impervious to an influence] unsusceptibility, immunity, immovability, hardness, imperviousness, endurance, fixedness, fastness, stability, stableness, permanence. 3. [The power of holding back another substance] friction, attrition, resistance; see **reserve** 3. 4. [An opposition] underground movement, anti-Fascist, anti-Communist, anti-American, etc., movement; boycott, strike, walkout, slowdown, front, stand, guerrilla movement; see also **revolution** 2.

resister, *n.* adversary, antagonist, opponent; see **opposition** 2.

resolute, *a.* steadfast, firm, determined; see **determined 1.**

resolutely, *a.* with all one's heart, bravely, with a will; see **firmly 1, 2.**

resolution, *n.* 1. [Fixedness of mind] fortitude, perseverance, resolve; see **determination. 2.** [A formal statement of opinion] verdict, formal expression, decision, recommendation, analysis, elucidation, interpretation, exposition, presentation, declaration, recitation, assertion.

resolve, *v.* determine, settle (on), conclude, fix, purpose, propose, choose, fix upon, make up one's mind, take a firm stand, take one's stand, take a decisive step, make a point of, pass upon, decree, elect, remain firm, take the bull by the horns; see also **decide.**

resort, *n.* 1. [A relief in the face of difficulty] expedient, shift, makeshift, stopgap, substitute, surrogate, resource, device, refuge, recourse, hope, relief, possibility, opportunity. **2.** [A place for rest or amusement] Resorts include the following— seaside, mountain, rest, camping, skiing, sports, winter, lake, summer, gambling, amusement park, night club, restaurant, dance hall, club; see also **hotel, motel. —as a last resort,** in desperation, lastly, in the end; see **finally 1, 2.**

resort to, *v.* turn to, refer to, apply, go to, use, try, employ, utilize, have recourse to, benefit by, put to use, make use of, recur to, take up.

resource, *n.* reserve, supply, support, source, stock, store, means, expedient, stratagem, relief, resort, recourse, artifice, device, refuge.

resourceful, *a.* original, ingenious, capable; see **active, intelligent.**

resources, *n.* means, money, stocks, bonds, products, revenue, riches, assets, belongings, effects, capital, income, savings; see also **property 1, reserve 1, wealth.**

respect, *n.* esteem, honor, regard; see **admiration. —pay one's respects,** wait upon, show regard, be polite; see **visit 1.**

respect, *v.* 1. [To esteem] regard, value, look up to; see **admire. 2.** [To treat with consideration] appreciate, heed, notice, consider, note, recognize, defer *or* do honor *or* be kind *or* show courtesy to, spare, take into account, attend, uphold; see also **appreciate 1. —***Ant.* ridicule, mock, scorn.

respectability, *n.* integrity, decency, propriety; see **honesty 1, virtue 1.**

respectable, *a.* presentable, upright, fair, moderate, mediocre, tolerable, passable, ordinary, virtuous, modest, honorable,

worthy, estimable, decorous, seemly, proper; see **decent 2, honest 1.**

respected, *a.* regarded, appreciated, valued; see **honored.**

respectful, *a.* deferential, considerate, appreciative, courteous, admiring, reverent, attending, upholding, regarding, valuing, venerating, recognizing, deferring to, showing respect for; see also **polite.—***Ant.* rude, impudent, contemptuous.

respectfully, *a.* deferentially, reverentially, decorously, ceremoniously, attentively, courteously, considerately, with all respect, with due respect, with the highest respect, in deference to; see also **politely.—***Ant.* rudely, disrespectfully, impudently.

respecting, *a.* regarding, concerning, in relation to; see **about 2.**

respiration, *n.* inhalation, exhalation, expiration; see **breath.**

respite, *n.* reprieve, postponement, pause; see **delay.**

respond, *v.* reply, rejoin, acknowledge; see **answer 1.**

response, *n.* rejoinder, reply, acknowledgment; see **answer 1.**

responsibility, *n.* 1. [State of being reliable] trustworthiness, reliability, trustiness, dependableness, loyalty, faithfulness, capableness, capacity, efficiency, competency, uprightness, firmness, steadfastness, stability, ability; see also **honesty. 2.** [State of being accountable] answerability, accountability, liability, subjection, engagement, pledge, contract, constraint, restraint; see also **duty 1.—***Ant.* freedom, exemption, immunity. **3.** [Anything for which one is accountable] obligation, trust, contract; see **duty 1.**

responsible, *a.* 1. [Charged with responsibility] accountable, answerable (for), liable, subject, susceptive, bound, under obligation, constrained, tied, fettered, bonded, censurable, chargeable, obligated, obliged, compelled, contracted, hampered, held, pledged, sworn *or* bound to, under contract, engaged; see also **bound 2.** —*Ant.* free, unconstrained, unbound. **2.** [Capable of assuming responsibility] trustworthy, trusty, reliable, capable, efficient, loyal, faithful, dutiful, dependable, tried, self-reliant, able, competent, qualified, effective, upright, firm, steadfast, steady, stable; see also **able 2.—***Ant.* irresponsible, capricious, unstable.

rest, *n.* 1. [Repose] quiet, quietness, ease, tranquillity, slumber, calm, calmness, peace, peacefulness, relaxation, rest, recreation, coffee break, rest period, siesta, doze, nap, dreaminess, comfort, breathing spell, lounging period, loafing period, vacation, lull, leisure, respite, composure; see sense 2. 2. [State of inactivity] intermission, cessation, stillness, stop, stay, stand, standstill, lull, discontinuance, interval, hush, silence, dead calm, stagnation, fixity, immobility, inactivity, motionlessness, pause, full stop, deadlock, recess, noon hour; see sense 1.—*Ant*. continuance, **activity**, endurance. 3. [Anything upon which an object rests] support, prop, pillar; see **foundation** 2. 4. [The remainder] residue, surplus, remnant; see **remainder**. 5. [Death] release, demise, mortality; see **death**. —**at rest**, in a state of rest, immobile, inactive; see **resting** 1. —**lay to rest**, inter, assign to the grave, entomb; see **bury** 1.

rest, *v*. 1. [To take one's rest] sleep, slumber, doze, repose, compose oneself for sleep, lie (down), lounge, let down, ease off, recuperate, rest up, take a rest *or* a break, break the monotony, lean, recline, couch, pillow, relax, unbend, settle (down), dream, drowse, take one's ease, be comfortable, stretch out, nap, nod, *snooze. 2. [To depend upon] be supported *or* upheld, hang *or* lie upon, be seated on; see **depend** 2.

restaurant, *n*. eating house, eating place, dining room, café, *beanery, eatery. Types of restaurants include the following—café, hotel, dining room, inn, coffee shop, coffee house, coffee room, chophouse, tearoom, luncheon, luncheonette, lunch-wagon, sea-food grotto, coffee deck, creamery, diner, lunch bar, soda fountain, milk bar, hotdog stand, snack bar, automat, rotisserie, cabaret, night club, cafeteria, grill, oyster house, barbecue, spaghetti house, canteen.

rested, *a*. restored, refreshed, relaxed, strengthened, renewed, unwearied, unfatigued, untired, awake, revived, recovered, brought back, reanimated, revitalized, reintegrated, unworn.—*Ant*. **tired**, wearied, fatigued.

restful, *a*. untroubling, untroubled, tranquil, tranquilizing, calm, peaceful, quiet, reposeful, serene, comfortable, easy, placid, mild, still, soothing, relaxing, refreshing, restoring, revitalizing, reviving, renewing.—*Ant*. **loud**, irritating, agitating.

resting, *a*. 1. [Taking rest] relaxing, unbending, reposing, composing oneself, reclining, lying down, sleeping, stretched out, at ease, quiet, dormant, comfortable, lounging, loafing, taking a breathing spell *or* a breather, enjoying a lull, sleeping, dozing, drowsing, napping, taking a siesta, recessing, taking a vacation, having a holiday. 2. [Situated] located, set *or* settled on, seated; see **occupying** 1, **placed**.

resitution, *n*. compensation, return,

restoration; see **payment** 1, **reparation** 2.

restless, *a*. fidgety, skittish, feverish, sleepless, jumpy, nervous, unquiet, disturbed, uneasy, anxious, up in arms, discontented, vexed, excited, agitated, angry, disaffected, estranged, alienated, resentful, recalcitrant, insubordinate, flurried, roving, transient, wandering, discontented, unsettled, roaming, nomadic, moving, straying, ranging, gadding, restive, peeved, annoyed, impatient, flustered, twitching, trembling, tremulous, *rattled, *jittery; see also **active, excited, rebellious**.—*Ant*. quiet, sedate, calm.

restlessness, *n*. uneasiness, discomfort, excitability; see **excitement, nervousness**.

restoration, *n*. 1. [The act of restoring] revival, return, renewal; see **recovery** 1. 2. [The act of reconstructing] rehabilitation, reconstruction, reparation; see **repair**.

restore, *v*. 1. [To give back] make restitution, replace, put back; see **return** 2. 2. [To recreate] re-establish, revive, recover; see **renew** 1. 3. [To rebuild in a form supposed to be original] rebuild, alter, rehabilitate; see **reconstruct, repair**. 4. [To bring back to health] refresh, cure, make healthy; see **heal**.

restrain, *v*. check, control, curb, bridle, rein *or* hem *or* keep in, handle, regulate, keep in line, guide, direct, keep down *or* from, repress, harness, muzzle, hold in leash, govern, inhibit, hold, bind, deter, hold in *or* back, hamper, constrain, restrict, stay, gag, limit, impound, box *or* bottle up, tie *or* crack *or* pin down, hold *or* choke *or* pull back, contain, sit on, come down on.

restrained, *a*. under control, in check, on leash; see **held**.

restraint, *n*. 1. [Control over oneself] control, self-control, reserve, reticence, constraint, withholding, caution, coolness, forbearance, silence, secretiveness, stress, repression, self-government, self-restraint, stiffness, abstinence, self-denial, self-repression, unnaturalness, constrained manner, abstention, self-discipline, self-censorship; see also **attention**.—*Ant*. **laziness**, slackness, laxity. 2. [An influence that checks or hinders] repression, deprivation, limitation, hindrance, reduction, decrease, prohibition, confinement, check, barrier, obstacle, obstruction, restriction, bar, curb, blockade, order, command, instruction, coercion, impediment, compulsion, duress, force, violence, deterrence, determent, discipline, assignment, definition, moderation, tempering, qualifying.—*Ant*. liberty, license, **freedom**.

restrict, *v.* delimit, limit, circumscribe, assign, contract, shorten, narrow, decrease, inclose, keep in *or* within bounds, define, encircle, surround, shut in, tether, chain, diminish, reduce, moderate, modify, temper, qualify, come down on, pin down.—*Ant.* **increase,** extend, expand.

restricted, *a.* limited, confined, restrained, circumscribed, curbed, bound, prescribed, checked, bounded, inhibited, hampered, marked, defined, delimited, encircled, surrounded, shut in, hitched, tethered, chained, fastened, secured, bridled, held in *or* back *or* down, reined in, controlled, governed, deterred, impeded, stayed, stopped, suppressed, repressed, prevented, fettered, deprived, blocked, barred, obstructed, dammed, clogged, manacled, frustrated, embarrassed, baffled, foiled, shrunken, narrowed, shortened, decreased, diminished, reduced, moderated, tempered, modified, qualified, out of bounds; see also **bound 1, 2.**

restriction, *n.* custody, limitation, contraction; see **restraint 2.**

result, *n.* consequence, issue, event, execution, effect, outcome, end, finish, termination, consummation, completion, aftereffect, aftermath, upshot, sequel, sequence, fruit, eventuality, proceeds, emanation, outgrowth, outcropping, returns, backwash, backlash, repercussion, settlement, determination, decision, arrangement, *payoff; see also **end 2, 4.**—*Ant.* origin, source, root.

result, *v.* issue, grow *or* spring *or* rise *or* proceed *or* emanate *or* germinate *or* flow *or* accrue *or* arise *or* derive *or* come from, originate in, (be)come of, spring, emerge, rise, ensue, emanate, effect, produce, fruit, follow, happen, occur, come about *or* out *or* forth *or* of, pan *or* fall *or* crop *or* work out, appear, end, finish, terminate, conclude.

resume, *v.* take up again, reassume, begin again, recommence, reoccupy, go on (with), renew, recapitulate, return, keep *or* carry on, keep up; see also **continue 2.**—*Ant.* **stop,** cease, discontinue.

resurrection, *n.* return to life, transformation, rebirth; see **renewal 1.**

retain, *v.* **1.** [To hold] cling to, grasp, clutch; see **hold 1. 2.** [To reserve services] employ, maintain, engage; see **hire. 3.** [To remember] recall, recollect, recognize; see **remember 1.**

retained, *a.* **1.** [Kept] had, held, possessed, owned, enjoyed, secured, preserved, saved, maintained, restrained, confined, curbed, detained, contained, received, admitted, included, withheld, put away, treasured, sustained, celebrated, remembered, commemorated;

see also **kept 2.**—*Ant.* **lost,** wasted, refused. **2.** [Employed] hired, engaged, contracted; see **employed.**

retaliate, *v.* requite, return, repay; see **revenge.**

retaliation, *n.* vengeance, reprisal, punishment; see **revenge 1.**

retard, *v.* postpone, delay, impede; see **hinder.**

retarded, *a.* **1.** [*Said of persons*] backward, underachieving, stupid; see **dull 3. 2.** [*Said of activities*] delayed, slowed down *or* up, held back; see **slow 1, 2, 3.**

retire, *v.* **1.** [To draw away] withdraw, part, retreat; see **leave 1. 2.** [To go to bed] lie down, turn in, rest; see **sleep. 3.** [To cease active life] resign, give up work, sever one's connections, relinquish, make vacant, lay down, hand over, lead a quiet life, reach retirement age.

retired, *a.* resigned, relinquished, laid down, handed over, withdrawn, retreated, removed, reached retirement age, leading a quiet life, secluding oneself, separating oneself, aloof.—*Ant.* active, working, busy.

retirement, *n.* **1.** [The act of retiring] removal, vacating, separation; see **resignation 2. 2.** [The state of being retired] seclusion, aloofness, apartness, separateness, privacy, concealment, solitude, solitariness, isolation, remoteness, loneliness, quiet, retreat, tranquillity, refuge, serenity, inactivity; see also **silence 1.**—*Ant.* exposure, **activity,** association.

retort, *n.* counter, repartee, response; see **answer 1.**

retort, *v.* reply, rejoin, snap back; see **answer 1.**

retract, *v.* withdraw, draw away, take in; see **remove 1.**

retraction, *n.* denial, revocation, disowning; see **cancellation, denial 1.**

retreat, *n.* **1.** [The act of retreating] retirement, removal, evacuation, departure, escape, withdrawal, drawing back, reversal, retrogression, backing out, flight, recession, retraction, going, running away, eluding, evasion, avoidance, recoil.—*Ant.* **advance,** progress, progression. **2.** [A place to which one retreats] seclusion, solitude, privacy, shelter, refuge, asylum, safe place, defense, sanctuary, security, cover, ark, harbor, port, haven, place of concealment, hiding place, resort, haunt, habitat, hermitage, cell, convent, cloister.—*Ant.* **front,** exposed position, van.

retreat, *v.* recede, retrograde, back (out), retract, go, depart, recoil, shrink, quail, run, draw back, reel, start back, reverse, seclude oneself, keep aloof *or* apart, hide, separate from, regress, resign, relinquish, lay down, hand over, withdraw, backtrack, leave, back off or down, *chicken (out).—*Ant.* stay, remain, continue.

retribution, n. requital, reprisal, retaliation; see **revenge 1**.

retrieve, v. regain, bring back, reclaim; see **recover 1**.

return, a. coming back, repeat, repeating, repetitive, recurring, reappearing, sent back, answering, replying, retorting, rotating, turning, rebounding, recurrent; see also **repeated 1**.

return, n. 1. [The act of coming again] homecoming, arrival, reappearance; see sense 2. 2. [The act of being returned] restoration, restitution, rejoinder, recompense, acknowledgment, answer, reaction, reversion, repetition, reverberation, reappearance, reentrance, rotating, reoccurrence, rebound, recoil, reconsideration. 3. [Proceeds] profit, income, results, gain, avail, revenue, advantage, yield, accrual, acruement, interest.—*Ant.* failure, loss, disadvantage. —in return, in exchange, as payment or repayment, for or as a reward; see **pay 1, 2**.

return, v. 1. [To go back] go or come again, come back, recur, reappear, reoccur, repeat, revert, reconsider, re-enter, re-examine, reinspect, bounce back up, turn or hark back (to), retrieve or retrace one's steps, turn, rotate, revolve, renew, revive, recover, regain, rebound, circle or double or move or track or reel or turn or come back, reverberate, recoil, retrace, revisit, retire, retreat.—*Ant.* move, advance, go forward. 2. [To put or send something back] send or bring or toss or put or roll or hand or give back, restore, replace, restitute, render, reseat, re-establish, reinstate, react, recompense, refund, repay, make restitution.—*Ant.* hold, keep, hold back. 3. [To answer] reply, respond, retort; see **answer 1**. 4. [To repay] reimburse, recompense, refund; see **repay 1**. 5. [To yield a profit] pay off, show profit, pay dividends; see **pay 2**. 6. [To reflect] echo, sound, mirror; see **reflect 2, 3**.

returned, a. restored, restituted, given or gone or sent or brought or turned or come back, reappeared, recurred, reoccurred, repeated, reverted, re-entered, rotated, revolved, rebounded, reverberated, refunded, acknowledged, answered, rejoindered, repaid, yielded; see also **refused.**—*Ant.* kept, held, retained.

reunion, n. reuniting, meeting (again), rejoining, reconciliation, reconcilement, restoration, harmonizing, bringing together, healing the breach, *gettogether.

reunite, v. meet (again), reassemble, reconvene, join, rejoin, become reconciled,

have a reconciliation, be restored to one another, remarry, heal the breach, get together, patch it up, make up.—*Ant.* separate, go separate ways, be disrupted.

reveal, v. disclose, betray a confidence, make known, confess, impart, publish, lay bare, betray, avow, admit, acknowledge, give utterance to, bring or let or give or open out, make public, unfold, communicate, announce, declare, inform, notify, utter, make plain, break the news, broadcast, concede, come out with, explain, bring into the open, affirm, report, let the cat out of the bag, *blab, talk, *rat, *stool, make a clean breast of, put one's cards on the table, bring to light, show one's (true) colors, get (something) out of one's system, *give the low-down, *let on; see also **tell 1**.

revelation, n. 1. [A disclosure] discovery, announcement, betrayal; see **record 1**. 2. [Revealed divine truth] divine word, God's word, apocalypse; see **doctrine, faith 2**.

revenge, n. 1. [The act of returning an injury] vengeance, requital, reprisal, measure for measure, repayment, counterplay, sortie, retaliation, retribution, avenging, avengment, getting even; see also **attack, fight 1.**—*Ant.* **pardon,** forgiveness, excusing. 2. [The desire to obtain revenge] vindictiveness, rancor, malevolence; see **hatred**.

revenge, v. retaliate, vindicate, requite, take revenge, have accounts to settle, have one's revenge, pay back or off, make reprisal, get even with, punish for, repay (in kind), return (like for like or blow for blow), retort, match, reciprocate, square accounts, settle up, take an eye for an eye, turn the tables on, get or hit back at, fight back, be out for blood, give an exchange, give and take, give one his deserts, even (up) the score, *get, *fix, *give one his comeuppance, pay off old scores, get square with, *score off, give tit for tat, return the compliment.—*Ant.* forgive, condone, pardon.

revenue, n. 1. [Income] return, earnings, result, yield, wealth, receipts, proceeds, resources, funds, stocks, credits, dividends, interest, salary, profits, means, fruits, rents; see also **income, pay 1, 2.**—*Ant.* expenses, outgo, obligations. 2. [Governmental income] wealth, revenue, taxation; see also **income, tax 1**. Types of revenue include the following—direct tax, indirect tax, bonds, loans, customs, duties, tariff, tax surcharge, excise, property tax, income tax, inheritance and death tax, land tax, poll tax, gasoline tax, school tax, franchise, license, grants, rates, bridge and road tolls, harbor dues, special taxation, patent stamps, stamp duties, registration duties, internal revenue, tax on spirits, tobacco tax, revenue on fermented liquors, lease of land, sale of land, subsidy.

revere, *v.* venerate, regard, respect; see **admire 1.**

reverence, *n.* respect, admiration, love, regard, approval, approbation, esteem, deference, awe, fear, veneration, honor, devotion, adoration; see also **praise 2.—** *Ant.* hatred, contempt, disdain.

reverend, *n.* divine, (ordained) clergy (man), priest; see **minister 1.**

reverent, *a.* venerating, esteeming, honoring; see also **respectful.**

reversal, *n.* renunciation, repudiation, repeal; see **cancellation, refusal, withdrawal.**

reverse, *n.* 1. [The opposite] converse, other side, contrary; see **opposite.** 2. [A defeat] vanquishment, catastrophe, conquering; see **defeat.**

reverse, *v.* 1. [To turn] go back, shift, invert; see **turn 2.** 2. [To alter] turn around, modify, convert; see **change 2.** 3. [To annul] nullify, invalidate, repeal; see **cancel.** 4. [To exchange] transpose, rearrange, shift; see **exchange 1.** order.

reversed, *a.* turned (around *or* back), backward, end for end, inverted, contrariwise, out of order, regressive, retrogressive, undone, unmade.—*Ant.* ordered, established, in (proper) order.

revert, *v.* go back, reverse, recur to; see **return 1.**

review, *n.* 1. [A re-examination] reconsideration, second thought, revision, retrospection, second view, reflection, study, survey, retrospect. 2. [A critical study] survey, critique, criticism; see **examination 1.** 3. [A summary] synopsis, abstract, outline; see **summary.** 4. [A formal inspection] parade, inspection, dress parade, drill, march, procession, cavalcade, column, file, military display, march past, the once-over; see also **display.**

review, *v.* 1. [To correct] criticize, revise, re-edit; see **correct 1.** 2. [To inspect] analyze, re-examine, check thoroughly; see **examine.**

revise, *v.* reconsider, rewrite, correct; see **edit.**

revised, *a.* corrected, edited, revisioned, amended, overhauled, improved, altered, changed, rectified, polished, redone, rewritten, reorganized, restyled, emended.

revision, *n.* re-examination, edition, editing; see **correction.**

revival, *n.* 1. [The act of reviving] renewal, renascence *or* renaissance, refreshment, arousal, awakening, rebirth, reversion, resurrection, enkindling, resto-

ration, invigoration, vivification, resuscitation, reawakening, improvement, freshening, recovery, cheering, consolation. 2. [An evangelical service] evangelistic meeting, preaching; see **ceremony.**

revive, *v.* 1. [To give new life] enliven, enkindle, refresh, renew, vivify, animate, reanimate, resuscitate, recondition, rejuvenate, bring to *or* around, wake up, resurrect, make whole, exhilarate, energize, invigorate, put *or* breathe new life into, bring to, reproduce, regenerate, restore, touch up, repair.—*Ant.* **decrease,** wither, lessen. 2. [To take on new life] come around, freshen, improve, recover, flourish, awake, reawake, rouse, arouse, strengthen, overcome, come to life, grow well, be cured.—*Ant.* die, faint, weaken.

revoke, *v.* recall, retract, disclaim; see **cancel.**

revolt, *n.* uprising, mutiny, sedition; see **revolution 2.**

revolt, *v.* 1. [To rebel] mutiny, rise up, resist; see **rebel.** 2. [To repel] sicken, offend; nauseate; see **disgust.**

revolting, *a.* awful, loathsome, repulsive; see **offensive 2, shameful 1, 2.**

revolution, *n.* 1. [A complete motion about an axis] rotation, spin, turn, revolving, circuit, round, whirl, gyration, circumvolution, cycle, roll, reel, twirl, swirl, pirouette. 2. [An armed uprising] revolt, rebellion, mutiny, insurrection, riot, anarchy, outbreak, *coup (d'état)* (French), destruction, overturn, upset, overthrow, reversal, rising, crime, violence, bloodshed, turbulence, insubordination, disturbance, reformation, plot, underground activity, guerrilla activity, public unrest, upheaval, tumult, disorder, foment, turmoil, uproar, uprising, row, strife, strike, *Putsch* (German), subversion, breakup, secession; see also **change 2.—***Ant.* law, order, control.

revolutionary, *a.* 1. [Concerned with a revolution] rebellious, revolting, mutinous, insurrectionary, destructive, anarchistic, subverting, insurgent, overturning, upsetting, destroying, breaking up, convulsive, subversive, seceding, riotous, agitating, disturbing, working underground, treasonable.—*Ant.* **patriotic,** loyal, constructive. 2. [New and unusual] novel, advanced, forward; see **unusual 2.**

revolutionary, *n.* revolutionist, traitor, insurrectionist; see **rebel.**

revolutionize, *v.* recast, remodel, refashion; see **reform 1.**

revolve, *v.* spin, rotate, twirl; see **turn 1.**

revolver, *n.* automatic, gun, *rod; see **pistol.**

reward, *n.* 1. [Payment] compensation, remuneration, recompense; see **pay 1, 2.**

2. [A prize] premium, bonus, award; see prize.

reward, *v.* compensate, repay, remunerate; see **pay 1.**

rewrite, *v.* edit, fill out, cut; see edit.

rhyme, *n.* verse, rhyming verse, vowel-chime; see poetry.

rhythm, *n.* swing, accent, rise and fall; see beat **2.**

rhythmic, *a.* melodious, measured, balanced; see **musical 1, regular 3.**

rib, *n.* **1.** [One part of the bony frame of the thorax] true rib, false rib, floating rib; see bone. **2.** [A rod] girder, bar, strip; see **rod 1, support 2. 3.** [A ridge] fin, nervure, vaulting; see sense 2.

ribbon, *n.* strip, trimming, decoration; see band **1.**

rich, *a.* **1.** [Possessed of wealth] wealthy, moneyed, affluent, well-to-do, well provided for, worth a million, well off, well fixed, in clover, *swimming in gravy, *in the money.—*Ant.* poor, poverty-stricken, destitute. **2.** [Sumptuous] luxurious, magnificent, resplendent, lavish, embellished, ornate, costly, expensive, splendid, superb, elegant, gorgeous, valuable, precious, extravagant, grand; see also beautiful.—*Ant.* cheap, plain, simple. **3.** [Fertile] exuberant, lush, copious, plentiful, generous, fruitful, profuse, luxuriant, teeming, abundant, prolific, productive, fruit-bearing, bearing, propagating, yielding, breeding, superabounding, prodigal; see also fertile.—*Ant.* sterile, unfruitful, barren. **4.** [Having great food value] nourishing, luscious, sweet, fatty, oily, nutritious, sustaining, strengthening, satisfying; see also healthful.—*Ant.* inadequate, not nourishing, deficient.

riches, *n.* fortune, possessions, money; see wealth **2.**

richness, *n.* copiousness, bounty, abundance; see plenty.

rickety, *a.* infirm, shaky, fragile; see weak **2.**

ricochet, *v.* reflect, rebound, glance off; see bounce.

rid, *a.* relieved, quit, delivered; see free **2.** —be rid of, be freed, evade, have done with; see escape. —get rid of, clear, relieve, shed; see free.

rid, *v.* clear, relieve, shed; see free.

riddle, *n.* problem, question, knotty question, doubt, quandary, entanglement, dilemma, embarrassment, perplexity, enigma, confusion, complication, complexity, intricacy, strait, labyrinth, predicament, plight, distraction, bewilderment; see also puzzle **2.**—*Ant.* simplicity, clarity, disentanglement.

ride, *n.* drive, trip, transportation; see journey.

ride, *v.* **1.** [To be transported] be carried, tour, journey, motor, drive, go for an airing, go by automobile *or* train *or* plane, sail, go by boat *or* water. **2.** [To control a beast of burden by riding] manage, guide, handle; see drive **1. 3.** [*To treat with unusual severity] persecute, harass, hound; see bother **2.**

rider, *n.* **1.** [One who rides] driver, fare, passenger, motorist, horseman, hitchhiker. **2.** [An additional clause or provision, usually not connected with the main body of the work] amendment, appendix, supplement; see addition **1.**

ridge, *n.* **1.** [A long, straight, raised portion] rib, seam; see rim. **2.** [Land forming a ridge, sense 1] mountain ridge, range, elevation; see hill.

ridicule, *n.* scorn, contempt, mockery, disdain, derision, jeer, leer, disparagement, sneer, rally, flout, fleer, twit, taunt, burlesque, caricature, satire, parody, travesty, irony, sarcasm, persiflage, farce, buffoonery, horseplay, foolery, needle, razz, rib, roast, raspberry, horse laugh.—*Ant.* praise, commendation, approval.

ridicule, *v.* gibe *or* scoff *or* sneer *or* laugh *or* rail *or* point *or* grin at, mock, taunt, banter, mimic, jeer, deride, twit, quiz, disparage, flout, deride, scorn, make sport of, make fun of, rally, burlesque, caricature, satirize, parody, cartoon, travesty, run down, make fun of, put down, raz, rib, pull one's leg, roast, pan. —*Ant.* encourage, approve, applaud.

ridiculous, *a.* ludicrous, absurd, preposterous; see funny **1, unusual 2.**

rifle, *n.* repeating, twenty-two (rifle), carbine, automatic; see gun, machine gun.

rig, *n.* tackle, apparatus, gear; see equipment.

right, *a.* **1.** [Correct] true, precise, accurate, exact, sure, certain, determined, proven, factual, correct; see also accurate **2, valid 1. 2.** [Just] lawful, legitimate, honest; see fair **1. 3.** [Suitable] apt, proper, appropriate; see fit **1. 4.** [Sane] reasonable, rational, sound; see sane. **5.** [Justly] fairly, evenly, equitably, honestly, decently, sincerely, legitimately, lawfully, conscientiously, squarely, impartially, objectively, reliably, dispassionately, without bias, without prejudice; see also justly **1. 6.** [Straight] directly, undeviatingly, immediately; see direct **1. 7.** [Opposite to left] dextral, dexter, righthanded, clockwise, on the right.—*Ant.* left, sinistral, counterclockwise.

right, *n.* **1.** [A privilege] prerogative, immunity, exemption, license, benefit, advantage, favor, franchise, preference, priority; see also **freedom 2. 2.** [Justice] equity, freedom, liberty, independence, emancipation, enfranchisement, self-determination, natural expectation; see also **fairness. 3.** [The part opposite the left] right hand, dexter, right side, strong side, active side. —**by rights**, properly, justly, suitable; see **rightly.** —**in one's own right**, individually, acting as one's own agent, by one's own authority; see **independently. —in the right**, correct, true, accurate; see **valid 1.**

right, v. **1.** [To make upright] set or bring or put up, make straight, balance; see **straighten, turn 2. 2.** [To repair an injustice] adjust, correct, repair, restore, vindicate, do justice, recompense, reward, remedy, rectify, mend, amend, set right; see also **repair.**—Ant. **wrong,** hurt, harm.

right away, a. presently, directly, without delay; see **immediately, now.**

righteous, a. **1.** [Virtuous] just, upright, good, honorable, honest, worthy, exemplary, noble, right-minded, goodhearted, dutiful, trustworthy, equitable, scrupulous, conscientious, ethical, fair, impartial, fairminded, commendable, praiseworthy, guiltless, blameless, sinless, peerless, sterling, matchless, deserving, laudable, creditable, charitable, philanthropic, having a clear conscience; see also **reliable.**—Ant. **corrupt,** sinful, profligate. **2.** [Religiously inclined] devout, pious, saintly, godly, godlike, angelic, devoted, reverent, reverential, faithful, fervent, strict, rigid, devotional, zealous, spiritual; see also **holy 1, religious 2.**—Ant. **bad,** impious, irreligious. **3.** [Conscious of one's own virtue] self-righteous, hypocritical, self-esteeming; see **egotistic.**

righteousness, n. **1.** [Justice] uprightness, nobility, fairness; see **honor 1. 2.** [Devotion to a sinless life] piety, saintliness, godliness; see **devotion.**

rightful, a. proper, just, honest; see **fair 1, legal, permitted.**

rightfully, a. lawfully, justly, fairly, properly, truly, equitably, honestly, impartially, fittingly, legitimately, in all conscience, in equity, by right, in reason, objectively, according to his due, *fair and square, *on the level, by right(s); see also **legally.**

rightly, a. justly, properly, correctly; see **well 2.**

rigid, a. **1.** [Stiff] unyielding, inflexible, solid; see **firm 1. 2.** [Strict] exact, rigorous, firm; see **severe 1, 2. 3.** [Fixed] set, unmoving, solid; see **definite 1, determined.**

rigorous, a. harsh, austere, uncompromising; see **severe 1.**

rim, n. edge, border, verge, brim, lip, brink, top, margin, line, outline, band, ring, strip, brow, curb, ledge, skirt, fringe, hem, limit, confine, end, terminus. —Ant. **center,** middle, interior.

rind, n. peel, hull, shell, surface, coating, crust, bark, cortex, integument; see also **skin.**—Ant. **inside,** center, interior.

ring, n. **1.** [A circle] circlet, girdle, brim; see **circle 1, rim. 2.** [A circlet of metal] hoop, band, circle; see **jewelry.** Rings include the following—finger, wedding, engagement, guard, signet, organization, umbrella, ankle, nose, key, harness, napkin, bracelet, earring, ear drop. **3.** [A close association, often corrupt] cabal, combine, party, bloc, faction, group, gang, monopoly, cartel, corner, pool, trust, syndicate, *racket, *gang, *push, *string; see **organization 3. 4.** [Pugilism] prize fighting, boxing, professional fighting; see **sport 3. 5.** [A ringing sound] clank, clangor, jangle; see **noise 1.** —*give someone a ring**, call (up), phone, speak to or with; see **telephone.** —*run rings around**, excel, overtake, beat; see **pass 1.**

ring, v. **1.** [To encircle] circle, rim, surround, encompass, girdle, enclose or inclose, move around, loop, gird, belt, confine, hem in. **2.** [To cause to sound] clap, clang, bang, beat, toll, strike, pull, punch, buzz, play, resound, reverberate, peal, chime, tinkle, jingle, jangle, vibrate, chime, clang, *sound the brass; see also **sound 1. 3.** [To call by ringing] give a ring, call (out), ring (up); see **summon.**

rinse, v. clean, flush, dip (in water); see **soak 1, wash 2.**

riot, n. confusion, uproar, tumult; see **disorder 2, disturbance 2, protest.** —**run riot**, revolt, riot, fight; see **rebel 1.**

riot, v. revolt, stir up trouble, fight in the streets; see **rebel 1.**

rip, n. rent, cleavage, split; see **tear.**

rip, v. rend, split, cleave, rive, tear, shred; see also **cut 1.**

ripe, a. **1.** [Ready to be harvested] fully grown, fully developed, ruddy, red, yellow, plump, filled out, matured, ready. —Ant. **green,** undeveloped, half-grown. **2.** [Improved by time and experience] mellow, wise, perfected; see **mature. 3.** [Ready] prepared, seasoned, consummate, perfected, finished, usable, fit, conditioned, prime, available, on the mark, completed; see also **ready 2.**—Ant. **unfit,** unready, unprepared.

ripen, v. develop, evolve, advance; see **grow 2.**

ripple, v. fret, curl, break; see **wave 3.**

rise, n. **1.** [The act of rising] ascent,

mount, lift; see **climb. 2.** [An increase] augmentation, growth, enlargement, multiplication, heightening, intensifying, stacking up, piling up, addition, accession, inflation, acceleration, doubling, advance; see also **increase.—**_Ant._ reduction, decrease, lessening. **3.** [Source] beginning, commencement, start; see **origin 2.** —**"get a rise out of,** tease, provoke, annoy; see **bother 2.** —**give rise to,** initiate, begin, start; see **cause.**

rise, _v._ **1.** [To move upward] ascend, mount, climb, scale, surmount, soar, tower, rocket, surge, sweep upward, lift, get _or_ bob _or_ move _or_ push _or_ reach _or_ come _or_ go up, surge, sprout, grow, rear, uprise, blast off, curl upward; see also **fly 1.—**_Ant._ fall, drop, come down. **2.** [To get out of bed] get up, rise up, wake; see **arise 1. 3.** [To increase] grow, swell, intensify, mount, enlarge, spread, expand, augment, heighten, enhance, distend, inflate, pile _or_ stack up, multiply, accelerate, speed up, add to, wax, advance, raise, double; see also **increase.—**_Ant._ decrease, lessen, contract. **4.** [To begin] spring, emanate, issue; see **begin 2. 5.** [To improve one's station] prosper, flourish, thrive; see **improve 1. 6.** [To stand] be erected, be built, be placed, be located, be put up, go up, be founded, have foundation, be situated; see also **stand 1. 7.** [To swell; _said usually of dough or batter_] inflate, billow, bulge; see **swell.**

rising, _a._ climbing, ascending, going _or_ moving _or_ surging _or_ spiraling _or_ swinging _or_ slanting _or_ inclining up _or_ aloft, mounting, accelerating, on the rise, in ascension, upcoming, upswinging, *topping out; see also **growing.**

risk, _n._ **1.** [Danger] hazard, peril, jeopardy; see **danger. 2.** [The basis of a chance] contingency, opportunity, prospect; see **chance 1, uncertainty 1.** —**run a risk,** take a chance, gamble, venture; see **risk.**

risk, _v._ gamble (on), hazard, venture, run the risk _or_ chance _or_ hazard, do at one's own peril, hang by a thread, play with fire, go out of _or_ beyond _or_ over one's depth, be caught short, *bell the cat, make an investment, take the liberty, lay oneself open to, *pour money into, *go through fire and water, leave to luck, expose oneself, leap before one looks, *fish in troubled waters, *skate on thin ice, defy danger, *live in a glass house.

risky, _a._ perilous, precarious, hazardous; see **dangerous, unsafe.**

risque, _a._ indelicate, spicy, suggestive; see **lewd 2.**

rite, _n._ observance, service, ritual; see **ceremony 2, custom 2.**

ritual, _n._ observance, rite, act; see **ceremony 2, custom 2.**

rival, _a._ competing, striving, combatant, combatting, emulating, vying, opposing, disputing, contesting, contending, conflicting, battling, equal.—_Ant._ **helpful,** aiding, assisting.

rival, _n._ emulator, competitor, antagonist; see **opponent 1.**

rival, _v._ approach, match, compare with; see **equal.**

rivalry, _n._ competition, emulation, striving, contest, vying, struggle, battle, contention, opposition, dispute; see also **fight 1.—**_Ant._ **co-operation,** combination, conspiracy.

river, _n._ stream, flow, course, current, tributary, rivulet, river system, creek, brook, watercourse. Famous rivers include the following—Seine, Rhône, Loire, Thames, Severn, Avon, Clyde, Danube, Rhine, Elbe, Don, Volga, Vistula, Nile, Euphrates, Tigris, Ganges, Indus, Irrawaddy, Yellow, Yangste-Kiang, Congo, Zambesi, St. Lawrence, Saskatchewan, Mississippi, Missouri, Ohio, Platte, Delaware, Columbia, Gila, Colorado, Snake, Hudson, Rio Grande, Amazon, Orinoco, La Plata.

road, _n._ **1.** [A strip prepared for travel] path, way, highway, roadway, street, avenue, thoroughfare, boulevard, highroad, drive, terrace, parkway, byway, lane, alley, alleyway, crossroad, viaduct, subway, paving, slab, turnpike, trail, post road, post way, secondary road, market road, national highway, **state** highway, county road, military road, Roman road, freeway, *(the main) drag. **2.** [A course] scheme, way, plans; see **plan 2.** —**on the road,** on tour, traveling, on the way; see **en route.** —**"one for the road,** cocktail, nightcap, toast; see **drink 2.**

roam, _v._ ramble, range, stroll, rove, walk, traverse, stray, straggle, meander, prowl, tramp, saunter, knock _or_ bat around, scour, straggle, gallivant, struggle along, *traipse, hike; see also **travel.**

roar, _n._ bellow, shout, boom, thunder, howl, bay, bawl, yell, bluster, uproar, din, clash, detonation, explosion, barrage, reverberation, rumble; see also **cry 1, 2, noise 1.—**_Ant._ **silence,** whisper, sigh.

roar, _v._ bellow, shout, boom, thunder, howl, bay, bawl, yell, rumble, drum, detonate, explode, reverberate, resound, re-echo; see also **cry 3, sound 1.**

roast, _v._ toast, broil, barbecue; see **cook.**

rob, _v._ thieve, take, burglarize, strip, plunder, deprive of, withhold from, defraud, cheat, swindle, pilfer, break into, hold up, stick up, purloin, filch, lift, abscond with, embezzle, pillage, sack, loot, *snitch, *pinch, *swipe, *cop; see also **steal.**

robber, *n.* thief, burglar, cheat, plunderer, pillager, bandit, pirate, raider, forager, thug, desperado, forger, hold-up man, second-story man, privateer, buccaneer, swindler, highwayman, bank robber, pilferer, shoplifter, cattle-thief, housebreaker, pickpocket, freebooter, marauder, brigand, pickpurse, sharper, safecracker, fence, *rustler, *crook, *con man, *blaster, *clip artist, *chiseler, *paper hanger, *swagman, *stick-up man; see also **criminal, rascal.**

robbery, *n.* burglary, larceny, thievery; see **crime.**

robe, *n.* gown, dress, garment, costume, mantle, draperies, covering, cape, dressing gown, bathrobe, negligee, tea gown, kimono, house gown; see also **clothes.**

robot, *n.* 1. [A mechanical man] automaton, android, Frankenstein *or* mechanical monster, humanoid, thinking machine. 2. [A person who resembles a machine] slave, menial, scullion; see **laborer.**

robust, *a.* hale, hearty, sound; see **healthy.**

rock, *n.* 1. [A solidified form of earth] stone, mineral mass, dike, mineral body, earth crust; see also **metal, mineral.** Rocks include the following—igneous, sedimentary *or* stratified, metamorphic; concretion, gypsum, alabaster, limestone, freestone, sandstone, conglomerate, marble, dolomite, chalk, soapstone, slate, shale, granite, lava, pumice, basalt, quartz, obsidian, rhyolite, ironstone, gneiss, tufa, schist. 2. [A piece of rock, sense 1] stone, boulder, cobblestone, pebble, fieldstone, cliff, crag, promontory, scarp, escarpment, reef, chip, flake, sliver, building stone, paving block, slab. 3. [Anything firm or solid] defense, support, Rock of Gibralter; see **foundation 2.** 4. [Lively dance music] rock and roll, popular *or* modern *or* teenage dance, rhythm and blues; see **dance 1, music 1.** —*on the rocks,* 1. bankrupt, poverty-stricken, impoverished; see **poor 1, ruined 3,** 2. over ice cubes, undiluted, straight; see **strong 8.**

rock, *v.* sway, vibrate, reel, totter, swing, move, push and pull, agitate, roll, shake, shove, jolt, jiggle, quake, convulse, tremble, undulate, oscillate, quiver, quaver, wobble; see also **wave 3.**

rock-bottom, *a.* lowest, hopeless, way down; see **poor 2, worst.** —*hit rock bottom,* drop, not succeed, plunge; see **fail 1, fall 1.**

rocket, *n.* projectile, missile, retrorocket,

flying missile. Kinds of rockets include the following—intercosmic, air-to-ground (ATG), ground-to-air (GTA), barrage rocket, high velocity aircraft rocket (HVAR), ship-to-shore (STS), air-to-air, surface-to-air, lunar excursion module (LEM).

rocking chair, *n.* easy chair, arm chair, rocker; see also **chair 1, furniture.**

rocky, *a.* stony, flinty, hard, inflexible, solid, petrified, ragged, jagged, rugged; see also **stone.**—*Ant.* soft, flexible, sandy.

rod, *n.* 1. [A rodlike body] staff, bar, pole, wand, stave, baton, spike, pin, rodule, cylinder, bacillus, cylindrical object, rodlet, scepter, twig, switch, whip, stock, stalk, trunk; see also **stick.** 2. [A fishing rod] pole, rod and reel, tackle; see **equipment.**

rodent, *n.* Common varieties of rodents include the following— rat, mouse, squirrel, chipmunk, beaver, porcupine, rabbit, muskrat, prairie dog, gopher, marmot, ground hog, woodchuck, ground squirrel, chinchilla, mole, hare, guinea pig.

rodeo, *n.* riding unbroken horses, rounding up cattle, roundup, features of a roundup. Some rodeo events include the following—broncobusting, bulldogging, closed event, re-riding, calf-roping, cutting (out steers).

rogue, *n.* outlaw, problem, miscreant; see **criminal.**

role, *n.* function, task, part, character, title role, impersonation, leading man, leading woman, hero, heroine, ingenue, performance, presentation, acting, characterization, execution.

roll, *n.* 1. [The act of rolling] turn, turning over, revolution, rotation, wheeling, trundling, whirl, gyration. 2. [A relatively flat object rolled upon itself] scroll, volute, spiral, coil, whorl, convolution, fold, shell, cone, cornucopia. 3. [A long, heavy sound] thunder, roar, drumbeat; see **noise 1.** 4. [A small, fine bread] Types of rolls include the following— Parker House, potato, butter, finger, cinnamon, sweet, crescent, French, clover-leaf, poppy-seed, dinner, hot cross bun; see also **bread, pastry.** 5. [A list] register, table, schedule; see **catalogue, index 2, list, record 2.**

roll, *v.* 1. [To move by rotation, or in rotating numbers] rotate, come around, swing around, wheel, come in turn, circle, alternate, follow, succeed, be in sequence, follow in due course; see also **move 1, turn 1.** 2. [To revolve] turn (over), pivot, spin; see **sense 1.** 3. [To make into a roll] bend, curve, arch; see **twist.** 4. [To smooth with a roller] press, level, flatten, spread, pulverize, grind.—*Ant.* cut, roughen, toss up. 5.

[To flow] run, wave, surge; see also **flow. 6.** [To produce a relatively deep, continuous sound] reverberate, resound, echo; see also **roar, sound 1. 7.** [To function] work, go, start production; see **operate 2.**

rolled, *a.* **1.** [Made into a roll] twisted, folded, curved, bent, bowed, coiled, spiraled, arched, voluted, convoluted.—*Ant.* spread, unrolled, opened out. **2.** [Flattened] pressed, leveled, evened; see **flat 1, smooth 1.**

roll in, *v.* **1.** [To arrive] enter, land, disembark; see **arrive. 2.** [To accumulate] mass, collect, assemble; see **accumulate.**

Roman, *a.* Latin, classic, classical, late classic, Augustan, ancient, Italic.

romance, *n.* **1.** [A courtship] enchantment, passion, facsination; see **love 1. 2.** [A tale of love and adventure] adventure story, novel, fiction; see **story.**

romantic, *a.* **1.** [Referring to love and adventure] adventurous, novel, daring, charming, enchanting, lyric, poetic, fanciful, chivalrous, courtly, knightly. **2.** [Referring to languages descending from Latin; *often capital*] romanic, romance, Mediterranean, French, Italian, Spanish; see **language 1.**

romp, *v.* gambol, celebrate, frolic; see **play 1, 2.**

roof, *n.* cover, shelter, tent, house, habitation, home.

room, *n.* **1.** [Space] vastness, reach, sweep; see **extent. 2.** [An enclosure] chamber, apartment, cabin, cubicle, cubiculum, niche, vault. Rooms include the following—living, dining, sitting, drawing, reception, bed, music, play, bath, guest, family, furnace, waiting, board *or* conference, cupboard, foyer, vestibule, study, library, den, kitchen, hall, master bedroom, parlor, wardrobe, closet, press, pantry, basement, cellar, attic, garret, anteroom, dormitory, alcove, ward, office, breakfast nook, nursery, studio, schoolroom, loft. **3.** [The possibility of admission] opening, place, resignation; see **vacancy 2. 4.** [A rented sleeping room] quarters, lodgings, studio; see **apartment.**

roomer, *n.* lodger, occupant, dweller; see **renter, tenant.**

roommate, *n.* comrade, bed-fellow, roomie *or* roomy; see **friend.**

root, *n.* **1.** [An underground portion of a plant] Types of roots include the following—conical, napiform, fusiform, fibrous, moniliform, nodulose, tuberous, adventitious, prop, aerial, tap. **2.** [The cause or basis] source, reason, motive; see **origin 2, 3. —take root,** begin growing, start, commence; see **grow 3.**

rooted, *a.* grounded, based (on), fixed (in); see **firm 1.**

rope, *n.* cord, cordage, braiding, string, thread, strand, tape, cord, lace, cable, hawser, lariat, lasso, line, tow *or* towline *or* tow chain. **—at the end of one's rope,** desperate, despairing, in despair; see **extreme 2, hopeless 2. —*give someone enough rope,** permit, give freedom, concede; see **allow 1. —*know the ropes,** be experienced, comprehend, understand; see **know 1. —*on the ropes,** near collapse, close to ruin, in danger; see **endangered.**

rose, *a.* rose-colored, rosy, flushed; see **pink, red.**

rose, *n.* Classes of roses include the following—wild, tea, climbing tea, hybrid tea, hybrid perpetual, sweet briar, shrub, multiflora, floribunda, musk, cabbage, cinnamon, eglantine, rambler; see also **flower.**

roster, *n.* names, subscribers, program; see **catalogue, list, index 2.**

rosy, *a.* **1.** [Rose-colored] colored, deep pink, pale cardinal; see **pink, red. 2.** [Promising] optimistic, favorable, cheerful; see also **hopeful 2.**

rot, *n.* **1.** [The process of rotting] decomposition, corruption, disintegration; see **decay. 2.** [Nonsense] trash, silliness, foolishness; see **nonsense 1.**

rot, *v.* decay, disintegrate, decompose; see **spoil.**

rotate, *v.* twist, wheel, revolve; see **move 1, turn 1.**

rotation, *n.* turn, circumrotation, circle; see **revolution 1.**

rotten, *a.* **1.** [Having rotted] bad, rotting, putrifying, decaying, putrified, spoiled, decomposed, decayed, offensive, disgusting, rancid, fecal, rank, foul, corrupt, polluted, infected, loathsome, over-ripe, bad-smelling, putrid, crumbled, disintegrated, stale, noisome, smelling, fetid, noxious.—*Ant.* fresh, unspoiled, good. **2.** [Not sound] unsound, defective, impaired; see **weak 2. 3.** [Corrupt] contaminated, polluted, filthy, tainted, defiled, impure, sullied, unclean, soiled, debauched, blemished, morbid, infected, dirtied, depraved, tarnished; see also **dirty.**—*Ant.* pure, clean, healthy.

rough, *a.* **1.** [Not smooth] unequal, broken, coarse, choppy, ruffled, uneven, ridged, rugged, irregular; not sanded *or* smoothed *or* finished, etc.; unfinished, not completed, lacking *or* needing the finishing touches, bumpy, rocky, stony, jagged, grinding, knobby, sharpening, cutting, sharp, crinkled, crumpled, rumpled, scraggly, scraggy, hairy, shaggy, hirsute, bushy, tufted, bearded, woolly, unshaven, unshorn, gnarled, knotty, bristly.—*Ant.* level, flat, even. **2.** [Not gentle] harsh, strict, stern; see **severe** 2. 3. [Crude] boorish, uncivil, uncultivated; see **rude** 1. 4. [Not quiet] buffeting, stormy, tumultuous; see **turbulent**. 5. [Unfinished] incomplete, imperfect, uncompleted; see **unfinished**. 6. [Approximate] inexact, unprecise, uncertain; see **approximate**.

rough draft, *n.* outline, blueprint, first draft; see **plan** 1.

roughly, *a.* 1. [Approximately] about, in round numbers, by guess; see **approximately**. 2. [In a brutal manner] coarsely, cruelly, inhumanly; see **brutally**.

roughness, *n.* 1. [The quality of being rough on the surface] unevenness, coarseness, brokenness, bumpiness, break, crack, (ragged) edge, irregularity, scratch, nick, raggedness, jaggedness, wrinkledness, shagginess, bushiness, beardedness, hairiness, bristling, wooliness.—*Ant.* regularity, smoothness, evenness. 2. [The quality of being rough in conduct] harshness, severity, hardness; see **rudeness**.

round, *a.* 1. [Shaped like a globe *or* disk] spherical, globular, orbicular, globeshaped, ball-shaped, domical, circular, cylindrical, ringed, annular, oval, diskshaped. 2. [Curved] arched, rounded, bowed, looped, recurved, incurved, coiled, curled. 3. [Approximate] rough, in tens, in hundreds; see **approximate**.

round, *n.* 1. [A round object] ring, orb, globe; see **circle** 1, **rim**. 2. [A period of action] bout, course, whirl, cycle, circuit, routine, performance; see also **sequence** 1, **series**. 3. [A unit of ammunition] cartridge, charge, load; see **ammunition**, **bullet**, **shot** 1.

round, *prep.* about, near, in the neighborhood of, close to; see also **almost**, **approximately**, **around**.

round, *v.* 1. [To turn] whirl, wheel, spin; see **turn** 1. 2. [To make round] curve, convolute, bow, arch, bend, loop, whorl, shape, form, recurve, coil, fill out, curl, mold.—*Ant.* straighten, flatten, level.

roundness, *n.* fullness, completeness, circularity, oneness, inclusiveness, wholeness.

round off, *v.* approximate, round off by tens, hundreds, etc.; accept rough figure for; see **estimate**.

round out, *v.* expand, fill in *or* up *or* out, enlarge; see **grow** 1.

rouse, *v.* 1. [To waken] arouse, raise, awake; see **awaken**, **wake** 1. 2. [To stimulate] stimulate, urge, provoke; see **animate**, **excite**.

route, *n.* 1. [A course being followed] way, course, path, track, beat, tack, divergence, detour, digression, meandering, rambling, wandering, circuit, round,

rounds, range; see also **road** 1. 2. [A projected course] map, plans, plot; see **plan** 2, **program** 2.

routine, *a.* usual, customary, methodical; see **conventional** 1, **habitual** 1.

routine, *n.* round, cycle, habit; see **method** 2, **system** 2.

rove, *v.* walk, meander, wander; see **roam**.

row, *n.* series, order, file; see **line** 1. —in a row, in succession, successively, in a line; see **consecutive**.

rowdy, *a.* rebellious, rude, mischievous; see **lawless** 2, **unruly**.

royal, *a.* 1. [Pertaining to a king or his family] high, elevated, highborn, monarchic, reigning, regnant, regal, ruling, dominant, absolute, imperial, sovereign, supreme; see also sense 2, **noble** 3. 2. [Having qualities befitting royalty] great, grand, stately, lofty, illustrious, renowned, eminent, superior, worthy, honorable, dignified, chivalrous, courteous, kingly, great-hearted, large-hearted, princely, princelike, majestic, magnificent, splendid, courtly, impressive, commanding, aristocratic, lordly, august, imposing, superb, glorious, resplendent, gorgeous, sublime; see sense 1, **noble** 1, 2, **worthy**.

royalty, *n.* kingship, sovereignty, nobility, authority, eminence, distinction, blood, birth, high descent, rank, greatness, power, supremacy, primacy, the crown, mogul, suzerainty.

rub, *n.* 1. [A rubbing action] brushing, stroke, smoothing, scraping, scouring, grinding, rasping, friction, attrition; see also **touch** 2. 2. [A difficulty] impediment, hindrance, dilemma; see **difficulty** 1, **predicament**.

rub, *v.* 1. [To subject to friction] scrape, smooth, abrade, scour, grate, grind, wear away, graze, rasp, knead, fret, massage, polish, shine, burnish, scrub, erase, rub out *or* down, file, chafe, clean. 2. [To apply by rubbing; usually with *on*] brush, cover, finish; see **paint** 2.

rubber, *a.* elastic, rubbery, soft, stretchable, stretching, rebounding, flexible, ductile, lively, buoyant, resilient.

rubbish, *n.* litter, debris, waste; see **trash** 1.

rub out, *v.* 1. [To cancel] eradicate, erase, delete; see **cancel**, **eliminate** 2. 2. [*To kill] destroy, butcher, shoot; see **kill** 1.

rude, *a.* 1. [Boorish] rustic, ungainly, awkward, crude, coarse, gross, rough, harsh, blunt, rugged, common, barbarous, lumpish, ungraceful, hulking, loutish, antic, rowdy, disorderly, rowdyish, brutish, boorish, clownish, stupid, ill-proportioned, unpolished, uncultured, uncultivated, unrefined, untrained, indecorous, unknowing, untaught, uncouth, slovenly, ill-bred, inelegant, ignorant, inexpert, illiterate, clumsy, awkward, gawky, slouching, graceless, ungraceful, lumbering, green, unacquainted, unenlightened, uneducated, vulgar, indecent, ribald, homely, outlandish, disgraceful, inappropriate.—*Ant.* cultured, urbane, suave. 2. [Not polite] churlish, sullen, surly, sharp, harsh, gruff, snarling, ungracious, unkind, ungentle, obstreperous, overbearing, crabbed, sour, disdainful, unmannerly, ill-mannered, improper, shabby, ill-chosen, discourteous, ungentlemanly, fresh, abusive, forward, loud, loud-mouthed, bold, brazen, audacious, brash, arrogant, supercilious, blustering, impudent, crass, raw, saucy, crusty, pert, unabashed, sharp-tongued, loose, mocking, barefaced, insolent, impertinent, offensive, naughty, impolite, hostile, insulting, disrespectful, scornful, flippant, presumptuous, sarcastic, defiant, outrageous, swaggering, disparaging, contemptuous, rebellious, disdainful, unfeeling, insensitive, scoffing, disagreeable, domineering, overbearing, highhanded, hypercritical, self-assertive, brutal, severe, hard, cocky, bullying, cheeky, nervy, assuming, dictatorial, magisterial, misbehaved, officious, meddling, intrusive, meddlesome, bitter, uncivilized, slandering, ill-tempered, badtempered, *sassy, *snotty, *snooty, *uppity.—*Ant.* polite, courteous, mannerly. 3. [Harsh] rough, violent, stormy; see turbulent. 4. [Approximate] guessed, surmised, unprecise; see approximate. 5. [Coarse] rough, unrefined, unpolished; see crude. 6. [Primitive] ignorant, uncivilized, barbarous; see primitive 3.

rudely, *a.* crudely, impudently, coarsely, impolitely, indecently, barbarously, roughly, harshly, bluntly, decorously, insolently, contemptuously, brutally, dictatorially, churlishly, sullenly, gruffly, discourteously, impishly, loudly, brazenly, blusteringly, crassly, unabashedly, ribaldly, spunkily, mockingly, *sassily, *snootily, *snootingly.—*Ant.* kindly, politely, suavely.

rudeness, *n.* discourtesy, bad manners, vulgarity, incivility, impoliteness, impudence, disrespect, misbehavior, barbarity, ungentlemanliness, unmannerliness, ill-breeding, crudity, brutality, barbarism, tactlessness, boorishness, unbecoming conduct, conduct not becoming a gentleman, lack *or* want of courtesy, crudeness, grossness, coarseness, bluntness, effrontery, impertinence, insolence, audacity, boldness, shamelessness, presumption, officiousness, intrusiveness,

brazenness, sauciness, defiance, contempt, back talk, ill temper, irritability, disdain, bitterness, sharpness, unkindness, ungraciousness, harshness, *gall, *sass, *lip, *nerve, *brass, *crust, *cheek.

ruffle, *v.* 1. [To disarrange] rumple, tousle, rifle; see confuse, tangle. 2. [To anger] irritate, fret, anger; see bother 1, 2.

rug, *n.* carpet, carpeting, floor covering, linoleum, straw mat, floor mat, woven mat, drugget.

rugged, *a.* 1. [Rough; *said especially of terrain*] hilly, broken, mountainous; see rough 1. 2. [Strong; *said especially of persons*] hale, sturdy, hardy; see healthy, strong 1.

ruin, *n.* 1. [The act of destruction] extinction, demolition, overthrow; see destruction 1, wreck 1. 2. [A building fallen into decay; *often plural*] remains, traces, residue, foundations, vestiges, remnants, ruins, relics, wreck, walls, detritus, rubble; see also destruction 2. 3. [The state of destruction] dilapidation, waste, wreck; see destruction 2.

ruin, *v.* 1. [To destroy] injure, overthrow, demolish; see destroy, ravage. 2. [To cause to become bankrupt] impoverish, bankrupt, beggar; see wreck.

ruined, *a.* 1. [Destroyed] demolished, overthrown, torn down, extinct, abolished, exterminated, annihilated, subverted, wrecked, desolated, ravaged, smashed, crushed, crashed, extinguished, extirpated, dissolved, *totalled (out), *screwed up; see also destroyed.—*Ant.* protected, saved, preserved. 2. [Spoiled] pillaged, harried, robbed, plundered, injured, hurt, impaired, defaced, harmed, marred, past hope, mutilated, broken, *gone to the dogs *or* devil *or* deuce, *on the rocks, *done for. —*Ant.* repaired, restored, mended. 3. [Bankrupt] pauperized, poverty-stricken, beggared, reduced, left in penury, penniless, fleeced, brought to want, *gone under, *sold up, *through the mill.—*Ant.* rich, prosperous, well off.

ruins, *n.* remains, debris, wreckage; see destruction 2, wreck 2.

rule, *n.* 1. [Government] control, dominion, jurisdiction; see government 1, 2. 2. [A regulation] edict, command, commandment; see law 3. 3. [The custom] habit, course, practice; see custom 1, 2. —**as a rule,** ordinarily, generally, usually; see regularly.

rule, *v.* 1. [To govern] conduct, control, dictate; see govern. 2. [To regulate] order, decree, direct; see manage 1.

ruled, *a.* administered, controlled, managed; see governed.

rule out, v. eliminate, not consider, recant; see **abolish, cancel.**

ruler, n. 1. [One who governs] governor, commander, chief, manager, adjudicator, monarch, regent, director; for types of rulers, sense 1, see **dictator, king 1, leader 2.** 2. [A straightedge] Types of rulers, sense 2, include the following— foot rule, yardstick, carpenter's rule, slide rule, parallel rule, stationer's rule, T-square, try square, steel square, compositor's rule *or* ruler.

ruling, n. order, decision, precept; see **law 3.**

rumble, n. reverberation, resounding, roll; see **noise 1.**

rumble, v. resound, growl, thunder; see **sound 1.**

rumor, n. report, news, tidings, intelligence, dispatch, hearsay, gossip, scandal, tittle-tattle, notoriety, noise, cry, popular report, fame, repute, grapevine, *buzz, *breeze, hoax, fabrication, suggestion, supposition, story, tale, invention, fiction, falsehood; see also **lie.**

rumored, a. reported, told, said, noised, reputed, spread abroad, gossiped, given out, noised abroad, broadcast, as they say, all over town, current, circulating, in circulation, rife, prevailing, prevalent, persisting, general, going around *or* the rounds.

rump, n. posterior, buttocks, sacrum, hind end, tail end, posterior, butt end, bottom, croup, crupper, rear, back, seat, breech, hunkers, fundament, ass, *can.

rumple, v. crumple, crush, fold; see **wrinkle.**

run, n. 1. [The act of running] sprint, pace, bound, flow, amble, gallop, canter, lope, spring, trot, dart, rush, dash, flight, escape, break, charge, swoop, race, scamper, tear, whisk, flow, fall, drop. 2. [A series] continuity, succession, sequence; see **series.** 3. [In baseball, a score] record, tally, point; see **score 1.** 4. [The average] par, norm, run of the mill; see **average.** 5. [A course] way, route, field; see **track 1.** —**in the long run,** in the final outcome, finally, eventually; see **ultimately.** —**on the run,** 1. busy, in a hurry, running; see **hurrying.** 2. retreating, defeated, routed; see **beaten 1.**

run, v. 1. [To move, usually rapidly] flow in *or* over, cut *or* chase along, fall, pour, tumble, drop, leap, spin, whirl, whiz, sail. 2. [To go swiftly by physical effort] rush, hurry, spring, bound, scurry, skitter, scramble, scoot, travel, run off *or* away, dash ahead *or* at *or* on, put on a burst of speed, go on the double, light out, have a free play, make tracks, dart (ahead), gallop, canter, lope, spring, trot, single-foot, amble, pace, flee, speed, spurt, swoop, bolt, race, shoot, tear, whisk, scamper, scuttle. 3. [To function] move, work, go; see **operate 2.** 4. [To cause to function] control, drive, govern; see **manage 1.** 5. [To extend] encompass, cover, spread; see **reach 1, surround 1.** 6. [To continue] last, persevere, go on; see **continue 1.** 7. [To compete] oppose, contest, contend with; see **compete, race 2.**

run after, v. follow, chase, hunt; see **pursue 1.**

run amok, v. go crazy *or* insane, break down, kill in a frenzy; see **kill, rage 1.**

runaway, a. out of control, delinquent, wild; see **disorderly 1.**

runaway, n. juvenile offender, lawbreaker, truant; see **delinquent.**

run away, v. 1. [To empty] flow, wash, pour out; see **drain 3.** 2. [Escape] flee, depart, steal away; see **escape, leave 1.**

run-down, n. report, outline, review; see **summary.**

run down, v. 1. [To chase] hunt, seize, apprehend; see **pursue 1.** 2. [To ridicule] make fun of, belittle, depreciate; see **ridicule.**

run dry, v. dry up, stop running, cease to flow; see **dry 2.**

(a) run for one's money, n. one's money's worth, (adequate) payment, enough; see **pay 1.**

run into, v. 1. [To collide with] bump (into), crash, have a collision; see **hit 1.** 2. [To encounter] come across, see, contact; see **meet 6.** 3. [To blend with] mingle, combine with, osmose; see **enter, join 1.**

runner, n. racer, entrant, contestant, sprinter, dash man, (long) distance runner, middle distance runner, 220-man, cross-country runner *or* man, track man, hurdler, messenger, courier, express, dispatch bearer, *cinder artist; see **athlete.**

running, a. 1. [In the act of running] pacing, racing, speeding, galloping, cantering, trotting, scampering, fleeing, bounding, whisking, sprinting, flowing, tumbling, falling, pouring. 2. [In the process of running] producing, operating, working, functioning, proceeding, moving, revolving, guiding, conducting, administering, going, in operation, in action, executing, promoting, achieving, transacting, determining, bringing about. 3. [Extending] spreading, reaching, encompassing; see **extending.**

run-off, n. spring run-off, drainage, surplus water; see **flow, river, water 1.**

run off, v. 1. [To pour out] empty, exude, draw off; see **drain 3.** 2. [To abandon] depart, flee, go; see **leave 1.** 3.

[To produce] turn out, make, publish; see **manufacture, print 2.**

run-of-the-mill, *a.* popular, mediocre, ordinary; see **common 1.**

run out, *v.* 1. [To squander] lose, dissipate, exhaust; see **waste 2.** 2. [To stop] expire, finish, end; see **stop 2.** 3. [To become exhausted] weaken, wear out, waste away; see **tire 1.** 4. [To go away] go, depart, run away; see **abandon 2, escape, leave 1.** 5. [To pour out] flow, empty, leak; see **drain 3.** 6. [To pass] elapse, slip by, glide; see **pass 2.** 7. [To remove physically] dislodge, throw out, put out; see **eject.**

run over, *v.* trample on, drive over, run down; see **hit, kill.**

runt, *n.* little fellow, degenerate, whippersnapper; see **nobody 2.**

run through, *v.* 1. [To examine] check, inspect, look at; see **examine.** 2. [To spend] waste, squander, lose; see **spend 1.**

rupture, *n.* hole, separation, crack; see **break 1, tear.**

rupture, *v.* crack, tear, burst; see **break.**

rural, *a.* rustic, farm, agricultural, ranch, pastoral, bucolic, backwoods, country, agrarian, agronomic, suburban.—*Ant.* **urban,** industrial, commercial.

rush, *n.* haste, dash, charge; see **hurry 1.**

rush, *v.* hasten, speed, hurry up; see **hurry 1.**

rushed, *a.* hurried, pressed, pressured; see **driven.**

rushing, *a.* being quick, bestirring oneself, losing no time; see **hurrying.**

Russia, *n.* Union of Soviet Socialist Republics, U.S.S.R., Great Russia, Little Russia, White Russia, Muscovy, Russia in Europe, Siberia, the Soviets, Reds, Russian Bear; see also **Asia, Europe.**

Russian, *a.* Slavic, Slav, Muscovite, Siberian.

rust, *n.* decomposition, corruption, corrosion, oxidation, decay, rot, dilapidation, breakup, wear.

rust, *v.* oxidize, become rusty, degenerate, decay, rot, corrode.

rustic, *a.* agricultural, pastoral, agrarian; see **rural.**

rusty, *a.* 1. [Decayed] unused, neglected, worn; see **old 2, weak 2.** 2. [Unpracticed] out of practce, soft, ill-qualified; see **weak 5.**

rut, *n.* 1. [A deeply cut track] hollow, trench, furrow; see **groove.** 2. [Habitual behavior] custom, habit, course, routine, practice, performance, round, circuit, circle, usage, procedure.—*Ant.* **change,** veer, mutation.

ruthless, *a.* cruel, fierce, savage, brutal, merciless, inhuman, hard, cold, fiendish, unmerciful, pitiless, grim, unpitying, tigerish, ferocious, stony-hearted, cold-blooded, remorseless, vindictive, vengeful, revengeful, rancorous, implacable, unforgiving, malevolent, surly, hard-hearted, hard, cold, unsympathetic, unforbearing, vicious, sadistic, tyrannical, relentless, barbarous, inhuman, atrocious, flagrant, terrible, abominable, outrageous, oppressive, bloodthirsty, venomous, galling.—*Ant.* **kind,** helpful, civilized.

S

Sabbath, *n.* day of rest, Saturday, Sunday; see **weekend.**

sabotage, *n.* demolition, overthrow, treason; see **destruction 1, revolution 2.**

sabotage, *v.* subvert, siege, undermine; see **attack 1, destroy.**

sac, *n.* welt, pouch, cellblister; see **sore.**

sack, *n.* sac, pouch, pocket; see **bag, container.** —*hit the sack,** go to bed *or* to rest, go to sleep, retire; see **sleep.**

sack, *v.* bag, package, pocket; see **pack 1.**

sacrament, *n.* holy observance, ceremonial, liturgy, act of divine worship, mystery *or* the mysteries. In the Roman Catholic and Eastern Orthodox churches, the seven sacraments are as follows—baptism, confirmation *or* the laying on of hands, penance, Communion *or* the Eucharist, extreme unction, holy orders, matrimony.

sacramental, *a.* sacred, pure, solemn; see **holy 1, religious 1.**

sacred, *a.* 1. [Holy] pure, pious, saintly; see **holy 1.** 2. [Dedicated] consecrated, ordained, sanctioned; see **divine.**

sacrifice, *n.* 1. [An offering to a deity] offering, tribute, atonement; see **ceremony.** 2. [A loss] discount, deduction, reduction; see **loss 1.**

sacrifice, *v.* 1. [To offer to a deity] consecrate, dedicate, give up; see **bless.** 2. [To give up as a means to an end] forfeit, forgo, relinquish, yield, suffer the loss of, renounce, spare, give up, let go, resign oneself to, sacrifice oneself, surrender, part with, go astray from. 3. [To sell at a loss] cut, reduce, sell out; see **decrease 2, lose 2.**

sad, *a.* 1. [Afflicted with sorrow] unhappy, sorry, sorrowful, downcast, dismal, gloomy, glum, pensive, heavyhearted, dispirited, dejected, depressed, desolate, troubled, melancholy, morose, grieved, pessimistic, crushed, brokenhearted, heartbroken, heartsick, despondent, careworn, rueful, anguished, disheartened, lamenting, mourning, grieving, weeping, bitter, woebegone, doleful, spiritless, joyless, heavy, crestfallen, discouraged, moody, low-spirited, despairing, hopeless, worried, downhearted, cast down, in heavy spirits, morbid, oppressed, blighted, griefstricken, foreboding, apprehensive, horrified, anxious, wretched, miserable, mournful, disconsolate, forlorn, jaundiced, out of sorts, distressed, afflicted, bereaved, repining, harassed, dreary, (down) in the dumps, in bad humor, out of humor, *cut up, *in the depths, (looking) blue, stricken with grief, making a long face, in tears, *feeling like hell, *down in the mouth.—*Ant.* **happy,** gay, cheerful. 2. [Suggestive of sorrow] pitiable, unhappy, dejecting, saddening, disheartening, discouraging, joyless, dreary, dark, dismal, gloomy, moving, touching, mournful, disquieting, disturbing, somber, doleful, oppressive, funereal, lugubrious, pathetic, tragic, pitiful, piteous, woeful, rueful, sorry, unfortunate, hapless, heart-rending, dire, distressing, depressing, grievous.

sadden, *v.* oppress, dishearten, discourage, cast down, deject, depress, break one's heart.

saddle, *n.* seat, montura, leather; see **chair 1.**

sadly, *a.* unhappily, morosely, dejectedly, wistfully, sorrowfully, gloomily, joylessly, dismally, cheerlessly, in sorrow.

sadness, *n.* sorrow, dejection, melancholy, depression, grief, despondency, oppression, downs, gloom, *blues.

safe, *a.* 1. [Not in danger] out of danger, secure, in safety *or* security, free from harm *or* danger, unharmed, safe and sound, protected, guarded, housed, screened (from danger), unmolested, unthreatened, entrenched, impregnable, invulnerable, under the protection of, saved, safeguarded, secured, defended, supported, sustained, maintained, upheld, preserved, vindicated, shielded, nourished, sheltered, fostered, cared for, cherished, watched, impervious to, patrolled, looked after, supervised, tended, attended, kept in view *or* order, surveyed, regulated, (with one's head) above water, undercover, out of harm's way *or* reach, on the safe side, *on ice, at anchor, in harbor, snug (as a bug in a rug), under lock and key.—*Ant.* **dangerous,** unsafe, risky. 2. [Not dangerous] innocent, innocuous, innoxious; see **harmless.** 3. [Reliable] trustworthy, dependable, competent; see **reliable 1, 2.**

safe, *n.* strongbox, coffer, chest, repository, vault, case, reliquary, safe-deposit box.

safekeeping, *n.* supervision, care, guardianship; see **custody, protection 2.**

safely, *a.* securely, with safety *or* impunity, without harm *or* risk *or* mishap *or* danger, harmlessly, carefully, cautiously, reliably.

safety, *n.* **1.** [Freedom from danger] security, protection, impregnability, surety, sanctuary, refuge, shelter, invulnerability. **2.** [A lock] lock mechanism, safetycatch, safety lock; see **fastener, lock 1.**

sag, *n.* depression, dip, *slump; see **hole 1.**

sag, *v.* stoop, hang down, become warped; see **bend, lean 1.**

said, *a.* pronounced, aforesaid, forenamed; see **preceding, spoken.**

sail, *n.* **1.** [Means of sailing a vessel] sheet(s), canvas, cloth; see **goods.** Sails include the following—mainsail, foresail, topsail, jib, spanker, flying jib, trysail, balloon sail, spinnaker, balloon jib. **2.** [A journey by sailing vessel] voyage, cruise, trip; see **journey.** —**set sail,** go, depart, set out; see **leave 1, sail 1.**

sail, *v.* **1.** [To travel by sailing] cruise, voyage, go alongside, bear down on, bear for, direct one's course for, crowd *or* set sail, put on sail, put to sea, sail away from, navigate, travel, make headway, lie in, make at *or* for, heave to, lay in *or* for, fetch up, bring to, bear off, close with, run down *or* in, put off *or* in. **2.** [To fly] float, soar, ride the storm, skim, glide.

sailor, *n.* seaman, mariner, seafarer, pirate, navigator, pilot, boatman, yachtsman, able-bodied seaman, Jack Tar, tar, sea-dog, limey, salt, bluejacket. Kinds and ranks of sailors include the following—*crew:* (deck) hand, stoker, cabin boy, yeoman, purser; ship's carpenter, cooper, tailor; steward, navigator, signalman, gunner, afterguard; *officers:* captain *or* commander *or* skipper, navigating officer, deck officer; first, second, third, boatswain's mate; boatswain *or* *bo's'n.

saint, *n.* a true Christian, child of God, son of God, paragon, salt of the earth, godly person, martyr, man of God, unworldly person, altruist, the pure in heart, a believer.

saintly, *a.* angelic, pious, divine; see **holy.**

sake, *n.* **1.** [End] objective, consequence, final cause; see **result.** **2.** [Purpose] score, motive, principle; see **purpose 1.** **3.** [Welfare] benefit, interest, well-being; see **advantage, welfare 1.**

salad, *n.* (salad) greens, slaw, mixture, combination. Common salads include the following—green, tossed, vegetable, tomato, potato, macaroni, fruit, bean, combination, chef's, tuna, shrimp, lobster, crab, chicken, ham, Waldorf, Caesar, pineapple, banana, molded, frozen; cole slaw.

salary, *n.* wage(s), recompense, payroll; see **pay 2.**

sale, *n.* **1.** [The act of selling] commerce, business, traffic, exchange, barter, commercial enterprise, marketing, vending, trade. **2.** [An individual instance of selling] deal, transaction, negotiation, turnover, trade, purchase, auction, disposal; see also **buying, selling 1.** **3.** [An organized effort to promote unusual selling] bargain sale, clearance, stock reduction, fire sale, unloading, dumping, remnant sale, going out of business sale, bankruptcy sale. —**for** *or* **on** *or* **up for sale,** (put) on the market, to be sold, marketable, available, (offered) for purchase, not withheld. —**on sale,** reduced, at a bargain, cut; see **cheap 1.**

sales, *n.* (sales) receipts, day's *or* month's *or* week's *or* year's sales, business; see **income.**

salesman, *n.* **1.** [A sales clerk] salesperson, seller, counterman; see **clerk 1.** **2.** [A commercial traveler] (out-of-town) representative, agent, canvasser, solicitor, seller, businessman, itinerant, field worker, traveler, traveling man, traveling salesman, Fuller Brush man, sales manager.

salesperson, *n.* salesman, saleswoman, saleslady; see **clerk.**

saliva, *n.* water, spittle, salivation, excretion, phlegm, enzyme, spit.

saloon, *n.* bar, night club, cocktail lounge, pub, beer parlor, poor man's club, joint, hangout, place; see **restaurant.**

salt, *a.* alkaline, saline, briny; see **salty.**

salt, *n.* **1.** [A common seasoning and preservative] sodium chloride, common salt, table salt, savor, condiment, flavoring, spice, seasoning. Common types of flavoring salts include the following—garlic, sea, celery, onion, barbecue, salad, seasoning, (hickory) smoked; poultry seasoning, monosodium glutamate *or* MSG, salt substitute. **2.** [Anything that provides savor] relish, pungency, smartness; see **humor 1, wit 1.** —**not worth one's salt,** good-for-nothing, bad, worthless; see **poor 2.** —**with a grain** *or* **pinch of salt,** doubtingly, skeptically, lightly; see **suspiciously.**

salt, *v.* season, make tasty, make piquant; see **flavor.**

salty, *a.* briny, brackish, pungent, alkaline, well-seasoned, flavored, well-flavored, highly flavored, sour, acrid.

salute, *v.* snap to attention, dip the colors, touch one's cap, do honor to, recognize; see also **praise 1.**

salvage, v. retrieve, recover, regain; see **save 1.**

salvation, n. 1. [The act of preservation] deliverance, liberation, emancipation; see **rescue. 2.** [A means of preservation] buckler, safeguard, assurance; see **protection 2.**

salve, n. ointment, unguent, lubricant, balm, medicine, emollient, unction, remedy, help, cure, cream.

same, a. 1. [Like another in state] equivalent, identical, corresponding; see **alike, equal. 2.** [Like another in action] similarly, in the same manner, likewise; see **alike.**

same, pron. the very same, identical object, no other or different, substitute, equivalent, similar product, synthetic product, just as good.

sameness, n. uniformity, unity, resemblance, analogy, similarity, alikeness, identity, standardization, equality, unison, no difference.

sample, n. specimen, unit, individual; see **example.**

sample, v. taste, test, inspect; see **examine, experiment.**

sanction, n. consent, acquiescence, assent; see **permission.**

sanction, v. confirm, authorize, countenance; see **approve, endorse 2.**

sanctity, n. sanctification, sacredness, piety; see **virtue 1.**

sanctuary, n. 1. [A sacred place] shrine, church, temple; see **church 1. 2.** [A place to which one may retire] asylum, resort, haven; see **shelter.**

sand, n. 1. [Rock particles] sandy soil, sandy loam, silt, dust, grit, powder, gravel, rock powder, rock flour, debris, dirt; see also **earth 2. 2.** [The beach] strand, seaside, seashore; see **shore.**

sandal, n. slipper, thong, loafer; see **shoe.**

sandwich, n. lunch, light lunch, quick lunch. Sandwiches include the following—hamburger, *burger, cheeseburger, wiener, *(hot) dog, Denver, Western, club, tuna fish, ham, chicken, roast beef, ham and egg, cheese, deviled meat, steak, submarine, bacon and cheese, toasted cheese, tomato, egg salad, lettuce, open face, peanut butter and jelly, jelly, fruit and nut.

sandy, a. 1. [Containing sand; said especially of soil] light, loose, permeable, porous, easy to work, easily worked, granular, powdery, gritty. 2. [Suggestive of sand; said especially of the hair] fair-haired, fair, blond, light, light-haired, reddish, carrot-red, sandy-red, sun-bleached, flaxen, faded.

sane, a. 1. [Sound in mind] rational, normal, lucid, right-minded, sober, sound-minded, sound, in one's right mind,

with a healthy mind, mentally sound, balanced, healthy-minded, reasonable, in possession of one's faculties.—Ant. — insane, irrational, delirious. 2. [Sensible] reasonable, open to reason, wise; see **sensible.**

sanitary, a. hygienic, wholesome, sterile; see **healthful.**

sanity, n. sound mind, rationality, healthy mind, saneness, a clear mind, clearmindedness, wholesome outlook, common sense, intelligence, reason, reasonableness, prudence, good judgment, acumen, understanding, comprehension.

sap, n. 1. [The life fluid of a plant] fluid, secretion, essence; see **liquid. 2.** [*A dupe] dolt, gull, simpleton; see **fool.**

sapling, n. scion, seedling, slip, sprig, young tree; see also **tree.**

sappy, a. 1. [Juicy] lush, succulent, watery; see **juicy. 2.** [*Idiotic] foolish, silly, illogical; see **stupid 1.**

sarcasm, n. satire, irony, banter, derision, contempt, scoffing, flouting, ridicule, burlesque, disparagement, criticism, cynicism, invective, censure, lampooning, aspersion, sneering, mockery.—Ant. flattery, fawning, cajolery.

sarcastic, a. scornful, mocking, ironical, satirical, taunting, severe, derisive, bitter, saucy, hostile, sneering, snickering, quizzical, arrogant, disrespectful, offensive, carping, cynical, disillusioned, snarling, unbelieving, corrosive, acid, cutting, scorching, captious, sharp, pert, brusque, caustic, biting, harsh, austere, grim.

Satan, n. Mephistopheles, Lucifer, Beelzebub; see **devil 1.**

satanic, a. malicious, vicious, devilish; see **sinister.**

satellite, n. 1. [A small planet that revolves around a larger one] moon, planetoid, minor planet, secondary planet, inferior planet, asteroid. 2. [A man-made object put into orbit around a celestial body] space satellite, robot satellite, unmanned satellite, body satellite, orbital rocket, artificial moon, spacecraft, moonlet, man-made moon, sputnik, satellite station.

satire, n. mockery, ridicule, caricature; see **irony.**

satisfaction, n. 1. [The act of satisfying] gratification, fulfillment, achievement; see **achievement. 2.** [The state or feeling of being satisfied] comfort, pleasure, well-being, content, contentment, gladness, delight, bliss, joy, happiness, relief, complacency, peace of mind, ease, heart's ease, serenity, contentedness, cheerfulness. 3. [Something that contributes to satisfaction, sense 2] reward, prosperity, good fortune; see **blessing 2.**

satisfactorily, a. 1. [In a satisfactory

manner] convincingly, suitably, competently; see **adequately**. 2. [Productive of satisfactory results] amply, abundantly, thoroughly; see **agreeably**.

satisfactory, *a.* adequate, satisfying, pleasing; see **enough**.

satisfied, *a.* content, happy, contented, filled, supplied, fulfilled, paid, compensated, appeased, convinced, gratified, sated, at ease, with enough of, without care, satiated.

satisfy, *v.* 1. [To make content] comfort, cheer, elate, befriend, please, rejoice, delight, exhilarate, amuse, entertain, flatter, make merry, make cheerful, gladden, content, gratify, indulge, humor, conciliate, propitiate, capture, enthrall, enliven, animate, captivate, fascinate, fill, be of advantage, gorge. 2. [To pay] repay, clear (up), disburse; see **pay 1**, **settle 7**. 3. [To fulfill] do, fill, serve the purpose, be enough, observe, perform, comply with, conform to, meet requirements, keep a promise, accomplish, complete, be adequate, be sufficient, provide, furnish, qualify, answer, serve, equip, meet, avail, suffice, fill the want, come up to, content one, appease one, *fill the bill, *pass muster, get by, *go in a pinch.—*Ant.* neglect, leave open, fail to do.

satisfying, *a.* pleasing, comforting, gratifying; see **enough, pleasant 2**.

saturate, *v.* overfill, drench, steep; see **immerse, soak 1**.

saturated, *a.* drenched, full, soggy; see **soaked, wet 1**.

saturation, *n.* fullness, soaking, overload; see **excess 1**.

sauce, *n.* appetizer, gravy, seasoning; see **flavoring, food**.

saucepan, *n.* stewpan, vessel, utensil; see **pan**.

saucer, *n.* small bowl, sauce dish, cereal dish; see **dish**.

sausage, *n.* link sausage, salami, liverwurst; see **meat**.

savage, *a.* 1. [Primitive] crude, simple, original; see **crude**. 2. [Cruel] barbarous, inhuman, brutal; see **cruel**. 3. [Wild] untamed, uncivilized, uncultured; see **uncontrolled**.

savage, *n.* bully, ruffian, animal; see **beast 2**.

savagely, *a.* cruelly, viciously, indecently; see **brutally**.

save, *v.* 1. [To remove from danger] deliver, extricate, rescue, free, set free, liberate, release, emancipate, ransom, redeem, come to the rescue of, defend.—*Ant.* leave, desert, condemn. 2. [To assure an afterlife] rescue from sin, reclaim, regenerate; see **sense 1**. 3. [To hoard] collect, store, lay up *or* apart *or* in, invest, have on deposit, amass, ac-

cumulate, gather, treasure up, store up, pile up, hide away, cache, stow *or* sock away.—*Ant.* waste, spend, invest. 4. [To preserve] conserve, keep, put up; see **preserve 2**.

saved, *a.* 1. [Kept from danger] rescued, released, delivered, protected, defended, guarded, safeguarded, preserved, reclaimed, regenerated, cured, healed, conserved, maintained, safe, secure, freed, free from harm, free from danger, unthreatened.—*Ant.* ruined, lost, destroyed. 2. [Not spent] kept, unspent, unused, untouched, accumulated, deposited, on deposit, retained, laid away, hoarded, invested, amassed, stored, spared.—*Ant.* wasted, squandered, spent.

savings, *n.* means, property, resources, funds, reserve, investment, provision, provisions, accumulation, store, riches, harvest, hoard, saving(s) account, cache, nest egg, money in the bank, provision for a rainy day.

savior, *n.* 1. [One who saves another] deliverer, rescuer, preserver; see **protector**. 2. [Christ; *often capital; usually Saviour*] Redeemer, Messiah, Friend and Helper; see **Christ**.

savor, *v.* enjoy, relish, appreciate; see **like 1**.

saw, *n.* power, circular, concave, mill, ice, crosscut, band, rip, hand, pruning, whip, buck, keyhole, back, butcher's, hack, jig; see also **tool 1**.

say, *v.* tell, speak, relate, state, announce, declare, state positively, open one's mouth, have one's say, break silence, put forth, let out, assert, maintain, express oneself, answer, respond, suppose, assume. —**to say the least**, at a minimum *or* the (very) least, to put it mildly, minimally.

saying, *a.* mentioning, making clear, revealing; see **talking**.

saying, *n.* aphorism, (wise) saw, adage, maxim, byword, motto, proverb, precept.

scab, *n.* 1. [A crust over a wound] eschar, slough, crust. 2. [One who replaces a union worker on strike] strikebreaker, traitor, apostate, deserter.

scaffold, *n.* framework, stage, structure; see **building, platform 1**.

scald, *v.* char, blanch, parboil; see **burn**.

scale, *n.* 1. [A series for measurement] rule, computation, system; see **measure 2**. 2. [A flake or film] thin coating, covering, incrustation; see **flake, layer**. 3. [A device for weighing; *often plural*] steelyard, stilliard, balance, scale beam. Varieties of scales, sense 3, include the following—beam, automatic indicating, counter, cylinder, drum, barrel, platform, spring, computing, household, miner's, assayer's, truck, jeweler's. 4. [Musical tones] range, major *or* minor scale, harmonic *or* melodic scale; see **music**. **—on a large scale**, extensively, grandly, expansively; see **generously**. **—on a small scale**, economically, in a small limited way, with restrictions; see **inadequate 1, unimportant**.

scale, *v.* 1. [To climb] ascend, surmount, mount; see **climb**. 2. [To peel] exfoliate, strip off, flake; see **peel, skin**. 3. [To measure] compare, balance, compute; see **compare 1**.

scalpel, *n.* dissecting instrument, surgical tool, blade; see **knife**.

scamper, *v.* hasten, speed, haste; see **hurry 1, run 2**.

scan, *v.* browse, thumb over, consider; see **look 2**.

scandal, *n.* shame, disgrace, infamy, discredit, slander, disrepute, detraction, defamation, opprobrium, reproach, aspersion, backbiting, gossip, eavesdropping, rumor, hearsay.—*Ant.* **praise**, adulation, flattery.

scandalize, *v.* detract, defame, backbite; see **slander**.

scandalous, *a.* infamous, disreputable, ignominious; see **shameful**.

scanty, *a.* scarce, few, pinched, meager, little, small, bare, ragged, insufficient, inadequate, slender, narrow, thin, scrimp, scrimpy, tiny, wee, sparse, diminutive, short, stingy.—*Ant.* **much**, large, many.

scar, *n.* cicatrix *or* cicatrice, cat-face, mark, blemish, discoloration, disfigurement, defect, flaw, hurt, wound, injury.

scar, *v.* cut, pinch, slash; see **hurt 1**.

scarce, *a.* limited, infrequent, not plentiful; see **rare 2, uncommon**. **—*make oneself scarce**, go, depart, run (off); see **leave 1**.

scarcely, *a.* barely, only just, scantily; see **hardly**.

scarcity, *n.* deficiency, inadequacy, insufficiency; see **lack 2, poverty 1**.

scare, *n.* fright, terror, alarm; see **fear**.

scare, *v.* panic, terrify, alarm; see **frighten**.

scared, *a.* startled, frightened, fearful; see **afraid**.

scare off *or* **away**, *v.* drive off *or* out *or* away, get rid of, dispose of; see **frighten**.

scarf, *n.* throw, sash, muffler, shawl, comforter, ascot, stole, wrapper; see also **clothes**.

scarlet, *a.* cardinal, royal red, vermilion; see **red**.

scat, *v.* be off, begone, out of the way, get out of my way *or* from under my feet, away *or* out with you, (be) off with you, get out of my sight, *scoot, get out, *beat it, get going.

scatter, *v.* 1. [To become separated] run apart, run away, go one's own way, diverge, disperse, disband, migrate, spread widely, go in different directions, blow off, go in many directions, be strewn to the four winds.—*Ant.* **assemble**, convene, congregate. 2. [To cause to separate] dispel, dissipate, diffuse, strew, divide, disband, shed, distribute, disseminate, separate, disunite, sunder, scatter to the wind, sever, set asunder.—*Ant.* **unite**, join, mix. 3. [To waste] expend, dissipate, fritter away; see **spend 1, waste 2**.

scatterbrained, *a.* silly, giddy, irrational; see **illogical, stupid 1**.

scattered, *a.* spread, strewed, rambling, sowed, sown, sprinkled, spread abroad, separated, disseminated, dispersed, strung out, distributed, widespread, diffuse, all over the place, separate, shaken out.—*Ant.* **gathered**, condensed, concentrated.

scene, *n.* spectacle, exhibition, display; see **view 1**.

scenery, *n.* landscape, prospect, spectacle; see **view 1, 2**.

scenic, *a.* beautiful, spectacular, dramatic; see **beautiful**.

scent, *n.* odor, fragrance, redolence; see **perfume, smell 1, 2**.

schedule, *n.* 1. [List] catalogue, inventory, registry; see **list, record 1**. 2. [Program] agenda, order of business, calendar; see **plan 2, program 2**. **—on** *or* **up to schedule**, on time, not lagging *or* behind, being pushed along; see **accepted, early 2, enough**.

schedule, *v.* record, register, catalogue; see **list 1**.

scheduled, *a.* listed, announced, arranged; see **planned, proposed**.

scheme, *n.* project, course of action, purpose; see **plan 2, system 2**.

scheme, *v.* intrigue, contrive, devise; see **plan 1**.

scholar, *n.* schoolboy, schoolgirl, learner; see **student**.

scholarly, *a.* erudite, cultured, studious; see **educated, learned 1**.

scholarship, *n.* scientific approach, learning, intellectualism; see **knowledge 1**.

scholastic, *a.* academic, literary, lettered; see **learned 1**.

school, *n.* 1. [An institution of learning] —Varieties of schools include the following—nursery school, elementary school, high school, secondary school, parochial school, preparatory *or* private *or* *prep school, public school, boarding school, military school, seminary, normal school, conservatory, trade school, technical school, graduate school, professional school, divinity school, art school, law school, college of arts and science *or* liberal arts *or* dentistry *or* engineering, etc., preparatory school, junior high school, senior high school, community college, junior college, the grades; see also **college, university.** 2. [Persons or products associated by common intellectual or artistic theories] party, following, circle; see **following.** 3. [A building housing a school, sense 1] schoolhouse, establishment, institution; see **building.** —**go to school,** attend school *or* kindergarten *or* college, etc.; of medicine *or* dentistry *or* liberal arts *or* pure science; matriculate; see **learn, register.**

school-age, *a.* youthful, old enough to go to school, of school age; see **childish, young 1.**

schoolbook, *n.* primer, textbook, assigned reading; see **book.**

schooling, *n.* teaching, nurture, discipline; see **education 1.**

schoolmate, *n.* roommate, comrade, classmate; see **friend.**

schoolteacher, *n.* educator, lecturer, instructor; see **teacher.**

school year, *n.* nine months, from September to June, period (that the) school *or* college *or* kindergarten, etc., is in session; see **year.**

science, *n.* 1. [An organized body of knowledge] classified information, department of learning, branch of knowledge, system of knowledge, body of fact. For commonly recognized sciences see **chemistry, mathematics, medicine 3, social science, zoology.** 2. [A highly developed skill] craftsmanship, art, deftness; see **ability.**

scientific, *a.* 1. [Objectively accurate] precise, exact, clear; see **accurate 2, objective 1.** 2. [Concerning science] experimental, deductive, methodically sound; see **logical.**

scientist, *n.* expert, specialist, investigator, laboratory technologist *or* technician, natural philosopher, student of natural history, student of natural phenomena, explorer, research worker, research assistant, learned man, serious student, Ph.D., scientific thinker. Scientists include the following—anatomist, astronomer, botanist, biologist, chemist, biochemist, geologist, geographer, mathematician, physicist, psychiatrist, psychologist, astrophysicist, ecologist, biophysicist, bacteriologist, marine botanist, oceanographer, pharmacist, chemical engineer, sanitary engineer, agronomist, entomologist, ornithologist, endocrinologist, radiologist, graphologist, geophysicist, neurologist, neurophysicist, paleontologist, mineralogist, metallurgist, anthropologist, ethnologist, archaeologist, sociologist, linguist; see also **doctor.**

scissors, *n.* shears, pair of scissors *or* shears, blades, hair scissors, paper scissors, garden shears, cutting instrument.

scoff, *v.* mock, deride, jeer; see **ridicule.**

scold, *v.* admonish, chide, **chew *or* *bawl out*, get after, lay down the law, jump on *or* all over, rebuke, censure, reprove, upbraid, reprimand, taunt, cavil, criticize, denounce, disparage, recriminate, rate, revile, rail, abuse, villify, find fault with, nag, lecture, have on the carpet, *rake over the coals, give one a talking to, chasten, preach, *tell off, keep after, *light into, put down; see also **punish.**—*Ant.* praise, commend, extoll.

scoop, *v.* ladle, shovel, bail; see **dip 1.**

scoot, *v.* dart, speed, rush; see **hasten 2, hurry 1.**

scope, *n.* reach, range, field; see **extent.**

scorch, *v.* roast, parch, shrivel; see **burn.**

scorching, *a.* fiery, searing, sweltering; see **burning, hot 1.**

score, *n.* 1. [A tally] stock, reckoning, record, average, rate, account, count, number, summation, aggregate, sum, addition, summary, amount, final tally, final account; see also **number, whole.** 2. [Written music] transcript, arrangement, orchestration; see **music 1, composition.** —**know the score,* grasp *or* know *or* understand a little *or* the elements, *etc.*; be aware (of), comprehend; see **know 1, understand 1.**

score, *v.* 1. [To make a single score] make a goal, gain *or* make *or* win a point, *rack *or* chalk up, total, calculate, reckon, tally, enumerate, count, add. 2. [To compose a musical accompaniment] orchestrate, arrange, adapt; see **compose 2.** 3. [*To purchase legally or illegally] get, procure, secure; see **buy.** 4. [A Boy Scout or Girl Scout] have (sexual) intercourse (with), sleep *or* lie with, fornicate; see **copulate.**

scorn, *v.* hold in contempt, despise, disdain; see **hate.**

scornful, *a.* contemptuous, disdainful, haughty; see **egotistic 2.**

scoundrel, *n.* rogue, scamp, villain; see **rascal.**

scour, *v.* scrub, cleanse, rub; see **clean, wash 1, 2.**

scout, *n.* 1. [One who gathers information] explorer, pioneer, outpost, runner, advance guard, precursor, patrol, reconnoiterer. 2. [A Boy Scout or Girl Scout] Degrees of scouts, sense 2, include the following—Cub, Tenderfoot, Second Class, First Class, Star, Life, Eagle, Queen's (British), bronze palm, gold palm, silver palm; Brownie, Junior, Cadette, Senior.

scowl, *v.* glower, disapprove, grimace; see **frown**.

scramble, *v.* 1. [To mix] combine, blend, interfuse; see **mix 1**. 2. [To climb hastily] clamber, push, struggle; see **climb**.

scrap, *n.* 1. [Junk metal] waste material, chips, cuttings; see **trash 1**. 2. [A bit] fragment, particle, portion; see **bit 1**, **piece 1**. 3. [*A fight] quarrel, brawl, squabble; see **fight 1**.

scrap, *v.* 1. [To discard] reject, forsake, dismiss; see **abandon 2**, **discard**. 2. [*To fight] wrangle, battle, squabble; see **fight**, **quarrel**.

scrapbook, *n.* portfolio, memorabilia, notebook; see **album**, **collection**.

scrape, *v.* abrade, scour, rasp; see **rub 1**.

scraper, *n.* grater, rasp, abrasive; see **tool 1**.

scratch, *n.* hurt, cut, mark; see **injury**, **scar**. —**from scratch**, from the start *or* the beginning, without preparation *or* a predecessor, solely; see **alone**, **original 1**.

scratch, *v.* scrape, scarify, prick; see **damage**, **hurt 1**.

scratching, *a.* grating, abrasive, rasping; see **rough 1**.

scratch the surface, *v.* touch on *or* upon, mention, skim; see **begin 1**, **2**.

scrawl, *v.* scribble, scratch, doodle; see **write 2**.

scrawled, *a.* scribbled, scratched, inscribed; see **written 2**.

scrawny, *a.* lanky, gaunt, lean; see **thin 2**.

scream, *n.* screech, outcry, shriek; see **cry 1**, **yell**.

scream, *v.* shriek, screech, squeal; see **cry 3**, **yell**.

screaming, *a.* shrieking, screeching, squealing; see **yelling**.

screen, *n.* 1. [A concealment] cloak, cover, covering, curtain, shield, envelope, veil, mask, shade. 2. [A protection] shelter, guard, security; see **cover 1**, **protection 2**.

screen, *v.* 1. [To hide] veil, conceal, mask; see **hide 1**. 2. [To choose] select, eliminate, sift; see **choose**.

screw, *n.* spiral, worm, bolt, pin; see also **fastener**. Screws include the following—jack, lead, double, drive, lag, male *or* outside, female *or* inside, right-handed, left-handed, metric, regulating, set, winged, thumb, spiral, triple, wood, machine.

*****screw**, *v.* 1. [To copulate] lie *or* sleep with, fornicate (with), seduce; see **copulate 2**. 2. [To trick *or* defeat] cheat, swindle, beat; see **defeat**, **hurt 2**, **trick**.

*****screwy**, *a.* odd, crazy, inappropriate; see **insane**, **wrong 2**.

scribble, *n.* scrawl, scrabble, scratch; see **handwriting**.

scribble, *v.* scrawl, scratch, scrabble; see **write 2**.

scrimp, *v.* limit, pinch, skimp; see **economize**.

script, *n.* 1. [Handwriting] writing, characters, chirography; see **handwriting**. 2. [Playbook] lines, text, dialogue, book, scenario.

scripture, *n.* 1. [Truth] reality, verity, final word; see **truth**. 2. [*Capital*; the Bible] the Word, Holy Writ, the Book; see **Bible**.

scrub, *a.* second-rate, unimportant, mediocre; see **poor 2**.

scrub, *v.* rub, cleanse, scour; see **clean**, **wash 1**, **2**.

scrubbed, *a.* cleaned, polished, immaculate; see **clean 1**.

scruple, *n.* compunction, qualm, uneasiness; see **doubt**.

scruples, *n.* overconscientiousness, point of honor, scrupulousness; see **attention**, **care 1**.

scrupulous, *a.* exact, punctilious, strict; see **careful**.

scrutinize, *v.* view, study, stare; see **examine**, **watch**.

scrutiny, *n.* analysis, investigation, inspection; see **examination 1**.

scuffle, *n.* struggle, shuffle, strife; see **fight 1**.

sculptor, *n.* artist, modeler, carver, stone carver, wood carver, worker in bronze (*or* metal). Major sculptors include the following—Phidias, Ghiberti, Donatello, Luca della Robbia, Michelangelo, Giovanni da Bologna, Benvenuto Cellini, Gian Lorenzo Bernini, Auguste Rodin.

sculpture, *n.* carving, modeling, carving in stone, modeling in clay, kinetic sculpture, op art, casting in bronze, woodcutting, stone carving, plastic art; see also **art**, **statue**.

scum, *n.* froth, film, impurities; see **residue**, **trash 1**.

sea, *n.* Important seas include the following—Bering, Caribbean, Baltic, North, Irish, Mediterranean, Adriatic, Ionian, Aegean, Black, Caspian, Azov, Red, White, Tasman, Okhotsk, Japan, Yellow, South China, Arabian, East China, Java, Celebes, Coral; see also **ocean**.

sea bottom, *n.* ocean *or* deep-sea floor, depths *or* bottom of the sea, offshore land(s), ocean bottom, abyssal *or* ocean depths, continental shelf, undersea topography, marine farm, tidewater; see also **ocean**. Terms for undersea topography include the following—bands, sands, seamount *or* submarine mountain, ridge, guyot, hill, tablemount, escarpment, plateau, reef, basin, canal, province, shoal, sill, channel, deep, depth, plain, trench, trough, fracture zone, rift.

seacoast, *n.* seashore, seaboard, seaside; see **shore**.

sea food, *n.* halibut, mollusk, marine life; see **fish, shellfish**.

seal, *n.* 1. [Approval] authorization, permit, allowance; see **permission**. 2. [Fastener] adhesive tape, sticker, tie; see **fastener, tape**.

sealed, *a.* secured, fixed, held together; see **firm 1, tight 2**.

seal off, *v.* quarantine, close, segregate; see **forbid, restrict**.

seam, *n.* joint, line of joining, union, stitching, line of stitching, closure, suture.

seamstress, *n.* sewer, needleworker, designer; see **tailor**.

sear, *v.* scorch, brown, toast; see **cook**.

search, *n.* exploration, quest, research; see **hunting**. —**in search of**, looking for, seeking, on the lookout (for); see **searching**.

search, *v.* explore, examine, rummage, look up and down, track down, look for, go through, probe into, scrutinize, ransack; see also **hunt 1**. —*****search me**, I do not *or* don't know, who knows? how should *or* would I know?; see **uncertainty 1**.

searching, *a.* hunting, looking (for), seeking out *or* for, pursuing, in search of, ready for, in the market (for), in need of, needing, wanting, on the lookout (for), looking out (for), *****crazy about *or* for, *****all hot for.

searchlight, *n.* arc light, beam, Half-mile Ray (trademark); see **light 3**.

sea shell, *n.* Conch, clam, oyster; see **shell 1**.

seashore, *n.* seaboard, seaside, seacoast; see **shore**.

seasick, *a.* nauseated, miserable, uneasy; see **sick**.

seaside, *n.* seaboard, seashore, seacoast; see **shore**.

season, *n.* period, term, certain months of the year; see **fall 3, spring 2, summer, winter**.

seasonal, *a.* once a season, periodically, biennial; see **annual, yearly**.

seasoned, *a.* 1. [Spicy] tangy, sharp, aromatic; see **spicy 1**. 2. [Experienced] established, settled, mature; see **able, experienced**.

seasoning, *n.* sauce, relish, spice, pungency; see also **flavoring**.

seat, *n.* 1. [A structure on which one may sit] bench, chair, stool; see **furniture**. 2. [Space in which one may sit] situation, chair, accommodation; see **place 2**. 3. [The part of the body with which one sits] buttocks, rear, breech; see **rump**. —**have** *or* **take a seat**, be

seated, sit (down), occupy a place; see **sit**.

seated, *a.* situated, located, settled, installed, established, rooted, set, fitted in place, placed, arranged, accommodated with seats.

seating, *n.* places, reservations, chairs, seats, room, accommodation, arrangement, seating space.

seaward, *a.* offshore, out to sea, over the sea; see also **maritime**.

seaweed, *n.* kelp, tangle, sea tangle, sea meadow, algae, marine meadow; see also **plant**. Seaweed includes the following—sea moss, Irish moss, Sargasso weed, rockweed, sea lettuce, kelp, giant kelp, gulf-weed, sea cabbage.

seaworthy, *a.* fit for sea, navigable, secure; see **safe 1**.

secede, *v.* withdraw, retract, leave; see **retreat**.

secession, *n.* departure, seceding, retraction; see **withdrawal**.

seclude, *v.* screen out, conceal, cover; see **hide 1**.

secluded, *a.* screened, removed, sequestered; see **withdrawn**.

seclusion, *n.* solitude, aloofness, privacy; see **retirement 2**.

second, *a.* secondary, subordinate, inferior, next, next in order, following, next to the first, next in rank, another, other. —**play second fiddle (to)**, defer (to), be inferior (to), be less successful (than); see **fail 1**.

second, *n.* flash, trice, flash of an eyelid; see **moment 1**.

secondary, *a.* 1. [Derived] dependent, subsequent, subsidiary; see **subordinate**. 2. [Minor] inconsiderable, petty, small; see **trivial, unimportant**.

secondhand, *a.* used, not new, reclaimed, renewed, re-used, old, worn, borrowed, derived, not original.

secondly, *a.* in the second place, furthermore, also, besides, next, on the other hand, in the next place, for the next step, next in order, further, to continue; see also **including**.

secrecy, *n.* concealment, confidence, hiding, seclusion, privacy, retirement, solitude, mystery, dark, darkness, isolation, reticence, stealth.

secret, *a.* 1. [Not generally known] mysterious, ambiguous, hidden, unknown, arcane, cryptic, esoteric, occult, mystic, mystical, classified, dark, veiled, enigmatical, enigmatic, strange, deep, buried in mystery, obscure, clouded, shrouded, unenlightened, unintelligible, cabalistic.—*Ant.* **known**, revealed, exposed. 2. [Hidden] latent, secluded, concealed; see **hidden**. 3. [Operating secretly] clandestine, underhand, underhanded, stealthy, sly, surreptitious, close, furtive, disguised, undercover, backdoor, confidential, backstairs, incognito, camouflaged, enigmatic, under false pretense, unrevealed, undisclosed, dissembled, dissimulated, under wraps; see also **secretive.**—*Ant.* open, aboveboard, overt.

secret, *n.* mystery, deep mystery, something veiled, something hidden, confidence, private matter, code, telegram, personal matter, privileged information, top secret, enigma, puzzle, something forbidden, classified *or* confidential *or* inside information, an unknown, magic number, the unknown. **—in secret,** slyly, surreptitiously, quietly; see **secret 3.**

secretary, *n.* 1. [A secondary executive officer] director, manager, superintendent; see **executive. 2.** [An assistant] clerk, typist, stenographer, copyist, amanuensis, recorder, confidential clerk, correspondent.

secrete, *v.* 1. [To hide] conceal, cover, seclude; see **disguise, hide 1. 2.** [To perspire] discharge, swelter, emit; see **sweat.**

secretion, *n.* discharge, issue, movement; see **excretion, flow.**

secretive, *a.* reticent, taciturn, undercover, with bated breath, in private, in the dark, in chambers, by a side door, under the breath, in the background, between ourselves, in privacy, in a corner, under the cloak of, reserved.

secretly, *a.* privately, covertly, obscurely, darkly, surreptitiously, furtively, stealthily, underhandedly, slyly, behind one's back, intimately, personally, confidentially, between you and me, in (strict) confidence, in secret, behind the scenes, on the sly, behind closed doors, quietly, *hush-hush. —*Ant.* **openly,** obviously, publicly.

sect, *n.* denomination, following, order; see **church 3, faction.**

section, *n.* 1. [A portion] subdivision, slice, segment; see **part 1, share. 2.** [An area] district, sector, locality; see **region 1.**

sectional, *a.* local, narrow, separate; see **regional.**

sector, *n.* section, district, quarter; see **area, division 2.**

secure, *a.* 1. [Firm] fastened, adjusted, bound; see **firm 1, tight 1. 2.** [Safe] guarded, unharmed, defended; see **safe 1. 3.** [Self-confident] assured, stable, determined; see **confident.**

secure, *v.* 1. [To fasten] settle, adjust, bind; see **fasten, tighten 1. 2.** [To obtain] achieve, acquire, grasp; see **get 1.**

security, *n.* 1. [Safety] protection, shelter, safety, refuge, retreat, defense, safeguard, preservation, sanctuary, ward, guard, immunity, freedom from harm, freedom from danger, redemption, salvation.—*Ant.* **danger,** risk, hazard. **2.** [A guarantee] earnest, forfeit, token, pawn, pledge, surety, bond, collateral, assurance, bail, certainty, promise, warranty, pact, compact, contract, convenant, agreement, sponsor, bondsman, hostage; see also **protection 2.**—*Ant.* **doubt,** broken faith, unreliability.

sedative, *n.* tranquilizer, medication, narcotic; see **drug, medicine 2.**

sediment, *n.* silt, dregs, grounds; see **residue.**

seduce, *v.* decoy, allure, inveigle, entice, abduct, attract, tempt, bait, bribe, lure, induce, stimulate, defile, deprave, lead astray, violate, prostitute, rape, deflower.—*Ant.* **preserve,** protect, guide.

see, *v.* 1. [To perceive with the eye] observe, look at, behold, examine, inspect, regard, view, look out on, gaze, stare, eye, lay eyes on, mark, perceive, pay attention to, heed, mind, detect, (take) notice, discern, scrutinize, scan, spy, survey, contemplate, remark, *clap eyes on, make out, cast the eyes on, direct the eyes, catch sight of, cast the eyes over, *get a load of. 2. [To understand] perceive, comprehend, discern; see **recognize 1, understand 1. 3.** [To witness] look on, be present, pay attention, notice, observe, regard, heed; see **witness. 4.** [To accompany] escort, attend, bear company; see **accompany. 5.** [To have an appointment (with)] speak to *or* with, have a conference (with), get advice from; see **consult, discuss.**

see about, *v.* attend (to), look after *or* to, provide for; see **perform 1.**

seed, *n.* grain, bulbs, cuttings, ears, tubers, roots; seed corn, seed potatoes, etc.–Seeds and fruits commonly called seeds include the following–grain, kernel, berry, ear, corn, nut. **–go** *or* **run to seed,** decline, worsen, run out; see **waste 3.**

seed, *v.* scatter, sow, broadcast; see **plant.**

seeding, *n.* sowing, implanting, spreading; see **farming.**

see fit to, *v.* decide (to), be willing *or* determined (to), determine (to); see **want, wish.**

seeing, *a.* observing, looking, regarding, viewing, noticing, surveying, looking at, observant, wide awake, alert, awake, perceiving, inspecting, witnessing.

seek, *v.* search *or* delve *or* gun *or* bob *or* dig *or* ransack *or* fish *or* go gunning for, look around *or* about for, look *or* hunt up, sniff *or* dig *or* hunt *or* root out, smell around, go *or* run *or* see *or* prowl after, go in pursuit *or* search of.

seem, *v.* appear (to be), have the appearance, create *or* leave *or* give *or* convey the impression, impress one, appear to one, look, look like, resemble, make a show of, show, have the qualities *or* features *or* aspects of, lead one to suppose something to be, have all the evidence of being, be suggestive of, give the effect *or* feeling (of), sound like, make out to be, give the idea, have all the earmarks of, make a noise like.

seen, *a.* observed, evident, viewed; see **obvious 1.**

seep, *v.* leak, flow gently, trickle; see **drain 1, flow.**

seepage, *n.* drainage, infiltration, leakage; see **flow.**

seethe, *v.* simmer, stew, burn; see **boil, cook.**

see through, *v.* 1. [To complete] finish (up), bring to a (successful) conclusion, wind up; see **complete, end 1.** 2. [To understand] comprehend, penetrate, detect; see **understand 1.**

see to, *v.* do, attend (to), look to *or* after; see **understand 1.**

segment, *n.* section, portion, fragment; see **division 2, part 1.**

segregate, *v.* isolate, sever, split up; see **divide, separate 2.**

segregated, *a.* divided into racial groups *or* by race(s) *or* color *or* along racial lines, *etc.*, isolated, in line with *or* according to Jim Crow restrictions; see **racial, separated.**

segregation, *n.* dissociation, disconnection, separation; see **division 1.**

seize, *v.* 1. [To grasp] take, take hold of, lay hold of *or* hands on, catch up, catch hold of, hang on *or* onto, catch, grip, clinch, clench, clasp, embrace, grab, clutch, grapple, snag, pluck, appropriate, snatch, swoop up, enfold, enclose, pinch, squeeze, make *or* hold fast, possess oneself of, envelope.—*Ant.* leave, pass by, let alone. 2. [To take by force] capture, rape, occupy, win, take captive, pounce, conquer, take by storm *or* assault, subdue, overwhelm, overrun, overpower, ambush, snatch, incorporate, exact, retake, carry (off), apprehend, arrest, secure, commandeer, force, gain, take, recapture, appropriate, take possession of, take over, pounce on, usurp, overcome, impound, intercept, steal, abduct, *snap up, *nab, trap, throttle, lay hold of, lift, hook, *collar, fasten upon, wrench, claw, snare, bag, catch up, wring, get one's clutches *or* fingers *or* hands on, kidnap, *rustle, hold up, *swipe, scramble for, help oneself to, *jump a claim. 3. [To comprehend] perceive, see, know; see **understand 1.**

seized, *a.* confiscated, annexed, clutched; see **beaten 1, captured.**

seizure, *n.* 1. [Capture] seizing, taking, apprehending; see **capture.** 2. [A

spasm] spell, convulsion, breakdown; see **fit 1, illness 1.**

seldom, *a.* rarely, unusually, in a few cases, a few times, at times, seldom seen, usually, sporadically, irregularly, whimsically, sometimes, from time to time, on a few *or* several *or* rare occasions, infrequently, not often, not very often, occasionally, uncommonly, scarcely, hardly, hardly ever, scarcely ever, when the spirit moves, on and off, once in a while, once in a blue moon, once in a lifetime, every now and then, not in a month of Sundays.—*Ant.* frequently, often, frequent.

select, *v.* decide, pick, elect; see **choose.**

selected, *a.* picked, chosen, elected; see **named 2.**

selection, *n.* 1. [The act of selecting] choice, election, determination, choosing, preference, appropriation, adoption, reservation, separation. 2. [Anything selected] pick, collection, excerpt; see **choice.**

selective, *a.* discriminating, judicious, particular; see **careful.**

self, *a.* of one's self, by one's self, by one's own effort; see **alone, individual.**

self, *n.* oneself, one's being, inner nature; see **character 2.**

self-assurance, *n.* security, self-reliance, morale; see **confidence 1.**

self-centered, *a.* self-indulgent, self-conscious, egotistical; see **egotistic, selfish.**

self-confidence, *n.* assurance, courage, self-reliance; see **confidence 1.**

self-confident, *a.* fearless, secure, self-assured; see **confident.**

self-conscious, *a.* unsure, uncertain, shy; see **doubtful, humble 1.**

self-contained, *a.* self-sustaining, complete, independent; see **free 1, whole 1.**

self-control, *n.* poise, (self) restraint, self-government, reserve, reticence, discretion, balance, stability, sobriety, dignity, repression, constraint, self-regulation.—*Ant.* **nervousness,** timidity, talkativeness.

self-defense, *n.* self-protection, the manly art (of self-defense), putting up a fight; see **fight 1, protection 2.**

self-esteem, *n.* vanity, haughtiness, egotism; see **pride 1.**

self-evident, *a.* plain, visible, apparent; see **obvious 2.**

self-explanatory, *a.* plain, clear, distinct; see **obvious 2.**

self-imposed, *a.* accepted, self-determined, willingly adopted *or* enforced *or* established, *etc;* see **deliberate, voluntarily.**

selfish, *a.* self-seeking, self-centered, self-indulgent, indulging oneself, wrapped up in oneself, narrow, narrow-minded, prejudiced, egotistical, egotistic, looking out for number one; see also **greedy.**

selfishly, *a.* egotistically, miserly, stingily, greedily, in one's own interest, meanly, ungenerously, to gain private ends, from *or* because of selfish *or* interested motives.

selfishness, *n.* self-regard, self-indulgence, self-worship; see **greed.**

self-made, *a.* competent, self-reliant, audacious; see **able, confident.**

self-reliant, *a.* determined, resolute, independent; see **able, confident.**

self-respect, *n.* morale, worth, pride; see **confidence 1, dignity.**

self-restraint, *n.* patience, endurance, control; see **restraint 1.**

self-sacrifice, *n.* altruism, free-giving, benevolence; see **generosity, kindness 1, 2.**

self-satisfaction, *n.* complacency, smugness, conceit; see **egotism.**

self-satisfied, *a.* smug, vain, conceited; see **egotistic.**

self-sufficient, *a.* competent, self-confident, efficient; see **confident.**

sell, *v.* market, vend, auction, dispose of, put up for sale *or* on the market, barter, exchange, transfer, liquidate, trade, bargain, peddle, retail, merchandise, sell at the market, sell over the counter, contract, wholesale, retail, dump, clear out, have a sale, give title to *or* a deed for, put in escrow.—*Ant.* buy, obtain, get.

seller, *n.* dealer, tradesman, (door-to-door) salesman, retailer, agent, vender, merchant, auctioneer, shopkeeper, peddler, trader, marketer, storekeeper; see **businessman.**

selling, *n.* sale, auction, bartering, trading, vending, auctioning, transfer, transferring, commercial transaction, transacting, disposal, scoring, merchandising.—*Ant.* **buying**, acquiring, purchasing.

sell-out, *n.* betrayal, deception, deal; see **trick 1.**

sell out, *v.* thwart, trick, turn in, cop out; see also **deceive, disappoint.**

sell short, *v.* denigrate, derogate, belittle; see **insult, ridicule.**

semester, *n.* six-month period, eighteen weeks, four and one-half months; see **term 2.**

semifinal, *n.* next to the last, elimination test, elimination round; see **round 2.**

seminary, *n.* secondary school, institute, theological school; see **school 1.**

Senate, *n.* legislative body, upper branch of Congress, the Upper House; see **legislature.**

senate, *n.* legislative body, assembly, council; see **legislature.**

senator, *n.* statesman, politician, member of the senate; see **representative 2.**

send, *v.* 1. [To dispatch] transmit, forward, convey, advance, express, ship, mail, send forth *or* out *or* in, delegate, expedite, hasten, accelerate, post, address, rush (off), hurry off, get under way, put under sail, give papers, provide with credentials, send out for, address to, commission, consign, drop (a letter), convey, transfer, pack off, give, bestow, grant, confer, entrust, assign, impart, give out. 2. [To broadcast, usually electronically] transmit, relay, wire, cable, broadcast, televise, conduct, communicate.

send around, *v.* circulate, send to everybody *or* everyone, make available; see **distribute.**

send back, *v.* reject, mail *or* ship back, decide against; see **return 2.**

send (away) for, *v.* order, request, write away (for); see **ask, get 1.**

send in, *v.* submit, mail, deliver; see **offer 1.**

send word, *v.* get in touch, communicate, report; see **telephone.**

senile, *a.* aged, infirm, feeble; see **old 1, sick.**

senility, *n.* old age, dotage, feebleness; see **age 2, weakness 1.**

senior, *a.* elder, older, higher in rank; see **superior.**

seniority, *n.* (preferred) standing, rank(ing), station; see **advantage.**

sensation, *n.* 1. [The sense of feeling] sensibility, consciousness, perception; see **emotion, thought 1.** 2. [A feeling] response, sentiment, passion; see **feeling 1.**

sensational, *a.* 1. [Fascinating] exciting, marvelous, incredible; see **impressive, interesting.** 2. [Melodramatic] exaggerated, excessive, emotional; see **exciting.**

sense, *n.* 1. [One of the powers of physical perception] kinesthesia, function, sensation; see **hearing 3, sight 1, taste 1, touch 1.** 2. [Mental ability] intellect, understanding, reason, mind, spirit, soul, brains, judgment, wit, imagination, common sense, cleverness, reasoning, intellectual ability, mental capacity, knowledge; see also **thought 1.**—*Ant.* dullness, idiocy, feeble wit. 3. [Reasonable and agreeable conduct] reasonableness, fairmindedness, discretion; see **fairness.** 4. [Tact and understanding] insight, discernment, social sense; see **feeling 4, judgment 1.** —**in a sense,** in a way, to a degree, somewhat; see **some, somehow.** —**make sense,** be *or* appear to be reasonable *or* logical, look all right, add up; see **appear** 1, **seem**.

senseless, *a.* ridiculous, silly, foolish; see **illogical**, **stupid** 1.

senses, *n.* consciousness, mental faculties, feeling; see **awareness**, **life** 1, 2.

sensible, *a.* 1. [Showing good sense] reasonable, prudent, perceptive, acute, shrewd, sharp, careful, aware, sane, wise, cautious, capable, having a head of one's shoulders, endowed with reason, discerning, thoughtful; see also **rational** 1, **sane** 1. 2. [Perceptive] aware, informed, attentive; see **conscious**.

sensitive, *a.* 1. [Tender] delicate, sore, painful; see **sore** 1. 2. [Touchy] high-strung, tense, nervous; see **irritable**, **unstable** 2.

sensitivity, *n.* 1. [Susceptibility] allergy, irritability, ticklishness; see **feeling** 4. 2. [Emotional response or condition] delicacy, sensibility, sensitiveness, nervousness, (acute) awareness, consciousness, acuteness, subtlety, feeling(s), sympathetic response, sympathy.

sensory, *a.* 1. [Neurological] sensible, relating to sensation *or* the senses, conscious; see **sensual** 1. 2. [Conveyed by the senses] audible, perceptible, discernible; see **obvious** 1, 2, **tangible**.

sensual, *a.* 1. [Sensory] tactile, sensuous, stimulating, sharpened, pleasing, dazzling, feeling, being, heightened, enhanced, appealing, delightful, luxurious, emotional, fine, arousing, stirring, moving; see also **exciting**. 2. [Carnal] voluptuous, pleasure-loving, fleshly, lewd, unspiritual, self-loving, self-indulgent, epicurean, intemperate, gluttonous, rakish, debauched, orgiastic, sensuous, piggish, hoggish, bestial.

sensuality, *n.* sensationalism, appetite, ardor; see **desire** 2, **emotion**, **love** 1.

sensuous, *a.* passionate, physical, exciting; see **sensual** 2.

sent, *a.* commissioned, appointed, ordained, delegated, dispatched, directed, issued, transmitted, discharged, gone, on the road, in transit, uttered, sent forth, driven, impelled, forced to go, consigned, ordered, committed.—*Ant.* kept, restrained, held back.

sentence, *n.* 1. [A pronounced judgment] edict, decree, order; see **judgment** 3, **punishment**, **verdict**. 2. [An expressed thought] Types of sentences, sense 2, include the following—simple, complex, compound, compound-complex, kernel, transformed, declarative, interrogative, imperative, exclamatory, statement, question, command, exclamation.

sentence, *v.* pronounce judgment, judge, send to prison; see **condemn**, **convict**, **imprison**, **punish**.

sent for, *a.* applied for, written for, requested; see **ordered** 1.

sentiment, *n.* sensibility, predilection, tender feeling; see **emotion**, **feeling** 4, **thought** 2.

sentimental, *a.* emotional, romantic, romantical, silly, dreamy, idealistic, visionary, artificial, unrealistic, susceptible, overemotional, affected, simpering, insincere, overacted, schoolgirlish, *sappy, gushy.

sentimentality, *n.* sentimentalism, sentiment, melodramatics, bathos, melodrama, triteness, *mush, gush; see also **emotion**.

sentry, *n.* sentinel, watch, protector; see **watchman**.

separate, *v.* 1. [To keep apart] isolate, insulate, single out, sequester, seclude, rope off, segregate, intervene, stand between, draw apart, split *or* break up. 2. [To part company] take leave, go away, depart; see **leave** 1.

separated, *a.* divided, parted, apart, disconnected, partitioned, distinct, disunited, disjointed, sundered, disembodied, cut in two, cut apart, set apart, distant, disassociated, removed, distributed, scattered, put asunder, divorced, divergent, marked, severed, far between, in halves.—*Ant.* united, together, whole.

separately, *a.* singly, definitely, distinctly; see **clearly** 1, 2, **individually**.

separation, *n.* 1. [The act of dividing] disconnection, severance, division, cut, detachment. 2. [The act of parting] leave-taking, farewell, embarkation; see **departure**.

September, *n.* fall or autumn or summer (month), Indian summer, back-to-school season; see **fall** 3.

sequel, *n.* consequence, continuation, progression; see **sequence** 1, **series**.

sequence, *n.* 1. [Succession] order, continuity, continuousness, continuance, successiveness, progression, graduation, consecutiveness, flow, consecution, unbrokenness, subsequence, course. 2. [Arrangement] placement, distribution, classification; see **order** 3. 3. [A series] chain, string, array; see **series**.

serenade, *n.* melody, compliment, nocturne; see **music** 1, **song**.

serene, *a.* calm, clear, unruffled, translucent, undisturbed, undimmed, tranquil, composed, cool, cool-headed, sedate, level-headed, content, satisfied, patient, reconciled, easygoing, placid, limpid, comfortable, cheerful.—*Ant.* confused, disturbed, ruffled.

serenity, *n.* quietness, calmness, tranquility; see **peace** 2, 3.

sergeant, *n.* Types include the following—master sergeant, staff sergeant, technical sergeant, first sergeant, top sergeant, platoon sergeant, sergeant major, sergeant-at-arms, police sergeant, *top kick, *sarge; see also **officer 3, soldier.**

serial, *n.* installment, serial picture, continued story; see **movie.**

series, *n.* rank, file, line, row, set, train, range, list, string, chain, order, sequence, succession, group, procession, continuity, column, progression, category, classification, scale, array, gradation.

serious, *a.* 1. [Involving danger] grave, severe, pressing; see **dangerous, important 1.** 2. [Thoughtful] somber, reflecting, sincere; see **thoughtful 1.**

seriously, *a.* 1. [In a manner fraught with danger] dangerously, precariously, perilously, in a risky way, threateningly, menacingly, grievously, severely, harmfully.—*Ant.* safely, harmlessly, in no danger. 2. [In a manner that recognizes importance] gravely, soberly, earnestly, solemnly, thoughtfully, sternly, sedately, with great earnestness, all joking aside; see also **sincerely.**—*Ant.* lightly, thoughtlessly, airily.

seriousness, *n.* 1. [The quality of being dangerous] gravity, weight, enormity; see **importance.** 2. [The characteristic of being sober] earnestness, sobriety, solemnity, gravity, calmness, thoughtfulness, coolness, sedateness, sobermindedness; see also **sincerity.**—*Ant.* fun, gaiety, jollity.

sermon, *n.* lesson, doctrine, lecture; see **speech 3.**

serpent, *n.* reptile, viper, ophidian; see **snake.**

servant, *n.* attendant, retainer, helper, hireling, dependent, menial, domestic, drudge, slave; see also **assistant.** Servants include the following—butler, housekeeper, chef, cook, second maid, kitchenmaid, maid of all work, general maid, laundress, chambermaid, parlormaid, lady's maid, seamstress, nursemaid, nurse, valet, doorman, footman, squire, chauffeur, groom, gardener, yardman, kennelman.

serve, *v.* 1. [To fulfill an obligation] hear duty's call, obey the call of one's country, subserve, discharge one's duty, assume one's responsibilities. 2. [To work fór] be employed by, labor, be in the employ of; see **work 2.** 3. [To help] give aid, assist, be of assistance; see **help 1.** 4. [To serve at table] wait (on), attend, help one to food, help.

served, *a.* dressed, prepared, offered, apportioned, dealt, furnished, supplied, provided, dished up.

serve notice, *v.* inform, report, give word; see **tell 1.**

serve someone right, *v.* have it coming, get one's due(s) or just deserts, do justice to; see **deserve.**

serve time, *v.* stand committed, serve (out) a jail sentence, be incarcerated or in jail, pay one's debt to society, go to jail, *do a term, *be in stir, *be in the joint, *be sent up.

service, *n.* 1. [Aid] co-operation, assistance, aid; see **help 1.** 2. [Tableware] set, silver, setting; see **dish 1, pottery.** 3. [A religious service] rite, worship, sermon; see **ceremony 2.** 4. [Military service] army, duty, active service, stint. —**at one's service**, zealous, anxious to help or be of service, obedient; see **helpful 1, ready 1, willing.** —**of service**, useful, handy, usable; see **helpful 1.**

service, *v.* maintain, sustain, keep up; see **repair.**

serviceable, *a.* practical, advantageous, beneficial; see **helpful 1, usable.**

serving, *n.* plateful, course, portion; see **meal 2.**

session, *n.* assembly, concourse, sitting; see **gathering.**

set, *a.* 1. [Firm] stable, solid, settled; see **firm 2.** 2. [Determined] concluded, steadfast, decided; see **determined 1.**

set, *n.* 1. [Inclination] attitude, position, bearing; see **inclination 1.** 2. [A social group] clique, coterie, circle; see **faction, organization 2.** 3. [A collection of (like) items] kit, assemblage, assortment; see **collection.**

set, *v.* 1. [To place] insert, settle, put (in place), plant, store, situate, lay, deposit, arrange. 2. [To establish] anchor, fix, introduce; see **establish 2, install.** 3. [To become firm] jell, solidify, congeal; see **harden, stiffen, thicken.**

set about, *v.* start, begin a task, start doing; see **begin 1.**

set apart, *v.* isolate, segregate, make separate or distinct or individual, etc.; see **distinguish 1, separate 1.**

set aside, *v.* 1. [To save] put away, reserve, lay up; see **maintain 3, save 2.** 2. [To discard] abrogate, repeal, reject; see **cancel, discard.**

setback, *n.* hindrance, check, reversal; see **delay, difficulty 1.**

set off, *v.* 1. [To contrast] be different, appear different, be the opposite; see **contrast.** 2. [To explode] touch off, set the spark to, detonate; see **explode.**

set out, *v.* initiate, start, commence; see **begin 1.**

set sail, *v.* launch, shove off, weigh anchor; see **leave 1, sail 2.**

set straight, *v.* revise, inform (properly), provide the facts or the evidence or a new insight, *etc.*; see **correct, improve 2.**

setting, *n.* environment, surroundings, mounting, backdrop, frame, framework, background, context, perspective, horizon, shadow, shade, distance.—*Ant.* front, foreground, focus.

settle, *v.* **1.** [To decide] make a decision, form judgment, come to a conclusion; see **decide. 2.** [To prove] establish, verify, make certain; see **prove. 3.** [To finish] end, make an end of, complete; see **achieve. 4.** [To sink] descend, decline, fall; see **sink 1. 5.** [To establish residence] locate, lodge, become a citizen, reside, fix one's residence, abide, set up housekeeping, make one's home, establish a home, keep house; see also **dwell. 6.** [To take up sedentary life, *often used with* down] follow regular habits, live an orderly life, become conventional, follow convention, buy a house, marry, marry and settle down, raise a family, get in a rut, *hang up one's hat, mend one's fences. **7.** [To satisfy a claim] pay, compensate, make an adjustment, reach a compromise, make payment, arrange a settlement, get squared away, pay damages, pay out, settle out of court, settle *or* patch up, work out, settle *or* even the score, dispose of, account with.

settled, *a.* decided, resolved, ended; see **determined 1.**

settlement, *n.* **1.** [An agreement] covenant, arrangement, compact; see **agreement 1, contract. 2.** [A payment] compensation, remuneration, reimbursement; see **adjustment, pay 1. 3.** [A colony] principality, plantation, establishment; see **colony.**

settler, *n.* planter, immigrant, homesteader; see **pioneer 2.**

setup, *n.* structure, composition, plan; see **order 3, organization 2.**

set up, *v.* **1.** [To make arrangements] prearrange, inaugurate, work on; see **arrange 2. 2.** [To finance] patronize, promote, support; see **pay 1.**

sever, *v.* part, split, cleave; see **cut 1, divide.**

several, *a.* **1.** [Few] some, any, a few, quite a few, not many, sundry, two or three, a small number of, scarce, sparse, hardly any, scarcely any, half a dozen, only a few, scant, scanty, rare, infrequent, in a minority, a handful, more or less, not too many.—*Ant.* **many,** large numbers of, none. **2.** [Various] plural, a number, numerous; see **many, various.**

several, *n.* various ones, a small number, quite a few; see **few.**

severe, *a.* **1.** [Stern] exacting, uncompromising, unbending, inflexible, unchanging, unalterable, harsh, cruel, oppressive,

close, grinding, obdurate, resolute, austere, rigid, grim, earnest, stiff, forbidding, resolved, relentless, determined, unfeeling, with an iron will, strict, inconsiderate, firm, immovable, unyielding. **2.** [Difficult or rigorous] overbearing, tyrannical, sharp, exacting, drastic, domineering, rigid, oppressive, despotic, unmerciful, bullying, uncompromising, relentless, unrelenting, hard, rigorous, austere, grinding, grim, implacable, cruel, pitiless, critical, unjust, barbarous, crusty, gruff, stubborn, autocratic, hidebound; see also **difficult 1.**—*Ant.* **easy,** easygoing, indulgent.

severely, *a.* critically, harshly, rigorously; see **firmly 2, seriously 1.**

severity, *n.* hardness, hardheartedness, strictness; see **cruelty.**

sew, *v.* stitch, seam, fasten, work with needle and thread, tailor, tack, embroider, bind, piece, baste.

sewage, *n.* excrement, offal, waste matter; see **residue.**

sewer, *n.* drain, drainpipe, drainage tube, conduit, gutter, disposal *or* sewage system, septic tank, dry well, leech field *or* ditches, city sewer(s), sewage disposal, sanitary provisions *or* facility *or* facilities, *etc.*

sewing, *n.* stitching, seaming, tailoring, embroidering, darning, mending, piecing, patching, dressmaking.

sex, *n.* **1.** [Ideas associated with sexual relationships] sex attraction, sex appeal, magnetism, sensuality, affinity, love, courtship, marriage, generation, reproduction. **2.** [A group, either male or female] men, women, males, females, the feminine world, the masculine world. **3.** [Gender] sexuality, masculinity, femininity, womanliness, manhood, manliness. **4.** [Sexual intercourse] making love, (the) sexual act, going to bed (with someone); see **copulation, fornication.**

sexual, *a.* **1.** [Reproductive] generative, reproductive, procreative; see **original 1. 2.** [Intimate] carnal, wanton, passionate; see **sensual 2.**

sexuality, *n.* lust, sensuality, passion; see **desire 2.**

shabby, *a.* ragged, threadbare, faded, ill-dressed, dilapidated, decayed, deteriorated, poor, pitiful, worn, meager, miserable, wretched, poverty-stricken, scrubby, seedy, gone to seed, down at the heel.—*Ant.* **neat,** new, well-kept.

shack, *n.* hut, shed, hovel, cabin, shanty, shotgun shack.

shade, *n.* **1.** [Lack of light] blackness, shadow, dimness; see **darkness 1. 2.** [A degree of color] brilliance, saturation, hue; see **color, tint. 3.** [A slight difference] variation, proposal, hint; see

suggestion 1. 4. [An obstruction to light] covering, blind, screen; see **curtain**.

shade, v. 1. [To intercept direct rays] screen, cover, shadow; see sense 2, **shelter**. 2. [To make darker] darken, blacken, obscure, cloud, shadow, (make) dim, tone down, black out, make dusky, deepen the shade, overshadow, make gloomy, screen, shut out the light, keep out the light. 3. [To become darker] grow dark, grow black, become dark, grow dim, blacken, turn to twilight, deepen into night, become gloomy, be overcast, grow dusky, cloud up or over, overcloud, grow shadowy.

shadow, n. umbra, obscuration, adumbration; see **darkness** 1.

shadow, v. 1. [To shade] dim, veil, screen; see **shade** 2, **shelter**. 2. [To follow secretly] trail, watch, keep in sight; see **pursue** 1.

shady, a. dusky, shadowy, adumbral, in the shade, shaded, sheltered, out of the sun, dim, cloudy, under a cloud, cool, indistinct, vague; see also **dark** 1.

shaft, n. 1. [Rod] stem, bar, pole; see also **rod** 1. 2. [Light ray] wave, streak, beam of light; see **ray**.

shake, n. tremble, shiver, pulsation; see **movement** 1, 2.

shake, v. 1. [To vibrate] tremble, quiver, quake, shiver, shudder, palpitate, wave, waver, fluctuate, reel, flap, flutter, totter, thrill, wobble, stagger, waggle. 2. [To cause to vibrate] agitate, rock, sway, swing, joggle, jolt, bounce, jar, move, set in motion, convulse.

shaken, a. unnerved, upset, overcome; see **excited**.

shaky, a. 1. [Not firm] quivery, trembling, jellylike, unsettled, not set, yielding, unsteady, tottering, unsound, insecure, unstable, infirm, jittery, nervous.—Ant. firm, settled, rigid. 2. [Not reliable] uncertain, not dependable, questionable; see **unreliable** 2, **unstable** 1.

shall, v. intend, want to, must; see **will** 3.

shallow, a. 1. [Lacking physical depth] slight, inconsiderable, superficial, with the bottom in plain sight, with no depth, with little depth, not deep.—Ant. deep, bottomless, unfathomable. 2. [Lacking intellectual depth] simple, silly, trifling, insane, frivolous, superficial, petty, foolish, idle, unintelligent, piddling, *wishy-washy; see also **stupid** 1.

sham, a. misleading, lying, untrue; see **false** 3.

sham, n. fakery, pretense, pretext; see **fake**.

shame, n. 1. [A disgrace] embarrassment, stigma, blot; see **disgrace**. 2. [A sense

of wrongdoing] bad conscience, mortification, confusion, humiliation, compunction, regret, chagrin, discomposure, irritation, remorse, embarrassment, abashment, self-reproach, self-disgust; see also **guilt**. 3. [A condition of disgrace] humiliation, dishonor, degradation; see **disgrace**, **scandal**.

shame, v. humiliate, mortify, dishonor; see **disgrace**, **humble**.

shameful, a. 1. [Said of persons] immodest, corrupt, immoral, intemperate, debauched, drunken, villainous, knavish, degraded, reprobate, diabolical, indecent, indelicate, lewd, vulgar, impure, unclean, fleshly, carnal, sinful, wicked. 2. [Said of actions or conduct] dishonorable, disgraceful, scandalous, flagrant, obscene, ribald, infamous, outrageous, gross, infernal, disgusting, too bad, unworthy, evil, foul, hellish, disreputable, despicable; see also **wrong**.—Ant. **worthy**, admirable, creditable.

shameless, a. brazen, bold, forward; see **rude** 2, **lewd** 2.

shape, n. 1. [Form] contour, aspect, configuration; see **form** 1, **looks**. 2. [An actual form] pattern, stamp, frame; see **mold** 1. 3. [Condition] fitness, physical state, health; see **state** 2. —out of shape, distorted, misshapen, battered; see **bent**, **broken** 1, **flat** 1, **ruined** 1, 2, twisted 1. —take shape, take (on) form, grow (up), fill out; see **develop** 1, **improve** 2.

shape, v. 1. [To give shape] mold, cast, fashion; see **form** 1. 2. [To take shape] become, develop, take form; see **form** 4, **grow** 2.

shaped, a. made, fashioned, created; see **formed**.

shapeless, a. 1. [Formless] indistinct, indefinite, invisible, vague, without character or form or shape or definite form, lacking form, unformed, unmade, not formed or made or created, with no definite outline; see also **uncertain** 2. 2. [Deformed] misshapen, irregular, unshapely, unsymmetrical, mutilated, disfigured, malformed, ill-formed, abnormal; see also **deformed**.—Ant. regular, symmetrical, shapely.

shapely, a. symmetrical, comely, proportioned; see **trim** 2.

***shape up**, v. 1. [To obey] mind, conform, observe; see **behave**, **improve** 2, **obey**. 2. [To develop] enlarge, expand, refine; see **develop** 1.

share, n. division, apportionment, part, portion, helping, serving, piece, ration, slice, allotment, parcel, dose, fraction, fragment, allowance, dividend, percentage, commission, *cut, *whack, *rakeoff.

share, v. 1. [To divide] allot, distribute,

apportion, part, deal, dispense, assign, administer.—*Ant.* unite, combine, withhold. 2. [To partake] participate, share in, experience, take part in, receive, have a portion of, have a share in, go in with, take a part of, take a share of.—*Ant.* avoid, have no share in, take no part in. 3. [To give] yield, bestow, accord; see **give 1.**

sharp, *a.* 1. [Having a keen edge] acute, edged, razor-edged, sharpened, ground fine, honed, razor-sharp, sharp-edged, fine, cutting, knifelike, knife-edged.—*Ant.* dull, unsharpened, blunt. 2. [Having a keen point] pointed, sharp-pointed, spiked, spiky, peaked, needle-pointed, keen, fine, spiny, thorny, prickly, barbed, needlelike, stinging, sharp as a needle, pronged, tapered, tapering, horned. 3. [Having a keen mind] clever, astute, bright; see **intelligent.** 4. [Distinct] audible, visible, explicit; see **clear 2, definite 2, obvious 1.** 5. [Intense] cutting, biting, piercing; see **intense.** 6. [*Stylish] dressy, chic, in style; see **fashionable.**

sharpen, *v.* 1. [To make keen] grind, file, hone, put an edge on, grind to a fine edge, make sharp, make acute, whet, give an edge *or* a fine edge to, put a point on, give a fine point to. —*Ant.* flatten, thicken, turn. 2. [To make more exact] focus, bring into focus, intensify, make clear, make clearer, outline distinctly, make more distinct.—*Ant.* confuse, cloud, obscure.

sharply, *a.* piercingly, pointedly, distinctly; see **clearly 1, 2.**

shatter, *v.* shiver, split, burst; see **break 2.**

shattered, *a.* splintered, crushed, *in smithereens; see **broken 1.**

shave, *v.* shear, graze, barber, cut, use a razor, clip closely, strip, strip the hair from, tonsure, make bare.

she, *pron.* this one, this girl, this woman, that girl, that woman, a female animal; see also **woman 1.**

shears, *n.* cutters, clippers, snips; see **scissors.**

shed, *n.* shelter, outbuilding, hut, lean-to, woodshed.

shed, *v.* drop, let fall, send *or* give forth, shower down, cast, molt, slough, discard, exude, emit, scatter, sprinkle.

sheep, *n.* lamb, ewe, ram; see **animal 2, goat.**

sheer, *a.* 1. [Abrupt] abrupt, very steep, precipitous; see **steep.** 2. [Thin] transparent, delicate, fine; see **thin 1.**

sheet, *n.* 1. [A bed cover] covering, bed sheet, bedding; see **cloth, cover 1.** 2. [A thin, flat object] lamina, leaf, foil, veneer, layer, stratum, coat, film, ply, covering, expanse.

shelf, *n.* 1. [A ledge] rock, reef, sandbank; see **ledge.** 2. [A cupboard rack] counter, cupboard, mantelpiece, rack.

shell, *n.* 1. [A shell-like cover or structure] husk, crust, nut, pod, case, scale, shard, integument, eggshell. 2. [An explosive projectile] bullet, explosive, torpedo; see **weapon 1.** 3. [A crustaceous covering]—Varieties include the following—tortoise, conch, snail; see also **sea shell.**

shell, *v.* shuck, shell off, peel off; see **skin.**

shellfish, *n.* crustacean, mollusk, crustaceous animal, invertebrate, invertebrate *or* marine animal *or* creature, arthropod, gastropod, Arthropoda, molluskan type, bivalve, shell-meat. Creatures often called shellfish include the following—crab, lobster, clam, shrimp, prawn, crawfish, crayfish, mussel, whelk, cockle, abalone, snail.

shelter, *n.* refuge, harbor, haven, sanctuary, asylum, retreat, shield, screen, defense, security, safety, guardian, protector, house, roof, tent, shack, shed, hut, shade, shadow.

shelter, *v.* screen, cover, hide, conceal, guard, take in, ward, harbor, defend, protect, shield, watch over, take care of, secure, preserve, safeguard, surround, enclose, house.—*Ant.* expose, turn out, evict.

sheltered, *a.* 1. [Shaded] screened, protected, shady, veiled, covered, protective, curtained. 2. [Protected] guarded, ensured, shielded; see **safe, watched.**

sheriff, *n.* county officer, county administrator, peace officer; see also **policeman.**

shield, *n.* bumper, protection, guard; see **cover 1.**

shift, *n.* 1. [A change] transfer, transformation, substitution, displacement, fault, alteration, variation; see also **change 1.** 2. [A working period] turn, spell, working time; see **time 1.**

shift, *v.* 1. [To change position] move, turn, stir; see **change 2.** 2. [To cause to shift, sense 1] displace, remove, substitute; see **exchange 1.** 3. [To put in gear] change gears, downshift, put in drive; see **drive 2.**

shin, *n.* tibia, shankbone, limb; see **bone, leg 1.**

shine, *v.* 1. [To give forth light] radiate, beam, scintillate, glitter, sparkle, twinkle, glimmer, glare, glow, flash, blaze, shimmer, illumine, illuminate, blink, shoot out beams, irradiate, dazzle, flash, flicker. 2. [To reflect light] glisten, gleam, glow, look good, be *or* grow bright, give back, give light, deflect, mirror; see also **reflect 3.** 3. [To cause to shine, usually by polishing] scour, brush, polish, put a gloss *or* finish on, finish, burnish, wax, buff, polish up, make brilliant, make glitter; see also **clean, paint 2.**

shining, *a.* radiant, gleaming, luminous; see **bright 1, shimmering.**

shiny, *a.* polished, sparkling, glistening; see **bright 1.**

ship, *n.* Types of ships include the following—steamer, steamship, liner, freighter, landing barge, (refrigeration) trawler, floating cannery, factory ship, ferry, clipper, square-rigged vessel, sailing ship, transport, tanker, pilot boat, junk, galleon, sampan, battleship, cruiser, destroyer, aircraft carrier, whaling vessel, bark, schooner, windjammer, yacht, dragger, cutter, sloop, tug, three-master, four-master; see also **boat.**

ship, *v.* send, consign, ship out; see **send 1.**

shipment, *n.* consignment, carload, purchase; see **freight 2.**

shipped, *a.* consigned, exported, delivered; see **sent.**

shirk, *v.* elude, cheat, malinger; see **avoid, evade.**

shirt, *n.* Shirts include the following—dress, undershirt, sport, work, cowboy, Western, long-sleeved, short-sleeved, cotton, silk, flannel, T-shirt, jersey, pullover, turtleneck; see also **clothes.**

shiver, *v.* be cold, vibrate, quiver; see **shake 1, wave 3.**

shock, *n.* 1. [The effect of physical impact] crash, clash, wreck; see **collision.** 2. [The effect of a mental blow] excitement, hysteria, emotional upset; see **confusion.** 3. [The after-effect of physical harm] concussion, stupor, collapse; see **illness 1, injury.**

shock, *v.* 1. [To disturb one's self-control] startle, agitate, astound; see **disturb.** 2. [To disturb one's sense of propriety] insult, outrage, horrify, revolt, offend, appall, abash, astound, anger, floor, shake up, disquiet, dismay. 3. [To jar] rock, agitate, jolt; see **shake 2.**

shocked, *a.* startled, aghast, upset, astounded, offended, appalled, dismayed; see also **troubled.**

shocking, *a.* repulsive, hateful, revolting; see **offensive 2.**

shoe, *n.* footwear, foot covering. Footwear includes the following—Oxford, slipper, moccasin, low shoe, high shoe, boot, sandal, Roman sandal, pump, clog, galosh, plastic *or* rubber *or* leather *or* fabric shoe, tennis shoe, sneaker, loafer, heels, *tennies, wedgie. —in **another's shoes,** in the position or place of another, in changed *or* different *or*

other circumstances, reversal of roles; see **sympathetic, understood 1.**

shoo, *interj.* get away, begone, leave; see **get out.**

shoot, *v.* 1. [To discharge] fire, shoot off, expel, pull the trigger, set off, torpedo, explode, ignite, blast, sharpshoot, open fire, rake, gauntlet, pump full of lead. 2. [To move rapidly] dart, spurt, rush; see **hurry 1.** 3. [To kill by shooting] dispatch, murder, execute; see **kill 1.**

shoot at, *v.* 1. [To fire a weapon at] shoot, fire at, take a shot at; see **attack 1.** 2. [*To strive for] aim, endeavor, strive; see **try 1.**

*shoot the bull,** *v.* exaggerate grossly, carry on a lengthy conversation, converse; see **gossip.**

shop, *n.* store, department store, retail store, dry goods store, novelty shop. —**set up shop,** go into business, start, open (up) a shop *or* business *or* office, *etc.*; see **begin 1, 2.** —**shut up shop,** close (down *or* up), go out of business, cease functioning; see **close 4, stop 2.** —**talk shop,** talk business, exchange views, discuss one's speciality; see **gossip, talk 1.**

shop, *v.* shop for *or* around, look *or* hunt for, try to buy; see **buy 1.**

shopkeeper, *n.* manager, tradesman, storekeeper; see **businessman.**

shopper, *n.* bargain hunter, professional shopper, purchaser; see **buyer.**

shopping center, *n.* shops, trading center, parking lot; see **business 4, parking lot.**

shore, *n.* beach, strand, seaside, sand, coast, seacoast, brink, bank, border, seaboard, margin, sea beach, lakeside, lakeshore, river bank, riverside.

short, *a.* 1. [Not long in space] low, skimpy, slight, not tall, not long, undersized, little, abbreviated, dwarfish, stubby, stunted, stocky, diminutive, tiny, small, dwarf, dwarfed, close to the ground, dumpy, chunky, compact, stumpy, *sawed-off, runty. 2. [Not long in time] brief, curtailed, cut short, not protracted, concise, unprolonged, unsustained, condensed, terse, succinct, pithy, summary, pointed, precise, bare, abridged, summarized, epigrammatic, compressed, short-term, short-lived. 3. [Inadequate] deficient, insufficient, niggardly; see **inadequate.** —**be *or* run short** (of), lack, want, run out of; see **need.** —**fall short,** not reach, be unsuccessful *or* inadequate, fall down; see **fail 1, miss 3.** —**for short,** as a nickname, familiarly, commonly; see **named 1, so-called.** —**in short,** that is, in summary, to make a long story short; see **briefly, finally 1.**

shortage, *n.* short fall, scant supply, curtailment; see **lack 1.**

shortcoming, *n.* fault, deficiency, lapse; see **weakness 1.**

short cut, *n.* bypass, alternative, timesaver; see **means 1, why.**

shorten, *v.* curtail, abridge, abbreviate; see **decrease 2.**

shorter, *a.* smaller, lower, not so long, briefer, more limited, more concise, more abrupt, lessened, diminished, reduced, curtailed. —*Ant.* higher, longer, taller.

short-lived, *a.* brief, momentary, temporary; see **short 2.**

shortly, *a.* presently, quickly, right away; see **soon 1.**

shortness, *n.* brevity, briefness, conciseness; see **length 1.**

shorts, *n.* underpants, briefs, athletic underwear; see **clothes, underwear.**

shortsighted, *a.* unthinking, headlong, unwary; see **rash, stupid 2.**

shot, *n.* 1. [A flying missile] bullet, ball, pellet, lead, projectile, buckshot, grapeshot. 2. [An opportunity to shoot] range, chance, turn; see **opportunity 1.** 3. [One who shoots] gunner, huntsman, marksman; see **hunter.** —**call the shots,** direct, control, supervise; see **control.** —*have or take a shot at,* endeavor, attempt, do one's best (at or in); see **try 1.** —**like a shot,** rapidly, speedily, *like a bat out of hell; see **fast 1, quickly.** —**shot in the arm,** help, boost(er), assistance; see **encouragement.**

shoulder, *n.* upper arm *or* leg, shoulder cut, (shoulder) joint; see **arm 1, 2, joint 1.** —**cry on someone's shoulder,** weep, object, shed tears; see **cry 1, complain.** —**turn** *or* **give a cold shoulder to,** ignore, neglect, pass over; see **insult.**

shout, *n.* roar, bellow, scream; see **cry 1, yell.**

shout, *v.* screech, roar, scream; see **yell.**

shouting, *n.* cries, yelling, jeering; see **cry 1.**

shove, *v.* jostle, push out of one's way, shoulder; see **push 1.**

shovel, *n.* Shovels include the following—coal, snow, fire, miner's, irrigating, split, twisted, pronged, scoop, round-pointed; see also **tool 1.**

shovel, *v.* take up, pick up, take up with a shovel, clean out, throw, move, pass, shift, delve, muck; see also **dig 1, load 1.**

show, *n.* 1. [An exhibition] presentation, exhibit, showing, exposition, occurrence, sight, appearance, program, flower show, boat show, home show, dog *or* cat show, bringing before the public, bringing to public view, carnival, representation, burlesque, production, appearance,

concert, act, pageant, spectacle, light show, entertainment; see also **comedy, drama, movie.** 2. [Pretense] sham, make believe, semblance; see **pretense 1, 2.** —**for show,** for (sake of) appearances, ostensibly, ostentatiously; see **apparently.** —*get or put the show on the road,* start, open, get started; see **begin 1.** —**steal the show,** triumph, get the best of it, win (out); see **defeat, win 1.**

show, *v.* 1. [To display] exhibit, manifest, present; see **display.** 2. [To explain] reveal, tell, explicate; see **explain.** 3. [To demonstrate] attest, determine, confirm; see **prove.** 4. [To convince] teach, prove to, persuade; see **convince.** 5. [To indicate] register, note, point; see **record 1.**

showdown, *n.* crisis, exposé, unfolding; see **climax.**

shower, *n.* 1. [Water falling in drops] drizzle, mist, rainfall; see **rain 1.** 2. [Act of cleansing the body] bathing, washing, sponging; see **bath 1.**

shown, *a.* 1. [Put on display] displayed, demonstrated, advertised, exposed, set out, presented, exhibited, laid out, put up for sale, put up, put on the block.—*Ant.* withdrawn, concealed, held back. 2. [Proved] demonstrated, determined, made clear; see **obvious 2.**

show-off, *n.* boaster, exhibitionist, egotist; see **braggart.**

show off, *v.* brag, swagger, make a spectacle of oneself; see **boast.**

show up, *v.* 1. [To arrive] appear, come, turn up; see **arrive.** 2. [To expose] discredit, worst, belittle; see **expose 1.**

show window, *n.* display window, store window, picture window; see **display.**

showy, *a.* flashy, glaring, gaudy; see **ornate 1.**

shred, *n.* fragment, piece, tatter; see **bit 1.**

shred, *v.* slice, strip, cut into small pieces; see **tear.**

shrewd, *a.* astute, ingenious, sharp; see **intelligent 1.**

shrewdly, *a.* knowingly, cleverly, trickily, sagaciously, astutely, skillfully, ably, smartly, deceptively, cunningly, intelligently, judiciously, neatly, coolly, handily, facilely, adroitly, deftly, with skill *or* cunning *or* shrewdness *or* sagacity, in a crafty manner, in a cunning manner, with consummate skill, knowing one's way around; see also **carefully 1, deliberately.**

shriek, *n.* scream, screech, howl; see **cry 1, 3, yell 1.**

shriek, *v.* scream, screech, squawk; see **cry 1, 2, yell.**

shrill, *a.* high-pitched, piercing, penetrating, sharp, screeching, thin, deafening, earsplitting, blatant, noisy, clanging, harsh, blaring, raucous, metallic, discordant, cacophonous, acute; see also loud 1.—*Ant.* **soft, low, faint.**

shrine, *n.* sacred place, hallowed place, reliquary; see **church 1.**

shrink, *v.* withdraw, blench, flinch; see **contract 1.**

shrinkage, *n.* lessening, reduction, depreciation; see **loss 1, 3.**

shrivel, *v.* parch, dry up, shrink; see **contract 1, dry 1.**

shrub, *n.* scrub, fern, dwarf tree; see **plant.**

shrubbery, *n.* shrubs, bushes, hedge; see **brush 3.**

shrug (off), *v.* forget, ignore, disapprove; see **doubt, gesture.**

shrunken, *a.* withdrawn, withered, contracted; see **dry 1, wrinkled.**

shudder, *n.* tremor, shuddering, shaking, trembling.

shudder, *v.* quiver, quake, shiver; see **shake 1, wave 1.**

shun, *v.* dodge, evade, keep away from; see **avoid.**

shut, *a.* stopped, locked, fastened; see **tight 2.**

shut, *v.* close up, lock, seal; see **close 4.**

shut down, *v.* close up *or* down, shut up, abandon; see **stop 1.**

shut off, *v.* turn off, discontinue, put a stop to; see **close 4, stop 1.**

shut out, *v.* keep out, evict, fence out *or* off; see **refuse.**

shutter, *n.* blind, cover, shade; see **curtain, screen 1.**

shut up, *v.* 1. [To cease speaking] be quiet, stop talking, quiet, hush, quit (your) chattering, silence, *shut up. 2. [To close] padlock, close up *or* down *or* out, stop; see **close 4.**

shy, *a.* retiring, bashful, girlish, modest, diffident, submissive, timid, passive, reticent, fearful, tentative, subservient, docile, compliant, humble, coy, restrained, timorous.

shyness, *n.* bashfulness, reserve, timidity, modesty, timidness, coyness, demureness, sheepishness, diffidence, apprehension, backwardness, nervousness, insecurity, reticence; see also **restraint 1.**

sick, *a.* ill, ailing, unwell, disordered, diseased, feeble, weak, impaired, suffering, feverish, imperfect, sickly, declining, unhealthy, rabid, indisposed, distempered, infected, invalid, delicate, infirm, rickety, broken down, physically run down, confined, laid up, coming down with, under medication, bedridden, in poor health, at death's door, hospitalized, quarantined, incurable, *on the blink, *out of kilter, feeling poorly, *sick as a dog, in a bad way, *not so

hot, *under the weather.—*Ant.* **healthy, hearty, well.**

sicken, *v.* 1. [To contract a disease] become ill *or* sick, take sick, fall ill, become diseased, fall victim to a disease, be stricken, run a temperature *or* a fever, be taken with, come down with, get *or* catch *or* pick up a disease *or* illness, acquire, waste away, break out (with *or* in), *take *or* catch one's death, *pick up a bug. 2. [To offend] repel, nauseate, revolt; see **disgust.**

sickening, *a.* 1. [Contaminated] sickly, tainted, diseased; see **sick 2.** 2. [Disgusting] revolting, nauseous, putrid; see **offensive 2.**

sickly, *a.* ailing, weakly, feeble; see **sick.**

sickness, *n.* ill health, ailment, infirmity; see **illness 1.**

sick of, *a.* tired (of), disgusted, fed up; see **disgusted.**

side, *a.* at *or* to *or* from *or* by *or* into the side, indirect, roundabout; see **oblique.**

side, *n.* 1. [One of two opponents] party, contestant, combatant; see **faction.** 2. [A face] facet, front, front side, rear, surface, outer surface, inner surface, top, bottom, elevation, view; see also **plane 1.** —**on the side,** in addition (to), as a bonus, additionally; see **extra.** —**side by side,** adjacent, nearby, faithfully; see **loyally, near 1.** —**take sides,** join, fight for, declare oneself; see **help, support 2.**

side effect, *n.* influence, symptom, reaction; see **illness 1, result.**

side line, *n.* avocation, interest, trade; see **hobby.**

side-step, *v.* evade, elude, shun; see **avoid.**

sidewalk, *n.* footway, footpath, foot pavement; see **path.**

sideways, *a.* indirectly, sloping, sidelong; see **oblique.**

side with, *v.* join, aid, incline to; see **favor, help 1, support 2.**

siege, *n.* offense, onslaught, assault; see **attack.**

sieve, *n.* strainer, sifter, colander, screen, bolt, bolting cloth, mesh, hair sieve, drum sieve, flat sieve, quarter-inch sieve, half-inch sieve, gravel sieve, flour sieve.

sift, *v.* 1. [To evaluate] investigate, scrutinize, probe; see **examine.** 2. [To put through a sieve] bolt, screen, winnow, grade, sort, colander, size, strain; see also **clean, filter 2, purify.**

sigh, *n.* deep breath, sign of relief, expression of sorrow; see **cry 1.**

sigh, *v.* groan, moan, lament; see **cry 1, gasp.**

sight, *n.* 1. [The power of seeing] perception, apperception, eyesight, eyes (for), range of vision, apprehension, keen *or* clear *or* good sight; see **vision 1. 2.** [Something worth seeing; *often plural*] show, view, spectacle, display, scene, point of interest, local scene. **3.** [*An unsightly person*] eyesore, hag, ogre; see **slob.** —*a sight for sore eyes,* beauty, welcome sight, delight; see **blessing 2, friend, view 1.** —*at first sight,* hastily, without much *or* due consideration, provisionally; see **quickly.** —*by sight,* somewhat acquainted, not intimate(ly), superficially; see **unfamiliar 1.** —*catch sight of,* glimpse, notice, see momentarily *or* fleetingly *or* for a moment, etc.; see **see 1.** —*lose sight of,* miss, fail to follow, slip up on; see **forget, neglect 1.** —*on sight,* at once, without hesitation, precipitately; see **immediately, quickly 1, 2.** —*out of sight (of),* disappeared, vanished, indiscernible; see **gone 1, invisible.**

sight-seeing, *n.* vacationing, excursion, tour; see **travel.**

sight-seer, *n.* observer, wanderer, voyager; see **traveler.**

sign, *n.* **1.** [*A signal*] indication, clue, omen, divination, premonition, handwriting on the wall, foreshadowing, foreboding, foreknowledge, token, harbinger, herald, hint, symptom, assurance, prediction, portent, prophecy, mark, badge, symbol, caution, warning, beacon, flag, hand signal, wave of the arm, flash, whistle, warning bell, signal bell, signal light, *high sign. **2.** [*An emblem*] insignia, badge, crest; see **emblem. 3.** [*A symbol*] type, visible sign, token; see **sense 1.**

sign, *v.* **1.** [*Authorize*] endorse, confirm, acknowledge; see **approve 1. 2.** [*Indicate*] express, signify, signal; see **mean 1. 3.** [*Hire*] engage, contract, employ; see **hire 1.**

signal, *n.* beacon, flag, omen; see **sign 1.**

signature, *n.* sign, stamp, mark, name, written name, subscription, autograph, impression, indication, designation, trademark, *one's John Hancock.

signed, *a.* endorsed, marked, autographed, written, undersigned, countersigned, sealed, witnessed, subscripted, registered, enlisted, signed on the dotted line.

signer, *n.* cosigner, underwriter, endorser; see **witness.**

significance, *n.* weight, consequence, point; see **importance.**

significant, *a.* meaningful, notable, vital; see **important 1.**

signify, *v.* imply, import, purport; see **mean 1.**

silence, *n.* **1.** [*Absence of sound*] quietness, stillness (of death), hush, utter stillness, absolute quiet, calm, noiselessness, quiet, deep stillness, loss of signal, radio silence, security silence, security blackout, censorship, iron curtain.—*Ant.* **noise,** din, uproar. **2.** [*Absence of speech*] muteness, secrecy, reserve, reticence, inarticulateness, golden silence, respectful silence, sullen silence.

silence, *v.* overawe, quell, still; see **quiet 2.**

silenced, *a.* quieted, calmed, stilled, restrained, repressed, held down *or* back, restricted, subdued, inhibited, coerced, suppressed, under duress *or* compulsion *or* restraint, etc.; see also **interrupted.**

silent, *a.* **1.** [*Without noise*] still, hushed, soundless; see **calm 2, quiet. 2.** [*Without speech*] reserved, mute, speechless; see **dumb 1.**

silently, *a.* without noise, without a sound, as still as a mouse, like a shadow, in utter stillness, noiselessly, calmly, quietly, soundlessly, mutely, dumbly, in deathlike silence, like one struck dumb, speechlessly, wordlessly, as silently as falling snow.

silhouette, *n.* contour, shape, profile; see **form 1, outline 4.**

sill, *n.* threshold beam, bottom of the frame; see **ledge.**

silly, *a.* senseless, ridiculous, nonsensical, unreasonable, foolish, irrational, inconsistent, stupid, illogical, ludicrous, preposterous; see also **childish.**

silver, *a.* silvery, pale, white, lustrous, bright, silvery white, silverlike, white as silver.

silverware, *n.* silver, service, cutlery, flatware, hollow ware, silver plate. Common pieces of silverware include the following—knife, dinner knife, butter knife, fork, salad fork, cold meat fork, tablespoon, soup spoon, dessert spoon, ice-cream spoon, iced-tea spoon, coffee spoon, teaspoon, soup ladle, gravy ladle, sugar spoon, salt spoon, spatula.

silvery, *a.* shiny, glittering, brilliant; see **bright 1.**

similar, *a.* much the same, comparable, related; see **alike.**

similarity, *n.* correspondence, likeness, resemblance, parallelism, semblance, agreement, affinity, kinship, analogy, closeness, approximation, conformity, concordance, concurrence, coincidence, harmony, comparability, identity, community, relation, correlation, relationship, proportion, comparison, simile, interrelation, association, connection, similar form, similar appearance, like quality, point of likeness.—*Ant.* **difference,** variance, dissimilarity.

similarly, *a.* likewise, thus, furthermore, in a like manner, correspondingly, by the same token, in addition, then, as well, too; see also **so.**

simmer, v. seethe, stew, warm; see **boil, cook.**

simmer down, v. cool (off), be reasonable, become calm or quiet or sensible, etc.; see **calm down.**

simmering, a. broiling, heated, boiling; see **hot 1.**

simple, a. 1. [Not complicated] single, unmixed, unblended, mere, unadulterated, not complex, simplistic, not confusing, pure. 2. [Plain] unadorned, unaffected, homely; see **modest 2.** 3. [Easy] not difficult, mild, done with ease; see **easy 2.**

simple-minded, a. unintelligent, childish, moronic; see **dull 3, naive, stupid 1.**

simpleton, n. clod, idiot, bungler; see **fool.**

simplicity, n. 1. [The quality of being plain] plainness, stark reality, lack of ornament, lack of sophistication, bareness, homeliness, severity. 2. [Artlessness] naïveté, plainness, primitivenes; see **innocence 2.**

simplified, a. made easy, made plain, uncomplicated, clear, interpreted, broken down, cleared up, reduced; see also **obvious 2.**

simplify, v. clear up, clarify, interpret; see **explain.**

simplistic, a. simplest, naive, oversimplified; see also **childish, simple 1.**

simply, a. 1. [With simplicity] clearly, plainly, intelligibly, directly, candidly, sincerely, modestly, easily, quietly, naturally, honestly, frankly, unaffectedly, artlessly, ingenuously, without self-consciousness, commonly, ordinarily, matter-of-factly, unpretentiously, openly, guilelessly. 2. [Merely] utterly, just, solely; see **only 1.**

simulate, v. imitate, feign, lie; see **pretend 1.**

simultaneous, a. coincident, at the same time, concurrent, in concert, in the same breath, in chorus, at the same instant; see also **equally.**

simultaneously, a. at the same time, as one, concurrently; see **together 2.**

sin, n. error, wrongdoing, trespass, wickedness, evil-doing, iniquity, immorality, crime, ungodliness, unrighteousness, veniality, disobedience to the divine will, transgression of the divine law, violation of God's law; see also **crime.** Sins recognized as deadly include the following—pride, covetousness, lust, anger, gluttony, envy, sloth.

sin, v. err, do wrong, commit a crime, offend, break the moral law, break one of the Commandments, trespass, transgress, misbehave, go astray, fall, lapse, fall from grace or virtue, sow one's wild oats, *wander from the straight and narrow, backslide, *live in sin, *sleep around.

since, a. and prep. 1. [Because] for, as, inasmuch as, considering, in consideration of, after all, seeing that, in view of (the fact), for the reason that, by reason of, on account of, in view of; see also **because.** 2. [Between the present and a previous time] ago, from the time of, after, following, more recently than, until now.

sincere, a. truthful, faithful, trustworthy; see **honest 1, reliable.**

sincerely, a. truthfully, truly, really, genuinely, earnestly, aboveboard, seriously, naturally, candidly, frankly, profoundly, deeply, to the bottom of one's heart.

sincerity, n. openness, frankness, truthfulness; see **honesty, reliability.**

sinful, a. wicked, erring, immoral; see **bad 1, wrong 1.**

sinfully, a. wickedly, immorally, unjustly; see **wrongly 1.**

sing, v. chant, carol, warble, vocalize, trill, croon, twitter, chirp, raise a song, lift (up) the voice in song, burst into song.

singe, v. brand, sear, scorch; see **burn.**

singer, n. vocalist, songster, chorister, soloist, minstrel, chanter; see also **musician.**

singing, n. warbling, crooning, chanting; see **music 1.**

single, a. 1. [Unique] sole, original, exceptional, singular, only, without equal, unequaled, peerless, unrivaled; see also **rare 2, unique, unusual 1.**—Ant. many, numerous, widespread. 2. [Individual] particular, separate, indivisible; see **individual, private.** 3. [Unmarried] unwed, celibate, eligible, virginal, living alone, companionless, unattached, free, foot-loose, *on the loose, *in the market.—Ant. married, united, wed.

single-handed, a. without help or assistance, courageously, self-reliantly; see **alone, bravely.**

single-minded, a. stubborn, self-reliant, bigoted; see **selfish.**

singly, a. alone, by itself, by oneself, separately, only, solely, one by one, privately, individually, once.

singular, a. sole, one only, single; see **unique.**

sinister, a. evil, bad, corrupt, perverse, dishonest, foreboding, disastrous, malignant, hurtful, harmful, injurious, dire, poisonous, adverse, unlucky, unfortunate, unfavorable; see also **bad 1.**

sink, n. sewer, basin, cesspool, washbasin, tub, pan, bowl.

sink, v. 1. [To go downward] descend, decline, fall, subside, drop, droop, slump, go under, immerse, go to the bottom, be submerged, settle, go to Davy Jones's locker, touch bottom, go down (with the ship).—*Ant.* rise, float, come up. 2. [To cause to sink, sense 1] submerge, scuttle, depress, immerse, engulf, overwhelm, swamp, lower, bring down, force down, cast down, let down; see also **immerse**. 3. [To weaken] decline, fail, fade; see **weaken 1**. 4. [To decrease] lessen, diminish, wane; see **decrease 1**.

*sink in, *v.* impress, take hold, make an impression; see also **influence**.

sinner, *n.* wrongdoer, delinquent, lawbreaker; see **criminal**.

sip, *v.* taste, drink in, extract; see **drink 1**.

siren, *n.* horn, whistle, signal; see **alarm**.

*sissy, *a.* weak, afraid, *chicken; see **cowardly**.

sister, *n.* blood relative, member of the family, stepsister, half sister, big sister, *kid sister, *sis; see also **relative**.

sit, *v.* be seated, seat oneself, take a seat, sit down, sit up, squat, perch, *take a load off one's feet, have a place, have a chair, sit in, take a chair, take a seat, take a place.—*Ant.* rise, stand up, get up.

site, *n.* locality, section, situation; see **place 3, position 1**.

sit-in, *n.* demonstration, march, display; see **protest, strike 1**.

sit on *or* upon, *v.* sit in (on), take part (in), be a part of; see **cooperate, join 2**.

sit out, *v.* ignore, abstain (from), hold back; see **neglect 1, 2**.

sitter, *n.* baby sitter, attendant, companion; see **servant**.

situated, *a.* established, fixed, located; see **placed**.

situation, *n.* 1. [Circumstance] condition, state, state of one's affairs; see **circumstances 1, 2**. 2. [A physical position] location, site, spot; see **place 3, position 1**.

sit well with, *v.* please, be acceptable to, gratify; see **satisfy 1**.

size, *n.* 1. [Measurement] extent, area, dimension; see **measurement 2**. 2. [Magnitude] bulk, largeness, greatness, extent, vastness, scope, immensity, enormity, stature, hugeness, breadth, substance, volume, mass, extension, intensity, capacity, proportion; see also **extent, quantity**.

*size up, *v.* judge, survey, scrutinize; see **examine**.

sizzle, *v.* brown, grill, broil; see **cook, fry**.

skate, *v.* slide, glide, skim, slip, skid, go quickly, race, ice skate, roller skate.

skeleton, *n.* 1. [Bony structure] skeletal frame, bone *or* bony structure, support; see **bone**. 2. [Framework] draft, design, sketch; see **frame 1**.

skeptic, *n.* doubter, unbeliever, freethinker; see **cynic**.

skeptical, *a.* cynical, dubious, unbelieving; see **doubtful, suspicious 1**.

sketch, *n.* portrayal, picture, draft, design, outline, drawing, representation, painting, skeleton, figure, illustration, copy, likeness; see also **picture 2, plan 1**.

sketch, *v.* paint, describe, depict; see **draw 2**.

sketchily, *a.* hastily, patchily, incompletely; see **inadequately**.

sketchy, *a.* coarse, crude, preliminary; see **unfinished 1**.

skid, *v.* slip, glide, move; see **slide**.

skill, *n.* dexterity, facility, craft; see **ability**.

skilled, *a.* skillful, a hand at, proficient; see **able, experienced**.

skillful, *a.* skilled, practiced, accomplished; see **able, experienced**.

skim, *v.* 1. [To pass lightly and swiftly] soar, float, sail, dart; see also **fly 1**. 2. [To remove the top; especially, to remove cream] brush, scoop, separate; see **dip 2, remove 1**. 3. [To read swiftly] look through, brush over, scan; see **examine, read 1**.

skimp, *v.* scamp, slight, scrimp; see **sacrifice 2, save 2**.

skimpy, *a.* short, scanty, insufficient; see **inadequate**.

skin, *n.* epidermis, derma, cuticle, bark, peel, husk, rind, hide, coat, covering, surface, parchment. *—be no skin off one's back *or* nose, not hurt (one), do no harm, not affect one; see **survive 1**. —by the skin of one's teeth, barely scarcely, narrowly; see **hardly**. *—get under one's skin, irritate, disturb, upset; see **enrage**. *—save one's skin, get away *or* out, evade, leave (just) in time; see **escape, survive 1**.

skin, *v.* peel, pare, flay, scalp, shed, strip, strip off, pull off, remove the surface from, skin alive, husk, shuck, lay bare, bare.

skin-deep, *a.* shallow, desultory, ignorant; see **superficial, trivial**.

skin diver, *n.* scuba diver, submarine diver, deepsea diver, pearl diver, aquanaut, frogman; see also **diver**.

skinflint, *n.* scrimp, tightwad, hoarder; see **miser**.

skinny, *a.* lean, gaunt, slender; see **thin 2**.

skip, *v.* hop, spring, leap; see **jump 1**.

skirmish, *n.* engagement, encounter, conflict; see **battle, fight 1**.

skirt, *n.* kilt, petticoat, miniskirt; see **clothes, dress 2.**

skull, *n.* scalp, cranium, brain case; see **head 1.**

sky, *n.* firmament, atmosphere, the blue yonder; see **air 1, heaven. —out of a clear (blue) sky,** without warning, suddenly, abruptly; see **quickly, soon 1.**

skyscraper, *n.* tall building, high-rise (building), eyesore; see also **building.**

slab, *n.* slice, chunk, lump; see **part 1.**

slack, *a.* relaxed, lax, limp; see **loose 1.**

slack down *or* **off** *or* **up,** *v.* decline, lessen, become slower *or* quieter, *etc.*; see **decrease 1, slow 1.**

slam, *v.* 1. [To throw with a slam] thump, fling, hurl; see **throw 1.** 2. [To shut with a slam] bang, crash, push; see **close 2, 4.**

slander, *n.* defamation, calumny, scandal; see **lie 1.**

slander, *v.* defame, libel, defile, detract, depreciate, disparage, revile, dishonor, blaspheme, curse, attack, sully, tarnish, villify, blot, cast a slur on, scandalize, belittle, backbite, malign, speak evil of, give a bad name, *sling mud.—Ant.* praise, applaud, eulogize.

slang, *n.* cant, argot, colloquialism, pidgin English, vulgarism, lingo, bad grammar, dog Latin, *slanguage,* English as she is spoke, *Americanese;* see also **jargon 1, 3.**

slant, *v.* veer, lie obliquely, incline; see **bend, lean 1, tilt.**

slanting, *a.* inclining, sloping, tilting; see **bent.**

slap, *v.* strike, pat, spank; see **hit 1.**

slapdash, *a.* hasty, sluggish, impetuous; see **careless.**

slap down, *v.* rebuke, reprimand, worst; see **defeat 2, quiet 2.**

slap-happy, *a.* out of one's wit(s) *or* head, badly beaten, dizzy; see **beaten 1, silly.**

slapstick, *a.* absurd, droll, comical; see **funny 1.**

slash, *v.* slit, gash, sever; see **cut 1.**

slaughter, *n.* butchery, killing, massacre; see **murder.**

slaughter, *v.* slay, murder, massacre; see **butcher 1, kill.**

Slav, *n.* Slavs include the following—Russian, Bulgarian, Pole, Slovene, Slovak, Ukranian, Bohemian, Moravian, Czech, Serb, Croat, Sorb, Deniker.

slave, *n.* bondsman, bondservant, chattel, serf, toiler, menial, drudge, laborer, captive, bondsmaid, bondwoman, victim of tyranny, one of a subject people.

slavery, *n.* 1. [Bondage] subjugation, restraint, involuntary servitude; see **captivity.** 2. [Drudgery] toil, menial labor, grind; see **work 2.**

Slavic, *a.* Slav, Slavophile, Slavonic, Old Slavonic, Church Slavonic. Words referring to Slavic peoples include the following—Cyrillic, Glagolitic, Russian, Polish, Bulgarian, Czech, Ukrainian, Bohemian, Serbian, Croatian *or* Croat, Bosnian, Montenegrin, Yugoslavian.

slay, *v.* murder, slaughter, assassinate; see **kill 1.**

sleazy, *a.* shoddy, flimsy, slight; see **thin 1, weak 2.**

sled, *n.* hand sled, bobsled, sleigh, coasting sled, child's sled, toboggan, bellybumper, pig-sticker.

sleek, *a.* silken, silky, satin, see **smooth 1.**

sleep, *n.* slumber, doze, nap, rest, sound *or* deep sleep, siesta, catnap, dream, hibernation, the sandman, *snooze,* *shut-eye.*

sleep, *v.* slumber, doze, drowse, rest, nap, snooze, hibernate, dream, snore, nod, yawn, relax, go to bed, drop *or* fall asleep, *take forty winks, catnap, turn in, *hit the hay, *saw logs, *sack up *or* out.

sleeping, *a.* dormant, inert, inactive; see **asleep.**

sleep (something) off, *v.* get over it, improve, sober up; see **recover 3.**

***sleep on it,** *v.* think about it, consider, ponder; see **think 1.**

sleepy, *a.* dozy, somnolent, sluggish; see **tired.**

slender, *a.* slim, slight, spare; see **thin 1, 2.**

slice, *n.* thin piece, chop, chunk; see **part 1.**

slick, *a.* sleek, slippery, glossy; see **oily 2, smooth 1.**

slide, *v.* glide, skate, skim, slip, coast, skid, move along, move over, move past, pass along. —**let slide,** ignore, pass over, allow to decline *or* get worse *or* decay, *etc.;* see **neglect 1, 2.**

slight, *a.* 1. [Trifling] insignificant, petty, piddling; see **trivial, unimportant.** 2. [Inconsiderable] small, sparse, scanty; see **inadequate.** 3. [Delicate] frail, slender, flimsy; see **dainty.**

slightly, *a.* a little, to some *or* a small extent, hardly at all, scarcely any, not noticeably, unimportantly, inconsiderably, insignificantly, lightly, somewhat.

slim, *a.* slender, narrow, lank; see **thin 2.**

slime, *a.* fungus, mire, ooze; see **mud.**

slimy, *a.* oozy, miry, mucky; see **muddy 1, 2.**

sling, *v.* hurl, send, shoot; see **throw 1.**

slink, *v.* prowl, cower, lurk; see **sneak.**

slip, *n.* 1. [Error] lapse, misdeed, indiscretion; see **error.** 2. [Misstep] slide, skid, stumble; see **fall 1.** 3. [Undergarment] underclothing, panti-slip, bra-slip; see **clothes, underwear. —give some-**

one the **slip**, get away, slip away, escape (from); see **leave 1**.

slipper, n. house shoe, sandal, pump; see **shoe**.

slippery, a. glassy, smooth, glazed, polished, oily, waxy, soapy, greasy, slimy, icy, sleek, glistening, wet, unsafe, insecure, uncertain, tricky, shifty, slithery, *slippery as an eel.

slip-up, n. oversight, mishap, omission; see **error**.

slip up (on), v. overlook, miss, bungle; see **fail 1**.

slit, n. split, cleavage, crevice; see **hole 1**, **tear**.

slit, v. tear, slice, split; see **cut 1**.

sliver, n. splinter, thorn, fragment; see **bit 1**, **flake**.

*slob, n. pig, hog, slattern, tramp, bum, yokel, ragamuffin.

slobber, v. drip, salivate, dribble; see **drool**.

slogan, n. catchword, rallying cry, trademark; see **motto**, **proverb**.

slop, v. slosh, wallow, splash, drip, spill, run over; see also **drop 1**, **empty 1**.

slope, n. rising ground, incline, grade; see **hill**.

sloppy, a. clumsy, amateurish, mediocre; see **awkward**, **careless**.

slot, n. aperture, opening, cut; see **hole 1**.

slow, a. 1. [Slow in motion] sluggish, laggard, deliberate, gradual, loitering, leaden, creeping, inactive, slow moving, crawling, slow-paced, leisurely, *as slow as molasses in January.—Ant. fast, swift, rapid. 2. [Slow in starting] dilatory, procrastinating, delaying, postponing, idle, indolent, tardy, lazy, apathetic, phlegmatic, inactive, sluggish, heavy, quiet, drowsy, inert, sleepy, lethargic, stagnant, negligent, listless, dormant, potential, latent; see also **late 1**.—Ant. immediate, alert, instant. 3. [Slow in producing an effect] belated, behindhand, backward, overdue, delayed, long-delayed, behindtime, retarded, detained, hindered.—Ant. busy, diligent, industrious. 4. [Dull or stupid] stolid, tame, uninteresting; see **dull 3**.

slow, v. 1. [To become slower] slacken, slow up or down, lag, loiter, relax, procrastinate, stall, let up, wind down, ease up or off. 2. [To cause to become slower] delay, postpone, moderate, reduce, retard, detain, decrease, diminish, hinder, hold back, keep waiting, brake, curtail, check, curb, cut down, rein in, cut back.

slowly, a. moderately, gradually, nonchalantly, gently, leisurely, at one's leisure, *taking one's (own) sweet time.

slowness, n. sluggishness, apathy, lethargy; see **indifference**.

sluggish, a. inactive, torpid, indolent; see **lazy 1**, **slow 1**, **2**.

sluggishness, n. apathy, drowsiness, lethargy; see **fatigue**, **laziness**.

slum, a. ghetto, poverty-stricken, crowded; see **poor 1**.

slum, n. low-cost or cheap housing, poor district, tenement neighborhood, *rat-nest, *the wrong side of the tracks.

slump, n. depreciation, slip, descent; see **drop 2**.

slump, v. decline, depreciate, decay; see **sink 1**.

slush, n. (melting) snow, mire, refuse; see **mud**.

slut, n. wench, whore, *hooker; see **prostitute**.

sly, a. wily, tricky, foxy, shifty, crafty, shrewd, designing, deceitful, scheming, deceiving, intriguing, cunning, unscrupulous, deceptive, conniving, calculating, plotting, dishonest, treacherous, underhanded, sneaking, double-dealing, faithless, traitorous, sharp, smart, ingenious, *cagey, dishonorable, crooked, mean, dirty, *double-crossing, *slick, *smooth, slippery, *shady.

slyly, a. secretly, cunningly, furtively; see **cleverly**.

*smack down, v. rebuke, take aback, humiliate; see **defeat 2**, **3**, **humiliate**.

small, a. 1. [Little in size] tiny, diminutive, miniature; see **little 1**, **2**. [Little in quantity] scanty, short, meager; see **inadequate**. 3. [Unimportant] trivial, insignificant, unessential; see **shallow 2**, **unimportant**.

smaller, a. tinier, lesser, (more) petite; see **less**, **shorter**.

smallness, n. littleness, narrowness, small or little or minute or diminutive size or bulk or mass, shortness, brevity, slightness, scantiness, tininess.

smart, a. 1. [Intelligent] clever, bright, quick; see **intelligent**. 2. [Impudent] bold, brazen, forward; see **rude 2**.

smart, v. sting, be painful, burn; see **hurt 1**.

*smart aleck, n. show-off, boaster, life of the party; see **braggart**.

smash, n. crash, breakup, breaking; see **blow**.

smash, v. crack, shatter, crush, burst, shiver, fracture, break, demolish, destroy, batter, crash, wreck, break up, overturn, overthrow, lay in ruins, raze, topple, tumble.

smashed, a. wrecked, crushed, mashed; see **broken 1**.

smear, v. 1. [To spread] cover, coat, apply; see **paint 2**, **spread 3**. 2. [To slander] defame, vilify, libel; see **insult**, **slander**.

smell, *n*. 1. [A pleasant smell] fragrance, odor, scent, perfume, essence, aroma, bouquet. 2. [An unpleasant smell] malodor, stench, stink, mustiness, foulness, uncleanness, fume. 3. [The sense of smell] smelling, detection, olfaction; see **awareness**.

smell, *v*. 1. [To give off odor] perfume, scent, exhale, emanate, stink, stench. 2. [To use the sense of smell] scent, sniff, inhale, snuff, nose out, get a whiff of; see also **breathe**.

smelly, *a*. stinking, foul, fetid; see **rank 2**.

smile, *n*. grin, smirk, tender look, friendly expression, delighted look, joyous look; see also **laugh**.

smile, *v*. beam, be gracious, look happy *or* delighted *or* pleased, break into a smile, look amused, smirk, grin; see also **laugh**.

smiling, *a*. bright, with a smile, sunny, beaming; see also **happy**.

smirk, *n*. leer, grin, smile; see **sneer**.

smith, *n*. metalworker, forger, metallurgist; see also **craftsman**, **workman**.

smog, *n*. high fog, smoke haze, haze, mist, air pollution; see also **smoke**.

smoke, *n*. vapor, fume, gas, soot, reek, haze, smudge, smog.

smoke, *v*. 1. [To give off smoke] burn, fume, smudge, smoke up, smolder, reek. 2. [To use tobacco, especially from tobacco] puff, inhale, smoke a pipe, smoke cigarettes, use cigars.

smoked, *a*. cured, dried, kippered; see **preserved 2**.

smoke out, *v*. uncover, reveal, find; see **discover**.

smoky, *a*. smoking, smoldering, reeking; see **burning**.

smolder, *v*. fume, consume, steam; see **burn**, **smoke 1**.

smooth, *a*. 1. [Without bumps] flat, plane, flush, horizontal, unwrinkled, level, monotonous, unrelieved, unruffled, mirrorlike, quiet, still, tranquil, glossy, glassy, lustrous, smooth as glass. —*Ant.* **rough**, steep, broken. 2. [Without jerks] uniform, regular, even, invariable, steady, stable, fluid, flowing, rhythmic, constant, continuous. 3. [Without hair] shaven, beardless, whiskerless, cleanshaven, smooth-faced, smooth-chinned; see also **bald**.—*Ant.* **hairy**, bearded, unshaven.

smooth, *v*. even, level, flatten, grade, iron, polish, varnish, gloss, clear the way, smooth the path.

smoothly, *a*. flatly, sleekly, placidly; see **easily**, **evenly 1**.

smooth over, *v*. conceal, cover (up), hush (up); see **hide 1**.

smorgasbord, *n*. buffet, self-service (meal), salad course; see **food, lunch, meal 2**.

smother, *v*. stifle, suffocate, suppress; see **choke**, **extinguish**.

smothered, *a*. 1. [Extinguished] drenched, consumed, drowned, put out, not burning, quenched, snuffed. 2. [Strangled] choked, asphyxiated, breathless; see **dead 1**.

smudge, *n*. smirch, spot, soiled spot; see **blemish**.

smug, *a*. self-satisfied, complacent, conceited, pleased with oneself, snobbish, egotistical, self-righteous, *stuck up, *stuck on oneself.

snack, *n*. luncheon, slight meal, hasty repast; see **lunch, meal 2**.

snack bar, *n*. cafeteria, lunchroom, café; see **restaurant**.

snag, *n*. obstacle, hindrance, knot; see **barrier, difficulty 1**.

snake, *n*. reptile, serpent, vermin. Common snakes include the following–viper, water moccasin, copperhead, black snake, rattlesnake, python, cobra, blue snake, coral snake, blue racer, garter snake, gopher snake, king snake, milk snake, water snake, boa *or* boa constrictor, adder, puff adder, anaconda, *fer-de-lance* (French).

snap, *n*. clasp, fastening, catch; see **fastener**.

snap, *v*. catch, clasp, lock; see **close 4, fasten**.

snap at, *v*. vent one's anger (at), jump down one's throat, take it out on; see **get angry**.

snap out of it, *v*. pull through, get over, revive; see **recover 3**.

snapshot, *n*. *snap, candid camera shot, action shot; see **photograph, picture 2, 3**.

snare, *n*. trap, lure, decoy; see **trick 1**.

snarl, *n*. 1. [Confusion] tangle, entanglement, complication; see **confusion**. 2. [A snarling sound] grumble, gnarl, angry words; see **growl**.

snarl, *v*. growl, gnarl, grumble, mutter, threaten, bark, yelp, snap, gnash the teeth, bully, quarrel.

snatch, *v*. jerk, grasp, steal; see **seize 1, 2**.

sneak, *v*. skulk, slink, creep, slip away, move secretly, hide, prowl, lurk; see also **evade**.

sneaky, *a*. tricky, deceitful, unreliable; see **dishonest**.

sneer, *v*. mock, scoff, jeer, taunt, slight, scorn, decry, belittle, detract, lampoon, ridicule, deride, caricature, laugh at, look down, insult, disdain, satirize, condemn, *give the raspberry, *give the Bronx cheer.

sneeze, *n.* wheezing, suspiration, sniffle; see **cold 2, fit 1.**

snicker, *v.* giggle, titter, snigger; see **laugh.**

sniff, *v.* snuff, scent, inhale; see **smell 2.**

snip, *v.* clip, slice, nip (off); see **cut 1.**

snob, *n.* showoff, pretender, upstart; see **braggart.**

snobbish, *a.* ostentatious, pretentious, overbearing; see **egotistic.**

*****snooty,** *a.* conceited, nasty, egotistical; see **egotistic.**

snore, *v.* snort, wheeze, sleep; see **breathe.**

*****snotty,** *a.* impudent, like a (spoiled) brat, nasty; see **rude 2.**

snout, *n.* muzzle, proboscis, nozzle; see **nose 1.**

snow, *n.* **1.** [A snowstorm] blizzard, snowfall, snow flurry; see **storm. 2.** [Frozen vapor] snow crystal, snowflake, slush, sleet, snowdrift, snowbank, powder snow, snow pack, snowfall, fall of snow.

snow, *v.* storm, whiten, blanket, spit snow, blizzard, cover, pelt, shower, sleet.

snub, *v.* ignore, disregard, disdain; see **neglect 1.**

snug, *a.* **1.** [Cozy] homelike, secure, sheltered; see **comfortable 1, warm 1. 2.** [Close in fit] trim, well-built, close; see **tight 3.**

so, *a.* **1.** [To a degree] very, this much, so large, vaguely, indefinitely, extremely, infinitely, remarkably, unusually, so much, extremely, in great measure, in some measure; see also **such. 2.** [Thus] and so on *or* forth, in such manner, in this way, even so, in this degree, to this extent; see also **thus. 3.** [Accordingly] then, therefore, consequently; see **accordingly.**

soak, *v.* **1.** [To drench] wet, immerse, dip, water, percolate, permeate, drown, saturate, pour into, pour on, wash over, flood; see also **moisten. 2.** [To remain in liquid] steep, soften, be saturated, be pervaded, sink into, waterlog. **3.** [To absorb] dry, sop, mop; see **absorb.**

soaked, *a.* sodden, saturated, wet, wet through, drenched, soggy, dripping, immersed, steeped, dipped, flooded, drowned, sunk into, waterlogged.

soap, *n.* solvent, soapsuds. Varieties and forms of soap include the following—bar, liquid, glycerine, saddle, powdered, tar, green, perfumed, bath, laundry, soap flakes; see also **cleanser.**

sob, *n.* weeping, bewailing, convulsive sighs; see **cry 3.**

sob, *v.* lament, sigh convulsively, snivel; see **cry 1.**

sober, *a.* solemn, serious, sedate, clear-headed, not drunk *or* inebriated, calm, steady; see also **moderate 4.**

soberly, *a.* moderately, temperately, solemnly, gravely, sedately, in a subdued manner, quietly, regularly, steadily, calmly, coolly, seriously, earnestly, dispassionately, fairly, justly.

so-called, *a.* commonly named, doubtfully called, allegedly, thus termed, wrongly named, popularly supposed, erroneously accepted as, usually supposed.

sociable, *a.* affable, genial, companionable; see **friendly.**

social, *a.* genial, amusing, entertaining, companionable, pleasurable, civil, polite, mannerly, pleasure-seeking, hospitable, pleasant.

socialistic, *a.* Marxist, communist(ic), Fabian, social-democrat, non-capitalistic; see also **democratic, radical.**

socially, *a.* politely, civilly, courteously, hospitably, companionably, entertainingly, amusingly, cordially, genially, sociably.

social science, *n.* study of man and social phenomena, (the) humanities, study of society, social *or* humanistic studies; see also **economics, geography, history, politics 1, psychology, science 1, sociology.**

social security, *n.* social insurance, old age *or* disability *or* unemployment, *etc.,* insurance, (the) dole, social security payments *or* system, retirement; see also **welfare 2.**

social service, *n.* welfare work, aid for the needy, philanthropy; see **welfare 2.**

society, *n.* **1.** [Friendly association] friendship, social intercourse, fellowship; see **organization 2. 2.** [Organized humanity] the public, civilization, culture, nation, community, human groupings, the people, the world at large, social life.

sociology, *n.* study of society *or* human groups, social *or* cultural anthropology, social psychology, (systematic) analysis of human institutions *or* behavior; see also **social science.**

sock, *n.* stocking, hose, ankle-length stocking; see **hosiery.**

socket, *n.* holder, opening, standard; see **joint 1.**

soda, *n.* soda water, carbonated water, mineral water; see **drink 2.**

sofa, *n.* couch, divan, love seat; see **furniture.**

so far, *a.* thus far, up to now, to here; see **here, now 1.**

soft, *a.* **1.** [Soft to the touch] smooth, satiny, velvety, silky, delicate, fine, thin, flimsy, limp, fluffy, feathery, downy, woolly, doughy, spongy, mushy, soppy.—*Ant.* harsh, rough, flinty. **2.** [Soft to the eye] dull, dim, quiet, shaded, pale, light, pastel, faint, blond, misty, hazy, dusky, delicate, tinted; see also shady. *—Ant.* bright, glaring, brilliant. 3. [Soft to the ear] low, melodious, faraway; see **faint** 3. **—be soft on**, treat lightly, not condemn *or* oppose, fail to attack; see **favor, neglect** 1.

soften, *v.* dissolve, lessen, diminish, disintegrate, become tender *or* mellow, thaw, melt, moderate, bend, give, yield, relax, relent, mellow, modify, temper, tone down, tenderize, weaken.*—Ant.* **strengthen**, increase, tone up.

softness, *n.* mellowness, impressibility, plasticity; see **flexibility**.

soggy, *a.* mushy, spongy, saturated; see **soaked, wet** 1.

soil, *n.* dirt, loam, clay; see **earth** 2.

soil, *v.* stain, sully, spoil; see **dirty**.

soiled, *a.* stained, tainted, ruined; see **dirty** 1.

sold, *a.* 1. [Sold out] disposed of, gone, taken; see **sold out**. 2. [*Convinced] pleased (with), impressed, taken with; see **satisfied**.

soldier, *n.* warrior, fighter, private, enlisted man, draftee, volunteer, conscript, commando, mercenary, cadet, rank and file, ranks, selectee, commissioned officer, noncommissioned officer, recruit, veteran, militant, marine, infantryman, guerrilla, guardsman, artilleryman, gunner, engineer, airman, bomber pilot, fighter pilot, paratrooper, tanker, machine-gunner, *G.I. Joe.

sold out, *a.* out of, all sold, out of stock, not in stock, gone, depleted.

sole, *a.* only one, no more than one, remaining; see **individual, single** 1.

solely, *a.* singly, undividedly, singularly; see **individually, only** 1.

solemn, *a.* grave, serious, sober, earnest, intense, deliberate, heavy, austere, somber, dignified, staid, sedate, moody, grim, stern, thoughtful, reflective.

solemnly, *a.* sedately, gravely, impressively; see **seriously** 2.

solid, *a.* 1. [Firm in position] stable, fixed, rooted; see **firm** 1. 2. [Firm or close in texture] compact, hard, substantial; see **firm** 2, **thick** 1. 3. [Reliable] dependable, trustworthy, steadfast; see **reliable**. 4. [Continuous] uninterrupted, continued, unbroken; see **consecutive, regular** 3.

solid, *n.* cube, cone, pyramid, cylinder, block, prism, sphere.

solidification, *n.* hardening, petrification, stiffening, setting, crystallization, fossilization, compression, coagulation, concentration.

solidify, *v.* set, fix, crystallize; see **compress, harden, thicken**.

solitary, *a.* sole, only, alone, single, lonely, separate, individual, isolated, singular.*—Ant.* **accompanied**, thick, attended.

solitude, *n.* isolation, seclusion, retirement; see **silence** 1.

soluble, *a.* dissolvable, solvent, dissoluble, emulsifiable, dispersible, water-soluble, fat-soluble.

solution, *n.* 1. [Explanation] explication, resolution, clarification; see **answer**. 2. [Fluid] suspension, solvent, juice; see **liquid**.

solve, *v.* figure *or* work *or* reason *or* think *or* find *or* make *or* puzzle out, decipher, unravel, interpret, explain, resolve, answer, decode, get to the bottom of, get (right), hit upon a solution, work, do, settle *or* clear up, untangle, unlock, determine, *dope (out), hit the nail on the head, put two and two together, have it.

somber, *a.* melancholy, dreary, dire; see **dismal**.

some, *a.* few, a few, a little, a bit, part of, more than a few, more than a little, any.

some, *pron.* any, a few, a number, an amount, a part, a portion, more or less.

somebody, *pron.* someone, some person, a person, one, anybody, he, a certain person, this person, so-and-so, whoever.

someday, *a.* sometime, one time, one time or another, at a future time, anytime, one day, one of these days, after a while, subsequently, finally, eventually.

somehow, *a.* in some way, in one way or another, by some means, somehow or other, by hook or by crook, anyhow, after a fashion, with any means at one's disposal.

someone, *pron.* some person, one, individual; see **somebody**.

something, *pron.* event, object, portion, anything, being; see **thing** 1, 8.

sometime, *a.* one day, in a time to come, in the future; see **someday**.

sometimes, *a.* at times, at intervals, now and then; see **seldom**.

somewhat, *a.* a little, to a degree, to some extent; see **moderately, slightly**.

somewhere, *a.* in some place, here and there, around, in one place or another, someplace, about, around somewhere, *kicking around, *any (old) place.

son, *n.* male child, offspring, descendant, foster son, dependent, scion, heir, boy, *junior, chip off the old block, *his father's son.

song, *n.* melody, lyric, strain, verse, poem, musical expression; see also **music** 1. *—(big) song and dance**, drivel, boasting, pretense; see **nonsense** 1, 2. **—for a song**, cheaply, at a bargain, for (almost) nothing; see **cheap** 1.

sonic boom, *n.* report, crash, evidence of a pressure wave; see **explosion, sound** 2.

soon, *a.* before long, in a short time, shortly, forthwith, quickly, in a minute *or* second, in short order; see also **someday.**

sooner or later, *a.* eventually, inevitably, certainly; see **someday, surely.**

soot, *n.* carbon, smoke, grit; see **residue.**

soothe, *v.* quiet, tranquilize, alleviate, help, pacify, lighten, unburden, console, cheer; see also **comfort 1, ease 1, 2, relieve.**

sophisticated, *a.* refined, adult, well-bred; see **cultured, mature.**

sophistication, *n.* tact, refinement, finesse; see **composure.**

soppy, *a.* soaked, drippy, damp; see **wet 1, 2.**

sorcerer, *n.* witch, wizard, alchemist; see **magician.**

sorcery, *n.* enchantment, divination, alchemy; see **magic 1, witchcraft.**

sore, *a.* 1. [Tender] painful, hurtful, raw, sensitive, tender, irritated, irritable, distressing, bruised, angry, inflamed, burned, unpleasant, ulcerated, abscessed, uncomfortable. 2. [*Angry] irked, resentful, irritated; see **angry.**

sore, *n.* cut, bruise, wound, boil, ulcer, hurt, abscess, gash, stab, soreness, discomfort, injury; see also **pain 2.**

sorely, *a.* extremely, painfully, badly; see **so 1, very.**

sorrow, *n.* sadness, anguish, pain; see **grief.**

sorrow, *v.* bemoan, bewail, regret; see **mourn 1.**

sorrowful, *a.* grieved, afflicted, in sorrow, in mourning, depressed, dejected; see also **sad 1.**

sorrowfully, *a.* regretfully, weeping, in sorrow *or* sadness *or* dejection, *etc.*; see **sadly.**

sorry, *a.* 1. [Penitent] contrite, repentant, conscience-stricken, remorseful, regretful, sorrowful, apologetic. 2. [Inadequate in quantity or quality] poor, paltry, trifling, cheap, mean, shabby, scrubby, small, trivial, unimportant, insignificant, dismal, pitiful, worthless, despicable; see also **inadequate 1.**—*Ant.* plentiful, adequate, **enough.**

sort, *n.* species, description, class; see **kind 2, variety 2.**

sort, *v.* file, assort, class; see **classify, distribute, order 3.**

***sort of,** *a.* somewhat, to a degree, *kind of; see **moderately, slightly.**

so-so, *a.* ordinary, mediocre, average; see **common 1, dull 4, fair 2.**

sought, *a.* wanted, needed, desired; see **hunted.**

soul, *n.* 1. [Essential nature] spiritual being, heart, substance, individuality, disposition, cause, personality, force, essence, genius, principle, ego, psyche, life.

2. [The more lofty human qualities] courage, love, affection, honor, duty, idealism, philosophy, culture, heroism, art, poetry, reverence, sense of beauty. 3. [A person] human being, man, being; see **person 1.**

sound, *a.* 1. [Healthy] hale, hearty, well; see **healthy.** 2. [Firm] solid, stable, safe; see **reliable.** 3. [Sensible] reasonable, rational, prudent; see **sensible. 4.** [Free from defect] flawless, unimpaired, undecayed; see **whole 2.**

sound, *n.* 1. [Something audible] vibration, din, racket; see **noise 1.** 2. [The quality of something audible] resonance, note, timbre, tone, pitch, intonation, accent, character, quality, softness, loudness, reverberation, ringing, vibration, modulation, discord, consonance, harmony. 3. [Water between an island and the mainland] strait, bay, bight; see **channel.**

sound, *v.* vibrate, echo, resound, reverberate, shout, sing, whisper, murmur, clatter, clank, rattle, blow, blare, bark, ring (out), explode, thunder, buzz, rumble, hum, jabber, jangle, whine, crash, bang, reflect, burst, chatter, creak, clang, roar, babble, clap, patter, prattle, clink, toot, cackle, clack, thud, slam, smash, thump, snort, shriek, moan, quaver, trumpet, croak, caw, quack, squawk.

sounding, *a.* ringing, thudding, bumping, roaring, calling, thundering, booming, crashing, clattering, clinking, clanging, tinkling, whispering, pinging, rattling, rumbling, ticking, crying, clicking, echoing, pattering, clucking, chirping, peeping, growling, grunting, bellowing, murmuring, whirring, splattering, screeching, screaming, squealing, making a noise *or* a sound *or* a racket *or* a clatter, etc.

sound out, *v.* probe, feel out, feel, put out a feeler, send up a trial balloon, see how the land lies, get the lay of the land, see which way the wind blows; see also **examine, experiment.**

soundproof, *a.* soundproofed, silent, soundless; see **quiet.**

soup, *n.* Soups include the following—(mulligan, beef, Irish, etc.), stew, *soupe du jour* (French), beef broth, mutton broth, bouillon, consommé, oxtail *or* split pea *or* French onion *or* chicken *or* tomato *or* celery etc. soup; cream of tomato bisque, purée of peas, minestrone, borsch, clam broth, (clam *or* fish) chowder, Scotch broth, mulligatawny, bouillabaisse, Philadelphia pepperpot; see also **broth, food, stew.**

sour, *a.* acid, tart, vinegary, fermented, rancid, musty, turned, acrid, salty, bitter, caustic, cutting, stinging, harsh, irritating, unsavory, tangy, briny, brackish, sharp, keen, biting, pungent, curdled, unripe.

sour, *v.* turn, ferment, spoil, make sour, curdle.

source, *n.* beginning, cause, root; see **origin** 2, 3.

South, *n.* the Sunny South, South Atlantic States, the Confederacy *or* Confederate States of America, the Old South, Pre-Civil War *or* antebellum South, Southern United States, the New South, the Deep South, (way) down south, Dixie(land), southland; see also **United States**.

south, *a.* 1. [Situated to the south] southern, southward, on the south side of, in the south, toward the equator, southernmost, toward the South Pole, southerly, tropical, equatorial, in the torrid zone. 2. [Moving south] southward, to the south, southbound, headed south, southerly, in a southerly direction, toward the equator. 3. [Coming from the south] headed north, northbound, out of the south, from the south, toward the North Pole; see also **North** 2.

south, *n.* southland, southern section, southern region, tropics, tropical region, equatorial region, southern hemisphere.

southeast, *a.* Points of the compass between south and east include the following—east by south, east-southeast, southeast by east, southeast, southeast by south, south-southeast, south by east; see also **direction**.

southern, *a.* in the south, of the south, from the south, toward the south, southerly; see also **south** 1.

southwest, *a.* Points of the compass between south and west include the following—south by west, south-southwest, southwest by south, southwest, southwest by west, west-southwest, west by south; see also **direction**.

souvenir, *n.* memento, keepsake, relic; see **memorial**.

Soviet Union, *n.* USSR *or* CCCP (Russian) *or* Union of Soviet Socialist Republics, the Soviets, New Russia, Soviet Russia; see also **Europe, Russia**.

sow, *v.* seed, scatter, plant, broadcast, drill in, drill seed, use a drill seeder *or* broadcast seeder, strew, plant to wheat, barley, etc.; put in small grain, do the seeding.

sowed, *a.* scattered, cast, broadcast, spread, distributed, dispersed, strewn, planted.

spa, *n.* baths, spring, curative bath; see **resort** 2.

space, *n.* 1. [The infinite regions] outer space, infinite distance, infinity, interstellar *or* interplanetary space, the universe, cosmos, solar system, galaxy, the beyond; see also **expanse**. —*Ant.* limit, measure, definite area. 2. [Room] expanse, scope, range; see **extent**. 3. [A place] area, location, reservation; see **place** 2.

space-age, *a.* twentieth-century, contemporary, recent; see **modern** 1.

spacecraft, *n.* flying saucer, capsule, unidentified flying object (UFO), manned orbiting laboratory (MOL), space-age *or* orbiting vehicle, spaceship, rocket, space station *or* platform, weather satellite; see also **satellite** 2.

spaced, *a.* divided, distributed, dispersed; see **separated**.

spacious, *a.* capacious, roomy, vast; see **big** 1.

spade, *n.* implement, garden tool, digging tool; see **tool** 1.

Spanish, *a.* Spanish-speaking, Iberian, Romance, Hispanic, Catalan, Castilian, Galician, Andalusian, Basque, Spanish-American, Mexican, South American, Latin American.

spank, *v.* whip, chastise, thrash; see **beat** 1, **punish**.

spare, *a.* superfluous, supernumerary, additional; see **extra**.

spare, *v.* forbear, forgive, be merciful; see **pity, save** 1.

spark, *n.* glitter, glow, sparkle; see **fire** 1.

sparkle, *v.* glitter, glisten, twinkle; see **shine** 1.

sparse, *a.* scattered, scanty, meager; see **inadequate, rare** 1.

spasm, *n.* convulsion, seizure, contraction; see **fit** 1.

spatter, *v.* splash, spot, wet, sprinkle, scatter, stain, dash, dot, speck, speckle, shower, dribble, spray.

speak, *v.* 1. [To utter] vocalize, pronounce, express; see **utter**. 2. [To communicate] converse, articulate, chat; see **talk** 1. 3. [To deliver a speech] lecture, declaim, deliver; see **address** 2. —**so to speak**, that is to say, in a manner of speaking, *as the saying goes; see **accordingly**. —**to speak of**, somewhat, a little, not much; see **some** 1.

speaker, *n.* speechmaker, orator, lecturer, public speaker, preacher, spokesman, spellbinder, discussant, talker.

speak for itself, *v.* account for, be self-explanatory, vindicate; see **explain** 1.

speaking, *a.* oral, verbal, vocal; see **talking**.

speak out, *v.* insist, assert, make oneself heard; see **declare**.

speak well of, *v.* commend, recommend, support; see **praise** 1.

spear, *n.* lance, javelin, bayonet; see **weapon**.

special, *a.* specific, particular, appropriate, peculiar, proper, individual, unique, restricted, exclusive, defined, limited, reserved, specialized, determinate, distinct, select, choice, definite, marked, designated, earmarked; see also **unusual 1, 2.**

*special, n. sale or advertised item, feature, prepared dish; see **meal 2, sale 1, 2.**

specialist, n. expert, devotee, master, veteran, scholar, professional, authority, connoisseur, technician.—Ant. novice, amateur, beginner.

specialize, v. work in exclusively, go in for, limit oneself to; see **practice 1.**

specialized, a. specific, for a particular purpose, functional; see **special.**

specialty, n. practice, work, special interest; see **hobby, job 1.**

species, n. class, variety, sort; see **division 2, kind 2.**

specific, a. particular, distinct, precise; see **definite 1, 2, special.**

specifically, a. particularly, individually, characteristically; see **especially.**

specification, n. designation, stipulation, blueprint; see **plan 1, 2, requirement 1.**

specified, a. particularized, detailed, precise; see **necessary 1.**

specify, v. name, designate, stipulate; see **choose.**

specimen, n. individual, part, unit; see also **example.**

speck, n. spot, iota, mite; see **bit 1.**

speckled, a. specked, dotted, motley; see **spotted 1.**

spectacle, n. scene, representation, exhibition; see **display, view.** —make a spectacle of oneself, show off, act ridiculously or like a fool, play the fool; see **misbehave.**

spectacular, a. striking, magnificent, dramatic; see **impressive.**

spectator, n. beholder, viewer, onlooker; see **observer.**

speculate, v. contemplate, meditate, consider; see **think 1.**

speech, n. 1. [Language] tongue, mother tongue, native tongue; see **language 1.** 2. [The power of audible expression] talk, utterance, articulation, diction, pronunciation, expression, locution, enunciation, communication, prattle, conversation, chatter. 3. [An address] lecture, discourse, oration, *pep talk, harangue, sermon, dissertation, homily, recitation, talk, rhetoric, tirade, bombast, diatribe, commentary, appeal, invocation; see also **communication.**

speechless, a. aphonic, inarticulate, mum; see **dumb 1, mute.**

speed, n. swiftness, briskness, activity, eagerness, haste, hurry, acceleration, dispatch, velocity, readiness, agility, liveliness, quickness, momentum, promptness, expedition, rapidity, rush, urgency, headway, fleetness, *breeze, (good or lively) clip, *steam.

speed, v. ride hard, go like the wind, roll, bowl, *give it the gun, go fast, cover ground, *gun the motor, *step on or give her the gas, go all out, break the sound barrier; see also **race 1.**

speed up, v. 1. [To accelerate] go faster, increase speed, move into a higher speed; see **race 1.** 2. [To cause to accelerate] promote, further, get things going; see **urge 3.**

speedy, a. quick, nimble, expeditious; see **fast 1.**

spell, n. 1. [A charm] trance, talisman, amulet; see **charm 1.** 2. [A period of time] term, interval, season; see **time 1.**

spell out, v. make clear, go into (great or minute) detail, simplify; see **explain.**

spend, v. consume, deplete, waste, dispense, contribute, donate, give, liquidate, exhaust, squander, disburse, pay, discharge, lay out, pay up, settle, use up, throw away, *foot the bill, *ante up, open the purse, *shell out, *blow.— Ant. save, keep, conserve.

spent, a. used, consumed, disbursed; see **finished 1.**

sphere, n. ball, globule, orb; see **circle 1.**

spice, n. seasoning, pepper, cinnamon, nutmeg, ginger, cloves, salt, paprika, savor, relish; see **flavoring.**

spicy, a. pungent, piquant, keen, fresh, aromatic, fragrant, (highly) seasoned, tangy, savory, flavorful, tasty; see also **salty, sour 1.**

spider, n. Common spiders include the following—black widow, garden, grass, trapdoor, bird, wolf, jumping, burrowing, water, violin back; tarantula.

spigot, n. plug, valve, tap; see **faucet.**

spill, v. lose, scatter, drop, spill over, run out; see also **empty 2.**

spilled, a. poured out, lost, run out; see **empty.**

spin, n. circuit, rotation, gyration; see **revolution 1, turn 1.**

spin, v. revolve, twirl, rotate; see **turn 1.**

spine, n. 1. [A spikelike protrusion] thorn, prick, spike, barb, quill, ray, thistle, needle; see also **point 2.** 2. [A column of vertabrae] spinal column, ridge, backbone, vertebral process; see also **bone.**

spineless, a. timid, fearful, frightened; see **cowardly, weak 3.**

spinster, n. unmarried woman, virgin, single woman, old maid, *bachelor girl; see also **woman 1.**

spiny, a. pointed, barbed, spiked; see **sharp 1.**

spiral, a. winding, circling, coiled, whorled, radial, curled, rolled, scrolled, wound.

spirit, *n.* 1. [Life] breath, vitality, animation; see **life** 1. 2. [Soul] psyche, essence, substance; see **soul** 2. 3. [A supernatural being] vision, apparition, specter; see **ghost**, **god**. 4. [Courage] boldness, ardor, enthusiasm; see **courage** 5. 5. [Feeling: *often plural*] humor, tenor; see **feeling** 4, **mood** 1.

spirited, *a.* lively, vivacious, animated; see **active** 2.

spiritless, *a.* dull, apathetic, unconcerned; see **indifferent** 1.

spiritual, *a.* refined, pure, holy; see **religious** 1.

spit, *v.* splutter, eject, drivel, slobber, drool.

spite, *n.* malice, resentment, hatred; see **hate**.

splash, *n.* plash, plop, dash, spatter, sprinkle, spray, slosh, slop.

splash, *v.* splatter, dabble, get wet; see **moisten**.

splendid, *a.* premium, great, fine; see **beautiful**, **excellent**, **glorious**.

splendor, *n.* luster, brilliance, brightness; see **glory** 2.

splice, *v.* knit, graft, mesh; see **join** 1, **weave** 1.

splint, *n.* prop, rib, reinforcement; see **brace**, **support** 2.

splinter, *n.* sliver, flake, chip; see also **bit** 1.

split, *n.* 1. [A dividing] separating, breaking up, severing; see **division** 1. 2. [An opening] crack, fissure, rent; see **hole** 1.

split, *v.* burst, rend, cleave; see **break** 1, **cut** 1, **divide** 1.

split up, *v.* part, break up, isolate; see **divide**, **divorce**.

spoil, *v.* 1. [To decay] rot, blight, fade, wither, molder, crumble, mold, mildew, corrode, decompose, putrefy, degenerate, weaken, become tainted. 2. [To ruin] destroy, defile, plunder; see **destroy**.

spoiled, *a.* damaged, marred, injured; see **ruined** 2, **wasted**.

spoiling, *a.* rotting, breaking up, wasting away; see **decaying**.

spoils, *n.* plunder, pillage, prize; see **booty**.

spoke, *n.* rung, handle, crosspiece; see **rod** 1.

spoken, *a.* uttered, expressed, told, announced, mentioned, communicated, oral, voiced, unwritten.

spokesman, *n.* deputy, mediator, substitute; see **agent**, **speaker**.

sponsor, *n.* advocate, patron, supporter, champion; see **patron**.

spontaneous, *a.* involuntary, instinctive, casual, unintentional, impulsive, automatic, unforced, natural, unavoidable, unwilling, unconscious, uncontrollable.—*Ant.* deliberate, willful, intended.

spontaneously, *a.* instinctively, impulsively, automatically; see **unconsciously**.

spoof, *n.* trickery, *put on, satire; see **deception**.

spoof, *v.* fool, play a trick on, *kid; see **trick** 1.

spooky, *a.* weird, eerie, ominous; see **mysterious** 2, **uncanny**.

spoon, *n.* teaspoon, tablespoon, ladle; see **silverware**.

sport, *n.* 1. [Entertainment] diversion, recreation, play, amusement, merrymaking, festivity, revelry, pastime, pleasure, enjoyment; see also **entertainment**, **fun**, **game** 1. 2. [A joke] pleasantry, mockery, jest, mirth, joke, joking, antics, tomfoolery, nonsense, laughter, practical joke. 3. [Athletic or competitive amusement] Sports, sense 3, include the following—(deer, rabbit, duck, etc.,) hunting, shooting, (the) Olympics, horse racing, automobile racing, running, fishing, basketball, golf, tennis, squash, handball, volleyball, soccer, gymnastics, (professional, *pro, collegiate, high-school, etc.) football, baseball, track and field sports, cricket, lacrosse, hockey, skating, skiing, fencing, jumping, boxing, wrestling.

sporting, *a.* considerate, sportsmanlike, gentlemanly; see **generous**, **reasonable** 1.

sportsman, *n.* huntsman, big game hunter, woodsman; see **fisherman**, **hunter**.

sportsmanship, *n.* 1. [Skill] facility, dexterity, cunning; see **ability**. 2. [Honor] justice, integrity, truthfulness; see **honesty**.

spot, *n.* 1. [A dot] speck, flaw, pimple; see **bit** 1, **blemish**. 2. [A place] point, locality, scene; see **place** 3. —*hit the high spots, 1. hurry, travel rapidly, make (good) time; see **speed**. 2. treat hastily, go over lightly, touch up; see **neglect** 1, 2. —*hit the spot, please, delight, be (just) right; see **satisfy** 1. —*in a bad spot, in danger *or* trouble *or* difficulty, etc.; threatened, *on the spot; see **dangerous**.

spot, *v.* blemish, blotch, spatter; see **dirty**.

spotless, *a.* stainless, immaculate, without spot *or* blemish; see **clean**, **pure** 2.

spotted, *a.* 1. [Dotted] marked, dappled, mottled, dotted, speckled, motley, blotchy. 2. [Blemished] soiled, smudged, smeared; see **dirty** 1.

spouse, *n.* marriage partner, groom, bride; see **husband**, **mate** 3, **wife**.

sprain, *n.* twist, overstrain; strain; see **injury** 1.

sprained, *a.* wrenched, strained, pulled out of place; see **hurt, twisted 1.**

sprawl, *v.* slouch, relax, lounge; see **lie 3.**

spray, *n.* splash, steam, fine mist; see **fog.**

spray, *v.* scatter, diffuse, sprinkle; see **spatter.**

spread, *a.* expanded, dispersed, extended, opened, unfurled, sown, scattered, diffused, strewn, spread thin; see **distributed.** *—Ant.* restricted, narrowed, restrained.

spread, *n.* 1. [Extent] scope, range, expanse; see **extent, measure 1.** 2. [A spread cloth] blanket, coverlet, counterpane; see **cover 1.** 3. [A spread food] preserve, conserve, jelly; see **butter, cheese.** 4. [*A meal] feast, banquet, informal repast; see **dinner, lunch, meal 2.**

spread, *v.* 1. [To distribute] cast, diffuse, disseminate; see **radiate 1, scatter 2, sow.** 2. [To extend] open, unfurl, roll out, unroll, unfold, reach, circulate, lengthen, widen, expand, untwist, unwind, uncoil, enlarge, increase, develop, branch off, expand; see also **flow, reach 1.***—Ant.* close, shorten, shrink. 3. [To apply over a surface] cover, coat, smear, daub, plate, gloss, enamel, paint, spray, plaster, pave, wax, varnish. 4. [To separate] part, sever, disperse; see **divide 1, separate 1.**

spreading, *a.* extended, extensive, spread out, growing, widening.

spree, *n.* revel, frolic, *binge; see **celebration.**

sprightly, *a.* lively, gay, quick, alert; see **agile.**

spring, *n.* 1. [A fountain] flowing well, artesian well, sweet water; see **origin 2.** 2. [The season between winter and summer] springtime, seedtime, flowering, budding, vernal equinox, *blackberry winter; see also **season.**

sprinkle, *v.* dampen, bedew, spray; see **moisten.**

sprout, *v.* germinate, take root, shoot (up), bud, burgeon; see also **grow 1.**

spry, *a.* nimble, fleet, vigorous; see **agile.**

spurn, *v.* despise, disdain, look down on; see **evade.**

spurt, *n.* squirt, jet, stream; see **water 2.**

spurt, *v.* spout, jet, burst; see **flow 2.**

sputter, *v.* stumble, stutter, falter; see **stammer.**

spy, *n.* (secret *or* foreign) agent, scout, detective, plainclothes *or* undercover *or* CIA *or* FBI man, observer, watcher.

spy, *v.* scout, observe, watch, examine, *bug, tap, scrutinize, take note, search, discover, look for, hunt, peer, pry, spy out, set a watch on, hound, trail, *tail, follow; see **meddle 1, 2.**

squabble, *n.* spat, quarrel, feud; see **dispute.**

squabble, *v.* argue, disagree, fight; see **quarrel.**

squad, *n.* company, small company, crew; see **team 1.**

squalid, *a.* dirty, poor, foul; see **dirty 1.**

squall, *n.* blast, gust, gale; see **storm 1.**

squalor, *n.* ugliness, disorder, uncleanness; see **filth.**

squander, *v.* spend, spend lavishly, throw away; see **waste 2.**

square, *a.* 1. [Having right angles] right-angled, four-sided, equal-sided, squared, equilateral, rectangular, rectilinear. 2. [*Old-fashioned] dated, stuffy, out-of-date; see **conservative, old-fashioned.**

square, *n.* 1. [A rectangle] equal-sided rectangle, plane figure, rectilinear plane; see **rectangle.** 2. [A park] city *or* civic center, plaza, recreational area; see also **park 1.**

squat, *v.* stoop, hunch, cower; see **sit.**

squaw, *n.* female Indian, Indian woman, wife; see **Indian 1, woman 1.**

squawk, *v.* cackle, crow, yap; see **cry 3.**

squeak, *n.* peep, squeal, shrill sound; see **cry 2, noise 1.**

squeak, *v.* creak, peep, squeal; see **cry 3, sound 1.**

*squeak through,** *v.* manage, survive, pass; see **endure 2, succeed 1.**

squeal, *v.* shout, yell, screech; see **cry 1, 3.**

squeamish, *a.* finicky, fussy, delicate, hard to please, fastidious, particular, exacting, prim, prudish, queasy.

squeeze, *n.* influence, restraint, force; see **pressure 1, 2.** —put the squeeze on, compel, urge, use force *or* pressure *or* compulsion, *etc.* (with); see **force, influence.**

squeeze, *v.* clasp, pinch, clutch; see **hug, press 1.**

squeeze through, *v.* survive, accomplish, get by; see **endure 1, succeed 1.**

squint, *v.* give a sidelong look, screw up the eyes, peek, peep; see **look 2.**

squirm, *v.* wriggle, twist, fidget; see **wiggle.**

squirt, *v.* spurt, spit, eject; see **emit.**

stab, *n.* thrust, wound, puncture; see **cut.** —make a stab at, endeavor, try to, do one's best (to); see **try 1.**

stab, *v.* pierce, wound, stick, cut, hurt, run through, thrust, prick, drive, puncture, hit, bayonet, knife; see also **kill 1.**

stability, *n.* 1. [Firmness of position] steadiness, durability, solidity, endurance, immobility, suspense, establishment, balance, permanence. 2. [Steadfastness of character] stableness, aplomb, security, endurance, maturity, resoluteness, determination, perseverance, adherence, backbone, assurance, resistance; see also **confidence 1**.

stab in the back, *v.* deceive, undercut, turn traitor; see **trick**.

stable, *a.* 1. [Fixed] steady, stationary, solid; see **firm 1**. 2. [Steadfast] calm, firm, constant; see **determined**.

stable, *v.* barn, coop, corral; see **pen 1**.

stack, *n.* pile, heap, mound; see **bunch**.

stack, *v.* heap, pile (up), accumulate; see **load 1**.

stack up, *v.* become, work out (to *or* as), resolve (into); see **result**.

stadium, *n.* gymnasium, strand, amphitheater; see **arena**.

staff, *n.* 1. [A stick] wand, pole, stave; see **stick**. 2. [A corps of employees] personnel, assistants, men, women, force, help, workers, crew, organization, agents, operatives, deputies, servants.

stage, *n.* 1. [The theater] theater, limelight, spotlight; see **drama**. 2. [A platform] frame, scaffold, staging; see **platform 1**. 3. [A level, period, or degree] grade, plane, step; see **degree 1**. —**by easy stages**, easily, gently, taking one's time; see **slowly**.

stagger, *v.* totter, waver, sway, weave, bob, careen, vacillate.

staggering, *a.* monstrous, huge, tremendous; see **large 1**, **unbelievable**.

stagnant, *a.* inert, dead, inactive; see **idle**.

stagnate, *v.* deteriorate, rot, putrefy; see **decay**.

staid, *a.* sober, grave, steady; see **dignified**.

stain, *n.* blot, blemish, spot, splotch, stained spot, smudge, stigma, brand, blotch, ink spot, spatter, drip, speck.

stain, *v.* spot, discolor, taint; see **dirty**.

stairs, *n.* stairway, staircase, flight, steps, stair, escalator, ascent.

stake, *n.* rod, paling, pale; see **stick**. —**at stake**, at issue, in danger, risked; see **endangered**. —**pull up stakes**, depart, move, decamp; see **leave 1**.

stale, *a.* spoiled, dried, smelly; see **old 2**.

stalk, *n.* stem, support, upright, spire, shaft, spike, straw, stock.

stalk, *v.* approach stealthily, track, chase; see **hunt 1**, **pursue 1**.

stall, *v.* 1. [To break down] not start, conk out, go dead; see **break down 2**. 2. [To delay] postpone, hamper, hinder; see **delay**.

stamina, *n.* strength, vigor, vitality; see **endurance**.

stammer, *v.* falter, stop, stumble, hesitate, pause, stutter, repeat oneself, hem and haw; see also **speak 1**.

stamp, *n.* emblem, brand, cast; see **mark 1**.

stamp, *v.* impress, imprint, brand; see **mark 1**.

stamped, *a.* marked, branded, okayed; see **approved**.

stamp out, *v.* eliminate, kill out *or* off, dispatch; see **destroy**.

stand, *n.* notion, view, belief; see **attitude**, **opinion 1**. —**make or take a stand**, insist, assert, take a position; see **declare**.

stand, *v.* 1. [To be in an upright position] be erect, be on one's feet, stand up, come to one's feet, rise, jump up. 2. [To endure] last, hold, abide; see **endure 1**. 3. [To be of a certain height] be, attain, come to; see **reach 1**.

stand a chance, *v.* have a chance, be a possibility, have something in one's favor, have something on one's side, be preferred.

standard, *a.* regular, regulation, made to a standard; see **approved**.

standard, *n.* pattern, type, example; see **model 2**.

standardization, *n.* uniformity, sameness, likeness, evenness, levelness, monotony; see also **regularity**.

standardize, *v.* regulate, institute, normalize; see **order 3**, **systematize**.

standardized, *a.* patterned, graded, made alike; see **regulated**.

stand-by, *n.* upholder, supporter, advocate; see **patron**, **protector**.

stand by, *v.* 1. [To defend or help] befriend, second, abet; see **defend 2**, **help 1**. 2. [To wait] be prepared, be ready, be near; see **wait 1**.

stand for, *v.* 1. [To mean] represent, suggest, imply; see **mean 1**. 2. [To allow] permit, suffer, endure; see **allow**.

stand-in, *n.* double, second, understudy; see **substitute**.

standing, *n.* position, status, reputation; see **rank 3**.

standoff, *n.* stalemate, deadlock, dead end; see **delay**.

stand one's ground, *v.* oppose, fight (back *or* against), resist; see **fight**.

stand out, *v.* be prominent, be conspicuous, emerge; see **loom 2**.

standpoint, *n.* attitude, point of view, station; see **opinion 1**.

standstill, *n.* stop, halt, cessation; see **delay**.

stand up for, *v.* back, protect, champion; see **defend**.

stand up to, *v.* resist, oppose, challenge; see **fight**.

star, *n.* 1. [A luminous heavenly body] sun, astral body, pulsar, quasar, fixed star, variable star. Familiar stars include the following—individual stars: Betelgeuse, Sirius, Vega, Spica, Arcturus, Aldebaran, Antares, Atlas, Castor, Pollux, Capella, Algol, North Star *or*

Polaris; constellations: Great Bear *or* Ursa Major, Little Bear *or* Ursa Minor, Great Dipper, Little Dipper, Orion, Coma Berenices *or* Berenice's Hair, The Gemini *or* Castor and Pollux, Cassiopeia, Pleiades, Hyades, Taurus, Canis Major *or* the Great Dog, Canis Minor *or* the Little Dog, Scorpion, Sagittarius, Corona Borealis *or* the Northern Crown, Pegasus, Leo, Hercules, Boötes, Cetus, Aquila *or* the Eagle, Cygnus *or* the Swan, Corona Australis *or* the Southern Crown, the Southern Cross. 2. [A conventional figure] asterisk, six-pointed star, five-pointed star; see **form** 1. 3. [A superior performer] headliner, leading lady, leading man, movie actor, movie actress, actor, actress, matinee idol, chief attraction.

stare, *v.* gaze, gawk, look fixedly; see **look** 2, **watch**.

stark-naked, *a.* nude, without a stitch (of clothing), in the altogether; see **naked** 1.

start, *n.* inception, commencement, beginning; see **origin** 2.

start, *v.* commence, rise, spring; see **begin** 1, 2.

started, *a.* evoked, initiated, instituted; see **begun**.

start in, *v.* commence, open, make a start *or* a beginning *or* a first move, *etc.*; see **begin** 1, 2.

startle, *v.* alarm, shock, astonish; see **surprise**.

start up, *v.* make go *or* run, *crank (up), get (something) started; see **begin**, 1, 2.

starvation, *n.* deprivation, need, want; see **hunger**.

starve, *v.* famish, crave, perish; see **die**.

starving, *a.* famished, weakening, dying; see **hungry**.

state, *n.* 1. [A sovereign unit] republic, land, kingdom; see **nation** 1. 2. [A condition] circumstance, situation, welfare, phase, case, station, nature, estate, footing, status, standing, occurrence, occasion, eventuality, element, requirement, category, standing, reputation, environment, chances, outlook, position. —**in a state**, disturbed, upset, badly off; see **troubled**.

state, *v.* pronounce, assert, affirm; see **declare**.

stately, *a.* 1. [*Said of persons*] dignified, haughty, noble; see **proud** 1. 2. [*Said of objects*] large, imposing, magnificent; see **grand**.

statement, *n.* 1. [The act of stating] allegation, declaration, assertion, profession, acknowledgment, assurance, affirmation; see also **announcement**. 2. [A statement of account] bill, charge, reckoning, account, record, report, budget, audit, balance sheet.

statesman, *n.* legislator, lawgiver, administrator, executive, minister, official, politician, diplomat, representative, elder statesman, veteran lawmaker.

station, *n.* 1. [Place] situation, site, location; see **position** 1. 2. [Depot] terminal, stop, stopping place; see **depot**. 3. [Social position] order, standing, state; see **rank** 3. 4. [An establishment to vend petroleum products] gas *or* gasoline *or* service *or* filling *or* petrol station, pumps, petroleum outlet *or* retailer; see **garage** 2. 5. [A broadcasting establishment] (local) television *or* radio *or* transmission *or* transmitter *or* radar *or* microwave *or* broadcasting station, plant, studio(s), transmittor, Channel 1 *or* 2 *or* 3, etc.; see also **communications, radio, television**.

station, *v.* place, commission, allot; see **assign**.

stationary, *a.* fixed, stable, permanent; see **motionless** 1.

stationery, *n.* writing materials, office supplies, school supplies; see **paper** 5.

statue, *n.* statuette, cast, figure, bust, representation, likeness, image, sculpture, statuary, marble, bronze, ivory, icon.

statuesque, *a.* stately, beautiful, grand; see **graceful** 2.

stature, *n.* development, growth, tallness; see **height, size** 2.

status, *n.* situation, standing, station; see **rank** 3.

staunch, *a.* steadfast, strong, constant; see **faithful**.

stay, *n.* 1. [A support] prop, hold, truss; see **support** 2. 2. [A visit] stop, sojourn, halt; see **visit**.

stay, *v.* tarry, linger, sojourn; see **visit** 1. *stay put, *v.* remain, stand (still *or* fast *or* rigid *or* immovable, *etc.*), persist; see **wait** 1.

steadfast, *a.* staunch, stable, constant; see **faithful**.

steadily, *a.* firmly, unwaveringly, undeviatingly; see **regularly**.

steady, *a.* uniform, unvarying, patterned; see **constant, regular** 3. —*go steady (with), keep company (with), court *or* be courted, go with *or* together; see **court, love** 1, 2.

steak, *n.* filet mignon, sirloin, T-bone; see **food, meat**.

steal, *v.* take, filch, thieve, loot, rob, purloin, embezzle, defraud, keep, carry away *or* off, appropriate, take possession of, lift, remove, impress, abduct, shanghai, kidnap, make *or* run off with, hold up, strip, poach, swindle, plagiarize, misappropriate, burglarize, blackmail, fleece, plunder, pillage, ransack, *burgle, *stick up, *hijack, *skyjack, *pinch, *mooch, *gyp; see also **seize** 2.

stealing, *n.* piracy, embezzlement, shoplifting; see **crime, theft.**

steam, *n.* vaporized water, fume(s), fog; see **vapor.**

steam, *v.* heat, brew, pressure cook; see **cook.**

steamboat, *n.* steamer, steamship, liner; see **boat, ship.**

steep, *a.* precipitous, sudden, sharp, angular, craggy, uneven, rough, rugged, irregular, jagged, vertical, uphill, downhill, abrupt, sheer, perpendicular.

steer, *v.* point, head for, direct; see **drive 2.**

steer clear of, *v.* keep *or* stay away (from), miss, escape; see **avoid.**

stem, *n.* peduncle, petiole, pedice; see **stalk.** —**from stem to stern,** the full length, completely, entirely; see **everywhere, throughout.**

stench, *n.* odor, stink, foulness; see **smell 2.**

stenographer, *n.* office girl, typist, shorthand stenographer; see also **clerk, secretary.**

step, *n.* 1. [A movement of the foot] pace, stride, gait, footfall, tread, stepping. 2. [One degree in a graded rise] rest, run, tread, round, rung, level. 3. [The print of a foot] footprint, footmark, print, imprint, impression, footstep, trail, trace, mark; see also **track 2.** —**in step (with),** in agreement (with), coinciding (with), similar (to); see **alike, similarly.** —**keep step,** agree to *or* with, conform (to), keep in line; see **conform.** —**out of step,** inappropriate(ly), incorrect(ly), inaccurate(ly); see **wrong 2, wrongly.** —**take steps,** do (something), start, intervene; see **act 1.** —**watch one's step,** be careful, take precautions, look out; see **watch out.**

step, *v.* pace, stride, advance, recede, go forward *or* backward, *or* up *or* down, ascend, descend, pass, walk, march, move, hurry, hop; see also **climb, rise 1.**

step by step, *a.* by degrees, cautiously, tentatively; see **slowly.**

*****step on it,** *v.* go *or* travel (fast), make (good) time, speed (up); see **speed.**

steppingstone, *n.* help, agent, factor; see **means 1.**

step up, *v.* augment, improve, intensify; see **increase.**

stereotype, *n.* convention, fashion, institution; see **average, custom 2.**

stereotype, *v.* conventionalize, standardize, normalize; see **regulate 2, systematize.**

stereotyped, *a.* hackneyed, trite, ordinary; see **conventional 1, 3, dull 4.**

sterile, *a.* 1. [Incapable of producing young] infertile, impotent, childless,

barren.—*Ant.* **fertile,** productive, potent. 2. [Incapable of producing vegetation] desolate, fallow, waste, desert, arid, dry, barren, unproductive, fruitless, bleak; see also **empty.** 3. [Scrupulously clean] antiseptic, disinfected, decontaminated, germ-free, sterilized, uninfected, sanitary, pasteurized; see also **pure 2.**

sterilize, *v.* antisepticize, disinfect, pasteurize; see **clean, purify.**

stern, *a.* rigid, austere, strict; see **severe 1.**

stew, *n.* ragout, goulash, Hungarian goulash, fish *or* clam *or* sea food chowder, steak-and-kidney *or* oyster *or* beef *or* lamb *or* veal etc. stew; Irish *or* mulligan stew *or* *mulligan, casserole; see also **food, soup.**

stick, *n.* shoot, twig, branch, stem, stalk, rod, wand, staff, stave, walking stick, cane, matchstick, club, baton, drumstick, pole, bludgeon, bat, ruler, stock, cue, mast. —*****the sticks,** rural area(s), (the) back country, outlying district(s); see **country 1.**

stick, *v.* 1. [To remain fastened] adhere, cling, fasten, attach, unite, cohere, hold, stick together, hug, clasp, hold fast. —*Ant.* **loosen,** let go, fall, come away. 2. [To penetrate with a point] prick, impale, pierce; see **penetrate.**

*****stick around,** *v.* stay, continue, be present; see **wait 1.**

stick by (someone), *v.* be loyal (to), stand by, believe in; see **support 2.**

*****stick it out,** *v.* persist, endure, stay; see **wait 1.**

stick out, *v.* jut, show, come through; see **project 1.**

*****stick-up,** *n.* burglary, robbery, stealing; see **crime, theft.**

*****stick up for,** *v.* support, aid, fight for; see **support 2.**

sticky, *a.* ropy, viscous, adherent, sticking, gummy, waxy, pasty, gluey.

stiff, *a.* 1. [Not easily bent] solid, rigid, petrified, firm, tense, unyielding, inflexible, hard, hardened, starched, taut, thick, stubborn, obstinate, unbending, thickened, wooden, steely, frozen, solidified.—*Ant.* flexible, softened, soft. 2. [Formal] ungainly, ungraceful, unnatural; see **awkward.** 3. [Severe] rigorous, exact, strict; see **severe 1, 2. 4.** [Potent] hard, potent, powerful; see **strong 8.**

stiffen, *v.* jelly, harden, starch, petrify, brace, prop, cement, strengthen, thicken, clot, coagulate, solidify, congeal, condense, set, curdle, freeze, cake, crystallize.

stifle, *v.* smother, suffocate, extinguish; see **choke.**

still, *a.* 1. [Silent] calm, tranquil, noiseless; see **quiet 2. 2.** [Yet] nevertheless, furthermore, however; see **besides, but 1, yet 1.**

stimulant, *n.* tonic, bracer, energizer; see **drug 2.**

stimulate, *v.* support, foster, incite; see **urge 2.**

stimulated, *a.* keyed up, speeded up, accelerated; see **excited.**

stimulating, *a.* intriguing, enlivening, arousing, high-spirited, bracing, rousing, energetic, refreshing, exhilarating, enjoyable, health-building, sharp, evocative, exciting, inspiring, provoking, animating.—*Ant.* dull, dreary, humdrum.

sting, *n.* 1. [An injury] wound, cut, sore; see **injury.** 2. [Pain] prick, bite, burn; see **pain 2.**

sting, *v.* prick, prickle, tingle; see **hurt 1.**

stingy, *a.* parsimonious, niggardly, miserly, close, closefisted, greedy, covetous, tightfisted, grasping, penny-pinching, cheap, selfish, meagerly, meanly, skimpy.—*Ant.* **generous,** bountiful, liberal.

stink, *n.* stench, fetor, offensive odor; see **smell 2.**

stink, *v.* smell bad, emit a stench, be offensive; see **smell 1.**

stir, *v.* move, beat, agitate; see **mix 1.**

stir up trouble, *v.* cause difficulty, foment, agitate; see **bother 2, disturb.**

stitch, *v.* join, make a seam, baste; see **sew.**

stock, *n.* 1. [Goods] merchandise, produce, accumulation; see **produce.** 2. [Livestock] domestic animals, barnyard animals, farm animals; see **cattle.** 3. [A stalk] stem, plant, trunk; see **stalk.** —**in stock,** not sold out, stocked, not difficult to get; see **available.** —**out of stock,** sold (out or off), gone, not available; see **sold out.** —**take stock (of),** count up, inventory, figure; see **estimate.** —**take stock in,** invest (in), purchase, take a chance on; see **buy.**

stocking, *n.* hose, panty hose, nylons; see **hosiery.**

stock-still, *a.* frozen, stagnant, inactive; see **motionless 1.**

stock (up), *v.* replenish, supply, furnish; see **buy.**

stolen, *a.* taken, kept, robbed, filched, purloined, appropriated, lifted, abducted, kidnapped, run off with, poached, sacked, cheated, plagiarized, misappropriated.

stomach, *n.* paunch, belly, midsection, bowels, intestines, viscera, entrails; *insides, guts, tummy, *pot, middle, *breadbasket.

stomach-ache, *n.* indigestion, acute indigestion, gastric upset; see **illness 1, 2.**

stone, *a.* rock, stony, rocky, hard, rough, craggy, petrified, marble, granite.

stone, *n.* mass, crag, cobblestone, boulder, gravel, pebble, rock, sand, grain, granite, marble, flint, gem, jewel. —**cast the first stone,** criticize, blame, reprimand; see **attack, scold.** —**leave no stone unturned,** take (great) pains or care, be scrupulous, try hard; see **pursue 1, work 1.**

*stoned,** *a.* drugged, *high, *turned on; see also **drunk.**

stony, *a.* inflexible, cruel, unrelenting; see **firm 2, rough 1.**

stool, *n.* seat, footstool, footrest; see **furniture.**

stoop, *v.* incline, crouch, slant; see **lean 1.**

stop, *interj.* cease, *cut it out, quit it; see **stop,** *v.*, 1.

stop, *n.* 1. [A pause] halt, stay, standstill; see **end 2, pause.** 2. [A stopping place] station, passenger station, wayside stop; see **depot.** —**put a stop to,** halt, interrupt, intervene; see **stop 1.**

stop, *v.* 1. [To halt] pause, stay, stand (still), lay or stay over, break the journey, shut down, rest, discontinue, pull up, reach a standstill, hold, *stop dead in one's tracks, stop short, freeze (up), *call it a day, cut short; see also **end 1.** 2. [To cease] terminate, finish, conclude, withdraw, leave off, let or pull or fold or fetch or wind or bring up, relinquish, have done (with), desist, refrain, settle, discontinue, end, close, draw or tie or give up, call off, bring up, close down, break up, hold up, pull up, lapse, be at an end, cut out, die away, go out, defect, surrender, close, *peter out, *call it a day, *knock (it) off, *lay off, *throw in the towel, melt away, drop it, run out, write off, run its course.—*Ant.* begin, start, commence. 3. [To prevent] hinder, obstruct, arrest; see **prevent.**

stopover, *n.* layover, halt, pause; see **delay.**

stopped, *a.* at a halt, off the air, cut short; see **interrupted.**

storage, *n.* room, area, accommodation; see **storehouse.**

store, *n.* shop, mart, retail establishment, (sales) outlet, market, department store, specialty shop, chain store, drygoods, grocery, drug, men's furnishings, etc., store.

store, *v.* put, deposit, cache, stock, store or stow away, lay by or in or up or down, put away or aside, lock away, bank, warehouse, collect, pack away, set aside or apart, amass, file, *stash, *salt away, put in moth balls; see also **save 3.**—*Ant.* spend, draw out, withdraw.

stored, *a.* stocked, reserved, hoarded; see **saved 1.**

storehouse, *n.* depository, warehouse, granary, silo, store, storage space, corncrib, barn, depot, cache, grain elevator, safe-deposit vault, armory, arsenal, repository.

storekeeper, *n*. small businessman, purveyor, grocer; see **merchant**.

storm, *n*. tempest, downpour, cloudburst, disturbance, waterspout, blizzard, snowstorm, squall, hurricane, cyclone, tornado, twister, gust, blast, gale, blow, monsoon.

storm, *v*. blow violently, howl, blow a gale, roar, set in, squall, pour, drizzle, rain, *rain cats and dogs.

stormy, *a*. rainy, wet, damp, cold, bitter, raging, roaring, frigid, windy, blustery, pouring, turbulent, storming, wild, boisterous, rough, squally, dark, violent, threatening, menacing.

story, *n*. imaginative writing, fable, narrative, tale, myth, fairy tale, anecdote, legend, account, satire, burlesque, memoir, parable, fiction, novel, romance, allegory, epic, saga, fantasy; see also **literature 1**.

stout, *a*. corpulent, fleshy, portly; see **fat**.

stove, *n*. range, heater, cooking stove, furnace; see also **appliance**.

straight, *a*. **1**. [Not curved or twisted] rectilinear, vertical, perpendicular, plumb, upright, erect, in line with, unbent, in *or* on a line *or* row, inflexible, even, level.—*Ant*. bent, curved, curving. **2**. [Direct] uninterrupted, continuous, through; see **direct 1**.

straighten, *v*. order, compose, make straight, untwist, unsnarl, unbend, uncoil, unravel, uncurl, unfold, put straight, level, arrange, arrange on a line, align.—*Ant*. bend, twist, curl.

straighten out, *v*. conclude, set at rest, figure out; see **straighten**.

straighten up, *v*. **1**. [To make neat] tidy, arrange, fix; see **clean, straighten**. **2**. [To stand up] rise up, arise, be upright; see **stand 1**.

straightforward, *a*. sincere, candid, outspoken; see **frank, honest 1**.

strain, *n*. **1**. [Effort] exertion, struggle, endeavor; see **effort**. **2**. [Mental tension] anxiety, tension, pressure; see **stress 2**.

strain, *v*. **1**. [To exert] strive, endeavor, labor; see **try 1**. **2**. [To filter] refine, purify, screen; see **sift 2**.

strained, *a*. forced, constrained, tense; see **difficult 1**.

strainer, *n*. mesh, filter, colander; see **sieve**.

strait-laced, *a*. strict, severe, stiff; see **prudish**.

stranded, *a*. aground, beached, ashore; see **abandoned**.

strange, *a*. foreign, rare, unusual, uncommon, external, outside, without, detached, apart, faraway, remote, alien,

unexplored, isolated, unrelated, irrelevant; see also **unfamiliar 2, unknown 1, 2, 3, unnatural 1**.—*Ant*. familiar, present, close.

strangely, *a*. oddly, queerly, unfamiliarly, unnaturally, uncommonly, exceptionally, remarkably, rarely, fantastically, amazingly, surprisingly, singularly, peculiarly, unusually.—*Ant*. **regularly**, commonly, usually.

strangeness, *n*. newness, unfamiliarity, novelty, abnormality, eccentricity, remoteness.

stranger, *n*. foreigner, outsider, unknown *or* unexpected *or* uninvited person, visitor, guest, immigrant, intruder, interloper, new boy *or* girl in town *or* in school, drifter, squatter, migratory worker, perfect *or* complete stranger, *gate *or* party crasher.

strangle, *v*. asphyxiate, suffocate, kill; see **choke 1**.

strap, *n*. thong, strop, leash; see **band 1**.

strategy, *n*. approach, maneuvering, procedure; see **tactics**.

straw, *n*. Straws and strawlike fibers include the following—oat, wheat, barley, rye, rice, buckwheat, bean; see also **hay**. **—grasp at straws** *or* **a straw**, panic attempt, be desperate *or* excited *or* frightened; see **fear, try 1**. **—a straw in the wind**, evidence, indication, signal; see **sign 1**.

straw vote, *n*. opinion poll, unofficial ballot, *dry run; see **opinion 1, vote 1, 2**.

stray, *v*. rove, roam, go astray; see **walk 1**.

strayed, *a*. wandered, vagrant, roaming; see **lost 1**.

streak, *n*. stripe, strip, ridge; see **band 1**.

stream, *n*. current, rivulet, brook; see **river, water 2**.

stream, *v*. gush, run, flow; see **flow**.

street, *n*. highway, way, lane, path, avenue, thoroughfare, boulevard, terrace, place, road, route, artery, parkway, court, cross street, alley, passage.

streetcar, *n*. tram, trolley, bus; see **vehicle**.

streetwalker, *n*. whore, woman *or* girl of bad repute, harlot; see **prostitute**.

strength, *n*. vigor, brawn, energy, nerve, vitality, muscle, stoutness, health, toughness, sturdiness, hardiness, tenacity, soundness.—*Ant*. **weakness**, feebleness, loss of energy.

strengthen, *v*. intensify, add, invigorate, fortify, reinforce, encourage, confirm, increase, multiply, empower, arm, harden, steel, brace, buttress, stimulate, sustain, nerve, animate, reanimate, restore, refresh, recover, hearten, establish, toughen, temper, rejuvenate, tone up, build up, make firm, stiffen, brace up, rally, sharpen, enliven, substantiate, uphold, back, augment, enlarge, extend, mount, rise, ascend, wax, grow, back up, beef up.—*Ant.* weaken, cripple, tear down.

strenuous, *a.* vigorous, ardent, zealous; see **difficult 1.**

strenuously, *a.* hard, laboriously, energetically; see **vigorously.**

stress, *n.* 1. [Importance] significance, weight, import; see **importance 2.** [Pressure] strain, tension, force, burden, trial, fear, tenseness, stretch, tautness, pull, draw, extension, protraction, intensity, tightness, spring; see also **pressure 1.**

stress, *v.* accent, make emphatic, accentuate; see **emphasize.**

stretch, *n.* compass, range, reach; see **extent.**

stretch, *v.* 1. [To become longer] grow, expand, be extended, extend oneself, spread, unfold, increase, swell, spring up, shoot up, open.—*Ant.* contract, shrink, wane. 2. [To cause to stretch, sense 1] tighten, strain, make tense, draw, draw out, elongate, extend, develop, distend, inflate, lengthen, magnify, amplify, spread out, widen, draw tight.—*Ant.* relax, let go, slacken.

stretcher, *n.* litter, cot, portable bed; see **bed 1.**

strew, *v.* spread, toss, cover; see **scatter 2.**

stricken, *a.* wounded, injured, harmed; see **hurt.**

strict, *a.* stringent, stern, austere; see **severe 2.**

strictly, *a.* rigidly, rigorously, stringently; see **surely.**

stride, *n.* walk, pace, measured step; see **gait.** —**take in one's stride**, handle, do easily *or* naturally, deal with; see **manage 1.**

strife, *n.* quarrel, struggle, combat; see **fight 1.**

strike, *n.* 1. [An organized refusal] walkout, deadlock, work stoppage, quitting, sit-down (strike), tie-up, slowdown, confrontation, sit-in, *love-in; see also **revolution 2.** 2. [A blow] hit, stroke, punch; see **blow 1.** —(**out**) **on strike**, striking, protesting, on the picket line; see **unemployed.**

strike, *v.* 1. [To hit] box, punch, thump; see **beat 1, hit 1.** 2. [To refuse to work] walk out, tie up, sit down, slow down, go out, be on strike, sit in, arbitrate, negotiate a contract, picket, boycott, stop, quit, resist, hold out for; see also **oppose 1, 2.** 3. [To light] kindle, inflame, scratch; see **ignite.**

strike it rich, *v.* strike *or* find oil *or* gold *or* iron, *etc.*, become wealthy, make money; see **succeed 1.**

strike out, *v.* 1. [To begin something new] start (out), initiate, find a new approach; see **begin 1.** 2. [To cancel] obliterate, invalidate, expunge; see **cancel.**

striking, *a.* attractive, stunning, dazzling; see **beautiful, handsome.**

string, *n.* 1. [A sequence] chain, succession, procession; see **sequence 1, series 2.** [Twine] cord, twist, strand; see **rope.** —*string along (with)*, *v.* bow *or* accede to, accept, tolerate; see **follow 2.**

stringy, *a.* wiry, ropy, woody, pulpy, hairy, veined, coarse, threadlike.

strip, *n.* tape, slip, shred; see **band 1, layer.**

strip, *v.* 1. [Undress] divest, disrobe, become naked; see **undress.** 2. [Remove] displace, tear, lift off; see **peel.**

stripe, *n.* line, division, strip, contrasting color, band, border, ribbon; see also **layer.**

striped, *a.* lined, marked, graphed, barred, banded.

strive, *v.* endeavor, aim, attempt; see **try 1.**

stroll, *v.* ramble, saunter, roam; see **walk 1.**

strong, *a.* 1. [Physically strong; *said especially of persons*] robust, sturdy, firm, muscular, sinewy, vigorous, stout, hardy, big, heavy, husky, lusty, active, energetic, tough, virile, mighty, athletic, able-bodied, powerful, manly, brawny, burly, wiry, strapping, *made of iron.—*Ant.* weak, emaciated, feeble. 2. [Physically strong; *said especially of things*] solid, firm, staunch, well-built, secure, tough, durable, able, unyielding, steady, stable, fixed, sound, powerful, mighty, tough, rugged, substantial, reinforced.—*Ant.* unstable, insecure, tottering. 3. [Wielding power] great, mighty, influential; see **powerful 1.** 4. [Potent in effect] powerful, potent, high-powered, stiff, effective, hard, high-potency, stimulating, inebriating, intoxicating, *spiked. 5. [Intense] sharp, acute, keen; see **intense.** 6. [Financially sound] stable, solid, safe; see **reliable.**

strongest, *a.* mightiest, stoutest, firmest, hardiest, healthiest, most vigorous, most active, most intense, most capable, most masterful, sturdiest, most courageous, strongest-willed, most efficient.—*Ant.* weak, feeblest, most timid.

strongly, *a.* stoutly, vigorously, actively, heavily, fully, completely, sturdily, robustly, firmly, solidly, securely, immovably, steadily, heartily, forcibly, resolutely, capably, powerfully.

structure, *n.* arrangement, composition, fabrication; see **building.**

struggle, *n.* conflict, contest, strife; see **fight 1.**

struggle, *v.* strive, grapple, cope; see **fight.**

stub, *n.* stump, short end, snag, root, remainder, remnant.

stubborn, *a.* unreasonable, obstinate, firm, dogged, opinionated, contradictory, contrary, determined, resolved, bull-headed, mulish, fixed, hard, willful, dogmatic, prejudiced, unyielding, headstrong.

stubbornly, *a.* persistently, resolutely, willfully, doggedly, tenaciously; see **firmly 2.**

stubbornness, *n.* obstinacy, doggedness, inflexibility, pertinacity, perverseness, perversity, stupidity, bullheadedness; see also **determination.**

stuck, *a.* 1. [Tight] fast, fastened, cemented; see **tight 2.** 2. [Stranded] grounded, lost, high and dry; see **abandoned.**

student, *n.* learner, undergraduate, novice, high school *or* college *or* graduate student, pupil, docent, apprentice.

studious, *a.* industrious, thoughtful, well-read, well-informed, scholarly, lettered, learned, bookish, earnest, diligent, attentive.

study, *n.* research, investigation, examination; see **education 1.**

study, *v.* read, go into, refresh the memory, read up on, burn the midnight oil, *bone up, go over, cram, think, inquire, bury oneself in, dive *or* plunge into.

stuff, *v.* ram, pad, wad; see **fill 1, pack 2.**

stuffed, *a.* crowded, packed, crammed; see **full 1.**

***stuffed shirt,** *n.* *phony, pompous person *or* individual, incompetent; see **fake.**

stuffing, *n.* 1. [Material used to pad] packing, wadding, padding, quilting, filler, packing material. 2. [Material used to stuff fowl, fish, etc.] dressing, forcemeat, filling; see **dressing.**

stuffy, *a.* confined, stagnant, muggy; see **close 5.**

stumble, *v.* pitch, tilt, topple; see **fall 1, trip 1.**

stump, *n.* butt, piece, projection; see **end 4.**

***stumped,** *a.* puzzled, baffled, bewildered; see **uncertain 1, 2.**

stun, *v.* hit, put to sleep, knock out; see **deaden.**

stunned, *a.* dazed, astonished, amazed; see **shocked.**

stunning, *a.* striking, marvelous, remarkable; see **beautiful, handsome.**

stunt, *n.* act, skit, comic sketch; see **performance 2.**

stupid, *a.* senseless, brainless, idiotic, simple, shallow, imprudent, witless, irrational, inane, ridiculous, mindless, ludicrous, muddled, absurd, half-witted, funny, comical, silly, laughable, nonsensical, illogical, indiscreet, unintelligent, irresponsible, scatterbrained, crackbrained, addled, flirting, unwary, incautious, misguided, wild, injudicious, imbecile, addleheaded, lunatic, insane, mad, crazy, moronic, touched, freakish, comic, narrow-minded, incoherent, childish, senile, far-fetched, preposterous, unreasonable, asinine, unwise, thoughtless, careless, fatuous, light, lightheaded, flighty, madcap, giddy, *cuckoo, *bone-headed, *goofy, *cracked, *dumb, half-baked, in the dark, in a daze, wacky, harebrained, *screwy, *cockeyed, *loony, *batty, *nutty.—*Ant.* sane, wise, judicious.

stupidity, *n.* 1. [Dullness of mind] stupor, slowness, heaviness, obtuseness, sluggishness, feeble-mindedness, folly, weakness, silliness, nonsense, absurdity, imbecility, imprudence, lunacy, idiocy, brainlessness, shallowness, weakmindedness, impracticality, senility, giddiness, thick-headedness, asininity, slowness, lack of judgment, insensibility, *baloney, *bull, *hooey, *phooey.—*Ant.* wisdom, **intelligence,** judgment. 2. [Extreme folly] nonsense, absurdity, silliness; see **carelessness, nonsense.**

stupidly, *a.* imprudently, stubbornly, obtusely; see **foolishly.**

sturdy, *a.* firm, resolute, unyielding; see **strong 1, 2.**

stutter, *v.* stumble, falter, sputter; see **stammer.**

style, *n.* 1. [Distinctive manner] way, form, technique; see **method.** 2. [Fashion] vogue, habit, custom; see **fashion 2.**

stylish, *a.* chic, smart, in fashion; see **fashionable.**

suave, *a.* sophisticated, agreeable, urbane; see **cultured.**

subconscious, *a.* subliminal, innermost, inmost; see **mental 2.**

subconscious, *n.* (the) unconscious, psyche, mind; see **soul 2.**

subject, *a.* governed, ruled, controlled, directed, obedient, submissive, subaltern, servile, slavish, subservient, subjected, at one's feet, at the mercy of.

subject, *n.* substance, matter, theme, material, topic, question, problem, point, case, matter for discussion *or* in hand, item on the agenda, topic under consideration, field of inquiry, head, chapter,

proposition, argument, thought, discussion.

subject, *v.* control, dominate, restrain; see **govern.**

subjective, *a.* nonobjective, biased, personal; see **prejudiced.**

subjectively, *a.* internally, intrinsically, individually, mentally, nonobjectively, emotionally, inner, interior, inherently; see also **personally 2.**

sublime, *a.* exalted, lofty, stately; see **grand.**

submarine, *n.* undersea boat, submersible, sub; see **ship.**

submerge, *v.* submerse, engulf, swamp; see **immerse, sink 2.**

submission, *n.* obedience, meekness, assent; see **resignation 1.**

submissive, *a.* passive, tractable, yielding; see **docile.**

submit, *v.* 1. [To offer] tender, proffer, present; see **offer 1. 2.** [To surrender] capitulate, resign, relinquish; see **obey.**

subordinate, *a.* inferior, junior, smaller, low, insignificant, subnormal, paltry, not up to snuff, below par, unequal to, not comparable to, lower, minor, depending on, lower in rank, subject, subservient, submissive, subsidiary; see also **under 2.**—*Ant.* superior, higher, **excellent.**

subordination, *n.* subjection, submission, servitude; see **slavery 1.**

subsequent, *a.* succeeding, consequent, after; see **following.**

subsequently, *a.* after, consequently, in the end; see **finally 2.**

subside, *v.* recede, sink, dwindle; see **fall 1.**

subsidiary, *a.* assistant, auxiliary, subject; see **subordinate.**

subsidize, *v.* support, finance, back; see **promote 1.**

subsidy, *n.* allowance, support, scholarship; see **payment 1.**

subsist, *v.* stay alive, remain alive, live on; see **live 4.**

subsistence, *n.* 1. [The supporting of life] living, sustenance, maintenance, support, keep, necessities of life. 2. [The means of supporting life] means, circumstances, resources, property, money, riches, wealth, capital, substance, affluence, independence, gratuity, fortune, dowry, legacy, earnings, wages, salary, income, pension; see **funds.**—*Ant.* poverty, penury, pennilessness.

substance, *n.* matter, material, being, object, item, person, animal, something, element; see also **thing 1.**

substantial, *a.* 1. [Real] material, actual, visible; see **tangible.** 2. [Considerable] ample, abundant, plentiful; see **large 1, much 2.**

substantially, *a.* extensively, considerably, largely; see **much 1, 2.**

substitute, *n.* deputy, double, dummy, relief, stand-in, understudy, proxy, replacement, ringer, sub, pinch-hitter; see also **delegate.**

substitute, *v.* act for, do the work of, replace, supplant, displace, take another's place, double *or* answer *or* make way *or* count for, pass for, go for *or* as, step up, fill in for, pinch-hit for, *take the rap for, *go to bat for, front for, be in *or* fill someone's shoes.

substitution, *n.* replacement, change, swap; see **exchange 2.**

subterranean, *a.* subsurface, sunk, subterraneous; see **underground.**

subtle, *a.* indirect, implied, insinuated; see **mental 2.**

subtlety, *n.* fine distinction, nuance, innuendo; see **suggestion 1.**

subtract, *v.* deduct, take away, withhold; see **decrease 2.**

subtraction, *n.* deducting, subduction, diminution; see **discount, reduction 1.**

suburb, *n.* outlying district, residential district, outskirts; see **area.**

suburban, *a.* provincial, in the country, rural; see **district, local 1, rural.**

subversion, *n.* overthrow, subversive activities, un-American activities; see **defeat, revolution 2.**

subversive, *a.* ruinous, riotous, insurgent; see **rebellious 2.**

subway, *n.* Underground (British), tube, rapid transit; see **railroad, train.**

succeed, *v.* 1. [To attain success] achieve, accomplish, get, prosper, attain, reach, be successful, fulfill, earn, do well, secure, succeed in, score, obtain, thrive, profit, realize, acquire, flourish, be victorious, capture, reap, benefit, recover, retrieve, gain, receive, master, triumph, possess, overcome, win (out), work *or* carry out, surmount, prevail, conquer, vanquish, distance, outdistance, reduce, suppress, worst, work, outwit, outmaneuver, score a point, be accepted, be well-known, grow famous, carry *or* pull (something) off, go *or* come off, put *or* come through, make *or* work one's way, make one's fortune, satisfy one's ambition, make one's mark, hit it, hit the mark, live high, come out with flying colors, *beat the game, work well, overcome all obstacles, play one's cards well, crown, top, *do oneself proud, *make it, *make good, do all right by oneself, *be on top of the heap, *go *or* get places, *click, *set the world on fire, *cut the mustard, *make a killing, put across.—*Ant.* fail, give up, go amiss. 2. [To follow in time] follow after, come after, take the place of, ensue, supervene, supplant, supersede, replace, postdate, displace, come next, become heir to, result, be subsequent to, follow in order, bring up the rear.

succeeding, *a.* ensuing, following after, next in order; see **following.**

success, *n.* 1. [The fact of having succeeded to a high degree] fortune, good luck, achievement, gain, benefit, prosperity, victory, advance, attainment, progress, profit, end, completion, triumph, conclusion, accomplishment, *the life of Riley, *bed of roses, favorable outcome.—*Ant.* defeat, loss, disaster. 2. [A successful person *or* thing] celebrity, famous person, leader, authority, master, expert, man of fortune, somebody, star, *VIP, tops.—*Ant.* failure, loser, nonentity.

successful, *a.* prosperous, fortunate, lucky, victorious, triumphant, auspicious, happy, unbeaten, favorable, strong, propitious, advantageous, encouraging, contented, satisfied, thriving, flourishing, wealthy, up in the world, *ahead of the game, at the top of the ladder, out in front, *on the track, *over the hump.—*Ant.* unsuccessful, poor, failing.

successfully, *a.* fortunately, triumphantly, luckily, victoriously, happily, favorably, strongly, thrivingly, flourishingly, famously, propitiously, auspiciously, prosperously, contentedly, beyond all expectation.

succession, *n.* continuation, suite, set; see **sequence 1, series.**

successive, *a.* serial, succeeding, in line; see **consecutive.**

successor, *n.* heir, follower, replacement; see **candidate.**

such, *a.* so, so very, of this kind, of that kind, of the sort, of the degree, so much, before-mentioned.

such, *pron.* this, that, such a one, such an one, such a person, such a thing. —**as such,** in *or* of *or* in and of itself, by its (own) nature, more than in name only; see **accordingly, essentially.**

such as, *conj.* and *prep.* for example, for instance, to give an example *or* instance; see **including, similarly, thus.**

such as it is, *a.* as is, however poor it may be, for whatever it is worth; see also **inadequate, poor 2.**

suck, *v.* absorb, take up, swallow up; see **swallow.**

sucker, *n.* 1. [A fish] lumpfish, sand sucker, brook sucker; see also **fish.** 2. [*A victim] dupe, fool, cat's-paw; see **victim.** 3. [Candy] sweet, confectionary, lollipop; see **candy.**

suction, *n.* sucking, the force of air *or* the wind *or* a vacuum, effect of atmospheric pressures; see **attraction, power 2, pull 1.**

sudden, *a.* precipitate, swift, impromptu; see **immediate, unexpected.** —**all of a sudden,** unexpectedly, suddenly, precipitously; see **quickly.**

suddenly, *a.* without any warning, abruptly, swiftly; see **quickly.**

suds, *n.* foam, bubbles, lather; see **froth, soap.**

sue, *v.* prosecute, follow up, claim, demand, indict, solicit, beg, litigate, contest, pray, entreat, plead, petition, appeal, accuse, file a plea, enter a plea, claim damages, go to law, file suit, prefer a claim, enter a lawsuit, take one to court, file a claim, have the law on one, *law, haul into court.

suffer, *v.* 1. [To feel pain] undergo, experience, ache, smart, be in pain, be wounded, agonize, grieve, be racked, be convulsed, droop, flag, sicken, torture oneself, *get it (in the neck), look green about the gills, complain of, be affected with, go hard with, match it, flinch at, not feel like anything, labor under.—*Ant.* recover, be relieved, be restored. 2. [To endure] bear, sustain, put up with; see **endure 2.** 3. [To permit] admit, let, submit; see **allow.**

suffering, *n.* distress, misery, affliction; see **difficulty 1, 2, pain 2.**

sufficient, *a.* adequate, ample, satisfactory; see **enough 1.**

sufficiently, *a.* to one's satisfaction, enough, amply; see **adequately.**

suffocate, *v.* stifle, smother, strangle; see **choke.**

sugar, *n.* Common varieties and forms of sugar include the following—sucrose, cane sugar, brown sugar, beet sugar, grape sugar, dextrose, fruit sugar, levulose, maltrose, malt sugar, lactose, maple sugar, saccharose; see also **food.**

sugary, *a.* sticky, granular, candied; see **sweet 1.**

suggest, *v.* 1. [To make a suggestion] submit, advise, recommend; see **propose 1.** 2. [To bring to mind] imply, infer, intimate; see **hint.**

suggested, *a.* submitted, advanced, proposed, propounded, advised, recommended, counseled, tendered, reminded, prompted, summoned up, called up, offered, laid before, put forward.

suggestion, *n.* 1. [A suggested detail] hint, allusion, suspicion, intimation, implication, innuendo, insinuation, opinion, proposal, advice, recommendation, injunction, charge, instruction, submission, reminder, approach, advance, bid, idea, tentative statement, presentation, proposition. 2. [A suggested plan] scheme, idea, outline; see **plan 2.** 3. [A very small quantity] trace, touch, taste; see **bit 1.**

suicide, *n.* self-murder, self-destruction, hara-kiri; see also **death 1.**

suit, *n.* **1.** [A series] suite, set, group; see **series. 2.** [A case at law] lawsuit, action, litigation; see **trial 2. 3.** [Clothes to be worn together] costume, ensemble, outfit, livery, uniform; see also **clothes.** Kinds of suits include the following—women: sport suit, tailored suit, man-tailored suit, soft suit, dressmaker suit, cocktail suit, three-piece suit, jump suit, minisuit, slack suit, cardigan suit, evening suit, bathing suit, sun suit, play suit; men: sport suit, slack suit, business suit, full dress *or* *tails *or* *monkey suit *or* *soup and fish, dinner jacket, tuxedo *or* *tux, bathing suit, play suit, Eton suit. —**bring suit,** prosecute, start (legal) proceedings, initiate a case; see **sue.**

suit, *v.* **1.** [To be in accord with] befit, be agreeable, be appropriate to; see **agree. 2.** [To please] amuse, fill, gratify; see **entertain 1, satisfy 1. 3.** [To adapt] accommodate, revise, readjust; see **alter 1.**

suitable, *a.* fitting, becoming, proper; see **fit 1.**

suitably, *a.* well, all to the good, pleasantly; see **fit 1.**

suitcase, *n.* case, grip, satchel; see **bag.**

suited, *a.* adapted, satisfactory, fitted; see **fit 1.**

sullen, *a.* unsociable, silent, morose, glum, sulky, sour, cross, ill-humored, petulant, moody, grouchy, fretful, ill-natured, peevish, gloomy, gruff, churlish, sourpussed; see also **irritable.**—*Ant.* friendly, sociable, jolly.

sullenly, *a.* morosely, glumly, sourly; see **angrily, silently.**

sum, *n.* amount, value, worth; see **whole.**

summarily, *a.* promptly, readily, speedily; see **immediately.**

summarize, *v.* review, compile, shorten; see **decrease 2.**

summary, *n.* outline, epitome, digest, synopsis, recap, analysis, abstract, abbreviation, resume, précis, skeleton, brief, case, reduction, version, core, report, survey, sketch, syllabus, condensation, sum and substance, *wrap-up.

summer, *n.* summertime, summer season, dog days, sunny season, harvest, haying (time), vacation, picnic days; see also **season.**

summit, *n.* apex, zenith, crown; see **top 1.**

summon, *v.* request, beckon, send for, invoke, bid, ask, draft, petition, signal, motion, sign, order, command, direct, enjoin, conjure up, ring, charge, recall,

call in *or* for *or* out *or* forth *or* up *or* away *or* down *or* together, volunteer.

sum up, *v.* summarize, review, conclude; see **total.**

sun, *n.* day-star, solar disk, eye of heaven, light *or* lamp of the day, solar energy, source of light; see also **star 1.** —**under the sun,** on earth, terrestrial, mundane; see **earthly.**

sunburned, *a.* tanned, burned, sunburnt, brown, suntanned, bronzed, ruddy.—*Ant.* **pale,** white skinned, pallid.

Sunday, *n.* first day, day off, Lord's day; see **weekend.**

sunken, *a.* lowered, depressed, down; see **under 1.**

sunlight, *n.* daylight, sunshine, light of day; see **light 1.**

sunny, *a.* shining, brilliant, sunshiny; see **bright 1.**

sunrise, *n.* peep of day, daybreak, aurora; see **morning 1.**

sunset, *n.* sundown, evening, end of the day, close of the day, nightfall, twilight, dusk; see also **night 1.**—*Ant.* dawn, sunrise, **morning.**

sunshine, *n.* sunlight, the sun, sunbeams; see **light 1.**

superb, *a.* magnificent, splendid, elegant; see **excellent, grand.**

superficial, *a.* flimsy, cursory, hasty, shallow, short-sighted, ignorant, narrow-minded, prejudiced, partial, external, unenlightened.—*Ant.* **learned,** deep, profound.

superficially, *a.* lightly, on the surface, frivolously; see **carelessly.**—*Ant.* **carefully,** thoroughly, thoughtfully.

superfluous, *a.* unnecessary, excessive, exorbitant; see **extreme.**

superintendent, *n.* supervisor, inspector, director; see **executive.**

superior, *a.* higher, better, preferred, above, finer, of higher rank, *a cut above, more exalted; see also **excellent.**

superiority, *n.* supremacy, preponderance, advantage; see **perfection.**

supernatural, *a.* superhuman, spectral, ghostly, occult, hidden, mysterious, secret, unknown, unrevealed, dark, mystic, mythical, mythological, fabulous, legendary, unintelligible, unfathomable, inscrutable, incomprehensible, undiscernible, transcendental, obscure, unknowable, impenetrable, invisible, concealed.—*Ant.* **natural,** plain, common.

superstition, *n.* false belief, fear, superstitious fear; see **fear.**

superstitious, *a.* fearful, apprehensive, credulous; see **afraid.**

supervise, *v.* oversee, conduct, control; see **manage 1.**

supervised, *a.* directed, administered, superintended; see **manage 2.**

supervision, *n.* guidance, surveillance, direction; see **management 1.**

supervisor, *n.* director, superintendent, administrator; see **executive.**

supper, *n.* evening meal, tea, late refreshments; see **dinner.**

supplement, *n.* sequel, continuation, complement; see **addition 1.**

supplement, *v.* add to, reinforce, strengthen; see **increase.**

supplementary, *a.* additional, completing, supplemental; see **extra.**

supplied, *a.* provided, furnished, endowed; see **given.**

supply, *n.* stock, amount, number; see **quantity.**

supply, *v.* furnish, fulfill, outfit; see **satisfy 3.**

support, *n.* 1. [Aid] care, assistance, comfort; see **help 1.** 2. [A reinforcement] lining, coating, rib, stilt, stay, supporter, buttress, pole, post, prop, guide, backing, stiffener, rampart, stave, stake, rod, pillar, timber; see also **brace.** 3. [Financial aid] maintenance, livelihood, sustenance; see **payment 1.**

support, *v.* 1. [To hold up from beneath] prop, hold *or* buoy *or* keep *or* bolster *or* shore *or* bear up, bolster, buttress, brace, sustain, stay, keep from falling, shoulder, carry, bear.–*Ant.* drop, let fall, break down. 2. [To uphold] maintain, sustain, back up, abet, aid, assist, help, bolster, comfort, carry, bear out, hold, foster, shoulder, corroborate, cheer, establish, promote, advance, champion, advocate, approve, stick *or* stand by, stand behind, substantiate, verify, get back of, *stick up for, *go to bat for, confirm, further, encourage, hearten, strengthen, recommend, take care of, pull for, agree with, stand up for, keep up, stand back of, take the part of, rally round, give a lift to, boost. 3. [To provide for] take care of, keep an eye on, care for, attend to, look after, back, bring up, sponsor, put up the money (for), finance, pay for, subsidize, nurse, pay the expenses of, grubstake, stake, raise.–*Ant.* abandon, ignore, fail.

supported, *a.* 1. [Backed personally] financed, promoted, sustained; see **backed 2.** 2. [Supported physically] held up, propped (up), braced, bolstered, borne (up), floating (on *or* upon), floated, borne *or* buoyed *or* lifted (up), based *or* founded (upon *or* on), raised (up), having (an adequate *or* a sufficient) base *or* basis *or* foundation(s) *or* underpinning(s), etc.; see also **firm 1.**

supporter, *n.* advocate, sponsor, helper; see **patron.**

suppose, *v.* conjecture, surmise, deem; see **guess.**

supposed, *a.* assumed, presumed, presupposed; see **likely 1.**

supposedly, *a.* seemingly, supposably, believably; see **probably.**

supposing, *a.* and *conj.* if, in case that, in these circumstances, under these conditions, let us suppose, allowing that, presuming, assuming, taking for granted that.

suppress, *v.* crush, overpower, subdue; see **defeat.**

suppression, *n.* abolition, suppressing, overthrow; see **defeat.**

supremacy, *n.* domination, mastery, supreme authority; see **power 2.**

supreme, *a.* highest, greatest, paramount, chief; see also **best.**

sure, *a.* and *interj.* certainly, of course, by all means, positively, absolutely, but definitely; see also **surely.**

sure, *a.* positive, assured, convinced; see **certain 1.** –for **sure,** certainly, for certain, without doubt; see **surely.** –make **sure,** make certain, determine, establish; see **guarantee.** –to be **sure,** of course, certainly, obviously; see **surely.**

*sure-fire, *a.* dependable, good, infallible; see **excellent, reliable.**

surely, *a.* doubtlessly, certainly, undoubtedly, definitely, absolutely, evidently, explicitly, without doubt, beyond doubt *or* question, plainly, infallibly, most assuredly, decidedly, inevitably, indisputably, positively, unquestionably, without any doubt, admittedly, clearly, with assurance, beyond the shadow of a doubt, nothing else but, precisely, conclusively, distinctly, by all means, at any rate, with certainty, unerringly, unmistakable, at all events, undeniably, with confidence, as a matter of course, *rain *or* shine.

*sure thing, *n.* no gamble, certainty, safe venture *or* investment *or* project, etc.; see **winner.**

surf, *n.* breakers, rollers, combers; see **wave 1.**

surface, *n.* exterior, covering, superficies; see **cover 1, outside 1.**

surgeon, *n.* specialist (in surgery), surgical expert, internist; see **doctor 1.**

surgery, *n.* operative surgery, *the knife, (surgical) operation; see **medicine 3, operation 4.**

surname, *n.* cognomen, last name, patronymic; see **name 1.**

surpass, *v.* excel, outdo, better; see **exceed.**

surplus, *n.* residue, leftover, something extra; see **excess 1, remainder.**

surprise, *n.* 1. [A feeling] astonishment, wonderment, shock; see **wonder 1.** 2. [The cause of a feeling] something unexpected, blow, sudden attack, unexpected good fortune, sudden misfortune, unawaited event, unsuspected plot. — **take by surprise**, startle, assault, sneak up on; see **surprise**.

surprise, v. astonish, astound, bewilder, confound, shock, overwhelm, dumbfound, unsettle, stun, electrify, petrify, startle, stupefy, stagger, take aback, cause wonder, strike with wonder or awe, dazzle, daze, perplex, leave aghast, flabbergast, *floor, *bowl over, jar, take one's breath away, strike dumb, beggar belief, come or creep up on, catch unaware.

surprised, a. upset, taken unaware, astounded, caught short or napping, astonished, bewildered, taken by surprise, shocked, confounded, startled.

surprising, a. extraordinary, remarkable, shocking; see **unexpected**, **unusual 1, 2**.

surrender, n. capitulation, yielding, giving up, submission, giving way, unconditional surrender, abdication, resignation, delivery.

surrender, v. 1. [To accept defeat] capitulate, yield, give in; see **quit 2**. 2. [To relinquish possession] give up, let go, resign; see **abandon 1**.

surround, v. 1. [To be on all sides] girdle, circle, environ, enclose, shut or close in, close around, circle about, envelop, hem in, wall in. 2. [To take a position on all sides] encompass, encircle, inundate, flow around, close in or around, hem in, go around, beleaguer, blockade. —Ant. **abandon**, flee from, desert.

surrounded, a. girdled, encompassed, encircled, hemmed in, fenced in, hedged in, circled about, enclosed, fenced about, enveloped. —Ant. **free**, unfenced, agape.

surrounding, a. enclosing, encircling, encompassing; see also **around**.

surroundings, n. setting, environs, vicinity; see **environment**.

survey, n. study, critique, outline; see **examination 1**.

survey, v. 1. [To look upon] look over, take a view of, view; see **see 1**. 2. [To examine or summarize] study, scan, inspect; see **examine**.

survival, n. endurance, durability, continuance; see **continuation**.

survive, v. 1. [To live on] outlive, outlast, outwear, live down or out, weather the storm, make out, persist, persevere, last, remain, pull or live or come through, keep afloat, get on; see also **endure 1**. 2. [To endure] bear or suffer through, withstand, sustain; see **endure 2**.

survivor, n. descendant, heir, widow, widower, orphan.

suspect, a. dubious, questionable, suspected; see **suspicious 2**, **unlikely**.

suspect, v. 1. [To doubt someone] distrust, disbelieve, mistrust; see **doubt**. 2. [To suppose] presume, surmise, speculate; see **assume**.

suspected, a. doubtful, imagined, fancied; see **suspicious 2**.

suspend, v. 1. [To exclude temporarily] reject, exclude, drop, remove; see **bar 2**, **eject 1**, **refuse**. 2. [To cease temporarily] postpone, defer, put off, discontinue, adjourn, interrupt, delay, procrastinate, shelve, wave, retard, protract, lay on the table, file, lay aside, break up, restrain, desist, break off, halt, put a stop to, check, put an end to.—Ant. **continue**, carry on, proceed.

suspended, a. pensile, postponed, pendulous; see **hanging**.

suspense, n. apprehension, indecisiveness, dilemma; see **doubt**.

suspicion, n. misgiving, mistrust, surmise; see **doubt**. —**above suspicion**, honorable, cleared, gentlemanly; see **honest 1**, **innocent 1**. —**under suspicion**, suspected, held or apprehended or arrested, etc. (for questioning), dubious; see **suspicious 2**.

suspicious, a. 1. [Entertaining suspicion] jealous, distrustful, suspecting, doubting, questioning, doubtful, dubious, in doubt, skeptical, unbelieving, wondering.—Ant. **trusting**, trustful, without any doubt of. 2. [Arousing suspicion] not (quite) trustworthy, questionable, queer, suspect, irregular, unusual, peculiar, out of line, debatable, disputable.—Ant. **regular**, usual, common.

suspiciously, a. doubtingly, doubtfully, skeptically, dubiously, uncertainly, unbelievingly, questioningly, in doubt, having or entertaining doubt or uncertainty or skepticism, etc., causing or inducing or encouraging, etc.; suspicion; with caution, with (some) reservation(s) or allowance(s), with a grain or a pinch of salt.

sustain, v. 1. [To carry] bear, transport, pack; see **carry 1**, **support 1, 2**. 2. [To nourish] maintain, provide for, nurse; see **provide 1**, **support 2**.

swallow, v. consume, engulf, gulp, take, wash down, pour, swill, bolt, swig, choke down, swallow up, toss off; see also **drink 1**, **eat 1**.

swamp, n. bog, fen, quagmire, morass, marsh, slough, soft ground, wet ground, mire, (peat) bog, bottoms, river bottoms, lowland, bottomland, muskeg.

swampy, *a.* boggy, wet, miry; see **muddy** 2.

swanky, *a.* showy, elegant, *swank; see **excellent, expensive, ornate** 1.

***swap**, *v.* interchange, trade, barter; see **exchange**.

swarm, *n.* throng, crowd, multitude, horde, pack, troop, school.

swarm, *v.* rush together, crowd, throng; see **gather, run**.

swarthy, *a.* dark skinned, brown, tawny, dark hued, dark complexioned.

swat, *v.* beat, knock, slap; see **hit** 1.

sway, *n.* swaying, swinging, swing, leaning, oscillation, vibration, undulation, wave, wavering, pulsation.

sway, *v.* bend, oscillate, swagger; see **wave** 3.

swear, *v.* 1. [To curse] blaspheme, utter profanity, *cuss; see **curse**. 2. [To take an oath] avow, affirm, testify, state, vow, attest, warrant, vouch, assert, swear by, give witness, cross one's heart.

sweat, *n.* perspiration, beads of sweat, sweating, steam.

sweat, *v.* perspire, secrete, swelter, wilt, exude, break out in a sweat.

sweater, *n.* Types of sweaters include the following—coat, twin, evening, sport, long-sleeved, short-sleeved, barrel, sleeveless, crew neck, turtle neck; pullover, cardigan; see also **clothes**.

sweaty, *a.* perspiring, moist, wet with perspiration, glowing, bathed in *or* covered with sweat; see also **hot** 1.

sweep, *v.* brush up, clear, clear up; see **clean, mop**.

***sweep under the rug**, *v.* conceal, ignore, get *or* put something out of sight; see **hide** 1, **neglect** 1.

sweet, *a.* 1. [Sweet in taste] toothsome, sugary, luscious, candied, honeyed, saccharine, cloying, like nectar, delicious; see also **rich** 4.—*Ant.* sour, bitter, sharp. 2. [Sweet in disposition] agreeable, pleasing, engaging, winning, delightful, reasonable, gentle, kind, generous, unselfish, even-tempered, good-humored, considerate, thoughtful, companionable; see also **friendly**.—*Ant.* selfish, repulsive, inconsiderate. 3. [Sweet in smell] fragrant, sweet-smelling, fresh, delicate, delicious, spicy, rich, perfumed, clean.

sweeten, *v.* sugar, add sugar, make sweet, add sweetening; see **flavor**.

sweetheart, *n.* beloved, dear, loved one; see **lover** 1.

sweetly, *a.* agreeably, pleasantly, comfortably, gently, gratefully, softly, smoothly, kindly, in a winning manner, charmingly.

sweets, *n.* bonbons, candy, confection, sweetmeats, preserves, candied fruit; see also **candy**.

***swell**, *a.* just what one wants, desirable, fine; see **excellent**.

swell, *v.* dilate, expand, distend, increase, enlarge, grow, grow larger, puff up, be inflated, become larger, bulge, puff, inflate, bulge out, blister, round out, fill out.

swelling, *n.* welt, wart, pimple, carbuncle, boil, pock, pustule, inflammation, growth, corn, lump, bunion, tumor, blister, abscess; see also **injury**.

swerve, *v.* move, bend, turn aside; see **turn** 6.

swift, *a.* flying, sudden, speedy; see **fast** 1.

swiftly, *a.* speedily, rapidly, fast; see **quickly** 1.

swim, *n.* bath, dip, plunge, dive, jump, splash.

swim, *v.* bathe, float, glide, slip through the water, stroke, paddle, go swimming *or* for a swim, take a dip, train *or* practice for the swimming team, swim free style *or* the breast stroke *or* the Australian crawl, etc..

swimming, *n.* diving, aquatic, bathing; see **sport** 3.

swimmingly, *a.* successfully, smoothly, effectively; see **easily, quickly** 1.

swindle, *n.* imposition, deception, knavery; see **trick** 1.

swindle, *v.* dupe, victimize, defraud; see **deceive**.

swindler, *n.* cheat, cheater, thief, imposter, charlatan, trickster, deceiver, falsifier, counterfeiter, *card shark, forger, fraud, *conman, *fourflusher, sharper, gyp, *gyp(o); see also **criminal**.

swing, *n.* sway, motion, fluctuation, stroke, vibration, oscillation, lilt, beat, rhythm; see also **wave** 2. —**in full swing** lively, vigorous, animated; see **active, exciting**.

swing, *v.* sway, pivot, rotate, turn, turn about, revolve, fluctuate, waver, vibrate, turn on an axis; see also **wave** 3.

***swinger**, *n.* sex deviant, sophisticated *or* gay *or* lively *or* ultra-modern person, life of the party, mistress, cohabitant, not a marrying man.

switch, *v.* turnabout, shift, rearrange; see **alter** 1, **turn** 2.

swollen, *a.* distended, puffed, swelled; see **enlarged**.

swoop, *n.* plunge, fall, drop; see **descent** 2, **dive** 1.

swoop, *v.* slide, plummet, plunge; see **descend, dive, fall** 1.

sword, *n.* saber, rapier, weapon; see **knife**.

syllabus, *n.* digest, outline, synopsis; see **plan** 1, **program** 2.

symbol, *n.* type, representative, token, figure; see **sign 1.**

symbolic, *a.* representative, typical, indicatory, indicative, suggestive, symptomatic, characteristic.

symbolize, *v.* typify, signify, express; see **mean 1.**

symmetry, *n.* proportion, arrangement, order, equality, regularity, conformity, agreement, shapeliness, evenness, balance, equilibrium, similarity.

sympathetic, *a.* compassionate, loving, considerate; see **thoughtful 2.**

sympathetically, *a.* sensitively, perceptively, responsively, harmoniously, in accord *or* harmony *or* concert, understandingly, appreciatively, emotionally, with feeling, warmly, heartily, cordially, humanely.

sympathize, *v.* condole, pity, show mercy, comfort, understand, be understanding, love, be kind to, express sympathy.

sympathy, *n.* **1.** [Fellow feeling] understanding, commiseration, compassion; see **pity. 2.** [An expression of sympathy, sense 1] condolence, consolation, solace, comfort, cheer, encouragement, reassurance; see also **help 1.**

symptom, *n.* mark, sign, token; see **characteristic.**

synonymous, *a.* same, like, similar, equivalent, identical, correspondent, corresponding, alike, interchangeable, compatible, coincident; see also **equal.—*Ant.*** opposite, divergent, contrary.

synopsis, *n.* outline, digest, brief; see **summary.**

syntax, *n.* order (of words), arrangement, grammatical rules; see **grammar, language 2.**

synthetic, *a.* artificial, counterfeit, plastic; see **false 3.**

syrup, *n.* Kinds include the following— cane, corn, maple, simple, rock candy; glucose, molasses, honey; see also **sugar.**

system, *n.* orderliness, regularity, conformity, logical order, definite plan, arrangement, rule, systematic order *or* arrangement, logical *or* orderly process; see also **order 3.**

systematize, *v.* plan, arrange, organize; see **order 3.**

T

tab, *n.* loop, stop, clip; see **label, marker, tag** 2.

table, *n.* 1. [A piece of furniture] desk, pulpit, stand, board, counter, slab, dresser, bureau, lectern, sideboard, washstand, sink; see also **furniture**. Tables include the following—writing table, secretary, dining table, kitchen table, card table, drafting table, vanity table, operating table, altar table, end table, laboratory table, library table, refectory table. 2. [A statement in tabulated form] synopsis, report, record; see **summary**. —**turn the tables**, reverse, switch; see **alter** 1. —*under the table, covertly, surreptitiously, not obviously; see **secretly**.

tablecloth, *n.* covering, spread, place mats; see **cover** 1.

tablet, *n.* 1. [A thin piece of material bearing a legend] slab, stone, monument; see **memorial**. 2. [Writing paper] folder, pad, sheets; see **paper** 5. 3. [A pharmaceutical preparation] pill, dose, capsule; see **medicine** 2.

taboo, *a.* forbidden, out of bounds, reserved; see **illegal, restricted**.

taboo, *n.* restriction, reservation, limitation; see **restraint** 2.

taboo, *v.* inhibit, forbid, prevent; see **hinder, restrain** 1.

tabulate, *v.* formulate, arrange, index; see **list** 1, **record** 1.

tack, *n.* 1. [A short, broad-headed nail] thumbtack, push pin, carpet tack, copper tack; see ,also **nail, pin** 1. 2. [An oblique course] tangent, deviation, digression; see **turn** 6.

tack, *v.* 1. [To fasten lightly] pin, nail, stitch; see **fasten**. 2. [To steer ,an oblique course] go in zigzags, zigzag, change course; see **turn** 6.

tackle, *n.* 1. [Equipment] rigging, ropes and pulleys,. apparatus; see **equipment**. 2. [A contrivance having mechanical advantage] pulleys, block-and-tackle, movable pulley; see **tool** 1. 3. [In football, an attempt to down a ball-carrier] flying, running, shoulder, etc., tackle; plunge, lunge; see **defense** 1, **jump** 4. [In football, one who plays between end and guard] linesman, right tackle, left tackle; see **football player**. 5. [In fishing, equipment] gear, sporting goods, fishing apparatus *or* paraphernalia *or* outfit *or* machinery; see **equipment**. Fishing tackle includes the following—hook, line, fly, (casting) rod, (casting)

reel, (cut) bait, (live) bait, minnow, grasshopper, fish *or* salmon eggs, worm, lure, spinner, (fish) net, landing net, pole, float, cork, sinker, creel, tackle box, shot, deep-sea tackle, leader, number four *or* six *or* eight *or* ten hook, etc.; stringer, fish sack, basket.

tackle, *v.* 1. [To undertake] begin, turn to, make an attempt; see **try** 1, **undertake**. 2. [In football, to endeavor to down an opponent] seize, throw down, grab; see **upset** 1.

tact, *n.* perception, discrimination, judgment, acuteness, penetration, intelligence, acumen, common sense, perspicacity, subtlety, discernment, prudence, aptness, good tast, refinement, delicacy, the ability to get along with others, finesse, *horse sense.—*Ant.* rudeness, coarseness, misconduct.

tactful, *a.* diplomatic, civil, considerate; see **thoughtful** 2.

tactics, *n.* strategy, maneuvering, military art, generalship, plan of attack, plan of defense, procedure, approach, disposition, map work, chalk work.

tactless, *a.* stupid, unperceptive, inconsiderate, discourteous, unsympathetic, misunderstanding, impolite, rash, hasty, awkward, clumsy, imprudent, rude, rough, crude, unpolished, gruff, uncivil, vulgar.

tag, *n.* 1. [A remnant or scrap] rag, piece, patch; see **remnants**. 2. [A mark of identification] ticket, badge, card tab, trademark, stamp, stub, voucher, slip, label, check, emblem, insignia, tally, motto, sticker, inscription, laundry mark, price tag, identification number, button, pin. 3. [A children's game] cross tag, Chinese tag, squat tag; see **game** 1.

tag, *v.* 1. [To fit with a tag] check, hold, earmark; see **mark** 2. 2. [*To follow closely] chase, dog, trail; see **pursue** 1.

tail, *n.* rear end, rear appendage, extremity, stub, hind part, brush, tassel, *fly swatter, *wagger; see also **rear**. —**on one's tail**, behind, shadowing, trailing; see **following**. —**with one's tail between one's legs**, in defeat *or* fear, humbly, dejectedly; see **fearfully**.

tailor, *n.* garment maker, clothier, tailoress, dressmaker, seamstress, habitmaker, pants-presser.

take, *n.* 1. [Something that is taken] part, cut, proceeds; see **profit** 2, **share**. 2. [Scene filmed or televised] film, shot, motion picture; see **photograph**. 3.

[*Something that is seized] holding, catching, *haul; see **booty**.

take, *v.* 1. [To seize] appropriate, take hold of, catch, grip, grab, pluck, pocket, carry off; see also **seize** 1, 2. 2. [To collect] gather up, accept, reap; see **receive** 1. 3. [To catch] capture, grab, get hold of; see **catch** 1. 4. [To choose] select, settle on, opt for, make a selection, pick, decide on, prefer; see also **choose**, **decide**. 5. [To acquire] win, procure, gain, achieve, receive, attain, secure; see **earn** 2, **get** 1. 6. [To require] necessitate, demand, call for; see **need** 1. 7. [To contract; *said of a disease*] get, come down with, be seized with; see **catch** 4. 8. [To record] note, register, take notes; see **record** 1. 9. [To transport] move, drive, bear; see **carry** 1. 10. [To captivate] charm, delight, overwhelm; see **entertain** 1, **fascinate**. 11. [To win] prevail, triumph, beat; see **defeat** 2, 3. 12. [To buy] pay *or* contract for, select, procure; see **buy**. 13. [To rent] lease, hire, charter; see **rent** 2. 14. [To steal] misappropriate, purloin, filch; see **steal**. 15. [To undergo] tolerate, suffer, bear; see **endure** 2, **undergo**. 16. [To lead] guide, steer, pilot; see **lead** 1. 17. [To escort] conduct, attend, go with; see **accompany**. 18. [To admit] let in, welcome, give access to; see **receive** 4. 19. [To adopt] utilize, assume, appropriate; see **adopt** 2. 20. [To apply] put in practice, exert, exercise; see **practice** 1, **use** 1. 21. [To experience] sense, observe, be aware of; see **feel** 2. 22. [To cheat] defraud, cheat, swindle; see **deceive**. 23. [To grow] germinate, develop into, grow to be; see **become** 1.

*take a chance, *v.* venture, hazard, gamble; see **risk**, **try** 1.

take advantage of, *v.* dupe, fool, outwit; see **deceive**.

take after, *v.* 1. [To resemble] look like, be like, seem like; see **resemble**. 2. [To follow] follow suit, do like, emulate; see **follow** 2.

take a picture, *v.* shoot, snap, film; see **photograph**.

take away, *v.* 1. [To subtract] deduct, take from;, *minus; see **decrease** 2. 2. [To carry off] transport, cart off, carry away; see **remove** 1.

take back, *v.* 1. [To regain] retrieve, get back, reclaim; see **recover** 1. 2. [To restrict] draw in, retire, pull in; see **remove** 1, **withdraw**. 3. [To disavow] retract, back down, recall; see **deny**, **withdraw**.

take care, *v.* beware, heed, mind, take heed; see also **prepare** 1, **watch out**.

take care of, *v.* superintend, oversee, protect; see **guard**.

take down, *v.* 1. [To dismantle] disassemble, take apart, undo; see **dismantle**. 2. [To write down] inscribe, jot down, note down; see **record** 1, **write** 2.

take for, *v.* 1. [To mistake] misapprehend, misunderstand, err; see **mistake**. 2. [To assume] presuppose, infer, accept; see **assume**.

take from, *v.* take, grab, appropriate; see **seize** 2.

take in, *v.* 1. [To include] embrace, comprise, incorporate; see **include** 1. 2. [To understand] comprehend, apprehend, perceive; see **understand** 1. 3. [To cheat] swindle, lie, defraud; see **deceive**. 4. [To give hospitality] welcome, shelter, accept; see **receive** 1, 4. 5. [To shorten] reduce, lessen, cut down; see **decrease** 2.

take in (one's) stride, *v.* handle, do, manage; see **achieve**, **perform** 1, **succeed** 1.

take into account, *v.* ponder, study, take under *or* into consideration; see **consider**, **think** 1.

take into consideration, *v.* study, examine, ponder; see **consider**, **think** 1.

take into custody, *v.* jail, apprehend, imprison; see **arrest**.

take it, *v.* 1. [To assume] suppose, presume, gather; see **assume**. 2. [To endure] persevere, keep on, carry on; see **endure** 2.

*take it out on, *v.* get even with, get back at, settle with; see **revenge**.

taken, *a.* 1. [Captured] arrested, seized, appropriated; see **captured**. 2. [Employed or rented] occupied, reserved, held; see also **rented**.

take notice, *v.* heed, perceive, observe; see **see** 1.

take-off, *n.* ascent, upward flight, fly-off, climb, rise, hop, jump, vertical takeoff; see also **rise** 1.

take off, *v.* 1. [To undress] strip, divest, expose; see **undress**. 2. [To deduct] lessen, subtract, take away; see **decrease** 2. 3. [To leave the earth] blast off, ascend, soar; see **fly** 1, 4, **rise** 1. 4. [To leave] go (away), depart, *shove off; see **leave** 1.

take on, *v.* 1. [To hire] employ, engage, give work to; see **hire**. 2. [To acquire an appearance] assume, develop, turn; see **become**, **seem**. 3. [To undertake] attempt, handle, endeavor; see **try** 1, **undertake**. 4. [*To meet in fight or sport*] engage, battle, contest; see **attack** 1, **compete**.

take one's chance(s), v. hazard, jeopardize, try; see **chance, risk.**

take one's choice, v. pick out, discriminate between, make a decision; see **choose, decide.**

take out, v. 1. [To extract] cut out, pull out, draw out; see **remove 1. 2.** [To escort] lead, chaperon, attend; see **accompany.**

take over, v. 1. [To take control] take charge, take command, assume charge or control; see **lead 1. 2.** [To seize control] take the reins of, take the helm of, overthrow: see **seize 2. 3.** [To convey] transport, bear, move: see **carry 1, send 1.**

take pains, v. make an effort, care, endeavor; see **try 1.**

take part, v. associate, co-operate, follow; see **join 2, participate 1, share 2.**

take (someone's) part, v. aid, support, second; see **defend 2, help 1.**

take place, v. befall, (come to) pass, ensue; see **happen 2.**

take precautions, v. foresee, mind, adjust; see **prepare 1, watch out.**

take seriously, v. consider, calculate on, work on; see **believe, trust 1.**

take stock (of), v. 1. [To inventory] enumerate, audit, take account of; see **examine. 2.** [To consider] examine, study, review; see **consider, think 1.**

take the lead, v. direct, guide, head; see **lead 1.**

take the place of, v. replace, take over, supercede; see **substitute.**

take to, v. enjoy, be fond of, admire; see **favor, like 1, 2.**

take up, v. 1. [To begin] start, initiate, commence; see **begin 1. 2.** [To raise] lift, elevate, hoist; see **raise 1. 3.** [To shorten] tighten, reduce, lessen; see **decrease 2. 4.** [To occupy] consume, engage, fill; see **occupy 2, use 1. 5.** [To adopt as a cause] appropriate, become involved in or with, assume; see **adopt 2.**

tale, n. 1. [A story] anecdote, fairy tale, folk tale; see **story. 2.** [A lie] tall tale, fiction, exaggeration; see **lie 1.**

talent, n. aptitude, faculty, gift; see **ability.**

talented, a. gifted, capable, skilled; see **able.**

talk, n. 1. [Human speech] utterance, locution, parlance; see **communication, speech 2. 2.** [A conference] symposium, parley, consultation; see **conversation, discussion. 3.** [An address] lecture, oration, sermon; see **speech 3. 4.** [Gossip] report, hearsay, tittle-tattle; see **gossip 1, rumor. 5.** [Nonsense] bombast, rubbish, jive; see **jargon 1, nonsense 1.**

talk, v. 1. [To converse] discuss, confer, chat, interview, speak, communicate, talk together, engage or have or participate or indulge in a (meaningful) dialogue or a conversation or a meeting of the minds, chatter, gossip, yammer, remark, be on the phone with, be in contact with, talk over, reason with, visit with, parley, read, hold a discussion, confide in, argue, observe, notice, inform, rehearse, debate, have an exchange, exchange opinions, have a conference on or over or with, talk away, *go on, *gab, *chew the rag or fat, compare notes with, *talk an arm or a leg off of, *go over, *shoot off one's mouth, *spit out, *bat or shoot the breeze or bull, pass the time of day, engage in conversation. **2.** [To lecture] speak, give a talk, deliver a speech; see **address 2. 3.** [To inform] reveal, divulge, *sing; see **tell 1. 4.** [To utter] pronounce, express, speak; see **utter.**

talk about, v. treat, take under or into consideration, deal with; see **consider 1, discuss.**

talkative, a. wordy, verbal, long-winded; see **fluent.**

talk back, v. sass, retort, defy; see **answer 1.**

talk down to, v. stoop, snub, be overbearing; see **humiliate, patronize 2.**

talker, n. speaker, orator, speechmaker, mouthpiece, spokesman, lecturer, actor, performer, debater, story-teller, conversationalist, raconteur, barker, announcer, preacher, lawyer, reader, after-dinner speaker, gossip.

talking, a. eloquent, chattering, mouthing, repeating, echoing, pronouncing, expressing, articulating, enunciating, ranting, spouting, haranguing, speaking, vocalizing, verbalizing, orating, conversing, discussing, holding forth.

talk (one) into, v. win over, sway, affect; see **convince, influence, persuade 1.**

talk over, v. consider, consult, deliberate; see **discuss.**

tall, a. 1. [Lofty] big, great, towering; see **high 1. 2.** [Exaggerated] far-fetched, outlandish, unbelievable; see **exaggerated.**

tally, n. reckoning, summation, poll; see **score 1.**

tame, a. 1. [Domesticated] subdued, submissive, housebroken, harmless, trained, overcome, mastered, civilized, broken in, harnessed, yoked, acclimatized, muzzled, bridled.—Ant. wild, undomesticated, untamed. **2.** [Gentle] tractable, obedient, kindly; see **gentle 3. 3.** [Uninteresting] insipid, monotonous, routine; see **conventional 3, dull 4, uninteresting.**

tamper (with), v. alter, diversify, vary; see **alter 1, destroy.**

tan, *a.* brownish, sun-tanned, weathered; see **brown**.

tan, *n.* light-brown, beige, natural; see **brown**, **gold**, **yellow** 1.

tang, *n.* zest, flavor, savor; see **taste** 2.

tangible, *a.* perceptible, palpable, material, real, substantial, sensible, touchable, verifiable, physical, corporeal, solid, visible, stable, well-grounded, incarnated, embodied, manifest, factual, objective, tactile.—*Ant.* **spiritual**, ethereal, intangible.

tangle, *n.* snarl, snag, muddle; see **confusion**, **knot** 2.

tangle, *v.* involve, complicate, confuse, obstruct, hamper, derange, mix up, discompose, disorganize, upset, unbalance, unhinge, embarrass, perplex, tie up, trap, mess up.—*Ant.* **order**, fix, unravel.

tangled, *a.* tied up, confused, knit together, disordered, chaotic, out of place, mixed up, snarled, trapped, entangled, twisted, raveled, muddled, *messed up, *balled up, *screwy, *wires crossed.

tank, *n.* 1. [A large container for liquids] tub, basin, vat; see **container**. 2. [An armored caterpillar vehicle] caterpillar, land cruiser, *doodle-bug; see **weapon** 1.

tanned, *a.* brown, bronzed, tan-faced; see **brown**.

tantrum, *n.* conniption, outburst, animosity; see **anger**, **fit** 2.

tap, *n.* 1. [A light blow] pat, rap, dab; see **blow** 2. 2. [A spigot] faucet, petcock, bibcock; see **faucet**.

tap, *v.* 1. [To strike lightly] pat, touch, rap; see **hit** 1. 2. [To puncture in order to draw liquid] perforate, pierce, bore; see **penetrate**.

tape, *n.* ribbon, line, rope. Tapes include the following—recording *or* electronic tape, two-track, four-track, eight-track *etc.* tape; cartridge, cassette, braid, edging, beading, tapeline, tape measure, steel tape, surveyor's chain, adhesive tape, gummed tape, draftsman's tape, Scotch Tape (trademark), masking tape, videotape, mending tape.

tape, *v.* 1. [To fasten] tie up, bind, rope; see **fasten**. 2. [To record] register, make a recording, put on tape; see **record** 3. 3. [To bandage] tie, swathe, truss; see **bind** 1, **fasten**.

taper, *v.* narrow, lessen, thin out; see **decrease** 1, 2.

tape recorder, *n.* recording equipment, (monorial) recorder, stereo *or* stereophonic recorder, cassette *or* two-sided reel-to-reel cartridge recorder, dictaphone; see **record player**.

taper off, *v.* recede, rescind, diminish; see **decrease** 2.

tar, *n.* pitch, mineral pitch, coal tar; see **gum**.

tardy, *a.* overdue, too late, behindhand; see **late** 1, **slow** 2, 3.

target, *n.* 1. [A goal] objective, aim, purpose, end, destination, mark. 2. [Bull's-eye] point, spot, butt, mark, dummy. 3. [A prey] quarry, game, scapegoat; see **victim**.

tarnish, *v.* soil, smudge, smear; see **dirty**.

tart, *a.* bitter, acidulous, sharp; see **sour** 1.

task, *n.* chore, responsibility, business; see **duty** 1.

taste, *n.* 1. [The sense that detects flavor] tongue, taste buds, palate, gustation. 2. [The quality detected by taste, sense 1] flavor, savor, savoriness, aftertaste, tang, piquancy, suggestion, *zip, *wallop, *kick, *smack, *bang, *jolt, *zing, *punch. 3. [Judgment, especially esthetic judgment] discrimination, susceptibility, appreciation, good taste, discernment, acumen, penetration, acuteness, feeling, refinement, appreciation; see also **judgment** 1. 4. [Preference] tendency, leaning, attachment; see **inclination** 1. —**in bad taste**, pretentious, rude, crass; see **tasteless** 3. —**in good taste**, delicate, pleasing, refined; see **artistic**, **dainty**. —**to one's taste**, pleasing, satisfying, appealing; see **pleasant** 2.

taste, *v.* 1. [To test by the tongue] sip, try, touch, sample, lick, suck, roll over in the mouth, partake of. 2. [To recognize by flavor] sense, savor, distinguish; see **know** 3. 3. [To experience] feel, perceive, know; see **undergo**.

tasteful, *a.* 1. [Delicious] delectable, pleasing, tasty, savory, rich; see also **delicious** 2. [Esthetically pleasing] delicate, elegant, fine; see also **dainty**.

tasteless, *a.* 1. [Lacking flavor] unsavory, dull, unseasoned, vapid, flat, watery, flavorless, without spice; see also **dull** 4, **ordinary** 2.—*Ant.* **delicious**, seasoned, spicy. 2. [Plain] homely, insipid, trite; see **common** 1. 3. [Lacking good taste] pretentious, ornate, showy, trivial, artificial, florid, ostentatious, clumsy, makeshift, coarse, useless, rude, ugly, unsightly, unlovely, hideous, foolish, stupid, crass.—*Ant.* **simple**, effective, handsome.

tasty, *a.* savory, palatable, appetizing; see **delicious**.

tattle, *v.* prattle, tell on, chatter; see **gossip**.

tattler, *n.* busybody, tattletale, snoop; see **gossip 2, traitor.**

taught, *a.* instructed, informed, directed; see **educated, learned 1.**

tavern, *n.* taproom, alehouse, roadhouse; see **bar 2.**

tax, *n.* 1. [A pecuniary levy] fine, charge, rate, toll, levy, impost, duty, assessment, tariff, tribute, obligation, price, cost, contribution, expense; see also **dues.** 2. [A burden] strain, task, demand; see **burden 2.**

tax, *v.* 1. [To cause to pay a tax] assess, exact from, demand, exact tribute, charge duty, demand toll, require a contribution, enact a tax. 2. [To burden] encumber, weigh down, overload; see **burden.**

taxation, *n.* levying, assessment, money-gathering; see also **tax 1.**

taxed, *a.* 1. [Paying taxes] levied upon, demanded from, required from, assessed, imposed upon, subjected to tax. 2. [Burdened] overtaxed, strained, harassed, fatigued; see also **tired.**

taxicab, *n.* taxi, cab, sightseeing car; see **automobile.**

tea, *n.* 1. [An infusion made from tea leaves] beverage, brew, infusion, decoction; see also **drink 2.** Tea and tealike drinks include the following—black, green, Lapsang, Souchong, Oolong, Darjeeling, orange pekoe, pekoe, Gunpowder or Pearl, Earl Grey, basket fired, mixed, jasmine, blended, orange flower, sassafras, sage, mint, camomile, herb. 2. [A light afternoon or evening meal] snack, refreshment, tea party; see also **lunch, meal 2.**

teach, *v.* instruct, tutor, coach, educate, profess, explain, expound, lecture, direct, give a briefing, edify, enlighten, guide, show, give lessons in, ground, rear, prepare, fit, interpret, bring up *or* out, instill, inculcate, indoctrinate, brainwash, develop, form, address to, initiate, inform, nurture, illustrate, imbue, implant, break in, give the facts, give an idea of, improve one's mind, open one's eyes, *knock into someone's head, *bring home to, *cram, *stuff; see also **influence, motivate.**—*Ant.* learn, gain, acquire.

teacher, *n.* schoolmaster, schoolmistress, schoolman, educator, public school teacher, high school teacher, tutor, mentor, pedagogue, master, guru, swami, mistress, kindergarten teacher, pupil teacher, teacher-in-training, substitute teacher, professor, lecturer, instructor, faculty member, graduate assistant.

teaching, *n.* pedagogy, instruction, normal training; see **education 1, 3.**

team, *n.* 1. [People working together, especially on the stage] partners, combi-

nation troupe, company, duo, trio, foursome; see also **organization 2.** 2. [An organization, especially in sport] squad, crew, club; see **organization 2.**

team up with, *v.* attach oneself to, collaborate, corroborate; see **accompany, co-operate, help.**

teamwork, *n.* partisanship, collaboration, union; see **alliance 1, co-operation, partnership.**

tear, *n.* teardrop, droplet, *eye-wash; see **drop 1.**

tear, *n.* rent, rip, hole, slit, laceration, split, break, gash, rupture, fissure, crack, cut, breach, damage, imperfection. — *Ant.* repair, patch, renovation.

tear, *v.* rend, rip, shred, cut, mangle, split, lacerate; see also **cut 1.**

tears, *n.* sobbing, sob, crying, cry, weeping, lamenting, whimpering, grieving, mourning, *waterworks; see also **grief.**

tease, *v.* taunt, tantalize, torment; see **bother 2, ridicule.**

teaspoon, *n.* kitchen utensil, measuring spoon, 1/3 of a tablespoon, stirrer, sugar, silver, soup, desert, etc. spoon; see also **utensils.**

technical, *a.* specialized, special, scientific, professional, scholarly, mechanical, methodological, restricted, highly versed, technological, industrial.—*Ant.* **artistic,** nontechnical, simplified.

technician, *n.* practitioner, professional, engineer; see **craftsman, specialist.**

technique, *n.* procedure, system, routine; see **method.**

tedious, *a.* slow, wearisome, tiresome; see **dull 4.**

tedium, *n.* boredom, tediousness, dullness; see **monotony.**

teen-age, *a.* immature, youthful, adolescent; see **young 1, 2.**

teens, *n.* boyhood, girlhood, adolescence, early adolescence, late adolescence, teen age, *awkward age; see also **youth 1.**

teeter, *v.* seesaw, totter, wobble; see **shake 1.**

teeth, *n.* dentition, fangs, tusks; see **tooth.**

telegram, *n.* wire, cable, cablegram, message, teletype copy, radiogram, call, report, summons, night message, night letter, day letter, news message, code message, signal, flash, *buzzer; see also **communication.**

telegraph, *n.* Morse telegraph, wireless, transmitter; see **communication, radio 2.**

telegraph, *v.* wire, send a wire, send a cable; see **communicate 2.**

telepathy, *n.* insight, premonition, extrasensory perception; see **communication.**

telephone, *n.* phone *or* 'phone, private phone, extension phone, radiophone, radio telephone, wireless telephone,

French phone, Princess Phone (trademark), mouthpiece, line, party line, long distance, extension, pay phone.

telephone, v. call, call up, phone, ring, ring up, make a call to, dial, call on the phone, put in a call to, *phone up, give a ring, *give a buzz.

telephoned, a. phoned, radiophoned, called, communicated by telephone, reached by phone.

telescope, n. field glasses, binoculars, opera glass, glass, optical instrument, reflecting telescope, refracting telescope, helioscope, equatorial telescope; see also **glasses.**

television, n. T.V., teevee, video, color television, home entertainment center, *(boob) tube, the box; see also **station 5.**

tell, v. 1. [To inform] communicate, explain, instruct, direct, order, divulge, reveal, make known, utter, speak, report, recite, cue in, reel off, spit it out, put before, name over, let in on, let into, open up, give the facts, blow upon, lay open, fill one in, let on, let slip, level with, leave word, hand it to, lay before, break it to, break the news, add up, keep one posted, let know, give out, leak out, give notice, declare, acquaint, advise, confess, impart, notify, represent, assert, mention, tell all, break down with, give away, *cough up, *come across with, *shoot, *come clean, make a clean breast of; see also **discuss, say.**—*Ant.* hide, keep secret, be silent. 2. [To deduce] know, understand, make out, perceive, ascertain, find out, recognize, be sure, differentiate, discriminate, determine, know for certain.

teller, n. cashier, clerk, bank clerk; see **workman.**

telling, a. crucial, conspicuous, significant; see also **effective, important 1.**

tell off, v. rebuke, reprimand, chide; see **scold.**

temper, n. 1. [State of mind] disposition, frame of mind, humor; see **mood 1.** 2. [An angry state of mind] furor, ire, passion; see **anger, rage 1.** 3. [The quality of being easily angered] impatience, excitability, touchiness, sourness, sensitivity, fretfulness, peevishness, irritability, ill-humor, petulence, irascibility, crossness, churlishness, pugnacity, sullenness, grouchiness, huffiness.—*Ant.* **patience,** calmness, equanimity. 4. [The quality of induced hardness or toughness in materials] tensile strength, sturdiness, hardness; see **firmness, strength. —lose one's temper,** become angry, get mad, fly off the handle; see **rage 1.**

temper, v. 1. [To soften or qualify] mitigate, pacify, moderate; see **ease 1, 2, soften 2.** 2. [To toughen or harden] steel, stiffen, cement; see **strengthen.**

temperament, n. character, disposition, constitution, nature, inner nature, quality, temper, spirit, mood, attitude, type, structure, make-up, humor, mood, outlook, peculiarity, individuality, idiosyncrasy, distinctiveness, psychological habits, mentality, intellect, susceptibility, ego, inclination, tendency, turn of mind.

temperamental, a. moody, sensitive, touchy; see **irritable.**

temperance, n. moderation, abstinence, self-control; see **restraint 1.**

temperate, a. 1. [Moderate] regulated, reasonable, fair; see **moderate 4.** 2. [Neither hot nor cold] medium, warm, balmy; see **fair 3, mild 2.** 3. [Not given to drink] abstemious, abstinent, restrained; see **moderate 5.**

temperature, n. heat, warmth, cold, body heat, weather condition, climatic characteristic, thermal reading, degrees of temperature, degrees above *or* below zero.

temple, n. house of prayer, synagogue, pagoda; see **church 1.**

temporarily, a. momentarily, briefly, tentatively, for a while, for the moment, for a time, provisionally, transitorily, for the time being, pro tempore *or* pro tem.—*Ant.* **forever,** perpetually, perennially.

temporary, a. transitory, transient, fleeting, short, brief, ephemeral, fugitive, volatile, shifting, passing, summary, momentary, stopgap, makeshift, substitute, for the time being, overnight, *ad hoc* (Latin), impermanent, irregular, changeable, unenduring, unfixed, unstable, perishable, provisional, short-lived, mortal, pro tem, *on the go, *on the fly, on the wing, *here today and gone tomorrow.—*Ant.* **permanent,** fixed, eternal.

tempt, v. lure, fascinate, seduce, appeal to, induce, intrigue, incite, provoke, allure, charm, captivate, entice, draw out, bait, stimulate, move, motivate, rouse, instigate, wheedle, coax, inveigle, vamp, *make a play for, make one's mouth water.

temptation, n. lure, attraction, fascination; see **appeal 2.**

tempted, a. desiring, inclined, enticed; see **charmed.**

tempting, a. appetizing, attractive, fascinating; see **charming.**

ten, a. tenth, tenfold, decuple, denary, decimal.

tenant, n. renter, lessee, householder, rent payer, dweller, inhabitant, occupant, resident, roomer, lodger, holder, possessor, leaseholder, tenant farmer;

see also **resident.**—*Ant.* **owner,** proprietor, landlord.

tend, *v.* 1. [To watch over] care for, manage, direct, superintend, do, perform, accomplish, guard, administer, minister to, oversee, wait upon, attend, serve, nurse, mind; see also **manage 1.** 2. [To have a tendency (toward)] lead, point, direct, make for, result in, serve to, be in the habit of, favor, be disposed *or* predisposed (to) *or* biased *or* prejudiced (in favor of), be apt to, gravitate toward, incline (to), verge on.

tendency, *n.* 1. [Direction] aim, bent, trend; see **drift 1.** 2. [Inclination] leaning, bias, bent; see **inclination 1.**

tender, *a.* 1. [Soft] delicate, fragile, supple; see **soft 2.** 2. [Kind] loving, solicitous, compassionate; see **kind.** 3. [Touching] moving, pathetic, affecting; see **pitiful.** 4. [Sensitive] touchy, ticklish, oversensitive; see **raw 5, sore 1.**

tenderly, *a.* 1. [Softly] gently, carefully, delicately; see **lightly.** 2. [Lovingly] fondly, affectionately, appreciatively; see **lovingly.**

tenderness, *n.* love, consideration, care; see also **friendship, kindness 1.**

tending, *a.* 1. [Inclined (toward)] apt to, likely to, working toward; see **likely 4.** 2. [Giving attention to] caring for, managing, directing; see **managing.**

tennis, *n.* lawn tennis, court tennis, tennis tournament; see **sport 3.**

tense, *a.* 1. [Nervous] agitated, anxious, high-strung, on edge, fluttery, jumpy, jittery; see also **excited.**—*Ant.* calm, unconcerned, indifferent. 2. [Stretched tight] rigid, stiff, firm; see **tight 1.**

tension, *n.* 1. [Stress] tautness, force, tightness; see **balance 2, stress 2.** 2. [Mental stress] pressure, strain, anxiety; see **stress 2.**

tent, *n.* shelter, canvas, canopy, tarpaulin, covering; see also **cover 1.** Tentlike coverings include the following—umbrella tent, awning, marquee, wigwam, tepee, booth, pavilion, pup tent, fly tent, fly, canoe tent, lean-to tent, circus tent, *rag, *top, *big top, *round top.

tentative, *a.* provisional, probationary, makeshift; see also **experimental.**

tentatively, *a.* experimentally, conditionally, provisionally; see **temporarily.**

tepee, *n.* Indian tent, wigwam, wickiup; see also **tent.**

term, *n.* 1. [A name] expression, terminology, phrase, word, locution, indication, denomination, article, appellation, designation, title, head, caption, nomenclature, *moniker; see also **name 1.** 2. [A period of time] span, interval, course, cycle, season, duration, phase, quarter, course of time, semester, school period, session, period of confinement; see also **time 2.** —**come to terms,** compromise, arrive at an agreement, arbitrate; see **agree.** —**in terms of,** in reference to, about, concerning; see **regarding.**

terminate, *v.* complete, end, perfect; see **achieve.**

termination, *n.* finish, close, terminus; see **end 2.**

terminology, *n.* nomenclature, technology, specification; see **jargon 2, language 1.**

terms, *n.* 1. [Conditions] details, items, points, particulars; see also **circumstances 2.** 2. [An agreement] understanding, treaty, conclusion; see **agreement 1.**

terrace, *n.* patio, garden, lawn; see **garden, yard 1.**

terrain, *n.* ground, region, territory; see **area.**

terrible, *a.* 1. [Inspiring terror] terrifying, appalling, fearful, awesome, horrifying, ghastly, awe-inspiring, petrifying, revolting, gruesome, shocking, unnerving; see also **frightful.**—*Ant.* happy, joyful, pleasant. 2. [Unwelcome] unfortunate, disastrous, inconvenient, disturbing, *atrocious, *lousy; see also **offensive 2.**—*Ant.* welcome, good, attractive.

terribly, *a.* horribly, frightfully, drastically; see **badly 1, very.**

terrific, *a.* shocking, immense, tremendous; see **great 1, large 1.**

terrify, *v.* shock, horrify, terrorize; see **frighten.**

territorial, *a.* regional, sectional, provincial; see **national 1.**

territory, *n.* 1. [A specified area] region, township, empire; see **area.** 2. [An area organized politically under the central government] commonwealth, colony, dominion; see **nation 1.** 3. [An indefinite area] section, area, boundary; see **region 1.**

terror, *n.* fright, horror, panic; see **fear.**

terrorist, *n.* subversive, revolutionary, incendiary; see **rebel.**

terrorize, *v.* coerce, intimidate, browbeat; see **threaten.**

test, *n.* 1. [A check for adequacy] inspection, analysis, countdown, probing, inquiry, inquest, elimination, proving ground(s), training stable, search, *dry run; see also **examination 1, experiment.** Tests include the following—engineering, technical, structural, mechanical, chemical, countdown, psychological, mental, intelligence, IQ *or* intelligence quotient, aptitude, vocational, qualifying, comprehensive, written, true-false, multiple choice, objective, diagnostic, semester, term, association, psychiatric. 2. [A formal examination] quiz, questionnaire, essay; see **examination 2.**

test, *v.* inquire, question, try out; see **examine, experiment.**

tested, *a.* examined, tried, proved; see **established 2, reliable.**

testify, *v.* 1. [To demonstrate] indicate, show, make evident; see **prove.** 2. [To bear witness] affirm, give evidence, swear, swear to, attest, witness, give witness, give one's word, certify, warrant, depose, vouch, give the facts, stand up for, say a good word for. 3. [To declare] assert, attest, claim; see **declare.**

testimony, *n.* 1. [The act of stating] attestation, statement, assertion; see **declaration.** 2. [Evidence] grounds, facts, data; see **proof.** 3. [Statement] deposition, affidavit, affirmation; see **declaration.**

Texas, *n.* Lone Star State, Jumbo State, Longhorn State; see **South, United States.**

text, *n.* 1. [A textbook] required reading, manual, handbook; see **book.** 2. [A subject, especially a verse from the Bible] quotation, stanza, passage; see **subject.** 3. [Writing, considered for its authenticity] lines, textual evidence, document; see **manuscript, writing 2.**

texture, *n.* 1. [Quality] character, disposition, fineness, roughness, coarseness, feeling, feel, sense, flexibility, stiffness, smoothness, taste; see also **fiber.** 2. [Structure] composition, organization, arrangement; see **construction 2, form 2.**

thank, *v.* be obliged, show gratitude, give thanks, acknowledge, show appreciation, be obligated to, be indebted to, bless, praise, bow down to, kiss, smile on, show courtesy, express one's obligation to; see also **appreciate 1.**—*Ant.* **neglect,** ignore, show indifference.

thanked, *a.* blessed, applauded, appreciated; see **praised.**

thankful, *a.* obliged, grateful, gratified, contented, satisfied, indebted to, pleased, kindly disposed, appreciative, giving thanks, overwhelmed.

thankless, *a.* 1. [Not returning thanks] unappreciative, ungrateful, self-centered; see **cruel, rude 2.** 2. [Not eliciting thanks] poorly paid, unappreciated, unrewarded; see **useless 1.**

thanks, *n.* appreciation, thankfulness, acknowledgement, recognition, gratitude, gratefulness.—*Ant.* blame, censure, criticism.

Thanksgiving, *n.* Thanksgiving Day, last Thursday in November, *turkey day; see **celebration, feast, holiday.**

that, *conj.* in that, so, so that, in order

that, to the end that, for the reason that; see also **because.**

that, *a.* the, this, one, a certain, a (well) known, a particular, such.

that, *pron.* the one, this one, the one in question, that fact, that other, who; see also **which.** —*all that,** so very, so, rather less; see **not.** —*at that,** even so, all things considered, anyway; see **anyhow 1.**

thaw, *v.* dissolve, liquefy, flow, run, liquate, fuse, become liquid; see also **dissolve, melt 1.**—*Ant.* freeze, congeal, refrigerate.

the, *a.* 1. [The definite article] some, a few, a particular one, a special one, a specific one, a certain one, an individual one, this, that, each, every, these, those, the, the whole, the entire. 2. [Special or unique; *often italics*] pre-eminent, outstanding, particular, unparalleled, unequaled, supreme, unsurpassed, unusual, uncommon, rare, singular, unprecedented, exceptional, one, sole, single, significant, distinguished, specific, choice, individual, peculiar, exceptional, occasional, unfamiliar, strange, spectacular, phenomenal, unheard of, unknown, unattainable, invincible, almighty, all-powerful; see also **special 1, unique 1.**—*Ant.* common, usual, ordinary.

theater, *n.* 1. [A building intended for theatrical productions] playhouse, concert hall, coliseum; see **auditorium.** 2. [The legitimate stage] stage, drama, Broadway; see **comedy, movies 2.**

theatrical, *a.* ceremonious, meretricious, superficial; see **affected 2.**

theft, *n.* robbery, racket, thievery, larceny, stealing, swindling, swindle, cheating, defrauding, fraud, piracy, burglary, pillage, pilfering, plunder, vandalism, pocket-picking, safecracking, extortion, embezzlement, looting, appropriation, shoplifting, fleece, holdup, mugging, *stickup; see also **crime.**

their, *a.* belonging to them, belonging to others, theirs, of them.

them, *pron.* those (other) (persons *or* things), the others, the above, some people, he and she; see also **everybody.**

theme, *n.* 1. [A subject] topic, proposition, argument, thesis, text, subject matter, matter in hand, problem, question, point at issue, affair, business, point, case, thought, idea, line; see also **subject.** 2. [A recurrent melody] melody, motif, strain; see **song.** 3. [A short composition] essay, report, paper; see **review 4, statement 1.**

then, *a.* at that time, formerly, before, years ago, at that point, suddenly, all at once, soon after, before long, next, later, thereupon; see also **when 1, 2.** — **but then,** but at the same time, on the other hand, however; see **but 1, 2**. — **what then?**, in that case? and then? as a result?; see **what 1**.

theology, *n*. dogma, creed, theism; see **belief 1, faith 2**.

theoretical, *a*. ideal, analytical, academic; see **assumed**.

theory, *n*. 1. [Principles] method, approach, philosophy; see **law 4**. 2. [Something to be proved] assumption, conjecture, speculation; see **opinion 1**.

therapy, *n*. remedy, healing, cure; see **medicine 3**.

there, *a*. in that place, not here, beyond, over there, yonder, in the distance, at a distance, over yonder, just there, where I point, in that spot, at that point; see also **where 2**. —*not all there*, crazy, eccentric, demented; see **insane**.

thereafter, *a*. from there on, from that day on, after that; see **following, hereafter**.

thereby, *a*. by way of, how, by which; see **through 4, whereby**.

therefore, *a*. and *conj*. accordingly, consequently, hence, wherefore, for, since, inasmuch as, for this reason, on account of, to that end, on the ground, in that event, in consequence, as a result.

thermometer, *n*. mercury, thermostat, thermo-regulator; see **measure 2**.

these, *a*. those, the indicated, the present, the aforementioned, the already stated, the referred to, hereinafter described, the previously mentioned, the well-known, the aforesaid, the above, the below; see also **certain 4**.

they, *pron*. people, men, those people, all, others, he and she, both; see also **everybody**.

thick, *a*. 1. [Dense] compact, impervious, condensed, compressed, multitudinous, numerous, rank, crowded, close, solid, packed, populous, profuse, populated, swarming, heaped, abundant, impenetrable, concentrated, crammed, packed together, closely packed, *like sardines in a can, jam-packed.—Ant*. **scattered**, spacious, wide-open. 2. [Deep] in depth, third-dimensional, edgewise; see **deep 2**. 3. [Of heavy consistency] compact, heavy, viscous, viscid, dense, syrupy, ropy, coagulated, curdled, turbid, gelatinous, glutinous, gummy, opaque, clotted; see also **stringy.—Ant**. light, porous, filmy. 4. [Not clear] cloudy, turbid, indistinct; see **dull 2, muddy 1, obscure 1**. 5. [Stupid] obtuse, ignorant, doltish; see **dull 3**. 6. [*Intimate] cordial, familiar, fraternal; see **friendly**. — *through thick and thin*, faithfully, devotedly, in good and bad times; see **loyally**.

thicken, *v*. coagulate, curdle, petrify, ossify, solidify, freeze, clot, set, congeal, jelly, grow thick; see also **harden, stiffen**.

thickheaded, *a*. stupid, ignorant, idiotic; see **dull 3**.

thickness, *n*. density, compactness, solidity, closeness, heaviness, stiffness, condensation, concentration, clot.—*Ant*. frailty, thinness, slimness.

thief, *n*. burglar, highwayman, holdup man; see **criminal**.

thieve, *v*. loot, rob, filch; see **steal**.

thievery, *n*. burglary, robbery, pilfering; see **crime, theft**.

thigh, *n*. thigh bone, femur, ham; see **leg 1**.

thin, *a*. 1. [Of little thickness] flimsy, slim, slight, diaphanous, sheer, rare, sleazy, permeable, paper-thin, wafer-sliced. —*Ant*. thick, heavy, coarse. 2. [Slender] slim, lean, skinny, scraggy, lank, spare, gaunt, bony, wan, rangy, skeletal, scrawny, lanky, delicate, wasted, haggard, emaciated, rawboned, shriveled, wizened, rickety, spindling, pinched, starved.—*Ant*. fat, obese, heavy. 3. [Sparse] scarce, insufficient, deficient; see **inadequate 1**. 4. [Having little content] sketchy, slight, insubstantial; see **shallow 1, 2**. 5. [Having little volume] faint, shrill, weak; see **light 7**.

thin, *v*. thin out, weed out, dilute; see **decrease 2, weaken 2**.

thing, *n*. 1. [An object] article, object, item, lifeless object, commodity, device, gadget, material object, being, entity, body, person, something, anything, everything, element, substance, piece, shape, form, figure, configuration, creature, stuff, goods, matter, *thingumajig, *doohickey, *thingumabob. 2. [A circumstance] matter, condition, situation; see **circumstance 1**. 3. [An act] deed, feat, movement; see **action 2**. 4. [A characteristic] quality, trait, attribute; see **characteristic**. 5. [An idea] notion, opinion, impression; see **thought 2**. 6. [A pitiable person] wretch, poor person, sufferer, urchin; see also **patient, refugee**. 7. [Belongings; *usually pl*.] possessions, clothes, personals; see **property 1**. 8. [Something so vague as to be nameless] affair, matter, concern, business, occurrence, anything, everything, something, stuff, point, information, subject, idea, question, indication, intimation, contrivance, word, name, shape, form, entity. 9. [Something to be done] task, obligation, duty; see **job 2**. —*do one's own thing*, live according to one's own principles, do what one likes, live fully; see **live 1**.

things, *n.* possessions, luggage, belongings; see **baggage, property 1.**

think, *v.* 1. [To examine with the mind] cogitate, muse, ponder, consider, contemplate, deliberate, stop to consider, study, reflect, examine, think twice, estimate, evaluate, appraise, resolve, ruminate, scan, confer, consult, meditate, meditate upon, take under consideration, have on one's mind, brood over, speculate, weigh, have or keep in mind, bear in mind, *mull over, turn over, *sweat over, stew, *bone, beat one's brains, rack one's brains, *use the old bean, figure out, *put on one's thinking cap, use one's head, hammer away at, hammer out, bury oneself in.—*Ant.* neglect, take for granted, accept. 2. [To believe] be convinced, deem, hold; see **believe 1.** 3. [To suppose] imagine, guess, presume; see **assume. 4.** [To form in the mind] conceive, invent, create; see **imagine. 5.** [To remember] recollect, recall, reminisce; see **remember 1, 2.**

thinking, *a.* pensive, introspective, reflective; see also **thoughtful 1.**

thinking, *n.* reasoning, reason, contemplation; see **thought 1.**

think twice (about), *n.* reconsider, weigh, pause, be uncertain; see also **hesitate.**

thinness, *n.* slenderness, slimness, shallowness; see **lightness 2.**

third, *a.* part, after the second, next but one; see **three.**

thirst, *n.* dryness, need for liquid, longing, craving, *cobweb throat.

thirsty, *a.* dry, parched, arid, eager, hankering for, burning for, craving, longing for, partial to, hungry for, itching for, inclined to, *bone dry, *crazy for, wild for; see also **hungry. —*Ant.* satisfied, full, replete.

this, *a.* the, that, the indicated, the present, here, aforementioned, already stated.

this, *pron.* the one, this one, that one, the one in question, the aforementioned one, this person, the thing indicated; see also **that.**

thorn, *n.* spine, briar, nettle; see **point 2, spine 1.**

thorough, *a.* 1. [Painstaking] exact, meticulous, precise; see **accurate 2, careful. 2.** [Complete] thoroughgoing, out-and-out, total; see **absolute 1.**

thoroughly, *a.* fully, wholly, in detail; see **completely.**

those, *a.* these, the indicated, the above-mentioned; see also **the 1.**

those, *pron.* the others, they, them, not these; see also **that.**

though, *conj.* despite, even if, if; see **although, but 1.**

thought, *n.* 1. [Mental activity] speculation, reflection, deliberation, meditation, rumination, perceiving, apprehending, seeing, consideration, reasoning, intuition, logical process, perception, insight, understanding, viewpoint, concept, brainwork, thinking, knowing, realizing, discerning, rationalizing, drawing conclusions, concluding, inferring, deducing, deriving, deduction, inducing, logic, judging, rationalization, judgment, argumentation, cogitation, contemplation, cognition, intellection, *brainstorm. 2. [The result of mental activity] idea, plan, view, fancy, notion, impression, image, understanding, appreciation, conception, observation, belief, feeling, opinion, guess, inference, theory, hypothesis, supposition, assumption, intuition, conjecture, deduction, postulate, premise, knowledge, evaluation, assessment, appraisal, estimate, verdict, finding, decision, determination, reflection, consideration, abstraction, conviction, tenet, presumption, intellectualization, surmise, doctrine, principle, drift, calculation, caprice, reverie, sentiment, care, worry, anxiety, uneasiness, dream. 3. [Care or attention] heed, thoughtfulness, solicitude; see **attention.**

thoughtful, *a.* 1. [Notable for thought] thinking, meditative, engrossed, absorbed, rapt in, pensive, considered, seasoned, matured, studied, philosophic, contemplative, studious, cogitative, examined, pondered, speculative, deliberative, reflective, introspective, clear-headed, level-headed, keen, wise, well-balanced, judged, far-sighted, reasoning, rational, calculating, discerning, penetrating, politic, shrewd, careful, sensible, retrospective, intellectual, *brainy, deep.—*Ant.* thoughtless, unthinking, irrational. 2. [Considerate] heedful, polite, courteous, solicitous, friendly, kind, kindly, unselfish, concerned, anxious, neighborly, regardful, social, cooperative, responsive, aware, sensitive, benign, indulgent, obliging, careful, attentive, gallant, chivalrous, charitable.—*Ant.* selfish, boorish, inconsiderate.

thoughtfulness, *n.* understanding, helpfulness, indulgence; see **kindness 1.**

thoughtless, *a.* 1. [Destitute of thought] irrational, unreasoning, unreasonable, inane, incomprehensible, witless, undiscerning, foolish, doltish, babbling, bewildered, confused, puerile, senseless, driveling, inept, dull, heavy, obtuse, feeble-minded, flighty; see also **stupid 1. 2.** [Inconsiderate] heedless, negligent, inattentive, careless, neglectful, self-centered, egocentric, selfish, asocial, antisocial, unmindful, unheeding, deaf, blind, indifferent, unconcerned, listless, apathetic, boorish, discourteous, primitive, unrefined; see also **rude 2.**—Ant. careful, thoughtful, unselfish.

thoughtlessness, *n.* inattention, oversight, heedlessness; see **carelessness, neglect 1.**

thought (over) *or* **through,** *a.* studied, thought about, revised; see **considered 1,** investigated.

thousand, *a.* ten hundred, millenary, thousandfold; see **many.**

thrash, *v.* trounce, whip, chasten; see **beat 1, punish.**

thread, *n.* yarn, string, strand; see **fiber.**

thread, *v.* attach, weave together, string together; see **join 1.**

threat, *n.* menace, fulmination, intimidation; see **warning.**

threaten, *v.* intimidate, caution, admonish, hold over, scare, torment, push around, forewarn, bully, abuse, bluster, endanger, be dangerous, be gathering, be in the offing, imperil, be brewing, approach, come on, advance; see also **frighten, warn.**—Ant. help, mollify, placate.

threatened, *a.* warned, endangered, imperiled, jeopardized, in bad straits, insecure, unsafe, unprotected, vulnerable, exposed, in a crucial state, in danger, besieged, surrounded, under attack, set upon, in a bad way.—Ant. **safe,** invulnerable, protected.

threatening, *a.* alarming, dangerous, aggressive; see **ominous, sinister, unsafe.**

three, *a.* triple, treble, threefold, third, triform, triune, tertiary, thrice, triply.

threshold, *n.* sill, gate, door; see also **entrance 1.**

thrift, *n.* saving, parsimony, frugality; see **economy.**

thrifty, *a.* saving, careful, frugal; see **economical 1.**

thrill, *n.* pleasant sensation, stimulation, tingle; see **excitement, fun.**

thrill, *v.* animate, inspire, rouse; see **excite.**

thrilled, *a.* inspired, moved, touched; see also **excited, happy.**

thrilling, *a.* overwhelming, exciting, breathtaking; see **stimulating.**

thrive, *v.* flourish, increase, succeed; see **grow 1.**

throat, *n.* neck, windpipe, larynx, trachea, esophagus, jugular region, gullet, gorge. —*cut each other's throats,* ruin each other, fight, feud; see **destroy.** — *cut one's own throat,* harm *or* damage *or* ruin oneself, cause one's own destruction, act contrary to one's best interest(s); see **commit suicide, damage.** —*ram down someone's throat,* impose, pressure, coerce; see **force.** —

stick in one's throat, be difficult to say, not come easily, be disturbing; see **disturb.**

throng, *n.* multitude, mass, concourse; see **crowd, gathering.**

throttle, *v.* strangle, stifle, silence; see **choke.**

through, *a.* and *prep.* 1. [Finished] completed, over, ended; see **done 1, finished 1.** 2. [From one side to the other] straight through, through and through, clear through; see in **2, into, within.** 3. [During] throughout, for the period of, from beginning to end; see **during.** 4. [By means of] by, by way of, by reason, in virtue of, in consequence of, for, by the agency of, at the hand of. 5. [Referring to continuous passage] nonstop, unbroken, one-way; see **consecutive, constant, regular 3.**

through and through, *a.* permeating, pervasive, enduring; see **completely, throughout.**

throughout, *a.* and *prep.* all through, during, from beginning to end, from one end to the other, everywhere, all over, in everything, in every place, up and down, on all accounts, in all respects, inside and out, at full length, every bit, to the end, down to the ground, *hide and hair, head and shoulders, from the word go, *up to the brim; see also **completely.**

through thick and thin, *a.* devotedly, loyally, constantly; see **regularly.**

throw, *v.* 1. [To hurl] fling, butt, bunt, pitch, fire, let go, sling, toss, heave, lob, dash, launch, chuck, bowl, cast, heave *or* hurl at, let fly, deliver, *cast off, *lay across.—Ant. catch, receive, grab. 2. [To connect or disconnect] turn a switch, connect, start; see **turn off, turn on 1.** 3. [To force to the ground] *pin, *nail, flatten; see **defeat 3.** 4. [*To permit an opponent to win] submit, yield, surrender; see **lose 3.**

throw away, *v.* reject, refuse, turn down; see **discard.**

throw in, *v.* add, expand, give; see **increase 1.**

throw in the towel or *sponge,* *v.* give up, surrender, bow to; see **quit 2.**

thrown, *a.* 1. [Hurled] pitched, tossed, heaved; see **sent.** 2. [Beaten] knocked over, sent sprawling, heaved; see **beaten 1.**

throw out, *v.* discharge, throw away, reject; see **discard.**

throw up, *v.* 1. [To vomit] regurgitate, retch, *barf; see **vomit.** 2. [To quit] give up, cease, terminate; see **stop 2.** 3. [To construct, usually hastily] build overnight, patch up, knock together; see **build 1.**

throw together, *v.* make (quickly) do in

a hurry, do a rush job; see **build**, **manufacture** 1.

thrust, n. 1. [A jab] punch, stab, poke; see **blow** 1. 2. [An attack] onset, onslaught, advance; see **attack**. 3. [A strong push] drive, impetus, momentum; see **push**.

thrust, v. poke, push, shove; see **hit** 1.

thud, n. fall, dull sound, plop; see **noise** 1.

thumb, ʍ. pollex, first digit, preaxial digit; see **finger**. —**all thumbs**, fumbling, clumsy, inept; see **awkward** 1. —**under one's thumb**, under one's control, controlled, governed; see **managed**.

thump, n. thud, knock, rap; see **noise** 1.

thump, v. pound, knock, rap, wallop, slap, strike, whack, hit; see **beat** 1.

thunder, n. crash, peal, outburst, explosion, boom, booming, roar, rumble, clap, crack, discharge, thunderbolt, uproar, blast; see also **noise** 1.

thunder, v. peal, boom, rumble, resound, roll, deafen, crash, clamor, clash; see also **sound** 1, **storm**.

thunderstorm, n. electric storm, squall, downpour; see **thunder**, **storm**.

thus, a. in this manner, so, consequently, hence, in such a way, just like that, in kind, along these lines; see also **therefore**.

thwart, v. stop, impede, frustrate; see **confuse**, **prevent**.

tick, n. 1. [A light beat] beat, click, ticktock; see **beat** 1, 2. 2. [An insect] parasite, louse, mite; see **insect**, **pest** 1.

ticket, n. 1. [A valid token] check, certificate, notice, badge, label, voucher, stub, countercheck, rain-check, tag, slip, note, card, pass, receipt, record, license, permit, passage, credential, visa, passport, document. 2. [Candidates representing a political party] party list, choice, ballot; see **candidate**, **faction**, **party** 3.

tickle, v. rub, caress, stroke, see **touch** 1.

ticklish, a. sensitive, unsteady, touchy; see **irritable**, **unstable** 2.

tidbit, n. morsel, mouthful, bite; see **bit** 1.

tide, n. current, flow, flux, stream, course, sluice, undercurrent, undertow, drag, whirlpool, eddy, vortex, torrent, wave, tidal wave. Tides of the sea include the following—low, neap, ebb, spring, full, high, flood.

tidiness, n. neatness, spruceness, uniformity; see **cleanliness**.

tidy, a. orderly, trim, spruce; see **neat** 1.

tie, n. 1. [A fastening] band, strap, bandage, zipper; see **fastener**. 2. [A necktie] cravat, neckerchief, bow, knot, scarf, neckcloth, choker. 3. [Affection] bond, relation, kinship; see **affection**, **love** 1.

4. [An equal score, or a contest having that score] deadlock, draw, even game, dead heat, drawn battle, neck-and-neck contest, *even-Stephen, stalemate, *nose finish, standoff.¹

tie, v. 1. [To fasten] bind, make fast, attach; see **fasten**, **join** 1. 2. [To tie a knot in] knot, make a bow, make a tie, make a knot, do up, fix a tie, make a hitch; see also sense 1. 3. [To equal] match, keep up with, parallel; see **equal**.

tied, a. 1. [Firm] fixed, bound, made firm; see **firm** 1. 2. [Even] evenly matched, (running) neck and neck, in a dead heat; see **alike**, **equal**.

tie up, v. wrap, package, fasten; see **close** 4, **enclose**.

tight, a. 1. [Firm] taut, secure, fast, bound up, close, clasped, fixed, steady, stretched thin, established, compact, strong, stable, enduring, steadfast, unyielding, unbending, set, stuck hard, hidebound, invulnerable, snug, sturdy; see also **firm** 1.—*Ant.* loose, tottery, shaky. 2. [Closed] sealed, airtight, impenetrable, impermeable, impervious, watertight, hermetically sealed, padlocked, bolted, locked, fastened, shut tight, clamped, fixed, tied, snapped, swung to, tied up, nailed, spiked, slammed, obstructed, blocked, blind, shut, stopped up, plugged.—*Ant.* open, penetrable, unprotected. 3. [Close-fitting] pinching, shrunken, snug, uncomfortable, cramping, skintight, short, crushing, choking, smothering, cutting.—*Ant.* loose, ample, wide. 4. [*Intoxicated] inebriated, drunken, tipsy; see **drunk**. 5. [*Stingy] miserly, parsimonious, close; see **stingy**. 6. [Difficult to obtain, *said especially of money*] scarce, frozen, tied up; see **rare** 2. —**sit tight**, do nothing, refrain from action, stay (put); see **wait** 1.

tighten, v. 1. [To make tight] compress, condense, squeeze, bind, contract, strangle, constrict, crush, cramp, pinch, grip more tightly, clench, screw down, add pressure; see also **stretch** 2.—*Ant.* loosen, relax, unloose. 2. [To become tight] contract, harden, congeal, stiffen, toughen, become more disciplined *or* stricter.—*Ant.* melt, soften, liquefy.

tightfisted, a. thrifty, niggardly, frugal; see **stingy**.

tile, n. baked clay, flooring, roofing; see also **clay**, **flooring**.

till, v. cultivate, work, raise crops from; see **farm** 1.

tilt, n. slant, slope, slide; see **inclination** 2.

tilt, v. slant, tip, turn, set at an angle, lean, slope, slouch, shift, dip, sway, make oblique, deviate, turn edgewise;

see also bend. *—Ant.* **straighten,** level, bring into line.

timber, *n.* 1. [Standing trees] wood, lumber, timberland; see **forest.** 2. [A beam] stake, pole, club; see **beam 1, lumber.**

time, *n.* 1. [Duration] continuance, lastingness, extent, past, present, future, infinity, space-time; see also **today.** Units of measuring time include the following—second, minute, hour, day, term, millisecond, week, month, year, decade, generation, lifetime, century, millennium, eon. 2. [A point in time] incident, event, occurrence, occasion, time and tide, instant, term, season, tide, course, sequence, point, generation. 3. [A period of time] season, era, interval; see **age 3.** 4. [Experience] background, living, participation; see **experience.** 5. [Leisure] opportunity, free moment, chance; see **freedom 2. 6.** [Circumstances: *usually plural; used with* the] condition, the present, nowadays; see **circumstance 1, circumstances 2. 7.** [A measure of speed] tempo, rate, meter; see **beat 2.**

time, *v.* register, distance, clock, measure time; see **measure 1.** —**ahead of time,** ahead of schedule, fast, earlier than expected; see **early 1.** —**at one time,** simultaneously, concurrently, at once; see **together 2.** —**at the same time,** simultaneously, concurrently, at once; see **together 2.** —**at times,** occasionally, sometimes, once in a while; see **seldom.** —**behind the times,** out of date, archaic, antediluvian; see **old-fashioned.** —**behind time,** tardy, delayed, coming later; see **late 1.** —**between times,** now and then, occasionally, sometimes; see **seldom.** —**do time,* serve a prison term, go to jail, be imprisoned; see **serve time.** —**for the time being,** for the present, for now, under consideration; see **temporarily.** —**from time to time,** occasionally, sometimes, once in a while; see **frequently.** —**in no time,** instantly, rapidly, without delay; see **quickly, soon 1.** —**in time,** eventually, after the proper time, inevitably; see **finally 2.** —**lose time,** go too slow, tarry, cause a delay; see **delay 1.** —**make time,** gain time, act hastily, hasten; see **hurry 1.** —**many a time,** often, regularly, consistently; see **frequently.** —**on time, 1.** at the appointed time, punctually, correct; see **punctual.** 2. by credit, in installments, on account; see **unpaid 1.** —**out of time,** out of pace, unreasonable, improper; see **untimely.** —**pass the time of day,** exchange greetings, chat, converse; see **greet.**

timely, *a.* opportune, seasonable, in good time, fitting the times, suitable, appropriate, convenient, favorable, propitious,

well-timed, modern, up-to-date, newsworthy.*—Ant.* **untimely,** ill-timed, inappropriate.

timepiece, *n.* timekeeper, chronometer, sundial; see **clock, watch 1.**

timid, *a.* 1. [Irresolute] indecisive, vacillating, wavering; see **irresponsible.** 2. [Cowardly] fainthearted, spiritless, weak; see **afraid, cowardly.** 3. [Reticent] shy, withdrawn, modest; see **humble 1.**

tinge, *n.* nib, shade, hint; see **trace 1.**

tingle, *v.* shiver, prickle, sting, itch, creep, grow excited, **get goose pimples all over.*

tinker, *v.* try to mend, play with, take apart; see **repair.**

tint, *n.* tinge, hue, shade, color value, cast, flush, dye, tinct, taint, glow, pastel color, luminous color, pale hue, tone, tincture, dash, touch, color tone, coloration, pigmentation, ground color, complexion; see also **color 1.**

tinted, *a.* tinged, painted, touched up; see **colored.**

tiny, *a.* small, miniature, diminutive; see **little 1.**

tip, *n.* 1. [The point] apex, peak, top; see **point 2.** 2. [A gratuity] reward, gift, compensation, fee, small change, money, handout; see also **pay 2.** 3. [**A bit of information*] hint, clue, warning; see **knowledge 1, news 1.**

tip, *v.* slant, incline, shift; see **bend, lean 1, tilt.**

tiptop, *a.* superior, prime, choice; see **best, excellent.**

tire, *n.* casing, tire and tube, one of a set or a pair; see **wheel 1.** Terms for types of tires, include the following—tubeless, belted, radial, snow, mud, punctureproof, recapped, low-pressure, synthetic, natural rubber, solid rubber, pneumatic, oversize, airplane, motorcycle, bicycle, recap.

tire, *v.* 1. [To become exhausted] grow weary, break down, droop, flag, pall, faint, drop, puff, sink, yawn, collapse, give out, wilt, go stale, **poop out, *burn out.—Ant.* **rest,** awake, relax. 2. [To make a person exhausted] tax, overtax, harass, fatigue, exhaust, overwork, strain, overstrain, overburden, depress, dispirit, pain, vex, worry, distress, deject, dishearten, wear out, run a person ragged, **do up or* in.

tired, *a.* fatigued, weary, run-down, exhausted, overworked, overtaxed, wearied, worn, spent, wasted, wornout, drooping, distressed, unmanned, drowsy, droopy, sleepy, haggard, faint, prostrated, brokendown, drained, consumed, empty, collapsing, **all in,* finished, stale, fagged, **dog-tired, *dead on one's feet, *pooped, *done in or for, *worn to a* frazzle, *played out, *tuckered out, *fed up.—*Ant.* active, lively, energetic.

tireless, *a.* unwearied, unwearying, untiring; see **active.**

tiresome, *a.* irksome, wearying, monotonous; see **dull 4.**

tissue, *n.* 1. [A network] web, mesh, filigree; see **network 2.** 2. [Thin fabric] gauze, gossamer, lace; see **veil, web 1.** 3. [Protective layer, especially in living organisms] film, membrane, intercellular substance; see **muscle.**

title, *n.* 1. [A designation] indication, inscription, sign; see also **name 1.** 2. [Ownership or evidence of ownership] right, claim, license; see **ownership.** 3. [Mark of rank or dignity] commission, decoration, medal, ribbon, coat of arms, crest, order, authority, privilege, degree; see also **emblem.** Titles include the following—Sir, Doctor, Mr., Ms., Mrs., Miss, Reverend, Monsignor, Dame, King, Prince, Baron, Viscount, Earl, Marquis, Marquise, Duke, Grand Duke, Knight, Count, Sultan, Queen, Duchess, Lady, Princess, Countess, Monsieur, Madame, Mademoiselle, Don, Doña, Herr, General, Colonel, Major, Captain, Lieutenant, Admiral, Commander, Ensign, President, Vice-president, Secretary, Speaker, Governor, Mayor, Representative, Senator.

to, *prep.* 1. [In the direction of] toward, via, into, facing, through, directed toward, traveling to, along the line of. 2. [Indicating position] over, upon, in front of; see **on 1.** 3. [Until] till, up to, stopping at; see also **until.** 4. [So that] in order to, intending to, that one may, for the purpose of. 5. [Indicating degree] up to, down to, as far as, in that degree, to this extent. 6. [Indicating result] becoming, until, back, ending with.

to and fro, *a.* seesaw, zigzag, back and forth, backward(s) and forward(s), in and out, up and down, from side to side, from pillar to post, off and on, round and round, forward and back.

toast, *n.* 1. [A sentiment or person drunk to] pledge, salute, acknowledgment; see **honor 1.** Invitations for toasts include the following—here's to you, good luck, lest we forget, your health, *prosit* (German), *skoal* (Scandinavian), *salud* (Spanish), *a votre sante* (French), *down the hatch, here's how, mud in your eye, here's looking at you. 2. [Browned bread] Varieties of toast include the following—Melba, French, cinnamon; see **bread.**

toast, *v.* 1. [To honor by drinking liquor] drink to, compliment, propose a toast; see **drink 2, praise 1.** 2. [To brown bread] put in a toaster, heat, crisp; see **cook.**

to blame, *a.* at fault, culpable, censurable; see **guilty.**

to date, *a.* so far, as yet, up to now; see **now 1.**

today, *n.* this day, the present, our time, this moment; see also **now 1.**

to-do, *n.* commotion, stir, fuss; see **disorder 2, fight 1.**

toe, *n.* digit, front of the foot, tip of a shoe; see **foot 2.** —*on ones toes,* alert, aware, attentive; see **careful.** —*step or tread on someone's toes,* annoy, offend, disturb; see **anger 1.**

together, *a.* 1. [Jointly] collectively, unitedly, commonly; see **sense 2.** 2. [Simultaneously] at the same time, concurrently, coincidentally, contemporaneously, at once, in connection with, at a blow, in unison, at one jump.

toil, *n.* labor, occupation, drudgery; see **work 2.**

toil, *v.* sweat, labor, slave; see **work.**

toilet, *n.* water closet, lavatory, washroom, rest-room, men's room, women's room, powder room, gentlemen's room, ladies' room, comfort station, bathroom, bath, *little boy's room, *little girl's room, *head, potty, *can, *pot, *john.

token, *n.* mark, favor, sample; see **gift 1.** —*by the same token,* following from this, similarly, thus; see **therefore.** —*in token of,* evidence of, by way of, as a gesture; see **by 2.**

told, *a.* recounted, recorded, set down, reported, known, chronicled, revealed, exposed, made known, said, published, printed, announced, released, described, stated, set forth, included in the official statement, made public property, become common knowledge, related, depicted, enunciated, pronounced, given out, handed down, telegraphed, broadcast, telecast, confessed, admitted, well-known, discovered; see also **spoken.**—*Ant.* **secret,** concealed, unknown.

tolerable, *a.* endurable, sufferable, sustainable; see **bearable.**

tolerance, *n.* 1. [Open-mindedness] concession, liberality, permission, forbearance, indulgence, mercy, compassion, license, sufferance, grace, understanding, sensitivity, charity, benevolence, humanity, endurance, altruism, patience, good will; see also **kindness 1.** 2. [Saturation point] threshold, tolerance level, end; see **limit 2.**

tolerant, *a.* understanding, receptive, sophisticated; see **liberal, patient 1.**

tolerate, *v.* 1. [To allow] permit, consent to, put up (with); see **allow.** 2. [To endure] bear, undergo, abide; see **endure 2.**

toll, *n.* 1. [Charges] duty, fee, customs, exaction, tollage; see also **price, tax.** 2.

[Loss] casualties, deaths, losses; see **damage 2**.

tomb, *n.* vault, crypt, mausoleum; see **grave**.

tombstone, *n.* monument, gravestone, headstone, footstone, stone, marker, cross, funerary statue.

tomorrow, *n.* the morrow, next day in the course of time, the future, *mañana* (Spanish); see also **day 1**.

ton, *n.* twelve hundredweight, two thousand pounds, short ton, metric ton, long ton, shipping ton, displacement ton, measurement ton, freight ton; see also **weight 1, 2**.

tone, *n.* 1. [A musical sound] pitch, timbre, resonance; see **sound 2**. 2. [Quality] nature, trend, temper; see **character 1**. 3. [Manner] expression, condition, aspect; see **mood 1**. 4. [A degree of color] hue, tint, color value; see **color 1**.

tone down, *v.* subdue, moderate, temper; see **soften 2**.

tongs, *n.* pinchers, pliers, tweezers; see **utensils**.

tongue, *n.* 1. [The movable muscle in the mouth] organ of taste or speech, lingua; see also **muscle, organ 2**. Parts of the tongue used in speech are—tip, apex, front, center, back. 2. [Speech] speech, utterance, discourse; see **language 1**. —**hold one's tongue**, refrain from speaking, hold back, keep silent, see **restrain 1**. —**on the tip of one's tongue**, forgotten, not quite remembered, not readily recalled; see **familiar, forgotten**.

tongue-tied, *a.* 1. [Mute] silent, speechless, aphonic; see **dumb 1, mute 1**. 2. [Inarticulate] reticent, nervous, inarticulate; see **reserved 3**.

tonight, *n.* this evening, this p.m., this night, later; see **night 1**.

too, *a.* 1. [Also] as well, likewise, in addition, additionally, moreover, furthermore, further, besides; see also **also**. 2. [In excess] excessively, extremely, over and above; see **besides**.

tool, *n.* 1. [An implement] utensil, machine, instrument, mechanism, weapon, apparatus, appliance, engine, means, contrivance, gadget; see also **device 1**. Common tools include the following—can opener, hammer, knife, jack, crank, pulley, wheel, bar, crowbar, lever, sledge, winch, cam, loom, shuttle, chisel, plane, screw, brace, bit, file, saw, screwdriver, ax, corkscrew, jimmy. 2. [One who permits himself to be used] accomplice, hireling, dupe; see also **servant**.

too much, *n.* excess, waste, extravagance, overabundance, superfluity, preposterousness, overgoing, overcharge, ever so much, more than can be used, vastness, prodigiousness, immensity; see also **excess 1**.—*Ant.* lack, want, shortage.

tooth, *n.* 1. [A dental process] fang, tusk, saber-tooth, tusk, ivory, snag, artificial tooth, false tooth, bony appendage. Human teeth include the following—incisor, canine or cuspid or eyetooth, biscuspid or premolar, first biscuspid, second bicuspid, molar (grinder), first molar, second molar, third molar or wisdom tooth. 2. [A toothlike or tooth-shaped object] point, stub, projection; see **root 1**. —**get** or **sink one's teeth into**, become occupied with, involve oneself in, be busy at; see **act 1**.

toothache, *n.* swollen gums, abscessed tooth, decayed tooth; see **pain 2**.

tooth and nail, *a.* energetically, fervently, forcefully; see **eagerly, fiercely**.

toothbrush, *n.* electric (toothbrush), nylon or natural bristle toothbrush, Water Pik (trademark); see **brush 1**.

top, *a.* 1. [Highest] topmost, uppermost, highest, on the upper end; see also **highest**. 2. [Best] prime, head, first, among the first; see also **best 1**.

top, *n.* 1. [The uppermost portion] peak, summit, crown, head, crest, tip, apex, cap, crowning point, headpiece, capital, pinnacle, zenith, consummation, spire; see also **height**.—*Ant.* bottom, lower end, nadir. 2. [A cover] lid, roof, ceiling; see **cover 1**. 3. [A spinning toy] spinner, musical top, whistling top; see **toy 1**. 4. [The leader] head, captain, chief; see also **leader 2**. —***blow one's top**, lose one's temper, become angry, be enraged; see **rage 1**. —**off the top of one's head**, speaking offhand, chatting, casually; see **spontaneous**. —**on top**, prosperous, thriving, superior; see **successful**.

top, *v.* 1. [To remove the top] prune, lop off, trim; see **cut 1**. 2. [To exceed] better, beat, excel; see **exceed**. 3. [To apply topping] cover, screen, coat; see **paint 2**.

top-heavy, *a.* overweight, unstable, unbalanced; see **shaky 1**.

topic, *n.* question, theme, material; see **subject**.

topless, *a.* almost nude, bare to the waist, exposed; see **naked 1**.

top-level, *a.* leading, superior, supreme; see **excellent, important 1**.

top off, *v.* finish, end, bring to a conclusion; see **complete**.

top-secret, *a.* restricted, kept (very) quiet, *hush-hush; see **secret 1**.

topsy-turvy, *a.* confused, upside down, disordered; see **disorderly 1**.

torch, *n.* beacon, light, flare; see **light 3**.

torment, *n.* agony, suffering, misery; see pain 1, 2, **torture.**

torment, *v.* abuse, mistreat, torture, irritate; see also **hurt 1.**

tormentor, *n.* oppressor, persecutor, tormentress; see **enemy.**

torn, *a.* ripped, slit, split, severed, lacerated, mutilated, broken, rent, fractured, cracked, slashed, gashed, ruptured, snapped, sliced, burst, cleaved, wrenched, divided, pulled out, impaired, damaged, spoiled; see also **ruined 1.**— *Ant.* whole, repaired, adjusted.

torrent, *n.* overflow, deluge, downpour; see also **flood, flow, storm.**

torrid, *a.* blazing, fiery, sweltering; see hot 1.

torture, *n.* pain, anguish, agony, torment, crucifixion, cruciation, martyrdom, pang, ache, twinge, physical suffering, mental suffering; see also **cruelty.**—*Ant.* comfort, enjoyment, delight.

torture, *v.* annoy, irritate, disturb; see abuse, **bother 2.**

toss, *v.* 1. [To throw easily] hurl, fling, cast; see **throw 1.** 2. [To move up and down] bob, buffet, stir, move restlessly, tumble, pitch, roll, heave, sway, flounder, rock, wobble, undulate, swing, rise and fall; see also **wave 3.**

toss-up, *n.* deadlock, bet, draw; see **tie 4.**

tot, *n.* child, infant, youngster; see **baby.**

total, *a.* 1. [Whole] entire, inclusive, every; see **whole 1.** 2. [Complete] utter, gross, thorough; see **absolute 1.**

total, *n.* sum; entirety, result; see **whole.**

total, *v.* 1. [To add] figure, calculate, count up, ring up, tag up, sum up, add up; see also **add 1.** 2. [To amount to] consist of, come to, add up to; see **amount to, equal.**

totality, *n.* everything, oneness, collectivity; see **whole.**

totally, *a.* entirely, wholly, exclusively; see **completely.**

totem, *n.* fetish, symbol, crest; see **emblem.**

to the contrary, *a.* in disagreement with, in opposition to, in contradiction of *or* to; see **against 1, on the contrary.**

totter, *v.* shake, rock, careen, quake, tremble, stumble, falter, trip, weave, zigzag, reel, rock, roll, walk drunkenly, wobble, waver, hesitate, seesaw, teeter, dodder, crumple, sway, be loose, be weak; see also **wave 3.**

touch, *n.* 1. [The tactile sense] feeling, touching, feel, perception, tactility, taction. 2. [Contact] rub, stroke, pat, fondling, rubbing, stroking, licking, handling, graze, scratch, brush, taste, nudge, kiss, peck, embrace, cuddling, caress. 3. [A sensation] sense, impression, pressure; see **feeling 2.** 4. [Skill] knack,

technique, finish; see **ability, method.** 5. [A trace] suggestion, scent, inkling; see **bit 1.**

touch, *v.* 1. [To be in contact] stroke, graze, rub, nudge, thumb, finger, paw, lick, taste, brush, kiss, glance, sweep, fondle, smooth, massage, sip, partake; see also **feel 1.** 2. [To come into contact with] meet, encounter, reach; see **meet 1.** 3. [To relate to] refer to, regard, affect; see **concern 1.**

touch-and-go, *a.* 1. [Hasty] rapid, casual, superficial; see **shallow 2.** 2. [Risky] ticklish, hazardous, tricky; see **dangerous, uncertain 2.**

touched, *a.* 1. [Having been in slight contact] fingered, nudged, used, brushed, handled, rubbed, stroked, rearranged, kissed, grazed, licked, tasted, fondled. 2. [Affected] moved, impressed, stirred; see **affected 1.**

touching, *a.* and *prep.* 1. [Referring to] regarding, in regard to, in reference to; see **about 2.** 2. [Affecting] moving, pathetic, tender; see **pitiful 3.** 3. [Adjacent] tangent, in contact, against; see **near 1, next 2.**

touch off, *v.* 1. [To cause to explode] detonate, light the fuse, set off; see **explode.** 2. [To cause to start] start, initiate, release; see **begin 1, cause.**

touch on, *v.* treat, refer to, mention; see **discuss.**

touch up, *v.* renew, modify, rework; see **remodel, repair.**

touchy, *a.* 1. [Irritable] ill-humored, testy, irascible; see **irritable 2.** 2. [Delicate] harmful, hazardous, risky; see **unsafe.**

tough, *a.* 1. [Strong] robust, wiry, mighty; see **strong 1, 2.** 2. [Cohesive] solid, firm, sturdy, hard, hardened, adhesive, leathery, coherent, inseparable, molded, tight, cemented, unbreakable, in one piece, dense, closely packed.— *Ant.* weak, fragile, brittle. 3. [Difficult to chew] uncooked, half-cooked, sinewy, indigestible, inedible, fibrous, old, hard as nails, *tough as shoe-leather.*—*Ant.* soft, tender, overcooked. 4. [Difficult] hard, troublesome, laborious; see **difficult 1, severe 1.** 5. [Hardy] robust, sound, capable; see **healthy.** 6. [Rough and cruel] savage, fierce, ferocious; see **cruel.**

tour, *n.* trip, voyage, travel; see **journey.**

tour, *v.* voyage, vacation, take a trip; see **travel.**

tourist, *n.* sight-seer, vacationist, visitor; see also **traveler.**

tournament, *n.* meet, tourney, match; see **sport 3.**

tow, *v.* haul, pull, drag; see **draw 1.**

toward, *a.* and *prep.* to, in the direction of, pointing to, via, on the way to, proceeding, moving, approaching, in relation to, close to, headed for, on the road to; see also **near** 1.

towel, *n*. wiper, drier, absorbent paper, sheet, toweling, napkin, cloth, rag. Towels include the following—linen, cotton, terry, guest, face, Turkish, hand, bath, dish, tea, paper, napkin. **—*throw in the towel**, admit defeat, give in, surrender; see **quit** 2.

tower, *n*. spire, mast, steeple, bell tower, belfry, monolith, radio tower, skyscraper, obelisk, pillar, column, minaret.

tower, *v*. look over, extend above, mount; see **overlook** 1.

town, *a*. civic, community, civil; see **municipal, urban**.

town, *n*. 1. [In the United States, a small collection of dwellings] hamlet, county seat, municipality, borough, *hick town, *falling-off place, *wide place in the road, *the sticks. 2. [The people in a city, especially the prominent people] townspeople, inhabitants, society; see **population**.

toxic, *a*. noxious, virulent, lethal; see **deadly, poisonous**.

toy, *a*. childish, miniature, small; see **little** 1.

toy, *n*. 1. [Something designed for amusement] game, plaything, pastime; see **doll, game** 1. Toys include the following—dolls, games, balls, toy weapons, blocks, jacks, tops, bicycles, tricycles, roller skates, marbles, skateboards, hobby horses. 2. [Anything trivial] trifle, bauble, gadget; see **knickknack**.

trace, *n*. 1. [A very small quantity] indication, fragment, dash, dab, sprinkling, tinge, pinch, crumb, trifle, shred, drop, speck, shade, hint, shadow, nuance, iota, particle, jot, suggestion, touch, tittle, suspicion, minimum, smell, spot; see also **bit** 1. 2. [A track] evidence, trail, footprint; see **track** 2.

trace, *v*. 1. [To track] smell out, track down, run down; see **track** 1. 2. [To draw] sketch, outline, copy; see **draw** 2.

tracing, *n*. imitation, reproduction, duplicate; see **copy**.

track, *n*. 1. [A prepared way] path, course, road; see **railroad**. 2. [Evidence left in passage] footprint, trace, vestige, impression, tire track, mark, footmark, spoor, trail, imprint, remnant, record, indication, print, sign, remains, token, symbol, clue, scent, wake, monument. **—keep track of**, keep an account of, stay informed about, maintain contact with; see **track** 1, **watch**. **—lose track of**, lose sight of, lose contact with, abandon; see **forget** 1. **—*make tracks**, run away, abandon, depart quickly; see **leave** 1. **—off the track**, deviant, variant, deviating; see **mistaken** 1. **—the**

wrong side of the tracks, ghetto, poor side of town, lower class neighborhood; see **slum**.

track, *v*. 1. [To follow by evidence] hunt, pursue, smell out, add up, put together, trail, follow, trace, follow the scent, follow a clue, follow footprints, draw an inference, piece together, dog, be hot on the trail of, tail, shadow. 2. [To dirty with tracks] leave footprints, leave mud, muddy, stain, filth, soil, spatter, leave a trail of dirt; see also **dirty**.

track down, *v*. pursue, hunt (down), find; see **catch** 1, **discover**.

tracks, *n*. 1. [*An injection scar] needlemarks, punctures, injection marks; see **mark** 1, **scar**. 2. [Means of passage] road, way, path; see **track** 1. 3. [Evidence of passage] trail, (foot)prints, marks; see **track** 2.

trade, *n*. 1. [Business] commerce, sales, enterprise; see **business** 1. 2. [A craft] occupation, profession, position; see **job** 1. Common trades include the following—auto mechanic, accountant, boilermaker, baker, barber, butcher, bookbinder, bricklayer, carpenter, draughtsman, cabinetmaker, cameraman, dressmaker, electrician, embalmer, engraver, jeweler, locksmith, metallurgist, millwright, miner, machinist, optician, operator, painter, plumber, printer, shoemaker, textile worker, technician, toolmaker, welder. 3. [An individual business transaction] deal, barter, contract; see **sale** 2.

trade, *v*. 1. [To do business] patronize, shop, purchase; see **buy, sell**. 2. [To give one thing for another] barter, swap, give in exchange; see **exchange**. **—trade in**, turn in, make part of a deal, get rid of; see **sell**.

trader, *n*. salesman, dealer, tradesman; see **businessman**.

trademark, *n*. brand, tag, commercial stamp; see **label**.

tradesman, *n*. storekeeper, shopkeeper, merchant; see **businessman**.

trade union, *n*. union, organized labor, guild; see **labor** 4.

tradition, *n*. 1. [The process of preserving orally] folklore, legend, fable; see **story**. 2. [Cultural heritage] ritual, mores, law; see **culture** 2, **custom** 2.

traditional, *a*. folkloric, legendary, mythical, epical, ancestral, unwritten, balladic, told, handed down, fabulous, anecdotal, proverbial, inherited, folkloristic, old, acknowledged, customary, habitual, widespread, usual, widely used, popular, acceptable, established, fixed, sanctioned, universal, taken for granted, rooted, classical, prescribed, conventional; see also **common** 1, **regular** 3.

traffic, *n*. 1. [The flow of transport]

travel, passage, transportation, flux, movement, transfer, transit, passenger service, freight shipment, influx. 2. [Dealings] commerce, transactions, exchange; see **business**.

tragedy, *n.* 1. [Unhappy fate] lot, bad fortune, misfortune, doom, bad end, no good end.—*Ant.* **happiness,** fortune, success. 2. [A series of tragic events] adversity, affliction, hardship; see **difficulty** 1, 2.—*Ant.* **success,** prosperity, good fortune. 3. [An artistic creation climaxed by catastrophe] play, tragic drama, *pic; see **drama, movie, novel.**

tragic, *a.* catastrophic, fatal, disastrous; see **unfortunate.**

trail, *n.* trace, tracks, path; see **way** 2.

trail, *v.* 1. [To follow] track, trace, follow a scent; see **hunt** 1, **pursue** 1. 2. [To lag behind] fall back, loiter, tarry; see **wait** 1.

trailer, *n.* house trailer, auto home, mobile home; see **home** 1.

train, *n.* 1. [A sequence] string, chain, succession; see **series.** 2. [A locomotive and attached cars] transport train, passenger, freight train, local train, limited, supply train, express train, excursion train, commuters' train, troop train, boat train, mail train, subway, underground, elevated, electric, diesel; see also **railroad.**

train, *v.* 1. [To drill] practice, exercise, discipline; see **reach** 2. 2. [To educate] instruct, tutor, enlighten; see **teach** 1. 3. [To toughen oneself] prepare, inure, grow strong, get into practice, reduce, make ready, fit out, equip, qualify, bring up to standard, *whip into shape, get a workout.—*Ant.* **weaken,** break training, be unfit. 4. [To direct growth] rear, lead, discipline (oneself), mold, bend, implant, guide, shape, care for, encourage, infuse, imbue, order, bring up, nurture, nurse, prune, weed; see also **raise** 1.—*Ant.* **neglect,** ignore, disdain. 5. [To aim] cock, level, draw a bead; see **aim** 2.

trained, *a.* prepared, qualified, cultured, initiated, skilled, informed, schooled, primed, graduated, disciplined, enlightened; see also **educated** 1.—*Ant.* **inexperienced,** untrained, raw.

trainer, *n.* teacher, tutor, instructor, coach, manager, mentor, officer, master, boss, handler, pilot.

training, *n.* drill, practice, exercise, preparation, instruction, foundation, schooling, discipline, basic principles, groundwork, coaching, indoctrination, preliminaries, *tune-up, *build up; see also **education.**

trait, *n.* habit, manner, peculiarity; see **characteristic.**

traitor, *n.* betrayer, traducer, deserter, renegade, Judas, informer, spy, hypocrite, imposter, plotter, conspirator, turncoat, sneak, backslider, *double-crosser, *fink, *rat, *stool pigeon, *two-timer; see also **rebel**—*Ant.* **supporter,** follower, partisan.

tramp, *n.* 1. [Vagrant] vagrant, wanderer, bum; see **beggar** 1. 2. [A long walk, often in rough country] hike, ramble, stroll; see **walk** 3. 3. [Prostitute] whore, harlot, slut; see **prostitute.**

trample, *v.* stamp on, crush, tread on, grind underfoot, injure, squash, bruise, tramp over, overwhelm.

trance, *n.* coma, daze, insensibility; see **confusion.**

tranquil, *a.* composed, agreeable, gentle; see **serene.**

tranquilize, *v.* calm, pacify, quell; see **calm down, quiet** 1, **soothe.**

tranquilizer, *n.* sleeping pill, depressant, mitigator, moderator, temperer, assuager, alleviator, alleviative, palliative, soother, mollifier, calmative, sedative, placebo, anodyne, soporific, sedative; see **drug, medicine** 2.

tranquillity, *n.* calmness, peacefulness, serenity; see **peace** 2, 3.

transact, *v.* accomplish, carry on, conclude; see **buy, sell.**

transaction, *n.* doing, proceeding, deal; see **business** 4.

transcend, *v.* rise above, transform, excel; see **exceed.**

transcontinental, *a.* trans-American, trans-Siberian, trans-Canadian, trans-European, cross-country, intracontinental.

transcribe, *v.* reprint, reproduce, decipher; see **copy.**

transcriber, *n.* copyist, copier, translator; see **secretary** 2.

transcript, *n.* record, fair copy, reproduction; see **copy.**

transfer, *n.* 1. [Ticket] token, fare, check; see **ticket** 1. 2. [A document providing for a transfer, sense 2] (new) orders, instructions, (new) assignment; see **command, directions.**

transfer, *v.* 1. [To carry] transport, convey, shift; see **carry** 1. 2. [To assign] sell, hand over, *pass the buck; see **assign** 1, **give** 1.

transferred, *a.* moved, removed, shifted, transported, relocated, transmitted, turned over, sent, relayed, transplanted, reassigned, transposed, restationed, conveyed, transmuted; see also **sent.** —*Ant.* **fixed,** left, stationed.

transform, v. convert, mold, reconstruct; see **alter 1**.

transform or **transformational grammar**, n. generative grammar, new grammar, string grammar; see **grammar**.

transformation, n. 1. [A change] alteration, transmutation, conversion; see **change 1**. 2. [A grammatical construction] transform, transformed or transformational structure or construction, equivalent or alternative grammatical sequence or string; see **adjective, phrase, sentence 2**.

transfusion, n. transmission, blood exchange, bleeding; see also **exchange 1**.

transgress, v. trespass, rebel, infringe; see **disobey**.

transgression, n. misbehavior, trespass, infraction; see **crime, sin, violation**.

transgressor, n. offender, sinner, rebel; see **criminal**.

transient, a. provisional, ephemeral, transitory; see **temporary**.

transistor, n. portable, pocket radio, batterypowered radio; see **radio 2**.

transition, n. shift, passage, flux, passing, development, transformation, turn, realignment; see also **change 2**.—*Ant.* stability, constancy, durability.

translate, v. decode, transliterate, interpret, decipher, paraphrase, render, transpose, turn, gloss, do into, put in equivalent terms.

translated, a. interpreted, adapted, rendered, transliterated, glossed, paraphrased, reworded, transposed, transferred, transplanted, reworked, rewritten.

translation, n. transliteration, version, adaptation, rendition, rendering, interpretation, paraphrase, rewording, gloss, reading.

transmission, n. 1. [The act of transporting] transference, conveyance, carrying; see **delivery 1, transportation 2**. [The carrying of sound on radio waves] broadcast, telecast, frequency; see **broadcasting**. 3. [A mechanism for adapting power] gears, gear box, overdrive; see **device 1**.

transmit, v. 1. [To send] dispatch, forward, convey; see **send, 1, 2**. 2. [To carry] pass on, transfer, communicate; see **send 2**.

transmitter, n. conductor, aerial, wire; see **communication, electronics**.

transparent, a. 1. [Allowing light to pass through] translucent, lucid, crystalline, gauzy, thin, permeable, glassy, cellophane, diaphanous; see also **clear 2**.—*Ant.* dark, black, smoky. 2. [Obvious] easily seen, plain, clear; see **obvious 1**.

transplant, n. skin graft, heart or cardiac transplant, kidney transplant, eye transplant, etc.; see **operation 4**.

transplant, v. reset, reorient, remove; see **alter 1**.

transport, v. convey, move, bring; see **carry 1**.

transportation, n. conveying, conveyance, carrying, hauling, shipping, carting, moving, transferring, truckage, freightage, air lift, transference, transit, passage.

transported, a. conveyed, forwarded, carried; see **moved 1**.

trap, n. 1. [A device to catch game or persons] net, cul-de-sac, snare, mousetrap, deadfall, spring, pit, blind, noose, trapfall, maneuver. 2. [A trick] prank, practical joke, snare; see **trick 1**.

trap, v. ensnare, seduce, fool; see **ambush, deceive**.

trapped, a. ambushed, cornered, with one's back to the wall; see **captured**.

trash, n. 1. [Rubbish] garbage, waste, refuse, dregs, filth, litter, debris, dross, oddments, sweepings, rubble, odds and ends, stuff, frippery, rags, scraps, scrap, scourings, fragments, pieces, shavings, loppings, slash, rakings, slag, parings, rinsings, deads, shoddy, residue, offal, junk, sediment, leavings, droppings. —*Ant.* money, goods, riches. 2. [Nonsense] drivel, twaddle, prating; see **nonsense 1**.

travel, n. riding, roving, wandering, rambling, sailing, touring, biking, hiking, cruising, driving, wayfaring, going abroad, seeing the world, sight-seeing, voyaging, trekking, flying, globe-trotting, space travel, rocketing, moon shot, orbiting, manning a space station, interstellar or intercontinental travel, jet travel.

travel v. tour, cruise, voyage, roam, explore, jet (to), rocket (to or toward), orbit, go into orbit, take a jet, go by jet, migrate, trek, vacation, motor, visit, jaunt, wander, adventure, quest, trip, rove, inspect, make an expedition, cross the continent, cross the ocean, encircle the globe, make the grand tour, sail, see the country, go camping, go abroad, take a trip, take a train or boat or plane (for), cover, go walking or riding or bicycling, etc., make a train trip, drive, fly, sail, set out, set forth, sight-see; see also **walk 1**.

traveled, a. 1. [Said of persons] worldly, cosmopolitan, urbane; see **cultured 2**. [Said of roads] well-used, busy, operating, in use, frequented, widely known, sure, safe, well-trodden, accepted.—*Ant.* abandoned, little-used, unexplored.

traveler, n. voyager, adventurer, tourist, explorer, nomad, wanderer, truant, roamer, rambler, wayfarer, migrant, excursionist, sight-seer, straggler, vagabond, vagrant, hobo, tramp, gypsy, wandering Jew, gadabout, itinerant, pilgrim, rover, passenger, commuter, globe-trotter.

traveling, *a.* passing, en route, on board, shipped, freighted, transported, moving, carried, conveyed, consigned, wandering, touring, roving, on tour, vagrant, migrant, nomadic, wayfaring, itinerant, cruising, excursioning, commuting, driving, flying, sailing, riding, on vacation, migrating, voyaging; see also **moving 2.**

tray, *n.* platter, plate, tea wagon; see **dish 1.**

treacherous, *a.* deceptive, undependable, dangerous, risky, misleading, tricky, ensnaring, faulty, precarious, unstable, insecure, shaky, slippery, ticklish, difficult, ominous, alarming, menacing. — *Ant.* reliable, dependable, steady.

treachery, *n.* faithlessness, disloyalty, betrayal; see **dishonesty, treason.**

tread, *v.* walk, step, step on; see **trample.**

treason, *n.* sedition, disloyalty, perfidy, treachery, seditionary *or* seditious act, aid and comfort to the enemy, factious revolt; see also **dishonesty, deception 1, revolution 2.**

treasure, *n.* richness, riches, nest egg; see **wealth.**

treasure, *v.* prize, value, appreciate, guard; see also **love 1.**

treasurer, *n.* receiver, cashier, banker; see **clerk.**

treasury, *n.* exchequer, safe, depository; see **bank 2.**

treat, *n.* entertainment, surprise, amusement, feast, source of gratification, gift, *drinks for the crowd, setup, spree.

treat, *v.* 1. [To deal with a person or thing] negotiate, manage, have to do with, have business with, behave toward, handle, make terms with, act toward, react toward, use, employ, have recourse to.—*Ant.* neglect, ignore, have nothing to do with. 2. [To assist toward a cure] attend, administer, prescribe, dose, operate, nurse, dress, minister to, apply therapy, care for, *doctor; see also **heal.** 3. [To pay for another's entertainment] entertain, indulge, satisfy, amuse, divert, play host to, escort, set up, *stake to.

treatment, *n.* 1. [Usage] handling, processing, dealing, approach, execution, procedure, method, manner, proceeding, way, strategy, custom, habit, employment, practice, mode, line, angle. 2. [Assistance toward a cure] diet, operation, medical care, surgery, therapy, remedy, prescription, regimen, hospitalization, *doctoring; see also **medicine 2.**

treaty, *n.* agreement, pact, settlement,

covenant, compact, convention, alliance, charter, sanction, bond, understanding, arrangement, bargain, negotiation, *deal.

tree, *n.* Trees include the following—ash, elm, oak, maple, evergreen, birch, tulip, fir, cypress, juniper, larch *or* tamarack, pine, cedar, beech, chestnut, eucalyptus, hickory, walnut, sycamore, palm, willow, locust, sequoia, redwood, poplar, acacia, cottonwood, box elder, apple, cherry, peach, plum, pear, prune, banyan, bamboo, mahogany, ebony, bo, ironwood, bottle; see also **wood 1. —up a tree**, cornered, in difficulty, trapped; see in **trouble 1.**

trees, *n.* wood, woods, windbreak; see **forest.**

trek, *v.* hike, migrate, journey; see **travel 2.**

tremble, *v.* quiver, shiver, vibrate; see **shake 1.**

tremendous, *a.* huge, great, colossal; see **large 1.**

tremor, *n.* trembling, shaking, shivering; see **earthquake.**

trench, *n.* rut, hollow, gully, depression, gutter, tube, furrow, drainage canal, creek, moat, dike, drain, channel, main, gorge, gulch, arroyo. Military trenches include the following—dugout, earthwork, intrenchment, fortification, breastwork, pillbox, excavation, bunker, machine-gun nest, foxhole.

trend, *n.* bias, bent, leaning; see **inclination 1.**

trespass, *v.* encroach, invade, infringe; see **meddle 1.**

trespasser, *n.* encroacher, invader, infringer; see **intruder.**

trial, *a.* tentative, test, preliminary; see **experimental.**

trial, *n.* 1. [An effort to learn the truth] analysis, test, examination; see **experiment.** 2. [A case at law] suit, lawsuit, fair hearing, hearing, action, case, contest, indictment, legal proceedings, claim, cross-examination, litigation, counterclaim, arraignment, prosecution, citation, court action, judicial contest, seizure, bill of divorce, habeas corpus, court-martial, impeachment. 3. [An ordeal] suffering, misfortune, heavy blow; see **difficulty 1, 2. —on trial**, being tried *or* considered *or* tested *or* examined, under consideration, not yet accepted; see **on trial 1.**

triangle, *n.* Triangles include the following—equilateral, isosceles, right-angled, obtuse-angled, scalene, acute-angled.

triangular, *a.* three-cornered, three-sided, trigonal; see also **angular.**

tribal, *a.* tribular, racial, kindred; see **racial.**

tribe, *n.* primitive group, ethnic group, association; see **race 2**.

tributary, *n.* stream, branch, sidestream; see **river**.

tribute, *n.* 1. [Recognition] applause, memorial service, eulogy; see **recognition 2**.

trick, *n.* 1. [A deceit] wile, fraud, deception, ruse, cheat, cover, feint, hoax, artifice, decoy, trap, stratagem, intrigue, fabrication, double-dealing, forgery, fake, illusion, invention, subterfuge, distortion, delusion, ambush, snare, blind, evasion, plot, equivocation, concealment, treachery, swindle, feigning, impersonation, duplicity, pretense, falsehood, falsification, perjury, disguise, conspiracy, circumvention, quibble, trickery, beguiling, chicanery, humbug, maneuver, sham, counterfeit, *gyp, *touch, *phoney, *come-on, *fast one, *dodge, *plant, *clip, *sucker deal, *con game, bluff, *shakedown, *sell-out, *con, *funny business, *dirty work, crooked deal, *front, *gimmick; see also **lie 1.**—*Ant.* honesty, truth, veracity. 2. [A prank] jest, sport, practical joke; see **joke**. 3. [A practical method or expedient] skill, facility, *know-how; see **ability, method**.

trick, *v.* dupe, outwit, fool; see **deceive**.

trickle, *v.* drip, leak, run; see **flow**.

tricky, *a.* 1. [Shrewd] clever, sharp, keen-witted; see **intelligent 1**. 2. [Delicate or difficult] complicated, intricate, critical, touchy, involved, perplexing, knotty, thorny, complex, unstable, ticklish, catchy, likely to go wrong, *hanging by a thread; see also **difficult 1, 2.**—*Ant.* easy, clearcut, simple.

tricycle, *n.* *trike, *wheel, three-wheeler; see **vehicle**.

tried, *a.* dependable, proved, used; see **used 1**.

trifle, *n.* particle, piece, speck; see **bit 1**.

trifling, *a.* petty, small, insignificant; see **trivial, unimportant**.

trim, *a.* 1. [Neat] orderly, tidy, spruce; see **clean 1, neat 1**. 2. [Well-proportioned] shapely, well-designed, streamlined, clean, slim, shipshape, delicate, fit, comely, well-formed, symmetrical, well-made, clean-cut, well-balanced, graceful, well-molded, harmonious, beautiful, classical, compact, smart; see also **handsome.**—*Ant.* **disordered**, shapeless, straggly.

trim, *v.* 1. [To cut off excess] prune, shave, lop; see **cut 1**. 2. [To adorn] ornament, embellish, deck; see **decorate**. 3. [To prepare for sailing] ballast, rig, outfit; see **sail 1**.

trimming, *n.* 1. [Ornamentation] accessory, frill, tassel; see **decoration 2**. [The act of cutting off excess] shearing,

lopping off, shaving off; see **reduction 1**.

trinity, *n.* trio, trilogy, triplet, triplicate, threesome, triad, set of three, three-personed God, the Godhead; Father, Son, and Holy Ghost; the Triune God, Trinity, the Trinity in Unity, Threefold Unity, Three in One and One in Three; see also **god 1**.

trinket, *n.* gadget, novelty, bauble; see **jewel, jewelry**.

trio, *n.* 1. [A combination of three] threesome, triangle, triplet; see **trinity**. 2. [Three musicians performing together] string trio, vocal trio, swing trio; see **band 3**.

trip, *n.* 1. [A journey] voyage, excursion, tour; see **journey**. 2. [A psychedelic experience] hallucinations; LSD *or* heroin *or* mescaline, etc.; trip, being turned on; see **drug**.

trip, *v.* 1. [To stumble] tumble, slip, lurch, slide, founder, fall, pitch, fall over, slip upon, plunge, sprawl, topple, go head over heels.—*Ant.* arise, ascend, get up. 2. [To cause to stumble] block, hinder, bind, tackle, overthrow, push, send headlong, kick, shove, mislead.—*Ant.* help, pick up, give a helping hand.

triple, *a.* in triplicate, by three, threefold; see **three**.

trite, *a.* hackneyed, prosaic, stereotyped; see **common 1, dull 4**.

triumph, *n.* conquest, achievement, success; see **victory**.

triumphant, *a.* victorious, successful, lucky, winning, conquering, in the lead, triumphal, jubilant, dominant, laurel-crowned, champion, unbeaten, topseeded, out front, triumphing, victorial, elated, in ascendancy, with flying colors.—*Ant.* **beaten**, defeated, overwhelmed.

trivial, *a.* petty, trifling, small, superficial, piddling, wee, little, insignificant, frivolous, irrelevant, unimportant, nugatory, skin-deep, meaningless, mean, diminutive, slight, of no account, scanty, meager, inappreciable, microscopic, atomic, dribbling, nonessential, flimsy, inconsiderable, vanishing, momentary, immaterial, indifferent, beside the point, minute, unessential, paltry, inferior, minor, small-minded, beggarly, useless, inconsequential, worthless, mangy, trashy, pitiful, of little moment, *dinky, *small-town, *cutting no ice, cut and dried; see also **shallow 2.**—*Ant.* **important**, great, serious.

troops, *n.* soldiers, armed forces, fighting men; see **army 1**.

trophy, *n.* citation, medal, cup; see **prize**.

tropic, *a.* 1. [Related to the tropics] tropical, equatorial, jungle; see **hot 1**. 2.

[Hot] thermal, torrid, burning; see **hot 1**.

tropics, *n.* torrid zone, equator, Equatorial Africa; South America, Amazon, the Congo, the Pacific Islands, hot countries, jungle(s); see **jungle**.

trot, *v.* single-foot, jog, amble; see **run 2**.

trouble, *n.* 1. [A person or thing causing trouble] annoyance, difficult situation, bother, bind, hindrance, difficulty, task, puzzle, predicament, plight, problem, fear, worry, concern, inconvenience, nuisance, disturbance, calamity, catastrophe, crisis, delay, quarrel, dispute, bad news, affliction, intrusion, irritation, trial, pain, ordeal, discomfort, injury, adversity, hang-up, case, bore, gossip, problem child, meddler, pest, tease, tiresome person, talkative person, inconsiderate person, intruder, troublemaker, fly in the ointment, *headache, brat, *holy terror, *peck of trouble.—*Ant.* aid, **help**, comfort. 3. [Illness] malady, ailment, affliction; see **illness 1, 2**. 4. [Civil disorder] riot, turmoil, strife; see **disturbance 2**. 5. [A quarrel] argument, feud, bickering; see **dispute, fight 1**. —**in trouble**, unfortunate, having trouble, in difficulty; see **in trouble**.

trouble, *v.* 1. [To disturb] disconcert, annoy, irritate; see **bother 2, disturb**. 2. [To take care] be concerned with, make an effort, take pains; see **bother 1**.

troubled, *a.* disturbed, agitated, grieved, apprehensive, pained, anxious, perplexed, afflicted, confused, puzzled, overwrought, *aggravated, uptight, bothered, harassed, vexed, plagued, teased, annoyed, concerned, uneasy, discomposed, harried, careworn, mortified, badgered, baited, inconvenienced, put out, upset, flurried, flustered, bored, tortured, goaded, irritated, displeased, tried, roused, disconcerted, pursued, chafed, galled, rubbed the wrong way, ragged, tired, molested, crossed, thwarted, fazed, distressed, wounded, sickened, griped, restless, irked, pestered, heckled, persecuted, frightened, alarmed, terrified, scared, anguished, harrowed, tormented, provoked, stung, ruffled, fretting, perturbed, afraid, shaky, fearful, unsettled, suspicious, in turmoil, full of misgivings, shaken, careworn, dreading, *bugged, in a quandary, between the devil and the deep blue sea, in a stew, *on pins and needles, *all hot and bothered, worried stiff, *in a tizzy, *burned up, *miffed, *peeved, *riled, *behind the eight ball, *floored, *up a tree, *hung-up, *up the creek without a paddle. —*Ant.* **calm**, at ease, settled.

troublemaker, *n.* rogue, knave, recreant; see **criminal**.

troublesome, *a.* bothersome, annoying, difficult, irritating, oppressive, repressive, distressing, upsetting, painful, dangerous, damaging.

trough, *n.* dip, channel, hollow; see **hole 2**.

trousers, *n.* slacks, breeches, knickerbockers; see **clothes**.

trout, *n.* Trout include the following—speckled, brook, rainbow, cutthroat, lake, salmon, steelhead, blue-backed, brown; see **fish**.

trowel, *n.* blade, scoop, implement; see **tool 1**.

truant, *a.* missing, straying, playing hooky; see **absent**.

truce, *n.* armistice, peace agreement, lull; see **peace 1**.

truck, *n.* carriage, van, lorry, car; see also **vehicle**. Types of trucks include the following—delivery wagon, moving van, police van, patrol wagon, laundry truck, pickup truck, freight truck, logging truck, army truck, trailer, piggyback trailer, truck trailer, truck and trailer, truck train, cement *or* transit mixer, refrigerator truck, four-wheel drive (truck), freighter, garbage truck, dump truck, diesel-powered truck, chain-drive truck, half-track.

trudge, *v.* plod, step, tread; see **walk 1**.

true, *a.* 1. [Accurate] precise, verified, proved, certain, certified, definite, checked, exact, correct; see also **valid 1**. 2. [Loyal] sure, reliable, trustworthy, faithful, dependable, sincere; see also **faithful, reliable**. 3. [Genuine] authentic, virtual, substantial, tangible, genuine, actual, pure; see also **real 2, valid 2**. —**come true**, become a fact, be actualized, come about; see **develop 1, happen 2**.

truly, *a.* honestly, exactly, definitely, reliably, factually, correctly, unequivocally, sincerely, scrupulously, fairly, justly, validly, rightfully, righteously, faithfully, worthily, scientifically, unbiasedly, without bias *or* prejudice, *fairly and squarely. —*Ant.* **wrongly**, dishonestly, deceptively.

trumped up, *a.* falsified, concocted, magnified; see **exaggerated, false 2**.

trumpet, *n.* horn, bugle, cornet; see **musical instrument**.

trump up, *v.* think up, devise, concoct, present fraudulent evidence, misrepresent, falsify; see also **deceive, lie 1**.

trunk, *n.* 1. [A container for goods] chest, case, foot locker; see **container**. 2. [The torso] body, soma, thorax; see **back 1, stomach**. 3. [The stem of a tree] column, stock, log; see **stalk**. 4.

[The proboscis] prow, snoot, snout; see nose 1.

trust, n. 1. [Reliance] confidence, dependence, credence; see faith 1. 2. [Responsibility] guardianship, account, liability; see duty 1. 3. [A large company] corporation, monopoly, institution; see business 4. —in trust, in another's care, held for, reserved; see saved 2.

trust, v. 1. [To believe in] swear by, believe in, place confidence in, confide in, esteem, depend upon, expect help from, presume upon, lean on, have no doubt, rest assured, be sure about, have no reservations, rely on, put faith in, look to, count on, assume that, presume that, be persuaded by, be convinced, put great stock in, set great store by, *bank on, take at one's word; see also believe 1.—Ant. doubt, mistrust, disbelieve. 2. [To hope] presume, take, imagine; see assume, hope. 3. [To place in the protection of another] lend, put in safekeeping, entrust; see sense 1. 4. [To give credit to] advance, lend, loan, let out, grant, confer, let, patronize, aid, give financial aid to.—Ant. borrow, raise money, pawn.

trusted, a. trustworthy, dependable, reliable, trusty, tried, proved, intimate, close, faithful, loyal, true, constant, stanch, devoted, incorruptible, safe, honorable, honored, inviolable, *on the level, *regular, right, *sure-fire.—Ant. dishonest, questionable, unreliable.

trustee, n. guardian, custodian, controller, lawyer, custodian, guarantor, regent, board member, appointee, administrator, member of the directorate.

trusting, a. trustful, credulous, confiding, gullible, unsuspecting, easygoing, open, candid, indulgent, obliging, well-meaning, good-natured, tenderhearted, green, *with a glass jaw; see also naive.—Ant. critical, suspicious, skeptical.

trustworthiness, n. integrity, uprightness, loyalty; see honesty.

trustworthy, a. accurate, honest, true; see reliable.

trusty, n. trusted person, trustworthy convict, prison attendant, privileged prisoner; see also prisoner.

truth, n. 1. [Conformity to reality] truthfulness, correctness, sincerity, verity, candor, openness, honesty, fidelity, frankness, revelation, authenticity, exactness, infallibility, precision, perfection, certainty, genuineness, accuracy, fact, *the gospel truth, *straight dope, *inside track, *the nitty-gritty, the facts, the case.—Ant. lie, deception, falsehood. 2. [Integrity] trustworthiness, honor, probity; see honesty 1. —in truth, in fact, indeed, really; see truly.

truthful, a. correct, frank, just; see honest 1.

truthfully, a. honestly, honorably, veraciously; see sincerely, truly.

truthfulness, n. integrity, frankness, accuracy; see honesty.

try, v. 1. [To endeavor] attempt, undertake, exert (oneself), contend, strive, make an effort, risk, have a try (at), contest, wrangle, labor, work, aspire, propose, try to reach, do what one can, tackle, venture, struggle for, compete for, speculate, make every effort, put oneself out, vie for, aspire to, attack, make a bid for, *beat one's brains, bear down, *shoot at or for, drive for, *chip away at, do one's best, make a pass at, go after, go out of the way, *give a workout, do all in one's power, buckle down, lift a finger, *break an arm, lay (oneself) out, lay to, do oneself justice, *have a go at, *make a go of it, go all out, leave no stone unturned, move heaven and earth, go all lengths, *go to market, *knock oneself out, *break one's neck, *bust a gut, *take a crack at, *give it a whirl. 2. [To test] assay, investigate, put to the proof; see analyze, examine. 3. [To conduct a trial] hear (a case), examine, decide; see judge.

trying, a. troublesome, bothersome, irritating; see difficult 1, 2.

try on, v. fit, have a fitting, try on for size; see wear 1.

tryout, n. test, demonstration, rehearsal; see examination 1.

try out for, v. go out for, read or audition (for), compete; see rehearse 3.

tub, n. keg, bucket, tank; see container.

tube, n. 1. [A pipe] conduit, hose, test tube, tubing, tunnel, loom, subway; see also pipe 1. 2. [A metal container] package, paste tube, squeeze tube; see container. 3. [An electronic device] cell, electric eye, vacuum or radio or television or photoelectric or X-ray or electron or electronic, etc. tube; see device 1, machine.

tuck, n. crease, folding, pleat; see fold 1, 2.

tuck in, v. insert, put or squeeze in, add; see include 2.

tuft, n. clump, cluster, group; see bunch.

tug, v. pull, haul, tow; see draw 1.

tuition, n. fee, cost, expenditure; see price.

tumble, v. drop, plunge, descend; see fall 1, trip 1.

tumor, n. neoplasm, tumefaction, cyst; see swelling.

tumult, n. agitation, uproar, turbulence; see confusion, disturbance 2, fight 1.

tune, n. melody, air, strain; see song. — change one's tune, change one's mind, alter one's actions, be transformed; see **alter 1.** —sing a different **tune,** change one's mind, alter one's actions, be transformed; see **alter 1.**

tune, v. adjust the pitch, attune, put in tune, tune up, tighten the strings, use the tuning fork, set the tune; see also **harmonize 1.**

*tune in (on), v. participate, become part of, enter into; see **join 1, 2, listen.**

*tune up, v. enliven, refine, make better; see **repair.**

tunnel, n. hole, burrow, underground passage, subway, tube, crawl space, crawlway, shaft, mine, pit.

turbulence, n. disorder, commotion, fracas; see **confusion, disturbance 2, fight 1.**

turbulent, a. riotous, violent, stormy, disturbed, noisy, restless, raging, howling, buffeting, thunderous, tumultuous, excited, passionate, uncontrolled, vehement, roaring, tempestuous, rampant, rowdy, lawless, disorderly, untamed, disordered, chaotic, agitated, fierce, wild, rude, rough, blustering, angry, storming, uproarious, clamorous, mutinous, rebellious, destructive, hard, stern, bitter, fiery, rabid, boisterous, perturbed, foaming, shaking, demonstrative.—*Ant.* **peaceful,** tranquil, at ease.

turf, n. earth, peat, lawn; see **grass 1.**

turkey, n. turkey cock or hen, bird, fowl, Thanksgiving bird, Christmas bird, gobbler, turkey gobbler, wild turkey, domestic turkey.

turmoil, n. agitation, turbulence, riot; see **confusion, disturbance 2.**

turn, n. 1. [A revolution] rotation, cycle, circle, round, circulation, pirouette, gyre, gyration, spin, round-about-face, roll, turning, circumrotation, spiral; see also **revolution 1, 2.** 2. [A bend] curve, winding, twist, wind, hook, shift, angle, corner, fork, branch. 3. [A turning point] climax, crisis, juncture, emergency, critical period, crossing, change, new development, shift, twist. 4. [A shock] fright, jolt, blow; see **surprise 2.** 5. [An action] deed, accomplishment, service; see **help 1.** 6. [A change in course] curve, detour, deviation, corner, ground loop, stem turn, jump turn, Telemark (turn), kick turn, inside loop, outside loop, left or right wing spin, tight spin, tight spiral. —at every **turn,** in every instance, constantly, consistently; see **regularly.** —by **turns,** taking turns, in succession, alternately; see **consecutive.** —call the **turn,** anticipate, predict, foretell; see **expect 1.** —take **turns,** do by turns, do in succession, share; see **alternate 1.** —to a **turn,** correctly, properly, to the right degree; see **perfectly 1.**

turn, v. 1. [To pivot] revolve, rotate, roll, spin, wheel, whirl, gyre, circulate, go around, swivel, round, twist, twirl, gyrate, ground, loop; see also **swing.** 2. [To reverse] go back, recoil, change, upset, retrace, face around, turn around, capsize, shift, alter, vary, convert, transform, invert, subvert, return, alternate. 3. [To divert] deflect, veer, turn aside or away, sidetrack, swerve, put or call or turn off, deviate, dodge, twist, avoid, shift, switch, avert, zigzag, shy away, redirect, draw aside. 4. [To become] grow into, change into, pass into; see **become.** 5. [To sour] curdle, acidify, become rancid; see **sour.** 6. [To change direction] swerve, swing, bend, veer, tack, round to, incline, deviate, detour, loop, curve. 7. [To incline] prefer, be predisposed to, favor; see **lean 1, tend 2.** 8. [To sprain] strain, bruise, dislocate; see **hurt 1.** 9. [To nauseate] sicken, make one sick, revolt; see **disgust.** 10. [To bend] curve, twist, fold; see **bend.** 11. [To transform] transmute, remake, transpose; see **alter 1.** 12. [To make use of] apply, adapt, utilize; see **use 1.** 13. [To point] direct, set, train; see **aim.** 14. [To repel] repulse, push back, throw back; see **repel 1.**

turn about, v. turn around, pivot, reverse; see **turn 1.**

turn against, v. revolt, disobey, defy; see **oppose 1, 2, rebel.**

turn aside, v. avert, deflect, divert; see **turn 3.**

turn back, v. retrogress, retrograde, revert; see **return 1, 2.**

turn down, v. 1. [To decrease in volume, etc.] hush, lower, curb; see **decrease 2.** 2. [To refuse] reject, decline, rebuff; see **refuse.**

turned, a. 1. [Revolved] spun, rounded, circled, circulated, rotated, rolled, whirled, gyrated, set going. 2. [Deflected] switched, twisted, dodged, avoided, shied away from, shifted, shunted, changed.

turn in, v. 1. [To deliver] hand over, transfer, give up; see **give 1.** 2. [*To go to bed] lie down, retire, *hit the hay; see **rest 1.**

turning, a. twisting, shifting, whirling, rotating, revolving, bending, curving, shunting; see also **growing, changing.**—*Ant.* **permanent,** static, fixed.

turning, n. whirling, revolving, rotating; see **revolution 1.**

turning point, n. peak, juncture, culmination; see **climax, crisis.**

turn into, v. 1. [To change] transform, alter, transmute; see **alter 1.** 2. [To become changed] be converted, transform, modify; see **change 2.**

turn loose, v. liberate, emancipate, set free; see **free**.

turn off, v. stop, shut off, close, shut, extinguish, shut down, kill the light *or* engine *or* motor, turn off the juice, cut the light *or* engine *or* motor, hit the switch.

turn on, v. 1. [To start the operation of] set going, switch on, set in motion, put in gear; see also **begin** 1. 2. [To attack] strike, assail, assault; see **attack**. 3. [*To take drugs] take LSD, smoke marijuana, *get high, *take a trip, *smoke pot, *get stoned, *blow pot, *trip out, *get wasted. 4. [*To arouse] titillate, stimulate, stir up; see **excite** 1. 5. [*To depend on *or* upon] hinge on, be dependent on, be based on; see **depend** 2.

turnout, n. 1. [Production] output, aggregate, volume; see **production** 1. 2. [A gathering] assembly, attendance, group; see **gathering**.

turn out, v. 1. [To stop the operation of] extinguish, shut off, stop; see **turn off** 1. 2. [To dismiss] discharge, evict, send away; see **dismiss**, **oust**. 3. [To produce] make, put out, build; see **manufacture**, **produce** 2. 4. [To get out of bed] get up, rise, wake up; see **arise** 1, **wake** 2. 5. [To finish] end, complete, perfect; see **achieve** 1.

turn over, v. 1. [To invert] overturn, reverse, subvert; see **upset** 1. 2. [To transfer] hand over, give over, deliver; see **assign**, **give** 1.

turn over a new leaf, v. get better, change for the better, make (New Year's) resolutions; see **improve** 2, **reform** 1.

turn sour, v. putrefy, rot, spoil; see **spoil**.

turn the tables, v. reverse conditions, reverse circumstances, give one his own medicine; see **alter** 1, **upset** 1.

turn to, v. 1. [To rely upon] confide, appeal to, depend upon; see **trust** 1. 2. [To start] start to work, become interested in, take up; see **begin** 1.

turn up, v. 1. [To find] disclose, learn, come across; see **discover**, **find**. 2. [To arrive] enter, come, roll in; see **arrive**. 3. [To increase the volume, etc.] amplify, augment, boost; see **increase**, **strengthen**.

tusk, n. canine (tooth), fang, incisor; see **tooth** 1.

tutor, n. instructor, tutorial assistant, private tutor; see **teacher**.

tutoring, n. coaching, training, instruction; see **education** 1.

T.V., n. video, *(boob) tube, *idiot box; see **television**.

tweak, v. twitch, squeeze, jerk; see **pinch**.

tweezers, n. forceps, nippers, tongs; see **tool** 1.

twelve, a. dozen, twelvefold, twelfth, duodecimo, duodecimal, uncial.

twenty, a. twentieth, vicenary, twentyfold, vicennial.

twice, a. double, doubly, once and again, over again, once over.

twig, n. offshoot, limb, sprig; see **branch** 2.

twilight, n. dusk, nightfall, late afternoon, early evening, sunset, dawn, break of day; see also **night** 1.

twin, a. identical twin, identical two, fellow, twofold, second, accompanying, joint, coupled, matched, copied, duplicating; see also **second**, **two**.—*Ant.* single, lone, solitary.

twine, n. braid, cord, string; see **rope**.

twinge, v. twitch, shiver, smart; see **tingle**.

twinkle, v. shimmer, flicker, sparkle; see **shine** 1.

twinkling, a. sparkling, glimmering, flashing; see **bright** 1.

twirl, v. spin, rotate, twist; see **turn** 1.

twist, v. wring, wrap, twine, twirl, turn around, wrap around; see also **turn** 1.

twisted, a. 1. [Crooked] contorted, wrenched, bent, knotted, braided, twined, wound, wreathed, writhing, convolute, twisting.—*Ant.* straight, even, regular. 2. [Confused] erroneous, perplexing, wrongheaded, awry, puzzling, unintelligible, disorganized, perverted; see also **wrong** 2.—*Ant.* clear, simple, logical.

twitch, v. 1. [To pluck] pull, tug, snatch; see **pull** 2. 2. [To jerk] shiver, shudder, have a fit, kick, work, palpitate, beat, twinge, pain.

two, a. twin, dual, binary, both, double, bifid.

two, n. two of a kind, brace, couple; see **pair**. —**in two**, halved, divided, split; see **separated**. —**put two and two together**, reason, sum up, reach a conclusion; see **decide**.

two-faced, a. deceitful, caviling, treacherous; see **false** 1.

tycoon, n. administrator, boss, director; see **businessman**, **executive**.

type, n. 1. [Kind] sort, nature, character; see **kind** 2, **variety** 2. 2. [Representative] model, sample, example, copy order; see **model** 1, 2. 3. [Letter] symbol, emblem, figure, character, sign; see also **letter** 1. Styles of types include the following—Gothic *or* black letter, old style, new style, modern, roman, italic, script, sans serif, text. Sizes of types include the following—Excelsior *or* 3-point, Brilliant *or* 3-1/2-point, Diamond *or* 4-1/2-

point, Pearl *or* 5-point, Agate *or* 5-1/2-point, Non-pareil *or* 6-point, Minion *or* 7-point, Brevier *or* 8-point, Bourgeois *or* 9-point, Long Primer *or* 10-point, Small Pica *or* 11-point, Pica *or* 12-point, English *or* 14-point, Columbian *or* 16-point, Great Primer *or* 18-point. Fonts of types include the following—standard, lightface, boldface, extrabold, cursive, open, extended, condensed, shaded, upright, expanded, wide.

type, *v.* **1.** [To use a typewriter] typewrite, copy, transcribe, teletype, touchtype, hunt and peck. **2.** [To classify] categorize, normalize, standardize; see **classify.**

typed, *a.* **1.** [Set down on a typewriter] typewritten, copied, set up, written, transcribed; see also **printed. 2.** [Classified] labeled, characterized, analyzed, symbolized, classed, prefigured, sampled, exemplified, made out to be, patterned, standardized, stylized, cast, formalized.

typewriter, *n.* typing machine, office typewriter, portable, noiseless, electric typewriter, ticker, teletypewriter.

typewritten, *a.* written on a typewriter, transcribed, copied; see **printed.**

typical, *a.* characteristic, habitual, usual, representative, symbolic, normal, illustrative, conventional, archetypical, ideal, expected, suggestive, standardized, patterned, ordinary, average, common, everyday, regular.—*Ant.* **superior,** exceptional, extraordinary.

typify, *v.* exemplify, symbolize, embody; see **mean 1.**

typing, *n.* typescript, typewriting, typed copy; see **writing 1.**

typist, *n.* secretary, typewriter operator, teletyper, office girl, *key pounder, *typer, typewriter.

tyrannical, *a.* dictatorial, fascistic, totalitarian; see **absolute 2.**

tyranny, *n.* oppression, cruelty, severity, reign of terror, despotism, absolutism.

tyrant, *n.* despot, absolute ruler, inquisitor; see **dictator.**

U

ugliness, *n.* unsightliness, homeliness, hideousness, repulsiveness, loathsomeness, unseemliness, offensiveness, deformity, bad looks, ill looks, ill-favored countenance, plainness, disfigurement, grim aspect, foulness, horridness, inelegance, frightfulness, fearfulness. —*Ant.* beauty, fairness, attractiveness.

ugly, *a.* 1. [Ill-favored] unsightly, loathsome, hideous, homely, repulsive, unseemly, uncomely, deformed, bad-looking, plain, disfigured, monstrous, foul, horrid, frightful, revolting, repellent, unlovely, appalling, haglike, misshapen, misbegotten, grisly, *having a face that would stop a clock, *looking a mess or fright, *looking like the devil, *not fit to be seen.—*Ant.* handsome, beautiful, graceful. 2. [Dangerous] pugnacious, quarrelsome, bellicose, rough, cantankerous, violent, vicious, evil, sinister, treacherous, wicked, formidable. —*Ant.* mild, reasonable, complaisant.

ulcer, *n.* boil, abscess, running sore; see sore.

ultimate, *a.* final, terminal, latest; see last 1.

ultimately, *a.* eventually, at last, in the end, sooner or later, as a conclusion, to cap the climax, sequentially, after all, at the close, in conclusion, conclusively, in due time, after a while, in after days, presently, by and by; see also finally.— *Ant.* early, in the beginning, at present.

ultimatum, *n.* demands, requirements, terms.

ultraviolet, *a.* beyond violet, having wavelengths of more than 4,000 angstroms, beyond or out of the range of sight; see invisible.

umbrella, *n.* parasol, sunshade, *bumbershoot; see hat.

umpire, *n.* referee, moderator, mediator; see judge 1.

unable, *a.* incapable, powerless, weak, incompetent, unskilled, impotent, not able, inept, incapacitated, inefficacious, helpless, unfitted, inefficient, unqualified, inadequate, ineffectual, inoperative. —*Ant.* able, capable, effective.

unaccompanied, *a.* sole, solitary, deserted; see alone 1.

unaccustomed, *a.* 1. [Unfamiliar] strange, unknown, unusual; see unfamiliar 1. 2. [Unpracticed] unskilled, incompetent, untrained; see naive.

unacquainted, *a.* ignorant, unfamiliar, unknown; see unfamiliar 1.

unaffected, *a.* 1. [Genuine] spontaneous, natural, simple; see natural 3. 2. [Uninfluenced] unmoved, unaltered, unchanged; see calm 1.

un-American, *a.* undemocratic, fascistic, subversive; see foreign.

unanimous, *a.* united, single, collective, combined, unified, concerted, concurrent, public, popular, undivided, of one accord, agreed, common, communal, shared, universal, accepted, unquestioned, undisputed, uncontested, consonant, consistent, of a piece, with one voice, homogeneous, accordant, assenting.—*Ant.* different, dissenting, irreconcilable.

unanimously, *a.* with one voice or one accord, harmoniously, all together, universally, unitedly, singly, collectively, without a dissenting voice, by common consent, by oral or written ballot or vote, in unison, co-operatively, concurrently, popularly, commonly, undisputedly, consonantly, consistently, in agreement.

unanswered, *a.* without reply, unrefuted, not responded to, unnoticed, unchallenged, unquestioned, demanding an answer, filed, ignored, unsettled, undecided, in doubt, disputed, moot, debatable, tabled, up in the air, vexed, open, pending, under consideration, undetermined.—*Ant.* determined, answered, responded to.

unapproachable, *a.* withdrawn, hesitant, aloof; see distant.

unarmed, *a.* weaponless, defenseless, peaceable; see weak 5.

unasked, *a.* uninvited, not asked or invited, unwelcome(d); see unpopular.

unattached, *a.* independent, unbound, ungoverned; see free 1, 2, 3.

unavoidable, *a.* inescapable, impending, sure; see certain 2.

unaware, *a.* uninformed, oblivious, ignorant, not cognizant, unmindful, heedless, negligent, careless, insensible, forgetful, unconcerned, blind, deaf, inattentive, without notice, deaf or dead to, caught napping, in a daze, *not seeing the forest for the trees.—*Ant.* conscious, aware, cognizant.

unbalance, *v.* 1. [To upset] capsize, overturn, tumble; see upset 1. 2. [To derange] dement, craze, obsess; see disturb.

unbalanced, *a.* 1. [Deranged] unsound,

crazy, psychotic; see **insane, troubled.**
2. [Unsteady] wobbly, shaky, treacherous; see **unstable 1.**

unbearable, a. inadmissible, unacceptable, *too much; see **terrible 2.**

unbeaten, a. victorious, thriving, winning; see **successful.**

unbecoming, a. unsuited, unfitted, awkward; see **improper.**

unbelievable, a. beyond or past belief, staggering, unimaginable, not to be credited, dubious, doubtful, improbable, questionable, implausible, open to doubt, *a bit thick; see also **unlikely.** —Ant. likely, believable, probable.

unbelievably, a. remarkably, horribly, badly; see **strangely.**

unbend, v. become more natural or casual or nonchalant, be informal or at home, relax; see **rest 1.**

unbind, v. unfasten, disengage, unchain; see **free.**

unborn, a. embryonic, incipient, expected, future, prospective, potential, latent, enwombed, anticipated, awaited.

unbound, a. loose, untied, unfastened; see also **free** 1, 2, 3. —Ant. bound, stapled, tied.

unbreakable, a. indestructible, durable, everlasting, brass-bound, cast-iron, lasting, unshakeable, solid, firm, unchangeable, invulnerable, incorruptible, resistant, rugged, tight, unyielding. —Ant. dainty, fragile, brittle.

unbroken, a. 1. [Whole] entire, intact, unimpaired; see **whole 2.** 2. [Continuous] uninterrupted, continuous, even; see **regular 3, smooth 1, 2.**

unburden, v. 1. [To unload] dump, dispose of, relinquish; see **lighten, relieve.** 2. [To reveal] disclose, unbosom, divulge; see **admit 2.**

unbutton, v. undo, open (up), unfasten; see **open 2.**

uncalled for, a. unjustified, redundant, not needed; see **unnecessary.**

uncanny, a. weird, unnatural, supernatural, preternatural, superhuman, ghostly, mystifying, incredible, mysterious, magical, devilish; see also **magic 1.**

uncertain, a. undecided, undetermined, unsettled, doubtful, changeable, unpredictable, improbable, unlikely, unfixed, unsure, indeterminate, haphazard, random, chance, casual, provisional, contingent, alterable, subject to change, possible, vague, conjectural, questionable, problematic, suppositional, hypothetical, theoretical, open to question, equivocal, perplexing, debatable, dubious, indefinite, unascertained, ambiguous, unresolved, debated, conjecturable, unknown, unannounced, up in the air, in doubt.

uncertainty, n. 1. [The mental state of being uncertain] perplexity, doubt, puzzlement, quandary, mystification, guesswork, conjecture, indecision, dilemma.— Ant. opinion, belief, decision. 2. [The state of being undetermined or unknown] incertitude, questionableness, contingency, obscurity, vagueness, ambiguity, difficulty, incoherence, intricacy, involvement, darkness, inconclusiveness, indeterminateness, improbability, unlikelihood, low probability, conjecturability; see also **doubt 2.**—Ant. determination, sureness, necessity. 3. [That which is not determined or not known] chance, mutability, change, unpredictability, possibility, emergence, contingency, blind spot, puzzle, enigma, question, blank, vacancy, maze, theory, risk, blind bargain, leap in the dark.—Ant. fact, **truth,** matter of record.

unchangeable, a. fixed, unalterable, inevitable; see **firm 1.**

unchanged, a. unaltered, the same, unmoved, constant, fixed, continuing, stable, permanent, durable, unvarying, invariable, consistent, persistent, firm, unvaried, resolute, perpetual, continuous, maintained, uninterrupted, fast.—Ant. **changed,** altered, modified.

uncivilized, a. barbarous, uncontrolled, barbarian; see **primitive 3.**

unclassified, a. not classified or ordered or put in order, disordered, out of order; see **confused 2, unknown 1.**

uncle, n. father's brother, mother's brother, elder; see **relative.**

unclean, a. soiled, sullied, stained, spotted, filthy, bedraggled, smeared, befouled, nasty, grimy, polluted, rank, unhealthful, defiled, muddy, stinking, rotten, vile, decayed, contaminated, tainted, rancid, putrid, putrescent, moldy, musty, mildewed, besmirched, smirched, filmed over, bleary, dusty, sooty, smudgy, scurvy, scurfy, clogged, slimy, mucky, tarnished, murky, smudged, daubed, blurred, spattered; see also **dirty 1, impure 1.**—Ant. pure, clean, white.

uncomfortable, a. 1. [Troubled in body or mind] distressed, ill at ease, uneasy, disturbed, pained, miserable, wretched, restless, annoyed, angry, in pain, smarting, suffering, upset, vexed, on pins and needles, weary, tired, fatigued, exhausted, strained, worn, aching, sore, galled, stiff, chafed, cramped, agonized, hurt, anguished.—Ant. **quiet,** rested, happy. 2. [Causing discomfort] illfitting, awkward, annoying, irritating, galling, wearisome, difficult, hard, thorny, troublesome, harsh, grievous, dolorous, bitter, excruciating, afflictive, distressing, torturing, painful, agonizing, disagreeable.—*Ant.* **easy,** pleasant, grateful.

uncomfortably, *a.* distressfully, uneasily, painfully, miserably, wretchedly, restlessly, sadly, fretfully, annoyingly, disturbingly, awkwardly, irritatingly, troublesomely, harshly, grievously, bitterly, poignantly, sharply, keenly, excruciatingly, disagreeably, unhappily, dismally, in anguish.

uncommitted, *a.* 1. [Neutral] unpledged, unaffiliated, free; see **neutral 1.** 2. [Reserved] evasive, reticent, shy; see **withdrawn.**

uncommon, *a.* unusual, out of the ordinary, different, extraordinary, unheard of, unique, rare, exceptional, out of the way, strange, exotic, remarkable, startling, surprising, fantastic, unaccustomed, unfamiliar, freakish, irregular, uncustomary, unconventional, unorthodox, abnormal, peculiar, odd, bizarre, eccentric, original, nondescript, prodigious, fabulous, monstrous, curious, wonderful, unaccountable, noteworthy, queer, unparalleled, unexampled, outlandish, extreme.—*Ant.* **common,** usual, ordinary.

uncompromising, *a.* strong, inflexible, determined; see **firm 1.**

unconcern, *n.* apathy, aloofness, coldness; see **indifference.**

unconcerned, *a.* indifferent, careless, apathetic, inattentive, cold, impassive, callous; see also **nonchalant.**

unconditional, *a.* positive, definite, absolute, unconstrained, without reserve, final, certain, complete, entire, whole, unrestricted, unqualified, unlimited, actual, thorough, thoroughgoing, genuine, indubitable, assured, determinate, unequivocal, full, categorical, decisive, unmistakable, clear, unquestionable.

unconditionally, *a.* absolutely, thoroughly, unreservedly; see **completely.**

unconnected, *a.* 1. [Separate] divided, detached, disconnected; see **separated.** 2. [Irrelevant] impertinent, unrelated, inapplicable; see **irrelevant.**

unconscious, *a.* insensible, swooning, in a state of suspended animation, torpid, lethargic, inanimate, senseless, drowsy, numb, inert, paralyzed, palsied, tranced, entranced, in a stupor *or* coma *or* trance, raving, out of one's head, *out like a light, knocked out.—*Ant.* **conscious,** vivacious, awake.

unconscious (*usually used with* the) *n.* psyche, instinct, motive force; see **memory 1,** mind 1.

unconsciously, *a.* abstractedly, mechanically, carelessly, automatically, habitually, by rote, unintentionally, inattentively, heedlessly, without reflection, negligently, disregardfully, thoughtlessly, neglectfully, hurriedly, without calculation, unguardedly. —*Ant.* **deliberately,** intentionally, willfully.

unconstitutional, *a.* un-American, undemocratic, lawless; see **illegal.**

uncontrollable, *a.* ungovernable, lawless, insurgent; see **unruly.**

uncontrolled, *a.* open, clear, free, unchecked, unhindered, boundless, ungoverned, unsuppressed, limitless, unbridled, unfettered, unobstructed, independent, unburdened, unbounded, unhampered, unlimited, uncurbed, unconstrained, unconfined.

unconventional, *a.* anarchistic, individual, different; see **unique 1, unusual 2.**

uncouth, *a.* ungainly, clumsy, crude; see **rude 1, 2.**

uncover, *v.* unseal, uncork, unscrew, pry open, lift the lid, dig up, reveal, tap, lay open, unclose, fish up; see also **open 2.** —*Ant.* **close,** cover, seal up.

uncovered, *a.* exposed, conspicuous, unsafe; see **open 4.**

undamaged, *a.* uninjured, safe, unharmed; see **whole 2.**

undecided, *a.* undetermined, in the middle *or* balance, unsettled; see **doubtful, uncertain 2.**

undefeated, *a.* unbeaten, victorious, winning; see **successful.**

undefined, *a.* 1. [Infinite] limitless, boundless, forever; see **infinite.** 2. [Vague] dim, unclear, indistinct; see **irregular 4,** obscure 1.

undeniable, *a.* proven, sound, sure; see **accurate 1.**

undependable, *a.* careless, unsound, inconstant; see **irresponsible, unreliable 1.**

under, *a.* and *prep.* 1. [Referring to physical position] on the bottom of, below, covered by, 'neath, concealed by, held down by, supporting, pinned beneath, on the underside of, pressed down by, beneath.—*Ant.* **above,** over, on top of. 2. [Subject to authority] governed by, in the power of, obedient to; see **subordinate.** 3. [Included within] belonging to, subsequent to, following; see **below 3.**

under-achiever, *n.* slow learner, retarded child, underprivileged person, backward *or* problem child, misfit, pupil from the ghetto *or* the back country *or* the hinterlands, etc.; foreigner, foreign-born pupil, nonnative speaker; see also **fool.**

underage, *a.* juvenile, youthful, minor; see **young 1.**

under arrest, *a.* arrested, caught, taken into custody, seized, taken (in), handcuffed, confined, jailed, imprisoned, detained, shut up *or* penned up, put in irons, sent to prison *or* to jail, *busted, *pinched, booked, *collared, *nabbed, *sent up the river.

underbrush, *n.* thicket, brush, brushwood, jungle, (second) growth, tangle, hedge, cover, scrub, bush; see also **forest.**

underclothes, *n.* lingerie, *undies, underthings; see **clothes, underwear.**

under construction, *a.* in production, in preparation, being built, going up.

undercover, *a.* 1. [Secret] hidden, surreptitious, clandestine; see **secret 3.** 2. [Secretly] privately, surreptitiously, stealthily; see **secretly.**

underdeveloped, *a.* backward, retarded, slowed down; see **weak 1, 2, 3, 5.**

underdog, *a.* loser, underling, *low man on the totem pole; see **failure 2, victim.**

underestimate, *v.* miscalculate, come short of, undervalue, depreciate, underrate, disparage, slight, minimize, think too little of, hold too lightly, make light of, deprecate.

under fire, *a.* in action, at the front, embattled; see **fighting.**

underfoot, *a.* 1. [Beneath] down, at bottom, below; see **under 1.** 2. [In the way] annoying, tiresome, impeding; see **disturbing.**

undergo, *v.* sustain, submit to, support, experience, feel, know, be subject to, bear, meet with, endure, go through, encounter, bear up under, put up with, share, withstand.—*Ant.* **avoid, escape, resist.**

undergone, *a.* sustained, submitted to, supported, experienced, felt, suffered, borne, met (with), known, endured, gone through, encountered, put up with, shared, seen, withstood.

underground, *a.* subterranean, buried, covered, earthed over, under the sod, in the recesses of the earth, hidden from the eye of day, gone to earth; see also **under 1.**

undergrowth, *n.* underwood, tangle, scrub; see **brush 3.**

underhanded, *a.* secret, sneaky, secretive; see **sly.**

underlie, *v.* carry, bear, hold up; see **hold 7.**

underline, *v.* 1. [Emphasize] stress, mark, indicate; see **emphasize.** 2. [To make a line under] underscore, mark, interlineate, bracket, check off, italicize.

undermine, *v.* impair, ruin, threaten; see **weaken 2.**

underneath, *a.* and *prep.* beneath, below, lower than; see **under 1.**

undernourished, *a.* underfed, mistreated, afflicted with malnutrition; see **hungry.**

underpass, *n.* bridge, culvert, cave; see **tunnel.**

underprivileged, *a.* indigent, destitute, educationally handicapped; see **poor 1.**

undershirt, *n.* shirt, T-shirt, turtleneck; see also **clothes, underwear.**

underside, *n.* underneath, base, root; see **bottom, foundation 2.**

understand, *v.* 1. [To comprehend] apprehend, fathom, take in, grasp, figure out, seize, take (one's meaning), identify with, know, perceive, appreciate, follow, master, conceive, be aware of, sense, recognize, grow aware, explain, interpret, see through, learn, find out, see (into), catch, note, be conscious of, have cognizance of, realize, discern, read, distinguish, infer, deduce, induce, make out, be apprized of, become alive to, have been around, experience, have knowledge of, be instructed in, get to the bottom of, get at the root of, penetrate, possess, be informed of, come to one's senses, see the light, make out, *register, *savvy, get the gist of, catch on, get the point of, *dig, read between the lines, *be with it, get the idea. 2. [To suppose] guess, conjecture, surmise; see **assume.** 3. [To accept] concede, take for granted, count on; see **agree.**

understandable, *a.* comprehensible, conceivable, appreciable, expected, to be expected, natural, normal, regular, making sense, intelligible, in harmony with, readable, reasonable, logical, right, customary, recognizable, justifiable, imaginable, acceptable, apprehensible, credible.

understanding, *n.* 1. [The power to understand] sharpness, intelligence, comprehension; see **judgment 1.** 2. [The act of comprehending] recognition, knowing, perception; see **judgment 2, thought 1.** 3. [That which comes from understanding, sense 2] conclusion, knowledge, perception; see **belief, opinion 1.** 4. [Informal agreement] meeting of minds, common view, harmony; see **agreement 1.** 5. [The intellect] head, brain, mentality; see **mind 1.**

understood, *a.* 1. [Comprehended] penetrated, realized, appreciated, known, discovered, grasped, reasoned out, rationalized, explained, experienced, discerned, distinguished, made out, learned, fathomed, searched, explored, analyzed, mastered, conned, taken to heart.—*Ant.* unknown, overlooked, uncomprehended. 2. [Agreed upon] concerted, ratified, (reciprocally) approved, assumed, stipulated, pledged, tacitly agreed upon, engaged for, settled, concluded, fixed upon, endorsed, subscribed to, accepted.

undertake, *v.* endeavor, engage, set out, promise, try out, try, begin, offer, set in motion, volunteer, initiate, commit one-self to, embark upon, venture, take upon oneself, answer for, hazard, stake, move, devote or pledge oneself to, take up (for), take on or upon, set about, go into or about or in for, put one's hand to, have one's hands in, have in hand, launch (into or upon or forth), address oneself to, enter on or upon, busy oneself with, tackle, *pitch into, fall into, buckle down, take on, take the plunge, fall to, have a try at, go for (in a big way).

undertaken, a. set in motion, begun, launched, embarked upon, initiated, pushed forward, ventured, started, en-deavored, assumed, taken up, promised, offered, volunteered, hazarded, chanced, risked, pledged, tackled, essayed, tried, aimed at, attempted, striven for, en-gaged for.

undertaker, n. mortician, funeral direc-tor, embalmer, *body snatcher.

undertaking, n. enterprise, attempt, en-gagement; see **action 1, 2**.

undertone, n. buzz, murmur, hum; see **whisper 1**.

undertow, n. whirlpool, undercurrent, riptide; see **flow, tide**.

underwater, a. submarine, sunken, ma-rine; see **under 1**.

under way, a. initiated, started, under construction; see **begun**.

underwear, n. undergarments, under-clothing, unmentionables, lingerie, inti-mate things, underlinen, underclothes; see also **clothes**. Types of underwear include the following—*men*: shirt, shorts, drawers, red flannels, union suit, jockey shorts, T-shirt, boxer shorts, long under-wear; *women*: underskirt, slip, petticoat, girdle, brassiere, garter belt, bra-slip, bra, panty slip, halfslip, corset, corselet, briefs, bodice, *cache-sexe* (French), vest, briefs, foundation garment, panty girdle, panties, shorts, knickers (British), *fal-sies; *infants*: shirt, drawers, pants, diaper, slip, rubber pants.

underweight, a. skinny, undersized, puny; see **thin 2**.

underworld, n. 1. [Hell] Hades, Inferno, netherworld; see **hell**. 2. [Crime] gang-dom, rackets, organized crime; see **crime**.

undesirable, a. objectionable, shunned, disliked, (to be) avoided, unwanted, out-cast, rejected, defective, disadvanta-geous, inexpedient, inconvenient, trou-blesome, unwished for, repellent, loathed, unsought, dreaded, annoying, insufferable, unacceptable, scorned, dis-pleasing, distasteful, loathsome, abomi-nable, obnoxious, unpopular, bother-some, unlikable, unwelcome, unapprova-ble, useless, inadmissible, unsatisfactory,

disagreeable, awkward, embarrassing, unfit.—*Ant.* **welcome**, proper, suitable.

undeveloped, a. potential, incipient, unactualized; see **hidden**.

undisputed, a. unchallenged, unques-tioned, assured; see **certain 2**.

undisturbed, a. settled, unruffled, un-troubled; see **calm 1, 2**.

undivided, a. 1. [Unified] united, full, collective; see **whole**. 2. [Undistracted] exclusive, complete, entire; see **whole 1**.

undo, v. mar, destroy, ruin, wreck, break, bring to naught, subvert, injure, over-throw, unsettle, turn topsy-turvy, upset, defeat.

undoing, n. ruination, downfall, reversal, destruction, misfortune, calamity, over-throw, trouble, grief, catastrophe, defeat, shipwreck, smash, wrack, subversion, collapse, casualty, accident, mishap, misadventure, misstep, mischance, bad luck, adversity, reverse, blow, trial, af-fliction, stroke of fate, slip, blunder, fault, omission, difficulty, failure, error, miscalculation, trip, stumble, fumble, blunder, repulse, discouragement, death-blow, last straw.—*Ant.* **advantage**, good omen, godsend.

undone, a. 1. [Unfinished] left, incom-plete, unperformed; see **unfinished 1**. 2. [Distraught] upset, disturbed, agitated; see **troubled**. 3. [Ruined] betrayed, de-stroyed, killed; see **dead 1, ruined 1, 2**.

undoubtedly, a. assuredly, without doubt, of course; see **unquestionably**.

undress, v. strip, take off one's clothes, disrobe, dismantle, divest, become naked, *peel, *pile out of one's clothes.—*Ant.* **dress**, put on one's clothes, attire oneself.

undue, a. improper, illegal, indecorous, unfair, unseemly, unjust, underhanded, sinister, forbidden, excessive, unneces-sary, extreme, extravagant, dispropor-tionate, immoderate.—*Ant.* **necessary**, proper, requisite.

unduly, a. improperly, excessively, ex-tremely; see **unnecessarily**.

undying, a. everlasting, perpetual, death-less; see **eternal**.

unearned, a. won, gratis, unmerited; see **free 4**.

unearth, v. reveal, find, uncover; see **learn**.

unearthly, a. frightening, ghostly, super-natural; see **unnatural 1**.

uneasiness, n. disquiet, restlessness, agi-tation; see **fear**.

uneasy, a. unquiet, anxious, fearful, iras-cible, troubled, harassed, vexed, per-turbed, alarmed, upset, afraid, appre-hensive, nervous, frightened, shaky, per-plexed, agitated, unsettled, suspicious, peevish, irritable, fretful, worried, an-guished, in turmoil, disquieted, shaken, full of misgivings, fidgety, jittery, on edge, all nerves, jumpy, snappish, uncomfortable, molested, tormented, in distress.—*Ant.* quiet, placid, soothed.

uneducated, *a.* illiterate, unschooled, untaught; see **ignorant 2.**

unemotional, *a.* reticent, apathetic, insensitive; see **indifferent, quiet.**

unemployed, *a.* out of work, in the bread lines, receiving charity, jobless, idle, inactive, loafing, unoccupied, without gainful employment, on the dole, *cooling one's heels, on the shelf.—*Ant.* busy, employed, at work.

unemployment, *n.* work stoppage, layoff, strike conditions; see **idleness.**

unending, *a.* everlasting, infinite, neverending; see **eternal.**

unequal, *a.* 1. [Not alike] odd, illmatched, dissimilar; see **unlike.** 2. [One-sided] uneven, unbalanced, inequitable; see **irregular 1.**

unequaled, *a.* unmatched, unrivaled, supreme; see **unique.**

unethical, *a.* sneaky, immoral, unfair; see **dishonest, wrong 1.**

uneven, *a.* 1. [Rough] bumpy, rugged, jagged; see **rough 1.** 2. [Irregular] notched, jagged, serrate; see **irregular 4.** 3. [Variable] intermittent, spasmodic, fitful; see **irregular 1.** 4. [Odd] remaining, leftover, additional; see **odd 5.**

unevenly, *a.* roughly, intermittently, irregularly, spottily, bumpily, with friction, haphazardly, wobbling, bumping, stumbling, hopping, jumpily, jumping, all up and down, staggering.

unexpected, *a.* unforeseen, surprising, unlooked for, sudden, startling, unpredicted, coming unaware, astonishing, staggering, stunning, electrifying, amazing, not in the cards, not on the books, unanticipated, not bargained for, left out of calculation *or* reckoning, wonderful, unprepared for, instantaneous, eyeopening, like a bolt from the blue.—*Ant.* **expected,** predicted, foreseen.

unexpectedly, *a.* surprisingly, instantaneously, suddenly, startlingly, without warning, like a bolt from the blue; see also **quickly.—*Ant.* regularly,** according to prediction, as anticipated.

unfair, *a.* 1. [Unjust] wrongful, wrong, unrightful, low, base, injurious, unethical, bad, wicked, culpable, blamable, blameworthy, foul, illegal, inequitable, improper, unsporting, shameful, cruel, shameless, dishonorable, unreasonable, grievous, vicious, vile, undue, unlawful, petty, mean, inexcusable, unjustifiable, immoral, injurious, criminal, forbidden, irregular.—*Ant.* **fair,** proper, sporting 2. [Not in accord with approved trade practices] unethical, criminal, discriminatory; see sense 1.

unfairly, *a.* unjustly, unreasonable, irregularly; see **brutally.**

unfaithful, *a.* 1. [Not faithful] false, untrue, deceitful; see **unreliable 1. 2.** [Having broken the marriage vow] adulterous, incontinent, unchaste; see **bad 1.**

unfamiliar, *a.* 1. [Unacquainted] not introduced, not associated, unknown, not on speaking terms, not versed in, not in the habit of, out of contact with.—*Ant.* **friendly,** intimate, acquainted. 2. [Strange] alien, outlandish, exotic, remote, novel, original, different, unusual, extraordinary, unaccustomed, unexplored, uncommon. —*Ant.* **common,** ordinary, usual.

unfashionable, *a.* outmoded, antiquated, obsolete; see **old-fashioned.**

unfasten, *v.* unsnap, untie, unlock; see **loosen 1.**

unfavorable, *a.* inopportune, untimely, unseasonable, adverse, calamitous, unpropitious, inexpedient, bad, ill-chosen, ill-fated, ill-suited, ill-timed, unsuitable, improper, wrong, abortive, untoward, inauspicious, unlucky, ill, unfortunate, regrettable, premature, tardy, late, unfit, inadvisable, objectionable, inconvenient, disadvantageous, damaging, destructive, unseemly, ill-advised, obstructive, troublesome, embarrassing, unpromising, awkward.

unfavorably, *a.* adversely, negatively, opposingly, oppositely, conflictingly, antagonistically, obstructively, malignantly, counteractively, contrarily, in opposition (to), in the negative, on the contrary, by turning thumbs down, giving the red light (to); see also **against 3.**

unfilled, *a.* vacant, void, drained; see **empty 1.**

unfinished, *a.* 1. [Not completed] uncompleted, undone, half done, incomplete, under construction, unperformed, imperfect, unconcluded, deficient, unexecuted, unaccomplished, in preparation, in the making, not done, in the rough, sketchy, tentative, shapeless, formless, unperfected, unfulfilled, undeveloped, unassembled, defective, found wanting, cut short, immature, faulty, crude, rough.—*Ant.* **done,** completed, perfected. 2. [Without a finish] unpainted, unvarnished, bare, raw, rough, crude, unprotected, uncovered, plain, undecorated, unadorned.

unfit, *a.* 1. [Incompetent] unqualified, feeble, unpracticed, inexperienced, weak, impotent, inept, clumsy, debilitated, incapacitated, badly qualified, incompetent, unable, unprepared, ineffective, unapt.—*Ant.* **able,** fit, effective. 2. [Unsuitable] improper, ill-adapted, wrong, ill-advised, unlikely, unpromising, inexpedient, inappropriate, inapplicable, useless, valueless, mistaken, incorrect, inadequate, flimsy.—*Ant.* fit, suitable, correct.

unfold, *v.* shake out, straighten, release, display, unwind, spread out, uncurl, unwrap, reel out, unbend, open, flatten, loosen, unroll.—*Ant.* fold, roll, lap.

unforeseen, *a.* surprising, abrupt, sudden; see **unexpected.**

unforgettable, *a.* notable, exceptional, extraordinary; see **impressive.**

unforgivable, *a.* inexcusable, unpardonable, unjustifiable, indefensible, inexpiable; see also **wrong 1.**

unformed, *a.* not formed, formless, incomplete; see **unfinished 1.**

unfortunate, *a.* unlucky, luckless, unhappy, afflicted, troubled, stricken, unsuccessful, without success, burdened, pained, not prosperous, in adverse circumstances, out of fortune, forsaken by fortune, broken, shattered, ill-fated, on the road to ruin, in a desperate plight, ruined, out of luck, in a bad way, *jinxed, *behind the eight ball, *gone to the dogs, down on one's luck; see also **sad 1.**—*Ant.* happy, lucky, prosperous.

unfortunately, *a.* unluckily, unhappily, miserably, sadly, grievously, disastrously, dismally, calamitously, badly, sickeningly, discouragingly, catastrophically, horribly, if worst comes to worst. —*Ant.* happily, favorably, prosperously.

unfounded, *a.* baseless, unproven, groundless; see **untrue.**

unfriendly, *a.* 1. [Hostile] opposed, alienated, ill-disposed, against, opposite, contrary, warlike, competitive, conflicting, antagonistic, estranged, at variance, irreconcilable, not on speaking terms, turned against, *with a chip on one's shoulder.—*Ant.* friendly, intimate, approving. 2. [Lacking friendly qualities] grouchy, bearish, surly, misanthropic, gruff, ill-disposed, envious, uncharitable, faultfinding, combative, quarrelsome, grudging, malignant, spiteful, malicious, vengeful, resentful, hateful, peevish, aloof, unsociable, suspicious, sour.—*Ant.* generous, frank, open.

ungainly, *a.* clumsy, gawky, inexpert; see **awkward 1, rude 1.**

ungodly, *a.* dreadful, atrocious, immoral; see **bad 1.**

ungovernable, *a.* unmanageable, wild, uncontrollable; see **unruly.**

ungrateful, *a.* thankless, selfish, lacking in appreciation, grasping, demanding, self-centered, unmindful, forgetful, heedless, careless, insensible, dissatisfied, grumbling, unnatural, faultfinding,

oblivious.—*Ant.* thankful, grateful, obliged.

unguarded, *a.* thoughtless, frank, careless; see **careless.**

unhandy, *a.* awkward, ill-arranged, unwieldy, ill-contrived, clumsy; see **troublesome.**

unhappily, *a.* regrettably, lamentably, unluckily; see **unfortunately.**

unhappiness, *n.* sorrow, woe, sadness; see **depression 2, grief.**

unhappy, *a.* 1. [Sad] miserable, sorrowful, wretched; see **troubled 1. 2.** [Unfortunate] afflicted, troubled, in a desperate plight; see **unfortunate.**

unharmed, *a.* unhurt, uninjured, intact; see **safe 1, whole 2.**

unhealthy, *a.* sickly, sick, in a decline, in ill health, infirm, delicate, feeble, shaky, undernourished, rickety, spindling, ailing, weak, in a run-down condition.—*Ant.* healthy, robust, hale.

unheard, *a.* noiseless, soundless, hushed; see **quiet.**

unheard-of, *a.* unprecedented, unique, new; see **unknown 1.**

unhinge, *v.* 1. [To detach] dislodge, disjoint, disunite; see **remove 1. 2.** [To upset] unbalance, disorder, derange; see **upset 1.**

unhoped-for, *a.* incredible, unforeseen, unexpected; see **unimaginable.**

unhurried, *a.* leisurely, deliberate, nonchalant; see **slow 1.**

unhurt, *a.* uninjured, all right, whole; see also **safe 1.**

unidentified, *a.* nameless, unnamed, not known; see **unknown 1, 2.**

unified, *a.* made one, united, joined, combined, concerted, synthesized, amalgamated, conjoined, incorporated, blended, identified, coalesced, federated, centralized, intertwined, consolidated, associated, cemented, coupled, allied, wedded, married, confederated. —*Ant.* separated, distinct, disjoined.

uniform, *a.* 1. [Even] symmetrical, smooth, straight; see **regular 3. 2.** [Alike] equal, well-matched, similar; see **alike.**

uniform, *n.* costume, suit, dress; see **clothes.**

uniformity, *n.* 1. [Regulation] steadiness, sameness, evenness; see **regularity. 2.** [Harmony] unity, accord, concord; see **agreement 1.**

unify, *v.* consolidate, ally, conjoin; see **unite.**

unimaginable, *a.* inconceivable, incomprehensible, incredible, inapprehensible, unbelievable, unheard of, indescribable, unthinkable, improbable; see also **impossible.**

unimaginative, *a.* barren, tedious, usual; see **common 1, dull 4.**

unimportance, *n.* immateriality, triviality, worthlessness; see **insignificance.**

unimportant, *a.* trifling, inconsiderable, slight, worthless, inconsequential, insignificant, unnecessary, immaterial, indifferent, beside the point, frivolous, useless, of no account, worthless, trivial, paltry.—*Ant.* important, weighty, great.

unimproved, *a.* ordinary, in a natural state, untutored; see **natural 3.**

uninformed, *a.* unenlightened, naive, unacquainted; see **ignorant 1, 2.**

unintentional, *a.* unthinking, involuntary, erratic; see **aimless.**

unintentionally, *a.* involuntarily, casually, inadvertently; see **accidentally.**

uninterested, *a.* apathetic, impassive, detached; see **indifferent 1.**

uninteresting, *a.* tedious, boring, tiresome, dreary, wearisome, prosaic, fatiguing, monotonous, dull, stale, trite, commonplace, irksome, stupid, humdrum, prosy, flat, depressing, insipid, unentertaining, dismal, banal.—*Ant.* interesting, exciting, lively.

uninterrupted, *a.* continuous, unending, unbroken; see **consecutive, constant.**

uninvited, *a.* unasked, unwanted, not asked *or* invited; see **unpopular.**

Union, *n.* 1. [The United States] the States, Columbia, America; see **United States.** 2. [The North in the American Civil War] the Free States, Anti-slavery States, the Northern States; see **North.**

union, *n.* 1. [The act of joining] unification, junction, meeting, uniting, joining, coupling, embracing, coming together, merging, fusion, mingling, concurrence, symbiosis, amalgamation, confluence, congregation, reconciliation, conciliation, correlation, combination, connection, linking, attachment, coalition, conjunction, consolidation, incorporation, centralization, affiliation, confederation, copulation, coition.—*Ant.* divorce, separation, severance. 2. [A closely knit group] association, federation, society; see **organization 2.** 3. [A marriage] wedlock, conjugal ties, matrimony, cohabitation, nuptial connection, match, matrimonial affiliation. 4. [A labor union] laborers, workingmen, employees; see **labor 4.**

unique, *a.* single, peerless, matchless, unprecedented, unparalleled, novel, individual, sole, unexampled, lone, different, unequaled. —*Ant.* common, frequent, many.

unison, *n.* concert, unity, harmony; see **unity 1.**

unit, *n.* 1. [A whole] entirety, complement, total, totality, assemblage, assembly, system. 2. [A detail] section, segment, part, fraction, piece, joint, block,

square, layer, link, length, digit, member, factor.

unite, *v.* join, meet, ally, combine, solidify, harden, strengthen, condense, confederate, couple, affiliate, merge, band together, blend, mix, become one, concentrate, consolidate, entwine, intertwine, grapple, amalgamate, league, band, embody, embrace, copulate, associate, assemble, gather together, conjoin, keep together, tie in, pull together, hang together, join forces, coalesce, fuse, wed, marry, mingle, stick together, stay together.—*Ant.* divide, separate, part.

united, *a.* unified, leagued, combined, affiliated, federal, confederated, integrated, amalgamated, co-operative, consolidated, concerted, congruent, associated, assembled, linked, banded, in partnership; see also **organized.**—*Ant.* separated, distinct, individual.

United Kingdom, *n.* England, Scotland, Ireland, Wales; the British Isles, Britain, Great Britain, the mother country, U.K., G.B.; see **Europe.**

United Nations, *n.* UN, peace-keeping force, international society, community of nations. Divisions and function of the United Nations include the following— General Assembly, Security Council, Economic and Social Council, Trust and Non Self-Governing Territories Trusteeship, Trusteeship Council, International Court of Justice, Secretariat.

United States, *n.* America, US, United States of America, U.S.A., Columbia, the Union, these States, the States, the land of the Stars and Stripes, US of A, *the land of liberty, *the land of the free and the home of the brave, *God's country, the melting pot, *stateside, the mainland.

unity, *n.* 1. [The quality of oneness] homogeneity, homogeneousness, sameness, indivisibility, identity, inseparability, singleness, similarity, uniqueness, integration, uniformity, universality, all-togetherness, ensemble, wholeness; see also **whole.** —*Ant.* difference, diversity, divorce. 2. [Union] federation, confederation, compact, combination, correspondence, alliance, agreement, concord, identity of purpose, unification, aggregation; see also **organization 2.** 3. [Harmony] concord, agreement, accord; see **harmony 1.**

universal, *a.* 1. [Concerning the universe] cosmic, stellar, celestial, sidereal, astronomical, cosmogonal. 2. [Worldwide] mundane, earthly, terrestrial, sublunary, terrene, human, wordly.—*Ant.* local, restricted, district. 3. [General] entire, all-embracing, prevalent, customary, usual, whole, sweeping, extensive, comprehensive, total, unlimited, limitless, endless, vast, widespread, catholic, common, regular, undisputed, accepted, unrestricted.—*Ant.* special, limited, peculiar.

universally, *a.* entirely, prevailingly, comprehensively; see completely.

universe, *n.* cosmos, creation, the visible world, astral system, universal frame, all created things, everything, nature, the natural world.

university, *a.* professional, advanced, graduate, college, collegiate, undergraduate, freshman, sophomore, junior, senior, learned, academic, educational.

university, *n.* educational institution, institution of higher learning, multiversity, megaversity, normal school, state *or* municipal *or* provincial university; see also college, school 1.

unjust, *a.* wrong, inequitable, wrongful; see unfair.

unjustifiable, *a.* unallowable, unforgivable, unjust; see wrong 1.

unjustly, *a.* brutally, cruelly, meanly; see wrongly 1.

unkind, *a.* malignant, spiteful, mean, malicious, inhuman, inhumane, sadistic, cruel, hateful, malevolent, savage, barbarous; see also rude 1, 2.—*Ant.* kind, benevolent, helpful.

unknown, *a.* 1. [Not known; *said of information*] uncomprehended, unapprehended, undiscovered, untold, unexplained, uninvestigated, unexplored, unheard of, unperceived, concealed, hidden, unrevealed.—*Ant.* known, established, understood. 2. [Not known; *said of people*] alien, unfamiliar, not introduced, unheard of, obscure, foreign, strange, unacknowledged, ostracized, outcast, friendless, private, retired, aloof, out of the world, forgotten. 3. [Not known; *said of terrain*] unexplored, far-off, remote, far, distant, foreign, undiscovered, exotic, transoceanic, transmarine, at the far corners of the earth, faraway, outlandish, unheard-of, unfrequented, untraveled, desolate, desert, unvisited, legendary, strange.

unlawful, *a.* forbidden, illicit, outlawed; see illegal.

unlawfully, *a.* illegally, unjustly, unjustifiably; see wrongly 1, 2.

unlearned, *a.* unlettered, rude, boorish, uneducated, ignorant, illiterate, clownish, untutored, untaught, unread, savage, uncivilized, doltish, crass, half-taught, half-educated, uninitiated, ill-bred, unversed, uninstructed, unguided, unenlightened, dull, misguided, empty, unaccomplished, backward, superficial, pedantic, *low-brow. —*Ant.* learned, educated, adept.

unless, *prep.* saving, without the provi-

sion that, if not, except, except that, excepting that.

unlike, *a.* dissimilar, different, incongruous, contradictory, hostile, opposed, inconsistent, heterogeneous, diverse, contrasted, conflicting, contrary, disparate, dissonant, discordant, clashing, separate, opposite, divergent, various, variant.—*Ant.* like, similar, correspondent.

unlikely, *a.* improbable, unheard-of, incredible, implausible, not to be thought of, unbelievable, absurd, unconvincing, not likely, scarcely possible, apparently false, contrary to expectation, inconceivable, doubtful, dubious, questionable, extraordinary, marvelous, out of the ordinary, strange.—*Ant.* likely, probable, credible.

unlimited, *a.* infinite, limitless, boundless, unending, extensive, universal, unrestricted, unconditional, unfathomable, inexhaustible, unconfined, immense, illimitable, measureless, incalculable, interminable, without number, unfathomed, unsounded, untold, countless, numberless, incomprehensible, immeasurable, endless.

unload, *v.* disburden, discharge, dump, slough, lighten, cast, unpack, relieve, remove cargo, disgorge, empty, deplane, unburden, break bulk.—*Ant.* fill, load, pack.

unlock, *v.* unbar, unfasten, open the lock; see open 2.

unlocked, *a.* free, unbarred, unlatched; see open 1, 2.

unloved, *a.* disliked, detested, despised; see hated.

unlucky, *a.* 1. [Unfortunate] luckless, unhappy, afflicted; see unfortunate. 2. [Unpropitious] ill-chosen, ill-fated, untimely; see unfavorable.

unmanageable, *a.* uncontrollable, irrepressible, ungovernable; see unruly.

unmarried, *a.* celibate, unwed, single, virgin, maiden, eligible, chaste, unwedded, spouseless, footloose and fancy-free.—*Ant.* married, wed, wedded.

unmistakable, *a.* conspicuous, distinct, evident; see clear 2, obvious 1.

unmoved, *a.* 1. [Not moved physically] firm, stable, motionless, static, solid, durable, immovable, firm as a rock, staunch, fast, moveless, statuelike, rooted, steady, immobile, unshaken, changeless, unwavering. 2. [Not moved emotionally] impassive, stoic, quiet, cold, cool, calm, collected, deliberate, resolute, dispassionate, calculating, unaffected, unemotional, indifferent, judicious, unflinching, nerveless, cool as a cucumber.

unnatural, *a.* 1. [Contrary to nature] monstrous, phenomenal, malformed, unaccountable, abnormal, preposterous, marvelous, uncanny, wonderful, strange, incredible, sublime, freakish, unconforming, inhuman, outrageous, unorthodox, miraculous, contrary to known laws. — *Ant.* common, ordinary, usual. 2. [Artificial] synthetic, imitation, manufactured, ersatz, concocted, made-up, fabricated, false, pseudo, mock, spurious, phoney.—*Ant.* natural, occurring naturally.

unnecessarily, *a.* needlessly, causelessly, without occasion, by chance, carelessly, fortuitously, casually, haphazardly, wantonly, accidentally, unessentially, redundantly, inexpediently, uselessly, exorbitantly, superfluously, undesirably, objectionably, disadvantageously, optionally, avoidably, without cause, without reason, gratuitously; see also foolishly.—*Ant.* necessarily, indispensably, unavoidably.

unnecessary, *a.* needless, causeless, fortuitous, casual, chance, haphazard, wanton, accidental, unessential, nonessential, beside the point, irrelevant, futile, extraneous, additional, redundant, useless, exorbitant, superfluous, worthless, undesirable, optional, avoidable, objectionable, disadvantageous, noncompulsory, random, dispensable, adventitious, without compulsion, uncalled for, gratuitous.—*Ant.* necessary, essential, required.

unnoticed, *a.* unobserved, unseen, unheeded, overlooked, inconspicuous, secret, hidden, passed by, unobtrusive, disregarded, unconsidered, unattended, neglected, unmarked, unremembered, unscrutinized, unremarked, unrecognized, slurred over, uninspected, winked at, glossed over, lost sight of, ignored, shoved into the background, undistinguished, unexamined, unwatched, unlooked at. —*Ant.* watched, noticed, seen.

unoccupied, *a.* 1. [Vacant] uninhabited, empty, deserted, unfurnished, void, voided, disfurnished, blank, untenanted.—*Ant.* full, inhabited, tenanted. 2. [Idle] loitering, inactive, unemployed; see idle.

unofficial, *a.* unconstrained, personal, casual; see informal.

unopposed, *a.* unchallenged, unrestricted, unhampered; see free 1, 2, 3.

unorganized, *a.* chaotic, random, disorganized; see confused 2.

unorthodox, *a.* unconventional, irregular, eccentric; see unusual 2.

unpack, *v.* unload, uncrate, unwrap; see remove 1.

unpaid, *a.* 1. [Owed; *said of debts*] due, payable, not discharged, past due, overdue, delinquent, unsettled, unliquidated, undefrayed, outstanding.—*Ant.* paid, discharged, defrayed. 2. [Working without

salary] voluntary, unsalaried, amateur, freewill, donated, contributed.

unpleasant, *a.* 1. [Not pleasing in society] disagreeable, obnoxious, boring; see rude 2. 2. [Not pleasing to the senses] repulsive, obnoxious, abhorrent; see offensive 2.

unpopular, *a.* disliked, despised, out of favor, abhorred, loathed, shunned, avoided, ostracized, scorned, detested, unloved, unvalued, uncared for, obnoxious.—*Ant.* popular, liked, agreeable.

unprecedented, *a.* unparalleled, novel, original; see unique.

unpredictable, *a.* random, inconstant, variable; see irregular 1.

unprepared, *a.* unready, unwarned, unwary, unexpectant, surprised, taken aback, unguarded, unnotified, unadvised, unaware, unsuspecting, taken off guard, napping, in the dark, going off half-cocked.

unproductive, *a.* unprolific, impotent, barren; see sterile 1, 2.

unprofitable, *a.* ill-requited, ill-paid, profitless, costly, expensive, unlucrative, unremunerative.—*Ant.* profitable, gainful, productive.

unpromising, *a.* discouraging, unfavorable, adverse; see unlikely.

unprotected, *a.* defenseless, unarmed, unguarded; see unsafe.

unpublished, *a.* unprinted, (still) in manuscript, manuscript; see unknown 1.

unqualified, *a.* 1. [Absolute] downright, utter, outright; see certain 2. 2. [Incompetent] inexperienced, unprepared, incapable; see unfit.

unquestionable, *a.* 1. [Certain] sure, obvious, clear; see certain 2. 2. [Faultless] unexceptionable, superior, flawless; see excellent.

unquestionably, *a.* certainly, without a doubt, surely, indubitably, indisputably, definitely, reliably, absolutely, positively, incontrovertibly, indefensibly, indeed, assuredly, of course, undoubtedly, certes, undeniably, past a doubt, beyond doubt, beyond a shadow of a doubt, past dispute.

unravel, *v.* unwind, disengage, undo; see free 1.

unreal, *a.* visionary, delusive, deceptive, illusory, imagined, hallucinatory, ideal, dreamlike, unsubstantial, nonexistent, fanciful, misleading, fictitious, theoretical, hypothetical, fabulous, notional, whimsical, fantastic; see also unbelievable.—*Ant.* genuine, real, substantial.

unrealistic, *a.* unworkable, not sensible *or* practical *or* workable *or* applicable, etc., nonsensical; see unreliable 1, 2.

unreasonable, *a.* 1. [Illogical] irrational, biased, fatuous; see illogical 2. 2. [Immoderate} exorbitant, extravagant, inordinate; see **extreme.** 3. [Senseless] foolish, silly, thoughtless; see **stupid 1.**

unreasonably, *a.* illogically, irrationally, stupidly; see **foolishly.**

unregulated, *a.* uncontrollable, unchecked, chaotic; see **uncontrolled.**

unrelated, *a.* independent, unattached, irrelative; see **separate.**

unreliable, *a.* undependable, unstable, wavering, deceitful, tricky, shifty, furtive, underhanded, untrue, fickle, giddy, untrustworthy, vacillating, fallible, weak, unpredictable; see also **dishonest.**

unrest, *n.* 1. [Lack of mental calm] malaise, distress, discomfort, perturbation, agitation, worry, sorrow, anxiety, grief, trouble, annoyance, tension, ennui, disquiet, soulsearching, irritation, harassment, upset, vexation, chagrin, mortification, perplexity, unease, disease, stour, moodiness, disturbance, bother, dither, *tizzy. 2. [Social or political restlessness] disquiet, agitation, turmoil, strife, disturbance, uproar, debate, contention, bickering, change, altercation, crisis, confusion, disputation, contest, controversy, quarrel, sparring, uncertainty, insurrection, suspicion, dissatisfaction.

unrestricted, *a.* allowable, not forbidden, free; see **open 3.**

unripe, *a.* green, tart, immature; see **raw 1.**

unroll, *v.* display, uncover, present; see **expose 1.**

unruffled, *a.* collected, smooth, serene; see **calm 1, 2.**

unruly, *a.* uncontrollable, willful, headstrong, forward, violent, impulsive, uncurbed, impetuous, ill-advised, rash, reckless, dashing, heedless, perverse, intractable, recalcitrant, self-assertive, refractory, rebellious, wayward, inexorable, restive, impervious, hidebound, inyielding, incorrigible, intemperate, drunken, lawless, vicious, brawling, unlicensed, rowdy, bawdy, quarrelsome, immovable, unwieldy, resolute, inflexible, forceful, dogged, mulish, fanatic, irrational, unreasonable, irrepressible, high-spirited, in.pudent, abandoned, profligate, stubborn, obstinate, turbulent, disorderly, self-willed, opinionated, bullheaded, ungovernable, stiff-necked, *ornery, mean, skittish, dangerous.

unsafe, *a.* hazardous, perilous, risky, threatening, treacherous, fearsome, unreliable, insecure, venturesome, unstable, alarming, precarious, ticklish, giddy, dizzy, slippery, uncertain, unpromising, shaky, explosive.—*Ant.* safe, harmless, proof.

unsaid, *a.* unspoken, not spoken *or* expressed *or* uttered, etc., unstated; see **quiet.**

unsatisfactorily, *a.* poorly, crudely, inefficiently; see **badly 1.**

unsatisfactory, *a.* disappointing, below expectation, displeasing, undesirable, regrettable, disconcerting, disquieting, vexing, distressing, upsetting, disturbing, offensive, unacceptable, disagreeable, unwelcome, shocking, deficient; see also **poor 2.** —*Ant.* excellent, satisfactory, gratifying.

unsavory, *a.* disagreeable, unpleasant, revolting; see **offensive 2.**

unscientific, *a.* irrational, impulsive, inconclusive; see **illogical.**

unscrew, *v.* screw out *or* off, unfasten, untwist; see **loosen 1.**

unscrupulous, *a.* unprincipled, bad, wicked; see **dishonest.**

unseal, *v.* free, remove, crack; see **open 2.**

unseemly, *a.* 1. [In bad taste; *said of conduct*] improper, unbecoming, inept; see **rude 1. 2.** [In bad taste; *said of things*] vulgar, tawdry, cheap; see **poor 2.**

unseen, *a.* imagined, imaginary, hidden, obscure, unobserved, veiled, occult, sensed, unperceived, unnoticed, unsuspected, curtained, unobtrusive, viewless, invisible, sightless, dark, shrouded, impalpable, imperceptible, inconspicuous, undiscovered, impenetrable, dense.

unselfish, *a.* disinterested, selfless, charitable; see **kind.**

unselfishly, *a.* openhandedly, bountifully, lavishly; see **freely 1, 2, generously 1, 2.**

unselfishness, *n.* charity, kindness, liberality; see **generosity.**

unsettle, *v.* disrupt, displace, disarrange; see **bother 2, disturb.**

unsettled, *a.* 1. [Undetermined] undecided, unfixed, unresolved; see **uncertain 2. 2.** [Unstable] confused, agitated, troubled, changing, explosive, shifting, precarious, ticklish, unpredictable, uneasy, unbalanced, perilous, complex, complicated, fluid, kinetic, active, busy, critical. —*Ant.* simple, stable, solid.

unshaken, *a.* unmoved, unaffected, undaunted; see **firm 1.**

unsheltered, *a.* unprotected, exposed, uncovered; see **unprepared, unsafe.**

unsightly, *a.* hideous, deformed, homely; see **repulsive 1, ugly 1.**

unskilled, *a.* untrained, uneducated, amateur; see **ignorant 2.**

unsophisticated, *a.* ingenuous, innocent, simple; see **inexperienced, naive.**

unsound, *a.* 1. [False] ill-founded, erroneous, incongruous; see **illogical 2. 2.** [Insecure] unreliable, unbacked, weak; see **unstable 2.**

unspeakable, *a.* horrid, unutterable, abominable, horrible, fearful, inexpressible, unimaginable, dreadful, dire, shocking, appalling, frightful, frightening, alarming, beastly, inhuman, calamitous.

unspeakably, *a.* greatly, unbelievably, terribly; see **much 1, 2.**

unspecified, *a.* general, undefined, indefinite; see **vague 2.**

unspoiled, *a.* unblemished, spotless, faultless; see **perfect 2, pure 2.**

unspoken, *a.* tacit, implicit, inferred; see **understood 1.**

unstable, *a.* **1.** [Having a high center of gravity] unsteady, wavering, unbalanced, giddy, wobbly, wiggly, weaving, shifty, precarious, top-heavy, teetering, shifting, uncertain, rattletrap, beetling, jutting, lightly balanced.—*Ant.* **firm,** steady, solid. **2.** [Easily disturbed] variable, changeable, giddy, capricious, fluctuating, shifty, volatile, rootless, dizzy, unpredictable, uncertain, sensitive, oversensitive, thinskinned, timid, delicate.

unsteady, *a.* **1.** [Wobbly] wiggly, wavering, shaky, treacherous, unbalanced, top-heavy, leaning, ramshackle, giddy, weaving, heaving, precarious, teetering, uncertain; see also **irregular 1. 2.** [Inconstant] changeable, fluctuating, vacillating, variable, uncertain, unfixed, capricious, volatile, unreliable, tricky, shifty, shaky, jerky, fluttering.

unstuck, *a.* unfastened, unglued, rattling; see **loose 1.**

unsubstantiated, *a.* unconfirmed, unattested, unsupported; see **false 2.**

unsuccessful, *a.* defeated, disappointed, frustrated, aborted, disastrous, unprosperous, unfortunate, unlucky, futile, (in)vain, failing, fruitless, worthless, sterile, bootless, unavailing, ineffectual, ineffective, immature, useless, foiled, shipwrecked, overwhelmed, overpowered, broken, ruined, destroyed, thwarted, crossed, disconcerted, dashed, circumvented, premature, inoperative, of no effect, balked, *left holding the sack, *skunked, stymied, *jinxed, out of luck, *stuck.—*Ant.* **successful,** fortunate, lucky.

unsuitable, *a.* inadequate, improper, malapropos, disagreeable, discordant, incongruous, inharmonious, incompatible, clashing, out of place, jarring, dissonant, discrepant, irrelevant, uncalled-for, dissident, inappropriate, ill-suited, unseemly, conflicting, opposite, contrary, unbecoming, unfitting, unfit, disparate, disturbing, mismatched, disproportionate, divergent, mismated, inapplicable, inconformable, unassimilable, inconsistent, intrusive, amiss, interfering, disagreeing, inept, unbefitting, inadmissible, absurd,

senseless, unseasonable, unfortunate, ill-timed, unsympathetic, not in keeping, out of joint, at odds, at variance, repugnant, *out of kilter, *cockeyed.—*Ant.* **fit,** suitable, proper.

unsure, *a.* unreliable, hesitant, doubtful; see **uncertain 1.**

unsurpassed, *a.* unexcelled, unequaled, matchless; see **unique.**

unsuspecting, *a.* **1.** [Gullible] undoubting, confiding, credulous; see **trusting 1. 2.** [Naive] innocent, inexperienced, simple; see **naive.**

unsympathetic, *a.* unmoved, apathetic, cold; see **indifferent 2.**

untangle, *v.* clear up, put in order, disentangle; see **order 3.**

unthinkable, *a.* inconceivable, unimaginable, improbable; see **unlikely.**

unthinking, *a.* heedless, rude, inconsiderate; see **careless 1.**

untidy, *a.* slovenly, unkempt, disorderly; see **dirty 1.**

untie, *v.* unlace, unknot, loosen, unfasten; see **loosen 1.**

untied, *a.* unfastened, slack, unbound; see **free 2, 3, loose 1.**

until, *prep.* till, to, between the present and, in anticipation of, prior to, during the time preceding, down to, continuously, before the coming of, in expectation of, as far as; see also **unto.**

untimely, *a.* unseasonable, awkward, ill-timed, inauspicious, badly timed, too early, abortive, too late, unpromising, ill-chosen, improper, unseemly, inappropriate, wrong, unfit, disagreeable, mistimed, intrusive, badly calculated, inopportune, out-of-date, malapropos, premature, unlucky, unfavorable, unfortunate, inexpedient, anachronistic.—*Ant.* **early,** timely, seasonable.

untiring, *a.* inexhaustible, powerful, persevering; see **strong 1.**

unto, *prep.* to, toward, till, until, contiguous to, against, up to, next to, beside, in the direction of, to the degree of, to the extreme of.

untold, *a.* uncounted, countless, unnumbered, many, innumerable, beyond measure, inexpressible, incalculable, undreamed of, staggering, unimaginable, multitudinous, manifold, multiple.

untouchable, *a.* taboo, forbidden, denied; see **illegal.**

untouched, *a.* **1.** [Not harmed] intact, whole, secure, unbroken, in good order, unharmed, in good condition, in a good state of preservation, safe and sound, out of danger, shipshape. **2.** [Not contaminated] virgin, clear, pure; see **clean 1.**

untrained, *a.* green, new, novice; see **inexperienced.**

untried, *a.* untested, uninitiated, new; see **inexperienced.**

untroubled, *a.* composed, serene, placid; see **calm 1, 2.**

untrue, *a.* false, misleading, specious, lying, hollow, deceptive, delusive, untrustworthy, deceitful, sham, spurious, incorrect, prevaricating, wrong.

untruth, *n.* falsehood, misrepresentation, evasion; see **lie.**

untruthful, *a.* insincere, crooked, deceitful; see **dishonest 1.**

unused, *a.* 1. [Not used] fresh, available, usable; see **new 1.** 2. [Surplus] additional, remaining, superfluous; see **extra.**

unusual, *a.* 1. [Remarkable] rare, extraordinary, strange, outstanding, great, uncommon, special, distinguished, prominent, important, noteworthy, awe-inspiring, awesome, unique, fine, unheard of, unexpected, seldom met with, surprising, superior, astonishing, amazing, prodigious, incredible, inconceivable, atypical, conspicuous, exceptional, eminent, significant, memorable, renowned, refreshing, singular, fabulous, unprecedented, unparalleled, unexampled, unaccountable, stupendous, unaccustomed, wonderful, notable, superior, marvelous, striking, overpowering, electrifying, dazing, fantastic, startling, astounding, indescribable, appalling, stupefying, ineffable, *out of sight.—Ant.* common, familiar, customary. 2. [Different] unique, extreme, uncommon, particular, exaggerated, distinctive, choice, little-known, out of the ordinary, marked, forward, unconventional, radical, exceptional, peculiar, strange, foreign, unnatural, puzzling, perplexing, confounding, disturbing, novel, advanced, startling, shocking, staggering, uncustomary, breaking with tradition, infrequent, mysterious, mystifying, surprising, extraordinary, unparalleled, deep, profound, aberrant, singular, unorthodox, unconformable, not to be expected, eccentric, unbalanced, unprecedented, inconsistent, individual, original, refreshing, newfangled, new, modern, recent, late, fresh, curious, unfamiliar, irregular, odd, unaccountable, alien, queer, quaint, freakish, bizarre, far-fetched, neurotic, exotic, outlandish, old-fashioned, out-of-the-way, abnormal, irrational, monstrous, anomalous, fearful.—*Ant.* common, ordinary, normal.

unusually, *a.* 1. [Not usually] oddly, curiously, peculiarly; see **especially 1.** 2. [To a marked degree] extraordinarily, remarkably, surprisingly; see **very.**

unveil, *v.* uncover, reveal, make known; see **expose 1.**

unwanted, *a.* undesired, rejected, outcast; see **hated, unpopular.**

unwarranted, *a.* unjust, wrong, groundless; see **unfair 1.**

unwelcome, *a.* uninvited, unwished for, repellent; see **unpopular.**

unwholesome, *a.* unhealthful, toxic, dangerous; see **poisonous.**

unwieldy, *a.* awkward, clumsy, cumbersome; see **heavy 1.**

unwilling, *a.* backward, resistant, reluctant, recalcitrant, unenthusiastic, doubtful, wayward, unready, indisposed, disinclined, averse, opposed, against, contrary, indifferent, indocile, intractable, demurring, shrinking, flinching, hesitating, shy, slack, evasive, loath, shy of, malcontent, slow, remiss, grudging, unco-operative, contrary, against the grain.—*Ant.* ready, willing, eager.

unwillingly, *a.* grudgingly, resentfully, involuntarily; see **angrily.**

unwind, *v.* 1. [To undo] separate, loose, undo; see **unwrap.** 2. [To uncoil] untwist, unravel, untwine; see **free 1, loosen 2.** 3. [To relax] recline, get rid of one's tensions, calm down; see **relax.**

unwise, *a.* ill-considered, ill-advised, rash; see **stupid 1.**

unwitting, *a.* chance, inadvertent, accidental; see **aimless.**

unwittingly, *a.* ignorantly, in ignorance, without knowledge *or* awareness; see **unconsciously.**

unworthy, *a.* undeserving, reprehensible, contemptible; see **offensive 2.**

unwrap, *v.* untie, undo, unpack, take out of wrappings, unroll, disclose, free, uncover, strip, lay bare, divest, dismantle, peel, husk, shuck, flay, expose, lay open, unclothe, denude.—*Ant.* wrap, pack, cover.

unzip, *v.* unfasten, undo, free; see **open 3.**

up, *a.* and *prep.* 1. [Situated above] at the top of, at the crest of, at the summit of, at the apex of, nearer the top of, nearer the head of, nearer the source of.—*Ant.* down, nearer the bottom of, farther from the head of. 2. [Moving from the earth] upward, uphill, skyward, heavenward, away from the center of gravity, perpendicularly, into the air, higher, away from the earth. 3. [Expired] lapsed, elapsed, run out, terminated, invalid, ended, come to a term, outdated, exhausted, finished, done. 4. [Happening] under consideration, being scrutinized, moot, live, current, pertinent, timely, relevant, pressing, urgent. 5. [Next] after, in order, prospective; see **following.**

up, *v.* elevate, raise up, boost; see **increase.**

up and around, *a.* improved, improving, getting better; see **well 1.**

up and coming, *a.* industrious, prospering, alert; see **active 2.**

upbringing, *n.* rearing, bringing up, instruction; see **childhood, training.**

upcoming, *a.* expected, future, imminent; see **forthcoming.**

update, *v.* modernize, bring up to date, refresh; see **renew 1.**

*up for grabs, *a.* ready, open to applications, not allocated; see **free 4.**

upheaval, *n.* outburst, explosion, eruption; see **outbreak 1.**

upheld, *a.* supported, maintained, advanced; see **backed 2.**

uphill, *a.* up, toward the summit, toward the crest, skyward, ascending, climbing.—*Ant.* down, downhill, descending.

uphold, *v.* 1. [To hold up] brace, buttress, prop; see **support 1.** 2. [To maintain] confirm, sustain, back up; see **support 2.**

up in arms, *a.* agitated, alarmed, riotous; see **excited, rebellious.**

up in the air, *a.* undecided, confused, uncertain; see **uncertain 2.**

upkeep, *n.* 1. [Maintenance] conservation, subsistence, repair; see **care 1.** 2. [Cost of maintenance] expense(s), outlay, expenditure; see **price.**

upon, *a.* and *prep.* 1. [On] on top of, in, attached to, visible on, against, affixed to, above, next to, located at, superimposed, above. 2. [At the time of] consequent to, beginning with, at the occurrence of; see **simultaneous.**

upper, *a.* top, topmost, uppermost, above, higher, more elevated, loftier, overhead.—*Ant.* under, lower, bottom.

upper-class, *a.* highbred, wellborn, genteel; see **noble 3.**

upper hand, *n.* sway, dominion, superiority; see **advantage.**

upright, *a.* 1. [Vertical] erect, perpendicular, on end; see **straight 1.** 2. [Honorable] straightforward, honest, fair; see **honest 1.**

uprising, *n.* rebellion, riot, upheaval; see **revolution 2.**

uproar, *n.* babble, confusion, turmoil, clamor, disturbance, tumult, din, racket, clatter, hubbub, fracas, clangor, jangle, bustle, bickering, discord, row.

uproot, *v.* tear up by the roots, pull up, weed out; see **remove 1.**

ups and downs, *n.* troubles, complications, uncertainties; see **difficulty 1, 2.**

upset, *a.* disconcerted, amazed, shocked; see **confused 2.**

upset, *n.* overthrow, destruction, reversion; see **defeat.**

upset, *v.* 1. [To turn over] overturn, upturn, subvert, turn bottom-side up, turn inside out, upend, reverse, keel over, overset, topple, tip over, turn topsy-turvy, over-balance, invert, capsize, tilt, pitch over, overthrow.—*Ant.* stand, erect, elevate. 2. [To disturb] agitate, fluster, perturb; see **bother 2.** 3. [To beat] conquer, outplay, overpower; see **defeat 2, 3.**

upside-down, *a.* topsy-turvy, tangled, bottomside up, inverted, rear-end foremost, backward, the wrong way, wrong-side uppermost, cart-before-the-horse, ***heels-over-head.**—*Ant.* upright, right-side up, **steady.**

upstairs, *a.* in the upper story, above, up the steps; see **upper.**

upstairs, *n.* the upper story, the penthouse, the rooms above the ground floor; see **floor 2.**

upstanding, *a.* honorable, upright, straightforward; see **honest 1.**

upswing, *n.* growth, boom, acceleration; see **increase 1.**

*up tight, *a.* 1. [Troubled] worried, concerned, apprehensive; see **troubled 1, 2.** [Cautious] conventional, strict, old-fashioned; see **conservative.**

up to, *prep.* 1. [Until] before, preceding, previous; see **until.** 2. [Against] contrary to, opposing; in disagreement with; see **against 1.** 3. [Dependent upon] assigned to, expected of, enjoined upon; see **depending on.**

up-to-date, *a.* in vogue, in fashion, fashionable, conventional, stylish, modern, modernistic, streamlined, popular, faddish, brand new, current, according to the prevailing taste, modish, the latest, all the rage.

up to one's ears *or* **neck in** *or* **with,** *a.* occupied, busy (with), absorbed (in); see **busy 1.**

upturned, *a.* tilted, tipped, upside-down, inclined, sloped, slanted, expectant, upward looking, turned up, extended.

upward, *a.* up, higher, skyward, in the air, uphill, away from the earth, up the slope, on an incline, up north.

urban, *a.* 1. [Concerning city government] city, metropolitan, civil; see **public 2.** 2. [Concerning city living] (big) city, civic, municipal, metropolitan, within the city limits, inner-city, downtown, zoned, planned, business-district, civil, nonrural, ghetto, shopping, residential, apartment-dwelling.

urban renewal, *n.* rebuilding the inner city, modernization, bringing up to date; see **improvement 2.**

urge, *v.* 1. [To present favorably] favor, further, support; see **approve.** 2. [To induce] charge, beg, plead, adjure, influence, beseech, implore, ask, command, entreat, desire, request, press, inveigle, talk into, incite, move, allure, tempt, attract, influence, prompt, instigate, exhort, advise, solicit, inspire, stimulate, conjure, coax, wheedle, maneuver, draw, put up to, prevail upon.—*Ant.* restrain, deter, discourage. 3. [To drive] compel, drive, propel, impel, force, coerce, constrain, press, push, make, oblige, goad, prod, spur.—*Ant.* deny, block, withhold.

urged, *a.* 1. [Supported] favored, furthered, proposed; see **backed** 2. 2. [Pressed] begged, charged, implored, asked, commanded, entreated, desired, requested, inveigled, talked into, incited, moved, motivated, allured, lured, tempted, seduced, attracted, influenced, prompted, instigated, exhorted, advised, solicited, inspired, whipped up, stimulated, coaxed, wheedled, maneuvered, put up to, prevailed upon, compelled, obliged, propelled, driven, induced, impelled, coerced, forced, constrained.

urgency, *n.* exigency, need, seriousness; see **importance, necessity** 3.

urgent, *a.* 1. [Of immediate importance] pressing, critical, necessary, imperative, important, indispensable, momentous, wanted, required, called for, demanded, salient, chief, paramount, essential, primary, vital, principal, absorbing, all-absorbing, not to be delayed, crucial, instant, leading, capital, overruling, foremost, exigent, crying. 2. [Insistent] compelling, persuasive, imperious, solemn, grave, weighty, impressive, earnest, importunate, clamorous, hasty, breathless, precipitate, frantic, impetuous, imperative, convincing, beseeching, seductive, commanding, imploring, eager, zealous, anxious, moving, excited, impulsive, vigorous, enthusiastic, overpowering, masterful.

urgently, *a.* 1. [Critically] pressingly, instantly, imperatively, necessarily, indispensably, momently, requisitely, essentially, primarily, crucially, capitally. 2. [Insistently] compellingly, persuasively, solemnly, gravely, weightily, impressively, earnestly, importunately, clamorously, hastily, breathlessly, precipitately, frantically, impetuously, convincingly, beseechingly, seductively, commandingly, imploringly, eagerly, anxious, zealously, movingly, emotionally, excitedly, impulsively, vigorously, irresistibly, enthusiastically, overpoweringly, masterfully, compulsively.

urging, *n.* begging, persuading, pleading; see **request.**

urinate, *v.* go to the restroom *or* bathroom, have to go, excrete, use the urinal *or* bedpan, make water, *tinkle, *wizz, *peepee, *go to the little boy's *or* girl's room.

usable, *a.* available, at hand, useful, unused, good, serviceable, applicable, ready, subservient, helpful, utile, valuable, beneficial, profitable, advantageous, fit, desirable, efficacious, instrumental, fitting, comfortable, suitable, proper, practical, convenient.—*Ant.* **useless,** worthless, no good.

usage, *n.* 1. [Custom] practice, rule, habit; see **use** 1. 2. [Accepted language] good usage, grammatical usage, approved diction; see **grammar.**

use, *n.* 1. [The act of using] practice, employment, application, usage, appliance, effecting, manner, adoption, utilization, manipulation, bringing to bear, management, handling, performance, conduct, recourse, resort, exercise, treatment, method, technique, control, resolution, realization, **association.**—*Ant.* **neglect,** disuse, dismissal. 2. [The state of being useful] utility, usefulness, employment, application, value, advantage, excellence, helpfulness, convenience, suitability, expedience, aid, serviceability, merit, profit, practicability, practicality, fitness, subservience, effectiveness, applicability.

use, *v.* [To make use of] avail oneself of, employ, put to use, exercise, exert, put forth, utilize, apply, bring to bear, practice, play on, do with, draw on, adopt, take advantage of, make do, accept, work, put in practice, relate, make with, put to work, make shift with.—*Ant.* **discard,** reject, refuse. 2. [To make a practice of; *now used principally in the past tense*] be accustomed to, practice, adapt, conform, habituate, regulate, suit, familiarize, attune. 3. [To behave toward] deal with, handle, bear oneself toward; see **manage** 1.

used, *a.* 1. [Employed] put to use, utilized, applied, adopted, adapted, accepted, put in service, practiced, turned to account.—*Ant.* **discarded,** rejected, unused. 2. [Accustomed] practiced, customary, suited; see **habitual.** 3. [Secondhand] castoff, depreciated, repossessed; see **old** 2.

useful, *a.* valuable, beneficial, serviceable; see **helpful** 1.

usefulness, *n.* application, value, advantage, excellence, convenience, suitability, range, versatility, helpfulness, utility, serviceability, merit, profitableness, practicality, practicability, fitness, propriety, adaptability; see also **use** 2.

useless, *a.* 1. [Unserviceable] worthless, unusable, ineffectual, expendable, incompetent, of no use, ineffective, inoperative, dysfunctional, counterproductive, inefficient, *no damn good.—*Ant.* efficient, usable, operative. 2. [Futile] vain, unavailing, fruitless; see hopeless.

use up *v.* consume, exhaust, squander; see **spend** 1, **waste** 1, 2.

using, *a.* employing, utilizing, applying, adopting, taking advantage of, accepting, working, practicing, manipulating, controlling, putting in service, trying out, testing, proving, wearing out.

usual, *a.* 1. [Ordinary] general, frequent, normal; see **common** 1. 2. [Habitual] wonted, accustomed, customary; see **conventional** 1.

usually, *a.* ordinarily, customarily, habitually; see **regularly.**

utensils, *n.* [Implements; *especially for the kitchen*] equipment, tools, appliances, conveniences, ware(s); see also **tool** 1. Kitchen utensils include the following—sieve, egg beater, knife, fork, spoon, measuring cup, grater, spatula, pancake turner, can opener, egg slicer, meat grinder, butcher knife, paring knife, pastry cutter, lemon squeezer, knife sharpener, coffee grinder, vegetable brush, pan scourer, frying pan, saucepan, cake pan, pie pan, roaster, bottle brush, dishpan, draining pan, sink strainer, dishmop, mixing bowl, pan lid, rolling pin, pastry board, coffee pot, bread pan, cookie sheet.

utilities, *n.* services, public utilities, conveniences, current necessities of modern life, household slaves. Utilities include the following—heat, light, power, gas, water, bus, street car, telephone, electricity, garbage disposal, sewage disposal.

utility, *n.* 1. [Usefulness] service, advantage, convenience; see **use** 2. 2. [Utility company] gas company, electricity company, water company; see **business** 4.

utilize, *v.* employ, appropriate, turn to account; see **use** 1.

utmost, *a.* ultimate, chief, entire, whole, full, unreserved, complete, unstinted, total, absolute, unlimited, unsparing, thorough, exhaustive, highest, maximum, most, top, undiminished, undivided, thoroughgoing, unmitigated, sheer, unqualified, unconditional, all-out.

utter, *a.* complete, total, thorough; see **absolute** 1.

utter, *v.* pronounce, talk, express, come out with, articulate, voice, whisper, enunciate, air, speak, tell, disclose, declare, say, assert, affirm, ejaculate, vocalize, proclaim, give tongue to, recite, blurt (out), let fall, announce, come out with.

utterance, *n.* declaration, saying, assertion, announcement, pronouncement, ejaculation, vociferation, talk, speech, query, expression, sentence, proclamation, recitation, spiel, rant, jargon, response, reply, oration.

uttered, *a.* asserted, expressed, announced; see **oral.**

utterly, *a.* wholly, thoroughly, entirely; see **completely.**

V

vacancy, *n.* **1.** [A vacated position] opening, vacated post, post without an incumbent, unfilled position, unheld office, job. **2.** [A vacated residence] empty house *or* room *or* apartment, tenantless house, uninhabited house, vacant house, unoccupied house, deserted house, house for rent *or* for sale.

vacant, *a.* **1.** [Without contents] devoid, void, unfilled; see **empty 1. 2.** [Without an occupant] unoccupied, untenanted, tenantless, uninhabited, idle, free, deserted, abandoned, without a resident, not lived in.—*Ant.* **inhabited,** occupied, tenanted.

vacate, *v.* go away, relinquish, depart; see **leave 1.**

vacation, *n.* respite, rest, recreation time, intermission, recess, nonterm, holiday, leave of absence, sabbatical, *time off.

vaccinate, *v.* inoculate, immunize, prevent, treat, mitigate, protect, inject, shoot.

vaccinated, *a.* immunized, inoculated, given (hypodermic) injections; see **protected.**

vaccination, *n.* **1.** [The act of administering vaccine] injection, inoculation, shots; see **treatment 2. 2.** [A result of vaccination, sense 1] protection, immunization, inoculation; see **immunity 2.**

vacuum, *n.* space, void, exhaustion; see **emptiness.**

vacuum cleaner, *n.* vacuum (sweeper), carpet sweeper, cleaning device; see **appliance.**

vagrant, *a.* **1.** [Having no home] roaming, itinerant, nomadic; see **traveling. 2.** [Having no occupation] begging, idling, prodigal, loafing, beachcombing, *panhandling, *bumming, *mooching. **3.** [Having no fixed course] wayward, capricious, erratic; see **aimless.**

vagrant, *n.* begger, idler, loafer; see **traveler.**

vague, *a.* **1.** [Not clearly expressed] indefinite, unintelligible, superficial; see **obscure 1. 2.** [Not clearly understood] uncertain, undetermined, unsure, doubtful, dubious, questionable, misunderstood, enigmatic, puzzling, inexplicable, unsettled, bewildering, perplexing, problematic.—*Ant.* **certain,** sure, positive. **3.** [Not clearly visible] dim, nebulous, dark; see **hazy.**

vaguely, *a.* uncertainly, unclearly, not clearly *or* certainly *or* reliably, hazily, foggily, confusedly, shiftily, unreliably, dubiously, eccentrically, unsurely, ille-

gally, evasively, unpredictably, without (clear) outlines, incapable of being fixed *or* determined *or* outlined *or* pinned down.

vagueness, *n.* ambiguity, obscurity, double entendre; see **confusion, uncertainty 1, 2.**

vain, *a.* **1.** [Possessing unwarranted self-esteem] proud, arrogant, haughty; see **egotistic. 2.** [Useless] worthless, unavailing, profitless; see **futile, useless 1.**

valentine, *n.* sentimental letter, St. Valentine's Day greeting, love verse; see also **letter 2.**

valiant, *a.* courageous, unafraid, dauntless; see **brave.**

valiantly, *a.* courageously, boldly, fearlessly; see **bravely.**

valid, *a.* **1.** [Capable of proof] sound, cogent, logical, conclusive, solid, well-grounded, well-founded, tested, accurate, convincing, telling, correct, determinative, compelling, persuasive, potent, stringent, strong, ultimate, unanswerable, irrefutable.—*Ant.* **wrong,** erring, misleading. **2.** [Genuine] true, original, factual, real, actual, pure, uncorrupted, authentic, confirmed, authoritative, trustworthy, credible, attested, efficient, legitimate, adequate, substantial, proved *or* proven, unadulterated.—*Ant.* **false,** fictitious, counterfeit.

validate, *v.* confirm, sanction, legalize; see **approve.**

validity, *n.* soundness, efficacy, gravity; see **originality.**

valley, *n.* vale, glen, canyon, depression, trough, notch, channel, lowland, river valley, stream valley, plain, dell, valley floor, coulee, dale, river bottom; see also **gap, ravine.**—*Ant.* **mountain,** ridge, hilltop.

valor, *n.* bravery, heroism, boldness; see **courage.**

valuable, *a.* saleable, marketable, in demand, high-priced, commanding a good price, costly, expensive, dear, of value, in great demand, hardly obtainable, scarce, without price, *good as gold.—*Ant.* **cheap,** unsaleable, unmarketable.

value, *n.* **1.** [Monetary value] price, expense, cost, profit, value in exchange, equivalent, rate, amount, market price, charge, face value, assessment, appraisal. **2.** [The quality of being desirable] use, benefit, advantage; see sense **3. 3.** [Quality] worth, merit, significance, consequence, goodness, condition, state, excellence, distinction, desirability, grade, finish, perfection, eminence, superiority, advantage, power, regard, importance, mark, caliber, repute. 4. [Precise signification] significance, force, sense; see **meaning**.

value, v. 1. [To believe to be valuable] esteem, prize, appreciate; see **admire**. 2. [To set a price upon] estimate, reckon, assess, appraise, fix the price of, place a value on, assay, rate, figure, compute, evaluate, judge, repute, consider, enumerate, account, charge, levy, ascertain, price.

valued, a. evaluated, appraised, charged; see **marked 2**.

valve, n. flap, lid, plug; see also **pipe 1**. Valves include the following–automatic, alarm, check, cutoff, side, overhead, dry-pipe, gate, lift, piston, rocking, safety, slide, throttle, sleeve, intake, exhaust, butterfly.

vandal, n. despoiler, rapist, thief; see **pirate**.

vandalism, n. piracy, demolition, spoilation; see **destruction 1**.

vanish, v. fade (out), go away, dissolve; see **disappear**.

vanishing, a. disappearing, going, fading; see **hazy 1**.

vanity, n. ostentation, display, show, self-love, self-glorification, self-applause, pretension, vainglory, conceitedness, affection, foppishness, complacency, smugness.

vanquish, v. conquer, overcome, subdue; see **defeat 2, 3**.

vapor, n. mist, steam, condensation, smog, exhalation, breath, fog, gas, haze, smoke.

vaporize, v. exhale, sublimate, volatize; see **evaporate**.

variable, a. inconstant, mutable, unsteady; see **irregular 1, 4**.

variance, n. change, fluctuations, deviation; see **variation 2**.

variation, n. 1. [Change] modification, alteration, mutation; see **change 1**. 2. [Disparity] inequality, difference, dissimilarity, distinction, disproportion, exception, contrast, contradistinction, unconformity, irregularity, aberration, abnormality, disparity.–Ant. **similarity**, conformity, likeness.

varied, a. discrete, different, diverse; see **mixed 1, various**.

variety, n. 1. [Quality or state of being diverse] diversity, change, diversification, difference, variance, medley, mixture, miscellany, disparateness, divergency, variation, incongruity, fluctuation, shift, change, modification, departure, many-sidedness, unlikeness. 2. [Sort] kind, class, division, species, genus, race, tribe, family, assortment, type, stripe, nature, ilk, character, description, rank, grade, category, classification, quality.–Ant. **equality**, equalness, similarity.

various, a. different, disparate, dissimilar, diverse, diversified, variegated, varicolored, many-sided, several, manifold, numerous, unlike, many, sundry, divers, variable, changeable, inconstant, uncertain, of any kind, all manner of, of every description, distinct; see also **multiple 1**.–Ant. **alike**, undiversified, identical.

variously, a. varyingly, inconsistently, unpredictably; see **differently**.

varnish, v. finish, paint, shellac, lacquer, wax, size, enamel, japan, surface, coat, luster, polish, gloss, adorn, refinish, glaze, gloss over.–Ant. **expose**, remove the finish, give a natural finish.

vary, v. dissent, diverge, differ, deviate, digress, swerve, depart, fluctuate, alternate, diverge from, be distinguished from, range, be inconstant, mutate, be uncertain.–Ant. **remain**, be steady, hold.

varying, a. diverse, differing, diverging; see **changing**.

vase, n. vessel, urn, jar, pottery, porcelain, receptacle, flower holder, ornament.

vast, a. 1. [Large] huge, enormous, immense; see **large 1**. 2. [Extensive] broad, far-flung, wide, spacious, expansive, spread-out, ample, far-reaching, widespread, comprehensive, detailed, all-inclusive, astronomical, prolonged, stretched out, expanded. –Ant. **narrow**, limited, confined.

vastness, n. hugeness, extent, enormity; see **expanse, size 2**.

vat, n. vessel, tub, barrel; see also **container**.

vault, n. 1. [A place for the dead] tomb, crypt, grave; see **monument 1**. 2. [A place for preserving valuables] safe-deposit box, time vault, burglar-proof safe; see **safe**.

veal, n. calf, bob veal, baby beef; see also **meat**. Cuts of veal include the following–chops, leg, loin, rack, neck, breast, chuck. Veal dishes include the following–(breaded) veal cutlet, veal stew, calf's liver, Wiener schnitzel, veal Parmigiano, (veal) scallopini.

veer, v. swerve, bend, divert; see **turn 1, 2, 3**.

vegetable, a. plantlike, herblike, floral, blooming, blossoming, growing, flourishing.

vegetable, n. plant, herbaceous plant, herb, edible root. Common vegetables include the following–cabbage, potato, turnip, bean, carrot, pea, celery, lettuce, parsnip, spinach, squash, tomato, pumpkin, asparagus, onion, corn, lentil, leek, garlic, radish, cucumber, artichoke, egg-plant, beet, scallion, pepper, okra, kohl-rabi, parsley, chard, rhubarb, cauli-flower, Brussels sprouts, broccoli, endive, Chinese cabbage, (water) cress, rutabaga.

vegetate, v. 1. [To germinate] sprout, bud, blossom; see **bloom, grow** 1. 2. [To stagnate] hibernate, stagnate, languish; see **weaken** 1.

vegetation, n. plants, plant growth, trees, shrubs, saplings, flowers, wild flowers, grasses, herbage, herbs, pasturage, weeds, vegetables, crops.

vehicle, n. Vehicles include the following—carriage, buggy, wagon, sleigh, cart, motor car, jeep, rover, automobile, truck, van, motorcycle, taxicab, railroad car, cab, hack, taxi.

veil, n. 1. [A thin fabric] scarf, kerchief, mask; see **web.** 2. [A curtain] screen, cover, shade; see **curtain.**

vein, n. 1. [A fissure] cleft, aperture, opening, channel, cavity, crack, cranny, rift, chink, break, breach, slit, crevice, flaw, rupture. 2. [A persistent quality] strain, humor, mood, temper, tang, spice, dash; see also **characteristic, temperament.** 3. [A blood duct leading to the heart] Important veins include the following—jugular, pulmonary, subclavian, portal, iliac, hepatic, renal.

velocity, n. quickness, rapidity, impetus; see **speed.**

velvet, a. silken, shining, plushy; see also **soft** 2.

velvet, n. cotton velvet, rayon, corduroy; see **goods.**

veneer, n. surface, exterior, covering; see **cover** 1.

venerable, a. revered, old, aged, ancient, hoary, reverenced, honored, honorable, noble, august, grand, esteemed, respected, dignified, imposing, grave, serious, sage, wise, philosophical, experienced.—*Ant.* **inexperienced,** callow, raw.

venerate, v. revere, reverence, adore; see **love** 1, **worship.**

veneration, n. respect, adoration, awe; see **reverence, worship** 1.

vengeance, n. retribution, return, retaliation; see **revenge** 1.

vengeful, a. spiteful, revengeful, rancorous; see **cruel.**

venom, n. poison, virus, toxin, bane, microbe, contagion, infection.

vent, n. ventilator, vent hole, venting hole, ventiduct, liquid-vent, vent faucet, molding, touchhole, drain, smoke hole, flue, aperture.

vent, v. let out, drive out, discharge; see **free.**

ventilate, v. freshen, let in fresh air, circulate fresh air, vent, air cool, air out, free, oxygenate; see also **air.**

ventilated, a. aired (out), having (adequate) ventilation, not close *or* closed (up); see **air** 1, **cool** 1, **open** 1.

ventilation, n. airing, purifying, oxygenating, freshening, opening windows, changing air, circulating air, air-conditioning.

venture, n. adventure, risk, hazard, peril, stake, chance, speculation, dare, experiment, trial, attempt, test, gamble, undertaking, enterprise, investment, leap in the dark, *plunge, *flyer, *crack, *fling.

venture, v. attempt, experiment, try out; see **try** 1.

ventured, a. risked, chanced, dared; see **done** 1.

verb, n. Verbs include the following—finite, active, neuter, passive, transitive, intransitive, media, modal, auxiliary, linking, reciprocal, copulative, reflexive, strong, weak, regular, irregular.

verbal, a. told, unwritten, lingual; see **oral, spoken.**

verbal, n. Verbals in English include the following—infinitive, gerund, participle, gerundive, verbal noun, present participle, verbal adjective, past participle, verbal phrase, absolute *or* independent construction.

verbally, a. orally, by word of mouth, person-to-person; see **spoken.**

verbatim, a. exactly, literatim, to the letter; see **literally.**

verdict, n. judgment, finding, decision, answer, opinion, sentence, determination, decree, conclusion, deduction, adjudication, arbitrament.

verge, n. edge, brink, terminus; see **boundary.**

verge, v. end, edge, touch; see **approach** 2.

verification, n. verifying, attestation, affirmation; see **confirmation** 1.

verify, v. establish, substantiate, authenticate, prove, check, test, validate, settle, corroborate, confirm.

veritable, a. authentic, true, real; see **genuine** 1.

vermin, n. flea, louse, mite; see also **insect.**

versatile, a. many-sided, adaptable, dexterous, varied, ready, clever, handy, talented, gifted, adroit, resourceful, ingenious, accomplished; see **able.**

versatility, a. flexibility, utility, adjustability; see **adaptability.**

verse, n. 1. [Composition in poetic form] poetry, metrical composition, versification, stanza, rhyme, lyric, sonnet, ode, heroic verse, dramatic poetry, blank verse, free verse. 2. [A unit of verse, sense 1] line, verse, stanza, stave, strophe, antistrophe, hemistich, distich, quatrain.

version, *n*. 1. [One of various accounts] report, account, tale; see **story**. 2. [A translation] paraphrase, redaction, transcription; see **translation**.

vertebrae, *n*. spine, spinal column, backbone, chine. Parts of the vertebra include the following—atlas, axis, cervical, thoracic, lumbar, caudal, disk, spinous process, neural arch, anterior *and* posterior zygapophysis, transverse process.

vertical, *a*. perpendicular, upright, on end; see **straight** 1.

very, *a*. extremely, exceedingly, greatly, acutely, indispensably, just so, surprisingly, astonishingly, incredibly, wonderfully, particularly, certainly, positively, emphatically, really, truly, pretty, decidedly, pressingly, notably, uncommonly, extraordinarily, prodigiously, highly, substantially, dearly, amply, vastly, extensively, noticeably, conspicuously, largely, considerably, hugely, excessively, imperatively, markedly, enormously, sizeably, materially, immensely, tremendously, superlatively, remarkably, unusually, immoderately, quite, indeed, somewhat, rather, simply, intensely, urgently, exceptionally, severely, seriously, in a great measure, to a great degree, beyond compare, on a large scale, ever so, beyond measure, by far, in the extreme, in a marked degree, to a great extent, without restraint, more or less, in part, infinitely, very much, *real, right, pretty, *awfully, *good and, *powerful, *powerfully, *hell of a, *precious, *so, to a fault, a bit of, *no end.

vessel, *n*. 1. [A container] pitcher, urn, kettle; see **container**. 2. [A ship] boat, craft, bark; see **ship**. 3. [A duct; *especially for blood*] blood vessel, artery, capillary; see **vein** 2.

vest, *n*. waistcoat, jacket, garment; see **clothes**.

vestige, *n*. trace, remains, scrap; see **remainder**.

veteran, *n*. 1. [An experienced person] master, one long in service, old hand, one of the old guard, *old bird, *old dog, *old timer.—*Ant*. amateur, new man, youngster. 2. [An experienced soldier] ex-soldier, seasoned campaigner, ex-service man, re-enlisted man, old soldier, *war horse, vet, *ex-G.I.

veterinarian, *n*. animal specialist, vet, animal doctor; see **doctor**.

veto, *n*. prohibition, declination, negative; see **denial, refusal**.

veto, *v*. interdict, prohibit, decline; see **deny, refuse**.

vetoed, *a*. declined, rejected, disapproved; see **no, refused**.

via, *prep*. by way of, by the route passing through, on the way to, through

the medium of; see also **by** 2, **through** 4.

vibrant, *a*. energetic, vigorous, lively; see **active** 1.

vibrate, *v*. 1. [To quiver] fluctuate, flutter, waver; see **wave** 3. 2. [To sound] echo, resound, reverberate; see **sound** 1.

vibration, *n*. quake, wavering, vacillation, fluctuation, oscillation, quiver, shake; see also **wave** 3.

vice, *n*. corruption, iniquity, wickedness; see **evil** 1.

vice versa, *a*. conversely, in reverse, the other way round, turn about, about face, in opposite manner, far from it, on the contrary, in reverse.

vicinity, *n*. proximity, nearness, neighborhood; see **environment, region** 1.

vicious, *a*. bad, debased, base, impious, profligate, demoralized, faulty, vile, foul, impure, lewd, indecent, licentious, libidinous; see also **bad** 1.—*Ant*. noble, **pure**, virtuous.

vicious circle, *n*. chain of events, cause and effect, interreliant problems; see **difficulty** 1. 2.

viciously, *a*. cruelly, spitefully, harmfully; see **brutally, wrongly**.

victim, *n*. prey, sacrifice, immolation, sufferer, wretch, quarry, game, hunted, offering, scapegoat, martyr.

victimize, *v*. cheat, swindle, dupe, trick, fool; see **deceive**.

victor, *n*. conqueror, champion, prize winner; see **winner**.

victorious, *a*. winning, triumphant, mastering; see **successful**.

victory, *n*. conquest, mastery, subjugation, overcoming, overthrow, master stroke, lucky stroke, winning, gaining, defeating, subduing, destruction, killing, knockout, pushover.

vie, *v*. contend, strive, rival; see **compete**.

view, *n*. glimpse, look, panorama, aspect, show, appearance, prospect, distance, opening, stretch, outlook, way, extended view, long view, avenue, contour, outline, scene, spectacle. —**in view**, visible, in sight, not out of sight, perceptible, perceivable; see **obvious** 1. —**on view**, displayed, on display, exposed; see **shown** 1. —**with a view to**, in order that *or* to, so that, anticipating; see **to** 4.

view, *v*. observe, survey, inspect; see **see** 1.

viewer, *n*. spectator, watcher, onlooker; see **observer**.

viewpoint, *n*. point of view, perspective, standpoint, angle, slant, position, stand, aspect, light, respect, attitude, ground, point of observation, outlook.

vigor, *n*. 1. [Activity] exercise, action,

energy; see **vitality**. 2. [Health] well-being, endurance, vitality; see **health**.

vigorous, a. 1. [Done with vigor] energetic, lively, brisk; see **active**. 2. [Forceful] powerful, strong, potent; see **effective**.

vigorously, a. energetically, alertly, eagerly, quickly, nimbly, agilely, strenuously, resolutely, firmly, forcibly, forcefully, urgently, unfalteringly, purposefully, actively, boldly, adventurously, zealously, lustily, robustly, stoutly, hardily, wholeheartedly, earnestly, warmly, fervidly, passionately, sincerely, devoutly, appreciatively, with heart and soul, healthily, fearlessly, mightily, decidedly, by brute force, *like blazes; see also **powerfully**.—*Ant.* calmly, aimlessly, slowly.

vile, a. sordid, corrupt, debased; see **shameful** 1, 2.

village, n. hamlet, crossroads town, small town; see **town** 1.

villain, n. scoundrel, knave, brute; see **criminal**.

vindicate, v. 1. [To clear] acquit, free, absolve; see **excuse**. 2. [To justify] prove, bear out, warrant; see **prove**.

vindication, n. defense, acquittal, clearance; see **proof** 1.

vindictive, a. revengeful, resentful, spiteful; see **cruel**.

vine, n. creeper, climbing plant, creeping plant, trailing plant, stem climber, leaf climber, tendril climber; see also **plant**. Vines include the following—grapevine, honeysuckle, trumpet vine, English ivy, Virginia creeper, poison ivy, blackberry, raspberry, briar, rambler, teaberry, dewberry, morning-glory, hopvine, bougainvillea, jasmine, pea vine, watermelon, canteloupe, cucumber, wild cucumber, passion flower.

violate, v. 1. [To transgress] outrage, disrupt, infringe, break, tamper (with); see also **meddle** 1, 2. 2. [To rape] dishonor, profane, defile, ravish.

violation, n. infringement, negligence, misbehavior, nonobservance, violating, shattering, transgressing, (forcible) trespass, trespassing, contravention, breach, breaking, rupture, flouting; see also **crime**.

violence, n. 1. [Violent disturbance] rampage, tumult, disorder, clash, onslaught, struggle; see also **confusion**, **disturbance** 2, **uproar**. 2. [Violent conduct] fury, force, vehemence, frenzy, savagery; see also **intensity**.

violent, a. strong, powerful, forceful, forcible, rough, mighty, great, potent, coercive, furious, mad, savage, fierce, passionate, splitting, vehement, frenzied, demoniac, frantic, fuming, enraged, disturbed, agitated, impassioned, impetuous, urgent, maddened, aroused, inflamed, distraught, infatuated, hysterical, great, vehement, extreme, unusual, destructible, murderous, homicidal, rampageous.—*Ant.* calm, gentle, quiet.

violently, a. destructively, forcibly, forcefully, combatively, powerfully, strongly, coercively, flagrantly, outrageously, overwhelmingly, compellingly, disturbingly, turbulently, stormily, ruinously, stubbornly, with violence, in a violent manner, abruptly, noisily, with a vengeance, like fury, rebelliously, riotously, furiously, angrily, vehemently, frantically, fiercely, hysterically, hilariously, passionately, urgently, madly, frenziedly, ardently, enthusiastically, impulsively.—*Ant.* mildly, gently, undisturbedly.

violet, a. lavender, mauve, purplish; see **purple**.

violin, n. fiddle, viola, Stradivarius; see **musical instrument**.

*****V.I.P.**, n. very important person, notable, important figure; see **leader** 2.

virgin, n. Madonna, Blessed Virgin Mary, Queen of Saints, Our Lady, Mother of God, Mary, the Queen of Heaven, Queen of Angels, Star of the Sea, The Virgin Mother, Immaculate Conception, Immaculate Mary; see also **saint** 1.

virgin, a. 1. [Chaste] pure, modest, virginal; see **chaste**. 2. [Original or natural] undisturbed, new, untamed; see also **natural** 3, **original** 1, 3.

virginity, n. maidenhood, girlhood, celibacy; see **virtue** 1.

virile, a. masculine, potent, manlike; see **male**, **manly**.

virility, n. potency, masculinity, manliness; see **manhood** 2.

virtually, a. for all practical purposes, practically, implicitly; see **essentially**.

virtue, n. 1. [Moral excellence] ideal, ethic, morality, goodness, righteousness, uprightness, ethical conduct, good thing, respectability, rectitude, honor, honesty, candor, merit, fineness, character, excellence, value, chastity, quality, worth, kindness, innocence, generosity, trustworthiness, faithfulness, consideration, justice, prudence, temperance, fortitude, faith, hope, charity *or* love.—*Ant.* evil, immorality, depravity. 2. [An individual excellence] quality, characteristic, attribute, temper, way, trait, feature, accomplishment, achievement, property, distinction, capacity, power.—*Ant.* lack, inability, incapacity. 3. [Probity in sexual conduct] virginity, purity, decency; see **chastity**. —**by virtue of**, on (the) grounds of, because of, looking toward; see **because**.

virtuous, *a.* good, upright, moral; see honest 1, worthy.

virus, *n.* 1. [An infection] sickness, communicability, illness; see illness 2. 2. [An organism] micro-organism, bacillus, phage; see germ.

vise, *n.* clamp, holder, universal vise; see also fastener.

visibility, *n.* perceptibility, discernibility, distinctness; see clarity.

visible, *a.* apparent, evident, noticeable; see obvious 1.

vision, *n.* 1. [The faculty of sight] sight, perception, perceiving, range of view, optics, eyesight. 2. [Understanding] foresight, discernment, breadth of view, insight, penetration, intuition, divination, astuteness, keenness, foreknowledge, prescience, farsightedness. 3. [Something seen through powers of the mind] imagination, poetic insight, fancy, fantasy, image, concept, conception, ideality, idea; see also thought 1, 2. 4. [Something seen because of an abnormality] revelation, trance, ecstasy, phantom, apparition, ghost, wraith, specter, apocalypse, nightmare, spirit, warlock; see also illusion 1.

visionary, *a.* 1. [Impractical] ideal, romantic, utopian; see impractical. 2. [Imaginary] chimerical, delusory, dreamy; see imaginary.

visit, *n.* social call, call, appointment, interview, formal call, talk, evening, stay, weekend, holiday, visitation.

visit, *v.* stay, *or* dwell with, stop with *or* by, call at *or* on *or* upon, come around, be the guest of, make a visit, sojourn awhile, revisit, make one's compliments to, look in on, visit with, call for, stop off *or* in *or* over, have an appointment (with), pay a visit (to), tour, take in, drop in on, hit, *look around, look up, go over to, look in, drop over, pop in, have a date.

visitor, *n.* caller, visitant, official inspector; see guest.

visual, *a.* seen, optic, of the vision; see obvious 1.

visualize, *v.* see in the mind's eye, picture mentally, conceive; see imagine.

vital, *a.* 1. [Necessary] essential, indispensable, requisite; see necessary. 2. [Alive] live, animate, animated; see alive. 3. [Vigorous] lively, energetic, lusty; see active 1.

vitality, *n.* life, liveliness, animation, vim, vigor, intensity, continuity, endurance, energy, spirit, ardor, audacity, spunk, fervor, verve, venturesomeness.

vitals, *n.* organs, intestines, entrails; see insides.

vitamin, *n.* Types of vitamins include the following—vitamin A, vitamin B complex (vitamin B_1, vitamin B_2,

vitamin B_6, vitamin B_{12}), vitamin C, vitamin D (vitamin D_1, vitamin D_2), vitamin E, vitamin K (vitamin K_1, vitamin K_2), vitamin L_1, vitamin L_2, vitamin P, riboflavin, lacoflavin, flavin, nicotine acid, Betalin compound, ascorbic acid, thiamin, thiamine hydrochloride, thiamine chloride, betataxin, betalin, niacinamide, niacin, calcium pantothenate, pantothenic acid, nicotinamide, pyridoxine, tocopherol; see also medicine 2.

vivid, *a.* 1. [Brilliant] shining, rich, glowing; see bright 1. 2. [Distinct] strong, vigorous, lucid; see clear 2, definite 2.

vividly, *a.* glowingly, strikingly, flamingly; see brightly.

vocabulary, *n.* wordbook, dictionary, lexicon, thesaurus, stock of words, glossary, scientific vocabulary, literary vocabulary, *word-hoard; see also diction.

vocal, *a.* 1. [Verbal] expressed, uttered, voiced; see oral, spoken. 2. [Produced by the voice; *said especially of music*] sung, scored for voice, vocalized; see musical 1.

vocalist, *n.* chorister, songstress, caroler; see musician, singer.

vocation, *n.* calling, mission, pursuit; see profession 1.

voice, *n.* 1. [A vocal sound] speech, sound, call, cry, utterance, tongue, whistle, moan, groan, song, yell, hail, howl, yowl, bark, whine, whimper, mutter, murmur, shout, bleat, bray, neigh, whinny, roar, trumpet, cluck, honk, meow, hiss, quack; see also noise 1.—*Ant.* silence, dumbness, deaf-mutism. 2. [Approval or opinion] decision, conclusion, assent, negation, approval, recommendation, wish, view; see also choice, opinion 1. —with one voice, all together, by unanimous vote, without dissent; see unanimously.

voice, *v.* assert, cry, sound; see talk 1, tell 1.

voiced, *a.* vocal, sonant, sounded; see oral, spoken.

void, *a.* barren, sterile, fruitless, meaningless, useless, invalid, vain, voided, unconfirmed, unratified, null and void, worthless, unsanctioned, set aside, avoided, forceless, voted out, ineffectual, ineffective, voidable.—*Ant.* valid, in force, used.

volatile, *a.* 1. [Having the qualities of a gas] gaseous, airy, buoyant; see light 5. 2. [Having a sprightly temperament] lively, vivacious, playful; see active.

volley, *n.* round, discharge, barrage; see fire 2.

voltage, *n.* electric potential, potential difference, charge; see energy 2.

volume, *n.* 1. [Quantity] bulk, mass, amount; see extent, size 2. 2. [Contents] cubical, size, dimensions; see **capacity**. 3. [A book] printed document, tome, pamphlet; see **book**. 4. [Degree of sound] loudness, amplification, strength; see **sound 2**.

voluntarily, *a.* by preference, willingly, deliberately, optionally, spontaneously, freely, intentionally, at *or* by choice, of one's own choice, on one's own, in one's own sweet way, heart in hand, of one's own free will, on one's own hook, to one's heart's content, at one's discretion, on one's own initiative, with all one's heart.

voluntary, *a.* willing, freely, spontaneous; see **optional**.

volunteer, *n.* enlistee, enlisted man, taker; see **candidate, recruit**.

volunteer, *v.* come forward, enlist, sign (up), submit oneself, take the initiative, present *or* offer oneself, do on one's own volition *or* accord *or* account *or* of one's (own) (free) will *or* upon one's own responsibility, *or* authority, take the initiative, take upon oneself, speak up, stand up and be counted, *go in, *chip in, *do on one's own hook, take the bull by the horns, stand on one's own feet, take the bit between one's teeth, paddle one's own canoe, take the plunge; see also **join 2**.

volunteered, *a.* offered, proffered, signed-up; see **joined**.

volunteers, *n.* all comers, everybody, anyone; see **recruit**.

vomit, *v.* throw up, eject, bring up, spit up, dry heave, be seasick, hurl forth, retch, ruminate, regurgitate, give forth, discharge, belch forth, spew out *or* up.

vote, *n.* 1. [A ballot] tally, ticket, slip of paper, ball, yes *or* no, rising vote, Australian ballot, secret ballot. 2. [A decision] referendum, choice, majority; see **election**. 3. [The right to vote] suffrage, the franchise, manhood suffrage, universal suffrage, woman suffrage; see also **right 1**.

vote, *v.* ballot, cast a vote *or* ballot, give a vote, enact, establish, determine, bring about, effect, grant, confer, declare, suggest, propose; see also **decide**.

voted, *a.* decided, willed, chosen; see **named 2**.

vote down, *v.* decide against, refuse, blackball; see **deny**.

vote for, *v.* give one's vote *or* ballot to, cast a ballot for, second; see **support 2**.

vote in, *v.* elect, put in, put in office; see **choose**.

vote out, *v.* reject, remove from office, vote down; see **defeat, dismiss**.

voter, *n.* elector, balloter, registered voter, Republican *or* Democratic *or* Independent voter, member of a *or* one's constituency *or* of the electorate, part of the farm vote, labor vote, urban vote, etc.; vote caster, native, naturalized citizen, poll-tax payer, taxpayer, resident (voter), stay-at-home voter, proxy (voter), *one of the folks back home *or* at the grass-roots level *or* on the campaign trail, *ballot-box stuffer; see also **citizen**.

vouch, *v.* assert, attest, affirm; see **endorse 2**.

vow, *n.* pledge, solemn assertion, asseveration; see **promise 1**.

vowel, *n.* vocoid, open-voiced sound, vowel sound, glide, diphthong, digraph; see also **letter 1**. Linguistic terms referring to vowel sounds include the following—high, mid, low, front, back, rounded, unrounded, tense, slack, stressed, unstressed, nasal, nasalized, clipped, diphthongized. In English spelling symbols to represent vowels include the following: a,e,i,o,u and sometimes y.

voyage, *n.* tour, trip, excursion; see **journey**.

vulgar, *a.* sordid, ignoble, mean, base, obscene, indecent, gross, filthy, villainous, dishonorable, unworthy, fractious, inferior, disgusting, base-minded, mean-spirited, malicious, ill-tempered, sneaking, deceitful, slippery, loathsome, odious, foul-mouthed, brutish, debased, contemptible, abhorrent, profane, nasty.—*Ant.* noble, high-minded, lofty.

vulgarity, *n.* impudence, discourtesy, crudity; see **rudeness**.

vulnerable, *a.* woundable, exposed, assailable; see **unsafe, weak 2, 5**.

W

wad, *n.* 1. [A little heap] bundle, pile, gathering; see **bunch.** 2. [*A considerable amount of money] fortune, purse, bankroll; see **wealth.**

wad, *v.* stuff, pad, cushion; see **pack 2.**

wade, *v.* walk in the surf, paddle, get one's feet wet; see **swim.**

wafer, *n.* biscuit, hardtack, slice; see **bread.**

wag, *v.* waggle, swing, sway; see **wave 3.**

wage, *v.* conduct, make, carry on; see **do 1.**

wager, *n.* risk, hazard, challenge; see **bet.**

wages, *n.* salary, earnings, payment; see **pay 2.**

wagon, *n.* pushcart, buggy, truck, coach, carriage, caravan, car, covered wagon (prairie schooner), Conestoga wagon, cab.

wail, *v.* moan, weep, lament; see **mourn.**

waist, *n.* waistline, middle, midriff; see **stomach.**

wait, *n.* halt, interim, time wasted; see **delay 1,** pause.

wait, *v.* 1. [To await] expect, anticipate, tarry, pause, wait *or* look *or* delay *or* watch *or* pray for, abide, dally, remain, idle, bide one's time, mark *or* fill time, wait *or* sit *or* stay up for, lie in wait (for), ambush, *lie low, *hole up, *hang *or* stick around, *cool one's heels.—*Ant.* leave, hurry, act. 2. [To attend at table] serve, deliver, tend, act as waiter *or* waitress, arrange, set, ready, place on the table, help, portion, bus (the) dishes.

waiter, *n.* headwaiter, steward, attendant, footman, boy, servant, innkeeper, host, proprietor, lackey, counterman, soda jerk.

wait for, *v.* await, expect, stay *or* sit up for; see **wait 1.**

waiting, *a.* standing, languishing, in line, next in turn, expecting, hoping for, marking time, in wait, *cooling one's heels. —*Ant.* moving, hurrying, acting.

waiting room, *n.* restroom, salon, lounge, terminal, reception (room), hall, antechamber, foyer, preparation room, depot, station.

wait on, *v.* accommodate, provide, attend; see **wait 2.**

waitress, *n.* female attendant, servant, maidservant, hostess, (counter) girl, soda dispenser, restaurant employee, car hop.

wait up (for), *v.* wait for, expect, stay awake; see **wait 1, worry 2.**

waive, *v.* forgo, neglect, reject; see **abandon 1.**

wake, *v.* 1. [To waken another] call, rouse, bring to life, arouse, awaken, wake up, prod, shake, nudge, break into one's slumber. 2. [To become awake] get up, awake, be roused, get out of bed, open one's eyes, rise, arise, stir, stretch oneself.

wake up, *interj.* rise and shine, arise, get up, awake(n), *get going *or* cracking.

walk, *n.* 1. [Manner of walking] gait, tread, stride; see **step 1.** 2. [Course over which one walks] pavement, sidewalk, pathway, footpath, track, sheepwalk, boardwalk, pier, promenade, avenue, street, road, alley, dock, platform, gangway; see also **street.** 3. [A short walking expedition] stroll, ramble, turn, hike, promenade, airing, saunter, tramp, constitutional, march, circuit, jaunt, tour.

walk, *v.* 1. [To move on foot] step, pace, march, tread, amble, stroll, hike, saunter, wander, ramble, go out for an airing *or* outing, take a walk, promenade, trudge, tramp, trek, tour, take a turn, roam, rove, meander, traipse (about), patrol, file off, *knock about *or* around, *hoof *or* jog it, toddle along, shuffle, wend one's way, cruise. 2. [To cause to move on foot] lead, drive, exercise, train, order a march, escort, accompany, take for a walk.

*walk (all) over, *v.* subdue, trample on, beat down *or* up; see **abuse.**

walk away, *v.* vanish, depart, *split; see **abandon 1, 2,** leave 1.

walkie-talkie, *n.* portable transmitter and receiver, field radio, battery-operated two-way communication; see **radio 2.**

walking, *a.* strolling, rambling, trudging, hiking, touring, ambling, sauntering, tramping, marching, promenading, passing, roaming, wandering, wayfaring, *trekking.

walk off *or* **out on,** *v.* desert, leave, walk off from; see **abandon 2.**

walk off with, *v.* take, appropriate, pick up; see **steal.**

walkout, *n.* sit-down, boycott, demonstration; see **strike 1.**

wall, *n.* 1. [A physical barrier] dam, embankment, dike, ditch, bank, levee, stockade, fence, parapet, retainer, rampart, bulwark, palisade, fort, cliff, barricade, floodgate, sluice, paling. 2. [An obstacle; *figurative*] barrier, obstruction, bar, cordon, entanglement, hurdle, resistance, defense, snag, hindrance, impediment, difficulty, limitation, restriction, retardation, knot, hitch, drawback, stumbling block, check, stop, curb, red tape, fly in the ointment, bottleneck, red herring, detour.

wallet, *n*. billfold, purse, moneybag; see **bag, folder**.

wallop, *v*. thump, thrash, strike; see **hit 1**.

wallow, *v*. grovel, welter, flounder, lie in, move around *or* roll about in, bathe in, toss, immerse, be immersed in, besmirch oneself.

wall up, *v*. close up, surround, wall in *or* out; see **enclose**.

wander, *v*. 1. [To stroll] hike, ramble, saunter; see **walk 1. 2.** [To speak *or* think incoherently] stray, shift, digress; see **ramble 2**.

wanderer, *n*. adventurer, voyager, gypsy; see **traveler**.

wandering, *a*. 1. [Wandering in space] roving, roaming, nomadic, meandering, restless, traveling, drifting, straying, going off, strolling, ranging, prowling, ambulatory, straggling, on the road, peripatetic, itinerant, roundabout, circuitous.— *Ant.* idle, home-loving, sedentary. 2. [Wandering in thought] discursive, digressive, disconnected; see **incoherent**.

wane, *v*. decline, subside, fade away; see **decrease 1, fade 1**.

want, *n*. 1. [Need] privation, dearth, shortage; see **lack 2. 2.** [Desire] wish, craving, demand; see **desire 1**.

want, *v*. 1. [To desire] require, aspire, hanker after, have an urge for, incline toward, covet, crave, long *or* lust for, have a fondness *or* passion for, have ambition, thirst *or* hunger after, be greedy for, *ache, *have a yen *or* an itch for. 2. [To lack] be deficient in, be deprived of, require; see **need**.

wanted, *a*. needed, necessary, desired, in need of, sought after, in demand, requested, asked for.—*Ant.* **satisfied**, fulfilled, filled.

***want in** *or* **out**, *v*. want to get *or* go in *or* out *or* leave *or* come in, anxious to go *or* come, be impatient; see **arrive, leave 1**.

wanting, *a*. 1. [Deficient] destitute, poor, in default *or* deprived *or* denuded *or* bereft *or* devoid *or* empty of, bankrupt in, cut off, lacking, short, inadequate, defective, remiss, incomplete, missing, needed, unfulfilled, on the short end. 2. [Desiring] desirous of, convetous, longing for; see **envious, greedy**.

wanton, *a*. 1. [Unrestrained] extravagant, capricious, reckless, unreserved, unfet-

tered, free, wayward, fluctuating, changeable, whimisical, fitful, variable, fanciful, inconstant, fickle, frivolous, volatile. 2. [Lewd] libidinous, lustful, licentious; see **lewd 2**.

war, *n*. fighting, hostilities, combat. Types of wars include the following–air, guerrilla, shooting, ground, sea, amphibious, three-dimensional, trench, naval, aerial, land, push-button, hot, cold, total, limited, civil, revolutionary, religious, preventive, world, offensive, defensive, biological, bacteriological, germ, chemical, atomic, psychological, war to end all wars, war of nerves, campaign, crusade, *Blitzkrieg* (German).

war, *v*. fight, battle, go to war, wage *or* make war (on *or* against), engage in combat, take the field against, contend, contest, meet in conflict, march against, attack, bombard, shell, kill, shoot, murder.

ward, *n*. 1. [A territorial division] district, division, territory; see **region 1. 2.** [A juvenile charge] protégé, foster child, adopted child; see **child. 3.** [Hospital room] convalescent chamber, infirmary, emergency ward; see **hospital**.

warden, *n*. official, officer, overseer, guardian, tutor, keeper, head keeper, jailer, bodyguard, guard, governor, prison head.

wardrobe, *n*. 1. [A closet] chest, bureau, dresser; see **closet. 2.** [Clothing] apparel, garments, vestments; see **clothes**.

warehouse, *n*. wholesale establishment, storehouse, stockroom, storage place, distributing center, repository, depot, shed, stockpile, depository, bin, elevator, storage loft.

wares, *n*. goods, lines, stock, products, commodities, manufactured articles, merchandise, range, stuff.

warfare, *n*. military operations, hostilities, armed struggle *or* combat; see **war**.

warlike, *a*. attacking, hostile, offensive; see **aggressive**.

warm, *a*. 1. [Moderately heated] heated, sunny, melting, hot, mild, tepid, lukewarm, summery, temperate, clement, glowing, perspiring, sweaty, sweating, flushed, warmish, *snug as a bug in a rug.—*Ant.* cool, chilly, chilling. 2. [Sympathetic] gracious, cordial, empathetic; see **friendly**.

warm, *v*. heat (up), warm up *or* over, put on the fire; see **cook, heat 2**.

warmth, *n*. 1. [Fervor] fervor, passion, feeling; see **emotion. 2.** [Affection] friendliness, kindness, sympathy; see **friendship. 3.** [Heat] light, glow, warmness; see **heat 1, temperature**.

warn, *v*. forewarn, give notice, put on guard, give fair warning, signal, advise, prepare, alert, inform, remind, hint, prepare for the worst, offer a word of caution, admonish, counsel, exhort, dissuade, reprove, threaten, forbid, predict, remonstrate, deprecate, prescribe, urge, recommend, prompt, suggest, advocate, cry wolf, *tip off, give the high sign, *put a bug in one's ear.

warned, *a.* informed, admonished, made aware, cautioned, advised, given warning, prepared for the worst, told, forewarned, *tipped off, on the lookout.

warning, *n.* caution, admonition, notice, advice, forewarning, alert, intimation, premonition, notification, sign, alarm, indication, token, hint, lesson, information, example, distress signal(s), prediction, signal, injunction, exhortation, high sign, word to the wise, tip-off, *SOS, handwriting on the wall.

warp, *v.* curve, twist, pervert; see **bend.**

warrant, *n.* authorization, certificate, credential, official document, summons, subpoena, security, pass, testimonial, passport, credentials, permit, permission, verification, authentication.

warrant, *v.* 1. [To guarantee] assure, insure, vouch for; see **guarantee** 1. 2. [To justify] bear out, call for, give grounds for; see **explain.**

warrior, *n.* battler, fighter, hero; see **soldier.**

warship, *n.* fighting ship, armored vessel, gunboat, man-of-war, frigate, ship-of-the-line; see also **boat, ship.** Warships include the following—battleship, cruiser, destroyer, destroyer escort, submarine, submarine chaser, aircraft carrier, escort carrier, corvette, torpedo boat, PT-boat, raider, flagship.

wart, *n.* protuberance, spots, mole, projection, blemish, growth, bulge, tumor.

wary, *a.* circumspect, cautious, alert; see **careful, sly.**

wash, *n.* 1. [Laundry] wet wash, washing, linen, family wash, soiled clothing, clean clothes, washed clothing, roughdry wash, flat pieces, finished laundry. 2. [The movement of water] swishing, lapping, roll, swirl, rush, surging, eddy, wave, undulation, surge, heave, flow, murmur, gush, spurt. 3. [A stream bed that is usually dry] arroyo, gulch, canyon; see **gap** 3. 4. [A prepared liquid] rinse, swab, coating; see **liquid.**

wash, *v.* 1. [To bathe] clean, cleanse, lave, shine, immerse, douse, soak, take a bath, (take a) shower, soap, rub the dirt off, scour, scrub, rinse, wipe, sponge, dip, *fresh up, wash up, clean up, brush up. 2. [To launder] clean, starch, scrub, put in a washing machine, boil, soap, send to the laundry, scour, rinse out, soak, drench. —*Ant.* dirty, stain, smirch. 3. [To brush with a liquid] swab,

whitewash, color; see **paint** 2. 4. [To be convincing] be plausible *or* reasonable *or* acceptable, stand up, endure examination; see **endure** 1, **succeed** 1.

washable, *a.* tubfast, fast, unfading, launderable, colorfast, pre-shrunk, Sanforized (trademark), *tubbable, *sudsable.

washed, *a.* 1. [Laundered] cleaned, scrubbed, bleached, boiled, put through the wash, soaped. —*Ant.* dirty, soiled, foul. 2. [Laved] bathed, dipped, drenched, sponged, doused, soaked, cleansed, submerged, watered, showered. —*Ant.* dry, scorching, desert.

***washed up,** *a.* finished, defeated, *done for; see **ruined** 1, 2.

washer, *n.* electric dishwasher, washing machine, laundry machine, electric washer, gasoline washer, power-driven washer; see also **appliance, machine.**

washing, *n.* laundry, soiled clothes, dirty clothes; see **wash** 1.

Washington, *n.* the (nation's) capital, the national *or* Federal government, the Establishment; see **administration** 2, **city, United States.**

***washout,** *n.* disaster, disappointment, mess; see **failure** 1, 2.

waste, *a.* futile, discarded, worthless, valueless, useless, empty, barren, dreary, uninhabited, desolate, profitless, superfluous, unnecessary, functionless, purposeless, pointless, unserviceable.

waste, *n.* 1. [The state of being wasted] disuse, misuse, dissipation, consumption, uselessness, devastation, ruin, decay, delapidation, loss, exhaustion, extravagance, squandering, wear and tear, wrack and ruin; see also **wear.** —*Ant.* use, profit, value. 2. [Refuse] rubbish, garbage, scrap; see **excess** 4, **trash** 1, 3. 3. [Unused land] desert, wilds, wilderness, wasteland, tundra, marsh, marshland, bog, moor, quagmire, swamp, wash.

waste, *v.* 1. [To use without result] dissipate, spend, consume, lose, be of no avail, come to nothing, go to waste, misuse, throw away, use up, misapply, misemploy, labor in vain, cast pearls before swine, carry coals to Newcastle. —*Ant.* profit, use well, get results. 2. [To squander] burn up, lavish, scatter, splurge, spend, be prodigal, indulge, abuse, empty, drain, fatigue, spill, impoverish, misspend, exhaust, fritter *or* fool away, ruin, be spendthrift, divert, go through, gamble away, *throw (money) into a well, run through, *hang the expense, *blow *or* scatter to the winds, *blow, burn the candle at both ends. —*Ant.* save, be thrifty, manage wisely. 3. [To be consumed gradually] decay, thin out, become thin, wither, dwindle, lose weight, be diseased, run dry, run to seed, wilt, droop, decrease, disappear, drain, empty, wear, wither.—*Ant.* grow, develop, enrich.

wasted, *a.* squandered, spent, destroyed, lost, consumed, eaten up, thrown away, shriveled, gaunt, emaciated, decayed, depleted, scattered, drained, gone for nothing, missapplied, useless, to no avail, down the drain, unappreciated, of no use, worthless.

wasteful, *a.* extravagant, profligate, dissipated, prodigal, liberal, immoderate, overgenerous, incontinent, thriftless, lavish, squandering, profuse, unthrifty, improvident, careless, reckless, wild, fullhanded, without stint, destructive, *with money to burn, easy come easy go, out of bounds.

wastefully, *a.* extravagantly, carelessly, wildly, immoderately, thriftlessly, recklessly, prodigally, destructively, foolishly, lavishly, inconsiderately, openhandedly, imprudently, ruthlessly, profusely, overgenerously, with no thought for tomorrow, without a second thought; without restraint *or* good sense *or* consideration, etc.

waste time, *v.* malinger, dawdle, drift; see **loaf**.

watch, *n.* 1. [A portable timepiece] wrist watch, pocket watch, stopwatch, chronometer; see also **clock**. 2. [Strict attention] lookout, observation, observance, surveillance, awareness, attention, vigilance, guard, heed, watchfulness.—*Ant.* neglect, sleepiness, apathy. 3. [A period of duty *or* vigilance] patrol, guard duty, nightwatch; see **guard**. 4. [Those who keep a watch, sense 3] guard, sentry, sentinel; see **guardian 1**.

watch, *v.* 1. [To be attentive] observe, see, scrutinize, follow, attend, mark, regard, listen, wait, attend, take notice, contemplate, mind, view, pay attention, concentrate, look closely. 2. [To guard] keep an eye on, patrol, police; see **guard**.

watched, *a.* guarded, spied on, followed, held under suspicion, scrutinized, observed, marked, kept under surveillance, noticed, noted, *bugged.

watchful, *a.* on guard, vigilant, prepared; see **careful**.

watchfulness, *n.* vigilance, alertness, caution; see **attention**.

watching, *a.* vigilant, wary, alert; see **careful**.

watchman, *n.* day watchman, watcher, sentinel, scout, spy, ranger, observer, spotter, signalman, flagman, shore patrol, night watchman, curator, guard, detective, policeman, sentry, keeper, caretaker, flagman, lookout.

watch out, *v.* take care, heed, be cautious, proceed carefully, mind, go on tiptoe, take precautions, be on one's guard, make sure of, be doubly sure, keep an eye peeled, *handle with kid gloves.

watch over, *v.* protect, look after, attend to; see **guard**.

water, *n.* 1. [Water as a liquid] rain, rainwater, liquid, drinking water, city water, mineral water, salt water, spa water, distilled water, limewater, H2O, aqua pura. 2. [Water as a body] spring, lake, ocean, dam, sea, puddle, pond, basin, pool, river, lagoon, reservoir, brook, stream, creek, waterfall, bayou.

water, *v.* sprinkle, spray, irrigate; see **moisten**.

water down, *v.* dilute, restrict, make weaker *or* less potent *or* less effective, etc.; see **weaken 2**.

watered, *a.* 1. [Given water] sprinkled, showered, hosed, sprayed, washed, sluiced, bathed, drenched, wetted, irrigated, flooded, baptized, doused, soused, sodden, slaked, quenched; see also **wet 1**.—*Ant.* dry, arid, thirsty. 2. [Diluted] thinned, weakened, adulterated, lessened, contaminated, mixed, debased, impure, corrupt, blended, weakened, spread out, inflated, cheapened.

water power, *n.* hydraulics, water works, electricity, electric power; see also **energy 2**.

waterproof, *a.* impermeable, tight, airtight, vacuum-packed, oiled, rubbercoated, watertight, insulated, impervious, hermetically sealed.

watery, *a.* moist, damp, humid, soggy, sodden, wet, thin, colorless, washed, waterlike.—*Ant.* dry, parched, baked.

wave, *n.* 1. [A wall of water] comber, swell, roller, heave, tidal wave, billow, tide, surge, crest, bore, breaker, white cap, *curl. 2. [A movement suggestive of a wave] surge, gush, swell, uprising, onslaught, influx, tide, flow, stream, come and go, swarm, drift, rush, crush, fluctuation. 3. [Undulating movement] rocking, bending, winding; see sense 2.

wave, *v.* 1. [To flutter] stream, pulse, flow, shake, fly, dance, flap, swish, swing, tremble, whirl.—*Ant.* droop, fall, hang listless. 2. [To give an alternating movement] motion, beckon, call, raise the arm, signal, greet, return a greeting, hail. 3. [To move back and forth] falter, waver, oscillate, vacillate, fluctuate, pulsate, vibrate, wag, waggle, sway, lurch, bend, swing, dangle, seesaw, wobble, reel, quaver, quiver, swing from side to side, palpitate, move to and fro; see also **rock**.

waver, *v.* fluctuate, vacillate, hesitate, dillydally, seesaw, deliberate, reel, teeter, totter, hem and haw, pause, stagger.

wavy, *a*. 1. [Sinuous] bumpy, crinkly, curved; see **rough** 1, **twisted** 1. 2. [Unsteady] wavering, fluctuating, vibrating; see **unstable** 1.

wax, *n*. Waxes include the following—paraffin, resin, spermaceti, oxocerite, beeswax, honeycomb, sealing wax, earwax *or* cerumen, carnauba wax, automobile wax, floor wax, furniture polish.

waxy, *a*. slick, glistening, polished, smooth, glazed, sticky, tacky, glassy; see **smooth** 1.

way, *n*. 1. [Road] trail, walk, byway; see **highway**. 2. [Course] alternative, direction, progression, trend, tendency, distance, space, extent, bearing, orbit, approach, passage, gateway, entrance, access, door, gate, channel. 3. [Means] method, mode, means, plan, design, system, procedure, process, measure, contrivance, stroke, step, move, action, idea, outline, plot, policy, instrument. 4. [Manner] form, fashion, gait, tone, guise, habit, custom, behavior, style. — by the way, casually, by the by, as a matter of fact; see **incidentally**. —by way of, routed (through), detoured (through), utilizing; see **through** 4. —get out of the *or* one's way, go, remove oneself; retire; see **leave** 1, **remove** 1. —make one's way, progress, succeed, do well; see **succeed** 1. —make way, draw *or* pull back, give way, withdraw; see **leave** 1. —on the way out, declining, no longer fashionable, going (out); see **old-fashioned**, **unpopular**. —out of the way, disposed of, terminated, taken out; see **gone** 1. —parting of the ways, break-up, agreeing to disagree, difference of opinion; see **fight** 1, **separation** 1. —under way, going, prospering, making headway; see **moving** 1.

way-out, *a*. very different, revolutionary, strange; see **extreme**.

way out, *n*. means of escape, salvation, loophole; see **escape**.

ways and means, *n*. methods, approaches, devices; see **means** 1.

wayward, *a*. unruly, disobedient, perverse, head-strong, capricious, delinquent, refractory, willful, unruly, self-indulgent, changeable, stubborn.—*Ant*. obedient, stable, resolute.

we, *pron*. you and I, he and I, she and I, they and I, us.

weak, *a*. 1. [Lacking physical strength; *said of persons*] delicate, puny, flabby, flaccid, effeminate, frail, sickly, senile; see also **sick**.—*Ant*. strong, healthy, robust. 2. [Lacking physical strength; *said of things*] flimsy, makeshift, brittle, unsubstantial, jerry-built, rickety, tum-

bledown, sleazy, shaky, unsteady, ramshackle, rotten, wobbly, tottery.—*Ant*. strong, shatter-proof, sturdy. 3. [Lacking mental firmness or character] weak-minded, nerveless, fainthearted, nervous, spineless, unstrung, palsied, wishy-washy, hesitant, vacillating, frightened.—*Ant*. brave, courageous, adventurous. 4. [Lacking in volume] thin, low, soft, indistinct, feeble, faint, dim, muffled, whispered, baited, inaudible, light, stifled, dull, pale.—*Ant*. loud, strong, forceful. 5. [Lacking in military power] small, paltry, ineffectual, ineffective, inadequate, impotent, ill-equipped, insufficiently armed, limited, unorganized, undisciplined, untrained, vulnerable, exposed, assailable, unprepared. 6. [Lacking in capacity or experience] unsure, untrained, young; see **unstable** 2.

weaken, *v*. 1. [To become weaker] lessen, lose, decrease, relapse, soften, relax, droop, fail, crumble, halt, limp, languish, fade, decline, totter, tremble, flag, faint, wilt, lose spirit, become disheartened, fail in courage, slow down, break up, *crack up, *wash out.—*Ant*. revive, strengthen, straighten. 2. [To make weaker] reduce, minimize, enervate, debilitate, exhaust, cripple, unman, emasculate, castrate, devitalize, undermine, impair, sap, enfeeble, unnerve, incapacitate, impoverish, thin, dilute, take the wind out of, *wash up; see also **decrease** 2.—*Ant*. revive, quicken, animate.

weakling, *n*. puny person, feeble creature, dotard, coward, crybaby, invertebrate, mollycoddle, milksop, *jellyfish, *sissy, *pushover, nambypamby.

weakness, *n*. 1. [The state of being weak] feebleness, senility, anility, delicacy, invalidity, frailty, faintness, prostration, decrepitude, debility, effeminacy, impotence, enervation, dizziness, infirmity.—*Ant*. strength, good health, vitality. 2. [An instance or manner of being weak] fault, failing, deficiency, defect, disturbance, lapse, vice, sore point, gap, flaw, instability, indecision, inconstancy, vulnerability.—*Ant*. virtue, good, strength. 3. [Inclination] liking, tendency, bent; see **hunger, inclination** 1.

wealth, *n*. capital, capital stock, economic resources, stock, stocks and bonds, securities, vested interests, land, property, labor power, commodities, cash, money in the bank, money, natural resources, assets, means, riches, substance, affluence, belongings, property, fortune, hoard, treasure, resources, revenue, cache, cash, competence, luxury, prosperity, abundance, *money to burn.—*Ant*. poverty, pauperism, straits.

wealthy, *a.* opulent, moneyed, affluent; see **rich 1.**

weapon, *n.* armament, protection, weaponry, deadly weapon, (military) hardware, sophisticated hardware, lethal weapon, defense. Weapons include the following—club, spear, arrow, knife, catapult, bullet, dart, missile, ABM (antiballistic missle), MRV (multiple re-entry vehicle), MIRV (multiple independently-targetable re-entry vehicle), CAM (cybernetic anthropomorphic machine), CBW (chemical and biological warfare), bomb, stick, ax, firearm, cannon, gun, musket, rifle, blackjack, whip, sword, pistol, revolver, bayonet, machine gun, warhead, airplane, tank, destroyer.

wear, *n.* depreciation, damage, loss, erosion, wear and tear, loss by friction, diminution, waste, corrosion, impairment, wearing away, disappearance, result of friction.—*Ant.* growth, accretion, building up.

wear, *v.* 1. [To use as clothing or personal ornament] bear, carry, effect, put on, don, be clothed, slip *or* get *or* have on, dress in, attire, cover, wrap, harness, *get into; see also **dress 1.**—*Ant.* **undress,** take off, disrobe. 2. [To consume by wearing] use up, use, consume, wear thin *or* out, waste, diminish, cut down, scrape off, exhaust, fatigue, weather down, impair. 3. [To be consumed by wearing] fade, go to seed, decay, crumble, dwindle, shrink, decline, deteriorate, decrease, waste, become threadbare.

wear and tear, *n.* depletion, wearing, effect of use; see **damage 1, 2, destruction 2.**

wear down, *v.* wear out, get thin(ner), get worn out; see **decrease 1, waste 3.**

weariness, *n.* tiredness, exhaustion, dullness; see **fatigue.**

wear off, *v.* go away, get better, decline; see **stop 2.**

wear out, *v.* become worn, be worthless, get thinner *or* weaker *or* softer, etc.; see **waste 1, 3.**

weary, *a.* exhausted, fatigued, overworked; see **tired.**

weary, *v.* 1. [To make weary] annoy, vex, distress, irk, tax, strain, overwork, exhaust, fatigue, tire, harass, bore, disgust, dishearten, dispirit, wear out, cause ennui, leave one cold, depress, glut, overstuff, burden, sicken, nauseate. 2. [To become weary] pain, flag, be worn out, sink, droop, lose interest, fall off, tire, grow tired, drowse, doze, sicken.—*Ant.* excite, enjoy, be amused.

weather, *n.* climate, atmospheric conditions, air conditions, drought, clear weather, sunny weather, foul weather, tempest, calm, windiness, the elements, cloudiness, heat, cold, warmth, chilliness.

weather, *v.* 1. [To expose to the weather] dry, bleach, discolor, blanch, whiten, pulverize, tan, burn, expose, harden, petrify. 2. [To pass through adversity successfully] overcome, stand up against, bear the brunt of; see **endure 1, succeed 1.**

weather-beaten, *a.* decayed, battered, weathered; see **old 2, 3, worn 2.**

weatherman, *n.* weather reporter, weather prophet, weather forecaster, meteorologist, climatologist, weather bureau, weather station, newsman.

weather report, *n.* weather picture, weathercast, meteorological forecast; see **forecast.**

weave, *n.* pattern, design, texture; see **web.**

weave, *v.* 1. [To construct by interlacing] knit, sew, interlace, spin, twine, intertwine, crisscross, interlink, wreathe, mesh, net, knot, twill, fold, interfold, ply, reticulate, loop, splice, braid, plait, twist. 2. [To move in and out] sidle through, make one's way, twist and turn, snake, zigzag, beat one's way, insinuate oneself through, wedge through.

web, *n.* cobweb, lacework, netting, plait, mesh, mat, matting, wicker, weft, warp, woof, network, interconnection, reticulation, intermixture, entanglement, tracery, filigree, interweaving, trellis.

wed, *v.* espouse, join in wedlock, give *or* take *or* receive in marriage; see **marry 1, 2.**

wedded, *a.* married, espoused, in holy matrimony; see **married.**

wedding, *n.* wedlock, nuptials, matrimony; see **marriage.**

wedge, *n.* spearhead, prong, drive; see **machine 1, tool 1.**

weed, *n.* 1. [Wild plant] noxious weed, unwanted plant, prolific plant; see **plant.** Common weeds include the following—ragweed, nettle, wild morning-glory, pigweed, buckthorn, dandelion, lamb's quarters, buttonweed, dog fennel, plantain, quack grass, jimson weed, ironweed, wild sunflower, wild hemp, horsemint, foxtail, milkweed, wild barley, wild buckwheat, mullein, cheat grass, Russian thistle *or* tumbleweed, burdock, wild carrot, wild parsley, tarweed, vervain, wild mustard. 2. [*Cigarette or cigar] *coffin nail, *fag, *joint; see **tobacco.** 3. [*Marijuana] *pot, *boo, *grass; see **marijuana.**

week, *n.* wk., seven days, six days, forty-hour week, forty-four hours, working week, work week.

week after week, *a.* continually, right along, regularly; see **regularly**.

weekday, *n.* working day, Mondays, Tuesdays, Wednesdays, etc.; not a Sunday *or* the Sabbath; see also **day 1**.

weekend, *n.* end of the week, Saturday to Monday, short vacation, English weekend.

weekly, *a.* once every seven days; every Monday, regularly every Tuesday, etc.; once a week, occuring every week.

weep, *v.* wail, moan, lament; see **cry 1**.

weigh, *v.* 1. [To take the weight of] measure, scale, put on the scales, hold the scales, put in the balance, counterbalance, *heft; see also **measure 1**. 2. [To have weight] be heavy, carry weight, be important, tell, count, show, register, press, pull, be a load, burden, *tip the beams. 3. [To consider] ponder, contemplate, balance; see **consider 1**.

weigh down, *v.* push *or* pull *or* hold, etc., down; burden, oppress; see **depress 2**.

weight, *n.* 1. [Heaviness] pressure, load, gross weight, net weight, dead weight, molecular weight, gravity, burden, mass, density, ponderability, tonnage, ballast, substance, *G-factor; see **measurement 2**, **pressure 1**.—*Ant.* **lightness**, buoyancy, airiness. 2. [An object used for its weight] counterbalance, counterweight, counterpoise, ballast, paperweight, stone, rock, leadweight, sinker, anchor, plumb, sandbag. Common weights include the following—ounce, pound, ton, long ton, kilogram, centigram, gram, gram molecule, milligram, metric ton, metric carat, carat (grain), assay ton. 3. [Importance] influence, authority, sway; see **importance 1**.

weird, *a.* uncanny, ominous, eerie; see **mysterious 2**.

welcome, *interj.* greetings: come right in, make yourself at home, how do you do? glad to see you, won't you come in?

welcome, *a.* gladly received *or* admitted, desired, appreciated, honored, esteemed, cherished, desirable, agreeable, pleasant, grateful, good, pleasing, joy-bringing, delightful.—*Ant.* **undesirable**, disagreeable, unpleasant.

welcome, *n.* greetings, salute, salutation, a hero's welcome, handshake, (warm) reception, free entrance, entree, hospitality, friendliness, *the glad hand.—*Ant.* rebuke, snub, cool reception. —**wear out one's welcome**, bore (others), stay (too long), make others tired *or* weary *or* bored, etc. (with one); see **weary 1**.

welcome, *v.* embrace, hug, take in; see **greet**.

welcomed, *a.* received, accepted, initiated; see **welcome**.

weld, *v.* fuse, unite, seam; see **join 1**.

welfare, *n.* 1. [Personal condition] health, happiness, well-being, prosperity, good, good fortune, progress, state of being. 2. [Social service] poverty program, social insurance, health service; see **insurance**.

well, *a.* 1. [In good health] fine, sound, fit, trim, healthy, robust, strong, hearty, high-spirited, vigorous, hardy, hale, blooming, fresh, flourishing, rosycheeked, whole, in fine fettle, *hunkydory, *great, fit as a fiddle, *chipper.—*Ant.* **sick**, ill, infirm. 2. [Satisfactorily] up to the mark, suitably, adequately, commendable, excellently, thoroughly, admirably, splendidly, favorably, rightly, properly, expertly, strongly, irreproachably, ably, capably, soundly, competently.—*Ant.* **badly**, poorly, unsatisfactorily. 3. [Sufficiently] abundantly, adequately, completely, fully, quite, entirely, considerably, wholly, plentifully, luxuriantly, extremely.—*Ant.* **hardily**, insufficiently, barely. —**as well**, in addition, additionally, along with; see **also**. —**as well as**, similarly, alike, as much *or* high *or* good, etc., as; see **equally**.

well, *n.* 1. [A source of water] spring, fountain, font, spout, geyser, wellspring, mouth, artesian well, reservoir. 2. [A shaft sunk into the earth] pit, hole, depression, chasm, abyss, oil well, gas well, water well. 3. [Any source] beginning, derivation, fountainhead; see **origin 3**.

well-balanced, *a.* steady, sensible, welladjusted; see **reliable**.

well-behaved, *a.* mannerly, courteous, civil; see **polite**.

well-being, *n.* prosperity, happiness, fortune; see **health**, **welfare 1**.

*well-fixed, *a.* well-to-do, wealthy, in comfortable circumstances; see **rich 1**.

well-informed, *a.* informed, advised, well-read; see **educated**, **learned 1**.

well-known, *a.* famous, reputable, recognized, renowned, familiar, widely known, noted, acclaimed, popular, public, celebrated, in the public eye.—*Ant.* **unknown**, obscure, undiscovered.

well-off, *a.* prosperous, well-to-do, wealthy; see **rich 1**.

well-rounded, *a.* well-informed, built up, having a good background; see **balanced**.

well-to-do, *a.* wealthy, well-off, prosperous; see **rich 1**.

welt, *n.* wound, bruise, weal; see **injury**.

West, *n.* 1. [Western Hemisphere] New World, the Americas, North and South America; see **America 1**, **2**. 2. [European and American Culture] Occident,

Western civilization, Christian society; see **Europe, United States. 3.** [Western United States; *especially the cowboy and mining culture*] the range, the prairies, Rocky Mountain country, Far West, Northwest, Southwest, *where men are men, *wild-and-woolly country, *the wide open spaces, *Cow Country, *buffalo range.

west, *a.* facing west, westerly, westward(s); see **western 1, 2.**

western, *a.* **1.** [In or toward the west] westward(s), westerly, occidental, in the west, on the west side, where the sun sets, facing west, from the east, westernly, westernmost, westbound. *—Ant.* **eastern,** easterly, oriental. **2.** [*Sometimes capital*; having characteristics of the western part of the United States] cowboy, middle-western, southwestern, far-western, in the sagebrush country, on the Western plains, in the great *or* wide open spaces, in the wild west, in the Rockies, in God's country, *in the wild and woolly West, *out where the men are men.

westward, *a.* to the west, in a westerly direction, westbound; see **western 1.**

wet, *a.* **1.** [Covered or soaked with liquid] moist, damp, soaking, soaked, drenched, soggy, muggy, dewy, watery, dank, slimy, dripping, saturated, sodden.*—Ant.* **dry,** dried, clean. **2.** [Rainy] drizzly, slushy, snowy, slippery, muddy, humid, foggy, damp, clammy, showery, drizzling, cloudy, misty.*—Ant.* **clear,** sunny, cloudless.

wet, *v.* sprinkle, dampen, splash; see **moisten.**

whack, *n.* stroke, thump, wham; see **blow 1. —*out of whack,** out of order, not working, spoiled; see **ruined 1, 2.**

wham, *n.* hit, knock, whack; see **blow 1.**

wharf, *n.* (boat) landing, quay, pier; see **dock.**

what, *pron.* **1.** [An indication of a question] which? what sort? what kind? what thing? what means? **2.** [Something indefinite] that which, whatever, something, anything, everything, whichever, anything at all. **—and what not,** etc. *or* and so forth *or* etcetera, and other things (too numerous to mention), (some) more; see **anything, everything.**

what about, *conj.* and *prep.* but what, remember, and then; see **but 1, 2, 3.**

whatever, *pron.* anything, everything, no matter what, whatsoever.

what for, *conj.* (but) why, to what end, for what purpose; see **why.**

*what have you, *n.* (other) things, (almost) anything (else), the rest; see **anything, everything.**

what if, *conj.* but suppose, imagine, supposing; see **but 1, 2, 3, if.**

*what it takes, *n.* capacity, competence, aptitude; see **ability 1.**

*what's what, *n.* (the) fact(s) (in the case), (the) truth, *the lowdown; see also **answer 1, 2.**

wheat, *n.* staff of life, breadstuff, wheat flour; see **grain 1.**

wheel, *n.* **1.** [A thin circular body that turns on an axis] disk, ratchet, ring, hoop, roller, caster, drum, ferris wheel, wheel trolley, flywheel, cogwheel, steering wheel, sprocket, wheel, chain wheel, water wheel. **2.** [*An important person*] personage, VIP, *big shot; see **celebrity, executive. —at the wheel,** driving, in control, running things; see **running 1, 2.**

*wheel and deal, *v.* play fast and loose, take chances, cut corners; see **operate 2, 3.**

*wheels, *n.* car, vehicle, *buggy; see **automobile.**

wheeze, *v.* breath heavily, puff, pant; see **gasp.**

when, *a.* and *conj.* **1.** [At what time?] how soon? how long ago? in what period? just when? at which instant? **2.** [Whenever] if, at any time, at the moment that, just as soon as, in the event that, on the condition that; see also **if. 3.** [During] at the same time that, immediately upon, just as, just after, at, while, meanwhile; see also **during.**

whenever, *conj.* at any time *or* moment *or* minute *or* hour, etc.; on *or* at any occasion *or* the first opportunity, etc.; if, when, should.

where, *a.* and *conj.* **1.** [A question as to position] in what place? at which place? at what moment? whither? in what direction? toward what? **2.** [An indication of position] wherever, anywhere, in whatever place, at which point, in which, to which, to what end.

whereabouts, *n.* location, spot, site; see **place 3.**

whereas, *conj.* since, inasmuch as, insomuch as, forasmuch as, considering that, when in fact, while, while on the contrary.

whereby, *a.* by which, through which, in accordance with which, with the help of which, how.

wherefore. *a.* why? for what? for which reason? therefore, so, accordingly, thereupon.

whereupon, *a.* at which point, thereupon, at the conclusion of which, whereon, upon which, consequently.

wherever, *a.* and *conj.* where, in whatever place, anywhere, in any place that, wheresoever, regardless of where, in any direction.

whether, *conj.* if, either, even if, if it follows that.

whether or not, *a.* and *conj.* 1. [Surely] in any case, certainly, positively; see **surely.** 2. [If] whether, yes or no, whichever; see **if.**

which, *conj.* what, whichever, that, whatever, and that, and which.

which, *pron.* what, that, one, who.

whichever, *a.* and *conj.* whatever, which, whichsoever, no matter which, whoever.

whiff, *n.* scent, puff, fume; see **smell 1, 2.**

whiff, *v.* inhale, sniff, scent; see **smell 2.**

while, *conj.* 1. [As long as] during, at the same time that, during the time that, whilst, throughout the time that, in the time that. 2. [Although] whereas, though, even though; see **although.**

whim, *n.* notion, vagary, caprice; see **inclination 1.**

whimper, *v.* fuss, weep, object; see **complain 1, whine.**

whimsical, *a.* playful, capricious, comical; see **funny 1.**

whine, *v.* sing, hum, whistle, whimper, drone, cry, moan, murmur, grumble, complain, *gripe, *beef.

whip, *n.* switch, strap, rod, cane, lash, scourge, knotted cord, knout, cat-o-nine-tails, thong, blacksnake, dog whip, ox whip, bull whip, horsewhip, buggy whip, riding whip, quirt.

whip, *v.* thrash, strike, scourge; see **beat 2, punish.**

whipping, *n.* beating, thrashing, strapping; see **punishment.**

whir, *v.* whiz, swish, vibrate; see **hum.**

whirl, *n.* 1. [Rapid rotating motion] swirl, turn, flurry, spin, gyration, reel, surge, whir; see also **revolution 1, 2.** [Confusion] hurry, flutter, fluster, ferment, agitation, tempest, storm, rush, tumult, turbulence, commotion, hurlyburly, bustle.

whirl, *v.* turn around, rotate, spin; see **turn 1.**

whiskers, *n.* beard, mustache, sideburns, goatee, hair, face hair, bristles, muff, chin armor, weeds.

whiskey, *n.* bourbon (whiskey), rye (whiskey), corn (whiskey), Scotch (whiskey), Irish (whiskey), Canadian (whiskey), hard liquor, spirits, aqua vitae, *firewater, *hooch, home-brew, *moonshine, *mountain dew; see also **drink 2.**

whisper, *n.* 1. [A low, sibilant sound] rustle, noise, murmur, hum, buzz, drone, undertone, hissing. 2. [A guarded utterance] disclosure, divulgence, rumor; see **secret.**

whisper, *v.* speak softly, speak in a whisper, speak under one's breath, speak in an undertone, tell, talk low, speak confidentially, mutter, murmur,

speak into someone's ear.—*Ant.* yell, speak aloud, shout.

whispering, *a.* rustling, sighing, buzzing, humming, murmuring, droning, hissing.

whistle, *n.* 1. [A shrill sound] cry, shriek, howl, blast, piping, siren call, fire alarm, birdcall, signal, toot, blare; see also **noise 1, 2.** [An instrument that produces a shrill sound] fife, pipe(s), siren; see **alarm.**

whistle, *v.* 1. [To produce a shrill blast] fife, pipe, flute, trill, hiss, whiz, wheeze, shriek, howl, blare, toot, tootle; see also **sound 1, 2.** [To call with a whistle] signal, summon, warn; see **summon.**

white, *a.* 1. [The color of fresh snow] ivory, silvery, snow-white, snowy, frosted, milky, milky-white, chalky, pearly, blanched, ashen, pale, wan, albescent.—*Ant.* dark, black, dirty. 2. [Colorless] clear, transparent, clean, blank, spotless, pure, unalloyed, neutral, achromatic, achromic. 3. [Concerning the white race] fair-skinned, light-complexioned, Caucasian; see also **European, Western 2.** 4. [Pale] ashen, wan, pallid; see **pale 1.**

whiten, *v.* 1. [To become white] grow hoary, blanch, turn white, turn gray, (grow) pale, be covered with snow, be silvered, change color, fade. 2. [To make white] bleach, blanch, silver, paint white, whitewash, apply powder, chalk.—*Ant.* dirty, smudge, blacken.

whitewash, *v.* 1. [To cover with a lime wash] whiten, apply a white coating, wash; see **paint 2.** 2. [To give the appearance of innocence] gloss over, cover up, prove innocent; see **excuse.**

whittle, *v.* pare, carve, shape, fashion, shave, model, chip off, lessen, diminish, shave, decrease, pare (down).

who, *pron.* what, that, which, he, she, they, I, you, whoever, whichever.

whoever, *pron.* he who, the one who; whatever person, whatever man, no matter who.

whole, *a.* 1. [Entire] all, every, inclusive, full, undivided, integral, complete, total, aggregate, indivisible, organismic, inseparable, indissoluble, gross, undiminished, utter.—*Ant.* unfinished, partial, incomplete. 2. [Not broken or damaged] thorough, mature, developed, unimpaired, unmarred, full, unbroken, undamaged, entire, in one piece, sound, solid, untouched, without a scratch, intact, uninjured, undecayed, completed, preserved, perfect, complete, safe, in A-1 condition, shipshape, in good order, together, unified, exhaustive, conclusive, unqualified, fulfilled, accomplished, consummate.—*Ant.* broken, mutilated, defective. 3. [Not ill or injured] hale, hearty, sound; see **healthy, well 1.**

whole, *n.* unity, totality, everything, one-ness, entity, entirety, collectivity, sum, unity, assemblage, aggregate, aggrega-tion, body, lump, gross, entire stock, length and breadth, generality, mass, amount, bulk, quantity, universality, combination, complex, assembly, gross amount.—*Ant.* part, portion, fraction.

wholehearted, *a.* sincere, earnest, can-did; see **hearty.**

wholesale, *a.* 1. [Dealing in large lots] large-scale, in the mass, quantitative, in bulk, bulk, to the retailer, by the car-load, loose, in quantity, in job lots; see also **commercial.** 2. [Indiscriminate] sweeping, widespread, comprehensive; see **whole 1.**

wholesome, *a.* nutritive, nourishing, beneficial; see **healthful.**

wholly, *a.* totally, entirely, fully; see **completely.**

whom, *pron.* that, her, him; see **who, what 2.**

whoops, *interj.* *oh-oh, sorry, oh, no; see **no.**

whore, *n.* call girl, harlot, streetwalker; see **prostitute.**

whose, *pron.* to whom, belonging to what person, of the aforementioned one, from these.

why, *a, conj.* and *interrog.* for what rea-son? how so? how? how is it that? on whose account? what is the cause that? to what end? for what purpose? on what foundation? how do you explain that? *how come?

whys and wherefores, *n.* reason(s), explanation(s), cause(s); see **reason 3.**

wicked, *a.* sinful, immoral, corrupt, evil, base, foul, gross, dissolute, wayward, ir-religious, blasphemous, profane, evil-minded, vile, bad, naughty, degenerate, depraved, incorrigible, unruly, heartless, shameless, degraded, debauched, hard, toughened, disreputable, infamous, inde-cent, mean, remorseless, scandalous, atrocious, contemptible, nasty, vicious, fiendish, hellish, villainous, rascally, devilish, malevolent, plotting, con-spiratorial, flagrant, criminal, heinous, murderous, tricky, sinister, ignoble, monstrous, *rotten, *low-down, good-for-nothing, dirty, felonious, dangerous, cut-throat, *ratty, slippery, crooked.—*Ant.* honest, just, kind.

wickedness, *n.* evil, depravity, immoral-ity; see **evil 1.**

wide, *a.* 1. [Broad] extended, spacious, deep; see **broad 1.** 2. [Loose] broad, roomy, full; see **loose 1.** 3. [Extensive] large-scale, all-inclusive, universal; see **general 1.**

wide-awake, *a.* alert, watchful, vigilant; see **careful.**

widely, *a.* extensively, generally, publicly, nationally, internationally, universally, in many places, broadly, comprehen-sively.

widen, *v.* 1. [To make wider] add to, broaden, stretch, extend, increase, en-large, distend, spread out, give more space, augment. 2. [To become wider] unfold, grow, open, stretch, grow larger, increase, swell, multiply.

widespread, *a.* extensive, general, sweep-ing, broad, comprehensive, far-reaching, widely accepted, boundless, popular, public, unrestricted, unlimited, on a large scale, over-all.—*Ant.* secret, ob-scure, limited.

widow, *n.* widow woman, dowager, divorcée, husbandless wife, dead man's wife; see also **wife.**

widower, *n.* surviving husband, grass widower, *widowman; see **husband.**

width, *n.* breadth, wideness, girth, diam-eter, distance across, amplitude, cross dimension, cross measurement, ex-panse.—*Ant.* length, height, altitude.

wield, *v.* handle, manipulate, exercise; see **hold 1.**

wiener, *n.* frankfurter, sausage, *hot dog; see also **meat.**

wife, *n.* married woman, spouse, lady, dame, madam, matron, squaw, help-mate, consort, mate, housewife, *better half, *the missis, *(the little) woman, *wifey, *the old lady.—*Ant.* **widow,** spinster, old maid.

wig, *n.* artificial hair, fall, hairpiece; see **hair 1.**

wiggle, *v.* wag, waggle, wriggle, squirm, shimmy, shake, flounce, dance sensu-ally.

wild, *a.* 1. [Not controlled] unrestrained, unmanageable, boisterous; see **unruly.** 2. [Uncivilized] barbarous, savage, un-domesticated; see **primitive.** 3. [Not cultivated] luxuriant, lush, exuberant, dense, excessive, desolate, waste, desert, weedy, untrimmed, impenetrable, unin-habited, native, natural, untouched, vir-gin, overgrown, uncultivated, untilled, uncared for, neglected, overrun, free, rampant. 4. [Inaccurate] erratic, off, un-sound; see **wrong 2.** 5. [Stormy] dis-turbed, raging, storming; see **turbulent.** 6. [Excited] hot, eager, avid; see ex-cited. 7. [Dissolute] loose, licentious, profligate; see **lewd 2.** 8. [Imprudent] reckless, foolish, incautious; see **care-less.**

wilderness, *n.* primitive area, waste-lands, back country, the woods, the North woods, primeval forest, uninhab-ited region; see also **desert, forest.**

wildly, *a.* hastily, rashly, fiercely, violently, ferociously, uncontrollably, carelessly, quixotically, savagely, unwittingly, recklessly, confusedly, pellmell.—*Ant.* **carefully**, prudently, judiciously.

will, *n.* **1.** [Desire] inclination, wish, disposition, pleasure, yearning, craving, longing, hankering. **2.** [Conscious power] resolution, volition, intention, will power, preference, mind, determination, self-determination, decisiveness, moral strength, discretion, conviction, willfulness.—*Ant.* **doubt**, vacillation, indecision. **3.** [Testament for the disposition of property] bequest, disposition, instructions, last wishes, bestowal, dispensation, last will and testament. —**at will**, whenever one wishes, at any time, *ad libitum* (Latin); see **anytime**.

will, *v.* **1.** [To exert one's will] decree, order, command, demand, authorize, request, make oneself felt, decide upon, insist, direct, enjoin. **2.** [To wish] want, incline to, prefer; see **wish**. **3.** [An indication of futurity] shall, would, should, expect to, anticipate, look forward to, hope to, await, foresee, propose.

willful, *a.* intentional, premeditated, contemplated; see **deliberate**.

willing, *a.* energetic, prompt, reliable, active, obedient, enthusiastic, responsible, agreeable, prepared, voluntary, ready, compliant, tractable, feeling, like, in accord with.—*Ant.* **opposed**, averse, unwilling.

willingly, *a.* gladly, readily, obediently, voluntarily, with relish, at one's pleasure, on one's own account, of one's own accord, with open arms, with good cheer, freely, with pleasure, cheerfully, with all one's heart, *at the drop of a hat, *like a shot.

willingness, *n.* zeal, enthusiasm, readiness, earnestness, eagerness, cordiality, hospitality, courteousness, compliance, good will, geniality.

wilt, *v.* droop, wither, weaken, flag, dry up, fade, become flaccid, lose freshness, faint.—*Ant.* **grow**, stiffen, stand.

*win, *n.* triumph, conquest, gain; see **success 1**.

win, *v.* **1.** [To gain a victory] be victorious, prevail, get the best of, come out or be first, conquer, overwhelm, triumph; see also **succeed 1**. **2.** [To obtain] obtain, acquire, gain; see **get 1**. **3.** [To reach] attain, accomplish, effect; see **approach 2, 3**.

wind, *n.* draft, air current, breeze, gust, gale, blast, flurry, whisk, whiff, puff, whirlwind, flutter, wafting, zephyr, trade wind, northeaster, southwester, tempest, blow, cyclone, typhoon, twister, hurricane, sandstorm, prevailing westerlies, stiff breeze, Chinook. —**get or have**

wind of, hear of or about or from, have news of, trace; see **hear 1**. —**take the wind out of one's sails**, best, get the better of, overcome; see **defeat 2, 3**.

wind, *v.* **1.** [To wrap about] coil, reel in, entwine, wreathe, shroud, fold, cover, bind, tape, bandage. **2.** [To twist] convolute, screw, wind up; see **bend 2**. **3.** [To meander] zigzag, weave, snake, twist, loop, turn, twine, ramble, swerve, deviate.

winding, *a.* turning, gyrating, gyring, spiraling, twisting, snaky, serpentine, convoluted.—*Ant.* **straight**, direct, vertical.

window, *n.* skylight, porthole, bay window, bow window, picture window, casement, fenestration, dormer, embrasure, stained-glass, show window, bull's eye, transom, peephole.

windowpane, *n.* pane, square of glass, glass; see **window**.

windpipe, *n.* airpipe, gullet, trachea; see **throat**.

windshield, *n.* windscreen, protection (against the wind), wrap-around; see **screen 1**.

wind up, *v.* conclude, be through with, come to the end of; see **end 1**.

windy, *a.* breezy, blustery, raw, stormy, wind-swept, airy, gusty, blowing, fresh, drafty, wind-shaken, tempestuous, boisterous.—*Ant.* **calm**, quiet, still.

wine, *n.* Wines include the following—fine, sparkling, still, fortified, dry, sweet, heavy, light, white, rose, red, green (Hungarian), blackberry, cherry, currant, gooseberry, dandelion; sacramental, dessert, dinner, medicinal, aperitif, cooking; California, New York State, French, Italian, sherry, Tokay, port, muscatel, Burgundy, Bordeaux, Champagne, (Haut) Sauterne, Rhine wine, Riesling, Traminer, Chablis, Chardonnay, white Chianti, red Chianti, Pinot, Concord, Sauvignon blanc; see also **drink 2**.

wing, *n.* **1.** [An organ or instrument of flight] appendage, pinion, aileron, airfoil; see also **feather**. **2.** [An architectural unit or extension] annex, ell, addition, projection, hall, section, division, part. **3.** [An organized group of aircraft] flying unit, formation, air squadron; see **unit**. —**take under one's wing**, favor, help, guarantee; see **adopt 2**.

wink, *v.* squint, blink, nictate, flirt, make eyes at, bat the eyes.

winner, *n.* victor, conqueror, prize winner, champion, winning competitor, hero, victorious or successful contestant, leading entrant; grand or national or Olympic champion, etc.; title-holder, *champ, front runner.

winning, *a.* **1.** [Engaging] attractive, appealing, agreeable; see **charming**. **2.**

[Victorious] champion, conquering, leading; see **successful**.

winter, *n.* cold season, frosty weather, wintertime, Christmastime, Jack Frost, *King Winter, *squaw winter, *blackberry winter.

wintry, *a.* chilly, frosty, icy, snowy, frigid, cold, bleak, raw, biting, cutting.—*Ant.* warm, summery, balmy.

wipe, *v.* rub, clean, dry, dust, mop, clear, wash, swab, soak up, obliterate.

wipe out, *v.* slay, annihilate, eradicate; see **destroy, kill 1, remove 1**.

wire, *n.* 1. [A metal strand] line, electric wire, cable, aerial, circuit, wiring, live wire, coil, conductor, filament, musical string, wire tape, wire cord. 2. [A metal net] barbed wire, wire fence, wire cage; see **fence**. 3. [A telegraphic message] cablegram, message, night letter; see **telegram**. —**down to the wire**, to the (very) end, at (the) last, eventually; see **finally 2**. —**get (in) under the wire**, (just) make it, succeed, *(just) squeak through; see **arrive**.

wire, *v.* 1. [To install wire] set up a circuit, install electricity, lay wires, connect electric cables, prepare for electric(al) service, *pipe; see also **electrify**. 2. [To send a message by wire] flash, telegraph, file; see **tell 1**.

wiring, *n.* wirework, electric line, cable work, cables, electric *or* electrical installations, facilities for electric power *or* light, circuit system, filamentation, electrical wire distribution, tubing, circuit pattern, circuiting, threading, process, route, line, path, pattern, trail.

wiry, *a.* agile, sinewy, tough; see **strong 1**.

wisdom, *n.* prudence, astuteness, sense, reason, clear thinking, good judgment, understanding, sanity, shrewdness, experience, practical knowledge, carefulness, vigilance, tact, balance, poise, stability, caution, solidity, hardheadedness, common sense, *horse sense, *savvy.—*Ant.* stupidity, irrationality, rashness.

wise, *a.* 1. [Judicious] clever, sagacious, witty; see **thoughtful 1**. 2. [Shrewd] calculating, cunning, crafty; see **sly 1**. 3. [Prudent] tactful, sensible, wary; see **careful**. 4. [Erudite] taught, scholarly, smart; see **educated 1, learned 1**. 5. [Informed] *wise to, acquainted with, aware (of); see **familiar with**.

wisely, *a.* tactfully, prudently, circumspectly, sagaciously, shrewdly, judiciously, discreetly, carefully, admirably, discerningly, sagely, knowingly, reasonably, sensibly, intelligently. —*Ant.* foolishly, stupidly, unthinkingly.

***wise up**, *v.* become informed, get acquainted (with), learn one's way around; see **learn 1**.

wish, *n.* longing, yearning, hankering, desire, thirst, disposition, request, hope, intention, preference, choice, want, prayer, invocation, liking, pleasure, injunction, command, order.

wish, *v.* 1. [To desire] covet, crave, envy; see **want 1**. 2. [To express a desire] hope, request, entreat, prefer, want, pray for, invoke, command, order, solicit, beg, look forward to, need; see also **need**.

wishful, *a.* desirous, longing, eager; see **zealous**.

wishy-washy, *a.* cowardly, mediocre, feeble; see **weak 3**.

wit, *n.* 1. [Clever humor] wittiness, smartness, whimsicality, pleasantry, drollery, banter, burlesque, satire, badinage, witticism, sally, whimsy, repartee, joke, aphorism, jest, quip, epigram, pun, *wisecrack, gag. —**at one's wits' end**, downhearted, desperate, helpless; see **troubled**. —**have** *or* **keep one's wits about one**, be ready *or* alert, take precautions, be on one's guard; see **watch out**. —**live by one's wits**, use sharp practices, live dangerously, take advantage (of all opportunities); see **trick**.

witch, *n.* sorcerer, warlock, magician, enchantress, charmer, hag, crone.

witchcraft, *n.* sorcery, magic, black magic, necromancy, witchery, divination, enchantment, spell, bewitchment, voodooism, shamanism, demonology.

with, *prep.* by, in association, in the midst of, among, amidst, along with, in company with, arm in arm, hand in glove, in conjunction with, among other things, beside, alongside of, including.

withdraw, *v.* 1. [To retire] depart, draw back, take leave; see **retreat**. 2. [To remove from use or circulation] revoke, rescind, abolish, repeal, annul, abrogate, veto, suppress, repress, retire, stamp out, declare illegal, ban, bar, nullify, repudiate, reverse, retract, throw overboard, invalidate, quash, dissolve.

withdrawal, *n.* removal, retreat, retraction, resignation, alienation, abandonment, recession, revulsion, abdication, relinquishment, departure.—*Ant.* progress, advance, appearance.

withdrawn, *a.* retired, secluded, isolated, removed, departed, cloistered, recluse, drawn back, gone into retirement, taken out, absent, retreated.—*Ant.* active, involved, progressing.

wither, *v.* shrivel, shrink, droop, wilt, decay, die, grow brown, dry up *or* out, fade, lose freshness, deteriorate, fall away. —*Ant.* revive, reawaken, bloom.

withered, *a.* shriveled, wilted, decayed, deteriorated, shrunken, dead, browned faded, parched, dried up, drooping, wrinkled.—*Ant.* **fresh**, blooming, alive.

withheld, *a.* concealed, held back, hidden, checked, restrained, delayed, denied, kept on leash, *on ice.—*Ant.* **free**, opened, made visible.

withhold, *v.* hold back *or* out, reserve, keep; see **deny**.

within, *a.* and *prep.* (on the) inside, indoors, in, not further than, not beyond, not over, in reach of, in a period of, not outside; see also **inside 2**.

***with it**, *a.* up to date, informed, contemporary; see **modern 1**.

without, *a.* and *prep.* 1. [Outside] out, outdoors, outwardly, externally, on the outside, standing outside, left out. 2. [Lacking] not with, not having, in the absence of, free from, deprived of.

withstand, *v.* face, confront, oppose, resist, endure, stand up to *or* against, hold out.

witness, *n.* observer, onlooker, eyewitness, bystander, deponent, testifier, beholder, signatory.

witness, *v.* see, observe, be a witness, be on the scene, behold, be present, testify, vouch for, stand for, look on, say under oath, depose, be on hand.

witnessed, *a.* sworn to, vouched for, alleged, borne out, validated, valid, established, verified, authenticated, substantiated, supported, upheld, endorsed, brought forward.

witty, *a.* quick-witted, clever, bright; see **intelligent 1**.

wizard, *n.* magician, soothsayer, witch, witch doctor, necromancer, fortuneteller, astrologer, medicine man, conjurer, shaman, enchanter, hypnotist, diviner, seer, clairvoyant, palmist, augurer, medium.

wobble, *v.* shake, quaver, flounder, vacillate, tremble, quiver, move unsteadily (from side to side), dodder, teeter, totter, be unsteady, waver, quake, stagger, shuffle, waggle.

wobbly, *a.* wavering, unbalanced, precarious; see **unstable 1**.

wolf, *n.* wild dog, coyote, timber wolf; see **dog**.

woman, *n.* 1. [An adult female] lady, dame, matron, gentlewoman, maid, spinster, debutante, nymph, virgin, girl, old woman, squaw, *chick, *doll, *broad. 2. [A wife or mistress] love, lover, wife; see **wife**. 3. [Womankind] femininity, fair sex, womanhood, eternal feminine, the world of women, *the female of the species.

womanhood, *n.* 1. [The state of being a woman] adulthood, maturity, majority, womanliness, sexual prime, nubility, marriageable age, maidenhood, matronhood, spinsterhood.

womanly, *a.* effeminate, ladylike, feminine, female, gentle, modest, compassionate, wifely, sisterly, motherly, protective, womanish, fair.—*Ant.* **manly**, virile, masculine.

womb, *n.* uterus, female cavity, belly; see **stomach**.

won, *a.* gained, achieved, conquered, taken, got, triumphed, overwhelmed.—*Ant.* **beaten**, lost, failed.

wonder, *n.* 1. [Amazement] surprise, awe, stupefaction, admiration, wonderment, astonishment, wondering, stupor, bewilderment, perplexity, fascination, consternation, perturbation, confusion, shock, start, jar, jolt, incredulity. 2. [A marvel] miracle, curiosity, oddity, rarity, freak, phenomenon, sensation, prodigy, act of God, portent, wonderwork, spectacle, perversion, monstrous birth, prodigious event, something unnatural, the unbelievable.

wonder, *v.* 1. [To marvel] be surprised *or* startled *or* fascinated *or* amazed *or* dumbfounded *or* confounded *or* dazed *or* awestruck *or* astonished *or* agape *or* dazzled, stand *or* look aghast, be struck by, be unable to take one's eyes off, admire, gape, be taken aback, stare, be flabbergasted. 2. [To question] be curious, query, hold in doubt; see **ask 1**.

wonderful, *a.* fine, enjoyable, pleasing; see **pleasant 2**.

wonderfully, *a.* beautifully, admirably, excellently; see **well 2**.

wood, *a.* woodlike, made of wood, hard; see **wooden**.

wood, *n.* 1. [A forest; *often plural*] grove, woodland, copse; see **forest**. 2. [The portion of trees within the bark] log, timber, lumber, sapwood, heartwood. Varieties of wood include the following—oak, chestnut, mahogany, sugar maple, red maple, cherry, cedar, walnut, hickory, butternut, hemlock, spruce, bass wood *or* linden, beech, birch, poplar, tamarack, white pine, yellow pine, gumwood, elm, cocobolo, cypress, redwood, fir, Douglas fir, ash, red oak, live oak, white oak, willow, cottonwood, bamboo.

wooded, *a.* timbered, forested, tree-covered, wild, tree-laden, treed, reforested, woody, jungly, having cover, timber-bearing, lumbering, uncut, not lumbered, not cut over *or* off, with standing timber, primeval, below the timberline, jungle covered.

wooden, *a.* wood, frame, frame-built, log-built, boarded, clapboarded, plank, built of slabs, pine, oak, elm, ash, mahogany, etc.

woodwork, *n.* molding, fittings, paneling, stairway, wood finishing, doors, window frames, sashes, jambs, wood trim.

wool, *n.* fleece, lamb's wool, Angora

wool, Berlin or German wool, Shetland wool, Australian or Botany wool, glass wool, mineral wool, tweed, flannel, gabardine, worsted, woolen, suiting, serge, broadcloth, frieze, mohair, felt, blanketing, carpeting; see also **goods 1.**

word, n. 1. [A unit of expression] term, name, expression, designation, concept, vocable, utterance, sound, a voicing, form of speech, speech, locution, free morpheme. Classes of words include the following—common noun, proper noun, personal pronoun, possessive pronoun, demonstrative pronoun, relative pronoun, interrogative pronoun, indefinite pronoun, definite article, indefinite article, transitive verb, intransitive verb, descriptive adjective, quantitative adjective, participial adjective, adverb, coordinating conjunction, subordinate or relative conjunction, preposition, modifier, subject, predicate, root, primitive word, parent word, source word, synonym, antonym, cognative word, analogous word, derivative, slang, colloquialism, jargon, slang word, dialect word, provincialism, translation, native word, foreign word, idiom, connotative word, denotative word. 2. [Promise] pledge, commitment, word of honor; see **promise 1.** 3. [Tidings] report, message, information; see **news 1. —a good word,** favorable comment, recommendation, support; see **praise 2. —by word of mouth,** orally, verbally, spoken; see **oral. —have words with,** argue (with), differ with or from, bicker; see **argue 1, fight. —in so many words,** succinctly, cursorily, economically; see **briefly. — take at one's word,** trust (in), have faith or confidence in, put one's trust in; see **believe 1. —the word,** information, the facts (in the case), *the lowdown; see **knowledge 1.**

word-for-word, a. exactly, accurately, verbatim; see **literally.**

wordiness, n. redundance, redundancy, diffuseness, circumlocution, repetition, verbiage, verbosity, tautology, indirectness, vicious circle, flow of words, rhetoric, copiousness, tediousness.—*Ant.* silence, conciseness, succinctness.

wordy, a. tedious, bombastic, longwinded; see **dull 4.**

work, n. 1. [Something to be done] commitment, task, obligation; see **job 2.** 2. [The doing of work, sense 1] performance, endeavor, employment, production, occupation, practice, activity, manufacture, industry, operation, transaction, toil, labor, exertion, drudgery, functioning, stress, struggle, slavery, trial, push, attempt, effort, pains, *elbow grease, *muscle. 3. [The result of labor; *often plural*] feat, accomplish-

ment, output; see **achievement. 4.** [Occupation] profession, craft, business; see **job 1. —at work,** working, on the job, engaged; see **busy 1. —*in the works,** prepared for, budgeted, approved; see **ready 2. —make short or quick work of,** finish (off), deal with, dispose of; see **do 1. —out of work,** not hired, dismissed, looking for a job; see **unemployed.**

work, v. 1. [To labor] toil, slave, sweat, do a day's work or the chores, exert or apply oneself, do one's best, overexert, overwork, overstrain, get to work, work overtime or day and night or early and late, work or fight one's way (up), tax one's energies, pull, plod, tug, chore, struggle, strive, carry on, do the job, *punch a time clock, put in time, *pour it on, *work one's fingers to the bone, buckle or bear down, *work like a horse or a dog or a slave, keep at it, stay with it, put one's shoulder to the wheel, burn the candle at both ends, burn the midnight oil. 2. [To be employed] earn one's or a living, have or hold or occupy a position or job or post, report for work, be off the dole or the welfare rolls, be among the (gainfully) employed, be on the job, *be a wage slave. 3. [To function] go, run, serve; see **operate 2. 4.** [To handle successfully] control, accomplish, manage; see **achieve 1, operate 3. 5.** [To fashion] give form to, sculpture, mold; see **form 1.**

workable, a. useful, practicable, functional; see **working 1.**

work at, v. attempt, endeavor, do one's best; see **try 1.**

worker, n. laborer, toiler, mechanic; see **workman.**

work in, v. introduce, find a place for, squeeze in; see **include 1.**

working, a. 1. [Functioning] toiling, laboring, moving, in process, in good condition, in force, in gear, in collar, in exercise, going, twitching, effective, practical, on the job, never idle, on (the) fire. 2. [Employed] with or having a job, engaged, on the staff; see **busy 1.**

workings, n. innards, mechanism, parts; see **insides, works 1.**

workman, n. operator, mechanic, machinist, craftsman, artist, artisan, journeyman, master worker, handworker, skilled workman, white-collar worker, field workman. Skilled workers include the following—carpenter, cabinetmaker, upholsterer, paper hanger, plasterer, bricklayer, plumber, pipefitter, coppersmith, sheet-metal worker, auto sheetmetal worker, printer, pressman, linotype operator, glassworker, automobile mechanic, punch press operator, addressograph operator, multigraph operator, cost accountant, clerk, file clerk, stenographer, bookkeeper, salesman, packager, darkroom operator, photographer, proofreader, railroad freight clerk, division clerk, conductor, brakeman, locomotive engineer, fireman, barber, baker, butcher, farm worker, cowboy, dairyman, waiter, waitress, laundry worker, welder, drill operator, die sink operator, mason, lathe operator, gearcutting machine operator, threading machine operator, telegrapher, teletype operator, telephone girl, radio operator, radio repairer, pattern builder, textile worker, tool designer, postal clerk, painter, galvanizer, draftsman, furrier, jewelry repairman.

workmanship, *n.* craftsmanship, skill, quality of work, performance, handicraft, working ability, handiwork, achievement, manufacture, execution.

work on *or* **upon,** *v.* try to dissuade *or* encourage, use one's influence with, talk to; see **influence**.

workout, *n.* work, conditioning, gymnastics; see **discipline 2**.

work out, *v.* 1. [To solve] come to terms, compromise, reach an agreement; see **agree**. 2. [To satisfy a requirement] finish, do what is necessary, get something done; see **achieve**.

work over, *v.* 1. [To repair] fix (up), go over, redo; see **repair, repeat 1**. 2. [*To beat *or* punish] thrash, *beat up (on), abuse; see **beat 1, punish**.

works, *n.* 1. [Working parts] cogs, wheels, gears, pistons, springs, coils, chains, rods, pulleys, wires; see also **insides**. 2. [*Punishment] beating, thrashing, wallop; see **abuse 3, attack 1**. 3. [*Everything] totality, entirety, the whole; see **all, everything**.

world, *n.* 1. [The earth] globe, wide world, terrestrial sphere; see **earth 1**. 2. [The universe] cosmos, nature, creation; see **universe**. 3. [A specific group] realm, division, system; see **class 1**. 4. [All one's surroundings] environment, atmosphere, childhood, adolescence, adulthood, experience, life, inner life, memory, idealization. **—bring into the world,** give birth (to), bear, have a baby; see **produce 1**. **—in the world,** anywhere at all, wheresoever, in the universe; see **anywhere, wherever**. **—on top of the world,** feeling fine *or* wonderful *or* happy, etc.; exuberant, successful; see **happy 1**. **—out of this world,** extraordinary, strange, remarkable; see **usual 1, 2**.

worldly, *a.* mundane, earthly, ungodly, matter-of-fact, practical, secular, strategic, grubbing, money-making, unprincipled, power-loving, self-centered, oppor-

tunistic, sophisticated, terrestrial, sublunary, human, natural, temporal.

worldwide, *a.* global, universal, extensive; see **general 1**.

worm, *n.* caterpillar, grub, larva, maggot, leech, parasite, helminth. Common worms include the following—angleworm, earth-worm, threadworm, tapeworm, galleyworm, silkworm, flatworm, blindworm, roundworm, annelid worm, cutworm, army worm, cotton worm, wire worm.

worm, *v.* inch, insinuate oneself, sidle; see **crawl, sneak**.

worm out of, *v.* evade, get out of, slip out (of); see **avoid, escape**.

worn, *a.* 1. [Used as clothing] carried, put on, donned, displayed, exhibited, used, *sported. 2. [Showing signs of wear] frayed, threadbare, old, secondhand, ragged, impaired, used, consumed, deteriorated, torn, patched, the worse for wear.—*Ant.* fresh, new, whole.

worn-out, *a.* used (up), gone, destroyed; see **ruined 1, 2, useless 1**.

worried, *a.* troubled, bothered, perturbed, vexed, distressed, annoyed, concerned, upset, suffering, torn, in conflict, pained, burdened, ill at ease, racking one's brains, *uptight, *all hot and bothered, anxious, *hung up.

worry, *n.* 1. [The state of anxiety] concern, anxiety, misery; see **distress**. 2. [A cause of worry] problem, upset, disturbance; see **fear, trouble 1**.

worry, *v.* 1. [To cause worry] annoy, trouble, bother, *bug; see **disturb**. 2. [To indulge in worry] fret, chafe, grieve, take to heart, break one's heart, worry oneself, have qualms, wince, agonize, writhe, suffer, turn gray with worry, become sick with worry, *sweat out; see also **bother 1**.

worse, *a.* more evil, not so good, deteriorated; see **poor 2**.

worship, *n.* 1. [Adoration] prayer, devotion, homage, adulation, benediction, invocation, supplication, beatification, veneration, (burnt) offering, reverence, honor, religious ritual. 2. [A religious service] Mass, vespers, devotions; see **church 2**.

worship, *v.* sanctify, pray to, invoke, venerate, glorify, praise, exalt, offer one's prayers to, pay homage to, recite the rosary, give thanks, offer thanks to, sing praises to, reverence, celebrate, adore, revere, laud, extol, magnify, chant, sing, bow down, canonize; see also **pray 1**.

worshiper, *n.* churchgoer, communicant, pilgrim, suppliant, devotee, devotionalist, adorer, pietist, pious *or* devout person, celebrant, saint, priest, priestess.—*Ant.* skeptic, atheist, agnostic.

worst, *a.* most terrible *or* harmful *or* lethal, poorest, lowest, least, most ghastly *or* horrible *or* pitiful, least meaningful, meanest, least understanding, least effective.

worst, *n.* calamity, catastrophe, ruin; see **destruction** 2. —**at worst,** under the worst (possible) circumstances, unluckily, grievously; see **badly** 1, **unfortunately.** —**(in) the worst way,** unluckily, disastrously, horribly; see **unfortunately.**

worth, *a.* deserving, meriting, equal in value to, priced at, exchangeable for, valued at, worth in the open market, pegged at, cashable for, good for, appraised at, having a face value of, reasonably estimated at, bid at, held at. —**for all one is worth,** greatly, mightily, hard; see **powerfully.**

worth, *n.* goodness, value, quality, character, importance, significance, meaning, estimation, benefit, excellence, merit; see also **value** 1, 3.

worthless, *a.* profitless, counterproductive, barren, unprofitable, unproductive, unimportant, insignificant, counterfeit, bogus, cheap, sterile, waste, wasted, no good, trashy, inconsequential, petty, piddling, paltry, trivial, trifling, unessential, beneath notice, empty, good-for-nothing, *no-account, *not worth a damn, *not worth the trouble, *not worth speaking of, *not able to say much for.

worthlessness, *n.* uselessness, impracticality, inefficiency; see **waste** 1.

worthwhile, *a.* good, serviceable, useful, important, profitable, valuable, remunerative, estimable, worthy, helpful, beneficial, meritorious, excellent, rewarding, praiseworthy.

worthy, *a.* good, true, honest, honorable, reliable, trustworthy, dependable, noble, charitable, dutiful, philanthropic, virtuous, moral, pure, upright, righteous, decent, incorruptible, meritorious, creditable, deserving, right-minded, worthy of, model, exemplary, sterling, sinless, stainless, blameless.—*Ant.* **worthless,** bad, evil.

would-be, *a.* anticipated, assuming, supposed; see **hopeful** 1.

wound, *a.* twisted, coiled, wrapped; see **woven.**

wound, *n.* bruise, hurt, scar; see **injury** 1.

wound, *v.* 1. [To hurt the body] gash, scrape, injure; see **hurt** 1. 2. [To hurt the feelings] trouble, upset, pain; see **bother** 2, **disturb.**

wounded, *a.* injured, hurt, disabled, stabbed, cut, shot, scratched, bitten, gashed, hit, beaten, attacked, winged, nicked, *pipped.

woven, *a.* spun, interlinked, netted, net-like, dovetailed, wreathed, sewn, intertwined, united, interlaced, interwoven, worked into.

*****wow (them),** *v.* triumph, overcome, be a success; see **defeat** 2, 3.

wrap, *v.* roll up, swathe, muffle, bind, fold about, encircle, coil, enclose, swaddle, bandage, envelop, enwrap, protect, encase, sheathe, cover (up), shelter, clothe, cover with paper, enclose in a box.—*Ant.* unwrap, unsheathe, open up.

wrapped, *a.* covered, sheathed, swaddled, swathed, enclosed, papered, protected, enveloped, encased, shrouded, concealed, hidden, clothed, done up.—*Ant.* open, unwrapped, uncovered.

wrapped up in, *a.* in love (with), devoted (to), affectionate; see **loving.**

wrapper, *n.* envelope, folder, book cover; see **cover** 1.

*****wrap up,** *v.* finish (off), bring to an end or a conclusion, *polish off; see **complete.**

wrath, *n.* fury, vengeance, madness; see **anger.**

wreck, *n.* 1. [Anything wrecked] junk, ruins, skeleton, hulk, stubble, collapse, bones, scattered parts, rattletrap, relic, litter, pieces, shreds, waste, wreckage, debris. 2. [A person in poor physical condition] incurable, invalid, consumptive, nervous case, overworked person, cripple, *mess, *goner,. *washout, shadow, *skin-and-bones, *(walking) nightmare.

wreck, *v.* spoil, ruin, destroy, disfigure, mangle, smash, tear down, break, split, efface, batter, torpedo, tear to pieces, put out of order, impair, injure, bash in, mess up, *play hell with, put out of commission.—*Ant.* **repair,** restore, rebuild.

wreckage, *n.* remains, ruins, hulk, remnants; see **wreck** 1.

wrecked, *a.* demolished, destroyed, broken (up), knocked to pieces, ruined, smashed (to bits), shipwrecked, stranded, beached, grounded, scuttled, capsized, (put) out of order, blown to bits, junked, dismantled, shattered, *on the rocks, gone to pot, shot to hell.

wrench, *n.* 1. [A violent twist] jerk, strain, sprain, tug, pull, dislodgement, extrication, dislocation. 2. [A spanner] Wrenches include the following—monkey, single-head, double-head, pipe, Stillson, plumber's crescent, sparkplug, hubcap, flat, S-socket, connecting-rod, bearing; see also **tool** 1.

wrench, *v.* twist, strain, distort; see **bend.**

wrestle, *v.* grapple, struggle with, contend with, perform in a wrestling bout, *wrassle, *tangle, tussle; see also **fight** 2.

wrestling, *n.* contention, grappling, bout; see **fight 1.**

wretched, *a.* 1. [Afflicted] distressed, woeful, sorrowful; see **sad 1. 2.** [Poor in quality] weak, faulty, cheap; see **poor 2.**

wring, *v.* press *or* squeeze out, compress, press; see **twist.**

wrinkle, *n.* crease, furrow, crinkle, ridge, fold, corrugation, line, crow's foot, pucker, pleat.

wrinkle, *v.* rumple, crease, furrow, screw up, pucker, twist, crumple, compress, crinkle.—*Ant.* **straighten,** smooth out, iron.

wrinkled, *a.* creased, rumpled, furrowed, puckered, warped, twisted, crumpled, crinkled, dried up, withered, unironed, unpressed, shrivelled.—*Ant.* **smooth,** ironed, pressed.

write, *v.* 1. [To compose in words] set forth, record, formulate, draft, turn out, give a report, note down, transcribe, pen, put in writing, comment upon, go into, indite, typewrite, communicate, rewrite, produce poetry *or* plays *or* novels, do imaginative writings, correspond, scribble. 2. [To set down in writing] inscribe, sign, scrawl, address, print, letter, autograph, reproduce, *knock *or* dash off, put in black and white. — **write off,** charge off, take a loss on, recognize as a bad debt; see **lose 2.** — **write up,** expand, work up, deal at length with; see **write 1, 2.**

writer, *n.* author, journalist, reporter, newspaperman, magazine writer, contributor, poet, novelist, essayist, biographer, dramatist, playwright, literary critic, (foreign) correspondent, feature writer, sports writer, fashion writer, shorthand writer, stenographer, anecdotist, amanuensis, ghost writer, song writer, copyist, scribe, editor, contributing editor, war correspondent, special writer, freelance writer, representative, member of the Fourth Estate, scribbler, *pen pusher, hack, *newshound. Major writers include the following—British: Henry Fielding, Sir Walter Scott, Charlotte Brontë, George Eliot, Jane Austen, Charles Dickens, Thomas Hardy, D. H. Lawrence, James Joyce, Joseph Conrad; American: James Fenimore Cooper, Edgar Allan Poe, Ralph Waldo Emerson, Henry David Thoreau, Nathaniel Hawthorne, Herman Melville, Samuel Langhorne Clemens (Mark Twain), Henry James, Stephen Crane, Theodore Dreiser, William Faulkner, John Steinbeck, Ernest Hemingway; French: (François-Marie Arouet de) Voltaire, Jean Jacques Rosseau, Victor Hugo, Honoré de Balzac, Gustave Flaubert, Alexandre Dumas, Jules Verne, Albert Camus; Italian: Niccolo Machiavelli, Giovanni Boccaccio; German: Thomas Mann, Franz Kafka; Russian: Fyodor Dostoevsky, Leo Tolstoy, Boris Pasternak; Spanish: Miguel de Cervantes.

*write-up, *n.* report, account, publicity; see **writing 2.**

writhe, *v.* contort, move painfully, squirm, distort, suffer, twist (and turn), undergo agony, turn with pain, *throw a fit.—*Ant.* **rest,** be at ease, move easily.

writing, *n.* 1. [The practice of writing] transcribing, inscribing, reporting, corresponding, letter-writing, copying, typewriting, penmanship, lettering, printing, graphology, signing, autographing, stenography. 2. [Anything written] literature, written matter, document, composition, article, poem, prose, paper, theme, editorial, discourse, essay, thesis, dissertation, book, manuscript, novel, play, literary production, scenario, drama, piece, work, signature, letter, pamphlet, tract, treatise, disquisition, comment, commentary, review, recitation, certificate, record, bill, *bit, item, piece. 3. [The occupation of a writer] journalism, reporting, literature, authorship, freelance, writing, professional writing, auctorial pursuits, the pen, the Fourth Estate, creative writing; novelwriting, verse-writing, feature-writing, etc.; newspaper work, the writers' craft, pencil-pushing, hack writing, *writing for the slicks, ghost-writing.

written, *a.* 1. [Composed] set forth, authored, penned, drawn up, reported, signed, turned out, fictionalized, arranged, rearranged, adapted, ghostwritten, recorded, dictated. 2. [Inscribed] copied, scriptural, transcribed, printed, lettered, autographed, signed, put in writing, in black and white, under one's hand.

wrong, *a.* 1. [Immoral] evil, sinful, wicked, naughty, salacious, base, indecent, risqué, blasphemous, ungodly, amoral, dissolute, dissipated, wanton, profane, sacrilegious, depraved, corrupt, profligate, *shady, *low-down, smutty.— *Ant.* righteous, virtuous, **good. 2.** [Inaccurate] inexact, erroneous, mistaken, in error, incorrect, fallacious, untrue, erring, astray, amiss, ungrounded, spurious, unsubstantial, unsound, erratic, deceiving oneself, in the wrong, under an error, beside the mark, laboring under a false impression, out of line, at fault, to no purpose, not right, awry, faulty, mishandled, miscalculated, misfigured, misconstructed, misconstrued, misfashioned, mismade, altered, not precise, perverse, wide of the mark, not according to the facts, badly estimated, *a mile off, all off, *crazy. 3. [Inappropriate] unfitted, ill-fitting, disproportionate; see **improper.**

wrong, *n.* vice, sin, misdemeanor, crime, immorality, indecency, transgression, unfairness, imposition, oppression, foul play, prejudice, bias, favor, unlawful practice, villainy, delinquency, misdoing, error, miscarriage, mistake, blunder, offense, wrongdoing, violation, tort, hurt, persecution, malevolence, cruelty, libel, abuse, harm, damage, spite, slander, false report, slight, misusage, outrage, inhumanity, over-presumption, insult, discourtesy, *raw deal, *bum steer, dirt.—*Ant.* **kindness,** good deed, consideration.

wrong, *v.* hurt, oppress, defame; see **abuse.**

wrongdoer, *n.* lawbreaker, rogue, fugitive; see **criminal.**

wrongly, *a.* unfairly, prejudicially, wrongfully, partially, badly, unjustifiably, illegally, disgracefully, sinfully, unreasonably, unlawfully, criminally, inexcusably, unsuitably, improperly, awkwardly, incongruously, incorrectly, unbecomingly, indecorously, out of the question, imprudently, rashly, unnaturally, illogically; see also **inadequately.**—*Ant.* **appropriately,** tastefully, prudently.

wrung, *a.* twisted, squeezed out, pressed; see **twisted 1.**

X

x, *n.* unknown quantity, unknown, y; see **quantity**.
Xerox (trademark), *v.* reproduce, make a copy of, ditto; see **copy**.
Xmas, *n.* the Nativity, Christmas holiday, Yule; see **holiday**.
X-rays, *n.* Roentgen rays, radioactivity, radium emanation, actinic rays, actinism, encephalogram, ultraviolet rays, refractometry, radiant energy, cathode rays; see also **energy 2, ray**.
xylophone, *n.* carillon, vibraphone, *vibes, glockenspiel, marimba; see also **musical instrument**.

Y

yacht, *n.* pleasure boat, sloop, racing boat; see **boat, ship**.
Yale, *n.* Yale University, old Eli, (the) Blue; see **university**.
yammer, *v.* nag, whine, whimper; see **complain**.
yank, *n.* twitch, jerk, wrench; see **jerk 1**.
***Yank,** *n.* American, soldier, Yankee, *doughboy, *GI (Joe).
***yank,** *v.* haul, tug, drag, jiggle, *jerk, flip, wrench, twitch; see also **draw 1, pull 2**.
Yankee, *a.* 1. [Having New England qualities] homespun, individualistic, conservative; see **moderate 3, 4, 5, practical**. 2. [Concerning the United States] North American, Western, Americanized; see **American**.
Yankee, *n.* 1. [A New Englander] Northerner, Easterner, early settler, Abolitionist, Unionist. 2. [A person from the United States] American, American citizen, North American, westerner, Occidental, *Yank.
***yap,** *v.* jabber, rant, chatter; see **babble, talk 1**.
yard, *n.* 1. [An enclosure, usually about a building] court, courtyard, barnyard, backyard, corral, fold, patch, patio, terrace, play area, lawn, grass, garden, clearing, quadrangle, lot; see also **playground**. 2. [An enclosure for work] brickyard, coalyard, junkyard, navy yard, dockyard, railroad yard, stockyard, lumberyard. 3. [*Often plural*; tracks for making up trains] railroad yard, switchyard, railway yard, marshalling yard, terminal. 4. [A unit of measurement]

three feet, pace, step, arm-span, thirty-six inches; see also **measure 1**.
yardstick, *n.* 1. [A rule three feet long] thirty-six-inch ruler, measuring stick, molding rule, yard, yard measure; see also **ruler 2**. 2. [A unit for comparison] criterion, basis for judgment, standard; see **measure 2**.
yarn, *n.* 1. [Spun fiber] spun wool, twist, flaxen thread, cotton fiber, rug yarn, crochet thread, knitting yarn, alpaca yarn; see also **fiber**. 2. [A tale] anecdote, sea story, adventure story, fictional account; see also **story**. 3. [A lie] fabrication, tall story, alibi, *fish story, *cock-and-bull story; see also **lie 1**.
yawn, *v.* 1. [To open wide] gape, split open, spread out; see **divide, grow 1**. 2. [To give evidence of drowsiness] gape, be sleepy, make a yawning sound, show weariness; see also **sleep, tire 1**.
yea, *interj.* okay, aye, well; see **yes**.
year, *n.* twelve months, cycle, continuum of days; see **age 3, time 1, 2**. Kinds of years include the following—civil, legal, calendar, lunar, solar, astronomical, natural, sidereal, tropical, equinoctial, leap, school, fiscal.
year after year, *a.* year by year, annually; year in, year out; see **yearly**.
yearbook, *n.* annual, almanac, yearly report; see **catalogue, record 1**.
yearling, *n.* suckling, nursling, weanling; see **animal, baby**.
yearly, *a.* annually, once a year, every winter, every spring, every summer, every autumn, year by year; see also **regularly 1**.
yearn, *v.* want, crave, long for, fret,

chafe, grieve, mourn, droop, pine, languish, be eager for, be desirous of, be ardent *or* fervent *or* passionate, wish (for), thirst *or* hunger for, aspire to, set one's heart upon, hanker after *or* for, *have a yen for; see also try 1.—*Ant.* avoid, be content, be indifferent.

yearning, *n.* want, longing, craving; see desire 1, wish.

years, *n.* agedness, oldness, senescence; see age 2.

yell, *n.* 1. [A shout] bellow, cry, yelp, roar, whoop, howl, screech, shriek, squeal, *holler, hoot, *yawp, hubbub, hullabaloo, hue and cry, protest; see also noise 1, 2. 2. [Organized cheering] hip-hip-hurrah, rooting, cheer; see encouragement.

yell, *v.* bellow, cry out, scream, shout, yelp, yap, bawl, roar, halloo, vociferate, whoop, howl, screech, shriek, shrill, squeal, squall, yammer, hoot, cheer, call, yip, give encouragement, call down, raise one's voice, holler, whoop it up; see also sound 1.

yelling, *a.* boisterous, clamorous, noisy, bawling, uproarious, turbulent, drunken, aroused, riotous, cantankerous, blatant, vociferous; see also harsh 1, loud 2.—*Ant.* quiet, subdued, silent.

yelling, *n.* cry, scream, shout, outcry, vociferation, screeching, bawling, yowling, bellowing, howling, yelping; see also noise 1, 2, yell.

yellow, *n.* 1. Tints and shades of yellow include the following —cream color, ivory color, old ivory, ivory-yellow, tan, lemon color, orange-yellow, saffron, jasmine, tawny, sand, gold, sallow, buff, brilliant yellow, chrome yellow, Dutch pink-yellow, Dutch yellow, golden yellow, Imperial yellow, platinum yellow, yellow carmine, yellow madder, yellow ocher; see also color, gold. 2. [*Cowardly] tricky, deceitful, low, cringing, sneaking, white-livered, craven, treacherous; see also cowardly, vulgar 1. 3. [Sensational; *said especially of some newspapers*] tabloid, unethical, unprincipled; see exciting, offensive 2.

yellow, *a.* yellowish, golden, jaundiced-looking; see yellow *n.*

yelp, *v.* howl, screech, hoot; see cry 2, sound 1.

yes, *interj.* surely, of course, certainly, good, fine, aye, true, granted, very well, all right, *O.K. *or* *okay *or* *oke *or* *okey-dokey, Roger, we copy, over (to you), most assuredly, by all means, agreed, oh yes! amen, naturally, without fail, just so, good enough, even so, (in) the affirmative, *you bet (you).

yesterday, *a.* recently, previously, earlier; see before.

yesterday, *n.* the other day, the day before, recently, last day, not long ago; see also past 1.

yet, *a.* 1. [Nevertheless] notwithstanding, however, in spite of, despite, still, but, though, although, at any rate, on the other hand. 2. [Thus far] until now, till, hitherto, prior to, still; see also until 3. [In addition] besides, additionally, further; see besides.

yield, *v.* 1. [To surrender] give up, capitulate, succumb, resign, abdicate, relinquish, quit, cede, bow, lay down arms, cease from, let go, submit, give oneself over, relent, admit *or* suffer defeat, forgo, humble oneself, waive, *throw in the towel, *call quits, *back down, *holler uncle, *eat crow; see also abandon 1.—*Ant.* resist, withstand, repulse. 2. [To produce] bear, bring forth, blossom; see bloom, produce 1, 2. 3. [To grant] accede, concur, acquiesce; see admit 2, agree.

yielding, *a.* 1. [Producing] green, fruitful, productive; see fertile, rich 3. 2. [Flexible] pliant, plastic, malleable; see flexible. 3. [Docile] submissive, pliable, tractable; see humble 1, obedient 1.

yogi, *n.* mystic, fakir, anchorite, ascetic, practitioner of yoga, guru, devotee.

yokel, *n.* rustic, bumpkin, hayseed; see boor.

yolk, *n.* yellow, egg-yellow, egg yolk; see center 1, egg.

yonder, *a.* farther, away, faraway; see distant, remote 1.

you, *pron.* yourself, you yourself, thee, thou, all of you, you too, you alone, *you all.

young, *a.* 1. [In the early portion of life] puerile, boyish, girlish, adolescent, juvenile, budding, in one's teen's, childlike, youthful, pubescent, boylike, girllike, new-fledged, blooming, burgeoning, childish, half-grown, growing, blossoming, at the breast, (babe) in arms, knee high to a grasshopper.—*Ant.* old, aged, senile. 2. [Inexperienced] callow, green, immature, tender, raw, untutored, unlearned, junior, subordinate, inferior, unfledged, ignorant, undisciplined, tenderfoot, not dry behind the ears; see also inexperienced, naïve.—*Ant.* experienced, veteran, expert. 3. [New] fresh, modern, recent, newborn; see also fashionable.

youngster, *n.* child, boy, girl, pupil; see youth 3.

you're welcome, *interj.* my pleasure, forget it, think nothing of it, don't mention it, it's nothing.

youth, *n.* 1. [The state or quality of being young] boyhood, adolescence, girlhood, childhood, early manhood or womanhood or adulthood, puberty, tender age, juvenescence, minority, youthfulness, teen age, virginity, bloom, teens, age of ignorance, age of indiscretion, awkward age, salad days.—*Ant.* maturity, old age, senility. **2.** [Young people] the younger generation, the rising generation, the next generation, juvenility, children, the young, college youth, working youth. **3.** [A young person] boy, junior, teenager, lad, youngster, stripling, minor, young man, miss, girl, maiden, fledgling, juvenile, urchin, adolescent, student, *kid, teen, pre-teen, gosling, pup, calf; see also child.

youthful, *a.* **1.** [Possessing youth] young childlike, adolescent; see active, young 1, 2. **2.** [Suited to youth] keen, enthusiastic, zestful, vigorous, active, buoyant, lighthearted, prankish, fresh, lithe, full-blooded, full of life, full of animal spirits, limber, athletic, lightfooted, bubbling over, full of the devil; see also modern 1.—*Ant.* slow, cautious, serious.

yowl, *n.* howl, yelp, wail; see cry 1, yell 1.

yule, *n.* Christmas, Xmas, Nativity, Christmas season, Christmastide.

Z

zeal, *n.* **1.** [Enthusiasm] ardor, eagerness, fervor; see enthusiasm 1. **2.** [Industry] earnestness, hustle, hustling, bustle, bustling, intensity, industry, willingness, inclination, application, determination, promptitude, dispatch, diligence, perseverance, intentness, readiness, aptitude, enterprise, initiative, *push, *what it takes, *stick-to-itiveness; see also attention 2, care 1, co-operation 1.—*Ant.* idleness, slackness, indolence.

zealot, *n.* partisan, fan, bigot, fanatic, lobbyist, devotee, dogmatist, opinionist, missionary, fighter, cultist, follower, disciple, propagandist, *bitterender, *crank, addict, *bug, faddist, fiend.

zealously, *a.* with zeal, assiduously, fiercely; see industriously, vigorously.

zealous, *a.* fervent, earnest, intense, fanatic, industrious, diligent, intent, dogmatic, devoted, ardent; see also enthusiastic.

zero, *n.* **1.** [A cipher] naught, nothing, nadir, love, below freezing, the lowest point, *goose or duck egg, *nix. **2.** [Nothing] nullity, oblivion, void; see blank 1.

zest, *n.* **1.** [Relish] gusto, enjoyment, pleasure; see happiness 1. **2.** [Savor] taste, tang, piquancy, spice, bite, nip, pungency, punch, snap, ginger, kick, guts, body; see also flavor.

zigzag, *a.* oblique, inclined, sloping, awry, crooked, sinuous, twisted, askew, transverse, diagonal, curved, bent, crinkled, serrated, jagged, straggling, meandering, devious, erratic, rambling, oscillating, fluctuating, waggling, undulatory, vibratory, indirect, spiral, tortuous; see also angular, irregular 4.—*Ant.* straight, parallel, undeviating.

zodiac, *n.* celestial meridian, sign(s) of the zodiac, sky sign(s), group(s) of stars or planets, constellation(s); see also planet, star 1. The twelve signs of the zodiac are as follows—Aquarius or Water Bearer, Pisces or Fish, Aries or Ram, Taurus or Bull, Gemini or Twins, Cancer or Crab, Leo or Lion, Virgo or Virgin, Libra or Scales, Scorpio or Scorpion, Sagittarius or Archer, Capricorn or Goat.

zone, *n.* **1.** [A band] circuit, meridian, latitude; see band 1, stripe. **2.** [An area] region, district, territory; see place 3, position 1. Specific zones include the following—Torrid, Frigid, Temperate, Variable, Canal, traffic, parking, danger, building, quiet, school; Tropic of Cancer, Tropic of Capricorn, Arctic Circle, Antarctic Circle.

zoo, *n.* menagerie, terrarium, aquarium, aviary, vivarium, zoological garden.

zoological, *a.* animal, mammalian, marsupial, zoologic, mammalogical, ornithological, herpetological, ichthyological, ascidiological, echinological, conchological, entomological, arachnological, crustaceological, zoophytological, spongiological, protozoological, helminthiological; see alive 1, biological.

zoology, *n.* life science, biological science, natural history; see life 1, science.

zoom, *v.* speed, rush, hum; see climb, hurry 1, rise 1.

SYNONYMIES

The following paragraphs, listing and discriminating groups of closely related terms, are arranged alphabetically under those words which may generally be considered the most basic or comprehensive for each group. Although synonyms have similar, sometimes even identical, meanings, they are not always interchangeable with one another in every context. The subtle differences that distinguish such synonyms are briefly stated here, and typical examples of usage are given where they may be helpful.

able implies power or ability to do something [*able* to make payments] but sometimes suggests special power or skill [an *able* speaker]; **capable** usually implies that only ordinary requirements are met [a *capable* machinist]; **competent** and **qualified** both imply that the necessary qualifications for something are met, but **qualified** emphasizes that certain specified requirements are complied with [a *competent* critic of modern art; a *qualified* voter]

abridgment describes a work that is shortened from a larger work, but that keeps the main contents more or less unchanged; an **abstract** is a short statement of the main contents as of a court record or a technical writing; a **summary** usually restates the main points of the matter that has gone before; a **synopsis** is a condensed, orderly treatment, as of the plot of a novel; a **digest** is a concise, systematic treatment, generally broader in scope than a synopsis

absurd means so inconsistent with what is judged as reasonable or true as to be laughable [an *absurd* hypothesis]; **ludicrous** is applied to what is so incongruous or exaggerated as to be laughable [a *ludicrous* facial expression]; **preposterous** is used to describe anything extremely absurd or ludicrous; **foolish** describes that which shows lack of good judgment or of common sense [I don't take *foolish* chances]; **ridiculous** applies to whatever causes amusement or contempt because of its extreme foolishness

adjacent things may or may not be in actual contact with each other, but they are not separated by things of the same kind [*adjacent* angles; *adjacent* buildings]; that which is **adjoining** something else touches it at some point or along some line [*adjoining* rooms]; things are **contiguous** when they touch along the whole or most of one side [*contiguous* lots]; **tangent** implies contact at a single point on a curved line or surface [a line *tangent* to a circle]

agile and **nimble** both imply quickness and lightness of movement, but **agile** stresses general skill and ease in the use of the limbs, while **nimble** suggests quick sureness in carrying out a particular act [*nimble* fingers at the keyboard]; **quick** implies speed or promptness with no indication of the degree of skill; **spry** suggests nimbleness, esp. as displayed by a vigorous, elderly person; **sprightly** suggests liveliness, gaiety, etc.

agree is the general term used to express a fitting or going together without conflict; **conform** emphasizes agreement in form or basic character [specifications must *conform* to the building code]; **accord** emphasizes fitness for each other of the things being considered together [his story does not *accord* with the facts]; **harmonize** implies a combining of different things in an orderly or pleasing arrangement [*harmonizing* colors]; **correspond** is applied to that which matches, complements, or is comparable to something else [their Foreign Office *corresponds* to our State Department]; **coincide** stresses that the things being considered are identical [their interests *coincide*]

amiable and **affable** both suggest friendliness and an easygoing temperament that make one likeable, **affable** also implying a readiness to talk and be sociable; a **good-natured** person is one who tends to like others as well as to be liked by them, and is sometimes easily imposed on; **obliging** implies a ready, often cheerful, desire to be helpful [the *obliging* clerk answered my questions]; **genial** suggests cheerful sociability [our *genial* host]; **cordial** suggests sincerity and warmth [a *cordial* welcome]

appreciate implies enough understanding and judgment to see the value or to enjoy [he *appreciates* good music]; to **value** is to rate highly because of worth [I *value* your friendship]; to **prize** is to think highly of or take great satisfaction in [he *prizes* his art collection]; to **treasure** is to regard as precious and implies special care and protection; to **esteem** is to hold in high regard or respect [an *esteemed* statesman]; to **cherish** is to prize or treasure, but connotes greater affection for the thing cherished [he *cherished* his family]

argument refers to a discussion in which there is disagreement and suggests the use of reasoning and the bringing forth of facts to support or disprove a point; **dispute** basically refers to a disagreement involving debate in which there is strong feeling or anger [an international boundary *dispute*]; **controversy** suggests a disagreement that lasts a long time and has to do with a matter of some importance [the continuing *controversy* over some of Freud's theories]

avenge and **revenge** both refer to the inflicting of punishment for a wrong done, but **avenge** suggests that the motive is a wish to see justice done, whereas **revenge** implies that one wishes to get even, usually for an injury against oneself, and suggests bitter feelings of hatred and resentment

banish means to force to leave a country (not necessarily one's own) as a punishment; **exile** implies being forced to leave one's own country, either because the government has ordered it or events have made it necessary; **expatriate** suggests more strongly exile by one's own choice and often implies the getting of citizenship in another country; to **deport** is to send (an alien) out of the country, either because he entered unlawfully or because he is considered undesirable

base implies a putting of one's own interests ahead of all else, as because of

greed or cowardice [*base* motives]; **mean** suggests a pettiness of character or conduct [his *mean* attempts to slander her]; **ignoble** suggests a lack of high moral qualities [to work for an *ignoble* end]; **abject** implies lowness of character and a lack of self-respect [an *abject* coward]; **sordid** suggests a depressing drabness of something mean or base [a *sordid* scheme to cheat others]; **vile** suggests disgusting foulness or wickedness [*vile* language]; **low** suggests coarseness and corruption, esp. in reference to taking unfair advantage [so *low* as to rob the poor]

beautiful is applied to that which gives the most pleasure and suggests that the thing that delights one comes close to one's ideal; **lovely** refers to that which delights by causing one to feel affection or warm admiration; **handsome** is used of that which attracts by its pleasing proportions, elegance, etc. and suggests a masculine quality; **pretty** implies daintiness or gracefulness and suggests a feminine quality; **comely** applies to persons only and suggests a wholesome attractiveness rather than great beauty; **fair** suggests beauty, esp. of complexion or features, that is fresh, bright, or perfect; **good-looking** generally equals either **handsome** or **pretty**; **beauteous**, a poetical synonym for **beautiful**, is now often used in a joking or belittling way

belief is the general term for the acceptance of something as true, even without being completely certain; **faith** implies complete acceptance, even without proof and, esp., of something not supported by reason; **trust** implies assurance, often based on intuition, that someone or something is reliable; **confidence** also suggests such assurance, esp. when based on reason or proof

belligerent implies a taking part in war or fighting or in warlike actions [*belligerent* nations]; **bellicose** implies a warlike nature, suggesting a readiness to fight [a *bellicose* mood]; **pugnacious** and **quarrelsome** both suggest eagerness to start a fight, but **quarrelsome** more often suggests willingness to fight for no good reason; **contentious** suggests a readiness to keep on arguing or quarreling in an annoying way

bodily refers to the human body as apart from the mind or spirit [*bodily* organs]; **physical** is often used like **bodily**, but may suggest less directly the organs or parts, etc. of the body [*physical* labor]; **corporeal** refers to the matter that makes up the body and is opposed to *spiritual* [his *corporeal* remains]; **corporal** refers to the effect of something upon the body [*corporal* punishment]; **somatic** is the word used, as in a scientific description, to refer to the body as distinct from the mind [the *somatic* differences between individuals]

bright implies in a general way the giving forth or reflecting of light, or a being filled with light [a *bright* day, star, shield, etc.]; **radiant** emphasizes the sending out of rays of light; **shining** implies a steady, continuous brightness [the *shining* sun]; **brilliant** implies strong or flashing brightness [*brilliant* sunlight, diamonds, etc.]; **luminous** is used of objects that are full of light or give off phosphorescent light; **lustrous** is used of objects whose surfaces gleam by reflected light and suggests glossiness [*lustrous* silk]

bulk, **mass**, and **volume** all refer to a quantity of matter or number of units making up a whole; **bulk** implies a body of great size, weight, or numbers [the lumbering *bulk* of an elephant; the *bulk* of humanity]; **mass** suggests a group or number of parts forming a single, unified body [an egg-shaped *mass*; the *mass* of workers]; **volume** implies a moving or flowing mass, often one that keeps changing [*volumes* of smoke; the *volume* of production]

calm, basically applied to the weather, suggests a lack of movement or excitement [a *calm* sea; a *calm* reply]; **tranquil** implies a deeper or more permanent peace and quiet than calm [a *tranquil* old age]; **serene** suggests a dignified tranquillity, as of a person who is at peace with himself; **placid** implies total calmness, often to the point of being dull and uninteresting [she's as *placid* as a cow]; **peaceful** suggests freedom from disorder or from a show of strong feeling [a *peaceful* gathering]

caricature refers to an imitation or drawing of a person, as in a cartoon, that exaggerates outstanding features in a comical way; **burlesque** implies the handling of a serious subject in a light and flippant way or of a trivial subject in a way that pretends to be serious; a **parody** imitates the style of a writer or of some writing very closely, but makes fun of it by using an absurd subject or a nonsensical approach; a **travesty**, on the other hand, deals with the same subject as the original but in a ridiculous style or laughable language; **satire** refers to writing in which evil, stupid, or wicked persons or institutions are ridiculed or dealt with sarcastically

cause refers to something that produces an effect or result [carelessness is often a *cause* of accidents]; **reason** implies

thinking that is engaged in to explain some act or idea [she had a *reason* for laughing]; a **motive** is a thought, emotion, or desire that leads to action [the *motive* for the crime]; an **antecedent** is an event or thing that comes before, and is responsible for, a later event or thing [war always has its *antecedents*]; an **occasion** is a situation or event that allows a cause to have an effect [the court case was an *occasion* for stating a new legal principle]

cheat implies the use of dishonesty in dealing with someone, in order to get something he has; **defraud** stresses the use of deliberate deception in taking away a person's rights, property, etc. in a way that is against the law; **swindle** stresses the winning of a person's trust in order to cheat or defraud him of money, etc.; **trick** implies the use of a clever scheme or device to mislead someone, but does not necessarily suggest dishonesty; **dupe** suggests the tricking of someone who is foolish and too willing to trust others; **hoax** implies the use of a complicated scheme to dupe others, often simply in fun

childlike and **childish** are both applied to persons of any age in referring to qualities considered typical of a child, **childlike** suggesting the favorable qualities such as innocence, honesty, curiosity, zest, etc., and **childish** the unfavorable ones such as immaturity, foolishness, lack of self-control, self-centeredness, etc.

clever implies a quickness of mind or wit, as in solving a problem, in conversation, etc. [a *clever* idea; a *clever* reply]; **cunning** implies cleverness of a sly, tricky, or crafty kind [*cunning* as a fox]; **ingenious** suggests cleverness in thinking up or inventing something [an *ingenious* explanation; an *ingenious* designer]; **shrewd** suggests cleverness or sharpness in dealing with practical matters [a *shrewd* analysis; a *shrewd* bargainer]

comfort suggests any attempt to make someone less sorrowful or unhappy as by trying to cheer him up or inspire him with hope; **console** suggests the offering of help or relief to someone who has lost someone or something or has been disappointed [to *console* someone whose best friend has died]; **solace** suggests any thing or any action that makes a person less sad, depressed, bored, lonely, etc. [he *solaced* himself by playing the guitar]; **relief** suggests the easing, often just for a time, of misery or discomfort so that one can bear it more easily [to *relieve* the poor on welfare]; **soothe** implies trying to calm or lessen pain or distress [she *soothed* the child with a lullaby]

compare implies a noting of likenesses and differences and an examining of features side by side to see how they are alike or different [to *compare* Shaw with Chekov]; **contrast** implies a comparing for the express purpose of showing differences [to *contrast* city life with living in the country]

concise stresses briefness in speaking or writing so that no more words are used than are needed to express something clearly [a *concise* statement]; **terse** suggests extremely clipped and abrupt expression, as when one must be brief and to the point [the captain's *terse* command]; **laconic** implies a very brief, sometimes vague statement, as by someone who habitually says very little [the cowboy's *laconic* reply]; **succinct** indicates very brief, clear, and compact expression in which only what is essential is dealt with [a *succinct* record of the proceedings]; **pithy** suggests that what is stated in highly compressed form is important and full of meaning [a *pithy* proverb]

consent implies giving in to something proposed or requested when one has the power to do so or not [to *consent* to serve as chairman]; to **assent** is to express one's acceptance or approval of something [he *assented* to the plan favored by the others]; **agree** implies accord reached by settling differences of opinion or overcoming resistance [to *agree* on a fair price for the property]; **concur** implies agreement arrived at formally on a specific matter, often with regard to a line of action [all the doctors *concurred* in the decision to operate]; to **accede** is to yield one's assent to a proposal [he *acceded* to the union's request for arbitration]; **acquiesce** implies a giving in quietly when one may have some doubts

continual applies to that which happens again and again or goes on without stopping over a long period of time [*continual* arguments]; **continuous** applies to that which goes on without a break in either space or time [a *continuous* area of land]; **constant** stresses being steady or regular in happening or happening again and again [the *constant* beat of the heart]; **incessant** implies activity that goes on without being stopped or interrupted [*incessant* chatter]; **perpetual** applies to that which lasts or remains for an indefinitely long period of time [a *perpetual* nuisance]; **eternal** stresses an endless or timeless quality [the *eternal* truths]

copy is the broadest of the terms here

referring to anything that is made to be like the original or patterned after it [a carbon *copy*; a *copy* of a designer's dress]; **reproduction** implies a close imitation of the original, often, however, with differences, as of material, size, or quality [a *reproduction* of a painting]; **facsimile** is an exact reproduction, sometimes one differing in scale [a photostated *facsimile* of a document]; a **duplicate** is a double, or counterpart, of something, serving all the purposes of the original [all the books of a single printing are *duplicates*]; a **replica** is an exact reproduction of a work of art

criticize, in this comparison, is the general term for finding fault with or disapproving of a person or thing; **reprehend** suggests severe disapproval, usually of faults, errors, etc. rather than of people; **blame** stresses the fixing of responsibility for an error, fault, etc. [don't *blame* your laziness on the heat]; **censure** implies the expression of severe criticism or disapproval, as by a person in authority; **condemn** suggests the passing of harsh, final judgment on a person or thing considered guilty or to blame; **denounce** implies a speaking out publicly against persons or actions thought to be immoral, corrupt, evil, etc.

danger is the general word for any kind of exposure to injury, loss, etc. [the *danger* of falling on icy walks]; **peril** suggests great danger that is near at hand [flood waters put the town in *peril*]; **jeopardy** emphasizes exposure to extreme danger [reckless driving puts one's life in *jeopardy*]; **hazard** implies danger of which one may be aware but over which one has little control [the *hazards* of combat duty]; **risk** implies willingness to take a dangerous chance [he saved the day at the *risk* of his life]

deceive implies a deliberate telling of lies or acting dishonestly, usually by one who expects to gain something for himself [he was *deceived* by the salesman into paying too much for the car]; to **mislead** is to cause to follow the wrong course or do the wrong thing, although not always on purpose [misled by the sign into going to the wrong floor]; **beguile** implies the use of charm, tempting promises, etc. in deceiving or misleading [she *beguiled* him into believing her lies]; to **delude** is to fool someone so completely that he accepts as true or real something that is false; **betray** implies a breaking of faith while seeming to be loyal, true, or friendly

delusion implies belief in something that

is contrary to fact or reality, resulting from trickery, a misunderstanding, or a mental disorder [to have *delusions* of grandeur]; **illusion** suggests or gives an appearance of something real as by copying it or making something that looks like it [movies give us the *illusion* of seeing and hearing real people]; **hallucination** gives one the impression of experiencing as though it were real something that is not actually there, as when one is drugged or has a mental disorder

dexterous implies an ability to do things with skill and precision [a *dexterous* weaver]; **adroit** adds to this the idea of cleverness, now esp. in dealing with people, ideas, etc. [they admired her *adroit* handling of an awkward situation]; **deft** suggests a nimbleness and sureness of touch [a seamstress *deft* with the needle]; **handy** suggests skill, usually without training, at a large variety of tasks [he is very *handy* around the house]

discern implies a making out of something or recognizing it clearly with the eyes or in the mind [to *discern* one's motives]; **perceive** implies a recognizing by means of any of the senses and, often, in addition, implies keen understanding or insight [to *perceive* differences in pitch; to *perceive* a change in attitude]; **distinguish** implies a perceiving clearly by sight, hearing, etc. [he *distinguished* the voices of men and women down the hall]; **observe** and **notice** both connote paying attention to some degree, and usually suggest use of the sense of sight [to *observe* an eclipse; to *notice* a sign]

disparage means to cast doubt on the worth or reputation of someone or something, often in subtle ways, as by praising with little enthusiasm or making an unfair comparison [to *disparage* a modern dramatist by comparing him with Shakespeare]; to **depreciate** is to suggest that something has less value than it is generally supposed to have; to **belittle** is to indicate, often spitefully or scornfully, one's low opinion of something's or someone's worth [always *belittling* his fellow scientist's achievements]; to **minimize** is to make seem as small as possible [a biased biographer who *minimized* his subject's faults]

distinguish implies a recognizing or setting apart from others by means of special features or characteristic qualities [to *distinguish* the Asian elephant from the African elephant]; **discriminate** suggests a distinguishing of minute or subtle differences between similar things [to *discriminate* between synonyms];

differentiate suggests noticing or pointing out specific differences between things by comparing them in detail [his duties as a son as *differentiated* from those as a brother]

dwarf refers to an individual that is much smaller than the usual kind and sometimes implies that the parts are deformed or not in normal proportion; **midget** refers to a very small human being who has normal form and proportions; **Pygmy**, in strict use, refers to a member of any of several small-sized African or Asian peoples, but it is sometimes used (written **pygmy**) as a synonym for **dwarf** or **midget**

ecstasy implies very strong feeling, now usually intense delight, that overpowers one's senses and lifts one into a kind of trance; **bliss** implies a state of happiness and contentment so great as to suggest the joys of heaven; **rapture** now generally suggests the intense feeling one has when something causing great joy or pleasure captures all of one's attention; **transport** implies a being carried away by any powerful feeling

eject implies generally a throwing or casting out from within [to *eject* saliva from the mouth]; **expel** suggests a driving out, as by force, specif., a forcing out of a country, organization, etc., often in disgrace [*expelled* from school]; **evict** refers to a forcing out by the use of legal means [to *evict* a tenant]; **oust** implies the getting rid of something that is not wanted, as by the use of force or the action of the law [to *oust* corrupt officials]

enormous implies a going far beyond what is normal in size, amount, or degree [an *enormous* room; *enormous* expenses]; **immense** implies size beyond the usual measurements but suggests that great size is normal for the thing described [redwoods are *immense* trees]; **huge** usually suggests a great mass or bulk [a *huge* building; *huge* profits]; **gigantic, colossal,** and **mammoth** originally implied a likeness to a *giant,* the *Colossus* of Rhodes, and an extinct elephant (the *mammoth*), and therefore these words emphasize the idea of great size, force, importance, etc., now often in an exaggerated way; **tremendous** literally suggests that which causes awe or amazement because of its great size

epicure refers to a person whose taste in food and drink is highly refined and who takes great pleasure in eating and drinking good things; a **gourmet** is one who is very fond of fine things to eat and drink, has expert knowledge about their selection and preparation, and takes pride in his ability to appreciate subtle differences in flavor and quality; **gourmand**, occasionally used to mean the same thing as **gourmet**, is more often applied to a person who has such a hearty appetite for good food that he tends to overeat

essential is applied to that which is the basic essence or fundamental nature of a thing and therefore must be present for the thing to exist, function, etc. [food is *essential* to life]; an **indispensable** person or thing cannot be done without if the specified purpose is to be achieved; **requisite** is applied to that which is required by the circumstances or for the purpose and often suggests a requirement that is demanded or insisted upon [the *requisite* skills for the job]; **necessary** implies an urgent or pressing need but not always for something that is indispensable

excessive applies to that which goes beyond what is needed, right, or usual [*excessive* demands]; **exorbitant** is applied esp. to charges, prices, etc. that are unreasonably or unfairly high [*exorbitant* profits]; **extravagant** and **immoderate** both imply excessiveness resulting from a lack of control or careful judgment [*extravagant* praise; *immoderate* smoking]; **inordinate** implies a going beyond the orderly limits of convention or good taste [his *inordinate* pride]

explain implies a making clear of something that is not known or understood [to *explain* how a machine operates]; **expound** implies an orderly and thorough explanation, often one made by a person having expert knowledge [to *expound* a theory]; **explicate** implies a scholarly analysis or explanation that is developed in detail [the *explication* of a Biblical passage]; **elucidate** implies a shedding light upon by clear and specific explanation, illustration, etc. [to *elucidate* the country's foreign policy]; to **interpret** is to bring out meanings not immediately clear, as by translation, personal insight, or special knowledge [how do you *interpret* his silence?]; **construe** suggests a particular interpretation of something that can be understood in several ways [his statement is not to be lightly *construed*]

extract implies a drawing out of something, as if by pulling [to *extract* testimony from an unwilling witness]; **educe** suggests a bringing out or evolving of something that is undeveloped [to *educe* a theory from the known facts]; **elicit** suggests difficulty or skill in drawing forth something [his jokes *elicited* laughter from the angry crowd];

evoke implies a calling forth, as of a mental image, by stimulating the mind or emotions [the odor *evoked* a memory of childhood]

fantastic implies a completely free use of the imagination, and suggests that which is unreal or dreamlike in a striking way [*fantastic* stage sets]; **bizarre** suggests that which is extremely strange or unusual because it is startling or unexpected [a *bizarre* combination of costumes]; **grotesque** suggests something that appears comic or frightening because it is a distortion of the real or natural [pain twisted his face into a *grotesque* mask]

fatal implies that death or disaster has occurred or will surely occur [a *fatal* disease; a *fatal* mistake]; **deadly** is applied to a thing that can and probably will cause death [a *deadly* poison]; **mortal** is applied to that which has just caused or will soon cause death [a *mortal* wound]; **lethal** is applied to that which is intended or designed to cause death [a *lethal* weapon]

flagrant applies to anything that is so clearly bad or wrong that it deserves to be criticized or condemned [a *flagrant* violation of the law]; **glaring** is used of something bad that stands out even more clearly so that it is noticed immediately [a *glaring* error in arithmetic]; **gross** implies badness or wrongness which is so extreme or disgusting that it cannot be excused or forgiven [*gross* neglect of a child]

flash implies a sudden, brief, brilliant light; **gleam** suggests a steady, narrow ray of light shining through darkness; **sparkle** implies a number of brief, bright flashes from many points of light; **glitter** implies the reflection of such bright flashes, as from metal or a jewel; **glisten** suggests the reflection of a bright light, as from a wet surface; **shimmer** refers to a soft, wavering reflection of light, as from the surface of gently moving water

frank applies to a person, remark, etc. that is free or blunt in expressing the truth or an opinion and is not held back by the usual restraints [a *frank* criticism]; **candid** implies a basic honesty that makes it impossible for one to deceive or be sly, sometimes to the point where the listener could be embarrassed [a *candid* opinion]; **open** implies a lack of secrecy and often suggests a genuine and innocent quality [her *open* admiration for him]; **outspoken** suggests a lack of restraint in offering opinions, esp. when it might be better to keep quiet

funny is the simple, general term for

anything that appeals to one's sense of humor or causes laughter; **laughable** is a usually scornful term for that which is fit to be laughed at [what a *laughable* excuse!]; something that is amusing brings laughter or smiles by its pleasant, entertaining quality; that which is **droll** amuses one because it is quaint or strange or because of its twisted humor; **comic** is applied to that which is like a comedy in amusing one in a thoughtful way; **comical** is used of that which brings on uncontrolled laughter; **farcical** suggests a comical quality that is based on nonsense, broad humor, etc.

gaudy applies to that which is brightly colored and highly decorated but which is regarded as being in bad taste [*gaudy* furniture]; **tawdry** is used of something cheap and poorly made that is also gaudy [a *tawdry* wall hanging]; **garish** implies a glaring brightness of color and too much decoration [*garish* wallpaper]; **flashy** and **showy** imply a brightness or display that attracts attention, but **flashy** implies that it is offensive to those with more conservative tastes [a *flashy* sport coat], while **showy** does not always imply this [*showy* blossoms]

ghastly suggests the horror caused by the sight or suggestion of death [a *ghastly* smile on the dead man's face]; **grim** implies extremely disagreeable or even terrifying aspects [the *grim* life of the very poor]; **grisly** suggests an appearance or nature that causes one to be horrified [the *grisly* sights of the concentration camp]; **gruesome** suggests the fear and disgust caused by something horrible and evil [the *gruesome* details of a murder]; **macabre** implies a being concerned or fascinated with the gruesome aspects of death [a *macabre* tale]

greedy implies a desire to get or have much or more of something than is one's share or than one needs; **avaricious** stresses greed for money or riches and often suggests a being miserly; **grasping** suggests a strong eagerness for gain that shows itself in a seizing of every opportunity to get what one wants; **acquisitive** stresses the drive to keep gathering more and more wealth or possessions; **covetous** implies a strong desire for something that belongs to another person

group is the basic, general word expressing the simple idea of an assembly of persons, animals, or things without any added meaning; **herd** is applied to a group of cattle, sheep, or similar large animals feeding, living, or moving together; **flock**, to goats, sheep, or birds; **drove**, to cattle, hogs, or sheep;

pack, to hounds or wolves; **pride**, to lions; **swarm**, to insects; **school**, to fish, porpoises, whales, etc.; **bevy**, to quails; **covey**, to partridges or quails; **flight**, to birds flying together. In extended use, **flock** connotes guidance and care, **herd**, **drove**, and **pack** are used as terms of contempt for people, **swarm** suggests a large mass or throng moving together, and **bevy** and **covey** are used of girls or women

happy generally suggests a feeling of great pleasure, contentment, etc. [a *happy* marriage]; **glad** more strongly implies a feeling of joy [your letter made her so *glad!*], but both **glad** and **happy** are commonly used in merely polite phrases expressing pleasure [I'm *glad*, or *happy*, to have met you]; **cheerful** implies a steady display of bright spirits, optimism, etc. [she is always *cheerful* in the morning]; **joyful** and **joyous** both imply very high spirits and rejoicing, the former generally because of a particular event [the good news made them *joyful*], and the latter usually because of a continuing situation [they were a *joyous* family]

hate implies a feeling of great dislike or a strong wish to avoid, and, with persons as the object, suggests a wish to harm them; **detest** implies extreme dislike; **despise** suggests a looking down with great contempt upon the person or thing one hates; **loathe** implies intense dislike together with extreme disgust; **abhor** implies great dislike or disgust joined with feelings of moral disapproval

hesitate implies a temporary stopping because of feeling uncertain, unwilling, or confused [he *hesitated* before entering]; **vacillate** implies a shifting back and forth in a decision, opinion, etc. [she *vacillates* in her affection]; **waver** is often applied to a holding back or hesitating after a decision has been made [do not *waver* in your determination]; **falter** suggests a pausing or slowing down, as in fear or indecision [they never *faltered* in the counterattack]

high and **tall** both refer to something which extends farther upward than is normal for its kind, and **high** also refers to something in a place far above a given level [a *high* mountain; *high* clouds], but **tall** is usually applied to people, animals, and other growing things [a *tall* woman; a *tall* tree]; **lofty** and **towering** suggest great, imposing, or very noticeable height [*lofty* peaks; a *towering* castle]

ignorant implies a lack of knowledge, either in general [an *ignorant* man] or on some particular matter [*ignorant* of the reason for their quarrel]; **illiterate** implies an inability to read or write; **unlettered** is sometimes used as a milder substitute for **illiterate**, but often implies unfamiliarity with fine literature [although a graduate engineer, he is relatively *unlettered*]; **uneducated** and **untutored** imply a lack of formal schooling [he had a brilliant, though *uneducated*, mind]

impertinent is used of speech or behavior that shows a lack of respect by not following the usual rules of politeness and good manners; **impudent** suggests bold, open, deliberate rudeness or impertinence; **insolent** implies extreme disrespect shown in speech or behavior that is deliberately insulting or filled with contempt; **saucy** suggests a light, flippant manner and improper informality in dealing with someone to whom respect should be shown

include implies a containing as part of a whole; **comprise**, in careful use, means to consist of and takes as its object the various parts that make up the whole [his library *comprises* 2,000 volumes and *includes* many first editions]; **comprehend** suggests that the object is contained within the total scope or range of the subject, sometimes by being implied [the word "beauty" *comprehends* various qualities]; **embrace** emphasizes the variety of objects comprehended [he had *embraced* a number of hobbies]; **involve** implies that an object is included because of its connection with the subject as a cause or result [acceptance of high office *involves* responsibilities]

infer suggests the arriving at a decision or opinion by reasoning from known facts or evidence [from your smile, I *infer* that you are pleased]; **deduce** stresses the use of logical and systematic reasoning in inferring something [the existence of the planet Neptune was *deduced* before its actual discovery]; **conclude** strictly implies an inference that is the final, logical result in a process of reasoning [I must, therefore, *conclude* that you are right]; **judge** stresses the careful checking and weighing of statements, arguments, etc. in reaching a conclusion; **gather** is an informal substitute for **infer** and **conclude** [I *gather* that you don't care]

instance refers to a person, thing, or event that is given as proof or support of something [the gift is an *instance* of his generosity]; **case** is applied to a happening or situation of a specified kind [a *case* of mistaken identity]; **example** is applied to something that is mentioned as typical of the members of its group [his novel is an *example* of science fiction]; **illustration** is used of an instance or example that helps to explain or make something clear [this sentence is an *illustration* of the use of a word]

intrude implies the forcing of oneself or something upon another without being asked or wanted or without having the right to do so [to *intrude* upon another's privacy]; **obtrude** suggests even more strongly that the intrusion causes an unwanted distraction or great unpleasantness [side issues keep *obtruding*]

irritate is the most general of the words here and may suggest mild impatience, continued annoyance, or a flare-up of anger [their smugness *irritates* her]; **provoke** suggests the causing of strong feelings of annoyance, resentment, or anger, often with a wish to get even [*provoked* by the insult]; **nettle** implies irritation caused as by petty, nagging remarks or actions that hurt one's pride [subtle taunts that *nettled* him]; **exasperate** implies great irritation caused by something that makes one lose one's patience or self-control [*exasperated* by the clerk's many careless mistakes]

join is the general term meaning a bringing or coming together of two or more things and may suggest direct contact, becoming a member of a group, etc.; **combine** implies a mingling together of things or a complete merging of distinct elements [to *combine* milk and water]; **unite** implies a joining or combining of things to form a single whole [the *United* States]; **connect** implies attachment by some fastening or relationship [roads *connected* by a bridge; the duties *connected* with a job]; **link** stresses firmness of a connection [*linked* together in a common cause]; **consolidate** implies a merger of distinct and separate units into a single whole for making something compact, strong, efficient, etc. [to *consolidate* one's debts]

laugh is the general word for the sounds made in expressing happiness, amusement, ridicule, etc.; **chuckle** implies the soft laughter in low tones that expresses mild amusement or inner satisfaction; **giggle** and **titter**, both often associated with children or girls, refer to a half-suppressed laugh consisting of a series of rapid, high-pitched sounds, suggesting embarrassment, silliness, etc.; **snicker** is used of a sly, half-suppressed laugh, as at another's embarrassment, confusion, etc.; **guffaw** refers to loud, hearty, coarse laughter

liberal implies tolerance of others' views as well as open-mindedness to ideas that challenge tradition, established institutions, etc.; **progressive** is the opposite of *reactionary* or *conservative* and is applied to persons who favor progress and reform in politics, education, etc. and are inclined to take direct action; **radical** is applied to those who favor fundamental or extreme change, specifically of the social structure; **left** is applied to those who are liberal or radical in their political views

liquid refers to a substance that flows readily and takes on the form of its container but stays the same in volume [water that is neither ice nor steam is a *liquid*]; **fluid** applies to any substance that flows [all liquids, gases, and viscous substances are *fluids*]

loiter implies either staying around a place without having anything to do there or moving along in a slow, rambling way [to *loiter* on street corners]; **dawdle** implies wasting time over trifles or taking more time to do something than is necessary [to *dawdle* over dinner]; **dally** suggests spending time in silly or pointless activity; **idle** suggests laziness or avoidance of work [to *idle* away the hours]

love implies intense fondness or deep devotion and may apply to various relationships or objects [sexual *love*, brotherly *love*, *love* of one's work, etc.]; **affection** suggests warm, tender feelings, usually not as powerful or as deep as those implied by **love** [he has no *affection* for children]; **attachment** implies connection by ties of affection, loyalty, devotion, etc. and may be felt for non-living things as well as for people [an *attachment* for an old hat]; **infatuation** implies a passion or affection that is foolish or shows poor judgment, often one that lasts only a short time [an elderly man's *infatuation* with a young girl]

lure suggests a strong force, as desire, greed, curiosity, etc., that attracts someone, often to something harmful or evil [*lured* into the plot by their false promises]; **entice** implies a clever or skillful luring [he *enticed* the squirrel to eat from his hand]; **decoy** implies the use of false appearances in luring into a trap [artificial birds are used to *decoy* wild ducks]; **beguile** suggests the use of subtle tricks in leading someone on [*beguiled* by her sweet words]; **tempt** suggests a powerful attraction that tends to overcome doubts or judgment [*tempted* by a chance for profit to invest his savings]

malice implies a deep hatred or dislike causing one to get pleasure from hurting others or seeing them suffer; **ill**

will implies unfriendly feelings that lead one to wish harm, unhappiness, etc. to others; **malevolence**, a formal term for **ill will**, may also suggest that the unfriendly feelings are stronger and more evil; **spite** suggests a mean desire to get back at others by hurting or annoying them, esp. in nasty, petty ways; **rancor** implies bitter, long-lasting ill will; **malignity** suggests great malevolence that shows itself in acts of cruelty without pity

material is applied to anything that is formed of matter or substance [chairs are *material* objects]; **physical** applies either to material things known through the senses or to forces that can be measured scientifically [the *physical* world; the *physical* properties of sound]; **corporeal** applies only to material objects that have bodily form and can be touched [a house is *corporeal* property]

meaning is the general word for what is intended to be expressed or understood by something [the *meaning* of a sentence]; **sense** refers especially to any of the various meanings of a word or phrase [this word has several slang *senses*]; **import** refers to all of what is being implied by something said or done, including any subtle or hidden meanings [the full *import* of his remark came to me later]; **purport** refers to the general meaning, or main point, of something [what was the *purport* of her letter?]; **signification** is applied especially to the meaning that a certain sign, symbol, character, etc. commonly suggests to people [the *signification* of the ace of spades in fortunetelling]

memory refers to the ability or power of keeping in or bringing to mind past thoughts, images, ideas, etc. [to have a good *memory*]; **remembrance** applies to the act or process of having such events or things come to mind again [the *remembrance* of things in the past]; **recollection** implies a careful effort to remember the details of some event [his *recollection* of the campaign is not too clear]; **reminiscence** implies the thoughtful or nostalgic recollection of long-past events, usually pleasant ones, or the telling of these [he entertained us with *reminiscences* of his childhood]

mirth implies gaiety, gladness, or great amusement, esp. as expressed by laughter; **glee** implies a great, open display of joy, or it may suggest delight over another's suffering or unhappiness; **jollity** and **merriment** imply very great mirth or joy like that displayed at an especially lively and merry party or celebration; **hilarity** implies noisy and lively merriment and sometimes suggests an excessively loud display of high spirits

mix implies a combining of things so that the resulting substance is the same throughout, whether or not the separate elements can be distinguished [to *mix* paints]; **mingle** usually implies that the separate elements can be distinguished [*mingled* feelings of joy and sorrow]; **blend** implies a mixing of different varieties to produce a desired quality [a *blended* tea, whiskey, etc.] or the mingling of different elements to form a pleasing whole [a novel *blending* fact and fiction]

mood refers to a temporary state of mind and emphasizes a specified feeling [she's in a happy *mood*]; **humor** emphasizes an uncertain or unchanging quality in the mood [he wept and laughed as his *humor* moved him]; **temper** applies to a mood marked by a single, strong emotion, especially that of anger [my, he's in a nasty *temper*]

moral implies living according to accepted standards of goodness or rightness in conduct or character, especially in sexual conduct [a *moral* woman]; **ethical** implies following a carefully planned ideal code of moral principles, often the code of a particular profession [an *ethical* lawyer]; **virtuous** implies a morally excellent character concerned about justice, integrity, and, often, chastity; **righteous** implies taking a moral stand based on good or just reasons [*righteous* anger]

murmur implies a steady flow of words or sounds in a low, indistinct voice and may suggest either a contented or discontented feeling [to *murmur* a prayer]; **mutter** usually suggests angry or complaining words or sounds of this kind [to *mutter* curses]; to **mumble** is to utter words or sounds in low tones and with the mouth almost closed so that they are very hard to hear or understand [an old woman *mumbling* to herself]

naive implies a being simple and innocent in a trusting way, but sometimes suggests an almost foolish lack of worldly wisdom [his *naive* belief that all advertising is honest]; **ingenuous** suggests a childlike frankness or straightforwardness [her *ingenuous* delight in any kind of flattery]; **artless** implies the appealing open and natural quality of one who is indifferent to the effect he has on others [a simple, *artless* style of folk singing]; **unsophisticated** implies a lack of poise, worldliness, subtlety, etc. resulting from a limited experience of life [an *unsophisticated* farm boy]

need is the simple, direct word and necessity the more formal term referring to a lack of something that is wanted or must be had, or to the thing that is required [they are in *need* of food; food is a *necessity* for all living things]; **exigency** refers to a necessity brought about by some emergency or by specific events [the *exigencies* created by the flood]; **requisite** applies to something that cannot be done without in order to carry out some activity [a sense of rhythm is a *requisite* in a dancer]

new is applied to that which has never existed before or which has only just come into being, possession, use, etc. [a *new* coat, plan, etc.]; **fresh** is used of something so new that it still has its original appearance, quality, strength, etc. [*fresh* eggs, a *fresh* start]; **novel** implies a newness that is very strange or unusual [a *novel* idea, combination, etc.]; **modern** and **modernistic** refer to that which is associated with the present time rather than an earlier period and imply up-to-dateness, with **modernistic** sometimes being used to suggest contempt as well [*modern* dance, a *modernistic* painting]; **original** is used of that which not only is new but is also the first of its kind [an *original* plan, melody, etc.]

obscure applies to that which is unclear to the senses or to the mind either because it is concealed, veiled, or imprecisely stated or because of dullness or lack of insight in the perceiver [his motives remain *obscure*]; **vague** applies to that which is so lacking in precision or exactness that it is indistinct or unclear [a *vague* notion]; **enigmatic** and **cryptic** are used of that which baffles or bewilders, the latter word implying a deliberate intention to puzzle [his *enigmatic* behavior, a *cryptic* warning]; **ambiguous** applies to that which puzzles because it can be understood in more than one way ["The Lead Horse" is an *ambiguous* title]; **equivocal** is used of something ambiguous that is used to mislead or confuse [the politician's *equivocal* answer]

offend implies a causing displeasure or resentment in another, either on purpose or without meaning to, by hurting his feelings or by behaving in a way he considers improper [she will be *offended* if she is not invited]; **affront** implies an open and deliberate showing of disrespect or contempt [his uncalled-for criticism of their school *affronted* the graduates]; **insult** implies an affront so insolent or rude that it causes deep humiliation and resentment [to *insult* someone by calling him a liar]

ominous is used of something that seems to threaten but does not necessarily suggest that a disaster will result [his request was met by an *ominous* silence]; **portentous** is applied literally to a sign or warning, esp. of evil, but is now more often used of that which causes awe or amazement because of its wonderful or extraordinary character [the first landing on the moon was a *portentous* event]; **fateful** may imply control by or as if by fate, but is now usually applied to that which is of very important or crucial significance [a *fateful* truce conference]; **foreboding** implies a feeling that something evil or harmful will happen [a *foreboding* anxiety]

opinion is used of a conclusion or judgment which seems true or probable to one's own mind even though it may still be argued [it's my *opinion* that he'll agree]; **belief** refers to the acceptance by the mind of an idea, esp. a doctrine or dogma that others accept [religious *beliefs*]; a **view** is an opinion affected by the personal way one looks at things [she gave us her *views* on life]; a **conviction** is a strong belief about whose truth one has no doubts [I have a *conviction* of his innocence]; **sentiment** refers to an opinion that is the result of careful thought but that is influenced by emotion; **persuasion** refers to a strong belief that cannot be shaken because one wishes to believe in its truth

oppose implies attacking something that threatens or interferes with one; **resist** implies defending against something that is already actively opposed to one [one *opposes* a legislative action under consideration, one *resists* a law already passed by refusing to obey it]; **withstand** usually implies resistance that keeps the attack from being successful [can they *withstand* the heavy bombing?]

oral refers to that which is spoken, rather than written, to communicate something [an *oral* promise, request, etc.]; **verbal**, though sometimes used in the same way as *oral*, in careful discrimination refers to the use of words, either written or oral, rather than pictures, symbols, etc., to communicate an idea or feeling [a *verbal* image, portrait, etc.

origin is applied to that from which a person or thing has its very beginning [the word "rodeo" has its *origin* in Spanish]; **source** is applied to the point or place from which something arises,

comes, or develops [the sun is our *source* of energy]; **beginning** is the general term for a starting point or place [the *beginning* of a friendship]; **inception** is specifically applied to the beginning of an undertaking, organization, etc. [Smith headed the business from its *inception*]; **root** suggests an origin so deep and basic as to be the very first cause from which something stems [an error in arithmetic was the *root* of all our trouble]

pacify implies a making quiet and peaceful that which has become noisy or disorderly [to *pacify* a crying child]; **appease** suggests a pacifying by giving in to demands [to *appease* one's hunger]; **mollify** suggests a soothing of wounded feelings or calming of anger [his compliments failed to *mollify* her]; **placate** implies the changing of an unfriendly or angry attitude to a friendly or favorable one [to *placate* an offended colleague]; **propitiate** implies a calming or preventing of hostile feeling by winning the good will of a higher power [to *propitiate* a deity]; **conciliate** implies the use of arbitration, concession, persuasion, etc. in an attempt to win someone over

part is the general word for any of the components of a whole [a *part* of one's life]; **portion** often suggests a part given or assigned as a share [his *portion* of the inheritance]; a **piece** is either a part separated from the whole [a *piece* of pie] or a single unit from a collection of related things [only one *piece* missing from her set of china]; a **division** is a part formed by cutting, partitioning, classifying, etc. [the fine-arts *division* of a library]; **section** means much the same as **division** but usually suggests a smaller part [a *section* of a bookcase]; **segment** implies a part separated along natural lines of division [a *segment* of a tangerine]; a **fraction** is strictly a part contained by the whole a certain number of times without remainder, but generally it suggests a small, unimportant part [he received only a *fraction* of the benefits he was entitled to]; a **fragment** is a relatively small part separated as by breaking [a *fragment* of rock]

pay is the simple, direct word meaning to give money, etc. due for services provided, goods received, etc.; **compensate** implies a return, whether of money or something else, thought of as equal to the service given, the effort made, or the loss suffered [he could never be *compensated* for the loss of his son]; **remunerate** emphasizes the idea of payment for a service provided, but it often also implies a reward [a bumper crop *remunerated* the farmer for his labors]; to **reimburse** is to pay back what has been spent [the salesman was *reimbursed* for his traveling expenses]

perseverance implies a continuing to do something in spite of difficulties, obstacles, etc.; **persistence** may imply either steadfast perseverance that is usually admired or stubborn continuance that is usually annoying; **tenacity** and **pertinacity** both imply firmness in holding to some purpose, action, or belief, but **tenacity** suggests that such firmness is admirable, while **pertinacity** suggests a being obstinate in a way that annoys

petty is applied to that which is small, minor, unimportant, etc. compared with others of its kind, and it is often used to imply small-mindedness [*petty* cash, a *petty* grudge]; **trivial** applies to that which, because it is both petty and ordinary, has no special value [a *trivial* remark]; **trifling** applies to something so small and unimportant that it can be ignored [a *trifling* matter]; **paltry** is applied to something so small or worthless that it deserves contempt [a *paltry* wage]; **picayune** is used of a person or thing thought of as small, mean, or insignificant [a *picayune* objection]

pity implies sorrow felt for another's suffering or misfortune and sometimes suggests slight contempt as well, because the person's troubles are considered to be the result of his own weakness or inferiority [she felt *pity* for a person so ignorant]; **compassion** implies pity along with an urge to help or spare [he was moved by *compassion* and did not demand payment of the debt]; **sympathy** implies a feeling of such closeness to another that one is able to understand and even share emotionally his sorrow, etc. [he always turned to his wife for *sympathy*]

pleasant and **pleasing** are both applied to the effect of giving satisfaction or delight, but **pleasant** stresses the effect produced [a *pleasant* smile] and **pleasing**, the ability to produce such an effect [her *pleasing* ways]; **agreeable** is used of that which suits one's personal likes, mood, etc. [*agreeable* music]; **enjoyable** implies the ability to give enjoyment or pleasure [an *enjoyable* picnic]; **gratifying** implies the ability to give pleasure by satisfying one's wishes, hopes, etc. [a *gratifying* experience]

plentiful implies a large or full supply [a *plentiful* supply of books]; **abundant** implies a very plentiful or very large supply [a forest *abundant* in wild game]; **copious**, now used chiefly to re-

fer to quantity produced, used, etc., implies a rich or continuing abundance [a *copious* harvest, discharge, etc.]; **profuse** implies a giving or pouring forth abundantly or very generously, often beyond what is needed or wanted [*profuse* in his thanks]; **ample** applies to that which is large enough to meet all demands [his savings are *ample* to see him through this crisis]

pliable and **pliant** both suggest something that can be easily bent, as a thin wooden stick, and in a more general way, a nature that gives in or adapts easily; **plastic** is used of substances, such as plaster or clay, that can be molded into various shapes which they keep after they become hard, and is also used of persons who can be easily influenced or persuaded; **ductile** suggests that which can be drawn or stretched out [copper is a *ductile* metal]; **malleable** suggests that which can be hammered, beaten, or pressed into various forms [copper is *malleable* as well as ductile]

ponder implies a weighing mentally and suggests careful consideration of a matter from all sides [to *ponder* over a problem]; **meditate** suggests quiet, deep study or thought [he *meditated* on the state of the world] or careful thinking about some plan [to *meditate* revenge]; **muse** implies a dreamlike series of thoughts [to *muse* over the past]; **ruminate** suggests turning a matter over and over in the mind [the loser *ruminated* on the cause of his defeat]

position is used of any kind of work done for salary or wages, but often only of work done by a white-collar or professional worker; **situation** now usually refers to a position that needs to be filled or to one that is desired [*situation* wanted as salesman]; **office** refers to a position that gives one authority or power, esp. in government, a corporation, etc.; a **post** is a position or office that carries important responsibilities, esp. one to which a person is appointed; **job** is now the common, basic term which can be used in place of any of the preceding terms

possible is used of anything that may exist, occur, be done, etc., depending on circumstances [a *possible* solution to a problem]; **practicable** applies to that which can easily be brought about under the existing conditions or by the means available [a *practicable* plan]; **feasible** is used of anything that is likely to be carried through to a successful conclusion and, thus, may seem worth doing [a *feasible* enterprise]

praise is the simple, basic word that refers to the expressing of approval, respect, or admiration [to *praise* a student's work]; **laud** implies great, sometimes excessive praise [the critics *lauded* the actor to the skies]; **extol** implies high, often formal praise that is meant to make the one who receives it feel proud and happy [the scientist was *extolled* for his work]; **eulogize** suggests formal praise in a speech or writing, esp. of someone who has recently died **presume** implies a taking something for granted or accepting it as true, usually on the basis of probable evidence in its favor and the absence of proof against it [the man is *presumed* to be of sound mind]; **presuppose** suggests a taking something for granted without good reason [this writer *presupposes* too large a vocabulary in children]; **assume** implies the taking of something for granted as a basis for argument or action [let us *assume* his motives were good]; **postulate** implies the assuming of something as an underlying factor, often something that cannot be proved [his argument *postulates* the natural goodness of man]

previous generally implies a coming before in time or order [a *previous* meeting]; **prior** adds to this the idea of greater importance or claim as a result of being first [a *prior* obligation]; **preceding**, esp. when used with the definite article, implies a coming just before [the *preceding* night]; **antecedent** adds to the meaning of **previous** the idea of directly causing what follows [events *antecedent* to the war]; **foregoing** applies specif. to something previously said or written [the *foregoing* examples]; **former** always implies a comparison between the first and the last (called *latter*) of two persons or things just mentioned

prone, in strict use, implies a position in which one lies on one's belly [he fell *prone* upon the ground and drank from the brook]; **supine** implies a position in which one lies on one's back, and may suggest a listless feeling or passive attitude [lying *supine* on the grass and gazing lazily at the clouds]; **prostrate** implies the position of one thrown or lying flat in a prone or supine position or the state of one completely beaten, helpless, exhausted, etc. [the victim lay *prostrate* at his attacker's feet]; **recumbent** suggests a lying down or back in any position one might assume for rest or sleep [she was *recumbent* upon the couch]

punish implies making a wrongdoer suffer for his wrongdoing by paying a penalty, usually with no idea of reform-

ing or correcting him [to *punish* a murderer by hanging him]; **discipline** suggests punishment that is intended to control the wrongdoer or to establish in him habits of self-control [to *discipline* a naughty child]; **correct** suggests punishment of a wrongdoer for the purpose of overcoming his faults [to *correct* unruly pupils]; **chastise** implies punishment, usually physical punishment, along with an attempt to correct the wrongdoer

push implies the use of force or pressure by a person or thing in contact with the object to be moved ahead, aside, etc. [to *push* a baby carriage]; **shove** implies a pushing of something so as to force it to slide along a surface, or it suggests rough handling in pushing [*shove* the box into the corner]; to **thrust** is to push with sudden, often violent force, sometimes so as to put one thing into another [he *thrust* his hand into the water]; **propel** implies a driving forward of something by a force that makes it move [the wind *propelled* the sailboat]

puzzle implies that a problem, situation, etc. is so involved or complicated that it is very hard or difficult to understand or solve; **perplex**, in addition, implies uncertainty or even worry as to what to think, say, or do; **confuse** implies a being mixed up mentally to a greater or lesser degree; **confound** implies a being so confused that one is completely frustrated or greatly astonished; **bewilder** implies such complete confusion in one's mind that one can no longer think clearly

quarrel implies a sharp disagreement full of angry words and feeling and often suggests that those arguing become unfriendly; **wrangle** suggests a noisy, fairly lengthy dispute in which each person stubbornly refuses to change his mind; **altercation** suggests a heated argument which may or may not come to blows; **squabble** implies undignified, childish arguing over a small matter; **spat** is the colloquial word for a petty quarrel and suggests a brief, angry outburst that has little lasting effect

range refers to the full extent over which something is recognizable, effective, etc. [the *range* of his knowledge]; **reach** refers to the furthest limit of effectiveness, influence, etc. [beyond the *reach* of my understanding]; **scope** is used of the area covered by a particular activity, written work, etc. having set limits [does it fall within the *scope* of this dictionary?]; **compass** suggests completeness within limits thought of as the outer edge of a circle [he did all within the *compass* of his power]; **gamut**, in this connection, refers to the full range of shades, tones, etc. within the limits of something [the full *gamut* of emotions]

rational implies the ability to reason in an orderly, carefully controlled way so as to reach conclusions logically without being swayed by emotion [Holmes's *rational* explanation of the mysterious events]; **reasonable** suggests the calm, careful use of the mind in making decisions, choices, etc. that are fair and practical [the teacher was *reasonable* in the amount of homework she required]; **sensible** implies the use of common sense based on sound judgment and practical experience [a *sensible* man who bought no more than he needed]

rebellion implies organized, armed, open resistance to the authority or government in power, and, when applied to a historical event, suggests that it failed [Shay's *Rebellion*]; **revolution** applies to a rebellion that succeeds in overthrowing an old government and establishing a new one [the American *Revolution*] or to any movement that brings about a drastic change in society [the Industrial *Revolution*]; **insurrection** suggests an outbreak that is smaller in scope and less well organized than a rebellion [the Philippine *Insurrection*]; **revolt** stresses a casting off of allegiance or a refusal to submit to established authority [a *revolt* of students against the dress code]; **mutiny** applies to a forcible revolt of soldiers or, especially, sailors against their officers [*mutiny* on the Bounty]; **uprising** is a simple, direct term for any outbreak against a government and applies specifically to a small, limited action or to the beginning of a general rebellion [local *uprisings* against the Stamp Act]

recover implies a finding or getting back something that one has lost in any manner [to *recover* stolen property, one's self-control, etc.]; **regain** emphasizes a struggle to win back something that has been taken from one [to *regain* a hill from the enemy]; **retrieve** suggests that something is beyond easy reach and requires some effort to get it back [he was determined to *retrieve* his honor]

regard usually implies a judging of someone or something according to its worth or value [the book is highly *regarded* by critics]; **respect** implies a judging of how great worth or high value, as shown by courtesy or honor [a jurist *respected* by lawyers]; **esteem**, in addition, suggests that the person or object is highly prized or desired [a

friend *esteemed* for his loyalty]; **admire** suggests a feeling of enthusiastic delight in appreciating something or someone that is superior [one must *admire* such courage]

relevant implies a close, logical relationship with, and importance to, the matter being considered [*relevant* testimony]; **germane** implies such close natural connection as to be highly suitable or fitting [your memories are not really *germane* to this discussion]; **pertinent** implies an immediate and direct bearing on the matter at hand [a *pertinent* suggestion]; **apposite** applies to that which is both relevant and happily suitable or fitting [referring to an *apposite* passage in Shakespeare]; **apropos** is used of that which is right for the purpose as well as relevant [an *apropos* remark]

reliable is used of a person or thing that can be counted upon to do what is expected or required [his *reliable* assistant]; **dependable** refers to a person or thing that can be depended on, as in an emergency, and often suggests personal loyalty, levelheadedness, or steadiness [she is a *dependable* friend]; **trustworthy** applies to a person, or sometimes a thing, whose truthfulness, honesty, carefulness, etc. one has complete confidence in [a *trustworthy* source of information]; **trusty** applies to a person or thing that has in the past always been trustworthy or dependable [his *trusty* horse]

reluctant implies an unwillingness to do something, as because of dislike, uncertainty, etc. [she was *reluctant* to marry]; **disinclined** suggests a lack of desire for something, as because it fails to suit one's taste [I feel *disinclined* to argue]; **hesitant** implies a holding back from action, as because of caution, uncertainty, etc. [don't be *hesitant* about asking]; **loath** suggests a strong feeling of unwillingness [I am *loath* to depart]; **averse** suggests a deep-seated, long-lasting unwillingness [she is *averse* to borrowing money]

remark applies to a brief, more or less casual statement of opinion, etc., as in calling attention to something [a *remark* about her clothes]; an **observation** is an expression of opinion on something to which one has given special attention and thought [the warden's *observations* on prison reform]; a **comment** is a remark or observation made in explaining, criticizing, or interpreting something [*comments* on a novel]

remember implies a putting oneself in mind of something, often suggesting that the thing stays so vividly alive in the memory that one becomes conscious of it without effort [he'll *remember* this day]; **recall** and **recollect** both imply some effort to bring something back to mind, **recall**, in addition, often suggesting that one tells others what is brought back [let me *recall* what was said; to *recollect* the days of one's childhood]

replace implies a taking the place of someone or something that is now lost, gone, destroyed, worn out, etc. [we *replace* defective tubes]; **displace** suggests the forcing or driving out of a person or thing by another that replaces it [he had been *displaced* in her affections by another man]; **supersede** implies a replacing with something superior, more up-to-date, etc. [the steamship *superseded* the sailing ship]; **supplant** suggests a displacing that involves force, trickery, or an introduction of new methods [the prince had been *supplanted* by an imposter]

restrain suggests the use of strong force or authority either in preventing, or in putting down or controlling, some action [try to *restrain* your enthusiasm]; **curb**, **check**, and **bridle** get their meanings from the various uses of a horse's harness, **curb** implying a sudden, sharp action to bring something under control [to *curb* one's tongue], **check** implying a slowing up of action or progress [to *check* inflationary trends], and **bridle** suggesting a holding in of emotion, feelings, etc. [to *bridle* one's envy]; **inhibit**, as used in psychology, implies a holding down or keeping back of some thought or emotion [her natural warmth and affection had become *inhibited*]

ridicule implies a making fun of a person or thing by way of showing disapproval [he *ridiculed* her new hat]; **deride** suggests contempt for or a strong dislike of what is being made fun of [to *deride* another's beliefs]; **mock** suggests a ridiculing by the unkind imitation of another's mannerisms or habits [it is cruel to *mock* his lisp]; **taunt** implies insulting ridicule, esp. as shown by jeering at another and harping on something that makes him feel ashamed [they *taunted* him about his failure]

rise and **arise** both imply a coming into being, action, notice, etc., but **rise** carries an added suggestion of upward movement [empires *rise* and fall] and **arise** is often used to show a cause-and-effect relationship [accidents *arise* from carelessness]

roam implies a traveling about without a fixed goal over a large area and carries

suggestions of freedom, pleasure, etc. [to *roam* about the country]; **ramble** implies an idle moving or walking about, esp. in a carefree or aimless way [we *rambled* through the woods]; **rove** suggests a wandering over a wide area, but usually implies a special purpose or activity [a *roving* reporter, *roving* bands of looters]; **range** stresses the wide area covered and sometimes suggests a search for something [hunters *ranging* the western plains]; **meander** is used of streams, paths, etc., and, less often, of people and animals, that follow a winding, seemingly aimless course

rural is the general word referring to life on the farm or in the country as distinguished from life in the city [*rural* schools]; **rustic** emphasizes the contrast between the supposed crudeness and lack of sophistication of country people and the polish and refinement of city people [*rustic* humor]; **pastoral** suggests an ideally simple sort of life as lived in the country, originally by shepherds; **bucolic**, in contrast, suggests a down-to-earth, rustic simplicity or crudeness [her *bucolic* suitor]

sarcastic implies a deliberate attempt to hurt by ridicule, mocking, sneers, etc. [a *sarcastic* reminder that work begins at 9:00 A.M.]; **ironical** or **ironic** is used of a form of sarcasm in which the meaning of what is said is directly opposite to the usual sense ["My, you're early," was his *ironical* taunt to the latecomer]; **sardonic** implies sneering or mocking bitterness in a person, or, more often, in what he says or how he looks [a *sardonic* smile]; **caustic** implies a cutting, biting, or stinging wit or sarcasm [a *caustic* tongue]

satisfy implies the fact of meeting wishes, needs, expectations, etc. fully; **content** implies a filling of needs to the degree that one is not disturbed by a desire for something more [it takes great wealth to *satisfy* him, but she is *contented* with their modest but steady income]

scream is the general word for a loud, high, piercing cry, made as in fear, pain, or anger; **shriek** suggests a sharper, more sudden or anguished cry than scream and is also used of loud, high-pitched, uncontrolled laughter; **screech** suggests a shrill or harsh cry that is painful or unpleasant to hear

sentimental suggests emotion of a kind that is felt in a longing or tender mood [*sentimental* music] or emotion that is exaggerated, artificial, foolish, etc. [a trashy, *sentimental* novel]; **romantic** suggests emotion stirred up by that which appeals to the imagination as it is influenced by stories of love and adventure [a *romantic* girl waiting for her knight in shining armor]; that is **mawkish** which is sentimental in a disgustingly weak, insincere, or exaggerated way [the *mawkish* lyrics of a popular love song]; that is **maudlin** which is tearfully or weakly sentimental in a foolish way [to become *maudlin* when drunk]

sharp and **keen** both apply to that which is cutting, biting, penetrating, or piercing, as because of having a very thin edge, but **sharp** may imply a harsh, disagreeable cutting quality [a *sharp* pain, tongue, etc.] and **keen**, a pleasantly biting or stimulating quality [*keen* wit, delight, etc.]; **acute** is used literally to describe an angle or end formed by lines or edges that meet in a sharp point, but may be used to suggest a very clear awareness of small differences [*acute* hearing, an *acute* intelligence] or the quality of being sharply painful to the feelings [*acute* distress]

shrewd implies a keen mind, sharp insight, and often a crafty approach in practical matters [a *shrewd* comment, businessman, etc.]; **sagacious** implies a keen insight and farsighted judgment [a *sagacious* adviser]; **perspicacious** suggests the keen mental vision or judgment that helps one clearly to see and understar.d what is vague, hidden, etc. [a *perspicacious* judge of character]; **astute** implies shrewdness combined with wisdom [an *astute* politician]

silly implies ridiculous or unthinking behavior that seems to show a lack of common sense, good judgment, or seriousness [it was *silly* of you to dress so lightly]; **stupid** implies slowness in thinking or a lack of normal intelligence [he is *stupid* to believe that]; **fatuous** suggests stupidity or dullness joined with smug, mistaken satisfaction with the way things are [a *fatuous* smile]; **asinine** implies the extreme stupidity traditionally thought of as characteristic of the ass, or donkey [an *asinine* argument]

small and **little** are often used interchangeably, but **small** is preferred in referring to something of slightly less than the usual size, amount, value, importance, etc. [a *small* man, tax, matter, etc.] and **little** is more often used when no comparison is being stressed [he has his *little* faults], in expressing tenderness [his *little* sister], and in suggesting unimportance, pettiness, etc. [of *little* interest]; **diminutive** implies extreme, sometimes delicate, smallness or littleness [a *diminutive* teacup]; **minute** and the more informal **tiny** suggest that

which is extremely diminutive, often to the degree that it can be noticed only by looking very closely [a *minute*, or *tiny*, difference]; **miniature** applies to a copy, model, etc. on a very small scale [*miniature* paintings]; **petite** refers specifically to a girl or woman who is small and trim in figure

sorrow refers to the deep, long-lasting mental pain caused by loss, disappointment, etc. [his secret, life-long *sorrow*]; **grief** suggests briefer, more intense mental pain resulting from a particular misfortune, disaster, etc. [her *grief* over the loss of her child]; **woe** suggests grief or misery so intense that it cannot be relieved [the war-torn nation's *woe*]

speech is the general word for a piece on some subject spoken before an audience, with or without preparation; **address** implies a formal, carefully prepared speech and usually suggests that the speaker or the speech is important [an *address* to a legislature]; **oration** suggests an eloquent, sometimes merely pompous and showy speech, esp. one delivered on some special occasion [a Fourth of July *oration*]; a **lecture** is a carefully prepared speech intended to inform or instruct the audience [a *lecture* to a college class]; **talk** suggests informality and is applied either to an unprepared speech or to an address or lecture in which the speaker purposely uses a simple, conversational approach

steep suggests a slope so sharp that it makes going up or down difficult [a *steep* hill]; **abrupt** implies a very sharp incline in a surface that breaks off suddenly from the level [an *abrupt* bank at the river's edge]; **precipitous** suggests the sudden, almost vertical drop of a precipice [*precipitous* canyon walls that few men could climb]; **sheer** indicates an incline that is straight up and down, or almost so, with a surface that is smooth and unbroken [cliffs falling *sheer* to the sea]

strong is the most general of these terms, implying power that can be used actively as well as power that resists destruction [a *strong* body, fortress, etc.]; **stout** implies ability to stand strain, pressure, wear, etc. without breaking down or giving way [a *stout* rope, heart, etc.]; **sturdy** suggests the strength of that which is solidly developed or built and thus difficult to shake, weaken, etc. [*sturdy* oaks, faith, etc.]; **tough** suggests the strength of that which is firm and resistant in quality [*tough* leather, opposition, etc.]; **stalwart** emphasizes firmness, loyalty, or reliability [a *stalwart* supporter]

stupid implies such lack of intelligence

or inability to understand, learn, etc. as might be shown by one in a mental daze [a *stupid* answer]; **dull** implies a mental slowness that may be in one's makeup or may result from overfatigue, illness, etc. [the fever left him *dull* and listless]; **dense** suggests lack of sensitivity or an irritating failure to understand quickly or to react intelligently [too *dense* to take a hint]; **slow** suggests that the quickness to learn, but not necessarily the ability to learn, is below average [a pupil *slow* in his studies]

summit refers to the topmost point of a hill or similar high place or to the highest reachable level, as of achievement or rank; **peak** refers to the highest of a number of high points, as in a mountain range or in some changing action or condition [at the *peak* of his powers as a writer]; **climax** applies to the highest point in interest, force, excitement, etc. in a scale of rising values; **acme** refers to the highest possible point of perfection in the development or progress of something; **apex** suggests the highest point of a geometric figure or of a career, process, etc.; **pinnacle**, in its figurative uses, can be substituted for **summit** or **peak**, but sometimes suggests a dizzy or unsteady height [the *pinnacle* of success]; **zenith** refers to the highest point in the heavens and thus suggests fame or success reached by a spectacular rise

surprise, in this connection, implies a causing wonder because unexpected, unusual, etc. [I'm *surprised* at your concern]; **astonish** implies a surprising with something that seems unbelievable [to *astonish* with magic tricks]; **amaze** suggests an astonishing that causes confusion [*amazed* at the sudden turn of events]; **astound** suggests shocking astonishment that leaves one unable to act or think [I was *astounded* when he offered me a bribe]

talent implies a natural ability to do a certain thing and suggests that the ability has been or can be developed through training, practice, etc. [a *talent* for drawing]; **gift** suggests a special ability that is thought of as having been given, as by nature, rather than gotten through effort [a *gift* for making friends]; **aptitude** implies a special ability which makes it likely that one can do a certain kind of work easily and well [*aptitude* tests]; **faculty** implies a special ability or skill that is either natural or acquired [she has developed the *faculty* of getting along with others]; **knack** implies an ability, gained through practice or experience, to do

something easily and cleverly [the *knack* of writing limericks]; **genius** may imply any great natural ability [he has a *genius* for always saying the right thing], but more often suggests an extraordinary natural power to do creative, original work in the arts or sciences [the *genius* of Leonardo da Vinci]

theory, as compared here, implies a general principle for which there is much evidence explaining how something works or comes to be [the *theory* of evolution]; **hypothesis** implies an explanation which, although there is little evidence for it, is assumed to be true, esp. as a basis for further experimenting [the nebular *hypothesis*]; **law** implies an exact principle that has been worked out by observing how certain events in nature occur over and over again under the same conditions [the *law* of the conservation of energy]

throw is the general word meaning to cause to move through the air by a rapid movement of the arm, etc.; **cast**, the preferred word in special uses [to *cast* a fishing line], generally has a more archaic or formal quality [they *cast* stones at him]; to **toss** is to throw lightly or carelessly and, usually, with an upward or sidewise motion [to *toss* a coin]; **hurl** and **fling** both imply a throwing with force or violence, but **hurl** suggests that the object thrown moves swiftly for some distance [to *hurl* a spear], while **fling** suggests that the object is thrust sharply so that it strikes a surface with considerable force [she *flung* the plate to the floor]; **pitch** implies a throwing with a definite aim or in a definite direction [to *pitch* a baseball]

transform implies a change either in outer form or inner nature, in use, etc. [she was *transformed* into a happy girl]; **transmute** suggests a change in basic nature that seems almost like a miracle [*transmuted* from a shy youth into a man about town]; **convert** implies a change in details so as to be suitable for a new use [to *convert* an attic into an apartment]; **metamorphose** suggests a surprising change produced as if by magic [a tadpole is *metamorphosed* into a frog]; **transfigure** implies a change in outward appearance which seems to make splendid or glorious [her plain features were *transfigured* with tenderness]

trite is applied to an expression or idea which has been used so often that it has lost its original freshness and force (e.g., "like a bolt from the blue"); **hackneyed** refers to expressions which through constant use have become just about meaningless (e.g., "last but not least"); **stereotyped** applies to those fixed expressions which seem almost sure to be used in certain situations (e.g., "I point with pride" in a political speech); **commonplace** is used of any obvious remark or idea that is familiar to just about everybody and is used merely as a matter of course and without any real thought (e.g., "it isn't the heat, it's the humidity")

turn, the most general word here, implies motion around, or partly around, a center or axis [a wheel *turns*]; **rotate** implies movement of a body around its own center or axis [the earth *rotates* on its axis]; **revolve** is sometimes substituted for **rotate**, but in exact use it suggests movement, usually circular or elliptical, around a center outside itself [the earth *revolves* around the sun]; **gyrate** implies movement in a spiral course, as by a tornado; **spin** and **whirl** suggest very fast and continuous rotation or revolution [a top *spins*; the leaves *whirled* about the yard]

universal is used of that which applies to every case or individual, without exception, in the class, category, etc. concerned [a *universal* practice among primitive peoples]; **general** refers to that which applies to all or nearly all of the members of a group or class [a *general* favorite among college students]; **generic** is used of that which applies to every member of a class or, specif. in biology, of a genus [a *generic* name]

use implies the putting of a thing into action or service for a given purpose, esp. its intended purpose, or, in the case of a person treated as a thing, for one's own selfish purposes [to *use* a pencil, a suggestion, etc.; he *used* his brother to advance himself]; **employ**, a more formal term, implies the putting to useful work of something not in use at that moment [to *employ* a vacant lot as a playground] and with reference to persons, suggests a providing of work and pay [he *employs* five mechanics]; **utilize** implies the putting of something to a practical or profitable use [to *utilize* byproducts]

vagrant refers to a person without a fixed home who wanders about from place to place, supporting himself by begging, etc., and in legal usage refers to any person, as a prostitute or disorderly person, whose way of living may cause him to be arrested; **vagabond**, orig. implying laziness, roguishness, etc., now often suggests no more than a carefree, roaming existence; **bum**, **tramp**, and **hobo** are informal substitutes for **vagrant** and **vagabond**, in some senses, but **bum** specifically brings to mind a homeless drunkard who never works, **tramp**, a vagrant who lives by begging or by doing odd jobs, and **hobo**, a migratory laborer who follows seasonal work

view is the general word for that which can be seen [the *view* is cut off by the next building]; **prospect** suggests a view from a position that allows one to look out over a wide area and to a great distance [a grand *prospect* of snowy mountains and deep valleys]; **scene** suggests an attractive or dramatic view of objects, persons, etc. placed or arranged as they might be in a painting or a play [a peaceful country *scene*]; **vista** suggests a distant view seen through a long, narrow passage [at the end of the valley lay a *vista* of rolling hills and winding rivers]

wage (or **wages**) applies to money paid an employee at regular periods of time, as at hourly or piecework rates, esp. for skilled or manual labor; **salary** applies to fixed amounts usually paid monthly or twice a month, esp. to clerical or professional workers; **stipend** is a somewhat overly formal substitute for **salary**, or it is applied to a fixed payment, as an amount of money granted to a student; **fee** applies to the payment requested or given for professional services, as of a doctor, lawyer, etc.; **pay** is the general term that may be substituted for any of these words

weak, the most general of these words, implies having very little, or less than normal, physical, mental, or moral strength [a *weak* muscle, mind, character, etc.]; **feeble** is used of that which is so weak or ineffective as to be pitiable [a *feeble* old man, a *feeble* joke]; **frail** refers to that which is extremely delicate or weak, or easily broken or shattered [a *frail* body, *frail* support]; **infirm** suggests a loss of strength or soundness, as through illness or old age [his *infirm*, old grandfather]; **decrepit** implies a being broken down or worn out, as by old age or long use [a *decrepit* old horse, a *decrepit* sofa]

wise implies the ability to judge and deal with persons, situations, etc. rightly, based on a broad range of knowledge, experience, and understanding [a *wise* parent]; **sage** suggests the great wisdom of age, experience, and philosophical thought [*sage* advice]; **judicious** implies the ability to make wise decisions based on sound judgment [a *judicious* approach to a problem]; **prudent** suggests the wisdom of one who is able to recognize the most suitable or careful course of action in practical matters [a *prudent* policy]

wit refers to the ability to see contradictions, weaknesses, etc. in people and things and to make quick, sharp, often sarcastic remarks about them that delight or entertain; **humor** is applied to the ability to see and express that which is comical, or ridiculous, but suggests a kindly or sympathetic quality in the use of this ability to amuse others; **irony** refers to the humor that is implied in the difference between what is actually said and the meaning that is intended, or in the difference between appearance and reality in life

worth and **value** both refer to the amount of money or goods a thing can be exchanged for [the *worth* or *value* of the jewels]; when the terms are distinguished, **worth** refers to the basic excellence of a thing as judged by its moral or cultural qualities and the like, while **value** refers to excellence as measured by how useful, important, profitable, etc. a thing is [the true *worth* of Shakespeare's plays cannot be measured by their *value* to the commercial theater]

zealot implies great, often too great, devotion to a cause and intense activity in its support [*zealots* of reform]; **fanatic** suggests the unreasonable attitude of one who goes to any length to preserve or carry out his beliefs [an anti-smoking *fanatic*]; an **enthusiast** is one who shows a strong, eager, lively interest in an activity, cause, etc. [a sports *enthusiast*]